Contemporary Intellectual Assessment

Contemporary Intellectual Assessment

Theories, Tests, and Issues

Edited by

Dawn P. Flanagan
Judy L. Genshaft
Patti L. Harrison

THE GUILFORD PRESS
New York   London

©1997 The Guilford Press
A Division of Guilford Publications, Inc.
72 Spring Street, New York, NY 10012

Printed in the United States of America

This book is printed on acid-free paper.

Last digit is print number: 9 8 7 6 5 4 3

Library of Congress Cataloging-in-Publication Data

Contemporary intellectual assessment : theories, tests, and issues /
    edited by Dawn P. Flanagan, Judy L. Genshaft, Patti L. Harrison.
        p.   cm.
    Includes bibliographical references and index.
    ISBN 1-57230-147-3
    1. Intelligence tests. 2. Intelligence tests—History.
  I. Flanagan, Dawn P. II. Genshaft, Judy L. III. Harrison, Patti L.
  BF431.C66 1997   96-22622
  153.9′3—dc20   CIP

Contributors

Vincent C. Alfonso, Ph.D., Graduate School of Education, Fordham University, New York, NY

Ted Andrews, Ph.D., Children's Seashore House, University of Pennsylvania School of Medicine, Philadelphia Center for Health Care Sciences, Philadelphia, PA

Bruce A. Bracken, Ph.D., Department of Psychology, University of Memphis, Memphis, TN

John B. Carroll, Ph.D., University of North Carolina, Chapel Hill, NC

Jie-Qi Chen, Ph.D., Erikson Institute, Chicago, IL

John Driscoll, Department of Educational Psychology, University of Connecticut, Storrs, CT

Colin D. Elliott, Ph.D., American Guidance Service, Inc., Circle Pines, MN

Irvin Esters, Ph.D. Lyon College, Batesville, AR

Rafi Feuerstein, The Benehev Institute for Dynamic Assessment, The International Center for the Enhancement of Learning Potential, Jerusalem, Israel

Reuven Feuerstein, Ph.D., The International Center for the Enhancement of Learning Potential, Jerusalem, Israel

Dawn P. Flanagan, Ph.D., Department of Psychology, St. John's University, Jamaica, NY

Howard Gardner, Ph.D., Harvard Graduate School of Education, Developmental Psychology, Harvard University, Cambridge, MA

Judy L. Genshaft, Ph.D., Office of Academic Affairs, State University of New York at Albany, Albany, NY

Joseph J. Glutting, Ph.D., Department of Educational Studies, School of Education, University of Delaware, Newark, DE

Stephen Greenspan, Ph.D., Department of Educational Psychology, University of Connecticut, Storrs, CT

Stephen Gross, Ph.D., International Services, The International Center for the Enhancement of Learning Potential, Jerusalem, Israel

Patti L. Harrison, Ph.D., The Educational and School Psychology Program, University of Alabama, Tuscaloosa, AL

Janet E. Helms, Ph.D., Department of Psychology, University of Maryland, College Park, MD

John L. Horn, Ph.D., Department of Psychology, University of Southern California, Los Angeles, CA

Richard F. Ittenbach, Ph.D., Educational Psychology, School of Education, University of Mississippi, University, MS

Randy W. Kamphaus, Ph.D., Department of Educational Psychology, University of Georgia, Athens, GA

Alan S. Kaufman, Ph.D., Yale University School of Medicine, New Haven, CT

Nadeen Kaufman, Ed.D., Yale University School of Medicine, New Haven, CT

Timothy Z. Keith, Ph.D., The Graduate School Division of School Psychology, Alfred University, Alfred, NY

Timothy Konold, Ph.D., University of Virginia, Charlottesville, VA,

Carol S. Lidz, Psy.D., School Psychology Program, Touro College, New York, NY

Emilia Lopez, Ph.D., Graduate Program in School Psychology, Department of Educational and Community Programs, Queens College, City University of New York, Flushing, NY

John J. McArdle, Ph.D., Department of Psychology, University of Virginia, Charlottesville, VA

R. Steve McCallum, Ph.D., Psychoeducational Studies Unit, University of Tennessee at Knoxville, Knoxville, TN

Paul McDermott, Ph.D., Graduate School of Education, University of Pennsylvania, Philadelphia, PA

Kevin S. McGrew, Ph.D., Department of Applied Psychology, St. Cloud State University, St. Cloud, MN

Anna Walters Morgan, M.Ed., Department of Educational Psychology, University of Georgia, Athens, GA

Jack Naglieri, Ph.D., Department of Educational Services and Research, Ohio State University, Columbus, OH

Jennie Noll, Ph.D., National Institute of Health, Unit on Developmental Traumatology, Bethesda, MD

Martha D. Petoskey, M.Ed., Department of Educational Psychology, University of Georgia, Athens, GA

Sarah Pratt, M.A., Fordham University, Bronx, NY

Carol A. Prescott, Ph.D., Virginia Institute for Psychiatric and Behavioral Genetics, Medical College of Virginia, Virginia Commonwealth University, Richmond, VA

Daniel J. Reschly, Ph.D., Department of Psychology, Iowa State University, Ames, IA

Robert J. Sternberg, Ph.D., Department of Psychology, Yale University, New Haven, CT

Robert M. Thorndike, Ph.D., Department of Psychology, Western Washington University, Bellingham, WA

Howard Wainer, Ph.D., Educational Testing Service, Princeton, NJ

Kathryn C. Walker, M.A., Psychoeducational Studies Unit, University of Tennessee at Knoxville, Knoxville, TN

Richard W. Woodcock, Ph.D., Department of Psychology, University of Virginia, Charlottesville, VA

Preface

———◦∞◦———

THE HISTORY OF INTELLIGENCE TESTING has been well documented from the early period of mental measurement (e.g., Peterson, 1925) to present day conceptions of the structure of intelligence and its operationalization (e.g., Carroll, 1982, 1993; DuBois, 1970; Jensen, 1987; Thorndike & Lohman, 1990). The foundations of psychometric theory and practice were established in the late 1800s and set the stage for the ensuing enterprise in the measurement of human cognitive abilities. The technology of intelligence testing was apparent in the early 1900s, when Binet and Simon (1905) developed a test that adequately distinguished children with mental retardation from children with normal intellectual capabilities, and well-entrenched by the late 1900s, when the Wechsler–Bellevue (Wechsler, 1939) was published. In subsequent decades, significant refinements and advances in intelligence testing technology were made and the concept of individual differences was a constant focus of scientific inquiry.

Although several definitions and theories of intelligence have been offered in the past century, the nature of this concept continues to be elusive. Perhaps the most popular definition was that offered by Wechsler in 1958. According to Wechsler, intelligence is "[t]he aggregate or global capacity of the individual to act purposefully, to think rationally and to deal effectively with his environment" (p. 7). It is on this conception of intelligence that the current Wechsler tests were built. Because for decades the Wechsler batteries were the dominant intelligence tests in the field of psychology, were found to measure global intelligence validly, and for many years were largely without rival, they assumed number one status and remain in that position today. As such, Wechsler's (1958) definition of intelligence continues to guide and influence the present day practice of intelligence testing. Despite the influx of new and revised intelligence batteries in recent years, such as the Kaufman Adolescent Battery for Children (K-ABC), Stanford-Binet Intelligence Scale: Fourth Edition (SB:IV), and Woodcock-Johnson Psycho-Educational Battery-Revised (WJ-R) in the 1980s, and the Differential Abilities Scale (DAS) and Kaufman Adolescent and Adult Intelligence Test (KAIT) in the 1990s, psychologists continue to rely almost exclusively on the Wechsler batteries. In light of recent theoretical and empirical advances in cognitive psychology, however, it is clear that the Wechsler tests are not based on the most dependable and current evidence of science and that over-reliance on these instruments, especially in the past decade, served to widen the gap between intelligence testing and cognitive science.

Notwithstanding the significant contributions that the Wechsler scales have made to research and practice in school and clinical psychology as well as special education over the past six decades, the information presented in this text on intelligence theory and assessment technology suggests that it is time for clinicians to either augment the Wechsler batteries to include measures of important abilities and processes that are not currently assessed by these scales or to use alternative instruments and approaches to assessing intelligence. In order for the field of intellectual assessment to advance, clinicians must use instruments that operationalize contemporary and empirically supported theories of intelligence or employ assessment techniques that are designed to measure the broad array of cognitive abilities represented in current theory. It is only through a broader measurement of intelligence, grounded in a well-validated theory of the nature of human cognitive abilities, that professionals can gain a better understanding of the relationship between intelligence and important outcome criteria (e.g., school achievement, occupational success) and begin to narrow the gap between intelligence testing and cognitive science.

Purpose and Objectives

The purpose of this text is to provide a comprehensive conceptual and practical overview of the current state of the art of intellectual assessment. This text describes contemporary theories of the structure of intelligence and personal competencies, new assessment technology, and current scientific knowledge of the validity of cognitive constructs and measures of intelligence. The three primary objectives of this book are as follows: (1) to present in-depth descriptions of a wide variety of prominent theories of intelligence, tests and techniques for assessing human cognitive abilities, and issues related to the utility of current intelligence batteries for special populations (e.g., preschoolers, culturally and linguistically diverse); (2) to provide critical information related to the construct, predictive, and diagnostic validity of contemporary intelligence tests that could be used by professionals to make informed decisions regarding their assessment practices and research programs; and (3) to demonstrate the utility of and the growing need for an empirically supported theoretical foundation to guide intelligence assessment, interpretation, research, and test development. The ultimate goal of this book is to provide professionals with the knowledge necessary to effectively use new intelligence batteries that are grounded in contemporary theory and research and make up-to-date, empirically supported interpretations of older tests, thereby providing a bridge between research and practice.

Organization and Theme

This book consists of 27 chapters, organized into four parts. The theme of this text is "*beyond traditional* intellectual assessment." Part I, "The Origins of Intellectual Assessment," traces the historical roots of test conceptualization, development, and interpretation up to modern day. This part of the book provides a necessary foundation for understanding and elucidating contemporary and emerging theories, tests, and issues in the field of intellectual assessment. Part II, "Contemporary and Emerging Theoretical Perspectives," introduces recently revised, new, and emerging theories of intelligence and personal competence. Each theory represents a more comprehensive view of the structure of human cognitive abilities and competencies than traditional general and dichotomous views of intelligence. These theories are described in terms of (1) how they reflect recent advances in psychometrics, neuropsychology, and/or cognitive psychology, (2) the empirical evidence that exists to support them, (3) how they have been operationalized, and (4) their relationship to other competing theoretical models. The theories presented in Part II represent a significant departure from traditional views and conceptualizations of the structure of intelligence and provide a viable foundation for building more broad-based and culturally sensitive intelligence test batteries.

Part III, "New Tests and Alternative Techniques for Assessing Intelligence," presents new and soon-to-be-published tests and alternative methods of assessing intelligence that move beyond the tradition established by the Binet and Wechsler scales, primarily through their incorporation of strong theoretical foundations. The test developers who have written chapters for this volume provide a description of how their tests reflect advances in intellectual assessment and offer recommendations for interpreting the general, broad, and specific abilities measured by their instruments. Part IV, "Emerging Issues and New Directions in Intellectual Assessment," focuses mainly on issues related to the construct, predictive, and diagnostic validity of current intelligence batteries. Each validity issue is discussed in terms of its implications for the general use and interpretation of cognitive ability tests, particularly with regard to special populations, including culturally and linguistically diverse. Suggestions and recommendations regarding the appropriate use of intelligence tests with diverse groups as well as future research directions are provided throughout this section of the book. Part IV culminates with an integration and synthesis of contemporary theories, tests, and issues in the field of intellectual assessment, highlighting the salient ways in which the field has moved beyond traditional paradigms.

Intended Audience

Practitioners, university trainers, researchers, students, and other professionals in the fields of school, clinical, counseling, and educational psychology will find this book interesting and useful. This volume would be appropriate as a primary text in any graduate (masters or doctoral level) course or seminar on cognitive assessment, intelligence, psychoeducational assessment, or measurement and assessment. This book also would be appropriate as a primary text for graduate level courses or seminars on theories of intelligence.

Acknowledgments

The editors wish to thank a number of individuals who have contributed to or assisted in the preparation of this book.

We are extremely appreciative of the authors' significant contributions. It has been a rewarding experience to work with a dedicated group of authors who are nationally recognized authorities in their respective areas.

Appreciation is extended to our colleague, Dr. Kevin S. McGrew, for his thoughtful and insightful comments and suggestions during the conceptualization of this text.

We are deeply grateful to Christine Brown for her competent assistance throughout the preparation of this text. She spent countless hours preparing tables and figures for production, checking references, and aiding in other important editorial tasks. Her valuable assistance greatly facilitated the editorial process. We also appreciate the diligent editing work of Mary Macedonio whose computer skills and technical assistance guided us through the final stages of preparing the book manuscript for submission to the publisher.

Finally, the contributions of Sharon Panulla and Rowena Howells and the rest of the staff at Guilford Publications are gratefully acknowledged. Their expertise and pleasant and cooperative working style made this project an enjoyable and productive endeavor.

DPF
JLG
PLH

REFERENCES

Binet, A., & Simon, T. (1905). Methodes nouvelles pour le diagnostic du niveau intellectuel des anormaux. *L'Annee Psychologique, 11,* 191–244.

Caroll, J. B. (1982). The measurement of intelligence. In R. J. Sternberg (Ed.), *Handbook of human intelligence* (pp. 29–120). New York: Cambridge University Press.

Carroll, J. B. (1993). *Human cognitive abilities. A survey of factor-analytic studies.* New York: Cambridge University Press.

DuBois, P. H. (1970). *A history of psychological testing.* Boston: Allyn & Bacon.

Jensen, A. R. (1987). Individual differences in mental ability. In J. A. Glover & R. R. Ronning (Eds.), *Historical foundations of educational psychology* (pp. 61–88). New York: Plenum.

Thorndike, R. M., & Lohman, D. F. (1990). *A century of ability testing.* Chicago: Riverside Publishing.

Wechsler, D. (1939). *The measurement of adult intelligence.* Baltimore: Williams & Wilkins.

Contents

⎯⎯⎯◦◦◦⎯⎯⎯

PART III

PART I

⸺⬥⸺

THE ORIGINS
OF INTELLECTUAL ASSESSMENT

PART I OF THIS TEXTBOOK consists of three chapters that describe the historical and theoretical origins of intellectual assessment. In the first chapter, "The Early History of Intelligence Testing," Robert M. Thorndike traces the history of intelligence tests from the latter part of the 19th century to the present day. In addition, he explores the increased interest in intelligence and its measurement in the late 1800s and early 1900s with particular emphasis on the work of Alfred Binet. Other pertinent aspects of the scientific movement that resulted in the emergence of psychology as a separate discipline are also discussed in Chapter 1. In Chapter 2, "The History of Test Development," Richard F. Ittenbach, Irvin G. Esters, and Howard Wainer place the modern period of testing and assessment into a temporal, historical, and professional context, beginning with the earliest thinkers of the Western world. In addition, the authors discuss the operationalization and implementation of the original ideas of Alfred Binet and David Wechsler and compare traditional test theory to today's sophisticated measurement theories. They also discuss the early clash between theory and practice, the reliability and stability of modern measurement, and the evolution of test validity. Chapter 2 concludes with a discussion of the most significant advances in test conceptualization and development since the publication of the Binet–Simon Scale in 1905. In Chapter 3, "A History of Intelligence Test Interpretation," Randy W. Kamphaus, Martha D. Petoskey, and Anna Walters Morgan provide an historical account of dominant methods of test interpretation, including the "dipstick approach," designed to quantify a general level of intelligence, clinical and psychometric approaches to interpreting profiles of cognitive performance, and a theory-based approach to test interpretation. The discussion of these approaches provides readers with an understanding of how current practices evolved as well as a basis for improving contemporary approaches to test interpretation. Overall, the chapters included in Part I trace the historical roots of test conceptualization, development, and interpretation to modern day, providing the necessary foundation from which to understand and elucidate the contemporary and emerging theories, tests, and issues in the field of intellectual assessment that are presented in subsequent sections of this volume.

DPF

CHAPTER 1

The Early History
of Intelligence Testing[1]

ROBERT M. THORNDIKE

IT IS CRITICALLY IMPORTANT to understand contemporary events in terms of contemporary realities, but there is also value in understanding how we got to where we are. Those who do not learn from history are forced to repeat it. In this opening chapter of a book on the state of the art and the future of the assessment of human cognitive abilities, it is appropriate to look back on some of the forces that led to the development of the measures of intellectual ability that are so controversial today with a view to understanding why they have the form and substance they do.

EARLY INFLUENCES

We can trace attempts to measure human cognitive abilities to a time early in the history of imperial China. Because the Chinese had no hereditary aristocracy, they developed a standardized civil service testing program that was in operation for about 4,000 years, a program they discontinued the same year Alfred Binet first displayed his scale for measuring intelligence. The United States and England adopted civil service ability testing during the latter portion of the 19th century as people came to believe that appointments should be based on talent rather than patronage. These testing programs did not have much direct influence on the development of intelligence tests, but throughout much of the United States intelligence tests have had an effect on developments in civil service testing. It is worth noting that even at this early stage, fairness was an explicitly stated objective of the application of ability tests. What has changed more than almost anything else in the testing enterprise during the past century is our notion of what constitutes fair assessment practice.

Universal Education

The late 19th century saw many changes in Western civilization and technology, but two developments were critical for the introduction of measures of intelligence. First was a move toward universal compulsory education. Thomas Jefferson believed that only an educated electorate could make sound self-governing decisions, and he was a proponent of universal education, but it was not until nearly the end of the century that, state by state, the necessary laws were passed and modest public funding was provided. The trend continued also in Europe. France, for example, enacted universal compulsory education legislation in the 1880s.

One consequence of the new laws in the United States was to bring into the schools for the first time large numbers of children whose parents did not have an education or were not native English speakers. Previously, only children who were interested in an education or who were from families that valued education received more than minimal schooling. Of course, these were also the families from the higher social strata, those who could pay for an education. In the United States, compulsory education was also seen as a way to make Americans out of the large numbers of immigrants coming into the country each year. The result was heterogeneity in the student body on a scale never before experienced.

Educators of the era had some quaint ideas about the role that education played in the process of intellectual development. For example, an English physician lecturing at Cambridge told his students, "Good mental training diminishes the amount of subsequent brain wear" (Warner, 1890, p. 24). He also suggested that "a well-made brain in a well-made body is likely to give the best results under good and wise training. The less good the physiognomy may be, the more the need for good education" (p. 30).

The new waves of pupils were exposed to curricula and academic standards that had been developed for a more selected group of students, so the rate of failure rose dramatically, sometimes reaching 50%. In the years before and just after World War I, it was not uncommon to find students who were 3 or 4 years older than the average for their grade. High failure rates were seen as a waste of resources, so leaders of the period sought ways to apportion the resources to those who could benefit most. Intelligence testing was one alternative.

The Mind Can Be Measured

The second important development that precipitated tests to measure intellectual abilities was the rise of a belief that psychology was on the verge of becoming a quantitative science based on the model of physics. During the second half of the 19th century the work of such German psychologists as Gustav Fechner and Hermann Ebbinghaus was making it possible to quantify various psychological characteristics. Fechner felt he had discovered a physics of the mind, a procedure for relating the qualities of physical stimuli quantitatively with the mental representations they created. Ebbinghaus demonstrated that memory and mental fatigue could be studied empirically.

Charles Darwin's cousin, Francis Galton, combined some of Fechner's ideas with the associationism of John Locke to produce a theory of human ability and its measurement. Galton believed that each person is a blank slate at birth and that sensory experience writes on the slate to produce knowledge. He reasoned that because we experience our environment through our senses, a person with greater sensory acuity and more rapid sensory information processing would be able to profit more from experience. Thus, he reasoned that measures of sensory acuity and reaction time should provide an index of intelligence. James McKeen Cattell, who, in 1890, coined the term "mental test," brought Galton's ideas to the United States and proposed a widespread program of mental testing to provide a standard metric for the assessment of human intellectual ability.

ENTER ALFRED BINET

While Galton and Cattell were presenting their ideas about the nature and measurement of intellectual abilities, Alfred Binet, a Frenchman of independent means, was in the process of recovering from a professional thrashing. He had been doing research on the effects of magnetism on hypnotic suggestion (he argued that electromagnetic fields could affect mental acts) and had published results that others found difficult to believe. After a debate in the journals, Binet had to acknowledge that he was wrong; his findings were a methodological artifact resulting from his overzealous belief in the theory he was trying to prove. As a result of this encounter, Binet became a convinced empiricist; he would never again tamper with or venture beyond his data. This made him exceptionally careful when he came to create his tests of intelligence.

Licking his wounds, Binet set out on a new career, the study of the development of intelligence. His subjects were his two daughters, and during the 1890s he published a series of papers in which he reported his findings and argued that the Galton/Cattell approach was wrong. To measure complex mental processes, Binet argued, it is necessary to observe the performance of complex mental acts. He created a series of brief games that he played with his daughters, tasks that were graded in difficulty and that he believed measured their intellectual development.

By 1904 Binet had become involved with the Free Society for the Psychological Study of the Child, a group of concerned parents and educational professionals who formed what we might call a scientifically oriented Parent–Teachers Association. This group was particularly interested in improving the effectiveness and efficiency of the schools by identifying the causes of school failure. Two kinds of children failed: those who could learn the material but would not do so and those who could not learn. The former were referred to in the Society's publications as "malicious," the latter, "stupid." The objective of the Society, then, was to differentiate the stupid from the malicious. We have changed the terminology dramatically in the intervening 90 years, but a major application of intelligence tests remains to make the same basic distinction that concerned Binet, to determine whether a child's low level of academic achievement is due to mental retardation or some other cause.

In a move foreshadowing modern grantsmanship, Binet and his colleagues submitted a proposal in February 1904, to the minister of public instruction for Paris, suggesting the appointment of a committee to develop a measure to make the desired differentiation. After an interval of 8 months, the minister formed the committee, with Binet and others from the Society as members. The following April, at the International Congress of Psychology in Rome, the Binet–Simon scale was presented for the first time. The scale consisted of 30 brief tasks arranged in order of difficulty. A child's intellectual level was defined by the most difficult tasks he or she could perform correctly. This scale was similar in many ways to one introduced 2 years earlier by Henri Damaye, but the ordering of Damaye's items had not been empirically verified, a critical shortcoming in Binet's empiricist view, and Damaye did not have the personal publishing outlet, *L'Annee Psychologique*, that Binet used to disseminate his ideas.

We need to be clear about Binet's objective in this work. Information was available on the abilities of the children who were failing; their teachers found them unable to master school subjects at the same rate as other pupils. But teachers were known to be biased, and Binet viewed his scale as a way to assess ability in an unbiased manner. He intended his test to provide objective corroboration or refutation of the teacher's opinion and to eliminate low motivation and personality problems as explanations for poor scholarship. Of course, learning disabilities had not yet been identified as a reason for low achievement, but without a measure of ability that was independent of (which is not to say uncorrelated with) achievement, these impediments to learning might still await discovery.

OTHER CONTEMPORARY WORK

One often gets the impression that Binet's developments occurred in a vacuum, but such was definitely not the case. As early as 1891, anthropologist Franz Boas had measured 1,500 American school children on a variety of traits and related these measures to teachers' judgments of intellectual acuteness. Shortly thereafter, Gilbert found that older children showed better performance on measures of reaction time and memory, suggesting that age might provide a metric for ability development (cited in Peterson, 1925). In Germany, Ebbinghaus was finding that older children were better at completing mutilated sentences. Finally, in 1903, Blin and Damaye had developed their set of standard questions that were ordered by apparent difficulty and that they claimed could be used to identify the mentally retarded (cited in Wolf, 1973). The genius of Binet was to bring these ideas together into a measuring device which related increasing ability to maturation and was based on empirical results with children.

American psychologists also were in active pursuit of a measure of mental ability. Psychological testing got a strong boost from the American Psychological Association (APA) in 1895 with the appointment of a committee on testing. In 1899, Kirkpatrick (1900), addressing the APA, called for tests "of such a nature that they can be taken by children as well as adults, that they shall be such that all persons tested will have had about an equal opportunity for the exercise of the power tested, and that in the interest of economy of time the tests so far as possible shall be so planned that they can be given to a whole class or school at once" (pp. 279–280). This sounds very much like a call for unbiased group tests of ability, something we still strive for.

Among the early leaders in the American effort to find measures of intelligence was Edward L. Thorndike, a student of Cattell. After first making a name for himself with his studies of problem solving by cats in puzzle boxes, Thorndike devoted much of his effort for the next 40 years to the measurement of human intellect. He and his students, who were always active collaborators in his research, explored many aspects of measurement and intelligence.

One of Thorndike's early students was Naomi Norsworthy. Her name does not appear in many histories of testing, but for her doctoral dissertation in 1903 (Thorndike, 1903; Norsworthy, 1906) she conducted a study of tests of mental and scholastic ability in which she contrasted the performance of two groups of girls. One group was judged by their teachers to be unable to profit from regular school work; the other group, from the same school, was considered normal. Her study, which predated Binet's scale by 2 years, pointed to symbolic reasoning as the main difference between the two groups. Binet would have agreed completely, but probably he was unaware of her study.

There were so many people working on the problem of measuring intelligence between 1900 and 1920 that by 1931, Rudolph Pintner, a pioneer in ability measurement for the handicapped, wrote that although Binet had made a major contribution, the state of the discipline would be little different if he had never lived. The widely perceived needs of the schools to deal with the problems created by universal compulsory education combined with an intellectual climate of naive optimism about the measurability of mental processes produced an atmosphere in which measures of intellectual ability were almost certain to be developed. Of course, once such measures were available, it did not take long for them to be widely applied.

Two Influential Pioneers

Although the measurement of intelligence was being actively pursued in the United States by several people before 1910, two individuals became particularly influential in applied measurement. The first was Henry Goddard, the man responsible for bringing Binet's test to the United States, who might well be considered the first school psychologist. The second was a young graduate student named Lewis Terman.

Goddard was appointed research director of the Vineland Training School for retarded children in 1905. Immediately he set out to find a way to measure the abilities of his charges. His search took him to France in 1906, where he met Binet and became familiar with the 1905 version of Binet's scale. Goddard was skeptical at first, but he took the materials home, translated them into English, and used them in his work at Vineland. When Binet's revised scale was published in 1908, Goddard became an enthusiastic advocate. He quickly produced an American version and began to promote the use of the Binet method widely and for various purposes.

If Goddard was Binet's St. Paul, a convert preaching the gospel of mental testing, the role of St. Augustine, the systematizer of the doctrine, fell to Lewis Terman. For his doctoral research Terman had been working on tasks similar to those Binet had developed. The two corresponded during the 1904–1906 period and Terman adapted tests from the 1905 scale for his own studies. Binet was at work on his 1908 revision and it is not clear whether Terman adopted some of Binet's new tasks, Binet adopted some of Terman's, or, more likely, there was mutual influence. At any rate, Terman applied several Binet-like tasks in his dissertation, which he published in 1906 under the title "Genius and Stupidity: A Study of the Intellectual Process of Seven Bright and Seven Stupid Boys." The scale that Binet released in 1908 contained many tasks that Terman had also used in his study.

After earning his degree, Terman worked in the public schools of Los Angeles for about 4 years before accepting a position at Stanford University. During that time he continued developing tests of the Binet type for use in the schools. In 1911 he published the results of his study of 400 children with his own expansion of Binet's 1908 scale. Five years later he produced the Stanford revision of the Binet–Simon scale (Terman, 1916), which became known as the Stanford–Binet in its 1937 revision.

At the same time that Terman was completing the Stanford revision, Robert Yerkes was working on the forerunner of the major competitor to the Stanford–Binet. In Binet-type scales the items were arranged by mental age or mental level (Binet's preferred term). The items were sorted into groups by the age at which the average child could pass them. Yerkes proposed to abandon the age placement of items entirely and use what he called a point scale. In the Yerkes Point Scale (Yerkes, Bridges, & Hardwick, 1915), items were grouped by type and ordered by difficulty. The examinee was given a score on each type of item based on the number of correct answers given, with bonus points for exceptionally quick or insightful answers. The score could then be converted into an overall mental level. This is the same format that David Wechsler adopted for the Wechsler–Bellevue (Wechsler, 1939) and its successors.

INTRODUCTION OF THE IQ

Several important factors loom in these early developments. First, Binet's major insight was to relate level of ability to age. The primary criterion for whether a task was suitable as a measure of intellectual ability was whether it showed a pattern of decreasing difficulty with age. Binet ordered the 30 tasks in his original scale by the age at which the average child could successfully complete them. This relationship was formalized in the 1908 revision of the scale by placing each item at a mental level defined by the age where half of the children would get the item correct. The examiner would determine the child's mental level by finding the level where the child could complete all the items and adding a year for each five items passed beyond the base.

One of the problems with Binet's method was that although it told at what level the child was functioning, it gave no indication of how good that functioning was. Two children, both testing at the 8-year level, were seen as having the same intellectual development, but if one child was 6 years old and the other was 10, the conclusions drawn about them should be quite different. In 1912 Wilhelm Stern attempted to solve this problem by proposing that a child's mental level, or mental age as he called it, be divided by the child's chronological age to produce an intelligence quotient. The 6-year-old with a mental age of 8 would then have a quotient of 1.33, whereas the 10-year-old would rate a .75. A child who was average would have a quotient of 1.00. It was not until the 1920s that these quotients were multiplied by 100 to get rid of the decimal and yield the metric we know today.

Although the intelligence quotient, or IQ, was endorsed by many, particularly Terman, who adopted it enthusiastically and defended it against all criticism, it also was the source of much controversy and misunderstanding. Binet's concept of mental level emphasized growth, because a child's placement would change from year to year. The IQ, or any other strictly norm-referenced index, emphasizes the stability of relative position. Although the reality of the child's ability level is the same in either case, the impression is a little like seeing the cup as half empty rather than half full. The impression of stasis conveyed by the IQ as an index of relative position is taken as a message of doom by those who do not understand it.

Another unfortunate result of using age as the metric for ability is that in the normal course of human development, the *rate of growth* in ability drops dramatically during the teenage years. There is still much debate about the precise course of change in abilities, but there is no debate about the overall pattern. The result is that we get such statements as Terman's observation that the average American adult has the mental age of a 14-year-old. Given knowledge of the pattern of human development, this statement may make some sense. It makes exactly the same amount of sense as saying that the average American adult has the height of a 16-year-old. The difficulty is that people will draw dramatically different conclusions from the two statements. Although a wealth of evidence leads to the conclusion that intellectual growth in terms of test scores generally levels off in the late teens or early twenties, just as physical growth does, the reality seems normal in the latter case and unacceptable in the former.

Criticism of the IQ and Testing

Even before the 1916 Stanford–Binet was published critics of the IQ metric spoke out. Binet rejected it because it was norm referenced rather than growth referenced. Yerkes rejected it in favor of what he called the coefficient of intelligence (Yerkes & Wood, 1916). This was the ratio of a person's score on the Yerkes Point Scale to the mean score for people of the same age as the examinee. Others, notably Truman Kelley and Arthur Otis, advocated using what we now call the deviation IQ, but Terman insisted on the ratio IQ for the Stanford–Binet, and his power and prestige won out. It was not until 4 years after his death that the 1960 edition of the Stanford–Binet switched to a different index.

Binet never claimed that his tests measured all there was to intelligence. He had a rather narrow concern, and so have most other test developers: the prediction of academic performance. Binet was trying to identify those who did not have the ability to succeed at a minimal level under the ordinary conditions of French public schools. Terman had the same basic objective, although he later let his enthusiasm carry him beyond his data to argue that mental tests reflected a biological reality. It has been common practice to criticize intelligence tests because they correlate better with success in schooling than they do with success in other endeavors, but this criticism is similar to saying that a ruler does a poor job of measuring weight. What happened is that the public, often with the aid and encouragement of overly optimistic psychologists, started expecting tests to do things they were never intended to do.

One of the most frequently voiced criticisms of tests of mental abilities is that they are simplistic and do not reflect the way the human mind really works. That criticism is certainly valid, but it is probably also irrelevant. Intelligent behavior is much more than making marks on a piece of paper. It is also much more than answering vocabulary questions, solving matrix analogies or number series problems, or performing any of the other tasks that are used as indicators of intellectual functioning. What nobody has been able to do yet is come up with a procedure for diagnosing problems related to school performance that is superior to the tests currently in use. Later chapters in this volume review our most recent attempts, some of which seem to be leading to workable assessment devices.

INTELLIGENCE TESTING IN WORLD WAR I
AND ITS AFTERMATH

Although there is no causal relationship, the United States entered World War I shortly after Terman published his version of the Binet–Simon scale. For a number of reasons, some patriotic and some personal, Robert Yerkes, the president of the APA in that year of 1917, worked hard to get the army to accept the services of psychologists in support of the war effort. Psychologists served in a number of capacities, but the one that drew the greatest attention and has had by far the greatest subsequent impact was the development of group tests to screen recruits for intellectual fitness. One of Terman's graduate students at Stanford, Arthur Otis, had been working on a group-administered test of intellectual ability, and this test served as the prototype for what became known as the Army Alpha. Because a significant number of recruits were illiterate in English, a nonverbal instrument using tests such as mazes, picture completion problems, and digit-symbol tasks was also prepared and given the name Army Beta. Workable forms of both tests were completed by November 1917, and before the war's end more than 1.7 million men had been tested.

The Army Alpha, like Terman's own Binet test, was heavily loaded with a verbal component. Although it seems obvious to us now, the test constructors did not see this fact as biasing the test results against individuals who were not native English speakers or who had little formal education. They were living in a time characterized by widespread hostility toward the large number of immigrants who were coming into the country. The prevailing scientific opinion also favored biological rather than experiential explanations for individual differences in ability. The result of this combination was that some very unfortunate conclusions were drawn from the data that resulted from the army testing program. However, it is important for us to realize as we approach the opposite end of the current century, in a climate when such conclusions seem particularly repugnant, that the authors of those studies and opinions were living at a time closer to the Civil War, and a national character that could tolerate slavery, than they were to the present. It was a time when internationally famous educators believed that removing the adenoids improved intelligence (Terman, 1919) and otherwise competent physicians (Warner, 1890) were suggesting that a good education reduced brain wear. It is little wonder that some psychologists of the era were willing, even seeking, to draw racial conclusions from the army testing data.

Testing and the Millennium

After the war, the testing movement took off. As early as 1909, Binet called for universal measurement of the intelligence of school pupils. He was even willing to entrust the task of testing to parents, and his purpose was to identify both those of weak intellect and the "supernormal."

Terman (1919) suggested that the real cause of low achievement was the practice of putting all students of the same age in the same classes. He stated that "innate differences in intelligence are chiefly responsible for the problem of the school laggard" (p. 24) and went on to claim that "90 percent, at least, of school retardation is due to mental inferiority" (p. 303). Mental tests should be used, he claimed, to put children in the proper classes.

Terman had great plans for mental testing in the schools. He believed that a mental age of 7 was necessary for a child to do average first-grade work. In 1920, as the first group-administered tests for use in the schools were being published, he stated that "the greatest usefulness [of intelligence tests] will be found in their universal application to school children. . . . 'A mental test for every child' is no longer an unreasonable slogan" (Terman, 1920, p. 20). As a start, he proposed that "all the pupils in the fourth grade and beyond should be given a test by the group method every year, and those whose scores are either very high or very low in the group examination should be given a Binet test.

. . . It is [also] highly desirable that every pupil be given a mental test within the first half-year of his school life" (Terman, 1919, pp. 15–16).

The use of intelligence tests in the schools grew rapidly. Again, quoting Terman, "Probably a million children in the schools of the United States were given a group mental test during the year 1919–1920. In 1920–1921 the number was probably not less than two million. We may expect the number to exceed five million within a few years" (Terman et al., 1922, p. 3). How right he was.

The 1920s were a decade of boundless enthusiasm for testing in psychology. Tests were seen as measuring innate talent and as providing a way to solve society's problems. Terman was very active, and under his influence some California school districts took the lead in applying tests in the schools. The first was Oakland, which instituted a three-track program in 1918. Berkeley followed in 1920, and many others soon joined the parade. The purpose was to solve the costly problem of keeping children in a single grade for more than one year and to let all children work at their optimum pace. The idea sounds quite contemporary except that we would now prefer to achieve this objective by individualization within a single classroom.

There was a widespread fear among educators in the 1920s that standards would be lowered so the less able could be promoted. The Oakland Plan was based on the premise that "the high school must classify according to brightness and must offer modified courses of study, or the present standards for academic work will fall" (Dickson, 1922, p. 50). All across the country school districts were trying out variants of this plan, and intelligence tests were used to place students in the appropriate track.

The possibility of bias was a major concern among early test developers. As we have already seen, tests originally were intended to replace or supplement other, more biased sources of information for making educational decisions. Even one of the major critics of testing at that time, Walter Lippmann of the *New Republic*, acknowledged that the tests being developed for use in the schools were better than what occurred when tests were not used.

At the time that tests began to infiltrate the schools, E. L. Thorndike, recognizing that some children would have greater access to testing experiences than others and that this might affect their scores, suggested that a huge pool of items be developed from which all tests would be constructed. He argued that this pool should be made public in order to equate examinees on the opportunity to become familiar with test content. He also put a large number of practice items at the beginning of each of his tests in an effort to eliminate differences among students in test-taking experience. Contemporary concerns with bias have become much more sophisticated, but the problem was recognized early.

DEBATE OVER THE NATURE OF INTELLIGENCE

Throughout the first quarter of this century E. L. Thorndike was also engaged in an ongoing theoretical debate with the British psychologist Charles Spearman over the fundamental nature of intelligence. In 1904, Spearman proposed a two-factor theory of intellect that held that performance on any intelligence measure was composed of two parts: one part due to the individual's level on the trait of general intelligence, which he called g, and the other on an ability specific to the particular test, which he called s. The correlation between any two tests was attributed to the presence of g in both.

In 1909, Thorndike, Lay, and Dean tested the hypothesis of g on a set of measures similar to those Spearman used in his original study and found no support for the two-factor theory. Rather than finding g, they concluded that "in general there is evidence of a complex set of bonds between the psychological equivalents of both what we call the formal side of thought and what we call its content, so that one is almost tempted to replace Spearman's statement by the equally extravagant one that there is *nothing whatever* common to all mental functions, or to any half of them" (Thorndike et al., 1909, p. 368).

Spearman responded to this criticism in 1912 (Hart & Spearman, 1912), pointing out that his critics had not satisfied one of the conditions for testing the two-factor theory–that the test battery not contain more than one test of a particular type. This work also presented the derivation of the mathematical criterion for the theory: Spearman's famous tetrad equation. Spearman asserted that Thorndike's data satisfied the criterion when redundant variables (those measuring functions that were too similar) were eliminated.

In the same year, B. R. Simpson, one of Thorndike's students, conducted a further test of Spearman's hypothesis. He gave 15 tests to 17 "good men" (bright college students and Columbia faculty) and 20 "poor men" (unemployed men and laborers) and concluded that "it is quite evident that Spearman's theory is not in harmony with the facts we have secured" (Simpson, 1912, p. 91). But he added that on one hand "there is a close inter-relation among certain mental abilities, and consequently a something that may be called 'general mental ability' or 'general intelligence'; and that on the other hand certain capacities are relatively specialized, and do not necessarily imply other abilities except to a very limited extent" (p. 109).

After a break for World War I, the argument over the nature of intelligence was resumed. In America the widespread acceptance of the Stanford–Binet as the standard defining general intelligence helped Spearman (1920) to conclude that "among the most unexpected events in the psychology of the last dozen years has been the sudden spring of 'general intelligence' from an almost universal incredulity to no less universal investment with the highest importance" (p. 159). He further asserted, "As regards the fundamental theory [of two factors], I venture to maintain that this has now been demonstrated with finality. . . . it becomes a bed of Procrustes, into which all our doctrines must somehow or other be made to fit" (p. 172).

Thorndike also resumed the debate over the theory of two factors. In 1919, he severely criticized Binet-type tests because of their coachability. Noting that coaching seriously impaired the validity of intelligence tests, he advocated creating a large number of alternate forms of tests and making the test items public in order to equate knowledge about the content of the tests. He and his students worked on a set of tests that would meet these criteria to be used for admission to Columbia University.

Bucking a trend led by Spearman and, to a certain extent, Terman, who suggested the testing millennium was just around the corner, Thorndike saw the problem of defining and measuring intelligence as increasingly complex and the solution as receding farther into the distance. He argued that the separate functions measured by different types of intellectual tasks could not be explained with a single construct. "The primary fact is that intelligence is not one thing but many. The abilities measured by a speed test with language and mathematics are not identical with, or even very similar to, those measured by a test with pictures and less exacting in speed" (Thorndike, 1920a, p. 287). Intelligence tests, he asserted, really measured only a limited aspect of intelligent behavior, which he labeled "abstract intelligence." In addition, he said, intelligence comprises at least two other major kinds: *social,* the ability to understand and work successfully with people, and *mechanical,* the ability to understand and deal with concrete things and spatial concepts.

In some ways Thorndike's theory of intelligence was becoming more like Binet's, an integration of many aspects of the person. That same year he argued, "In human nature good traits go together. To him who hath a superior intellect is given also on the average a superior character. . . . There is no principle of compensation whereby a weak intellect is offset by a strong will. . . ." (Thorndike, 1920b, pp. 233–234). However, he categorically rejected *g.* "Everybody will agree that many complexities of individual differences are superadded by likenesses and differences in training. I fear, however, that even if we did dissect out all the consequences of nurture, leaving only a skeleton of inborn capacities, the organization of these would still be much more complex than that required by Spearman's theory" (Thorndike, 1921, p. 151).

The Spearman–Thorndike debate never reached a firm resolution. In 1926, Strasheim constructed a set of test exercises to measure the mental functions postulated by Spearman and found evidence of a single dimension of intellect. This test, and the Comprehension Arithmetic Vocabulary Directions Test (CAVD; Thorndike, Bregman, Cobb, & Woodyard, 1926), which Thorndike designed to measure comprehension, arithmetic, vocabulary, and directions, important indicators of intelligence as he conceived it, were the only instruments specifically derived from the two competing theories. (With the CAVD, Thorndike also introduced the first primitive approximation to item response theory in test construction.) Each antagonist continued to believe in his own theory, but in the late 1920s the controversy shifted to a higher mathematical level and Thorndike left others, notably L. L. Thurstone, to attack the two-factor theory with the theory of multiple factors.

MIDCENTURY (1925–1975)

The period from the 1920s to the 1960s saw an explosion in the use of tests in every phase of American life. Group tests of intelligence became common in the schools and the growing field of clinical psychology, led by David Wechsler, began applying measures of intellect to adults in various civilian contexts outside of education. The debate over the number of dimensions or types of intelligence focused on technical details in the application of factor analysis.

Factorial Theories and Test Batteries

In the 1930s, a series of mathematical developments led to the development of batteries of ability tests. Using his new method of multiple factor analysis, Thurstone (1938) proposed that there was a small number of "primary mental abilities." The exact number became the subject of much debate. Thurstone identified seven factors in his pioneering study, but others argued for more or fewer, with Spearman retaining the extreme position of only one. Theories of ability were constructed from the results of these analyses, and the most extreme version was proposed by Guilford (1959). This theory, based almost exclusively on factor-analytic studies, eventually called for 150 distinct factors organized along three dimensions.

The factor analyses led to batteries of tests designed to measure the several factors. One of the first was the Primary Mental Abilities Battery (Thurstone & Thurstone, 1941), which measured seven factors. Others included the Differential Aptitude Tests and the Flanagan Aptitude Classification Tests. The idea behind all of these tests was that the pattern of a subject's scores would permit more accurate prediction of academic or occupational criteria than a single overall score would. It is one of the surprising developments of the last 30 years that these tests have largely dropped out of use, primarily because the hope that they would yield more accurate prediction has been unfulfilled.

Development of the Wechsler Scales

Wechsler served as an enlisted man in the military testing program of World War I. After the war he earned his doctorate under Robert Woodworth (a close friend and associate of Thorndike) at Columbia and went on to hold various jobs relating to psychometrics in the New York area. It may have been while working for Cattell at the Psychological Corporation or later while serving as a staff psychologist at Bellevue hospital that Wechsler started working out the organization of a new intelligence test specifically designed for testing adults.

Wechsler felt that the Binet scales were too verbally loaded for use with adults, so he designed an instrument with subtests to measure both verbal and nonverbal abilities. He relied heavily on the work of others, borrowing many of his verbal items and subtests from the Army Alpha, whereas the performance subtests came from the Army Beta and the Kohs Blocks Test. His point scale design and variable credit scoring system came from Yerkes and the deviation score format for IQ from Otis. Because the Stanford–Binet IQ metric was universally accepted, he adopted a mean score of 100. As a measure of variability he chose a probable error of 10, which produced a standard deviation of 15 and the metric we know today. It probably would have been better if Wechsler had chosen a scale that differed from that of the Binet because by using such a similar metric he gave added credibility to the reification of the intelligence quotient.

The original test, the Wechsler–Bellevue (Wechsler, 1939), proved quite successful in both civilian and military applications. In 1949, Wechsler moved into direct competition with the Stanford–Binet with the introduction of a version for children, the Wechsler Intelligence Scale for Children (WISC). A few years later, in 1955, he produced a revision of the adult scale, renamed the Wechsler Adult Intelligence Scale (WAIS). This was followed in 1967 with a downward extension of the WISC, the Wechsler Preschool and Primary Scale of Intelligence (WPPSI). All these scales have since been revised, but all still show a distinct family resemblance to the original 1939 scale.

A Period of Stagnation and Criticism

Over the middle decades of the century, intelligence tests themselves changed relatively little. In fact, one of the great disappointments in the career of the well-known critic of tests and testing practice, Oscar Buros, was the lack of progress he saw from 1925 to 1975. The middle half of the century could be characterized as a period of consolidation, almost entrenchment, of the methods that had been developed in the first 25 years. Although testing became big business and an almost universal part of the American experience, little real progress was made. The tests produced by the factor analysts explored some new content areas, but mostly without fruitful result. The Wechsler scales and the revisions of the Stanford–Binet broke no new ground. A single bright spot in the area of theory is found in the work of Raymond B. Cattell (1943, 1963) and his student, John Horn (Horn & Cattell, 1966; Horn, 1985) with the theory of fluid and crystallized intelligence (see Horn & Noll, Chapter 4, this volume).

What did happen during this period was that testing came under violent attack. In the 1960s, the movement to gain equality of civil rights for all Americans finally found a receptive audience. Because psychological tests, particularly tests of cognitive ability, showed differences in mean scores between racial/ethnic groups, and because these tests were seen as restricting access for some groups to better education and better-paying jobs, they became the focus of an attack in the courts and the public press that went well beyond the usual debate between academics. Congressional hearings were held in 1965 to determine whether psychological tests were an invasion of privacy. Equal rights legislation also targeted tests, particularly tests of intelligence, because they showed racial/ethnic group differences. Lawsuits in California and Illinois challenged the use of the WISC and Stanford–Binet for placing students in special education classrooms. (The courts reached the interesting conclusion that the tests were biased in California but not in Illinois.) Psychologists who defended the tests, such as Arthur Jensen and Richard Herrnstein, were excoriated in the press and occasionally threatened with physical violence.

The psychological community responded to the criticism with increased efforts at self-regulation and a careful and extended debate over the issue of test bias. Self-regulation took the form of a series of professional guidelines for test development and use, most recently revised in 1985, but currently under review again. Jensen (1980) published a detailed study of bias in mental testing, concluding that well-constructed modern tests of intellectual ability were not systematically biased against any group, and his conclusions have been supported by most other well-conducted studies (e.g., Hartigan & Wigdor, 1989).

All recently published intelligence tests have been developed with a careful view to racial/ethnic and gender bias. Nevertheless, group differences persist. The reasons for these differences are unclear, but the fact remains that decisions reached with the sensitive aid of good measures of cognitive ability are more likely to be unbiased than decisions made without the benefit of the tests.

ENTERING THE SECOND CENTURY

The centennial of mental testing has seen some fairly dramatic recent developments in the theory and measurement of intellectual abilities. A sampling of new theoretical developments is given in Part II of this volume. Some of these chapters (e.g., 4 and 7) reflect the most up-to-date versions of theoretical perspectives with long histories, whereas the others represent more recent offerings.

There has also been an effort in the last few years to develop tests out of theory rather than using the blunt empirical approach of Binet, Terman, and Wechsler. One notable example is the attempt to operationalize the neuropsychological model of A. R. Luria, first by Alan and Nadeen Kaufman with their Kaufman Ability Battery for Children (K-ABC) and then by J. P. Das and Jack Naglieri (see Naglieri, Chapter 13, this volume). If we can attach cognitive functions to identifiable neurological structures, as Das and Naglieri attempt to do, we will have answered some of the major skeptics' criticisms of intelligence as a scientific concept.

Another significant advance has been the production of tests using item response theory and adaptive testing. Many of the newer tests, such as the Woodcock–Johnson Psycho-Educational Battery–Revised (see Woodcock, Chapter 12, this volume) and the Differential Ability Scales (see Elliott, Chapter 10, this volume), as well as the radically revised Stanford–Binet Intelligence Scale: Fourth Edition (SB:IV; Thorndike, Hagen, & Sattler, 1986), are based on this technology. Once we have fully implemented these psychometric developments, we should be able to be more efficient and more accurate in our assessments.

But even with these advances, the basic method for measuring a child's ability remains little different than it was 65 years ago. What has changed far more than the general strategy and format of testing are the fine-grained details of the items and, more important, the way that test scores are used. The application and interpretation of test scores have changed more in the last 15 years than they did in the preceding 50, and to condemn current testing practice, as some critics do, on the basis of 20-year-old evidence is to do tests and test users a great injustice. It is true that tests were used in the past in ways that we now consider impermissible. It is also true that the laws governing the use of tests called for applications that we now see as inappropriate. But the tests still give information that can be of great value in educational and clinical diagnosis, personnel selection and placement, and vocational counseling. It is the responsibility of test users to see that current practices ensure that all people receive benefit, not harm, from testing. It is toward these issues that the final chapters in Part IV of this book are directed.

NOTE

1. This chapter has been written in an informal style, with a minimum of citations. A more complete discussion of the issues included here can be found in Thorndike (1990). A brief list of other useful reference works on the history of the assessment of human abilities and individual differences is included at the end of the chapter.

REFERENCES

Cattell, R. B. (1943). The measurement of adult intelligence. *Psychological Bulletin, 40,* 153–193.

Cattell, R. B. (1963). Theory of fluid and crystallized intelligence: A critical experiment. *Journal of Educational Psychology, 54,* 1–22.

Dickson, V. E. (1922). The Oakland plan. In L. M. Terman, V. E. Dickson, A. H. Sutherland, R. H. Franzen, C. R. Tupper, & G. Fernald (Eds.), *Intelligence tests and school reorganization* (pp. 30–50). Yonkers, NY: World Book.

Guilford, J. P. (1959). Three faces of intellect. *American Psychologist, 14,* 459–479.

Hart, B., & Spearman, C. (1912). General ability, its existence and nature. *British Journal of Psychology, 5,* 51–84.

Hartigan, J. A., & Wigdor, A. K. (Eds.). (1989). *Fairness in employment testing: Validity generalization, minority issues, and the General Aptitude Test Battery.* Washington, DC: National Academy Press.

Horn, J. L. (1985). Remodeling old models of intelligence. In B. B. Wolman (Ed.), *Handbook of intelligence* (pp. 267–300). New York: Wiley.

Horn, J. L., & Cattell, R. B. (1966). Refinement and test of the theory of fluid and crystallized ability intelligences. *Journal of Educational Psychology, 57,* 253–270.

Jensen, A. R. (1980). *Bias in mental testing.* New York: Free Press.

Kirkpatrick, E. A. (1900). Individual tests of school children. *Psychological Review, 7,* 274–280.

Norsworthy, N. (1906). The psychology of mentally deficient children. *Archives of Psychology, 1.*

Peterson, J. (1925). *Early conceptions of tests of intelligence.* Yonkers, NY: World Book.

Pintner, R. (1931). *Intelligence testing* (2nd ed.). New York: Holt.

Simpson, B. R. (1912). *Correlations of mental abilities.* (Contributions to Education No. 53). New York: Teachers College Bureau of Publications.

Spearman, C. (1904). "General intelligence," objectively determined and measured. *American Journal of Psychology, 15,* 201–293.

Spearman, C. (1920). Manifold sub-theories of "the two factors." *Psychological Review, 29,* 159–172.

Terman, L. M. (1916). *The measurement of intelligence.* Boston: Houghton Mifflin.

Terman, L. M. (1919). *The intelligence of school children.* Boston: Houghton Mifflin.

Terman, L. M. (1920) The use of intelligence tests in grading school children. *Journal of Educational Research, 1,* 20–32.

Terman, L. M., Dickson, V. E., Sutherland, A. H., Franzen, R. H., Tupper, C. R., & Fernald, G. (Eds.). (1922). *Intelligence tests and school reorganization.* Yonkers, NY: World Book.

Thorndike, E. L. (1903). *Educational psychology.* New York: Science Press.

Thorndike, E. L. (1920a). The reliability and significance of tests of intelligence. *Journal of Educational Psychology, 11,* 284–287.

Thorndike, E. L. (1920b). Intelligence and its uses. *Harper's Magazine, 140,* 227–235.

Thorndike, E. L. (1921). On the organization of intellect. *Psychological Review, 28,* 141–151.

Thorndike, E. L., Bregman, E. O., Cobb, M. V., & Woodyard, E. (1926). *The measurement of intelligence.* New York: Teachers College Bureau of Publications.

Thorndike, E. L., Lay, W., & Dean, P. R. (1909). The relation of accuracy in sensory discrimination to general intelligence. *American Journal of Psychology, 20,* 364–369.

Thorndike, R. L., Hagen, E. P., & Sattler, J. M. (1986). *Stanford–Binet Intelligence Scale: Fourth Edition.* Chicago: Riverside.

Thorndike, R. M. (1990). *A century of ability testing.* Chicago: Riverside.

Thurstone, L. L. (1938). Primary mental abilities. *Psychometric Monographs* (No. 1).

Thurstone, L. L., & Thurstone, T. G. (1941). Factorial studies of intelligence. *Psychometric Monographs,* (No. 2).

Warner, F. (1890). *A course of lectures on the growth and means of training the mental faculty.* Cambridge, England: Cambridge University Press.

Wechsler, D. (1939). *The measurement of adult intelligence.* Baltimore: Williams & Wilkins.

Wolf, T. H. (1973). *Alfred Binet.* Chicago: University of Chicago Press.

Yerkes, R. M., Bridges, J. W., & Hardwick, R. S. (1915). *A point scale for measuring ability.* Baltimore: Warwick & York.

Yerkes, R. M., & Wood, L. (1916). Methods of expressing results of measurements of intelligence: Coefficient of intelligence. *Journal of Educational Psychology, 7,* 593–606.

SUGGESTED FURTHER READING

Anastasi, A. (1958). *Differential psychology* (3rd ed.). New York: Macmillan.

Anastasi, A. (1965). *Individual differences.* New York: Wiley.

DuBois, P. H. (1970). *A history of psychological testing.* Boston: Allyn & Bacon.

Jenkins, J. J., & Paterson, D. G. (1961). *Studies in individual differences.* New York: Appleton-Century-Crofts.

Rogers, T. B. (1995). *The psychological testing enterprise.* Pacific Grove, CA: Brooks/Cole.

Tyler, L. E. (1965). *The psychology of human differences* (3rd ed.). New York: Appleton-Century-Crofts.

CHAPTER 2

The History
of Test Development

RICHARD F. ITTENBACH

IRVIN G. ESTERS

HOWARD WAINER

THE HISTORY OF TEST DEVELOPMENT

"We understand best," said Aristotle in his *Metaphysics*, "those things we see grow from their very beginnings." Thus, to understand fully the status and future of intellectual assessment one must appreciate the forces shaping the origins and evolution of the field from its formal inception in the 1880s to the practice-oriented accomplishments of today. Better still, one should put the modern period of testing and assessment into a temporal, historical, and professional context that begins with the earliest thinkers of the Western world. Test development, like so many other professions within psychology and education, is a product of many contributors and disciplines throughout history.

From the origins of measurement to the multitrait, multifactor theories of today, tests designed to reveal important aspects of human intelligence have changed markedly little over the centuries. However, no longer are the topics of intelligence and intellectual assessment the sole province of academics and psychological service providers. The discipline's veil of protective anonymity has long since disappeared. The field of intellectual assessment and the test development industry, have moved quickly and unashamedly into the spotlight of the national media and into the mainstream of American business. Developers of intellectual tests must now respond to the many educational, psychological, and sociological forces that shape all aspects of American life, forces that extend well beyond what the early theorists ever intended.

The purpose of this chapter is to lay a foundation for a more complete discussion of contemporary and emerging trends in the field of intellectual assessment by tracing the development of tests from the earliest of times to the technically more sophisticated scaling methods of today. The chapter is organized into three broad sections: historical and philosophical foundations, the practice of testing, and advances in technology. A discussion of these topics follows.

HISTORICAL AND PHILOSOPHICAL FOUNDATIONS

If a system for assigning values to intellectual abilities lies at the heart of the assessment process, it seems prudent to first present a foundational account of measurement and the measurement process. Measurement is considered to be the process by which numerical values are assigned to the characteristics or conditions of people, places, or events according to some rule. *According to some rule,* in this case, represents socially and scientifically agreed on criteria for classification.

As early as 3000 B.C., efforts to understand the world and its events were guided by a mixture of science, magic, and religion. It was not until the arrival of fixed units of measurement that common ground was found for the widespread and consistent use of measurement principles. When the Babylonians first defined a foot equal to 20 fingers and a cubit equal to 30 fingers, they began the process of standardizing units of measurement. It was not until approximately 2000 B.C., however, that a year was held to consist of 12 months or 360 days (Dampier, 1948). So much time and so many important breakthroughs have evolved since these early discoveries, yet the world of mental abilities continues to remain a challenging if not daunting task some 5,000 years later.

Once early measurement principles moved from discovery to application, advances came more quickly. Navigation on water and land, the production of food, clothing, and medicine, and the benefits of mercantilism marked many of the early applications of rudimentary measurement principles. Formalized testing procedures were present in China as early as 2000 B.C. (e.g., Anastasi, 1988; DuBois, 1970; Teng, 1943; Wainer, 1990). There is evidence as early as the 11th century B.C. of multistage evaluations and the notion that observations of performances made under controlled conditions could be generalized to other less formal settings (Teng, 1943). Moreover, there is an account in the Old Testament of a one-item military test, with a cut score, devised to help Gideon reduce the size of his army before entering battle with the Midianites. Gideon took the soldiers of his army to the Jordan River and ordered them to drink. Those who lowered their heads and "lapped up the water like a dog" were discharged; the 300 who maintained a watchful posture, raising the water to their mouths with their hands, heads up and eyes open, were retained (*Judges, 7:1–8*). As with many performance assessments, there is no record of the reliability or validity of the test.

Psychologists and educators trained in the practice of assessment will readily recognize the link between the aforementioned example and today's rationale for generalization of observations across settings. Less well-known, perhaps, is the rationale behind the practice of assessment and the dry, rather formal, routine manner in which it typically occurs. Philosophically and scientifically, the act of assessment is a quest for truth and reality. It is a means by which the examiner's hypotheses are identified and then tested within the context of the scientific method (Messick, 1988). In the spirit of true Cartesian philosophy, if the method of inquiry can be made correct, truth will reveal itself; in this case, the true pattern of an individual's underlying skills and abilities. At the most basic level, it is this quest for revealing the fundamentals of truth and reality that served as the point of origin for all scientific thought.

Do test results represent the reality of underlying abilities? The answer to that question will likely depend on who is asked. The early Greeks believed that an accurate and orderly interpretation of natural events was possible, and that not all natural events were the results of the random and unpredictable will of the gods. Thales (c. 585 B.C.), for instance, is considered to be a major philosophical figure in the history of Western thought. When Thales offered his explanation for a solar eclipse as the product of a consistent, natural order that was both predictable and observable, he was abandoning the practice of mythological explanations of naturally occurring events. Moreover, when he offered his ideas for public scrutiny, allowing them to be accepted or rejected on their own merits, he was opening the door for other Greek thinkers to begin the struggle for the discovery of the fundamental concepts of truth and reality (Ittenbach & Swindell, 1993). Thales would have had an ally in many of the later, post-Renaissance thinkers such as Albert Einstein, whose familiar phrase, "I shall never believe that God plays dice with the world," tacitly represents his notion that "reality is invariant, [and] that a real external world exists to be discovered by scientific research" (Paul, 1982, p. 56).

Although the influence of such prominent classical philosophers as Socrates, Plato, and Aristotle on everyday life is important, their influence is even more profound for students of research. Not only did these early thinkers extend and further strengthen the importance of truth and reason to epistemology, but, with Aristotle, they established the ground rules for contemporary scientific inquiry. In contrast to his immediate predecessors, the Sophists, Socrates believed in fixed and stable truths. Leading a virtuous life meant pursuing knowledge, a knowledge that was synonymous with truth. Many of today's service providers would, through their work as educational and psychological investigators, like to view themselves as operating in a similar vein.

But would it not be possible to pursue these unobservable truths without resorting to numbers and mathematical operations? Perhaps, but Plato (Socrates' premier student) believed in the importance of math to the curriculum, and the importance of formalized instruction. For Plato, genuine knowledge was made possible only through a "systematic, coherent account of reality in which each conclusion is rationally justified," and that "what is particular, observable, and concrete must be understood in terms of higher-level principles that are comprehensive, theoretical, and abstract" (Ittenbach & Lawhead, in press). Similar to his philosophical contemporaries, the Pythagoreans, and his later scientific descendants, Copernicus, Kepler, and Galileo, Plato believed that mathematical reasoning allowed one to look beyond physical appearances to timeless ideas and ultimate reality. Even at this early time in recorded history, math was beginning to play a prominent role in the quest for better understanding unobservable truths and realities. "To count is modern practice," Samuel Johnson summarized, "the ancient method was to guess." But, of course, Seneca was aware of the difference: "*Magnum esse solem philosophus probabit, quantus sit mathematicus*" (Epistulae, 88.27).

Aristotle, the greatest scientist of the classical era, offered early science the most profound contributions. It was Aristotle who made the distinction between the applied and theoretical sciences. He believed theoretical science was the pursuit of science for its own sake while practical science consisted of knowledge that could be used to influence a particular course of events. One can easily see the origin of the distinction between basic and applied science in this taxonomy. In this regard, intellectual assessment represents a key factor in both the applied and theoretical sides of psychology's quest to understand human intellectual functioning. Aristotle, an ardent inductivist, believed that in all observable phenomena were general properties and essences that could be observed and attributed to all members of a class. He would very likely have allies in the differential psychologists of today. For example, the famous psychometrician Harold Gulliksen (personal communication, 1965) pointed out that the "difference between basic and applied research is that basic research has so many more applications."

THE PRACTICE OF TESTING

Any historical treatment of intellectual assessment must, out of necessity, weave together a number of seemingly disparate topics ranging from the formal beginnings of testing to the highly sophisticated measurement theories of today. Serving as the bridge between these supporting structures of intellectual assessment are brief discussions of the early clash between theory and practice, the reliability and stability of modern measurement, and the evolution of test validity, topics that present a rather technical side of what is supposed to be a humanistic, service-oriented activity.

Birth of Standardized Testing

British mathematician and physician Sir Francis Galton (1822–1911) is generally recognized as the founder of formal testing. However, it is the American psychologist James McKeen Cattell (1860–

1944) who is given credit for coining the term "mental tests." Though both worked together to propel the field of mental testing forward in large and definable units, it is Cattell's work under the renowned German experimental psychologist Wilhelm Wundt (1832–1920) that provided him with the notion that testing needed to occur. Wundt, like so many physiologists before him, was interested in discovering laws of behavior responsible for human sensation and perception. Cattell was interested in the latency of mental operations, even to the point of seeking a position in Wundt's laboratory in Leipzig, but had neither the will nor the inclination to study the physiology of perception at the deep, organic level of Wundt and his other colleagues. Instead, Cattell proposed studying perceptual differences between individuals.

Cattell believed that general laws of behavior were most likely to be revealed by examining differences among individuals. This belief did not mesh well with those of other colleagues in the German laboratory. However, he did find support from his next colleague, Galton, a researcher with a vast array of interests and abilities, and the first person to study individual differences systematically (Minton & Schneider, 1980). Galton's interest in the inheritance of mental abilities stems largely from the evolutionary work of his cousin, Charles Darwin (1809–1882), and Darwin's interest in the new theory of natural selection. If Darwin could find evidence to suggest the inheritance of physical traits, could Galton not do the same for mental abilities? Galton not only believed that he could generate such evidence but believed sufficiently enough in the laws of heredity to begin the process of large-scale testing by recruiting and paying people at the 1884 International Exposition in London to provide him with their sensory data.

Galton's early influence on Cattell extended well beyond their shared interests in eugenics and the measurement of mental abilities. In addition, Galton's laboratory had something that Wundt's laboratory did not have, a mathematician and statistician of the first order, Karl Pearson (1857–1936). Pearson was able to derive the mathematical underpinnings of regression (then referred to as reversion), correlation, and covariation of observable phenomena in a manner that allowed Galton to make inferences about unobservable phenomena. In this case, the unobservable phenomena represented higher-order abilities that Galton believed were both latent and responsible for variations in sensorimotor performances. As a team, Galton and Pearson have rewritten the rules by which psychologists evaluate their subjects. Their correlation coefficients continue to be used as the basis for reliability and validity coefficients in educational and psychological testing today.[1] Galton had the ideas and rationale for explaining how abilities covaried in nature, but his student Karl Pearson had the mathematical acumen to sell it to the world (Ittenbach & Lawhead, in press).

On his return to the United States in 1988, Cattell tested and analyzed the abilities of his students in an experimental psychology class at the University of Pennsylvania using his new *mental tests* (Dahlstrom, 1985). Were it not for the early influence of Wundt, the insight of Galton, the statistical deftness of Pearson, and the persistence and determination of the then up-and-coming young American psychologist James McKeen Cattell, the field of intellectual assessment might have evolved along very different lines. For it is in his paper, *Mental Tests and Measurements,* that Cattell first proposed that mental abilities could be objectively measured through formalized testing (French & Hale, 1990). Consistent with the spirit of American functionalism, the field of experimental psychology now had a proponent for "a practical, test oriented approach to the study of mental processes" (Schultz & Schultz, 1987, p. 146).

Theory vs. Practice

Theories of intelligence are useful to the extent that they provide psychologists and educators with a means of understanding the intellectual functioning of children, adolescents, and adults. For some, intelligence is an intricate and highly sophisticated construct replete with specifications for accomplishment. These are the explicit theories of intelligence. For others, the implicit theories of intelligence are often little more than an intuitively understood set of ideas. Formal, commercially produced instruments are used to investigate the former with casual and informal methods used to better understand the latter. According to Weinberg (1989), far more assessments of intelligence take place in the real world than in the laboratories, classrooms, and diagnostic test centers of the world.

Most psychologists involved in assessment at any level can recall that the first actual test of intelligence was developed by the French psychologist Alfred Binet. Lost among many students of the discipline is the realization that two other French clinicians, Victor Henri and Theodore Simon, also played a major role in the development of the first scale (Schultz & Schultz, 1987). The first edition of the Binet scale was published in 1905 as a 30-item *Measuring Scale of Intelligence* (Binet & Simon, 1905) and resulted from Binet's belief that most tests prior to that time were far too narrow in scope to reveal much about the learning process. Four formal revisions of the Binet scale (Terman, 1916; Terman & Merrill, 1937, 1960; Thorndike, Hagen, & Sattler, 1986) were subsequently published in the United States, and all four of the psychometric descendants have done much to define the way intelligence has been conceptualized and defined in America and throughout the world.

Binet's original scale was not theory driven, which reinforces Boring's (1923) contention that up to that time, intelligence could be defined most succinctly as what the tests test. The 1905 Binet version represented a collection of tasks and activities that extended far beyond traditional reading and writing, skills typically assessed through normal academic channels. Although the "Stanford–Binet has served as the standard of intellectual assessment for nearly a century," it may be ironic to many that the "Wechsler intelligence scales have served as the workhorse" (Beirne-Smith, Patton, & Ittenbach, 1994, p. 111). Similar to Binet, Wechsler was also a clinician, first and foremost. Weschler believed that intelligence was a unitary trait and was best explained through performances over a wide range of intellectual activities. Neither the original Binet scale nor the original Wechsler scales (Wechsler Intelligence Scale for Children [WISC; Wechsler, 1949], Wechsler Adult Intelligence Scale [WAIS; Wechsler, 1955], Wechsler Preschool and Primary Scale of Intelligence [WPPSI; Wechsler, 1967]) were built on any theoretical base; they were simply a collection of tasks divided along verbal and motoric lines. They were a clinician's test. That is, they provided the information needed for optimum service delivery at the time.[2]

Most tests developed since publication of the original Binet and Wechsler scales, and most certainly those developed within the past 10 to 15 years, have been theory driven or at least based on a preexisting theory of intellectual functioning. Factor-analytic research conducted using theories developed over the past century have emphasized one of two models: a hierarchical one-factor theory (*g*) espoused by such researchers as Jensen (1980), Spearman (1927), and Vernon (1950), or a multifactored theory proposed by such investigators as Gardner (1983), Guilford (1967), Horn (1985), Sternberg (1985), Thorndike (1927), and Thurstone (1938). Most practitioners, however, place these models on a continuum and conceptualize intelligence as some combination of the two. That is, they respect the notion of *g* but accept the premise of multidimensionality (Urbach, 1974).

Despite the practical and beguiling nature of the aforementioned theories, Cattell (1957) contended that any systematic treatment of important psychological constructs must also take into account the nuances of the observers and the instruments used to gather the information. That is, the construct of interest cannot be explained without also addressing other, naturally occurring forces and factors that serve to influence the status of the presumed effect. Psychologists' preoccupation with measurement and measurement error likely stems from early theoreticians' work advancing the discipline of psychology while defining measurement principles in mathematical and statistical terms. Underlying latent factors represented by correlation coefficients represented a major theoretical advancement for early psychometrists. Defining an instrument's credibility using those correlation coefficients represented quite another. Spearman's (1904) early work in the reliability of measurement is considered seminal in this regard.

Since Spearman's time, psychologists and educators have been trained to identify a test's reliability using three basic markers: internal consistency, alternate forms, and test–retest. As recently as the 1950s, there was evidence to suggest that "test reliability" and "trait stability" were not synonymous terms (Cattell, 1957). For Cattell, understanding the characteristics of a trait (or construct) was very different from understanding how a test behaved under similar conditions. According to McGrew, Werder, and Woodcock (1991), some traits, such as those associated with long-term fund of information (e.g., quantitative ability and verbal ability), remain stable over time whereas other skills such as short-term memory, visual processing, and attention skills may fluctuate markedly. According to McGrew et al., highly valid tests should reflect these phenomena.

Recent developments in statistical methodology and computer technology have demonstrated that the three historical measures of reliability may be too simplistic to represent changes in human traits as adequately as desired. Worse, the measures may even misrepresent a test's ability to reliably track those changes. McArdle and Woodock (1991) have taken Cattell's (1957) notion of a *stability coefficient* well beyond what the original author ever intended. Through the use of linear structural (LISREL) modeling relations, McArdle and Woodock have demonstrated that such factors as test reliability, test stability, trait change, and trait stability can all be accounted for within the framework of a single statistical model. Even in the context of the most sophisticated models, however, if the conditions change (either internal or external), the likelihood of true replicability also changes. Hence, even when the probability of error approaches zero, no guarantee of validity remains.

Psychometric Validity

The textbook definition provided in many testing classes typically presents validity as a version of Garrett's original definition: "The degree to which a test measures what it was intended to measure" (Garrett, 1937, p. 324). Although this definition is no longer adequate to judge the validity of the testing process, at the turn of the century it was sufficient. For example, who was better able to determine the value and usefulness of Cattell's scale with college students in 1886 than the author? Or, who better to judge the utility of Binet and Simon's early scale with children experiencing learning problems in 1904 than the architects of the instruments themselves? Probably no one. Until the 1930s and 1940s, when it became apparent that all tests were not appropriate for all persons, the authors and publishers of the instruments were considered the experts on the validity of their instruments. After all, they were the ones who lived with the constructs represented by their instruments. If others did not agree with their approach, they were free to design their own instruments, which many did. For example, many versions of the first American Binet never took hold before Louis Terman's 90-item *Stanford Revision and Extension of the Binet-Simon Intelligence Scale* in 1916.

Guilford's (1946) claim that validity was demonstrated anytime an instrument correlated with a measure similar to the one of interest, but external to the test itself, represented another important perspective on the early concept of validity. Guilford's view was important in that it reflected both the spirit of the times and the empirical, associationist position of his ideological predecessors Galton, Pearson, and Spearman. In short, the proof was in the correlations. That psychometricians worldwide continue to demand correlation-based validity coefficients nearly a century after their development speaks highly of their perceived value to practitioners and professionals alike. Much of that preference has to do with the fact that testing and correlation evolved at the same time and emanated from the same (Galton's) laboratory. The discipline of statistics was quick to find alternatives to Pearson's correlations; psychology and education have been much slower to respond.[3]

Among the more recent perspectives on validity is content validity. Historically, the concept of matching test items to a prescribed curriculum is older than the correlational method. However, content validity did not receive equal status with criterion and construct validity (to be mentioned in subsequent paragraphs) until the American Psychological Association (APA) listed it in its 1954 edition of *Technical Recommendations for Psychological Tests and Diagnostic Techniques* as one of the four principal types of test validity (content, predictive, concurrent, construct). Content validity's contribution to the broader construct of test validity is in the breadth and adequacy with which a test measures a construct (Nunnally, 1978). Levine (1976) credits Rice (1915) and Riley (cited in Trabue, 1924) with establishing the practice of matching standardized items and tests with curricular content to produce grade-by-grade standards for achievement. It appears that early test theorists conceptualized content validity even if they did not have the name.

By 1966, the number of different types of validity mentioned in the APA's new standards manual had decreased from four to three, putting two specific types of validity, predictive and concurrent, under one broader category referred to as criterion-related validity. For purposes of this chapter, criterion validity is defined as a test score's tendency to relate systematically to one or more outcome criteria. The most obvious difference between the two specific cases, predictive and concurrent, relates to the time the outcome criteria are obtained. If a test score correlates with a future measure of performance, the test is said to have predictive criterion validity. If a test score correlates with a measure of performance obtained simultaneously, the test has concurrent criterion validity. As with content validity, the practice of establishing criterion validity must have existed prior to its official name. As indicated previously, underlying abilities inferred from a high calculated covariation of observable phenomena served as the conceptual basis for Pearson's correlation coefficient. Equally important, however, is the notion that a valid test should also have a *low* (zero) correlation with irrelevant variables. For example, as described in Flanagan (1948), Fredriksen found that verbal ability had a high correlation with performance in an armed forces machinist's training program whereas mechanical aptitude had a low correlation. These early psychometricians found that the grade in a machinist's training was given on the basis of a paper-and-pencil test. Consequently, Fredriksen developed a more "hands-on" test in which aviation students actually had to do things *mechanically,* thereby yielding a correlation with mechanical aptitude that soared and a correlation with verbal ability that dropped.

Construct validity remains the third and broadest type of test validity. Described simply as a test score's tendency to relate systematically with the construct of interest, it remains a difficult concept for new students of psychometrics. Although students of psychology can comprehend the notion of correlating one variable with another (criterion validity), the concept of correlating a set of test performances with an unobservable construct is a bit more elusive. In practice, and using the simplest-case scenario, construct validity is established by correlating test scores with an operationally defined representative of the construct, such as a well-accepted measure of IQ (e.g., Stanford–Binet Intelligence Scale: Fourth Edition [SB-IV; Thorndike et al.,1986]; WISC-III, [Wechsler,1991]) for the construct of human intelligence. Though the term "construct validity" and a brief explanation of it first appeared in the APA's 1954 standards manual, Cronbach and Meehl's (1955) article, "Construct Validity in Psychological Tests," represents the foundational presentation of this concept (Angoff, 1988).

A trend has been building within the psychometric community for over a decade in which all types of validity presented here, and others mentioned elsewhere (e.g., face validity, convergent validity, and divergent validity) are all subsumed under the broader heading of construct validity. Messick (1993) labeled this phenomenon "unified validity." Unified validity is considered an extension of construct validity and operates on the realization that test validity is not the property of a test per se, but of the inferences made from the test scorers. The verification of a test's validity must include all the uses to which the test scores will be put. At a deeper level, the process of validation represents a verification of the inferences and interpretations that are drawn from a test's results (Angoff, 1988). Messick (1993) summarizes the mission of unified validity well, stating that "the essence of unified validity is that the appropriateness, meaningfulness, and usefulness of score-based inferences are inseparable and that the unifying force behind this integration is the trustworthiness of empirically grounded score interpretation" (p. i).

Increasingly, the aim of assessment instruments is to use score-based inferences. The goal of some modern tests is to aid in the development of diagnoses and subsequent treatment plans based on strengths and weaknesses evidenced by subtest scores. Although many professionals and practitioners have been critical of this use of intelligence tests, the practice persists. This type of validity is commonly known as diagnostic-treatment validity, and although not considered an example of a classical measure of validity, it has been addressed in the technical manual of at least one major assessment instrument (cf. Kaufman & Kaufman, 1993b). Diagnostic validity has been evident in the differential diagnoses of right or left brain-lobe impairment, depression, and Alzheimer's-type dementia. With the movement of intelligence tests toward the testing of multiple intelligences and thus becoming broader in scope, the demonstration of diagnostic-treatment validity may become more prevalent.

Currently, a popular application of diagnostic-treatment validity is in the formulation and administration of learning prescriptions based on aptitude, or *aptitude-treatment interaction* (ATI). This is most evident in the *learning styles* movement seen in some areas of education. The application of learning styles to improve students' learning has received little support in the literature. In fact, "no ATI is as yet understood well enough to be practically reliable for prescriptive use" (R. E. Snow, personal communication, August 28, 1996).

Measurement Theory

If the chronology of human intelligence is short by historical standards, the history of its measurement is even shorter. A special committee of the British Association for the Advancement of Science was assembled in 1932 to study problems of measurement. The final report came out 8 years later in 1940 (Stevens, 1946). Not that investigators were not using and applying measurement principles prior to that time; undoubtedly they were. The techniques used to analyze the measurement components of the various instruments were far less sophisticated than their current counterparts.

Even Binet looked for age-related differences in test performance—that children of average intellect who were 10 years old should score higher than children of average intellect who were 9 years old. Shortly after the turn of the century, Courdis was applying the same rationale to children of different grades for arithmetic performance (cited in Levine, 1976). By 1914, William Stern had developed the quotient Terman would later popularize as the IQ score (mental age ÷ chronological age × 100), and by 1915, Yerkes, Bridges, and Hardwick had developed the first point scale, a forerunner of today's standard scores (French & Hale, 1990). However, these scales were appropriate for norming purposes only and did not tell the test authors anything about the relationship between the items, the abilities of the persons taking the tests, or the constructs themselves.

Traditional test theory has gone under many names, true score theory being the most predominant. The key notion in true score theory is that a person's obtained score on a test, expressed perhaps as a percentage of items answered correctly, is only the observed manifestation of what might have occurred if the test had been much longer. Thus, the score that is observed is composed of the person's true score obtained from a hypothetical test of infinite length plus some error. Two joint goals of test theory were to suggest ways to minimize that error within the bounds of practicality and to characterize the size of the error honestly. As should be clear from this brief description, true score theory is closely tied to the examinee's responses on the total test. Although it is virtually never called by such a name, an evocative, alternative name for such a theory might be test response theory.

The focus on the total test as the unit of measurement led naturally to summary measures with the same focus. Examinees' scores are expressed as a percentage of items on the test answered correctly, with error being in the same metric. Measures of the stability of scores, usually called reliability, are essentially correlations of observed scores with hypothetical replicates of themselves. Although there are measures of the performance of individual items, they too are keyed to the performance on the total test. For example, it is usually considered important that each item be related to the total test score. The extent to which this occurs is often measured by a correlation of one's performance on the item with one's overall performance on the test (biserial or point biserial correlations). Just as a person's score is represented by the proportion of items answered correctly, an item's difficulty is characterized by the proportion of people who answered it correctly.

The weakness of true score theory is that it is tied to the specific test and to the specific group of people who take it. Thus, both kinds of measures are always relative. There is nothing explicit in true score theory that allows it to separate the two possible explanations for any result. An examinee could be very able or the test could be very easy. An item could have been very hard, or those who answered it very dim—or anything in between. These kinds of indeterminacies are reduced through practical constraints on the testing situation. Alternative test forms are constructed to be parallel in content and difficulty; different examinee samples are equated through statistical adjustments to a common population. But such adjustments, though eminently workable, are extratheoretical. If only for esthetic reasons, a more graceful theoretical structure is desirable.

Esthetics joined with practicality as the widespread availability of modern high-speed computing became a reality. The computer meant that mass testing could also be individualized. The challenge of accomplishing individualized mass testing held out the possibility of increasing precision while staying within practical constraints for test administration. It also meant that by crafting a test for each examinee individually, the effects of irrelevant items could be at least reduced if not eliminated entirely. However, to accomplish this, a theoretical structure had to be built that had as its center a smaller unit than the entire test. That unit would have to be characterized by some statistics that could describe its performance in various unforeseen contexts. To do this required the development of an item-based test theory. Such a theory grew, and its various versions have come to be called item response theory (IRT). ✻

An IRT model mixes parameters that characterize each item with those that characterize each person and tell us what will happen when a person of a certain ability level meets an item. It surmounts the true score problems associated with being tied to a particular test by hypothesizing the existence of a latent trait (e.g., reading proficiency, mathematics proficiency, general intelligence, and skeletal maturity). Each item is merely a specific manifestation generated by the examinee's (unobserved) position on this latent trait. Examinees' positions on this trait are commonly termed their "proficiency." Similarly, each item has a position on this same trait, but the item's location is its *difficulty*. If an item is much more difficult than the examinee is able, the IRT model predicts a low likelihood of a correct response. If a person is much more able than the item is difficult, the likelihood of a correct response is great. For each item there is a curve that relates examinee proficiency to the likelihood of a correct response to that item. The functional form of the curve is a graphical representation of the IRT model and is termed the item's characteristic curve (ICC).

Automated test construction chooses items on the basis of their ICCs to build a test that is, in some sense, optimized for the circumstance. It tries to choose items that are neither too hard nor too easy and, as the testing process progresses, constantly updates its estimate of the examinee's proficiency and so chooses the next item more wisely still. Finally, but most important, it can stop testing when it has reached a prespecified level of accuracy. This allows fairer testing because each individualized test will be as accurate as necessary for that individual rather than only on average over the entire examinee population.

IRT not only simplifies many of the problems of testing but also provides a measure of its own efficacy. Through various kinds of statistical fit statistics, it tells us whether its underlying assumptions (principally unidimensionality) are correct. Thus, although one might argue that a complex trait such as general intelligence cannot be well characterized by a single trait, the results of fitting the IRT model will provide an empirical test of that hypothesis. IRT also gracefully solves the problems of scaling, inherent in all testing, by tying everything to the metric of the underlying trait. This has profound implications. For example, suppose we have a test that consists of one essay and a set of 50 multiple-choice items. Further suppose that we have allowed 30 minutes for the essay and 30 minutes for the multiple-choice section. Tradition would have it that we give 1 point each for the multiple-choice questions and 50 points for the essay. Is this right? We are all familiar with the kinds of arguments that would support this sort of weighting, yet IRT offers empirical guidance on this point (remember Seneca's comment quoted earlier) by telling us quite precisely what the relative weights ought to be to ensure maximal precision. For nonpsychometric reasons we may want to deviate from this suggestion, but at least we will know the costs of such deviance.

IRT models provide us with a scale. This scale can be transformed to other, perhaps more convenient metrics. An ingenious utilization of these properties is the National Assessment of Educational Progress (NAEP) Scale. The NAEP Scale uses expert judges to characterize the level of accomplishment for key items in each of its testing areas. This characterization is then transformed numerically to match the IRT item difficulties. The scale is pieced together to be continuous for children over the entire range of school ages, thus providing us with a ruler that does not change as a child grows older. Having a single scale, a common currency if you will, has allowed the remarkable feat of placing the results of international assessments on the same scale. Such precision in measurement has only just begun to show its effects (Johnson & Zwick, 1988).

Lord and Novick (1968) provide the definitive source on true score theory,[4] as well as the first rigorous statement of the most general IRT models.[5] The Danish statistician George Rasch (1960/1980) describes a special case of an IRT model that, when appropriate, is both beautiful and useful. The most popular IRT models are based on a specific form of the ICC—the logistic function. The Rasch model is among the simplest characterizations of the logistic function because, under the Rasch model, all items count equally (their ICCs have equal slopes). More complex models allow items to have differential weights in the calculation of total score and allow for the possibility that an examinee can get an item correct by chance (guessing). The numerical simplicity that the Rasch model yields is only available when neither guessing nor differential item value is appreciable. The practical appeal of the Rasch model has declined with the availability of cheap, high-speed computing and improved numerical estimation algorithms, although the sweetness of its epistemological elegance lingers on.

IRT also provides us with a more natural way of assessing precision than the indirect correlational approach in use since Galton. The correlational approach to both test reliability and criterion validity is essentially a measure of similarity of ordering. If two forms of a test both order a group of examinees in essentially the same way, it is said to have high test–retest reliability. If test scores order examinees in about the same way as they are ordered on the criterion, it is said to have high predictive validity. Although such measures are undoubtedly useful, they have flaws. How does one obtain an ordering for just one examinee? Does this mean that if a test is administered to just one person it has no reliability? Or, perhaps that the accuracy of a bathroom scale depends on who else gets weighed? In addition, if a group of people are close together on some trait, reordering them in the same way on a second measurement is much more difficult than if the group was more heterogeneous. Learning that your salary will increase by 16 next year is worth much less than knowing if it is 16¢, $16, or 16%.

IRT provides a more attractive alternative: a standard error. Each estimate of item difficulty, examinee proficiency, or any other parameter is accompanied by a standard error. Thus we know that a score is, for example, 6 ± 2. Such a measure remains true regardless of who else is tested with you, even if you are the only one tested. Of course, more accurate tests are those with smaller standard errors. Standard errors can also be displayed as a function of score. For example, one test may be especially accurate for lower-scoring individuals, whereas another might be more accurate at the high end, and thence one may choose the most desirable test for the given situation.

How is the standard error determined? It consists of several factors:

1. The variability observed in an individual's behavior (in fatigue over the course of a test, idiosyncratic knowledge, etc.).
2. Variability introduced by human judges (i.e., in scoring an essay there will be variation across raters).
3. Variability due to specific choice of items asked (i.e., would an examinee get the same score on one essay topic as another?).

Of course, variability may also be due to various combinations of these and other factors. Through carefully designed studies one can estimate the amount of variation associated with each of these factors. This allows one an understanding of the causal path that must be taken to reduce error. For example, increasing the number of items on a test is likely to reduce the effect of item 3 on the list, better training for judges might reduce the likelihood of contamination related to the item 2 listed previously, and highly motivated examinees might minimize item 1. The decomposition of observed variation into its component parts is a well-understood statistical methodology (variance components analysis). Its application within the confines of testing and the design of experiments that allows the estimation of all the parts have been dubbed "generalizability theory" by its proponents (Cronbach, Gleser, Nanda, & Rajaratnam, 1972).

ADVANCES IN TECHNOLOGY

As alluded to previously, early tests of intelligence were heavily dependent on psychophysical equipment and manipulatives. Some examples include the equipment needed in the measurement of reaction times and other sensory and motor abilities and the use of tachistoscopes and formboards. The Binet–Simon Scale of 1905, the first formally published intelligence test, was also heavily dependent on observation and equipment. In this test, lighted matches, wooden cubes, food, and various weights used for comparison were commonplace. This reliance on equipment became less salient with the development of such tests as those used during the World War I era: namely, the Army Alpha and Army Beta, the Otis Group Intelligence Test, and the National Intelligence Test. The primary benefit of these paper-and-pencil tests was their applicability to large groups. Fass (1980) describes an unprecedented mass testing of 1.7 million men using the Army Alpha and Army Beta, alone.

A review of today's most popular IQ tests suggests that the move toward group testing did little to diminish the popularity of manipulatives and other forms of equipment. This is evident in the Wechsler scales (Wechsler, 1949, 1955, 1967, 1974, 1981, 1989, 1991), the Binet scales (Binet & Simon, 1905; Terman, 1916; Terman & Merrill, 1937, 1960; Thorndike et al., 1986), and the Kaufman scales (Kaufman & Kaufman, 1983, 1993a) over the past few decades. Manipulatives such as bead memory (Stanford–Binet IV), magic window (Kaufman Assessment Battery for Children [K-ABC; Kaufman & Kaufman, 1983]), picture arrangement and block design (WISC-III) exemplify this point. In addition, there is a move toward the use of computers in the administration, scoring, and report writing of not only intelligence tests but other measures, such as attitude, achievement, personality, and aptitude. Indeed, the rise of the computer revolution has been slow but deliberate with regard to testing over the last several decades (McCullough, 1990).

What might the future hold regarding intellectual assessment instruments? Let us first concede that predicting the future is a monumental task not without a considerable measure of uncertainty. That is, we can only draw from the past and the present, all the while acknowledging that speculation is just that—speculation. We must even consider the possibility of a future without intellectual assessment. It may be that the desire and need to assess intellectual abilities will be nonexistent in the future. In our predictions we must also be cognizant of emerging trends in the field. Many scientists have suggested that the advent of the computer ranks among the most important discoveries of the past century (Hammond, 1984). There is little reason to doubt a less than similar contribution to the field of intellectual assessment.

A logical argument at this point might be that the use of computers will anchor the format of future tests to what is essentially *paper and pencil,* with the only difference being the transposition of the test content onto the computer screen and the use of the keyboard as a replacement for the pencil. Others may argue that computer-assisted testing, especially adaptive testing, uses technology in a way that has revolutionized the practice of assessment and is likely to become increasingly popular in the future (Wainer, 1990). Essentially, computerized adaptive testing makes use of the best parts of both the group-administered tests (uniformity of situation and reduced cost) and individually administered tests (few inappropriately chosen items producing a *tailored* testing experience). With the assistance of computer technology, the actions of a well-trained test examiner can be emulated. As discussed earlier in this chapter, more is learned about test takers who are asked questions equal to their proficiency level in a given content area, computerized adaptive testing utilizes the following procedure: (1) a question is asked in the middle of the prospective ability range, (2) the next question is based on the examinee's response (if correct, the next question is harder, if incorrect, the next question is easier), and (3) this process continues until the examinee's proficiency level is established. The entire process may be likened to establishing *basals* and *ceilings* in such individually administered tests as the Binet and Weschler scales (cf. Wainer, 1990). As indicated previously, one would be hard pressed to identify one factor more crucial to the future of intelligence testing than the application of IRT as facilitated by the use of computers.

Given the increasing sophistication of computer technology in the 1980s and 1990s alone, it is clear that we are witnessing only the tip of the iceberg in regard to the use of technology in intellectual assessment. The introduction of CD-ROM guided interactive programs, presently seen only in high-tech entertainment systems, has the potential of assessing many of the skills presently observable in social contexts only. For example, social scenarios could be directed by answers keyed in by the respondent, with each answer guiding the future course of action. At the risk of delving into the realm of science fiction, it may be possible that one day technology will advance to the extent that the examiner and examinee will operate in virtual space or, for that matter, the examiner may not be human but a computer-generated *virtual examiner.* More realistically, the use of technology also has the potential for enabling examiners to interpret response patterns, thereby formulating a strategy analysis for different types of items as well as different types of examinees.

With our expanding knowledge of the link between the brain and human behavior and subsequent developments in measuring brain function come an interest in observable neurological pathways and their involvement in intellectual thought processes. Jensen (1981) reported that intelligence (g) was correlated with the speed and amplitude of electrical potentials evoked in the brain, as well as with other individual characteristics. Although little is known about the biochemical or physiological substrate of intelligence, it is exactly here that Jensen proposes to search for the very essence of g. Brain mapping, the recording of brain wave activities during various tasks, has great potential for contributing to the assessment process. Although not presently used in an intellectual assessment capacity, the emerging technologies in medicine, particularly positron emission tomography and computed axial tomography, may prove valuable in future avenues of intellectual assessment. Advances in medication must not be overlooked either. Nootropics, the *smart drugs* used in the treatment of Alzheimer's disease, may actually increase the normal brain's capabilities. Imagine the implications this might have for the accurate measurement of attempts to increase human intelligence! Regardless of one's confidence in these technologies as elements of progress, it is almost certain that cognitive theories coupled with neuropsychological perspectives will change the face of intellectual assessment as it is presently known.

Furthermore, one must not discount the contributions and implications of behavioral genetics. Could the future of intellectual assessment lie in the hands of a skilled geneticist? Might we expect someday for an analysis of DNA to render as much or more information about the intellect as today's paper-and-pencil tests? If this is so, will genetic engineering allow us to optimize the intellect of the unborn? Such a practice would also be accompanied by equally important discussions as to the ethics and morality of its use.

Regardless of the evolutionary path intellectual assessment pursues, one point is certain: Change will occur. This is especially true when we consider that intellectual assessment is a field in which change is one of the most salient constants. Whether or not this change will be in a predictable direction is unknown. We can only hope and await with eager anticipation the next generation of the tools to be wielded by the psychometrists of the future.

Acknowledgments

A special thanks is due to George McCloskey of The Psychological Corporation for his helpful suggestions regarding the direction of this chapter.

NOTES

1. Modern item response theory and generalizability theory provide better measures of precision and have now begun to supplant the now outdated correlational methods.

2. The reader is referred to R. M. Thorndike (Chapter 1, this volume) for a more complete description of the history and role of the Binet and Weschler scales in intellectual assessment.

3. Readers are referred to Cowles (1989) for a more complete discussion of the separation of many experimental psychologists from the associationists position of Galton and Pearson in favor of the classical position of Fisher.

4. As an easy introduction, Harold Gulliksen's (1950) book remains remarkably practical and accessible despite being 45 years old.

5. More details on IRT are available in Wainer's (1983) short, readable introduction, and Chapter 4 of his *Primer* (1990) on computerized adaptive testing. However, Lord's (1980) text remains the definitive source on this topic.

REFERENCES

American Psychological Association. (1954). *Technical recommendations for psychological tests and diagnostic techniques.* Washington, DC: Author.

American Psychological Association. (1966). *Standards for educational and psychological tests and manuals.* Washington, DC: Author.

Anastasi, A. (1988). *Psychological testing* (6th ed.). New York: Prentice-Hall.

Angoff, W. H. (1988). Validity: An evolving concept. In H. Wainer & H. I. Braun (Eds.), *Test validity* (pp. 19–32). Hillsdale, NJ: Erlbaum.

Beirne-Smith, M., Patton, J. R., & Ittenbach, R. F. (1994). *Mental retardation* (4th ed.). New York: Merrill/Prentice-Hall.

Binet, A., & Simon, T. (1905). Methodes nouvelles pour le diagnostic du niveau intellectuel des anormaux [A new method for the diagnosis of intellectual level of abnormal persons]. *L'annee Psychologique, 11,* 191–244.

Boring, E. G. (1923). Intelligence as the tests see it. *New Republic, 35,* 35–36.

Cattell, R. B. (1957). *Personality and motivation: Structure and measurement.* New York: World Book.

Cowles, M. (1989). *Statistics in psychology: An historical perspective.* Hillsdale, NJ: Erlbaum.

Cronbach, L. J., Gleser, G. C., Nanda, H., & Rajaratnam, N. (1972). *The dependability of behavioral measurements: Theory of generalizability for scores and profiles.* New York: Wiley.

Cronbach, L. J., & Meehl, P. E. (1955). Construct validity in psychological tests. *Psychological Bulletin, 52,* 281–302.

Dahlstrom, W. G. (1985). The development of psychological testing. In G. A. Kimble & K. Schlesinger (Eds.), *Topics in the history of psychology* (pp. 63–113). Hillsdale, NJ: Erlbaum.

Dampier, W. C. (1948). *A history of science: And its relations with philosophy and religion.* London: Cambridge University Press.

DuBois, P. H. (1970). *A history of psychological testing.* Boston: Allyn & Bacon.

Fass, P. S. (1980). The IQ: A cultural and historical framework. *American Journal of Education, 88,* 431–458.

Flanagan, J. C. (1948). *The Aviation Psychology Program in the Army Air Forces.* (Report 1, AAF Aviation Psychology Program Research Reports). Washington, DC: U.S. Government Printing Office.

French, J. L., & Hale, R. L. (1990). A history of the development of psychological and educational testing. In C. R. Reynolds & R. W. Kamphaus (Eds.), *Handbook of psychological and educational assessment of children: Intelligence and Achievement* (pp. 3–28). New York: Guilford Press.

Gardner, H. (1983). *Frames of the mind: The theory of multiple intelligences.* New York: Basic Books.

Garrett, H. E. (1937). *Statistics in psychology and education.* New York: Longmans, Green.

Guilford, J. P. (1946). New standards for test evaluation. *Educational and Psychological Measurement, 6,* 427–438.

Guilford, J. P. (1967). *The nature of human intelligence.* New York: McGraw-Hill.

Gulliksen, H. O. (1950). *Theory of mental tests.* New York: Wiley. (Reprinted in 1987, Hillsdale, NJ: Erlbaum)

Hammond, A. (Ed.). (1984). Century of sciences: 20 Discoveries that changed our lives. *Science '84, 5*(9).

Horn, J. L. (1985). Remodelling old models of intelligence. In B. B. Wolman (Ed.), *Handbook of intelligence: Theories, measurements, and applications* (pp. 267–300). New York: Wiley.

Ittenbach, R. F., & Lawhead, W. F. (in press). Historical and philosophical foundations of single-case research. In R. D. Franklin, D. B. Allison, & B. S. Gorman (Eds.), *Design and analysis of single-case research.* Hillsdale, NJ: Erlbaum.

Ittenbach, R. F., & Swindell, L. K. (1993, December). Empiricism and early scientific thought. *Teaching Statistics in the Health Sciences,* p. 1–4.

Jensen, A. R. (1980). *Bias in mental testing.* New York: Free Press.

Jensen, A. R. (1981). *Straight talk about mental tests.* New York: Free Press.

Johnson, E. G., & Zwick, R. J. (1988). *The NAEP technical report.* Princeton, NJ: Educational Testing Service.

Kaufman, A. S., & Kaufman, N. L. (1983). *Kaufman Assessment Battery for Children* (K-ABC). Circle Pines, MN: American Guidance Service.

Kaufman, A. S., & Kaufman, N. L. (1993a). *Kaufman Adolescent and Adult Intelligence Test* (KAIT). Circle Pines, MN: American Guidance Service.

Kaufman, A. S., & Kaufman, N. L. (1993b). *Kaufman Adolescent and Adult Intelligence Test Manual.* Circle Pines, MN: American Guidance Service.

Levine, M. (1976). The academic achievement test: Its historical context and social functions. *American Psychologist, 31,* 228–237.

Lord, F. M. (1980). *Applications of item response theory to practical testing problems.* Hillsdale, NJ: Erlbaum.

Lord, F. M., & Novick, M. R. (1968). *Statistical theories of mental test scores.* Reading, MA: Addison-Wesley.

McArdle, J. J., & Woodcock, R. W. (1991). *A repeated measures reliability analysis of the Woodcock–Johnson Psycho-Educational Battery—Revised.* Unpublished manuscript, University of Virginia.

McCullough, C. S. (1990). Computerized assessment. In C. R. Reynolds & R. W. Kamphaus (Ed.), *Handbook of psychological and educational assessment of children: Intelligence and achievement* (pp. 723–747). New York: Guilford Press.

McGrew, K. S., Werder, J. K., & Woodcock, R. W. (1991). *WJ-R Technical manual.* Chicago: Riverside.

Messick, S. (1988). The once and future issues of validity: Assessing the meaning and consequences of measurement. In H. Wainer & H. I. Braun (Eds.), *Test validity* (pp. 33–45). Hillsdale, NJ: Erlbaum.

Messick, S. (1993). *Foundations of validity: Meaning and consequences in psychological assessment.* Princeton, NJ: Educational Testing Service.

Minton, H. L., & Schneider, F. W. (1980). *Differential psychology.* Prospect Heights, IL: Waveland.

Nunnally, J. C. (1978). *Psychometric theory* (2nd ed.). New York: McGraw-Hill.

Paul, I. (1982). *Science, theology, and Einstein.* New York: Oxford University Press.

Rasch, G. (1980). *Probabilistic models for some intelligence and attainment tests.* Chicago: University of Chicago Press. (Original work published 1960)

Rice, J. M. (1915). *Scientific management in education.* London: Harrap.

Schultz, D. P., & Schultz, S. E. (1987). *A history of modern psychology* (4th ed.). San Diego, CA: Harcourt Brace Jovanovich.

Snow, R. E., & Yalow, E. (1982). Education and intelligence. In R. J. Sternberg (Ed.), *Handbook of human intelligence* (pp. 493–585). London: Cambridge University Press.

Spearman, C. E. (1904). "General intelligence" objectively determined and measured. *American Journal of Psychology, 15,* 201–292.

Spearman, C. E. (1927). *The abilities of man.* New York: Macmillan.

Sternberg, R. J. (1985). *Beyond IQ: A triarchic theory of intelligence.* London: Cambridge University Press.

Stevens, S. S. (1946). On the theory of scales of measurement. *Science, 103*(2684), 677–680.

Teng, S. (1943). Chinese influence on the western examination system. *Harvard Journal of Asiatic Studies, 7,* 267–312.

Terman, L. M. (1916). *The measurement of intelligence.* Boston, MA: Houghton Mifflin.

Terman, L. M., & Merrill, M. A. (1937). *Measuring intelligence.* Boston, MA: Houghton Mifflin.

Terman, L. M., & Merrill, M. A. (1960). *Stanford–Binet Intelligence Scale, Form L-M.* Boston, MA: Houghton Mifflin.

Thorndike, E. L. (1927). *The measurement of intelligence.* New York: Columbia University, Teachers College, Bureau of Publications.

Thorndike, R. L., Hagen, E. P., & Sattler, J. M. (1986). *Stanford–Binet Intelligence Scale: Fourth Edition.* Chicago: Riverside.

Thurstone, L. L. (1938). Primary mental abilities. *Psychometric Monographs* (Whole No. 1).

Trabue, M. R. (1924). *Measuring results in education.* New York: American Book.

Urbach, P. (1974). Progress and degeneration in the "IQ debate." *British Journal of the Philosophy of Science, 25,* 99–135.

Vernon, P. E. (1950). *The structure of human abilities.* New York: Wiley.

Wainer, H. (1983). On item response theory and computerized adaptive tests: The coming technical revolution in testing. *Journal of College Admissions, 28,* 9–16.

Wainer, H. (1990). *Computerized adaptive testing: A primer.* Hillsale, NJ: Erlbaum.

Wechsler, D. (1949). *Wechsler Intelligence Scale for Children.* San Antonio, TX: Psychological Corporation.

Wechsler, D. (1955). *Wechsler Adult Intelligence Scale.* San Antonio, TX: Psychological Corporation.

Wechsler, D. (1967). *Wechsler Preschool and Primary Scale of Intelligence.* San Antonio, TX: Psychological Corporation.

Wechsler, D. (1974). *Wechsler Intelligence Scale for Children–Revised.* San Antonio, TX: Psychological Corporation.

Wechsler, D. (1981). *Wechsler Adult Intelligence Scale–Revised.* San Antonio, TX: Psychological Corporation.

Wechsler, D. (1989). *Wechsler Preschool and Primary Scale of Intelligence–Revised.* San Antonio, TX: Psychological Corporation.

Wechsler, D. (1991). *Wechsler Intelligence Scale for Children–Third edition.* San Antonio, TX: Psychological Corporation.

Weinberg, R. A. (1989). Intelligence and IQ: Landmark issues and great debates. *American Psychologist, 44,* 98–104.

Ysseldyke, J. E., & Mirkin, P. K. (1982). The use of assessment information to plan instructional interventions: A review of the research. In C. R. Reynolds & T. B. Gutkin (Eds.), *The handbook of school psychology* (pp. 395–409). New York: Wiley.

CHAPTER 3

A History of Intelligence Test Interpretation

R. W. KAMPHAUS

MARTHA D. PETOSKEY

ANNA WALTERS MORGAN

A HISTORY OF INTELLIGENCE TEST INTERPRETATION

The first formal methods of intelligence test interpretation emerged subsequent to Binet's creation of the first successful intelligence scale (Kamphaus, 1993). These first methods, sometimes referred to colloquially as the "dipstick approach" to intelligence test use and interpretation, attempted primarily to quantify a general level of intelligence. Upon the introduction of subtest scores to clinical tests and the emergence of group tests measuring differential abilities, *clinical profile analysis* replaced the "dipstick approach" as the dominant heuristic for intelligence test interpretation. *Psychometric profile analysis* soon followed. However, as measurement approaches to intelligence test interpretation developed, psychometric problems with profile analysis surfaced. More recently, *theory-based interpretations* have shaken the foundation of purely quantitative and empirical approaches to test interpretation.

Our aim in this chapter is to provide a discussion of these four major approaches to intelligence test interpretation. Such information, we hope, will act as a springboard for the development of new methods and variants of these approaches that may be applied in the future.

Our treatise is necessarily incomplete. We do not address such issues as clinical versus empirical methods of psychiatric diagnosis, logical flaws associated with various types of test interpretation and use, or other potentially germane issues. We focus exclusively on providing a historical account of dominant methods of intelligence test interpretation. Fortunately, there is much to be learned from such an overview. As E. G. Boring (1929) wisely observed in the case of the experimental psychologist, "Without such [historical] knowledge he sees the present in distorted perspective, he mistakes old facts and old views for new, and he remains unable to evaluate the significance of new movements and new methods" (p. vii).

1) QUANTIFICATION OF A GENERAL LEVEL—THE FIRST WAVE

The process of analyzing human abilities has intrigued scientists for centuries. Indeed, some form for analyzing people's abilities has existed since the Chinese, more than 2,000 years ago, instituted civil service exams and formulated a system to classify individuals according to their abilities. Their system provided an elegant way of associating ability with a profession in a way that also met the needs of society (French & Hale, 1990).

The early work in interpretation of intelligence tests used, extensively, methods for the classification of individuals into groups. This section provides a brief description of the early attempts to interpret information obtained on intelligence tests. Emphasis is placed on the early work related to test instruments and the use of classification systems based on instrument scores.

Early classification provided a way to organize individuals into specified groups, based on scores obtained on intelligence tests. This organization was dependent on the acceptance of the intelligence tests by laypersons as well as by professionals. Today, professionals in the fields of psychology and education may benefit from the use of well-researched and objective instruments that were derived through periods of investigation and development. The following discussion is a brief description of some of the early work leading to the development of appropriate instrumentation.

The Impact of the Work of Early Investigators

At the turn of the century, practitioners in the field of psychology and education were beginning to feel the compelling influence of Alfred Binet and his colleagues in France. Binet's experiments involved studies into the mental qualities of children, and these experiments led to the first genuinely successful method for classifying persons with respect to their cognitive abilities (Goodenough, 1949). Indeed, the development, by Binet and Theophilius Simon, of the first acceptable intelligence test for applied use in the classification of students, represented a "technological breakthrough" (Kamphaus, 1993; p. 6) in the field of intelligence assessment. The first Binet–Simon scale (Binet & Simon, 1905) would lead to future scales and, according to Anastasi (1988), an overall increase in the use of intelligence tests.

Binet's efforts reflected great interest in certain forms of cognitive activity. These forms included the abilities related to thinking and reasoning, the development of strategies for complex problem solving, and the use of adaptation for success in novel experiences (Pintner, 1923). This work of Binet appeared to stem from an interest in the complex cognitive processes of children (Kamphaus, 1993). His work would eventually lead to a series of popular instruments, most recently represented in the *Stanford–Binet Intelligence Scale: Fourth Edition* (SB-IV; Thorndike, Hagen, & Sattler, 1986).

In contrast to the interests of Binet and Simon, scientists such as James McKeen Cattell in the United States were conducting equally important work of a different kind. The investigations made in Cattell's laboratory were often measures of perception and motor skills. Although different in scope and purpose from that of Binet and Simon, Cattell's work would ultimately have a profound effect on the popularization and use of intelligence tests (Pintner, 1923). Indeed, Cattell's experimentation resulted in the appointment, with the assistance of the American Psychological Association, of a special committee charged with developing a series of mental ability tests for use in the classification and guidance of college students (Goodenough, 1949). The development of these tests would place great emphasis on the need for standardized procedures.

Procedures for standardization had been introduced with the idea that measurements would be even more informative when they could be compared to the measurements of someone in the same age group, who is administered the test under the same conditions (Pintner, 1923). Indeed, the conditions of test administration must be controlled for everyone if the goal is the scientific interpretation of the test data (Anastasi, 1988). Some of the earliest attempts at scientific test interpretation included the classification of individuals into groups, with descriptive terminology, based on their test scores. The following section provides a description of popular classification systems used before and during World War II.

Classification Schemes

The first well-documented efforts at intelligence test interpretation emphasized the assignment of a classification to an overall intelligence test composite score. This practice seems a reasonable first step given that (1) the dominant scale of the day, the SB-IV (Thorndike et al., 1986), yielded only one score, and (2) Spearman's (1927) general intelligence theory emphasized the preeminence of an underlying "mental energy."

According to Goodenough (1949), the identification of mental ability was regarded as a purely physical/medical issue until the beginning of the 20th century. Wechsler (1944) made a similar statement, claiming that the vocabulary of choice included medical/legal terms such as "idiot", "imbecile", and "moron." Levine and Marks (1928, p. 131) provided an example of a classification system utilizing the above-mentioned terms. Their system is shown in Table 3.1.

This classification system is notable for the descriptive terms used, as well as for the bands of scores. The descriptive terms are evaluative and could possibly lead to abuse of the terms. Regarding the bands of scores, there are many levels of scores. The top and bottom three levels comprise bands of 24 score points each. Those in the middle, from borderline to very bright, comprise bands of 9 points each. Although the band comprising the average range is not far from our present conceptions of average (except for this example's upper limit), the use of numerous uneven levels could be confusing to the layperson.

Another classification scheme, provided by Wechsler at the time of World War II, is significant for its purpose. Apparently, Wechsler wished to formulate a classification scheme that contained a specific structural rationale. Specifically, the system proposed by Wechsler was based on a definition of intelligence levels related to statistical frequencies, and each level of intelligence was based on a range of intelligence scores lying a certain distance from the mean (Wechsler, 1944). The following classification scheme, in an effort to move from the arbitrary qualities of classification, incorporated

TABLE 3.1. Levine and Marks Intelligence Test Score Classification System

Level	Range in IQ
Idiots	0–24
Imbeciles	25–49
Morons	50–74
Borderline	75–84
Dull	85–94
Average	95–104
Bright	105–114
Very bright	115–124
Superior	125–149
Very superior	150–174
Precocious	175 and above

estimates of the prevalence of certain intelligence levels in the country at that time (Wechsler, 1944, p. 40; see Table 3.2).

This system is notable for its attempt at departure from evaluative terminology and for bands of IQ limits that are somewhat closer to those we use at the present time. These two systems, that of Levine and Marks as well as the scheme provided by Wechsler, provide a glimpse at the procedures used in early attempts at interpretation. In the period since World War II, and especially in the last 20 years, scientists and practitioners have moved to a less evaluative vocabulary that incorporates parallel terminology around the mean (Kamphaus, 1993). Examples of the more recent schemes may be found in Kaufman and Kaufman (1983b) and Fish (1990).

Considerations for Interpretation

We have learned to use calculation of intelligence test scores, or IQs, as a way of describing cognitive ability. The calculation of the intelligence test score is only the first step in the interpretive process, and this has been the case since the early days of testing (Goodenough, 1949). Indeed, even though the scores may fall neatly into the categories, there is often additional data to consider when discussing an individual's abilities. This axiom was made clear by the clarification that those individuals in the population possessing below-average abilities do not manifest the same degree of retardation (Goodenough, 1949).

In a similar statement, Wechsler (1958) related that a clear advantage to using scores in the classification process has been the fact that it keeps us from forgetting that intelligence tests are completely relative. Moreover, we have been warned to remember that we are not assessing absolute quantities (Wechsler, 1958).

These concerns of Goodenough and Wechsler have affected intelligence test interpretation for many years. We continue to use classification schemes, based on global IQ scores, for diagnosis and interpretation, and the concerns of Goodenough and Wechsler are alive today. With the understanding that global IQ scores represent the most robust estimate of ability, we frequently use them in the diagnosis of mental retardation, learning disabilities, and other disorders. Still, we are charged with remembering that global cutoff scores may not always be appropriate in the decisions made based on intelligence test scores (Kaufman, 1990). In addition to the intelligence test data, one must examine any additional data related to the individual's cognitive functioning.

The structure of classification schemes appears to be more stable today than in the past. In the past, according to Wechsler (1944), Terman's classification system was in general use. Practitioners often applied the scheme, originally developed for the interpretation of the Stanford–Binet, in their interpretation of many different tests that measured a variety of different abilities (Wechsler, 1944).

TABLE 3.2. **Wechsler's Intelligence Classifications According to IQ**

Classification	IQ limits	% included
Defective	65 and below	2.2
Borderline	66–79	6.7
Dull normal	80–90	16.1
Average	91–110	50.0
Bright normal	111–119	16.1
Superior	120–127	6.7
Very superior	128 and over	2.2

Fortunately, today we have the opportunity to choose the most appropriate test and interpret the results of that test accordingly. Many test batteries today provide their own classification schemes within the test manual. In addition, because these classification schemes are often based on deviation from the mean of 100, there is consistency across most tests. Clearly, we have made much progress regarding the use of classification schemes in the evaluation of human abilities.

2) CLINICAL PROFILE ANALYSIS—THE SECOND WAVE

Rapaport, Gill, and Schafer's (1945/1946) seminal work exerted a profound influence on intelligence test interpretation until the present day. The authors seized on the opportunity that the publication of the Wechsler–Bellevue scales provided (Wechsler, 1939)—the interpretation of the newly introduced subtest scores to achieve a more thorough understanding of an individuals cognitive skills.

Profiles of Subtest Scores

To that end, Rapaport et al. (1945/1946) espoused a new and additional emphasis in the interpretation of intelligence tests, focusing on the shape of score profiles in addition to an overall general level. Whereas the pre-World War II psychologist was primarily dependent on the Binet scales and the determination of a general level of cognitive attainment, the post-Rapaport et al. (1945/1946) psychologist became equally concerned with the shape of a persons profile of subtest scores. Specifically, patterns of high and low subtest scores could presumably reveal diagnostic and psychotherapeutic considerations.

In their own words Rapaport et al. (1945/1946) put forth this new approach to intelligence test interpretation:

> In our opinion, one can most fully exploit intelligence tests neither by stating merely that the patient was poor on some and good on other subtests, nor by trying to connect directly the impairments of certain subtest scores with certain clinical-nosological categories; but rather only by attempting to understand and describe the psychological functions whose impairment or change brings about the impairment of scores. . . . Every subtest score—and especially the relationship of every subtest score to the other subtest scores—has a multitude of determinants. If we are able to establish the main psychological function underlying the achievement, then we can hope to construct a complex psychodynamic and structural picture out of the interrelationships of these achievements and impairments of functions. . . . (p. 106)

Rapaport et al. (1945/1946) went even further, suggesting that item responses may warrant interpretation as well. An emphasis on subtest and item level interpretation stands in direct contrast to the pre-World War II efforts to simply establish an overall general level of intelligence.

The Rapaport et al. (1945/1946) system had five major emphases, the first of which involved interpretation of item responses. The second emphasis involved comparing a subjects item responses within subtests. Differential responding to the same item type (e.g., Information subtest items assessing U.S. vs. international knowledge) was thought to be of some diagnostic significance. The third emphasis suggested that meaningful interpretations can be made based on within subject comparisons of subtest scores. Rapaport et al. (1945/1946) also ushered in the era of gleaning diagnostic information from comparisons of Verbal and Performance scales, which represents the fourth interpretive emphasis. The authors went so far as to suggest that a Verbal Performance profile could be diagnostic of depression (Rapaport et al., 1945/1946, p. 68). The fifth and final emphasis involved the comparison of intelligence test findings to other test findings. Rapaport et al.

(1945/1946) noted in this regard, "Thus, a badly impaired intelligence test achievement has a different diagnostic implication if the Rorschach test indicates a rich endowment or a poor endowment" (p. 68).

Rapaport et al.'s (1945/1946) work is a considerable landmark due to its scope. It provided diagnostic suggestions at each interpretive level for a variety of adult psychiatric populations. Furthermore, their work ushered in the era of interpretive emphasis on intraindividual differences that, at times, took preeminence over interindividual comparison in clinical work with clients.

In addition to breadth of approach, the structure of the Rapaport et al. (1945/1946) method is noteworthy as well. Their method gave clinicians a logical, step-by-step method for assessing impairment of function and for making specific diagnostic hypotheses. They directed clinicians to calculate a mean subtest score that could be used for identifying intraindividual strengths and weaknesses, and they gave desired difference score values for determining significant subtest fluctuations from the mean subtest score.

The case of "simple schizophrenia" (see Table 3.3) provides an example of the specificity of some of the diagnostic considerations that could be gleaned from the text. According to the authors, this diagnosis might be warranted when the noted set of responses and results was observed (Rapaport et al., 1945/1946).

Because of its logical, thorough, and intuitive approach the Rapaport et al. (1945/1946) volume provided an ideal structure for training post-World War II clinical psychologists in the interpreta-

TABLE 3.3. Diagnostic Considerations for the Case of "Simple Schizophrenia"

Subtest	Considerations
Vocabulary	Many misses on relatively easy items, especially if harder items are passed
	Relatively low weighted scores
	Parallel lowering of both the mean of the Verbal subtest scores (excluding Digit Span and Arithmetic) and the Vocabulary score
Information	Two or more misses on the easy items
	Relatively well-retained score 2 or more points above Vocabulary
Comprehension	Complete failure on any (especially more than one) of the seven easy items
	Weighted score 3 or more points below the Vocabulary score (or below the mean of the other verbal subtests: Information, Similarities, and Vocabulary)
	Great positive Comprehension scatter (2 or more points superior to Vocabulary) is not to be expected
Similarities	Failure on easy items
	Weighted score 3 points below Vocabulary
Picture Arrangement	Tend to show a special impairment of Picture Arrangement in comparison to the other Performance subtests
Picture Completion	Weighted score of 7 or less
Object Assembly	Performance relatively strong
Block Design	No significant impairment from Vocabulary level
	Tends to be above the Performance mean
Digit Symbol	May show some impairment, but some bland schizophrenics may perform well

tion of intelligence test (i.e., Wechsler scale) results. Today's clinician commonly regards the shape of intelligence test results as important for interpretation (Kamphaus, 1993).

Verbal/Performance Differences and Subtest Profiles

Wechsler (1944) reinforced the influence of Rapaport et al. (1945/1946) by offering a method of interpretation that also placed a premium on shape (i.e., profile analysis) over level, with particular emphasis on subtest profiles and Verbal/Performance differences (scatter). Wechsler's (1944) similar interpretive method is highlighted in a case example presented as a set of results for "adolescent psychopaths" (see Table 3.4).

It is noteworthy that Wechsler does not provide a Full Scale IQ for this case example, which is consistent with the *zeitgeist* in that it emphasized interpretation of shape rather than general level. Wechsler (1944) offered the following interpretation of the above set of scores:

> White, male, age 15, 8th grade. Continuous history of stealing, incorrigibility and running away. Several admissions to Bellevue Hospital, the last one after suicide attempt. While on wards persistently created disturbances, broke rules, fought with other boys and continuously tried to evade ordinary duties. Psychopathic patterning: Performance higher than Verbal, low Similarities, low Arithmetic, sum of Picture Arrangement plus Object Assembly greater than sum of scores on Blocks and Picture Completion. (p. 164)

This case exemplifies the second wave of intelligence test interpretation. Although this second wave is more sophisticated than the first in that it suggests that intelligence test interpretation should involve more than mere designation of a general level of intelligence, methodological problems remain. One central question is elicited by such approaches—how do we know that these various subtest profiles accurately differentiate between clinical samples thus demonstrating diagnostic utility? The next wave sought to answer this central question by applying measurement science to the process of intelligence test interpretation, but, as the reader will see, profile analysis continues to be the dominant interpretive method.

TABLE 3.4. Wechsler's Case Example for "Adolescent Psychopaths"

Subtest	Standard score
Comprehension	11
Arithmetic	6
Information	10
Digits	6
Similarities	5
Picture Arrangement	12
Picture Completion	10
Block Design	15
Object Assembly	16
Digit Symbol	12
Verbal IQ	90
Performance IQ	123

3) PSYCHOMETRIC PROFILE ANALYSIS—THE THIRD WAVE

The availability of computers and statistical software packages provided researchers of the 1960s and 1970s greater opportunity to assess the validity of various interpretive methods and the psychometric properties of popular scales. Two research traditions—factor analysis and psychometric profile analysis—have had a profound effect on intelligence test interpretation.

Factor Analysis

Cohen's (1959) seminal investigation shook the foundation of the second wave of intelligence test interpretation by questioning the measurement basis of so-called clinical methods of profile analysis. Cohen (1959) conducted one of the first comprehensive factor analyses of the Wechsler Intelligence Scale for Children (WISC; Wechsler, 1949) standardization sample, analyzing the results for 200 children from three age groups of the sample. Initially, five factors emerged, as shown in Table 3.5.

It is noteworthy that Cohen's labels for the first three factors have been retained as names for the Index scores of the Wechsler Intelligence Scale for Children—Third Edition (WISC-III; Wechsler, 1991). More important, it appears that Cohen's study popularized the Freedom from Distractibility label for the controversial third factor (Kamphaus, 1993). Cohen observed that prior to his study, this factor was commonly viewed as a measure of memory because it was marked by loadings for Digit Span and Arithmetic. His 1959 study identified additional loadings for Mazes, Picture Arrangement, and Object Assembly. Noting an absence of an obvious memory component in these latter tests, Cohen argued that performance on this group of measures was more aptly subsumed under the Freedom from Distractibility label. Subsequent studies of the Wechsler Intelligence Scale for Children—Revised (WISC-R; Wechsler, 1974) and WISC-III, on the other hand, have only identified significant factor loadings for Digit Span and Arithmetic (and, in the case of the WISC-R, Coding) (Kamphaus, 1993), yet Cohen's label for the factor has been retained through the decades.

Cohen (1959) chose not to interpret the fourth and fifth factors and to subsume their loadings and subtests under the first three factors. Hence, the common three-factor structure of the WISC was established as the de facto standard for conceptualizing the factor structure of the Wechsler scales. Eventually, Kaufman (1979) provided a systematic method for utilizing the three factor scores of the WISC-R to interpret the scales as an alternative to interpreting the Verbal and Performance IQs, hence, calling into question the common clinical practice of interpreting the Verbal and Performance scores as if they were measures of valid constructs.

Cohen (1959) also popularized the notion of considering subtest specificity prior to making subtest score interpretations. The investigation of subtests' measurement properties was crucial, as Cohen (1959) noted: "A body of doctrine has come down in the clinical use of the Wechsler scales,

TABLE 3.5. WISC Factors Emerging from Cohen's Analysis

Factor	Label
A	Verbal Comprehension I
B	Perceptual Organization
C	Freedom from Distractibility
D	Verbal Comprehension II
E	(quasi specific)

which involves a rationale in which specific intellective and psychodynamic trait-measurement functions are assigned to each of the subtests (e.g., Rapaport, 1945). Implicit in this rationale lies the assumption that a substantial part of a test's variance is associated with these specific measurement functions" (p. 289).

Cohen (1959) described his concept of subtest specificity and its computation as follows. Subtest specificity refers to the computation of the amount of subtest variance that is reliable (not error), and specific to it (Cohen, 1959). Put another way, a subtest's reliability coefficient represents both reliable specific and shared variance. When shared variance is removed, the clinician may be surprised to discover that little reliable specific variance remains to support interpretation. A clinician may draw a diagnostic or other conclusion based on a subtest with a reliability estimate of .80 and feel confident of the interpretation. Cohen (1959) cautioned that this coefficient may be illusory because the clinicians interpretation is assuming that the subtest is measuring an ability that is only measured by this subtest of the battery. The subtest specificity value for this same subtest may be rather poor if it shares considerable variance with other subtests. In fact, its subtest specificity value may be lower than its error variance (< .20).

Cohen (1959) correctly concluded that few of the WISC subtests can attribute one third or more of their variance to subtest specific variance. This finding has been replicated for subsequent reincarnations of the WISC (Kaufman, 1979; Kamphaus, 1993). Cohen pointedly concluded, adherents to the "clinical" rationales can find no support in the factor analytic studies of the Wechsler scales (p. 290). He then singles out many of the subtests for criticism and, in the case of the Coding subtest, concluded that taken by themselves, Coding scores are of limited utility (p. 295).

This important study set the stage for a major shift in intelligence test interpretation—toward an emphasis on test interpretation that is supported by measurement science. Several hallmarks of this approach are exemplified in Cohen's work, including the following:

1. Renewed emphasis on interpretation of the Full Scale IQ (harkening clinicians back to the first wave) as a large second-order factor accounts for much of the variance of the Wechsler scales
2. Reconfiguration of the Wechsler scales that proposes the three factor scores as alternatives or supplements to interpretation of the Verbal and Performance scales
3. Deemphasis of individual subtest interpretation due to limited subtest specificity.

Kaufman's Psychometric Approach

Further evidence of the influence of measurement science on intelligence test interpretation and problems associated with profile analysis can be found in the influential work of Kaufman (1979) as presented in his widely cited first edition of his text, *Intelligent Testing with the WISC-R*. Kaufman (1979) provided a logically appealing and systematic method for WISC-R interpretation that is rooted in sound measurement theory. For example, he created a hierarchy of WISC-R interpretation based on the basic premises of reliability and validity. His hierarchy, as interpreted by Kamphaus (1993), is summarized in Table 3.6. This hierarchy is noteworthy in that it emphasizes drawing conclusions based on the most reliable and valid scores yielded by the WISC-R.

The interpretive scheme offered by Kaufman (1979) is apparently an extension of the seminal work of Cohen (1959). Although such interpretive methods remain "clinical" in the sense that interpretation of the child's results is still dependent on the child's unique profile of results (Anastasi, 1988), the infusion of measurement science into the interpretive process creates new standards for assessment practice. Applying such methods requires knowledge of the basic psychometric properties of the instrument and thus creates a need for greater psychometric expertise on the part of the clinician.

These measurement-based interpretive options contrasted sharply with the approach espoused by Rapaport et al. (1945/1946), which elevated subtest scores and item responses—presumably the most unreliable and invalid scores and indicators—to prominence in the interpretive process. The measurement science approach, however, was unable to conquer some lingering validity problems. Most notably, the lack of validity support for profile analysis remained unsolved (Kamphaus, 1993). These frustrations set the stage for a fourth wave of intelligence test interpretive practice wherein theory and measurement science are intermingled.

Diagnostic and Validity Problems

The publication of the Wechsler scales and their associated subtest scores created the opportunity for the typical clinician to analyze score profiles as opposed to merely gauging an overall intellectual level via a sole composite score. Rapaport et al. (1945/1946) seized on this opportunity and popularized the method they labeled "scatter analysis," which they define as follows: "Scatter is the pattern or configuration formed by the distribution of the weighted subtest scores on an intelligence test . . . the definition of scatter as a configuration or pattern of all the subtest scores implies that the final meaning of the relationship of any two scores, or of any single score to the central tendency of all the scores, is derived from the total pattern" (p. 75).

Kamphaus (1993) provided a more modern definition of the method, typically referred to as profile analysis. Profile analysis is intended to identify intraindividual strengths and weakness, a process often referred to as ipsative interpretation (Kamphaus, 1993). In ipsative interpretation, the individual client is used as his or her own normative standard as opposed to making comparisons to the national normative sample.

Rapaport et al. (1945/1946) began to identify problems with profile analysis early on in their research efforts. In one instance they expressed their frustration with the Wechsler scales as a tool for profile analysis, observing that "the standardization of the W-B left a great deal to be desired so that the average scatter-grams of normal college students, Kansas highway patrolmen . . . and applicants to the Meninger School of Psychiatry . . . all deviated from a straight line in just about the same ways" (p. 161).

Similarly, although Kaufman (1979) provided detailed advice for conducting profile analysis, he expressed considerable misgiving based on a review of research designed to show links between particular profiles of subtest scores and child diagnostic categories. The profiles proved to be far less than diagnostic. As he noted:

> The apparent trends in the profiles of individuals in a given exceptional category can sometimes provide one piece of evidence to be weighed in the diagnostic process. When there is ample support for a diagnosis from many diverse background, behavioral, test-related (and in some cases medical) criteria, the emergence of a reasonably characteristic profile can be treated as one ingredient in the overall stack of evidence. However, the lack of a characteristic profile should not be considered

TABLE 3.6. Kaufman's Hierarchy for WISC-R Interpretation

Source of conclusion	Definition	Reliability	Validity
Composite scores	Wechsler IQs	Good	Good
Shared subtest scores	Two or more subtests combined to draw a conclusion	Good	Fair to Poor
Single subtest scores	A single subtest score	Fair	Poor

as disconfirming evidence. In addition, no characteristic profile, in and of itself, should ever be used as the primary basis of a diagnostic decision. We do not even know how many normal youngsters display similar WISC-R profiles. Furthermore . . . the extreme similarity in the relative strengths and weaknesses of the typical profiles for mentally retarded, reading-disabled, and learning-disabled children renders differential diagnosis based primarily on WISC-R subtest patterns a veritable impossibility. (Kaufman, 1979, pp. 204–205)

Recently, Kamphaus (1993) summarized considerable research subsequent to the publication of Kaufman's work regarding profile analysis. He noted continuing problems with the validation of particular profiles, including in this case, recategorizations of the WISC that were designed to assist in the diagnostic and/or prescriptive process.

Bannatyne (1974) offered one of the more appealing and hallowed recategorizations of the WISC subtests into presumably more meaningful profiles. His recategorizations are shown in Table 3.7. Matheson, Mueller, and Short (1984), however, called into question the validity of Bannatyne's recategorizations. They studied the validity of Bannatyne's recategorization of the WISC-R using a multiple group factor analysis procedure with three age ranges of the WISC-R and data from the WISC-R standardization sample. They found that the acquired knowledge, conceptualization, sequencing, and spatial categories of the WISC-R had high reliabilities but problems with validity. Matheson et al. (1984) found, for example, that although the acquired knowledge category had sufficiently high reliabilities, it was not independent of the other three categories, particularly conceptualization. This finding is sensible given that the conceptualization and acquired knowledge categories have one subtest in common (i.e., Vocabulary) and that previous factor-analytic studies of the WISC-R revealed three instead of four factors. The subtests from the conceptualization and acquired knowledge categories form the large first factor, Verbal Comprehension. As a result, Matheson et al. (1984) advised that the acquired knowledge category not be interpreted as a unique entity. These results suggest that the acquired knowledge and conceptualization categories are best interpreted as one measure of verbal intelligence, which is more consistent with the factor-analytic research on the WISC-R.

Other Measurement Problems

Measurement issues loom large with profile analysis. Even such seemingly intuitive practices as comparing subtest scores to the mean subtest score and comparing pairs of subtest scores are fraught with measurement problems. The clinical interpretation literature, for example, infrequently mentions the poor reliability of difference scores—the difference between two subtest scores. Anastasi (1985) reminds clinicians that the standard error of the difference between two scores is larger than the standard error of measurement of the two scores being compared. Such knowledge makes a 3- or 5-point difference between two subtest scores less dependable for hypothesis generation or making conclusions about a child's cognitive abilities.

TABLE 3.7. **Bannatyne's Recategorization of WISC Subtests**

Spatial	Conceptualization	Sequencing	Acquired knowledge
Block Design	Vocabulary	Digit Span	Information
Object Assembly	Similarities	Coding	Arithmetic
Picture Completion	Comprehension	Arithmetic	Vocabulary
		Picture Arrangement	

The long-standing practice of comparing a child's subtest scores to his or her own mean subtest score in order to draw conclusions about intraindividual strengths and weaknesses has also been called into question based on measurement cautions. An often-cited problem with this practice is the fact that the correlations among subtests are positive and often high, suggesting that the individual subtests provide little differential information about a child's cognitive skills (Anastasi, 1985). Furthermore, McDermott, Fantuzzo, Glutting, Watkins, and Baggaley (1992) assessed the internal and external validity of subtest strengths and weaknesses and found these measures to be wholly inferior to basic norm-referenced information (for a more complete discussion of this criticism, see Glutting, McDermott, & Konold, Chapter 19, in this volume).

The application of psychometric rigor to profile analysis methods of intelligence test interpretation has been less than satisfactory. Measurement problems remain, many of which are endemic to the type of measure used (variations on the Wechsler tradition), necessitating the need for the fourth wave and other attempts to enhance the meaningfulness of interpretive practice.

4) APPLYING THEORY TO INTELLIGENCE TEST INTERPRETATION—THE FOURTH WAVE

Merging Research, Theory, and Intelligence Testing

Kaufman (1979) was among the first to cogently argue the case that intelligence tests lack theoretical clarity and support. We think that this lack of theoretical clarity of the measures adversely affects the ability of the examiner to draw clear and useful conclusions. Kaufman (1979) proposed reorganizing subtests into clusters that may conform to a variety of theories, which would allow the clinician to produce more meaningful conclusions. Profile analysis, as we have seen, has not fared well in numerous empirical tests of its application.

Integrating Theory and Hypothesis Validation

Kamphaus (1993) suggested several approaches for dealing with the meager reliability and validity of score profiles. He espoused an "integrative" method of interpretation that had two central premises. First, intelligence test results can only be interpreted meaningfully in the context of other test results (e.g., clinical findings, background information, and other sources of quantitative and qualitative information). Second, all interpretations made should be supported by research evidence and/or theory. Presumably, these two approaches would mitigate against uniform interpretations that do not possess validity for the particular case (i.e., applying a uniform interpretation to case data that are at odds with information unique to the individual) and promote interpretations that are supported rather than refuted by research findings (i.e., interpretations based on clinical evidence that are refuted by research findings).

There is a long history of failure to integrate intelligence test results with other case data that yield flawed interpretations. Matarazzo (1990) gives the following example from a neuropsychological evaluation in which the clinician failed to integrate test results with background information:

> There is little that is more humbling to a practitioner who uses the highest one or two Wechsler subtest scores as the only index of a patients "premorbid" level of intellectual functioning and who therefore interprets concurrently obtained lower subtest scores as indexes of clear "impairment" and who is then shown by the opposing attorney elementary and high school transcripts that contain several global IQ scores, each of which were at the same low IQ levels as are suggested by the currently obtained lowest Wechsler subtest scaled scores. (p. 1003)

To protect against failure to integrate information, Kamphaus (1993) further advised the intelligence test user to set a standard for integrating intelligence test results with other findings. He suggested that the test user adhere to a standard of at least two pieces of corroborating evidence for each test interpretation made. Such a standard "forces" the examiner to carefully consider other findings and information prior to offering conclusions.

A clinician, for example, may see a Full Scale score of 84 (below average) for a child and conclude that she possesses below-average intelligence. Even this seemingly obvious conclusion should be corroborated by two external sources of information. If the majority of the child's achievement scores are in this range and her teacher says that she seems to be progressing more slowly than the majority of the children in her class, the conclusion of below-average intelligence has been corroborated by two sources of information external to the WISC-III. On the other hand, had this child previously been diagnosed as having attention-deficit hyperactivity disorder and had she missed her dosage of medication prior to testing, the veracity of the WISC-III scores would be in question. If she were also extremely active during the testing session, the obtained scores would be even more in question.

The requirement of research (i.e., validity) support for test-based interpretations is virtually mandatory in light of the publication of the *Standards for Educational and Psychological Tests* (American Educational Research Association, American Psychological Association, and National Council on Measurement in Education, 1985) and the increased expectations of consumers for assessment accuracy (Kamphaus, 1993). The "clinical impressions" of examiners are no longer adequate for supporting interpretations of a child's intelligence test scores (Matarazzo, 1990). Consider again the above example in which the child with persistent school problems obtained a WISC-III Full Scale score of 84. Given the data showing the positive relationship between intelligence and achievement scores, the results seem consistent with the research literature and lend support to the interpretation of below average intelligence. If necessary to support the conclusion of below-average intelligence, the clinician could give testimony citing studies supporting the correlational relationship between intelligence and achievement test scores (Matarazzo, 1990).

Knowledge of theory is important above and beyond research findings, as theory allows the clinician to do a better job of conceptualizing a child's scores. Having a clearer conceptualization of the child's cognitive status allows the clinician to better explain the child's test results to parents, teachers, colleagues, and other consumers of the test findings. Parents will often want to know the etiology of the child's scores. They will question, "Is it my fault for not reading to her?" or "Did he inherit this problem—my father had the same problems in school?" Clinicians will find themselves unprepared to give reasonable answers to such questions without adequate theoretical knowledge.

Confirmatory Methods of Hypothesis Validation

The interpretive method advocated by Kamphaus (1993) also advises offering a priori (confirmatory) hypotheses prior to the calculation of the child's scores as a method of informing the interpretive process with theory and/or research findings. This method is a powerful one for encouraging the integration of test results with other information. The traditional interpretive method in clinical assessment has been a posteriori (exploratory) in nature.

Confirmatory hypotheses are based on previous information about the child, including reports from teachers, clinicians, and parents; previous school grades, medical and developmental histories; and observations during the test session. The clinician, for example, may observe that a child entered the test session angrily because she had to leave her favorite playmate to attend the test session. She had a noticeable scowl on her face during administration of some of the subtests, and she offered minimal effort with no elaboration of her verbal answers. After a few subtests the examiner was able to more firmly establish rapport, and thereafter the child's effort improved substantially. The examiner may then hypothesize, based on these observations, that the child will score lower on the earlier subtests of the battery than on others because of her poor initial motivation. If in fact this finding obtains, the examiner can feel confident that the hypothesis is confirmed. This method virtually guarantees integration of intelligence test results with other findings because the hypotheses are already based on non–intelligence test findings.

The confirmatory approach espoused by Kamphaus (1993) also forces consideration of research and theory because the clinician is operating from a basis of research and theory when the hypothesis is drawn. Another example clarifies the element of an application of previous research. A child is referred for psychological evaluation because of a failure to make academic gains in the first grade. He does not yet know such basic concepts as letters and numbers, and he is being retained in first grade while receiving remedial assistance. Based on the known correlation between intelligence and academic achievement, the examiner would hypothesize below-average intelligence test scores. If the child obtains a WISC-III Full Scale in the 80s or below, the hypothesis would be confirmed and, in addition, the examiners conclusion would be based on research findings.

This approach to interpretation is analogous to one of the differences between exploratory and confirmatory factor analysis wherein, in the latter procedure, theories about the factor structure are offered a priori (Kamphaus, 1993). Traditional "exploratory" methods of interpretation give the clinician a data set consisting of intelligence test scores and ask the clinician to make sense of them, similar to what a researcher does when labeling exploratory factors post hoc. Kamphaus (1993) concluded that "*a priori* hypotheses should receive priority in the interpretive process because these hypotheses are already based on substantial information suggesting that they are likely to be highly meaningful in the context of the child's referring problem(s)" (p. 168).

CONCLUSION

What will be the fifth wave of intelligence test interpretation? We think that the fifth wave will have to be contributed not by researchers using quantitative or qualitative methods of interpreting existing tests but, rather, by the publication of new tests with stronger evidence of content validity. If the ultimate purpose of intelligence testing is to take a sample of behavior that represents a construct and then draw inferences about the construct (Anastasi, 1988), the process of interpretation is limited by the clarity of the definition of the construct being measured. Ultimately, we must move away from the oft-cited notion that intelligence is "what the test measures," as such a nebulous and circular conception of intelligence leads to equally unclear interpretations and/or inferences.

Kaufman (1979) not only cited this problem, suggesting that it results from a lack of infusion of theory into the test development process, but also offered his Kaufman Assessment Battery for Children (K-ABC; Kaufman & Kaufman, 1983) as a solution. More recently, Woodcock advanced the effort to enhance the meaningfulness of intelligence test results by fully applying the fluid/crystallized theory to the development of the Woodcock–Johnson Tests of Cognitive Ability (Woodcock–Johnson Psycho-Educational Battery—Revised [WJ-R; Woodcock & Johnson, 1989]). The content validity of these two popular measures, however, was not clearly established using such traditional means as developing a content blueprint based on the opinions of numerous experts and then clearly specifying item-writing parameters based on that blueprint (Hambleton & Jurgensen, 1990). The K-ABC and WJ-R primarily utilized factor-analytic means to develop a set of subtests related to their a priori specified theories, with an emphasis on the use of two or more subtests to measure a particular latent trait. Although the factor-analytic validity of such measures is impressive, and probably better than that of the WISC-III (Kamphaus, 1993), the lack of clear specification of the skills or abilities assessed by each of the subtests and item types hinders interpretation.

It is time to broaden the concept of content validity and to apply it to intelligence test interpretation (e.g., Flanagan & McGrew, Chapter 17, this volume). Cronbach (1971) suggested such an expansion of the term more than two decades ago, observing: "Whether the operations that finally constitute the test correspond to the specified universe is the question of content validity. It is so common in education to identify 'content' with the subject matter of the curriculum that the broader application of the word here must be stressed" (p. 452).

Although it is difficult to draw inferences about an undefined "universe" of cognitive function, it is also *de rigueur.* Psychologists make such interpretations about an ill-defined universe of human functioning on a daily basis. Just as it is nearly unimaginable to have nonpolluting cars with an internal combustion engine, it is equally difficult to imagine that the scores offered by Wechsler-like intelligence tests will eventually be readily interpretable. A new technology is likely needed to solve the problem of interpretability. In the case of intelligence measures, we think that content validity is a solution analogous to that of the electric-powered automobile.

REFERENCES

American Educational Research Association, American Psychological Association, and National Council on Measurement in Education. (1985). *Standards for educational and psychological testing.* Washington, DC: American Psychological Association.

Anastasi, A. (1985). Interpreting results from multiscore batteries. *Journal of Counseling and Development, 64,* 84–86.

Anastasi, A. (1988). *Psychological testing* (6th ed.). New York: Macmillan.

Bannatyne, A. (1974). Diagnosis: A note on recategorization of the WISC scale scores. *Journal of Learning Disabilities, 7,* 272–274.

Binet, A., & Simon, T. (1905). Methodes nouvelles pour le diagnostic du niveau intellectuel des anormaux. [A new method for the diagnosis of the intellectual level of abnormal persons]. *L'annee Psychologique, 11,* 191–244.

Boring, E. G. (1929). *A history of experimental psychology.* New York: Century.

Cohen, J. (1959). The factorial structure of the WISC at ages 7-6, 10-6, and 13-6. *Journal of Consulting Psychology, 23,* 285–299.

Cronbach, L. J. (1971). Test validation. In R. L. Thorndike (Ed.), *Educational measurement, 2nd edition* (pp. 443–506). Washington, DC: American Council on Education.

Fish, J. M. (1990). IQ terminology: Modification of current scheme. *Journal of Psychoeducational Assessment, 8,* 527–530.

French, J. L., & Hale, R. L. (1990). A history of the development of psychological and educational testing. In C. R. Reynolds & R. W. Kamphaus (Eds.), *Handbook of psychological and educational assessment of children* (pp. 3–28). New York: Guilford Press.

Goodenough, F. L. (1949). *Mental testing: Its history, principles, and applications.* New York: Rinehart & Company.

Hambleton, R. K., & Jurgensen, C. (1990). Criterion-referenced assessment of school achievement. In C. R. Reynolds & R. W. Kamphaus (Eds.), *Handbook of psychological and educational assessment of children* (pp. 456–477). New York: Guilford Press.

Kamphaus, R. W. (1993). *Clinical assessment of children's intelligence.* Needham Heights, MA: Allyn & Bacon.

Kaufman, A. (1979). *Intelligent testing with the WISC-R.* New York: Wiley-Interscience.

Kaufman, A. S. (1990). *Assessing adolescent and adult intelligence.* Needham, MA: Allyn & Bacon.

Kaufman, A. S., & Kaufman, N. L. (1983a). *Administration and scoring manual for the Kaufman Assessment Battery for Children.* Circle Pines, MN: American Guidance Service.

Kaufman, A. S., & Kaufman, N. L. (1983b). *Interpretive manual for the Kaufman Assessment Battery for Children.* Circle Pines, MN: American Guidance Service.

Levine, A. J., & Marks, L. (1928). *Testing intelligence and achievement.* New York: Macmillan.

Matarazzo, J. D. (1990). Psychological assessment versus psychological testing? Validation from Binet to the school, clinic, and courtroom. *American Psychologists, 45*(9), 999–1017.

Matheson, D. W., Mueller, H. H., & Short, R. H. (1984). The validity of Bannatyne's acquired knowledge category as a separate construct. *Journal of Psychoeducational Assessment, 2,* 279–291.

McDermott, P. A., Fantuzzo, J. W., Glutting, J. J., Watkins, M. W., & Baggaley, A. R. (1992). Illusions of meaning in the ipsative assessment of children's ability. *Journal of Special Education, 25,* 504–526.

Pintner, R. (1923). *Intelligence testing.* New York: Holt, Rinehart & Winston.

Rapaport, D., Gill, M., & Schafer, R. (1945/1946). *Diagnostic psychological testing* (2 vols.). Chicago: Year Book.

Spearman, C. (1927). *The abilities of man.* New York: Macmillan.

Thorndike, R. L., Hagen, E. P., & Sattler, J. M. (1986). *Stanford–Binet Intelligence Scale: Fourth Edition.* Chicago: Riverside.

Wechsler, D. (1939). *The measurement of adult intelligence.* Baltimore: Williams & Wilkins.

Wechsler, D. (1944). *Measurement of adult intelligence* (3rd ed.). Baltimore: Williams and Wilkins.

Wechsler, D. (1949). *Wechsler Intelligence Scale for Children.* San Antonio, TX: Psychological Corporation.

Wechsler, D. (1958). *The measurement and appraisal of adult intelligence* (4th ed.). Baltimore: Williams & Wilkins.

Wechsler, D. (1974). *Wechsler Intelligence Scale for Children—Revised.* San Antonio, TX: Psychological Corporation.

Wechsler, D. (1991). *Wechsler Intelligence Scale for Children—Third edition.* New York: Psychological Corporation.

Woodcock, R. W., & Johnson, M. B. (1989). *Woodcock–Johnson Psycho-Educational Battery—Revised.* Allen, TX: DLM Teaching Resources.

PART II

───◦◦◦───

CONTEMPORARY AND EMERGING THEORETICAL PERSPECTIVES

P ART II OF THIS TEXTBOOK includes several chapters that introduce recently revised, new, and emerging theories of intelligence and personal competence. The theories described in this section were authored or coauthored by the individuals who developed them. Each theory represents a more comprehensive view of the structure of human cognitive abilities and competencies than traditional general and dichotomous views of intelligence. A comprehensive description of these theories is provided, focusing specifically on how they reflect recent advances in psychometrics, neuropsychology, and/or cognitive psychology. Each theory is described in terms of its historical origins as well as the rationale and impetus for its development. In addition, the component parts of each theory are enumerated followed by a discussion of the mechanisms through which the model has been operationalized. A summary of the empirical support for each theoretical model is provided as well, and the relationship between the theoretical model and other models of intelligence is reviewed vis-à-vis content or empirically guided analyses. Each chapter concludes with a brief description of the most salient ways in which the respective theoretical model departs from traditional paradigms.

The first chapter in this section of the book (Chapter 4), "Human Cognitive Capabilities: Gf-Gc Theory," coauthored by John L. Horn and Jennie Noll, provides an historical overview of the development and refinement of structural theories of intelligence, beginning with Spearman's functional unity theory of general ability and ending with the Gf-Gc theory of multiple intelligences. In addition, these authors provide an examination of the developmental, genetic and heritability evidence for nine broad Gf-Gc constructs, including Fluid Reasoning (Gf), Acculturation Knowledge (Gc), Short-Term Memory (Gsm), Long-Term Memory (Glr), Visual Processing (Gv), Auditory Processing (Ga), Processing Speed (Gs), Correct Decision Speed (CDS), and Quantitative Knowledge (Gq).

Another expanded theory of intelligence is presented in Chapter 5, "The Triarchic Theory of Intelligence," by Robert J. Sternberg. In this chapter Sternberg describes how intelligence functions as a *system*. He presents three interrelated subtheories of intelligence that are subsumed in his triarchic theory, including (1) the componential subtheory, which explains the relationship between intelligence and the individual's internal world; (2) the experiential subtheory, which explains the relationship between intelligence and the individual's immediate experience with tasks and situations; and (3) the contextual subtheory, which explains the relationship between intelligence and the individual's external world. According to Sternberg, one distinctive aspect of this theory is that its operationalization followed rather than preceded the development of the theory. Sternberg concludes his chapter with a description of how the triarchic theory can be used as a foundation for planning educational interventions that lead to improved student performance.

A third alternative theory, and one that encompasses many distinct intelligences, is Gardner's theory of multiple intelligences (or MI theory). This theory is described by Jie-Qi Chen and Howard Gardner in Chapter 6, "Alternative Assessment from a Multiple Intelligences Theoretical Perspective." MI theory consists of seven different and equally important intelligences, including linguistic, logical–mathematical, musical, spatial, bodily–kinesthetic, interpersonal, and intrapersonal. Following a description of the theory, Chen and Gardner contrast MI theory with traditional psychometric views of intelligence. In addition, they demonstrate how MI theory can be applied to educational settings and describe research projects that led to the development of domain-specific tasks and observational guidelines for assessing the seven areas of intelligence. Chen and Gardner conclude that MI theory takes into consideration psychological, biological, and cultural dimensions of cognition and, therefore, presents a scientifically compelling understanding of intelligence that provides an impetus for an alternative approach to assessing cognitive capabilities.

A fourth expanded and extended version of previous theoretical models of intelligence is presented by John B. Carroll in Chapter 7, "The Three-Stratum Theory of Cognitive Abilities." Carroll summarizes his development of the three-stratum theory, which is based on his seminal book, *Human Cognitive Abilities: A Survey of Factor Analytic Studies* (1993). He describes his review of the factor-analytic research on the structure of cognitive abilities which encompasses nearly all of the more important and classic factor-analytic studies of the past 50–60 years. In addition, he explains his analysis and reanalysis of more than 460 datasets in which he applied a consistent exploratory factor analytic methodology. Based on his comprehensive survey of the relevant research, Carroll proposes the existence of a large number of distinct cognitive abilities, the relationship among which can be understood by classifying them according to three different strata: stratum level I comprises approximately 70 "narrow" abilities, stratum level II comprises approximately eight "broad" abilities (that are similar to Horn's Gf-Gc abilities described in Chapter 4), and stratum level III comprises a single "general" ability. Carroll refers to his theory as a "map" of virtually all known cognitive abilities that can be used as a guide to interpreting scores on many tests used by clinical, school, and industrial psychologists.

A fifth alternative to traditional theoretical conceptions of intelligence is the Luria–Das model of information processing. Although described in the next part of this textbook, this model deserves mention here because it is a prominent theory in the field and may play a role in the interpretation of new cognitive ability tests. The Luria–Das model is based on the premise that the cognitive activity of the brain is divided into three functional units. The first functional unit (associated with the subcortex and brain stem) is described as a unit for regulating tone or waking and is measured by attention tasks; the second functional unit (located in the lateral regions of the neocortex, including the occipital, temporal, and parietal regions) is responsible for obtaining, processing, and storing information as it arrives from the outside world and is measured by simultaneous and successive processing tasks; and the third functional unit (associated with the anterior regions of the hemispheres, anteriorly to the precentral gyrus) is described as a unit for programming, regulating, and verifying mental activity and is measured by planning tasks. Each unit is described as having a distinct role to play in mental processing; however, the collective participation of all three structures necessitates any type of mental activity. (A detailed description of this theoretical model as well as its operationalization, is provided by Jack A. Naglieri in Chapter 13 of this volume.)

In Chapter 8, "The Role of Intelligence in a Broad Model of Personal Competence," Stephen Greenspan and John Driscoll describe the relationship between concepts of intelligence and personal competence. In this chapter, they present a model of personal competence that can be used as a framework for understanding the role of intelligence in human functioning and adaptation. The model is composed of four elements: physical competence, affective competence, everyday competence (which subsumes social intelligence and practical intelligence), and academic competence (which subsumes conceptual intelligence and language). The applications of this model are described in detail, particularly as they relate to research and practice in the areas of developmental disabilities and special education. Greenspan and Driscoll conclude their chapter with a summary of validity evidence for the model of personal competence and offer suggestions for future research.

Part II culminates with an "Analysis of the Major Intelligence Batteries According to a Proposed Comprehensive Gf-Gc Framework" (Chapter 9), by Kevin S. McGrew. In this chapter, McGrew follows Carroll's (Chapter 7) suggestion that psychologists use his three-stratum theory as a "map" to guide their selection and interpretation of intelligence tests. To achieve this goal, McGrew classified the tests of all the major intelligence batteries (Wechsler Scales, Stanford–Binet: Fourth Edition, Kaufman Assessment Battery for Children, Kaufman Adolescent and Adult Intelligence Scale, Differential Ability Scales, and Woodcock–Johnson Tests of Cognitive Ability—Revised) that were published at the time this textbook was being prepared following a synthesized Carroll and Horn–Cattell Gf-Gc framework. These tests were classified at the stratum II (broad) ability level following the results of several joint factor-analytical studies and at the stratum I (narrow) ability level. McGrew's classification system represents a major step toward providing a much needed "bridge" between the theoretical and empirical research and the practice of assessing and interpreting human cognitive abilities.

The theories presented in Part II represent a significant departure from traditional views and conceptualizations of the structure of intelligence. Although the theories included in this section have undergone varying degrees of empirical validation, they all represent viable foundations from which to construct new measures of intelligence—measures that may lead to greater insights into the nature, structure, and neurobiological substrates of cognitive functioning and that may be more appropriate for assessing the cognitive abilities of individuals from culturally, linguistically, and ethnically diverse backgrounds. The utilization of contemporary theories to build broader and more culturally sensitive cognitive ability tests has only just begun, as illustrated in Parts III and IV of this volume, respectively.

DPF

CHAPTER 4

Human Cognitive Capabilities: Gf-Gc Theory[*]

JOHN L. HORN

JENNIE NOLL

T HIS IS A PROGRESS REPORT on a theory of human cognitive abilities. It is an account of the development and current form of Gf-Gc theory. Earlier versions of this theory have guided many studies of human cognitive capabilities. Findings from these studies have indicated how the theory is incorrect and inadequate and thus have suggested modifications of the theory. Our aim in this chapter is to bring statement of the theory up-to-date: to describe what the theory can now say about the development and organization of cognitive capabilities.

The theory is, first, a description of thinking capabilities that characterize humans in contrast to other creatures. Humans believe, and they produce evidence to support their belief, that they have abilities of thinking that are notably different from the abilities of other animals: Either these abilities are more advanced than comparable abilities of other creatures—as, for example, the span of immediate memory—or different in kind from abilities of other animals—as, for example, the abilities of verbal communication. Early in history the term "intelligence" was used to refer to these kinds of abilities (Spearman, 1937).

The theory is, second, a description of abilities in respect to which there are individual differences within the human species. Among the capabilities that characterize humans in contrast to other animals are some that allow for description of one individual as different from another. This was recognized from an early point in history. In all languages of the world there are words used to describe thinking abilities in which people differ. These abilities also, like those that distinguish the human from other animals, are referred to as intelligence.

Gf-Gc theory is thus a theory of intelligence. There is a problem in describing the theory in this way, however. "Intelligence" is a singular word. But the accumulated evidence indicates that there is more than one kind of ability that can be called intelligence—that has the qualities said to be characteristic of human intelligence. Cattell (1941, 1957) recognized this in a theory of two intelligences—fluid (Gf) and crystallized (Gc). With the accumulation of evidence, this theory evolved

[*]The writing and research of this chapter was aided by grants from the National Institute on Aging, AG00156 and AG09936.

into a description of several kinds of intelligence—in what is referred to as extended Gf-Gc theory (Horn, 1968). These several kinds of intelligence are positively correlated, but no unifying principle (such as the principle that unites different forms of energy—kinetic, heat, chemical, etc.) has been found that unites different forms of intelligence. The problem is that use of the singular word "intelligence" fosters belief that different abilities are all forms of one thing, intelligence, but this does not seem to be the case. It is thus better to use the plural of intelligence and describe Gf-Gc theory as a theory of (several) intelligences. Better yet, the theory can be described simply as a theory of human cognitive abilities.

The theory is largely descriptive—an account of the abilities that characterize the human's capacities in generating and coping with complexities. But it is also a description of variables with which abilities correlate, and an account of how and why such relationships come about. Thus it is also explanatory.

Any theory that purports to be scientific should account for the extant evidence—ideally all the evidence. It should also give indications of where to seek new evidence that can test the theory and lead to modifications.[1]

Gf-Gc theory was developed in response to five principal kinds of evidence, namely (1) that of covariation and organization among human cognitive capabilities, called structural evidence; (2) that of developmental change from infancy to old age, called developmental evidence; (3) that of relationships to indicators of physiological and neurological functioning, called neurocognitive evidence; (4) that of predictions of school performance, educational levels, and occupational performance, called achievement evidence; and (5) that of relationships among persons related biologically to different degrees, called heritability or behavioral–genetic evidence.

STRUCTURAL EVIDENCE

Structural evidence is based on the logic of concomitant variation: If different operations of measurement yield measures that vary together, there is suggestion that a common function is, or several common functions are, measured with the different operations. This is not necessarily true—measures can vary together and not indicate common functions—but empirically concomitant variation is often indicative of common functions, and so a finding of such covariation indicates the likelihood of common functions. If findings of concomitant variation are replicated in different samples of people, at different times, in different places, and, in general, under a variety of circumstances, it becomes increasingly plausible that a common function is (or possibly several common functions are) indicated by the different measurement operations. This is the principle of concomitant variation.

Many measures of intelligence or essential features of intelligence have been developed. The results from many studies have now well established that, with few exceptions, most of these measures of cognitive capabilities are positively correlated. There is concomitant variation among different kinds of cognitive abilities. A few exceptions have been found in samples of young children and samples that are highly homogeneous in terms of age and education, in each case for measures obtained under highly speeded conditions, on the one hand, and measures obtained under conditions in which speed is not a factor, on the other hand (Guilford, 1964; Horn, 1972). But, generally, the intercorrelations among ability measures are positive. This is the finding of "positive manifold."

In accordance with the principle of concomitant variation, the well-replicated finding of positive manifold indicates a single common function or more than one common function. Whether there is one or more than one common function is important for the study of human abilities. It distinguishes two major kinds of theories. One kind of theory interprets positive manifold as indicating, at some level of analysis, a single common factor and a concept of general intelligence.

The second kind of theory considers the same evidence as indicating more than one common factor—more than one kind of intelligence.

The same evidence thus spawns two different theories. Is there a basis for choosing which theory is more nearly correct? There is, and it is spelled out in the sections that follow. In general, the choice between the two theories derives partly from structural findings that one factor is not adequate to describe the organization of human capabilities and partly from additional evidence of construct validation. Collectively the evidence suggests that there is more than one intelligence. But the evidence is not definitive. It is possible that there is one organizing principle indicating general intelligence, but it has not yet been discovered. Studies that can lead to such discovery must be based on a thorough understanding of current evidence.

Structural Theories of General Intelligence

There are two classes of theories in which positive manifold is interpreted as indicating general intelligence. In one class, a single process is specified: The single process may be either an essence or a functional unity. In the other class of general intelligence theories a mixture of processes is specified. Mixture theories are also referred to as conglomerate theories. A particular form of mixture theory emerges in hierarchical analyses.

Spearman (1927) described a model for an essence theory of general intelligence, which, to avoid unwarranted connotations, he relabeled *g*. He also put forth a substantive theory that illustrates the concept of functional unity. Spearman's model and theory indicate how positive manifold can, but may not, indicate a single, general organization of cognitive capabilities.

Spearman's Essence Theory and Model

Essence theories stipulate that all distinct intellectual abilities stem from one basic process (i.e., a single essence). Depending on the theory, the essence may come from any of several possible sources. The essence might be genetic, for example, or it might be neural speed, or it could be a factor of environmental determination. The main feature of essence theory is not whence comes the essence but the idea that one thing determines what is seen.

Spearman presented a model in which the capacity he referred to as *g* produces (what is seen in) the intercorrelations among cognitive ability measures. The model specifies that all measures of (individual differences in human) cognitive capabilities involve (1) one, and only one, common factor, g_i, representing individual i's amount of the common factor, and (2) a specific factor unique to each particular measure, s_{ij}, representing individual i's amount of the specific factor measured in test j. Thus, for any $i = 1, 2, \ldots N$ individuals and $j = 1, 2, \ldots, m$ measures of cognitive capabilities, there are m specific factors, $s_{i1}, s_{i2}, \ldots, s_{ij}, \ldots, s_{im}$, but only one g_i factor. Tests vary in the proportions of the specific factor, S_j, and common factor, G_j, they measure. Then, according to the model, an observed score, T_{ij}, of person i on test j will be a sum of the specific and general factors, thus

$$T_{ij} = S_j s_{ij} + G_j g_i. \tag{1}$$

On another test, k, the observed score for person i will be

$$T_{ik} = S_k s_{ik} + G_k g_i. \tag{2}$$

In these specifications we see concretely that each person's g_i is the same no matter what test is used for measure (all tests j and k), but the extent to which this common factor is measured in different tests (G_j and G_k) varies from one test to another. A person's specific factors (s_{ij} and s_{ik}) vary from one test to another, as do the weights, S_j and S_k, indicating the extent to which tests measure the test-unique specific factors.

The model also requires that (to within chance) the intercorrelations among the specific factors are zero and the specific factor correlations with the common factor are zero. Given these requirements, it follows that the correlation between any two tests (for which the model is correct) is quite simply[2]

$$r_{jk} = G_j G_k. \tag{3}$$

The result in (3) indicates that the specific factors of different tests produce none of the observed test intercorrelation (because they are uncorrelated with g and other specific factors). The manifest variable correlations are produced only by the common factor and the magnitude of this correlation is the product of the proportions indicating the extent to which the tests measure the common factor.

The Spearman model does not require that the correlations among tests be large (contrary to what is sometimes said); the requirement of the model is simply that the observed correlations be due to the one common factor and only to that factor.

Spearman's Functional Unity Theory

In the theory just described the G_j proportions ($j =1, 2, \ldots, m$) indicate the extent to which different tests measure the same thing, rather as if all tests measured neural speed but some tests are more sensitive indicators of this speed than are other tests. But a Spearman model can obtain under an assumption that the different G_j of different tests represent different features of a functional unity of separate processes working together (Cattell, 1957).[3]

The operations of the human heart illustrate a functional unity. The separate processes that work together are those of the right and left atria and the right and left ventricles. Different manifest measures of heart activities can indicate this unity.

Spearman's substantive theory specified a functional unity of three separate processes. One process was described as apprehension of experience, or introspection. Spearman (1927) reasoned that "clear introspection may well lie within the power of one person more than another [indicating] individual differences of ability" (p. 164). A second essential process described by Spearman (1927) is one of "eduction of relations." This specifies that "when a person has in mind two or more ideas, [that person] has more or less power to bring to mind any relations that essentially hold between them" (p. 165). A third process was described as "eduction of correlates [whereby] when a person has in mind any idea together with a relation, [that person] has more or less power to bring up into mind the correlative idea" (p. 166).

In cognition, these three processes are inextricably linked together to form a unity of function: g_i. The quality of an outcome in function depends on the quality of the working together of all three processes. The three processes do not reliably measure any specific factor separate from this working together, but different tests may involve one process more than another. One test may better indicate eduction of relations G_j and another be more indicative of eduction of correlates G_k, for example.

Thus, a theory that general intelligence is a functional unity of separate processes can be represented by the same kind of one-common-factor model for g as that described for an essence theory of general intelligence. The difference is that each measure of a functional unity indicates a different feature integral to the function, whereas all measures of an essence theory measure (in different degrees) the same thing.

It is logical that separate processes of apprehension, retention, induction, evaluation, deduction, and production work together to enable one to produce answers that are judged to be correct in cognitive tests. One must first apprehend stimuli before one can retain awareness of the stimuli; one must hold information in awareness in order to perceive relationships among elements of information; one must apprehend such relationships in order to inductively comprehend relations; one must comprehend relations in order to deductively draw conclusions. Other basic processes probably contribute to the function of producing a response that is judged to indicate human intelligence in action.

Such processes may form a functional unity, but this is not necessarily true. Even if it is true, it does not follow that just any set of cognitive measures will indicate the unity—in the sense of the Spearman model. Tests must indicate only the unity in common, not any other factor in common.

The concept of functional unity comes from the study of anatomy and physiology, where it is used to describe separate bodily functions. The functional unity of the heart is described as separate from (although related to) functional unities of the liver, the kidneys, the lungs, and so on. Features of the heart covary in a manner that is distinct from the covariation in features of other organs.

Analogously, the question raised by an hypothesis that general intelligence is a functional unity is one of whether different manifestations of cognitive abilities are indicative of one function that is distinct from other psychological functions. The answer to this question should be based on evidence. One form of evidence derives from test of the Spearman model.

Tests of Spearman's Model

For any sizable number of variables (e.g., six or more) the Spearman model is very demanding. Fit to the model requires not only that different tests measure g but also that they measure nothing in common except g: they must not measure any other common factor. It is difficult in measurement to avoid what Spearman called "swollen specifics"—the same specific factor measured in more than one test. When the same specific factor is measured in more than one test it becomes a common factor—S, say, measured in tests j and k, S_j and S_k. The test intercorrelations are then due in part to this common factor, as seen in this equation

$$r_{jk} = G_j G_k + S_j S_k,\tag{4}$$

and so do not conform to the Spearman specifications of equation (3). If several tasks of a battery measured short-term memory (perhaps in rather different ways), even if all these tasks also involved g and the other tests of the battery involved g, the g-factor model would not fit the data because the several measures of short-term memory would form a common factor separate from g.

The Spearman mathematical model (evaluated statistically) thus provides a powerful test of an hypothesis that different measures of cognitive abilities all measure a g factor of general intelligence. If the observed intercorrelations among m cognitive ability measures were found to be proportional (to within chance variation) as specified in equation (3) and seen concretely in Figure 4.1, the result would provide support for the central hypothesis of a g theory. If replicated and shown to be true for different batteries of tests representing the range of capabilities that indicate individual differences in human intelligence, the evidence would be compelling indeed.[4]

The g hypothesis is falsifiable, which is as it should be. Good scientific theory should be falsifiable. Spearman's theory exemplifies how good, testable theory is found to be inadequate and thus calls for improved theory.

Shortly after Spearman first proposed his model in 1904, Burt (1909, 1911) found evidence that failed to support the central hypothesis. His results suggested at least two common factors. Burt's results were repeated by several investigators between 1910 and 1920. In 1924, Burt reported substantial support for three common factors additional to the two he had identified in his early studies. In the 1930s, results from several studies of large batteries of tests indicated as many as five additional

The correlations in accordance with the model

	1	2	3	4	5	6
1	G_1G_1	G_1G_2	G_1G_3	G_1G_4	G_1G_5	G_1G_6
2	G_2G_1	G_2G_2	G_2G_3	G_2G_4	G_2G_5	G_2G_6
3	G_3G_1	G_3G_2	G_3G_3	G_3G_4	G_3G_5	G_3G_6
4	G_4G_1	G_4G_2	G_4G_3	G_4G_4	G_4G_5	G_4G_6
5	G_5G_1	G_5G_2	G_5G_3	G_5G_4	G_5G_5	G_5G_6
6	G_6G_1	G_6G_2	G_6G_3	G_6G_4	G_6G_5	G_6G_6

Column totals:

$(\mathrm{Sum}\,G_j)G_1$	$(\mathrm{Sum}\,G_j)G_2$	$(\mathrm{Sum}\,G_j)G_3$	$(\mathrm{Sum}\,G_j)G_4$	$(\mathrm{Sum}\,G_j)G_5$	$(\mathrm{Sum}\,Gj)G_6$

The sum of column totals $= (\mathrm{Sum}\,G_j)\,(G_1+G_2+G_3+G_4+G_5+G_6) = (\mathrm{Sum}\,G_j)\,(\mathrm{Sum}\,G_j) = (\mathrm{Sum}\,G_j)^2$

Dividing column totals by square root of the sum of column totals solves for G_j

$$\frac{G_1(\mathrm{Sum}\,G_j)}{(\mathrm{Sum}\,G_j)} \quad \frac{G_2(\mathrm{Sum}\,G_j)}{(\mathrm{Sum}\,G_j)} \quad \frac{G_3(\mathrm{Sum}\,G_j)}{(\mathrm{Sum}\,G_j)} \quad \frac{G_4(\mathrm{Sum}\,G_j)}{(\mathrm{Sum}\,G_j)} \quad \frac{G_5(\mathrm{Sum}\,G_j)}{(\mathrm{Sum}\,G_j)} \quad \frac{G_6(\mathrm{Sum}\,G_j)}{(\mathrm{Sum}\,G_j)}$$

$$= G_1 \qquad = G_2 \qquad = G_3 \qquad = G_4 \qquad = G_5 \qquad = G_6$$

The manifest (obtained) correlations

Measurement numbers

	1	2	3	4	5	6
1	r_{11}	r_{12}	r_{13}	r_{14}	r_{15}	r_{16}
2	r_{21}	r_{22}	r_{23}	r_{24}	r_{25}	r_{26}
3	r_{31}	r_{32}	r_{33}	r_{34}	r_{35}	r_{36}
4	r_{41}	r_{42}	r_{43}	r_{44}	r_{45}	r_{46}
5	r_{51}	r_{52}	r_{53}	r_{54}	r_{55}	r_{56}
6	r_{61}	r_{62}	r_{63}	r_{64}	r_{65}	r_{66}

Column totals:

$(\mathrm{Sum}\,r_{j1})$	$(\mathrm{Sum}\,r_{j2})$	$(\mathrm{Sum}\,r_{j3})$	$(\mathrm{Sum}\,r_{j4})$	$(\mathrm{Sum}\,r_{j5})$	$(\mathrm{Sum}\,r_{j6})$

The sum of column totals from $j = 1$ to $j = 6$ yields $(\mathrm{Sum}\,r_{jk})^2$. If the data conform with the model, dividing the column totals by the square root of the sum of column totals solves for G_j

$$\frac{(\mathrm{Sum}\,r_{j1})}{(\mathrm{Sum}\,r_{jk})} \quad \frac{(\mathrm{Sum}\,r_{j2})}{(\mathrm{Sum}\,r_{jk})} \quad \frac{(\mathrm{Sum}\,r_{j3})}{(\mathrm{Sum}\,r_{jk})} \quad \frac{(\mathrm{Sum}\,r_{j4})}{(\mathrm{Sum}\,r_{jk})} \quad \frac{(\mathrm{Sum}\,r_{j5})}{(\mathrm{Sum}\,r_{jk})} \quad \frac{(\mathrm{Sum}\,r_{j6})}{(\mathrm{Sum}\,r_{jk})}$$

$$= G_1 \qquad = G_2 \qquad = G_3 \qquad = G_4 \qquad = G_5 \qquad = G_6$$

Notice that $\quad (G_5G_1)\,(G_6G_2) - (G_6G_1)\,(G_5G_2) = G_1G_2G_5G_6 - G_1G_2G_5G_6 = 0$

$(r_{51}) \quad (r_{62}) \;-\; (r_{61}) \quad (r_{52}) \;=\; 0$

In general, any $\quad (r_{kj}) \quad (r_{mn}) \;-\; (r_{mj}) \quad (r_{kn}),$ tetrad difference $= 0$

FIGURE 4.1. Structure of a manifest intercorrelation matrix if one (and only one) common factor operates to produce the variations of different measurements.

common factors (Alexander, 1935; Brown, 1933; Brigham, 1932; Cox, 1928; El Koussy, 1935; Kelley, 1928; Patterson & Elliott, 1930).

Spearman (1927) criticized many of these studies on grounds that they were not carefully designed to avoid swollen specifics, and he put together small batteries of tests that did satisfy the conditions of the *g* model. These batteries did not, however, well represent the full range of abilities recognized as indicating human intelligence. Results from studies carefully designed to both sample a large section of the range of cognitive capabilities and avoid swollen specifics (Alexander, 1935; Cattell, 1941; El Koussy, 1935; Eysenck, 1939; Rimoldi 1948; Willoughby, 1927) failed to support Spearman's theory. Efforts in these studies to modify the theory by respecifying the samples of tests also were unsuccessful in indicating a *g* factor.

Thus, the results from studies done in the 1930s and 1940s did not support the hypothesis of *g* for any substantial sampling of the abilities identified as indicating human intelligence. Results suggested that more than one kind of common factor was needed to describe the relationships among such abilities.

But this was not to be the end of the matter. Belief that there was a *g* factor persisted. Indeed, as of this writing, it is still widely accepted that in basic respects the results of research are consistent with Spearman's theory (e.g., Eysenck, 1982; Jensen, 1992).

Other Structural Theories

Support for a theory of general intelligence has been claimed three major ways, namely, (1) by fiat, simply ignoring the logical, mathematical, and statistical requirements; (2) by interpretation of positive manifold and, in some cases, appeal to sampling; and (3) by appeal to results from hierarchical studies in which common factors are specified at different levels and a factor at the highest level is interpreted as indicating general intelligence. In this section we consider these claims in the order listed.

In the course of considering hierarchical studies we describe primary mental abilities theory, and theories that have derived from this formulation, including particular hierarchical theories. We describe, also, theories in which Spearman's substantive theory is regarded as a theory of one kind of intelligence in a system of several intelligences, and formulations of Spearman's model for *g* are applied to variable sets that do not encompass all tasks that have been said to indicate human intelligence.

By-Fiat Theories of General Intelligence

Two kinds of theories claim to measure of general intelligence or *g* but do not propose or test any major hypothesis for this claim. In one kind of theory it is simply asserted that a particular test measures *g* or general intelligence. Such theories can be called one-test theories. The other kind of theory asserts that particular collections of cognitive abilities define general intelligence. These have been called mixture theories.

One-Test Theories. Statements about the Raven (1938) matrices test illustrate this kind of theory. The Raven is said to be an almost pure measure of *g* (Eysenck, 1979; Jensen, 1982; Raven, 1938, revised 1956). The Porteus (1946) maze test also has been regarded as a measure of general intelligence.

There is little basis for testing such theories. Nevertheless, the theories are often accepted as indicating that a scientific concept of general intelligence has been established and that a particular test represents this scientific finding. In fact, such tests measure only narrow samples of the abilities that scientists have identified as indicating human intelligence.

Mixture Theories. Most of the most widely used tests of intelligence are mixtures of items and/or subtests designed to measure different cognitive abilities. The different mixtures are all said to be measures of general intelligence, or *g.* The theories guiding the particular choices of items or subtests are merely statements that the abilities assessed are the abilities of general intelligence. Particularly well-known examples of such theories are those of the Wechsler Adult Intelligence Scale (WAIS, 1955), the Wechsler Intelligence Scale for Children (WISC, 1974), and the Stanford–Binet Intelligence Scale (Terman & Merrill, 1973). Herrnstein and Murray (1994) who invoke the idea that the mixture tests of the National Longitudinal Survey of Youth, National Assessment of Educational Progress, Scholastic Assessment Test, and American College Test are all measures of general intelligence and good indicators of *g.*

Positive Manifold Theories of General Intelligence

As we noted previously, in almost any sample of people older than 5 years of age, almost all tests that reliably measure a cognitive ability correlate positively with all other such tests. This finding of positive manifold has been used to justify by-fiat theories, sampling theories, and hierarchical theories of general intelligence.

Further By-Fiat Theories. In one kind of theory of general intelligence it is reasoned that positive intercorrelations among cognitive abilities indicate that one thing is measured by all cognitive tests, and almost any mixture of such tests provides measure of this one thing. Such theories are thus essentially by-fiat mixture theories. Jensen (1992, 1984, 1982) is a strong advocate for this kind of theory. The sum of scores on any broad collection of cognitive tests, Jensen argues, will provide a good "working definition" of Spearman's *g.*

A major problem with this working definition is that different broad collections of cognitive tests (items, subtests) are, in a word, different. They measure different abilities that have different relationships with other variables. Even if all ability tests measured one thing (say, *g*)—and the evidence of positive manifold does not necessitate this—they measure other abilities as well, and these other abilities are in different proportions of the total in different mixtures. The orders of people from high to low on different mixture measures are different. Decisions made on such different tests thus will vary with the mixture used. It is rather like thinking that mixtures of orange juice and vodka, milk and honey, benzine, and gasoline all measure a *q* factor of liquidity. Well, yes, but mixture measures of these substances have different relations to other variables (construct validities) and no one of them is a particularly good measure of liquidity, per se. Different mixtures represent different things.

Sampling Theories. These forms of positive manifold theory provide a theoretical basis for specifying a stable concept of general intelligence. Humphreys (1979, 1985) is the principal proponent of this kind of theory. He defined intelligence as a mixture of "the entire repertoire of acquired skills, knowledge, learning sets, and generalization tendencies considered intellectual in nature that are available at any one period of time" (Humphreys, 1979, p. 106). He proposed that a measure of intelligence should be a representative sample from this repertoire. Such a sample would not necessarily satisfy the conditions of Spearman's one-and-only-one common factor of *g.* Still, representative sampling would provide a stable basis for specifying one (mixture) concept of general intelligence.

Thus, if different mixture measures are based on representative samples of the abilities of intelligence, they can be said to measure the same intelligence. But how does one of circumscribe and sample from the universe of abilities that make up intelligence? What is the entire repertoire of abilities? How does one draw a representative sample from this repertoire? How can one know when such a sample has been drawn? There are no answers to these questions and thus the theory, while plausible, is not testable. There is no clear way to circumscribe a universe of the "entire repertoire" to which Humphreys refers and thus there is no way to representatively sample from it. We can neither designate the population of abilities for such sampling nor specify the criteria with which to evaluate the extent to which a sample is representative of such a population.

An additional problem with sampling theories is that the number of abilities that must be sampled to form a representative mixture is too large to hope to sample comprehensively. Thousands of human abilities have been identified; thousands more can be identified.

Sampling theories thus indicate, in theory, a basis for specifying general intelligence, but there is no way to apply the theories or check them for falsifiability. The samples of abilities of mixture measures of general intelligence are not known to be representative of the universe of the entire repertoire to which Humphreys refers.

Different samples of cognitive tests measure different things. Indeed, mixtures for the same test used at different ages measure different things. The Stanford–Binet for infants, for example, measures abilities that are different from those measured with the Stanford–Binet for 13-year-old children. Different mixture measures represent different theories of intelligence.

Early Hierarchical Theories of General Intelligence

The discovery that intercorrelations among cognitive abilities are almost always positive was made early in this century and repeatedly confirmed. It was repeatedly found, too, that a single common factor would not account for the shared (common) variability indicated by the positive intercorrelations among ability measures. As this evidence accumulated, theories for several common factors were developed. Three kinds of such theories have been particularly influential: (1) hierarchical theories, (2) primary mental ability (PMA) theories, and (3) multiple-level theories that are not fully hierarchical, the best known being a theory of several intelligences known as Gf-Gc theory. Mathematical–statistical models for each of these kinds of theories specify several common factors to account for covariability that is not accounted for by one common factor.

The models for the first hierarchical theories were extensions of Spearman's model. A factor specified in accordance with Spearman's *g* model was calculated. In early work this was a centroid factor, which accounts for a major (but not a maximum) proportion of the common variance; in later work, a factor of maximum variance was calculated. In either case, the common variance of the first factor was removed from (partialed out of) the intercorrelations, and additional common factors were calculated on the residual correlations in much the same way as the first factor was calculated. Factors were extracted in this manner until nearly all the common variance was accounted for—the residual intercorrelations were reduced to approximately zero.

The first factor was usually interpreted as indicating general intelligence. Additional factors were calculated without appreciably altering this first factor. A necessary bipolarity among these residual factors was interpreted as indicating contrasts. A bipolar residual factor that correlated positively with verbal tests and negatively with mathematical tests, for example, might be interpreted as indicating opposition in the development of verbal and quantitative abilities—after general intelligence was controlled. If one spent intellectual resources developing verbal abilities, the theory would argue, this would take resources away from developing quantitative abilities. Hence, verbal indicators would be "expected" to correlate negatively with the factor when quantitative variables correlated positively.

The idea that abilities are in opposition generally did not meet with favor, largely because the abilities found to be in opposition on a bipolar factor in one study were not found to be similarly opposed in other studies: The results of bipolar factor analysis did not replicate dependably.

Other methods were developed in which the contrast of bipolar residual factors was eliminated by reducing the variance of the general factor and calculating two factors in place of each bipolar factor (Holzinger & Harman, 1941). Most of the hierarchical theories developed in the first two-thirds of this century were based on calculations of this kind (Burt, 1949; Vernon, 1969).

Under the aegis of this kind of calculation Burt's (1941, 1949a, 1949b) hierarchical theory became particularly influential. In this theory, the mind was said to be

> organized on what can be called a hierarchical basis [in which] the processes of the lowest level are assumed to consist of simple sensations or simple movements, such as can be artificially isolated and measured by tests of sensory "thresholds" and by the timing of "simple reactions." The next level includes the more complex processes of perception and coordinated movement, as in experiments on the apprehension of form and pattern or on "compound reactions." The third is the associative level—the level of memory and of habit formation. the fourth and highest of all involves the apprehension or application of relations. "Intelligence," as the "integrative capacity of the mind" is manifested at every level, but these manifestations differ not only in degree, but also (as introspection suggests) in their qualitative nature (Burt, 1949a, p. 46)

Much of this kind of thinking was incorporated into later-developed hierarchical theories (Carroll, 1989, 1993; Gustafsson, 1985; Hakstian & Cattell, 1978; Horn, 1965, 1972; Undheim & Gustafsson, 1987), but the hierarchical analyses for these other theories were based either on higher-order analysis (e.g., Carroll, 1993; Horn, 1965) or on direct specification in structural equation modeling analysis (e.g., Undheim, 1987; Undheim & Gustafsson, 1987; McArdle & Horn, 1986).

Higher-order analysis stems from Thurstone's (1938, 1947) influential theory of primary mental abilities. To a considerable extent, modern hierarchical theories derive from this theory.

Theory of Primary Mental Abilities (PMA)

A metatheory of simple structure among common factors is at the core of Thurstone's theory. This metatheory provides an objective basis for evaluating replications of factor-analytic studies. Prior to Thurstone's invention of simple structure, factors (better regarded as components) were defined as linear combinations of variables, each combination designed to maximize (a principal component) or almost maximize (a centroid component) the variance of the measurement. The number of variables of a particular kind, and the variances of these variables, determined the character of the components (factors). As the number of variables of particular kinds varied from one study to another, the results seen in the components varied. The results, therefore, often were not stable. They did not replicate.

Thurstone's model and methods required variables to be linear combinations of factors (rather than the other way around). Measured abilities were regarded as manifestations of the influences of underlying (in theory) factors. The model encouraged investigators to design studies in which each of a small number of common factors affected only a small number of clearly specified variables. The metatheory specified that primary abilities largely influence performances on only some tests, not all or even most tests (so there is no general ability pervading performance on all intellectual tests), and most tests indicate (in measurement) only a few primary abilities, not all abilities. Common factors were calculated in accordance with this metatheory by means of a procedure of rotation to simple structure. This is a mathematical calculation designed to maximize the possibility that the following three conditions will obtain:

1. That all (of several) common factors have approximately equal variance.
2. That tests correlate at non-chance levels with only few common factors—ideally, only one.
3. That common factors correlate at nonchance level with only a few tests. For a common

factor to be overdetermined it is necessary that it correlate at a nonchance level with at least three variables, and the stability of the factor in cross-validation is enhanced if it has nonchance correlations with four or five variables, but beyond this it should, in accordance with Thurstone's principle of simple structure, correlate near zero with all other variables.

There are several somewhat different procedures for achieving this kind of factor solution, Varimax (Kaiser, 1958) and Equimax (Saunders, 1976) being the most commonly used. Each such procedure is designed to (in somewhat different ways) approximate the three conditions of simple structure as closely as a given set of data will permit. For the approximation to be really good, the data must have a simple structure. Usually this means that a study must be designed to demonstrate simple structure. The operative word is "design." To demonstrate a simple structure, a sample of subjects must be selected *by design* to ensure that variables selected *by design* correlate primarily with only a few—ideally one—common factors, and common factors are specified (i.e., hypothesized) in accordance with *design* to correlate at a nonchance level with only a few marker variables and correlate near zero (at a chance level) with most variables. Thus, studies must be designed to reveal simple structure. If they are and the hypotheses of simple structure are supported, results can replicate if there is reality represented by the simple structure. If there is no such reality, this will be indicated by not finding simple structure and lack of replication. Thurstone thus introduced the principle of falsifiability into multiple factor analysis.

Thurstone designed several studies in the 1930s and 1940s that demonstrated a simple structure of nine common factors that collectively accounted for most of the reliable individual differences variance obtained with different tests said to be indicative of major features of intelligence. The process features of these factors suggested that they indicated primary abilities of inductive reasoning (I), deductive reasoning (Rs), practical problem reasoning (R), verbal comprehension (V), associative short-term memory (Ma), spatial relations (S), perceptual speed (P), numerical facility (N), and word fluency (Fw).

Many studies were designed to replicate the findings of Thurstone and most did. This follow-up research also indicated new common factors that very much expanded the primary mental abilities system. The system went from nine primary abilities to over 60 such abilities. Summaries of replicated common factors indicating such abilities have been provided (Carroll, 1993; Eckstrom, French, & Harman, 1979; French, 1951; French, Eckstrom, & Price, 1963; Guilford, 1967; Hakstian & Cattell, 1974; Horn, 1972). Table 4.1 provides short descriptions of the best known among these factors.

The evidence of replicated primary ability factors thus suggests that a system of more than 60 different abilities is needed to describe human cognitive capabilities. Some investigators have opined that intelligence comprises many more than this number of capabilities (Commons, 1985).

Guilford's Structure-of-Intellect Theory

As evidence of more and more primary abilities accumulated, it became increasingly clear that a system of so many primary abilities is too cumbersome to guide most research. The resources needed to develop construct validity for more than 60 separate abilities were beyond the means of researchers. A rationale for a smaller number of basic cognitive processes was needed. This rationale should accurately take account of the evidence indicating the many factors of the PMA system.

Much of the theory put forth in accordance with this need for parsimony stemmed from an armchair (i.e., theorists speculated about the organization among abilities and thought up a more parsimonious systems). Unfortunately, the rationale for such systems often originated only in the armchair and remained there. The systems did not build on extant empirical evidence or demon-

TABLE 4.1. Primary Mental Abilities

	Symbols used to represent ability	
	Eckstrom et al.	Guilford
Abilities of acculturational knowledge: Acculturation knowledge (Gc).		
General information: Science, humanities, social sciences, business	Vi	
Verbal comprehension: Demonstrate understanding of words, sentences, and paragraphs	V	CMU
Sensitivity to problems: Suggest ways to deal with problems (e.g., improvement for a toaster)	Se	EMI
Syllogistic reasoning. Given stated premises, draw logically permissible conclusions even when these are nonsensical	Rs	EMR
Behavioral relations: Judgments about how people interact and behave; estimate others' feelings		CBI
Semantic relations: Esoteric concepts; demonstrate awareness of analogic relationships among abstruse bits of information		CMRe
Number facility: Do basic operations of arithmetic quickly and accurately	N	NSI
Estimation: Use incomplete information to estimate what is required for problem solution		CMI
Mechanical knowledge: Demonstrate knowledge about industrial arts (mechanics, electricity, etc.)	Mk	
Verbal closure: Show comprehension of words and sentences when parts are omitted		CSU
Abilities of reasoning under novel conditions: Fluid Reasoning (Gf).		
Induction: Indicate a principle of relationships among elements	I	NSR
General reasoning: Find solutions for problems having an algebraic quality	R	CMS
Figural relations: Demonstrate awareness of relationships among figures		CFR
Semantic relations: Common concepts; Demonstrate awareness of analogic relationships among common bits of information		CMRc
Symbolic classifications: Show which symbol does not belong in a class of several symbols		CSC
Concept formation: Given several examples of a concept, identify new instances		CFC
Short-term apprehension and retrieval abilities (SAR).		
Associative memory: When immediately presented with one element of previously associated but otherwise unrelated elements, recall the associated element after up to about a minute	Ma	MSR
Span memory: Immediately recall a series of randomly related elements (letters, numbers) after a few seconds (up to about a minute)	Ms	MSU
Meaningful memory: Immediately recall a set of items that are meaningfully related	Mm	MSR
Chinking memory: Immediately recall elements by categories into which elements can be classified		MC
Memory for order: Immediately recall the position of an element within a set of elements		MASS

TABLE 4.1. *(cont.)*

	Symbols used to represent ability	
	Eckstrom et al.	Guilford
Long-term storage and retrieval abilities (TSR).		
Delayed retrieval: Recall material learned several minutes or hours before	Dr	
Associational fluency: Produce words similar in meaning to a given word	Fa	DIR
Expressional fluency: Produce different ways of saying much the same thing	Fe	DDS
Ideational fluency: Produce ideas about a stated condition or object (e.g., a lady holding a baby)	F	DMZ
Word fluency: Produce words meeting particular structural requirements (e.g., ending with a particular suffix)	F	DIR
Originality: Produce "clever" expressions or interpretations (e.g., titles for a story plot)	O	DDT
Spontaneous flexibility: Produce diverse functions and classifications (e.g., uses for a pencil)	Xs	DMC
Visualization and spatial orientation abilities (Gv).		
Visualization: Mentally manipulate forms to "see" how they would look under altered conditions	Vz	CFT
Spatial orientation: Visually imagine parts out of place and put them in place (solve jigsaw puzzles)	S	CFS
Speed of closure: Identify Gestalt when parts of whole are missing	Cs	CFU
Flexibility of closure: Find a particular figure embedded within distracting figures	Cs	NFT
Spatial planning: Survey a spatial field and find a path through the field (e.g., pencil mazes)	Ss	CFI
Figural adaptive flexibility: Try out possible arrangements of elements of visual pattern to find one arrangement that satisfies several conditions	Xa	DFT
Length estimation: Estimate lengths or distances between points	Le	
Figural fluency: Produce different figures using the lines of a stimulus figure	DFI	
Seeing illusions: Report illusions of such tests as Muller-Lyer, Sanders, and Poggendorff	DFS	
Abilities of listening and hearing (Ga).		
Listening verbal comprehension: Show understanding of oral communications	Va	
Temporal tracking: Demonstrate understanding of sequence of auditory information (e.g., reorder a set of tones)	Tc	
Auditory cognitive relations: Show understanding of relations among tones (e.g., identify separate notes of a chord)	Acor	
Discriminate sound patterns: Show awareness of differences in different arrangements of tones	DASP	
Auditory span memory: Immediately recall a set of notes played 10 to 30 seconds previously	Msa	
Perception of distorted speech: Demonstrate comprehension of speech against a background of noise or when distorted in several ways	SPUD	
Maintain and judge rhythms: Continue an established beat; judge whether two beats are the same or different	MaJR	

(cont.)

TABLE 4.1. *(cont.)*

	Symbols used to represent ability	
	Eckstrom et al.	Guilford
Speed of thinking abilities		
Perceptual speed: Under highly speeded conditions, distinguish similar visual patterns and find instances of a particular pattern	*P*	*ESU*
Numerical facility: Do simple arithmetic operations (adding, subtracting) as quickly as possible	*N*	*NSI*
Writing and printing speed: As quickly as possible, write cursive letters or print printed letters	*Ws*	
Choice reaction time: As quickly as possible, press a lever or button to indicate one among several possible patterns presented tachistoscopically	*CRT*	
Decision speed: Speed in finding correct answers to problems of low difficulty level	*CDS*	
Simple reaction time: As quickly as possible, press a lever or button to indicate a stimulus presented tachistoscopically	*SRT*	
Abilities of quantitative thinking		
Applied problems: Given information about a quantitative problem, indicate the analyses that need to be done to solve the problem	*APP*	
Sensitivity to problems: Given information about desired outcomes, indicate the nature of the quantitative problems that must be solved to yield the desired outcomes	*SEP*	
Quantitative concepts: Demonstrate understanding of quantitative concepts	*CA*	
Number facility: Do basic operations of arithmetic quickly and accurately	*N*	*NSI*
General reasoning: Find solutions for problems having an algebraic quality	*R*	*CMS*

Note. Symbols from "Cognitive factors: Their identification and replication," by R. B. Eckstrom, J. W. French, and M. H. Harman, 1979, *Multivariate Behavioral Research Monographs, 79;* Guilford (1956).

strate the support of other evidence. In particular, little use was made of research results such as those of the PMA studies. Refutable tests of the theories were not described or carried out.

Guilford's (e.g., 1967) work in developing a structure-of-intellect model (SIM) is an important exception to this generalization. Guilford based this theory on the results of PMA studies, specified refutable hypotheses, and gathered data to test these hypotheses. The theory developed in Guilford's research is summarized in schematic form in Figure 4.2.

The basic idea of Guilford's theory is that each of the many abilities humans display can be described as an expression of one of five separate mental operations—cognition, memory, divergent production, convergent production, evaluation—operating on one of four separate contents—figural, symbolic, semantic, behavioral—to produce one of six separate kinds of products—units, classes, relations, systems, transformations, implications. As shown in Figure 4.2, such an organizational system implies that there are $5 \times 4 \times 6 = 120$ separate abilities. The 60 or so primary abilities are, according to this theory, particular exemplars of the model. The model is thus parsimonious in the number of organizing concepts (operations, contents, products) it requires, not in the number of abilities it specifies.

Although there were many studies of the SIM in the 1960s and 1970s, the implications of the system have yet to be fully explored in research that provides a sound basis for rejecting or retaining

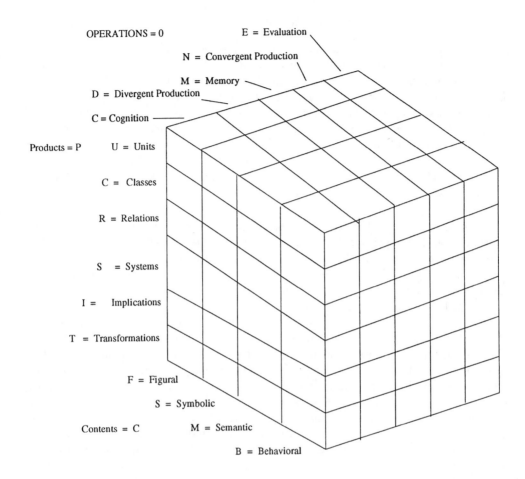

FIGURE 4.2. Schematic representation of Guilford's structure of intellect model. *Note.* The ability in the cell defined by the ineresection of DBI is referred to as divergent production of behavioral implications. See Table 4.1 for other examples.

most of its basic hypotheses. Studies designed to provide support for the theory often lacked objectivity (Carroll, 1972; Horn, 1967; Horn & Knapp, 1973, 1974; Humphreys, 1962; Undheim & Horn, 1977), so the results could not be taken as evidence in support of hypotheses of the theory. Over all of many studies, the results add up to suggest that some of the three-way combinations of the Guilford system represent empirically based distinctions between established primary mental abilities, but many are only logical indications of ways to construct tests, not indications of distinct human abilities. As Humphreys (1962, p. 428) pointed out, the facets of the Guilford system "are not psychological as defined. They should be useful to the test constructor, [but] they do not need to make a behavioral difference."

The facet of "products," particularly, does not appear to correspond to systematic structural or developmental features of human behavior. On the other hand, the facets of "operations," particularly, and "contents" work better: They point to functions of reasoning (cognition), short-term apprehension (memory), retrieval (divergent production), and visualization (figural content). These are among the functions of modern-day theory.

Later Hierarchical Theories of General Intelligence

As mentioned previously, the analyses for hierarchical theories are based either on higher-order analysis or on direct specification in structural equation modeling (SEM) analysis. In higher-order analysis common factors are derived from the intercorrelations among common factors. Oblique, which is to say correlated, common factors are calculated at the first order, usually by a procedure that approximates a simple structure. Second-order common factors are calculated on the basis of the intercorrelations among the first-order factors. The second-order factors, too, are calculated to be oblique and to approximate simple structure. Third-order, or even fourth- or fifth-order factors can be calculated in the same manner if there are enough factors at the lower order to allow definition of factors at a higher order. The relationship of each test to each of the factors at all levels can be calculated by means of what is called a Schmid–Leiman (1957) transformation.

Schmid–Leiman Theory. The major theory based on these kinds of analyses is the three-stratum theory of Carroll (1993). This specifies more than 60 primary mental abilities, eight broad abilities at the second order, and one very broad ability at the third order. The second-order factors are the same as are identified in Gf-Gc theory, which will be described in the next section. The third-order factor is interpreted as measuring general intelligence.

Carroll (1993) identified a general factor at the third stratum in 33 separate analyses in his reanalysis of the data of 461 studies. These factors are general in the sense that they are defined at the highest order in higher-order analyses, and each is defined by nonchance correlations with many different cognitive tests. The problem for theory of general intelligences is that the factors are not the same from one study to another. For example, in one case (an analysis labeled ARNO01) the factor is defined by lexical knowledge, spatial relations, memory span, general interest, and an unidentified first-order factor, whereas in another case (analysis DENT01) the factor is defined by reasoning, number, word fluency, short-term memory, and perceptual speed. The different general factors do not meet the requirements for the weakest form of invariance (Horn & McArdle, 1992) or satisfy the conditions of the Spearman model. The general factors represent different mixture measures, not one general intelligence.

Structural Equation Modeling Theory. In hierarchical theories based on SEM (Gustafsson, 1984, 1985; Undheim, 1987; Undheim & Gustafsson, 1987), a general factor is specified in terms of relationships to second-order factors, which in turn are specified in terms of relationships to first-order factors, which are related to tests. The entire model is tested for goodness of fit.

In principle. results from these analyses could test an hypothesis of general intelligence. The factor at the highest order could meet the conditions of a Spearman model for factors at the next order down that are representative of the abilities that have been identified as indicating human intelligence. The results of the Undheim and Gustafsson studies do not meet these conditions, however. The results from these analyses demonstrate an identity of a factor of fluid intelligence and a factor at the highest order—similar to the third order in Carroll's three-stratum analyses. This identity of Gf and the third-order factor indicates that the third-order factor is underdetermined. It must line up with one of the factors at the second order, and the Gf factor is chosen. That factor does not account for the common variance among the other factors at the second order. The Gf factor does not include all the features of cognitive capability that are accepted as indicating human intelligence; it is not a general factor. In particular, it does not include the features of intelligence represented in the second-order factors of crystallized intelligence, auditory intelligence, visual intelligence, and quantitative intelligence. The alignment between the Gf factor of the second order and a factor at the third order is a demonstration that no factor at the third order accounts for all factor intercorrelations at the second order. The results thus do not provide support for a theory of general intelligence.

Gf-Gc Theory

This theory specifies a simple structure organization of broad abilities among primary abilities. The parsimony of the system is thus built on the established findings of the PMA system. Substantively, the theory incorporates many ideas and measures derived from Spearman's studies of *g*, Burt's hierarchical analyses, and Guilford's ideas about what ability tests measure. But the evidence that mainly distinguishes Gf-Gc theory from other structural theories is evidence from studies of cognitive development and neurological functioning, particularly studies suggesting how abilities change with age in adulthood and with brain damage. The structural evidence provides a basis for analyses of development and neurological functioning.

Structural Indications of Several Intelligences. The patterns of intercorrelations among estimates of primary mental abilities point to a system of nine broad abilities. The evidence for this system can be seen in many studies (reviewed in, e.g., Carroll, 1989, 1993; Horn, 1968, 1976, 1988, 1989; Horn & Donaldson, 1980). The major results are exemplified in the early studies of Horn and Cattell (1966, 1967), several follow-up studies by these two investigators (e.g., Cattell & Horn, 1978; Hakstian & Cattell, 1978; Horn & Bramble, 1967; Horn & Stankov, 1982; Rossman & Horn, 1972), and the recent studies of Carroll (1989), Gustafsson (1984), Undheim (1987), and Woodcock (1990). The recent studies, particularly, indicate the generality of the system. Carroll's results stem from 461 separate studies done by almost as many investigators. Woodcock's findings are based on a standardization sample of 6,359 subjects spanning an age range from childhood to elderly. Gustafsson's sample is Swedish, Undheim's Norwegian. The results indicate that the PMA system can be organized in terms of nine dimensions that are almost as broad as the sets of abilities people refer to when they use terms such as intelligence or IQ. Described in capsule form, these abilities are:

Fluid reasoning (Gf), measured in tasks requiring inductive, deductive, conjunctive, and disjunctive reasoning to arrive at understanding relations among stimuli, comprehend implications, and draw inferences—abilities of reasoning in Table 4.1.

Acculturation knowledge (Gc), measured in tasks indicating breadth and depth of the knowledge of the dominant culture—abilities of acculturation in Table 4.1.

Short-term apprehension-retention (SAR), also called short-term memory (Gsm), measured in a variety of tasks that mainly require one to maintain awareness of, and be able to recall, elements of immediate stimulation (i.e., events of the last minute or so).

Fluency of retrieval from long-term storage (TSR), also called long-term memory (Glr), measured in tasks that indicate consolidation for storage and mainly require retrieval, through association, of information stored minutes, hours, weeks, and years before.

Visual processing (Gv), measured in tasks involving visual closure and constancy and fluency in "imaging" the way objects appear in space as they are rotated and flip-flopped in various ways—abilities of Visualization in Table 4.1.

Auditory processing (Ga), measured in tasks that involve perception of sound patterns under distraction or distortion, maintaining awareness of order and rhythm among sounds, and comprehending elements of groups of sounds, such as chords and the relations among such groups—abilities of listening and hearing in Table 4.1.

Processing speed (Gs), although involved in almost all intellectual tasks (Hertzog, 1989), measured most purely in rapid scanning and responding in intellectually simple tasks (in which almost all people would get the right answer if the task were not highly speeded).

Correct decision speed (CDS), measured in quickness in providing answers in tasks of nontrivial difficulty.

Quantitative knowledge (Gq), measured in tasks requiring understanding and application of the concepts and skills of mathematics.

The abilities measured in IQ tests and neuropsychological batteries of tests are accounted for by these nine abilities (McGrew & Flanagan, 1996). That is, although IQ tests and neuropsychological batteries are not necessarily described as involving these abilities, nevertheless that which is reliably measured in such tests is measured in some of the nine factors of Gf-Gc theory and thus can be estimated by some combination of these nine factors (different combinations in different IQ tests).

The structural part of Gf-Gc theory is similar to Thurstone's early statement of the theory of PMA. It differs primarily in the fact that each Gf-Gc factor is broader than any somewhat similar factor of Thurstone's system. For example, Gc involves the abilities of the PMA factors of Verbal Comprehension, Deductive Reasoning, and Numerical Facility, as well as abilities measured in various achievement test batteries (Woodcock & Johnson, 1990). Other Gf-Gc factors similarly involve the abilities of several PMA factors.

The component abilities within each Gf-Gc factor are different. This gives breadth to definition of the ability. But the different abilities of a factor are similar relative to the abilities of other Gf-Gc factors. This similarity, this conjunction, is responsible for the common factor and indicates the similar and related processes of the ability.

Identifying each factor and replicating this finding in different studies helps to indicate the distinctiveness of each cognitive function. This distinctiveness is demonstrated, also, by showing that in particular samples, the factors are construct independent, that is, the best-weighted linear combination of any set of eight of the factors does not fully predict the reliable covariance among the component abilities of the ninth factor. This evidence indicates that each factor measures a function that is not measured in the other factors.

Gf Related to Spearman's Theory. The fact that a Spearman model does not well represent all abilities indicative of human intelligence does not mean that such a model cannot represent some of these abilities. Indeed, ideally every common factor of multiple common factor analysis should fit a Spearman model. Demonstration of such a fit indicates either the redundancy of a process or the working together of separate processes of a functional unity.

Functional unities are usually of most value for scientific explanation. A common factor that indicates redundancy in measurement of the same thing demonstrates only that parallel measurements can be constructed. Such factors are what Spearman referred to as swollen specifics. A common factor indicating the working together of different processes, on the other hand, provides a basis for understanding function.

Structural studies of Gf-Gc theory have been designed to measure different features of each broad ability (Cattell & Horn, 1978; Horn, 1972, 1980; Horn, Donaldson, & Engstrom, 1981; Horn & Stankov, 1982; Hundal & Horn, 1977; Stankov & Horn, 1980). Particular attention has been paid to identifying distinct processes of Gf, fluid intelligence.

The central processes of Gf were thought to be ordered along a continuum from elementary awareness to immediate memory to working memory to inductive reasoning to deductive reasoning. Hypotheses specified that one must first become aware of stimuli, then hold the stimuli in immediate memory and manipulate the stimuli in working memory to inductively perceive the relations that must be perceived in order to draw the inferences required to produce answers to problems. Cognitive speed, attention, concentration, and carefulness were also hypothesized to be indicative of Gf.

The guiding theory thus is similar to Spearman's substantive theory of *g*. As in Spearman's studies, careful attention was given to avoiding swollen specifics in devising operational definitions of the hypothesized processes. Modeling analyses, also derived from Spearman's work, were directed at demonstrating that the interrelationships among the process variables fit a Spearman model for a *g* factor.

In one study that illustrates this approach, the intercorrelations among the following seven measures were obtained in a sample of 146 adults ranging from 26 to 61 years of age:

1. Immediate awareness, measured with an adaptation of the Sperling (1960) paradigm.
2. Primacy memory, measured as immediate recall of the first two elements—numbers and letters—of serial recall tests.
3. Working memory, measured as recall in reverse order after 5 seconds of elements presented in serial order.
4. Inductive reasoning measured under power conditions with a letter series test.
5. Cognitive speed, measured with a cross-out test.
6. Concentration, measured with a slow tracing test.
7. Carefulness, measured as few of incorrect answers in various speed tests in which the items are of non trivial difficulty.

A test of the Spearman model for *g* in these data require the estimation of 14 free parameters with 28 degrees of freedom. For this test the chi square was 32.4, indicating fit of a *g* model with probability greater than .90. The variables of the model thus indicate processes of a functional unity labeled "fluid intelligence."

These results provide support for an hypothesis of a *g* factor. A case can be made that this factor represents a substantive theory of intelligence; indeed, that it is a theory similar to that of Spearman. But the theory is limited. It represents only a few highly selected measures of the capabilities that have been identified as indicative of human intelligence. Missing in the factor are indicators of verbal comprehension, Gestalt closure, breadth of information, visualization, arithmetical skill, and quantitative reasoning.

When a task that primarily defines Gc was introduced into the battery of Gf indicators, the fit to a Spearman model for *g* was lost. When two or three such Gc indicators were included in the battery, a model that would approximate fit to the intercorrelations required at least two common factors. These results are consistent with the results of early studies designed to test Spearman's model (Alexander, 1935; El Koussy, 1935; Rimoldi, 1948). The evidence thus indicates that a *g* factor of fluid intelligence is not a *g* factor of general intelligence.

Support for a *g* factor probably can be adduced for carefully chosen selections of tests that are not indicative of Gf but are indicative of what is described as crystallized intelligence. A second theory of intelligence thus could be indicated. This theory would be limited in the same way that the theory of Gf is limited. The process variables that indicate the Gc factor are different from tests that define Gf. The evidence indicting a *g* factor among measures of Gc would not be support for a theory of general intelligence.

EVIDENCE FROM STUDIES OF DEVELOPMENT AND FUNCTION

Structural evidence (factor analysis) provides a basis for understanding individual differences in abilities and gives some indications of how abilities are organized within individuals, but it does not indicate how abilities develop, how individual differences in abilities come about, or how abilities relate to important human adjustments, adaptations and achievements. Other evidence is needed. Some other evidence has been adduced. It indicates how the different abilities relate to age, other indicators of development, and variables of personality. It suggests that different abilities stem from different sets of determinants, such as those of heritability, and are affected in different ways by influences associated with injuries, childrearing, education, and factors of lifestyle. It indicates different patterns of achievement associated with the different abilities. Most of this evidence converges toward indicating several forms of what is referred to as intelligence.

Adult Development and Aging

The results of Figure 4.3 illustrate how mixture measures of g, coupled with an assumption that the same g is measured in different mixtures, can be misleading. From young adulthood to old age there is (on the average across many individuals) a decrease in some intellectual abilities, namely, Gf, Gs, and SAR. Over much of this period, in the same samples of individuals, there are increases in the averages for other abilities, in this case Gc and TSR.[5] If these different abilities are combined in a mixture measure of what might be called general intelligence, g, or IQ, the mixture might, depending on which abilities were combined, indicate decline or improvement or neither decline nor improvement in the averages. Results from studies using different measures of g might thus appear to be contradictory. Many pages in the literature of adult development were devoted to explanations for a finding that cross-sectional studies show aging decrease in intelligence and thus contradict longitudinal results that indicated no such decline. This contradiction vanished when it was seen that the two kinds of studies were based on different mixture measures of intelligence.

   Comparisons of averages for cross-sectional data can reflect what are called age-cohort effects. People born and living through the same period of history are, in a sense, a cohort,[6] and differences between people born at different times might mainly reflect different influences operating on different such cohorts rather than age differences (Baltes & Schaie, 1974; Schaie, 1973; Schaie & Baltes,

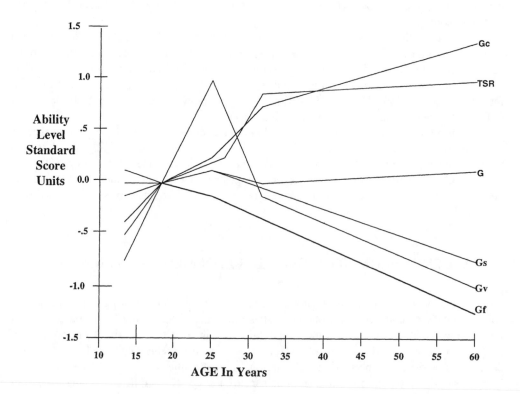

FIGURE 4.3. Adulthood age differences in dimensions of human intellect.

1977). On the basis of such reasoning, cross-sectional results showing declines in the averages for measures of intelligence were interpreted as indicting cohort differences, and longitudinal results (argued to be more dependable) showing no significant age differences were interpreted as indicating no decline. Then it was realized that different mixture measures of intelligence were used in the different studies: mixtures heavy with indicators of Gf, SAR and Gs—the vulnerable abilities—were used in cross-sectional studies; mixtures loaded with tests of Gc and TSR—the maintained abilities—were used in longitudinal studies.[7] When separate measures of the vulnerable and maintained abilities were analyzed what seemed to be a contradiction between the cross-sectional and longitudinal results was found to be mainly a difference in what had been measured.

It is now realized that longitudinal and cross-sectional data-gathering methods have limitations and strengths that are somewhat different and complementary (Donaldson & Horn, 1992; Flynn, 1984, 1994; Horn & Donaldson, 1980; Lindenberger & Baltes, 1994; McArdle & Epstein, 1987; McArdle & Hamagami, 1992; Siegler & Botwinick, 1979). Practice effects and selective attrition effects (dropout and survival) may influence results obtained with longitudinal data. Different kinds of age–cohort effects can influence results obtained with cross-sectional data. Neither the cross-sectional method alone nor the longitudinal method alone provides a royal road to truth. That road is more nearly reached by gathering both kinds of data and using methods of analysis that take into account the different possible influences that can operate longitudinally and cross-sectionally (Donaldson & Horn, 1992; Horn & Donaldson, 1976; McArdle & Epstein, 1987; McArdle & Hamagami, 1992; Schaie & Hertzog, 1982).

The cross-sectional and longitudinal results are similar when comparable measures are used in the two kinds of studies (Horn, 1968, 1976; Horn & Donaldson, 1980; Horn & Hofer, 1992; Schaie, 1983, 1994). Over an age range from the 20s into the 60s both kinds of studies point to age-related declines in Gf, SAR, and Gs, and improvements for Gc and TSR. Convergence in the two kinds of results becomes particularly close when there is control for selective dropout and attrition in longitudinal data and for historical time effects in cross-sectional data (Lindenberger & Baltes, 1994; Schaie, 1983, 1994).

Schaie (1994) reported that age changes for individuals are in some cases notably different from the age changes or differences seen in averages. The results summarized in Figure 4.4 illustrate how this can be true, particularly for measures of Gc.

The figure depicts age differences in the variances for an estimate of Gc that was obtained with the WAIS (Matarazzo, 1972). The middle curve in the plots depicts the average at each age; the two curves on either side of the middle curve represent the variance around the average at each age.

The plots for the means in these cross-sectional data are consistent with results for longitudinal data. Up to 60 to 65 years of age, the slope for the curve of the averages for the Gc estimate is near zero or positive; thereafter it is negative (a quadratic component is needed to well define the curve).

Most prominent in the results depicted in Figure 4.4, however, are the age-related changes in variances for Gc. These increases substantially over the developmental period from 40 to 80 years of age, which indicates that many individuals are not well represented by the averages. A considerable subsample of quite elderly individuals perform on tests indicating Gc at a level that is substantially above the level for substantial numbers of younger individuals, but a considerable subsample of elderly individuals also perform below the average of younger individuals. Schaie (1994) found these kinds of results in studies of individual cases.

The differences in variances indicate also how a sample drawn from these data could rather easily contain an overrepresentation of people on either the upper or the lower side of the line for the averages and thus suggest either age-related improvement or decline in Gc. If the sampling were on the upper side, the results would suggest that Gc increases with age, whereas if the sampling tended toward the lower side of the trend line, the results would suggest a decrease of Gc in older ages.

For the WAIS estimate of Gf, the variances at different ages are approximately the same. The averages thus better represent the individuals for Gf than for Gc. In this case, too, there can be notable individual variations from the average, but these are expected to be infrequent relative to the possibilities for Gc.

The data from Schaie's studies of gender differences in the age changes for vulnerable and maintained abilities suggest that vulnerable abilities appeared to decline earlier in women than in men and crystallized abilities appeared decline earlier in men than in women (Schaie, 1983). With comparable although different measures, however, Kaufman, Kaufman-Packer, McLean, and Reynolds (1991) found no such gender differences when they introduced control for educational differences.

Analyses of Aging Decline

Findings indicating adulthood decline in the averages for the vulnerable abilities raise concerns about why. The hope that the age differences might represent little more than test-taking age–cohort differences (as suggested by the results of Flynn, 1994) has been shattered by results from longitudinal data and from the analyses of mixed longitudinal and cross-sectional data. These results indicate a decline similar to that found for cross-sectional data.

There has been hope, too, that the decline of vulnerable abilities is due mainly to aging loss of relatively unimportant physical capabilities (e.g., those of sensory acuity) or largely reflects age increases in carefulness and disinclination to hurry. The evidence does little to sustain this hope.

There is ample evidence that with the increase in age in adulthood, there is a corresponding increase in slowness in performance on a variety of cognitive measures (Birren, 1965, 1974;

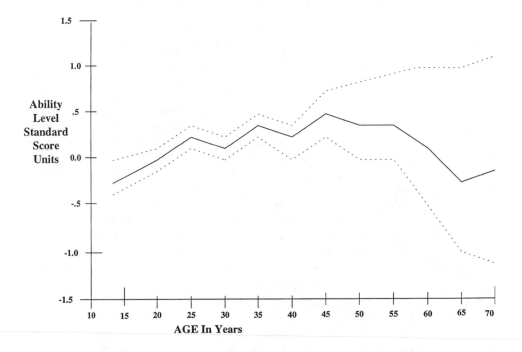

FIGURE 4.4. Factor means and variances for Gc estimate derived from the WAIS census data ($N = 2,977$).

Salthouse, 1985, 1991, 1992; Horn & Bramble, 1967). This evidence has spawned theory that cognitive slowing results because there is slowing with age in neural processing, which quite generally affects cognitive processing and thus almost all measures of cognitive capabilities. This is referred to as the general slowing hypothesis.

Not necessarily orthogonal to the general slowing hypothesis is the theory that individual differences in slowness are reflections of individual differences in test-taking strategy. Here the hypothesis is that age differences in slowness mainly indicate age increase in adopting a slow and circumspect testing-taking strategy.

Detailed process analyses of age declines in vulnerable abilities suggest that neither the general slowing hypothesis nor the test-taking strategy hypothesis is entirely correct. Results from some of these analyses are summarized in Figure 4.5.

The rationale for the analyses of Figure 4.5 can be illustrated by first considering the claim that the aging decline of Gf is due to loss of a simple function represented by speed in getting correct answers to problems of nontrivial difficulty (correct decision speed, or CDS). It can be seen in Figure 4.5 that CDS does indeed decline with age, to about the same extent as Gf declines. This establishes a prima facie case. Because there is a decline in CDS, which is about the same as the decline for Gf, performances on Gf tasks could involve CDS and, therefore, a decline of the Gf could result from a decline of CDS.

Missing in this argument, however, is a demonstration that the loss of CDS is, indeed, associated with the loss of Gf. When this missing link is introduced by controlling for the part of Gf decline

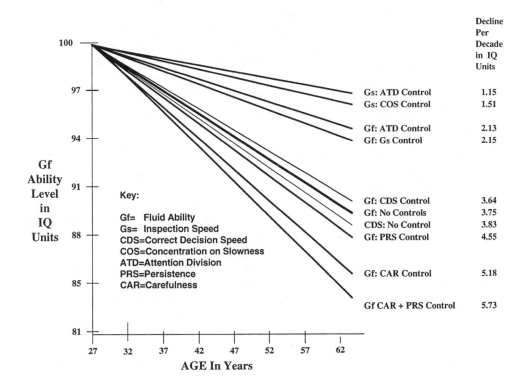

FIGURE 4.5. Age differences in fluid reasoning (Gf) and information processing (Gs) after control for information-processing speed (CDS), concentration on slowness (COS), dividing attention (ATD), persistence (PER), and carefulness (CAR).

that can be accounted for with measure of CDS, the result (illustrated with the curve labeled Gf:CDS Control) provides no support for the hypothesis. The loss of the CDS that accompanies aging does not predict the loss of Gf capabilities. CDS correlates at a very low level with Gf. Therefore, control for decline of CDS in the decline of Gf does not bring about a significant change. The change from 3.75 to 3.64 units of decline per decade is small in absolute terms and not statistically significant. This same kind of result has been obtained with measures of basic auditory and visual processes and acuities.

The results are different for Gs (information processing speed), which is measured in tests of speed of searching for a particular symbol or speed in deciding whether two stimuli are the same or different. Gs appears to represent a simple cognitive function. Yet the results from partialing analyses suggest that it is involved in the Gf function and, in particular, in the aging decline of Gf. Controlling for Gs in Gf (in the manner described above for CDS), there is change from 3.75 to 2.15 units of decline of Gf per decade (the Gf:Gs Control curve in the figure); this change is statistically significant. This result thus seems to support an hypothesis that an aging decrease in cognitive speed is responsible for at least some of the observed Gf decline with age. But there is more to the story.

As seen in the curves labeled Gs:COS Control and Gs:ATD Control in Figure 4.5, most of the aging decline of Gs itself is accounted for by control with a measure of close concentration (COS) and/or a measure of dividing attention (ATD). Yet, neither COS nor ATD involves speed of performance. Indeed, COS is a measure of how slowly one can behave. It is measured by calibrating how slow one can trace a line of a simple figure.

When COS or ATD is controlled in Gf, much of the decline of Gf is removed (as seen in the curve labeled Gf:ATD Control in Figure 4.5. The Gf:COS Control curve is at practically the same place). Because these two unspeeded tasks correlate substantially with the highly speeded Gs tasks, control for COS or ATD in Gf also controls for a part of Gs that is associated with the decline of Gf. The results thus suggest that it is not processing speed per se that declines with age and results in decline of Gf but a process (or processes) indicated by unspeeded tasks (COS and ATD) as well as by speeded tasks. One such process is a capacity for focusing and maintaining concentration. This appears to be involved both in the measure of ability to behave slowly and in the measure of ability to behave quickly. Such a process may also be involved in the core capacity for dividing attention.

Also summarized in Figure 4.5 are results suggesting that the decline of Gf does not result because older adults are more careful and/or persistent than younger adults. Indeed, the results suggest the opposite. Older adults work longer than younger adults before abandoning a difficult problem. Summed over a number of tasks, this is the PRS (persistence) variable of Figure 4.5.

When tests are speeded, so that the number of correct answers does not correlate -1.00 with the number of incorrect answers, it is found that over a number of such tests older adults tend to give fewer incorrect answers than do younger adults. Fewness of incorrect answers is the CAR (carefulness) variable of the figure.

Because older adults are more persistent and careful, they are slower. Thus, it could be that this is why they score lower on measures of Gf. This would be trivially true if the measure of Gf were the number of correct answers given in speeded tests. Because older adults tend to work more slowly in a speeded test, they would work on fewer problems than would the young and thus get fewer correct. However, the Gf measure obtained for studies of the kind summarized in Figure 4.5 was not number of correct answers given in speeded tests. Rather, it was a measure of the level of difficulty correctly resolved regardless of number of problems worked.

The problems for the Gf measure were given in sets of 5. One item of each set was at an easy level of difficulty: Somewhat more than 80% of a standardization sample got it correct. Another item was at a high level of difficulty: somewhat fewer than 20% of people in the standardization sample got it correct. The difficulty levels for the other the three items of each set were ranged in approximately equal steps between these extremes of low and high difficulty.

In the instructions for this kind of test, subjects were taught that there are no correct answers for some problems. This was done by introducing trial questions in which there was no solution. Subjects were taught that when a problem of this kind was encountered in the test, they should select a "no answer" (NA) option and move on to the next item.

Thus, a subject learned that a problem might have no good answer. This enabled the person to abandon a problem for which there was a good solution if that solution could not be comprehended. The score, then, was the level of difficulty of the problems for which correct answers were given. The same score could be obtained by working slowly through a few sets of 5 problems or by working quickly through many sets of 5 problems.

Figure 4.5 illustrates that for Gf measured under these conditions, control by CAR and PRS does not reduce the age decline; it increases it. This is seen in the increase in negative slope for curves of Gf in which CAR and PRS have been controlled (change from 3.75 to 5.18 and 5.73 units of decline, respectively). The findings thus indicate that carefulness and persistence are qualities that enable older adults to perform better on untimed Gf tasks than if these qualities are not allowed to operate. When advantages associated with carefulness and persistence are removed by statistical control, there is significant increase in the aging decline of Gf.

These findings thus again question an hypothesis that it is primarily speed of thinking that declines with age and accounts for decline in the reasoning abilities of Gf. It appears that Gf decline reflects inability to resolve complexities even under conditions in which there is no press to behave quickly and individuals, particularly older individuals, are not penalized for being persistent in seeking correct answers and for being careful to avoid incorrect answers.

Results consistent with those summarized in Figure 4.5 have been obtained in five separate studies based on different samples of subjects. In these studies, somewhat different sets of cognitive process variables were used to effect control in analyses of age differences. Besides those described in Figure 4.5, process variables to estimate encoding organization (EOG), incidental memory (ICM), eschewing irrelevancies (EIR), hypothesizing (HYP), working memory (WOM), and associative memory (ASM) were studied.

It was found that there is considerable functional overlap in operationally independent measures of such process variables. Although measures such as those obtained with COS and ATD, are based on quite different operations of measurement, they nevertheless intercorrelate in a manner that suggests that to some extent they measure common processes—processes that are implicated in the decline of Gf. Perhaps in the case of COS and ATD, the process is a capacity for concentration.

In general, when several separate process variables were entered in multiple regression control analyses, it was found that the process variables did not carry entirely independent variance in accounting for the aging loss of Gf. Although as many as nine quite separate process variables were considered in some analyses, and each on its own accounted for some of the age decline of Gf, no more than four variables independently accounted for some portion of the age differences in Gf. Different sets of four variables accounted for essentially the same amount of the age differences in Gf.

Also, no combination of the process variables accounted for all the observed decline of Gf. The precise proportion of the decline accounted for by different process variables varied with the reliabilities of the measures and the extent of the variability in the subject sample, but, roughly, only about half the aging loss of Gf could be reliably accounted for with the process variables thus far studied.

Studies of Achievements

In reviewing evidence of prediction of educational and occupational achievements, it is important to recognize that the abilities measured with tests, referred to as aptitudes and regarded as predictors of important outcomes, are themselves achievements and at the upper extremes indicate expertise: Aptitude tests are achievement tests (Humphreys, 1974).

A substantial body of evidence indicates that outstanding ability achievements in a variety of different areas are realized through deliberate practice that starts at a young age, extends over a long period of development (10 years or more to reach the highest levels), and is well guided and encouraged by good instruction and coaching (Ericsson & Charness, 1994; Ericsson, Krampe, & Tesch-Romer, 1993; Ericsson & Lehmann, 1996). The differences between those who reach the highest levels of expert performance and those at lower levels are in knowledge, skills, and physiological adaptations that are affected by intensive and extended training. What is seen most clearly at the extremes of developing expertise is seen also at lower levels in the distributions of achievements: The more sustained, deliberate, and well-guided the practice, the higher the level of achievement attained in both narrow and broad abilities (Charness, 1991; Ericsson & Lehmann, 1996; Ericsson, Krampe, & Heizmann, 1993; Ericsson, Krampe, & Tesch-Romer, 1993; Hoffman, 1992; Radford, 1990).

In evaluating the evidence on the prediction of achievement outcomes, it is important, also, to attend to whether or not distinct features of outcomes are measured. What are regarded as achievement criteria are often ratings that are mixtures of different factors—conglomerates of overall performance. Raters are not helped to, or even allowed to, distinguish between and separately assess different qualities of outcome. Similarly, when measured with tests, outcomes are often composed of several component abilities and other qualities all mixed together in an overall assessment.

If an outcome is measured as a mixture of different capabilities, a conglomerate predictor that mirrors the mixture will best predict it (Anastasi, 1989; Austin & Hanisch, 1990; Hartigan & Wigdore, 1990; Larson & Wolfe, 1995; Schmidt, Hunter, & Larson, 1988; Schmidt, Ones, & Hunter, 1992; Welsh, Watson, & Ree, 1990). For example, if performance in electrical engineering is an expression of abilities of visualization (Vz), numerical skill (N), and verbal comprehension (V), and the criterion measure is simply a global rating of job performance, the best predictor is likely to be a conglomerate that contains or predicts all three components—Vz, N, and V—not any one of these components as such. In this kind of prediction situation, it has been found again and again (e.g., Campbell, 1990; Schmidt et al., 1988) that broad conglomerate measures are better predictors than a primary or second-stratum factor and usually are as good as a best-weighted linear combination of several such factors. Also, after the prediction obtained with the conglomerate measure is taken into account, primary or second-strata abilities provide little or no additional predictability. Such results are necessary consequences of not distinguishing separate components of outcome in criterion measurements.

It is difficult to identify the separate abilities involved in educational and occupational achievements and difficult in practice to measure them. It is not done in most studies of predicting important outcomes. In the majority of prediction studies, therefore, a conglomerate measure, often unfortunately referred to as representing *g*, has been found to be the best predictor of important outcomes. But when, and to the extent that, different dimensions of outcome are distinguished, these distinct features usually are best predicted by separate predictor dimensions—dimensions that are most similar to the separate features of outcome (Ackerman, 1992; Anastasi, 1989; Carretta, 1989; Colberg & Nestor, 1987; Larson & Wolfe, 1995; Prediger, 1989; Schmidt et al., 1992). Different kinds of achievements are themselves different cognitive abilities and combinations of abilities (Berman, 1989; Lave, 1989; Nunes, Carraher, & Schliemann, 1993). To most accurately predict such outcomes, it is necessary to measure different abilities reliably in both the outcome and the predictors.

In general, the best predictor of educational and occupational achievements are similar achievements (regarded as predictors) (Glaser & Bassock, 1989; Perkins & Solomon, 1989; Reif & Allen, 1992). Vocabulary and information learned in high school social studies are the best predictors of performance in college social studies courses. Mathematics achievement at one level is the best predictor of mathematics achievement at the next level. The best predictors of component abilities of achievements are similar abilities measured in predictors. For example, in a study of performance in physics, Levidow, Hunt, and Hinman (1996) distinguished in the outcome between knowledge and reasoning, and they found that Gc best predicted knowledge and Gf best predicted reasoning.

Over short periods of time—few years between predictor measurement and assessment of criterion achievement—the best second-stratum ability predictors of academic criteria are usually conglomerate estimates containing much Gc, TSR, and Gq; measures that indicate Gf, SAR, and Gs are among the weaker predictors. This order of predictor validities tends to become reversed as length of time increases between measurement of predictors and measurement of outcome—measures containing or indicating Gf and SAR become better predictors relative to measures that primarily indicate Gc and TSR (Ackerman, 1987, 1989; Austin, Humphreys, & Hulin, 1989; Cattell, 1957, 1971).

Overall, the results from prediction studies indicate that usually only broad conglomerate measures of outcome are obtained and that the best predictors of such outcomes are broad conglomerate measures of predictor abilities, but when different abilities are distinguished in criterion measures, predictors that are most similar to these achievements are the best predictors.

Studies of Heritability

Heritability evidence derives from comparison studies of samples of people of different degrees of biological relationship: identical (monozygotic, or MZ) twins compared with fraternal twins and/or ordinary siblings, children compared with parents. The variance in measurements of individual differences is partitioned into estimates of two proportions: a proportion, interpreted as heritability, associated with the differences in biological relatedness (MZ twins compared with siblings) and a nonerror proportion remaining, interpreted as representing environmental influences (Loehlin, Lindzey, & Spuhler, 1975; Plomin, DeFries, & McClearn, 1980; Plomin & Loehlin, 1989; Chipuer, Rovine, & Plomin, 1990). Although it is impossible to fully separate heredity and environment with such partitioning, and heritability is a population statistic that depends very much on the reliability of measures and the variability of environmental opportunities within the society where the estimates are obtained (e.g., Herrnstein, 1973; Schonemann, 1990), the results from heritability analyses are useful in suggesting how different kinds of measures are more and less associated with degrees of biological relationship.

Heritability might be estimated for any cognitive ability, and some of the primary abilities have been so studied (DeFries, Kuse, & Vandenberg, 1979; Plomin et al., 1980; Nichols, 1978; Vandenberg, 1962, 1971), but most of the research and discussion of heritability has centered on mixture measures of general intelligence. In this research it has been found that for samples of identical twins (who basically have the same genetic structure) reared in the same home, the correlation between the twins' IQ scores is about .8 to .9. The comparable correlation for fraternal twins (who share genes to the same extent as ordinary siblings, or a child and parent), has been about .6 to .7. The correlation between IQs of MZ twins reared apart is smaller than the correlation for MZ twins reared together but larger than the correlation for fraternal twins reared together (Bouchard & Propping, 1993). For samples of ordinary siblings and parent child pairs, the correlations have hovered around .5. For half siblings, the correlations have been roughly .3 to .4. The correlations for pairings of first cousins, uncle–nephew, aunt–niece, and child–grandparent have been a bit lower than this. For unrelated people raised in the same home, the correlations have ranged between .0 and .3.

The results thus suggest that some of the individual differences in variability of IQ measures stems from genetic factors—the greater the degree of biological relationship, the higher the correlation. But the inseparability and thus confounding of genetic and environmental influences sully this interpretation. For the greater the degree of biological relationship, the more similar are the environments in which people develop. The environments for identical twins are most similar, for fraternal twins next most similar, for ordinary siblings next after this, and for other comparisons, the similarities expected for environments decrease monotonically with decrease in similarities in genetic structure. Genetic and environmental influences thus are mixed. The influences are not unmixed by partitioning the variance into the part representing the similarity of biologically related people and a residual. The extent of the confounding is unknown, but it is there.

If people of the same degree of biological relationships could be assigned at random to different environments, if MZ twins separated at birth (or ideally before this) could be randomly assigned to childrearing environments, for example, the confounding of genetic and environmental influences would be eliminated. But this is not possible and thus is not done in research. MZ twins separated at birth are placed in similar kinds of homes, usually with relatives, usually with people of the same religion, similar economic circumstances, and so on. The assignment is not random. Heritability estimates thus always reflect to some unknown degree both environmental and genetic determination of individual differences.

Heritability estimates based on measures of IQ are ambiguous, because these mixture measures contain different proportions of Gf, Gc, and other cognitive capabilities. Heritability studies of different intelligences have been motivated primarily by Cattell's (1941, 1957) theory stipulating different heritabilities for Gf and Gc. Three critical hypotheses stem from this theory.

The first hypothesis stipulates that Gf reflects, primarily, genetic influences. These influences interact with environmental influences to produce Gc, which reflects, primarily, environmental influences. Thus, the heritability of Gf should be substantially larger than the heritability of Gc.

The second hypothesis stipulates that Gc stems from Gf, which is "invested" in the development of Gc. Gc becomes independent from Gf as individual differences in environmental influences accumulate through childhood. Gf precedes development of Gc and can predict it, but Gc follows development of Gf and so should not predict it. Rather, environmental individual differences should predict Gc, but not Gf.

The third hypothesis follows from the first two. Because, in the earliest period of life there would have been few individual differences in environmental influences and little time for such influences to operate, there should be virtually no distinction between Gf and Gc, but as development proceeds beyond the earliest years, the distinction between Gf and Gc should become clearer and clearer, and the correlation between these abilities should become smaller and smaller.

The evidence does not support these hypotheses, but neither does it provide an unequivocal basis for rejecting them.

First, the evidence does not clearly indicate that the heritability of Gf is larger than the heritability of Gc. In two samples, one of 647 people for whom Gf measures were obtained and one in which a Gc measure was obtained on 1,024 people, each sample involving identical and fraternal twins reared together, siblings reared together and apart, and unrelated persons raised together, Cattell (1982, 1987) found the difference between the heritability for Gf and Gc to be .04. Although statistically significant in large samples, the difference is too small to indicate that Gc is due mainly environmental influences and Gf due mainly to genetic influences. Results from further analyses suggested that the difference might be somewhat larger than .04 but still too small to provide good support. The difference in the heritability estimates based on twins alone was only .02. Moreover, results and summaries of results provided by DeFries et al. (1979), Plomin et al. (1980), Nichols (1978), and McArdle, Goldsmith, and Horn (1981) suggest that the average of the heritabilities for abilities that define Gf is no larger than the corresponding average for the abilities of Gc.

Results from the pioneering study of Schmidt and Crano (1974) appeared to support the second hypothesis of Cattell's theory, the investment hypothesis. It turned out, however, that when differences in the reliabilities of measures were taken into account, Gf was no more predictive of Gc than Gc was predictive of Gf.

In another study of this hypothesis, the sampling was across a major portion of the life span (McArdle, 1995). Results indicated that Gf was not a precursor of Gc in either childhood or adulthood. However, the span of age in childhood was a jump from early childhood to adolescence. It would seem that the major investments of Gf in the development of Gc would occur in the earliest period of childhood—a period from birth to early childhood. A more thorough analysis of this period of development might yield support for the investment hypothesis.

McArdle (1995) found that in adulthood Gc was a precursor to Gf. This was not predicted by Cattell's statement of the investment hypothesis, but it is consistent with another form of this hypothesis. That form of the hypothesis states that knowledge developed in Gc includes knowledge about how to maintain health and avoid conditions that destroy neurons and decrease Gf abilities (conditions of exposure to inebriation, carbon monoxide, anesthetics, drugs, etc.). Development of Gc, therefore, is the precursor investment in maintenance of Gf.

The evidence generally does not support the third hypothesis of Cattell's theory, namely, the idea that the distinction between Gf and Gc (and other intelligences) will not be seen in early childhood. Few distinctions in cognitive capabilities can be measured in infants, but distinctions between Gf, Gc, SAR, and TSR functions can be seen in samples of children as young as 4 years old (Ellison, Horn, & Browning, 1983; Horn, 1985; Stankov, 1978). The correlations among these dimensions were no smaller in samples of young children than in samples of older children and samples of adults.

The results from studies of heritability and from studies of early childhood differentiation between cognitive capabilities thus lead to a conclusion that the outlines for different intelligences can be seen in early childhood. The different intelligences appear to stem from separate genetic determiners and separate environmental determiners. It follows logically that the observed distinctions probably mirror distinctions in neurological functions.

Neurological Evidence

All in all, results from studies of heritability suggest that measures of what is called general intelligence are mixtures of attributes that are inherited separately rather in the way that eye, ear, cheekbone, lip, and nose characteristics of the face are inherited separately. It appears that different sets of genes determine structures and functions of the brain and that these different structures and functions support cognitive capabilities.

For example, the norepinephrine system of the brain, which centers around the locus coeruleus and branches largely into the hypothalamus and adjacent areas, is associated with neurological arousal such as is characteristic of Gf (see Iverson, 1979; Horn, 1982, 1985, for review). The dopamine system, on the other hand, centered around the *substantia nigra* and *corpus striatum*, is linked to a complex of events associated with coordination abilities and Parkinson's disease. The serotonin system also has a distinct place of function in the brain and distinct associations in behavior.

Anatomical analyses also indicate distinct functions associated with different sections of the brain. The left hemisphere, for example, is associated with different aspects of intellectual function than is the right hemisphere, and a growing mound of evidence suggests that the top-to-bottom and front-to-back divisions of the brain are even more important indicators of distinct ability functions than is the left-to-right division (Bourne, Ekstrand, & Dominowski, 1971; Blackwood & Coresellis, 1976; Prohovnik, 1980).

The structures and functions of the brain thus are distinct and derive from different genetic determinants. The different structures and functions have a different role to play in sensation, perception, and learning. Different configurations of these distinct features produce different cognitive capacities, different perceptions, and different ways to process the same information. Just as there are many different configurations of facial features that provide examples of a "beautiful face," so there are many configurations of features of brains that exemplify the "good brain" that underlies good intelligence. The terms "intelligence" and "beauty" unite diversity in a single word in colloquial language, but this is not the language of science. The words are not expressions of lawful functions. Studies of how the brain functions and of different brains do not support any known theory of general intelligence. To the contrary, this evidence suggests that there should be several intelligences.

SUMMARY

Evidence accumulated over the course of this century has made it clear that the phenomenon of human intelligence is multidimensional. Abilities that characterize this phenomenon are found at several levels of generality. A huge number of tests are regarded as indicating intelligence, or basic features of intelligence. The common factors among these tests are known as primary mental abilities. Redundancy among the PMAs indicates nine broad abilities, several of which appear to represent intelligence. This evidence of common factors, plus evidence indicating different patterns of developmental change for the different factors and evidence from considerations of neurological functioning and heritability, suggests that although one word, "intelligence," is used to refer to human cognitive capabilities, a single scientific concept does not represent the phenomenon. There appear to be several intelligences.

A description and system for explaining this evidence is Gf-Gc theory. This theory has changed over the years to accommodate to emerging evidence. At first it was a theory of two intelligences. Today, it would be better labeled the theory of several intelligences: reasoning intelligence (Gf), the intelligence of knowledge stemming from acculturation (Gc), visual intelligence (Gv), auditory intelligence (Ga), the intelligence of short-term apprehension and retention (SAR), the intelligence of fluency and retrieval from long-term storage (TSR), and quantitative intelligence (Gq). Also part of the system are broad process of intellectual speed (Gs), and speed of decision making (QDS) that may be forms of intelligence. Narrower processes of sensory detection (auditory, visual), carefulness, concentration, attention, hypothesis formation, and incidental memory are also important descriptors of the system.

Evidence obtained in many kinds of studies suggest that the structural organization relates to (1) organization in central nervous system, (2) distinctions between genetic and environmental influences, and (3) age differences and age changes. The broad intelligences are construct independent: No one of them is fully predicted by a best-weighted linear combination of the others. They stem from different combinations of genetic and environmental determinants. They are affected in different ways by influences associated with injuries, childrearing, and education. They are brought about by different patterns of practice that vary over individuals in intensity, length, and quality. They increase with learning, practice, and use. Without use (practice) they decline. They decline also with loss of neurological base. Over the ages of childhood all increase. As development continues through adulthood, increases in Gc and TSR—maintained abilities—are sufficient to show up in averages for samples of people of different ages. In the same samples, averages for Gf, SAR, and Gs—vulnerable abilities—decrease. These differences in averages are seen in both cross-sectional and longitudinal data. The maintained and vulnerable abilities appear to be linked to separate organizations within the central nervous system.

QUALIFICATIONS AND OTHER POINTS OF PERSPECTIVES

It is important to recognize that whereas Gf-Gc theory provides an empirically based system for describing the phenomena of human cognitive capabilities, it is by no means a definitive theory and has a number of important limitations. These limitations should be kept in mind by researchers as they work to develop better theory.

Gf-Gc theory is largely a descriptive empirical generalization of research findings; it is much less a deductive explanation of these findings (Sternberg, 1985). The findings of previous factor analyses largely determined the choice of variables and hypotheses that have gone into building the evidence from which the theory derives. In successive studies over the course of this century, tests used to indicate a factor in one study were chosen, or designed, to be similar to tasks that had been used to indicate such a factor in previous studies. A kind of tradition thus was built, and Gf-Gc theory grew out of this tradition. Sternberg points out that this does not constitute an a priori, theoretical basis for establishing evidence for a theory. This point is well taken.

Although important, this point should not detract from awareness that all scientific theory necessarily is a product of history and culture (Kuhn, 1970), and good theory should be based on "the tradition" of what has been established as known. Theory should summarize and describe: It should be inductive. It should be deductive, too. This is the feature to which Sternberg points. The best of scientific theory is both inductive and deductive. As described by Cattell (1957), it evolves out of a repetitive spiral of building on what is known (induction), which leads to deductions that generate empirical studies and more induction, which leads to further deductions, which spawn further induction, and so on.

Although mainly inductive, Gf-Gc structural theory is also deductive. Many of the paradigms, tests, and items that were studied over this century and that form the structural basis for the theory were derived from hypotheses about the nature of intelligence. Tests were designed to test hypotheses about functions. For example, verbal reasoning tasks were selected in the Horn–Cattell (1967) study to test hypotheses that fluid reasoning (Gf) can involve verbal abilities as well as spatial abilities and is distinctly different from visual processing (Gv). The results from factor-analytic research are distillations of many theories of intelligence. The results confirm and disconfirm many hypotheses.

A major limitation of the theory is inherent in its structure. The capabilities of the theory are described in terms of Cartesian coordinates or factors. These factors may be rotated into an infinity of different positions, each equally adequate for describing the relationships among abilities, but each calling for different concepts—different language, different theory substantively—for describing abilities.

A metatheory of simple structure has guided the rotation that has been accepted as the basic structure of Gf-Gc theory. This metatheory requires that at the primary and second-strata levels manifest abilities relate to few factors and factors relate to few abilities. This is a reasonable requirement for studies designed to indicate it (and many studies have been so designed), but it is not an indication of how abilities must be organized to account for relationships or how they must function in the practice of thinking.

Similarly, the order of factors (as primary factors and second-strata factors) is not intrinsic to the phenomenon; it is a matter of the design of studies (Humphreys, 1976). For example, a primary factor, F, defined by tests of the form x, y, and z can be identified as a second-stratum factor if the study is designed at the primary level to have three tests of the x type—x_1, x_2, x_3—three tests of the

y type—y_1, y_2, y_3—and three of the z type—z_1, z_2, z_3. Three primary factors—x, y, and z—will then be identified at the primary level, and these will define the factor F at the second stratum.

A fundamental limitation of any theory built on a rectilinear system of factors is that it is not of a form that well describes natural phenomena. It is thus unlikely to be fully adequate. It is a system that can accurately describe rectangular structures built by humans (the right angles of city streets or rooms of buildings) but not the rounded and irregular structures of mother nature. The phenomena of nature are not usually well described by the linear equations of a Cartesian coordinate system. A system of factors is not a system for representing rounded structures such as we see in the configurations of plants and animals or the human brain. Nor is it a set of structural formulas such as those for the hydrocarbons, the chief constituents of living things. The equations that describe the outer structure and convolutions of brains must be parabolas, cycloids, cissoids, spirals, foliums, exponentials, hyperboles, and the like. It is likely that the equations that best describe the inner organizations and workings of brains—human capabilities—are of the same forms, not those that describe city blocks and buildings.

Gf-Gc theory provides few details about how abilities develop or about how cognitive processes interact and work together to produce the behavior seen in abilities. The test for a functional unity g factor model for Gf is illustrative of functional theory, but no such models have been developed for most of the constructs of the theory. The theory does little to indicate the dynamic processing of human cognition.

The kind of system that ultimately will best describe human abilities and their development will be functional and more nearly of the form of carbon compounds. It will map on to brain functions. To represent development mathematically, it will be more nearly of the form of a spiral of Archimedes or equiangular spiral.

In the long run, knowing that science is a never-ending search for better explanations and that no model of reality is reality, we can be confident that Gf-Gc theory will be replaced by a better theory.

NOTES

1. No theory quite reaches such an ideal, but all should be judged against it. The best theory is one that accounts for the most and most important evidence. Lesser theories may account for some evidence but fail to explain important evidence that is well documented. Some theories that are quite appealing to common sense account for little evidence other than that of common sense. Such theories often appear in popular books and magazines. They are not necessarily incorrect; they are simply unproven and in that sense are not or have yet to become scientific theories.

2. This can be seen by plugging T_{ij} and T_{ik} into the calculation formula for the product moment correlation and deriving the theory side of the equation. That is, with the total scores and factor scores in standard score form, the correlation between tests j and k is

    $$r_{jk} = \text{Sum}(T_{ij})(T_{ik})/N = \text{Sum}(S_j s_{ij} + G_j g_{ij})(S_k s_{ik} + G_k g_{ik})/N$$

    which is

    $$= S_j S_k \text{Sum}(s_{ij})(s_{ik})/N + S_j G_k \text{Sum}(s_{ij})(g_{ik})/N + G_j S_k \text{Sum}(g_{ij})(s_{ik})/N + G_j G_k \text{Sum}(g_{ij})(g_{ik})/N$$

    $$= 0 + 0 + 0 + G_j G_k \,(1.0)$$

    $$= G_j G_k$$

    That is, each of the Sum( )( )/N terms containing specific factor scores is a correlation that the model requires to be zero, while the Sum$(g_{ij})(g_{ik})/N$ is a variance for the common factor of theory, which is in standard score form and thus has variance equal to 1.00.

3. Thomson's (1919) theory of bonds is also an account of how tests measuring different things may be linked together in a common factor.

4. Such evidence alone would not provide a basis for full understanding of *g* any more than the identification of black holes in the universe, in itself, provides full understanding of these phenomena. Additional structural evidence would be needed to establish the distinctiveness of a particular unity relative to other unities (as in distinguishing heart, liver, kidneys, etc.) and thus structural evidence alone would not be sufficient. There would need to be evidence indicating the unity in development, in sequence of processes, in responses to manipulations. Many forms of evidence would be needed to provide full understanding of the functional unity.

   Although structural evidence alone is not adequate to provide a basis for full understanding, evidence indicating fit of a *g* model would be important. It would indicate lawful order among measures and a basis for seeking further evidence.

5. In the oldest ages (beyond 70) there may be some decline in these abilities that increase throughout most of adulthood (Lindenberger & Baltes, 1994; Schaie & Baltes, 1977; Schaie, 1994).

6. "Cohort," from Latin, meaning "1. In the Roman army, one of the ten divisions of a legion. 2. A company or band, esp. of warriors." *Webster's New Collegiate Dictionary.*

7. Gf, SAR, and Gs are said to be vulnerable abilities not only because they decline first and most with age in adulthood but also because they are most irreversibly affected by (are most vulnerable to) injuries to the central nervous system. Gc and TSR are said to be maintained abilities because they do not decline with age in adulthood and because, although depressed immediately following by brain damage (e.g., that produced by stroke), they "spring back" to nearly preinjury level in the weeks of the recovery period.

REFERENCES

Ackerman, P. L. (1987). Individual differences in skill learning: An integration of psychometric and information processing perspectives. *Psychological Bulletin, 102,* 3–27.

Ackerman, P. L. (1989). Within-task intercorrelations of skill performance: Implications for predicting individual differences? *Journal of Applied Psychology, 74,* 360–364.

Ackerman, P. L. (1992). Predicting individual differences in complex skill acquisition: Dynamics of ability determinants. *Journal of Applied Psychology, 77,* 598–614.

Alexander, W. P. (1935). Intelligence, concrete and abstract. *British Journal of Psychology* (Monograph Suppl. No. 19).

Anastasi, A. (1989). Ability testing in the 1980's and beyond: Some major trends. *Public Personnel Management Journal, 18,* 471–484.

Austin, J. T., & Hanisch, K. A. (1990). Occupational attainment as a function of abilities and interests: A longitudinal analysis using project TALENT data. *Journal Applied Psychology, 75,* 77–86.

Austin, J. T., Humphreys, L. G., & Hulin, C. L. (1989). Another view of dynamic criteria: A critical reanalysis of Barrett, Caldwell, Alexander. *Personnel Psychology, 42,* 593–596.

Baltes, P. B., & Schaie, K. W. (1974). The myth of the twilight years. *Psychology Today, 40,* 35–40.

Birren, J. E. (1965). Age changes in speed of behavior: Its central nature and physiological correlates. In A. T. Welford & J. E. Birren (Eds.), *Behavior aging and the nervous system.* Springfield, IL: Charles C. Thomas.

Birren, J. E. (1974). Psychophysiology and speed of response. *American Psychologist, 29,* 808–815.

Blackwood, W., & Coresellis, J. A. (Eds.). (1976). *Greenfield's neuropathology.* London: Arnold.

Bouchard, T. J., & Propping, P. (1993). *Twins as a tool of behavioral genetics.* West Sussex, England: Wiley.

Bourne, L. R., Ekstrand, B. R., & Dominowski, R. L. (1971). *The psychology of thinking.* Englewood Cliffs, NJ: Prentice-Hall.

Brigham, C. C. (1932). *The study of error.* New York: College Entrance Examination Board.

Brown, W. (1933). The mathematical and experimental evidence for the existence of a central intellective factor. *British Journal of Psychology, 23,* 171–179.

Burt, C. (1909). Experimental tests of general intelligence. *British Journal of Psychology, 3,* 94–177.

Burt, C. (1911). Experimental tests of higher mental processes and their relation to general intelligence. *Journal of Experimental Pedagogy, 1,* 93–112.

Burt, C. (1941). *Factors of the mind.* London: University of London Press.

Burt, C. (1949a). The structure of the mind: A review of the results of factor analysis. *British Journal of Psychology, 19,* 176–199.

Burt, C. (1949b). Subdivided factors. *British Journal of Statistical Psychology, 2,* 41–63.

Campbell, J. P. (1990). An overview of the army selection and classification project (Project A). *Personnel Psychology, 43,* 231–239.

Carretta, T. R. (1989). USAF pilot selection and classification systems. *Aviation Space Environment, 60,* 46–49.

Carroll, J. B. (1972). Stalking the wayward factors. *Contemporary Psychology, 17,* 321–324.

Carroll, J. B. (1989). Factor analysis since Spearman: Where do we stand? What do we know? In R. Kanfer, P. L. Ackerman, & R. Cudeck (Eds.), *Abilities, motivation, and methodology: The Minnesota symposium on learning and individual differences* (pp. 43–67). Hillsdale, NJ: Erlbaum.

Carroll, J. B. (1993). *Human cognitive abilities: A survey of factor analytic studies.* New York: Cambridge University Press.

Cattell, R. B. (1941). Some theoretical issues in adult intelligence testing. *Psychological Bulletin, 38,* 592.

Cattell, R. B. (1957). *Personality and motivation structure and measurement.* New York: World Book.

Cattell, R. B. (1971). *Abilities: Their structure, growth and action.* Boston: Houghton Mifflin.

Cattell, R. B. (1982). *The inheritance of personality and ability.* New York: Academic Press.

Cattell, R. B. (1987). *Intelligence: Its structure, growth and action.* New York: North-Holland.

Cattell, R. B., & Horn, J. L. (1978). A check on the theory of fluid and crystallized intelligence with description of new subtest designs. *Journal of Educational Measurement, 15,* 139–164.

Charness, N. (1991). Expertise in chess: The balance between knowledge and search. In K. A. Ericsson & J. Smith (Eds.), *Toward a general theory of expertise: Prospects and limits* (pp. 30–62). Cambridge, England: Cambridge University Press.

Chipuer, H. M., Rovine, M. J., & Plomin, R. (1990). LISREL modeling: Genetic and environmental influences on IQ revisited. *Intelligence, 14*(1), 11–29.

Colberg, M., & Nestor, M. A. (1987). *The use of illogical biases in psychometrics.* Eighth International Congress on Logic, Methodology & Philosophy of Science, Moscow.

Commons, M. (1985). *How novelty produced continuity in cognitive development within a domain and accounts for unequal development across domains.* Toronto: SRCD.

Cox, G. W. (1928). *Mechanical aptitude.* London: Methuen.

DeFries, J. C., Kuse, A. R., & Vandenberg, S. G. (1979). Genetic correlations, environmental correlations and behavior. In J. R. Royce & L. P. Mos (Eds.), *Theoretical advances in behavior genetic* (pp. 389–421). Alpen aan den Rijn, Netherlands: Sijthoff Noordhoff Internalional.

Donaldson, G., & Horn, J. L. (1992). Age, cohort, and time developmental muddles: Easy in practice, hard in theory. *Experimental Aging Research, 18,* 213–222.

Eckstrom, R. B., French, J. W., & Harman, M. H. (1979). Cognitive factors: Their identification and replication. *Multivariate Behavioral Research Monographs, 79*(2).

El Koussy, A. A. H. (1935). The visual perception of space. *British Journal of Psychology* (Monograph Suppl. 7, No. 20).

Ellison, P. H., Horn, J. L., & Browning, C. (1983). A large-sample, many variable study of motor dysfunction of infancy. *Journal of Pediatric Psychology, 8,* 345–357.

Ericsson, K. A., & Charness, N. (1994). Expert performance: Its structure and acquisition. *American Psychologist, 49,* 725–747.

Ericsson, K. A., Krampe, R. T., & Heizmann, S. (1993). Can we create gifted people? In CIBA Foundation Symposium, *The origins and development of high ability* (pp. 22–249). Chichester, England: Wiley.

Ericsson, K. A., Krampe, R. T., & Tesch-Romer. (1993). The role of deliberate practice in the acquisition of expert performance. *Psychological Review, 100,* 363–406.

Ericsson, K. A., & Lehmann, A. C. (1996). Expert and exceptional performance. *Annual Review, 47,* 273–305.

Eysenck, H. J. (1939). Primary mental abilities. *British Journal of Educational Psychology, 9,* 270–275.

Eysenck, H. J. (1979). *The structure and measurement of intelligence.* New York: Springer-Verlag.

Eysenck, H. J. (Ed.). (1982). *A model for intelligence.* Berlin: Springer-Verlag.

Flynn, J. R. (1984). The mean IQ of Americans: Massive gains 1932 to 1978. *Psychological Bulletin, 95,* 29–51.

Flynn, J. R. (1994). IQ gains over time. In R. J. Sternberg (Ed.), *Encyclopedia of intelligence* (pp. 617–623). New York: Macmillan.

French, J. W. (1951). The description of aptitude and achievement tests in terms of rotated factors. *Psychometric Monographs* (No. 5).

French, J. W., Eckstrom, R. B., & Price, L. A. (1963). *Manual and kit of reference tests for cognitive factors.* Princeton, NJ: Educational Testing Service.

Glaser, R., & Bassock, M. (1989). Learning theory and the study of instruction. *Annual Review of Psychology, 40,* 631–666.

Guilford, J. P. (1956). The structure of the intellect. *Psychological Bulletin, 53,* 276–293.

Guilford, J. P. (1964). Zero intercorrelations among tests of intellectual abilities. *Psychological Bulletin, 61,* 401–404.

Guilford, J. P. (1967). *The nature of human intelligence.* New York: McGraw-Hill.

Gustafsson, J. E. (1984). A unifying model for the structure of intellectual abilities. *Intelligence, 8,* 179–203.

Gustafsson, J. E. (1985). Measuring and interpreting *g. Behavioral and Brain Sciences, 8,* 231–232.

Hakstian, A. R., & Cattell, R. B. (1974). The checking of primary ability structure on a broader basis of performances. *British Journal of Educational Psychology, 44,* 140–154.

Hakstian, A. R., & Cattell, R. B. (1978). Higher stratum ability structure on a basis of twenty primary abilities. *Journal of Educational Psychology, 70,* 657–659.

Hartigan, J. A., & Wigdore, A. K. (Eds.). (1990). *Fairness in employment testing: Validity generalization, minority issues, and the general aptitude test battery.* Washington, DC: National Academic Press.

Herrnstein, R. J., & Murray, C. (1994). *The bell curve: Intelligence and class structure in American life.* New York: Free Press.

Herrnstein, R. J. (1973). *IQ in the meritocracy.* Boston: Little, Brown.

Hertzog, C. (1989). Influences of cognitive slowing on age differences. *Developmental Psychology, 25,* 636–651.

Hoffman, R. R. (1992). *The psychology of expertise: Cognitive research and empirical results.* New York: Springer-Verlag.

Holzinger, K. J., & Harman, H. H. (1941). *Factor analysis: A synthesis of factorial methods.* Chicago: University of Chicago Press.

Horn, J. L. (1965). *Fluid and crystallized intelligence: A factor analytic and developmental study of the structure among primary mental abilities.* Unpublished doctoral dissertation, University of Illinois, Champaign.

Horn, J. L. (1967). On subjectivity in factor analysis. *Educational and Psychological Measurement, 27,* 811–820.

Horn, J. L. (1968). Organization of abilities and the development of intelligence. *Psychological Review, 75,* 242–259.

Horn, J. L. (1972). The structure of intellect: Primary abilities. In R. M. Dreger (Ed.), *Multivariate personality research* (pp. 451–511). Baton Rouge, LA: Claitor's.

Horn, J. L. (1976). Human abilities: A review of research and theory in the early 1970s. *Annual Review of Psychology, 27,* 437–485.

Horn, J. L. (1980). Concepts of intellect in relation to learning and adult development. *Intelligence, 4,* 285–317.

Horn, J. L. (1982). The theory of fluid and crystallized intelligence in relation to concepts of cognitive psychology and aging in adulthood. In F. I. M. Craik & S. Trehub (Eds.), *Aging and cognitive processes* (pp. 237–278). New York: Plenum Press.

Horn, J. L. (1985). Remodeling old models of intelligence: Gf-Gc theory. In B. B. Wolman (Ed.), *Handbook of intelligence* (pp. 267–300). New York: Wiley.

Horn, J. L. (1988). Thinking about human abilities. In J. R. Nesselroade (Ed.), *Handbook of multivariate psychology* (pp. 645–685). New York: Academic Press.

Horn, J. L. (1989). Models for intelligence. In R. Linn (Ed.), *Intelligence: Measurement, theory and public policy* (pp. 29–73). Urbana, IL: University of Illinois Press.

Horn, J. L. (1989). Cognitive diversity: A framework for learning. In P. L. Ackerman, R. J. Sternberg, & R. Glaser (Eds.), *Learning and individual differences: Advances in theory and research* (pp. 61–114). New York: Freeman.

Horn, J. L., & Bramble, W. J. (1967). Second order ability structure revealed in right and wrong scores. *Journal of Educational Psychology, 58,* 115–122.

Horn, J. L., & Cattell, R. B. (1966). Refinement and test of the theory of fluid and crystallized intelligence. *Journal of Educational Psychology, 57,* 253–270.

Horn, J. L., & Cattell, R. B. (1967). Age differences in fluid and crystallized intelligence. *Acta Psychologica, 26,* 107–129.

Horn, J. L., & Donaldson, G. (1976). On the myth of intellectual decline in adulthood. *American Psychologist, 31*(10), 701–719.

Horn, J. L., & Donaldson, G. (1977). Faith is not enough: A response to the Baltes–Schaie claim that intelligence does not wane. *American Psychologist, 32*(5), 369–373.

Horn, J. L., & Donaldson, G. (1980). Cognitive development in adulthood. In O. G. Brim & J. Kagan (Eds.), *Constancy and change in human development* (pp. 445–529). Cambridge, MA: Harvard University Press.

Horn, J. L., Donaldson, G., & Engstrom, R. (1981). Apprehension, memory, and fluid intelligence decline in adulthood. *Research on Aging, 3*(1), 33–84.

Horn, J. L., & Hofer, S. M. (1992). Major abilities and development in the adult period. In R. Sternberg & C. Berg (Eds.), *Intellectual development* (pp. 44–91). New York: Cambridge University Press.

Horn, J. L., & Knapp, J. R. (1973). On the subjective character of the empirical base of Guilford's e-of-Intellect model. *Psychological Bulletin, 80,* 33–43.

Horn, J. L., & Knapp, J. R. (1974). Thirty wrongs of not make a right: Reply to Guilford. *Psychological Bulletin, 81,* 502–504.

Horn, J. L., & McArdle, J. J. (1992). A practical and theoretical guide to measurement invariance in aging research. *Experimental Aging Research, 18,* 117–144.

Horn, J. L., & Stankov, L. (1982). Auditory and visual factors of intelligence. *Intelligence, 6,* 165–185.

Humphreys, L. G. (1962). The organization of human abilities. *American Psychologist, 17,* 475–483.

Humphreys, L. G. (1974). The misleading distinction between aptitude and achievement tests. In D. R. Green (Ed.), *The aptitude achievement distinction* (pp. 262–274). Monterey, CA: CTB/McGraw-Hill.

Humphreys, L. G. (1976). A factor model for research on intelligence and problem solving. In L. B. Resnick (Ed.), *The nature of intelligence* (pp. 329–340). New York: Wiley.

Humphreys, L. G. (1979). The construct of general intelligence. *Intelligence, 3,* 105–120.

Humphreys, L. G. (1985). General intelligence: An integration of factor, test, and simplex theory. In B. B. Wolman (Ed.), *Handbook of intelligence: Theories, measurement, and applications* (pp. 201–224). New York: Wiley.

Humphreys, L. G. (1992). Commentary: What both critics and users of ability tests need to know. *Psychological Science, 3,* 271–274.

Hundal, P. S., & Horn, J. L. (1977). On the relationships between short-term learning and fluid and crystallized intelligence. *Applied Psychological Measurement, 1,* 11–21.

Iverson, L. L. (1979). The chemistry of the brain. *Scientific American, 241,* 134–149.

Jensen, A. R. (1980). *Bias in mental testing.* New York: Free Press.

Jensen, A. R. (1982). Reaction time and psychometric *g.* In J. J. Eysenck (Ed.), *A model for intelligence* (pp. 93–132). New York: Springer-Verlag.

Jensen, A. R. (1984). Test validity: *g* versus the specificity doctrine. *Journal of Social and Biological Structures, 7,* 93–118.

Jensen, A. R. (1992). Commentary: Vehicles of *g. Psychological Science, 5,* 275–278

Kaiser, H. F. (1958). The varimax criterion for analytic rotation in factor analysis. *Psychometrika, 23,* 187–200.

Kaufman, A. S., Kaufman-Packer, J. L., McLean, J. E., & Reynolds, C. R. (1991). In the pattern of intellectual growth and decline across the adult life span different for men and women? *Journal of Clinical Psychology, 47*(6), 801–812.

Kelley, T. L. (1928). *Crossroads in the mind of man: A study of differentiable mental abilities.* Stanford, CA: Stanford University Press.

Kuhn, T. S. (1970). *The structure of scientific revolutions* (2nd ed.). Chicago: University of Chicago Press.

Larson, G. E., & Wolfe, J. H. (1995). Validity results for *g* from an expanded test base. *Intelligence, 20,* 15–25.

Lave, J. (1989). Cognition in practice: Mind, mathematics and culture in everyday life. New York: Wiley.

Levidow, B. B., Hunt, E., & Hinmann, A. (1996). *The relation between fluid and crystallized intelligence and learning in introductory high school physics.* Seattle, WA: University of Washington, Department of Psychology.

Lindenberger, U., & Baltes, P. B. (1994). Aging and intelligence. In R. B. Sternberg (Ed.), *Encyclopedia of intelligence* (pp. 52–63). New York: Macmillan.

Loehlin, J. C., Lindzey, G., & Spuhler, J. N. (1975). *Race differences in intelligence.* San Francisco: Freeman.

Matarazzo, J. D. (1972). *Wechsler's measurement and appraisal of adult intelligence* (5th ed.). Baltimore: Williams & Wilkins.

McArdle, J. J. (1988). A dynamic and structural equation modeling with repeated measures data. In J. R. Nesselroade & R. B. Cattell (Eds.), *Handbook of multivatiariate experimental psychology* (Vol. II, pp. 561–614). New York: Plenum Press.

McArdle, J. J. (1995). A modeling examination of Cattell's investment theory of human abilities. *Proceedings European Congress of Psychology.* University of Athens, Greece.

McArdle, J. J., & Epstein, D. (1987). Latent growth curves within developmental structural equation models. *Child Development, 58,* 110–133.

McArdle, J. J., Goldsmith, H. H., & Horn, J. L. (1981). Genetic Structural equation models of fluid and crystallized intelligence. *Behavior Genetics, 60,* 607.

McArdle, J. J., & Hamagami, F. (1992). Modeling incomplete longitudinal and cross-sectional data using latent growth structural models. *Experimental Aging Research, 18,* 145–166.

McArdle, J. J., & Horn, J. L. (1983). *Validation by systems modeling of WAIS-R abilities.* Washington, DC: National Institute of Aging.

McArdle, J. J., & Horn, J. L. (1986). *Growth curves of adult intelligence modeled in the WAIS.* Unpublished manuscript, University of Virginia.

McGrew, K. S., & Flanagan, D. P. (1996). *An intelligence test desk reference (ITDR): A cross-battery approach to intelligence test interpretation.* Boston: Allyn & Bacon.

Nichols, R. (1978). Twin studies of ability, personality, and interests. *Homo, 29,* 158–173.

Nunes, T., Carraher, D. W., & Schliemann, A. D. (1993). *Street mathematics and school mathematics.* New York: Cambridge University Press.

Patterson, D. G., & Elliott, R. N. (1930). *Minnesota mechanical ability tests.* Minneapolis: University of Minnesota Press.

Perkins, D. N., & Solomon, G. (1989). Are cognitive skills context-bound? *Educational Research, 18,* 16–25.

Plomin, R., DeFries, J. C., & McClearn, G. E. (1980). *Behavioral genetics.* San Francisco: Freeman.

Plomin, R., & Loehlin, J. C. (1989). Direct and indirect IQ heritability estimates: A puzzle. *Behavior Genetics, 19*(3), 331–342.

Porteus, S. D. (1946). *The Porteus maze test: Revised.* New York: Psychological Corporation. (Original work published 1914)

Prediger, D. J. (1989). Ability differences across occupations: More than *g. Journal Vocational Behavior, 34,* 1–27.

Prohovnik, I. (1980). *Mapping brainwork.* Malmo, Sweden: CWK Gleerup.

Radford, J. (1990). *Child prodigies and exceptional early achievers.* New York: Free Press.

Raven, J. C. (1938). *Guide to using progressive matrices* (rev. 1954, 1956). London: H. K. Lewis.

Reif, F., & Allen, S. (1992). Cognition for interpreting scientific concepts: A study of acceleration. *Cognitive Instruction, 9,* 1–44.

Rimoldi, H. J. A. (1948). Study of some factors related to intelligence. *Psychometrika, 13,* 27–46.

Rossman, B. B., & Horn, J. L. (1972). Cognitive, motivational and temperamental indicants of creativity and intelligence. *Journal of Educational Measurement, 9,* 265–286.

Salthouse, T. A. (1985). Speed of behavior and its implications for cognition. In J. E. Birren & K. W. Schaie (Eds.), *Handbook of the psychology of aging* (2nd ed., pp. 400–426). New York: Van Nostrand Reinhold.

Salthouse, T. A. (Ed.). (1991). *Theoretical perspectives on cognitive aging.* Hillsdale, NJ: Erlbaum.

Salthouse, T. A. (1992). Influence of processing speed on adult age differences in working memory. *Acta Psychologica, 79,* 155–170.

Saunders, D. R. (1976). *Collected papers on the Personality Assessment System.* Princeton, NJ: Mathematica.

Schaie, K. W. (1973). Methodological problems in descriptive developmental research on adulthood and aging. In J. R. Nesselroade & H. W. Reese (Eds.), *Life-span developmental psychology: Developmental issues* (pp. 253–280). New York: Academic Press.

Schaie, K. W. (Ed.). (1983). *Longitudinal studies of adult psychological development.* New York: Guilford Press.

Schaie, K. W. (1994). The course of adult intellectual development. *American Psychologist, 49,* 304–314.

Schaie, K. W., & Baltes, P. B. (1977). Some faith helps see the forest: A final comment on the Horn and Donaldson myth of the Baltes–Schaie position on adult intelligence. *American Psychologist, 32,* 1118–1120.

Schaie, K. W., & Hertzog, C. (1982). Longitudinal methods. In B. B. Wolman, (Ed.), *Handbook of developmental psychology* (pp. 91–115). New York: Prentice Hall.

Schmid, J., & Leiman, J. M. (1957). The development of hierarchical factor solutions. *Psychometrika, 22,* 53–61.

Schmidt, F. L., & Crano, W. D. (1974). A test of the theory of fluid and crystallized intelligence in middle- and low-socioeconomic-status children: A cross-lagged panel analysis. *Journal of Educational Psychology, 66,* 255–261.

Schmidt, F. L., Hunter, J. E., & Larson, M. (1988). *General cognitive ability versus general and specific aptitudes in the prediction of training performance: Some preliminary findings.* Report for Navy Personnel Research Development Center.

Schmidt, F. L., Ones, D. S., & Hunter, J. E. (1992). Personnel selection. *Annual Review of Psychology, 43,* 627–670.

Schonemann, P. H. (1990). New questions about old heritability estimates. *Bulletin of the Psychonomic Science, 27,* 175–178.

Siegler, I. C., & Botwinick, J. (1979). A long-term longitudinal study of intellectual ability of older adults: The matter of selective subject attrition. *Journal of Gerontology, 34,* 242–245.

Spearman, C. (1927). *The abilities of man: Their nature and measurement.* London: Macmillan.

Spearman, C. (1937). *Psychology down the ages.* London: Macmillan.

Sperling, G. (1960). The information available in brief visual presentations. *Psychological Monographs, 74,* 498–450.

Stankov, L. (1978). Fluid and crystallized intelligence and broad perceptual factors among the 11 to 12 year olds. *Journal of Educational Psychology, 70*(3), 324–334.

Stankov, L. (1988). Aging, intelligence and attention. *Psychology of Aging, 3*(2), 59–74.

Stankov, L., & Horn, J. L. (1980). Human abilities revealed through auditory tests. *Journal of Educational Psychology, 72,* 21–44.

Sternberg, R. J. (1985). *Beyond IQ: A triarchic theory of human intelligence.* Cambridge, MA: Cambridge University Press.

Sternberg, R. J., & Detterman, D. K. (Eds.). (1986). *What is intelligence? Contemporary viewpoints on its nature and definition.* Norwood, NJ: Ablex.

Terman, L. M., & Merrill, M. (1973). Stanford–Binet Intelligence Scale, Form L-M: 1972 norms edition. Boston: Houghton Mifflin.

Thomson, G. A. (1919). On the cause of hierarchical order among correlation coefficients. *Proceedings of the Royal Society, A, 95,* 400–408.

Thurstone, L. L. (1938). Primary mental abilities. *Psychometric Monographs* (No. 1). Chicago: University of Chicago Press.

Thurstone, L. L. (1947). *Multiple factor analysis.* Chicago: University of Chicago Press.

Undheim, J. O., & Gustafsson, J. E. (1987). The hierarchical organization of cognitive abilities: Restoring general intelligence through the use of linear structural relations (LISREL). *Multivariate Behavioral Research 22,* 149–171.

Undheim, J. O., & Horn, J. L. (1977). Critical evaluation of Guilford's e-of-intellect theory. *Intelligence, 1,* 65–81.

Vandenberg, S. G. (1962). The hereditary abilities study: Hereditary components in a psychological test battery. *American Journal of Human Genetics, 14,* 20–237.

Vandenberg, S. G. (1971). What do we know today about the inheritance of intelligence and how do we know it? In R. Cancro (Ed.), *Intelligence: Genetic and environmental influences* (pp. 182–218). New York: Grune & Stratton.

Vernon, P. E. (1969). *Intelligence and Cultural Environment.* London: Methuen.

Vernon, P. E. (1979). *Intelligence, heredity, and environment.* San Francisco: Freeman.

Wechsler, D. (1955). *Manual for the Wechsler Adult Intelligence Scale.* New York: Psychological Corporation.

Wechsler, D. (1958). *The measurement and appraisal of adult intelligence* (4th ed.). Baltimore: Williams & Wilkins.

Wechsler, D. (1974). *Wechsler Intelligence Scale for Children—Revised.* New York: Psychological Corporation.

Wechsler, D. (1981). *Wechsler Adult Intelligence Scale—Revised.* New York: Psychological Corporation.

Welsh, J. R., Watson, T. W., & Ree, M. J. (1990). *Armed Services Vocational Battery (ASVAB). Predicting military criteria from general and specific abilities.* Brooks Air Force Base, TX: Air Force Human Resources Laboratory.

Willoughby, R. R. (1927). Family similarities in mental-test abilities. *Genetic Psychology Monographs, 2,* 235–277.

Woodcock, R. W. (1990). Theoretical foundations of the WJ-R measures of cognitive ability. *Journal of Psycho-Educational Assessment, 8,* 231–258.

Woodcock, R. W., & Johnson, M. B. (1990). *Woodcock–Johnson Psycho-Educational Battery—Revised.* Allen, TX: DLM Teaching Resources.

CHAPTER 5

The Triarchic Theory
of Intelligence

ROBERT J. STERNBERG

SOME PEOPLE SEEM TO DO what they do better than others, and so various cultures have created roughly comparable psychological constructs to try to explain, or at least to describe, this fact. The construct we have created we call intelligence. It is our way of saying that some people seem to adapt to the environments we both create and confront better than do others.

There have been numerous approaches to understanding the construct of intelligence, based on somewhat different metaphors for understanding the construct (Sternberg, 1990). For example, some investigators seek to understand intelligence via what I have referred to as a geographic model, in which intelligence is conceived as a map of the mind. Such researchers have used psychometric tests to uncover the latent factors alleged to underlie intellectual functioning. Other investigators have used a computational metaphor, viewing intelligence in much the way one views the symbolic processing of a computer. Still others have followed an anthropological approach, viewing intelligence as a unique cultural creation. The approach I take in the triarchic theory proposed here can be viewed as a systems approach in which many different aspects of intelligence are interrelated to each other in an attempt to understand how intelligence functions as a system.

The triarchic theory of human intelligence (Sternberg, 1985a, 1988) explains in an integrative way the relationship between intelligence and (1) the internal world of the individual, or the mental mechanisms that underlie intelligent behavior; (2) experience, or the mediating role of one's passage through life between the internal and external worlds of the individual; and (3) the external world of the individual, or the use of these mental mechanisms in everyday life in order to attain an intelligent fit to the environment.

A crucial difference between this theory and others is that the operationalizations (measurements) follow rather than precede the theory. Thus, rather than deriving the theory from factor or other analyses of tests, the tests are chosen on the basis of the tenets of the theory. We have used many different kinds of tests (see Sternberg, 1985a, 1988, for reviews), such as analogies, syllogisms, verbal comprehension, prediction of future outcomes, and decoding of nonverbal cues. In every case, though, the choice of tasks was dictated by the aspects of the theory that were being investigated rather than the other way around.

A. INTELLIGENCE AND THE INTERNAL WORLD OF THE INDIVIDUAL

Psychometricians, Piagetians, and information-processing psychologists have all recognized the importance of understanding the mental states or processes that underlie intelligent thought. In the triarchic theory, they seek this understanding by identifying and understanding of three basic kinds of information-processing components, referred to as metacomponents, performance components, and knowledge-acquisition components.

1) Metacomponents

Metacomponents are higher-order, executive processes used to plan what one is going to do, to monitor it while one is doing it, and evaluate it after it is done. These metacomponents include (1) recognizing the existence of a problem, (2) deciding on the nature of the problem confronting one, (3) selecting a set of lower-order processes to solve the problem, (4) selecting a strategy into which to combine these components, (5) selecting a mental representation on which the components and strategy can act, (6) allocating one's mental resources, (7) monitoring one's problem solving as it is happening, and (8) evaluating one's problem solving after it is done. Consider some examples of these higher-order processes.

Deciding on the nature of a problem plays a prominent role in intelligence. For example, the difficulty for young children as well as older adults in problem solving often lies not in actually solving a given problem but in figuring out just what the problem is that needs to be solved (see, e.g., Flavell, 1977; Sternberg & Rifkin, 1979). A major feature distinguishing people with mental retardation from normal persons is the need of the former to be instructed explicitly and completely as to the nature of the particular task they are solving and how it should be performed (Butterfield, Wambold, & Belmont, 1973; Campione & Brown, 1979). The importance of figuring out the nature of the problem is not limited to persons with mental retardation. Resnick and Glaser (1976) have argued that intelligence is the ability to learn from incomplete instruction.

Selection of a strategy for combining lower-order components is also a critical aspect of intelligence. In early information-processing research on intelligence, including my own (e.g., Sternberg, 1977), the primary emphasis was simply on figuring out what subjects do when confronted with a problem. What components do subjects use and into what strategies do they combine these components?

Soon, information-processing researchers began to ask why subjects use the strategies they choose. For example, Cooper (1982) reported that in solving spatial problems, and especially mental-rotation problems, some subjects seem to use a holistic strategy of comparison whereas others use an analytic strategy. She sought to figure out what leads subjects to the choice of one strategy over another. Siegler (1986) proposed a model of strategy selection in arithmetic computation problems that links strategy choice to both the rules and mental associations one has stored in long-term memory. MacLeod, Hunt, and Mathews (1978) found that high-spatial subjects tend to use a spatial strategy in solving sentence–picture comparison problems, whereas high-verbal subjects are more likely to use a linguistic strategy. In my own work, I have found that subjects tend to prefer certain strategies for analogical reasoning over others because they place fewer demands on working memory (Sternberg & Ketron, 1982). Similarly, subjects choose different strategies in linear–syllogistic reasoning (spatial, linguistic, mixed spatial–linguistic), but in this task, they do not always capitalize on their ability patterns to choose the strategy most suitable to their respective levels of spatial and verbal abilities (Sternberg & Weil, 1980). In sum, the selection of a strategy seems to be at least as important for understanding intelligent task performance as the efficacy with which the chosen strategy is implemented.

Intimately tied up with the selection of a strategy is the selection of a mental representation for information. In the early literature on mental representations, the emphasis seemed to be on understanding how information is represented. For example, can individuals use imagery as a form of mental representation (Kosslyn, 1980)? In more recent research, investigators have realized that people are quite flexible in their representations of information. The most appropriate question to ask seems to be not how such information is represented but which representations are used in what circumstances. For example, Sternberg (1977) found that analogy problems using animal names can draw on either spatial or clustering representations of the animal names. In the studies of strategy choice mentioned earlier, it was found that subjects can use either linguistic or spatial representations in solving sentence–picture comparisons (MacLeod et al., 1978) or linear syllogisms (Sternberg & Weil, 1980). Sternberg and Rifkin (1979) found that the mental representation of certain kinds of analogies can be either more or less holistic, depending on the ages of the subjects.

As important as any other metacomponent is one's ability to allocate one's mental resources. Different investigators have studied resource allocation in different ways. Hunt and Lansman (1982), for example, have concentrated on the use of secondary tasks in assessing information processing and have proposed a model of attention allocation in the solution of problems that involves both a primary and a secondary task. In my work, I have found that better problem solvers tend to spend relatively more time in global strategy planning (Sternberg, 1981). Similarly, in solving analogies, better analogical reasoners seemed to spend relatively more time encoding the terms of the problem than do poorer reasoners but relatively less time in operating on these encodings (Sternberg, 1977; Sternberg & Rifkin, 1979). In reading as well, the superior readers are better able than poorer readers to allocate their time across reading passages as a function of the difficulty of the passages to be read and the purpose for which the passages are being read (see Brown, Bransford, Ferrara, & Campione, 1983; Wagner & Sternberg, 1987).

Finally, monitoring one's solution process is a key aspect of intelligence (see also Brown, 1978). Consider, for example, the missionaries and cannibals problem, in which the subjects must "transport" a set of missionaries and cannibals across a river in a small boat without allowing the cannibals an opportunity to eat the missionaries, an event that can transpire only if the cannibals are allowed to outnumber the missionaries on either side of the river bank. The main kinds of errors that can be made are either to return to an earlier state in the problem space for solution or to make an impermissible move (Simon & Reed, 1976; also see Sternberg, 1982). Neither of these errors would result if a given subject closely monitored his or her solution processes. For young children learning to count, a major source of errors in counting objects is to count a given object twice, an error that, again, can result from a failure in solution monitoring (Gelman & Gallistel, 1978). The effects of solution monitoring are not limited, of course, to any one kind of problem. One's ability to use the strategy of means–ends analysis (Newell & Simon, 1972)—that is, reduction of differences between where one is solving a problem and where one wishes to get in solving that problem—depends on one's ability to monitor just where one is in problem solution.

Performance Components

Performance components are lower-order processes that execute the instructions of the metacomponents. These lower-order components solve the problems according to the plans laid out by the metacomponents. Whereas the number of metacomponents used in the performance of various tasks is relatively limited, the number of performance components is probably quite large. Many of these performance components are relatively specific to narrow ranges of tasks (Sternberg, 1979, 1983, 1985a).

One of the most interesting classes of performance components is that found in inductive reasoning of the kind measured by tests such as matrices, analogies, series completions, and classifications. These components are important because of the importance of the tasks into which they enter: Induction problems of these kinds show the highest loading on the so-called *g*, or general intelligence factor (Jensen, 1980; Snow & Lohman, 1984; Sternberg & Gardner, 1982). Thus, identifying these performance components can give us some insight into the nature of the general factor. I am not arguing for any one factorial model of intelligence (i.e., one with a general factor) over others: To the contrary, I believe that most factor models are mutually compatible, differing only in the form of rotation that has been applied to a given factor space (Sternberg, 1977). The rotation one uses is a matter of theoretical or practical convenience, not of truth or falsity.

The main performance components of inductive reasoning are encoding, inference, mapping, application, comparison, justification, and response. They can be illustrated with reference to an analogy problem, such as LAWYER : CLIENT :: DOCTOR :(a) PATIENT, (b) MEDICINE. In encoding, the subject retrieves from semantic memory semantic attributes that are potentially relevant for analogy solution. In inference, the subject discovers the relation between the first two terms of the analogy, here, LAWYER and CLIENT. In mapping, the subject discovers the higher-order relation that links the first half of the analogy, headed by LAWYER, to the second half of the analogy, headed by DOCTOR. In application, the subject carries over the relation inferred in the first half of the analogy to the second half of the analogy, generating a possible completion for the analogy. In comparison, the subject compares each of the answer options to the mentally generated completion, deciding which, if any, is correct. In justification, used optionally if none of the answer options matches the mentally generated solution, the subject decides which, if any, of the options is close enough to constitute an acceptable solution to the examiner. In response, the subject indicates an option, whether by means of pressing a button, making a mark on a piece of paper, or whatever.

Two fundamental issues have arisen regarding the nature of performance components as a fundamental construct in human intelligence. The first, mentioned briefly here, is whether their number simply keeps expanding indefinitely. Neisser (1982), for example, suggested that it does. As a result, he views the construct as of little use. But this expansion results only if one considers seriously those components that are specific to small classes of problems or to single problems. If one limits one's attention to the more important, general components of performance, the problem simply does not arise, as shown, for example, in Sternberg and Gardner's (1982) analysis of inductive reasoning or in Pellegrino and Kail's (1982) analysis of spatial ability. The second issue is one of the level at which performance components should be studied. In so-called cognitive-correlates research (Pellegrino & Glaser, 1979), theorists emphasize components at relatively low levels of information processing (Hunt, 1978, 1980; Jensen, 1982). In so-called cognitive-components research (Pellegrino & Glaser, 1979), theorists emphasize components at relatively high levels of information processing (e.g., Mulholland, Pellegrino, & Glaser, 1980; Snow, 1980; Sternberg, 1977). Because of the interactive nature of human information processing, it would appear that there is no right or wrong level of analysis. Rather, all levels of information processing contribute to both task and subject variance in intelligent performance. The most expeditious level of analysis depends on the task and subject population: Lower-level performance components might be more important, for example, in studying more basic information-processing tasks, such as choice reaction time, or in studying higher-level tasks in children who have not yet automatized the lower-order processes that contribute to performance of these tasks.

Knowledge-Acquisition Components

Knowledge-acquisition components are used to *learn how to do* what the metacomponents and performance components eventually do. Three knowledge-acquisition components appear to be central in intellectual functioning: (1) selective encoding, (2) selective combination, and (3) selective comparison.

Selective encoding involves sifting out relevant from irrelevant information. When new information is presented in natural contexts, relevant information for one's given purpose is embedded in the midst of large amounts of purpose-irrelevant information. A critical task for the learner is that of sifting the "wheat from the chaff," recognizing just what among all the pieces of information is relevant for one's purposes (see Schank, 1980).

Selective combination involves combining selectively encoded information in such a way as to form an integrated, plausible whole. Simply sifting out relevant from irrelevant information is not enough to generate a new knowledge structure. One must know how to combine the pieces of information into an internally connected whole (see Mayer & Greeno, 1972).

My emphasis on components of knowledge acquisition differs somewhat from the focus of some contemporary theorists in cognitive psychology, who emphasize what is already known and the structure of this knowledge (e.g., Chase & Simon, 1973; Chi, 1978; Keil, 1984). These various emphases are complementary. If one is interested in understanding, for example, differences in performance between experts and novices, clearly one would wish to look at the amount and structure of their respective knowledge bases. But if one wishes to understand how these differences come to be, merely looking at developed knowledge would not be enough. Rather, one would have to look as well at differences in the ways in which the knowledge bases were acquired. It is here that understanding of knowledge-acquisition components will prove to be most relevant.

We have studied knowledge-acquisition components in the domain of vocabulary acquisition (e.g., Sternberg, 1987; Sternberg & Powell, 1983). Difficulty in learning new words can be traced, at least in part, to the application of components of knowledge acquisition to context cues stored in long-term memory. Individuals with higher vocabularies tend to be those who are better able to apply the knowledge-acquisition components to vocabulary-learning situations. Given the importance of vocabulary for overall intelligence, almost without respect to the theory or test one uses, utilization of knowledge-acquisition components in vocabulary-learning situations would appear to be critically important for the development of intelligence. Effective use of knowledge-acquisition components is trainable. I have found, for example, that just 45 minutes of training in the use of these components in vocabulary learning can significantly and fairly substantially improve the ability of adults to learn vocabulary from natural-language contexts (Sternberg, 1987).

To summarize, then, the components of intelligence are an important part of the intelligence of the individual. The various kinds of components work together. Metacomponents activate performance and knowledge-acquisition components. These latter kinds of components in turn provide feedback to the metacomponents. Although one can isolate various kinds of information-processing components from task performance using experimental means, in practice, the components function together in highly interactive, and not easily isolable, ways. Thus, diagnoses as well instructional interventions need to consider all three types of components in interaction rather than any one kind of component in isolation. But understanding the nature of the components of intelligence is not, in itself, sufficient to understand the nature of intelligence because there is more to intelligence than a set of information-processing components. One could scarcely understand all of what it is that makes one person more intelligent than another by understanding the components of processing on, say, an intelligence test. The other aspects of the triarchic theory address some of the other aspects of intelligence that contribute to individual differences in observed performance, outside testing situations as well as within them.

☙ • INTELLIGENCE AND EXPERIENCE

Components of information processing are always applied to tasks and situations with which one has some level of prior experience (including the null level). Hence, these internal mechanisms are closely tied to one's experience. According to the experiential subtheory, the components are not equally good measures of intelligence at all levels of experience. Assessing intelligence requires one to consider not only components but the level of experience at which they are applied.

In recent years, there has been a tendency in cognitive science to study script-based behavior (e.g., Schank & Abelson, 1977), whether under the name of "script" or under some other name, such as "schema" or "frame." There is no longer any question that much of our behavior is scripted in some sense. However, from the standpoint of the present subtheory, such behavior is nonoptimal for understanding intelligence. Typically, one's actions when going to a restaurant, doctor's office, or movie theater do not provide good measures of intelligence, even though they do provide good measures of scripted behavior. What, then, is the relation between intelligence and experience?

According to the experiential subtheory, intelligence is best measured at those regions of the experiential continuum that involve tasks or situations that are either relatively novel, on the one hand, or in the process of becoming automatized, on the other. As Raaheim (1974) pointed out, totally novel tasks and situations provide poor measures of intelligence: One would not want to administer, say, trigonometry problems to a first-grader roughly 6 years old. But one might wish to administer problems that are just at the limits of the child's understanding, in order to test how far this understanding extends. Related is Vygotsky's (1978) concept of the zone of proximal development, in which one examines a child's ability to profit from instruction to facilitate his or her solutions of novel problems. To measure automatization skill, one might wish to present a series of problems—mathematical or otherwise—to see how long it takes for their solution to become automatic, and to see how automatized performance becomes. Thus, both slope and asymptote (if any) of automatization are of interest.

Ability to Deal with Novelty

Several sources of evidence converge on the notion that the ability to deal with relative novelty is a good way of measuring intelligence. Consider three such sources of evidence. First, we have conducted several studies on the nature of insight, both in children and in adults (Davidson & Sternberg, 1984; Sternberg & Davidson, 1982). In the studies with children (Davidson & Sternberg, 1984), we separated three kinds of insights: insights of selective encoding, insights of selective combination, and insights of selective comparison. Use of these knowledge-acquisition components is referred to as insightful when they are applied in the absence of existing scripts, plans, or frames. In other words, one must decide what information is relevant, how to put the information together, or how new information relates to old in the absence of any obvious cues on the basis of which to make these judgments. A problem is insightfully solved at the individual level when a given individual lacks such cues. A problem is insightfully solved at the societal level when no one else has these cues either. In our studies, we found that children who are intellectually gifted are so in part by virtue of their insight abilities, which represent an important part of the ability to deal with novelty.

The critical finding was that providing insights to the children significantly benefited the nongifted, but not the gifted, children. (None of the children performed anywhere near ceiling, so that the interaction was not due to ceiling effects.) In other words, the gifted children spontaneously had the insights and hence did not benefit from being given these insights. The nongifted children did not have the insights spontaneously and hence did benefit. Thus, the gifted children were better able to deal with novelty spontaneously.

Another source of evidence for the proposed hypothesis relating coping with novelty to intelligence derives from the large literature on fluid intelligence, which is in part a kind of intelligence that involves dealing with novelty (see Cattell, 1971). Snow and Lohman (1984; see also Snow, Kyllonen, & Marshalek, 1984) have multidimensionally scaled a variety of such tests and found the dimensional loading to follow a radex structure. In particular, tests with higher loadings on *g*, or general intelligence, fall closer to the center of the spatial diagram. The critical thing to note is that those tests that best measure the ability to deal with novelty fall closer to the center, and tests tend to be more removed from the center as their assessment of the ability to deal with novelty becomes more remote. In sum, evidence from the laboratories of others as well as mine supports the idea that the various components of intelligence that are involved in dealing with novelty, as measured in particular tasks and situations, provide particularly apt measures of intellectual ability.

Ability to Automatize Information Processing

There are several converging lines of evidence in the literature to support the claim that automatization ability is a key aspect of intelligence. For example, Sternberg (1977) found that the correlation between People–Piece (schematic picture) analogy performance and measures of general intelligence increased with practice, as performance on these items became increasingly automatized. Skilled reading is heavily dependent on automatization of bottom-up functions, and the ability to read well is an essential part of crystallized ability, whether as viewed from the standpoint of theories such as Cattell's (1971) or Vernon's (1971) or from the standpoint of tests of crystallized ability, such as the verbal portion of the Scholastic Assessment Test. Poor comprehenders often are those who have not automatized the elementary, bottom-up processes of reading and hence who do not have sufficient attentional resources to allocate to top-down comprehension processes. Ackerman (1987; Kanfer & Ackerman, 1989) has provided a three-stage model of automatization in which the first stage is related to intelligence although the latter two appear not to be.

Theorists such as Jensen (1982) and Hunt (1978) have attributed the correlation between such tasks as choice reaction time and letter matching to the relation between speed of information processing and intelligence. Indeed, there is almost certainly some relation, although I believe it is much more complex than these theorists seem to allow for. But a plausible alternative hypothesis is that at least some of that correlation is due to the effects of automatization of processing: Because of the simplicity of these tasks, they probably become at least partially automatized fairly rapidly and hence can measure both rate and asymptote of automatization of performance. In sum, then, although the evidence is far from complete, there is at least some support for the notion that rate and level of automatization are related to intellectual skill.

The ability to deal with novelty and the ability to automatize information processing are interrelated, as shown in the example of reading in this section. If one is well able to automatize, one has more resources left over for dealing with novelty. Similarly, if one is well able to deal with novelty, one has more resources left over for automatization. Thus, performance at the various levels of the experiential continuum are related to one another.

These abilities should not be viewed in a vacuum with respect to the componential subtheory. The components of intelligence are applied to tasks and situations at various levels of experience. The ability to deal with novelty can be understood in part in terms of the metacomponents, performance components, and knowledge-acquisition components involved in it. Automatization refers to the way these components are executed. Hence, the two subtheories considered so far are closely intertwined. Now we need to consider the application of these subtheories to everyday tasks in addition to laboratory ones.

℃ INTELLIGENCE AND THE EXTERNAL WORLD OF THE INDIVIDUAL

According to the contextual subtheory, intelligent thought is directed toward one or more of three behavioral goals: *adaptation to an environment, shaping of an environment,* or *selection of an environment.* These three goals may be viewed as the functions toward which intelligence is directed:

Intelligence is not aimless or random mental activity that happens to involve certain components of information processing at certain levels of experience. Rather, it is purposefully directed toward the pursuit of these three global goals, all of which have more specific and concrete instantiations in people's lives.

Adaptation

Most intelligent thought is directed toward the attempt to adapt to one's environment. The requirements for adaptation can differ radically from one environment to another—whether environments are defined in terms of families, jobs, subcultures, or cultures. Hence, although the components of intelligence required in these various contexts may be the same or quite similar and although all of them may involve, at one time or another, dealing with novelty and automatization of information processing, the concrete instantiations that these processes and levels of experience take may differ substantially across contexts. This fact has an important implication for our understanding of the nature of intelligence. According to the triarchic theory, in general, and the contextual subtheory in particular, the processes, experiential facets, and functions of intelligence remain essentially the same across contexts, but the particular instantiations of these processes, facets, and functions can differ radically. Thus, the content of intelligent thought and its manifestations in behavior will bear no necessary resemblance across contexts. As a result, although the mental elements that an intelligence test should measure do not differ across contexts, the vehicle for measurement may have to differ. A test that measures a set of processes, experiential facets, or intelligent functions in one context may not provide equally adequate measurement in another context. To the contrary, what is intelligent in one culture may be viewed as unintelligent in another.

Different contextual milieus may result in the development of different mental abilities. For example, Puluwat navigators must develop their large-scale spatial abilities for dealing with cognitive maps to a degree that far exceeds the adaptive requirements of contemporary Western societies (Gladwin, 1970). Similarly, Kearins (1981) found that aboriginal children probably develop their visuospatial memories to a greater degree than do Anglo-Australian children, who are more likely to apply verbal strategies to spatial memory tasks than are the aborigines, who employ spatial strategies. In contrast, participants in Western societies probably develop their abilities for thinking abstractly to a greater degree than do societies in which concepts are rarely dealt with outside their concrete manifestations in the objects of the everyday environment.

One of the most interesting differences among cultures and subcultures in the development of patterns of adaptation is in the matter of time allocation, a metacomponential function. In Western cultures, in general, careful allocation of one's time to various activities is a prized commodity. Our lives are largely governed by careful scheduling at home, school, work, and so on. There are fixed hours for certain activities and fixed lengths of time within which these activities are expected to be completed. Indeed, the intelligence tests we use show our prizing of time allocation to the fullest. Almost all of them are timed in such a way as to make completion of the tests a nontrivial challenge. A slow or cautious worker is at a distinct disadvantage.

Not all cultures and subcultures view time in the same way that we do. For example, among the Kipsigi, schedules are much more flexible and, hence, these individuals have difficulty understanding and dealing with Western notions of the time pressure under which people are expected to live (Super & Harkness, 1982). In Hispanic cultures, such as Venezuela, my own personal experience indicates that the press of time is taken with much less seriousness than it is in typical North American cultural settings. Even within the continental United States, though, there can be major differences in the importance of time allocation (Heath, 1983).

The point of these examples has been to illustrate how differences in environmental press and people's conception of what constitutes an intelligent response to it can influence just what counts as adaptive behavior. To understand intelligence, one must understand it, not only in relation to its internal manifestations in terms of mental processes and its experiential manifestations in terms of facets of the experiential continuum but also in terms of how thought is intelligently translated into action in a variety of different contextual settings. The differences in what is considered adaptive and intelligent can extend even to different occupations within a given cultural milieu. For example, Sternberg (1985b) has found that individuals in different fields of endeavor (art, business, philosophy, physics) view intelligence in slightly different ways that reflect the demands of their respective fields.

Shaping

Shaping of the environment is often used as a backup strategy when adaptation fails. If one is unable to change oneself to fit the environment, one may attempt to change the environment to fit oneself. For example, repeated attempts to adjust to the demands of one's romantic partner may eventually lead to attempts to get the partner to adjust to oneself. But shaping is not always used in lieu of adaptation. In some cases, shaping may be used before adaptation is ever tried, as in the case of the individual who attempts to shape a romantic partner with little or no effort to shape him- or herself so as better to suit the partner's wants or needs.

In the laboratory, examples of shaping behavior can be seen in strategy-selection situations where one essentially molds the task to fit one's preferred style of dealing with tasks. For example, in comparing sentence statements, individuals may select either a verbal or a spatial strategy, depending on their pattern of verbal and spatial ability (MacLeod et al., 1978). The task is "made over" in conformity to what one does best.

In some respects, shaping may be seen as the quintessence of intelligent thought and behavior. One essentially makes over the environment rather than allowing the environment to make over oneself. Perhaps it is this skill that has enabled humankind to reach its current level of scientific, technological, and cultural advancement (for better or for worse). In science, the greatest scientists are those who set the paradigms (shaping), rather than those who merely follow them (adaptation). Similarly, in art and in literature, the individuals who achieve greatest distinction are often those who create new modes and styles of expression rather than merely following existing ones. It is not their use of shaping alone that distinguishes them intellectually but, rather, a combination of their willingness to do it with their skill in doing it.

Selection

Selection involves renunciation of one environment in favor of another. In terms of the rough hierarchy established so far, selection is sometimes used when both adaptation and shaping fail. After attempting to both adapt to and shape a marriage, one may decide to deal with one's failure in these activities by "deselecting" the marriage and choosing the environment of the newly single. Failure to adjust to the demands of work environments, or to change the demands placed on one to make them a reasonable fit to one's interests, values, expectations, or abilities, may result in the decision to seek another job altogether. But selection is not always used as a last resort. Sometimes one attempts to shape an environment only after attempts to leave it have failed. Other times, one may decide almost instantly that an environment is simply wrong and feel that one need not or should not even try to fit into or to change it. For example, every now and then we get a new graduate student who realizes almost immediately that he or she came to graduate school for the wrong reasons or who finds that graduate school is nothing at all like the continuation of undergraduate school he or she expected. In such cases, the intelligent thing to do may be to leave the environment as soon as possible to pursue activities more in line with one's goals in life.

Environmental selection is not usually directly studied in the laboratory, although it may have relevance for certain experimental settings. Perhaps no research example of its relevance has been more salient than the experimental paradigm created by Milgram (1974), who, in a long series of studies, asked subjects to "shock" other subjects (who were actually confederates and who were not actually shocked). The finding of critical interest was how few subjects shaped the environment by refusing to continue with the experiment and walking out of it. Milgram has drawn an analogy to the situation in Nazi Germany, where obedience to authority created an environment whose horrors continue to amaze us to this day and always will. This example is a good one in showing how close matters of intelligence can come to matters of personality.

To conclude, adaptation, shaping, and selection are functions of intelligent thought as it operates in context. They may, although they need not, be employed hierarchically, with one path followed when another one fails. It is through adaptation, shaping, and selection that the components of intelligence, as employed at various levels of experience, become actualized in the real world. In this section, it has become clear that the modes of actualization can differ widely across individuals and groups, so that intelligence cannot be understood independently of the ways in which it is manifested.

INSTRUCTIONAL INTERVENTIONS BASED ON THE THEORY

The triarchic theory has been applied to instructional settings in various ways, with considerable success. The componential subtheory has been applied in teaching the learning of vocabulary from context to adult subjects (Sternberg, 1987), as mentioned earlier. Experimental subjects were taught components of decontextualization. There were three groups, corresponding to three types of instruction that were given based on the theory (see Sternberg, 1987, 1988). Control subjects either received no relevant material at all or else received practical items but without theory-based instruction. Improvement occurred only when subjects were given the theory-based instruction.

The experiential subtheory was the basis for the program of Davidson and Sternberg (1984), which successfully taught insight skills (selective encoding, selective combination, and selective comparison) to children roughly 9 to 11 years of age. The program lasted 6 weeks and involved insight skills as applied to a variety of subject-matter areas. An uninstructed control group, like experimental subjects, received a pretest and posttest but no instruction. We found that the experimental subjects improved significantly more than the controls, both for subjects previously identified as gifted and for those not so identified. Moreover, we found durable results that lasted even 1 year after the training program, and we found transfer to types of insight problems not specifically used in the program.

The contextual subtheory served as the basis for a program on Practical Intelligence for Schools, developed in collaboration with a team of investigators from Harvard (Gardner, Krechevsky, Sternberg, & Okagaki, 1994; Sternberg, Okagaki, & Jackson, 1990). The goal of this program is to teach practical intellectual skills to children roughly 9 to 11 years of age in the areas of reading, writing, homework, and test taking. The program is completely infused into existing curricula. Over a period of years, we studied the program in a variety of school districts and obtained significant improvements for experimental versus uninstructed control subjects in a variety of criterion measures, including study-skills measures and performance-based measures of performance in the areas taught by the program.

Each program described here utilizes a part of the triarchic theory. However, we investigated the implementation of the theory as a whole in an instructional setting. The program, *Intelligence Applied,* is an instructional program for increasing intellectual skills based on the whole of the theory (Sternberg, 1986). It is a separate program taught as a course in itself. Indeed, I have taught the course in my own university. The program is usable for high school or college-level students.

A more ambitious program attempts to infuse the whole of the triarchic theory into already existing subject matter. I have described how the triarchic theory can be successfully implemented in a number of different subject-matter areas and, in particular, in psychology (Sternberg, 1994). We have taught an introductory-level psychology course at Yale that infuses analytical, creative, and practical thinking. An evaluation of the program shows that it can improve educational outcomes. Moreover, my own textbook on introductory psychology (Sternberg, 1995) uses a triarchic approach to the teaching of the introductory psychology course.

In sum, the triarchic theory serves as a useful basis for educational interventions and, in our own work, has shown itself to be a basis for interventions that improve students performance relative to controls who do not receive the theory-based instruction.

BEYOND TRADITIONAL THEORIES OF INTELLIGENCE

The triarchic theory consists of three interrelated subtheories that attempt to account for the bases and manifestations of intelligent thought and as such represents an expanded view of intelligence that departs from traditional, general, and dichotomous theoretical perspectives. The componential subtheory relates intelligence to the internal world of the individual. The experiential subtheory relates intelligence to the experience of the individual with tasks and situations. The contextual subtheory relates intelligence to the external world of the individual.

The elements of the three subtheories are interrelated: The components of intelligence are manifested at different levels of experience with tasks and in situations of varying degrees of contextual relevance to a person's life. The components of intelligence are posited to be universal to intelligence: Thus, the components that contribute to intelligent performance in one culture do so in all other cultures as well. Moreover, the importance of dealing with novelty and automatization of information processing to intelligence are posited to be universal. But the manifestations of these components in experience is posited to be relative to cultural contexts. What constitutes adaptive thought or behavior in one culture is not necessarily adaptive in another culture. Moreover, thoughts and actions that would shape behavior in appropriate ways in one context might not shape them in appropriate ways in another context. Finally, the environment one selects will depend largely on the environments available to one and the fit of one's cognitive abilities, motivation, values, and affects to the available alternatives.

ACKNOWLEDGMENTS

The work reported herein was supported under the Javits Act program (Grant #R206R50001) as administered by the Office of Educational Research and Improvement, U.S. Department of Education. The findings and opinions expressed in this report do not reflect the positions or policies of the Office of Educational Research and Improvement or the U.S. Department of Education.

REFERENCES

Ackerman, P. L. (1987). Individual differences in skill learning: An integration of psychometric and informa-
    tion processing perspectives. *Psychological Bulletin, 102,* 3–27.
Brown, A. L. (1978). Knowing when, where, and how to remember: A problem of metacognition. In R. Glaser
    (Ed.), *Advances in instructional psychology* (Vol. I, pp. 77–165). Hillsdale, NJ: Erlbaum.
Brown, A. L., Bransford, J., Ferrara, R., & Campione, J. (1983). Learning, remembering, and understanding. In
    P. H. Mussen (Series Ed.) & J. Flavell & E. Markman (Vol. Eds.), *Handbook of child psychology* (4th ed.,
    Vol. 3, pp. 77–166). New York: Wiley.
Butterfield, E. C., Wambold, C., & Belmont, J. M. (1973). On the theory and practice of improving short-term
    memory. *American Journal of Mental Deficiency, 77,* 654–669.

Campione, J. C., & Brown, A. L. (1979). Toward a theory of intelligence: Contributions from research with retarded children. In R. J. Sternberg & D. K. Detterman (Eds.), *Human intelligence: Perspectives on its theory and measurement* (pp. 139–64). Norwood, NJ: Ablex.

Cattell, R. B. (1971). *Abilities: Their structure, growth, and action.* Boston: Houghton Mifflin.

Chase, W. G., & Simon, H. A. (1973). The mind's eye in chess. In W. G. Chase (Ed.), *Visual information processing* (pp. 215–281). New York: Academic Press.

Chi, M. T. H. (1978). Knowledge structure and memory development. In R. S. Siegler (Ed.), *Children's thinking: What develops?* (pp. 73–96). Hillsdale, NJ: Erlbaum.

Cooper, L. A. (1982). Strategies for visual comparison and representation: Individual differences. In R. J. Sternberg (Ed.), *Advances in the psychology of human intelligence* (Vol. I, pp. 77–124). Hillsdale, NJ: Erlbaum.

Davidson, J. E., & Sternberg, R. J. (1984). The role of insight in intellectual giftedness. *Gifted Child Quarterly, 28,* 58–64.

Flavell, J. H. (1977). *Cognitive development.* Englewood Cliffs, NJ: Prentice-Hall.

Gardner, H., Krechevsky, M., Sternberg, R. J., & Okagaki, L. (1994). Intelligence in context: Enhancing students' practical intelligence for school. In K. McGilly (Ed.), *Classroom lessons: Integrating cognitive theory and classroom practice* (pp. 105–127). Cambridge, MA: Bradford Books.

Gelman, R., & Gallistel, C. R. (1978). *The child's understanding of number.* Cambridge, MA: Harvard University Press.

Gladwin, T. (1970). *East is a big bird.* Cambridge, MA: Harvard University Press.

Heath, S. B. (1983). *Ways with words: language, life, and work in communities and classrooms.* New York: Cambridge University Press.

Hunt, E. B. (1978). Mechanics of verbal ability. *Psychological Review, 85,* 109–130.

Hunt, E. B. (1980). Intelligence as an information-processing concept. *British Journal of Psychology, 71,* 449–474.

Hunt, E. B., & Lansman, M. (1982). Individual differences in attention. In R. J. Sternberg (Ed.), *Advances in the psychology of human intelligence* (Vol. I, pp. 207–254). Hillsdale, NJ: Erlbaum.

Jensen, A. R. (1980). *Bias in mental testing.* New York: Free Press.

Jensen, A. R. (1982). The chronometry of intelligence. In R. J. Sternberg (Ed.), *Advances in the psychology of human intelligence* (Vol. I, pp. 255–310). Hillsdale, NJ: Erlbaum.

Kanfer, R., & Ackerman, P. L. (1989). Dynamics of skill acquisition: Building a bridge between intelligence and motivation. In R. J.Sternberg (Ed.), *Advances in the psychology of human intelligence* (Vol. 5, pp. 83–134). Hillsdale, NJ: Erlbaum.

Kearins, J. M. (1981). Visual spatial memory in Australian Aboriginal children of desert regions. *Cognitive Psychology, 13,* 434–460.

Keil, F. C. (1984). Transition mechanisms in cognitive development and the structure of knowledge. In R. J. Sternberg (Ed.), *Mechanisms of cognitive development* (pp. 81–99). San Francisco: Freeman.

Kosslyn, S. M. (1980). *Image and mind.* Cambridge, MA: Harvard University Press.

MacLeod, C. M., Hunt, E. B., & Mathews, N. N. (1978). Individual differences in the verification of sentence-picture relationships. *Journal of Verbal Learning and Verbal Behavior, 17,* 493–507.

Mayer, R. E., & Greeno, J. G. (1972). Structural differences between learning outcomes produces by different instructional methods. *Journal of Educational Psychology, 63,* 165–173.

Milgram, S. (1974). *Obedience to authority.* New York: Harper & Row.

Mulholland, T. M., Pellegrino, J. W., & Glaser, R. (1980). Components of geometric analogy solution. *Cognitive Psychology, 12,* 252–284.

Neisser, U. (1982). *Memory observed.* New York: Freeman.

Newell, A., & Simon, H. A. (1972). *Human problem solving.* Englewood Cliffs, NJ: Prentice-Hall.

Pellegrino, J. W., & Glaser, R. (1979). Cognitive correlates and components in the analysis of individual differences. In R. J. Sternberg & D. K. Detterman (Eds.), *Human intelligence: Perspectives on its theory and measurement* (pp. 61–88). Norwood, NJ: Ablex.

Pellegrino, J. W., & Kail, R. (1982). Process analyses of spatial aptitude. In R. J. Sternberg (Ed.), *Advances in the psychology of human intelligence* (Vol. 1, pp. 311–365). Hillsdale, NJ: Erlbaum.

Raaheim, K. (1974). *Problem solving and intelligence.* Oslo: Universitetsforlaget.

Resnick, L. B., & Glaser, R. (1976). Problem solving and intelligence. In L. B. Resnick (Ed.), *The nature of intelligence* (pp. 205–230). Hillsdale, NJ: Erlbaum.

Schank, R. C. (1980). How much intelligence is there in artificial intelligence? *Intelligence, 4,* 1–14.

Schank, R. C., & Abelson, R. P. (1977). *Scripts, plans, goals, and understanding.* Hillsdale, NJ: Erlbaum.

Siegler, R. S. (1986). Unities across domains in children's strategy choices. In Perlmutter (Ed.), *Perspectives on intellectual development: The Minnesota symposia on child psychology* (Vol. 19, pp. 1–48). Hillsdale, NJ: Erlbaum.

Simon, H. A., & Reed, S. K. (1976). Modeling strategy shifts in a problem solving task. *Cognitive Psychology, 8,* 86–97.

Snow, R. E. (1980). Aptitude process. In R. E. Snow, P. A. Frederico, & W. E. Montague (Eds.), *Aptitude, learning, and instruction: Cognitive process analyses of aptitude* (Vol. 1, pp. 27–63). Hillsdale, NJ: Erlbaum.

Snow, R. E., Kyllonen, P. C., & Marshalek, B. (1984). The topography of ability and learning correlations. In R. J. Sternberg (Ed.), *Advances in the psychology of human intelligence* (Vol. 2, pp. 47–103). Hillsdale, NJ: Erlbaum.

Snow, R. E., & Lohman, D. F. (1984). Toward a theory of cognitive aptitude for learning from instruction. *Journal of Educational Psychology, 76,* 347–376.

Sternberg, R. J. (1977). *Intelligence, information processing, and analogical reasoning: The componential analysis of human abilities.* Hillsdale, NJ: Erlbaum.

Sternberg, R. J. (1979). The nature of mental abilities. *American Psychologist, 34,* 214–230.

Sternberg, R. J. (1981). Intelligence and nonentrenchment. *Journal of Educational Psychology, 73,* 1–16.

Sternberg, R. J. (1982). Reasoning, problem solving, and intelligence. In R. J. Sternberg (Ed.), *Handbook of human intelligence* (pp. 225–307). New York: Cambridge University Press.

Sternberg, R. J. (1983). Components of human intelligence. *Cognition, 15,* 1–48.

Sternberg, R. J. (1985a). *Beyond IQ: A triarchic theory of human intelligence.* New York: Cambridge University Press.

Sternberg, R. J. (1985b). Implicit theories of intelligence, creativity, and wisdom. *Journal of Personality and Social Psychology, 49,* 607–627.

Sternberg, R. J. (1986). *Intelligence applied: Understanding and increasing your intellectual skills.* San Diego, CA: Harcourt Brace Jovanovich.

Sternberg, R. J. (1987). Most vocabulary is learned from context. In M. G. McKeown & M. E. Curtis (Eds.), *The nature of vocabulary acquisition* (pp. 89–105). Hillsdale, NJ: Erlbaum.

Sternberg, R. J. (1988). *The triarchic mind: A new theory of human intelligence.* New York: Viking.

Sternberg, R. J. (1990). *Metaphors of mind.* New York: Cambridge University Press.

Sternberg, R. J. (1994). A triarchic model for teaching and assessing students in general psychology. *General Psychologist, 30*(2), 42–48.

Sternberg, R. J. (1995). *In search of the human mind.* Orlando, FL: Harcourt Brace.

Sternberg, R. J., & Davidson, J. E. (1982, June). The mind of the puzzler. *Psychology Today, 16,* 37–44.

Sternberg, R. J., & Gardner, M. K. (1982). A componential interpretation of the general factor in human intelligence. In H. J. Eysenck (Ed.), *A model for intelligence* (pp. 231–254). Berlin: Springer-Verlag.

Sternberg, R. J., & Ketron, J. L. (1982). Selection and implementation of strategies in reasoning by analogy. *Journal of Educational Psychology, 74,* 399–413.

Sternberg, R. J., Okagaki, L., & Jackson, A. (1990). Practical intelligence for success in school. *Educational Leadership, 48,* 35–39.

Sternberg, R. J., & Powell, J. S. (1983). Comprehending verbal comprehension. *American Psychologist, 38,* 878–893.

Sternberg, R. J., & Rifkin, B. (1979). The development of analogical reasoning processes. *Journal of Experimental Child Psychology, 27,* 195–232.

Sternberg, R. J., & Weil, E. M. (1980). An aptitude–strategy interaction in linear syllogistic reasoning. *Journal of Educational Psychology, 72,* 226–234.

Super, C. M., & Harkness, S. (1982). The infants' niche in rural Kenya and metropolitan America. In L. L. Adler (Ed.), *Cross-cultural research at issue* (pp. 47–55). New York: Academic Press.

Vernon, P. E. (1971). *The structure of human abilities.* London: Methuen.

Vygotsky, L. S. (1978). *Mind in society: The development of higher psychological processes.* Cambridge, MA: Harvard University Press.

Wagner, R. K., & Sternberg, R. J. (1987). Executive control in reading comprehension. In B. K. Britton & S. M. Glynn (Eds.), *Executive control processes in reading* (pp. 1–21). Hillsdale, NJ: Erlbaum.

CHAPTER 6

Alternative Assessment from a Multiple Intelligences Theoretical Perspective

‹━━━✦✦✦━━━›

JIE-QI CHEN

HOWARD GARDNER

HOW SMART ARE YOU? "I'm pretty smart," you may be thinking. When we ask this question at meetings and workshops, we also hear such responses as the following: "That's not an easy question. If I compare myself to my colleagues, I'd have to say I'm about average." "I'm not sure. I have a hard time with some job demands and sometimes have doubts about my competence."

Consider a second question: *How are you smart?* This question tends to elicit such answers as the following: "I'm an articulate speaker and I enjoy writing, but I have trouble with math, especially statistics." "I'm good at designing charts and other graphics, but it's hard for me to express my ideas in words." "I learn to play musical instruments easily, because I have a good sense of pitch."

Although both questions concern human capability or competence, they provoke different responses that reflect different models of intelligence. The underlying notion of the first question is that intelligence is a single overall property with one dimension, along which everyone can be arrayed. Moreover, this general mental ability can be measured reasonably well by a variety of standardized tests, especially by IQ tests designed specifically for this purpose (Eysenck, 1979; Snyderman & Rothman, 1988). In this view, IQ and scores on other standardized tests of intelligence have predictive value for many educational, economic, and social outcomes (Herrnstein & Murray, 1994; Jensen, 1969, 1987).

In contrast, the second question suggests a theoretical view that recognizes many discrete facets of cognition and acknowledges that people have different cognitive strengths and contrasting cognitive styles. In this view, the array of intelligences cannot be assessed adequately with a brief sampling of short-answer psychological tasks in a decontextualized situation. Rather, they are more validly documented by the use of contextually rich instruments and an authentic assessment approach that sample a range of discrete cognitive capacities.

In this chapter, we describe the theory of multiple intelligences (MI; Gardner, 1993b) and present it as a source of an alternative approach to assessment. We begin by reviewing the origins of the theory and its distinctive characteristics. We then chart its challenges to traditional conceptions of intelligence, particularly the psychometric view of intelligence and Piaget's theory of cognitive development. Moving from theory to practice, we identify general features of an MI-style assessment, including descriptions of measures, materials, and contexts. We also describe a research project that has developed and piloted domain-specific assessment tasks and observational guidelines as an example of the application of MI theory to assessment. Finally, we report on an empirical study that offers evidence for the notion that intellect is structured in terms of specific, relatively independent abilities.

THE THEORY OF MULTIPLE INTELLIGENCES: ITS ORIGINS AND CLAIMS

MI theory grew from the efforts of one of the authors of this chapter, Howard Gardner, to reconceptualize the nature of intelligence. Gardner began by considering the range of adult end states that are appreciated in diverse cultures around the world and then asking what kind of mind–brain would be needed to realize these various end states. Gardner's assumption was that *any* set of adult competence that may be valued in a culture merits consideration as a potential intelligence (Gardner, 1994).

Most studies of intelligence are based on short-answer psychological tests and correlations among these tests. Gardner proceeded in a different investigative fashion. He surveyed bodies of information and knowledge that had never been considered together for the purpose of defining intelligence (Gardner, 1993b). One aspect of the research focused on atypical populations, such as prodigies, idiot savants, autistic children, and children with learning disabilities. These populations tend to exhibit jagged cognitive profiles with level of performance. Such profiles are inconsistent with a unitary view of intelligence. Gardner also scrutinized research on patients who had suffered isolated loss of cognitive function through brain damage; the highly specific nature of their deficits provides strong evidence that humans possess discrete kinds of intelligence. Further evidence for MI theory came from studies of skill development in normal children and from investigations that evaluated the effectiveness of skill training efforts. A central question that emerged from research on skill training cannot be ignored in the study of intelligence: Does training in skill A transfer to skill B? For example, does training in mathematics enhance one's musical abilities? Finally, cross-cultural studies revealed that intelligence may be manifested differently in different cultures; a society in the South Seas may value the ability to navigate through island passages using the stars, just as Western society values the ability to write a symphony, perform open heart surgery, or carry a football across an opponent's goal line.

These diverse sources provided converging evidence that in describing intelligence, one must consider not only abstract thinking skills and problem-solving abilities but also the applications of such skills and abilities. Pursuing this line of argument, Gardner (1993b) defines intelligence as "the ability to solve problems, or to create products, that are valued within one or more cultural settings" (p. x). With this definition of intelligence, a variety of skills valued in different cultures and historical settings become objects of study (Gardner & Hatch, 1989; Walters & Gardner, 1986).

As a species, human beings have evolved over the millennia to carry out several distinct, relatively independent forms of competence, geared to meet the specific demands of everyday life. Based on his study of the sources mentioned previously, Gardner proposes seven different intelligences: linguistic, logical–mathematical, musical, spatial, bodily–kinesthetic, interpersonal, and intrapersonal. Though the linguistic and logical–mathematical intelligences have been emphasized in psychometric testing and school settings, the seven intelligences in the MI framework have equal claims to priority and are seen as equally valid and important (Gardner, 1987a, 1987b, 1993b).

Gardner does not claim that this roster of intelligences is exhaustive; rather, his aim is to establish support for a pluralistic view of intelligence. MI theory is based wholly on empirical evidence and can be revised on the basis of new empirical findings (Gardner, 1994). There are probably numerous intelligences and even more "subintelligences," but, Gardner would argue, this list of seven more adequately characterizes human intellect than previous unitary and pluralistic schemes (Gardner, 1987b; 1993b).

According to MI theory, the seven intelligences are to a significant extent independent of one another. Each exhibits particular problem-solving features, information-processing capacities, and developmental trajectories. As a function of this independence, the development of the intelligences may proceed at different rates and individuals can display an uneven profile of abilities across intelligences.

Although relatively autonomous, the intelligences do not work in isolation. The fact that nearly every cultural role requires a combination of intelligences suggests the importance of considering that individuals possess various aptitudes rather than a singular problem-solving faculty. With a combination of skills, an individual can become competent in certain tasks or fields even though he or she may not be particularly gifted in any specific intelligence (Gardner, 1991; Walters & Gardner, 1986).

Intelligences do not function as abstract entities. Each intelligence is expressed through one or more symbol systems, such as spoken or written language, numbers, music notation, picturing, or mapping. Through symbol systems, intelligences are applied in specific *domains* or bodies of knowledge within a culture, such as mathematics, art, basketball, and medication. An intelligence may be deployed in many domains (e.g., spatial forms of intelligence may operate in the domains of visual arts, navigation, and engineering). Similarly, performance in a domain may require the use of more than one intelligence. For example, the domain of musical performance involves bodily–kinesthetic and personal as well as musical intelligences (Gardner, 1993b).

As noted, MI theory emphasizes the relative independence of the intelligences. MI theory does not question the existence, but challenges the explanatory and utility power of *g* (general intelligence). One can make *g* higher or lower by varying the kinds of tests given. Moreover, evidence for *g* is provided almost entirely by tests of linguistic or logical intelligence. As such, even if *g* reflects the capacities of certain individuals as they operate in certain contexts, it unduly constricts the definition of intelligence. It treats a particular form of scholastic performance as if it encompassed the entire range of human capacities and leads to disdain for those who are not psychometrically bright (Gardner, 1995a).

Consider the diverse cognitive profiles that individuals exhibit. Gardner claims that intelligences, to a great extent, are shaped by cultural influences and refined by educational processes. Although all humans exhibit the range of intelligences, individuals differ—presumably for both hereditary and environmental reasons—in the extent to which these intelligences are developed in various settings. It is through the process of education that "raw" intellectual competencies are developed and individuals are prepared to assume mature cultural roles. Rich educational experiences, including the use of appropriate forms of assessment, are essential for the development of each individual's particular configuration of interests and abilities (Adams & Feldman, 1993; Gardner, 1991, 1993a).

CHALLENGES TO TRADITIONAL CONCEPTS OF INTELLIGENCE

Challenges to the Psychometric View of Intelligence

MI theory challenges the psychometric view of intelligence on several fronts. First, MI theory questions the conception of intelligence as a single entity which is general, stable, and representative of the entire range of cognitive behaviors (Herrnstein & Murray, 1994; Snyderman & Rothman,

1987; for a critical review, see Gould, 1981). As previously noted, research on both typical and atypical populations produced evidence that is inconsistent with the position of a general intelligence. MI theory argues that it is dangerous to single out one dimension and array individuals on that ability, particularly if the implication is that this rank ordering indicates how smart people are in a global sense. Such a notion gives rise to the idea of a cognitive elite and encourages the notion that some people are special from the start and that those who are not in the elite cause our social problems (Gardner, 1995b; Gould, 1994).

We are aware that based on correlations among psychological tests and subtests, numerous studies support the idea of a positive manifold—the idea that an underlying factor exists that contributes to performance of all measures of intellect. However, many of the measures used in these studies are short-answer, paper-and-pencil tests, and most of the tests measure primarily logical–mathematical and linguistic intelligences. Given that the tests measure only two intelligences and rely on the same means of measurement, it is not surprising that scores on the tests are correlated. MI theory predicts, however, that if a wide range of areas is assessed, individuals will display an uneven profile of abilities, and correlations among diverse abilities will not be high (Gardner & Walters, 1993).

Noting that intelligence tests focus primarily on linguistic and logical–mathematical forms of thinking, we recognize that some current intelligence tests do measure more than two cognitive abilities. In fact, some tests measure up to seven different intellectual components, including crystallized intelligence, visual ability, auditory intelligence, short-term memory, long-term retrieval, speed of processing, and fluid intelligence (see Carroll, 1993; Woodcock, 1990). Guilford (1967) claims that there are 120 or even 150 components of intelligence. These intelligence tests, however, are based on "horizontal" theories of intelligence. That is, mental faculties measured in these tests putatively function similarly in all content areas and operate according to one general law. MI theory is a "vertical" conceptualization of intelligence. According to MI theory, the mind is organized in terms of content areas. There is no single "horizontal" capacity, such as memory, perception, or speed of processing that cuts across domains. Accordingly, individuals can be rapid or slow learners or exhibit novel or stereotypical thinking in any one of the seven intelligences without there being predictable consequences for any of the other intelligences (Gardner, 1993d).

With regard to how intelligence is measured, we acknowledge that there is a continuum of testing instruments from those that are mass produced, standardized, paper-and-pencil–based to those that feature interaction between test takers and test administrators and use a variety of materials, such as blocks, pictures, and geographic shapes. Despite this range, tests based on the psychometric view tend to be one-shot experience and exclude capacities that cannot be measured through the use of such tasks as short-answer questions, block design, or picture arrangement. MI theory argues that the capacities excluded, such as artistic ability, athletic competence, and interpersonal skills, must be measured directly. MI theory calls for measuring intelligences by asking individuals to solve problems in the contexts in which they naturally occur. This approach expands the range of what is measured and permits assessment of the intelligences as an individual applies them in meaningful ways.

Challenging the psychometric assumption regarding biological determinism or racially based intelligence (Jensen, 1969; Herrnstein & Murray, 1994), MI theory argues that intelligence, or intelligences, should be viewed as an interaction between biological proclivities and the opportunities for learning that exist in a culture (Kornhaber, Krechevsky, & Gardner, 1990). In MI theory, intelligences are expressed as abilities valued within a cultural setting. Thus the theory switches the focus of study from individuals to interactions between individuals and societies. Genes regulate all human behavior, but no form of behavior will emerge without the appropriate environmental triggers or supports (Gardner, 1995b).

Challenges to Piaget's Theory of Cognitive Development

Piaget's account of cognitive development is a theoretically distinct perspective. Departing from the psychometric view, Piaget emphasizes the developmental, rather than static, nature of intelligence and the qualitatively, rather than quantitatively, different mind of the child. However, Piaget's theory is also similar to the psychometric view in its claim that the mental structures that characterize developmental stages are best represented as a single entity or unified set of processes. In Piaget's theory, mental structures are general rather than specific and universal rather than cultural. In this limited respect, Piaget views intelligence as a single entity.

The universal or general quality of mind in Piaget's theory is defined in terms of logical–mathematical thought about the physical aspects of the world, including the understanding of causality, time, and space. However, logical–mathematical thinking is only one kind of human intelligence, and it does not reflect the core operations of other forms of intelligence. In contrast to Piaget's belief, MI theory holds that there are no general structures that are applied to every domain. Rather, what exists in the mind of the child at a moment in time is a variety of skills in a variety of domains, each skill functioning at a certain level of mastery with respect to that domain (Chen, 1993; Feldman, 1994; Krechevsky & Gardner, 1990).

Piaget's theory assumes that cognitive development is essentially the result of the child's spontaneous tendencies to learn about the world, with the environment playing a minor role in the process. In contrast, MI theory argues that for progressive and productive change to occur in any intellectual domain, specific environmental conditions must be systematically presented and sustained over time. These environmental forces may be material, technological, social, or cultural in character. The role of education is not to wait passively for cognition to develop by itself but, rather, to orchestrate a variety of environment conditions that will catalyze, facilitate, and enable developmental progress in diverse intellect domains (Feldman, 1994; Gardner, 1993c).

ASSESSMENT FROM A MULTIPLE INTELLIGENCES PERSPECTIVE

MI theory calls for a significant departure from traditional concepts of intelligences. Although not its initial intention, MI theory has also led to the development of alternative forms of assessment. A risk to any innovation is the danger that it will be assimilated into traditional forms and distorted in the process (Adams & Feldman, 1993). In fact, there have been repeated requests for standardized paper-and-pencil MI tests (Gardner, 1993d). To avoid inadvertently producing another psychometrically inspired tracking approach, in the section that follows we describe the central features of an MI approach to assessment, including measures, instruments, materials, context, and purposes.

Measures: Valuing Intellectual Capacities in a Wide Range of Domains

As described earlier, MI theory maintains that human intelligence is pluralistic, each intelligence is relatively autonomous, and all the intelligences are of potentially equal import. Assessment based on MI theory incorporates a range of measures designed to tap the different facets of each intellectual capacity.

In emphasizing the measurement of intellectual capacities in a wide range of domains, it is important to note that we do not deny the existence of some correlation among cognitive abilities, nor do we propose that standard psychometric measures be abolished overnight. Instead, we advocate the investigation of alternative methods of assessment as well as the assessment of a broader range of skills and abilities. MI approach to assessment recognizes those students who excel in linguistic and logical pursuits as well as those students who have cognitive and personal strengths in other intelligences. By virtue of the wider range it measures, MI types of assessment identify more students who are "smart," albeit in different ways (Gardner, 1984, 1986, 1993a).

Students who have trouble with some academic subjects, such as reading or math, are not necessarily inadequate in all areas (Chen, 1993; Levin, 1990). The challenge is to provide comparable opportunities for these students to demonstrate their strengths and interests. When the students recognize that they are good at something, and when this accomplishment is acknowledged by teachers and classmates, the students experience success and feel valued. In some instances, the sense of success in one area may make the students more likely to engage in areas in which they feel less comfortable. At that point, the use of multiple measures goes beyond its initial purpose of identifying diverse cognitive abilities and begins to serve as a means of bridging a student's strengths in one area to other areas of learning (Chen, 1993).

Instruments: Using Media Appropriate to the Domain

Because it emphasizes that each intelligence exhibits particular problem-solving features and operational mechanism, MI theory argues that "intelligence-fair" instruments are needed in order to assess the unique capacities of each intelligence. Intelligence-fair instruments engage the key abilities of particular intelligences, allowing one to look directly at the functioning of each intellectual capacity rather than forcing the individual to reveal his or her intelligence through the customary lens of a linguistic or logical instrument.

For example, bodily intelligence can be assessed by recording how a person learns and remembers a new dance or physical exercise. To consider a person's interpersonal intelligence, it would be necessary to observe how that person interacts with and influences others in different social situations. It is important to note that what is being assessed here is not intelligence in pure form. Intelligences are always expressed in the context of specific tasks, domains, and discipline. For example, there is no "pure" spatial intelligence; instead, there is spatial intelligence as expressed in a child's puzzle solution, route finding, blocking building, or basketball passing (Gardner, 1993b).

Unfortunately, until now nearly all intelligence assessment has depended directly or indirectly on the measurement of linguistic and logical mathematical abilities. This kind of test ignores that distinct domains and symbol systems require different kinds of sensory processing and present unique constraints and problems. As a consequence, if students are not strong in linguistic-logical areas, their abilities in other areas would be more likely obscured. However, if we can assess an individual's ability to solve problems or create products using the materials of the domain, we are confident that many students will reveal their strengths in different areas, and the notion of general brightness will become greatly attenuated (Gardner, 1987a, 1993a).

Materials: Engaging Children in Meaningful Activities and Learning

The design of MI types of assessment is responsive to the fact that children have had different environmental and educational experiences. Considering that each intelligence is an expression of the interplay among genetic and environmental factors, children's prior experience with assessment materials directly affects their performance on tasks. For example, children who have little experience with blocks are less likely to do well in a block design task. Similarly, it would be unfair to assess a child's musical ability by asking the child to play a xylophone if he or she has never seen such a musical instrument. In recognition of the role that experience plays, the MI approach to assessment aims to provide materials with which children are familiar. To the extent that children are not familiar with materials, they are given ample opportunities to explore the materials prior to the assessment.

Many current intelligence tests use blocks, pictures, and geometric shapes. These materials are familiar to most children in industrial societies. Yet they provide little intrinsic incentive for children to engage the activity, and they have little meaning to children's daily lives. For assessment to be meaningful for students and instructive for teachers, it should occur in the context of students working on problems and projects that genuinely engage them and that hold their interest and motivate them to do well. Such assessments may not be as easy to design as the standard multiple-choice test, but they are more likely to elicit a student's full repertoire of skills and to yield information that is useful for subsequent learning and instruction (Gardner, 1993a).

Context: Assessment as an Ongoing Process

Learning is not a one-shot experience. Assessment should not be either; instead, it should be an ongoing process fully integrated into the natural learning environment. When a child's ability is measured through a one-shot experience, the child's profile is often incomplete and possibly distorted. In contrast, when assessment is naturally embedded in the learning environment, it allows teachers to observe children's performances in various situations over time. Such observations make it possible to gain multiple samples of a child's ability, document the dynamics and variation of the child's performances within a domain and across domains, and therefore more accurately portray the child's intellectual profile.

MI types of assessment emphasize blurring the traditional distinction between assessment and instruction. A teacher uses the results of assessment to plan instruction; as instruction proceeds, the teacher has new opportunities to assess a child's developing competence. In this process, assessment and instruction inform and enhance each other. Initially, methods for ongoing assessment would be introduced explicitly, but, over time, assessment would occur spontaneously with little need for explicit recognition or labeling by either the student or the teacher (Gardner, 1993a).

Purpose of Assessment: Identifying Strengths as Well as Weaknesses

The development of MI theory started with the question, "What basic cognitive abilities account for what people can do?" The question implies that intelligence should be viewed as a profile of strengths, interests, and weaknesses. As well, the question stimulates the design of assessment vehicles that simultaneously help uncover and foster an individual's competence. Further, the question suggests that human beings have unique combinations of abilities that are qualitatively different and cannot be quantitatively ranked and sorted.

Traditional tests—achievement, readiness, intelligence, and the like—are often designed to rank and sort students based on a single score. Reference to single test scores leads to an almost exclusive focus on deficits when test scores are relatively low. Consequently, psychologists often spend too much time ranking individuals and not nearly enough time helping them, and educators often focus too much on remediating students deficits rather than bridging their strengths to other areas of learning.

Instead of ranking, sorting, and remediating, the purpose of MI types of assessment is to support students on the basis of their complete intellectual profile—strengths and weaknesses. The assessor provides feedback to the student that is helpful immediately, such as suggestions about what to study or work on and pointers on which habits are productive and which are not, as well as explanations of what can be expected in terms of assessments. It is especially important that feedback include concrete suggestions and information about which relative strengths the students should build on, independent of their rank within a comparable group of students (Gardner, 1993a).

PROJECT SPECTRUM: DOMAIN-SPECIFIC ASSESSMENT

Armed with findings about human cognition and its development and in light of perceived need for an alternative to formal testing, Gardner and his colleagues at Harvard Project Zero began to design programs that feature new approaches to assessment. Project Spectrum, one of these efforts attempted to tap a wide range of cognitive abilities in young children.

Project Spectrum was a collaborative research project codirected by Howard Gardner at Harvard Project Zero and David Feldman at Tufts University. The name of the project, Spectrum, reflects its mission to recognize diverse intellectual strengths in children. From 1984 to 1993, Spectrum researchers completed a number of programs, including the development of new means of assessing the cognitive abilities of preschool children, implementation of an intervention program for first-graders based on the Spectrum approach, and coordination of a mentorship program for inner-city first- and second-grade students. All these programs—whether they were done in preschools or elementary schools or whether they involved teachers or community members—included a rich assessment component designed to identify children's areas of strength and use them as the basis for an individualized educational program.

Over the 9 years of work, Spectrum researchers developed two kinds of domain-specific assessment instruments: Preschool Assessment Activities and Observational Guidelines (Chen, Isberg, & Krechevsky, in press; Krechevsky, 1994). The Spectrum Preschool Assessment Activities include 15 activities in seven different domains of knowledge: language, math, music, art, social understanding, mechanical science, and movement. Rather than attempting to look at intelligences in pure form when developing assessment activities, Spectrum researchers looked at the domains that are compatible with school curricula.

The assessments are embedded in meaningful, hands-on activities that share a number of distinctive features. The activities give children inviting materials to manipulate, such as toy figures or a playdough birthday cake; they are intelligence-fair, using materials appropriate to the domain rather than relying on language and math as assessment vehicles; and they examine abilities relevant to achieving fulfilling adult roles. Although Spectrum assessment activities measure skills that are valued by adult society, these skills are used in a context that is meaningful to the child. For example, to assess social understanding skills, children are encouraged to manipulate figures in a scaled-down, three-dimensional replica of their classroom; to assess math skills, children are asked to keep track of passengers getting on and off a toy bus. (For detailed descriptions of Spectrum preschool assessment activities, see Adams & Feldman, 1993; Krechevsky, 1994; Krechevsky & Gardner, 1990).

A majority of these Spectrum assessment activities are structured tasks that can be administered in a one-on-one setting. Each task measures specific abilities, often requires particular materials, and is accompanied by written instructions for task administration. These instructions include a score sheet detailing the skills exercised in each activity and how to evaluate them, so that the child's performance on many activities is quantifiable (Krechevsky, 1994).

Like the score sheets, the Observational Guidelines are designed to highlight the distinct skills required for achievement in different cognitive domains. Unlike the score sheets, they can be used in a range of situations and invite observers to make qualitative as well as quantitative evaluations. Created for early elementary teachers to use in their classrooms, the guidelines consist of eight sets of key abilities in the domains of language, math, natural science, mechanical science, art, social understanding, music, and movement (see Table 6.1).

Key abilities are the abilities that children need to perform tasks successfully in each domain. In the case of music, key abilities include music perception, production, and composition. Spectrum researchers further identify a set of core elements or specific cognitive skills that help children exercise and execute the designated key ability. For example, core elements for music production include the abilities to maintain accurate pitch, tempo, and rhythmic patterns; to exhibit expres-

TABLE 6.1. Domain-Specific Observational Guidelines

Components	Guidelines
	Visual Arts
Perception	• Is aware of visual elements in the environment and in artwork (e.g., color, lines, shapes, patterns, detail) • Is sensitive to different artistic styles (e.g., can distinguish abstract art from realism, impressionism, etc.)
Production	
Representation	• Is able to represent visual world accurately in two or three dimensions • Is able to create recognizable symbols for common objects (e.g., people, vege-tation, houses, animals) and coordinate elements spatially into unified whole • Uses realistic proportions, detailed features, deliberate choice of color
Artistry	• Is able to use various elements of art (e.g., line, color, shape) to depict emotions, produce certain effects, and embellish drawings or three-dimensional work • Conveys strong mood through literal representation (e.g., smiling sun, crying face) and abstract features (e.g., dark colors or drooping lines to express sadness); produces drawings or sculptures that appear "lively," "sad," or "powerful" • Shows concern with decoration and embellishment • Produces drawings that are colorful, balanced, and/or rhythmic
Exploration	• Is flexible and inventive in use of art materials (e.g., experiments with paint, chalk, clay) • Uses lines and shapes to generate a wide variety of forms (e.g., open and closed, explosive and controlled) in two- or three-dimensional work • Is able to execute a range of subjects or themes (e.g., people, animals, buildings, landscapes)
	Mechanical Science
Visual–spatial abilities	• Is able to construct or reconstruct physical objects and simple machines in two or three dimensions • Understands spatial relationships between parts of a mechanical object
Problem-solving approach with mechanical objects	• Uses and learns from trial-and-error approach • Uses systematic approach in solving mechanical problems • Compares and generalizes information
Understanding of causal and functional relationships	• Infers relationships based on observation • Understands relationship of parts to whole, the function of these parts, and how parts are put together
Fine motor skills	• Is adept at manipulating small parts or objects • Exhibits good eye–hand coordination (e.g., hammers on head of nail rather than on fingers)
	Movement
Body control	• Shows an awareness of and ability to isolate and use different body parts • Plans, sequences, and execute moves efficiently, movements do not seem random or disjointed • Is able to replicate one's own movements and those of others

(cont.)

TABLE 6.1. (*cont.*)

Components	Guidelines
Movement (*cont.*)	
Sensitivity to rhythm	• Moves in synchrony with stable or changing rhythms, particularly in music (e.g., child attempts to move with the rhythm, as opposed to being unaware of or disregarding rhythmic changes) • Is able to set a rhythm of one's own and regulate it to achieve a desired effect
Expressivity	• Evokes moods and images through movement using gestures and body postures; stimulus can be a verbal image, a prop, or music • Is able to respond to mood or tonal quality of an instrument or music selection (e.g., uses light and fluid movements for lyrical music versus strong and staccato movements for a march)
Generation of movement ideas	• Is able to invent interesting and novel movement ideas, verbally and/or physically, or offer extensions of ideas (e.g., suggesting that children raise their arms to look like clouds floating in the sky) • Responds immediately to ideas and images with original movements • Choreographs a simple dance, perhaps teaching it to others
Responsiveness to music	• Responds differently to different kinds of music • Shows sensitivity to rhythm and expressiveness when responding to music • Explores available space (vertical and horizontal) comfortably using different levels, moving easily and fluidly around the space • Anticipates others in a shared space • Experiments with her body in space (e.g., turning and spinning)
Music	
Music perception	• Is sensitive to dynamics (loud and soft) • Is sensitive to tempo and rhythmic patterns • Discriminates pitch • Identifies musical and musicians' styles • Identifies different instruments and sounds
Music production	• Is able to maintain accurate pitch • Is able to maintain accurate tempo and rhythmic patterns • Exhibits expressiveness when singing or playing instrument • Can recall and reproduce musical properties of songs and other compositions
Music composition	• Creates simple compositions with some sense of beginning, middle, and end • Creates simple notation system
Social Understanding	
Understanding of self	• Identifies own abilities, skills, interests, and areas of difficulty • Reflects on own feelings, experiences, and accomplishments • Draws on these reflections to understand and guide own behavior • Shows insight into the factors that enable an individual to do well or have difficulty in an area
Understanding of others	• Demonstrates knowledge of peers and their activities • Attends closely to others • Recognizes others' thoughts, feelings, and abilities • Draws conclusions about others based on their activities

TABLE 6.1. (*cont.*)

Components	Guidelines
Social Understanding (*Cont.*)	
Assumption of distinctive social roles	
Leader	• Often initiates and organizes activities • Organizes other children • Assigns roles to others • Explains how activity is carried out • Oversees and directs activities
Facilitator	• Often shares ideas, information, and skills with other children • Mediates conflict • Invites other children to play • Extends and elaborates other children's ideas • Provides help when others need attention
Caregiver/friend	• Comforts other children when they are upset • Shows sensitivity to other children's feelings • Shows understanding of friends' likes and dislikes
Mathematics	
Numerical reasoning	• Adept at calculations (e.g., find shortcuts) • Able to estimate • Adept at quantifying objects and information (e.g., by recordkeeping, creating effective notation, graphing) • Able to identify numerical relationships (e.g., probability, ratio)
Spatial reasoning	• Finds spatial patterns • Adept with puzzles • Uses imagery to visualize and conceptualize a problem
Logical problem solving	• Focuses on relationships and overall structure of problem instead of isolated facts • Makes logical inferences • Generalizes rules • Develops and uses strategies (e.g., when playing games)
Science	
Observational skills	• Engages in close observation of materials to learn about their physical characteristics; uses one or more of the senses • Often notices changes in the environment (e.g., new leaves on plants, bugs on trees, subtle seasonal changes) • Shows interest in recording observations through drawings, charts, sequence cards, or other methods
Identification of similarities and differences	• Likes to compare and contrast materials and/or events • Classifies materials and often notices similarities and/or differences between specimens (e.g., compares and contrasts crabs and spiders)
Hypothesis formation and experimentation	• Makes predictions based on observations • Asks "what if"-type questions and offers explanations for why things are the way they are • Conducts simple experiments or generates ideas for experiments to test own or others' hypotheses (e.g., drops large and small rocks in water to see if one size sinks faster than the other; waters plant with paint instead of water)

(cont.)

TABLE 6.1. (*cont.*)

Components	Guidelines
	Science (*cont.*)
Interest in/knowledge of nature/scientific phenomena	• Exhibits extensive knowledge about various scientific topics; spontaneously offers information about these topics or reports on own or others' experience with natural world • Shows interest in natural phenomena, or related materials such as natural history books, over extended periods of time • Regularly asks questions about things observed
	Language
Invented narrative/storytelling	• Uses imagination and originality in storytelling • Enjoys listening to or reading stories • Exhibits interest in plot design and development, character elaboration and motivation, descriptions of settings, scenes or moods, use of dialogue, etc. • Brings a sense of narrative to different tasks • Shows performing ability or dramatic flair, including a distinctive style, expressiveness, or an ability to play a variety of roles
Descriptive language/reporting	• Provides accurate and coherent accounts of events, feelings and experiences (e.g., uses correct sequence and appropriate level of detail; distinguishes fact from fantasy) • Provides accurate labels and descriptions for things • Shows interest in explaining how things work, or describing a procedure • Engages in logical argument or inquiry
Poetic use of language/word play	• Enjoys and is adept at word play such as puns, rhymes, metaphors • Plays with word meanings and sounds • Demonstrates interest in learning new words • Uses words in a humorous fashion

siveness when singing or playing an instrument; and to recall and reproduce musical properties (Chen et al., in press). By directing observations in terms of domains, key abilities, and core elements, the guidelines provide teachers with a means of organizing and recording their observations of individual children and of systematizing information they may already be gleaning in a more intuitive way.

The Spectrum Preschool Assessment Activities and Observational Guidelines are valuable additions to the classroom because they cover a wide range of intellectual domains, including such areas as mechanical science, creative movement, music, and visual arts, which usually are ignored in traditional tests of intelligence. Further, in contrast to many traditional forms of assessment that are designed to identify deficits, Spectrum assessment instruments aim to identify children's strengths and interests. Spectrum's work is based on the assumption that every individual has strengths; the challenge is to sample a wide enough range of possibilities so that they can be detected (Adams & Feldman, 1993).

We now have data from a number of empirical studies that grow out of the Spectrum framework. For example, when we worked with four public first-grade classrooms in Somerville, Massachusetts, we identified areas of strength for 13 of the 15 at-risk students (about 87%) on the basis of their demonstrated competence and interest in an area. These children's strengths spanned many areas, including art, mechanical science, social understanding, math, language, science, and movement. Identification of strengths in such diverse areas would not have been possible had these children been in a classroom environment that did not provide them opportunities to explore different intellectual domains (Chen, 1993).

The example cited above leads to another characteristics shared by the Spectrum Preschool Assessment Activities and the Observational Guidelines. To use the instruments appropriately, one must first supply opportunities for intelligences or sets of intelligences to be activated. For example, to help identify areas of strength for at-risk students in our Somerville project, teachers first introduced eight learning centers into the classroom. These learning centers were stocked with inviting materials, from dress-up clothes to magnifying glasses, that students used for structured exercises as well as open-ended play. Only after the children had ample opportunity to explore diverse areas and become immersed in their own areas of interest could we begin to assess their intellectual strengths.

Stressing the importance of learning experiences for the development of intelligences, the Spectrum Preschool Assessment Activities and the Observational Guidelines are designed to dissolve the traditional boundary between assessment and curriculum or learning. For example, teachers can use the key abilities and core elements in the Observational Guidelines not only to observe and identify a child's intellectual strengths but also to generate further learning experiences and plan an individualized curriculum for that child. The Observational Guidelines thus can be used to help nurture, as well as identify, the child's intellectual strengths.

The Spectrum Preschool Assessment Activities and the Observational Guidelines are domain-specific assessment instruments that can be used independently. However, when used together, they provide a more comprehensive approach to assessing children's performance and documenting their performance. The assessment activities help describe the child's place in a developmental process at a particular point in time, whereas the guidelines direct ongoing observations in a natural learning environment, so that a child's developmental progress can be tracked over time. Furthermore, the Observational Guidelines can be used to obtain a rough approximation of the ways in which children differ from one another and to identify those children who might benefit from a structured assessment activity that more closely examines a particular domain.

INTELLIGENCE AS DOMAIN-SPECIFIC: EVIDENCE FROM AN EMPIRICAL STUDY

MI theory has attracted much attention in the fields of cognition and education (Kornhaber & Krechevsky, 1995). It is concordant with many people's implicit belief about the nature of human intelligence. From its inception, MI theory has been based on massive amounts of empirical data. Gardner and his colleagues are continuing to monitor the considerable body of new data relevant to the claims of the theory. Some of the work is being done at Harvard Project Zero (Gardner, 1993d; Krechevsky, 1991; Winner, Rosenblatt, Windmueller, Davidson, & Gardner, 1986); some of it is being done by other researchers, either explicitly investigating MI theory (Adams, 1993; Rosnow, 1991; Rosnow, Skleder, Jaeger, & Rind, 1994; Rosnow, Skleder, & Rind, 1995) or implicitly touching on its claims (Rauscher, Shaw, & Ky, 1993). Adams's study (1993), briefly described below, examines the relationship among diverse cognitive abilities (For a more detailed description of the study see Adams, 1993).[1]

The sample in Adams's study consisted of 42 subjects, including 22 girls and 20 boys. The subjects were predominantly white and from middle- to upper-income families. The age range of the subjects was 4.2 to 4.8 years, with a mean of 4.45 years. All subjects were seen in their homes for two 1-hour sessions and completed three tasks per session. The tasks were designed to measure mathematical, linguistic, artistic, social, musical, and mechanical abilities in 4-year-olds (see Table 6.2). The development of the tasks was based on the early work of Project Spectrum. The set of tasks

TABLE 6.2. Spectrum Field Inventory[a]

Task	Description
Dinosaur game	Measures understanding of number concepts, and counting skills
Storytelling	Measures a range of language skills including complexity of sentence structure, use of descriptive language, use of expressive dialogue, and ability to pursue a story line
Art portfolio	Measures representational ability, extent of exploration, and level of artistry as these abilities are expressed through the medium of drawing
Pretend birthday party (social analytical task)	Assesses understanding of friendship, conflict situations, and others' needs and feelings
Singing	Assesses the ability to maintain accurate pitch and rhythm and recall a song's musical properties
Assembly	Measures mechanical ability which involves visual–spatial abilities as well as a range of observational and problem-solving skills

[a]From Adams (1993). Reprinted by permission.

is called the Spectrum Field Inventory. The tasks were administered by a trained experimenter in a game-like atmosphere.

The Box test (Mardia, Kent, & Bibby, 1979) was used to assess the joint independence of the group scores on the six tasks. The null hypothesis that all scores were uncorrelated with one another was rejected ($F = 35.76, p < .01$). That is, overall, Adams found that the cognitive abilities measured were not independent of each other. The sense in which they are not independent is defined in statistical terms. Meeting the statistical criterion for independence is an either/or proposition, yet Gardner does not claim there is no relation among the intelligences. His claim is that multiple intelligences are *relatively* independent. The Box test does not provide information about the degree of dependence in the structure of the scores that are analyzed, nor is there another multivariate technique that does yield such information (Adams, 1993).

To identify possible sources of covariation that contributed to the overall result, Adams generated a Pearson correlation matrix of all possible pairings of the task scores (see Table 6.3). As indicated in Table 6.3, 10 of the 15 correlations in the matrix were not significant. This finding runs counter to the repeated reports of substantial positive correlations among IQ tests (Detterman & Daniel, 1989; Gould, 1981; Humphreys, 1982; Sattler, 1992).

To explore further the potential specificity of intellectual abilities, Adams (1993) also analyzed each individual's levels of performance in relation to the group. Using the standard deviation as a criterion, Adams defined three levels of performance. Strong, weak, and average performances were defined as scores above +1 standard deviation, below -1 standard deviation, and between +1 and -1 standard deviations, respectively. Defining the three levels of performance in relation to the standard deviation provides a set of objective criteria for determining the degree of variability within an individual's set of scores.

Of the 42 subjects in Adams' study, three children completed fewer than half the six tasks and were eliminated from the analysis. In the remaining 39 profiles, only four subjects (10%) exhibited the same level of performance on all tasks. Thirty-five subjects (90%) performed varying levels of tasks. Of these 35 subjects, 16 (46%) earned scores that scattered over a range of 3 to 5 standard deviations. These results suggest that an individual's level of performance often varies when a diverse set of abilities is measured (Adams, 1993).

The results of the study are based on a sample of 42, drawn from a predominately white middle- to upper-income population. This limits their generalizability. Nonetheless, taken as a whole, the results of Adams's study offer some support for the position that intelligence is domain-specific.

TABLE 6.3. Correlation Matrix of Group Scores on Tasks[a]

Tasks	Story	Art	Birthday	Singing	Assembly
Dinosaur	.44**	.20	.25	.21	.41**
Story		.43*	.26	-.14	.15
Art			.51**	-.37	.48**
Birthday				-.03	.23
Singing					.06

$^*p < .05. ^{**}p < .01.$
[a]From Adams (1993). Reprinted by permission.

BEYOND TRADITIONAL THEORIES OF INTELLIGENCE: IMPLICATIONS FOR ASSESSMENT

Assessment, as much current literature points out, provides top levers for affecting educational practice. Many people criticize current educational practices; a significant part of our educational malaise, however, lies in the instruments that are used to assess student learning and, not incidentally, to signal what learning is. This kind of instrument is often presented in a standard pencil-and-paper short-answer fashion, sampling only a small proportion of intellectual abilities and often rewarding a certain kind of decontextualized facility. In other words, it may be a better indicator of test-taking skill than understanding central aspects of the disciplines. Because this kind of instrument systematically ignores the wide range of abilities that are valued in our culture, it does little to help us recognize and nurture individuals potential. By constraining the curriculum and taking control of the learning process away from teachers and students, this kind of instrument in fact discourages many students from discovering activities they can enjoy and at which they can achieve some success (Hatch & Gardner, 1990).

Taking into account psychological, biological, and cultural dimensions of cognition, MI theory presents a more empirically sensitive and scientifically compelling understanding of human intelligences as compared to traditional, general, and dichotomous conceptions of intelligence and provides an impetus for alternative assessment. Based on MI theory, assessments can be designed to examine and build on the range of an individual's cognitive potentials or competence. This kind of assessment is sensitive to what individuals are capable of accomplishing; it also suggest alternative routes to the achievement of important educational goal (learning mathematics via spatial relations; learning music through linguistic techniques).

The ultimate goal of MI approach to assessment is to help create environments that foster individual as well as group potential. Clearly, such assessments will require concerted efforts over a long period to develop quality instruments and carefully trained individuals who can administer and interpret them in a sensitive manner. However, when one ponders on the enormous human potential currently wasted in our society because it labels as "intelligence" only a small subset of human talents, such an investment seems worthwhile (Gardner, 1993d).

ACKNOWLEDGMENTS

Preparation of this paper was aided by grants from the MacArthur Foundation, the Rockefeller Foundation, and the Spencer Foundation. We would like to thank Margaret Adams and Emily Isberg for their helpful comments on an earlier version of the paper.

NOTE

This study was supported by the National Institute of Child Health and Human Development and is one component of a longitudinal study being conducted by Dr. Marc Bornstein and Dr. Cathy Tamis-LeMonda.

REFERENCES

Adams, M. (1993). *An empirical investigation of domain-specific theories of preschool children's cognitive abilities.* Unpublished doctoral dissertation, Tufts University, Medford, MA.

Adams, M., & Feldman, D. H. (1993). Project Spectrum: A theory-based approach to early education. In R. Pasnak & M. L. Howe (Eds.), *Emerging themes in cognitive development: Vol. II: Competencies* (pp. 53–76). New York: Springer-Verlag.

Carroll, J. B. (1993). *Human cognitive abilities: A survey of factor-analytic studies.* Cambridge, England: Cambridge University Press.

Chen, J. Q. (1993, April). *Building on children's strengths: Project Spectrum intervention program for students at risk for school failure.* Paper presented at biennial conference of Society for Research of Child Development, New Orleans, LA.

Chen, J. Q., Isberg, E., & Krechevsky, M. (in press). *Project Spectrum Early Learning Activities.* Cambridge, MA: Harvard Project Zero.

Detterman, D. K., & Daniel, M. H. (1989). Correlations of mental tests with each other and with cognitive variables are highest for low IQ groups. *Intelligence, 13,* 349–359.

Eysenck, H. J. (1979). *The structure and measurement of intelligence.* Berlin: Springer-Verlag.

Feldman, D. H. (1994). *Beyond universals in cognitive development* (2nd ed.). Norwood, NJ: Ablex.

Gardner, H. (1984). Assessing intelligence: A comment on "Testing intelligence without IQ test" by R. J. Sternberg. *Phi Delta Kappa, 65*(10), 699–700.

Gardner, H. (1986). The waning of intelligence tests. In R. Sternberg & D. Detterman (Eds.), *The acquisition of symbolic skills* (pp. 19–42). London: Plenum Press.

Gardner, H. (1987a). Beyond the IQ: Education and human development. *Harvard Educational Review, 57,* 187–193.

Gardner, H. (1987b). The theory of multiple intelligences. *Annals of Dyslexia, 37,* 19–35.

Gardner, H. (1991). *The unschooled mind: How children think and how schools should teach.* New York: Basic Books.

Gardner, H. (1993a). Assessment in context: The alternative to standardized testing. In H. Gardner (Ed.), *Multiple intelligences: The theory in practice* (pp. 161–183). New York: Basic Books.

Gardner, H. (1993b). *Frames of mind: The theory of multiple intelligences* (10th-anniversary ed.). New York: Basic Books.

Gardner, H. (1993c). Intelligence in seven phases. In H. Gardner (Ed.), *Multiple intelligences: The theory in practice* (pp. 213–230). New York: Basic Books.

Gardner, H. (1993d). *Multiple intelligences: The theory in practice.* New York: Basic Books.

Gardner, H. (1994). Multiple intelligences theory. In R. J. Sternberg (Ed.), *Encyclopedia of human intelligence* (pp. 740–742). New York: Macmillan.

Gardner, H. (1995a). Reflect on multiple intelligences: Myths and messages. *Phi Delta Kappan, 11*(77), 200–209.

Gardner, H. (1995b, Winter). Cracking open the IQ box. *The American Prospect, (20),* pp. 20, 71–80.

Gardner, H., & Hatch, T. (1989). Multiple intelligences go to school: Educational implications of the theory of multiple intelligences. *Educational Research, 18,* 4–10.

Gardner, H., & Walters, J. M. (1993). A rounded version. In H. Gardner (Ed.), *Multiple intelligences: The theory in practice* (pp. 13–34). New York: Basic Books.

Gould, S. J. (1981). *The mismeasure of man.* New York: Norton.

Gould, S. J. (1994, November 28). Curveball. *The New Yorker,* pp. 139–149.

Guilford, J. P. (1967). *The nature of human intelligence.* New York: McGraw-Hill.

Hatch, T., & Gardner, H. (1990). If Binet had looked beyond the classroom: The assessment of multiple intelligences. *International Journal of Educational Research, 14*(5), 415–429.

Herrnstein, R. J., & Murray, C. (1994). *The bell curve: Intelligence and class structure in American Life.* New York: Free Press.

Humphreys, L. G. (1982). The hierarchical factor model and general intelligence. In N. Hirschberg & L. G. Humphreys (Eds.), *Multivariate applications in the social sciences* (pp. 223–239). Hillsdale, NJ: Erlbaum.

Jensen, A. R. (1969). How much can we boost IQ and scholastic achievement? *Harvard Educational Review, 39*(1), 1–123.

Jensen, A. R. (1987). The "g" beyond factor analysis. In R. R. Ronning, J. A. Glover, J. C. Conoley, & J. C. Witt (Eds.), *The influence of cognitive psychology on testing. Buros-Nebraska Symposium on Measurement and Testing* (Vol. 3, pp. 87–142). Hillsdale, NJ: Erlbaum.

Kornhaber, M., & Krechevsky, M. (1995). Expanding definition of learning and teaching: Notes from the MI underground. In P. W. Cookson & B. Schneider (Eds.), *Transforming schools* (pp. 181–208). New York: Garland Press.

Kornhaber, M., Krechevsky, M., & Gardner, H. (1990). Engaging intelligence. *Educational Psychologist, 25*(3–4), 177–199.

Krechevsky, M. (1991). Project Spectrum: An innovative assessment alternative. *Educational Leadership, 2,* 43–48.

Krechevsky, M. (1994). *Project Spectrum preschool assessment handbook.* Cambridge, MA: Harvard Project Zero.

Krechevsky, M., & Gardner, H. (1990). The emergence and nurturance of multiple intelligences: The Project Spectrum approach. In M. J. Howe (Ed.), *Encouraging the development of exceptional skills and talents* (pp. 222–245). Leicester, England: British Psychological Society.

Levin, H. M. (1990). Accelerated schools: A new strategy for at risk students. *Policy Bulletin, 6,* 1–7.

Mardia, K. V., Kent, J. T., & Bibby, J. M. (1979). *Multivariate analysis.* New York: Academic Press.

Rauscher, F., Shaw, G. L., & Ky, K. N. (1993, October 14). Music and spatial task performance. *Nature, 365*(6447), p. 611.

Rosnow, R. L. (1991). Inside rumor: A personal journey. *American Psychologist, 46*(5), 484–496.

Rosnow, R. L., Skleder, A. A., Jaeger, M., & Rind, B. (1994). Intelligence and epistemics of interpersonal acumen: Testing some implications of Gardner's theory. *Intelligence, 19,* 93–116.

Rosnow, R. L., Skleder, A. A., & Rind, B. (1995). Reading other people: A hidden cognitive structure? *General Psychologist, 31,* 1–10.

Sattler, J. M. (1992). *Assessment of children* (4th ed.). San Diego: Sattler.

Snyderman, M., & Rothman, S. (1987). Survey of expert opinion on intelligence and aptitude testing. *American Psychologist, 42,* 137–144.

Snyderman, M., & Rothman, S. (1988). *The IQ controversy, the media and public policy.* New Brunswick, NJ: Transaction.

Walters, J. M., & Gardner, H. (1986). The theory of multiple intelligences: Some issues and answers. In R. Sternberg & R. Wagner (Eds.), *Practical intelligences* (pp. 163–183). New York: Cambridge University Press.

Winner, E., Rosenblatt, E., Windmueller, G., Davidson, L., & Gardner, H. (1986). Children's perceptions of "aesthetic" properties of the arts: Domain specific or pan artistic? *British Journal of Developmental Psychology, 4,* 149–160.

Woodcock, R. W. (1990). Theoretical foundations of the WJ-R measures of cognitive ability. *Journal of Psychoeducational Assessment, 8,* 231–258.

C H A P T E R   7

The Three-Stratum Theory
of Cognitive Abilities

JOHN B. CARROLL

T HE THREE-STRATUM THEORY of cognitive abilities is an expansion and extension of previous theories. It specifies what kinds of individual differences in cognitive abilities exist and how those kinds of individual differences are related to one another. It provides a map of all cognitive abilities known or expected to exist and can be used as a guide to research and practice. It proposes that there are a fairly large number of distinct individual differences in cognitive ability, and that the relationships among them can be derived by classifying them into three different strata: stratum I, "narrow" abilities; stratum II, "broad" abilities; and stratum III, consisting of a single "general" ability.

ORIGIN OF THE THEORY

The theory was developed in the course of a major survey (Carroll, 1993a, 1994) of research over the past 60 or 70 years on the nature, identification, and structure of human cognitive abilities. That research involved the use of the mathematical technique known as factor analysis. Necessarily, the work also involved the analysis of correlations among scores on psychological tests and other kinds of assessments of individuals. This is because factor analysis concerns the structure of correlations among such variables; that is, the question of how many "factors" or "latent traits" are indicated by a set of correlations arranged in a matrix such that all the correlations among variables are shown systematically.

In my survey, I used factor analysis to examine more than 460 sets of data (hereafter, datasets) from the relevant literature. In most cases these datasets had been previously analyzed by the original investigators, but I felt it necessary to reanalyze them because I wanted to take advantage of important technical advances in factor-analytic methodology that were not used by the original investigators, usually because they were not yet available at the time of the original data analysis. I also considered it desirable to analyze the datasets in as consistent a way as possible to facilitate making valid general conclusions.

Before beginning my survey, I considered how best to select datasets because it was going to be impossible to reanalyze all of what I estimated as more than 2,000 datasets available in the relevant literature published over the years 1930–1985 (approximately) in many countries, mainly English-speaking countries such as the United States, Canada, Great Britain, and Australia, but also other countries such as France, Germany, Japan, Spain, and even Russia. I established several criteria for selecting datasets: (1) each dataset should contain a substantial number of variables reflecting performance on cognitive tasks typical of those used in intelligence and aptitude tests or in research in cognitive psychology, (2) the dataset should be based on a substantial number of individuals (preferably more than, say, 100) taken from a defined population of children, adolescents, or adults that had been tested in a consistent way, (3) the published form of the dataset should present the matrix of correlations among its variables, thus permitting reanalysis, and (4) sufficient information about the sample and the variables must have been available to permit at least tentative interpretation of the findings.

In the end, more than 480 datasets were selected, but a small number (about 15) turned out to contain mathematical inconsistencies that could not be resolved. Thus, reanalysis of these datasets was not feasible. Many of the datasets were from research by prominent investigators of cognitive abilities such as Thurstone (1938), Thurstone and Thurstone (1941), Guilford (1967), Guilford and Hoepfner (1971), Cattell (1971), Horn (1965), and Vernon (1961); for this reason, the three-stratum theory has similarities to certain theories espoused by some of these investigators (e.g., Horn's fluid-crystallized theory) (see Horn & Noll, Chapter 4, this volume).

At this point it is necessary to introduce the concept of *stratum* and to describe certain features of the reanalyses performed in my survey. It was probably Thurstone (1947) who created a related concept—the *order* of a factor analysis. A *first-order* factor analysis is the application of factor-analytic techniques directly to a correlation matrix of the original variables in the dataset; it results in one or more *first-order factors*. A *second-order* factor analysis is the application of factor-analytic techniques to the matrix of correlations among the first-order factors (if there are two or more, and if the correlations are other than zero) of a dataset; it results in one or more *second-order factors*. A *third-order* factor analysis is the application of factor-analytic techniques to the matrix of correlations among the second-order factors (if there are two or more) of a dataset; usually it results in a single *third-order factor*, but it could result in more than one such factor. This process could be repeated at still higher orders, but it would rarely be necessary because at each successive order the number of resulting factors becomes ever smaller. (A large number of original variables would be necessary to permit analysis at the fourth order, for example.)

The concept of order (of a factor, or of a factor analysis) is therefore tied to operations in the application of factor analysis to a particular dataset. Usually, the variables in a dataset are scores on a variety of psychological tests; the factor analysis produces first-order factors that correspond to clusters of tests such that within each cluster, the tests are similar in the contents or psychological processes they involve. A dataset might, for example, yield three first-order factors, one being a "verbal factor" with loadings on vocabulary and reading comprehension tests, another being a "spatial" factor with loadings on formboard and paperfolding tests, and still another being a "memory span" factor with loadings on a series of memory span tests. If these factors are correlated, a second-order factor might be interpreted as a "general intelligence" factor.

Suppose, however, the variables in a dataset are individual test items (e.g., the individual items on a vocabulary test). A first-order factor analysis of the matrix of correlations among vocabulary items might produce one or more factors; if one factor were found, it might indeed be a "vocabulary" or "verbal" factor, but if two or more factors were found, the investigator might be prompted to identify these factors by their different contents (a factor of "literary vocabulary," a factor of "scientific vocabulary," etc.). A second-order factor analysis of the correlations among such factors would probably produce a "general vocabulary factor," which might be similar to the first-order vocabulary or verbal factor produced in the analysis of a more typical battery of psychological tests. Thus, a vocabulary factor might be a first-order factor in one case but a second-order factor in another case. Similarly, a "general" factor might be a second-order factor in one case but a third-order factor in another case.

As factor analysis is essentially a technique of classifying abilities, Cattell (1971) introduced the term "stratum" to help in characterizing factors, in an absolute sense, in terms of the narrowness or breadth of their content. In the conduct of my survey and in interpreting results, I called the first-order factors resulting from analysis of typical sets of psychological tests *factors at the first stratum*, or *stratum I factors*. (Almost all the datasets were composed of typical sets of psychological tests.) *Stratum II factors* were second-order factors from such datasets, and *stratum III factors* were third-order factors from such datasets. Frequently, however, datasets did not produce third-order factors; they produced only one second-order factor, which was often interpretable as a *general* factor similar to the general factor that occurred as a third-order factor in some other datasets. Thus the stratum of a factor is relative to the variety and diversity of the variables covered by it. Sometimes it is the same as the order of a factor, but in other cases it is not; its stratum is assigned in terms of its perceived breadth or narrowness. It is possible that some factors are so narrow or specific (in content) that their stratum is less than 1. This would be the case for highly specific kinds of vocabulary knowledge identified by factor analysis of the items of a vocabulary test, as mentioned previously. For convenience, however, the three-stratum theory omits mention of such narrow factors, of which there could be many.

The three-stratum theory thus postulates that most factors of interest can be classified as being at a certain stratum, and that the total array of cognitive ability factors contains factors at three strata, namely, first, second, and third. At the third or highest stratum is a general factor (often called *g*). The second stratum is composed of a relatively small number (perhaps about 10) of "broad" factors, including *fluid intelligence, crystallized intelligence, general memory and learning, broad visual perception, broad auditory perception, broad retrieval ability, broad cognitive speediness,* and *processing speed.* At the first stratum (or stratum I), there are numerous first-order factors, roughly grouped under the second-stratum factors as shown in Figure 7.1. Some are "level" factors in the sense that their scores indicate the level of mastery, along a difficulty scale, that the individual is able to demonstrate. Others are "speed" factors in the sense that their scores indicate the speed with which the individual performs tasks or the individual's rate of learning in learning and memory tasks.

Rationale and Impetus for Generating the Theory

The theory was intended to constitute a provisional statement about the enumeration, identification, and structuring of the total range of cognitive abilities known or discovered thus far. In this way it was expected to replace, expand, or supplement previous theories of the structure of cognitive abilities, such as Thurstone's (1938) theory of primary mental abilities, Guilford's (1967) structure-of-intellect theory, Horn and Cattell's (1966) Gf-Gc theory, or Wechsler's (1974; see also Matarazzo, 1972) theory of verbal and performance components of intelligence.

OPERATIONALIZATION AND APPLICATION OF THE THEORY

Component Parts of the Theory

The theory consists of an enumeration of the cognitive abilities that have been found thus far, with statements concerning the nature and generality of these abilities, the types of tasks that require them, and the types of tests that can be used to measure them. In effect, it also consists of statements about the structure of the abilities in terms of the assignment of abilities to one of three strata of different degrees of generality. Second-order factors subsumed by the third-order general factor are related to each other by virtue of their loadings on the general factor, some of these are more related to the general factor than others. Similarly, first-order factors subsumed by a given second-order factor are related to each other by virtue of their loadings on that second-order factor.

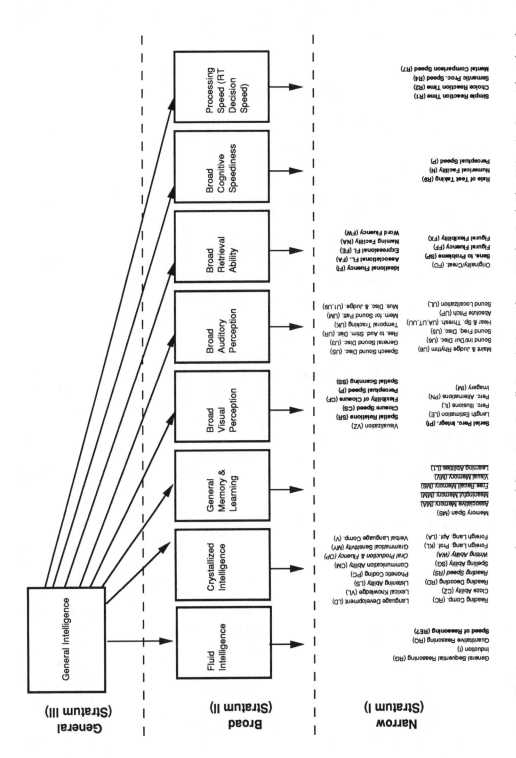

FIGURE 7.1. The three-stratum structure of cognitive abilities. From Carroll (1993a). Copyright © 1993 by Cambridge University Press. Adapted and reproduced by permission. *Note.* Stratum I factors are differentiated as "level" (plain type), "speed" (bold type), "speed and level" (italics type), and "rate" (underlined") factors.

125

All the abilities covered by the theory are assumed to be "cognitive" in the sense that cognitive processes are critical to the successful understanding and performance of tasks requiring these abilities, most particularly in the *processing of mental information.* In many cases, they go far beyond the kinds of intelligences measured in typical batteries of intelligence tests. The abilities are roughly classified as follows:

Abilities in the domain of language
Abilities in the domain of reasoning
Abilities in the domain of memory and learning
Abilities in the domain of visual perception
Abilities in the domain of auditory reception
Abilities in the domain of idea production
Abilities in the domain of cognitive speed
Abilities in the domain of knowledge and achievement
Miscellaneous domains of ability (e.g., abilities in the sensory domain, attention abilities, cognitive styles, and administrative abilities)

It must be stressed that this theory is only provisional. Further research may suggest that it should be revised, either in small or in radical ways. It is becoming clear that present methods of measuring abilities may not adequately cover all the abilities that exist or that are important in practical life.

Operationalization of the Theory

Thus far, the three-stratum theory has not been operationalized in any formal sense, in terms of either actual batteries of tests or other assessment procedures that are specifically designed to measure the abilities specified by the theory. A detailed description of the theory, as it pertains to the different domains of ability, including higher-stratum abilities, can be found in relevant chapters of my book, *Human Cognitive Abilities* (Carroll, 1993a). Most of these chapters describe representative tests or other procedures drawn from research studies or from well-known batteries of tests whereby the relevant factors of ability can be measured. Other sources of information about tests for measuring the abilities specified by the three-stratum theory are handbooks by Jonassen and Grabowski (1993) and Fleishman and Reilly (1992).

Applications of the Theoretical Model for Practice and Research

The three-stratum theory is intended chiefly to provide guidance for further research concerning cognitive abilities and their structure. For example, if new abilities are identified, the theory provides guidance as to where such abilities should fit in the structure already established—whether they are truly new or merely subvarieties of abilities previously identified.

In research, also, the theory plays an important role in presentation of factor-analytic results. Matrices of factor loadings show the loadings of tests (or other variables) on the different factors, at different strata. Most often it is found that a given test has significant loadings (say, greater than .3) on more than one factor; for example, a test might have such a loading on the general factor (at stratum III), a significant loading on one or more of the stratum II factors, and a significant loading on one or more of the stratum I factors. In other cases, a test's significant loadings might occur only on a general factor and one of the stratum I factors. In either case the display of the test's loadings provides useful information about what the test measures and the extent to which it measures different factors. It is important to realize that the scores of most tests reflect influences of more than one factor, usually factors at different strata.

The theory has similar uses in professional practice. As was mentioned previously, it provides what is essentially a "map" of all known cognitive abilities. Such a map can be used in interpreting scores on the many tests used in individual assessment by clinical psychologists, school psychologists, industrial psychologists, and others. Such scores can be assessed in terms of the abilities they most probably measure. The map also suggests what abilities may need to be assessed in particular cases that require selection of appropriate tests (see McGrew, Chapter 9, this volume; Flanagan & McGrew, Chapter 17, this volume).

EMPIRICAL SUPPORT FOR THE THEORY

The empirical support for this theory resides in the reanalyses of the more than 460 datasets that were presented in Carroll (1993a), where I offered arguments to justify the procedures I used. The reanalyses themselves were presented in the form of detailed hierarchical orthogonalized factor matrices contained in a set of computer disks (Carroll, 1993b). Reviews of the book have been highly favorable (Brand, 1993; Brody, 1994; Burns, 1994; Eysenck, 1994; Nagoshi, 1994; Sternberg, 1994); thus it would seem that experts in the field have entered no serious objections to the results or the theory. It is possible, however, that more critical reviews will eventually appear, raising questions about certain features of the theory.

Relations with Other Theories

The three-stratum theory is an expansion and extension of most of the previous theories of cognitive abilities, in particular (in rough chronological order), those of Spearman (1927), Thurstone (1938), Vernon (1961), Horn and Cattell (1966; see Horn & Noll, Chapter 4, this volume), Hakstian and Cattell (1978), and Gustafsson (1989). Even in 1927, Spearman offered what was essentially a two-stratum theory; the latter authors presented further and more detailed evidence of the hierarchical structure of abilities.

The three-stratum theory differs more radically from the structure-of-intelligence theory offered by Guilford (1967) and Guilford and Hoepfner (1971). These investigators initially did not accept the notion of higher-order factors of intelligence; only in more recent papers did Guilford (1981, 1985) admit the possibility of higher-order factors, and some of Guilford's former colleagues have started to reanalyze his data in terms of higher-order factors (Bachelor, Michael, & Kim, 1994). The three-stratum theory has resemblances to the theory of multiple intelligences offered by Gardner (see Chen & Gardner, Chapter 6, this volume). The various "broad abilities" show rough correspondences to Gardner's seven "intelligences"; however, Gardner seems not to accept the concept of an overarching general ability, nor does he accept the notion of a hierarchical structure of abilities. Apparently he regards his seven intelligences as being completely independent of each other, despite a plethora of evidence that this is not the case.

BEYOND TRADITIONAL THEORIES OF INTELLIGENCE

The three-stratum theory reflects advances in the behavioral sciences in a number of ways.

The Influence of Recent Advances in Psychometrics

In psychometrics, research over the past 50 years has increasingly emphasized that "intelligence," or IQ, is not a single thing, but a complex, composite structure of a number of intelligences. A psychometric technique put forward by Schmid and Leiman (1957), the orthogonalization of hierarchical factor matrices, made it possible to formulate more exactly how this composite structure of intelligences could be conceptualized. The Schmid and Leiman technique has become popular only in recent years, but it has become one of the major bases of the three-stratum theory.

Other major bases of the three-stratum theory have been improvements in measurement theory and computational methods. A major advance in measurement theory has been the so-called item-response theory (see mainly Lord & Novick, 1968), which presents a model of the relation of ability to test item performance and assists in the design of more valid and reliable ability tests. Although the conduct of a comprehensive factor-analytic study requires large logistic resources in assembling tests, test subjects, and test data, analysis of data has become increasingly easier with the advent of modern high-speed computers, particularly personal computers. The availability of personal computers enormously facilitated the reanalyses of large numbers of datasets in Carroll's studies (1993a, 1993b).

Influence of Recent Advances in Cognitive Psychology

The three-stratum theory reflects advances in cognitive psychology because these advances make it easier to interpret findings from factor analysis in terms of the properties of cognitive tasks (as represented in the psychological tests studied by factor analysis). Also, cognitive research has made it possible to focus attention on various cognitive tasks that were largely ignored in psychometrics (e.g., the sentence verification task and category-sorting tasks).

How the Three-Stratum Theory Departs from Traditional Paradigms

Above all, the three-stratum theory emphasizes the multifactorial nature of the domain of cognitive abilities and directs attention to many types of ability usually ignored in traditional paradigms. It implies that individual profiles of ability levels are much more complex than previously thought, but at the same time it offers a way of structuring such profiles, by classifying abilities in terms of strata. Thus, a general factor is close to former conceptions of intelligence, whereas second-stratum factors summarize abilities in such domains as visual and spatial perception. Nevertheless, some first-stratum abilities are probably of importance in individual cases, such as the phonetic coding ability that is likely to describe differences between normal and dyslexic readers.

Future Directions in Research and Application

Much work remains to be done in the factor-analytic study of cognitive abilities. The map of abilities provided by the three-stratum theory undoubtedly has errors of commission and omission, with gaps to be filled in by further research, including the development of new types of testing and assessment and the factorial investigation of their relationships with each other and with better established types of assessment.

The theory needs to be further validated by acquiring information about the importance and relevance of the various abilities it specifies. In this endeavor, cognitive psychology can help by investigating the basic information-processing aspects of such abilities. Developmental and educational psychology can assist by investigating the development, stability, and educability of abilities—not only those such as IQ, which has been studied extensively, but also the other types of abilities in different domains specified by the theory.

Moreover, the three-stratum theory has implications for studies in neuropsychology and human genetics. For example, the theory specifies, on the basis of factor-analytic studies, a certain structure for memory abilities. Does this structure have parallels in theories of brain function (Crick, 1994; Schacter & Tulving, 1994)? Similarly, the structure of abilities specified by the theory currently says little about the relative roles of genetic and environmental influences on these abilities; such influences can be investigated by considering them in relation to different strata of abilities (Plomin & McClearn, 1993). Thus far, we have a considerable amount of information on the heritability of the third-stratum factor *g* but relatively little on how much genes influence the development of lower-stratum abilities such as broad visual perception and perceptual speed.

The theory has major implications for practical assessment of individuals in clinical. educational, or industrial settings. It appears to prescribe that individuals should be assessed with regard to the *total range* of abilities the theory specifies. Any such prescription would of course create enormous problems; generally there would not be sufficient time to conduct assessments (by tests, ratings, interviews, personal observations, etc.) of all the abilities that exist. Even if there were, there is a lack of appropriate tests for many abilities. Research is needed to spell out how the assessor can select what abilities need to be tested in particular cases. The conventional wisdom is that abilities close to *g* are the most important to test or assess, but if this policy is followed too strictly, many abilities that are important in particular cases would probably be missed. Only the future will enable us to appreciate these possibilities adequately.

REFERENCES

Bachelor, P., Michael, W. B., & Kim, S. (1994). First-order and higher-order semantic and figural factors in structure-of-intellect divergent production measures. *Educational and Psychological Measurement, 54,* 608–619.

Brand, C. (1993, October 22). The importance of the *g* factor [Review of Carroll, 1993a]. *Times Higher Educational Supplement,* p. 22.

Brody, N. (1994). Cognitive abilities [Review of Carroll, 1993a]. *Psychological Science, 5,* 63, 65–68.

Burns, R. B. (1994). Surveying the cognitive terrain [Review of Carroll, 1993a]. *Educational Researcher, 23*(2), 35–37.

Carroll, J. B. (1993a). *Human cognitive abilities: A survey of factor-analytic studies.* New York: Cambridge University Press.

Carroll, J. B. (1993b). *Human cognitive abilities: A survey of factor-analytic studies.* Appendix B: Hierarchical factor matrix files. New York: Cambridge University Press.

Carroll, J. B. (1994). Cognitive abilities: Constructing a theory from data. In D. K. Detterman (Ed.), *Current topics in human intelligence, Vol. 4: Theories of intelligence* (pp. 43–63). Norwood, NJ: Ablex.

Cattell, R. B. (1971). *Abilities: Their structure, growth, and action.* Boston: Houghton Mifflin.

Crick, F. (1994). *The astonishing hypothesis: The scientific search for the soul.* New York: Scribner's.

Eysenck, H. J. (1994). [Special review of Carroll, 1993a.] *Personality and Individual Differences, 16,* 199.

Fleishman, E. A., & Reilly, M. E. (1992). *Handbook of human abilities: Definitions, measurements, and job task requirements.* Palo Alto, CA: Consulting Psychologists Press.

Guilford, J. P. (1967). *The nature of human intelligence.* New York: McGraw-Hill.

Guilford, J. P. (1981). Higher-order structure-of-intellect abilities. *Multivariate Behavioral Research, 16,* 411–435.

Guilford, J. P. (1985). The structure-of-intellect model. In B. B. Wolman (Ed.), *Handbook of intelligence: Theories, measurements, and applications* (pp. 225–266). New York: Wiley.

Guilford, J. P., & Hoepfner, R. (1971). *The analysis of intelligence.* New York: McGraw-Hill.

Gustafsson, J. E. (1989). Broad and narrow abilities in research on learning and instruction. In R. Kanfer, P. L. Ackerman, & R. Cudeck (Eds.), *Abilities, motivation, and methodology: The Minnesota Symposium on Learning and Individual Differences* (pp. 203–237). Hillsdale, NJ: Erlbaum.

Hakstian, A. R., & Cattell, R. B. (1978). Higher-stratum ability structures on a basis of twenty primary abilities. *Journal of Educational Psychology, 70,* 657–669.

Horn, J. L. (1965). *Fluid and crystallized intelligence: A factor analytic study of the structure among primary mental abilities.* Unpublished doctoral dissertation, University of Illinois, Urbana/Champaign.

Horn, J. L., & Cattell, R. B. (1966). Refinement of the theory of fluid and crystallized general intelligences. *Journal of Educational Psychology, 57,* 253–270.

Jonassen, D. H., & Grabowski, B. L. (Eds.). (1993). *Handbook of individual differences, learning, and instruction.* Hillsdale, NJ: Erlbaum.

Lord, F. M., & Novick, M. R. (1968). *Statistical theories of mental test scores.* Reading, MA: Addison-Wesley.

Matarazzo, J. D. (1972). *Wechsler's measurement and appraisal of adult intelligence* (5th ed.). Baltimore: Williams & Wilkins.

Nagoshi, C. T. (1994). The factor-analytic guide to cognitive abilities [Review of Carroll, 1993a]. *Contemporary Psychology, 39,* 617–618.

Plomin, R., & McClearn, G. E. (Eds.). (1993). *Nature, nurture, and psychology.* Washington, DC: American Psychological Association.

Schacter, D. L., & Tulving, E. (Eds.). (1994). *Memory systems 1994.* Cambridge, MA: MIT Press.

Schmid, J., & Leiman, J. M. (1957). The development of hierarchical factor solutions. *Psychometrika, 22,* 53–61.

Spearman, C. (1927). *The abilities of man: Their nature and measurement.* New York: Macmillan.

Sternberg, R. J. (1994). 468 factor-analyzed data sets: What they tell us and don't tell us about human intelligence [Review of Carroll, 1993a]. *Psychological Science, 5,* 63–65.

Thurstone, L. L. (1938). Primary mental abilities. *Psychometric Monographs* (No. 1).

Thurstone, L. L. (1947). *Multiple factor analysis: A development and expansion of the vectors of mind.* Chicago: University of Chicago Press.

Thurstone, L. L., & Thurstone, T. G. (1941). Factorial studies of intelligence. *Psychometric Monographs* (No. 2).

Vernon, P. E. (1961). *The structure of human abilities* (2nd ed.). London: Methuen.

Wechsler, D. (1974). *Wechsler Intelligence Scale for Children—Revised.* New York: Psychological Corporation.

CHAPTER 8

The Role of Intelligence in a Broad Model of Personal Competence

STEPHEN GREENSPAN

JOHN DRISCOLL

THE CONCEPTS OF INTELLIGENCE and personal competence are closely intertwined (Ford, 1994; McClelland, 1973). Both relate to ability to achieve valued and/or desired goals and solve particular tasks or challenges. The difference is that personal competence is a broader construct, incorporating all the skills that contribute to attaining goals or solving challenges, whereas the term "intelligence" refers to that subset of skills that involves thinking and understanding. In spite of the centrality of intelligence to psychological research and practice throughout this century, where intelligence fits into the larger picture of human competencies has attracted relatively little attention until recently. As various observers have noted, research on the construct validity of intelligence has been limited mainly to investigation of the structure of existing tests.

Intelligence is, undoubtedly, among the most important aspects of human personal competence. It is a prerequisite to success in virtually all forms of human endeavor. However, other aspects of personal competence also contribute to success in attaining goals and solving problems. For example, no matter how sophisticated one's understanding of mountain-climbing technique may be, one is not likely to be able to conquer a peak such as Anapurna without such exceptional physical attributes as strength, endurance, and tolerance of high altitude, as well as such exemplary personality attributes as perseverance, courage, work ethic, and ability to cooperate with others. Furthermore, contextual variables undoubtedly enter into the equation as well. Thus, a climber not up to Anapurna may still attain considerable success on less formidable peaks, and even the most exceptional of climbers will need more than a little luck (e.g., with weather) to scale a peak as challenging as Anapurna.

Although intelligence is usually viewed mainly as an input (independent variable) contributing to various outcomes (dependent variables) such as school success, personal competence can be viewed in terms of either inputs or outcomes. Thus, competent individuals can be defined in terms of both the qualities they bring to various goals and challenges as well as their relative degree of success in meeting those goals and challenges. For example, a climber may be described as highly competent either because of the exceptional talents and attributes that he or she possesses or (more usually) because of the success he or she has had in climbing notably difficult peaks or routes. This dual nature of competence as both input and outcome has, undoubtedly, contributed to some confusion regarding how best to define or measure this elusive construct.

The title of this chapter implies an emphasis on the input (independent variable) approach to competence. Such an emphasis (which we have previously termed "content-oriented") has, in fact, characterized much of the first author's work in this area, as it has the work of others. Such an approach has potential value, both for the field and for this volume, in putting the construct of intelligence in a broader perspective, as well as in identifying aspects of competence (particularly in the socioemotional domain) that may have been underemphasized both in theory and in practice. A content-oriented approach has its limitations, however.

One limitation of a content-oriented approach to competence is the tendency to reify particular inputs (especially intelligence) and lose sight of what Silvern (1984) characterized as the "principle of equifinality," namely, that different people can attain the same outcome through different pathways. For example, although shyness is generally an impediment to success in American society, it need not be, as reflected in the fact that at least two recent Presidents of the United States (Nixon and Carter) could be described as somewhat shy. In a similar vein, whereas hard training and long preparation are considered essential prerequisites for greatness as a mountain climber, one of America's most successful mountaineers is notorious for doing almost none of either.

In addition to contributing to the tendency to overemphasize particular inputs, a limitation of a content-oriented approach to competence is that it rests on a somewhat artificial division of human capabilities into discrete domains. For example, whereas "character" and "intelligence" both make separate contributions to an outcome such as "staying out of jail," it is probably the case that important aspects of character (e.g., delay of gratification) are partly cognitive in nature (i.e., involve an understanding of social consequences) and vice versa (Baron, 1989).

A content-oriented approach contributes to what Sameroff and Chandler (1975) termed a "main effects" or "interactional" view of competence, whereas an outcome-oriented approach offers the possibility of an approach that is more "transactional." Nevertheless, a content-oriented model of human competence is still potentially useful given that clinical practice is largely grounded in mechanistic assumptions. One of these potential uses is to identify aspects of competence that may be underemphasized in current clinical practices.

The bulk of this chapter is devoted to a discussion of a model of personal competence and the role of intelligence, broadly defined, within that model. Various implications of the model are discussed, particularly those relevant to study and practice in the field of disabilities. In a later section, we present some ideas regarding steps toward a more outcome-oriented or transactional approach to the relationship between intelligence and competence.

DESCRIPTION OF THE MODEL

The model described in this section is a heuristic device, intended to guide speculation about the role of intelligence in the broad spectrum of human abilities. Based in large part on previous theoretical and empirical work by various investigators, it, like the work of Guilford, Gardner, and other model-builders, represents a creative integration—what Gardner (1993), referring to his own model, termed a "subjective factor analysis"—on the part of the first author and his colleagues.

The model, as depicted in this chapter, may be considered a "broad framework theory" geared to a relatively molar level of specificity. Thus, whereas Greenspan (1979) previously specified seven components of social intelligence, grouped into the three domains of social sensitivity, social insight, and social communication, in this chapter we deal with social intelligence and the other constructs in the model as relatively global entities. It should be understood, however, that each of the major elements depicted in Figure 8.1 can be further divided into several subcomponents. The list of eight subcomponents portrayed at the lowest level of Figure 8.1 suggests the types of content subsumed under the four major domains (the middle level) of the model. Our intent in devising this model was to create a broad umbrella under which all the major elements of competence could be placed without necessarily specifying all of those elements.

The model has been fleshed out and modified over several years. Although refinement of the model has involved some increase in specification of subcomponents, the greatest amount of change has involved rearrangement of elements at the middle (relatively molar) level. Such rearrangement has been driven partly by esthetic considerations (i.e., to make the model more elegant and symmetrical). As in any classificatory scheme, groupings of elements are somewhat arbitrary and can be changed depending on whether one focuses on "intensional" or "extensional" (or, in this case, intellectual or social) features (Blashfield, 1993). However, we recognize that the manner in which elements are grouped sometimes does make a difference. Thus, there is the danger that the combination of social and practical intelligence in the current version of the model into "everyday competence" may be used—inappropriately, in our view—as justification for continuing to deemphasize the importance of social intelligence.

The last published version of the model (Greenspan & Granfield, 1992), "version 2," was a somewhat radical departure from the previous (Greenspan, 1981a) presentation ("version 1b"), which itself represented a minor modification of the initial ("version 1a") portrayal (Greenspan, 1979) of the model. Although the major elements in the model have remained fairly constant across these various versions, the manner in which the elements have been grouped and organized hierarchically has changed somewhat. The current version of the model ("version 3") is depicted in Figure 8.1. It represents a synthesis of versions 1a and 1b and version 2, although it is closer in spirit to versions 1a and 1b, which are the versions most widely cited in the literature.

Version 1a of the model contained three major components: (1) "adaptive intelligence," (2) "socioemotional adaptation" and (3) "physical competence"; the first two components were subdivided, whereas physical competence was presented in an undifferentiated manner. Adaptive Intelli-

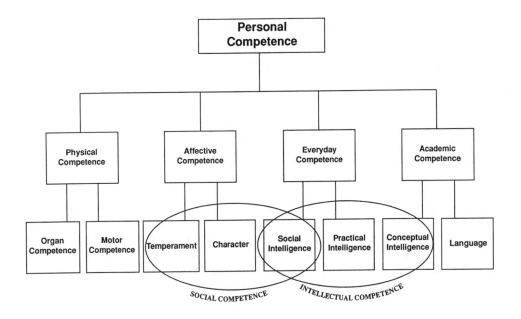

FIGURE 8.1. Content model of personal competence.

gence contained three domains: conceptual intelligence, practical intelligence, and social intelligence. Socioemotional adaptation contained two domains: temperament and character. Version 1b is identical to 1a with some minor changes in terminology: "intellectual competence" (with the same three components) is substituted for "adaptive intelligence") and "emotional competence" (with the same two components) is substituted for "socioemotional competence." Another minor difference is that social intelligence was linked with temperament and character in version 1b by having a dotted line drawn around these three domains indicating that these three variables constitute the construct of social competence.

In version 2, the role of social competence was incorporated more formally into the model. Competence was divided into social and instrumental, with each of these further divided into intellectual and nonintellectual aspects. Temperament and character together comprise the nonintellectual aspects of social competence, whereas practical intelligence and social intelligence together formed the intellectual aspects of social competence. Analogous to the widely used notions of crystallized and fluid intelligence, conceptual intelligence and "processing" were grouped under the rubric of intellectual aspects of instrumental competence. The nonintellectual aspects of instrumental competence contained the two domains of "state" and "motor functioning," which together comprise (in somewhat more differentiated fashion) what was termed in versions 1a and 1b "physical competence."

In retrospect, we realize that version 2 was probably a mistake. In attempting to highlight the role of social competence, and to create greater symmetry, Greenspan and Granfield (1992) deconstructed the natural category of intelligence and created artificial constructs of intellectual aspects and nonintellectual aspects of social and instrumental competence (with this latter term itself an artifice). In version 3, therefore, we return to a view that is closer to the spirit of versions 1a and 1b, a version that has shown evidence of both social and empirical validity while keeping some of the symmetry of version 2. This symmetry is reflected in the fact that there are now four domains of competence: physical competence, affective competence, everyday competence and academic competence, each of which is further subdivided, producing eight subdomains at the bottom level of the model. Each of these, of course, can be broken into more discrete elements, although we do not do so here.

The main difference between versions 1a and 1b and 3 is that the two earlier versions contained three major domains (physical, emotional, and intellectual competence), while the current version contains four major domains, a result of dividing intellectual competence into everyday and academic components. Unlike version 2, we do not attempt to create an artificial grouping of the four major domains, say, into intellectual aspects (everyday and academic) and physiological aspects (physical and affective) of competence. Although such an approach has a certain appeal, it is somewhat forced (e.g., character is largely nonphysiological whereas language is largely nonintellectual), lacks empirical support, and serves no real purpose.

Everyday competence refers to one's ability to think about and understand problems found in such real-world settings as work, play, social relationships, and home. It contains two of the three elements (practical and social intelligence) contained in the original construct of adaptive intelligence. Practical intelligence refers to the ability to think about and understand mechanical, technical, or physical problems found in everyday settings. Social intelligence refers to the ability to think about and understand problems found in relationships with other people.

The term "academic competence" contains the third element (conceptual intelligence) contained in the 1979 model of adaptive intelligence, along with an additional element, language. It refers to the skills that are most prized and relevant to success in school. Conceptual intelligence (the element tapped by IQ measures) refers to the ability to think about and understand problems found in formal learning settings. Language refers to the ability to understand and participate in the communication process.

The terms "academic competence" and "everyday competence" were borrowed and adapted from Sternberg's (1984) typology of academic and everyday intelligence. We changed the second word in the terms to "competence," to create a broader framework that could include language. This was necessary because language is a vital contributor to school success, is related to (but different from) conceptual intelligence (Stanovich, 1993), is a key aspect of any typology of disability, and was a serious omission from earlier versions of the model.

Because one of the potential uses of the model is to provide a framework (discussed in the next section) for a dimensional approach to classifying disorders, the bottom level of the model is meant to be as all-inclusive as possible. For the most part, these elements are as depicted in former versions, with no real changes other than terminology. Temperament and character constitute the domain of affective (formerly emotional) competence. Temperament refers to such biologically mediated aspects of personality as calmness–emotionality and attentiveness–distractability, whereas character refers to such environmentally mediated aspects of personality as gregariousness–timidity and prosocial versus antisocial orientation. Motor competence and "organ competence" ("state" in version 2) constitute physical competence. The term organ competence refers to the functioning of such various bodily systems as vision, hearing, heart, lungs, and so on. Motor competence refers to such things as size, strength, coordination, and mobility.

As in version 1a, social competence is not formally depicted hierarchically, but we do represent it (as in 1b) by drawing a line around temperament, character, and social intelligence. We do the same to represent the construct of intelligence, by drawing a line around academic, practical, and social intelligence. The intersecting ovals in Figure 8.1 form a Venn diagram, with social intelligence falling within the intersection. This depiction supports the view expressed by Cantor and Kihlstrom (1989) that social intelligence is the link between intelligence and personality.

HISTORICAL ORIGINS

There have been various attempts to develop multifaceted taxonomies of intelligence, personality and physical ability. The current model is based, to a significant extent, on those earlier efforts. For the most part, however, these aspects of functioning have been treated as separate systems, and have not been put together into a single overarching framework. For example, Guilford (1967, 1975) developed models of both intelligence and personality, respectively, but did not, to our knowledge, put them together into a single model.

One likely reason for the failure to combine intelligence and personality is that personality has typically been framed in dispositional terms, whereas intelligence has been framed in ability terms. These perspectives have been viewed as operating on different planes and not, therefore, capable of being combined into a single system. The relative paucity of efforts to build comprehensive models of competence, while understandable within this context, is nonetheless surprising given the tremendous amount of debate throughout this century over the meaning and importance of intelligence.

For the first author, the effort to recast personality in ability terms was aided greatly by familiarity with the literature on "social competence" in childhood. Various efforts were made to define this elusive construct, some as a part of efforts to identify alternative criteria (other than IQ) for evaluating early intervention programs such as Head Start (Zigler & Trickett, 1978). Taxonomies of childhood social competence (e.g., Baumrind, 1967; Kohn, 1977) show great similarity to factorial models of adult personality (e.g., Eysenck, 1967; Guilford, 1975). Social competence thus provided the opportunity to recast the personality domain in ability terms.

The construct of character is derived from the so-called two-factor model of social competence (Kohn, 1977), which contains two components, which might be termed "niceness" and "gregarious- ness." The construct of temperament is derived from Schaefer's (1976) expansion of the definition of social competence from one grounded solely in character to one that also takes into account biologically grounded competencies having to do with self-regulation of attention and emotion. As noted by Kagan (1994), temperament is the aspect of personality considered most susceptible to biological influences such as heritability and neurological abnormalities.

Although there have been various taxonomies of physical competence (Bruininks, 1974; Fleishman, 1954, 1958), this is the least developed aspect of our model, reflecting the fact that the model grew out of our interest in social competence and gradually expanded to incorporate more peripheral aspects. Development of a differentiated model of intelligence was more central to this interest in social competence because the first author's starting point was an interest in social cognition (cf. Chandler & Greenspan, 1972). This construct (which Greenspan later came to refer to as social intelligence) falls as noted previously at the intersection of social competence and intelligence; although it is included in some taxonomies of both intelligence and social competence, this construct's importance has only recently begun to be recognized. For example, although O'Mal- ley (1977) added social cognition (social intelligence) to character and temperament to create a three-factor model of social competence, most taxonomies of social competence still emphasize its nonintellective components.

The notion of multiple intelligences, although brought to public awareness through the work of Gardner (1983), was in fact initially popularized by E. L. Thorndike (1920) more than 75 years ago. He proposed a tripartite model of intelligence, consisting of abstract intelligence (the aspect tapped by IQ), mechanical intelligence, and social intelligence. Various other prominent intelligence theorists have proposed factor models of intelligence to illustrate their conviction that the IQ measure should not be viewed as synonymous with the whole of intelligence. Ironically, one of the more outspoken advocates for this point of view was David Wechsler (1974), who used Thorndike's model to argue against the absurdity of calls, by critics who considered IQ culturally biased, to substitute equally (if not more) biased measures of educational achievement for use with minority children. Instead of discarding IQ (which Wechsler considered a good measure of Thorndike's abstract intelligence), Wechsler argued for the development of equally good measures of the other areas of intelligence, areas that IQ was never intended to tap.

Multiple models of intelligence are typically defended as a necessary counterbalance to the fact that the Binet–Simon (1905) scale, after which all current IQ tests are modeled, was initially intended only as a screen for academic failure. It is interesting to note, therefore, that the very earliest effort by Binet and Simon (which relied largely on a questionnaire format) reflected a view of intelligence that was much broader than adopted in their later more famous test and emphasized what we and others term "practical intelligence" (Haywood & Paour, 1992; Switzky, 1995).

Various multifaceted models of intelligence have been proposed, most bearing some resem- blance to Thorndike's tripartite model. Guilford's cube model of "ability," for example, contained four types of intelligence in the content plane: semantic, symbolic, figural and behavioral, with the first two equivalent to Thorndike's abstract intelligence and the last two tapping Thorndike's me- chanical and social intelligences, respectively. Sternberg's triarchic theory of intelligence also contains a content dimension, and he used the terms "academic intelligence" (Thorndike's abstract), "practi- cal intelligence" (Thorndike's mechanical), and "social intelligence" to identify the content domains in his model. Gardner (1983; Chen & Gardner, Chapter 6, this volume) has been one of the most outspoken advocates for a multidimensional view of intelligence, although his seven-part model (which contains such components as musical, artistic, and kinesthetic intelligences) contains many more elements than are included in other models (Brody, 1992). Despite differences in emphasis, the various proponents of multiple intelligence models all share a common belief, namely, that one's IQ score does not adequately capture all of the ways in which one can manifest intelligence in the real world.

The broad umbrella term "personal competence" has been used to designate the sum total of human abilities (Sundberg, Snowden, & Reynolds, 1978), although the term is sometimes used much more narrowly (e.g., Reynolds, 1981). Conversely, although both Zigler and Trickett (1978) and Anderson and Messick (1974) used the more delimited term "social competence," their proposed frameworks are quite comprehensive and more in line with our notion of personal competence. Anderson and Messick (1974), summarizing a consensus conference addressing the meaning of social competence, provided a shopping list of 23 competencies that are fairly all-inclusive but differ from our proposed framework in two ways: (1) they lack any hierarchical organization, and (2) they give little or no emphasis (in line with general practice) to the domain of social intelligence. Zigler and Trickett (1978) devised a more limited framework that contained four components: IQ, educational achievement, physical health/competence, and emotional and motivational factors. The Zigler and Trickett typology, although not organized hierarchically, has obvious similarities to the model depicted in Figure 8.1, with IQ and achievement together corresponding to our academic competence domain, physical health corresponding to our physical competence domain, and emotional/motivational factors corresponding to our affective competence domain. A major limitation of the Zigler and Trickett typology, however, is that in spite of being motivated largely by a feeling that IQ is overrelied on, Zigler and Trickett failed to incorporate everyday (i.e., social and practical) aspects of intelligence into their model.

Industrial psychology is another area in which taxonomies of competence have been devised. These taxonomies are comprehensively reviewed by Fleishman and Quaintance (1984). Although work in this area would appear to be most relevant to that aspect of competence we term "practical intelligence," models have been relatively narrow in scope and have given greater emphasis to conceptual than to everyday aspects of intelligence. One of the few content-based occupational competence models that is at all comprehensive was described by Rabideau (1964), adapted from work by Berliner and colleagues. This taxonomy is similar to our model, with four categories of behavior noted: motor processes (physical competence), communication processes (everyday competence), and mediational and perceptual processes (academic competence). A glaring omission from this taxonomy is any mention of affective aspects of competence, an omission that is true of the majority of vocationally based taxonomies.

One of the few research programs cited by Fleishman and Quaintance (1984) that includes personality and cognitive variables in the same taxonomy was the work of Harman (1975) and colleagues for the Office of Naval Research, in which they identified 23 cognitive factors and 28 "temperament" factors. A limitation of this work, however, is that, like the work of Anderson and Messick (1974) on social competence, it is essentially a shopping list, without any attempt at hierarchical grouping. Furthermore, in line with most taxonomies of human competence, the domain of social intelligence is given virtually no emphasis in the cognitive or personality sides of their model.

A final area in which models of personal competence have been constructed and tested is the study and assessment of "adaptive behavior." Widamin and McGrew (1996), in a recent review of work on structural aspects of adaptive behavior, note (somewhat disapprovingly) that the term has been used synonymously with personal competence. Measures of adaptive behavior are used mainly to assess individuals who may have mental retardation (MR) because adaptive behavior deficit is one of two diagnostic criteria for MR. Because the term was introduced in the absence of an adequate constitutive definition, questions have been raised about the wisdom of using the construct (Zigler, Balla, & Hodapp, 1984). Because research on the structure and meaning of adaptive behavior has been influenced by the first author's writings, literature dealing with adaptive behavior will be reviewed in subsequent sections.

APPLICATIONS OF THE MODEL
FOR PRACTICE AND RESEARCH

The model of personal competence has been used primarily by researchers and practitioners in developmental disabilities and special education. This is because papers describing the model have been published mainly in disability-related books and journals and have emphasized mainly issues of interest to people in the disability field. However, a model of personal competence that incorporates intelligence has a much wider range of research, policy, and clinical applications. In this section, we review briefly some of the major ways in which the model has been used. In a later section, we touch on some possible future applications and directions.

Assessment Framework

A major impetus for devising the model was concern over the lack of an overarching framework to guide psychoeducational assessment. This is reflected both in individual assessment practices (i.e., tendency to use standard batteries, regardless of relevance to referring question) and in practices used to validate measures (i.e., failure to address the issue of content validity). It has been noted by several authors that the model of personal competence has potential utility in both these areas.

Simeonsson (1986), in a book advocating a developmental approach to assessment in special education, used the model to demonstrate its potential utility for devising nontraditional forms of psychoeducational assessment. A particularly promising application involves compiling competence profiles of children and youth with a variety of referring problems. Such profiles provide information not only about deficits but also about strengths, which may result in a greater acceptance of nonrestrictive placement recommendations in settings such as schools (Javel & Greenspan, 1983) and residences (Granfield, 1990). Such profiles also provide information about the extent to which services provided are congruent with needs. Dunaway, Granfield, Norton and Greenspan (1992), using the model to assess appropriateness of individual residential placements for mentally retarded adults, found that individuals were typically overserved in relation to their levels of physical competence and practical intelligence and typically underserved in relation to their levels of social intelligence and emotional competence.

Another area in which the model has potential utility is as a framework for addressing the often underemphasized matter of content validity for tests and batteries. An example of this can be found in a book by McGrew (1994), in which he used the model to establish the validity of content coverage of the combined Woodcock–Johnson/Scales of Independent Behavior (WJ/SIB) assessment system. Specifically, he noted that all the elements in the model, with the exception of social intelligence, were tapped by the WJ/SIB system. Similarly, Ittenbach, Spiegel, McGrew, and Bruininks (1992) used the model to explore content domains of early childhood ability measures. Perhaps the most widespread application of the model has been as a framework for validating measures of adaptive behavior and adaptive skills, constructs central to recent efforts to redefine MR.

A major source of confusion about the construct of adaptive behavior and its relationship to personal competence is that it is sometimes used as a counterbalance to IQ (i.e., to refer to aspects of personal competence other than intelligence) and sometimes as a broad umbrella (essentially synonymous with personal competence) including both IQ and other aspects of competence. Reschly (1990) referred to the model's utility in helping to clarify the nature of content coverage in particular measures of adaptive behavior.

Reschly (1990) portrayed the personal competence model in a chapter on adaptive behavior in a book on best practices in school psychology. He noted that the model contributed to his views on competence and adaptive behavior. However, Reschly's depiction of the model is not entirely accurate. His figure (cited as the 1979 version) shows four components: physical competence, intellectual competence, social competence, and emotional competence. In fact, social competence was not depicted in the 1979 model and only indirectly in the 1981 version. Reschly (1990), furthermore, gives no indication that there is an intellectual component to social competence, or that social intelligence and practical intelligence are contained within intellectual competence.

Gresham and Reschly (1988) embed adaptive behavior within a model of social competence in which adaptive behavior is portrayed as overlapping with Greenspan's notion of cognitive competence while social skills are seen as overlapping with Greenspan's notion of emotional competence. Gresham and Reschly's model has merit and, in fact, resembles closely the social competence side of the model of personal competence portrayed in Greenspan and Granfield (1992). A major point of difference, however, has to do with the fact that Gresham and Reschly see only adaptive behavior (i.e., practical intelligence) as having overlap with intelligence. The concept of social skills is depicted as if it involves external behaviors, with no mention of mediating cognitive processes implied by the term "social intelligence."

This lack of emphasis on cognitive processing in social skills assessment and training is evident in reviews by Gresham (1990) and Elliot and Ershler (1990). Elliot and Ershler (1990) note that "social skills comprise specific and discrete verbal and nonverbal behaviors" (p. 597) that are acquired through learning. Gresham (1990) defines social skills as "situationally specific behaviors that predict important social outcomes" (p. 696) and meet social expectations. The five domains of socially skilled behaviors listed by Gresham and Elliot (1990) from their rating measure are all located within the construct of affective competence, with four of them (cooperation, assertion, responsibility and empathy) tapping aspects of character and one (self control) tapping aspects of temperament. This view of social skills as isolated behaviors with little emphasis on cognitive processes reflects what Spitz (1988) termed a "learning," as contrasted to a "thinking," approach to competence and disability.

The work of Reschly and Gresham on adaptive behavior and social skill exemplifies a common theme throughout the literature, namely, the tendency to emphasize emotional competence and deemphasize social intelligence. This tendency is commented on by Widamin and McGrew (1996) in a review of the empirical literature on the structure of adaptive behavior scales. They note that empirical studies using factor-analytic methods have tended to confirm the general outlines of the Greenspan (1979, 1981a) personal competence model. The main exception is the failure of a social intelligence factor to emerge. Widamin and McGrew (1996) attribute this exception to the relative absence of social intelligence items in adaptive behavior scales rather than to the invalidity of that part of the model. In fact, research by McGrew, Bruininks, and Johnson (1996) supplementing adaptive behavior with social intelligence content found support for the full Greenspan model.

Interventions and Individual Programming

An obvious extension of the model's utility for guiding assessment is its potential role in guiding educational and other interventions. Javel and Greenspan (1983) and Greenspan (1982) illustrate use of the model for devising individualized education plans (IEPs). In contrast, standard IEP formats, in line with the emphasis on curricular issues in schools, give relatively little emphasis to issues of emotional competence or everyday intelligence. This is in spite of the fact that behavioral difficulties are known to be responsible for most special education referrals, and acquisition of everyday competence is especially important for transition to adult life and services.

The model has been found to have particular utility in the area of vocational habilitation of people with mild disabilities. Specifically, the model has been used to ask whether vocational programming addresses all relevant areas of vocational need. As is true in other applied areas, there has been a tendency for vocational programs to focus on academic, practical, and physical competencies and to pay little or no attention to social competence (i.e., social intelligence and emotional competence). In a study that has been widely cited and replicated in the vocational literature, Greenspan and Shoultz (1981) explored reasons for involuntary job terminations ("firings") from competitive employment of people with MR. They found that problems of social incompetence were a frequent reason for failure in competitive employment, with socially unintelligent behaviors (e.g., a bellhop talking incessantly to hotel guests about his bleeding hemorrhoids) constituting a major reason for such failures. In a related study, Greenspan, Shoultz, and Weir (1981) found that vocational trainees with MR did poorly on a work-related social problem-solving task, compared to trainees with other diagnoses. Such findings imply that opponents of social programming in vocational training (e.g., Wolfensberger, 1967) may be mistaken in arguing that it is a form of psychotherapy and, therefore, inappropriate for work settings. In fact, interventions aimed at social intelligence deficits are more educational in nature and are quite appropriate for vocational habilitation programs.

A related application of the model is in the area of residential programming. Two studies were conducted by our research group, one examining residential models in the state of Connecticut (Dunaway, Granfield et al. 1992), the other in Washington State (Dunaway, Norton, Bear, Greenspan, & Granfield, 1992). A profile of residential needs and supports was compiled, based on the model of competence. Using this method, it was possible to compile a measure of service/needs congruence and to identify those who were overserved, underserved, or appropriately served, in terms of both overall score and need profile. Interestingly, underservice was associated with better outcomes (e.g., consumer satisfaction) than was (more expensive) overservice. This finding can be explained most likely by the fact that underservice means fewer staff persons "in one's face," whereas overservice often means that one is being prevented from moving into a desired less restrictive setting such as a supported apartment. An interesting ancillary finding is that persons are generally overserved in the areas of practical and physical competence (around such issues as cooking, cleaning, and budgeting) and underserved in the three social competence domains of social intelligence, temperament, and character. Ignoring social and emotional needs is associated with outcomes ranging from loneliness and isolation on the one hand to loss of placement and incarceration on the other.

Defining Mental Retardation and Other Disabilities

Underlying the development and refinement of the model has been our interest in its potential usefulness in the ongoing effort to define MR and other disorders. This is an obvious application of a model grounding intelligence in a broader framework because (1) initial popularity of intelligence testing, especially in England and America, was fueled largely by a search for a scientifically respectable method for segregating from society those considered to be incompetent (Trent, 1994); and (2) even in the early years of intelligence testing, there were outspoken critics of the tendency to base the definition of MR so heavily on performance on intelligence tests.

Scholars such as Doll (1936) and Tredgold (1922) pointed out earlier in this century that, before the advent of intelligence tests, MR was diagnosed on the basis of social incompetence; a consequence of the rise of formal intelligence testing is that social functioning began to be overlooked as a criterion for defining and diagnosing MR. This state of affairs was decried, not just on theoretical grounds but because of the injustice of committing many thousands of otherwise competent individuals to newly constructed residential institutions on the basis of low IQ. Similar problems in the overassignment of poor minority children to special classes on the basis of IQ caused the American Association on Mental Deficiency (AAMD, now AAMR) to devise a definition of MR (Heber, 1961) based on two criteria: (1) low IQ and (2) deficits in adaptive behavior.

This second criterion was devised in the absence of a model of competence; as a consequence, it was operationally defined as a mishmash of practical intelligence (activities of daily living) and absence of psychopathology (good affective competence). A more logically defensible strategy (Greenspan, 1981b) would have been to redefine MR as a condition marked by deficits in both academic and everyday competence (i.e., by low social, practical, and conceptual intelligence). Presence or absence of psychopathology would be viewed as relevant for programming but irrelevant for purposes of definition and diagnosis (except when a secondary mental health diagnosis might be indicated). An advantage of such an approach is that it would have kept the definition of MR in line with the historical view of MR as marked by deficits in intelligence, but a view of intelligence that is broader and more ecologically valid than one based solely on IQ. In fact, one could make a plausible case (Greenspan, Switzky, & Granfield, 1996; Kramer, 1986) for dropping IQ altogether, especially when diagnosing adults, and basing the definition entirely on everyday competence.

Writings about the model of personal competence were cited and used in the most recent effort by AAMR to revise the definition of MR (Luckasson et al., 1992). The new AAMR definition is based on the dual criteria of low IQ (raised from 70 to 75) and deficits in two out of 10 "adaptive skills." In line with the earlier recommendation by Greenspan (1979, 1981b), presence of psychopathology (poor affective competence) is no longer part of the definition. However, the AAMR continued the mistake (in the view of Greenspan et al., 1996) of relying on an artificial invented construct (adaptive skills) that reflects overt behaviors (most involving practical skills) rather than any underlying broad-based model of intelligence. A consequence of this is that social intelligence, an aspect of competence that is critical for successful community adaptation, continues to be given little emphasis.

Support for the view that the 1992 AAMR definition of MR is based on a flawed application of the model of personal competence was provided by a confirmatory factor-analytic study by McGrew et al. (in press); in that study, using a battery intended to measure all aspects of personal competence, they found greater support for the model of competence hypothesized by Greenspan and colleagues than for the model reflected in the 1992 AAMR definition. Support for the model as a framework for defining MR was also provided in an earlier study by Greenspan and Delaney (1983), in which they found that adults with Down syndrome are more competent in emotional competence (in line with what has been called the "classical personality stereotype" or "happy puppy" view of Down syndrome) than others with MR matched on age and IQ but equally incompetent in the area of everyday intelligence, including social intelligence. This suggests that even for persons with Down syndrome who have good social competence, deficiencies in social intelligence (the intellectual aspect of social competence) still are found, which is what one would expect if one adhered to a definition of MR that is grounded in everyday intelligence.

Classificatory implications of the model have been explored mainly for MR, but the model is also useful for addressing definitional controversies in other areas of disability. Implications of the model were discussed in a recent paper by Greenspan and Love (in press) for definitional issues in MR as well as two related disability areas: learning disabilities (LD) and autism. All three disability categories can be conceptualized in relation to the model as follows: (1) people with MR have deficits in conceptual, social, and practical intelligence, and may (but do not necessarily) have deficits in affective competence; (2) people with LD have deficits in academic competence (although conceptual intelligence is typically normal), typically have normal practical intelligence, and may or may not have deficits in social intelligence; and (3) people with autism always have deficits in social intelligence, usually have deficits in affective competence, and may have normal conceptual and practical intelligence (e.g., in cases of Asperger's syndrome) although they typically do not. Such an approach to classification has been dubbed a "dimensional taxonomy" (Blashfield, 1993; Reynolds, 1991) but has been rarely used because of the absence of a model for translating competence deficits and patterns into disability/disease categories.

A related application of the model may be as a basis for deriving an index of disability severity that cuts across diagnoses (Greenspan, 1991). Such an index might have utility for determining fiscal and resource needs, given that traditional diagnoses correlate weakly with service needs (Braddock, Hemp, Fujiura, Bachelder, & Mitchell, 1990). Although global assessment scales as Axis V of the fourth edition of the *Diagnostic and Statistical Manual of Mental Disorders* (American Psychiatric Association, 1994) have been proposed for such a use, a more differentiated measure would appear to have advantages, such as better reliability and the possibility of assigning different weights for different outcomes. Preliminary demonstration of such a use has been explored in a number of studies.

In one study, Gregory (1989) derived an overall index of disability severity by summing relative competence of subjects across all aspects of the model, using a Likert-type rating measure in which raters were asked to judge the relative competence of subjects on each of 16 variables. She found that this index (based on relatively molar ratings which took only 10 minutes to do) was a better predictor of level of independence in supported-living settings for persons with MR than the Vineland Adaptive Behavior Scale, a much lengthier measure to administer.

Dunaway and colleagues (Dunaway, Granfield et al., 1992; Dunaway, Norton et al., 1992) used a somewhat different index of disability severity based on the model. Instead of rating competence, they rated one's relative intensity of need for services and supports, for each of eight domains. Thus, disability severity was operationally defined in a manner directly translatable into resource needs. The resulting index was found to be significantly related to expenditures for residential services for adults with MR in contrast to the generally weak correlations between personal characteristics and service costs.

In another study aimed at exploring implications of the model for better understanding of what it means to be "normal," Greenspan and Delaney (1985) composed overall competence–disability scores for all of the residents of a large wing of a state residential institution, using as a norming group the staff who worked in the institution. All participants (residents and staff) were classified into four categories (normal, minor disability, serious disability, extreme disability) depending on their normalized standard overall personal competence score. The results suggested that normality is a fuzzy construct, as reflected in the finding of some overlap in the distributions of residents (all with a label of MR) and staff. Some residents (who dressed and acted like staff) were significantly more competent than some staff, with these residents falling in the normal or minor disability category and these staff (who tended to have behavior problems) falling in the minor or serious disability category. Similar findings were obtained in a school setting, with tremendous variability found in overall competence levels of students, both unlabeled and with various labels (Greenspan & Javel, 1983). Interestingly, students with the label of LD could be found in all disability levels from "normal" to "extreme disability," which supports those (e.g., Kavale, 1993) who argue that the LD label as actually used has little predictive value because of its lack of grounding in a theory or model of disability.

VALIDATIONAL RESEARCH

A number of studies have been conducted aimed at testing the validity of the competence model. These studies have been generally supportive, although controversy continues around some aspects of the model. In line with the general tendency to discount the importance of social intelligence, a major point of dispute has been over the extent to which social intelligence should be included as a distinct element in the model.

Mathias (1990) and Mathias and Nettelbeck (1992a, 1992b) have written several papers exploring the validity of the model based on a dissertation by Mathias (1988). In a study using a sample of youths with MR in Australia, Mathias and Nettelbeck (1992a) found support for the basic structure of the model, with the major exception that social and practical intelligence formed one factor rather than separate factors. A limitation of their study, however, is that they used only one good measure of practical intelligence as opposed to the recommended minimum of three. Furthermore, they used exploratory factor analysis, whereas confirmatory methods are considered more appropriate for comparison of theoretically or empirically derived models. Greenspan and McGrew (1996) reanalyzed Mathias and Nettelbeck's original correlation matrix using confirmatory (linear structural relations) methods; the results indicated that Mathias and Nettelbeck's data fit well with a model in which social and practical intelligence form separate factors.

Even stronger support for the model can also be found in a series of studies conducted by McGrew and Bruininks (1989, 1990) and McGrew et al. (1996). In only one of these studies were measures of social intelligence included. In that study, McGrew et al. (1996) tested the relative merits of two models of personal competence, one that combined social and practical intelligence into a single factor (like Mathias and Nettelbeck, and the 1992 AAMR construct of adaptive skills) and the other with separate social and practical intelligence factors. Using confirmatory factor-analytic methods, McGrew et al. (1996) found considerable support for all aspects of the Greenspan model of personal competence, including the separation of social and practical intelligence into separate factors.

FUTURE DIRECTIONS

In this chapter we have discussed the potential utility of a model of personal competence that includes four elements: academic competence (including conceptual intelligence), everyday competence (practical and social intelligence), physical competence, and affective competence. Such a model, which can be further differentiated into composite elements, has a wide range of potential uses, some of which have been discussed. Underlying development of the model, and of most of the related research, is a belief that such a model can help to provide a better and truer understanding of the role of intelligence in human functioning and adaptation.

Pervading the literature is a fair amount of resistance to the idea of incorporating nonacademic aspects of intelligence into concepts of intelligence and disorders based on the concept of intelligence. This resistance has been particularly strong with respect to everyday competence, especially social intelligence. Thus, even some advocates for an expanded notion of intelligence limit their enthusiasm mainly for aspects (e.g., artistic or musical skills) that have clear implications for schooling or creativity. This is reflected, for example, in the fact that Gardner (1993) makes only a single passing reference to the "personal intelligences" (two of the seven intelligences in his theory) in a recent book dealing with applications of the theory.

Resistance to everyday (especially social) aspects of intelligence probably reflects three factors: (1) a tendency to emphasize academic and creative activities in broadened conceptions of intelligence, (2) an unwillingness on the part of many (clearly not including Gardner) to give up the idea that intelligence is isomorphic with IQ, and (3) a widespread perception (e.g., Enright & Lapsley, 1980; Ford, 1979, 1982) that the construct of social intelligence has not been validated and that psychometrically adequate measures have yet to be developed.

Goodnow (1986) has taken psychologists to task for what she believes is their mistaken belief that personological and intellectual constructs exist only to the extent that they can be reliably measured. Writing in a book (Sternberg & Wagner, 1986) purporting to deal with practical intelligence but actually dealing as much with what we term "social intelligence," Goodnow (1986) wonders why psychologists do not raise methodological objections against the use of such everyday terms as "ugliness" and "shyness" but raise such strenuous methodological objections against the use of terms relating to an individual's smartness or stupidity in the everyday world. Goodnow believes that part of the explanation is that intelligence (and other personality traits) is viewed by psychologists as existing within persons rather than as labels attached to people on the basis of their externally observed behavior. By the latter standard, social stupidity–intelligence has equal if not greater construct validity than academic stupidity–intelligence, regardless of the psychometric evidence.

Interest in everyday (particularly social) intelligence has existed for many decades (Eysenck, 1994) and undoubtedly reflects an understanding that the power of intelligence in explaining success or failure lies partly in areas not tapped directly by traditional measures. Opposition to use of the construct has centered, however, on such psychometric arguments as high correlations with IQ measures and subscales (Thorndike & Stein, 1937), the failure to predict social outcomes in a manner substantially more powerful than obtained by IQ (Walker & Foley, 1973), the failure of supporting factors to emerge in studies of construct structure (Thorndike, 1936), and the low to moderate reliability of existing measures (Keating, 1978). Persistence in pursuing this construct reflects, however, the belief of many psychologists and most laypeople that social intelligence exists (Barnes & Sternberg, 1989). Such persistence appears to be paying off, as new methods, less resembling traditional IQ tests, appear promising. Among these methods are use of rating measures (Ford & Tisak, 1983) and electronic media (Bryan, 1991).

Although we agree that better measures of social intelligence are needed, it should be kept in mind that even with the use of makeshift measures, researchers (e.g., McGrew et al., 1996) have found some support for the validity and utility of the construct. Predictive validity in the social domain, furthermore, needs to be guided by more sophisticated theories. For example, it makes perfect sense for an aspect of social intelligence such as moral reasoning to correlate moderately with actual behavior (e.g., altruism) if one understands that behavior reflects a complex interaction among many personal and contextual factors (Gibbs & Widamin, 1992).

In this chapter, we have viewed personal competence largely in nomothetic and static terms. However, as noted earlier, the model may also prove useful in providing a basis for ideographic understanding of how certain desired or undesired outcomes come about for particular individuals. Although we do not share the strong resistance expressed by Cantor and Kihlstrom (1989) to the development of tests of social intelligence, we share their view that measurement should not be for the sole purpose of ranking people normatively. In a dynamic use of the model of personal competence, intelligence might be viewed as the mediator between the person and the attainment of short- and long-term goals in various settings.

As in Thomson's (1939) theory of intelligence, different aspects of personal competence ("bands" in Thomson's theory) would come into play, depending on the setting and goals. Thus, particular social outcomes, both on a macro- and microlevel, could be attained through alternative or overlapping means, and persons could often compensate for deficits in certain areas (e.g., everyday competence) with strengths in other areas (e.g., affective competence) in attaining certain objectives such as stable employment (Ford & Lerner, 1992). Obviously, one's ability to do this would depend to some extent on the nature and complexity of demands in the particular setting or task. Use of a model of personal competence in a dynamic outcome-oriented fashion requires that one analyze the full array of task demands, social expectations, and success routes operating in specific situations. Intelligence (broadly defined) might be viewed in such a model not as one of the elements contributing to competent (or incompetent) outcomes but as the central mechanism through which a person's resources are mobilized in a particular situation.

The central role of a cognitive mechanism in a dynamic model intended to explain human action is, of course, found in various theories. It has been pointed out (R. Shilkret, personal communication, April 12, 1983), for example, that the social competence component of the model resembles the Freudian structural model. In such an analogy, id is temperament, superego is character, and ego (the gatekeeper which maintains balance between the elements and mediates the person's interactions with people and objects) is social intelligence.

Various other dynamic models of human action, such as those of Parsons (1978), Goffman (1974), Garfinkel (1967), and Lewin (1951), have been devised. In a review of such models, most devised by sociologists or social psychologists, Turner (1988) notes that these tend to be aimed at a relatively macro- or social level of analysis, which explains why, with the exception of Lewin's field theory, they have been relatively ignored by psychologists.

A micro-oriented dynamic model has achieved considerable popularity recently in Europe, and is known as "action theory," the same term used by Parsons. Action theory has been widely used by scholars interested in occupational (Boesch, 1991), clinical (Semmer & Frese, 1985), and developmental (Silbereisen, 1985) psychology. According to Oppenheimer (1991), action theory originated out of a concern over the failure of existing cognitive measures and theories (especially of what we have termed "social intelligence") to explain how people develop competence in attaining specific contextual goals. In a paper spelling out the implications of action theory for the growth of social competence, Oppenheimer (1989) included a graphic depiction of the Greenspan (1979, 1981a) content model of personal competence and portrayed it as an example of a static "conformist" (i.e., normative) as opposed to a dynamic action–explanatory model.

An outcome-oriented application of our model of personal competence to an analysis of action is just beginning to be explored (Driscoll & Greenspan, 1995). Because of the preliminary nature of this work and space considerations, we only list some features of this work here: (1) outcomes can be conceptualized in terms of success in either macrosituations (e.g., in general tasks or roles such as holding a job) or on a microlevel (e.g., success in coping with specific critical tasks or transactions in the job setting); (2) the study of failure and of incompetence is generally more informative about action processes than is the study of success and competence (Langer & Park, 1990); (3) one can descriptively analyze how a particular individual has come to a particular successful or unsuccessful outcome (on either a macro- or microlevel), based on the contribution of all components of personal competence in relation to that particular task or context, (4) emphasis is placed on the role of intellectual processes (broadly defined) in the selection and use of schemas or strategies in those contexts; (5) these processes need not be viewed solely in terms of the relative "success" or utility of actual outcomes but are worthy of being studied and valued in themselves; (6) in valuing the processes used in adapting to real-world tasks and contexts, more weight should be attached to what Spitz (1988) termed "thinking" (judging and reasoning about the environment) than to what he termed "learning" (acquisition and storage of isolated skills); and (7) isolated skills and schemas often make important contribution to success in routine tasks or situations, but it should not be assumed that competence is nothing more than the sum total of such skills.

This emphasis on the distinction between thinking and learning has implications for any discussion of the meaning of intelligence and its relationship to a broader model of personal competence. The basic message of most of the authors in this volume is that one should approach intelligence less in terms of isolated products and more in terms of integrated processes. The study of everyday competence, and personal competence generally, has been dominated (as exemplified, for example, in checklists of adaptive behavior) by an approach heavily oriented toward measuring atomistic snippets of behavior, with little emphasis on the processes by which children and adults adapt to the world around them. Incorporation of current more process-oriented approaches derived from the study of academic and everyday competence can help greatly in advancing our understanding of what it means to be personally competent.

REFERENCES

American Psychiatric Association. (1994). *Diagnostic and statistical manual of mental disorders* (4th ed.). Washington, DC: Author.

Anderson, S., & Messick, S. (1974). Social competency in young children. *Developmental Psychology, 10,* 282–293.

Barnes, M. L., & Sternberg, R. J. (1989). Social intelligence and decoding of nonverbal cues. *Intelligence, 13,* 263–287.

Baron, J. (1989). Why a theory of social intelligence needs a theory of character. In R. S. Wyer & T. K. Srull (Eds.), *Advances in social cognition, Vol. 2: Social intelligence and cognitive assessments of personality* (pp. 61–70). Hillsdale, NJ: Erlbaum.

Baumrind, D. (1967). Child care practices anteceding three patterns of preschool behavior. *Genetic Psychology Monographs, 75,* 43–88.

Binet, A., & Simon, T. (1905). Methodes nouvelle pour le diagnostic du niveau intellectuel des anormaux [A new meethod for the diagnosis of intellectual level of abnormal persons]. *Annee Psychologique, 11,* 191–244.

Blashfield, R. K. (1993). Models of classification as related to a taxonomy of learning disabilities. In G. R. Lyon, D. B. Gray, J. F. Kavanaugh, & N. A. Krasnegor (Eds.), *Better understanding learning disabilities: New views from research and their implications for education and public policies* (pp. 17–26). Baltimore: Brookes.

Boesch, E. E. (1991). *Symbolic action theory and cultural psychology.* Berlin: Springer-Verlag.

Braddock, D., Hemp, R., Fujiura, G. Bachelder, L., & Mitchell, D. (1990). *The state of the states in developmental disabilities.* Baltimore: Brookes.

Brody, N. (1992). *Intelligence* (2nd ed.). San Diego, CA: Academic Press.

Bruininks, R. H. (1974). Physical and motor development of retarded persons. In N. R. Ellis (Ed.), *International review of research in mental retardation* (Vol. 7). New York: Academic Press.

Bryan, T. (1991). Assessment of social cognition: Review of research in learning disabilities. In H. L. Swanson (Ed.), *Handbook on the assessment of learning disabilities: Theory, research, and practice* (pp. 285–311). Austin, TX: Pro-Ed.

Cantor, N., & Kihlstrom, J. F. (1989). Social intelligence and cognitive assessments of personality. In R. S. Wyer, Jr. & T. K. Srull (Eds.), *Social intelligence and cognitive assessments of personality* (pp. 1–60). Hillsdale, NJ: Erlbaum.

Chandler, M. J., & Greenspan, S. (1972). Ersatz egocentrism: A reply to H. Borke. *Developmental Psychology, 7,* 104–106.

Doll, E. A. (1936). President's address. *Journal of Psycho-Asthenics, 18,* 40–41.

Driscoll, J., & Greenspan, S. (1995). *Social skills versus social intelligence: A theoretical analysis.* Unpublished manuscript, University of Connecticut, Storrs.

Dunaway, J., Granfield, J., Norton, K., & Greenspan, S. (1992). *Costs and benefits of privately-operated residential services for persons with mental retardation in Connecticut.* Storrs: Pappanikou Center of the University of Connecticut.

Dunaway, J., Norton, K., Bear, J. D., Greenspan, S., & Granfield, J. (1992). *Residential services for persons with developmental disabilities in the State of Washington.* Storrs: Pappanikou Center of the University of Connecticut.

Elliot, S. N., & Ershler, J. (1990). Best practices in preschool social skills training. In A. Thomas & J. Grimes (Eds.), *Best practices in school psychology—II* (pp. 591–606). Washington, DC: National Association of School Psychologists.

Enright, R. D., & Lapsley, D. K. (1980). Social role-taking: A review of the constructs, measures, and measurement properties. *Review of Educational Research, 50,* 647–674.

Eysenck, H. J. (1967). *The biological basis of personality.* Springfield, IL: Charles C. Thomas.

Eysenck, H. J. (1994). Personality and intelligence: Psychometric and experimental approaches. In R. J. Sternberg & P. Ruzgis (Eds.), *Personality and intelligence* (pp. 3–31). Cambridge, England: Cambridge University Press.

Fleishman, E. A. (1954). Dimensional analysis of psychomotor abilities. *Journal of Experimental Psychology, 48,* 437–454.

Fleishman, E. A. (1958). Dimensional analysis of movement reactions. *Journal of Experimental Psychology, 55,* 438–453.

Fleishman, E. A., & Quaintance, M. K. (1984). *Taxonomies of human performance: The description of human tasks.* New York: Academic Press.

Ford, D. H., & Lerner, R. M. (1992). *Developmental systems theory: A synthesis of developmental contextualism and the living systems framework.* Newbury Park, CA: Sage.

Ford, M. E. (1979). The construct validity of egocentrism. *Psychological Bulletin, 86,* 169–188.

Ford, M. E. (1982). Social cognition and social competence in adolescence. *Developmental Psychology, 18,* 323–340.

Ford, M. E. (1994). A living systems approach to the integration of personality and intelligence. In R. J. Sternberg & P. Ruzgis (Eds.), *Personality and intelligence* (pp. 188–220). Cambridge, England: Cambridge University Press.

Ford, M. E., & Tisak, M. (1983) A further search for social intelligence. *Journal of Educational Psychology, 75* 196–206.

Gardner, H. (1983). *Frames of mind.* New York: Basic Books.

Gardner, H. (1993). *Multiple intelligences: The theory in practice.* New York: Basic Books.

Garfinkel, H. (1967). *Studies in ethnomethodology.* Englewood Cliffs, NJ: Prentice-Hall.

Gibbs, J. C., & Widamin, K. (1992). *Social intelligence: Measuring moral reasoning.* Englewood Cliffs, NJ: Prentice-Hall.

Goffman, E. (1974). *Frame analysis.* New York: Harper & Row.

Goodnow, J. J. (1986). A social view of intelligence. In R. J. Sternberg & D. K. Detterman (Eds.), *What is intelligence? Contemporary viewpoints on its nature and definition* (pp. 85–90). Norwood, NJ: Ablex.

Granfield, J. M. (1990). *Factors affecting decisions regarding community placements for people with mental retardation.* Unpublished doctoral dissertation, University of Connecticut, Storrs.

Greenspan, S. (1979). Social intelligence in the retarded. In N. R. Ellis (Ed.), *Handbook of mental deficiency, psychological theory and research* (2nd ed., pp. 483–531). Hillsdale, NJ: Erlbaum.

Greenspan, S. (1981a). Defining childhood social competence: A proposed working model. In B. K. Keogh (Ed.), *Advances in special education* (Vol. 3, pp. 1–39). Greenwich, CT: JAI Press.

Greenspan, S. (1981b). Social competence and handicapped individuals: Implications of a proposed model. In B. K. Keogh (Ed.), *Advances in special education* (Vol. 3, pp. 41–82). Greenwich, CT: JAI Press.

Greenspan, S. (1982). Personal competence as a guide to educational placement. *New Perspectives in Special Education, 3,*(3), 1–3.

Greenspan, S. (1991). A universal approach to measuring disability severity: Implications of a model of general competence. In F. Hafferty, S. C. Hey, G. Kiger, & D. Pfeiffer (Eds.), *Translating disability: At the individual, institutional and societal levels* (pp. 127–132). Portland, OR: Society for Disability Studies.

Greenspan, S., & Delaney, K. (1983). Personal competence of institutionalized adult males with and without Down syndrome. *American Journal of Mental Deficiency, 88,* 218–220.

Greenspan, S., & Delaney, K. (1985). *Disability severity levels of staff and residents of an institution for persons with mental retardation.* Unpublished manuscript, University of Connecticut, Storrs.

Greenspan, S., & Granfield, J. M. (1992). Reconsidering the construct of mental retardation: Implications of a model of social competence. *American Journal on Mental Retardation, 96,* 442–453.

Greenspan, S., & Javel, M. E. (1983). *Categorizing exceptional students by overall competence levels.* Unpublished manuscript, Boys Town Center for the Study of Youth Development, Omaha, NE.

Greenspan, S., & Love, P. (in press). Social intelligence and developmental disorder: Mental retardation, learning disabilities and autism. In W. MacLean (Ed.), *Handbook of mental deficiency* (3rd ed.). Mahwah, NJ: Erlbaum.

Greenspan, S., & McGrew, K. S. (1996). Response to Mathias and Nettlebeck on the structure of competence: Need for theory-based methods to test theory-based questions. *Research in Developmental Disabilities, 17,* 145–152.

Greenspan, S., & Shoultz, B. (1981). Why mentally retarded adults lose their jobs: Social competence as a factor in work adjustment. *Applied Research in Mental Retardation, 2,* 23–38.

Greenspan, S., Shoultz, B., & Weir, M. M. (1981). Social judgment and work success of mentally retarded adults. *Applied Research In Mental Retardation, 2,* 335–346.

Greenspan, S., Switzky, H., & Granfield, J. (1996). Everyday intelligence and adaptive behavior: A theoretical framework. In J. Jacobson & J. Mulick (Eds.), *Manual on diagnosis and professional practice in mental retardation* (pp. 127–135). Washington, DC: American Psychological Association.

Gregory, S. (1989). *The social competence and work performance of persons with mental retardation.* Unpublished doctoral dissertation, University of Connecticut, Storrs.

Gresham, F. M. (1990). Best practices in social skills training. In A. Thomas & J. Grimes (Eds.), *Best practices in school psychology—II* (pp. 695–709). Washington, DC: National Association of School Psychologists.

Gresham, F. M., & Elliot, S. N. (1990). *Social skills rating system.* Circle Pines, MN: American Guidance Service.

Gresham, F. M., & Reschly, D. J. (1988). Issues in the conceptualization, classification, and assessment of social skills in the mildly handicapped. In T. R. Kratochwill (Ed.), *Advances in school psychology* (Vol. 6, pp. 203–247). Hillsdale, NJ: Erlbaum.

Guilford, J. P. (1967). *The nature of human intelligence.* New York: McGraw-Hill.

Guilford, J. P. (1975). Factors and factors of personality. *Psychological Bulletin, 84,* 802–814.

Harman, H. F. (1975). *Final report of research on assessing human abilities (PR-75-20).* Princeton, NJ: Educational Testing Service.

Haywood, H. C., & Paour, J. (1992). Alfred Binet (1857–1922): Multifaceted pioneer. *Psychology in Mental Retardation and Developmental Disabilities, 18,* 1–4.

Heber, R. (1961). *A manual on terminology and classification in mental retardation* (rev. ed.). Washington, DC: American Association of Mental Deficiency.

Ittenbach, R. F., Spiegel, A. N., McGrew, K. S., & Bruininks, R. H. (1992). Confirmatory factor analysis of early childhood ability measures within a model of personal competence. *Journal of School Psychology, 30,* 307–323.

Javel, M. E., & Greenspan, S. (1983). Influence of personal competence profiles on mainstreaming recommendations of school psychologists. *Psychology in the Schools, 20,* 459–465.

Kagan, J. (1994). *Galen's prophecy: Temperament in human nature.* New York: Basic Books.

Kavale, K. (1993). A science and theory of learning disabilities. In G. R. Lyon, D. B. Gray, J. F. Kavanaugh, & N. A. Krasnegor (Eds.), *Better understanding learning disabilities: New views from research and their implications for education and public policies* (pp. 171–195). Baltimore: Brookes.

Keating, D. P. (1978). A search for social intelligence. *Journal of Educational Psychology, 70,* 218–223.

Kohn, M. (1977). *Social competence, symptoms; and underachievement in childhood: A longitudinal perspective.* Washington, DC: Winston.

Kramer, D. A. (1986). Practical intelligence and adult development: A world views perspective. *Newsletter of the International Society for the Study of Behavioural Development, 9,* 1–2.

Langer, E. J., & Park, K. (1990). Incompetence: A conceptual reconsideration. In R. J. Sternberg, & J. Kolligan (Eds.), *Competence considered* (pp. 149–166). New Haven: Yale University Press.

Lewin, K. (1951). *Field theory in social sciences.* New York: Harper.

Luckasson, R., Counter, D. L., Polloway, E. A., Reiss, S., Schalock, R. L., Snell, M. E., Spitalnik, D. M., & Stark, J. A. (1992). *Mental retardation: Definition, classifications and systems of support* (9th ed.). Washington, DC: American Association of Mental Retardation.

Mathias, J. L. (1988). *Social intelligence and personal competence in mentally retarded adolescents.* Unpublished doctoral dissertation, University of Adelaide, South Australia.

Mathias, J. L. (1990). Social intelligence, social competence, and interpersonal competence. *International Review of Research in Mental Retardation, 16,* 125–160.

Mathias, J. L., & Nettelbeck, T. (1992a). Validity of Greenspan's models of adaptive and social intelligence. *Research in Developmental Disabilities, 13,* 113–129.

Mathias, J. L., & Nettelbeck, T. (1992b). Reliability of seven measures of social intelligence in a sample of adolescents with mental retardation. *Research in Developmental Disabilities, 3,* 131–143.

McClelland, D. C. (1973). Testing for competence rather than for "intelligence." *American Psychologist, 28,* 1–14.

McGrew, K. S. (1994). *Clinical interpretation of the Woodcock–Johnson tests of cognitive ability—Revised.* Boston: Allyn & Bacon.

McGrew, K., & Bruininks, R. (1989). The factor structure of adaptive behavior. *School Psychology Review, 18,* 64–81.

McGrew, K., & Bruininks, R. (1990). Defining adaptive and maladaptive behavior within a model of personal competence. *School Psychology Review, 19,* 53–73.

McGrew, K. S., Bruininks, R. H., & Johnson, D. R. (1996). A confirmatory factor analysis investigation of Greenspan's model of personal competence. *American Journal on Mental Retardation, 100,* 533–545.

O'Malley, J. M. (1977). Research perspectives on social competence. *Merrill-Palmer Quarterly, 23,* 29–44.

Oppenheimer, L. (1989). The nature of social action: Social competence versus social conformist. In B. H. Schneider, G. Attili, J. Nadel, & R. P. Weissberg (Eds.), *Social competence in developmental perspective* (pp. 41–70). Dordrecht, The Netherlands: Kluwer.

Oppenheimer, L. (1991). The concept of action: A historical perspective. In L. Oppenheimer, & J. Valsiner (Eds.), *The origins of action: Interdisciplinary and international perspectives* (pp. 1–36). New York: Springer-Verlag.

Parsons, T. (1978). *Action theory and the human condition.* New York.

Rabideau, G. F. (1964). Field measurement of human performance in man-machine systems. *Human Factors, 6,* 663–672.

Reschly, D. J. (1990). Best practices in adaptive behavior. In A. Thomas & J. Grimes (Eds.), *Best practices in school psychology—II* (pp. 29–42). Washington, DC: National Association of School Psychologists.

Reynolds, M. C. (1991). Classification and labeling. In J. W. Lloyd, N. N. Singh, & A. C. Repp (Eds.), *The regular education initiative: Alternative perspectives on concepts issues. and models* (pp. 29–41). Sycamore, IL: Sycamore Publishing.

Reynolds, W. M. (1981). Measurement of personal competence of mentally retarded individuals. *American Journal of Mental Deficiency, 85,* 368–376.

Sameroff, A. J., & Chandler, M. J. (1975). Reproductive risk and the continuum of caretaking casualty. In F. D. Horowitz (Ed.), *Review of child development research* (Vol. 4). Chicago: University of Chicago Press.

Schaefer, E. S. (1976). Factors that impede the process of socialization. In M. J. Begab & S. A. Richardson (Eds.), *The mentally retarded and society: A social science perspective.* Baltimore: University Park Press.

Semmer, N., & Frese, N. (1985). Action theory in clinical psychology. In M. Frese & J. Sabini (Eds.), *Goal directed behavior: The concept of action in psychology* (pp. 296–310). Hillsdale, NJ: Erlbaum.

Silbereisen, R. K. (1985). Action-theory perspective in research on social cognition. In M. Frese & J. Sabini (Eds.), *Goal directed behavior: The concept of action in psychology* (pp. 215–229). Hillsdale, NJ: Erlbaum.

Silvern, L. E. (1984). Emotional-behavioral disorders: A failure of system functions. In E. S. Gollin (Ed.), *Malformations of development: Biological and psychological sources and consequences* (pp. 95–152). New York: Academic Press.

Simeonsson, R. J. (1986). *Psychological and developmental assessment of special children.* Boston: Allyn & Bacon.

Spitz, H. H. (1988). Mental retardation as a thinking disorder: The rationalist alternative to empiricism. In N. Bray (Ed.), *International review of research in mental retardation* (Vol. 15, pp. 1–32). New York: Academic Press.

Stanovich, K. E. (1993). Does reading make you smarter? Literacy and the development of verbal intelligence. In H. W. Reese (Ed.), *Advances in child development and behavior* (Vol. 24, pp. 134–181). San Diego, CA: Academic Press.

Sternberg, R. J. (1984). Macrocomponents and microcomponents of intelligence: Some proposed loci of mental retardation. In P. Brooks, R. Sperber, & C. McCauley (Eds.), *Learning and cognition in the mentally retarded* (pp. 89–114). Hillsdale, NJ: Erlbaum.

Sternberg, R. J., & Wagner, R. K. (1986). *Practical intelligence: Nature and origins of competence in the everyday world.* Cambridge, England: Cambridge University Press.

Sundberg, N. D., Snowden, L. R., & Reynolds, W. M. (1978). Toward assessment of personal competence and incompetence in life situations. *Annual Review of Psychology, 29,* 179–221.

Switzky, H. N. (1995). The changing roles of psychologists: The influence of paradigm shifts. In O. Karan & S. Greenspan (Eds.), *Rehabilitation services in the community* (pp. 399–419). Newton, MA: Butterworth-Heinemann.

Thomson, G. H. (1939). *The factorial analysis of human ability.* London: University of London Press.

Thorndike, E. L. (1920). Intelligence and its uses. *Harper's Magazine, 140,* 227–235.

Thorndike, R. (1936). Factor analysis of social and abstract intelligence. *Journal of Educational Psychology, 27,* 231–233.

Thorndike, R. L., & Stein, S. (1937). An evaluation of the attempts to measure social intelligence. *Psychological Bulletin, 34,* 275–285.

Tredgold, A. F. (1922). Mental deficiency. New York: Wood.

Trent, J. W. (1994). *Inventing the feeble mind: A history of mental retardation in the United States.* Berkeley: University of California Press.

Turner, J. H. (1988). *A theory of social interaction.* Stanford, CA: Stanford University Press.

Walker, R. E., & Foley, J. M. (1973). Social intelligence: Its history and measurement. *Psychological Reports, 33,* 839–864.

Wechsler, D. (1974). Cognitive, conative, and non-intellective intelligence. In *Selected papers of David Wechsler.* New York: Academic Press.

Widamin, K. F., & McGrew, K. S. (1996). The structure of adaptive behavior. In J. W. Jacobson & J. A. Mulick (Eds.), *Manual of diagnosis and professional practice in mental retardation* (pp. 97–110). Washington, DC: American Psychological Association.

Wolfensberger, W. (1967). Vocational preparation and occupation. In A. A. Baumeister (Ed.), *Mental retardation: Appraisal education and rehabilitation.* Chicago: Aldine.

Zigler, E., Balla, D.,, & Hodapp, R. (1984). On the definition and classification of mental retardation. *American Journal of Mental Retardation, 89,* 215–230.

Zigler, E., & Trickett, P. K. (1978). IQ, social competence, and evaluation of early childhood intervention programs. *American Psychologist, 33,* 789–798.

CHAPTER 9

Analysis of the Major Intelligence Batteries According to a Proposed Comprehensive Gf-Gc Framework

KEVIN S. McGREW

SIGNIFICANT PROGRESS has been made during the past 60 to 70 years in understanding the structure of human intelligence. More important, this knowledge is now beginning to influence the development and interpretation of psychoeducational assessment instruments.

I predict that this progress has been particularly energized by the publication of *Human cognitive abilities: A survey of factor-analytic studies* by John Carroll (1993). Carroll summarizes his review and reanalysis of more than 460 different data sets that included nearly all the more important and classic factor analytic studies of human cognitive abilities. On the book cover, Richard Snow states that "John Carroll has done a magnificent thing. He has reviewed and reanalyzed the world's literature on individual differences in cognitive abilities . . . no one else could have done it . . . it defines the taxonomy of cognitive differential psychology for many years to come." Burns (1994) was similarly impressed when he stated that Carroll's book "is simply the finest work of research and scholarship I have read and is destined to be *the classic study and reference work* on human abilities for decades to come" (p. 35).

Simply put, all scholars, test developers, and users of intelligence tests need to become familiar with Carroll's treatise on the factors of human abilities. Unfortunately, this is a daunting task. Each of Carroll's chapters is a major literature review in a specific cognitive domain (Burns, 1994). The book is lengthy and, for those not well versed in the language and literature of factor analysis of cognitive variables, a challenge to read.

The purpose of this chapter is to facilitate the infusion of this important knowledge into psychoeducational assessment practice. My goal is to advocate for Carroll's suggestion (Chapter 7, this volume) that clinicians use his "map" of known cognitive abilities to guide their selection and interpretation of tests in intelligence batteries. Further, my goal further is to provide a "bridge" between the theoretical and empirical research on the factors of intelligence and the development and interpretation of psychoeducational assessment batteries.

CARROLL'S THREE-STRATUM MODEL

Carroll has proposed a three-tier model of human cognitive abilities that differentiates abilities as a function of breadth. At the broadest level (stratum III) is a *general* intelligence factor conceptually similar to Spearman's and Vernon's *g*. Next in breadth are eight *broad* abilities that represent "basic constitutional and long-standing characteristics of individuals that can govern or influence a great variety of behaviors in a given domain" (Carroll, 1993, p. 634). Stratum level II includes the abilities of Fluid Intelligence, Crystallized Intelligence, General Memory and Learning, Broad Visual Perception, Broad Auditory Perception, Broad Retrieval Ability, Broad Cognitive Speediness, and Reaction Time/Decision Speed. Finally, stratum level I includes 69 *narrow* abilities that are subsumed by the stratum II abilities, which in turn are subsumed by the single stratum III *g* factor. Carroll's work in this volume provides a detailed treatment of his model.

THE HORN–CATTELL Gf-Gc MODEL

After reviewing the major historical and contemporary theories and models of intelligence, Carroll concludes that the Horn–Cattell Gf-Gc model is the closest approximation to his three-stratum level model. Carroll states that the Horn–Cattell Gf-Gc model "appears to offer the most well-founded and reasonable approach to an acceptable theory of the structure of cognitive abilities" (Carroll, 1993, p. 62).

Horn (1991) has extended the work of Cattell (1941) by identifying 9 to 10 broad Gf-Gc abilities: Fluid Intelligence, Crystallized Intelligence, Short-Term Acquisition and Retrieval, Visual Intelligence, Auditory Intelligence, Long-Term Storage and Retrieval, Cognitive Processing Speed, Correct Decision Speed, and Quantitative Knowledge. A "newcomer" factor vying for inclusion in the Horn–Cattell Gf-Gc model is associated with the comprehension and expression of reading and writing skills (Grw) (Horn, 1988; McGrew, Werder, & Woodcock, 1991; Woodcock, 1993, in press). A thorough treatment of the Horn–Cattell Gf-Gc model is presented by Horn and Noll (Chapter 4, this volume).

A SYNTHESIZED CARROLL AND HORN–CATTELL
Gf-Gc FRAMEWORK

There are strong similarities between the Carroll and Horn–Cattell models. Both include the similarly defined broad abilities of fluid (Gf) and crystallized (Gc) intelligence, short-term memory (i.e., General Memory and Learning and Short-Term Acquisition and Retrieval—Gsm), visual (Gv) and auditory (Ga) processing or intelligence, storage and retrieval (i.e., Broad Retrieval Ability and Long-Term Associative Storage and Retrieval—Glr), and two speed abilities (i.e., Broad Cognitive Speediness or Cognitive Processing Speed—Gs, and Reaction Time/Decision Speed or Correct Decision Speed—Gt).

The most obvious difference between the two models is the presence or absence of a higher-order *g* factor in Carroll's and Horn's models, respectively. A careful reading of Carroll's and Horn's writings reflect other differences in the placement of narrow factors under the broad factors. The most salient differences are (1) the inclusion of reading and writing abilities under crystallized intelligence (Carroll) versus their existence under a separate broad reading and writing (Grw) ability (Horn–Cattell), (2) the inclusion of quantitative abilities under fluid intelligence (Carroll) versus their placement under a separate broad quantitative (Gq) ability (Horn–Cattell), and (3) and the inclusion of phonological awareness (e.g., phonetic coding) under crystallized intelligence (Carroll) versus broad auditory intelligence or perception (Ga) (Horn–Cattell).

Finally, Carroll includes short-term memory abilities and associative, meaningful, and free recall memory abilities together with learning abilities under a General Memory and Learning factor. In contrast, Horn (1991) makes a distinction between immediate apprehension (e.g., short-term memory span) and storage and retrieval abilities. Carroll includes both classes of memory abilities under a single factor. Horn indicates that it is often difficult to distinguish short-term memory and storage and retrieval abilities (Horn, 1988). Although he has included associative memory under short-term memory (Horn, 1994), Horn (1988) has also mentioned measures of associative memory (e.g., the Woodcock–Johnson Tests of Cognitive Ability—Revised [WJ-R COG] Delayed Recall tests) as clear measures of long-term storage and retrieval abilities (Glr) (Horn, 1988). Both Carroll and Horn place the fluency abilities (i.e., naming facility and word fluency) under their respective retrieval factors.

Before attempting to classify the individual tests from the major intelligence batteries according to a synthesized Carroll and Horn perspective, I felt that it was important to first resolve (at least to my satisfaction) the most notable differences between the Carroll and Horn–Cattell models. Using 37 measures from the standardization sample of the complete WJ-R battery, I used confirmatory factor analysis procedures to test a number of alternative models that operationalized the Carroll and Horn–Cattell model differences (see Appendix and Table 9.10 in this chapter for a brief description and summary of the results). The WJ-R battery is particularly well suited to a comparison of the Carroll and Horn model differences, as evidenced by Bickley, Keith, and Wolfes's (1995) use of the WJ-R norm data to evaluate the stability of Carroll's model across the lifespan. The specified models benefited from information provided by a separate analysis of the complete WJ-R by Carroll with the same factoring procedures he used in his massive review (see Appendix and Table 9.11 in this chapter for Carroll's results).

From these analyses, I conclude that a feasible framework would be one that (1) retains a quantitative reasoning/knowledge factor (Gq) distinct from fluid intelligence (Gf), (2) places reading and writing abilities under a separate broad reading and writing factor (Grw), (3) places phonological awareness abilities under auditory processing or intelligence (Ga), and (4) retains short-term memory abilities under a separate broad ability (Gsm) and places storage and retrieval abilities (e.g., associative memory) under a broad retrieval (Glr) ability. No attempt was made to resolve the existence of a *g* factor, a long-standing theoretical debate that does not bear directly on the purpose of this chapter.

As a result, the comprehensive Gf-Gc framework presented in Figure 9.1 was used to structure the remainder of my analyses. Using this framework, I then placed most of the first-order narrow ability factors summarized by Carroll under the 10 broad Gf-Gc abilities. Brief definitions of each of these abilities are presented in Table 9.1.[1]

THE Gf-Gc CLASSIFICATION OF TESTS IN INTELLIGENCE BATTERIES

Armed with the framework and the narrow ability definitions, I classified the individual tests in the Differential Ability Scales (DAS; Elliott, 1990), the Kaufman Assessment Battery for Children (K-ABC; Kaufman & Kaufman, 1983), the Kaufman Adolescent and Adult Intelligence Test (KAIT; Kaufman & Kaufman, 1993), the Stanford–Binet Intelligence Scale: Fourth Edition (SB-IV; Thorndike, Hagen, & Sattler, 1986), the three Wechsler Batteries (Wechsler, 1981, 1989, 1991), and the Woodcock–Johnson Psycho-Educational Battery—Revised (WJ-R; Woodcock & Johnson,

1989) at the narrow ability level. The Das–Naglieri Cognitive Assessment System (DN:CAS; Das, Naglieri, & Kirby, 1994) was not included as it was only in the development stages at the time I conducted these analyses.

The classification of each individual test as a measure of one or more of the narrow and/or broad Gf-Gc abilities was guided by a review of results of joint confirmatory factor analysis studies conceptualized from the modern Gf-Gc framework (not the older and simpler Gf-Gc dichotomy). The primary studies were those of Flanagan and McGrew (1995), McGhee (1993), and Woodcock (1990). Woodcock's (1990) comprehensive synthesis of a series of joint confirmatory factor studies was the cornerstone of my broad Gf-Gc test classifications for the WJ-R, K-ABC, SB-IV, and Wechsler batteries (researchers are encouraged to read Woodcock's article to gain an appreciation for the significance of his work and why it played such a pivotal role in my classifications). McGhee's (1993) study was the primary source of the DAS test classifications because it was the only study to include this instrument in a Gf-Gc–based confirmatory factor analysis. Flanagan and McGrew's (1995) Gf-Gc–based confirmatory factor study provided the primary classification information for the KAIT tests. The McGhee (1993) and Flanagan and McGrew (1995) studies are important because they used the modern Gf-Gc framework for their confirmatory factor analyses and they used tests from the WJ-R, two design features that provided a link with Woodcock's analyses. All three sources (Flanagan & McGrew, 1995; McGhee, 1993; Woodcock, 1990) were linked through the use of the WJ-R as Gf-Gc marker tests and the use of a common Gf-Gc confirmatory factor analysis framework. Although the primary contribution of the McGhee (1993) and Flanagan and McGrew (1995) studies is the provision of information about the DAS and KAIT tests, these studies also supported or clarified Woodcock's (1990) WJ-R test classifications.

Woodcock's empirically based criteria for classifying tests as strong, moderate, or mixed measures of Gf-Gc factors were the primary basis for my broad Gf-Gc classifications. If a test was classified as a strong or moderate Gf-Gc measure and it showed no other secondary loadings (was not found to be a factorially complex test), the broad Gf-Gc classifications implied by these findings were accepted. For example, the WJ-R Visual–Auditory Learning test was classified by Woodcock (1990) as a strong measure of Glr based on a median factor loading of .697 across 14 different analyses. Another example of a clear classification was the SB-IV Vocabulary test as a strong measure of Gc, based on a median factor loading of .810 across four analyses. Broad Gf-Gc factor classifications for tests with such consistent strong or moderate factor loadings across analyses were made with relative ease. Tests that showed evidence of measuring more than one broad Gf-Gc ability were classified accordingly. For example, across 15 different analyses, the WJ-R Memory for Sentences test displayed median factor loadings of .335 (Gc) and .554 (Gsm) (Woodcock, 1990). Thus, the WJ-R Memory for Sentences test was classified as an indicator of both Gc and Gsm.

In most cases the broad Gf-Gc test classifications provided by Woodcock (1990), or those classifications based on the application of the same criteria and logic to the McGhee (1993) or Flanagan and McGrew's (1995) studies, were made with little difficulty. However, this was not always the case. For example, Woodcock's (1990) analyses suggested that the WJ-R Picture Recognition test should be classified as a mixed measure of Gv (median loading of .378) and Glr (median loading of .248). McGhee's (1993) analyses found this test to have a relatively low, but significant, loading of .156 on a short-term (Gsm) visual memory factor. More important, when the Picture Recognition test was jointly analyzed with the KAIT tests, it formed a robust visual memory factor with the KAIT Memory for Block Designs test, with a factor loading in the .90s (Flanagan & McGrew, 1995). Flanagan and McGrew's results suggested that Woodcock's classification for this test may need modification, especially in light of the fact that none of the joint confirmatory factor studies he reported included other tests that might measure visual memory abilities. Thus, the Flanagan and McGrew results suggested that Woodcock's classification of this test should be modified. Because Flanagan and McGrew's (1995) results represented only one study, and Woodcock's Picture Recog-

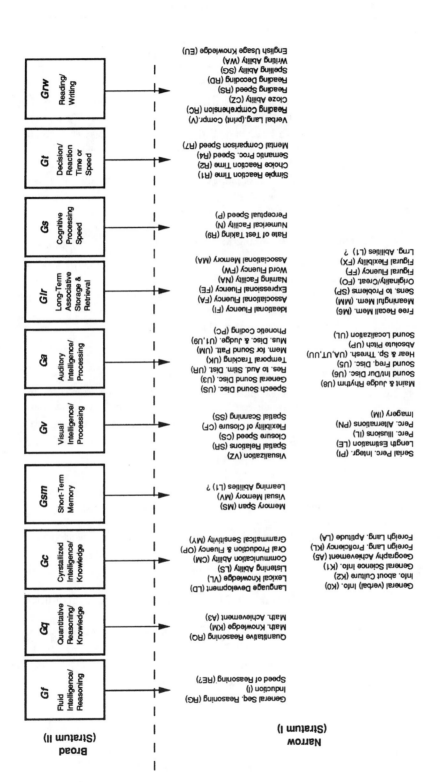

FIGURE 9.1. A proposed comprehensive Gf-Gc framework relevant to the interpretation of psychoeducational assessment batteries.

TABLE 9.1. First-Order Gf-Gc Narrow Stratum Level I Ability Definitions

Gf-Gc Broad Stratum Level II Ability	
Narrow stratum level I name (code)	Definition

Fluid Intelligence/Reasoning (Gf)

General Sequential Reasoning (Seq Reas: RG)	Ability to start with stated rules, premises, or conditions, and to engage in one or more steps to reach a solution to a problem
Induction (Ind: I)	Ability to discover the underlying characteristic (e.g., rule, concept, process, trend, class membership) that governs a problem or a set of materials
Piagetian Reasoning (RP)	Seriation, conservation, classification and other cognitive abilities as defined by Piaget
Speed of Reasoning (RE)	(Not clearly defined by existing research)

Quantitative Reasoning/Knowledge (Gq)

Quantitative Reasoning (Quan Reas: RQ)	Ability to inductively and deductively reason with concepts involving mathematical relations and properties
Mathematical Knowledge (Math Know: KM)	Range of general knowledge about mathematics
Mathematical Achievement (Math Ach: A3)	Measured mathematics achievement

Crystallized Intelligence/Knowledge (Gc)

Language Development (Lng Dev: LD)	General development, or the understanding of words, sentences, and paragraphs (*not* requiring reading), in spoken native language skills
Lexical Knowledge (Lex Know: VL)	Extent of vocabulary that can be understood in terms of correct word meanings
Listening Ability (Lst Abl: LS)	Ability to listen and comprehend oral communications
General (verbal) Information (Gnrl Info: KO)	Range of general knowledge
Information about Culture (Info Cltr: K2)	Range of cultural knowledge (e.g., music, art)
General Science Information (Sci Info: K1)	Range of scientific knowledge (e.g., biology, physics, engineering, mechanics, electronics)
Geography Achievement (Geo Ach: A5)	Range of geography knowledge
Communication Ability (CM)	Ability to speak in "real life" situations (e.g., lecture, group participation) in an adult-like manner
Oral Production and Fluency (OP)	More specific or narrow oral communication skills than reflected by Communication Ability (CM)
Grammatical Sensitivity (MY)	Knowledge or awareness of the grammatical features of the native language
Foreign Language Proficiency (KL)	Similar to LD but for a foreign language
Foreign Language Aptitude (LA)	Rate and ease of learning a new language

Short-Term Memory (Gsm)

Memory Span (Mem Span: MS)	Ability to attend to and immediately recall temporally ordered elements in the correct order after a single presentation

TABLE 9.1. (*Cont.*)

Gf-Gc Broad Stratum Level II Ability	
Narrow stratum level I name (code)	Definition

Short-Term Memory (Gsm) (*cont.*)

Visual Memory (Vis Mem: MV)	Ability to form and store a mental representation or image of a visual stimulus and then recognize or recall it later
Learning Abilities (L1) (also listed under Glr)	(Not clearly defined by existing research)

Visual Intelligence/Processing (Gv)

Visualization (Vis: VZ)	Ability to mentally manipulate objects or visual patterns and to "see" how they would appear under altered conditions
Spatial Relations (Spt Rel: SR)	Ability to rapidly perceive and manipulate visual patterns or to maintain orientation with respect to objects in space
Closure Speed (Cls Spd: CS)	Ability to quickly combine disconnected, vague, or partially obscured visual stimuli or patterns into a meaningful whole, *without knowing in advance* what the pattern is
Flexibility of Closure (Flex Cls: CF)	Ability to identify a visual figure or pattern embedded in a complex visual array, *when knowing in advance* what the pattern is
Spatial Scanning (Spt Scan: SS)	Ability to accurately and quickly survey a spatial field or pattern and identify a path through the visual field or pattern
Serial Perceptual Integration (SerP Int: PI)	Ability to identify a pictorial or visual pattern when parts of the pattern are presented rapidly in order
Length Estimation (LE)	Ability to accurately estimate or compare visual lengths and distances without using measurement instruments
Perceptual Illusions (IL)	Ability to resist being affected by perceptual illusions involving geometric figures
Perceptual Alternations (PN)	Consistency in the rate of alternating between different visual perceptions
Imagery (IM)	Ability to vividly mentally manipulate abstract spatial forms (not clearly defined by existing research)

Auditory Intelligence/Processing (Ga)

Phonetic Coding (Phn Cod: PC)	Ability to process speech sounds, as in identifying, isolating, and blending sounds; phonological awareness
Speech Sound Discrimination (SpSd Disc: US)	Ability to detect differences in speech sounds under conditions of little distraction or distortion
Resistance to Auditory Stimulus Distortion (Res AdDS: UR)	Ability to understand speech and language that has been distorted or masked in one or more ways
Memory for Sound Patterns (Mem Sndp: UM)	Ability to retain on a short-term basis auditory events such as tones, tonal patterns, and voices
General Sound Discrimination (U3)	Ability to discriminate tones, tone patterns, or musical materials with regard to pitch, intensity, duration, and rhythm
Temporal Tracking (UK)	Ability to track auditory temporal events so as to be able to count or rearrange them
Musical Discrimination and Judgment (U1, U9)	Ability to discriminate and judge tonal patterns in music with respect to phrasing, tempo, and intensity variations

(*cont.*)

TABLE 9.1. (*Cont.*)

Gf-Gc Broad Stratum Level II Ability	
Narrow stratum level I name (code)	Definition

Auditory Intelligence Processing (Ga) (*cont.*)

Maintaining and Judging Rhythm (U8)	Ability to recognize and maintain a musical beat.
Sound-Intensity/Duration Discrimination (U6)	Ability to discriminate sound intensities and to be sensitive to the temporal/rhythmic aspects of tonal patterns
Sound-Frequency Discrimination (U5)	Ability to discriminate frequency attributes (pitch and timbre) of tones
Hearing and Speech Threshold factors (UA, UT, UU)	Ability to hear pitch and varying sound frequencies
Absolute Pitch (UP)	Ability to perfectly identify the pitch of tones
Sound Localization (UL)	Ability to localize heard sounds in space

Long-Term Associative Storage and Retrieval (Glr)

Associative Memory (Assc Mem: MA)	Ability to recall one part of a previously learned but unrelated pair of items when the other part is presented (i.e., paired-associative learning)
Meaningful Memory (Mng Mem: MM)	Ability to recall a set of items where there is a meaningful relation between items or the items comprise a meaningful story or connected discourse
Free Recall Memory (FrRe Mem: M6)	Ability to recall as many unrelated items as possible, in any order, after a large collection of items is presented
Ideational Fluency (FI)	Ability to rapidly produce a series of ideas, words, or phrases related to a specific condition or object
Associational Fluency (FA)	Ability to rapidly produce words or phrases associated in meaning (semantically associated) with a given word or concept
Expressional Fluency (FE)	Ability to rapidly think of and organize words or phrases into meaningful complex ideas
Naming Facility (NA)	Ability to rapidly produce names for concepts
Word Fluency (FW)	Ability to rapidly produce words that have specific phonemic, structural, or orthographic characteristics
Figural Fluency (FF)	Ability to rapidly draw or sketch several examples or elaborations when given a starting visual stimulus
Figural Flexibility (FX)	Ability to change set in order to generate new and different solutions to figural problems
Sensitivity to Problems (SP)	Ability to rapidly think of solutions to practical problems
Originality/Creativity (FO)	Ability to rapidly produce original, clever, or uncommon responses to specified tasks
Learning Abilities (L1)	[Also listed under Gsm] (Not clearly defined by existing research)

Cognitive Processing Speed (Gs)

Perceptual Speed (Prc Spd: P)	Ability to rapidly search for and compare visual symbols presented side by side or separated in a visual field
Rate-of-Test-Taking (Rate TsTk: R9)	Ability to rapidly perform tests which are relatively easy or that require very simple decisions

TABLE 9.1. (*Cont.*)

Gf-Gc Broad Stratum Level II Ability	
Narrow stratum level I name (code)	Definition

Cognitive Processing Speed (Gs) (*cont.*)

Number Facility (N)	Ability to rapidly and accurately manipulate and deal with numbers, from elementary skills of counting and recognizing numbers to advanced skills of adding, subtracting, multiplying, and dividing numbers

Decision/Reaction Time or Speed (Gt)

Simple Reaction Time (R1)	Reaction time to the presentation of a single stimulus
Choice Reaction Time (R2)	Reaction time to one of two or more alternative stimuli, depending on which alternative is signaled
Semantic Processing Speed (R4)	Reaction time when the decision requires some encoding and mental manipulation of stimulus content
Mental Comparison Speed (R7)	Reaction time where the stimuli must be compared for a particular attribute

Reading/Writing (Grw)

Reading Decoding (Rdg Dec: RD)	Ability to recognize and decode words or pseudowords in reading
Reading Comprehension (Rdg Cmp: RC)	Ability to comprehend connected discourse during reading
Verbal (printed) Language Comprehension (Vrbl Cmp: V)	General development, or the understanding of words, sentences, and paragraphs in native language, as measured by *reading* vocabulary and *reading* comprehension tests
Cloze Ability (Clz Abl: CZ)	Ability to supply words deleted from prose passages that must be read
Spelling Ability (Spl Abl: SG)	Ability to spell (not clearly defined by existing research)
Writing Ability (Wrt Abl: WA)	Ability to write with clarity of thought, organization, and good sentence structure (not clearly defined by existing research)
English Usage Knowledge (Eng UsKn: EU)	Knowledge of writing in the English language with respect to capitalization, punctuation, usage, and spelling
Reading Speed (RS)	Time required to silently read a passage as quickly as possible

Note. Most of the definitions were derived from *Human Cognitive Abilities: A Survey of Factor-Analytic Studies,* by J. B. Carroll, 1993. New York: Cambridge University Press. Copyright 1993 by Cambridge University Press. Two-letter factor codes (e.g., RG) are from Carroll (1993). Factor label abbreviations are those of the author and correspond to factor names used in Tables 9.2 through 9.8.

nition classification was based on 12 different analyses, radical changes were not made to Woodcock's initial classification. The Picture Recognition test was not simply classified as a measure of Gsm based on the Flanagan and McGrew study. Their findings, together with logical task analysis of the test, resulted in the WJ-R Picture Recognition test being classified as an indicator of Gsm, Gv, and Glr. There were other such modifications made to the classifications of Woodcock, but they all cannot be described in detail in this chapter. The above example illustrates the logic used when modifications were made to Woodcock's primary Gf-Gc test classifications.

Once the broad Gf-Gc test classifications were made based on the synthesis of the empirical studies of Flanagan and McGrew (1995), McGhee (1993), and Woodcock (1990), I asked 10 scholars with experience in the development and/or interpretation of intelligence tests for assistance in verifying these classifications and, more important, extending the classifications to the narrow ability level.[2] These individuals were asked to logically classify the tests contained in one or more of the intelligence batteries according to the narrow ability factor definitions (see Table 9.1). For each test in the battery they reviewed, they were asked to indicate the primary ability (based on the narrow ability definitions provided) measured by the test by giving the ability a rating of "1." If they felt that they could not discriminate between two major abilities measured by the test, they were instructed to give each a rating of "1." If the experts felt that the test measured a secondary ability (to a lesser degree than the primary ability), they were instructed to record a rating of "2." The individuals were requested to focus on the primary abilities measured by each test, not unique or specific abilities. Two or three individuals independently completed the task for each test. These ratings, together with my blind ratings of the same tests, were then summarized.

In most cases the expert ratings were consistent and reinforced the broad Gf-Gc factor classifications. The most important result from this expert consensus process was the classification of each test at the narrow ability level. Although no interrater reliability figures were calculated, the independent narrow ability classifications were typically consistent across individuals. When noticeable differences were observed, I made a decision based on a detailed review of Carroll's narrow ability definitions and my task analysis of the test. Thus, the narrow ability test classifications presented in this chapter are based primarily on an expert consensus process.

SUMMARY OF Gf-Gc TEST CLASSIFICATIONS

The classification summaries for the individual test batteries are presented in Tables 9.2 through 9.8. The amount of information is extensive and cannot be discussed in detail in a single chapter. Thus, I will only make general comments that should allow readers the ability to pursue the information desired in the tables.

Breadth of Gf-Gc Coverage by Intelligence Batteries

As would be expected given its theoretical grounding in the Horn–Cattell Gf-Gc model, the WJ-R battery (Tables 9.7 and 9.8) provides for the broadest coverage of the Gf-Gc abilities used in this analysis. The only broad Gf-Gc ability not represented by at least one narrow ability test in the WJ-R, which was also not present in any of the other batteries, is reaction time/decision speed (Gt). Next in breadth of coverage is the DAS (Table 9.2), which includes measures of narrow abilities under all but the broad Ga and Gt factors (the complete battery also includes Grw measures).

The remaining four test batteries all provide coverage of narrow abilities under six broad Gf-Gc domains. All include tests that measure narrow abilities under Gc, Gsm, and Gv. All but the Wechsler batteries (Table 9.6) include some measures of narrow Gf abilities, and all but the KAIT (Table 9.4) have tests that measure some aspect of Gq. Similar to the DAS, the K-ABC (Table 9.3), KAIT, SB-IV (Table 9.5), and Wechsler batteries all do not include measures of Ga abilities. The KAIT is the only battery besides the DAS and WJ-R to include tests of Glr abilities. Finally, similar to the DAS and WJ-R, the Wechsler batteries are the only other battery to include tests of abilities under the broad Gs domain.

These results indicate that the DAS, KAIT, and WJ-R make the most unique contributions to psychoeducational assessment. The WJ-R is the only battery that includes tests of such narrow Ga abilities as awareness of and access to the sounds of language (i.e., phonological awareness). This is an important contribution given that "one of the most compelling and well established findings in the research on beginning reading is the important relation between phonological awareness and reading acquisitions" (Baker, Kameenui, Simmons, & Stahl, 1994, p. 379). The DAS, KAIT, and WJ-R

TABLE 9.2. Broad and Narrow Gf-Gc Factor Classification of the DAS Individual Cognitive and Achievement Tests

Broad Gf-Gc Factors

	Gf	Gq			Gc				Gsm		Gv		Glr	Gs		Grw	
Narrow Factor Name:	Ind	Quan Reas	Math Know	Math Ach	Lng Dev	Lex Know	Lst Abl	Gnrl Info	Mem Span	Vis Mem	Vis	Spt Rel	FrRe Mem	Prc Spd	Rate TsTk	Spl Abl	Rdg Dec
Narrow Factor Code:	I	RQ	KM	A3	LD	VL	LS	KO	MS	MV	VZ	SR	M6	P	R9	SG	RD
Pic. Similarities (gf)	x																
Matrices (Gf)	X																
Seq. & Quan. Reas. (Gf/Gq)	X	X															
Verbal Comprehension (gc)					x	x	x										
Naming Vocabulary (gc)					x	x		o									
Word Definitions (Gc)					X	X											
Similarities (Gc)					X	O		O									
Copying (gv)											o						
Recall of Designs (Gsm)										X	X						
Pattern Construction (Gv)											X	X					
Block Building (gv)											x	x					
Mat. Letter-Like Forms (gv)											x	x					
Recall of Digits (gsm)									x								
Recall of Objects (glr/gsm)										o			x				
Recognition of Pict. (gsm/gv)										x	o						
Speed of Info. Proc. (gs)														x	x		
Early Num. Concepts (gq)		x	x	o													
Basic Number Skills (gq)		o	x	x													
Spelling (grw)																x	
Word Reading (grw)																	x

Note. Tests in bold are "strong" indicators of their respective Gf-Gc factors; tests not in bold are either "moderate" measures of a Gf-Gc factor or "mixed" measures of more than one Gf-Gc factor as reported by McGhee (1993) and McGrew (1994), or, cannot be so classified due to no appropriate joint factor-analytic studies. Gf-Gc notations in parentheses correspond to primary factor classifications as reported by McGhee (1993) and McGrew (1994). "Xs" indicate most "probable" narrow factor classifications; "Os" indicate "possible" narrow factor classifications. Lower case "xs", "os", and Gf-Gc notation (e.g., gf for Picture Similarities) indicate classifications that are primarily logically based due to either limited or no appropriately designed research studies. Detailed definitions of the factor names, with their respective factor codes, are presented in Table 9.1. Joint confirmatory factor studies and logical content analysis indicate that the DAS does not contain indicators of the Ga and Gt factors.

TABLE 9.3. Broad and Narrow Gf-Gc Factor Classification of the K-ABC Individual Cognitive and Achievement Tests

	Gf	Gq			Gc				Gsm		Gv				Grw		
Narrow Factor Name:	Ind	Quan Reas	Math Know	Math Ach	Lng Dev	Lex Know	Gnrl Info	Info Cltr	Mem Span	Vis Mem	Vis	Spt Rel	Cls Spd	SerP Int	Rdg Dec	Rdg Cmp	Vrbl Cmp
Narrow Factor Code:	I	RQ	KM	A3	LD	VL	KO	K2	MS	MV	VZ	SR	CS	PI	RD	RC	V
Hand Movements (Gsm/Gq)		O							X	X							
Number Recall (Gsm)									X								
Word Order (Gsm)									X								
Magic Window (gv)											o		o	x			
Face Recogn. (gsm/gv)										x	x						
Gestalt Closure (Gv)													X				
Triangles (Gv)											X	X					
Matrix Anal. (Gv/Gf)											X						
Spatial Memory (Gv/gsm)									x	x		O					
Photo Series (Gv/Gf)	X										X						
Expressive Voc. (Gc)					X	X	O										
Faces and Places (Gc)						X	X	X									
Riddles (Gc)					X	X	O										
Arithmetic (Gq)		X	O	X													
Reading/Decoding (grw)															x		
Reading/Understanding (grw)																x	x

Note. Tests in bold are "strong" indicators of their respective Gf-Gc factors; tests not in bold are either "moderate" or "mixed" measures of a Gf-Gc factor or "mixed" measures of more than one Gf-Gc factor as empirically defined by Woodcock (1990). Gf-Gc notations in parentheses correspond to primary factor classifications as reported by McGrew (1994) and Woodcock (1990). "X's" indicate most "probable" narrow factor classifications; "O's" indicate "possible" narrow factor classifications. Lower case "x's", "o's" and Gf-Gc notation (e.g., grw for reading tests) indicate classifications that are primarily logically based due to either limited or no appropriately designed research studies. Detailed definitions of the factor names, with their respective factor codes, are presented in Table 9.1. Joint confirmatory factor studies and logical content analysis indicate that the K-ABC does not contain indicators of the Ga, Glr, Gs, and Gt factors.

162

TABLE 9.4. Broad and Narrow Gf-Gc Factor Classification of the KAIT Individual Tests

Broad Gf-Gc Factors

Narrow Factor Name:	Gf		Gc					Gsm		Glr		Grw		
	Seq Reas	Quan Ind	Lng Know	Lex Dev	Lst Know	Gnrl Abl	Info Cltr	Mem Span	Vis Mem	Assc Mem	Mng Mem	Rdg Dec	Spl Abl	Vrbl Cmp
Narrow Factor Code:	RG	I	LD	VL	LS	KO	K2	MS	MV	MA	MM	RD	SG	V
Definitions (Gc/Grw)			X	X								O	X	
Auditory Compr. (Gc/Gsm)			X		X			X						
Double Meanings (Gc/Grw)				X										X
Famous Faces (Gc)						X	X							
Del. Rec. -AdCm. (Glr/Gc)			O								X			
Rebus Learning (Glr)										X				
Logical Steps (Gf)	X	O												
Mystery Codes (Gf)		X												
Mem. Blk. Des. (Gsm)									X					
Del. Rec. -Relrn. (Glr)										X				

Note. Tests in bold are "strong" indicators of their respective Gf-Gc factors; tests not in bold are either "moderate" measures of a Gf-Gc factor or "mixed" measures of more than one Gf-Gc factor as empirically defined by Flanagan and McGrew (1995). Gf-Gc notations in parentheses correspond to primary factor classifications as reported by Flanagan and McGrew (1995). "X's" indicate most "probable" narrow factor classifications; "O's" indicate possible narrow factor classifications. Detailed definitions of the factor names, with their respective factor codes, are presented in Table 9.1. Joint confirmatory factor studies and logical content analysis indicate that the KAIT does not contain indicators of the Gq, Gv, Ga, Gs, and Gt factors.

TABLE 9.5. Broad and Narrow Gf-Gc Factor Classification of the SB:IV Individual Tests

	Gf	Gq		Gc			Gsm		Gv	
Narrow Factor Name:	Ind	Quan Reas	Math Know	Lng Dev	Lex Know	Gnrl Info	Mem Span	Vis Mem	Vis	Spt Rel
Narrow Factor Code:	I	RQ	KM	LD	VL	KO	MS	MV	VZ	SR
Vocabulary (Gc)				X	X					
Comprehension (Gc)				X		X				
Absurdities (Gc)				X		O				
Verbal Relations (Gc)				X	O	O				
Pattern Analysis (Gv)									O	X
Copying (Gv)									X	
Matrices (Gf)	X									
Paper Fold. & Cut. (Gv/Gq)		O							X	
Quantitative (Gq)		X	O							
Number Series (Gq)		X								
Equation Building (Gq)		X	O							
Bead Memory (Gsm/Gv)								X		
Mem. for Sent. (Gsm/Gc)							X			
Memory for Digits (Gsm)							X			
Memory for Objects (Gsm)								X		

Note. Tests in bold are "strong" indicators of their respective Gf-Gc factors; tests not in bold are either "moderate" or "mixed" measures of more than one Gf-Gc factor as empirically defined by Woodcock (1990). Gf-Gc notations in parentheses correspond to primary factor classifications as reported by McGrew (1994) and Woodcock (1990). "X's" indicate most "probable" narrow factor classifications; "O's" indicate "possible" narrow factor classifications. Detailed definitions of the factor names, with their respective factor codes, are presented in Table 9.1. Joint confirmatory factor studies and logical content analysis indicate that the SB:IV does not contain indicators of the Ga, Glr, Gs, and Gt factors.

TABLE 9.6. Broad and Narrow Gf-Gc Factor Classification of the Wechsler Individual Tests

	Broad Gf-Gc Factors												
	Gq		Gc			Gsm	Gv					Gs	
Narrow Factor Name:	Quan Reas	Math Know	Lng Dev	Lex Know	Gnrl Info	Mem Span	Vis	Spt Rel	Cls Spd	Flex Cls	Spt Scan	Prc Spd	Rate TsTk
Narrow Factor Code:	RQ	KM	LD	VL	KO	MS	VZ	SR	CS	CF	SS	P	R9
Information (Gc)					X								
Similarities (Gc)			X	O	O								
Vocabulary (Gc)			X	X									
Comprehension (Gc)			X		X								
Pict. Completion (Gv/Gc)					O		O						
Pict. Arrangement (Gv/Gc)			O				O			O			
Block Design (Gv)							X	X					
Object Assembly (Gv)							X		X				
Mazes (Gv)											X		
Coding/Digit Symbol (Gs)												X	X
Symbol Search (gs)												x	x
Arithmetic (Gq)	X	O											
Digit Span (Gsm)						X							

Note. Tests in bold are "strong" indicators of their respective Gf-Gc factors; tests not in bold are either "moderate" measures of a Gf-Gc factor or "mixed" measures of more than one Gf-Gc factor as empirically defined by Woodcock (1990). Gf-Gc notations in parentheses correspond to primary factor classifications as reported by McGrew (1994) and Woodcock (1990). "X's" indicate most "probable" narrow factor classifications; "Os" indicate "possible" narrow factor classifications. Lower case "x's", "os" and Gf-Gc notation (e.g., gs for Symbol Search) indicate classifications that are primarily logically based due to either limited or no appropriately designed research studies. Detailed definitions of the factor names, with their respective factor codes, are presented in Table 9.1. Joint confirmatory factor studies and logical content analysis indicate that the Wechsler batteries do not contain indicators of the Gf, Ga, Glr, and Gt factors.

165

TABLE 9.7. Broad and Narrow Gf-Gc Factor Classification of the WJ-R Individual Cognitive Tests

	Gf	Gf	Gq	Gc	Gc	Gc	Gc	Gsm	Gsm	Gv	Gv	Gv	Gv	Ga	Ga	Ga	Ga	Glr	Gs	Gs
Narrow Factor Name:	Seq Reas	Ind	Quan Reas	Lng Dev	Lex Know	Lst Abl	Gnrl Info	Mem Span	Vis Mem	Vis	Spt Rel	Cls Spd	Spt Scan	Phn Cod	SpSd Disc	Res AdDs	Mem SndP	Assc Mem	Prc Spd	Rate TsTk
Narrow Factor Code:	RG	I	QR	LD	VL	LS	KO	MS	MV	VZ	SR	CS	SS	PC	US	UR	UM	MA	P	R9
Analysis-Synthesis (Gf)	X		O																	
Concept Formation (Gf)		X	O																	
Verbal Analogies (Gf-Gc)		X		X																
Picture Vocabulary (Gc)				X	X		O													
Oral Vocabulary (Gc)				X	X															
List. Comprehension(Gc)				X		X														
Mem. for Sent. (Gsm/Gc)				X				X												
Memory for Words (Gsm)				O				X												
Numbers Reversed (Gsm/Gf)	X							X												
Visual Closure (Gv)												X								
Pict. Recogn. (Gsm/Gv)									X	O										
Spatial Relations (Gv/Gf)	X									X	X									
Incomplete Words (Ga)														X		O				
Sound Blending (Ga)														X						
Sound Patterns (Ga/Gf)	O														O		O	O		
Memory for Names (Glr)																		X		
Vis-Aud Learning (Glr)																		X		
Delayed Recall - MN (Glr)																		X		
Delayed Recall - VAL (Glr)																		X		
Visual Matching (Gs)																			X	X
Cross-Out (Gs)													O						X	X

Note. Tests in bold are "strong" indicators of their respective Gf-Gc factors; tests not in bold are either "moderate" measures of a Gf-Gc factor or "mixed" measures of more than one Gf-Gc factor as empirically defined Woodcock (1990). Gf-Gc notations in parentheses correspond to primary factor classifications as reported by McGrew (1994) and Woodcock (1990) and modified by new WJ-R analyses reported in this chapter and that reported by Flanagan and McGrew (1995). "X's" indicate most "probable" narrow factor classifications; "O's" indicate "possible" narrow factor classifications. Detailed definitions of the factor names, with their respective factor codes, are presented in Table 9.1. Tests of the Grw factor, and additional tests of the Gq, Gf, Gc, Ga, and Gs

TABLE 9.8. Broad and Narrow Gf-Gc Factor Classification of the WJ-R Individual Achievement Tests

Narrow Factor Name:	Gf	Gq			Gc						Ga	Gs	Grw						
	Seq Reas	Quan Reas	Math Know	Math Ach	Lng Dev	Lex Know	Gnrl Info	Info Cult	Sci Info	Geo Ach	Phn Cod	Rate TsTk	Rdg Dec	Rdg Cmp	Vrbl Cmp	Clz Abl	Spl Abl	Wrt Abl	Eng UsKn
Narrow Factor Code:	RG	RQ	KM	A3	LD	VL	KO	K2	K1	A5	PC	R9	RD	RC	V	CZ	SG	WA	EU
Calculation (Gq)			O	X															
Applied Problems (Gq)	O	X	X	X	O														
Quant. Concepts (Gq)		O	X	X		O													
Science (Gc)						O	X		X										
Social Studies (Gc)						O	X			X									
Humanities (Gc)						O	X	X											
Letter-Word Iden. (Grw)													X						
Passage Comp. (Grw)					O									X	X	X			
Word Attack (Grw)											X		X						
Rdg. Vocabulary (Grw/Gc)						X							X		X				
Writing Samples (Grw)															O	O		X	
Writing Fluency (Grw/Gs)												X						X	
Punctuation (Grw)															O				X
Spelling (Grw)															O		X		
Usage (Grw)															O				X
Handwriting (Grw)																		X	

Note. Tests in bold are "strong" indicators of their respective Gf-Gc factors; tests not in bold are either "moderate" measures of a Gf-Gc factor or "mixed" measures of more than one Gf-Gc factor as empirically defined by Woodcock (1990) and modified by new WJ-R analyses reported in this chapter. Gf-Gc notations in parentheses correspond to primary factor classifications as reported by McGrew (1994) and Woodcock (1990) and modified by new WJ-R analyses reported in this chapter. "X's" indicate most "probable" narrow factor classifications; "O's" indicate "possible" narrow factor classifications. Detailed definitions of the factor names, with their respective factor codes, are presented in Table 9.1. Tests of the other Gf-Gc factors from the cognitive section of the complete WJ-R battery are reported in Table 9.7.

all provide for measurement of some narrow Glr abilities which are not covered by traditional intelligence tests such as the Wechslers and SB-IV.

Breadth of Coverage of the Gf-Gc Framework

A frequency count of measures of the different narrow ability factors is presented in Table 9.9.

A review of Table 9.9 indicates that narrow abilities under Gc (67) and Gv (36) are the most frequently represented abilities in our current collection of individual intelligence batteries. There is no shortage of tests of narrow abilities that can be considered indicators of the broad Gc and Gv abilities. The Gq (28) and Grw (27) abilities are next, but these results cannot accurately be compared with the other broad Gf-Gc abilities because they include measures from three achievement batteries that accompany only three of the intelligence batteries (i.e., DAS, K-ABC, and WJ-R). Narrow abilities under the Gsm (22) domain are also represented by a good number of tests.

Gs (11), Glr (9), and especially Ga (6) are the broad Gf-Gc abilities that have the smallest number of tests of narrow abilities under each broad domain. Given the significant relationship between some of the narrow abilities within these broad Gf-Gc domains and school achievement (McGrew, 1993, 1994; McGrew & Hessler, 1995; McGrew & Knopik, 1993; Baker et al., 1994), this ability "undercoverage" will most likely change in the future with the development of new, and revisions to old, tests.

The finding that Gf (17) abilities are fourth from the bottom in Table 9.9 is important. Fluid intelligence or reasoning is often considered the essence of intelligence by both scholars and laypeople. One would think that Gf abilities would be prominently featured in all intelligence batteries. This finding appears due to the fact that tests that have been historically considered to be good measures of Gf abilities (e.g., Wechsler Block Design and Similarities) are now found to primarily be measures of other constructs. In particular, many nonverbal visual-spatial tasks (e.g., Wechsler Block Design and Object Assembly) are measures of narrow abilities in the broad domain of Gv and not Gf (McGrew & Flanagan, 1996).

A final word of caution: Not all the classifications presented in Tables 9.2 to 9.8 are made with equal confidence. For most of the individual tests the empirical factor-analytic data were clear and the expert classifications consistent. I found the test classifications the easiest for the DAS, KAIT, SB-IV, and WJ-R. This is not unexpected given that each of these test batteries has been either directly or indirectly, or completely or partially, influenced by the Gf-Gc–related factor-analytic research literature. Therefore, with a few exceptions the reader can place more confidence in the Gf-Gc classifications of the DAS, KAIT, SB-IV, and WJ-R batteries.

I found the K-ABC battery, and a number of the simultaneous processing tests in particular (i.e., Magic Window, Photo Series, and Spatial Memory), to be some of the most difficult tests to classify. The classifications for the DAS and SB-IV Copying tests should also be viewed cautiously. Although they have Gv-related classifications, performance on these tests is probably related to motor abilities not included in the Gf-Gc framework. The WJ-R Sound Patterns test has always been a "maverick" test in available joint factor-analytic studies. There is still a significant portion of the Sound Patterns test variance that is not yet understood from the Gf-Gc perspective. One hypothesis is that performance on the Sound Patterns test may be influenced by attention and concentration abilities (McGrew et al., 1991).

Finally, the classification of the Wechsler Picture Arrangement test was difficult. In joint factor-analytic studies, this test showed only relatively low to moderate factor loadings (i.e., from approximately .10 to .35) on Gv- and Gc-related factors. Although expert classifications often suggested some narrow abilities under the Gf domain, the empirical studies reviewed never supported this logical claim. The Picture Arrangement test may be influenced by other abilities outside the domain of Gf-Gc theory. Possibly some aspects of practical or social intelligence from a larger model of

TABLE 9.9. Number of Tests from Reviewed Batteries That Measure Gf-Gc Factors

Gf-Gc broad/narrow factors	Code	Number
Crystallized Intelligence/Knowledge (Gc)		(67)
Language Development	LD	26
Lexical Knowledge	VL	19
General (verbal) Information	KO	17
Information about Culture	K2	3
Listening Ability	LS	3
General Science Information	K1	1
Geography Achievement	A5	1
Visual Intelligence/Processing (Gv)		(36)
Visualization	VZ	20
Spatial Relations	SR	8
Closure Speed	CS	4
Spatial Scanning	SS	2
Flexibility of Closure	CF	1
Serial Perceptual Integration	PI	1
Quantitative Reasoning/Knowledge (Gq)		(28)
Quantitative Reasoning	RQ	14
Mathematical Knowledge	KM	8
Mathematical Achievement	A3	6
Reading/Writing (Grw)		(27)
Verbal (printed) Language Compr.	V	
Reading Decoding	RD	6
Spelling Ability	SG	3
Writing Ability	WA	3
English Usage Knowledge	EU	3
Reading Comprehension	RC	2
Cloze Ability	CZ	2
Short-Term Memory (Gsm)		(22)
Memory Span	MS	12
Visual Memory	MV	10
Fluid Intelligence/Reasoning (Gf)		(17)
Induction	I	10
General Sequential Reasoning	RG	7
Cognitive Processing Speed (Gs)		(11)
Rate-of-Test-Taking	R9	6
Perceptual Speed	P	5
Long-Term Associative Storage & Retrieval (Glr)		(9)
Associative Memory	MA	7
Meaningful Memory	MM	1
Free Recall Memory	M6	1
Auditory Intelligence/Processing (Ga)		(6)
Phonetic Coding	PC	3
Speech Sound Discrimination	US	1
Resistance to Aud. Stimulus Distortion	UR	1
Memory for Sound Patterns	UM	1

personal competence (see Greenspan & Driscoll, Chapter 8, this volume) may account for the unexplained variance in Picture Arrangement.

Unique Test Contributions at the Gf-Gc Narrow Ability Level

Because there is considerable overlap within and across test batteries in the assessment of some Gf-Gc abilities (e.g., 19, 20, and 26 tests classified as Gc measures of Lexical Knowledge, General or Cultural Information, and Language Development, respectively, see Table 9.9), it is more informative to look at which tests make unique contributions. From a review of Table 9.9, the following unique contributions are noted.

In the domain of Gc, the DAS Verbal Comprehension, KAIT Auditory Comprehension, and WJ-R Listening Comprehension tests are the only measures of Listening Ability (LA) in the six batteries reviewed. The Gv domain is adequately represented by measures of Visualization (VZ) and Spatial Relations (SR). Unique Gv contributions are made by the K-ABC Magic Window and Gestalt Closure, Wechsler Object Assembly, and WJ-R Visual Closure tests in the area of Closure Speed (CS). The Wechsler Mazes and WJ-R Cross-Out tests may assist in the measurement of Spatial Scanning (SS), whereas the Wechsler Picture Completion test may measure some aspects of Flexibility of Closure (CF). Finally, the K-ABC Magic Window test may be a unique measure of Serial Perceptual Integration (PI) abilities.

There appears to be no unique test contributions in the broad Gsm, Gf, and Gs ability domains. A review of Table 9.9 finds a relatively equal representation of Memory Span (MS) and Visual Memory (MV) abilities in the Gsm domain, Induction (I) and General Sequential (deductive) Reasoning (RG) abilities for Gf, and Rate-of-Test-Taking (R9) and Perceptual Speed (P) abilities for Gs.

As noted previously, all the tests that measure narrow abilities within the broad Glr and Ga domains make unique contributions to intellectual assessment. The KAIT Rebus Learning and Delayed Recall–Rebus Learning tests and the four WJ-R Long-Term Retrieval tests all appear to provide coverage of the Glr Associative Memory (MA) ability. Even more unique contributions within the Glr domain are made in the assessment of Meaningful Memory (MM) and Free Recall Memory (M6) by the KAIT Delayed Recall–Auditory Comprehension and DAS Recall of Objects tests, respectively.

Finally, the WJ-R Incomplete Words and Sound Blending tests make unique contributions in the domain of Ga by their assessment of Phonetic Coding (PC) abilities. In addition, the Incomplete Words test may provide unique coverage of Resistance to Auditory Distortion (UR) abilities. The Sound Patterns test also appears to make a contribution by measuring Speech Sound Discrimination (US) and Memory for Sound Patterns (UM) abilities.

Gf-Gc Abilities in Tests of Achievement

The distinction between intelligence and achievement distinction is largely an artificial dichotomy used in educational settings. With this caveat in mind, it is informative to examine the Gf-Gc analysis of tests traditionally considered to measure "achievement."

For example, the WJ-R Passage Comprehension reading test has its primary narrow ability classifications under the Grw factor. A review of Table 9.8 indicates that it also has a "possible" Language Development classification under Gc. The WJ-R Applied Problems test, although primarily classified under Gq, also has General Sequential Reasoning (Gf) and Language Development (Gc) classifications. The Phonetic Coding (Ga) classification of the WJ-R Word Attack reflects another "cognitive" influence on an achievement task. These results suggest that both researchers and clinicians need to be sensitive to the fact that achievement tests may be more factorially complex than their test names suggest. Competent interpretation of achievement tests requires the same attention to multiple Gf-Gc influences as that suggested for the more traditionally labeled tests of intelligence.

IMPLICATIONS FOR RESEARCH AND PRACTICE

The implications of the information presented in this chapter are numerous and only limited by how long one studies and digests the results in the various tables. At a minimum, this form of analysis has six major implications.

First, the use of consistent ability terminology can only improve the interpretation of intelligence tests. The clinical literature is replete (including my own book on the WJ-R; McGrew, 1994) with the use of test interpretation terms such as "fund of information," "verbal concept formation," "visual perception of meaningful stimuli," and the "ability to distinguish essential from nonessential details," to list but a few. The origin of most of these terms would be difficult to trace, with most being passed down through the clinical literature, often without empirical support. I believe that test developers, scholars, and clinicians should anchor the dialogue on what different individual tests measure in terminology that is empirically grounded. The consistent use of the first-order narrow ability factor definitions (Table 9.1) might go far in helping us all better understand what we are measuring, facilitate better communication between and among professionals and scholars, and increase our ability to compare individual tests across and within intelligence batteries.

Second, it is clear that a *cross-battery* approach to assessment (McGrew & Flanagan, 1995; Flanagan & McGrew, Chapter 17, this volume; Woodcock, in press) is necessary to competently assess the major Gf-Gc human abilities. For example, clinicians who are strong advocates of the Wechsler batteries need to consult Table 9.6 to identify those Gf-Gc abilities that are not assessed by the Wechsler batteries. Strong measures of Gf abilities (e.g., SB-IV Matrices, KAIT Mystery Codes and Logical Steps, and WJ-R Concept Formation and Analysis-Synthesis), Ga abilities (e.g., WJ-R Auditory Processing tests), and Glr abilities (e.g., KAIT Rebus Learning and WJ-R Long-Term Retrieval tests) should be added to the Wechsler batteries to better "round out" a complete assessment (i.e., including tests that measure at least one narrow ability factor under each broad Gf-Gc domain). As another example, the WJ-R does not include "strong" measures of Gv abilities (Table 9.7). Thus, users of the WJ-R should seriously entertain the augmentation of their assessments with one or more strong measures of at least one narrow ability under the broad Gv domain (e.g., Wechsler Block Design or Object Assembly).

Not only is this cross-battery approach useful in performing more complete assessments, it can help when following up interpretive hypotheses (McGrew, 1994; McGrew & Flanagan, 1995; Flanagan & McGrew, Chapter 17, this volume). For example, a clinician may observe a relatively low score on the SB-IV Matrices test, a strong measure of Induction (I) abilities under Gf. However, because the SB-IV does not include other strong Gf measures (Table 9.5), the clinician could seek additional verification of this weakness by selecting a strong Inductive Gf measure from another battery (e.g., DAS Matrices, KAIT Mystery Codes, or WJ-R Concept Formation). Or, because the SB-IV Matrices test is primarily a measure of Induction, the clinician may want to augment it with a strong test of General Sequential (deductive) Reasoning (e.g., WJ-R Analysis–Synthesis) to more comprehensively sample the person's broad Gf abilities. By consulting the test classifications presented in Tables 9.2 to 9.8, clinicians should be able to improve their clinical interpretation of tests.

Third, the classification of individual tests by narrow abilities can help clinicians understand why a person may perform differently on two tests that have the same broad Gf-Gc label. I am frequently asked such questions as, "Why do I often get different scores on the WJ-R Analysis–Synthesis and Concept Formation tests if they are both measuring fluid intelligence [Gf]?" The analyses presented in this chapter indicate that the broad Gf-Gc abilities are second-order abilities that subsume narrower abilities that are strongly related but are still different in many respects. In the case of the two WJ-R tests, a review of Table 9.7 finds that although both tests are considered measures of Gf, the difference in test scores may be due to Analysis–Synthesis being more a measure of deductive (General Sequential Reasoning) reasoning whereas Concept Formation is more a measure of Inductive reasoning. The test summary tables should help clinicians understand why tests of narrow abilities in the same broad Gf-Gc ability often produce different scores.

Fourth, the availability of a comprehensive, empirically supported Gf-Gc model, together with theory-based data-analytic techniques such as confirmatory factor analysis (see Keith, Chapter 20, this volume), should help researchers and test developers design and conduct better studies. Theory-driven analyses with known narrow and/or broad Gf-Gc "marker" tests from across batteries should help researchers and test developers design better assessment batteries and increase our understanding of what existing assessment batteries measure. The studies of Flanagan and McGrew (1995), McGhee (1993), and Woodcock (1990) are illustrative of this approach to assessment research.

By focusing on the first-order narrow ability level, test developers can design test batteries that provide for more valid measurement of the broad Gf-Gc abilities by including measures of more than one narrow ability under a broad Gf-Gc ability. Also, it is now possible with appropriately designed studies to examine the advertising claims and clinical lore of what the individual tests in intelligence batteries measure (e.g., Wechsler Block Design is primarily a measure of narrow visual processing abilities, not fluid reasoning abilities) (McGrew & Flanagan, 1996). Maybe future versions of the Wechsler batteries will include good measures of Induction or General Sequential Reasoning (Gf) modeled after other good Gf tests (e.g., KAIT Mystery Codes and Logical Steps, DAS and SB-IV Matrices, and WJ-R Analysis–Synthesis and Concept Formation).

Fifth, the summary analyses across intelligence batteries highlight abilities that are well represented by existing tests (e.g., Language Development, Lexical Knowledge, and General Information areas in Gc) and abilities that are not assessed, or are assessed by a limited number of tests. These results suggest fruitful avenues for the development of new measures. Test developers need to consider developing new and innovative measures within the Ga and Glr domains. Examining the complete narrow ability definition list (Table 9.1) for abilities not measured by any intelligence battery (Table 9.9) suggests areas for future test development (e.g., Communication Ability under Gc, all the fluency abilities under Glr, and Sensitivity to Problems under Glr).

Finally, I have found the Gf-Gc framework and list of narrow ability definitions to be effective teaching tools. Students (or one's self, if pursuing self-study) can be required to classify the individual tests in an assessment battery according to the narrow ability definition list (Table 9.1). Such detailed task analysis of tests forces an individual to take a serious look at the task demands of individual tests. At the same time, the process increases an individual's understanding of the narrow and broad abilities within the Gf-Gc framework.

SUMMARY

These are exciting times for those involved in research, development, and the use of intelligence test batteries. Within the last decade the predominant verbal–nonverbal assessment model (i.e., the Wechsler batteries), a model that has remained largely unchanged since the 1939 publication of the Wechsler–Bellevue, has been challenged by instruments based on more contemporary theories and data. Although arguments may exist between different theoretical camps (e.g., the Luria–Das processing theories, Gardner's multiple intelligences theory, factor analytically based structural theories, and the more complete or modern Gf-Gc theories that include 9 to 10 abilities versus the older Gf-Gc dichotomy), there is little doubt that the seminal work of Carroll cannot be ignored, regardless of one's theoretical orientation. Only the most rigid of individuals would suggest that the emerging picture of the structure of human abilities derived from a systematic synthesis of 60 to 70 years of factor-analytic research should be ignored. Ignoring the seminal work of Carroll, which provides strong support for the Horn–Cattell Gf-Gc theory, would be akin to burying one's head in the sand.

Although my analyses highlight assessment batteries that may provide for the most comprehensive assessment of the narrow and/or broad Gf-Gc abilities, my goal is not to argue for reliance on a particular battery. Researchers and clinicians should use the information summarized in this chapter and the extension of this work by McGrew and Flanagan (1995), and Flanagan and McGrew (Chapter 17, this volume) to improve their research and clinical practice by cutting across batteries to conduct more thorough assessments. In particular, I want clinicians to become more true scientist–practitioners by using the best available empirical knowledge to inform their clinical assessment practice.

My classification of the individual tests in the major intelligence batteries is only an initial attempt in light of the emerging Gf-Gc models articulated by Carroll and Horn and are at best informed and reasoned hypotheses that need to be tested. The final Gf-Gc framework that I used to organize the test classifications was based partially on the Carroll versus Horn model analyses that I described in the Appendix, analyses that are based on limited sets of data and indicators. However, any errors in the placement of narrow abilities under the broad Gf-Gc abilities do not affect the narrow ability test classifications reported in this chapter. Future research and scholarly discussions will find that some of my classifications (most of them, I hope) are accurate, whereas others need modification. I fully expect this to happen. What is important is that this initial attempt begins to engage scholars and clinicians in a structured dialogue within a common framework and set of terms. If this is the end result of this chapter, I will be pleased. The monumental works of Carroll and Horn must begin to inform psychoeducational assessment practice, a professional activity that is too often influenced by arm-chair speculation and the inertia of tradition.

NOTES

1. A document with more detailed first-order narrow ability definitions can be obtained by contacting the author.

2. The following individuals provided their time and expertise in this activity: Vinny Alfonso, Ted Andrews, Colin Elliott, Dawn Flanagan, Patti Harrison, Gary Hessler, Rick Ittenbach, Alan Kaufman, Tim Keith, and Ron McGhee.

REFERENCES

Baker, S. K., Kameenui, E. K., Simmons, D. C., & Stahl, S. (1994). Beginning reading: Educational tools for diverse learners. *School Psychology Review, 23,* 372–391.

Bickley, P. G., Keith, T. Z., & Wolfe, L. M. (1995). The three-stratum theory of cognitive abilities: Test of the structure of intelligence across the life span. *Intelligence, 20,* 309–328.

Burns, R. B. (1994, April). Surveying the cognitive domain. *Educational Researcher,* 35–37.

Carroll, J. B. (1993). *Human cognitive abilities: A survey of factor-analytic studies.* New York: Cambridge University Press.

Cattell, R. B. (1941). Some theoretical issues in adult intelligence testing. *Psychological Bulletin, 38,* 592. [Abstract].

Das, J. P., Naglieri, J. A., & Kirby, J. R. (1994). *Assessment of cognitive processes: The PASS theory of intelligence.* Boston: Allyn & Bacon.

Elliott, C. D. (1990). *The Differential Ability Scales: Introductory and technical handbook.* San Antonio, TX: Psychological Corporation.

Flanagan, D. P., & McGrew, K. S. (1995). *Interpreting intelligence tests from modern Gf-Gc theory: Joint confirmatory factor analysis of the WJ-R and the Kaufman Adolescent and Adult Intelligence Test (KAIT).* Manuscript submitted for publication.

Gustafsson, J-E. (1984). A unifying model of the structure of intellectual abilities. *Intelligence, 8,* 179–203.

Horn, J. L. (1988). Thinking about human abilities. In J. R. Nesselroade & R. B. Cattell (Eds.), *Handbook of multivariate psychology* (2nd ed., pp. 645–685). New York: Academic Press.

Horn, J. L. (1991). Measurement of intellectual capabilities: A review of theory. In K. S. McGrew, J. K. Werder, & R. W. Woodcock, *WJ-R technical manual,* Chicago: Riverside.

Horn, J. L. (1994). Theory of fluid and crystallized intelligence. In R. J. Sternberg (Ed.), *Encyclopedia of human intelligence* (pp. 443–451). New York: Macmillan.

Kaufman, A. S., & Kaufman, N. L. (1983). *Kaufman Assessment Battery for Children.* Circle Pines, MN: American Guidance Service.

Kaufman, A. S., & Kaufman, N. L. (1993). *The Kaufman Adolescent and Adult Intelligence Test.* Circle Pines, MN: American Guidance Service.

McGhee, R. L. (1993). Fluid and crystallized intelligence: Confirmatory factor analysis of the Differential Abilities Scale, Detroit Tests of Learning Aptitude—3, and Woodcock–Johnson Psycho-Educational Assessment Battery—Revised. *Journal of Psychoeducational Assessment, Monograph Series: Woodcock–Johnson Psycho-Educational Battery—Revised,* 20–38.

McGrew, K. S. (1993). The relationship between the WJ-R Gf-Gc cognitive clusters and reading achievement across the life-span. *Journal of Psychoeducational Assessment, Monograph Series: Woodcock–Johnson Psycho-Educational Battery—Revised,* 39–53.

McGrew, K. S. (1994). *Clinical interpretation of the Woodcock—Johnson Tests of Cognitive Ability—Revised.* Boston: Allyn & Bacon.

McGrew, K. S., & Flanagan, D. P. (1996). *The intelligence test desk reference (ITDR): A Gf-Gc cross-battery approach to intelligence test interpretation.* Boston: Allyn & Bacon. Manuscript in preparation.

McGrew, K. S., & Flanagan, D. P. (1996). The Wechsler Performance Scale debate: Fluid intelligence (Gf) or visual processing (Gv)? *NASP Communique, 24*(4).

McGrew, K. S., & Hessler, G. L. (1995). The relationship between the WJ-R Gf-Gc cognitive clusters and mathematics across the lifespan. *Journal of Psychoeducational Assessment, 13,* 21–38.

McGrew, K. S., & Knopik, S. N. (1993). The relationship between the WJ-R Gf-Gc cognitive clusters and writing achievement across the life-span. *School Psychology Review, 22,* 687–695.

McGrew, K., Werder, J., & Woodcock, R. (1991). *WJ-R technical manual.* Chicago, IL: Riverside.

Thorndike, R. L., Hagen, E. P., & Sattler, J. M. (1986). *Stanford–Binet Intelligence Scale: Fourth Edition.* Chicago: Riverside.

Wechsler, D. (1981). *Wechsler Adult Intelligence Scale—Revised.* San Antonio, TX: Psychological Corporation.

Wechsler, D. (1989). *Wechsler Preschool and Primary Scale of Intelligence—Revised.* San Antonio, TX: Psychological Corporation.

Wechsler, D. (1991). *Wechsler Intelligence Scale for Children—Third Edition.* San Antonio, TX: Psychological Corporation.

Woodcock, R. W. (1990). Theoretical foundations of the WJ-R measures of cognitive ability. *Journal of Psychoeducational Assessment, 8,* 231–258.

Woodcock, R. W. (1993). An information processing view of Gf-Gc theory. *Journal of Psychoeducational Assessment, Monograph Series: Advances in Psychoeducational Assessment: Woodcock–Johnson Psycho-Educational Battery—Revised,* 80–102.

Woodcock, R. W. (in press). Extending Gf-Gc theory in practice. In J. J. McArdle & R. W. Woodcock (Eds.), *Human cognitive abilities in theory and practice.* Chicago: Riverside.

Woodcock, R. W., & Johnson, M. B. (1989). *Woodcock–Johnson Psycho-Educational Battery—Revised.* Chicago: Riverside.

APPENDIX

———————

To evaluate the differences between the Carroll and Horn models, I used 37 measures from the WJ-R in the kindergarten to adult ($n = 1291$) norm sample described by McGrew et al. (1991). Using confirmatory factor methods, I compared four different Gf-Gc models. The initial specification of the composition of the factors (i.e., what WJ-R measures loaded on the different factors) was based on a review of the factor loadings reported by McGrew et al. (1991), Woodcock (1990), and John Carroll (presented later in this appendix).

The factor labels used in this Appendix are consistent with the stratum level I narrow factor definitions provided by Carroll (1993). These factor labels differ from the Gf-Gc factor labels commonly used to describe the WJ-R factors (Gf, Gc, Glr, Gsm, etc.) as the interpretation of prior WJ-R confirmatory studies tended to confound Carroll's stratum level II broad Gf-Gc factors with stratum level I narrow factors (Flanagan & McGrew, 1995). I evaluated the breadth of each factor specified in these analyses against the definitions provided by Carroll and used either stratum level II broad Gf-Gc factor notations (e.g., Ga) or stratum level I factor labels followed by their respective stratum level II labels (e.g., Phonetic Coding or PC-Ga), depending on the diversity of tests represented by each factor. For example, five factors in these analyses (i.e., Gv, Gc, Gf, Gq, and Grw) retained the broad Gf-Gc factor labels because task analysis of the diversity of indicators defining these factors suggested that these are broader factors more consistent with Carroll's stratum level II Gf-Gc factors. Some factors that have been labeled as stratum level II Gf-Gc factors in previous studies (e.g., the WJ-R Sound Blending and Incomplete Words based factor label of Ga) have been given a stratum level I label in these analyses because the indicators that define these factors are measures of only a stratum level I or narrow factor (e.g., PC). For a factor to retain a stratum level II broad Gf-Gc factor label, it must be broad; that is, composed of two or more different stratum level I narrow abilities tests. Thus, a limitation of these analyses is that four of the broad Gf-Gc factors (i.e., Glr, Gsm, Gs, and Ga) specified in these analyses were defined by only one stratum level I narrow factor.

Model 1 was specified to approximate, to the extent possible with the given breadth of variables, the major features of Carroll's model. Based on the Carroll and Horn model differences discussed earlier in this chapter, this model included six factors: combined Associative Memory (MA-Glr) and Memory Span (MS-Gsm); combined Gc and Grw; combined Gf and Gq; separate Gv, Perceptual Speed (PS-Gs), and Phonetic Coding (PC-Ga) factors (Incomplete Words and Sound Blending had dual loadings on the PC-Ga and Gc+Grw factor). This was one of the poorest fitting models ($rmr = .05$; $GFI = .77$; $AGFI = .74$). The Incomplete Words and Sound Blending loadings on the Gc+Grw factor were nonsignificant, and the linear structural equation modeling (LISREL) modification indices suggested the need for separate Memory Span (MS-Gsm) and Associate Memory (MA-Glr) factors.

Models 2 and 3 used the results from Model 1 and did not have the phonetic coding tests (i.e.,

TABLE 9.10. John Carroll's Hierarchical Exploratory Factor Analysis Solution (Principal Factoring with Hierarchical Orthogonalization of Factors with Schmid–Leiman Technique) of the Complete WJ-R Battery in Kindergarten to Adult Sample ($n = 1,291$)

	First-order factors										Second-order factors		
	1A	1B	1C	1D	1E	1F	1G	1H	1I	1J	2A	2B	h^2[a]
1A: Auditory Processing											.74	—	.56
Sound Blending	.39	—	—	—	—	—	—	—	—	—	.45	—	.45
Incomplete Words	.37	—	—	—	—	—	—	—	—	—	.40	—	.32
Sound Patterns	.16	—	—	—	—	—	—	—	—	—	.33	—	.24
1B: Lexical Knowledge and Information											.66	**.45**	.63
Social Studies	—	.55	—	—	—	—	—	—	—	—	.57	**.34**	.77
Humanities	—	.47	—	—	—	—	—	—	—	—	.56	**.35**	.71
Science	—	.47	—	—	—	—	—	—	—	—	.59	**.35**	.66
Oral Vocabulary	—	.45	—	—	—	—	—	—	—	—	.64	**.35**	.77
Picture Vocabulary	—	.42	—	—	—	—	—	—	—	—	.62	—	.63
Listening Comprehension	—	.41	—	—	—	—	—	—	—	—	.59	—	.60
Quantitative Concepts	—	.39	—	—	—	—	—	—	—	—	.41	**.56**	.72
Reading Vocabulary	—	.36	—	—	—	—	—	—	—	—	.57	**.44**	.75
Punctuation & Capitalization	—	.30	—	—	—	—	—	—	—	—	.32	**.59**	.63
Verbal Analogies	—	.28	—	—	—	—	—	—	—	—	.55	**.41**	.62
1C: Inductive Reasoning											.63	—	.40
Concept Formation	—	—	.35	—	—	—	.31	—	—	—	.46	**.33**	.55
1D: Visual Processing											.57	—	.35
Visual Closure	—	—	—	.33	—	—	—	—	—	—	.29	—	.23
Picture Recognition	—	—	—	.32	—	—	—	—	—	—	.32	—	.27
1E: Associative Memory											.51	—	.31
Delayed Recall/Memory For Names	—	—	—	—	.70	—	—	—	—	—	.43	—	.72
Memory for Names	—	—	—	—	.68	—	—	—	—	—	.44	—	.71
Visual-Auditory Learning	—	—	—	—	.35	—	—	—	—	—	.45	**.30**	.48
Delayed Recall/Vis.-Aud. Learning	—	—	—	—	.30	—	—	—	—	—	.35	—	.37

176

												h2[a]
1F: Writing & Usage	—	—	—	—	—	—	—	—	—	—	.70	.52
Handwriting	—	—	.38	—	—	—	—	—	—	—	.32	.29
Writing Samples	—	—	.25	.38	—	—	—	—	—	—	.25	.60
Usage	—	—	.24	.37	—	—	—	—	—	—	.24	.61
1G: Quantitative Reasoning	—	—	—	—	—	—	—	—	—	—	.65	.48
Applied Problems	**.30**	**.43**	—	—	.38	—	—	—	—	—	.55	.72
Spatial Relations	**.33**	**.38**	—	—	.36	—	—	—	—	—	.31	.51
Calculation	—	—	—	—	.35	—	—	—	—	—	.63	.68
Analysis-Synthesis	—	**.40**	—	—	.34	—	—	—	—	—	.33	.44
1H: Perceptual Speed	—	—	—	—	—	—	—	—	—	—	.63	.44
Visual Matching	—	—	—	—	—	—	—	—	—	.61	.57	.74
Cross Out	—	—	—	—	—	—	—	—	—	.49	.45	.55
Writing Fluency	—	—	—	—	—	—	—	—	—	.23	.52	.49
1I: Orthography & Spelling	—	—	—	—	—	—	—	—	—	—	.57	.37
Word Attack	—	**.37**	—	—	—	—	—	—	.52	—	.46	.66
Letter-Word Identification	—	**.46**	—	—	—	—	—	—	.47	—	.52	.75
Spelling	—	**.33**	—	—	—	—	—	—	.30	—	.64	.72
Passage Comprehension	—	**.48**	—	—	—	—	—	—	.29	—	.45	.63
1J: Memory Span	—	—	—	—	—	—	—	—	—	—	.34	.13
Memory for Words	—	**.30**	—	—	—	—	—	.64	—	—	.30	.62
Memory for Sentences	—	**.46**	—	—	—	—	—	.49	—	—	.31	.64
Numbers Reversed	—	**.32**	—	—	—	—	—	.24	—	—	.43	.42
Sums of Squares	.42	2.20	.46	.56	1.21	.47	.88	.71	.99	.74	6.73	5.90

Note. To save on space, loadings for the tests on the first- and second-order factors are listed in the respective columns. Loadings for the first-order factors on the second-order factors are listed in the respective columns. Nonsalient factor loadings are omitted from the table. Factor loadings in bold were not salient for a given factor but were greater than .295 in absolute magnitude. Loadings in the oblique reference-vector matrices, rather than the loadings in the pattern matrices, were used to determine salient loadings. Sums of squares (SMSQ) for first-order factors on second-order factors are 2.16 (2A) and 2.03 (2B); sum of communalities for first-order factors is 4.19 (2A) and 2.03 (2B); sum of communalities for individual tests is 21.27. Second-order factors are labeled General Intelligence (2A) and Crystallized Intelligence (2B). This previously unpublished analysis was completed by John Carroll and is included here with his permission.

[a]h^2 = communality estimate.

TABLE 9.11. Final Confirmatory Factor Analysis Solution of 37 Measures from the Complete WJ-R Battery in Kindergarten to Adult Sample (*n* = 1,291)

Tests	Gf-Gc factor loadings								
	MA- Glr	MS- Gsm	PS- Gs	PC Ga	Gv	Gc	Gf	Gq	Grw
Mem. for Names	.67	—	—	—	—	—	—	—	—
Vis.-Aud. Lrng.	.80	—	—	—	—	—	—	—	—
Delayed Recall—MN	.59	—	—	—	—	—	—	—	—
Delayed Recall—VAL	.51	—	—	—	**.14**	—	—	—	—
Memory for Sentences	—	.51	—	—	—	.50	—	—	—
Memory for Words	—	.71	—	—	—	**.24**	—	—	—
Numbers Reversed	—	.33	—	—	—	—	.49	—	—
Visual Matching	—	—	.86	—	—	—	—	—	—
Cross Out	—	—	.64	—	.25	—	—	—	—
Incomplete Words	—	—	—	.50	—	—	—	—	—
Sound Blending	—	—	—	.73	—	—	—	—	—
Sound Patterns	—	—	—	.26	—	—	.29	—	—
Visual Closure	—	—	—	—	.54	—	—	—	—
Picture Recognition	.28	—	—	—	.32	—	—	—	—
Spatial Relations	—	—	—	—	.21	—	.51	—	—
Picture Vocabulary	—	—	—	—	—	.76	—	—	—
Oral Vocabulary	—	—	—	—	—	.69	—	—	**.23**
Listening Compr.	—	—	—	—	—	.74	—	—	—
Verbal Analogies	—	—	—	—	—	.41	.45	—	—
Science	—	—	—	—	—	.80	—	—	—
Social Studies	—	—	—	—	—	.84	—	—	—
Humanities	—	—	—	—	—	.78	—	—	—
Analysis-Synthesis	—	—	—	—	—	—	.64	—	—
Concept Formation	—	—	—	—	—	—	.67	—	—
Calculation	—	—	—	—	—	—	—	.84	—
Applied Problems	—	—	—	—	—	.21	**.18**	.54	—
Quant. Concepts	—	—	—	—	—	.33	—	.61	—
Letter-Word Iden.	—	—	—	—	—	—	—	—	**.85**
Passage Compr.	—	—	—	—	—	**.23**	—	—	**.60**
Word Attack	—	—	—	.22	—	—	—	—	**.58**
Reading Vocabulary	—	—	—	—	—	**.44**	—	—	**.48**
Writing Samples	—	—	—	—	—	—	—	—	**.74**
Writing Fluency	—	—	.31	—	—	—	—	—	**.47**
Punct. & Cap.	—	—	—	—	—	—	—	—	**.76**
Spelling	—	—	—	—	—	—	—	—	**.84**
Usage	—	—	—	—	—	—	—	—	**.76**
Handwriting	—	—	—	—	—	—	—	—	**.26**

Note. Factor loadings in bold indicate significant parameters not previously reported by McGrew et al. (1990) or Woodcock (1990). Residual parameters and latent factor correlations not reported in table.

Incomplete Words and Sound Blending) loading on both Phonetic Coding (PC-Ga) and Gc. Both models also maintained separate Associative Memory (MA-Glr) and Memory Span (MS-Gsm) factors. Model 3 differed from Model 2 in the separation of the Grw and Gc factors. Both models maintained the combined Gf+Gq factor. Model 3 (*rmr* = .04; *GFI* = .90; *AGFI* = .88) was a better-fitting model than Model 2 (*rmr* = .05; *GFI* = .79; *AGFI* = .75). This comparison indicated the need to maintain separate Grw and Gc factors.

Model 4 was identical to Model 3, except that Model 4 included separate Gq and Gf factors. The fit of Model 4 was almost identical (*rmr* = .04; *GFI* = .91; *AGFI* = .89) to that for Model 3, indicating that both models were equally plausible. To try to resolve the issue whether Gf and Gq should be separate factors, I tested the independence of the two factors by running a model where the Gf/Gq latent factor correlation was fixed at 1.0. Compared to Model 3, where the Gf/Gq correlation was free to vary (*r* = .84), the chi-square difference of 126.58 (*df* = 1) was significant (*p* < .05), a finding in favor of separate factors.

Although the formal test indicated that Gf and Gq were separate factors, I was still uncomfortable with their high latent factor correlation of .84. Thus, I looked for other non–factor-analytic validity information regarding the two factors. Inspection of the growth curves for the Gf and Gq WJ-R clusters in the WJ-R norm data (see McGrew et al., 1991) reveals that these two abilities have markedly different patterns of growth and decline over the lifespan. This finding, together with the confirmatory factor results, indicate that Gf and Gq, as operationally defined by the WJ-R battery, are separate factors. Altogether, the results of these WJ-R analyses resulted in my conclusion that the best model to use in the classification of tests would be one that includes separate Gf, Gq, Gc, Grw, Glr, Gsm, Ga, Gv, and Gs factors. To help with the classification of the WJ-R battery tests, I then examined the LISREL modification indices from the final model (Model 4), and went through a number of iterations of adding suggested parameters to the factors in the model. The final results, with significant parameters not previously reported by McGrew et al. (1991) or Woodcock (1990) clearly marked, are presented in Table 9.11. Carroll's previously unpublished analyses, which he graciously has allowed me to report in this appendix, are based on the same factoring procedures he used throughout his massive review of the extant factor analyses research literature (Carroll, 1993). Carroll's results, which used the same 37 WJ-R measures, are presented in Table 9.10.

PART III

⸺∘⚬∘⸺

NEW TESTS AND ALTERNATIVE TECHNIQUES FOR ASSESSING INTELLIGENCE

P ART III OF THIS TEXTBOOK focuses on recent standardized, norm-referenced intelligence tests and alternative intellectual assessment techniques. The methods of assessment used with the Binet and Wechsler scales dominated the 1900s. However, developers of new tests and alternative techniques for assessing intelligence have attempted to move beyond the tradition established by the Binet and Wechsler scales and to incorporate strong theoretical foundations into intellectual assessment.

Three chapters in Part III describe new intelligence tests published in the late 1980s and early 1990s and were written by the authors of the new tests. Chapter 10, "The Differential Ability Scales," was authored by Colin D. Elliott. The DAS was published in 1990, although an older version of the instrument, the British Ability Scales, was published in 1983. The DAS integrates several theoretical models of intelligence, instead of focusing on a single model. Chapter 11, "The Kaufman Adolescent and Adult Intelligence Test," was authored by Alan S. Kaufman and Nadeen L. Kaufman. The KAIT was published in 1993 and is based on the original Horn and Cattell model of fluid (Gf) and crystallized (Gc) intelligence. Chapter 12, "The Woodcock–Johnson Tests of Cognitive Ability—Revised," was authored by Richard W. Woodcock. The WJ-R COG was published in 1989 and measures eight broad cognitive abilities based on the most recent refinements to the Horn–Cattell Gf-Gc theory of intelligence.

Two chapters in Part III describe two intellectual assessment instruments under development at the time the textbook was being prepared. These chapters were written by the authors of the assessment instruments. Chapter 13, "Planning, Attention, Simultaneous, and Successive Theory and the Das–Naglieri Cognitive Assessment System: A Theory Based Measure of Intelligence," was authored by Jack A. Naglieri. The Das-Naglieri Cognitive Assessment System is based on Luria's neuropsychogical model of brain functioning. Chapter 14, "The Universal Nonverbal Intelligence Test," was authored by R. Steve McCallum and Bruce A. Bracken. The UNIT uses a model of

181

intelligence that includes two tiers (memory and reasoning) and two organizational strategies (symbolic and nonsymbolic) of intelligence.

Three chapters in Part III outline alternative techniques for assessing intelligence. Two of these chapters address dynamic assessment. Chapter 15, "Dynamic Assessment Approaches," by Carol S. Lidz, summarizes the general approach to assessment that utilizes a pretest–intervene–posttest administration format. Chapter 16, "The Learning Potential Assessment Device," by Reuven Feuerstein, Rafi Feuerstein, and Steven Gross, provides a comprehensive treatment of the LPAD, the most widely used dynamic assessment technique.

In general, the authors of Chapters 10 through 16 provide a description of their test (or technique) for assessing intelligence and discuss its theoretical underpinnings, organization and format, and psychometric characteristics. These authors also provide recommendations for interpreting the general, broad, and specific abilities measured by their instrument. Finally, each author concludes with a summary of the specific ways in which his or her intelligence test or assessment technique differs from traditional approaches and a description of how each one's test/technique reflects an advancement in intellectual assessment.

Chapter 17 also describes an alternative assessment technique. In "A Cross-Battery Approach to Assessing and Interpreting Cognitive Abilities: Narrowing the Gap Between Practice and Cognitive Science," Dawn P. Flanagan and Kevin S. McGrew contend that until new intelligence test batteries are developed, or existing batteries are revised substantially, an empirically supported and theory-driven "cross-battery" approach to assessment is needed to improve the validity of the practice of intelligence testing. In light of the research presented by John L. Horn and Jennie Noll (Chapter 4), John B. Carroll (Chapter 7), and Kevin S. McGrew (Chapter 9) in this textbook, Flanagan and McGrew offer empirically guided recommendations regarding how psychologists can augment any major intelligence test battery to ensure that a greater breadth of cognitive abilities is measured according to an integrated Carroll/Horn–Cattell Gf-Gc model. Flanagan and McGrew conclude with a summary of implications of the cross-battery approach for practice, research, and test development.

Part III concludes with a chapter that addresses training for the competent administration and interpretation of intelligence tests. In Chapter 18, "Issues and Suggestions for Training Professionals in Assessing Intelligence," Vincent C. Alfonso and Sarah I. Pratt integrate research and standards for professional practice and provide detailed recommendations for the best techniques to train new users of intelligence tests.

PLH

CHAPTER 10

The Differential Ability Scales

COLIN D. ELLIOTT

T HE DIFFERENTIAL ABILITY SCALES (DAS; Elliott, 1990a) is a relatively new cognitive assessment battery, developed and standardized in the United States. It has a longer history than this, however, as it is based on a predecessor, the British Ability Scales (BAS; Elliott, 1983a, 1983b). As its name suggests, the DAS was developed with a primary focus on specific abilities rather than on "intelligence."

STRUCTURE OF THE DAS

The DAS consists of (1) a cognitive battery of 17 subtests divided into two overlapping age levels, and (2) a short battery of three school achievement tests, conormed with the cognitive battery. The Preschool and School-Age Levels of the cognitive battery were conormed on children ages 5:0 through 6:11 (with most preschool subtests also conormed through 7:11).

The total age range covered by the instrument is 2:6 through 17:11. The DAS cognitive battery yields a composite score—General Conceptual Ability (GCA)—focused on reasoning and conceptual abilities, a Special Nonverbal Composite, and lower-level composite scores called cluster scores. These composites are derived from the *core* subtests, which are highly *g*-saturated. Diagnostic subtests measure other specific abilities that do not contribute to the composites. The overall structure is summarized in Table 10.1.

THEORETICAL UNDERPINNINGS

Two principles—self-evident truths to many practitioners—drove the development of the DAS. The first is that professionals assessing children with learning and developmental disabilities need information at a finer level of detail than an IQ score. IQ tests in the past have had a primary, disproportionate focus on global composite scores. The second principle is that psychometric assessment has much to offer the practitioner: Psychometric tests of cognitive abilities not only have well-established qualities of reliability, validity, time efficiency, objectivity, and lack of bias, but often give us information critical to our understanding of a child's learning styles and characteristics.

The first principle led to the major priority in the development of the DAS: to produce a battery

TABLE 10.1. Number of DAS Subtests and Composites at Each Age Level

Age level	Number of subtests	General Composite	Cluster scores
Lower Preschool level Age 2:6–3:5 (Extended Age 2:6-4:11)	4 core 2 diagnostic	1. GCA 2. Special Nonverbal	
Upper Preschool level Age 3:6–5:11 (Extended Age 3:6-6:11)	6 core 5 diagnostic	1. GCA 2. Special Nonverbal	1. Verbal Ability 2. Nonverbal Ability
School-Age level Age 6:0–17:11 (Extended Age 5:0-17:11)	6 core 4 diagnostic 3 achievement	1. GCA 2. Special Nonverbal	1. Verbal Ability 2. Nonverbal Reasoning Ability 3. Spatial Ability

in which subtests would be sufficiently reliable and measure sufficiently distinct cognitive functions to make them individually interpretable. Although it was expected that meaningful composites would be derived from the subtests, the primary focus in test development was at the subtest level. This emphasis distinguishes the DAS from most other batteries.

The DAS was not developed solely to reflect a single model of cognitive abilities but may be interpreted from a number of theoretical perspectives. It is designed to address processes that often underlie children's difficulties in learning and what we know of neurological structures underlying these abilities. As Carroll (1993) has shown, there are considerable similarities in the factor structures of cognitive batteries. A general factor (g) is an inescapable reality. It pervades all measures of ability and all relationships between cognitive abilities of any kind. It must therefore be represented in any test battery structure and in its theoretical model. In reviewing the many theories of the structure of abilities, it was apparent that no single theory is entirely persuasive and certainly no single theory has universal acceptance among theoreticians or practitioners. Even proponents of the Horn–Cattell theory, currently the most popular factor theory of the structure of abilities, do not all agree on the number of factors in the model or the precise nature of each factor (McGrew, Chapter 9, this volume).

Despite the fact that no single theory or model has universal acceptance, there is a common core of theory and research that is supportive of a number of propositions on which the development of the DAS was based:

- Human abilities are not explainable solely in terms of a single cognitive factor (g) or even in terms of two or three lower-order factors.
- Human abilities form multiple dimensions on which individuals show reliably observable differences (Carroll, 1993), and which are related in complex ways with how children learn, achieve, and solve problems.
- Human abilities are interrelated but not completely overlapping, thus making many of them distinct (Carroll, 1993).
- The wide range of human abilities represents a number of interlinked subsystems of information processing.
- Subsystems of information processing have structural correlates in the central nervous system, in which some functions are localized and others are integrated.

The relationship between cognitive abilities and neurological structure has long exercised the discipline of psychology because although it has been known for many years that there are cause-

and-effect relationships, their nature has not been clear. The following section of this chapter outlines some links between the factor structure of abilities and the neuropsychological evidence concerning the nature of structures underlying verbal and spatial abilities, fluid or general intelligence, and some aspects of memory. DAS measures (both subtests and composites) are mapped onto this structure.

Broad Verbal and Visual–Spatial Abilities

Two of the major ability clusters in the DAS and other cognitive batteries reflect two major systems through which we receive, perceive, remember, and process information. These systems are linked to the auditory and visual modalities. Factorially, the systems are represented by Verbal and Visualization (or Spatial) factors—Gc and Gv in the Horn–Cattell theory. Neuropsychologically, there is strong evidence for the existence of these systems. They tend to be localized in the left and right cerebral hemispheres, respectively, although there are individual differences in areas of localization of function. Moreover, the systems are doubly dissociated—that is, they represent two distinct, independent systems of information processing (McCarthy & Warrington, 1990; Springer & Deutsch, 1989). In the DAS, the *verbal* factor is measured by the Verbal cluster in both the Preschool and School-Age cognitive batteries. At the Preschool level, the Verbal cluster is formed by the Naming Vocabulary and Verbal Comprehension subtests, and at the School-Age level it is formed by Similarities and Word Definitions. The *visualization* or *spatial* factor is measured by the Spatial cluster at the School-Age level (consisting of the Pattern Construction and Recall of Designs subtests) and the Pattern Construction, Block Building, and Copying subtests at the Preschool age level.

Integration of Complex Information Processing

For normal cognitive functioning, the auditory–verbal and visual–spatial systems operate in an integrated fashion. Integration of the visual and auditory information-processing systems (and information from all subsystems) is probably a necessary underpinning for complex mental activity. Factorially, this integrative system is represented by the Fluid Reasoning (Gf) factor in the Horn–Cattell theory. Measures of Gf typically require integrated analysis of both verbal and visual information. Neuropsychologically, it seems that the integrative function of frontal lobe systems is central to complex mental functioning (Luria, 1973; discussed by McCarthy & Warrington, 1990, pp. 343–364), and it is therefore reasonable to hypothesize that it provides a structural correlate for Gf. In the DAS, the Gf factor is measured in the School-Age battery by the Nonverbal Reasoning cluster. Both subtests require integrated analysis and transformation of both visual and verbal information. For example, in the Matrices subtest, verbal mediation is critical for the solution of visually presented problems for most individuals. At the Preschool age level, the Picture Similarities subtest provides a measure of fluid reasoning.

There is some evidence that Gf forms the basis of the higher-order general factor (*g*). Although there are many factors at a lower order of generality that are related to *g*, the three that have the greatest contribution to defining *g* are the Gf, Gv, and Gc factors, discussed earlier. Carroll (1993) puts it this way: "There is abundant evidence for a factor of general intelligence . . . that dominates factors or variables that can be mastered in performing induction, reasoning, visualization, and language comprehension tasks" (p. 624). The central importance of Gf is also emphasized by Gustafsson (1988, 1989) and Härnqvist, Gustafsson, Muthén, and Nelson (1994), whose research indicates that the loading of Gf on *g* consistently has been found to be unity, which implies that *g* is equivalent to fluid intelligence. The hierarchical factor analyses of the DAS standardization data by Keith (1990), referred to later in this chapter, provide further support for this position. In the DAS, *g* is measured by an overall composite, General Conceptual Ability (a description of *g*). Because it is estimated from only those subtests that are the best estimators of g (i.e., those that measure Gf, Gc, and Gv), the GCA is a purer measure of g than the composites of most other batteries that include all cognitive subtests in the composite, irrespective of their g loading.

Verbal and Visual Short-Term Memory Systems

Some cognitive tests, such as the Stanford–Binet Intelligence Scale, Fourth Edition (SB-IV; Thorndike, Hagen, & Sattler, 1986), and the Woodcock–Johnson Psychoeducational Battery—Revised (WJ-R; Woodcock & Johnson, 1989), represent memory by a single factor. The Horn–Cattell theory of the structure of mental abilities also does not distinguish between separate, modality-related memory systems. However, there is much evidence from cognitive psychology and from neuropsychology that verbal and visual short-term memory systems are distinct and are doubly dissociated (Hitch, Halliday, Schaafstal, & Schraagen, 1988; McCarthy & Warrington, 1990, pp. 275–295). The DAS keeps visual and auditory short-term memory tasks as distinct measures and does not treat short-term memory as unitary. Visual short-term memory is represented at the Preschool level by Recognition of Pictures and at the School-Age level by Recall of Designs and Recognition of Pictures (out-of-level for ages 8 and over; a reliable and valid measure for older children of average to below-average ability). Auditory short-term memory is represented across the entire age range by Recall of Digits, a subtest designed to be a purer measure of this function than the Digit Span subtest of a number of other batteries.

The intermediate-term memory factor (Glr) in the Horn–Cattell model (associative storage and retrieval in McGrew, Chapter 9, this volume) is typically measured by tests that have both visual and verbal components. In the DAS Recall of Objects subtest, for example, pictures are presented, but they have to be recalled verbally. McCarthy and Warrington (1990, p.283) call this "visual–verbal" short-term memory and conclude that it is underpinned by another distinct information-processing system. In the DAS, the Recall of Objects subtest, which provides a measure of this factor, is for children 4 years of age and older.

ORGANIZATION AND FORMAT

Test Structure

The DAS has three major groups of component tests: the Preschool level of the cognitive battery, the School-Age level of the cognitive battery, and the brief achievement battery. These are listed in Tables 10.2, 10.3, and 10.4. In each table for the cognitive battery the subtests are grouped according to whether they are designated "core" subtests or "diagnostic" subtests. Each subtest has a brief description of the abilities it measures, including its relation to the Horn–Cattell factors. The core subtests are relatively strongly g-related and therefore measure complex processing and conceptual ability. The diagnostic subtests have a lower g saturation and measure such less cognitively complex functions as short-term memory and speed of information processing. Subtests have normative scores in a T score metric (mean = 50; SD = 10).

Tables 10.2 and 10.3 also show the composites that can be derived from the core subtests, and the subtests that contribute to those composites. Two types of composite are provided, all in a standard score metric (mean = 100; SD = 15). First are lower-order cluster scores. There are two of these at the Upper Preschool level (Verbal and Nonverbal), for children ages 3:6 to 5:11. There are three cluster scores at the School-Age level (Verbal, Nonverbal Reasoning, and Spatial). Note that at the lower Preschool level (ages 2:6 to 3:5) there are no cluster scores.

TABLE 10.2. Subtests of the DAS Preschool Cognitive Battery, Showing Abilities Measured (and Relation of Measures to Horn–Cattell Factors) and Their Contribution to Composites

Subtest	Abilities measured	Contribution to Composite
Core subtests:		
Block Building[a]	Visual–perceptual matching, especially of spatial orientation, in copying block patterns (Gv)	GCA
Verbal Comprehension	Receptive language: understanding oral instructions using basic language concepts (Gc)	Verbal, GCA
Naming Vocabulary	Expressive language: knowledge of names (Gc)	Verbal, GCA
Picture Similarities	Nonverbal Reasoning: matching pictures that have a common element or concept (Gf)	Nonverbal, GCA
Pattern Construction	Nonverbal, spatial visualization in reproducing designs with colored blocks and flat squares (Gv)	Nonverbal, GCA
Copying	Visual–spatial matching and fine-motor coordination in copying line drawings (Gv)	Nonverbal, GCA
Early Number Concepts[b]	Knowledge of prenumerical and numerical quantitative concepts (Gq)	GCA
Diagnostic subtests:		
Matching Letter-Like Forms	Visual discrimination of spatial relationships among similar shapes (Gv)	N/A
Recall of Digits	Short-term auditory–sequential memory for sequences of numbers (Gsma)	N/A
Recall of Objects	Short-term and intermediate-term learning and verbal recall of a display of pictures (Glr)	N/A
Recognition of Pictures	Short-term, nonverbal visual memory measured through recognition of familiar objects (Gsmv, Gv)	N/A

Note. N/A = not applicable. The DAS Preschool Cognitive Battery includes Verbal and Nonverbal/Special Nonverbal Composites as well as a GCA Composite.
[a]Used only for the GCA composite at the lower Preschool level. Used as a diagnostic subtest at the upper Preschool level.
[b]Not used for either cluster score because it has similar factor loadings on both the Verbal and Nonverbal factors.

Second are the higher-order composites. For most children, the most general composite will be the GCA score. For children for whom it is judged that the verbal component of that score is inappropriate, a Special Nonverbal Composite is provided. For the Upper Preschool age level, this is identical to the lower-order Nonverbal composite, formed from three subtests. For the School-Age battery, this is formed from the four subtests in the Nonverbal Reasoning and Spatial clusters.

Table 10.4 lists the three achievement tests. The normative scores on these tests are in a standard score metric (mean = 100; *SD* = 15), to facilitate comparison with composite scores from the cognitive battery. The achievement and cognitive batteries were fully conormed. Discrepancies between ability (as measured by GCA or Special Nonverbal Composite) may be evaluated taking either (1) the *simple difference* between the achievement score and the composite, or (2) the *difference between predicted and observed achievement,* with predicted achievement being based on the GCA or Special Nonverbal Composite score. The DAS *Handbook* provides information on both the statistical significance (or reliability) of discrepancies, and their frequency of occurrence (or unusualness) in the standardization sample.

The Preschool and School-Age levels of the cognitive battery were fully conòrmed for children in the age range of 5:0 to 7:11. This provides a major advantage for the professional examiner, who has the option of choosing which battery is most developmentally appropriate for a given child in this age range. Both the DAS handbook and an independent study by Keith (1990) demonstrated that the *g* factors measured at the Preschool and School-Age levels are identical.

Test Content

Developmental Appropriateness

The two levels of the DAS cognitive battery were deliberately designed to be developmentally appropriate and engaging for preschool and school-age children, respectively. By contrast, the practice of other test developers (e.g., in the Wechsler and Woodcock–Johnson scales) to push tasks originally designed for adults or older children into the preschool domain was considered undesirable. Such a practice leads to tasks that are less intrinsically interesting for preschoolers, resulting in poorer motivation and greater difficulty for the examiner in maintaining rapport.

TABLE 10.3. Subtests of the DAS School-Age Cognitive Battery, Showing Abilities Measured (and Relation of Measures to Horn–Cattell Factors) and Their Contribution to Composites

Subtest	Abilities measured	Contribution to Composite
Core subtests:		
Word Definitions	Expressive language: knowledge of word meanings (Gc)	Verbal, GCA
Similarities	Verbal, inductive reasoning and verbal knowledge (Gc)	Verbal, GCA
Matrices	Nonverbal, logical reasoning: perception and application of relationships among abstract figures (Gf)	Nonverbal Reasoning, GCA, Special Nonverbal
Sequential and Quantitative Reasoning	Detection of sequential patterns or relationships in figures or numbers (Gf)	Nonverbal Reasoning, GCA, Special Nonverbal
Recall of designs	Short-term recall of visual–spatial relationships through drawing abstract figures (Gv, Gsmv)	Spatial, GCA, Special Nonverbal
Pattern Construction	Nonverbal, spatial visualization in reproducing designs with colored blocks and flat squares (Gv)	Spatial, GCA, Special Nonverbal
Diagnostic subtests:		
Recall of Digits	Short-term auditory–sequential memory for sequences of numbers (Gsma)	N/A
Recall of Objects	Short-term and intermediate-term learning and verbal recall of a display of pictures (Glr)	N/A
Speed of Information Processing	Speed in performing simple mental operations (Gs)	N/A

Note. N/A = not applicable. The DAS School-Age Cognitive Battery contains Verbal, Nonverbal Reasoning, and Spatial Composites as well as a GCA and Special Nonverbal Composites.

Subtests as Specific Ability Measures

The chief aim in designing the content of the DAS was to produce subtests that are individually interpretable and can stand technically as separate, specific measures of various abilities. Once a specification was made of the desired tasks and dimensions to be measured, each subtest was designed to be unidimensional and homogeneous in content and distinct from other subtests, thus aiding the interpretation of children's performance. If a subtest score is to be interpreted as a measure of a specific, identifiable ability, the items within that subtest must be of similar content and must require the examinee to perform similar operations. In each item of the Naming Vocabulary subtest, a child is asked to name an object in a picture. All items are therefore homogeneous. Naming Vocabulary is distinct from Verbal Comprehension, another verbal subtest, because the former requires a verbal response and the latter does not.

In addition to having homogeneous content that focuses on a distinct ability, each subtest should also be reliable. Because the DAS emphasizes the identification of cognitive strengths and weaknesses, subtests must have a sufficient amount of reliable specificity to be separately interpretable (see later section, "Accuracy, Reliability, and Specificity").

Verbal Content

Although it was considered important to include measures of verbal ability in the DAS cognitive battery, too many verbal tasks would present problems for examiners wishing to assess children from multicultural or culturally disadvantaged backgrounds. In particular, we considered and rejected the inclusion of measures of general knowledge (either verbally or pictorially presented, as in the Wechsler Information Subtest or the Faces and Places subtest in the Kaufman Assessment Battery for Children [K-ABC; Kaufman & Kaufman, 1983]). In developing verbal items, considerable attention was paid to whether items and language would be usable throughout the English-speaking world. Colloquialisms or words with a specific meaning in the United States were eliminated as far as possible.

Because verbal abilities are a major component of cognition, it is certainly necessary to have some subtests, particularly at the School-Age Level, that are purely verbally presented. However, getting the balance right in a test battery is important, too. In developing the DAS content, only two core subtests were included with entirely verbal presentation and response (both at the School-Age level), plus the verbally administered Recall of Digits subtest as a measure of auditory short-term memory. Other than those subtests, the aim was to have subtests with varied tasks and materials. The following section shows the range and variety of DAS stimulus materials.

Timed or Speeded Items

The DAS content minimizes the use of timed or speeded items. The Speed of Information Processing subtest is an obvious exception as the nature of the task is to process information as speedily as

TABLE 10.4. DAS Achievement Tests

Achievement test	Skills measured
Basic Number Skills	Knowledge and written recall of spellings. Includes diagnostic performance analysis on items
Spelling	Recognition of printed numbers and performance of arithmetic operations. Includes diagnostic performance analysis of errors
Word Reading	Recognition and decoding of printed words

possible. Apart from that subtest only one subtest—Pattern Construction—gives extra points for correct completion of the designs within specified time limits. Of course, this feature of the subtest, which is appropriate for most individuals, is inappropriate for some children. Speed of response to the Pattern Construction items may not produce a valid measure for a child with a physical disability, such as cerebral palsy, or with an attentional problem, or one who takes an extremely deliberate approach to a task. For such children, an alternative procedure is provided, in which the score is based solely on accuracy within very liberal time limits. Confirmatory factor analyses reported in the DAS *Handbook* demonstrated the factorial equivalence of the Standard and Alternative versions of Pattern Construction.

Teaching Procedures

Finally, a major focus in the development of DAS subtest content was to ensure as far as possible that children who are being assessed understand what they are supposed to be doing. Young children and children with developmental and learning disabilities often have difficulty in "warming up" to a task, and initially understanding the task requirements. For this reason, most of the DAS subtests have demonstration and teaching procedures built in to the administration.

Test Materials

The DAS test kit includes two informational volumes: an *Administration and Scoring Manual,* and an *Introductory and Technical Handbook.* Separate Record Forms are provided for the Preschool and School-Age levels of the cognitive battery. The kit contains three stimulus books, and a variety of consumable booklets and manipulable materials. Materials vary for each subtest. The materials were specifically designed to be varied and engaging for children and students of all developmental levels. To this end, uniform presentation of subtests (e.g., in an easel format) was not considered acceptable in the design. As a result, the materials are colorful, manipulable, and varied, while being also easy to administer.

At the Preschool age level, only one subtest, Recall of Digits, is purely verbally presented, with no additional stimulus materials. At the School-Age level, three subtests are purely verbally presented, with no additional stimulus materials. These are Word Definitions and Similarities, which comprise the Verbal cluster and Recall of Digits.

PSYCHOMETRIC PROPERTIES

Norming Procedures and Standardization Characteristics

Quality of Norm Sample

The representativeness of the norm sample is crucial to any instrument, such as the DAS, that measures cognitive ability. The ultimate goal of sampling is to assemble a reference (or norm) group that has the same distribution of abilities as the population to which we want to generalize. For the DAS, the population was defined as all noninstitutionalized, English-proficient children ages 2:6–17:11 living in the United States. The target population excluded severely handicapped children, but included all others with handicaps provided the impairment would not prevent valid assessment.

The sampling plan for the DAS was constructed around the stratification variables of Age, Sex, Race/Ethnicity, Parent Education (as the variable representing socioeconomic status), Geographic Region, and (for preschool children) Educational Preschool Enrollment. In addition, three variables

. were monitored but not used as stratifying criteria: community size, special education status, and 16- and 17-year-old dropouts, who were included in the sample.

To match the population extremely accurately for race/ethnicity and parent education, computer tapes of census data for March 1988 were used to estimate target numbers. The census tape offered several important advantages. The most important of these was that it permitted the calculation of joint distributions of demographic variables. *Thus, for each sex and year of age (or half-year at the preschool level), the target matrix represented the joint distribution of parent education, race/ethnicity, and region.*

Another major advantage of the data tape is that it made possible the creation of demographic variables that were better suited to the needs of the project than were tables published by the Census Bureau. For example, the single dimension of race/ethnicity was created from two independent census dimensions of race (black, white, other) and Spanish origin. Consolidating these into a single dimension made it feasible to calculate the joint distributions of race/ethnicity with other variables. Another example is that the parent education levels of the children from one- and two-parent families in the DAS sample could be matched to the parent education levels of *children* from one- and two-parent families in the population. Neither of these estimates could have been made with any accuracy without the census data tape. Further details of the procedures, including the random selection of the sample through a multistage process, are provided in the DAS *Handbook* (Elliott, 1990b). These procedures made the DAS unique in its sampling accuracy.

Bias Oversample

Another unique feature of the DAS is that about 600 additional cases of black and Hispanic children were collected over and above the requirements of the norm sample. This was to enable statistical analyses of item bias and prediction bias to be conducted. Selected age groups were oversampled to ensure that every item would be administered to a sufficiently substantial number of children to enable accurate analyses of item bias to be conducted, and also to help ensure that item scoring rules would be sensitive to minority children's responses.

Results are reported in the DAS *Handbook* (Elliott, 1990b). Few examples of item bias were found—between-group differences in item difficulty were the grounds for a small number of item deletions. The prediction analyses showed no statistically significant differences in the strength of the relationship between achievement and GCA for either blacks or Hispanics compared with whites and no evidence that the DAS is biased against either minority group. When group-administered achievement-test scores were the criteria, Hispanics obtained lower group achievement-test scores than did whites for the same GCA scores. In other words, the DAS tends to overpredict Hispanic children's achievement test scores and in these terms is biased in their favor. The results underline the problem that, on the whole, Hispanic children tend to underachieve in school.

Accuracy, Reliability, and Specificity

Accuracy

Traditionally, reliability has been used as a means of evaluating the accuracy of a test, and the terms "reliability" and "accuracy" have often been used almost interchangeably. However, modern item response theory (IRT; typified by the Rasch model used in the DAS) provides a means of shifting the focus from reliability to accuracy. The DAS (and its predecessor, the BAS) is the first individually administered test battery in which IRT is used to make subtest administration more efficient and subtest scoring more accurate. Because the development of the DAS subtests is based on the Rasch model, the DAS enables accuracy rather than reliability to be our primary focus when we select tests for individual examinees and when we interpret test scores. This is illustrated in the next two sections.

Use of an Item Set Approach. Nearly all the DAS subtests employ an *item set* approach to test administration. The DAS item set approach entails administering a reasonably appropriate set of items to the examinee and obtaining an ability estimate from a table on the Record Form. This is illustrated in Figure 10.1, taken from the Sequential and Quantitative Reasoning subtest. From this table it is evident that there are a number of possible starting points (items 1, 8, 16, and 24) and a number of possible stopping points (items 15, 23, 30, or 39). Traditional basal and ceiling rules are not required (e.g., five consecutive passes for basal or five consecutive failures for ceiling). Instead, if a child obtains more than two passes and more than two failures in the set of items administered (it does not matter where those passes or failures occur), the test would normally be discontinued. The ability scores are equated across item sets, so an ability score obtained on any of the item sets may be interpreted normatively by reference to a single norm table.

In a traditional basal and ceiling approach, it is assumed that all items below basal would have been passed and all items above ceiling would have been failed. In contrast to this, the item set approach in the DAS makes no assumptions about the examinee's responses to items that were not taken. The use of an item set approach, allowing the child to move on to another task while still succeeding, is valuable when assessing students with learning disabilities. The development of poor self-esteem in such students results in a tendency to give up easily on tasks as soon as items are encountered that the student judges to be difficult or challenging.

Standard Errors of Measurement. In the DAS item set approach, every ability estimate made from raw scores on each set of items carries with it an associated standard error of measurement (*SEM*). These *SEM*s are shown in parentheses at the side of the ability estimate, as shown in Figure 10.1. Thus, for a child who obtained a raw score of 12 on items 1 to 15 in Sequential and Quantitative Reasoning, the ability estimate is 67, with a *SEM* of 7. Another child who got a raw score of 9 on items 8 to 23 would have the same ability estimate (67) but with an *SEM* of 5 points. Consider, too, the range of *SEM*s shown in Figure 10.1. Very low or very high raw scores on any item set are associated with correspondingly higher *SEM*s. Scores in the center of the raw score range carry the lowest *SEM*s. This is a function of the information contained in the item responses.

This approach lies in contrast to traditional reliability theory, in which a single *SEM* is estimated for all individuals of a given age and all scores obtained by them. Traditional *SEM*s provide an estimate of the mean error across all raw scores. We can see from IRT theory that this will tend to overestimate the *SEM* of individuals in the middle of the raw score range and underestimate the *SEM* of individuals at the extremes of the raw score range.

Reliability

A new method of estimating internal reliability was developed, based on IRT, which is described in detail in the DAS *Handbook*. Tables 10.5 and 10.6 show the mean internal reliability coefficients for each subtest in the Preschool and School-Age cognitive batteries. The mean internal reliabilities for the Achievement tests are .87 for Basic Number Skills, and .92 for both Spelling and Word Reading. For the Clusters, reliabilities range from .88 to .92 and for the GCA they are .94 (Preschool-Age) and .95 (School-Age).

Test–retest reliability values for the DAS subtests and composites were estimated for a retest interval of 2 to 6 weeks with two preschool and two school-age samples of varying age. Full results are given in the DAS *Handbook*. The test–retest results indicate that the scores are highly stable. For example, the composite test–retest reliabilities for 12- to 13-year-olds were as follows: Verbal Ability,

Sequential and Quantitative Reasoning
Raw Score to Ability Score

Raw Score	Item Set								
	1–15	1–23	1–30	8–23	8–30	8–39	16–30	16–39	24–39
0	$10_{(13)}$	$10_{(13)}$	$10_{(13)}$						
1	$13_{(11)}$	$12_{(11)}$	$12_{(11)}$	$35_{(10)}$	$35_{(10)}$	$34_{(10)}$	$45_{(11)}$	$45_{(11)}$	$66_{(11)}$
2	$21_{(8)}$	$21_{(8)}$	$20_{(8)}$	$43_{(8)}$	$42_{(8)}$	$42_{(8)}$	$54_{(8)}$	$54_{(8)}$	$75_{(8)}$
3	$27_{(7)}$	$26_{(7)}$	$26_{(7)}$	$48_{(7)}$	$47_{(7)}$	$47_{(7)}$	$60_{(7)}$	$59_{(7)}$	$81_{(7)}$
4	$32_{(7)}$	$31_{(7)}$	$31_{(7)}$	$52_{(6)}$	$51_{(6)}$	$51_{(6)}$	$64_{(7)}$	$64_{(6)}$	$86_{(7)}$
5	$37_{(7)}$	$35_{(6)}$	$35_{(6)}$	$55_{(6)}$	$54_{(5)}$	$54_{(5)}$	$68_{(6)}$	$68_{(6)}$	$90_{(6)}$
6	$41_{(7)}$	$39_{(6)}$	$38_{(6)}$	$58_{(5)}$	$57_{(5)}$	$57_{(5)}$	$72_{(6)}$	$71_{(6)}$	$94_{(6)}$
7	$45_{(6)}$	$42_{(6)}$	$42_{(6)}$	$61_{(5)}$	$60_{(5)}$	$60_{(5)}$	$75_{(6)}$	$74_{(6)}$	$98_{(6)}$
8	$49_{(6)}$	$46_{(6)}$	$45_{(6)}$	$64_{(5)}$	$62_{(5)}$	$62_{(5)}$	$79_{(6)}$	$78_{(6)}$	$102_{(6)}$
9	$53_{(6)}$	$49_{(5)}$	$48_{(5)}$	$67_{(5)}$	$65_{(5)}$	$64_{(5)}$	$82_{(6)}$	$81_{(6)}$	$106_{(6)}$
10	$58_{(6)}$	$52_{(5)}$	$51_{(5)}$	$70_{(5)}$	$67_{(5)}$	$67_{(5)}$	$86_{(6)}$	$84_{(5)}$	$110_{(7)}$
11	$62_{(7)}$	$54_{(5)}$	$54_{(5)}$	$73_{(6)}$	$69_{(5)}$	$69_{(5)}$	$90_{(6)}$	$87_{(6)}$	$114_{(7)}$
12	$67_{(7)}$	$57_{(5)}$	$56_{(5)}$	$76_{(6)}$	$72_{(5)}$	$71_{(5)}$	$94_{(7)}$	$90_{(6)}$	$119_{(7)}$
13	$72_{(8)}$	$60_{(5)}$	$59_{(5)}$	$80_{(7)}$	$74_{(5)}$	$74_{(5)}$	$100_{(8)}$	$93_{(6)}$	$124_{(8)}$
14	$81_{(11)}$	$62_{(5)}$	$61_{(5)}$	$86_{(8)}$	$77_{(5)}$	$76_{(5)}$	$108_{(11)}$	$96_{(6)}$	$131_{(9)}$
15		$65_{(5)}$	$63_{(5)}$	$94_{(11)}$	$79_{(5)}$	$78_{(5)}$		$99_{(6)}$	$142_{(12)}$
16		$67_{(5)}$	$65_{(5)}$		$82_{(5)}$	$81_{(5)}$		$103_{(6)}$	$152_{(16)}$
17		$70_{(5)}$	$68_{(5)}$		$85_{(5)}$	$83_{(5)}$		$107_{(6)}$	
18		$73_{(6)}$	$70_{(5)}$		$88_{(6)}$	$86_{(5)}$		$111_{(6)}$	
19		$77_{(6)}$	$72_{(5)}$		$91_{(6)}$	$88_{(5)}$		$115_{(7)}$	
20		$81_{(7)}$	$74_{(5)}$		$95_{(7)}$	$91_{(5)}$		$119_{(7)}$	
21		$86_{(8)}$	$77_{(5)}$		$101_{(8)}$	$94_{(5)}$		$125_{(8)}$	
22		$94_{(11)}$	$79_{(5)}$		$109_{(11)}$	$97_{(6)}$		$132_{(9)}$	
23			$82_{(5)}$			$100_{(6)}$		$142_{(12)}$	
24			$85_{(5)}$			$103_{(6)}$		$152_{(6)}$	
25			$88_{(6)}$			$107_{(6)}$			
26			$91_{(6)}$			$111_{(6)}$			
27			$96_{(7)}$			$115_{(7)}$			
28			$101_{(8)}$			$119_{(7)}$			
29			$109_{(11)}$			$125_{(8)}$			
30						$132_{(9)}$			
31						$142_{(12)}$			
32						$152_{(16)}$			

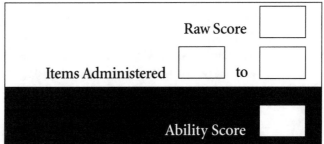

FIGURE 10.1. Equated ability estimates for various item sets in the DAS Sequential and Quantitative Reasoning subtest. From the Differential Ability Scales. Copyright © 1990 by The Psychological Corporation. Reproduced by permission. All rights reserved. *Differential Ability Scales* and *DAS* are registered trademarks of The Psychological Corporation.

.89; Nonverbal Reasoning Ability, .83; Spatial Ability, .90; Special Nonverbal Composite, .92; and GCA, .93.

Specificity

The variance of test scores can be partitioned into a number of components. As described earlier, the proportion of error variance may be estimated and is defined as the value of 1 minus the reliability of a test. The proportion of reliable variance (i.e., the reliability of the test) may itself be partitioned into two components: reliable common variance that is shared or overlapping with other tests in the battery and reliable specific variance that is not shared and does not overlap with other tests.

The proportion of common variance (often termed "communality") may be estimated by the squared multiple correlation between a subtest and all others in the battery (Kaufman, 1979; Silverstein, 1976). The proportion of specific reliable variance is usually termed the "specificity" of a test and is estimated by subtracting the communality from the reliability coefficient of the test.

McGrew and Murphy (1995) consider test specificity to be high when it is (1) .25 or more (indicating that it accounts for 25 percent or more of the total variance of the test), and (2) greater than the proportion of error variance. Tables 10.5 and 10.6 show specificities of each subtest in the Preschool and School-Age cognitive batteries. The first column in each table shows the proportion of common, or shared variance, denoted h^2, estimated by the squared multiple correlation between the specified subtest and all others in the battery. The second and third columns show the mean reliability (r_{tt}) and proportion of error variance (e), respectively. The fourth column shows the specificity (s) of each subtest. Results show every subtest in the DAS to have high specificity. All specificity values are above .25, the lowest being .30 and the highest .82. Moreover, all subtest specificities substantially exceed the proportion of error variance.

The same findings apply to the Cluster scores. For the Preschool cognitive battery, the specificities for the Verbal and Nonverbal clusters are .45 and .35, respectively. For the School-Age cognitive

TABLE 10.5. Specificity of DAS Preschool Cognitive Battery

Scale name	h^2	r_{tt}	e	s
Verbal Comprehension	0.50	0.84	0.16	0.34
Naming Vocabulary	0.44	0.78	0.22	0.34
Block Building	0.33	0.77	0.23	0.44
Picture Similarities	0.25	0.76	0.24	0.51
Pattern Construction	0.36	0.88	0.12	0.52
Copying	0.35	0.86	0.14	0.51
Early Number Concepts	0.55	0.86	0.14	0.31
Matching Letter-Like Forms	0.38	0.85	0.15	0.47
Recall of Digits	0.22	0.87	0.13	0.65
Recall of Objects—Immediate	0.10	0.71	0.29	0.61
Recognition of Pictures	0.22	0.73	0.27	0.51
Mean	0.34	0.81	0.19	0.47

Note: h^2 = Proportion of variance shared with other subtests (communality); r_{tt} = internal reliability (proportion of reliable variance); e = error variance; s = specificity (proportion of reliable specific variance).

battery, the specificities are .47 for the Verbal cluster, .39 for Nonverbal Reasoning, and .49 for Spatial Ability.

To compare the DAS with other popular cognitive batteries, precisely the same procedure was applied to the analysis of specificity in the Wechsler Preschool and Primary Scale of Intelligence—Revised (WPPSI-R; Wechsler, 1989), the Wechsler Intelligence Scale for Children—Revised (WISC-R; Wechsler, 1974), the Wechsler Intelligence Scale for Children—Third Edition (WISC-III; Wechsler, 1991), the K-ABC (Kaufman & Kaufman, 1983) at preschool and school age levels, the Kaufman Adolescent and Adult Intelligence Test (Kaufman & Kaufman, 1993) for ages 11 to 19, the SB-IV at ages 3 to 5, 7 to 11, and 12 to 17 years, and the Woodcock–Johnson Tests of Cognitive Ability—Revised (WJ-R COG; Woodcock & Johnson, 1989) at age 4 and at ages 6, 9, and 13 combined. Internal reliability coefficients and correlation matrices were obtained from the published manuals for the purpose of doing the analyses. Results are shown in Table 10.7. Those for the WJ-R COG are much the same as results reported in a similar study by McGrew and Murphy (1995). The results strongly support the conclusion that the DAS has approximately one-third more reliable specificity than the other batteries. The other batteries show remarkably similar mean specificities—all around 35% to 37% of the total variance. In comparison, the DAS mean specificities of .47 for the Preschool cognitive battery and .50 for the School-Age battery are very high. The lowest values of specificity for the DAS subtests are not much lower than the mean specificities for the other test batteries. These results show the DAS to have about one-third greater specificity than other batteries and strongly suggest that the original development goal of a battery with reliable, specific, individually interpretable subtests has been achieved.

Validity

The DAS *Handbook* contains extensive information on the validity of the instrument. This chapter presents three validity studies not published in the *Handbook*. These are (1) an independent confirmatory factor analysis of the DAS standardization data by Keith (1990), (2) joint factor analyses of the DAS and WISC-R, and (3) data on the relationship between DAS and WISC-III. Data on profiles of learning disabled (LD) students are presented later in this chapter.

TABLE 10.6. Specificity of DAS School-Age Cognitive Battery

Scale name	h^2	r_{tt}	e	s
Word Definitions	0.48	0.83	0.17	0.35
Similarities	0.49	0.79	0.21	0.30
Matrices	0.43	0.82	0.18	0.39
Sequential and Quantitative Reasoning	0.50	0.85	0.15	0.35
Recall of Designs	0.38	0.84	0.16	0.46
Pattern Construction	0.47	0.91	0.09	0.44
Recall of Digits	0.13	0.87	0.13	0.74
Recall of Objects—Immediate	0.12	0.76	0.24	0.64
Speed of Information Processing	0.09	0.91	0.09	0.82
Mean	0.34	0.84	0.26	0.50

Note: h^2 = Proportion of variance shared with other subtests (communality); r_{tt}= internal reliability (proportion of reliable variance); e = error variance; s = specificity (proportion of reliable specific variance).

TABLE 10.7. Specificity of Various Cognitive Batteries

Battery	Mean h^2	Mean e	Mean s	Range of s
DAS Pre-School	0.34	0.19	0.47	.31 to .65
DAS School-Age	0.34	0.16	0.50	.30 to .82
WPPSI-R	0.42	0.21	0.37	.24 to .47
WISC-R	0.42	0.22	0.36	.22 to .54
WISC-III	0.42	0.21	0.37	.21 to .63
K-ABC Pre-School	0.44	0.19	0.37	.23 to .53
K-ABC School-Age	0.48	0.17	0.35	.22 to .47
KAIT Ages 11-19	0.48	0.14	0.38	.29 to .47
SB-IV Ages 3-5	0.51	0.14	0.35	.22 to .45
SB-IV Ages 7-11	0.46	0.13	0.41	.23 to .55
SB-IV Ages 12-17	0.56	0.12	0.32	.15 to .42
WJ-R COG Age 4	0.53	0.12	0.35	.07 to .61
WJ-R COG Ages 6, 9, 13	0.46	0.19	0.35	.12 to .59

Note. h^2 = Proportion of variance shared with other subtests (communality); e = error variance; s = specificity (proportion of reliable specific variance).

Confirmatory Factor Analysis of the DAS

Keith (1990) reported a major study conducted independently on the DAS standardization data files. He found strong support for the invariance of measurement across ages and concluded that the constructs measured by the DAS are remarkably consistent across overlapping age levels of the test. Keith conducted confirmatory factor analyses of the hierarchical factor structure of the DAS. His final hierarchical solutions for the Preschool and School-Age levels of the cognitive battery are shown in the path diagrams in Figures 10.2 and 10.3. The figures show the subtests that contribute to Keith's factors, together with the correlations between the subtests and factors, and between the factors and second-order g. Keith called the DAS Spatial factor Nonverbal Reasoning and the Nonverbal Reasoning factor Gf. To avoid confusion in this chapter, the names of the factors have been made consistent with DAS terminology.[1] The Gf factor was almost indistinguishable from second-order g, a finding consistent with Gustafsson's research, discussed earlier.

Keith concluded that his results are quite consistent with those reported in the DAS *Handbook*, even though he approached the analyses in a very different manner. For the Preschool analysis, he found that the first-order Quantitative factor was indistinguishable from the second-order g factor, and that Early Number Concepts did not fit well in either the Verbal or Nonverbal factors. "Although Recall of Digits fit on a Quantitative/g factor with Early Number Concepts, its loading was small (.497), and thus a Quantitative composite probably is not justified. Furthermore, the extremely high loading of Early Number Concepts on the second-order g factor (.876) is consistent with the DAS author's inclusion of the subtest in the GCA" (Keith, 1990, pp. 401–402).

Joint Factor Analysis of DAS and WISC-R

Scores on the DAS and WISC-R were obtained from two samples of children ages 8–10 and 14–15 years. Means, *SD*s and selected correlations were published in the DAS *Handbook*. The data for the total group of 115 children were subsequently factor-analyzed. Stone (1992) reported a confirma-

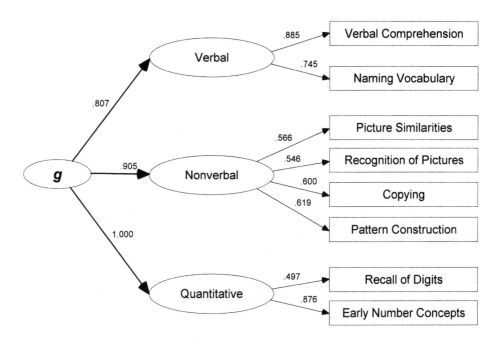

FIGURE 10.2. Hierarchical factor structure of the DAS, ages 3½ through 5 (after Keith, 1990). $\chi^2 = 30.37$, $df = 18$, Adjusted Goodness of Fit Index (*AGFI*) = .979, root mean square residual (*rms*) = .024. Original figure copyright ©1990 by the *Journal of Psychoeducational Assessment*. Modified and used by permission.

tory factor analysis, testing the fit of five models to the data. The best-fitting model was one that represented the three DAS factors (Verbal, Nonverbal Reasoning, Spatial), together with two other factors that Stone labeled Numeric Ability and Processing Speed (Stone, 1992, see Table 10.8). Interestingly, in light of Keith's findings concerning the high relationship between Gf and second-order *g*, Stone found that Factor 3: Nonverbal Reasoning (Gf) had a loading of .96 on second-order *g*, much higher than the loadings of the other first-order factors, which were: .79 (Factor 1), .70 (Factor 2), .81 (Factor 4), and .42 (Factor 5).

I have reanalyzed the data yet again, this time using exploratory principal factor analysis, with oblimin (oblique) rotation of a five-factor solution. Results are also shown in Table 10.8, within square brackets. Loadings are shown for all subtests having a loading over 0.3 on a given factor. Loadings of other subtests tend to be of zero order. The results are similar to those of Stone (1992) and indicate that (1) the first factor is a verbal or crystallized intelligence (Gc) factor, with the DAS Verbal and major WISC-R Verbal subtests all contributing; (2) the second factor is a Spatial or broad visualization (Gv) factor, with the DAS Spatial and four of the five major WISC-R Performance subtests contributing; and (3) the third factor is a Nonverbal Reasoning or fluid intelligence (Gf) factor. As Stone (1992) found, this factor is defined only by the DAS Nonverbal Reasoning subtests, and is not joined by any of the WISC-R subtests. The fourth and fifth factors are auditory short-term memory and speed of processing factors, respectively (auditory Gsm and Gs in the Horn–Cattell structure). In the exploratory factor analysis, where subtests are able to load freely on all factors, WISC-R Arithmetic had its strongest loading on the Verbal factor, and *not* on the fourth factor. This makes the interpretation of the fourth factor (auditory short-term memory) clearer.

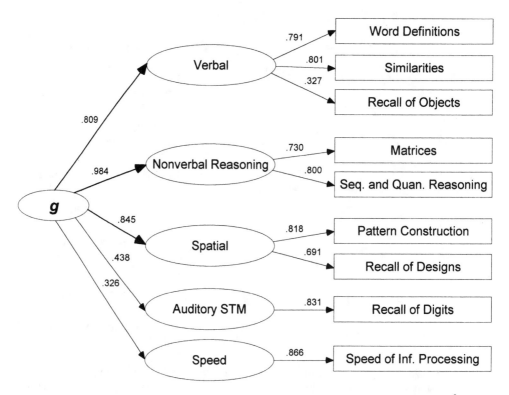

FIGURE 10.3. Hierarchical factor structure of the DAS, ages 6 through 17 (after Keith, 1990). $\chi^2 = 160.61$, $df = 24$, $AGFI = .973$, $rms = .032$. Original figure copyright ©1990 by the *Journal of Psychoeducational Assessment.* Modified and used by permission.

Relationship of DAS to WISC-III

Two limited data sources are currently available. First, the WISC-III manual (Wechsler, 1991) reports correlations between WISC-III composite scores and the DAS composite and achievement scores for a sample of 27 normal children between 7 and 14 years of age. These correlations, and the means and SDs of the composites for the two instruments, are shown in Table 10.9. There is a high correlation of .92 between the DAS GCA score and the WISC-III Full Scale IQ. From the joint factor analysis of the DAS and WISC-R, it would be expected that the DAS Verbal and Spatial clusters would have their highest correlations with WISC-III Verbal IQ and Performance IQ, respectively. This is clearly the case. The DAS Verbal cluster correlates .87 with WISC-III Verbal IQ but only .31 with Performance IQ. Conversely, the DAS Spatial cluster has a correlation of .82 with WISC-III Performance IQ but only .66 with Verbal IQ. The DAS Nonverbal Reasoning cluster has its highest correlation with WISC-III Performance IQ. The mean scores of the sample on the DAS and WISC-III are similar, which is to be expected because the batteries were normed at a similar time.

These results are supported by data from a study by Dumont, Cruse, Price, and Whelley (1996) of 53 New Hampshire children classified as learning disabled. All were given the WISC-III in 1992, and 3 years later were reevaluated with the DAS. Results showed that (1) the means for WISC-III Verbal and DAS Verbal were almost identical (89.4 and 90.5, respectively), and (2) the means for WISC-III Performance and DAS Spatial were almost identical (93.2 and 94.3, respectively). However, (3) the mean for the DAS Nonverbal Reasoning cluster (83.8) was markedly lower than the means of the other two clusters. Of the 16 students with statistically significant differences between

TABLE 10.8. Joint Factor Analysis of WISC-R and DAS: Stone's (1992) CFA Solution and Oblimin Factor Pattern[a] Showing Loadings of 0.3 or Greater ($N = 115$)

	Factors				
	1	2	3	4	5
DAS Word Definitions	.85 [.86]				
DAS Similarities	.85 [.80]				
DAS Recall of Objects	.48 [.40]				
WISC-R Information	.79 [.80]				
WISC-R Similarities	.81 [.77]				
WISC-R Arithmetic	[.37]			.65	
WISC-R Vocabulary	.93 [.87]				
WISC-R Comprehension	.74 [.70]				
DAS Recall of Designs		.63 [.60]			
DAS Pattern Construction		.85 [.77]			
WISC-R Picture Completion		.55 [.52]			
WISC-R Picture Arrangement		.37 [.28][b]			
WISC-R Block Design		.85 [.83]			
WISC-R Object Assembly		.63 [.58]			
DAS Matrices			.83 [.63]		
DAS Seq. & Quant. Reas.	[.32]		.82 [.39]		
DAS Recall of Digits				.78 [.77]	
WISC-R Digit Span				.77 [.81]	
DAS Speed of Inf. Proc.					.79 [.76]
WISC-R Coding					.55 [.56]

Note: Factor 1 = Verbal ability (Gc); Factor 2 = Spatial ability (Gv); Factor 3 = Nonverbal/Fluid Reasoning ability (Gf); Factor 4 = Auditory Short-Term Memory (Gsma); Factor 5 = Speed of Processing (Gs).
[a] Oblimin factor loadings are shown in square brackets.
[b] The highest loading for Picture Arrangement was .28 on Factor 2.

TABLE 10.9. Correlations between DAS and WISC-III Composites

DAS Composite	WISC-III Composite			DAS	
	VIQ	PIQ	FSIQ	Mean	SD
Verbal	0.87	0.31	0.71	104.1	11.2
Nonverbal Reasoning	0.58	0.78	0.81	99.8	13.3
Spatial	0.66	0.82	0.86	104.6	13.1
GCA	0.82	0.80	0.92	103.4	12.4
WISC-III Mean	105.4	104.7	105.5		
WISC-III *SD*	10.9	13.3	11.2		

Verbal and Nonverbal Reasoning cluster scores, 13 had Nonverbal Reasoning scores lower than Verbal. Of the 18 who had significant differences between Spatial and Nonverbal Reasoning cluster scores, 17 were lower on Nonverbal Reasoning. A similar finding was reported for a different sample of LD students in the DAS *Handbook*.

The relatively low scores of LD students on Nonverbal Reasoning suggests they tend to have a weakness in the integration and processing of complex information from the verbal and visual systems. Because the Wechsler scales do not have good measures of fluid reasoning (see previous section of this chapter on "Joint Factor Analysis of DAS and WISC-R," and also Carroll, 1993), they do not pick up this type of processing difficulty.

Finally, I turn to a more controversial aspect of validity. A number of critics of psychometric cognitive assessment have asserted that *treatment validity* is the acid test of an instrument's worth (Witt & Gresham, 1985; S. N. Elliott, 1990; Reschly & Grimes, 1995). According to the proponents of the concept of treatment validity, a test has treatment validity if its profile of test scores leads directly to the design of effective treatments. One of the obvious reasons why there can be no one-to-one mapping of test profiles to interventions is that two or more individuals with the same profile may have that profile for quite different reasons. With different causes, we ought to expect different treatments. Ability test profiles are designed to be helpful in reaching an understanding of a child's referred difficulties and can never provide an explanation or a prescription for intervention in themselves. These points have been ably and cogently argued elsewhere by Fagan and Bracken (1993), Keith (1994), and Kaufman (1994).

INTERPRETATION

Recommendations for Interpreting General, Broad, and Specific Cognitive Abilities

Chapters 4 and 5 in the DAS *Handbook* give detailed suggestions about cognitive processes underlying scores on the various DAS subtests and composites, and give a systematic procedure for test interpretation. The procedure is partly based on the identification of scores that are significantly high or low at the .05 probability level. This is greatly facilitated by the design of the Summary Page of the Record Form, which shows significant differences at the $p < .05$ level between achievement tests, composites and subtest scores.

Other comparisons are possible using tables in the DAS *Handbook*. In particular, the *Handbook* provides tables enabling discrepancies between observed and predicted achievement to be evaluated, as well as tables showing the frequency, or unusualness of discrepancies.

The following section of this chapter gives an overview of the strategy used in the interpretation of DAS scores, together with some basic interpretations of composite and subtest scores.

General Conceptual Ability

The GCA score, as its name suggests, is a measure of *g*. Overall, it provides a measure of complex mental processing. The GCA is a *well-saturated* measure of *g* because only those subtests that contribute best, and have the highest *g* loadings, contribute to its estimation. This is in contrast to most, if not all, other batteries, that seem to have adopted Wechsler's method of putting all subtests into the estimate.

The effect of removing such tests as Recall of Digits and other diagnostic subtests is to enhance the *g* estimates of many children with learning disabilities because it is often on such diagnostic subtests that they score low—that is the nature of their learning disability. Conversely, putting such diagnostic subtests with low *g* loadings into an overall composite tends to depress those composite scores for LD children, thereby reducing the size of discrepancies between estimates of *g* and achievement.

The general strategy for the analysis of scores on the DAS is to take the most general score, the GCA, and determine whether there are significant differences between any of the component Clusters (or their respective subtests). (*Note:* In the DAS standardization sample, 61% of children had 1 or more cluster scores that were significantly different ($p < .05$) from their GCA score.)

If there is no significant difference between the clusters, *and* if there is no significant difference between the subtests within each cluster, due weight may be given to the interpretation of the GCA score as a measure of *g*. However, *g* does not always tell the whole story about a child's cognitive abilities. There are, of course, a number of diagnostic subtests that should be administered and evaluated for significantly high or low scores. These should always be interpreted in addition to the GCA score.

If there is a significant difference between the cluster scores contributing to the GCA or the Special Nonverbal Composite, interpretive emphasis on the GCA should be reduced. Our attention then turns to the scores at the next lower level of generality—the cluster scores.

Cluster Scores

All cluster scores are highly *g* related, but they also have a good deal of specificity (see earlier section on "Specificity") to enable them to be interpreted separately and for differences between them to be evaluated.

A *Verbal Ability* cluster is found both at the upper preschool level and at the school-age level. At both age levels, its name is self-explanatory—it measures verbal ability, both receptive and expressive. It measures the same dimension as the Verbal subtests of the Wechsler scales and can also be considered to represent the Horn–Cattell crystallized intelligence (Gc) factor. In terms of the theoretical model described in the first section of this chapter, this cluster is a good measure of complex processing in the auditory–verbal information-processing system.

At the school-age level, the *Nonverbal Reasoning Ability* cluster is interpretable as a measure of fluid intelligence (Gf) in the Horn–Cattell model. Both subtests contributing to this cluster have visually presented problems, as the name of the cluster suggests. However, to solve the problems most effectively, a good deal of internalized verbal mediation is required. In terms of the theoretical model outlined in the first section of this chapter, this cluster is an excellent measure of complex integrative functioning between the two information processing systems associated with the visual and auditory modalities.

Finally, at the school-age level, the *Spatial Ability* cluster is interpretable as a measure of the Gv factor in the Horn–Cattell model; it is called broad visual perception by Carroll (1993) and visual intelligence/processing by McGrew (Chapter 9, this volume). This cluster is a good measure of complex processing in the visual information processing system. Similarly, at the Preschool level, the *Nonverbal Ability* cluster is self-explanatory—its subtests consist of measures of nonverbal reasoning, spatial ability, and fine motor ability, and as such it probably has components of both the Nonverbal Reasoning (Gf) and Spatial (Gv) Ability clusters at the school-age level. Indeed, for children ages 5 years 0 months (5:0) to 7:11, the correlations between the Preschool Nonverbal Ability cluster and the School-age Verbal, Nonverbal Reasoning, and Spatial Ability clusters are .52, .63, and .80, respectively, suggesting a somewhat higher weighting toward the spatial direction.

The strategy for the analysis of cluster scores on the DAS is similar to that for the GCA. In this case, each of the clusters is examined to determine whether their component subtests are significantly different. (*Note:* In the DAS standardization sample, 16% of children had significant differences between the two Verbal subtests, 27% between the Nonverbal Reasoning subtests, and 29%

between the Spatial subtests.) If there is a significant difference between the component subtests of a cluster, interpretive emphasis on that cluster score should be reduced. Our attention then turns to the scores at the lowest level of generality—the subtest scores.

Subtest Scores

Subtest scores are best evaluated ipsatively (i.e., in relation to the child's own pattern of scores) for significant strengths and weaknesses. In the DAS, this is done by obtaining the mean T score achieved by the child on the core subtests. All subtests are compared to this mean T score—both the core and the diagnostic subtests. Appropriate and different formulas for the significance of the difference were used to obtain statistically significant differences ($p < .05$) between each subtest T score and the mean T score on the core subtests.

The presence of significant strengths or weaknesses in subtest scores should always be interpreted at a subtest-specific level. Because the development of interpretable subtests was a primary goal of the DAS, the *Handbook* contains extensive interpretive guidelines for subtest scores. (*Note*: In the DAS standardization sample, 60% of children had one or more subtest scores that were significantly different from the mean core subtest T score, and 7% had 3 or more significantly high or low subtests.)

Studies Conducted with LD Students

The DAS, with its emphasis on cognitive processes and high subtest specificity, appears well suited to the identification of LD students. Federal regulations define a learning disability as "a disorder in one or more of the basic psychological processes involved in understanding or in using language, spoken or written" (Individuals with Disabilities Education Act [IDEA], 1991).

In practice, students are often identified as LD if they show a combination of low achievement and a severe ability–achievement discrepancy (IDEA, 1991). If these were the sole criteria for identifying LD students (without additional evidence of any psychological processing deficit), a significant proportion of LD students would have relatively flat cognitive profiles, indicating few, if any, specific strengths or weaknesses in cognitive abilities. For such students, ability–achievement discrepancies may have noncognitive causes, perhaps related to motivational or environmental factors. Mixed samples of LD students would be expected to contain one or more subgroups with flat cognitive profiles, reflecting noncognitive causative factors. This is so for each of the samples of LD students reported below.

Reading-Disabled Samples

The DAS *Handbook* reported a study in which a sample of 136 children were taken from the standardization sample. These students had the following characteristics: (1) GCA scores above 85, (2) Word Reading scores below 85, and (3) Word Reading scores at least 15 points below the score predicted from their GCA. It was known that 57 of these students were school-classified LD students, and a number of others were undoubtedly so classified.

A cluster analysis was performed on this sample using the FASTCLUS procedure (SAS Institute, 1985). Four clusters of students were identified. As expected, one of the profiles was relatively flat, this being for the largest cluster in the sample ($N = 45$). The remaining three groups had the following characteristics:

- Cluster 1 ($N = 26$): average Spatial ability, below-average Verbal and Nonverbal Reasoning ability, and particularly low scores on Recall of Digits and Speed of Information Processing, suggesting a verbal and sequential processing type of learning difficulty.

- Cluster 2 ($N = 34$): average Verbal ability, below-average Spatial ability, with particularly low scores on Speed of Information Processing and Recall of Objects, suggesting a visual processing type of learning difficulty.
- Cluster 3 ($N = 31$): below-average Verbal and above-average Spatial ability (mean difference of over 17 points between these cluster scores). Recall of Objects was particularly low, with low scores also for Recall of Digits and Speed of Information Processing, as in Cluster 1. The chief differences between Cluster 3 and Cluster 1 are that the Verbal and Spatial scores are wider apart in Cluster 3, and that Cluster 1 is high on Recall of Objects (a measure of Glr in Horn–Cattell terms) whereas Cluster 3 is low. Both groups appear to show generally weak verbal sequential information processing ability, a characteristic often found in poor readers (Goswami & Bryant, 1990).

Another study was reported by Kercher and Sandoval (1991), who compared the DAS scores of a carefully selected sample of 30 reading-disabled students with a matched control group of children from the standardization sample. Overall, the reading-disabled group had significantly lower scores ($p < .01$) on the DAS achievement tests (as expected) and also on the Recall of Objects and Recall of Digits subtests. This time, in a cluster analysis in which a three-cluster solution was obtained from the reading-disabled sample, *two* groups had relatively flat mean profiles. One of these groups ($N = 17$) had near-average mean scores on the subtests, and the other group ($N = 7$) had below-average mean scores. This illustrates one of the characteristics of cluster analysis, that it is sensitive to the elevation of scores as well as to the shape of the profile of scores.

The third cluster ($N = 6$) had average mean scores on the core subtests and much lower mean scores on the three diagnostic subtests of Speed of Information Processing, Recall of Digits, and Recall of Objects. Kercher and Sandoval's third cluster is similar to one identified as having *sequential processing problems* in a study reported by Tyler and Elliott (1988) and also by Elliott (1989), using the BAS. In that study of a sample of 121 children previously identified as dyslexic, three distinctive clusters were identified. One subgroup ($N = 30$) showed mixed linguistic and visuospatial problems. A second subgroup ($N = 39$) had low scores on Word Definitions and Recall of Designs but above-average scores on other subtests. This profile pattern suggested they had specific difficulties in retrieving holistic information. The third and largest subgroup ($N = 52$), which is similar to Kercher and Sandoval's third cluster, had average mean scores on all cognitive subtests except Speed of Information Processing, Recall of Objects (Immediate Visual Recall in the BAS), and Recall of Digits. The sequential processing problems of these children are similar in type to Boder's (1973) dysphonetic dyslexic subgroup.

A Learning-Disabled Sample

The DAS *Handbook* reported mean subtest and composite score for a total group of 110 LD students independently classified as LD by their school districts. McIntosh and Gridley (1993) reported a cluster analysis on the data, in which six clusters were identified. Four showed relatively flat cognitive profiles at high, average, below-average, and borderline mentally retarded levels. McIntosh and Gridley made the point that because of the various tests and criteria that are used for identifying LD children, it is not unlikely that many of the sample did not have learning disabilities, although needing help in school. The two remaining clusters yielded distinctive profiles. One cluster (McIntosh and Gridley's Cluster 4; $N = 17$) had a relatively low mean score on the Nonverbal Reasoning cluster and its component subtests, Matrices and Sequential and Quantitative Reasoning. This group seems to have similar characteristics to the LD sample of Dumont et al. (1995), referred to earlier in this chapter, with an apparent weakness in fluid reasoning and integrating complex information processed by the verbal and visual systems. The last cluster identified by McIntosh and Gridley

(Cluster 6; $N = 12$) was identified as a dyseidetic cluster, using Boder's (1973) term. This group had a mean Spatial cluster score 14 points below their mean Verbal score. They also scored at very low levels (an average of 2 standard deviations below the mean) on the Recall of Objects, Speed of Information Processing and Recognition of Pictures subtests, which all require processing of visual information.

The studies reviewed above provide further evidence of the ability of the DAS to identify distinctive profiles in individuals and groups of students with specific learning difficulties.

BEYOND TRADITIONAL INTELLECTUAL ASSESSMENT

This chapter has presented evidence on the advances in cognitive assessment represented by the DAS. There are various ways in which its conceptualization, its content, its technical quality, and its assessment procedures differ from traditionally developed test batteries. These are summarized in this concluding section.

Advances in Conceptualization

The DAS was conceived and designed to be radically different from other batteries. Although it is tied to theory, it is not bound or limited by a specific theory as are many modern test batteries. Because of this, its subtests, composites, and test scores can be interpreted from a number of theoretical perspectives. In its composites, the DAS recognizes the reality of second-order *g*. This is estimated only by those subtests that are the best estimators of *g*, in contrast to virtually all other cognitive batteries. The DAS does not refer to *g* by the terms "intelligence" and "IQ." They are ill-defined and commonly lead to misunderstanding and poor communication about human abilities (Elliott, 1990c).

The DAS lower-order composites reflect three major information-processing systems which are well documented in neuropsychological literature and research. These systems, concerned with verbal, visual–spatial, and integrative functions, are also well documented in research on the factor structure of abilities. Verbal, visualization (or spatial), and reasoning factors (Gc, Gv, and Gf in the Horn–Cattell structure) are the main contributors to second-order *g*, both in research and in the DAS.

The primary emphasis in developing the DAS was on subtests as interpretable measures of specific abilities. The composites were a secondary consideration (although those that were developed have theoretical and practical implications). Among the subtests, a clear distinction is made between visual and auditory memory systems, unlike the treatment of memory tasks in most other cognitive batteries. Speed of information processing, well researched in recent years as a variable underlying cognitive abilities, is also represented in the DAS. Subtests were avoided that placed a heavy emphasis on specific cultural knowledge.

Advances in Content

The DAS was deliberately designed to have separate but conormed Preschool and School-Age cognitive batteries that are developmentally appropriate for their respective age levels. The idea of finding materials that were appropriate for school-age children and adolescents, and extending these down into the preschool age range, was rejected. Also rejected was the notion of a standard format for item presentation. Materials vary considerably in content, including plenty of manipulables for younger children. Although there is so much that is new in the DAS, paradoxically it recaptures the child-centered approach and appeal of the old Stanford–Binet L-M (Terman & Merrill, 1960).

The DAS also includes a separate brief achievement battery completely conormed with the Preschool and School-Age cognitive batteries. This makes the evaluation of ability–achievement discrepancies both easy and objective.

The relative importance of purely verbal tests has been reduced in the DAS, in comparison with a battery such as the Wechsler. Apart from Recall of Digits, which is a specific measure of short-term auditory memory, there are no subtests for preschool children that are purely verbal (requiring only verbal input and an oral response). At the School-Age level, there are only two such subtests, Similarities and Word Definitions, both of them core (*g*-loaded) subtests of verbal ability. There are no tests of general knowledge, consistent with the aim of reducing culture-specific knowledge.

The number of DAS composites increases with age. At the youngest age level (2:6 to 3:5) only a GCA score may be estimated. Between 3:6 and 5:11 there are two first-order composites (Verbal and Nonverbal Ability) as well as GCA. From age 6 years and up there are three first-order composites (Verbal, Nonverbal Reasoning, and Spatial), again with the GCA and a Special Nonverbal Composite. The increase in the number of first-order composites with age is consistent with previous research to the effect that there is increasing cognitive differentiation with age (Anastasi, 1970; Keith, Cool, Novak, White, & Pottebaum, 1988).

The DAS Special Nonverbal Composite is formed from the two first-order Nonverbal Reasoning and Spatial clusters in the School-Age cognitive battery. It allows examiners additional flexibility in assessing children with limited verbal abilities, perhaps due to limited language experience, hearing impairments, or other difficulties that may have a negative effect on the administration of a verbal test. Its reliability is only marginally lower than that of the GCA, and its correlations with other tests and with achievement criteria are similar to the GCA.

Advances in Technical Quality

The DAS developers employed exceptionally careful and effective standardization and data-analytic procedures. No weighting was required to adjust the norms for lack of representativeness. The use of the Rasch IRT model enabled items to be tested for goodness of fit to the model and to be dropped if necessary. The use of the model thereby helped to produce unidimensional, focused subtests of specific abilities. The Rasch model also enabled realistic assessment to be made of the reliability of DAS subtests and composites, with emphasis on assessing the accuracy of individual scores.

The DAS subtests and cluster scores have higher specificity than those of other batteries, thus supporting their interpretation as measures of specific abilities. Extensive additional data were collected to address bias issues, and the *Handbook* provides good evidence of the lack of bias of the DAS against minorities.

Exploratory and confirmatory factor analyses of the DAS have helped to confirm the factor structure of the scales and to illuminate the relationship between the DAS, the WISC-R, and the WISC-III. The Wechsler Verbal and Performance IQs are equivalent to the DAS Verbal and Spatial Ability clusters, respectively. The DAS Nonverbal Reasoning cluster (a measure of fluid reasoning) has no parallel in the Wechsler scales.

Advances in Assessment Procedures

The item set approach to item administration makes the DAS relatively quick and more time-efficient to administer than scales that require traditional basals and ceilings. It helps with rapport because it enables subtests to be discontinued while the child is still succeeding. The DAS also contains a large number of teaching and unscored items, with modeling of correct responses. This enables children who are inexperienced or unsure of the task requirements to be encouraged to develop an appropriate "set" for the task and minimizes the number of children who fail because they do not understand the nature of the task.

Many of the children who will be evaluated using the DAS are those with learning and developmental disabilities. Out-of-level testing procedures and an extended GCA (taking the lowest GCA score down to 25) are provided for such children, with excellent test floors and ceilings. Thus, a school-age child may be assessed using the Preschool materials if these are considered by the examiner to be more developmentally appropriate.

Identifying high and low scores in the cognitive and achievement profiles is easy and objective. The design of scoring procedures on the Record Form enables statistically significantly high and low scores to be identified immediately. Thus, an examiner can have immediate knowledge of significant discrepancies between ability and achievement, between cluster scores, and between subtests. For differences between subtests, an ipsative approach is used, comparing the child's score on a given subtest with the mean of his or her scores on the core (*g*-loaded) subtests. All these discrepancy figures are provided on the Record Form, without the need for further look-ups in the manual. The *Handbook* also provides frequency information, so the examiner can evaluate the unusualness of discrepancies. The *Handbook* also contains extensive interpretive information and a framework for interpretation of each subtest and composite. Kamphaus (1993) notes that "this is an admirable characteristic of the DAS manual that is all too uncommon in intelligence test manuals" (p. 311).

Ability–achievement discrepancy analysis includes both simple differences between the GCA (or Special Nonverbal Composite) and each of the achievement tests and also differences between obtained and predicted achievement scores. In this case, predicted achievement is based on the child's GCA or Special Nonverbal Composite score.

CONCLUSION

This chapter has outlined various ways in which the DAS represents an advance in cognitive assessment. In a review of the British Ability Scales, the DAS forerunner, Embretson (1985) stated: "The BAS is an individual intelligence test with greater scope and psychometric sophistication than the major American individual tests. The test development procedures and norms are laudatory" (p. 232). In another review, Wright and Stone (1985) stated that the BAS "is a significant advance in mental measurement. . . . Its form and function are a model for contemporary test builders and a preview of the future of test construction" (p. 232). The future, in the form of the DAS, has now arrived! Kamphaus (1993), in summarizing his account of the battery, wrote: "There is every indication that the developers of the DAS erred in the direction of quality at every turn. The manual is extraordinarily thorough, the psychometric properties are strong, and the test materials are of high quality" (pp. 320–321). Sound theory, technical sophistication, and high-quality norms all characterize the DAS and are essential qualities in a good cognitive assessment instrument. Perhaps even more important, the DAS is also engaging for children and time-efficient for the examiner and yields a range of subtest and composite scores that are reliable, interpretable, and relevant to children's learning and development.

NOTE

1. Keith accepts that the DAS Verbal, Nonverbal Reasoning, and Spatial factors are good measures of Gc, Gf, and Gv, respectively, so there is no difference between us in our interpretation of the nature of the factors.

REFERENCES

Anastasi, A. (1970). On the formation of psychological traits. *American Psychologist, 25,* 899–910.

Boder, E. (1973). Developmental dyslexia: A diagnostic approach based on three atypical reading-spelling patterns. *Developmental Medicine and Child Neurology, 15,* 663–687.

Carroll, J. B. (1993). *Human cognitive abilities: A survey of factor-analytic studies.* New York: Cambridge University Press.

Dumont, R. P., Cruse, C. L., Price, L., & Whelley, P. (1996). The relationship between the Differential Ability Scales (DAS) and the Wechsler Intelligence Scale for Children, Third Edition (WISC-III) for students with learning disabilities. *Psychology in the Schools* (in press).

Elliott, C. D. (1983a). *The British Ability Scales. Manual 1: Introductory Handbook.* Windsor, England: NFER-Nelson.

Elliott, C. D. (1983b). *The British Ability Scales. Manual 2: Technical Handbook.* Windsor, England: NFER-Nelson.

Elliott, C. D. (1989). Cognitive profiles of learning disabled children. *British Journal of Developmental Psychology, 7,* 171–178.

Elliott, C. D. (1990a). *Differential Ability Scales.* San Antonio, TX: Psychological Corporation.

Elliott, C. D. (1990b). *Differential Ability Scales: Introductory and Technical Handbook.* San Antonio, TX: Psychological Corporation.

Elliott, C. D. (1990c). The nature and structure of children's abilities: Evidence from the Differential Ability Scales. *Journal of Psychoeducational Assessment, 8,* 376–390.

Elliott, S. N. (1990). The nature and structure of the DAS: Questioning the test's organizing model and use. *Journal of Psychoeducational Assessment, 8,* 406–411.

Embretson, S. (1985). Review of the British Ability Scales. In J. V. Mitchell (Ed.), *Ninth Mental Measurements Yearbook* (pp. 231–232). Lincoln: University of Nebraska Press.

Fagan, T., & Bracken, B. A. (1993). Reaction to Naglieri's "role of intelligence assessment." *The School Psychologist, 47,* 6–7.

Goswami, U., & Bryant, P. E. (1990). *Phonological skills and learning to read.* Hillsdale, NJ: Erlbaum.

Gustafsson, J. -E. (1988). Hierarchical models of individual differences in cognitive abilities. In R. J. Sternberg (Ed.), *Advances in the psychology of human intelligence* (Vol. 4, pp. 35–71). Hillsdale, NJ: Erlbaum.

Gustafsson, J. -E. (1989). Broad and narrow abilities in research on learning and instruction. In R. Kanfer, P. L. Ackerman, & R. Cudeck (Eds.), *Abilities, motivation, and methodology: The Minnesota Symposium on Learning and Individual Differences* (pp. 203–237). Hillsdale, NJ: Erlbaum.

Härnqvist, K., Gustafsson, J. -E., Muthén, B. O., & Nelson, G. (1994). Hierarchical models of ability at individual and class levels. *Intelligence, 18,* 165–187.

Hitch, G. J., Halliday, S., Schaafstal, A. M., & Schraagen, J. M. C. (1988). Visual working memory in young children. *Memory and Cognition, 16,* 120–132.

Individuals with Disabilities Education Act, 20 U.S.C. Ch. 33 (1991). (Department of Education Regulations for IDEA, to be codified at 34 C.F.R. § 300).

Kamphaus, R. W. (1993). *Clinical assessment of children's intelligence: A handbook for professional practice.* Boston: Allyn & Bacon.

Kaufman, A. S. (1979). *Intelligent testing with the WISC-R.* New York: Wiley.

Kaufman, A. S. (1994). *Intelligent testing with the WISC-III.* New York: Wiley.

Kaufman, A. S., & Kaufman, N. L. (1983). *Kaufman Assessment Battery for Children.* Circle Pines, MN: American Guidance Service.

Kaufman, A. S., & Kaufman, N. L. (1993). *Kaufman Adolescent and Adult Intelligence Test.* Circle Pines, MN: American Guidance Service.

Keith, T. Z. (1990). Confirmatory and hierarchical confirmatory analysis of the Differential Ability Scales. *Journal of Psychoeducational Assessment, 8,* 391–405.

Keith, T. Z. (1994). Intelligence is important, intelligence is complex. *School Psychology Quarterly, 9,* 209–221.

Keith, T. Z., Cool, V. A., Novak, C. G., White, L. J., & Pottebaum, S. M. (1988). Confirmatory factor analysis of the Stanford–Binet, Fourth Edition: Testing the theory-test match. *Journal of School Psychology, 26,* 253–274.

Kercher, A. C., & Sandoval, J. (1991). Reading disability and the Differential Ability Scales. *Journal of School Psychology, 29,* 293–307.

Luria, A. R. (1973). *The working brain.* New York: Basic Books.

McCarthy, R. A., & Warrington, E. K. (1990). *Cognitive neuropsychology: An introduction.* San Diego, CA: Academic Press.

McGrew, K., & Murphy, S. (1995). Uniqueness and general factor characteristics of the Woodcock–Johnson Tests of Cognitive Ability—Revised. *Journal of School Psychology, 33,* 235–245.

McIntosh, D. E., & Gridley, B. E. (1993). Differential Ability Scales: Profiles of learning-disabled subtypes. *Psychology in the Schools, 30,* 11–24.

Reschly, D. A., & Grimes, J. P. (1995). Best practices in intellectual assessment. In A. Thomas & J. Grimes (Eds.), *Best practices in school psychology* (pp. 763–773). Washington, DC: National Association of School Psychologists.

SAS Institute, Inc. (1985). *SAS user's guide: Statistics version 5 edition.* Cary, NC: Author.

Silverstein, A. B. (1976). Variance components in the subtests of the WISC-R. *Psychological Reports, 39,* 1109–1110.

Springer, S. P., & Deutsch, G. (1989). *Left brain, right brain* (3rd ed.). New York: Freeman.

Stone, B. J. (1992). Joint confirmatory factor analyses of the DAS and WISC-R. *Journal of School Psychology, 30,* 185–195.

Terman, L. M., & Merrill, M. A. (1960). *Stanford–Binet Intelligence Scale, Form L-M.* Boston: Houghton Mifflin.

Thorndike, R. L., Hagen, E. P., & Sattler, J. M. (1986). *Technical Manual for the Stanford–Binet Intelligence Scale: Fourth Edition.* Chicago: Riverside.

Tyler, S., & Elliott, C. D. (1988). Cognitive profiles of groups of poor readers and dyslexic children on the British Ability Scales. *British Journal of Psychology, 79,* 493–508.

Wechsler, D. (1974). *Wechsler Intelligence Scale for Children—Revised.* San Antonio, TX: Psychological Corporation.

Wechsler, D. (1989). *Wechsler Preschool and Primary Scale of Intelligence—Revised.* San Antonio, TX: Psychological Corporation.

Wechsler, D. (1991). *Wechsler Intelligence Scale for Children—Third edition.* San Antonio, TX: Psychological Corporation.

Witt, J. C., & Gresham, F. M. (1985). Review of the Wechsler Intelligence Scale for Children—Revised. In J. V. Mitchell (Ed.), *Ninth mental measurements yearbook* (pp. 1716–1719). Lincoln: University of Nebraska Press.

Woodcock, R. W., & Johnson, M. B. (1989). *Woodcock–Johnson Psycho-Educational Battery—Revised.* Chicago: Riverside.

Wright, B. D., & Stone, M. H. (1985). Review of the British Ability Scales. In J. V. Mitchell (Ed.), *Ninth mental measurements yearbook* (pp. 232–235). Lincoln: University of Nebraska Press.

CHAPTER 11

The Kaufman Adolescent and Adult Intelligence Test

ALAN S. KAUFMAN

NADEEN L. KAUFMAN

THEORY AND STRUCTURE

The Kaufman Adolescent and Adult Intelligence Test (KAIT; Kaufman & Kaufman, 1993), a new individually administered intelligence test for people between the ages of 11 and more than 85 years, provides Fluid, Crystallized, and Composite IQs, each with a mean of 100 and standard deviation of 15. The KAIT subtests are organized according to the theoretical model of Horn and Cattell (1966, 1967; Horn, 1985, 1989). The 60-minute Core Battery of the KAIT is composed of three crystallized (Gc) and three fluid (Gf) subtests, and these six subtests are used to compute the IQs. The Expanded Battery also includes two supplementary subtests (one Gc and one Gf) and two measures of delayed recall that evaluate the individual's ability to retain information that was learned previously in the evaluation during two of the Core subtests. Both supplements, as well as the measures of delayed recall, are of special neuropsychological interest; the 90-minute Expanded Battery of the KAIT, therefore, is recommended for use in neuropsychological batteries and for evaluation of the cognitive functioning of elderly adults in general.

Piaget's and Luria's Theories

Although Horn–Cattell theory forms the foundation of the KAIT and defines the constructs presumed to be measured by the separate IQs, other theories guided the test development process, specifically the construction of the subtests. Tasks were developed from the models of Piaget's formal operations (Inhelder & Piaget, 1958; Piaget, 1972) and Luria's (1980) planning ability in an attempt to include high-level, decision-making, adult-oriented tasks. Luria's notion of planning ability (Block 3 functions), associated with the tertiary areas of the prefrontal region of the frontal lobes of the brain, involves decision making, evaluation of hypotheses, and flexibility, and "represents the highest levels of development of the mammalian brain" (Golden, 1981, p. 285).

Similarly Piaget's concept of formal operations depicts a hypotheticodeductive abstract reasoning system that has as its featured capabilities the generation and evaluation of hypotheses and the testing of propositions. The prefrontal areas of the brain associated with planning ability mature at about ages 11–12 (Golden, 1981), the same ages that characterize the onset of formal operational thought (Piaget, 1972). The convergence of the Luria and Piaget theories regarding the ability to deal with abstractions is striking, and they provided the rationale for (1) having age 11 as the lower bound of the KAIT, and (2) striving to measure decision making and abstract thinking with virtually every task tried out for possible inclusion in the KAIT. As a further means of stressing the reasoning aspect of the KAIT subtests across a broad age range that spans preadolescence to old age (when physical handicaps can interfere with problem solving), visual–motor coordination and visual–motor speed were deemphasized.

Horn–Cattell Theory

The application of developmental (Piaget) and neuropsychological (Luria) models for KAIT task construction must, nonetheless, take a back seat to Horn–Cattell theory as the guiding principle for organizing and interpreting the KAIT intelligence scales. These scales were designed to measure broader, more general and correlated versions of Gf and Gc than were identified in the seminal studies of Horn and his coworkers (e. g., Horn, Donaldson, & Engstrom, 1981), and that have been cross-validated with expanded sets of tests throughout the world (Hakstian & Cattell, 1978; Horn & Stankov, 1982; Undheim, 1987).

The "purer" versions of Gf and Gc are delineated in Horn's expanded and refined version of Horn–Cattell Gf-Gc theory that encompasses about eight abilities in all (Horn, 1989; Horn & Hofer, 1992; see Horn & Noll, Chapter 4, this volume). The refined theory forms the basis for the seven-scale Woodcock–Johnson—Revised Tests of Cognitive Ability (WJ-R COG; Woodcock & Mather, 1989; see Woodcock, Chapter 12, this volume). However, pure tests of many specific abilities were deliberately avoided in the development of the KAIT subtests and scales. The Gc subtests include aspects of Gf, for example, because the aim in producing this clinical tool was to provide a measure of crystallized knowledge that would tap the abstract skills of Piagetian formal operations. Similarly, research results (e. g., Horn et al., 1981) indicate a distinction between the memory processes of short-term apprehension and retrieval (SAR) and the Gf construct. Both Gf and SAR decline with age and brain damage, and are called "vulnerable" abilities by Horn (1985). It is useful clinically to assess SAR as an aspect of Gf reasoning tasks, rather than in isolation, because pure measures of SAR (such as repeating digits forward) tend to assess simple—not complex—cognitive processes.

In constructing the KAIT, we followed the clinical teachings of Wechsler (1958) regarding the need to use complex tests to measure the complexities of adult intelligence and the desirability of measuring intellect across a diverse set of tasks that are grouped into a small number of clinically meaningful scales (two each for the KAIT and Wechsler tests) rather than into many specific scales.

These broad measures of Gc and Gf are defined as follows for the KAIT (Kaufman & Kaufman, 1993):

- Gc "measures acquisition of facts and problem solving ability using stimuli that are dependent on formal schooling, cultural experiences, and verbal conceptual development" (p. 7).
- Gf "measures a person's adaptability and flexibility when faced with new problems, using both verbal and nonverbal stimuli" (p. 7).

As we elaborate in a later section, these constructs are not the same as Wechsler's (1974, 1981, 1991) verbal–nonverbal split. In particular, the Gf scale is not the same as Wechsler's Performance Scale; KAIT Gf subtests stress reasoning rather than visual-spatial ability, include verbal comprehension or expression as key aspects of some tasks, and minimize the role played by visual–motor speed for correct responding.

Description of the Subtests

The 10 subtests that compose the KAIT Expanded Battery are described here, along with an eleventh, supplementary subtest (Mental Status). The number preceding each subtest indicates the order in which it is administered. Subtests 1–6 constitute the Core Battery; subtests 1–10 comprise the Expanded Battery. Each subtest except the supplementary Mental Status task yields age-based scaled scores with a mean of 10 and standard deviation of 3.

Crystallized Scale

1. *Definitions*—Figuring out a word based both on the configuration of the word (it is presented with some of its letters missing) and on a clue about its meaning (e. g., "It's awfully old. What word goes here?" ("_ N T _ Q _ _" Answer: ANTIQUE). In addition to measuring Gc, Definitions probably brings in Gf reasoning (Kaufman & Kaufman, 1993, Table 8.8).

4. *Auditory Comprehension*—Listening to a recording of a news story and then answering literal and inferential questions about the story. This subtest involves SAR to a considerable extent, as well as Gc.

6. *Double Meanings*—Studying two sets of word clues, and then thinking of a word with two different meanings that relates closely to both sets of clues (e.g., "BAT" goes with "animal and vampire" and also with "baseball and stick"). This subtest has a Gf component in addition to Gc, especially at ages 11–19 (Kaufman & Kaufman, 1993, Table 8.8).

10. *Famous Faces*—(Alternate)—Naming people of current or historical fame, based on their photographs and a verbal clue about them (e.g., pictures of Lucille Ball and Bob Hope are shown; the person is asked to "name either one of these comedians"). As an alternate subtest, Famous Faces is not included in the computation of Crystallized IQ.

Fluid Scale

2. *Rebus Learning*—Learning the word or concept associated with numerous rebus drawings, and then "reading" phrases and sentences composed of these rebuses. In addition to measuring Gf, this task has a Gc component, particularly at ages 35 and above.

3. *Logical Steps*—Attending to logical premises presented both visually and aurally, and then responding to a question by making use of the logical premises (e.g., "Here is a staircase with seven steps. Bob is always one step above Ann. Bob is on step 6. What step is Ann on?"). This verbal test is a strong measure of Gf across the age range (overall loading of .66). It involves Gc only to a small extent (overall loading of .13) (Kaufman & Kaufman, 1993, Table 8.8). The result is quite consistent with the findings of Horn and his colleagues for common word analogies.

5. *Mystery Codes*—Studying the identifying codes associated with a set of pictorial stimuli, and then systematically figuring out the code for a novel pictorial stimulus by using deductive reasoning. Harder items are highly speeded to assess speed of planning ability, so the test involves Gs (Broad Speediness) as well as Gf.

9. *Memory for Block Designs*—(Alternate for Fluid Scale)—Studying a printed abstract design that was exposed briefly, and then copying the design from memory using six cubes and a formboard. In addition to Gf, this task requires SAR and Broad Visualization (Gv). It does

not, however, contribute to Fluid IQ because of its status as an alternate subtest. Although it involves coordination for success, and has a 45-second time limit, individuals who are working slowly but accurately are given an extra 45 seconds of response time without penalty.

Additional Subtests

    7. *Rebus Delayed Recall*—"Reading" phrases and sentences composed of rebus drawings whose meaning was taught previously during subtest 2, Rebus Learning. These items include different phrases and sentences than the ones in subtest 2, but they are composed of the same symbols that correspond to the words or concepts that were taught during that task (the symbols are not retaught). This delayed recall subtest is administered, without prior warning, about 45 minutes after Rebus Learning, following the "interference" of subtests 3 through 6.

    8. *Auditory Delayed Recall*—Answering literal and inferential questions about the mock news stories that were presented by cassette during subtest 4, Auditory Comprehension. The questions are different from the ones asked in subtest 4, but they are based on the same news stories (which are not repeated). This task is administered without any warning about 25 minutes after Auditory Comprehension. Subtests 5 through 7 serve as interference tasks.

The two delayed recall subtests provide good measurement of Long-Term Storage and Retrieval ability (TSR; Horn, 1985, 1989). TSR, also abbreviated Glr, "involves the storage of information and the fluency of retrieving it later through association" (Woodcock, 1990, p. 234). "There can be difficulties in distinguishing TSR from SAR if the measures of TSR fail to tax ability to retrieve information stored at least several minutes or, preferably, several hours or days before" (Horn, 1989, p. 83). "Such retrieval indicates consolidation, 'making sense out of information,' and depth of processing" (Horn & Hofer, 1992, pp. 68–69). The TSR tasks on the KAIT assess the degree to which individuals were able to retain in long-term storage the symbols or facts that were learned about 25 to 45 minutes earlier and their ability to retrieve that learning from storage. The two delayed learning tasks, therefore, measure retrieval of information learned during both Gc (Auditory) and Gf (Rebus) items.

    Mental Status (supplement)—Answering 10 simple questions that assess attention and orientation to the world. Questions fit into the categories of general and personal information (e.g., the person's date of birth, the name of the current U. S. President), arithmetic (e.g., counting, telling time), and reading (e.g., identifying common words such as PUSH). For the Mental Status subtest, raw scores are converted into categories (e.g., Average and Lower Extreme). Most normal adolescents and adults pass at least 9 of the 10 items, but the task has special use with individuals diagnosed as retarded, neurologically impaired, and so forth. Mental Status also serves as a screener to determine if the KAIT can be validly administered.

ADMINISTRATION AND SCORING

The KAIT is organized into an easel format. Easel 1 includes the six Core subtests; Easel 2 includes the additional four subtests from the Expanded Battery plus Mental Status. Directions for administration and scoring appear on the easel pages facing the examiner and/or on the Individual Test

Record. Administration is basically straightforward and scoring is objective for nearly all subtests. Some subjectivity is required for scoring occasional items on Auditory Comprehension and Auditory Delayed Recall. Sample and Teaching items are included for most subtests to ensure that examinees understand what is expected of them for each subtest. Specific wording is provided for much of the teaching to encourage uniformity, especially for a learning task such as Mystery Codes, which requires individuals to master basic concepts before they can apply these concepts to higher-level items. The latter subtest, especially, requires practice to administer correctly, whereas another learning task (Rebus Learning) requires practice to score correctly as the examinee is responding.

An administration and scoring training video for the KAIT, available from the publisher, demonstrates each subtest with "clients" who span the age range and include a variety of presenting problems (Kaufman, Kaufman, Grossman, & Grossman, 1994). The video provides administration and scoring clues and hints and highlights most of the potential administration and scoring pitfalls for new examiners.

PSYCHOMETRIC PROPERTIES

An overview of the KAIT's psychometric properties follows (see Kaufman & Kaufman, 1993, Chs. 7, 8 for details).

Standardization Sample

The KAIT normative sample, composed of exactly 2,000 adolescents and adults between the ages of 11 and 94, was stratified on the variables of gender, racial/ethnic group, geographic region, and socioeconomic status (educational attainment). For the socioeconomic variable, parents' education was used for ages 11 to 24, and self-education was used for ages 25 to 94. Gender distributions matched U. S. Census proportions for 13 age groups between 11 and 75–94 years (Kaufman & Kaufman, 1993, Table 7.1). Race/ethnic proportions in the total sample are as follows (census percentages are presented following the sample percentages): white (77.4/77.4); African American (12.0/12.1); Hispanic (7.0/7.6); and "other" (3.6/2.9) (Kaufman & Kaufman, 1993, Table 7.4). The matches between the census and sample were close for the educational attainment variable for the total sample and for separate race/ethnic groups (Kaufman & Kaufman, 1993, Tables 7.3 & 7.5). The geographic region matches were close for the North Central and South regions, but the sample was underrepresented in the Northeast and overrepresented in the West (Kaufman & Kaufman, 1993, Table 7.2).

Reliability

Mean split-half reliability coefficients for the total normative sample were .95 for Crystallized IQ, .95 for Fluid IQ, and .97 for Composite IQ (Kaufman & Kaufman, 1993, Table 8.1). Mean test–retest reliability coefficients, based on 153 identified normal individuals in three age groups (11–19, 20–54, 55–85+), retested after a 1-month interval, were .94 for Crystallized IQ, .87 for Fluid IQ, and .94 for Composite IQ (Kaufman & Kaufman, 1993, Table 8.2). Mean subtest split-half reliabilities for the four Gc subtests ranged from .89 for Auditory Comprehension and Double Meanings to .92 for Famous Faces (median = .90). Mean values for the four Gf subtests ranged from .79 for Memory for Block Designs to .93 for Rebus Learning (median = .88) (Kaufman & Kaufman, 1993, Table 8.1). Median test–retest reliabilities for the eight subtests, based $N = 153$, ranged from .72 on Mystery Codes to .95 on Definitions (median = .78).

Validity

Factor analysis, both exploratory and confirmatory, gave strong construct validity support for the Fluid and Crystallized Scales and for the placement of each subtest on its designated scale. This support was provided for six age groups ranging from 11–14 to 70–94 years and for a mixed clinical sample. Crystallized IQs correlated .72 with Fluid IQs for the total normative group of 2,000 (Kaufman & Kaufman, 1993, Table 8.4), suggesting that rotational procedures that allow correlated factors is likely to offer the most accurate depiction of the factor structure. Therefore, Gc and Gf loadings from the oblimin (oblique) factor solution for the total standardization sample are shown in Table 11.1 as an overview of the KAIT's factor structure (Kaufman & Kaufman, 1993, Table 8.8).

Two-factor solutions corresponding to distinct Gc and Gf factors were also identified for separate groups of whites, African Americans, and Hispanics included in the standardization sample (Kaufman, Kaufman, & McLean, 1995) and for males and females within these three race/ethnic groups (Gonzalez, Adir, Kaufman, & McLean, 1995). Coefficients of congruence that were typically well above .90 for the diverse race/gender groups gave additional differential construct validity support for the Crystallized and Fluid Scales of the KAIT. Despite the factorial invariance, significant race/ethnic differences were observed, even when educational attainment was controlled: Whites scored higher than African Americans and Hispanics on most Gf and Gc variables; Hispanics outscored African Americans on Gf subtests (Kaufman, McLean, & Kaufman, 1995; Kaufman, McLean, Kaufman, & Kaufman, 1994).

KAIT Composite IQ correlated .83 to .88 with the Wechsler Adult Intelligence Scale—Revised (WAIS-R; Wechsler, 1981) Full Scale IQ for four samples of predominantly normal individuals from the ages of 16–19 to 50–83 (total N = 343); .83 with WAIS-R Full Scale IQ for 43 clinical cases (most of whom had right or left brain damage); .82 with the Wechsler Intelligence Scale Scale for Children—Revised (WISC-R; Wechsler, 1974) Full Scale IQ for 118 predominantly normal 11–16-year-olds; .66 with Kaufman Assessment Battery for Children (K-ABC; Kaufman & Kaufman, 1983) Mental Processing Composite and .82 with K-ABC Achievement for 124 predominantly normal children ages 11–12; and .87 with Stanford–Binet Intelligence Scale: Fourth Edition (Thorndike, Hagen, & Sattler, 1986) Test Composite for 79 predominantly normal individuals ages 11–42 (Kaufman & Kaufman, 1993, Ch. 8).

For these same samples, KAIT Fluid IQ and Crystallized IQ also correlated substantially (and about equally well) with the various global scores, typically correlating in the mid-.70s to low .80s. These values support the construct and criterion-related validity of the three KAIT IQs.

TABLE 11.1. Oblimin Factor Loadings of KAIT subtests on the Gc and Gf Factors

KAIT subtest	Gc	Gf
Crystallized Scale		
Definitions	**.80**	*.07*
Auditory Comprehension	**.69**	*.15*
Double Meanings	**.69**	*.16*
Famous Faces	**.84**	*−.11*
Fluid Scale		
Rebus Learning	*.23*	**.55**
Logical Steps	*.13*	**.66**
Mystery Codes	*.05*	**.71**
Memory for Block Designs	*−.09*	**.76**

Note. Loadings of .50 or greater are shown in bold.

INTERPRETATION

There is no clear dividing point between evidence of a test's validity and a description of how to interpret the scores yielded by the test. The sections that follow reflect aspects of the KAIT's validity but are included in this section on test interpretation because the obtained data are especially germane to the understanding of what the KAIT measures across its broad age range. Topics covered are (1) age-related differences, (2) clinical applications, and (3) relationship to Wechsler's verbal–nonverbal dichotomy.

Age-Related Differences

Additional construct validity support for the KAIT variables comes from studies of age differences on the tasks and IQs across the broad age range from adolescence through old age (Kaufman & Horn, 1996; Kaufman & Kaufman, 1993, Ch. 8). To investigate these differences, an "all-adult" norms sample was developed composed of the 1,500 individuals ages 17 to 94 from the normative sample. By combining all adults into a single sample, and controlling for education, it was possible to infer differences in Gc and Gf ability at different age groups from 17–19 to 75–94. The degree to which the age curves conform to the well-validated curves for the Gc and Gf constructs (Horn, 1985, 1989; Horn & Hofer, 1992) is the degree to which the aging data serve as support for the KAIT's construct validity. With a wide diversity of tasks, Gc abilities have shown small increases or maintenance across the lifespan through late middle age (often into the 60s) before declining slightly in old age; Gf abilities peak in late adolescence or early adulthood before dropping steadily throughout the lifespan.

Table 11.2 presents KAIT data for separate groups of males and females across the adult age range (Kaufman & Horn, 1996). These data support the construct validity of the two IQ scales, and also the validity of each separate Gc and Gf subtest. The results conform generally to the results of many previous investigations, including analyses of Wechsler's adult scales (Horn & Hofer, 1992; Kaufman, 1990, Ch. 7). Gc abilities increased or maintained through the 50s and did not drop precipitously until ages 75 and older. Gf abilities peaked in the early 20s, plateaued from the mid-20s

TABLE 11.2 Education-Adjusted Mean KAIT Crystallized IQs and Fluid IQs for Males ($N = 716$) and Females ($N = 784$) at Nine Age Groups

Age group	Crystallized IQ		Fluid IQ	
	Females	Males	Females	Males
17–19	99	98	108	106
20–24	102	103	110	110
25–29	98	105	101	107
30–34	100	102	101	103
35–44	102	101	100	101
45–54	103	102	102	102
55–64	100	98	95	96
65–74	98	95	91	92
75–94	91	88	86	83

Note. Means are derived from a special norms group composed of all individuals in the standardization sample ages 17 to 94. Data "Age Changes on Tests of Fluid and Crystallized Ability for Females and Males on the KAIT at Ages 17 to 94 Years," by A. S. Kaufman and J. L. Horn, 1996, *Archives of Clinical Neuropsychology.* Copyright © 1996 by Pergamon. Reprinted with permission.

to mid-50s, and did not drop steeply until age 55. The fact that KAIT Gc peaked in the late 40s instead of the 60s (as has been found in most of Horn's studies and in research with the WAIS and WAIS-R) may relate to the deliberate inclusion of some aspects of Gf in the Gc subtests in an attempt to measure Piaget's formal operations. The "vulnerability" of the Gf aspects of the KAIT Crystallized tasks may have accelerated the age-related decline in scores on the Gc tests. The plateau from the 20s to the 50s on KAIT Gf variables did not occur on Wechsler's Performance Scale (Kaufman, Reynolds, & McLean, 1989); Performance scaled scores declined steadily from the 20s to the 70s. The slight difference in the findings may relate to the inclusion of tests of visual–motor speed in the WAIS-R but not the KAIT. Research is needed, however, to aid in the interpretation of KAIT performance across the adult lifespan and to understand better the age-related similarities and differences that characterize the Gc and Gf constructs assessed by the KAIT, presumed to be assessed by Wechsler's Verbal and Performance Scales and measured by Horn's experimental tasks.

Clinical Applications

Clinical validity and applications of the KAIT were explored by examining the profiles obtained by several small samples of individuals with neurological impairment to the left hemisphere ($N = 18$), neurological impairment to the right hemisphere ($N = 25$), clinical depression ($N = 44$), Alzheimer's-type dementia ($N = 10$), and reading disabilities ($N = 14$). Each subsample was matched with a control group of individuals from the standardization sample on the variables of gender, race/ethnic group, age, and educational attainment (Kaufman & Kaufman, 1993, Ch. 8). The KAIT IQs and subtests discriminated effectively between the control samples and the samples of individuals with neurological impairment and Alzheimer's-type dementia. Auditory Comprehension, Famous Faces, Rebus Learning, Mental Status, and the delayed recall tasks tended to be the most discriminating subtests.

When comparing the KAIT profiles of neurologically impaired patients with right versus left hemisphere brain damage, the most discriminating subtests were Rebus Learning, Rebus Delayed Recall, Famous Faces, and Memory for Block Designs; patients with right damage scored higher on the first three tasks and lower on the block-design subtest. Most of the noteworthy differences in the clinical validity studies were on the subtests that are excluded from the Core Battery but are administered as part of the Expanded Battery. That result supports our contention that the Expanded Battery should prove especially useful for neuropsychological assessment.

The sample of patients with clinical depression, most of whom were hospitalized with major depression, averaged about 102 on the three KAIT IQs, and did not differ significantly from their matched control group on any subtest (Grossman, Kaufman, Mednitsky, Scharff, & Dennis, 1994). One significant difference was noted, however, and again it involved the Expanded Battery. When evaluating the mean difference between scaled scores earned on Auditory Comprehension and Auditory Delayed Recall (a comparison of immediate and delayed memory) the discrepancy was significantly larger for the depressed than the control group. (The depressed sample performed considerably higher on the delayed than the immediate task.) Also, virtually every KAIT subtest discriminated significantly between the total group of patients with neurological impairment versus those with depression (Kaufman & Kaufman, 1993).

The good performance by depressed patients on the KAIT is contrary to some research findings that have pinpointed deficiencies by depressed individuals in memory, both primary (Gruzelier, Seymour, Wilson, Jolley, & Hirsch, 1988) and secondary (Henry, Weingartner, & Murphy, 1973); in planning and sequential abilities (Burgess, 1991); in psychomotor tasks such as Wechsler's Performance subtests (Blatt & Allison, 1968; Pernicano, 1986); and, more generally, in cognitive tests that demand sustained, effortful responding (Golinkoff & Sweeney, 1989). The KAIT subtests require good skills in planning ability and memory and clearly require effortful responding for success.

The ability of patients with depression to cope well with the demands of the various KAIT subtests, and excel on measures of delayed recall, suggests that some of the prior research may have reached premature conclusions about these patients' deficiencies—in part because of weaknesses in experimental design (such as poor control groups) and inappropriate applications of statistics (Grossman et al., 1994; Miller, Faustman, Moses, & Csernansky, 1991). That notion is given support by the results of other recent investigations of patients with depression that have shown their intact performance on the Luria–Nebraska Neuropsychological Battery (Miller et al., 1991) and on a set of tasks that differed in its cognitive complexity (Kaufman, Grossman, & Kaufman, 1994).

The one area of purported weakness that may characterize depressed individuals is the "psychomotor retardation" (Blatt & Allison, 1968) that is sometimes reflected in low Performance IQs. As noted, the KAIT minimizes visual–motor speed for responding, and only Memory for Block Designs places heavy demands on coordination. Perhaps consistent with the so-called psychomotor retardation of depressed patients is the finding that the depressed patients in Grossman et al.'s (1994) study earned their lowest KAIT scaled score on Memory for Block Designs. However, speed per se was not a weak area for depressed patients, as they performed intactly on tests that require quick mental (as opposed to motor) problem-solving speed (Grossman et al., 1994; Kaufman, Grossman, & Kaufman, 1994).

Relationship to Wechsler's Verbal–Nonverbal Dichotomy

Despite the strong relationships in the mid-.80s between the KAIT Composite IQ and Wechsler's Full Scale IQ, reflecting a 70–75% overlap in their measures of global intelligence, the separate scales of the KAIT do not measure the same abilities as Wechsler's separate scales. The KAIT Crystallized IQ seems to measure the same ability as Wechsler's Verbal IQ, but KAIT Fluid IQ does not correspond very well to Wechsler's Performance IQ. These relationships are demonstrated by correlational and factor analysis. Coefficients of correlation between KAIT Crystallized IQ and Wechsler's V-IQ and P-IQ were .81 and .64, respectively, for 461 people ages 11 to 83 tested on either the WISC-R or WAIS-R; corresponding values for KAIT Fluid IQ were .71 and .70 (Kaufman & Kaufman, 1993, Table 8.21).

Crystallized IQ is closely related to V-IQ, but only moderately related to P-IQ. Fluid IQ relates about equally well to both IQs, which is sensible in view of the goal to measure fluid intelligence with both verbal and nonverbal stimuli and to avoid undue emphasis on visual–spatial ability. The KAIT Fluid Scale includes subtests that depend heavily on verbal comprehension (Logical Steps), verbal expression (Rebus Learning), and verbal mediation (Mystery Codes). Each KAIT Gf task stresses reasoning rather than visualization or coordination, producing a scale that seems distinct from Wechsler's Performance Scale. This distinction is made clearer by the results of joint factor analysis, based on essentially the same samples described previously.

Joint analyses of the WISC-R and KAIT ($N = 118$) and of the WAIS-R and KAIT ($N = 338$) each produced three interpretable factors based both on exploratory and confirmatory procedures (Kaufman & Kaufman, 1993, Tables 8.9–8.12). Factor loadings for the three factors identified in the oblimin (oblique rotation) solutions in each analysis are summarized in Table 11.3 (KAIT/WISC-R) and Table 11.4 (KAIT/WAIS-R).

The KAIT Crystallized and Wechsler Verbal Scales are measures of the same factor, but the KAIT Fluid Scale and Wechsler Performance Scale measure distinct abilities for adolescents and adults across a wide age span. The only Wechsler subtest that loads meaningfully on the Fluid factor is WISC-R Arithmetic, which emphasizes reasoning and is considered by Horn (1989) to have a Gf component. The only KAIT Fluid task to load on the Perceptual Organization factor is Memory for Block Designs, in the KAIT/WISC-R analysis. Whereas this meaningful loading is sensible in view of the visual–spatial and coordination aspects of this alternate Fluid subtest, it is nonetheless notable

TABLE 11.3. Oblimin Factor Loadings of KAIT and WISC-R Subtests on the Three Factors that Emerged in a Joint Analysis for 118 Individuals Ages 11–16

Crystallized/verbal	Fluid	Perceptual organization
K—Famous Faces (.78)	K—Mystery Codes (.88)	W —Object Assembly (.80)
W—Vocabulary (.75)	K—Rebus Learning (.64)	W—Block Design (.79)
W—Information (.62)	K—Logical Steps (.60)	W—Picture Completion (.43)
K—Aud. Comp. (.51)	W—Arithmetic (.59)	K—Mem. Block Designs (.41)
W—Similarities (.50)	K—Mem. Block Designs (.51)	W—Picture Arrange. (.36)
K—Definitions (.47)	K—Double Meanings (.48)	
K—Double Meanings (.47)	K—Definitions (.45)	
W—Comprehension (.46)		

Note. K = KAIT; W = WISC-R.

that Memory for Block Designs (1) loaded higher on the Fluid than Perceptual factor in the WISC-R analysis, and (2) had the highest Fluid loading in the WAIS-R analysis (loading negligibly on the Perceptual dimension).

For years, Wechsler's Verbal tests have been regarded as measures of Gc by most who have evaluated the evidence, and his Performance subtests have been regarded as measures of Gf (e. g., Dixon, Kramer, & Baltes, 1985; Horn, 1972; Matarazzo, 1972). More recently, that one-to-one association has been challenged, especially the correspondence between P-IQ and Gf. Horn still considers most Performance subtests to be markers for Gf but concedes that they also may have a broad visualization (Gv) component (Horn & Hofer, 1992).

Woodcock (1990) factor-analyzed a diversity of data sets that encompassed several cognitive test batteries, and reached a more extreme conclusion—that Wechsler's Performance subtests measure only Gv, and not Gf at all. He argues that P-IQ reflects the visualization skill required for gestalt closure and mind's-eye rotations but does not measure fluid reasoning. In a joint confirmatory analysis of the WISC-R and Differential Ability Scales (DAS; Elliott, 1990, see Elliott, Chapter 10, this volume), Stone (1992) observed that the WISC-R Performance subtests loaded on a factor with the DAS Spatial subtests (akin to Gv) and *not* with the Nonverbal Reasoning subtests (akin to Gf). These studies, along with the similar results of the KAIT analyses, may offer some support to Woodcock's contention that P-IQ is a measure of Gv that is devoid of a fluid component. Gv has many features of what is described as intelligence but it is distinctly different from Gf and Gc, and has relationships with age that are different from those for Gf and Gc. Further, it is difficult to define distinct measures of Gv and Gf; the distinction between the two is often not well drawn in research, and the difficulty in making this distinction has been recognized from the outset of research on Gf-Gc theory (Horn & Stankov, 1982; Humphreys, 1967).

The most likely explanation of what Wechsler's Perceptual Organization factor measures is a blend of Gf and Gv (Horn, personal communication, 1993), not the pure Gv that Woodcock (1990) contends. Some empirical support for the Gf/Gv interpretation is provided by the results of a joint factor analysis of the KAIT and K-ABC, which produced a Gv dimension that was separate from the Perceptual Organization factor (Kaufman, 1993); additional support for the Gf/Gv interpretation of P-IQ is provided by the results of another joint analysis involving the KAIT, WAIS-R, and other subtests (Kaufman, Ishikuma, & Kaufman, 1994); see A. S. Kaufman, 1994, pp. 50–51 and 167–180, for an in-depth discussion of this issue).

The most salient point for the present discussion is that the ability measured by the KAIT Fluid

TABLE 11.4. Oblimin Factor Loadings of KAIT and WAIS-R Subtests on the Three Factors that Emerged in a Joint Analysis for 336 Individuals Ages 16–83

Crystallized/verbal	Fluid	Perceptual organization
W—Vocabulary (.91)	K—Mem. Block Designs (.62)	W—Object Assembly (.80)
W—Information (.89)	K—Rebus Learning (.60)	W—Block Design (.76)
W—Comprehension (.78)	K—Logical Steps (.57)	W—Digit Symbol (.60)
K—Aud. Comp. (.69)	K—Mystery Codes (.56)	W—Picture Arrange. (.57)
K—Famous Faces (.69)	K—Double Meanings (.47)	W—Picture Completion (.49)
K—Definitions (.65)		
W—Similarities (.59)		
W—Arithmetic (.47)		
K—Double Meanings (.46)		

Note. K = KAIT; W = WAIS-R.

Scale is different from the ability measured by Wechsler's Performance IQ. Therefore, the KAIT Crystallized—Fluid dichotomy reflects a distinction that is different from the verbal–nonverbal split studied for years in countless investigations of normal and abnormal samples on Wechsler's various scales (Kaufman, 1979, 1990, 1994; Matarazzo, 1972). The KAIT Fluid Scale, with its emphasis on formal operational thought and abstract planning ability, seems to measure the fluid reasoning that is the defining element of Horn's Gf factor. In that respect, the KAIT factor is closely similar to the Nonverbal Reasoning tasks on the DAS and the Fluid Reasoning subtests on the WJ-R COG. As noted earlier, however, the KAIT Gf Scale was developed as a clinical scale, and is deliberately broader than the more pure measures of Gf that have been developed by Horn and his colleagues or that are included in the WJ-R COG and DAS.

BEYOND TRADITIONAL INTELLECTUAL ASSESSMENT

When speaking of traditional assessment, one is really speaking about assessment with Wechsler's scales. Moreover, as true as that maxim is for children's assessment, it is even more valid for adolescents and adults, the age range covered by the KAIT. For children, Wechsler's scales have always had competition of a sort from the various Binet tests and from a variety of tests for preschool and school-age children that have been published since the early 1970s, such as the McCarthy Scales of Children's Abilities (McCarthy, 1972), K-ABC, Woodcock–Johnson (WJ; Woodcock & Johnson, 1977), and WJ-R COG. For ages 16 or 17 and older, however, the WAIS-R and its ancestors have reigned supreme for more than a half century. Although the WJ (and now its revision) has provided well-normed assessment of the entire age range from preschool to old age, clinicians have not seemed to notice the potential value of the WJ/WJ-R COG cognitive battery for the adult age range. Therefore, when discussing the KAIT's contributions beyond traditional assessment, we have interpreted that to mean "beyond Wechsler assessment." In some instances, these contributions are not unique in the sense that other tests, most notably the WJ-R (which is also normed through old age), may also provide similar contributions.

Regarding the perceived benefits of the KAIT, one consideration applies to any new test: The Wechsler scales have the advantage of more than a half century of educational, clinical, and neuropsychological research conducted with a diversity of normal and abnormal samples, and a new test requires a solid research base to help establish an intuitive understanding of its presumed constructs. That research base has just begun with the KAIT, and the viability of the instrument is dependent, in large part, on a continuation of novel research investigations such as the study of the relationship of evoked potentials to the KAIT Gf and Gc constructs (J. Kaufman, 1995).

With the caveat about the need for broad-based research support in mind, as well as the similar need for examiners to gain clinical experience with the subtests, the main facets of the KAIT that expand assessment beyond the traditional scope are delineated in the sections that follow.

Provides Alternate to Verbal-Nonverbal Approach

The fact that the KAIT offers a different and potentially more valuable split than the verbal–nonverbal dichotomy was discussed earlier. The Gc-Gf distinction on the KAIT seems to measure a difference in human abilities that has been widely validated by Horn and his colleagues, and that relates to a person's skill at solving problems that are rooted in education and acculturation versus solving novel problems. This Horn distinction bears an important relationship to how individuals learn best, and how much they may have benefited or been handicapped by their cultural environments and formal education experiences. Research is needed to determine how remediation might be implemented to take advantage of each individual's problem-solving strengths while compensating for problem-solving weaknesses. The *content*-based distinction between verbal and nonverbal stimuli, as opposed to *process*-based abilities, does not have the theoretical validation support that is enjoyed by Horn's Gf and Gc constructs. Related to this issue is the degree to which the KAIT versus Wechsler constructs correspond to unitary dimensions. Both of Wechsler's separate scales include maverick subtests that bear little conceptual and empirical relationships to the factorial representation of the scale (Arithmetic and Digit Span on Verbal; Coding/Digit Symbol on Performance). As indicated previously, the KAIT includes robust Gc and Gf dimensions across the age range, without exception.

The aforementioned advantages of the KAIT regarding the theoretical meaningfulness of profile differences and the robustness of the factors are also enjoyed by the DAS and WJ-R.

Integrates Several Theoretical Approaches

The KAIT benefits from an integration of theories that unite developmental (Piaget), neuropsychological (Luria), and experimental–cognitive (Horn–Cattell) models of intellectual functioning. The theories interface well with each other, and do not compete; the Piaget and Luria approaches provided the rationale for task selection, whereas the Horn–Cattell model offered the most parsimonious explanation for the covariation among the subtests and, hence, of the resultant scale structure. Together, the theories give the KAIT a solid theoretical foundation that facilitates test interpretation across the broad 11–94-year age range on which the battery was normed.

Is Geared Specifically for Adolescent and Adult Age Range

One application of the use of the three specific theories to develop the KAIT is the fact that the end product is a test that is geared specifically for the adolescent and adult developmental level. It is not an upward extension of tests best suited to young children (which often require bonus points for speed to achieve sufficient difficulty for bright adolescents and adults). Instead, the KAIT includes adult-oriented tasks that place heavy demands on systematic, logicodeductive thinking; some tasks (most notably the mock news broadcast in Auditory Comprehension) are real-life, rather than artificial, mental tasks.

The Luria and Piaget theories deal with an aspect of human intellect whose onset at about ages

11–12 corresponds to neurological developments that occur in the prefrontal regions of the cerebral cortex and that are associated with the ability to deal with abstractions. The Horn–Cattell theory is also intimately related to adult development, as a bulk of the Gf-Gc research has been conducted to explore the differences in how these constructs rise and fall with increasing age from adolescence to old age.

By virtue of the adult orientation of the theoretical structure underlying the KAIT, it is sensible that no attempt was made to take the sequential–simultaneous theory that forms the foundation of the K-ABC and try to stretch it to adolescence and adulthood. The K-ABC extends to age $12\frac{1}{2}$, the age that marks the virtual starting point of the development of formal operations and planning ability; essentially the K-ABC was constructed for children who are within Piaget's preoperational and concrete operational stages. Not surprisingly, the constructs measured by the K-ABC and KAIT are quite different (Kaufman, 1993); just as the KAIT Fluid Scale is separate from Wechsler's Performance Scale, so too is it separate from the K-ABC Simultaneous Processing Scale.

Permits Reliable Measurement of Its Main Constructs in About an Hour

The Core Battery is composed of six subtests that yield the three IQs, each with an average reliability of .95 to .97, comparable to the values for Wechsler's scales or a bit better. In contrast to the 75 to 90 minutes that the WAIS-R requires to administer its 11 subtests (Kaufman, 1990, Chapter 4), the KAIT six-subtest Core Battery requires only about 1 hour to administer (as determined during the clinical validation of the KAIT). This savings of time without sacrificing measurement accuracy allows examiners to maximize the time spent with the client by administering additional, perhaps noncognitive, tests.

Offers Flexibility to Examiner

The inclusion of Core and Expanded Forms of the KAIT gives examiners a choice whenever they evaluate an adolescent or adult. The Core Battery is all that is needed for mandatory reevaluations when diagnostic issues are not involved, or for any type of evaluation for which possible neurological impairment or memory problems are not at issue. The 90-minute Expanded Battery has special uses for elderly clients, for anyone whose memory processes are suspect, and for individuals referred for possible neurological disorders. Like the WJ-R Standard and Supplementary Cognitive Batteries, clinicians are able to choose from two main administrative options that each have advantages depending on the purposes of the evaluation.

Provides Bridge between Intellectual and Neuropsychological Batteries

The inclusion of delayed recall subtests in the KAIT Expanded Battery, and the concomitant ability to compare statistically a person's immediate versus delayed recall of semantic information (Auditory tasks) and of verbal-coded symbols (Rebus tasks), resembles the kinds of memory functions that are tapped by subtests included in neuropsychological batteries. The supplementary Crystallized (Famous Faces) and Fluid (Memory for Block Designs) subtests both resemble tests that have rich neurological research histories, and the supplementary Mental Status task provides a well-normed alternative to the mental status exams that are routinely administered by neurologists and neuropsychologists. The KAIT Expanded Battery includes sets of tasks that resemble both conventional intelligence tests and neuropsychological batteries. Furthermore, the KAIT was conormed with two brief tests that are particularly useful for neuropsychological assessment—the Kaufman Short Neuropsychological Assessment Procedure (K-SNAP; Kaufman & Kaufman, 1994b) and the Kaufman Functional Academic Skills Test (K-FAST; Kaufman & Kaufman, 1994a). The K-SNAP measures neurological intactness and the K-FAST assesses functional reading and functional math ability (e.g., understanding the words and numbers in recipes and newspaper ads). The joint norming aids interpretation of the K-SNAP and K-FAST within the context of the Gf and Gc constructs.

The WJ-R also bridges the intellectual and neuropsychological domains by virtue of including an auditory perceptual scale among its seven cognitive scales (Auditory Processing) and by assessing immediate and long-term memory, including tests of delayed recall.

Permits Direct Evaluation of a Person's Learning Ability

Coding and Digit Symbol are often referred to as learning tasks, but they are more motor than mental and are too simplistic to be of much value as indices of learning ability. Indeed, the Wechsler scales have long been handicapped by their failure to include true learning tasks in tests that are intended to predict learning ability. The WJ-R COG and KAIT both include several subtests that assess a person's ability to learn new information and apply that information to new, more complex problems. In the KAIT, Rebus Learning, Mystery Codes, and Logical Steps all offer good assessment of a person's ability to learn new material and to apply that learning in a controlled learning situation. Because most KAIT tasks include teaching items with prescribed words to say, the KAIT tasks also enable examiners to observe individuals' ability to benefit from structured feedback. When this teaching occurs on a learning task, the examiner can obtain much clinical information about the person's learning ability.

The best example is Mystery Codes, which requires examiners to explain several initial answers, even when the person got the item right (to ensure that the person did not answer correctly by chance and to ensure that all examinees have equal amounts of instruction). A few experienced KAIT examiners have told us during KAIT workshops that they have found the administration of Mystery Codes to resemble the test–teach–test model that characterizes Feuerstein's work on dynamic assessment (see Feuerstein, Feuerstein, & Gross, Chapter 16, this volume; Lidz, Chapter 15, this volume). In addition, the focused attention and concentration that are necessary to solve the hypotheticodeductive items in tasks such as Mystery Codes and Logical Steps present special problems for children with attention-deficit disorders (ADD); clinical observations during these tasks can be quite useful for diagnosis of ADD (N. Kaufman, 1994).

Normed with Measures of Vocational Interests and Personality

Personality tests and vocational interest inventories are commonly administered with intelligence tests, but literature searches reveal few empirical investigations that explore relationships between personality/interest measures and individually administered intelligence tests. To better understand the relationships of the fluid and crystallized constructs with personality dimensions and aspects of vocational interests, and to facilitate the job of school psychologists and counselors who interpret intelligence tests alongside instruments that assess personality structure and vocational interests, virtually every person tested during the norming of the KAIT was administered self-report measures of personality and interests, usually the Myers–Briggs Typology Inventory (Myers & McCaulley, 1985), and Strong–Campbell Interest Inventory (Hansen & Campbell, 1985), respectively.

These other measures, which are noncognitive, provide alternate sources of meaningful context within which to evaluate a person's KAIT scores. Research findings on these measures and KAIT have indicated important differences among racial and cultural groups (e.g., Ford-Richards, 1992), which help make the KAIT a potentially valuable instrument for multicultural assessment. Among the research results are the following:

1. KAIT Composite IQ was significantly related to the Myers–Briggs Sensing–Intuition dimension at ages 14–94, with higher-IQ individuals tending to score at the Intuitive pole (i.e., those who perceive the world in terms of possibilities and relationships earned higher IQs than those who prefer to report observable facts through the five senses) (Kaufman, McLean, & Lincoln, in press).

2. Vocational interests were significantly related to intelligence—individuals with higher KAIT Composite IQs scored higher on Holland's Investigative and Artistic themes and on numerous Basic Interest Scales (notably Writing, Nature, Teaching, Mathematics, and Art) than did those with lower IQs (Kaufman & McLean, in press; McLean & Kaufman, 1992).

3. Individuals with High Crystallized—Low Fluid profiles earned relatively high scores on the Writing Basic Interest Scale, and individuals with low fluid ability scored low on the Mechanical Abilities scale (Kaufman & McLean, in press; McLean & Kaufman, 1992).

4. Whites and African Americans had distinctly different interest profiles (Kaufman, Ford-Richards, & McLean, in press; McLean & Kaufman, 1995), differences that have important implications for school psychologists and vocational counselors (Ford-Richards, 1992).

5. The Thinking–Feeling dimension of the Myers–Briggs produced race differences, with African Americans showing a greater preference than whites for basing judgments on "thinking" (impersonal analysis and logic) (Kaufman et al., 1992), although that race difference did not emerge at ages 11–15 (Kaufman & McLean, 1994a).

6. The interest and personality profiles of whites and Hispanics were remarkably similar, despite substantial differences in their educational attainment, and both whites and Hispanics differed markedly from African Americans in their interest and personality patterns (Kaufman, Ford-Richards, & McLean, in press; Kaufman, Kaufman, & McLean, 1993; Kaufman & McLean, 1994b).

KAIT CASE STUDY

Perhaps the best way to communicate the applicability of the KAIT for psychoeducational evaluation is to present an illustrative case study that uses the KAIT in conjunction with other instruments. The case report for "Tilden Dale," a 22-year-old male college student with learning problems who was evaluated at the clinic directed by the author (N.L.K.) from 1992 to 1994, facilitates a clinical and practical understanding of the KAIT (see also Table 11.5). The examiner was Paul W. Randolph, who completed his doctorate a few months after this evaluation. He was supervised by the author (N.L.K.). (For more information, the case report of Ira G., a 15-year-old with a specific learning disability in writing [A. S. Kaufman, 1994, pp. 371–382], presents an example of joint KAIT/WISC-III interpretation.)

Referral and Background Information

Tilden Dale, a 22-year-old college junior, referred himself to the clinic for evaluation because of concerns about a possible learning disability and the desire for remedial suggestions. He reported his frustration regarding his difficulties in Spanish class, describing himself as studying more than any other student. His problems with foreign languages have become worse this year, he said, and he believes that his memory "is not good." He said he is a slow reader and has difficulty when questioned orally in class. Past problems in college include math and chemistry, as well as his previous minor of philosophy, where he "got lost." His current area of interest is business finance. Although he reported that he did well in general education courses, he foresees difficulty in future math courses related to his major. Despite his varied concerns, Tilden indicated that he has main-

TABLE 11.5. KAIT Profile (Expanded Battery) for Tilden Dale

IQ's		90% conf.	Percentile	Subtests	Scaled score	Percentile
Crystallized	91	(86–96)	27th	Crystallized		
Fluid	100	(95–105)	50th	Definitions	12 - S	75th
Composite	95	(91–99)	37th	Auditory Comprehension	7	16th
				Double Meanings	6 - W	9th
Fluid > Crystallized ($p < .05$)				(Famous Faces)	(7)	16th
				Fluid		
Immediate vs. Delayed Recall				Rebus Learning	11	63rd
Rebus Learning (11) vs. Rebus Delayed Recall(10)—not significant				Logical Steps	12 - S	75th
				Mystery Codes	7 - W	16th
				(Memory for Block Designs)	(12)	75th
Auditory Comprehension (7) vs. Auditory Delayed Recall (3)—$p < .05$				Delayed Recall Rebus Delay	10	50th
				Auditory Delay	3	1st

tained approximately a 2.85 grade point average to date, and he identified writing as one of his specific strengths.

Tilden reported that he has five siblings, most of whom have dyslexia or some learning problems, and that his parents have wanted to have him tested for about a year. He was raised in Madison, Wisconsin, where he grew up with his biological parents and his siblings who are aged 26, 25, 19, 13, and 11. When not focusing on school, Tilden finds time to work out and kick-box.

Appearance and Behavioral Characteristics

Tilden is a brown-haired 22-year-old Caucasian adult male who presented himself in an appropriate, casually dressed manner. He was polite and friendly and spoke freely about his areas of academic difficulty. He was very serious about the evaluation, demonstrating motivation and active involvement. He had a keen sense of humor and was easy to relate to interpersonally.

On presentation of various tests, Tilden made multiple requests to have questions or directions repeated and, at times, he appeared not to be attending well or had difficulty immediately processing auditory stimuli. Further, he had problems remembering information that had previously been verbalized, and expressed the fact that he has trouble remembering details. He had trouble on memory tasks as he used circumlocutions on several occasions; he revealed much knowledge about objects and people but could not retrieve specific names. He had some difficulty changing mind-sets when the context in which he was working changed, and he had a hard time on a task that demanded flexibility (i.e., using sets of clues to identify a word with two different meanings).

Tilden was very verbal in responding to test items. In fact, he frequently used language to solve various types of problems. For example, on tasks that required him to learn new facts and integrate them, or to solve mathematical problems, he mouthed the words and numbers under his breath. When asked to repeat numbers, he used a rehearsal strategy to encode the information; it was apparent that he was compensating for memory difficulties.

Tilden was able to respond quickly when he was required to answer factual questions, whether or not he knew the correct answer. In contrast, he used time inefficiently when figuring out unfamiliar problems, although he was extremely persistent and rarely gave up, even if the task proved to be too difficult. When he could not answer questions or was confused, he would respond to these situations with a smile or laughter, acknowledging that he could not resolve the task. It was clear that he needed structure, feedback, and training to work most effectively on tasks that required him to learn new information, integrate it, and respond orally with his newly acquired learning.

The following tests were administered:

Kaufman Adolescent and Adult Intelligence Test (KAIT): Expanded Form
Woodcock–Johnson Psycho-Educational Battery Revised (WJ-R) Tests of Cognitive Ability (Six Subtests—Short-Term Memory and Auditory Processing clusters) and Tests of Achievement (Complete Battery)
Wechsler Adult Intelligence Scale—Revised (WAIS-R): Short Form (Information, Digit Span, Similarities, Picture Completion, Digit Symbol)

Test Results and Interpretation

On the KAIT, Tilden earned a Fluid IQ of 100 ± 5 (average level, 50th percentile), a Crystallized IQ of 91 ± 5 (average level, 27th percentile), and a Composite IQ of 95 ± 4 (average level, 37th percentile). His Average intelligence was also seen on a short form of the WAIS-R on which he earned an estimated Full Scale IQ of 108 ± 6 (70th percentile). All bands of error reflect 90% confidence.

On the KAIT Core Battery, Tilden performed significantly better when solving novel, non-school-related problems ("fluid" ability) than when answering questions that are aided by formal schooling and acculturation ("crystallized" ability). The 9-point difference, though significant, is not unusually large, and he performed at an average level on both types of tasks. Nonetheless, his better fluid than crystallized ability was reinforced by his performance on two supplementary KAIT subtests that were administered: He scored at the 75th percentile on a fluid test requiring him to copy abstract designs, from memory, using blocks, but only at the 16th percentile on a crystallized test (naming the famous person based on a verbal clue and a photo of the person). His better fluid than crystallized ability was displayed despite his inflexibility and inefficient use of time, described earlier.

Evaluation of Tilden's responses on the Famous Faces task indicated a long-term memory problem involving storage and/or retrieval of information; as indicated, he responded with circumlocutions on some items. Frequently, he was able to recognize and state true facts about the person (e.g., he knew that Woody Allen was "the guy accused of child molestation" and he could picture Joan of Arc burning), but he could not remember the person's name. Difficulty with long-term memory also surfaced on the KAIT on a pair of tests that required him to listen to a mock news broadcast and then answer questions about the news stories. For the first test of this type, the questions are asked immediately after the news stories are heard. For the second, or delayed, test, the questions are asked about a half hour after the news stories are heard. Tilden did not perform particularly well on the test of immediate recall (16th percentile), but he nevertheless scored significantly worse on the delayed recall task (1st percentile). In fact, he failed to answer a single question correctly on the delayed task. In contrast to his performance on these auditory memory tests, he performed at an average level (50th to 63rd percentile) on a similar immediate-delayed set of tests requiring him to learn, and later recall, the verbal meaning of numerous visual symbols.

Tilden's difficulty seems limited to long-term, rather than short-term, memory. Whereas his long-term memory for semantic material is impaired (both his secondary memory for information learned recently and his tertiary memory for information learned months or years previously), his immediate or primary memory of auditory stimuli is intact. That is, his compensatory strategies described previously seemed to work well for tests of immediate recall. He scored at the 75th percentile on a WAIS-R subtest requiring the repetition of digits forwards and backwards; he achieved the 50th percentile on the WJ-R Short-term Memory Scale (recall of sentences and words); and he scored at the 90th percentile on the WJ-R test of repeating digits backward. In addition, his ability to process auditory stimuli is good; he averaged the 78th percentile on three WJ-R auditory processing subtests. Further, he had a significant strength on a KAIT Fluid subtest that depends on the ability to process and comprehend complex verbal directions (Logical Steps). Therefore, despite the observations that Tilden needed questions and directions repeated and that he may have had difficulty processing auditory stimuli, his test scores suggest intact auditory functions.

Tilden's performance on the WJ-R Tests of Achievement ranged from average to very superior. His lowest standard score was 89 on both Humanities and Dictation (23rd percentile) and his highest was 146 on Writing Samples (99.9th percentile). The low scores reflect his long-term memory difficulties (knowledge related to art, music and literature; spelling and knowledge of rules of punctuation, capitalization, and grammar). Despite his relatively weak knowledge of the rules of writing, his exceptional performance was in the ability to demonstrate the quality of his written expression by writing responses to a variety of demands. Tilden's scores in the areas of reading and mathematics were consistently average; he earned standard scores of 99 in both Broad Reading and Broad Math. Overall, Tilden's scores on standardized achievement tests are entirely consistent with the average intelligence he evidenced on the KAIT and WAIS-R.

Because Tilden does not have discrepancies between his ability and achievement, he cannot be considered learning disabled in the conventional sense. He does have clear-cut deficits in his long-term memory capacities that impair his ability to learn and that make it more difficult for him to do well in college courses that stress memorization of facts rather than application of the course material. His memory problems, coupled with his exceptional writing skills, indicate that he is likely to perform much better on essay tests than on multiple-choice tests. He is likely to understand the material he studies but not to have mastered the small details. He will do worst in courses that require memorization of isolated facts, such as learning a foreign language.

Recommendations

Tilden's learning problems require modification of procedures for assessing his ability. He should be allowed to demonstrate his knowledge by writing short or long essays, even in courses in which the instructor only gives short-answer tests. In formulating these essay tests, the instructors should make efforts to assess understanding and application of the body of material, not just recall of specific details. If any of Tilden's remaining course requirements include courses that are primarily fact-oriented in nature, he should be permitted to take a relevant alternate course that stresses understanding. Specifically, rather than take a course in learning a foreign language he should be permitted to take a course on a foreign culture.

Tilden would also be wise to make self-accommodations to deal with his problems: (1) he should routinely use a cassette recorder in all lecture classes and listen to each recording a second time; (2) he should take notes on all material that he studies—organizing the facts in a meaningful way—and he should review these notes before exams; (3) he should choose courses and areas of study that stress understanding and application of material rather than mastery of specific facts, especially facts that are not part of a larger context; (4) rather than just reading and rereading pages, he should make up tests for himself and then write out the answers to these test questions; (5) he might do well to find a study partner to quiz him out loud and otherwise help him prepare for the memory components of his courses; and (6) when he does have a list of facts to memorize, he should break his study time up into several short segments rather than a single long period of time (e.g., he will learn new material better by studying three 20-minute periods spread out over a day instead of spending 1 straight hour studying at night).

REFERENCES

Blatt, S. J., & Allison, J. (1968) The intelligence test in personality assessment. In A. I. Rabin (Ed.), *Projective techniques in personality assessment* (pp. 421–460). New York: Springer.

Burgess, J. W. (1991). Neurocognition in acute and chronic depression: Personality disorder, major depression, and schizophrenia. *Biological Psychiatry, 30,* 305–309.

Dixon, R. A., Kramer, D. A., & Baltes, P. B. (1985). Intelligence: A life-span developmental perspective. In B. B. Wolman (Ed.), *Handbook of intelligence: Theories, measurements, and applications* (pp. 301–350). New York: Wiley.

Elliott, C. D. (1990). *Administration and scoring manual for the Differential Abilities Scale (DAS).* San Antonio, TX: Psychological Corporation.

Ford-Richards, J. M. (1992). *A comparison of the general occupational theme scores of black Americans and white Americans on the Strong Interest Inventory.* Unpublished doctoral dissertation, University of Alabama, Tuscaloosa.

Golden, C. J. (1981) The Luria–Nebraska Children's Battery: Theory and formulation. In G. W. Hynd and J. E. Obrzut (Eds.), *Neuropsychological assessment and the school-age child: Issues and procedures* (pp. 277–302). New York: Grune & Stratton.

Golinkoff, M., & Sweeney, J. A. (1989). Cognitive impairments in depression. *Journal of Affective Disorders, 17,* 105–112.

Gonzalez, J., Adir, Y., Kaufman, A. S., & McLean, J. E. (1995, February). *Race and gender differences in cognitive factors: A neuropsychological interpretation.* Paper presented at the meeting of the International Neuropsychological Society, Seattle.

Grossman, I., Kaufman, A. S., Mednitsky, S., Scharff, L., & Dennis, B. (1994). Neurocognitive abilities for a clinically depressed sample versus a matched control group of normal individuals. *Psychiatry Research, 51,* 231–244.

Gruzelier, J., Seymour, K., Wilson, L., Jolley, A., & Hirsch, S. (1988). Impairments on neuropsychologic tests of temporohippocampal and frontohippocampal functions and word fluency in remitting schizophrenia and affective disorders. *Archives of General Psychiatry, 45,* 623–629.

Hakstian, A. R., & Cattell, R. B. (1978). Higher stratum ability structure on a basis of twenty primary abilities. *Journal of Educational Psychology, 70,* 657–659.

Hansen, J. C., & Campbell, D. P. (1985). *Manual for the SVIB–SCII* (4th ed.). Stanford, CA: Stanford University Press (Distributed by Consulting Psychologists Press).

Henry, G. M., Weingartner, H., & Murphy, D. L. (1973). Influence of affective states and psychoactive drugs on verbal learning and memory. *American Journal of Psychiatry, 130,* 966–971.

Horn, J. L. (1972). State, trait, and change dimensions of intelligence. *British Journal of Educational Psychology, 42,* 159–185.

Horn, J. L. (1985). Remodeling old models of intelligence. In B. B. Wolman (Ed.), *Handbook of intelligence: Theories, measurements, and applications* (pp. 267–300). New York: Wiley.

Horn, J. L. (1989). Cognitive diversity: A framework of learning. In P. L. Ackerman, R. J. Sternberg, & R. Glaser (Eds.), *Learning and individual differences* (pp. 61–116). New York: Freeman.

Horn, J. L., & Cattell, R. B. (1966). Refinement and test of the theory of fluid and crystallized intelligence. *Journal of Educational Psychology, 57,* 253–270.

Horn, J. L., & Cattell, R. B. (1967). Age differences in fluid and crystallized intelligence. *Acta Psychologica, 26,* 107–129.

Horn, J. L., Donaldson, G., & Engstrom, R. (1981). Apprehension, memory, and fluid intelligence decline in adulthood. *Research on Aging, 3,* 33–84.

Horn, J. L., & Hofer, S. M. (1992). Major abilities and development in the adult period. In R. J. Sternberg & C. A. Berg (Eds.), *Intellectual development* (pp. 44–99). Boston: Cambridge University Press.

Horn, J. L., & Stankov, L. (1982). Auditory and visual factors of intelligence. *Intelligence, 6,* 165–185.

Humphreys, L. G. (1967). Critique of Cattell's "Theory of fluid and crystallized intelligence: A critical experiment." *Journal of Educational Psychology, 58,* 120–136.

Inhelder, B., & Piaget, J. (1958). *The growth of logical thinking from childhood to adolescence.* New York: Basic Books.

Kaufman, A. S. (1979). *Intelligent testing with the WISC-R.* New York: Wiley.

Kaufman, A. S. (1990). *Assessing adolescent and adult intelligence.* Boston: Allyn & Bacon.

Kaufman, A. S. (1993). Joint exploratory factor analysis of the Kaufman Assessment Battery for Children and the Kaufman Adolescent and Adult Intelligence Test for 11- and 12-year olds. *Journal of Clinical Child Psychology, 22,* 355–364.

Kaufman, A. S. (1994). *Intelligent testing with the WISC-III.* New York: Wiley.

Kaufman, A. S., Ford-Richards, J. M., & McLean, J. E. (in press). Black-white differences on the Strong Interest Inventory general occupational themes and basic interest scales at ages 16 to 65. *Journal of Clinical Psychology.*

Kaufman, A. S., Grossman, I., & Kaufman, N. L. (1994). Comparison of hospitalized depressed patients and matched normal controls on tests differing in their level of cognitive complexity. *Journal of Psychoeducational Assessment, 12,* 112–125.

Kaufman, A. S., & Horn, J. L. (1996). Age changes on tests of fluid and crystallized ability for females and males on the Kaufman Adolescent and Adult Intelligence Test (KAIT) at ages 17 to 94 years. *Archives of Clinical Neuropsychology, 11,* 97–121.

Kaufman, A. S., Ishikuma, T., & Kaufman, N. L. (1994). A Horn analysis of the factors measured by the WAIS-R, KAIT, and two brief tests for normal adolescents and adults. *Assessment, 1,* 353–366.

Kaufman, A. S., Kaufman, J. C., & McLean, J. E. (1995). Factor structure of the Kaufman Adolescent and Adult Intelligence Test (KAIT) for Whites, African-Americans, and Hispanics. *Educational and Psychological Measurement, 55,* 365–376.

Kaufman, A. S., & Kaufman, N. L. (1983). *K-ABC interpretive manual.* Circle Pines, MN: American Guidance Service.

Kaufman, A. S., & Kaufman, N. L. (1993). *Manual for the Kaufman Adolescent and Adult Intelligence Test (KAIT).* Circle Pines, MN: American Guidance Service.

Kaufman, A. S., & Kaufman, N. L. (1994a). *Manual for the Kaufman Functional Academic Skills Test (K-FAST).* Circle Pines, MN: American Guidance Service.

Kaufman, A. S., & Kaufman, N. L. (1994b). *Manual for the Kaufman Short Neuropsychological Assessment Procedure (K-SNAP).* Circle Pines, MN: American Guidance Service.

Kaufman, A. S., Kaufman, N. L., Grossman, D., & Grossman, I. (1994). *KAIT administration and scoring video.* Circle Pines, MN: American Guidance Service.

Kaufman, A. S., Kaufman, N. L., & McLean, J. E. (1993). Profiles of Hispanic adolescents and adults on the Myers–Briggs Typology Inventory. *Perceptual and Motor Skills, 76,* 628–630.

Kaufman, A. S., & McLean, J. E. (1994a). The relationship of the Murphy-Meisgeier Type Indicator for Children to sex, race, and fluid-crystallized intelligence on the KAIT at ages 11 to 15. *Research in the Schools, 1,* 37–47.

Kaufman, A. S., & McLean, J. E. (1994b). *Profiles of Hispanic adolescents and adults on the Holland themes and basic interest scales of the Strong Interest Inventory.* Manuscript submitted for publication.

Kaufman, A. S., & McLean, J. E. (in press). An investigation into the relationship between interest and intelligence. *Journal of Clinical Psychology.*

Kaufman, A. S., McLean, J. E., & Kaufman, J. C. (1995). The fluid and crystallized abilities of white, black, and Hispanic adolescents and adults, both with and without an education covariate. *Journal of Clinical Psychology, 51,* 637–647.

Kaufman, A. S., McLean, J. E., & Lincoln, A. (in press). The Relationship of the Myers-Briggs Type Indicator to IQ level and fluid-crystallized discrepancy on the Kaufman Adolescent and Adult Intelligence Test. *Assessment.*

Kaufman, A. S., Reynolds, C. R., & McLean, J. E. (1989). Age and WAIS-R intelligence in a national sample of adults in the 20- to 74-year age range: A cross-sectional analysis with education controlled. *Intelligence, 13,* 235–253.

Kaufman, J. C., McLean, J. E., Kaufman, A. S., & Kaufman, N. L. (1994). White-black and white-Hispanic differences on fluid and crystallized abilities by age across the 11- to 94-year range. *Psychological Reports, 75,* 1279–1288.

Kaufman, J. L. (1995). *Visual and auditory evoked brain potentials, the Hendricksons' pulse train hypothesis, and the fluid and crystallized theory of intelligence.* Unpublished doctoral dissertation, California School of Professional Psychology, San Diego.

Kaufman, N. L. (1994, September). *Behavioral and educational issues in childhood ADD: Psychoeducational assessment of ADD/ADHD.* Invited address presented at a workshop on Attention Deficit Disorder in childhood and adulthood, sponsored by the San Diego Psychiatric Society, San Diego.

Luria, A. R. (1980). *Higher cortical functions in man* (2nd ed.). New York: Basic Books.

Matarazzo, J. D. (1972). *Wechsler's measurement and appraisal of adult intelligence* (5th and enlarged ed.). New York: Oxford University Press.

McCarthy, D. (1972). *Manual for the McCarthy Scales of Children's Abilities.* San Antonio, TX: Psychological Corporation.

McLean, J. E., & Kaufman, A. S. (1992, November). *IQ level and scores on the Strong Interest Inventory.* Paper presented at the meeting of the Mid-South Educational Research Association, Knoxville, TN.

McLean, J. E., & Kaufman, A. S. (1995). The Harrington–O'Shea Career Decision-Making System (CDM) and the Kaufman Adolescent and Adult Intelligence Test (KAIT): Relationship of interest scale scores to Fluid and Crystallized IQs at ages 12 to 22 years. *Research in the Schools, 2,* 61–71.

Miller, L. S., Faustman, W. O., Moses, J. A., Jr., & Csernansky, J. G. (1991). Evaluating cognitive impairment in depression with the Luria–Nebraska Neuropsychological Battery: Severity correlates and comparisons with nonpsychiatric controls. *Psychiatry Research, 37,* 219–227.

Myers, I. B., & McCaulley, M. H. (1985). *Manual: A guide to the development and use of the Myers-Briggs Type Indicator.* Palo Alto, CA: Consulting Psychologists Press.

Pernicano, K. M. (1986). Score differences in WAIS-R scatter for schizophrenics, depressives, and personality disorders: A preliminary analysis. *Psychological Reports, 59,* 539–543.

Piaget, J. (1972). Intellectual evolution from adolescence to adulthood. *Human Development, 15,* 1–12.

Stone, B. J. (1992). Joint confirmatory factor analysis of the DAS and WISC-R. *Journal of School Psychology, 30,* 185–195.

Thorndike, R. L., Hagen, E. P., & Sattler, J. M. (1986). *Stanford–Binet Intelligence Scale: Fourth Edition.* Chicago: Riverside.

Undheim, J. O. (1987). The hierarchical organization of cognitive abilities: Restoring general intelligence through the use of linear structural relations (LISREL). *Multivariate Behavioral Research, 22,* 149–171.

Wechsler, D. (1958). *Measurement and appraisal of adult intelligence* (4th ed.). Baltimore: Williams & Wilkins.

Wechsler, D. (1974). *Manual for the Wechsler Intelligence Scale for Children—Revised.* San Antonio, TX: Psychological Corporation.

Wechsler, D. (1981). *Manual for the Wechsler Adult Intelligence Scale—Revised.* San Antonio, TX: Psychological Corporation.

Wechsler, D. (1991). *Manual for the Wechsler Intelligence Scale for Children—Third edition.* San Antonio, TX: Psychological Corporation.

Woodcock, R. W. (1990). Theoretical foundations of the WJ-R measures of cognitive ability. *Journal of Psychoeducational Assessment, 8,* 231–258.

Woodcock, R. W., & Johnson, M. B. (1977). *Woodcock–Johnson Psycho-Educational Battery.* Allen, TX: DLM/Teaching Resources.

Woodcock, R. W., & Mather, N. (1989). WJ-R Tests of Cognitive Ability—Standard and Supplemental Batteries: Examiner's Manual. In R. W. Woodcock & M. B. Johnson, *Woodcock–Johnson Psycho-Educational Battery—Revised.* Chicago: Riverside.

CHAPTER 12

The Woodcock–Johnson Tests of Cognitive Ability—Revised

⟨⟩

RICHARD W. WOODCOCK

Every tradition grows ever more venerable—the more remote is its origin, the more confused that origin is. The reverence due to it increases from generation to generation. The tradition finally becomes holy and inspires awe.

—NIETZSCHE (cited in Bartlett, 1992)

TRADITION AND VENERATION are not hallmarks of technological advancement; rather, progress evolves from the search to replace old ways with better ways. The technology of intelligence assessment should be no exception. The publication of the *Woodcock–Johnson Tests of Cognitive Ability* (WJ-COG) in 1977, and their revision in 1989 (WJ-R COG) represent a concerted effort to deviate from tradition and improve the technology of intelligence assessment.

The *Woodcock–Johnson Tests of Cognitive Ability* (Woodcock & Johnson, 1977b, 1989b) provide a wide-age-range comprehensive set of individually administered tests for measuring cognitive abilities, scholastic aptitudes, and oral language. Parallel versions of these tests have been translated/adapted into Spanish (Woodcock, 1982; Woodcock & Muñoz-Sandoval, 1996).

For independent reviews or descriptions of the Woodcock–Johnson Psycho-Educational Battery—Revised (WJ-R), see Cummings (1994), Kaufman (1990), Lee and Stefany (1994), McGhee and Buckhalt (1993), and McGrew (1994b). For a more thorough discussion about the WJ-R and its applications, see Hessler (1993), Mather (1991), Mather and Jaffe (1992), McGrew (1994a), and McGrew, Werder, and Woodcock (1991).

This chapter outlines the theoretical foundations of the 1977 and 1989 batteries and their major physical and interpretation features. The chapter draws attention to ways in which the WJ COG and WJ-R COG differ from the traditional intelligence batteries available in 1977, the publication date of the WJ COG. Individually administered intelligence batteries available in 1977 were limited essentially to three levels of the Wechsler scales (Wechsler Adult Intelligence Scale [WAIS], Wechsler Pre-School and Primary Scale of Intelligence [WPPSI], Wechsler Intelligence Scale for Children—Revised [WISC-R]; (Wechsler, 1955, 1967, 1974) and the Stanford–Binet, Form L-M, (Terman &

Merrill, 1973). Since 1977, the three Wechslers have been revised into the WAIS-R, WPPSI-R, and WISC-III, respectively, with minor changes. The Stanford–Binet also has been revised (SB-IV) (Thorndike, Hagen, & Sattler, 1986) and incorporates substantive changes from the earlier versions. A new entry into the field was the Kaufman Assessment Battery for Children (K-ABC; Kaufman & Kaufman, 1983). Since the 1989 release of the WJ-R we have seen the publication of at least two other significant intelligence batteries, the Differential Ability Scales (DAS; Elliot, 1990, Chapter 10, this volume) and the Kaufman Adolescent and Adult Intelligence Scale (KAIT; Kaufman & Kaufman, 1993, Chapter 11, this volume).

DESIGN OBJECTIVES

To meet the goal of developing a technologically advanced battery of intelligence tests, the first step was to review the existing batteries as well as concerns about their content and features. The purpose of the review was to identify aspects to be addressed and improved on with the new battery. After completing the review, seven broad design criteria for the WJ were prepared. These design criteria were retained during the revision effort that produced the 1989 WJ-R.

1. *Comprehensive content.* The new battery is to include a broader set of measures than available in any other intelligence battery. For the 1977 WJ COG, the objective was to develop tests measuring a wider variety of cognitive functions than either of the traditional batteries. The 1989 WJ-R COG formalized this objective into a model of Gf-Gc theory.
2. *Wide age range.* The battery is to provide a single set of tests usable from early childhood to the geriatric adult level.
3. *Physical convenience.* The battery is to be physically attractive and convenient for examiners to use. Tests are to be developed that measure all aspects of cognition without the use of cumbersome test materials. (The manipulatives used in many tests function as stimulus and/or response components and do not measure unique cognitive abilities.)
4. *Ease of administration.* Testing materials are to be designed with the user foremost in mind. Tests should not require examiners to make complex decisions while administering or scoring the tests. A tape player is to be used to ensure standard administration of all tests requiring auditory stimuli. Training activities, including practice exercises, are to be provided in the *Examiner's Manual.*
5. *Focused testing.* Test administration is to be focused in two ways. First, the user need only administer selected tests based on the referral question, unless a comprehensive intellectual assessment is required. Second, basal and ceiling rules are to be utilized with most tests to limit the range of items that must be administered to a given subject.
6. *Full array of interpretation options.* The interpretation plan is to include a full array of derived scores (developmental, proficiency level, and peer comparison). The most useful information for program planning is to be plotted on profiles. Further, performance may be evaluated against *either* age-based or grade-based norms.
7. *Conormed intelligence and achievement tests.* An important feature is that the norms for the cognitive tests are to be based on the same sample of subjects that provide norming data for the counterpart *Woodcock–Johnson Tests of Achievement* (WJ-ACH, WJ-R ACH) (Woodcock & Johnson, 1977a, 1989a). This allows direct comparison between the scores of cognitive ability and achievement with a degree of accuracy not possible when scores are compared from separately normed, or even equated, tests. Further, the analyses of aptitude/achievement discrepancies are to be based on true *discrepancy norms,* not estimates derived through regression.

The remainder of this chapter details the ways in which these criteria are operationalized in the WJ and WJ-R cognitive batteries.

THEORETICAL UNDERPINNINGS

At least one critic of the 1977 WJ COG berated the lack of a theoretical base for the battery (i.e., Kaufman, 1985). While designing the 1977 WJ COG, however, all major theories of intelligence extant at that time were reviewed. These included Gf-Gc theory, which I incorrectly perceived at that time to be a two-factor theory. Although Horn's research from the 1960s had been described in a book by Cattell (1971), the concept of multiple intelligences still was not well developed in the professional literature. My factor analyses of the early WJ COG data clearly indicated the presence of several common factors.

Building a model for the 1977 WJ COG, derived from some then current theory, was avoided intentionally. I felt that, *at that time,* no theory provided the model of cognitive functioning needed for a broad conceptualization of intelligence. Based on factor analyses of the WJ COG norming data and other information, a model of intelligence underlying the new cognitive battery was developed and presented in the technical manual (Woodcock, 1978, pp. 15–16). This model organized the 12 cognitive subtests into four broad functions (Discrimination–Perception, Memory–Learning, Knowledge–Comprehension, and Reasoning–Thinking) distributed along a continuum from lower to higher mental processes. This model, portrayed in Figure 12.1, is still instructive 20 years later.

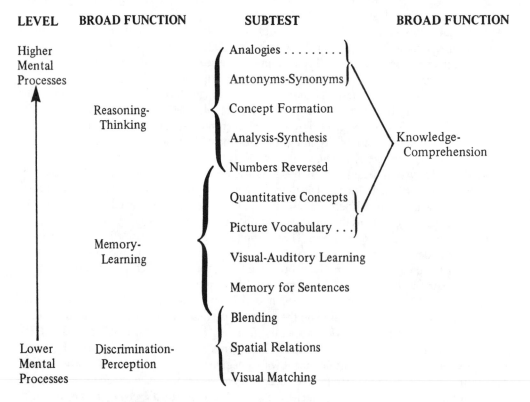

FIGURE 12.1. Theoretical model underlying the 1977 WJ-R COG.

The 1989 WJ-R COG extended the cognitive model underlying the 1977 WJ COG into an operational representation of a particular theory of intellectual processing, the Horn–Cattell Gf-Gc (fluid and crystallized abilities) theory (Horn & Noll, Chapter 4, this volume). Gf-Gc theory provides a data-based theoretical foundation for categorizing cognitive abilities. Gf-Gc theory has evolved from the statistical and logical analysis of hundreds of data sets involving many published and unpublished batteries of tests.

Working independently over many years, Carroll (1993, Chapter 7, this volume) has produced a landmark volume in which he proposes a three-stratum theory of intelligence. Carroll's stratum II is highly similar to what is described here as Gf-Gc theory.

The WJ-R COG closely models the major concepts of modern Gf-Gc theory and Carroll's stratum II. The core of the battery consists of fourteen tests with two measures falling under each of seven broad Gf-Gc abilities. Aspects of an additional Gf-Gc ability, quantitative ability, are measured by the mathematics tests included in the WJ-R ACH. These eight Gf-Gc broad abilities are described in Table 12.1. A further discussion about the composition of these broad abilities can be found in McGrew (Chapter 9, this volume).

Since the publication of the WJ-R, I have endeavored to develop more functional representations of Gf-Gc theory for assessment applications in general, and for WJ-R examiners in

TABLE 12.1. A Description of Eight Gf-Gc Broad Abilities

Gf-Gc ability	Description
Short-term memory (Gsm)	The ability to hold information in immediate awareness and then use it within a few seconds; Gsm deficits may result in difficulty in remembering just imparted instructions or information
Comprehension–knowledge (Gc)	The breadth and depth of knowledge including verbal communication, information, and reasoning when using previously learned procedures; Gc deficits are characterized by lack of information, language skills, and knowledge of procedures
Quantitative ability (Gq)	The ability to comprehend quantitative concepts and relationships and to manipulate numerical symbols; Gq deficits are reflected in difficulty with numerical tasks
Visual processing (Gv)	Spatial orientation and the ability to analyze and synthesize visual stimuli; Gv deficits may result in poor spatial orientation, misperception of object-space relationships, difficulty with art, and difficulty using maps
Auditory processing (Ga)	The ability to analyze and synthesize auditory stimuli; Ga deficits may be characterized by speech discrimination problems, poor phonological knowledge, and failure in recognizing sounds
Long-term retrieval (Glr)	The ability to store information and retrieve it later through association; Glr deficits may result in difficulty in recalling relevant information, and in learning and retrieving names
Fluid reasoning (Gf)	The ability to reason, form concepts, and solve problems that often include unfamiliar information or procedures; manifested in the reorganization, transformation, and extrapolation of information; Gf deficits may be characterized by difficulty in generalizing rules, forming concepts, and seeing implications
Processing speed (Gs)	The ability to rapidly perform automatic or very simple cognitive tasks; Gs deficits are characterized by slowness in executing easy cognitive tasks

particular. These efforts have included developing models of Gf-Gc theory that are more informative than the simple listing of abilities presented in Table 12.1.

Figure 12.2 presents a model of Gf-Gc abilities called the Gf-Gc Cognitive Performance Model (CPM; Woodcock, 1993, in press). The CPM implies that the several Gf-Gc abilities are not autonomous but fall into four functional categories. Further, the level and quality of an individual's cognitive performance results from the interaction of the four categories of ability:

1. *Short-term memory* (Gsm), sometimes called immediate awareness, involves the apprehension and almost immediate use of information. Most available tests of short-term memory measure the span of auditory awareness.

2. *Stores of acquired knowledge* (Gc, Gq, Grw). The stores of declarative and procedural knowledge are potentially available for access by short-term memory and subsequent processing. Declarative knowledge is the store of factual knowledge, including concepts, rules, and relationships. Procedural knowledge is applied in performing processes and routines. Current Gf-Gc research indicates that three psychometrically distinct stores of knowledge may exist—comprehension–knowledge (Gc), quantitative ability (Gq), and a

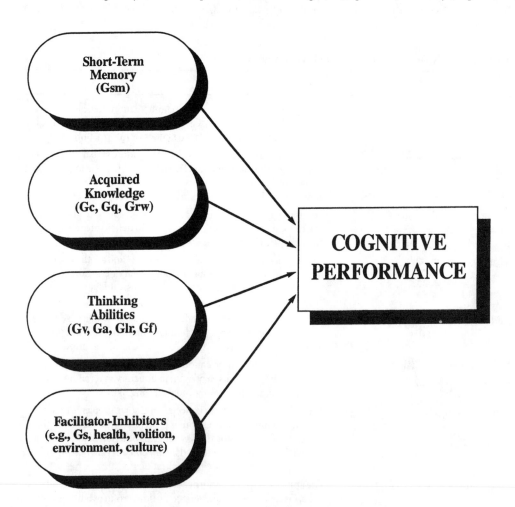

FIGURE 12.2. Gf-Gc Cognitive Performance Model.

reading–writing factor (Grw) that is not yet well identified in the literature (Woodcock, in press).

3. *Thinking abilities* (Gv, Ga, Glr, Gf) are probably the core of what many professionals and laypersons mean by "intelligence." Thinking abilities allow an individual to process information that has been placed in short-term memory but cannot be processed automatically. A subject performs very easy cognitive tasks automatically but must use one or more of the thinking abilities to perform difficult or novel tasks. New learning occurs primarily through the application of relevant thinking abilities. Current Gf-Gc research has identified at least four psychometrically distinct thinking abilities—visual processing (Gv), auditory processing (Ga), long-term retrieval (Glr), and fluid reasoning (Gf).

4. *Facilitator–inhibitors* (e.g., Gs) modify cognitive performance for better or for worse, often overriding strengths or weaknesses in the previously described cognitive abilities. The source of some facilitator–inhibitors is internal (e.g., processing speed [Gs], health, emotional state, and motivation/volition). The source of other facilitator–inhibitors is situational or environmental (e.g., the presence of visual and auditory distractions, the teaching method, or even the tests selected for an intelligence examination).

Each of these four categories includes Gf-Gc components that contribute in a common way to cognitive performance but also contribute differently from the common contributions of the other three categories. Note that the term "cognitive performance" is used on the outcome side of the CPM rather than "intelligence" or "cognitive ability." Intelligence can be inferred only from observations of performance. Further, experienced clinicians know that scores obtained from intelligence tests must often be interpreted with caution because the observed performance may be distorted by individual, environmental, or test situation variables.

The CPM provides a simple but useful description of certain relationships among the cognitive abilities measured by the WJ-R. The CPM has provided the organization on which some of the Hessler (1993) book is based, and it is the model followed by the narrative report produced by *Report Writer for the WJ-R* (Schrank & Woodcock, 1995). The results from confirmatory factor analysis studies by Woodcock (in press) and Keith (Chapter 20, this volume) provide support for the organization of Gf-Gc abilities into the CPM.

A second dynamic model of Gf-Gc theory that has been developed is called the Gf-Gc Information Processing Model (Woodcock, 1993, in press). It is more informative, though more complex, than the CPM. The Information Processing Model extends the CPM by displaying the functional relationships among Gf-Gc abilities and other features of cognition. The Gf-Gc Information Processing Model is not presented here, as it is beyond the scope of this chapter; however, a practical simplification of the model is presented next as the Gf-Gc Diagnostic Worksheet (see Figure 12.3).

The WJ-R is based on a philosophy that the primary purpose of testing should be to find out more about the problem—not to determine an IQ. Toward this end, the Gf-Gc Diagnostic Worksheet (Woodcock, in press) in Figure 12.3 may be used as a vehicle to aid test interpretation. This is an information-processing extension of the CPM described earlier. The horizontal dimension represents an input–processing–output cycle of information processing. The vertical dimension represents the complexity of mental processing, with the lower-order automatic processes represented at the bottom and the higher-order thinking and reasoning processes represented at the top.

The Cognitive Performance box in Figure 12.3 provides space for summarizing the problem or referral question. In the upper right-hand corner of the figure are spaces for recording pertinent information regarding potential facilitator–inhibitor influences. In addition, the scores obtained during a WJ-R assessment are recorded in the spaces provided. The letters "A" to "E" provided spaces to indicate possible facilitator–inhibitor effects. The test results are then evaluated with respect to their possible contribution to the referral problem. This evaluation may be aided by reference to the Gf-Gc ability and deficit descriptions presented earlier in this chapter and by the four implications for teaching and learning presented below.

Four diagnostic implications of the worksheet and its underlying Gf-Gc Information Processing Model have been proposed by Woodcock (1993, in press):

1. Automatic cognitive performance is constrained by a person's short-term memory (Gsm) and processing speed (Gs).
2. New learning is constrained by the person's thinking abilities (Gv, Ga, Glr, and Gf).
3. All performance, automatic processing or new learning, is constrained by the person's stores of knowledge (Gc, Gq, and Grw).
4. All performance, especially new learning, is constrained by the person's facilitator–inhibitors.

A case example illustrates how the diagnostic worksheet is used. Mike is a 17-year-old junior who has been referred by his Spanish teacher for persistent failure in class and because he does not "try hard enough." The school psychologist determined that Mike is in good health and there is no reason to suspect hearing or vision problems. Mike's performance is described typically as "low average" by his other teachers. After completing the worksheet in Figure 12.3, the psychologist noted the pattern of poor performance in Ga, Gsm, and Grw (Grw, in this case, is an average of Mike's scores on Letter–Word Identification and Dictation). This pattern could logically account for Mike's special problems in the Spanish class. Even though it was past the cutoff date for changing classes, Mike was allowed to make a change. Further, the school is providing some special reading and writing instruction in anticipation that this may improve performance in his other classes. The

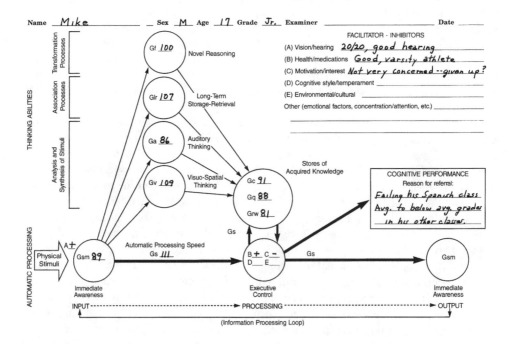

FIGURE 12.3. The Gf-Gc Diagnostic Worksheet completed for Mike, a 17-year-old high school junior who is failing Spanish.

school psychologist has alerted Mike's other teachers to his weaknesses in Ga, Gsm, and Grw and has discussed possible classroom accommodations with them.

This completes the discussion regarding the theoretical underpinnings of the WJ-R COG. The next section describes the physical characteristics of the battery.

ORGANIZATION AND MATERIALS

The WJ-R COG includes 21 tests, divided into a Standard Battery and a Supplemental Battery (see Figure 12.4). The Standard Battery, Tests 1–7, is included in one easel, and the Supplemental Battery, Tests 8–21, is included in a second easel. (The two tests for measuring aspects of Gq are located in the Standard Battery of the WJ-R ACH.)

In addition to the easel test books, other major components of the WJ-R COG include the *Examiner's Manual,* the book of Norm Tables, the Test Record, and the cassette tapes. *Compuscore for the WJ-R,* a computer scoring program, is available for examiners who wish to automate the scoring process and eliminate the need for reference to the printed norm tables.

Two report writing programs also are available. One of these is PEAR (*Psycho-Educational Assessment Reporter,* Frost, Hauger, & Read, 1992/1995). A second report writer is *Report Writer for the WJ-R* (Schrank & Woodcock, 1995). Both programs produce a report of several pages describing the subject's performance on the WJ-R and include an optional table listing the scores. To use the PEAR program the examiner first scores the WJ-R using *Compuscore* and then uses PEAR to read

FIGURE 12.4. Major components of the WJ-R COG.

the Compuscore output file and prepare the report. *Report Writer for the WJ-R* has both scoring and reporting integrated into a single program.

Description of Batteries and Tests

The Standard Battery of the WJ-R COG consists of seven tests, each of which measures a different intellectual ability. The Standard Battery covers the age range from 2 to 90+ years using a single easel test book.

The WJ-R COG Supplemental Battery includes 14 additional tests providing further information about the seven intellectual abilities. These 14 tests, which can be administered from kindergarten to 90+ years, are included in a second easel test book. Tests 8 to 14 measure a second aspect of each of the seven intellectual abilities and are required in the calculation of several cluster scores. Tests 15 to 21 can provide additional information about a subject's intellectual processing. These tests may be used selectively when an in-depth evaluation of a particular facet of cognitive ability is desired.

The 21 tests available from the Standard and Supplemental Batteries, along with the two quantitative ability tests from the WJ-R ACH, are described in Table 12.2. To emphasize certain interpretation implications, the test descriptions are organized with respect to the CPM (Figure 12.2) rather than by order of placement in the battery.

Description of Clusters

Whereas tests are the basic components of the WJ-R COG, clusters of tests provide the primary basis for test interpretation. Although cluster scores demonstrate higher reliability, their major advantage is that interpretation minimizes the danger of generalizing from a single, narrow behavior to a broad, multifaceted ability. All WJ-R cognitive clusters are based on equally weighted combinations of tests. Table 12.3 lists the WJ-R cognitive clusters and the tests each comprises.

Broad Cognitive Ability Clusters

Three broad cognitive clusters may be obtained from the WJ-R. The Early Development scale is designed to be administered as young as 24 months; the Standard and Extended scales usually are administered to subjects who are at the kindergarten level or older. All three scales provide norms up to 90 years of age or over. The three Broad Cognitive Ability scales are properly interpreted as measures of *general* problem solving and learning ability. In contrast, the scholastic aptitude clusters provide measures of *specific* learning abilities.

Scholastic Aptitude Clusters

Four scholastic aptitude clusters may be obtained after administering selected tests from the WJ-R COG. The scholastic aptitude clusters provide information regarding a subject's predicted achievement. Each of these clusters is based on an equally weighted combination of four tests and is the most technically appropriate cluster to use when determining the presence or extent of an aptitude/achievement discrepancy.

The development of the aptitude clusters was based on a set of stepwise multiple regression analyses. Within each achievement area, the combination of tests that was most consistently predictive of the criterion measure across age was selected to form the respective aptitude cluster. A detailed description of the development and technical characteristics of the aptitude clusters has been provided by McGrew (1994a) and McGrew et al. (1991).

TABLE 12.2. A Description of 23 WJ-R Tests Measuring Eight Cognitive Abilities and Structured according to the Cognitive Performance Model

	Functional category of the CPM
Test name	Definition

Short-Term Memory

Test 2: Memory for Sentences	Measures the ability to remember and repeat simple words, phrases, and sentences presented auditorily by a tape player; test is a measure of Short-Term Memory (Gsm)
Test 9: Memory for Words	Measures the ability to repeat lists of unrelated words in the correct sequence; words are presented by audiotape; test is a measure of Short-Term Memory (Gsm)
Test 17: Numbers Reversed	Measures the ability to repeat a series of random numbers backward; number sequences are presented by audiotape; test is a mixed measure of Short-Term Memory and Fluid Reasoning (Gsm and Gf)

Stores of Acquired Knowledge

Test 6: Picture Vocabulary	Measures the ability to name familiar and unfamiliar pictured objects; a measure of Comprehension–Knowledge (Gc)
Test 13: Oral Vocabulary	Measures knowledge of word meanings: in Part A: Synonyms, the subject must say a word similar in meaning to the word presented; in Part B: Antonyms, the subject must say a word that is opposite in meaning to the word presented; test is a measure of Comprehension-Knowledge (Gc)
Test 20: Listening Comprehension	Measures the ability to listen to a short tape-recorded passage and to verbally supply the single word missing at the end of the passage; test is a measure of Comprehension–Knowledge (Gc)
Test 24: Calculation	[WJ-R ACH] measures the subject's skill in performing mathematical calculations ranging from simple addition to calculus; subject is not required to make any decisions about what operations to use or what data to include; test is a measure of Quantitative Ability (Gq)
Test 25: Applied Problems	[WJ-R ACH] measures the subject's skill in analyzing and solving practical problems in mathematics; subject must decide not only the appropriate mathematical operations to use but also which of the data to include in the calculation; test is a measure of Quantitative Ability (Gq)

Thinking Abilities

Test 5: Visual Closure	Measures the ability to name a drawing or picture of a simple object that is altered or obscured in one of several ways; test is a measure of Visual Processing (Gv)
Test 12: Picture Recognition	Measures the ability to recognize a subset of previously presented pictures within a larger set of pictures; test is a measure of Visual Processing (Gv)
Test 19: Spatial Relations	Measures the ability to visually match and combine shapes; subject must select from a series of shapes, the component parts composing a given whole shape; test is a mixed measure of Visual Processing and Fluid Reasoning (Gv and Gf)
Test 4: Incomplete Words	An audiotape subtest that measures auditory closure: after hearing a recorded word with one or more phonemes missing, subject names the complete word; test is a measure of Auditory Processing (Ga)
Test 11: Sound Blending	Measures the ability to integrate and then say whole words after hearing parts (syllables and/or phonemes) of the word; audiotape presents word parts in their proper order for each item; test is a measure of Auditory Processing (Ga)

(cont.)

TABLE 12.2. (*Cont.*)

Test name	Definition
	Functional category of the CPM
	Thinking Abilities (*cont.*)
Test 18: Sound Patterns	Measures the ability to indicate whether pairs of complex sound patterns are the same or different: patterns may differ in pitch, rhythm, or sound content; sound patterns are presented by an audiotape; test is a mixed measure of Auditory Processing and Fluid Reasoning (Ga and Gf)
Test 1: Memory for Names	Measures the ability to learn associations between unfamiliar auditory and visual stimuli (an auditory–visual association task): task requires learning the names of a series of space creatures; test is a measure of Long-Term Retrieval (Glr)
Test 8: Visual–Auditory Learning	Measures the ability to associate new visual symbols (rebuses) with familiar words in oral language and to translate a series of symbols presented as a reading passage (a visual–auditory association task); test is a measure of Long-Term Retrieval (Glr)
Test 15: Delayed Recall—Memory for Names	Measures the ability to recall (after 1 to 8 days) the space creatures presented in Memory for Names; test is a measure of Long-Term Retrieval (Glr)
Test 16: Delayed Recall—Visual–Auditory Learning	Measures the ability to recall (after 1 to 8 days) the symbols (rebuses) presented in Visual–Auditory Learning; test is a measure of Long-Term Retrieval (Glr)
Test 7: Analysis-Synthesis	Measures the ability to analyze the components of an incomplete logic puzzle and to determine and name the missing components; test is a measure of Fluid Reasoning (Gf)
Test 14: Concept Formation	Measures the ability to identify and state the rule for a concept about a set of colored geometric figures when shown instances and noninstances of the concept; test is a measure of Fluid Reasoning (Gf)
Test 21: Verbal Analogies	Measures the ability to complete phrases with words that indicate appropriate analogies; although the vocabulary remains relatively simple, the relationships among the words become increasingly complex; test is a mixed measure of Fluid Reasoning and Comprehension–Knowledge (Gf and Gc)
	Facilitator–Inhibitors
Test 3: Visual Matching	Measures the ability to quickly locate and circle the two identical numbers in a row of six numbers: task proceeds in difficulty from single-digit numbers to triple-digit numbers and has a 3-minute time limit; test is a measure of Processing Speed (Gs)
Test 10: Cross Out	Measures the ability to quickly scan and compare visual information: subject must mark the five drawings in a row of 20 drawings that are identical to the first drawing in the row; subject is given a 3-minute time limit to complete as many rows of items as possible; test is a measure of Processing Speed (Gs)

Cognitive Factor Clusters

Seven cognitive factor cluster scores may be obtained from the WJ-R COG and one other (Gq) from the WJ-R ACH. The first 14 tests in the WJ-R COG and the 2 quantitative tests from the WJ-R ACH include two equally weighted measures for each of the eight cognitive factors. These 16 measures are identified as primary measures in the WJ-R of the eight Gf-Gc abilities through extensive factor analysis studies (McGrew et al., 1991; Woodcock, 1990; Woodcock & Mather, 1989).

TABLE 12.3. A Description of the WJ-R Cognitive Clusters

Cluster name	Cluster composition
Broad Cognitive Ability (BCA)	
Early Development Scale	Tests 1, 2, 4, 5, and 6 (can be administered to individuals as young as 24 months)
Standard Scale	Tests 1 to 7
Extended Scale	Tests 1 to 14
Cognitive Factors	
Short-Term Memory (Gsm)	Tests 2 and 9
Comprehension-Knowledge (Gc)	Tests 6 and 13
Quantitative Ability (Gq)	Tests 24 and 25 (from WJ-R ACH)
Visual Processing (Gv)	Tests 5 and 12
Auditory Processing (Ga)	Tests 4 and 11
Long-Term Retrieval (Glr)	Tests 1 and 8
Fluid Processing (Gf)	Tests 7 and 14
Processing Speed (Gs)	Tests 3 and 10
Scholastic Aptitudes	
Reading Aptitude	Tests 2, 3, 11, and 13
Mathematics Aptitude	Tests 3, 7, 13, and 14
Written Language Aptitude	Tests 3, 8, 11, and 13
Knowledge Aptitude	Tests 2, 5, 11, and 14
Oral Language	
Oral Language	Tests 2, 6, 13, 20, and 21
Oral Language Aptitude	Tests 12, 14, 17, and 18

Oral Language and Oral Language Aptitude Clusters

Two additional clusters may be obtained after administering selected tests from the WJ-R COG: Oral Language and Oral Language Aptitude. The Oral Language cluster provides a broad-based measure of an individual's oral language performance. It may also be used as a measure of "verbal ability." The Oral Language Aptitude cluster, which includes four nonlanguage measures, provides information regarding an individual's predicted achievement for oral language performance. It may also be used as a measure of "nonverbal" or nonlanguage-based ability.

SPECIAL FEATURES OF THE WJ AND WJ-R COG

This section highlights and describes several features of the WJ-R COG. The organization of this section parallels a table entitled "Comparative Features of Intelligence Batteries," presented in Harrison, Flanagan, and Genshaft (Chapter 27, this volume). Readers may wish to refer to this table for a more extended list of WJ-R COG features and for a listing of the features of six other cognitive batteries.

Content Features

Test content is important in dictating breadth of coverage and applicable age range (of usefulness). Four content features of the WJ-R COG are of special value to examiners.

- Provides measures of 8 multiple intelligences.
- The age range is from 2 to over 90 years.
- Five of the 21 tests may be used down to age 2; all 21 tests are used from the kindergarten level through age 90 and over. This is important, as a battery's scores obtained from one age to another cannot be validly compared if based on a different mix of tests.
- Other important content features include the provision of five differential aptitude measures, a measure of oral language ability, four controlled-learning tasks, and two measures of delayed recall.

Administration Features

Some features of a battery provide convenience and facilitate the standard administration of tests by the examiner. Four administration features of the WJ-R COG are directed toward those aims.

- Page-by-page directions are provided in the easel test books for all tests. These directions also include the keys for scoring the items and queries to invoke for certain responses that cannot be scored on the basis of the information initially given by the subject.
- The scoring table provided with each test in the Test Record provides instantly available age equivalents and grade equivalents.
- Critical auditory stimuli tests (e.g., auditory memory span) are presented by recorded audio-tape.
- Spanish-language versions are available and were developed with careful attention to translation and calibration/norming issues.

Interpretation Features

The interpretation of an intelligence battery is a complex process. Several features of the WJ-R COG make the interpretation process more efficient, adaptable, and precise.

- Scoring of the WJ-R COG can be completed efficiently, with minimum opportunity for clerical error, through use of *Compuscore for the WJ-R* (Woodcock & Johnson, 1990) or *Report Writer for the WJ-R* (Schrank & Woodcock, 1995).
- The WJ-R COG provides both age-based and grade-based norms (other batteries provide only age-based norms). The most appropriate set of norms to use for evaluating a subject's test performance are those norms based on the peer group for which comparison is the most relevant. For subjects attending school, from kindergarten to senior in college, grade mates are usually the most relevant reference group.
- The WJ-R COG is the only intelligence battery that provides norms for college and university students.
- Aptitude–achievement and intracognitive discrepancy analyses are based on *discrepancy norms*, not regression estimates. Discrepancy scores were calculated for all subjects in the norming sample and this data provided the basis for the discrepancy norm tables. As a consequence, interpretation is based on the actual distribution of discrepancies in the population.

- The WJ-R COG is fully conormed with the WJ-R ACH tests.
- The range of interpretive information for each test and cluster in the WJ-R COG includes developmental level (Age Equivalents, Grade Equivalents), proficiency level (Relative Mastery Index, Developmental Band), and status comparison with grade- or age-peers (Percentile Ranks, Standard Scores). The interpretive design of the WJ-R COG allows the clinician to capitalize on this full range of information.

Technical Features

The *Examiner's Manual* for the WJ-R COG includes a summary of the most important technical information underlying the battery. In addition, the WJ-R Technical Manual (McGrew et al., 1991) presents 350 pages of detailed information about the development, standardization, and technical characteristics of the WJ-R COG and WJ-R ACH. Selected features are highlighted here, but the *Technical Manual* should be consulted for in-depth information.

- Normative data for the WJ-R COG were gathered from 6,359 subjects in more than 100 geographically diverse U.S. communities. The preschool sample (2 to 5 years of age and not enrolled in kindergarten) comprises 705 subjects; the kindergarten-to-grade-12 sample comprises 3,245 subjects; the college/university sample comprises 916 subjects; and the adult nonschool sample (14 to over 90 years of age and not enrolled in secondary school or college) comprises 1,493 subjects.
- Subjects were randomly selected within a stratified sampling design that controlled for 10 specific community and subject variables.
- In addition to the traditional census region and community size variables, sites were further selected with respect to 13 socioeconomic status (SES) variables. Thus, the selection plan resulted in a distribution of communities that not only provided a cross section of U.S. communities but avoided a selection bias toward any specific type of community.
- Subsets of the norming sample representing populations with low percentages of occurrence in the United States (e.g., those classified as Asian-Pacific) were systematically oversampled and then weighted back to ensure more accurate contributions to the total norms.
- The sample to be tested in each chosen school was based on a quota-by-grade-level criterion. Subjects were *randomly* selected from the grade lists of students in each school. The sample drawn did not include severely handicapped students unless they were enrolled at least part-time in the mainstream of education, nor did it include any subject who had less than 1 year of experience in an English-speaking environment.
- The scores in the norm tables are based on the distribution of scores at the subject's *exact* chronological age or grade placement. Less precise norm tables, frequently found in other tests, include error to the extent that *average scores* for the reference group change (grow or decline) from the beginning of a wide age interval to the end.
- Reliability coefficients (r_{11}) and standard errors of measurement (SEMs) are reported in the *Technical Manual* for all tests and clusters across their range of intended use.
- The WJ-R *Technical Manual* includes extensive information regarding content validity, concurrent validity, and construct validity. A brief presentation of this information is also provided in Chapter 7 of the WJ-R COG *Examiner's Manual.*
- Comparative concurrent validity studies report matrices of results from the *same* samples among *all* major intelligence batteries. (If correlations between tests are reported from different samples, as in some technical reports, they cannot be meaningfully compared. Further, good concurrent validity studies should include all major competing tests.)
- The factor analysis studies, which are the foundation of the WJ-R COG construct validity

reports, include the necessary breadth and depth of measures to adequately describe the factorial structure of the battery and the construct validity of the tests.

There are two characteristics of a factor analysis study that make the results more meaningful. *First,* a breadth of human cognitive abilities should be represented in the factor analysis study, at least to the extent that the various abilities are required to perform any of the tests in the battery. *Second,* there must be a sufficient number (generally three or more) of reasonably clean measures, or markers, for each of the factors present so that the factor can be identified clearly.

A serious problem exists with many of the factor-analytic studies that have been reported on the major cognitive batteries. The variables in those studies routinely have been restricted to those subtests included within the battery itself. Any single cognitive battery, with the possible exception of the WJ-R, probably does not include enough markers for each embedded factor to allow an appropriate description of the factorial structure of that battery. As a result, factors present in the battery are not differentiated, or perhaps not even detected. Inappropriate conclusions then may be drawn about the factorial structure of the battery and about the construct validity of the individual subtests (Woodcock, 1990, p. 238).

Since publication of the WJ-R COG and its *Technical Manual,* several validity studies of the cognitive tests have been conducted. Among these are three important construct validity studies.

Woodcock (1990) reported the results from nine joint factor studies, including the WJ or WJ-R COG with combinations of the Wechsler batteries, SB-IV, and K-ABC. Altogether, 15 sets of exploratory and confirmatory factor analyses were conducted on a total of 68 subtests. The primary results are consolidated into a table (1990, pp. 242–243) reporting the relative loadings for each test in each battery on the eight Gf-Gc factors. The results of these joint factor studies all provide support for the WJ-R eight-factor model of Gf-Gc theory.

McGhee (1993) conducted a joint confirmatory factor analysis with a total of 30 variables from the WJ-R, the DAS, and the Detroit Tests of Learning Aptitude–3. McGhee also evaluated several alternative factor models to Gf-Gc. His results supported the factor structure previously reported for the WJ-R.

Bickley, Keith, and Wolfe (1995) report results from a hierarchical confirmatory factor analysis of the WJ-R norming data. Their purposes were to test Carroll's (1993) three-stratum level theory against this data and to investigate whether developmental changes in the structure of intelligence would be observed. Their results provided support for the three-stratum level theory, did not support developmental changes in the organization of cognitive ability, and suggested the possibility of intermediate factors between the second and third strata. They note that their intent was not to evaluate WJ-R construct validity but that the results can be used to provide such evidence.

Beyond Traditional Intellectual Assessment

Publication of the WJ COG in 1977 introduced numerous departures from traditional intellectual assessment as exemplified by the then current Wechsler and Stanford–Binet batteries. Since 1977, all these traditional batteries have been revised. How do they compare now?

- *Measures of multiple intelligences.* The 1989 WJ-R provides eight cognitive factor scores. The 1986 SB-IV provides four factor scores instead of the previous single score. The 1981 WAIS-R and 1989 WPPSI-R remain as two-factor batteries, but the 1991 WISC-III provides four factor scores.
- *Age range.* The WJ-R provides a wide age range of application allowing the same tests to be used at all age levels. The SB-IV and each of the Wechsler tests have restricted age ranges.

- *Conormed, or at least equated, intelligence and achievement measures.* The WJ-R provides fully conormed measures of intelligence and achievement. The 1992 Weschler Individual Achievement Test (WIAT, Psychological Corporation, 1992) provides *equated* norms with the 1991 WISC-III. The SB-IV supports no related measure of achievement.
- *Grade-based norms as well as age-based norms.* The WJ-R provides both. The SB-IV and Wechsler tests provide only age-based norms.
- *College/university level norms.* Provided in the WJ-R. The SB-IV and the Wechsler tests have none.
- *Differential scholastic aptitudes with discrepancy norms.* The WJ-R provides both. The SB-IV and the Wechsler tests do not provide differential scholastic aptitude scores.
- *Controlled learning tasks.* The WJ-R provides four such tests. The SB-IV and the Wechsler tests have none.
- *Measures of long-term retrieval (Glr).* The WJ-R provides four measures. The SB-IV and the Wechsler tests have none.
- *Measures of auditory processing (Ga).* The WJ-R has three. The traditional SB-IV and the Wechsler tests have none.

CONCLUSION

The 1977 WJ COG and the 1989 WJ-R COG represent a concerted effort to deviate from tradition and reduce the lag between intelligence test technology and cognitive science. This chapter has provided information about important features of content, administration, interpretation, and technical quality. The procedures followed in developing and standardizing the WJ-R COG have produced an instrument that may be used with confidence in a variety of educational and noneducational settings. In particular, the wide age range and breadth of coverage are especially important advantages underlying use of the WJ-R COG.

REFERENCES

Bartlett, J. (1992). *Familiar quotations* (16th ed.). Boston: Little, Brown.

Bickley, P. G., Keith, T. Z., & Wolfe, L. M. (1995). The three-stratum theory of cognitive abilities: Test of the structure of intelligence across the life span. *Intelligence, 20,* 309–328.

Carroll, J. B. (1993). *Human cognitive abilities: A survey of factor-analytic studies.* New York: Cambridge University Press.

Cattell, R. B. (1971). *Abilities: Their structure, growth, and action.* Boston: Houghton Mifflin.

Cummings, J. A. (1994). Review of the Woodcock–Johnson Psycho-Educational Battery—Revised. In L. L. Murphy (Ed.), *Supplement to the eleventh mental measurements yearbook* (pp. 283–287). Lincoln: Buros, University of Nebraska Press.

Elliott, C. (1990). *The Differential Ability Scales.* San Antonio, TX: Psychological Corporation.

Frost, J. M., Hauger, J., & Read, B. G. (1995). *Psycho-Educational Assessment Reporter.* Woodstock, VT: EDCS. (Original work published 1992)

Hessler, G. L. (1993). *Use and interpretation of the Woodcock–Johnson Psycho-Educational Battery—Revised.* Chicago: Riverside.

Kaufman, A. S. (1985). Review of the Woodcock–Johnson Psycho-Educational Battery. In J. F. Mitchell (Ed.), *The ninth mental measurements yearbook* (pp. 1762–1765). Lincoln: Buros, University of Nebraska Press.

Kaufman, A. S. (1990). *Assessing adolescent and adult intelligence.* Boston: Allyn & Bacon.

Kaufman, A. S., & Kaufman, N. L. (1983). *Kaufman Assessment Battery for Children.* Circle Pines, MN: American Guidance Service.

Kaufman, A. S., & Kaufman, N. L. (1993). *Kaufman Adolescent and Adult Intelligence Test.* Circle Pines, MN: American Guidance Service.

Lee, S. W., & Stefany, E. F. (1994). Review of the Woodcock–Johnson Psycho-Educational Battery—Revised. In L. L. Murphy (Ed.), *Supplement to the eleventh mental measurements yearbook* (pp. 287–288). Lincoln: Buros, University of Nebraska Press.

Mather, N. (1991). *An instructional guide to the Woodcock–Johnson Psycho-Educational Battery—Revised.* Brandon, VT: CPPC.

Mather, N., & Jaffe, L. E. (1992). *Woodcock–Johnson Psycho-Educational Battery—Revised: Recommendations and reports.* Brandon, VT: CPPC.

McGhee, R. L. (1993). Fluid and crystallized intelligence: Confirmatory factor analyses of the Differential Ability Scales, Detroit Tests of Learning Aptitude-3, and Woodcock–Johnson Psycho-Educational Battery—Revised. *Journal of Psychoeducational Assessment* [Monograph Series: WJ-R monograph], 20–38.

McGhee, R. L., & Buckhalt, J. A. (1993). Test review of the Woodcock–Johnson Psycho-Educational Battery—Revised. *Journal of Psychoeducational Assessment* [Monograph Series: WJ-R monograph], 136–149.

McGrew, K. S. (1994a). *Clinical interpretation of the Woodcock–Johnson Tests of Cognitive Ability—Revised.* Boston: Allyn & Bacon.

McGrew, K. S. (1994b). Woodcock–Johnson Tests of Cognitive Ability—Revised. In J. R. Sternberg (Ed.), *Encyclopedia of human intelligence* (pp. 1152–1158). New York: Macmillan.

McGrew, K. S., Werder, J. K., & Woodcock, R. W. (1991). *WJ-R technical manual: A reference on theory and current research.* Chicago: Riverside.

Psychological Corporation. (1992). *Weschler Individual Achievement Test.* San Antonio, TX: Psychological Corporation.

Schrank, F., & Woodcock, R. W. (1995). *Report Writer for the WJ-R.* Chicago: Riverside.

Terman, L. M., & Merrill, M. A. (1973). *Stanford–Binet Intelligence Scale, Form L-M: 1972 norms edition.* Chicago: Riverside.

Thorndike, R. L., Hagen, E. P., & Sattler, J. M. (1986). *Stanford–Binet Intelligence Scale: Fourth edition.* Chicago: Riverside.

Wechsler, D. (1955). *Wechsler Adult Intelligence Scale.* San Antonio, TX: Psychological Corporation.

Wechsler, D. (1967). *Wechsler Pre-school and Primary Scale of Intelligence..* San Antonio, TX: Psychological Corporation.

Wechsler, D. (1974). *Wechsler Intelligence Scale for Children—Revised.* San Antonio, TX: Psychological Corporation.

Woodcock, R. W. (1978). *Development and standardization of the Woodcock–Johnson Psycho-Educational Battery.* Chicago: Riverside

Woodcock, R. W. (1982). *Batera Woodcock Psico-Educativa en español.* Chicago: Riverside.

Woodcock, R. W. (1990). Theoretical foundations of the WJ-R measures of cognitive ability. *Journal of Psychoeducational Assessment, 8,* 231-258.

Woodcock, R. W. (1993). An information processing view of Gf-Gc theory. *Journal of Psychoeducational Assessment* [Monograaph Series: WJ-R monograph], 80–102.

Woodcock, R. W. (in press). Extending Gf-Gc theory into practice. In J. J. McArdle & R. W. Woodcock (Eds.), *Human cognitive abilities in theory and practice.* Mahwah, NJ: Erlbaum.

Woodcock, R. W., & Johnson, M. B. (1977a). *Woodcock–Johnson Psycho-Educational Battery.* Chicago: Riverside.

Woodcock, R. W., & Johnson, M. B. (1977b). *Woodcock–Johnson Tests of Cognitive Ability.* Chicago: Riverside.

Woodcock, R. W., & Johnson, M. B. (1989a). *Woodcock–Johnson Tests of Achievement—Revised.* Chicago: Riverside.

Woodcock, R. W., & Johnson, M. B. (1989b). *Woodcock–Johnson Tests of Cognitive Ability—Revised.* Chicago: Riverside.

Woodcock, R. W., & Johnson, M. B. (1990). *Compuscore for the WJ-R.* Chicago: Riverside.

Woodcock, R. W., & Mather, N. (1989). *WJ-R Test of Cognitive Ability, examiner's manual.* Chicago: Riverside.

Woodcock, R. W., & Muñoz-Sandoval, A. F. (1996). *Batera Woodcock-Muñoz Pruebas de habilidad cognoscitiva—Revisada.* Chicago: Riverside.

CHAPTER 13

Planning, Attention, Simultaneous, and Successive Theory and the Cognitive Assessment System: A New Theory-Based Measure of Intelligence

JACK A. NAGLIERI

THE PURPOSE OF SCIENCE is to develop and test theories to meet the needs of society. Theory development should be a major goal of any science because it provides a method for explaining observable events and predicting future ones. Theory is also important because it provides a way to construct a picture of complex phenomena from relatively simple components. Einstein (1956) noted this when he wrote, "When we say that we have succeeded in understanding a group of natural processes, we invariably mean that a constructive theory has been found which covers the processes in question" (p. 55). Whether we are studying physics, medicine, or psychology, the goal is the same—to develop a theory that can explain observable phenomena and make accurate predictions.

A theoretical basis is especially needed in an applied science such as psychology and most definitely in the area of intelligence. In this book, we are concerned about gaining an understanding of intelligence, or cognitive functioning, which goes beyond traditional methods. It is important to recognize that the selection of a particular approach (theory or IQ test) has a direct impact on the information obtained. Simply put, the test we use provides a view of intelligence as defined by that instrument. In addition, the more valid the test, the better the explanations, the better the explanations the more accurate the predictions. Because the method used defines what will and what will not be observed, it has a direct impact on the validity and utility of the information obtained. If a particular instrument measures constructs X, Y, and Z, then by definition, it will be insensitive to A through W. The scope of the technology can directly influence scientific thought. Sagan (1980) discussed this when he showed how scientists' understanding of the planet Venus changed as they interpreted information from a refracting telescope (from the 1600s to early 1900s), then using spectroscopic instruments (1920s), then using a radio telescope (1950s), then using the Magellan spacecraft's radar produced photographic-like images (1994). During each phase of exploration, the conclusions reached (initially very incorrect) were directly related to the quality of the instrument used to obtain information.

At each stage of the development of scientific instrumentation in any field, the type and scope of information obtained is directly related to the technology used. As technology improves, a corresponding improvement in our understanding results. Similarly, when we use "traditional IQ" tests, such as the Wechsler and Binet (Naglieri, 1996), we are using one approach to obtain information, which some suggest may limit our view (Naglieri & Das, 1990). I suggest that the field of intellectual assessment is at an important point in the evolution of our understanding of human cognitive functioning. We may choose to continue to use traditional technology, abandon the approach altogether for direct observation methods, or look to improved methods of obtaining information. If we look to newer improved technology then the evolution of the science of cognitive functioning can be facilitated. This will require the integration of evidence and theories in psychology presented over the past 50 years including the important works of, for example, Cattell (1963), Guilford (1967), Hunt (1990), Luria (1966), Neisser (1967), Piaget (1978), Pribram (1971), and many others. It also requires that we accept the idea that better intelligence tests can only be obtained through the development and operationalization of more valid theories of cognitive functioning.

This chapter encourages a step toward the use of newer technology. To achieve this step we have to be willing to reconceptualize human cognitive functioning to gain a thorough understanding of intra and interindividual differences. I suggest that the planning, attention, simultaneous, and successive (PASS) theory of cognitive functioning may be a viable new technology that may extend our understanding of intelligence in important ways. To discuss this new approach I first describe the PASS theory, then the test that J. P. Das and I have developed according to this theory, the Cognitive Assessment System (CAS; Naglieri & Das, 1996a), and, finally, I address a few relevant issues about our theory and the test.

PASS THEORY OF COGNITIVE PROCESSING

The PASS theory is the result of more than 25 years of theoretical and empirical work conducted in many countries around the world (Das, Naglieri, & Kirby, 1994). Das and his colleagues initiated the link between Luria's work (1966, 1970, 1973, 1976, 1980, 1982) and the field of intelligence when they suggested that intelligence should be seen as a cognitive construct (Das, Kirby, & Jarman, 1979). According to Naglieri and Sloutsky (1995), the theory of cognition incorporates neurophysiological findings (Anokhin, 1969, 1978; Luria, 1966), cognitive processing research (Broadbent, 1958; Das et al., 1994; Hunt & Lansman, 1986; Simon, 1981), and sociocultural components of human performance (Luria, 1976; Vygotsky, 1978; Vygotsky & Luria, 1993). In the initial stages, this work was described as an information-processing model (Das, 1973; Das, Kirby, & Jarman, 1975), then as the information–integration model (Das et al., 1979), and most recently as a cognitive functioning theory of intelligence called PASS (Naglieri, 1989; Naglieri & Das, 1990). The PASS theory, and the CAS, are the result of the synthesis of neuropsychology, cognitive psychology, and psychometrics with the emphasis on a theory-based theory of human cognitive functioning that includes a broad spectrum of measurement.

To improve instruments used to evaluate human intelligence, a few points warrant consideration. First, intelligence must be theoretically defined and more broadly measured if we are to overcome the limitations of traditional IQ tests. These considerations are intended to address the views held by some professionals that children's academic problems have not been adequately uncovered by traditional IQ tests, despite their general utility (see Kaufman, 1994, for a summary). To make these measures more useful, psychologists have developed elaborate interpretive schemes for tests such as the Wechsler scales to develop hypotheses about intellectual strengths and weaknesses. To develop these hypotheses, a seemingly endless number of articles and pages have been written that discuss what the Wechsler subtests and scales measure (e.g., Kaufman, 1979, 1990, 1994; Sattler, 1988; Wielkiewicz, 1990). Despite the clinical utility of these methods (Kaufman, 1994), IQ, factor, and subtest profiles have not been shown to be especially useful for differential diagnosis (see Glutting, McDermott, & Konold, Chapter 19, this volume; McDermott, Fantuzzo, & Glutting, 1990). Finally, there has been much less good experimental validity evidence (e.g., Lipsitz, Dworkin, & Erlenmeyer-Kimling, 1993; Stewart & Moely, 1983) to validate interpretive assertions (Naglieri, 1993) than logical analysis. These issues are all interrelated because if one has a sound theory of intelligence, practitioners are not left with the task of speculating about what the subtests measure and differential diagnosis can be conducted on both theoretical and practical levels.

The PASS Theory

The PASS theory provides the opportunity for several types of improvements. The following is a theory-based definition of intelligence:

> Intelligence consists of three components. First is *attentional processes* that provide focused cognitive activity; second is *information processes* of two types (simultaneous and successive); and third is *planning processes* that provide (a) the control of attention, (b) use of information processes, internal and external knowledge, and cognitive tools, and (c) self-regulation to achieve desired goals (Naglieri & Das, 1996b).

Planning

Planning processes provide the individual with the means to determine and use efficient solutions to problems using attention, simultaneous, and successive processes and the individual's base of knowledge. This includes the development of plans of action, evaluation of their effectiveness, impulse control, regulation of voluntary actions, and linguistic functions such as spontaneous speech. Planning processes provide an individual with the means to solve a problem for which no method of solution is apparent. It may be a complex or simple task and may involve attentional, simultaneous and successive processes, but the main requirement is to determine *how* to solve the problem. Once the need for a plan is apparent, the individual may search his or her base of knowledge for an approach. If one is not within the knowledge base, an initial plan of action is developed and the plan is examined to decide whether it is reasonable. If it is acceptable, the plan is carried out, or else a new plan is devised. If the plan is put into action, decisions are made to modify the effectiveness of the approach, continue to apply the plan, and modify it to achieve the most efficient approach to problem solving, or else generate another one.

Attention

Attentional processes allow the individual to respond to a particular stimulus and inhibit responding to competing stimuli. Although both arousal and selective attention comprise this component, selective attention is the dimension of interest because adequate arousal is assumed. Selective attention presumes selection of relevant stimuli while ignoring others and it becomes increasingly difficult when the nontarget stimuli are more salient than the target stimuli. Thus, attention refers to specifically directed cognitive activity as well as resistance to the distraction of competing stimuli.

Simultaneous

Simultaneous processing provides for the integration of stimuli into groups where each component of the stimulus array must be interrelated to every other. Simultaneous processing may take place when stimuli are perceived or remembered, or when dealing with conceptual aspects of stimuli. The essence of simultaneous processing is that the elements of the stimuli are interrelated (i.e., surveyable). Simultaneously processed information is said to be surveyable because the elements are interrelated and accessible to inspection either through examination of the actual stimuli during the activity or through memory of the stimuli. Simultaneous processes are involved in any tasks that demands the individual interrelate component parts of the question.

Successive

Successive processing provides for the integration of stimuli that are serial-ordered and form a chainlike progression. The distinguishing quality of successive processing is that the elements are only linearly related and each stimulus is only related to the one it follows. Successive coding is needed for skilled movements (e.g., writing) because this activity requires "a series of movements which follow each other in a strictly defined order . . . without surveyability" (Luria, 1966, p. 78). In the early stages of the formation of the skilled movement, each successive link exists as a separate unit and may be taught as a specific step in a larger behavior. Only when each aspect becomes automatic can the initial stimulus in the chain become the signal that leads to the automatic execution of the complete successive action.

Relationships among the PASS processes

The PASS processes are dynamic in nature, respond to the cultural experiences of the individual, are subject to developmental changes, and form an interrelated (correlated) interdependent system. Because the PASS processes are viewed as interactive, they act in concert to provide specific functions to nearly all tasks performed in everyday life. The use of the processes is a result of the demands of the task, the individual's experiences and preferences, and influences in the environment. These relationships are described in Figure 13.1.

Effective functioning is accomplished through the integration of knowledge with planning, attention, simultaneous, and successive processes. Although each type of process is an independent component with distinct functions, they are joined in cognitive activity as a complex functional system. Simultaneous and successive processes and planning interact to facilitate acquisition of knowledge and at the same time these higher functions depend on a proper state of arousal to provide the opportunity for learning. The information to be processed can arrive through any of the receptors (eyes, ears, skin, muscle movements, etc.) in a serial (i.e., over time) or synchronous (i.e., concurrent) manner. Despite the type of presentation, information is processed according to the requirements of the task and is not dictated by the method (serial or concurrent) of presentation.

The relationship between PASS and the sociocultural subsystem is described by Naglieri and Sloutsky (1995). They suggest that the sociocultural subsystem provides an individual with cognitive tools (symbols, signs, and technologies that have strong sociocultural components) and a base of knowledge for representation, processing, and acquiring new information (e.g., language, literacy, mathematical operations, and other semiotic systems, technologies, and procedural methods of problem solving). Sociocultural knowledge exists and is stored externally, but it undergoes the process of internalization in the course of development and education (e.g., Vygotsky, 1978). External knowledge, which is all the information the person has not acquired, but is available to the society for acquisition, has become increasingly available to modern societies, especially apparent today with the advanced communications and information systems. Internalized knowledge is stored in the subject's memory either on a short- or long-term basis. Internalized knowledge includes cognitive tools, which allows individuals to perform voluntary, intentional control over their cognitive processes. Cognitive tools play an essential role in development of planning of actions, voluntary attention, and subordinating simultaneous and successive processes to planning and attention

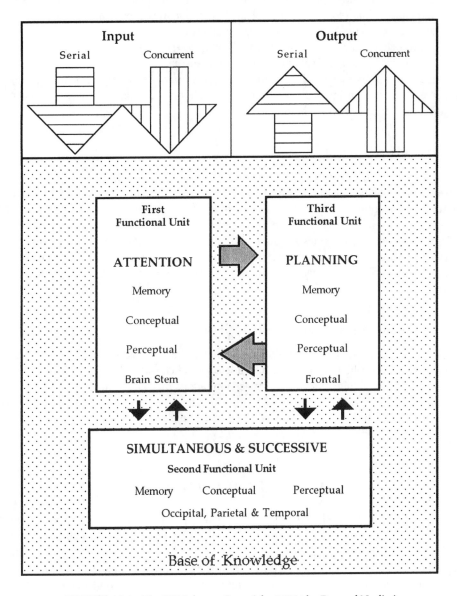

FIGURE 13.1. The PASS theory. Copyright ©1994 by Das and Naglieri.

(Naglieri & Sloutsky, 1995). Internalization of external knowledge and development of cognitive tools is a step-by-step process of developmental transformations (e.g., Galperin, 1989).

Operationalization of PASS in CAS

The four processes included in the PASS theory are represented in the Cognitive Processing Scales of the CAS. They are intended to represent a broad spectrum of the essential cognitive processes required for human performance. Subtests in each of the PASS scales were developed with both theoretical and practical issues in mind. For this reason, each of our scales has several dimensions that fall under the respective types of processing. For example, the planning tests vary in complexity across several dimensions (e.g., level of complexity), attention measures include those for which the attentional selection occurs at the point of receiving the stimuli (Receptive Attention) or making a verbal response (Expressive Attention); simultaneous subtests includes measures that have both nonverbal figural (Figure Memory) and verbal (Simultaneous Verbal) content, and the Successive scale includes measures that involve repetition and memory (Word Series), more complicated utilization and comprehension of syntax (Sentence Repetition and Questions), and minimal memory requirement (Successive Speech Rate).

PASS Subtest Development

Initially we selected subtests of the CAS on the basis of their consistency with the PASS theory. Tasks were selected as potential measures of a particular process if they corresponded to the theoretical framework and functional architecture we described elsewhere (Naglieri & Das, 1990). For example, planning tests had to be relatively easy to perform but require the individual to make decisions about *how* to solve the task. Attention tests should require the child to respond selectively only to those stimuli that have been identified as targets. Simultaneous tasks demand that the individual interrelate the component parts of the item, whereas successive tasks require appreciation of the serial relationships among stimuli.

Selected Cognitive Assessment Subtests

Subtests from the PASS scales of the CAS as they are currently configured in the standardization edition are briefly described in this section. Readers should consider these tests in relation to the section on functional architecture section. Space limitations preclude a thorough examination of each subtest, specifics about the methods of scoring, the developmental background, and why each task measures the particular processes. Further information is are presented in considerable detail in the *Cognitive Assessment System Interpretive Handbook* (Naglieri & Das, 1996b).

MEASURES OF PLANNING

Planning subtests included in the CAS were developed so that the child is required to create plans of action, regulate the application of these plans, and verify that these actions conform with the original goal, correcting any mistakes that are made (Luria, 1973, p. 80). Planning tests are, therefore, not especially difficult to complete, but it is how the child goes about completing the task that drives the scores. The child who better utilizes planning processes develops good strategies and applies them efficiently to solve the problems. It is the case, therefore, that these tasks do not have the same kind of progression of items on the basis of difficulty as those found in the simultaneous or successive scales. The hallmark of the planning tasks that have been used is that they require the completion of a relatively simple task through the development and utilization of efficient methods of problem solving.

Number Matching requires the individual to identify and underline two numbers on a row that are the same on each of eight rows on a page. There are six numbers per row, four rows per digit length, and numbers increase in length from one to seven digits over the several pages. The items were constructed so that the target numbers were balanced across all columns and the digit strings were written in particular ways so that clues may be detected to aid in the identification of the correct targets. For example, (1) many rows contain a number or two that start with a unique number (e.g., two of the six numbers may start with a 2 and the remaining numbers start with a 5); (2) the degree of serial confusability is high, which demands impulse control to avoid choosing the wrong answer too quickly; (3) the last numbers are typically differ more than the first numbers; and (4) location does not matter.

Planned Codes consists of two items that require the subject to write the sequence of XO, OO, OX, or XX in spaces under the letters A, B, C, or D. There are two pages administered and scored separately in which the codes an the position of the letters A–D are different. On the first page the codes corresponding to the A–D are XO, OO, OX, or XX and the codes are configured vertically on the page (all the As appear in the first column, the Bs in the second column, etc.). The second-page codes corresponding to the A–D are OX, XX, XO, or OO and the codes are configured in a diagonal pattern. In both administration events the child is encouraged to complete the page in any manner that seems efficient ("Fill in as many of these as you can, as fast as you can, using these answers . . . You do it any way you want . . . "; Naglieri & Das, 1996a). Our intent is to encourage the child to complete the code in a logical and efficient manner, which is, for example, to do the As first, then the Bs, and so on.

Planned Connections requires the child to connect sequential stimuli (e.g., the numbers 1-2-3-4-5) that appear in an apparently random manner on a page. The easy items require the child to connect a series of numbers in their proper numerical sequence (1 to 2, 2 to 3, etc.) and the harder items require that numbers and letters be connected alternately in their relative sequences (1 to A, A to 2, 2 to B, B to 3, etc.). The items are written so that at no point does the child complete the sequence by crossing one line over the other (this provides a means of reducing the areas to be searched when looking for the next number or letter).

The scoring methods used in the Planning subtests sometimes gives the impression that these tests may be measures of speed of processing, perceptual speed, or simply how fast a person can do something. There are two compelling reasons to reject this interpretation: (1) there are differences in the cognitive processing requirements of planning versus speed tests, and (2) there is considerable experimental evidence that does not support this hypothesis.

Analysis of tasks that are sensitive to planning processes shows activities that include the generation of a method to solve the problem, execution of the solution, monitoring of the solution, modification as needed, and so on. In the CAS we have used time as the best estimate of the *efficiency* with which these subtests are completed. Time is an excellent measure of how efficiently a child completes the subtest because disorganized execution, false starts, inadequate monitoring, and generation of bad plans consumes much time. Our experience in administering these tasks has shown this as well. Children who are poor planners solve Visual Search items by looking at the page in a disorganized manner, they choose incorrect targets impulsively and make many errors, and they are remarkably resistant to changing this inefficient method of solving these problems. Time is an excellent variable to measure of planning in these tasks because it is sensitive to the inefficiencies and efficiencies of plans subjects use.

A direct test of the hypothesis that planning and speed are separate has been examined in several investigations. Das and Dash (1983) and Naglieri, Prewett, and Bardos (1989) found clear factorial evidence that planning and speed tasks do not load on the same factor. These authors used a direct measure of speed—the time it took subjects to read four color words (red, yellow, green, and blue) and tell the color of objects (red, yellow, green, and blue Xs). When these speed scores were entered into the factorial analyses, they formed a distinct group from the planning tasks (Visual Search and Trail Making). Naglieri, Das, Stevens, and Ledbetter (1991) tested this hypothesis differently. In their study PASS was compared to a Verbal–Spatial–Speed (VSS) model using the linear structural relations (LISREL) confirmatory factor-analytic approach. Again, no support for the VSS model was found but the PASS model was supported.

MEASURES OF ATTENTION

The attention subtests included in the CAS were developed to measure selective attention (i.e., the specific detection of a particular stimulus and inhibition of responses to irrelevant competing stimuli). In contrast to the *general* arousal of cortical systems that prepares the brain for activity, selective attention is considered a "*specialized* directed form of activation" (Luria, 1973, p. 265). The CAS Attention subtests are designed to measure the latter and, therefore, require the individual to selectively focus cognitive activity on one and ignore the other aspects of multidimensional stimuli. Structural analysis of these tasks shows that the child must examine and detect target stimuli and respond to it while avoiding responding to competing stimuli. These tasks always involve a competing stimulus that is as salient or more salient than the target stimulus. It is important to note that attention and planning will be related because the inhibition of responses to irrelevant stimuli becomes central to the preservation of goal-directed, programmed behavior (the child's intention to follow the directions), which is how planning processes may become secondarily involved in attentional tasks (Luria, 1973, p. 274).

Expressive Attention is constructed differently for children 5–7 and 8–18 years of age, but only the version for those ages 8–18 is described here. This subtest is composed of three pages. On the first page the individual reads 40 words (blue, yellow, green, and red), and the second page requires the child to tell the colors of $1.25'' \times \frac{1}{8}''$ colored rectangles (printed in blue, yellow, green, and red) in varying order arranged in eight rows, five to a row. On page 3 the words "red," "blue," and "green" are printed in colors different than the word. The child is instructed to name the color used to print the word, rather than read the word, as fast as possible. The time needed to complete the last page is used as a measure of selective attention because only under this condition does the individual have to suppress the impulse to read the word and then name the color of the ink in which the word is written. Selecting to name the color rather than read the word makes this task a measure of selective attention. The impulse to read the word arrives first, as word reading is almost automatic at these ages.

Number Detection is constructed in two forms, one for children ages 5–7 and the other for those 8–18 years of age. For the 8–18-year-olds the task is to underline the numbers 1, 2, and 3 printed in this font, then on the second page to identify the numbers 1, 2, 3, 4, 5, 6 when they appear in this manner. There are 180 stimuli (numbers) with 45 targets (25% targets) on each of two pages. The child must compete the task working from left to right and top to bottom and may not go back to check the page upon completion.

Receptive Attention was also written in two versions, one that involves line drawings of six types of objects (a flower, house, tree, etc.) and one that involves six letters (t, T, b, B, etc.) each composed of two conditions. The first condition requires the child to underline pairs of objects (or letters) that are identical in appearance. The second requires the child to identify those pictures or letters that have the same name. In each condition there are 25% targets and the same distractors. The child must complete the task working from left to right and top to bottom and may not go back to check the page on completion.

MEASURES OF SIMULTANEOUS AND SUCCESSIVE PROCESSES

The CAS Simultaneous and Successive scales represent the "two basic forms of integrative activity of the cerebral cortex, by which different aspects of the outside world may be reflected" (Luria, 1966, p. 74). Simultaneous processes integrate individual stimuli into groups that typically have a spatial component and successive processes integrate individual stimuli into a temporally organized linear series. These two types of processes are typically associated with visual versus auditory stimuli because simultaneous synthesis is "associated with the visual, kinetic, and vestibular apparatuses, responsible for orientation of the body in space" and conversely, successive synthesis is "primarily associated with the motor . . . and the acoustic [systems]" (p. 79). For this reason, when a series of words is presented auditorily, the possibility of arranging them using simultaneous processing is minimized whereas if they are presented visually "the test becomes less pure" (p. 87). Therefore, the method of presentation of stimuli has a natural relation to the extent to which the task is an efficient measure of the process. In the CAS, we have balanced these dimensions to the extent reasonably possible.

Measures of Simultaneous Processing

Simultaneous processing subtests require the synthesis of separate elements into interrelated groups. This includes the conversion of "successively presented stimuli into simultaneously perceived structures" (Luria, 1966, p. 89), on information that is presented over time but is processed into a group. In each of the simultaneous tasks, efforts have been made to include a variety of tasks with additional requirements such as verbal, abstract figural, and memory. Despite the differences in the content of these subtests, they require the individual to interrelate the component parts of the particular item to arrive at the correct answer. The need to appreciate the relationships among all components of the item is the hallmark of a simultaneous task. The simultaneous subtest items range in difficulty from very easy to very difficult as a function of the complexity and number of the interrelationships that have to be incorporated into some complete pattern, idea, or group of ideas.

The Matrices subtest requires that the child choose one of six options which best completes the abstract figural analogy. To solve the problem, the child must recognize the relationships among the figures and combine them to predict what the missing element should be. The items are constructed using shapes and geometric designs in the colors white, black, blue, and yellow (to reduce the influence of color-impaired vision) that form a pattern that must be adequately understood for the child to choose which of six options completes the analogy.

Figure Memory requires the child to examine a diagram (e.g., a line drawing of a square) for 5 seconds and then identify that figure embedded within a more complex figure (a diagram of a square obscured by other lines and shapes). The child identifies the shape by writing over the appropriate lines within the more complex design that includes the original figure. For a response to be scored correct, all lines of the design have to be indicated without any additions or omissions.

Verbal-Spatial Relations is a subtest in which the child is shown six illustrations and asked to point to the picture that, for example, shows "the ball in a basket on the table." The question appears on the bottom of the stimulus page and is read by the examiner. The child must respond within the specified time limit. The items range from simple one-concept dimensions to multiconcept multidimensional questions (e.g., "Which picture shows a square above a triangle to the left of a circle below a cross?").

Measures of Successive Processing

Successive processing subtests demand the preservation of the serial organization of events (Luria, 1966, p. 108). These processes are involved in the perception, retention, and reproduction of serially organized stimuli, especially a series of speech sounds and of words (Luria, 1966, p. 110). These processes have been measured using tasks requiring (1) the repetition of a series of words or numbers, tasks that require the smooth performance of a serial activity; (2) learning poetry by memory; (3) differentiating between similar sounding phonemes (even though articulation is not impaired) (Luria, 1980, p. 508); (4) the serial organization of speech traces (Luria, 1966, p. 112), the combining of sounds with symbols (Luria, 1973, p. 140); and (5) the association of sounds and word meaning (Luria, 1970, p. 125). The CAS subtests demand that the individual appreciate the serial nature of stimuli. The successive tasks require the individual to reproduce a particular sequence of events, preserve the serial organization of speech sounds, or repeat and answer questions that require the linearity of events be correctly interpreted. These tests include items that are relatively easy (e.g., recalling a span of two words in order) to very difficult (comprehension of the syntax of a complex sentence).

Word Series consists of nine single-syllable high-frequency nouns which are presented (at the rate of one word per second) in series ranging in length from two to nine words. The child is asked to repeat the words in the same order as stated by the examiner. The nine words are consistently presented in a quasi-random fashion from the first item. The ordering of words was conducted using a balanced presentation of each possible word and each possible pair or words. The frequencies of each of the words used in the entire task and in the first and last positions were also balanced across the nine words. The raw score is the number of items correctly repeated in their entirety because this demands preservation of the linearity of the words and meets the functional architecture of successive processing.

Sentence Repetition and Sentence Questions involve sentences that are read to the child that use color words in place of nouns, verbs, and so on (e.g., the blue is graying). Color words are used to provide statements with minimal meaning. Sentence Repetition requires the child to repeat the sentence exactly as presented including word endings. Sentence Questions requires the subject to answer a question about the statement. For example, after hearing the sentence, "The blue is graying," the child is asked the question: "Who is graying?" (answer: "the blue"). These tasks demand appreciation of the syntax in the sentences for successful completion.

Speech Rate is a measure of successive processing that involves the repeated articulation of words in order. The total time taken to say three words in order ten times as fast as possible is sensitive to this process because repeating the words requires phonological decoding, producing the appropriate pronunciation, and executing the act of speech. The words are high imagery single and double syllable words presented in a series of three so that memory of the sequence is not at issue.

VALIDITY

Validity evidence for the PASS theory based on experimental tests has been presented in many research papers and summarized in two books (Das et al., 1979; Das et al., 1994). Research on the CAS's reliability and validity, however, cannot be presented here because the test is in standardization and validity studies are being conducted at the time of this writing. To provide the reader with a sample of the most current findings since the publication of the 1994 book, I present a discussion of some recent research studies. This includes a study involving the hearing impaired, based on a dissertation by Welch (1992), and an intervention study by Das, Mishra, and Pool (1995).

PASS and Wechsler with the Hearing Impaired

Welch (1992) conducted a study of the Wechsler Intelligence Scale for Children—Revised (WISC-R) Performance IQ and PASS cognitive processing tasks with the Stanford Achievement Test (SAT) for a sample of hearing-impaired students. The sample comprised 96 students (approximately equal numbers of males and females), age 8 years to 16 years 11 months (mean age = 12.4 years, $SD = 2.5$ years). Most of the subjects (59%) received instruction through total communication and the remaining 41% students were enrolled in oral educational programs. The children attended a public day school (73%) or a state residential school for the deaf (27%). The WISC-R Performance Scale and several PASS experimental tasks (Das & Naglieri, 1987) (WISC-R Digit Span Forward was given as an additional measure of successive processing) were administered (using visual or the combination of sign and oral instruction) in counterbalanced order, followed approximately 2 months later by the eighth edition of the Stanford Achievement Test (SAT-8; 1990).

The results of Welch's study showed PASS was a predictor of achievement in all areas assessed by the SAT-8 (see Table 13.1). The combination of the PASS scales correlated highly ($r = .75$, $p < .001$) with total achievement and all correlations between PASS and achievement were significant. These results showed that experimental PASS tasks were related to achievement for this low-incidence population in important ways. For example, the relationships between planning and successive processes with reading is consistent with other research with hearing-impaired (Ojile, 1991) and normally hearing individuals (e.g., Cummins & Das, 1977; Naglieri & Das, 1987). The correlations between PASS and math are also consistent with findings by Warrick (1989). Planning and successive processes each correlated higher with achievement than did the PIQ for this sample, suggesting that these two processes may play an important role in learning for this population. This finding also illustrates how PASS predicted achievement differently (planning and successive processes are not found in Wechsler) for this sample.

Welch also reported factor-analytic results for the PASS tests she used and found that the organization of tests was robust for this hearing-impaired sample as it has been in previous investigations involving normally hearing samples. These results, presented in Table 13.2, were more fully analyzed (using confirmatory factor analysis) by Naglieri, Welch, and Braden (1994) who also found support for the organization of PASS tasks according to the theory, as previously shown (Naglieri et

TABLE 13.1. Pearson Correlations Between PASS, WISC-R, and SAT-8 for Hearing-Impaired Students ($N = 96$)

	Plan.	Attent.	Sim.	Succ.	PASS	PIQ
Reading Comprehension	.54	.30	.40	.68	.68	.47
Spelling	.50	.38	.37	.45	.59	.44
Concepts of Number	.50	.23	.52	.55	.63	.44
Math Computation	.49	.32	.43	.50	.61	.37
Math Applications	.54	.23	.47	.62	.65	.43
Total Achievement	.61	.35	.52	.66	.75	.49

Note. All correlations are significant.

al., 1991; Naglieri, Braden, & Gottling, 1993; Naglieri, Braden, & Warrick, 1994). Naglieri, Welch, and Braden (1994) concluded that their results supported the PASS model as a viable explanation of cognitive processes for this sample of hearing-impaired students and that the PASS model provided a better fit to the data than a verbal–nonverbal solution. These results further suggested that PASS model may provide a method to measure intelligence more broadly, especially important for the hearing impaired.

An Intervention Based on PASS: PREP

The link between PASS and intervention is articulated by Das et al. (1994) and is illustrated in a recent paper by Das et al. (1995). Their study involved the *PASS Remedial Program* (PREP), which is designed to improve word decoding difficulties through the improved utilization of PASS, especially successive and simultaneous cognitive processes. Global process training provides children with the opportunity to internalize strategies through inductive reasoning and maximize generalization and transfer. Bridging processing tasks provide a means to make global tasks more relevant for academic skills of reading and spelling. Both components of PREP encourage the application of strategies to academic tasks by facilitating verbal mediation and internalization processes but focus on overcoming reading decoding problems related to successive processing difficulties.

In this study, Das et al. (1995) applied the PREP program in four elementary schools. Each child was seen about two times a week, 50–60 minutes per period, for a total of about 15 sessions. All students had word reading problems and were receiving special educational services. This groups was divided into control ($n = 31$) and experimental ($n = 20$) samples and administered the Woodcock Reading Mastery Test (Woodcock–Johnson, 1987) pre- and post-PREP. The results (see Figure 13.2) showed that the PREP group improved more than the control group and these differences were significant. This is an important finding because it is extremely difficult to show gains in standardized tests such as the Woodcock–Johnson Psycho-Educational Battery—Revised (WJ-R; Woodcock & Johnson, 1977). This finding is consistent with research by Brailsford, Snart, and Das (1984), Crawford and Das (1992), Krywaniuk and Das (1976), and Spencer, Snart, and Das (1989). Training processes and encouraging transfer via inductive reasoning and bridging tasks has been shown to have a possible beneficial influence on reading of real and pseudo-words.

TABLE 13.2. Principal Components Factor Analysis of PASS Tasks for Hearing-Impaired Students ($N = 87$)

	Successive	Simultaneous	Planning	Attention
Planned Search	−.271	.190	.657*	.071
Planned Connections	.223	.020	.403*	−.010
Planned Codes	−.006	−.239	.739*	−.055
Figure Memory	−.113	.869*	−.082	−.099
MAT-EF	.152	.454*	.022	.183
Number Finding	−.165	−.059	−.042	.843*
Receptive Attention	.059	−.019	−.031	.594*
Word Series	.702*	.001	−.079	−.114
Digit Span Forward	.776*	−.163	−.117	−.002
Sentence Questions	.557*	.060	.252	.037

Note. Highest loadings are noted with an asterisk.

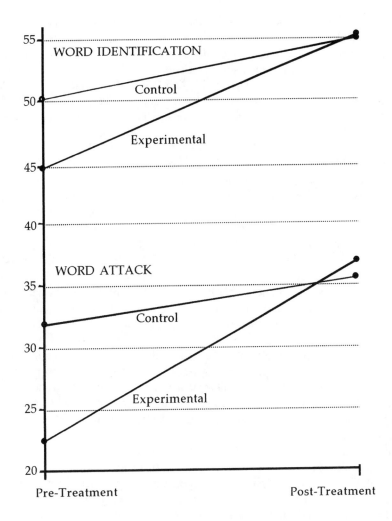

FIGURE13.2. Results of PREP Intervention Study. Data from Das, Mishra, and Pool, 1995.

HOW PASS AND CAS ARE DIFFERENT FROM TRADITIONAL IQ

To discuss how PASS and CAS differ from such traditional IQ tests as the Wechsler and the *Stanford–Binet: Fourth Edition* (SB-IV; Thorndike, Hagen, & Sattler, 1986), two issues have to be considered. First, I discuss the similarities and differences in what is assessed. Second, the implications of different coverage for identification of cognitive strengths and weaknesses of individuals with learning problems are examined.

Pass and Traditional IQ—Similarities and Differences

Traditional IQ Tests and the PASS Theory

The inclusion of tests that involve simultaneous processing is the area of greatest similarity between the CAS tasks and traditional IQ tests. Both the Wechsler scales and the SB-IV include tests often described as nonverbal spatial, such as Block Design (Pattern Analysis on the SB-IV), which have defined Perceptual Organization or Abstract–Visual factors. There is evidence that the Performance and Abstract–Visual Scales included in these IQ tests could be viewed as involving simultaneous processing. WISC-R Block Design and a similar task developed by Das and Naglieri have been used in studies involving the PASS theory. Hurt and Naglieri (1992) found WISC-R Block Design to be related to the PASS simultaneous tasks Figure Memory and Matrices, as did Naglieri et al. (1991) using a similar task. The results of these studies are consistent with the expectation that construction of a design to match a standard involves simultaneous processing because the component parts of the design must be interrelated in order to arrive at the correct solution. These may be the same processing demands placed on such tasks as Matrices and Figure Memory, which also demand interrelating component parts of the stimuli. Therefore, functional analysis of the cognitive processing demands of Block Design, along with some experimental evidence of the relationships between Block Design with Matrices and Figure Memory, support the view that this subtest may be considered one that demands simultaneous processes. Thus, simultaneous processes may be most similar to the nonverbal scales provided in the Wechsler and SB-IV tests.

In addition to nonverbal tasks, traditional IQ tests also have a large number of measures that involve verbal content (or verbal knowledge base) and numerical knowledge. This is evidenced by the Wechsler vocabulary subtest and Verbal Relations on the SB-IV, as well as arithmetic on the Wechsler and the Quantitative Scale on the on SB-IV. These verbal and quantitative tests which are either included in one overall scale (such as the WISC-R Verbal IQ) or subdivided into Verbal and Quantitative Scales on the SB-IV, all essentially measure counting and/or oral arithmetic problem solving. From the PASS theory, these tasks cannot be well represented by a single process. That is, some math tests, such as math computation, may be influenced considerably by planning processes (Garofalo, 1986), but others (e.g., Metropolitan Achievement Test) have been shown to require all PASS processes (Warrick, 1989). Therefore, to describe the verbal/achievement scales in the current IQ tests as particular processes does not seem warranted; instead, they should be conceptualized as measuring verbal/academic achievement.

Measures of memory or sequencing have been included as separate scales on some tests (Binet) or integrated into the Verbal Scale (WISC-R Digit Span) or included in an entire scale (SB-IV Memory Scale). These tests typically involve the repetition of some order of events for credit. So, for example, digits or words are repeated in order and the child is required to reproduce the sequence of stimuli. In general, the repetition of events in order may involve successive processing, but these tests are often confounded by increased complexity and therefore it should not be assumed that any task involving repetition in order will require successive processes. For example, the WISC-R Digit Span score is not a pure measure of successive processing for two reasons. First, the Digit Span comprises of Digits Forward and Backward. Second, forward and backward Digit Spans require different combinations of processes. Schofield and Ashman (1986) showed that forward span was significantly related to successive processing but backward span was related equally to both successive and planning processes. Thus, careful analysis of any task involving the serial repetition of events is needed when making decisions about the underlying processes involved.

This analysis of the form of traditional IQ tests leads me to suggest the following: (1) the Wechsler Performance scales may be considered to have some simultaneous processing demands, (2) successive processing may underlie tasks such as Digit Span Forward, and (3) verbal and quantitative scales may be best described as verbal–achievement involving a variety of the PASS processes. This leaves unassessed Planning and Attention, in many ways the most important components of human cognitive functioning, and partially assessed successive processes. This suggests that when viewed from the PASS perspective, traditional tests may offer a limited view of intelligence which is a significant and substantial difference between the methods, carrying important implications.

The K-ABC and the PASS Theory

The relationship between the PASS theory and the Kaufman Assessment Battery for Children (K-ABC) warrants clarification because of Kaufman and Kaufman's (1983) association of this test with the early research on simultaneous and successive processing (Das, 1973; Das et al., 1975). Although the position taken by Kaufman and Kaufman when they developed the K-ABC is not consistent with the entire PASS theory, the early work on simultaneous and successive processing is similar to the K-ABC Sequential/Simultaneous format. For example, it is apparent in their statement describing the Sequential/Simultaneous dichotomy that Kaufman and Kaufman chose to take an eclectic approach:

> Diverse avenues of research within cognitive psychology, neuropsychology, and related disciplines have come up with an intriguing variety of labels for the dichotomy between two basic types of information processing: sequential versus parallel or serial versus multiple (Neisser, 1967), successive versus simultaneous (Das, Kirby, & Jarman, 1975; Luria, 1966), analytic versus gestalt/holistic (Levy, 1972), propositional versus appositional (Bogen, 1969), verbal versus imagery or sequential versus synchronous (Paivio, 1975, 1976) controlled versus automatic (Schneider & Shiffrin, 1977, Shiffrin & Schneider, 1977), time-ordered versus time independent (Gordon & Bogen, 1974), and other dichotomous label associated with individuals such as Freud, Pavlov, Maslow, and James (Bogen, 1969). (Kaufman & Kaufman, 1983, p. 25)

The similarity of the various concepts of these theories is the essence of the view of ability Kaufman and Kaufman utilized in the K-ABC rather than any one of the theories in particular. Although the work of Das et al. (1975) on simultaneous and successive processing (one-half of the PASS theory) was one of many models that influenced Kaufman and Kaufman, their test was not designed to reflect any particular model. From the PASS perspective, the inclusion of simultaneous and successive-like tasks and the exclusion of planning and attention is a criticism of the K-ABC noted in past reviews (e.g., Das, 1984).

Evaluating Learning Disorders: The Planning and Successive Advantage

Past PASS research conducted by Das and me, as well as our affiliated colleagues, has suggested both planning and successive processing problems for those with general and specific (phonological decoding) reading failure (see Das et al., 1994; Kirby & WIlliams, 1991). This may give the PASS theory and the CAS advantages in uncovering the learning problem associated with impaired academic performance in reading as well as math (Naglieri & Gottling, 1995). For the purpose of identification of a cognitive weakness, PASS may have advantage over traditional IQ tests because of the scope of the processes evaluated. This was shown in the study by Welch described earlier and the focus of the study by Naglieri and Reardon (1993). They showed that if intelligence is redefined according to the PASS theory, a predictive relationship does exist with reading failure defined on the basis of phonological decoding of both familiar and pseudo-words. A study in investigating traditional IQ tests did not demonstrate such a relationship (Siegel, 1989). The CAS, therefore, may be useful as a tool that can help identify the cognitive processing problems associated with academic failure and, perhaps, may allow for a system of distinguishing among different kinds of learning disabilities such as reading disabilities related to decoding or comprehension, arithmetic disability, disabilities that primarily relate to attentional problems, planning-based academic problems, and so on. Separation of various learning problems based on the identification of specific cognitive difficulties and related academic failure may now be possible with PASS.

Evaluation of Individuals with Attention Deficit: The Planning and Attention Advantage

Attention-deficit disorder (ADD) is characterized by "developmentally inappropriate degrees of inattention, overactivity, and impulsivity" (Barkley, 1990, p. 47). Although well described in several sources, identification of children with ADD has been largely limited to thorough histories and behavioral rating scales (Barkley, 1990). However, with the carefully operationalized theory-based approach to assessment of attention provided by the CAS, improvement in the evaluation of individuals with ADD may be possible. Moreover, because the CAS includes measures of planning, sensitivity to the impulsivity problems sometimes displayed by children with attention deficits could be evaluated, thus allowing for differentiation of children who have primarily a difficulty in attention versus planning or both attention and planning. For example, if a child has an attentional deficit (this could be operationally defined in part, as a below-average standard score on the Attention scale) the opportunity for different interventions may be realized (e.g., drug therapy of different types or dosages or cognitive control programs described by Kirby & Williams, 1991).

Evaluating Individuals with Mental Retardation

There are two possible ways of using the CAS to help determine whether a person may be mentally retarded. First, the PASS view may provide the advantage of measuring a broader spectrum of human functioning than is available with previous IQ technology. Because students suspected of mental retardation typically have poor academic achievement and subtests with achievement content have been widely used to measure intelligence (e.g., Wechsler Verbal scale subtests such as Arithmetic or Information) but the PASS tests may not have such verbal/achievement content, the cognitive levels of those with mental retardation may be measured with less influence of academic knowledge. Second, because the CAS may measure cognitive processes not represented in other tests, specifically planning, and attention, the addition of these dimensions may provide important information when differential diagnosis and treatment planning decisions are made. For example, an individual with poor verbal–achievement (knowledge base) and Performance IQ (simultaneous processing) could have higher (perhaps low average) planning and/or attention scores. In such a case, this person may perform better than the IQ scores would predict on, for example, measures of adaptive functioning.

Das et al. (1994) have suggested that adequate functioning in planning would likely be seen with a similar level of adaptive functioning. The theoretical basis for suggesting that adaptive behavior and planning are related is discussed by Das et al. (1994). Essentially, planning may be at the base of adaptive behavior because it requires evaluation of the environment, development and use of appropriate actions, and control of words and deeds. These social judgments, necessary for adequate adaptive functioning, may require planning processes. Use of the CAS, therefore, may provide a more valid evaluation of persons suspected of having mental retardation because of its broader scope, especially sensitivity to planning processes.

BEYOND TRADITIONAL INTELLECTUAL ASSESSMENT

Theory Makes All the Difference

"Measurement, even though it is based on observable responses, would have little meaning or usefulness unless it could be interpreted in light of the underlying theoretical construct" (Crocker & Algina, 1986, p. 7). IQ scores, even though derived from tests that have a long history, have limited meaning and usefulness because they are based on an undifferentiated and truncated view of general ability. The CAS, because it is based on the well-articulated PASS theory, may have considerable meaning and usefulness because it provides information about a spectrum of cognitive processes that are related to human performance in many ways. Perhaps the most important way in which the CAS aims to advance the field of cognitive assessment is through its foundation in the well-articulated differentiated PASS theory.

Theory Informs Practice

Once we have a good theory, solutions to practical issues can flow from the theoretical perspective. For example, the problem of diagnostic differentiation has been poorly addressed by traditional IQ tests. In a paper in a special issue on intelligence in the *Journal of Psychoeducational Assessment* (Naglieri & Das, 1990), I described how early versions of the PASS tests may have differentiated reading disabled, mentally retarded, attention deficit, delinquent, and normal children. These different samples of children with different diagnoses had different PASS profiles from matched control groups. These data, which were a summary of several studies, illustrated the sensitivity of PASS and the advantages it may provide because some of the cognitive processes we measure are not assessed by traditional IQ tests. Thus, PASS may offer a viable method for solving the problem of differential diagnosis and may provide the opportunity to consider a theoretical view of what the disabilities may be.

PASS and Intervention

The relevance of PASS to instruction has been discussed in several sources (e.g., Das et al., 1994) and most recently by Das et al. (1995) and Naglieri and Gottling (1995; in press). The former study, presented earlier, provides data related to the utility of a specific remediation program, the latter illustrated how PASS could be applied on an individual basis to students with mathematics problems like those used in the classroom. Naglieri and Gottling modeled their studies after those published by Cormier, Carlson, and Das (1990) and Kar, Dash, Das, and Carlson (1992). These researchers showed that performance may be improved through instruction that encourages students to be more aware of their cognitive activities, to consider the problem in a broad context, and to use good problem-solving strategies. The results of their experiments showed that encouragement of strategy use was more effective for those with low planning scores than those with good scores on planning. The authors concluded that because planning controls and regulates cognitive processing, improving planning may optimize performance. In addition, because verbalization is one method to formulate and generate plans of action, it may help the student recognize the important parts of a problem, direct and control cognitive activity, and increase awareness of and attention to the problem.

Naglieri and Gottling (1995; in press) extended this research into the classroom using work sheets like those prepared by the teacher. We found that students with poor performance on CAS measures of planning improved substantially in mathematics as a result of an intervention that facilitated planfulness. In contrast, minimal improvements were apparent for those who were adequate in planning. Those students with a planning weakness benefited from an instruction that facilitated planfulness more than those who did not have a weakness in planning. This illustration and previous research cited earlier suggest that aptitude may interact with treatment if the aptitude is well defined.

When All Is Said and Done

It is my hope that the CAS will facilitate changes at both theoretical and practical levels, through the reconceptualization of intelligence as cognitive processes and the application of the PASS theory, to maximize the benefits to society. Through the application of a modern view of human cognitive functioning expressed within the context of PASS cognitive processes we may go beyond traditional IQ tests in several ways. First, because the CAS test development efforts intended to operationalize theoretical constructs that come directly from the PASS theory of cognitive processing, previous concepts of what intelligence may be did not limit the scope of constructs and tasks that are included. Second, although traditional IQ tests were developed essentially to categorize and classify individuals, our purpose is to measure important cognitive processes that underlie human performance and go beyond classification. Third, sensitivity to those cognitive processes that relate to academic failure has been a significant weakness of traditional IQ tests, but research has shown that PASS may not have this limitation (see Das et al., 1994). This means that instead of an IQ achievement discrepancy (which means that the test of intelligence failed to detect an intellectual problem related to the failure in achievement), a cognitive and academic similarity (an isolated PASS weakness that is related to, and similar to, the academic failure) may be discovered. In this case, then, the psychologist finds cognitive and academic weaknesses, and appropriate remediation, based on the knowledge of what the problem is, may be identified and implemented. If a cognitive problem is not uncovered, issues such as history of educational instruction, sensory difficulties, problems with motivation, emotional status, and so on, would be important to explore. Finally, if a cognitive difficulty is uncovered, methods such as the PREP, or those described by Kirby and Williams (1991), Naglieri and Gottling (1995; in press), or Ashman and Conway (1993) may be considered.

CONCLUSION

This chapter has emphasized how important it is for psychology to consider a modern theory of intelligence. In our work we started from a theory of human cognitive functioning that provided a definition of a spectrum of constructs (PASS). Next experimental tests were built according to the theory. The tests were standardized and their validity and reliability assessed. The results may be used to determine global (gifted, mentally retarded, etc.) and specific (attention deficits, planning failure, etc.) cognitive processing levels and may have value as a means of redefining the nature of various exceptional children. Informed about PASS processes, psychologists can then turn to the selection of appropriate interventions. At each step, the well-differentiated view based on the PASS theory guides the activity.

REFERENCES

Anokhin, P. K. (1969). Cybernetics and the integrative activity of the brain. In M. Cole & I. Maltzman (Eds.), *A handbook of contemporary Soviet psychology* (pp. 830–856). New York: Basic Books.

Anokhin, P. K. (1978). *Izbrannye trudy: Filosofskiye aspekty teorii funktzional'noy sistemy* [Selected papers: Philosophical aspects of the functional system's theory]. Moscow: Nauka.

Ashman, A. F., & Conway, R. N. F. (1993). *Using cognitive methods in the classroom.* London: Routledge.

Barkley, R. A. (1990). *Attention-deficit hyperactivity disorder: A handbook for diagnosis and treatment.* New York: Guilford Press.

Brailsford, A., Snart, F., & Das, J. P. (1984). Strategy training and reading comprehension. *Journal of Learning Disabilities, 17,* 287–290.

Broadbent, D. E. (1958). *Perception and communication.* Oxford, England: Pergamon.

Cormier, P., Carlson, J. S., & Das, J. P. (1990). Planning ability and cognitive performance: *The compensatory effects of a dynamic assessment approach. Learning and Individual Differences, 2,* 437–449.

Cattell, R. B. (1963). Theory of crystallized intelligence: A critical experiment. *Journal of Educational Psychology, 54,* 1–22.

Crawford, S. A. S., & Das, J. P. (1992). Teaching for transfer: A program for remediation in reading. In J. Carlson (Ed.), *Advances in cognitive and educational practice* (Vol.1B, pp. 73–103). Greenwich, CT: JAI Press.

Crocker, L., & Algina, J. (1986). *Introduction to classical and modern test theory.* New York: Holt, Rinehart & Winston.

Cummins, J. P., & Das, J. P. (1977). Cognitive processing and reading difficulties: A framework for research. *The Alberta Journal of Educational Research, 23,* 246–256.

Das, J. P. (1973). Structure of cognitive abilities: Evidence for simultaneous and successive processing. *Journal of Educational Psychology, 65,* 103–108.

Das, J. P. (1984). Simultaneous and successive processes and the K-ABC. *Journal of Special Education, 18,* 229–238.

Das, J. P., & Dash, U. N. (1983). Hierarchical factor solution of coding and planning processes: Any new insights? *Intelligence, 7,* 27–37.

Das, J. P., Kirby, J. R., & Jarman, R. F. (1975). Simultaneous and successive synthesis: An alternative model. *Psychological Bulletin, 82,* 87–103.

Das, J. P., Kirby, J. R., & Jarman, R. F. (1979). *Simultaneous and successive cognitive processes.* New York: Academic Press.

Das, J. P., Mishra, R. K., & Pool, J. (1995). An experiment on cognitive remediation of word-reading difficulty. *Journal of Learning Disabilities, 28,* 66–79.

Das, J. P., & Naglieri, J. A. (1987). Das–Naglieri: Cognitive Assessment System: Experimental Test Battery. Unpublished manuscript.

Das, J. P., Naglieri, J. A., & Kirby, J. R. (1994). *Assessment of cognitive processes: The PASS theory of intelligence.* Needham Heights, MA: Allyn & Bacon.

Einstein, A. (1956). *Out of my later years.* New York: Bonanza Books.

Galperin, P. Y. (1989). Study of the intellectual development of the child. *Soviet Psychology, 27,* 26–44.

Garofalo, J. F. (1986). Simultaneous synthesis, behavior regulation and arithmetic performance. *Journal of Psychoeducational Assessment, 4,* 229–238.

Guilford, J. P. (1967). *The nature of human intelligence.* New York: McGraw-Hill.

Hunt, E. B. (1990). A modern arsenal for mental assessment. *Educational Psychologists, 25,* 223–242.

Hunt, E., & Lansman, M. (1986). Unified model of attention and problem solving. *Psychological Review, 93,* 446–461.

Hurt, J., & Naglieri, J. A. (1992). Delinquent and normal males' performance on planning, attention simultaneous, successive cognitive processing tasks. *Journal of Clinical Psychology, 48,* 120–128.

Kar, B. C., Dash, U. N., Das, J. P., & Carlson, J. S. (1992). Two experiments on the dynamic assessment of planning. *Learning and Individual Differences, 5,* 13–29.

Kaufman, A. S. (1979). *Intelligent testing with the WISC-R.* New York: Wiley.

Kaufman, A. S. (1990). *Assessing adolescent and adult intelligence.* Boston: Allyn & Bacon.

Kaufman, A. S. (1994). *Intelligent testing with the WISC-III.* New York: Wiley.

Kaufman, A. S., & Kaufman, N. L. (1983). *Kaufman Assessment Battery for Children.* Circle Pines, MN: American Guidance Service.

Kirby, J. R., & Williams, N. H. (1991). *Learning problems: A cognitive approach.* Toronto: Kagan & Woo.

Krywaniuk. L. W., & Das, J. P. (1976). Cognitive strategies in native children: Analysis and intervention. *The Alberta Journal of Educational Research, 22,* 271–280.

Lipsitz, J. D., Dworkin, R. H., & Erlenmeyer-Kimling, L. (1993). Wechsler Comprehension and Picture Arrangement subtests and social adjustment. *JCCP: Psychological Assessment, 5,* 430–437.

Luria, A. R. (1966). *Human brain and psychological processes.* New York: Harper & Row.

Luria, A. R. (1970). The functional organization of the brain. *Scientific American, 222,* 66–78.

Luria, A. R. (1973). *The working brain: An introduction to neuropsychology.* New York: Basic Books.

Luria, A. R. (1976). *Cognitive development: Its cultural and social foundations.* Cambridge, MA: Harvard University Press.

Luria, A. R. (1980). *Higher cortical functions in man* (2nd ed., rev. and expanded). New York: Basic Books.

Luria, A. R. (1982). *Language and cognition.* New York: Wiley.

McDermott, P. A., Fantuzzo, J. W., & Glutting, J. J. (1990). Just say no to subtest analysis: A critique on Wechsler theory and practice. *Journal of Psychoeducational Assessment, 8,* 290–303.

Naglieri, J. A. (1989). A cognitive processing theory for the measurement of intelligence. *Educational Psychologist, 24,* 185–206.

Naglieri, J. A. (1993). Subtest and composite score comparisons for the Diagnostic Achievement Battery–Second Edition. *Journal of Psychoeducational Assessment, 11,* 139–143.

Naglieri, J. A. (1996). Cognitive assessment: Traditional intelligence tests (pp. 70–72). In T. Fagan & P. Warden, *Encyclopedia of school psychology.* Greenwood Group.

Naglieri, J. A., Braden, J., & Gottling, S. (1993). Confirmatory factor analysis of the Planning, Attention, Simultaneous, Successive (PASS) cognitive processing model for a kindergarten sample. *Journal of Psychoeducational Assessment, 11,* 259–269.

Naglieri, J. A., Braden, J. P., & Warrick, P. D. (1994). *Confirmatory factor analysis of the Planning, Attention, Simultaneous, Successive (PASS) Cognitive Processing Model.* Manuscript submitted for publication.

Naglieri, J. A., & Das, J. P. (1987). Construct and criterion related validity of Planning, Simultaneous and Successive cognitive processing tasks. *Journal of Psychoeducational Assessment, 4,* 353–363.

Naglieri, J. A., & Das, J. P. (1990). Planning, attention, simultaneous, and successive (PASS) cognitive processes as a model for intelligence. *Journal of Psychoeducational Assessment, 8,* 303–337.

Naglieri, J. A., & Das, J. P. (1996a). *Das Naglieri Cognitive Assessment System.* Chicago: Riverside.

Naglieri, J. A., & Das, J. P. (1996b). *Das Naglieri Cognitive Assessment System: Interpretive handbook.* Chicago: Riverside.

Naglieri, J. A., Das, J. P., Stevens, J. J., & Ledbetter, M. F. (1991). Confirmatory factor analysis of planning, simultaneous, successive cognitive processing tasks. *Journal of School Psychology, 29,* 1–17.

Naglieri, J. A. & Gottling, S. H. (1995). A study of planning and mathematics instruction for students with learning disabilities. *Psychological Reports, 76,* 1343–1354.

Naglieri, J. A. & Gottling, S. H. (in press). Mathematics instruction and PASS cognitive processes. *Journal of Learning Disabilities.*

Naglieri, J. A., Prewett, P. , & Bardos, A. N. (1989). An exploratory study of Planning, Attention, Simultaneous and Successive cognitive processes. *Journal of School Psychology, 27,* 347–364.

Naglieri, J. A., & Reardon, S. (1993). Traditional IQ is irrelevant to learning disabilities—Intelligence is not. *Journal of Learning Disabilities, 26,* 127–133.

Naglieri, J. A., & Sloutsky, V. N. (1995). Re-inventing intelligence: The PASS theory of cognitive functioning. *General Psychologist, 31,* 11–17.

Naglieri, J. A., Welch, J. A., & Braden, J. P. (1994). Factor structure of Planning, Attention, Simultaneous, Successive (PASS) Cognitive processing tasks and the Wechsler PIQ for a hearing impaired sample. *Journal of School Psychology, 32,* 371–384.

Neisser, U. (1967). *Cognitive psychology.* New York: Appleton-Century-Crofts.

Ojile, E. O. (1991). *A preliminary investigation of the use of the Cognitive Assessment System (CAS) with the deaf and hearing.* Unpublished doctoral dissertation, University of Alberta.

Piaget, J. (1978). *Behavior and evolution.* New York: Pantheon Books.

Pribram, K. H. (1971). *Languages of the brain: Experimental paradoxes and principles in neuropsychology.* Englewood Cliffs, NJ: Prentice-Hall.

Sagan, C. (1980). *Cosmos.* New York: Random House.

Sattler, J. M. (1988). *Assessment of children.* San Diego, CA: J. Sattler.

Schofield, N. J., & Ashman, A. F. (1986). The relationship between Digit Span and cognitive processing across ability groups. *Intelligence, 10,* 59–73.

Siegel, L. S. (1989). IQ is irrelevant to the definition of learning disabilities. *Journal of Learning Disabilities. 22,* 469–479.

Simon, H. (1981). Studying human intelligence by creating artificial intelligence. *American Scientist, 69,* 300–309.

Spencer, F., Snart, F., & Das, J. P. (1989). A process-based approach to the remediation of spelling in students with reading disabilities. *Alberta Journal of Educational Research, 35,* 269–282.

Stanford Achievement Test (SAT-8). (1990). San Antonio, TX: Psychological Corporation.

Stewart, K. J., & Moely, B. E. (1983). The WISC-R third factor: What does it mean? *Journal of Consulting and Clinical Psychology, 51,* 940–941.

Thorndike, R. L., Hagen, E. P., & Sattler, J. M. (1986). *Stanford–Binet Intelligence Scale: Fourth edition.* Chicago: Riverside.

Vygotsky, L. S. (1978). *Mind in society: the development of higher psychological processes.* Cambridge, MA: Harvard University Press.

Vygotsky, L. S., & Luria, A. R. (1993). *Studies on the history of behavior: Ape, primitive, and child.* Hillsdale, NJ: Erlbaum.

Warrick, P. D. (1989). *Investigation of the PASS Model of cognitive processing and mathematics achievement.* Unpublished doctoral dissertation, Ohio State University, Columbus.

Welch, J. A. (1992). *Predicting academic achievement of hearing impaired students using the Wechsler Intelligence Scale for Children—Revised and the Planning, Attention, Simultaneous, and Successive (PASS) Model of Cognitive Processing.* Unpublished doctoral dissertation, Ohio State University, Columbus.

Wielkiewicz, R. M. (1990). Interpreting low scores on the WISC-R third factor: It's more than distractibility. *JCCP: Psychological Assessment, 2,* 91–97.

Woodcock, R. W., & Johnson, M. B. (1977). *Woodcock–Johnson Psycho-Educational Battery.* Chicago: Riverside.

Woodcock, R. W., & Johnson, M. B. (1987). *Woodcock reading mastery tests—Revised.* Circle Pines, MN: American Guidance Service.

Woodcock, R. W., & Johnson, M. B. (1989). *Woodcock–Johnson Psycho-Educational Battery—Revised.* Chicago: Riverside.

CHAPTER 14

The Universal Nonverbal Intelligence Test

R. STEVE McCALLUM

BRUCE A. BRACKEN

DESCRIPTION OF THE UNIT

The Universal Nonverbal Intelligence Test (UNIT; Bracken & McCallum, in press) is scheduled to be published in early 1997. The UNIT is a language-free test that requires no receptive or expressive language from the examiner or the examinee. The need for the UNIT in the United States is obvious because of the increasing number of non–English-speaking individuals immigrating from other countries, especially Asia and Latin American. As a result, there is a concomitant increase in the number of non- or limited english proficient (LEP) children enrolled in the public schools. It was recently claimed that more than 200 languages are spoken in the Greater Chicago Area schools (Pasko, 1994). Included among the 200 spoken languages are such exotic and low-incidence languages as Akan, Fanti, Pima, Urdu, as well as many more common languages. This situation in our schools exists in many other countries because technology and travel have made the earth a much smaller planet. It is the complicated task of professionals in many urban settings to assess children who are not English proficient to determine whether they have existing psychological or educational difficulties that would hinder their acquisition of a new language (i.e., English). How do professionals assess such children and obtain valid assessments of their cognitive abilities when the children do not understand the spoken directions of traditional language-loaded intelligence tests? Because of the vast numbers of languages spoken by the students in the U.S. public schools and because our existing tests cannot be translated to accommodate all of these languages, nonverbal assessment of children's intelligence seems like the only viable solution.

Similar assessment-related problems exist for children with limited hearing abilities or receptive and expressive language disabilities. Children with severe language-related disabilities are at an unfair disadvantage when assessed by means of spoken language. Consequently, children with such impairments may be more fairly assessed with a comprehensive nonverbal intelligence test.

Historically, test developers have constructed nonverbal tests of intelligence to meet the needs of a linguistic minority (i.e., individuals who have limited proficiency with the language of the dominant culture). Typically these individuals are foreign-born or have hearing deficits. According to Robb, Bernardoni, and Johnson (1972), early efforts to assess intelligence nonverbally resulted in development of a formboard task by Sequin in 1866; just after the turn of the century, the Healy–Fernald tests were developed, and in 1914 the Knox performance tests were introduced. The first widespread application of nonverbal testing technology occurred during World War I. The army developed the group Army Alpha Test to screen the intellectual ability of recruits; however, because there was a need to screen significant numbers of recruits who were illiterate or unable to speak English, a nonverbal test was needed. The Army Beta Test was developed for use with that population. Since that time, the literature describing cognitive functioning of linguistic miniorities has shown higher cognitive ability scores when ability was assessed via nonverbal means relative to verbal measures (Figueroa, 1990). Recently, legal mandates for appropriate testing practices have resulted from misuse of verbal tests for minority populations, particularly when verbally laden intelligence test scores have been used as the sole or primary consideration for placement in special education classes. Special testing considerations for linguistic minority children have been developed by professional groups (e.g., the American Educational Research Association) and printed in the *Standards for Educational and Psychological Testing* (American Educational Research Association, American Psychological Association, & National Council for Measurement in Education, 1985). As a result of the need to provide appropriate assessment for children who have limited facility with the dominant language, several instruments have been developed. However, instruments that are currently available are seriously limited in various ways (e.g., standardized with verbal directions, unidimensional, and include outdated norms).

Unfortunately, the limitations of existing nonverbal or verbally reduced tests have left an undesirable impression on those who must use these instruments. One of the more popular tests, The Leiter International Performance Scale (Leiter, 1948), has been used for years and with considerable respect among psychologists. However, the Leiter was standardized in the 1940s and has extremely outdated stimulus materials and norms. Another test, the *Test of Nonverbal Intelligence—2* (Brown, Sherbenou, & Johnson, 1990), or TONI-2, has been somewhat successful, but it has a weak theoretical foundation and a unidimensional assessment focus. The *Kaufman Assessment Battery for Children* (K-ABC; Kaufman & Kaufman, 1983) purports to allow for a "nonverbal" administration of some of the subtests and provides a "nonverbal score"; however, the K-ABC was not normed using the nonverbal communication format advocated by its authors. Consequently, the nonverbal scores obtained on the K-ABC are of limited value or generalizability. Also, the Wechsler Performance scales are often used for nonverbal assessments, but even the Performance Scale subtest directions are wordy, presented in English, and tend to include difficult language concepts (Bracken, 1986).

Psychoeducational professionals need a measure of nonverbal intelligence that possesses a few essential elements. For example, a "good" nonverbal measure of intelligence should not require *any* receptive or expressive language for administration, it should assess multiple facets of intelligence, it should assess higher order cognitive processes, and it should provide materials and activities that are inherently interesting and motivating. The UNIT was designed with all these criteria in mind. The UNIT is administered completely nonverbally, requiring only gestures, pantomimed demonstrations, and modeling by the examiner. The examinee needs only to point or manually manipulate stimulus materials. Consequently, the UNIT can be employed easily with non–English-speaking populations without the traditional language demands of conventional intelligence tests or costly translations. The UNIT gestures (e.g., affirmative head nods and pointing) were chosen because they seem to be ubiquitous modes of communication across cultures. Also, an effort was made to employ universal item content (i.e., objects found in all industrialized cultures). Thus, use of the UNIT with children from other countries is facilitated.

Theoretical Underpinnings

The UNIT contains six subtests designed to assess functioning according to a *two-tier model of intelligence* (memory and reasoning), which incorporates *two organizational strategies* (symbolic and nonsymbolic organization). Within each of the two fundamental organizational strategies the two cognitive abilities of memory and reasoning are assessed in an hierarchical arrangement (see Bracken & McCallum, 1994; Bracken, McCallum, Reed, & Williams, 1993; McCallum & Bracken, 1993.) The three memory subtests include Object Memory (OM), Spatial Memory (Spa M), and Symbolic Memory (Sym M). Similarly, three subtests were developed to assess reasoning: Cube Design (CD), Mazes (M), and Analogic Reasoning (AR). Five of the subtests require motoric manipulation (i.e., CD, OM, M, Sym M, Spa M), and one requires only a pointing response (AR). With two exceptions (CD, M) the subtests that require motoric manipulation can be adapted to allow for a pointing response only if necessary.

Symbolic organization strategies require the use of concrete and abstract symbols to conceptualize the environment; these symbols typically are language-related (e.g., words), although the symbols may take on any form (e.g., numbers, statistical equations, Rebus characters, and flags). Symbols eventually are internalized and come to label, mediate, connote, and, over time, make our experiences meaningful. Nonsymbolic strategies require the ability to perceive and make meaningful judgments about the physical relationships within our environment; this ability is symbol-free, or relatively so, and is closer to fluid-like intellectual abilities. Specifically, nonsymbolical strategies require the ability to discern and to discriminate patterns and to complete abstract geometric patterning problems.

Within each of the two fundamental organizational categories included in the UNIT (nonsymbolic and symbolic), problem solution requires one of two types of abilities—memory or reasoning. That is, some of the items require primarily symbolic organization and rely heavily on memory (e.g., those included on the Symbolic Memory subtest). Other items require considerable symbolic organization and reasoning skills, but less memory (e.g., those included on the Analogic Reasoning subtest). Some items seem to require nonsymbolic organization strategies and memory (e.g., those on the Spatial Memory subtest). Finally, others may require nonsymbolic organization and reasoning and *little* memory (Cube Design). Consequently, the UNIT assesses four basic cognitive abilities operationalized by the six subtests (see Figure 14.1).

An existing body of literature supports the rationale for assessing intelligence using the four strategies operationalized by the UNIT. For example, Wechsler (1939) emphasized the importance of distinguishing between highly symbolic (verbal) versus nonsymbolic perceptual (performance) means of expressing intelligence. Jensen (1980) provides rationale for a two-tiered hierarchical conceptualization of intelligence consisting of the two subconstructs of memory (Level I) and reasoning (Level II). However, in contrast to many low *g*-loaded Level I memory tasks designed to require reproduction or recall of simple content, UNIT memory tasks were developed to require more complex memory functioning. UNIT reasoning tasks were designed to require the ability to comprehend, analyze, and synthesize the organizational aspects of concepts and ideas.

The theoretical organization of the UNIT is consistent with a number of newly developed instruments that adopt the Gf-Gc Model of fluid and crystallized abilities, as described by Cattell (1963), Horn (1968), and others (e.g., Woodcock, 1990). Memory and reasoning are two important subconstructs identified in the Gf-Gc Model. Memory and reasoning, as assessed by the UNIT, appear to correspond to the Gsm (short-term memory) and the Gf (fluid reasoning) factors, respectively. Similarly, the symbolic and nonsymbolic measures are akin to Gc (comprehension-knowledge) and Gv (visual processing), respectively. Therefore, in combination the UNIT subtests appear to assess four of the seven Gf-Gc subconstructs assessed by the Woodcock–Johnson Psycho-Educational Battery–Revised, Cognitive Battery (WJ-R; Woodcock & Johnson, 1989). Thus, operationalization of the relevant models of cognitive functioning produces a 2 (organization: symbolic vs. nonsymbolic) by 2 (function: memory vs. reasoning) theoretical conceptualization for the UNIT.

	Memory	Reasoning
Nonsymbolic Mediation (NSM)	Spatial Memory (NSM)	Cube Design (NSM)
Symbolic Mediation (SM)	Symbolic Memory (SM)	Analogic Reasoning (SM)
	Object Memory (SM)	Mazes (NSM)

FIGURE 14.1. Conceptual model for the UNIT.

Most importantly, we have designed the UNIT to be a measure of intelligence, obtained nonverbally. Intelligence consists primarily of a pervasive and fundamental ability, *g*, which provides a base for the development of somewhat unique specialized skills. Although there are many means of determining intelligence, it makes little sense to conceptualize intelligence as being either verbal or nonverbal. Rather, there are verbal and nonverbal means available to assess intelligence. Consequently, the UNIT should be considered a nonverbal measure of intelligence, not a measure of nonverbal intelligence. Even though the UNIT is designed to provide unique measures of cognitive organization (i.e., symbolic and nonsymbolic content) and function (memory and reasoning), it is anticipated that first and foremost, it will be a strong measure of *g*, general intellectual ability, because of the complex nature of the subtests. Even the memory subtests require considerable cognitive engagement (e.g., multiple salient features, multiple stimuli).

Organization and Format of the UNIT

Structure of the UNIT

As a result of the 2 by 2 structural scheme, we anticipate that several scores can be calculated for the UNIT total test, including a Full Scale score (FSIQ), Memory Quotient (MQ), Reasoning Quotient (RQ), Symbolic Quotient (SQ), and Nonsymbolic Quotient (NSQ). Finally, individual subtest scores can be derived for each of the six subtests for further analysis of examinee's performance. UNIT subtests are described below. The first three subtests are designed to assess memory, the second three, reasoning.

1. *Symbolic Memory.* The examinee recalls and recreates sequences of visually presented universal symbols (e.g., green boy, black woman).
2. *Spatial Memory.* The examinee must remember and recreate the placement of black and/or green chips on a 3 × 3 or 4 × 4 cell grid.
3. *Object Memory.* The examinee is shown a visual array of common objects (e.g., shoe, telephone, tree) for 5 seconds, after which the examinee identifies the pictured objects from a larger array of pictured objects.
4. *Cube Design.* The examinee completes a three-dimensional block design task using between one and nine green and white blocks.
5. *Analogic Reasoning.* The examinee completes a matrix analogies task using common objects (e.g., hand/glove, foot/_____?) and novel geometric figures.
6. *Mazes.* The examinee completes a maze task by tracing a path through each maze from the center starting point to an exit.

Completion of all six subtests requires approximately 45 minutes. UNIT norms will allow for two- and four-subtest short-form batteries in addition to the full six-subtest battery. The short-form batteries require approximately one-third to two-thirds less time than the full scale and may be useful for screening and research purposes (see Figure 14.1).

Content of the UNIT

Each UNIT subtest requires that the examiner present the stimulus material nonverbally. For the Symbolic Memory subtest, stimulus plates are presented on an easel. The easel contains plates showing pictures of one or more of the following universal human figures in a particular order: a green baby, a black baby, a green girl, a black girl, a green boy, a black boy, a green women, a black women, a green man, a black man. The examinee is presented the stimulus plate and then is instructed through gestures to replicate the order shown on the stimulus plate. The examinee uses $1\frac{1}{2}'' \times 11\frac{1}{2}''$ response cards, each containing one of the universal human figures, to reproduce the array depicted on the stimulus plate. The task has no time limits other than a 5-second exposure time.

For the Spatial Memory subtest the examiner briefly presents a series of grids on stimulus plates located on an administration easel. The grids show one or more green or black polka dots placed within cells (on the grid). The less difficult items use a 3 by 3 grid, the more difficult items require a 4 by 4 grid. The stimulus plate is shown for 5 seconds and then is removed from view. The examinee places response chips on a blank grid which is placed on the tabletop in front of the child. Spatial Memory has no time limits except for the 5-second exposure.

The Object Memory subtest requires presentation of pictures of common objects arranged on stimulus plates located on an administration easel. The easel is laid flat on the table and the examinee is shown a plate containing pictures of one or more objects for 5 seconds, then the examinee is shown a second plate containing pictures from the first plate *and* pictures of "distractor objects." The examinee identifies pictures on the second plate that were shown on the first plate; to create a semipermanent response, the examinee places black chips on the pictures selected. This memory task is not timed other than the 5-second exposure.

The Cube Design subtest requires the examinee to use up to nine cubes to replicate three-dimensional designs shown on a stimulus plate. Each cube contains six facets; two white sides, two green sides, and two sides which contain diagonals (triangles), one green and one white. These cubes can be arranged to replicate the three-dimensional figures depicted on the stimulus plates. This task is timed but the time limits are liberal to emphasize the power rather than speeded nature of the task.

The Analogic Reasoning subtest requires the examinee to solve analogies presented in a matrix format. The examinee is directed to indicate which one of several options best completes a two-cell or a four-cell analogy. Task solution requires the examinee to determine the relationships between objects. For example, in the four-cell matrix the first cell might depict a fish and the second water; the third cell might show a bird, and the fourth cell would be blank. The examinee would select from several options the picture that best completes the matrix. In this case a picture of the sky would be a correct response. This reasoning subtest is not timed.

The Mazes subtest requires the examinee to complete a maze using a number 2 lead pencil, minus the eraser. The examinee is presented a maze showing a mouse in the center and one or more pieces of cheese on the outside of the maze. The cheese depicts one or more possible exits from the maze. The task is to determine the correct path from the center to the (correct) piece of cheese. The examinee is stopped after the first error. The task is timed, though the time limits are quite liberal.

To communicate task demands, the UNIT administration instructions employ the use of eight fairly universal gestures to communicate to the examinee expected responses and conditions (e.g., pointing to stimuli to be addressed, raising hands, and shrugging shoulders to indicate a solution is sought). In addition to these gestures, the UNIT administration employs examiner demonstrations to illustrate the approach to each item type, sample items to allow the examiner to determine whether the examinee understands the problem, corrective responses when the examinee fails to respond appropriately to sample items, transitional checkpoint items, which are scored items that allow the examiner to correct examinee's incorrect responses, and scored items that do not permit examiner correction.

UNIT Materials

General materials required to administer the UNIT include a stopwatch, a number 2 lead pencil, and two test booklets, one for the Mazes subtest and one for recording the students' performance on the remaining five subtests and relevant demographic information. Except for Mazes, the stimulus plates for all subtests are contained in a stand-up easel. In addition to the general materials, each subtest requires some unique components. The Symbolic Memory subtest requires use of the stimulus plates on the easel *and* a set of response cards containing the Universal Human figures; the Spatial Memory subtest requires the stimulus plates from the easel, *and* green and black response chips, two laminated response grids, (one depicts a 3 by 3 matrix and one a 4 by 4 matrix); Cube Design requires the stimulus plates from the easel *and* green and white blocks, a response mat, and the stopwatch; Object Memory requires the stimulus plates from the easel *and* green and white response chips; Analogic Reasoning requires only the stimulus plates from the easel; and, Mazes requires the Mazes booklet, a number 2 lead pencil with no eraser, the stopwatch, and a red lead pencil.

PSYCHOMETRIC PROPERTIES

Norming Procedures and Standardization Characteristics

A pilot form of the test was prepared and administered to a sample in February and March 1992. These item-level data were analyzed using the Rasch model procedures to select the best set of items to be included in the norming edition. Standard error, infit and outfit indices, and conventional difficulty level indices were used to select the best items. The retained items composed the field study version and ultimately the standardization version.

Collection of standardization data produced U.S. norms for individuals ages 5 through 17 years, 11 months. The sampling procedure targeted communities and schools from all major U.S. geographic regions, as well as socioeconomic levels, racial and ethnic groups, and other demographic categories, in an attempt to accurately represent the U.S. population.

Several special studies are planned to assess UNIT technical adequacy and to provide reliability and validity data. For example, samples will include exceptional students (e.g., those with learning disabilities, deafness/hearing impairments, language impairments, mental retardation) and children in programs for English as a Second Language or those with LEP. Data will be gathered from additional samples to establish UNIT stability and concurrent validity with various established tests of intelligence such as the *Stanford–Binet Intelligence Scale: Fourth Edition* (Thorndike, Hagen, & Sattler, 1986) and the *Wechsler Intelligence Scale for Children—III* (Wechsler, 1991). Data from 104 cases have already been collected to examine concurrent validity with the WJ-R (Woodcock & Johnson, 1989), as well as construct validity. These data are presented below in the section on "Validity."

Reliability

Initial data from 707 cases from the UNIT field study show impressive internal consistency. For 177 5- to 7-year-old children from the field study, subtest alphas ranged from .74 (Analogic Reasoning) to .84 (Object Memory). For 530 older children from the field study (8 to 18 years of age), subtest alphas ranged from .83 (Analogic Reasoning) to .89 (Cube Design). Coefficient alphas were not generated for the Mazes subtest because the system used to score Mazes does not lend itself to calculation of internal consistency measures (i.e., very different scores can be obtained for adjacent items as difficulty level increases).

Alphas have not yet been generated for UNIT global scores for the field study samples but will most likely be higher than the reliabilities reported above for subtests because of the greater number of items included in such global calculations. Reliability data from an independent sample of 104 public school children (Reed & McCallum, 1994) across the age range also revealed strong coefficient alphas; values for five subtests (excluding Mazes) ranged from .83 (Object Memory) to .92 (Cube Design). As expected, global score coefficients were higher, ranging from .85 (Nonsymbolic Scale Quotient) to .94 (Memory Scale Quotient. Full scale reliability was .92 for this sample of 104 children.

Validity

Though still in the process of standardization, several indices of validity for the UNIT have been obtained. Several of the indices relate to the construct validity of the test. Intelligence as a psychological construct is known to be developmental in nature. That is, children gain knowledge and abilities as a function of maturation, assuming an intact nervous system and a nondetrimental environment. Consequently, on intelligence tests children should show raw score gains as a function of increasing age. Data from 707 children from the field study sample show nice raw score age progressions. For example, mean raw scores for Cube Design are about 13, 19, 26, and 33 for the 5–7, 8–10, 11–13, and 14–17-year-old groups, respectively. Additional data are available from 104 public school children, as reported by Reed and McCallum (1994); they obtained the following correlation coefficients between chronological age in months and raw scores: Symbolic Memory, .53; Spatial Memory, .69; Object Memory, .52; Cube Design, .53; Analogic Reasoning, .52; Mazes, .47; and Full Scale IQ, .65.

Additional evidence of construct validity can be obtained from scrutiny of correlational data taken from the 104 children mentioned earlier. A subtest correlation matrix showing coefficients between the six subtests reveals moderate coefficients, ranging from .23 between Mazes and Object Memory, to .56 between Object Memory and Spatial Memory. A confirmatory factor analyses performed on these data provide strong support for a two-factor model; the chi-square, Goodness of Fit Index (GFI), Adjusted Goodness of Fit Index (AGFI), and the Root Mean Square of the Residuals (RMSR) criteria support a two-factor model over one-factor and three-factor options. The chi-square, GFI, AGFI, and RMSR values for the two-factor solution were 7.84, .98, .94, and .35, respectively. Loadings from the confirmatory analyses for the two-factor solution show strong support for the two-factor solution and are presented in Table 14.1.

Data comparing UNIT scores with scores from the WJ-R Extended Cognitive Battery provide support for good concurrent validity (Reed & McCallum, 1994). Correlation coefficients between the UNIT global scores and the WJ-R Cognitive Ability Score (Extended) ranged from .60 (Memory Quotient and WJ-R) to .68 (UNIT Full Scale IQ and WJ-R) for 104 public school children. Coefficients showing the predictive relationship between the UNIT and the end-of-year Comprehensive Test of Basis Skills (CTBS/4, 1989)) scores for 104 school-age children are presented in Table 14.2; the coefficients are moderate and encouraging, particularly given the nonverbal nature of the UNIT and the verbal nature of academic achievement. The correlations ranged from .37 to .56 (Williams, McCallum, & Reed, 1994). Also, as one would predict, the Symbolic Organization Scale was a stronger predictor of academic achievement than the Nonsymbolic Organization Scale, which is analogous to the Wechsler Verbal scales serving as better predictors of achievement than the Per-

TABLE 14.1. Confirmatory Factor-Analytic Structure for the UNIT

Subtests	Factor 1 (memory)	Factor 2 (reasoning)
Object Memory	.72	
Spatial Memory	.77	
Symbolic Memory	.69	
Mazes		.50
Analogic Reasoning		.63
Cube Design		.67

Note. N = 104.

TABLE 14.2. Coefficients between UNIT and CTBS/4 Scores

Scales	Read.	Math.	Lang.	Total
Reasoning Scale	.42	.46	.37	.46
Memory Scale	.45	.42	.40	.48
Symbolic Scale	.52	.52	.48	.56
Nonsymbolic Scale	.40	.42	.34	.43
Full Scale	.48	.50	.42	.52

Note. N = 104.

formance scales. In general, predictive validity coefficients of this magnitude are comparable to the results of many IQ–Achievement comparisons (Sattler, 1988).

Interpreting the UNIT

Because the UNIT is multidimensional, a comprehensive nonverbal measure of intelligence, interpretation requires multiple steps. General steps for interpretation are discussed below, followed by a discussion of three specific interpretative procedures. Two cautions are necessary. First, the following guidelines are based on the expectation that the standardization data will support the UNIT model as defined, as have pilot data thus far. Second, because of space limitations the guidelines are presented in brief form. A more detailed discussion is available from the first author (R.S.M.) and will be presented in the *UNIT Examiner's Manual* when available (Bracken & McCallum, in press).

1. Interpret the UNIT composite or global score within a normative context. The most global score, the FSIQ, should be interpreted according to its relative standing in the population using standard scores, percentile ranks, age equivalents, and so on as indications of performance. For multidimensional tests like the UNIT it is useful to provide some statement regarding the representativeness of the score: That is, does the FSIQ represent the examinee's overall intellectual functioning well? Then, consider the next level of global scores, the scale scores (i.e., Reasoning Quotient, Memory Quotient, Symbolic Quotient, or NonSymbolic Quotient). Are these scores comparable or do they deviate significantly from one another? If these scores show considerable variability, the most global score may not represent the examinee's overall intellectual functioning very well. Considerable scatter in global and subtest scores reveal a profile with peaks and valleys and corresponding cognitive strengths and weaknesses. These weaknesses should be determined by examining the magnitude of differences using statistical significance and frequency of ocurrance data.

2. The band of error of the UNIT FSIQ should be communicated next. Typically, the most reliable single score from *any* multidimensional test is the total or composite score. This global score should be considered within a band of confidence framed by one or more standard errors of measure, determined by the level of significance desired.

3. Step 3 provides elaboration of step 1 and transition to the more specific interpretive procedures described below. In step 3, all UNIT standard scores should be compared *systematically*. As stated in step 1, if UNIT scale (global) scores are highly variable (i.e., if there are statistically significant differences among them), the composite score cannot be considered representative of the examinee's overall intellectual functioning. On the other hand, if there is little variability (i.e., nonsignificant amounts of variability), the composite score may be considered as a reasonable estimate of examinee's overall functioning.

Further description of the examinee's performance should also be addressed at this point. For example, the examiner may provide additional information about the nature of the UNIT and the abilities presumed to be measured by the instrument; in addition, the examiner may indicate that the examinee's abilities in particular areas as measured by the test (e.g., short-term memory and reasoning) are uniformly developed (or not, as the case may be). The examinee's overall level of ability should be described and inferences about the examinee's prognosis for achievement can be made. If qualitative (e.g., intrasubtest scatter) and quantitative (i.e., variable scores) data show variability in the examinee's performance, further analysis should be made to determine unique intrachild (ipsative) strengths and weaknesses.

Specific interpretation is possible using the following three procedures (after McCallum, 1991), depending on the nature of the score variability. The three interpretive procedures include (1) the pooled procedure, (2) the rational–intuitive procedure, and (3) the independent factors procedure. Each of the three procedures is described in a general way in the next section, after a discussion of *four* assumptions that underlie interpretation. Descriptions of the more specific interpretive steps used in the three procedures are available from the first author (R.S.M.).

The *first* assumption states that intelligence is a global and pervasive ability and is characterized by general intellectual ability (*g*). The essence of intelligence can be best conceptualized as pervasive and generalizable; it encompasses all activities and actions and it applies fairly robustly to multiple settings and tasks. Thus, test interpretation should proceed from the global to the more specific levels (i.e., consider the FSIQ first, then scale scores, then subtest scores).

The *second* assumption states that the psychometric properties of the test are acceptable. Bracken (1987) recommended basic rules of thumb for acceptable psychometric criteria. For example, global scores used for making placement decisions should evidence reliability at a level of .90 or better; scores used for screening purposes should have reliability at a level of .80 or better. Also, item gradients should be sufficiently sensitive to capture small differences in actual ability. That is, an increase in one raw score point should not yield a standard score increase of more than one-third standard deviation. In addition, each subtest and scale should be capable of yielding a ceiling and floor at least three standard deviations above and below the mean of the test, respectively. Finally, subtest specificity data must meet certain criteria before a particular subtest can be considered a unique measure of some ability. Because the Cube Design subtest, for example, contributes to the measurement of reasoning, it is included on the Reasoning Scale; however, it also assesses some unique ability that is not assessed by any other subtest on the UNIT. According to Kaufman (1979), if the unique variance on a particular subtest is greater than 25% of its total variance, and is larger than error, the subtest may be considered an interpretable measure of some unique ability.

The *third* assumption requires that any intepretation based on subtest analysis not be conducted in isolation; any hypotheses generated from subtest analysis should be considered tentative and should be subject to verification by extratest data. Of late, there has been considerable criticism of subtest analysis and intepretation, and with good reason. (See, for example, McDermott, Fantuzzo, & Glutting, 1990, for a good discussion of some of the problems associated with subtest analysis.) Because of the problems associated with subtest analysis these authors conclude that there is little support for the assertion that many constructs or subconstructs (of intelligence) are better than one. They recommend that practitioners just say "no" to subtest analysis. We agree with McDermott et al. that the use of a global score is more powerful and more defensible than relying on scores taken from hypothesized subconstructs; consequently, we recommend that practitioners rely heavily on the test's global score. (See the first assumption.) However, if there is considerable variability among scores that contribute to the global score, the total test score can be misleading. In that case we urge practitioners to interpret data showing scale and subtest strengths and weaknesses as obtained from subtest analysis. These data can be used to support tentative hypotheses, hypotheses to be supported (or not) from extratest data. Thus, data from subtests analysis should be used to generate tentative hypotheses and *never* in isolation.

The *fourth* assumption posits that the test under consideration, in this case the UNIT, is a reasonable measure of general intelligence. Jensen (1980) concludes that many of the measures used to assess intelligence perform reasonably well for that purpose. Jensen's working definition of intelligence is the *g* factor of an indefinitely large and varied battery of mental tests. Further, he defined "mental" capacities as those which produce individual variation in the population, other than sensory or motor abilities. According to Jensen a task measures *g* to the degree that it is complex and that one kind of task may measure *g* just as surely as some very different type of task. The capacity of a wide variety of tasks to assess *g* has been referred to by Spearman (1927) as the principle of the "indifference of the indicator." Based on the evidence presented by the early psychometric pioneers (e.g., Spearman, 1927; Thurstone, 1938; Thorndike, 1927) and more recent scholars such as Kaufman (1979) and Jensen (1980) we endorse the notion that currently available intelligence tests do a reasonable job of estimating intellectual functioning and of predicting future behavior, particularly academic performance. Further, we believe that it is possible to assess *g* as well as more specific intellectual abilities (e.g., memory, reasoning) through nonverbal assessment procedures.

The Pooled Procedure

The pooled interpretation procedure is the first of the three techniques discussed. It requires that the mean of all six UNIT subtests be computed and each subtest score is individually compared to that mean to identify "outliers" (i.e., scores that differ significantly from the overall subtest mean). If there are no significant differences between (among) the scale scores (e.g., the Memory Quotient of the UNIT is not significantly larger than the Reasoning Quotient), but there appears to be considerable variability within the two scales nonetheless, the pooled procedure should be used. In this case the assumption is that variability within the UNIT cannot be characterized more globally according to a model of abilities developed from rational or empirical bases.

The Independent Factors Procedure

This procedure is so named because it relies on interpretation based on a factor-analytic structure of the UNIT. Specifically, it is based on the factor structure obtained by maximizing the independence of the factors comprising the test. It is possible that the "independent factors" structure of a given test coincides with a given theoretical model underlying the test, but the independent factors model may not be consistent with any theoretical model. For example, the best independent factors solution for the WISC-III implies a four-factor solution (i.e., Verbal Comprehension,

Perceptual Organization, Freedom from Distractibility, and Perceptual Speed) rather than the "rational" or "intuitive" verbal–nonverbal categorization. When rational and empirical models differ for a particular test, a decision has to be made about which approach to follow for test interpretation. Will the first line of attack be based on the theoretical model underlying the test or will it be based on an awareness of the best empirically supported model? We suggest using the independent factors procedure first, because it has a stronger empirical basis. For the UNIT, the best factor-analytic solution from currently available data shows a good two-factor model, (i.e., the best factor solution appears to reveal a three-subtest memory factor and a three-subtest reasoning factor). The examiner should first look for the pattern of consistently higher memory (over reasoning) subtests, or the reverse. The difference between the two global scores may be compared to determine whether a significant difference exists. Factor-analytic data support a memory–reasoning model over a symbolic–nonsymbolic model for the UNIT. But a given child may show unique strengths and weaknesses according to a symbolic versus nonsymbolic split. The UNIT manual will provide the appropriate criteria to determine whether a particular difference between global scores is significant.

The Rational–Intuitive Procedure

The rational–intuitive procedure is so named because it relies on the interpretation of a multidimensional test based on the theoretical model that underpins the development of a test, or on other theoretical models of which the examiner is aware. To use a well-known example, results form the WISC-III could be interpreted solely from its foundational verbal–nonverbal perspective. The WISC-III yields two global scale scores (i.e., Verbal IQ and Performance IQ) as well as an overall Full Scale IQ. Based on his clinical experience, Wechsler believed that human cognitive performance could be categorized parsimoniously in that fashion (Wechsler, 1939). For some children their abilities can be divided along such dichotomous lines. For these children, the two global scale scores will differ significantly, but the subtests within the two scales will show little variability. For example, a child may have earned high scores on all the subtests that comprise the Verbal Scale, but (relatively) low scores on all the subtests that comprise the Performance Scale. For such a child, the rational–intuitive model explains cognitive functioning well. Users of the UNIT may find that some children perform well on all the symbolic subtests relative to the nonsymbolic subtests. Interpretations based on other rational or theoretical models may be useful to consider as well. For example, some children may perform better on subtests with a heavy visual–motor integration requirement relative to subtests requiring primarily visual perception.

Other Models of Interpretation

The three procedures described are valuable; all are systematic interpretation approaches that offer hypothesis generating strategies. Each should be considered and the one that seems most appropriate for the assessed child, depending on the referral problem and/or the particular pattern of scores exhibited, should be used over the remaining two procedures. In general, if little variability in subtest scores occurs the pooled procedure may offer the best fit to the data; for other children, the rational–intuitive model might best represent the child's strengths and weaknesses. In addition, other viable models may exist. For example, some subtests may require more of a successive problem-solving strategy (e.g., Symbolic Memory) and others may rely more on a simultaneous strategy (e.g., Cube Design); some subtests may require a moderate motoric ability (e.g., Cube Design) whereas others will not (Analogic Reasoning); some may require relatively strong planning (Mazes), and others may not (Object Memory). Examiners should keep these "models" in mind as they interpret patterns of scores from the UNIT.

BEYOND TRADITIONAL INTELLECTUAL ASSESSMENT: UNIQUE FEATURES OF THE UNIT

There are several features that set this nonverbal test apart from existing nonverbal scales. *First*, the UNIT is administered solely through the use of examiner demonstrations and gestures. The use of sample and demonstration/practice items ensures that the examinee understands the nature of the task prior to attempting the subtest for credit. *Second*, the test comprises a battery of subtests that will provide the opportunity for both motoric and motoric-reduced (i.e., pointing) responses. Administration of UNIT subtests can be modified so that only a pointing response is required on four of the six subtests. The use of motoric and motoric-reduced subtests facilitates administration by optimizing motivation and rapport. For example, a shy child may be encouraged initially to point only, and later, as rapport is gained, other more motorically involved responses may be possible. Also use of the motor reduced subtests may be indicated for children with limited motor skills. *Third*, the instrument's subtests contain items that are culturally fair, as much as possible. We have included line drawings and objects that are recognizable to most individuals from all cultures, *Fourth*, the test is model based. That is, we have included subtests designed to assess reasoning—a higher-order mental processing activity—as well as complex memory. Also, we have included symbolically loaded subtests as well as less symbolically laden ones. Interpretation of the UNIT is facilitated because of these theoretical underpinnings. *Fifth*, samples of non–English-speaking individuals are included for UNIT validation studies, collected by Riverside during the UNIT norming. Children from other cultures and children residing in the United States who have limited English facility were included in the norming and validation of the UNIT. *Sixth*, administration time can be controlled by the examiner, depending on the number of subtests administered. The UNIT will include two possible short forms, in addition to the six-subtest full scale. A two-subtest version and a four-subtest version short form will allow for abbreviated estimates of cognitive ability when a full scale score is not needed (e.g., screening, research).

Conclusion

Preliminary data analyses suggest that the UNIT will provide a psychometrically strong, examiner-friendly, and appropriate measure of intelligence for children who are limited in English proficiency or who are hearing impaired. The UNIT is model based and includes aspects of currently available instrumentation to provide examiners with familiar tasks and materials. The UNIT is being standardized on a nationwide sample without use of examiner or examinee verbalizations. The UNIT is intended to provide a good measure of *g* with two clear factor-based scales (i.e., Memory and Reasoning), and the subtests should possess sufficient subtest specificity to allow interpretation of more specific strengths and weakness.

REFERENCES

American Educational Research Association, American Psychological Association, & National Council for Measurement in Education. (1985). *Standards for educational and psychological testing.* Washington, DC: American Psychological Association.

Bracken, B. A. (1986). Incidence of basic concepts in the directions of five commonly used American tests of intelligence. *School Psychology International, 7,* 1–10.

Bracken, B. A. (1987). Limitations of preschool instruments and standards for minimal levels of technical adequacy. *Journal of Psychoeducational Assessment, 5,* 313–326.

Bracken, B. A., & McCallum, R. S. (November, 1994). *The Univeral Nonverbal Intelligence Test (UNIT): When a verbal test just won't do.* Paper presented at the Mid-South Conference on School Psychology, Huntsville, AL.

Bracken, B. A., & McCallum, R. S. (in press). *The Universal Nonverbal Intelligence Test.* Chicago: Riverside.

Bracken, B. A., McCallum, R. S., Reed, M., & Williams, P. (1993, November). *Cross-cultural Intellectual Assessment: The Universal Nonverbal Intelligence Test (UNIT).* Paper presented at the South Padre Island International Interdisciplinary Conference on the Cognitive Assessment of Children in School and Clinical Settings, South Padre Island, TX.

Brown, L., Sherbenou, R. J., & Johnson, S. K. (1990). *Test of Nonverbal Intelligence—2.* Austin, TX: Pro-Ed.

Cattell, R. B. (1963). Theory for fluid and crystallized intelligence: A critical experiment. *Journal of Educational Psychology, 54,* 1–22.

Comprehensive test of basic skills, fourth edition. (1989). Monterrey, CA: CTB MacMillan/McGraw-Hill.

Figueroa, R. A. (1990). Assessment of linguistic minority group children. In C. R. Reynolds & R. W. Kamphaus (Eds.), *Handbook of psychological and educational assessment of children: Intelligence and achievement* (Vol. 1, pp. 671–696). New York: Guilford Press.

Horn, J. L. (1968). Organization of abilities and the development of intelligence. *Psychological Review, 75,* 242–259.

Jensen, A. R. (1980). *Bias in mental testing.* New York: Free Press.

Kaufman, A. S. (1979). *Intelligent testing with the WISC-R.* New York: Wiley-Interscience.

Kaufman, A. S., & Kaufman, N. L. (1983). *Kaufman Assessment Battery for Children.* Circle Pines, MN: American Guidance Service.

Leiter, R. G. (1948). *Leiter International Performance Scale.* Chicago: Stoelting.

McCallum, R. S. (1991). The assessment of preschool children with the Stanford–Binet Intelligence Scale: Fourth Edition. In B. A. Bracken (Ed.), *The psychoeducational assessment of preschool Children* (2nd ed., pp. 107–132). Boston, MA: Allyn & Bacon.

McCallum, R. S., & Bracken, B. A. (1993, January). *The Universal Nonverbal Intelligence Test: A test for all people.* Paper presented at the International Testing Conference, Oxford, England.

McDermott, P. A., Fantuzzo, J. W., & Glutting, J. J. (1990). Just say no to subtest analysis: A critique on Wechsler theory and practice. *Journal of Psychoeducational Assessment, 3,* 290–302.

Pasko, J. R. (1994). Chicago—Don't miss it. *Communiqu, 23,* 2.

Reed, M. T., & McCallum, R. S. (1994). Construct validity of the Universal Nonverbal Intelligence Test (UNIT). *Psychology in the Schools, 32,* 276–290.

Robb, G., Bernardoni, L., & Johnson, R. (1972). *Assessment of individual mental ability.* Scranton: Intext.

Sattler, J. M. (1988). *Assessment of children.* San Diego, CA: Sattler.

Spearman, C. E. (1927). *The abilities of man.* New York: Macmillan.

Thorndike, E. L. (1927). *The measurement of intelligence.* New York: Bureau of Publications, Teachers College, Columbia University.

Thorndike, R. L., Hagen, E. P., & Sattler, J. M. (1986). *The Stanford–Binet Intelligence Scale: Fourth Edition.* Chicago: Riverside.

Thurstone, L. L. (1938). Primary mental abilities. *Psychometric Monographs* (No. 1).

Wechsler, D. (1939). *The measurement of adult intelligence.* Baltimore: Williams & Wilkins.

Wechsler, D. (1991). *Wechsler Intelligence Scale for Children—Third Edition.* San Antonio, TX: Psychological Corporation.

Williams, P. C., McCallum, R. S., & Reed, M. T. (1994). Predictive validity of the Cattell–Horn Gc-Gf constructs to achievement. *Assessment, 3,* 43–51.

Woodcock, R. W. (1990). Theoretical foundations of the WJ-R measures of cognitive ability. *Journal of Psychoeducational Assessment, 8,* 231–258.

Woodcock, R. W., & Johnson, M. B. (1989). *Woodcock–Johnson Psychoeducational Battery—Revised.* Chicago: Riverside.

CHAPTER 15

Dynamic Assessment Approaches

CAROL S. LIDZ

DYNAMIC ASSESSMENT REFERS to approaches to the development of decision-specific information that most characteristically involve interaction between the examiner and the examinee, focus on learner metacognitive processes and responsiveness to intervention, and follow a pretest–intervene–posttest administration format (Lidz, 1987, 1991). There is no one package of materials that "is" dynamic assessment. Rather, dynamic assessment is a model or an approach that has many interpretations, degrees of standardization, and applications to a wide variety of content.

THE CONCEPT OF DYNAMIC ASSESSMENT

The guiding principle of dynamic assessment is that if you wish to understand how a child learns, it is best to engage the child in the learning process. Related to this is the idea, attributed by Vygotsky to Marx, that the best understanding of a phenomenon or process derives from trying to change it. Dynamic assessment, in most interpretations, offers a situation in which the student engages in the learning process and the examiner actively attempts to facilitate the student's cognitive competence. The interaction serves to optimize rather than sample typical functioning. The result is in-depth information about the nature of the learner and hypotheses about effective (and ineffective) interventions. The assessment situation becomes a true laboratory of learning.

Dynamic assessment developed both as a reaction to dissatisfaction with existing procedures as well as a positive attempt to design a model that is theory-based, provides a meaningful description of cognitive functioning, and links assessment with instruction. So-called traditional, static, or status procedures tend to represent a one-instance sampling of behavior, assume common preparatory background of the examinee, focus on end products, and follow a standardized administration format.

The interest of most developers of dynamic assessment procedures is less in assessment of intelligence per se than in observation of the application of cognitive functions within learning situations. The intent is to provide information that can serve as the basis for enhancement of the cognitive functioning of the learner, regardless (but not independent) of the learner's independent level of performance. Most other procedures provide information only about the learner's independent level of performance and infer future from previous functioning. Dynamic assessors do not dismiss the relevance of past or independent level of performance but consider such information only a part of the total picture of a student's functioning or ability to learn. The assessment results of most traditional procedures represent the equivalent of the pretest of a dynamic assessment.

THEORETICAL BASES OF DYNAMIC ASSESSMENT

Dynamic assessment evolved from theories that highlight the importance of context and collaborative interaction to intellectual development, that is, a cultural–historical interpretation of development and learning.

The most influential theoretical bases for dynamic assessment are the works of Vygotsky (1978, 1986) and Feuerstein, Rand, and Hoffman (1979; 1980). Vygotsky's notion of the zone of proximal development (ZPD) as a necessary component of assessment, added to the zone of actual development, has been the most central guiding concept of this approach. The zone of actual development describes the learner's independent level of performance, whereas the zone of proximal development describes what the child is able to do with the help of a more experienced collaborator. This collaborator may be any other person with more experience in the domain of current engagement (e.g., a parent, a teacher, a peer, or a sibling).

Dynamic assessment then describes the interaction between a mediator (in this case, the assessor) and the student where the goal is to create and explore a ZPD; when the creation of such a zone is successful, the assessment closely approximates the process of cognitive development itself. The ZPD is the meeting place between the inner, mental world of the child and the external influences of the sociocultural environment, as represented by the assessor. The goal of the interaction is to promote, through such cognitive tools as language, internalization of the sociocultural environment. The instructional interaction of the classroom and of the assessment situation contain the same components as any developmental experience of the child, but schooling represents the child's exposure to the more formal, principle-based ("scientific") aspects of the sociocultural milieu.

Dynamic assessment represents Vygotsky's notion that both actual and proximal zones are necessary for more complete understanding and prognosis of the learner. Normed, standardized, and curriculum-based approaches provide information regarding the "actual," or independent, functioning of the learner, whereas dynamic approaches tap the "proximal," or facilitated, functioning. Dynamic assessment begins where traditional psychometric assessment ends. Instead of terminating the procedure with the establishment of a ceiling, the dynamic assessor views the ceiling as an area of functioning that warrants exploration. Although some dynamic approaches refer to learning potential, there is no need to introduce the concept of potential because proximal functioning is already available within the learner, requiring only the intervention of a social mediator.

Feuerstein and colleagues' (1979, 1980; Feuerstein, Feuerstein, & Gross, Chapter 16, this volume) conceptualization of mediated learning experience (MLE) delineate the specific components of the social interaction that help to create a ZPD. Feuerstein observes that children learn through both direct and mediated experiences. Mediated experiences promote self-regulation and representational thinking and result from specific types of interactions with experienced socializing agents; mediation occurs when experiences are selected, regulated, and interpreted for the child. Based on his clinical experiences with children with learning difficulties, Feuerstein describes the types of learning experiences that socializing agents need to provide within these selections and interpretations in order to optimize the cognitive development of children. Interactions characterized by mediation of intent (intent to influence, regulation of attention), meaning (attributions of value and importance), and transcendence (connections between present, past, and future experiences and thinking) are the most important among the 12 components comprising an MLE.

Feuerstein developed his ideas into a specific dynamic assessment procedure, the Learning

Potential Assessment Device (LPAD), which he discusses in this volume (Feuerstein et al., Chapter 16). The instruments in the LPAD serve to provide mediated learning experiences that create a zone of proximal development and allow observation of the student's facilitated functioning.

DYNAMIC ASSESSMENT IN ACTION

A description of an example of a dynamic assessment may provide a basis for a more complete comprehension of the uniqueness of this approach. This is the case of Daniel.

Daniel is a 4-year-old child who shows very high activity level and impulsive behavior in his preschool class. He has a seizure disorder, controlled with medication, and a speech disorder for which he receives speech therapy. He is not learning well in his preschool program and occasionally acts up in a disorganized way. His teacher seeks ideas for helping him learn more successfully. The assessment procedures for Daniel included standardized IQ and achievement measures, as well as interviews of his mother and teacher, multiple observations within his classroom, and a preschool dynamic procedure that included three tasks: figure drawing, block building, and parquetry design (Lidz, 1991). The drawing task is a standard human figure drawing; the instructions are to "draw a picture of a child; a boy or a girl." The block building task is adopted from the Gesell battery, and involves a stair structure with 10 blocks, beginning with four at the base and decreasing on one side by one at each of four levels to one at the top. The parquetry task involves copying a rocket-like design with large wooden multicolored parquetry pieces. Each of these tasks involves a pretest (no intervention), mediated intervention, and posttest (no intervention) administration format. Intervention follows the examiner's analysis, usually verbalized to the child, of the processing and skill areas intact and in need of improvement. The examiner proceeds to interact with the child and follows the child's responses in eliciting and providing the necessary concepts and strategies for the task. The primary targets of intervention for Daniel were his impulsive interaction with materials, his disorganized approach to tasks, and his difficulty with fine motor control. The dialogue with the child might sound something like the following:

> "Wow, Daniel. I can really tell that that's a boy. I see the head, two arms and two legs. He even looks like he could be running, because his legs are kind of bent. Now we're going to work together to see if we can get this picture to look even more like a boy. I think we need to think real hard about some more parts that people have and just where they need to go. I also noticed that you did this really fast, and that made this look kind of wobbly. So I'm going to help you slow down a bit so you can make this boy stand really straight. Also, I think if you learn to hold your pencil a little differently it will make you stronger."

In Daniel's case, the standardized procedures clearly documented average or above-average levels of functioning, with a strength in verbal development and a weakness in motor functioning. The dynamic assessment tasks revealed the need for intensive intervention effort to induce improvement with the drawing task, moderate effort to promote gains on block building, and minimal effort for the parquetry task. This corroborated the degree of difficulty Daniel experienced with tasks with high motor demands. With figure drawing, Daniel showed a great deal of resistance to engaging in the task, and the nature of his difficulty related to a combination of a poor pencil grasp and difficulty with part–whole analysis. Part–whole analysis became a focus of the intervention with block building, and Daniel responded well to provision of meaning to the parts; for example, the whole concept of "stairs" was discussed and broken down to show how these could be created by a series of piled up "trains." With the parquetry task, which has a strong visual–perceptual and low motor demand, Daniel showed excellent comparative behavior and ability to follow a model. He was able to use the demarcation of parts offered by the lines of the drawing, internalize these, and reproduce the model without the external structure. Daniel's impulsive behavior, which tended to interfere with his success with tasks, responded well to a repertory of interventions that varied physical control (e.g., occasional lap sitting or allowing him to choose between sitting and standing) with contingency management ("If you do this, then you can do . . . "), removing all but the necessary materials, reminders to look and think first, and verbalization of cause and effect ("you grabbed this block, and then the others fell over"). It was most effective to pair cause–effect questioning ("what happened when you . . . ?") with physical restraint (adult hand on his hands; arm around his shoulder). It also helped to cue him to say what he needed to do prior to proceeding with the task. Within his classroom, it was clear that Daniel became disorganized when there was a lot of noise and movement, and that he responded best when directed to and involved with a specific activity; an adult needed to be with him until he became involved in a task that he could carry on by himself. Without such guidance, his behavior looked wild. His disorganization was a particular issue during less structured, free-play times and in the physical education area where his class had their gross motor activities.

Thus, dynamic assessment added important information about the nature of Daniel's referred behaviors to the results of standardized procedures and other informal assessment approaches and permitted development of hypotheses about potentially effective interventions for use by his teacher. The dynamic procedure also provided an opportunity to experience Daniel's responsiveness to intervention attempts, as well as offering a window to view the degree of stress he experienced when asked to perform a motor task or when placed in a complex environment.

INTERVENTION (MEDIATION) TECHNIQUES

The most unique characteristic of dynamic assessment is the inclusion of intervention as an integral aspect of the assessment experience. The intervention typically follows a standard administration of a pretest, followed by a standard administration of a posttest. Dynamic assessment procedures differ primarily in the tasks involved in the pretest and posttest, as well as in the nature of the interventions. These interventions vary not only on a continuum of degree of standardization but also with regard to the content. Two contrasting approaches to both content and intervention are those of Feuerstein et al. (1979) and Campione and Brown (e.g., 1987).

Feuerstein chooses content that is not recognizably academic. This relates to his experiences with older learners who have accumulated lengthy histories of unsuccessful performance in school. He wishes to avoid the negative reaction of the learner to the assessment and, subsequently, to the remediation experiences. He also wishes to emphasize aspects of cognitive functioning that are generalizable across domains and are not domain-specific. Feuerstein's approach to intervention is clinical, nonstandardized and responsive to observations of the learner during the course of the assessment; his approach to intervention reflects his conceptualization of mediated learning experience. MLE refers to interactions with more experienced socializing agents that facilitate learning in the child. The specific behaviors that comprise MLE derive from the clinical experience of Feuerstein and his colleagues with low-functioning children from a variety of immigrant backgrounds; however, considerable evidence for the relationship of most of these components is available in the research literature (Lidz, 1992).

Feuerstein et al. (1979, 1980) suggests that children learn from either direct or mediated experiences but that optimal mediated experiences enhance their ability to profit from the direct, and it is the mediated experiences that are the most proximal influences of cognitive functioning. Following Feuerstein's theory, the assessment situation mimics natural developmental experiences in the attempt to provide an optimal mediated learning experience as a vehicle for learning and change in the child's cognitive functioning. Interventions based on MLE stress the need for a strategic approach and awareness of basic principles of task solution. The components of MLE also include induction of meaning; promotion of connections between present, past, and future; encouragement that includes information about the learner's performance; and promotion of self-regulation. Because the intervention offered depends on the response of the child, this approach involves considerable inference on the part of the examiner; there is much to observe but little to "count" except the evidence of improved application of learning by the child on subsequent measures.

In contrast to Feuerstein's clinical/diagnostic approach, Campione and Brown provide a series of graduated prompts that follow the commission of an error in the learner's solution of a task. The content of the Campione and Brown approach has increasingly approximated actual academic content, specifically, reading and math. The metric for this approach is the number of hints required to achieve mastery or success. Mastery is defined as three successful unprompted solutions. These prompts are predetermined, standardized, and graduated in terms of explicitness of approximation to the correct response. For example, the examiner may first merely bring the child's attention to important features of the task; if the child still makes an error, the examiner may remind the child of the necessary operation for completing the task; following another error, the examiner might move to providing partial task solution; finally, with continued error, the examiner might move to provision of complete task solution. This type of intervention is task, rather than child focused; that is, although the move from prompt to prompt is precipitated by the responses of the child, the type of prompt offered is predetermined and based on task analysis rather than relating to analysis of the basis for the child's error. Campione and Brown (1987) made a conscious choice to trade measurability for clinical sensitivity.

PSYCHOMETRIC ISSUES
OF DYNAMIC ASSESSMENT APPROACHES

Traditional measures typically define intelligence in terms of independent performance. Such definitions omit or ignore evidence of the learner's responsiveness to instruction or rate or profile of learning over time. Consideration of one instance of independent performance alone assumes that past level of acquisition is an accurate predictor of future performance, with products (rather than processes) of learning used as evidence of the learner's processing abilities. Although impressively robust correlations between IQ and achievement test scores have supported this assumption, these correlations have at best accounted for little more than half of the variance, with particularly problematic results for low performers and children from socioeconomically disadvantaged backgrounds (e.g., Jensen, 1961; Rohwer, Ammon, Suzuki, & Levin, 1971; Sewell & Severson, 1974). Product is not necessarily a strong predictor of process (e.g., Camp, 1973), and measures that were designed to be stable over time and to predict school achievement are not necessarily relevant to issues of determining response to intervention. The goal of intervention is, after all, to defy predictors of failure.

The dynamic approach reminds assessors of the need to consider the purpose of any assessment (Day & Hall, 1987). Good practice dictates that procedures reflect referral issues and decisions to be made. Static or status psychometric measures are most appropriate for selection and classification. Such measures rely on group evidence and are not sufficiently sensitive to individual performance to serve as a basis for program development. Moreover, most static measures were not designed to serve as a basis for individual programming decisions. What is error of measurement for a standardized measure may be of high diagnostic significance for an individual's intervention program. That is, variables such as stress, fatigue, inattention, and motivation, which account for fluctuations and ranges in scores for individuals, are relevant for individualizing program design and understanding the nature of the learner's functioning. Furthermore, even as a group measure, there is evidence (reviewed later) that the dynamic model improves predictive success of standardized measures, particularly for lower performing students.

Dynamic assessment to a significant extent represents a clinician's dream and a psychometrician's nightmare. What is valid for one approach is invalid for the other. The attempt to measure complex processes and change presents special challenges. The availability of pre- and posttest scores offers the temptation to use gain scores, which have been shown to be unreliable and subject to regression effects (e.g., Cronbach & Furby, 1970; Embretson, 1990). Although it is possible to use dynamic assessment clinically for diagnostic description and seemingly to reduce the problems of trying to quantify the results of an approach that incorporates inference and a focus on change, many have found quantification to be warranted both for research purposes, as well as for improved diagnosis. Some researchers use only the posttest scores (e.g., Guthke & Wingenfeld, 1992). Klauer (1993) argues for the need to norm posttests, and Schottke, Bartram, and Wiedl (1993) suggest a method for analysis of change that incorporates linear regression analysis. Campione and Brown (e.g., 1987) use the metric of graduated hints during the course of intervention, and Ferrara (cited in Campione, 1989) used the gain score as the criterion for comparing the results of static versus dynamic procedures. Embretson (1987a, b, 1990) and Sijtsma (1993) have been the most prominent in development of psychometric approaches and advocate the use of latent trait modeling. Embretson's data provide evidence for improved predictive validity and internal consistency of dynamic assessment scores and support the conclusion that pretest (static) and posttest (dynamic) results tap different processes: "Individual differences in ability on the posttest cannot be described by the pretest ability score" (Embretson, 1987b, p. 353). She also demonstrates the possibilities for combining dynamic and psychometric properties that can satisfactorily address the search for objectivity of measurement (Anastasi, 1993, p. 26).

Traditional notions of reliability are not automatically relevant to dynamic assessment, most notably, test–retest reliability. For example, although a case can be made for the importance of intratest reliability for pre- and posttests, high test–retest reliability would be an indication of low validity for a dynamic assessment because the goal of the assessment is to induce change and therefore defeat the assumption of stability. Alternatively, interobserver agreement regarding conclusions and recommendations from the assessment would be relevant, as would be predictions of the learner's response to instruction based on recommendations from the assessment (Gersten, Keating, & Irvin, 1995).

Claims for the inappropriateness of many of the traditional approaches to assessment evaluation is not a suggestion that the dynamic approach should be exempt from evaluation. Some of the psychometric parameters appear more appropriate than others, and, in some instances, the appropriate psychometrics for the dynamic model may need to be rethought, even reinvented. Because of the complexity introduced by the interactive nature of the assessment and the focus on change, issues of evaluation become considerably more challenging.

Predictive Validity

There is evidence that dynamic assessment tends to improve predictions of scores on standardized achievement tests for lower-performing students (Guthke, 1993; Guthke & Wingenfeld, 1992; Lidz & Greenberg, 1996). These authors document typically stronger relationships between posttests (following intervention) and achievement test scores than between pretests and achievement. However, there is a broader issue of determining the appropriate criteria for predictive validity. Feuerstein (1979) suggests that the only really valid criterion is the student's functioning *following exposure to instruction that incorporates the results of the dynamic assessment*. It would not make sense to place the whole case for validity on the evidence of achievement that followed teaching unaffected by assessment information; in such cases, it would not matter whether the assessment occurred or not, because it made no difference to the student. Dynamic assessment serves as a guide to intervention, not a predictor of stable rank order. The issue becomes one of "how" rather than "if."

CURRENT RESEARCH

The research on dynamic assessment up to 1990 is summarized in Lidz (1991). This research supports at least five general conclusions:

1. Mediational intervention is associated with improved performance on measures used for pre- and posttesting (e.g., Thompson, 1991).
2. Practice alone does not account for these effects; practice has been found to be most effective for the inexperienced and the more able (Linn, 1991), whereas mediation enhances the performance of the lower-functioning students (e.g., Tzuriel, 1989).
3. Two of the most powerful components of successful intervention or mediation seem to be verbalization of problem-solving processes by the student and elaborated feedback of performance results and nature of errors by the examiner (e.g., Carlson & Wiedl, 1991).
4. IQ scores show stronger relationships to achievement than process-based measures primarily when the criteria involve other static scores, but not when the criteria are process and change oriented, such as indications of learning rate (e.g., Camp, 1973).
5. Dynamic assessment results make an independent contribution even to prediction of "static" measures of achievement above and beyond IQ (Lidz, 1991, pp. 50–54).

The next section updates this evidence and reviews research from the early to mid-1990s. During this time, there have been significant applications of the dynamic assessment model in the areas of both reading and speech/language.

Research on Reading and Other Academic Achievement Areas

In the area of reading, several studies extend the clinical conclusions from such descriptive studies as Cioffi and Carney (1983) and Braun, Rennie, and Gordon (1987). In the first study, Bednar and Kletzien (1990), using 29 students from grades 9 through 12 (ages 14 to 17), adapted selected passages from three informal reading inventories into a four-step individually administered dynamic procedure that involved initial baseline pretest assessment, analysis of reading process and strategy utilization, involvement in a mediated learning lesson targeting strategy use, and posttest on an alternate form of the reading test. These subjects were reevaluated 6 months after this procedure and their teachers were interviewed. For the subjects who showed below-grade-level performance on their pretest, there was a .71 correlation between their posttest scores and their growth in reading. Their teachers reported having used the information provided to them and expressed positive attitudes about the usefulness of the information for their instruction. The researchers also reported substantial agreement regarding the strategies that were targeted for intervention during the assessment. This study did not include a control group.

Using multiple control groups and a group dynamic procedure with 196 sixth-grade suburban students, Valencia, Campione, Weiner, and Bazzi (1990) reported positive, though weak, results for their reading procedure. Merely orienting the students to the use of strategies increased only the scores involving multiple-choice test questions. Groups exposed to moderate and strong scaffolding (instructional support) during the intervention phase increased their scores on both a strategy use and reading comprehension measure immediately following the intervention, and maintained the increase in strategy utilization when retested 5 months later. Finally, the strongly scaffolded (dynamic) administration showed stronger association with the reading scores 5 months later than did the weaker scaffolding of the control group, though these differences did not reach significance. The authors note the possible lack of match between the interventions provided and the needs of the students because the scaffolding was standardized and not individualized according to need; this may have weakened the results, which were, nevertheless, in the direction of support for the dynamic condition.

Spector's (1992) study of phonemic awareness with 38 middle-class kindergarten children compared the ability of static and dynamic measures administered in the fall to predict spring scores on the static measures of reading and phonemic awareness. The dynamic procedure provided corrective feedback and graduated prompts for the students. The dynamic procedure showed the strongest correlations with all spring measures, and this relationship was considerably stronger than between fall Peabody Picture Vocabulary Test—Revised (PPVT-R; Dunn & Dunn, 1981) scores and spring scores. In multiple regression, the fall-administered dynamic procedure contributed an additional 12% to 14% of the variance to spring measures of phonemic awareness, above and beyond that contributed by the PPVT-R and the static measure of the same variable (phoneme segmentation). Finally, the dynamic procedure was the only significant predictor of spring scores on the word recognition test, used to estimate reading; the dynamic procedure added 21% to the variance of word recognition scores after PPVT-R and static segmentation scores were entered.

Meltzer's (1992) assessment for teaching (AFT) model combines the "how" to assess of dynamic assessment with the "what" to assess of both higher-order (metacognitive) and lower-order (automatized knowledge) skills related to curriculum content. Meltzer's work in the area of learning strategies offers evidence of the difference between product and process in learning, as students with apparently similar levels of product-based performance (what the student knows) may differ considerably in their approaches to task; specifically, students who are poor in determination and application of strategies tend to manifest learning difficulties. Meltzer places her model on the continuum between dynamic and curriculum-based assessment approaches. The AFT model adds observation of problem-solving strategies to evaluation of students with learning problems; this information derives from both guided observations of the student's approach to solving basic curriculum tasks as well as active probes by the examiner during the course of the assessment. Meltzer authored two measures that comprise the Surveys of Problem-Solving Skills and Educational Skills (SPES): the Survey of Problem-Solving Skills and the Survey of Educational Skills (Meltzer, 1987). The latter assesses educational tasks of reading, writing, spelling, and mathematics. The problem-solving skills include pattern analysis and memory, and conceptual/thematic flexibility, each applied both to linguistic and nonlinguistic content. Meltzer and her colleagues (Meltzer, Roditi, Paster, & Rudin, 1994) have most recently developed the Student Observation System as a way to assess the presence of learning strategies. Meltzer's research (e.g., Meltzer & Reid, 1994) documents that learning disabled students manifest less flexibility in the use of strategies than do successful learners, and cognitive inflexibility interacts with lack of automatization to characterize the functioning of children classified as learning disabled. Although Meltzer's approach includes observation and probes and shares a focus on metacognition with dynamic assessment, the model differs in that there is no explicit attempt to effect change in the student's functioning during the course of the assessment.

Swanson (1992, 1995b) has recently completed the standardization of his individually administered battery of 11 tests of intellectual abilities, the Swanson Cognitive Processing Test (S-CPT). Guided by information-processing theory, S-CPT includes measures of working memory, with specific subtests as follows: rhyming words, visual matrix, auditory digit sequencing, mapping and directions, story retelling, picture sequencing, phrase recall, spatial organization, semantic association, semantic categorization, and nonverbal sequencing. In addition to the standard scores, S-CPT yields a gain score that represents the highest possible assisted performance, a maintenance score that represents the stability of this asymptote when probes are discontinued, and an instructional efficiency index that reflects the amount of support needed to reach the asymptote. Swanson's procedure also reveals information about the examinee's strategic awareness.

Swanson (1992) documents the significant contribution of the gain score (achievement of an asymptote) above and beyond the significance of the initial scores to the relationship with reading; neither the maintenance score nor the number of hints made significant contributions. Swanson's (1995a) more recent data again corroborate the unique contribution of this dynamic testing to achievement (reading and math) and show that the S-CPT in fact provided better prediction of the achievement scores than did the WISC-R for this selected population (a portion chosen who were poor readers, a portion who were adequate readers, and a group of highly skilled readers, and all shown to have higher standardized gain scores than initial test scores on the S-CPT). Further, the gain scores were good predictors of educational classification, showing differentiation between those who appeared to be generally slow learners and those with learning disabilities; a large proportion of the minority children appeared better classified as instructionally deficient rather than learning disabled, as indicated by their high level of responsiveness to the graduated prompts.

Studies by Jitendra and Kameenui (1993b, 1996) apply dynamic assessment to the domain of math. In these studies, the authors demonstrated the ability of their procedure to differentiate between "novices" and "experts" among their third-grade subjects. They also showed the usefulness of dynamic assessment as a research vehicle for exploring the effectiveness of a variety of teaching strategies within the mathematics domain.

Research related to Speech and Language

Speech and language pathologists have been particularly receptive to the dynamic assessment model and some see the potential for use with children with limited English-language proficiency (LEP). One of the central issues for applications with LEP students is to differentiate between language difference and language deficiency; children with language deficiencies are at risk for determination of ineligibility for language services yet may be overrepresented in special education classes because of insensitive assessment procedures (Iglesias, 1984).

At least two groups of researchers have developed and evaluated specific procedures within the dynamic model (Oswang & Bain, 1991; Peña, Quinn, & Iglesias, 1992; Peña, 1993), and a third (Roseberry & Connell, 1991), though not using the word "dynamic," reported results that are supportive of the model. Olswang and Bain offer clinical support for the approach, and Peña and her associates provide research documentation. Peña et al. administered their procedure to 60 urban Head Start children from either Puerto Rican or African-American family backgrounds and demonstrated successful differentiation between those who were determined to be, by independent criteria, language deficient or language different. Similarly, Roseberry and Connell (1991) found that inclusion of intervention in their procedure increased the sensitivity of their assessment of 26 preschool children of Mexican descent, differentiating between children who were culturally different from those having genuine learning needs.

Further Applications of Dynamic Assessment

There are a number of applications of the dynamic model that are not domain-specific. Some of these tap general cognitive functions, while others span across content domains. For example, Lidz (1991) has joined dynamic with curriculum-based assessment to link a process-based conceptual model directly to academic content. According to this approach, called curriculum-based dynamic assessment, there is a pretest–mediate–posttest format with a focus on the mental processing of the learner and provision of an MLE during the course of the assessment. The description of mental processing is the Luria-based model designed by Das and Naglieri (Das, Naglieri, & Kirby, 1993; Naglieri, Chapter 13, this volume). This model addresses planning, attention, and simultaneous and successive processing (PASS) and includes perceptual and memory processes as well as representational thinking. Examiners learn to analyze both the task and the learner in terms of these processes and use Lidz's modification of Feuerstein's MLE to guide their interactions between the pre- and posttests. With this broad framework for assessment, any content relevant to the specific referral can be used for the assessment. Thus, there can be a dynamic assessment of reading, of math, of story listening, even of items from standardized and curriculum-based tests (following standardized administration), taking the assessment far beyond most assessors' ideas of testing the limits.

Whereas the curriculum-based dynamic assessment model is primarily a diagnostic clinical approach, the group procedure designed to reflect the same processing model is more standardized and has generated a number of research studies. Lidz and Greenberg (1996) designed the Group Dynamic Modification of the Cognitive Assessment System (CAS/GDM), which can be administered to small groups or full classrooms of students from first through third grade. CAS/GDM also follows the Das–Naglieri PASS model and uses one subtest from each of the processes included in their new battery, the Cognitive Assessment System (CAS) (see Naglieri, Chapter 13, this volume). Although the CAS is an individually administered procedure, Lidz and Greenberg have modified three of the four selected subtests for group administration. They include an intervention for each process (attention, planning, simultaneous, and successive coding), as well as a scale to record teacher observations of behavior of selected students during each of the four interventions. The CAS/GDM has been used with regular education first-grade students in rural Montana, with urban public school special education students in Detroit, and with private school special education students in New Jersey. The results from Montana have just been submitted for publication, and the reports of the data from the rest will soon follow. What these studies show is evidence of stronger prediction by process posttests, as compared with pretests, of both reading and math; significant relationships between the process tests and standardized tests of reading and math achievement; and strong test–retest reliability of the measures prior to intervention but significant changes from pretest to posttest on the process measures in response to intervention, primarily for low pretest performers. Teachers informally report that they find the information generated from the procedure relevant and useful for their instructional planning, and they appreciate the time for observation and focus on students of concern to them within their classrooms.

Specific dynamic procedures vary in their content and in the degree of standardization of their interventions. In the United States, the most well-known procedures are the LPAD of Feuerstein (1979), the learning potential assessment approach of Budoff (e.g., 1987), and the graduated prompting techniques of Campione and Brown (e.g., 1987). These procedures are described by their authors in Lidz (1987) and summarized and critiqued by Lidz (1991); research related to these procedures are included in these texts as well.

Tzuriel (1989; Tzuriel & Klein, 1985, 1986) has also developed specific tests within the dynamic model, and has discussed the contribution of nonintellective factors (motives, attitudes, feelings) to the results of dynamic assessment (Tzuriel, 1991; Tzuriel, Samuels, & Feuerstein, 1988; see also Carlson & Wiedl, 1991; Meijer, 1993; Rand, 1991). These authors suggest that some of the effects of dynamic assessment may be the response to and control of such nonintellective variables, and that such variables may account for lowered performance on cognitive procedures for children with disadvantaged backgrounds.

There is a substantial European contribution to the development of dynamic assessment procedures that has until recently not been accessible to English readers. Hamers of the Netherlands and Guthke of Germany have made particularly notable contributions. These procedures and discussions of issues are now available to the English-speaking audience in Hamers, Sijtsma, and Ruijssenaars (1993).

Also, Speece and Cooper (1990; Speece, Cooper, & Kibler, 1990) continue their work in this area, incorporating a graduated prompt procedure suitable for use with first-grade pupils into their research. Research showing effects of applications of dynamic procedures include determination of giftedness (e.g., Skuy, Kaniel, & Tzuriel 1988), assessment of metacognitive functioning (e.g., Clements & Nastasi, 1990) for use with adults (Kliegl, Smith, & Baltes, 1989; Samuels, Lamb, & Oberholtzer, 1991), and as an enhancement of neuropsychological evaluation (Wingenfeld, 1992). Practitioners report the usefulness of this approach in an urban public school setting (Draper, Hamilton, & Jones, 1987).

The studies of Day and her students and associates make important contributions to understanding the effects of specific variables within a dynamic assessment. For example, Day and Cordon (1993) compared two approaches to intervention on a balance task with 64 third-grade pupils, scaffolded (graduated prompt) and "swing strategy" (following verbal prompt with full demonstration). The pupils responded best to the scaffolded approach and maintained their gains on both the maintenance and transfer tasks, in contrast to the decline in scores for the contrast group. The scaffolded condition was the only significant predictor of the transfer task. In her investigation comparing the predictive validity of static and dynamic assessment of analogy and classification problems with 149 high school students, Kerwin (1989) found that the dynamic measures (practice time and mean latency of response to incorrect items from the first instructional session) predicted the same variables in a subsequent instructional session; however, the dynamic measures did not predict accuracy or pattern of learning. Static measures were the best predictors of static measures. This study also demonstrated the domain specificity of learning within the content areas of verbal and spatial analogies.

BEYOND TRADITIONAL INTELLECTUAL ASSESSMENT

It is a thesis of this chapter that the dynamic approach to assessment is genuinely different from traditional, status-oriented (or static) approaches, as well as the other models represented in this text, that it could be described as "going beyond" traditional approaches, and, mostly, that it is a viable approach that has a significant contribution to make to conceptualizations of assessment of intelligence. Although not totally independent of intelligence, as traditionally assessed (Bolig & Day, 1993), research documents the differential and unique contribution of learning scores to the prediction and understanding of scholastic achievement and supports the validity of a learning ability construct that may have relevance to the definition of intelligence.

However, it needs to be pointed out that dynamic assessment is not an assessment of intelligence per se. The types of content that are assessed within the dynamic model can vary considerably and may or may not include variables and domains that would be considered "intellective." Although the model suggests that application of cognitive functions is involved across domains, there is a difference between dynamic assessment of basic generalizable processes such as planning and assessment of specific domains such as reading or science. Both are dynamic, but neither is necessarily "intelligence."

Assessment within the dynamic model can most of all claim to be "authentic" in terms of providing a true sample of the learner in the act of learning. If administered as a group procedure, this sample can be even taken as representative of learning within a group context. If administered within a one to one setting, the sample still remains to be generalized to classroom instruction. Nevertheless, the assessment is of a learner in process and, therefore, more closely approximates instructional and developmental interactions than more traditional approaches. Although this may seem to some to be an instance of refueling an airplane in midflight, it is also evident that one cannot know the airplane without knowing how it flies. Thus, the first claim of dynamic assessment is that it can result in a more accurate description of the learner as learner than more traditional approaches. Therefore, one inference would be that dynamic assessment would lead to more accurate predictions of the learner's response to instruction than more product-oriented, standardized measures. However, there is at least one caveat to this claim: The criteria for prediction need to be dynamic, or process, measures, and the outcome measures should follow interventions based on assessment information. Even without such optimal criteria, there is still evidence that dynamic assessment provides better prediction of standardized achievement scores than preintervention pretest scores, particularly for lower-performing students (e.g., Lidz & Greenberg, 1996).

Dynamic assessment responds to the questions of how well and how much the learner responds to attempts at intervention (i.e., the issue of modifiability). This is truly unique to dynamic assessment. Modifiability and information regarding the intensity of input necessary to achieve it is information that is not provided by other approaches. Also, dynamic assessment holds the promise of improving the linkage between assessment and instruction. How well this is done remains to be demonstrated and would vary with the degree of overlap between the assessment and instruction situation, but the potential is clearly present and logic suggests that the inclusion of instruction within the assessment situation would provide the foundation for such a link.

It is time that we asked some basic questions about what we really want to be measuring. If we are interested in intelligence, do we have the best metaphor or paradigm? It seems that both teaching and testing have relied a great deal on right answers, with little concern either for how these answers were derived or for what the right answer implies regarding future ability to acquire the information. Perhaps this accounts for the close relationship between IQ tests and school achievement. However, it is not even the focus on right answers that is the biggest problem. When a student shows the ability to do something, we can at least assume that the student has the ability to do it, regardless of the process or route. What do we know when there is an error or a failure to respond? Static psychometric testing tempts us to equate lack of performance with lack of capacity; this is certainly the case if we follow testing with placement or classification decisions based on the test results. The static approach also relies on events that discriminate among rather than define or describe individual functioning; this is especially the case when measures are empirically, rather than theoretically, based.

There is also need to evaluate the criteria to which predictions are made in order to conclude that these are desirable. Such is the case for classroom assessment, where there is a major revolution in process calling for "authentic" assessment; such a challenge suggests that if ability to think and problem-solve is an educational objective, thinking and problem solving should be what is assessed. Similarly, if learning and ability to apply new learning independently are objectives, learning and the ability to apply (and maintain? and transfer?) new learning need to be assessed.

Dynamic assessment cannot be viewed or evaluated as if it were another instance of psychometric assessment. The term "paradigm shift" seems appropriately applied to this issue (Hilliard, 1982). Dynamic assessment is a genuinely different approach, not only with different methodology but with different assumptions. The model assumes that learning is a process of change and the result of interaction; the model is open-ended and makes no assumptions about how much can be learned, looking primarily at what it takes to promote competence. Outcomes for individuals cannot be predicted with confidence from current or previous status; pretests even for groups tend to correlate significantly, but only moderately with posttests. The model is generic, molar, and flexibly applied to a wide variety of specific procedures.

Yet, despite the logic and positive support, a survey of school psychology cognitive assessment course instructors in U.S. school psychology programs (Lidz, 1992) suggests that, although the concept of dynamic assessment is well-known and covered by lectures or readings, the procedures are rarely taught; few students graduate knowing how to do dynamic assessment. Comments from the respondents to the survey refer to a variety of reasons for this discrepancy, the first and foremost being perceptions of insufficient time, feelings of insufficient knowledge base, and concerns about technical adequacy. Dynamic assessment has also been critiqued regarding perceptions of lengthy time for administration, heterogeneity and "fuzziness" of model constructs, and insufficient relatedness to instructional domains (Jitendra & Kameenui, 1993a). These concerns need to be addressed.

Campione's (1989) explication of a taxonomy that includes the dimensions of focus, interaction, and target may help to reduce some of the fuzziness attributed to dynamic assessment approaches. Focus is subdivided into observations of actual improvements and the processes underlying these improvements; interactions are described in terms of degree of standardization involved in the intervention phase, and target addresses procedure content in terms of domain-specific versus domain-general skills and processes. Such dimensions can serve to describe and categorize the variety of procedures that have been and continue to be developed. Debate may then ensue to determine which approaches are "really" dynamic, but the thesis is advanced that there is room for a variety of approaches within the generic model of dynamic assessment.

To date, there is increasing attention to the relationship between the model and instructional domains, as evidenced by the studies discussed previously. The need to do this is highlighted by the equivocal results of studies that compare dynamic and static assessment reports (Delclos, Burns, & Vye, 1993; Hoy & Retish, 1984). More recent evidence from Schwager and Carlson (1994) suggests that receptivity of teachers to alternative assessment approaches relates to their beliefs and attitudes, or paradigms; their study of 252 teachers from 92 randomly sampled California elementary schools identified three distinct orientations to assessment. Teachers with a "cognitive learning paradigm" were the most receptive to alternative practices.

CONCLUSION

The information in this chapter supports dynamic assessment as a meaningful addition to the assessment repertory. Information from dynamic assessment is different from information yielded by other procedures and enhances the ability to predict and describe the learning and achievement of students in ways that are directly relevant for instruction. Such information, called learning ability or responsiveness to instruction or modifiability, appears to warrant inclusion in any construct called intelligence. It is difficult to conceive of a definition of intelligence that ignores such evidence of ability to profit from experience.

In his review of newly developing approaches to assessment, Kratochwill (1977) noted that procedures such as learning potential measures were beginning to move what had been "psychological extras" into the mainstream. The procedures he described were all in their formative stages but, in his view, were worthy of further development and research. Meltzer (1992) groups dynamic assessment as a participant in the "New and exciting zeitgeist [that] has begun to shape the face of assessment . . . the winds of change have been blown in . . ." (p. 93). Dynamic assessment has moved beyond the category of "extra" into a serious contender for attention and training.

REFERENCES

Anastasi, A. (1993). A century of psychological testing: Origins, problems, and progress. In T. K. Fagan & G. R. VandenBos (Eds.), *Exploring applied psychology: Origins and critical analyses (master lectures)* (pp. 13–36). Washington, DC: American Psychological Association.

Bednar, M. R., & Kletzien, S. B. (1990, November). *Dynamic assessment for reading: A validation.* Paper presented at the National Reading Conference, Miami, FL.

Bolig, E. E., & Day, J. D. (1993). Dynamic assessment and giftedness: The promise of assessing training responsiveness. *Roeper Review, 16,* 110–113.

Braun, C., Rennie, B. J., & Gordon, C. J. (1987). An examination of contexts for reading assessment. *Journal of Educational Research, 80,* 283–289.

Budoff, M. (1987). Measures for assessing learning In C. S. Lidz (Ed.), *Dynamic assessment: An interactional approach to evaluation of learning potential* (pp. 173–195). New York: Guilford Press.

Camp, B. W. (1973). Psychometric tests and learning in disabled readers. *Journal of Learning Disabilities, 6,* 512–517.

Campione, J. C. (1989). Assisted assessment: A taxonomy. *Journal of Learning Disabilities, 22,* 151–165.

Campione, J. C., & Brown, A. L. (1987). Linking dynamic assessment with school achievement. In C. S. Lidz (Ed.), *Dynamic assessment: An interactional approach to evaluating learning potential* (pp. 82–115). New York: Guilford Press.

Carlson, J. S., & Wiedl, K. H. (1991). The dynamic assessment of intelligence. In H. C. Haywood & D. Tzuriel (Eds.), *Interactive assessment* (pp. 167–186). New York: Springer-Verlag.

Cioffi, G., & Carney, J. J. (1983). Dynamic assessment of reading disabilities. *Reading Teacher, 36,* 764–768.

Clements, D. H., & Nastasi, B. K. (1990). Dynamic approach measurement of children's metacomponential functioning. *Intelligence, 14,* 109–125.

Cronbach, L. J., & Furby, L. (1970). How should we measure or should we? *Psychological Bulletin, 74,* 68–80.

Das, J. P., Naglieri, J. A., & Kirby, J. R. (1993). *Assessment of cognitive processes: The PASS theory of intelligence.* Boston: Allyn & Bacon.

Day, J. D., & Cordon, L. A. (1993). Static and dynamic measures of ability: An experimental comparison. *Journal of Educational Psychology, 85,* 75–82.

Day, J. D., & Hall, L. K. (1987). Cognitive assessment, intelligence, instruction. In J. D. Day & J. G. Borkowski (Eds.), *Intelligence and exceptionality: New directions for theory, assessment, and instructional practices* (pp. 57–80). Norwood, NJ: Ablex.

Delclos, V. R., Burns, M. S., & Vye, N. J. (1993). A comparison of teachers' responses to dynamic and traditional assessment reports. *Journal of Psychoeducational Assessment, 11,* 46–55.

Draper, I., Hamilton, A., & Jones, J. (1987). The Detroit Public Schools' experience with alternatives to I.Q. testing. *The Negro Educational Review, 38,* 173–189.

Dunn, L. M., & Dunn, L. M. (1981). *Peabody Picture Vocabulary Test—Revised.* Circle Pines, MN: American Guidance Service.

Embretson, S. (1990). Diagnostic testing by measuring learning processes: Psychometric considerations for dynamic testing. In N. Fredericksen, R. Glaser, A. Lesgold, & M. G. Shafto (Eds.), *Diagnostic monitoring of skill and knowledge acquisition* (pp. 407–432). Hillsdale, NJ: Erlbaum.

Embretson, S. E. (1987a). Toward development of a psychometric approach. In C. S. Lidz (Ed.), *Dynamic assessment: An interactional approach to evaluating learning potential* (pp. 141–170). New York: Guilford Press.

Embretson, S. E. (1987b). Improving the measurement of spatial aptitude by dynamic testing. *Intelligence, 11,* 333–358.

Feuerstein, R., Rand, Y., & Hoffmann, M. (1979). *Dynamic assessment of retarded performers.* Baltimore: University Park Press.

Feuerstein, R., Rand, Y., Hoffmann, M., & Miller, R. (1980). *Instrumental enrichment.* Baltimore: University Park Press.

Gersten, R., Keating, T., & Irvin, L. K. (1995). The burden of proof: Validity as improvement of instructional practice. *Exceptional Children, 61,* 510–519.

Guthke, J. (1993). Developments in learning potential assessment. In J. H. M. Hamers, K. Sijtsma, & A. J. J. M. Ruijssenaars (Eds.), *Learning potential assessment: Theoretical, methodological and practical issues* (pp. 43–67). Amsterdam/Berwyn, PA: Swets & Zeitlinger.

Guthke, J., & Wingenfeld, S. (1992). The learning test concept: Origins, state of the art, and trends. In H. C. Haywood & D. Tzuriel (Eds.), *Interactive assessment* (pp. 64–93). New York: Springer-Verlag.

Hamers, J. H. M., Sijtsma, K., & Ruijssenaars, A. J. J. M. (Eds.). (1993). *Learning potential assessment: Theoretical, methodological and practical issues.* Amsterdam/Berwyn, PA: Swets & Zeitlinger.

Hilliard, A. G. (1982). *The Learning Potential Assessment Device and instrumental enrichment as a paradigm shift.* (ERIC Document Reproduction Service No. ED 333 676)

Hoy, M. P., & Retish, P. M. (1984). A comparison of two types of assessment reports. *Exceptional Children, 51,* 225–229.

Iglesias, A. (1984, May). *Assessing communicative performance of LEP children in the classroom.* Paper presented at the Workshop on Communication Disorders and Language Proficiency: Assessment, Intervention, and Curriculum Implementation, Temple University, Philadelphia.

Jensen, A. R. (1961). Learning abilities in Mexican-American and Anglo-American children. *California Journal of Educational Research, 12,* 147–159.

Jitendra, A. K., & Kameenui, E. J. (1993a). An exploratory study of dynamic assessment involving two instructional strategies on experts and novices' performance in solving part–whole mathematical word problems. *Diagnostique, 18,* 305–324.

Jitendra, A. K., & Kameenui, E. J. (1993b). Dynamic assessment as a compensatory assessment approach: A description and analysis. *Remedial and Special Education, 14,* 6–18.

Jitendra, A. K., & Kameenui, E. J. (1996). *Experts and novices' error patterns in solving part-whole mathematical word problems: The role of dynamic assessment and instructional strategies.* Unpublished manuscript, Lehigh University, Bethlehem, PA.

Kerwin, M. E. (1989). *Static versus dynamic assessments of intelligence.* Unpublished doctoral dissertation, University of Notre Dame, IN.

Klauer, K. J. (1993). Learning potential testing: The effect of retesting. In J. H. M. Hamers, K. Sijtsma, & A. J. J. M. Ruijssenaars (Eds.), *Learning potential assessment: Theoretical, methodological and practical issues* (pp. 135–152). Amsterdam/Berwyn, PA: Swets & Zeitlinger.

Kliegl, R., Smith, J., & Baltes, P. B. (1989). Testing-the-limits and the study of adult age differences in cognitive plasticity of a mnemonic skill. *Developmental Psychology, 25,* 247–256.

Kratochwill, T. R. (1977). The movement of psychological extras into ability assessment. *Journal of Special Education, 11,* 299–311.

Lidz, C. S. (Ed.). (1987). *Dynamic assessment: An interactional approach to evaluation of learning potential.* New York: Guilford Press.

Lidz, C. S. (1991). *Practitioner's guide to dynamic assessment.* New York: Guilford Press.

Lidz, C. S. (1992). The extent of incorporation of dynamic assessment into cognitive assessment courses: A national survey of school psychology trainers. *Journal of Special Education, 26,* 325–331.

Lidz, C. S., & Greenberg, K. H. (1996). *Using a group dynamic assessment procedure to investigate the relationship between cognitive processes and academic achievement in rural first grade regular education students.* Manuscript submitted for publication.

Linn, R. L. (1991). Dimensions of thinking: Implications for testing. In L. Idol & B. F. Jones (Eds.), *Educational values and cognitive instruction: Implications for reform* (pp. 179–208). Hillsdale, NJ: Erlbaum.

Meijer, J. (1993). Learning potential, personality characteristics and test performance. In J. H. M. Hamers, K. Sijtsma, & A. J. J. M. Ruijssenaars (Eds.), *Learning potential assessment: Theoretical, methodological and practical issues* (pp. 341–362). Amsterdam/Berwyn, PA: Swets & Zeitlinger.

Meltzer, L. J. (1987). *The surveys of problem-solving and educational skills (SPES).* Cambridge, MA: Educator's Publishing Service.

Meltzer, L. J. (1992). Strategy use in students with learning disabilities: The challenge of assessment. In L. Meltzter (Ed.), *Strategy assessment and instruction students with learning disabilities: From theory to practice* (pp. 93–135). San Antonio, TX: Pro-Ed.

Meltzer, L. J., & Reid, D. K. (1994). New directions in the assessment of students with special needs: The shift toward a constructivist perspective. *Journal of Special Education, 28,* 338–355.

Meltzer, L. J. , Roditi, B., Paster, M., & Rudin, B. (1994). *The Student Observation System (S.O.S.).* Chelmsford, MA: Research Institute for Learning and Development.

Oswang, L. B., & Bain, B. A. (1991). Clinical forum: Treatment efficacy when to recommend intervention. *Language, Speech, and Hearing Services in Schools, 22,* 255–263.

Peña, E. (1993). *Dynamic assessment: A non-biased approach for assessing the language of young children.* Unpublished doctoral dissertation, Temple University, Philadelphia.

Peña, E., Quinn, R., & Iglesias, A. (1992). Application of dynamic methods of language assessment: A nonbiased approach. *Journal of Special Education, 26,* 269–280.

Rand, Y. (1991). Deficient cognitive functions and non-cognitive determinants- An integrating model: Assessment and intervention. In R. Feuerstein, P. S. Klein, & A. J. Tannenbaum (Eds.), *Mediated learning experience (MLE): Theoretical, psychosocial and learning implications* (pp. 71–94). London: Freund .

Rohwer, W. D., Jr., Ammon, M. S., Suzuki, N., & Levin, J. R. (1971). Population differences and learning proficiency. *Journal of Educational Psychology, 62,* 1–14.

Roseberry, C. A., & Connell, P. J. (1991). The use of an invented language rule in the differentiation of normal and language-impaired Spanish-speaking children. *Journal of Speech and Hearing Research, 34,* 596–603.

Samuels, M. T., Lamb, C. H., & Oberholtzer, L. (1991). Dynamic assessment of adults with learning disabilities. In H. C. Haywood & D. Tzuriel (Eds.), *Interactive assessment* (pp. 275–299) New York: Springer-Verlag.

Schottke, H., Bartram, M., & Wiedl, K. H. (1993). Psychometric implications of learning potential assessment: A typological approach. In J. H. M. Hamers, K. Sijtsma, & A. J. J. M. Ruijssenaars (Eds.), *Learning potential assessment: Theoretical, methodological and practical issues* (pp. 153–173). Amsterdam/Berwyn, PA: Swets & Zeitlinger.

Schwager, M. T., & Carlson, J. S. (1994). *Teacher perceptions in learning and assessment and their interrelationships.* Poster presentation for the International Association for Cognitive Education North American Regional Conference, Oxnard, CA.

Sewell, T. E., & Severson, R. A. (1974). Learning ability and intelligence as cognitive predictors of achievement in first-grade black children. *Journal of Educational Psychology, 66,* 948–955.

Sijtsma, K. (1993). Psychometric issues in learning potential assessment. In J. H. M. Hamers, K. Sijtsma, & A. J. J. M. Ruijssenaars (Eds.), *Learning potential assessment: Theoretical, methodological and practical issues* (pp. 175–193). Amsterdam/Berwyn, PA: Swets & Zeitlinger.

Skuy, M., Kaniel, S., & Tzuriel, D. (1988). Dynamic assessment of intellectually superior Israeli children in a low socio-economic status community. *Gifted Education International, 5,* 90–96.

Spector, J. E. (1992). Predicting progress in beginning reading: Dynamic assessment of phonemic awareness. *Journal of Educational Psychology, 84,* 353–363.

Speece, D. L., & Cooper, D. H. (1990). Ontogeny of school failure: Classification of first-grade children. *American Educational Research Journal, 27,* 119–140.

Speece, D. L., Cooper, D. H., & Kibler, J. M. (1990). Dynamic assessment, individual differences, and academic achievement. *Learning and Individual differences, 2,* 113–127.

Swanson, H. L. (1992). Generality and modifiability of working memory among skilled and less skilled readers. *Journal of Educational Psychology, 84,* 473–488.

Swanson, H. L. (1995a). Effects of dynamic testing on the classification of learning disabilities: The predictive and discriminant validity of the S-CPT. *Journal of Psychoeducational Assessment, 13,* 204–229.

Swanson, H. L. (1995b). Using the cognitive processing test to assess ability: Development of a dynamic assessment measure. *School Psychology Review, 24,* 672–693.

Thompson, E. K. (1991). Mediated learning versus direct instruction: An empirical study of the process of change in adolescent problem-solving. Unpublished doctoral dissertation, Columbia University, New York.

Tzuriel, D. (1989). Inferential thinking modifiability in young socially disadvantaged and advantaged children. *International Journal of Dynamic Assessment and Instruction, 1,* 65–80.

Tzuriel, D. (1991). Cognitive modifiability, mediated learning experience and affective-motivational processes: A transactional approach. In R. Feuerstein, P. S. Klein, & A. J. Tannenbaum (Eds.), *Mediated learning experience (MLE): Theoretical, psychosocial and learning implications* (pp. 95–120). London: Freund .

Tzuriel, D., & Klein, P. S. (1985). Analogical thinking modifiability in disadvantaged, regular, special education, and mentally retarded children. *Journal of Abnormal Child Psychology, 13,* 539–-552.

Tzuriel, D., & Klein, P. S. (1986). *The Frame Test of Cognitive Modifiability Manual.* Ramat Gan, Israel: Bar Ilan University (School of Education).

Tzuriel, D., Samuels, M. T., & Feuerstein, R. (1988). Non-intellective factors in dynamic assessment. In R.M. Gupta & P. Coxhead (Eds.), *Cultural diversity and learning efficiency: Recent developments in assessment* (pp. 141–163). New York: St. Martin's Press.

Valencia, S. W., Campione, J. C., Weiner, S., & Bazzi, S. (1990, November). *Dynamic assessment of reading achievement.* Paper presented at the National Reading Conference, Miami, FL.

Vygotsky, L. S. (1978). *Mind in society: The development of higher psychological processes* (M. Cole, V. John-Steiner, S. Scribner, & E. Souberman, Eds.). Cambridge, MA: Harvard University Press.

Vygotsky, L. (1986). *Thought and language* (A. Kozulin, Ed.). Cambridge, MA: MIT Press.

Wingenfeld, S. A. (1992). *Dynamic and neuropsychological assessment of the cognitive functioning of learning disabled and non-learning disabled adolescents.* Paper presented at the Third International Conference on Cognitive Education, Riverside, CA.

CHAPTER 16

The Learning Potential Assessment Device

REUVEN FEUERSTEIN

RAFI FEUERSTEIN

STEVEN GROSS

HISTORICAL ORIGINS

THE LEARNING POTENTIAL ASSESSMENT DEVICE (LPAD) plays a crucial role both historically and substantively in the development of the theory of structural cognitive modifiability (SCM) and its applied systems (Feuerstein, Feuerstein, & Schur, 1995). It acts both as the generator of the theory and as one of its products. The LPAD reflects a different view of human beings and their development, different from the way human beings have previously been described by psychological theories and the behavioral sciences. It represents a sharp departure from practices based on the assumption of the human being as an immutable and fixed entity and, therefore, accessible to study via psychometric methods of measurement. Ramey and MacPhee (1981), in their attempt to evaluate the LPAD program, stated that Feuerstein's book (Feuerstein, Rand, & Hoffman, 1979) represents a paradigmatic shift in intellectual assessment. They refer to the existence of three major conditions, which according to Kuhn (1970) and Feuerstein (Feuerstein et al., 1979) are required for the evolution of a new paradigm. The first condition is the disenchantment with the currently existent paradigm because of logical and empirical inconsistencies in its system. The second condition is social pressure due to the ways the existent paradigm affects the status of certain segments of the population. The third condition is the emergence of a new conception that is virtually free of previous paradigm inconsistencies and responses to social pressures. Because these three conditions are satisfied to the best of our knowledge, there is good reason to believe that a new paradigm of the assessment of cognitive, emotional and behavioral states of human beings is now available (see Lidz, Chapter 15, this volume, for a review of contemporary applications of dynamic assessment procedures).

Models and measurements of assessment affect masses of children and adults in determining educational and employment opportunities. These models have been developed for the norm; when alternative segments of a population are considered, they may not be able to respond to the model appropriately. In particular, the culturally different and the culturally deprived, including those whose lives were severely affected by conditions imposed on them by war, hunger, or other socially disorganizing factors, may not respond optimally to an assessment that was developed for a population with very different needs.

The inadequacy of the conventional psychometric model became clear to the first author (R.F.) in the late 1940s and early 1950s as he dealt with children from the Holocaust. These children witnessed the greatest atrocities a human being could imagine. Individuals who came through these deprived environments had very little preparation for confronting a new culture as they emigrated to Israel. Likewise, children and adults who came from culturally deprived or socially disorganized environments showed great difficulty in adapting to a new culture, one that confronted them with the need for higher mental processes to respond to modern technological requirements. Many of these children, regardless of individual etiology, were considered either mentally retarded, borderline or, at best, below average when their intelligence was measured with conventional, static, psychometric instruments. Following their categorization based on these tests, many children were considered ineligible for higher educational opportunities. Some of them were in danger of being denied the opportunity to benefit from the educational process and become integrated into the community. In short, they were being denied the chance to become active members of the occidental culture in Israel.

The first author (R.F.) has experienced a dilemma in making such vital decisions as educational eligibility based solely on the low manifest level of intellectual functioning as measured by traditional IQ tests, because these tests may reflect a lack of basic school skills or functional illiteracy rather than a true deficit in cognitive ability. The results of psychometric measures placed many of these children in the range of below average intelligence, and the prognosis for their adaptability was considered poor. Moreover, results of an IQ test or any static measure not only led policymakers and educators of these youngsters to question their educability and their accessibility to integration into society but actually made them decide in many cases to adhere to a "passive–acceptant" approach in their education (i.e., to accept their condition as it is reflected in a manifest level of functioning as immutable and unchangeable). Therefore, policymakers produced the kinds of special environments and educational systems that were considered accessible to these low-functioning children. Policymakers avoided any imposition on children's functioning that was considered beyond their low fixed capacities.

The dilemma described above created a strong need to do away with the existent methods of assessing intelligence, despite their scientific soundness and their strong theoretical and empirical basis. The disenchantment with these measurements made the first author (R.F.) consider both the fixists' theory of human intelligence and the social meaning of the psychometric method produced by this theory vis-á-vis an alternative dynamic assessment theory.

The evolution of a dynamic assessment theory and approach was very convoluted at first and had to go through many obstacles. It was evident from the outset that the types of mosaic tests, such as the Binet–Simon (1905) and later the Wechsler–Bellevue (Wechsler, 1939), were considered unacceptable for and irrelevant to the assessment of these children. Likewise, culturally free tests (e.g., Raven's Progressive Matrices; Raven, 1958), although considered by theoreticians to reflect the true potential of individuals, irrespective of educational history or cultural background, were found to be of limited utility with this population. The results obtained by these children on so-called culturally free tests were very similar to those obtained on other tests highly saturated in cultural determinants and educational requirements. An examination of culturally fair tests followed. Indeed, inspired and helped by Professor Andre Rey, the first author (R.F.) attempted to apply some specially produced tests which came closer to the criteria of culturally fair tests, using certain assessment procedures based on elements considered to be part of the cultural values and experiences of the individuals. However, these children were unable to respond better to these tests than to any of the aforementioned instruments.

Next, nonverbal measures of intelligence were evaluated, such as the Bender Visual Motor Gestalt Test (Bender, 1938) and human figure drawing tests. These tasks were considered less related to the educational background of the individual and to his or her direct, immediate experience. Furthermore, these tests were supposed to reveal evidence of certain developmental and maturational conditions of the individual. Once again, these measures proved to yield limited information regarding the cognitive and developmental capacities of the population in question. Specifically, little of the behaviorally visible capacities and abilities of these children to adapt to daily life were reflected in the (low) results obtained by nonverbal psychometric instruments.

One of the last attempts to identify an assessment device that would be sensitive to the capabilities of children from culturally deprived and/or socially disorganized environments was to examine Piagetian types of tasks. Feuerstein et al. (1979) considered Piagetian tasks to yield more universal manifestations of maturational processes and their developmental stages. There was a long list of tasks and a repertoire of modalities used in the early 1950s to evaluate culturally deprived children. Results of several studies showed that normally behaving individuals from diverse cultural backgrounds performed in the low-average range on these tasks (see Feuerstein et al., 1979, for more details). This kind of inconsistency of both an empirical and logical nature led the first author (R.F.) to consider the whole psychometric testing mechanism as belonging to a paradigm that does not respond to the goals of assessment, notably the evaluation of human potential and the understanding of the true nature of human intelligence irrespective of its immediate manifestation. This style of psychometric testing created conditions in which individuals were assessed on the basis of the modalities of their manifest functioning at a given time and did not really reflect what they could achieve if and when the various conditions responsible for their low functioning were avoided or corrected.

A Paradigm Shift

The dynamics of the shift from traditional cognitive assessment procedures to a new paradigm emerged from a real and stringent social condition. This condition, in essence, called for a better means to evaluate certain characteristics of each human being in order to decide on his or her destiny (e.g., educational placement and opportunities). As stated earlier, disenchantment with the existent methods was due mainly to the great gap between what was observed in a variety of behavioral dimensions and the results obtained on psychometric assessment instruments. This made one look for substitutions that might replace traditional methodologies. However, soon it became clear that replacing methodologies and techniques alone was not sufficient to solve these problems. A need also existed to evaluate the psychometric soundness of underlying theories of cognitive functioning (i.e., the foundation from which the assessment methods were built). The following inquiries then represented the fundamental basis for the paradigm shift: (1) Are observed psychometric behaviors *traits* of the individuals or are they *states*? (2) Do they reflect innate capacities or acquired ones? (3) Do they represent immutable and fixed characteristics or are they modifiable? and (4) Are low levels of manifest academic skills on psychometric tests truly representative of the individual's adaptive behaviors?

These questions generated new modalities and methodologies of application and experimentation. The development and observations of thousands of children gathered by the first author (R.F.) and his colleagues brought about a series of tentative answers that led to the formulation of the theory of SCM (see Feuerstein et al., 1995, for a complete discussion). Three core concepts of this theory are reflected in the LPAD.

First, the *learner's* behavior is represented in terms of a variety of cognitive deficiencies, found through clinical experience to typify the performance of children with low academic achievement.

Second, the *assessor's* behavior is characterized in terms of the components of the Mediated Learning Experience (MLE), hypothesized to represent the proximal (in contrast to distal) factors relating to development of cognitive functions. Third, the *task* is conceptualized in terms of a "cognitive map" that portrays the features distinguishing one task from another. (Lidz, 1991, pp. 10–11)

Each of these ideas is addressed below. The development of the LPAD and the direction it took in establishing the modality of dynamic assessment were, at an early point, the outcome of the formulation of goals different from those set by the static modalities of assessment.

Indeed, the goal of dynamic assessment is to *evaluate* (not *measure*) the *modifiability* of individuals, the extent of their modifiability, the preferred modalities of intervention required to reach the desired states of functioning, and the meaning of this modifiability for the adaptability of the individual. The rejection of psychometric tests as a means for evaluating individuals had to be followed by a generation of a more global and pervasive theoretical basis. That is, rather than just looking for ways to alleviate the difficulties encountered by the conventional tests, one had to shift in a meaningful way to a new paradigm.

This new paradigm, based on the theories of SCM and mediated learning experience (MLE) (see Lidz, Chapter 15, this volume), has generated three applied systems: the LPAD, the Feuerstein Instrumental Enrichment (FIE) program, and the Shaping of Modifying Environments (SME). These three applied systems reflect a set of underlying belief systems, or philosophical views, about the essence of human beings. These systems are the manifestation of theoretical elaborations about human beings as modifiable and modifying entities. They also represent the modality by which a concerted intervention is produced whose major goal is to ensure that this modifiability, which is uniquely human, can be shared by all individuals regardless of their cultural or ethnic background.

The LPAD is the first step toward the goal of the recognition and enhancement of human modifiability. It sets the theoretical condition and gives legitimacy and direction to the intervention necessary to produce the desired (and feasible) changes. It provides the data necessary to respond to the particular needs of an individual who is confronted with difficulties in his or her cognitive developmental and/or emotional structures which may be due to a variety of endogenic or exogenic barriers.

THE LPAD THEORY, INSTRUMENTS, AND TECHNIQUES

A description of the LPAD follows. Its conceptual framework, goals, and the way in which it structures the techniques of assessment will be compared with both conventional psychometric test techniques and a variety of dynamic methods that have been developed over the past 20 years. These dynamic assessment methods have been developed partly following the LPAD theory and model and were derived directly from the Vygotskian approach to dynamic assessment. The Vygotskian theory certainly preceded the theory of SCM; however it never actually became an applied system (see Feuerstein et al., 1979; Feuerstein et al., 1995; Lidz, Chapter 15, this volume). Therefore, those who subscribed to the Vygotskian theoretical model needed an operational apparatus for implementation.

Before beginning the description of the LPAD, a rectification is in place. Until now, the major goal of the Learning *Potential* Assessment Device was to discover the hidden potential of the individual, which was unrevealed by his or her manifest level of functioning. Presently in the development of the theory, however, the concept of potential has become somewhat ambiguous and yet restrictive. Potential, as it is often defined, consists of an individual's unrevealed innate capacities. By the very fact of their innate nature, these capacities are considered as existent in finite quantity which differs from individual to individual. Therefore, these capacities are considered to reflect more adequately an individual's true nature. Popularly said, someone's potential is different and greater than his or her manifest level of functioning.

The gap between the potential and the manifest level of functioning can be attributed to a variety of factors. The basic goal of dynamic assessment methods is to reveal the true potential of the individual via modalities of assessment that go beyond the manifest level of functioning. However, the *construct* of potential is limited, much as the concept of intelligence is limited, to a given quantum of an individual's functioning. Thus, the construct of potential becomes as reified a concept as intelligence, except that it is not totally identical with the manifestations of intelligence in the immediate behavior of an individual. To avoid this return to a reified, measurable, immutable and predictable construct of intelligence, the authors propose using the concept of propensity, instead of potential, which can be considered to describe a power, an energy, an orientation, and an inclination. Thus, by replacing the term "Learning *Potential* Assessment Device" with the term "Learning *Propensity* Assessment Device," the authors believe that greater justice to the mental construct of intelligence is achieved. Likewise, the authors propose further to replace the fixed terms of "traits" and "characteristics" with the term "states." States are dynamic and transient and can be changed, increased, reduced, developed, or deteriorated and more accurately reflect the constant change and changeability that are observed in human nature. This clarification, which represents a development of the theory, to a large extent, was provoked by the *contradictio in sensu* which the term "potential" produced (Sheffler, 1985).

We proceed now to describe the Learning *Propensity* Assessment Device (LPAD) and to examine its differential structure and meaning and compare it to various other dynamic assessment techniques. The LPAD has as its major goal to evaluate human "modifiability." This is to be contrasted with the major goal of conventional psychometric static measures, which is to detect the "hard-wired" traits—the immutable, unchangeable characteristics of an individual. The difference between these two goals (modifiability vs. immutability) is responsible for the course of testing, the design of instruments, the shaping of modalities of application, and the interpretation of results generated by these two approaches (dynamic assessment versus traditional psychometric approaches).

Whereas the LPAD attempts to assess modifiability of an individual, the goal of a number of other dynamic assessments is to unravel the "hidden potential" of an individual. Essentially, the goal of these other techniques is to look for modalities by which this "hidden potential" can be assessed via a test–teach–test technique (see Lidz, Chapter 15, this volume). Although there are many differences between the LPAD and other static or dynamic assessments, there are four major areas in which the LPAD greatly differs from these other methods. These areas include (1) the test instruments, (2) the test situation, (3) the goal of assessment (product versus process), and (4) the interpretation of results. The significant alterations within these areas (described later) represent a shift from the static paradigm of psychometric measures to the dynamic assessment of SCM.

The Test Instruments

The first difference between the LPAD and traditional psychometric measures, as well as other dynamic assessment devices, is the structure, nature and modality of the instruments used for the assessment and evaluation of the cognitive modifiability. Although the LPAD may well use certain instruments that have been created and used by the static, conventional, standardized methods, it presents and structures them in a different way. Following is an enumeration of the differences. First, the LPAD does not attempt to "measure" intelligence or even directly measure "modifiability" but rather attempts to "assess" and "evaluate" the process of change. The concept of measurement is carefully avoided in favor of the concept of evaluation because an attempt to measure something that is in a continuous state of change is an impossible task. Assessing elements that are in a constant state of change requires a different approach to observation than is often found in measuring phenomena in psychometrics and psychology. In effect, measurement represents a conventional fiction in that something that is constantly in flux ends up as a measured entity.

A second difference between the LPAD and other assessment techniques is that the tasks of the LPAD are able to detect changes. The instruments of conventional testing and many dynamic assessment techniques choose various cognitive and mental behaviors that represent immutable, stable, and reliable traits of the individual. These techniques are based on a set of empirical, mathematical and statistical procedures and therefore yield specific measures that are expected to reappear in any other reiteration of the measurement with a specific individual. In contrast, the LPAD attempts to measure the modifiability of an individual and therefore chooses those mental, motor, and emotional behaviors of an individual that are known to be amenable to change and are considered as reflecting the propensity of modifiability. The choice of tasks with highest reliability is, therefore, substituted by the LPAD with tasks of limited reliability because they are sensitive to intervention and are changed significantly by mediational interaction.

A third difference between LPAD and other assessment procedures is that the LPAD tasks were constructed from a model that allows a test–mediate–test sequence. This testing sequence yields the production of a sample of changes in the cognitive structure of the individual which may be considered to represent a universe of possible and necessary changes that form a profile of an individual's modifiability. This test–mediate–test technique calls on the examiner not only to observe the individual's behavior but to intervene, and assess the behavior again to know the outcome of the intervention. Therefore, the cognitive tasks to be used for assessment are chosen among those that offer an opportunity to mediate a specific function of the individual. As tasks become progressively more remote and less familiar from the initial one in which learning took place, there will be ample opportunity to demonstrate the effects of the mediational intervention. The type of tasks that are typically chosen for assessment reflect an individual's "fluid intelligence" (i.e., processes of cognitive behavior that are not only in a constant state of development but also overflow easily from one particular task to a variety of other tasks) (see Horn & Noll, Chapter 4, this volume). Tests for the LPAD's goal of assessing modifiability are not chosen from either activities that use stored information or previously learned behaviors such as reading, writing, computation, or other skills. Rather, the LPAD tasks require little automatization and do not appear to be influenced by cultural opportunities. Therefore, these tests are more able to reflect an individual's modifiability by reflecting the process of learning.

The fourth difference between LPAD and other assessment tools is that the LPAD tasks permit the detection of microchanges in behavior rather than only macrochanges. The microchanges have to be able to be detected within the framework of assessment. In the LPAD assessment procedure, the evaluator looks for immediate behavioral changes, in addition to those behaviors that point to the propensity of an individual's modifiability. To reach this end, the structure of the instruments are different from both the standard measures of the psychometric model and non-LPAD dynamic assessments, because both look for set criteria to serve as the basis for measurement. This structural difference also affects many other dimensions that are characteristic of the LPAD as compared to the two other types of measures. Here the search is not for a particular result but rather for the characteristics of the individual's functioning. That is, the search for those "mental conditions" that can be considered more as states than as traits and which can bring testimony and evidence of a process of change in the making. This last point calls for the construction of test instruments that act as a tight-knit net; that is, one that tries to capture any little behavioral changes that may be considered to be the few dynamic traces of the process rather than waiting for a major behavioral change, which may take much more time and effort to be produced.

This structure of tests is best described by the model presented in Figure 16.1, which has been proposed for the construction of the LPAD assessment instruments. As can be seen in the center of

L.P.A.D Model

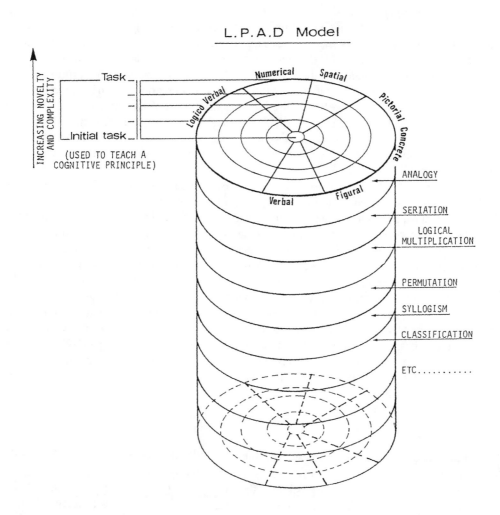

FIGURE 16.1. The LPAD model. From Feuerstein, Rand, & Hoffman, 1979. Copyright © 1979 by University Park Press. Reproduced by permission.

the cylinder, first a task is chosen to be used for the evaluation of the individual's functioning. This problem is then mediated to the individual after he or she has failed to solve it independently. The mediational intervention enables the individual to solve the problem. The question then is, "Has it really changed the structure and the cognitive processes of the individual, or has it affected only the knowledge or skills related to that particular task?"

To detect and understand the value of these changes, a series of variations on the same theme is offered to the individual. One attempts to see how slight changes in the task affect the propensity to solve the task. This enables the evaluator to define intelligence as the propensity of an individual to modify his or her level of functioning and adaptation to tasks that are becoming increasingly more different and more remote from the initial problem that was mediated. These variations represent a progressive change that is achieved by preserving certain components of the learned task while changing others. The subsequent task represents a variation of the initial task whose solution requires the rediscovery of an underlying principle or rule in the initial task that is different in certain dimensions from the task the individual previously learned. For example, a task that is initially presented in a figural modality may be presented to the examinee in either a logical, verbal, or numerical modality. The process of adaptation to this change in the modality of the task's presentation may be interpreted as reflecting the degree and nature of the structural change produced in an individual. The shift from one operation to a number of other operations, as seen in the vertical axis of the LPAD cylinder (see Figure 16.1), gives another dimension of the structural nature of the changes that have been produced in an individual through the mediational interaction. Using this approach, an individual can evaluate the level of change as a function of the distance he or she "carries" the cognitive structures that have been acquired through mediation to a variety of other situations to which he or she has to adapt.

The concept of adaptation presented here defines the major nature of human intelligence. Intelligence is not a static, reified notion but a "power" of adaptation. This power manifests itself in the changes that happen in the cognitive or emotional states of the individual. The model presented here takes into consideration the fluidity of those states that not only may affect the individual in a particular task but may overflow to a variety of other modalities in which that task or similar ones are presented. What is even more important to see is how this acquired state affects a variety of other processes and operations that differ from the one at hand (where the change has been produced), and thereby enables the individual to transcend what he or she has learned through the mediation. From this point of view, the choice of instruments is of vital importance in the attempt to evaluate the modifiability of the individual. Furthermore, other dimensions may be added to the definition of the nature of change. For instance, how much intervention is required for the modifiability of certain states as compared to others? What is the nature of the intervention that is required in order to produce the desired changes? Answers to these questions are crucial to the assessment of an individual's modifiability.

The Test Situation

The LPAD test situation differs greatly from both conventional tests and many other dynamic assessment procedures. It is necessary to shift the structure of the test situation from a static approach to a dynamic evaluation. The test situation in the LPAD is shaped differently from that of the psychometric one and is probably the most important aspect of dynamic assessment. We now examine the nature and structure of the LPAD test situation and compare it to other aspects and techniques of traditional testing situations.

Considering the goals of the LPAD, and in contrast to the psychometric model and other non-LPAD dynamic assessments, normative aspects of measurement are abandoned completely. For example, in the LPAD approach, there is no attempt to assess an individual compared to his or her peers. Conversely, the goal of the static psychometric approach, which has been conserved by some of the dynamic assessments, albeit not all of them, is to measure the individual by tools that permit comparisons of an individual's results to a normative scale. This requires a standardized approach to the assessment of the individual. The test situation, the instructions, and the interaction between the examiner and examinee must be free from any deviation from the normative testing condition so that the obtained results are comparable to the results of the group to which the individual is considered to belong. Any deviation from the standardized testing situation may invalidate the observed results.

This standardized testing procedure strongly affects the total interactive process between the examiner and the examinee. It is the contention of the authors that the sterilization of this relationship, as a result of standardized conditions, creates great barriers for the manifestation of the true propensity of the individual. It may even hamper the gathering of information on the true manifest level of skills and knowledge of the individual. Not only does the LPAD *not* require standardization of the testing situation, it actually encourages examiners to consider the particular needs of examinees in intensive and insightful ways. The LPAD also allows examiners to consider those methods that will lead to an optimal level of functioning and ultimately leads to a sample of changes in the individual's functioning that may be considered to reflect his or her modifiability.

When the goal of a flexible testing situation is to produce a sample of changes in an individual's functioning, these changes have to be interpreted in terms of their magnitude, meaning, and the amount and nature of the intervention that has produced them. This goal demands a change in the transactional process between the examiner and the examinee with a reciprocal modality of interaction. An effort is made to detect and define the individual's cognitive deficiencies that determine their low manifest level of functioning. Then an attempt is made to correct these deficiencies in order to produce the "sample of change," which then can be interpreted as reflecting the modifiability. Other approaches to testing limit the number of interventions so that various examinees can be compared on a fixed amount of intervention. Those who apply a dynamic assessment technique without changing the theoretical basis of the psychometric approach (i.e., without giving up the existent paradigm) do not necessarily look for, and therefore may never find, the structural change characteristic of the LPAD approach. Thus, other "dynamic" assessments stay within the framework of the "static" approach.

It should be noted here that the only thing the LPAD has preserved from traditional psychometric assessment is the use of samples of behavior to evaluate an individual's functioning. All other elements of traditional psychometric assessments have been abandoned. The LPAD compares individuals only to themselves, rather than to a norm group, and attempts to derive from this comparison samples of changes that have happened in their cognitive, emotional, and functional structure. Following this, one proceeds to interpret the sample of changes in terms of their specific meaning. Individuals are led to understand that what they are going to do is more a process of cooperative learning rather than a confrontation with problems in the absence of assistance to help them succeed. The major criterion for success in the LPAD situation is the individual's readiness and his or her propensity to benefit from mediation.

The constant feedback from the mediator in the assessment situation is of particular importance because the individuals who are being assessed have failed in a variety of areas in school and in society. For such children and adults, assessment may be a traumatic experience, especially when the standardized test situation creates a nonencouraging atmosphere that may lead to hostility and/or a feeling of helplessness on the part of the examinee that may ultimately serve to mask the skills and knowledge base of the individual. Conversely, the LPAD creates an atmosphere of encouragement that is followed immediately by a readiness to help to allow individuals to function at a higher or optimal level of performance. Also, in many respects, the LPAD testing situation creates the conditions for such success. Changes in an individual's emotional climate are often followed by changes in cognitive processes, which allow the individual to mobilize and apply themselves to accomplish successfully the task at hand.

The pivotal part of the test situation is the MLE (see Feuerstein et al., 1995; Lidz, Chapter 15, this volume). The goal of MLE is to produce structural changes that will equip individuals with tools of learning on a cognitive, emotional, and motivational level. The MLE has a corollary interaction of requiring the examiner to emit the appropriate stimuli and fostering mastery of the cognitive prerequisites for problem-solving behavior in a particular task. This is done with strong components of transcendence, which will accompany the transmission of the acquired skill with generalizable, transferable components and the orientation to proceed. For example, teaching the examinees an analogy on a figural dimension should be accompanied with mediating those elements of affinity between the analogy in the figural modality and the analogy task in a numerical modality. This can be accomplished by allowing examinees the opportunity to acquire the superordinate analogical skills that transcend the particularities of the language, content, and mode of presentation of a specific analogic modality.

Transcendence, an important criteria of MLE, is the major vital element in the mediational interaction in the LPAD. If the intervention offered takes on the form of prompting or coaching, the expectation to see structural changes in the examinee is not legitimate and is inappropriate. The LPAD, using MLE as the way to modify individuals, may produce cognitive structures that were previously nonexistent in an individual's repertoire.

The test–mediate–test model underlying the LPAD means that individuals are constantly given feedback about the nature of their responses. The insight and the reasons for the nature of their responses are given to examinees in a clinical approach. For example, the insight offered to individuals could be an orientation to the reasons for any dysfunction and the modalities by which they should change in order to be more successful.

The interaction between examiner and examinee in the LPAD testing situation optimizes an individual's functioning in a structural way by fostering an atmosphere in which the following goals may be achieved:

1. To endow individuals with the concepts, words, orientations, and operations they need to solve the problems with which they are confronted.
2. To offer an opportunity to reach out in a conscious way to those cognitive and motivational determinants that enable individuals to function and to mediate the insight necessary to successfully choose from among the functions they have previously employed which led to inadequate functioning.
3. To mediate the meaning of success in the particular task and the way by which it reflects an individual's true propensity to learn and to change.
4. To mediate to the examinees a self-image as a generator of information rather than a self-image as one who acts as a recipient, but not a producer, of information.

The interaction attempts to affect the individual in a more meaningful and pervasive way than simply coaching or prompting. Therefore, the differences between LPAD test results and those obtained by other static or dynamic assessment techniques can be explained by the different nature of the testing situation.

The Shift from Product to Process Orientation

In addition to the shift from a static to a dynamic approach to assessment is the shift from product to process. Psychometric methods of assessment that generate a resultant product have a major goal of obtaining reliability, validity, and the affinity between tasks. By contrast, the process orientation associated with the LPAD is the prominent goal of the assessment. The LPAD is not used as a way to categorize individuals but rather to see how far and in what way they become involved in the process of change and by what methods such changes are produced. To this end, one must have knowledge of the multitude of mental functions that are responsible for an individual's failure. Knowing the reason for failure enables an examiner to choose (1) the appropriate targets of intervention and (2) the most preferred modality of intervention for a particular individual.

A major goal of a process orientation is to achieve a better understanding of the components of human behavior and its relation to an individual's adaptive or nonadaptive behavior. Several questions arise in this regard. What function determines an individual's failure to use his or her "propensity" to adapt his or her "states" to respond better to the demands of a particular task? What makes one individual learn from an experience, while another individual fails to learn from that same experience? Understanding these processes is the major goal of assessment, not only for the immediate purpose of measurement but also for differentiating among mental states and understanding underlying human nature.

This shift from a static to a dynamic approach and from a product to a process orientation draws on two conceptual apparatuses as proposed by SCM theory. One is a list of deficient functions (see Appendix) as conceptualized on the input, elaboration, and output levels which describe the individual who is engaged in problem-solving behavior. The second is the cognitive map which includes the following components of the mental act: (1) the universe of content around which the mental act is centered, (2) the modality or language in which the mental act is expressed, (3) the phase of the cognitive functions required by the mental act (input, elaboration, output), (4) the cognitive operations required by the mental act, (5) level of complexity, (6) level of abstraction, and (7) the level of efficiency with which the mental act is performed. The major role of the cognitive map is to analyze the characteristics of tasks which, in combination with an individual's function, are considered responsible for the particularities of the individual's responses to a given task.

An individual may have the innate capacity to solve a problem but may be confronted with structural issues that interfere with his or her ability to perform the task. These structural issues include (1) a task whose content is totally unfamiliar or (2) a task whose language is unfamiliar, not only on a verbal level but also in regard to the preferred modality of response (e.g., written, verbal, symbolic, gestural, or motor behavior). The characteristics of the task analyzed by the cognitive map combined with an individual's cognitive states as described by the deficient functions determine the quality and adequacy of an individual's responses and his or her modifiability. Other dimensions of the task that should be considered include the amount of data the examinees have to handle on the input or output level, the type of operations used to solve the problems required by the tasks, and the degree of a task's complexity as defined by the number of units to be handled, or by the effects of familiarity.

The deficient functions and the cognitive map are tools that permit the examiner to gain a deeper understanding of an individual's behavior toward a certain type of task. Not only does an evaluation of the deficient functions and cognitive map suggest the intervention that should be applied to a given individual for a given task, but it helps to delineate the kind of interpretations that can be made following the completion of a particular task. For example, deficiencies on the input and the output phases of a mental act should be weighted differently than deficiencies that are related to the elaboration phase because the elaboration phase is the central process of thinking and is the central topic of interest in evaluating human modifiability. Although a deficiency in the amount of input may be responsible for many difficulties in handling certain tasks, it should be given lesser weight than that given to the elaboration processes.

Despite the peripheral place of the input and output phases of the mental act, the interaction between the three phases of input, elaboration, and output is very strong and codetermines the quality of functioning. Observations of the author's clinical cases show that the central elaboration process is often easier and more accessible to modifiability than the input and output processes. Although input and output processes such as reaction time and the modality of focusing impulsivity are difficult to change, they are not impossible. In general, the elaboration is marked by structural changes as well as the acquisition of such higher mental processes as analogical thinking, representational symbolic modes of functioning used in syllogistic and inferential operations, and planned, systematic modes of decision making.

Finally, one of the most important characteristics of the task that should be considered is the amount of efficiency a particular task requires to allow an individual to master it. The concept of efficiency implies three dimensions. Two dimensions, *rapidity* and *precision,* are measurable. The third dimension, the *degree of effort* that is required from an individual to perform the task, is a more subjective but powerful determinant of the nature and degree of an individual's success in mastering a particular task. These three dimensions act in a consonant way and determine an individual's persistence in an activity, the deterioration of an activity, and the degree of an individual's success.

Overall, the LPAD reflects an intricate relationship between the mental characteristics of the learners and the nature of the task. It appears to offer a better understanding of the network of determinants of human behavior than static or non-LPAD types of assessment. The LPAD avoids the global evaluation of individuals reflected by the IQ and allows a look into the more intimate dimensions of human functioning, including the attribution of specific weights to determinants in human learners, the characteristics of the task responsible for the nature of an individual's responses, and the subsequent results obtained from performing the tasks. The emphasis of the process orientation permits the shift in emphasis from the *performer* to the *performance*. When performance is analyzed, the specific reasons for successful or failed adaptation to a given task must be considered.

The heuristic goal of the shift from product to process is that it allows a way to outline preventive and remediational strategies that help individuals. In addition, it provides an examiner with the opportunity to choose from among various problematic topics (e.g., level of input, ability to focus, use of multiple sources of information for decisions, use of a systematic approach to solve a problem) and focus on those topics that are the most important in enhancing an individual's modifiability. An individual's cognitive deficiencies serve as the targets of "attack" and the focus of the MLE intervention. Once the topics have been selected, the examiner decides whether to mediate every deficient cognitive element or only select, pertinent elements.

Interpretation of Results

The interpretation of results in the LPAD differs radically from conventional psychometric methodologies that ascribe to the end product a representation of a "reified" form of intelligence. As in the case of dynamic methods that introduce a learning process as a modality of the assessment, the end product of the conventional, static assessment is considered to represent a universe of functioning. In this way, the measurements are compared to normative standards to determine the distance of the obtained results from the normative criterion of functioning.

The interpretation of results in the LPAD differs in a variety of ways from the static model. First, one attempts to interpret the *process* rather than the product. The detected process may be considered to represent a change even when the end product is not conclusive. For example, analyzing the errors that an individual makes in his or her answers results in an attempt to ascribe a meaning to those errors. Indeed, analyzing the changes that occur in an individual from pretest to posttest not only deals with the absolute changes in the end product (the extent to which the individuals have improved their functioning from erroneous responses to totally correct response) but also deals with the extent to which the nature of the errors has significantly and systematically improved. Moreover, answering the following questions may lead to an interpretation of results that is more explanatory and more revealing about an individual's functioning as well as the processes in which change has occurred: (1) Are the errors made closer to a proper elaborative process? and (2) Are the errors due to the peripheral or to the more central aspects of the task? In the case of the psychometric approach, only a limited number of errors are allowed to continue the measurement processes. If this limit is reached, the measurement of the particular task is discontinued.

A second way in which the interpretation of results in the LPAD differs from static approaches is as follows. The evaluation of an individual who is able to apply the elaboration system in an adequate way but fails to make the proper choices because of improper use of the input or output level yields a different meaning to the end result than when the individual lacks certain cognitive elaboration processes. Furthermore, the interpretation of results reveals those signs that serve as indicators of the existence of a propensity to change or a propensity to learn. The use of various tools such as MLE (the clinical method meant to discover the deficient functions) and the cognitive map (used to understand the nature of the task and its requirements) make it possible to ascribe even to minimal changes the propensity for modifiability. In certain cases, changes are detected that would normally pass unobserved by the product-oriented examiner. Once such changes are uncovered, they are magnified by a mediational process and become more attuned in analysis and interpretation.

A third difference between the LPAD and static approaches in regard to interpretation is that in the latter approach differential levels of the individual's functioning seldom become the object of an interpretation. In many cases, the global IQ does not reveal the underlying differences within an individual's functioning. In certain circumstances, a global score can create an obstructing view of the existence of outgrowths of an individual's functioning that are meaningfully higher in some areas than others. The LPAD uses "peaks" of an individual's functioning to reveal other areas of successful mastery.

A fourth difference between the LPAD and static approaches to interpretation is that in the former approach the examiner must sort out those results that represent and reflect peripheral behavioral changes versus those that represent changes in the individuals' structure of mental behavior. Examples of these structural changes include different ways of functioning cognitively and the way by which the process that has been developed with MLE might affect the cognitive structures. Here a dimension may be missing in the LPAD because the brevity of the intervention may not always allow for the changes to be "structural" in nature, but often the transcending elements that have been produced in the individual can be observed.

Overall, the clinical application of the LPAD takes into consideration the complexity of human beings and their functioning and presents the evaluator with a difficult task of interpretation. The elaboration of results obtained during a clinical period following the interaction of the examiner and the examinee does not easily yield a rigorous form of interpretation. One of the important conceptual elements that LPAD examiners have to adopt is the fact that they are not there to predict human development. Any attempt to fully predict the outcome of a confluence of human experiences, human behavior, and a system of intervening variables is ambitious and unrealistic. Of course, the need to predict human behavior is extremely great. This need is the one that has made even those among the dynamically oriented psychometricians give up on many of the basics of a dynamic approach in favor of some of the more static approaches relating to a "reified" objective element.

INDIVIDUAL PROFILE OF MODIFIABILITY

Another important conceptual tool that aids in evaluating the process of change and its products is a proposed *profile of modifiability*. Although the conceptual basis for this profile exists, the problem is how to construct a profile that corresponds to the LPAD and relates to components of process rather than the end results. The profile of modifiability deals with three facets in which structural change is considered to manifest itself.

The first facet is the attempt to locate changes in an individual's function and to define the magnitude of change. There are four possible types of changes in function: (1) changes in the deficient functions that have been responsible for the nonadaptive behavior, whose evaluation permits one to see the process of an individual's mental behavior; (2) the content aspect of mediational interaction which reflects the tools of thinking (e.g., verbal tools, spatial orientation, temporal elements, types of operations, relationships, and abstract thinking) that have to be evaluated according to the individual's propensity to use the newly acquired elements during and after the assessment;

(3) the energetic realm, notably the emotional, motivational, attitudinal elements that individuals experience during their mediational interaction and the way it has affected their emotional structures; and (4) the degree of efficiency, previously defined as rapidity, precision and subjective feelings of mastery.

A second facet of change to be evaluated is the quality and nature of the change that has been produced in the particular domain of content. Here the examiner tries to evaluate the prominence of the changed element and the resistance of the change to other conditions where it will be manifested including transferability, generalizability, and the capacity to go beyond certain modalities and certain levels of complexities. All these represent the quality, the magnitude, the intensity, and the permanence of the change.

Finally, the third facet of change in a profile of modifiability is the change in the nature and quantity of the mediational intervention necessary to produce a particular sample of modifiability. Here one looks for the changes in quantity and quality of mediation that were necessary at the beginning of the test situation and the quality and quantity of mediation necessary to produce the changes at the end of the assessment. This comes close to the Vygotskian concept of dynamic assessment in which the individual who is learning to do something with someone's help is then assessed according to his or her ability to do it independently at a later stage (Vygotsky, 1978, 1986). In general, the evaluation of change is meant to detect the structural nature of the learning process that took place in the individual during which time he or she approached or reached independence and autonomy.

BEYOND TRADITIONAL INTELLECTUAL ASSESSMENT

The LPAD is a new technique for assessing an individual's cognitive functions and represents a paradigmatic shift in the field of intellectual assessment. It is more than just a set of new instruments or a new way of measurement. It represents a change in the underlying assumptions and philosophy of intelligence. The recent innovations in the LPAD technique presented in this chapter are direct and necessary derivations of the original LPAD theory, philosophy, and belief system. It is our contention that the LPAD corresponds to the great needs of masses of populations for which the existent theories of human nature are unsatisfactory (e.g., culturally diverse and socially deprived).

What is even more important is that the need for this change in assessment theory and technique is strongly fueled and supported by real-life conditions. The existence of a theory that considers human nature as a changing, modifying, and modifiable entity and ascribes to this modifiability an important role in an individual's adaptability is an optimistic alternative to traditional theories, especially when one is engaged in the welfare of human beings. Guided and led by this optimism, psychology and education can turn into highly creative sciences that may find the most efficient ways to materialize the option of modifiability, something that individuals have irrespective of the etiology of their conditions, the age at which MLE is instituted, or even the severity of their conditions. The LPAD represents the first step toward such materialization.

ACKNOWLEDGMENTS

The authors would like to acknowledge that this chapter was written with the generous sponsorship of the supporters of the Benehev Bloomfield Institute, Neri Bloomfield, Harry Bloomfield, and Evelyn Bloomfield Schachter, as well as that of the rest of the Founding Members of the International Center for the Enhancement of Learning Potential, chaired by Sidney Corob, C.B.E., and Myer Deitcher, and thank them for their support. In addition, we would like to thank Hadassah Susson for her editorial assistance.

REFERENCES

Bender, L. (1938). A Visual Motor Gestalt Test and its clinical use. *American Orthopsychiatric Association Research Monograph* (No. 3).

Binet, A., & Simon, T. (1905). Methodes nouvelles pour le diagnostic du niveau intellectuel des anormaux [A new method for the diagnosis of intellectual level of abnormal persons]. *L'Anne Psychologique, 11,* 191–244.

Feuerstein, R., Feuerstein, R., & Schur, Y. (1995). *The theory of structural cognitive modifiability.* Unpublished manuscript.

Feuerstein, R., Rand, Y., & Hoffman, M. (1979). *The dynamic assessment of retarded performers: Learning potential assessment device, theory instruments, and techniques.* Baltimore: University Park Press.

Kuhn, T. S. (1970). *The structure of scientific revolutions.* Chicago: University of Chicago Press.

Lidz, C. S. (1991). *Practitioner's guide to dynamic assessment.* New York: Guilford Press.

Ramey, C. T., & MacPhee, D. (1981). A new paradigm in intellectual assessment? *Contemporary Psychology, 26*(7), 507–509.

Raven, J. C. (1958) *Standard Progressive Matrices.* London: H. K. Lewis.

Sheffler, I. (1985). *Of human potential: An essay in the philosophy of education.* London: Routledge & Kegan Paul.

Vygotsky, L. S. (1978). *Mind in society: The development of higher psychological processes* (M. Cole, V. John-Steiner, S. Scribner, & E. Souberman, Eds.). Cambridge, MA: Harvard University Press.

Vygotsky, L. S. (1986). *Thought and language* (A. Kozulin, Trans.). Cambridge, MA: MIT Press.

Wechsler, D. (1939). *The measurement of adult intelligence.* Baltimore: Williams & Wilkins.

APPENDIX

DEFICIENT COGNITIVE FUNCTIONS

The locus of the deficiencies resulting from the lack of mediated learning experience is peripheral rather than central. It reflects attitudinal and motivational deficiencies, lack of working habits, and learning sets *rather than* structural and elaborational incapacities. Evidence of the reversibility of the phenomena has been provided by clinical and experimental work—especially through dynamic assessment (Learning Propensity Assessment Device). The LPAD has also enabled the establishment of an *inventory of cognitive functions* that are undeveloped, poorly developed, arrested, and/or impaired. These cognitive functions are categorized into the input, elaboration, and output levels.

Impaired cognitive functions affecting the *input level* include those impairments concerning the quantity and quality of data gathered by the individual when confronted by a given problem, object, or experience:

1. Blurred and sweeping perception.
2. Unplanned, impulsive, and unsystematic exploratory behavior.
3. Lack of, or impaired, *receptive verbal tools* which affect discrimination (e.g., objects, events, relationships, etc., do not have appropriate labels).
4. Lack of, or impaired, spatial orientation; the lack of stable systems of reference impairs the establishment of topological and Euclidian organization of space.
5. Lack of, or impaired, temporal concepts.
6. Lack of, or impaired, conservation of constancies (size, shape, quantity, orientation) across variation in these factors.
7. Lack of, or deficient, need for precision and accuracy in data gathering.
8. Lack of capacity for considering two or more sources of information at once. This is reflected in dealing with data in a piecemeal fashion rather than as a unit of organized facts.

The severity of impairment at the input level may also affect ability to function at levels of elaboration and output, but not necessarily so.

Impaired cognitive functions affecting the elaboration level include those factors that impede the efficient use of available data and existing cues:

1. Inadequacy in the perception of the existence and definition of an actual problem.
2. Inability to select relevant versus nonrelevant cues in defining a problem.
3. Lack of spontaneous comparative behavior or limitation of its application by a restricted need system.
4. Narrowness of the psychic field.
5. Episodic grasp of reality.
6. Lack of, or impaired, need for pursuing logical evidence.
7. Lack of, or impaired, interiorization.
8. Lack of, or impaired, inferential–hypothetical "iffy" thinking.
9. Lack of, or impaired, strategies for hypothesis testing.
10. Lack of, or impaired, ability to define the framework necessary for problem-solving behavior.
11. Lack of, or impaired, planning behavior.
12. Nonelaboration of certain cognitive categories because the verbal concepts are not a part of the individual's verbal inventory on a receptive level, or they are not mobilized at the expressive level.

"Thinking" usually refers to the elaboration of cues. There may well be highly original, creative, and correct elaboration, which yields wrong responses because it is based on inappropriate or inadequate data on the input level.

Impaired cognitive functions on the output level include those factors that lead to an inadequate communication of final solutions. It should be noted that even adequately perceived data and appropriate elaboration can be expressed as an incorrect or haphazard solution if difficulties exist at this level.

1. Egocentric communicational modalities.
2. Difficulties in projecting virtual relationships.
3. Blocking.
4. Trial-and-error responses.
5. Lack of, or impaired, tools for communicating adequately elaborated responses.
6. Lack of, or impaired, need for precision in communicating one's responses.
7. Deficiency of visual transport.
8. Impulsive, acting-out behavior.

CHAPTER 17

A Cross-Battery Approach to Assessing and Interpreting Cognitive Abilities: Narrowing the Gap Between Practice and Cognitive Science

DAWN P. FLANAGAN

KEVIN S. McGREW

ALTHOUGH THE STANFORD–BINET INTELLIGENCE SCALE was the first widely used practical meas-ure of intelligence, the Wechsler batteries have dominated the field of individual intelligence testing for nearly six decades. Despite the Wechsler scales' rich research and clinical tradition (Kaufman, 1979, 1990, 1994), their well-entrenched number-one status has indirectly stifled the use of other intelligence test batteries. That is, as a result of the inertia of tradition, progress in the use of more theoretically and empirically defensible methods of assessing and interpreting human cognitive abilities has been limited (see Flanagan & McGrew, 1995a, 1995c).

Despite the fact that David Wechsler designed the Verbal and Performance scales of his tests to represent two different *ways intelligence can be expressed* (i.e., two different *languages*, not two different types of intellectual abilities) (Kamphaus, 1993; Reynolds & Kamphaus, 1990; Zachary, 1990), the prominence of the Wechsler scales in clinical practice has resulted in many psychologists believing that a verbal–nonverbal dichotomy represents *the* valid model of the structure of human intelligence. Psychological reports and professional conversations are replete with comments about a person's "verbal" and "nonverbal" abilities.

Although the dichotomous Wechsler interpretive framework was expanded to include a Free-dom-from-Distractibility factor in the Wechsler Intelligence Scale for Children—Revised (WISC-R; Wechsler, 1974) (Kaufman, 1979), and more recently a Processing Speed factor in the Wechsler Intelligence Scale for Children—Third Edition (WISC-III; Wechsler, 1991), even these interpretive additions failed to produce an intelligence test battery that reflects contemporary theoretically and empirically based knowledge regarding the structure of intelligence (Carroll, 1993b; Kamphaus, 1993; Shaw, Swerdlik, & Laurent, 1993; Sternberg, 1993). As a result, most of the extant literature cited in support of the clinical interpretation of intelligence test profiles is invalid (Glutting, McDer-mott, & Konold, Chapter 19, this volume; Kavale & Forness, 1984; McDermott, Fantuzzo, Glutting,

Watkins, & Baggaley, 1992; Mueller, Dennis, & Short, 1986; Reschly, Chapter 22, this volume) because it is based on theoretically impoverished instruments (viz., the Wechsler batteries) that are incomplete measures of the major domains of cognitive ability (see Carroll, 1993a).

Fortunately, we have come a long way in our understanding and measurement of the construct of intelligence since the Wechsler–Bellevue was published (Wechsler, 1939). A review of the chapters in this volume on contemporary theories and tests of intelligence reveals that the structure of cognitive abilities is much more complex and differentiated than a simple dichotomous (i.e., verbal–nonverbal) or four-factor (i.e., verbal, nonverbal, freedom from distractibility, processing speed) model. If the art and science of intelligence test interpretation is to survive and progress, it must be based on contemporary research and theory (see Kamphaus, Petoskey, & Morgan, Chapter 3, this volume).

Of all the prominent theories reviewed in this volume, we believe that an integration of the three-stratum level theory of cognitive abilities (Carroll, 1993a; Chapter 7, this volume) and the Horn–Cattell Gf-Gc theory (Horn, 1991, 1994; Horn & Noll, Chapter 4, this volume) provides the most comprehensive and *empirically supported* model of the structure of intelligence currently available. Therefore, we believe that all intelligence batteries should be interpreted from an integrated Carroll and Horn Gf-Gc theoretical framework (see McGrew, Chapter 9, this volume; Woodcock, in press).

Currently, no intelligence test battery adequately operationalizes the Gf-Gc theory of intelligence. All major intelligence batteries, including the Woodcock–Johnson Psycho-Educational Battery—Revised (WJ-R; Woodcock & Johnson, 1989), which was specifically designed to approximate the Horn–Cattell Gf-Gc model (see Woodcock, Chapter 12, this volume), fail to adequately measure all the major broad Gf-Gc abilities subsumed in an integrated Carroll and Horn Gf-Gc model. However, it is possible for clinicians to more closely approximate the measurement of the full range of empirically validated Gf-Gc cognitive abilities by moving beyond the boundaries of the intelligence test batteries they use most frequently. Through supplementing their preferred test battery with tests from other intelligence batteries, clinicians can conduct and interpret assessments that are more comprehensive and theoretically sound—a practice that effectively serves to narrow the gap between cognitive science and applied intelligence testing.

As first suggested by Woodcock (1990), and further expanded on by McGrew (Chapter 9, this volume) and McGrew and Flanagan (1995, 1996), clinicians can conduct and interpret intellectual assessments that more closely approximate the major Gf-Gc abilities by "crossing" intelligence test batteries in a systematic and empirically grounded manner. The remainder of this chapter describes the major features of this method, which we refer to as the "cross-battery" approach to assessing and interpreting cognitive abilities.

FOUNDATIONS OF THE "CROSS-BATTERY" APPROACH

Improving the Validity of Intellectual Assessment and Interpretation

A critical issue in psychological measurement is validity, or the inferences one can draw from test scores. In the assessment of intelligence the primary inferences of concern are (1) the extent to which test scores can be interpreted as indicators of important human cognitive constructs (i.e., construct validity) and (2) the degree to which the test scores are useful in making predictions about current or future performance (i.e., criterion-related validity). Now that Carroll and Horn have provided the field of intellectual assessment with a taxonomy or map of the important cognitive constructs that should be included in a complete assessment of intelligence, it is important for researchers and clinicians to attempt to measure these constructs more validly.

To improve our measurement of the *broad* (stratum level II) and *narrow* (stratum level I) Gf-Gc abilities included in the Carroll and Horn–Cattell models of the structure of intelligence, it is important to address two major sources of invalidity in measurement, namely, the presence of construct irrelevant variance and construct underrepresentation (Messick, 1995). According to Messick (1995), *construct irrelevant variance* occurs when an "assessment is too broad, containing excess reliable variance associated with other distinct constructs...that affects responses in a manner irrelevant to the interpreted constructs" (Messick, 1995, p. 742). Interpreting the Wechsler Verbal IQ as a measure of Crystallized Intelligence (Gc) is an example of construct irrelevant variance. The Wechsler Verbal scale includes the Arithmetic subtest which is a strong measure of Quantitative Reasoning (RQ), a narrow ability indicator of Quantitative Knowledge or Reasoning (Gq) (see McGrew's Table 6, this volume). Although the Wechsler Verbal IQ includes indicators of narrow abilities subsumed under Gc (e.g., Language Development and Lexical Knowledge), it also includes variance associated with the measurement of quantitative reasoning. Thus, interpretation of the Wechsler Verbal score as a measure of Gc is confounded by the presence of Gq abilities. The WISC-III Verbal Comprehension Index, which does not include the Arithmetic subtest, would be a measure with more construct relevant variance than the Verbal scale.

In contrast, *construct underrepresentation* is when an "assessment is too narrow and fails to include important dimensions or facets of the construct" (p. 742). An example of construct under-representation would be interpreting the WISC-III Information subtest as representing Carroll and Horn's broad ability of Gc. As summarized by McGrew (see Chapter 9, this volume, Table 9.1), Gc is a broad ability that includes Language Development (LD), Lexical Knowledge (VL), Listening Ability (LS), General Information (KO), Information about Culture (K2), and other abilities. Although the Information subtest measures an important component (viz., General Information) of Gc, this subtest only measures one narrow aspect of the broad Gc construct. The Information subtest *by itself* would be an example of underrepresentation of the broad Gc construct. In order for a construct to be well represented, at least two or more qualitatively different narrow indicators are needed.

Ensuring appropriate construct relevant variance and construct representation in the measurement of cognitive abilities is important if the field of intelligence testing is to progress. McGrew and Flanagan (1996) have used these important concepts of validity, together with an integrated Carroll and Horn–Cattell Gf-Gc theory, as the foundation of a "cross-battery" approach to the assessment and interpretation of tests of intelligence.

The Three Pillars of the Cross-Battery Approach

To measure intelligence more validly, researchers and clinicians first need a taxonomy or map of abilities to measure. In addition, researchers and clinicians must have the necessary information by which to select individual tests from intelligence batteries that will increase the validity of assessments and interpretation through the reduction of construct underrepresentation and construct irrelevant variance. To accomplish this goal, McGrew and Flanagan (1996) have outlined a cross-battery approach to assessment that is based on three foundational sources or pillars of information.

Pillar 1

The first pillar of the cross-battery approach is the use of a synthesized Carroll and Horn–Cattell Gf-Gc model of human cognitive abilities presented by McGrew (see Chapter 9, this volume, Figure 9.1). The Gf-Gc model is the most comprehensive and empirically supported model of the structure of cognitive abilities. Support for the Gf-Gc theory has been documented amply through the following types of empirical evidence: (1) individual differences in factor-analytic studies (i.e., structural evidence), (2) changes in abilities across the lifespan (i.e., developmental evidence), (3) relations to indicators of physiological and neurological functioning (i.e., neurocognitive evidence), (4) predictions of school performance and occupational levels (i.e., achievement evidence), and (5) relations among persons related biologically to different degrees (i.e., heritability evidence) (Horn, 1994). This model provides a map of the broad cognitive abilities or constructs that should be measured in a complete assessment of a person's intelligence.

Pillar 2

The second pillar is the use of construct relevant Gf-Gc abilities as the foundation from which assessments and interpretations may be conducted. Reducing the degree of construct irrelevant variance in intellectual assessment is the purpose of the second cross-battery pillar. This may be accomplished by organizing assessments and interpreting cognitive performance from the results of joint factor analyses that include a broad range of cognitive ability tests. Gf-Gc organized joint or cross-battery factor analysis studies of the major intelligence batteries (viz., McGhee, 1993; Flanagan & McGrew, 1996; Woodcock, 1990) have resulted in the classification of the individual tests in the batteries according to the broad Gf-Gc ability domains. The results of these studies are summarized in Table 17.1.

A number of conclusions can be gleaned from a review of Table 17.1. First, the need for a cross-battery approach is clear as almost all intelligence batteries are *incomplete* measures of the major broad Gf-Gc abilities. Second, most intelligence batteries have been *underfactored*. For example, the so-called WISC-R Freedom-from-Distractibility factor (comprised of Arithmetic, Digit Span, and Coding) disappears when the WISC-R tests are included in cross-battery factor analysis studies with indicators of all the major broad Gf-Gc abilities. Instead, the Arithmetic, Digit Span, and Coding tests are found to be strong indicators of the broad Gf-Gc abilities of Quantitative Ability (Gq), Short-Term Memory (Gsm), and Processing Speed (Gs), respectively. This is consistent with Carroll's (1993a) comment that "Kaufman's 'freedom from distractibility' factor is a complex factor, an artifact of the factor analysis of a severely limited battery of tests, and is not to be considered as a basic primary factor in mental organization" (p. 258).

Third, an understanding of the broad Gf-Gc classification of each test in a battery can reduce the confounding influence of construct irrelevant variance in test interpretation by making researchers and clinicians aware of tests that should or should not be combined to represent a broad Gf-Gc ability or construct. For example, from a review of Table 17.1 the conclusion is reached that clinicians are on solid ground when making interpretive statements about a person's quantitative reasoning from the combination of the Stanford–Binet Intelligence Scale: Fourth Edition (SB-IV; Thorndike, Hagen, & Sattler, 1986) Quantitative, Number Series, and Equation building subtests, subtests with similar shared construct variance (i.e., Gq). On the other hand, interpreting a person's WISC-III Performance Scale as a measure of visual processing (Gv) is confounded by the presence of construct irrelevant variance. As summarized in Table 17.1, some of the tests (e.g., Block Design and Object Assembly) that comprise the WISC-III Performance Scale are strong measures of Gv abilities, but other tests included in this composite score measure Gs (viz., Coding) and some aspects of Gc (viz., Picture Completion and Picture Arrangement). The presence of Gs and Gc abilities in the WISC-III Performance scale is an example of construct irrelevant variance that confounds the Gv interpretation of the Wechsler Performance scale.

Finally, the cross-battery factor studies summarized in Table 17.1 indicate that "all subtests are not created equal" (McGrew & Flanagan, 1996). That is, some tests are stronger or purer measures of their respective broad Gf-Gc constructs. This is reflected in the empirically based *strong, moderate*, and *mixed* Gf-Gc classifications of the individual tests. Those tests classified as either moderate or strong Gf-Gc measures are those that are the "purer" measures of their respective broad Gf-Gc ability. Inferences and interpretations based on the combination of two strong indicators of Gv

TABLE 17.1. Gf-Gc Factor Classifications of Six Major Intelligence Test Batteries

Gf-Gc Factor	WJ-R	Wechslers
Long-Term Retrieval (Glr)	**Memory for Names** **Vis-Aud Learning** **Delayed Recall-MN** Delayed Recall-VAL	----------
Short-Term Memory (Gsm)	**Memory for Words** Memory for Sent. (Gc*) Numbers Reversed (Gf*) Picture Recognition (Gv*)	**Digit Span**
Processing Speed (Gs)	**Visual Matching** **Cross Out**	**Coding/Digit Symbl** Symbol Search
Auditory Processing (Ga)	**Incomplete Words** **Sound Blending** Sound Patterns (Gf*)	----------
Visual Processing (Gv)	Visual Closure Spatial Relations (Gf*)	**Block Design** **Object Assembly** Mazes Picture Comp (Gc*) Picture Arrang (Gc*)
Comprehension-Knowledge (Gc)	**Picture Vocabulary** **Oral Vocabulary** **Listening Comp.**	**Information** **Similarities** **Vocabulary** **Comprehension**
Fluid Reasoning (Gf)	**Analysis-Synthesis** **Concept Formation** Verbal Analogies (Gc*)	----------
Quantitative Ability (Gq)	**Calculation** **Applied Problems**	**Arithmetic**

abilities (e.g., Wechsler Block Design and Object Assembly) are more valid than inferences based on a combination of two moderately classified Gv tests (e.g., WJ-R Visual Closure and Picture Recognition tests), which in turn is more valid than interpretation based on a combination of two mixed tests (e.g., Wechsler Picture Completion and Picture Arrangement that measure both Gv and Gc). Inferences based on tests classified as strong indicators of a Gf-Gc ability will minimize the influence of construct irrelevant variance.

Pillar 3

To guard against invalidity in assessment and interpretation due to construct underrepresentation, it is important to know the narrow Gf-Gc classification of tests in the major intelligence batteries. Tables 9.2 through 9.8 in Chapter 9 (McGrew, this volume) present the classification of tests at the narrow level of abilities (stratum level I). This information is provided to aid researchers and clinicians in selecting and interpreting specific combinations of tests, or a test composite score, at the appropriate broad or narrow stratum levels.

For example, drawing on the factor analysis rule of thumb that one needs at least two, and preferably three or more, indicators to adequately represent a factor (Carroll, 1993a), the interpre-

TABLE 17.1. *(continued)*

SB:IV	DAS[a]	K-ABC[a]	KAIT
----------	----------	----------	**Rebus Learning** **Del. Rec.-RebLrn.** Del. Rec-Aud Com (Gc*)
Memory for Digits Memory for Objects Mem. for Sent. (Gc*) Bead Memory (Gv*)	**Recall of Designs**	**Number Recall** **Word Order** Hand Move (Gq*)	**Mem. for Blk. Des.**
----------	----------	----------	----------
----------	----------	----------	----------
Pattern Analysis Copying Paper Fold. (Gq*)	Pattern Construction	**Triangles** Gestalt Closure Spatial Mem Mat. Analog. (Gf*) Photo Series (Gf*)	----------
Vocabulary **Verbal Relations** Comprehension Absurdities	**Word Definitions** **Similarities**	**Faces & Places** **Riddles** Expressive Voc.	**Famous Faces** Definitions (Go*) Dbl. Meanings (Go*) Auditory Comp. (Gsm*)
Matrices	**Matrices** Seq-Quant Reason (Gq)	----------	**Logical Steps** **Mystery Codes**
Quantitative **Number Series** **Equation Building**	----------	**Arithmetic**	----------

Note: Strong measures of Gf-Gc factors are reported in bold-faced type; measures not in bold type are moderate or mixed indicators of Gf-Gc abilities. Primary measures of Gf-Gc factors for the WJ-R are based on the empirical analyses of Woodcock (1990) and Flanagan and McGrew (1996); Gf-Gc factor classifications of the SB:IV, Wechslers, and K-ABC are reported in Woodcock (1990); Classifications for the DAS and KAIT are reported in McGhee (1993) and Flanagan and McGrew (1996), respectively. For additional information on Gf-Gc factor classifications of major intelligence test batteries see McGrew (1994, Chapter 9, this volume).
*Secondary factor loading.
[a]Only a subset of DAS and K-ABC subtests were joint factor analyzed by McGhee (1993) and Woodcock (1990), respectively. Therefore, only the subtests that were included in these analyses are reported in this Table. The Gf-Gc factor classifications of *all* DAS and K-ABC subtests following a logical task analysis and expert consensus are reported in McGrew (Chapter 9, this volume).

tation of the WISC-III Verbal Comprehension Index as a measure of Gc would be valid. McGrew (Chapter 9, this volume, Table 9.6) reveals that the four tests that comprise this index (i.e., Information, Similarities, Vocabulary, and Comprehension) measure at least three qualitatively different narrow abilities (viz., Language Development, Lexical Knowledge, and General Information) subsumed under the broad Gc construct. Thus, the broad Gc construct is represented adequately by at least three narrow Gc abilities.

In contrast, although the Memory for Names and Visual–Auditory Learning tests that comprise the WJ-R Long-Term Retrieval cluster are strong indicators of this factor, according to McGrew's classification (see Chapter 9, this volume, Table 9.7) these two tests are interpreted best as measuring the narrow ability of Associative Memory (MA). Associative memory is one of approximately 12 different narrow abilities included under Glr in McGrew's synthesized Carroll and Horn–Cattell model. With only one narrow ability measured by these two WJ-R tests, interpretation of the composite score formed by these two tests as representing the broad Glr ability is not appropriate. This composite score can be interpreted as measuring associative memory which is *a part* of Glr, but it should not be interpreted as representing Glr itself. Using the WJ-R Long-Term Memory cluster as a proxy of Glr would be an example of construct underrepresentation. Supplementing these two WJ-R measures of associative memory with tests that measure at least one other narrow Glr ability would be necessary before making statements or generalizations about a person's broad Glr ability. One possibility would be to cross batteries to include a measure of Meaningful Memory (e.g., Delayed Recall–Auditory Comprehension on the Kaufman Adolescent and Adult Intelligence Tests [KAIT], Kaufman & Kaufman, 1993) (see McGrew, Chapter 9, this volume, Table 9.4) with the WJ-R associate memory tests to better represent the construct of Glr. To guard against construct underrepresentation in intelligence test interpretation, researchers and clinicians need to be aware of the narrow Gf-Gc test classifications to ensure that tests of at least two different narrow abilities are combined before drawing inferences about a person's broad Gf-Gc ability.

OPERATIONALIZING THE CROSS-BATTERY APPROACH

Using the three pillars as a foundation, McGrew and Flanagan (1996) have operationalized the procedures necessary to translate the cross-battery concepts of intellectual assessment into practice. The essence of the cross-battery approach can be understood by reviewing Figure 17.1.

Figure 17.1 graphically summarizes how the three pillars of the cross-battery approach are translated into practice. The first pillar (an empirically supported theory of the structure of intelligence) is represented partially by the large rectangle labeled Gf (Fluid Intelligence). This is one of the 10 broad abilities included in the synthesized Carroll and Horn–Cattell Gf-Gc taxonomy of human cognitive abilities. It can be seen in Figure 17.1 that the broad Gf ability subsumes four narrower abilities including General Sequential Reasoning (RG), Induction (I), Piagetian Reasoning (RP), and Speed of Reasoning (RE). The broad and narrow levels seen in Figure 17.1 correspond to the model and definitions of human cognitive abilities presented in Figure 17.1 and Table 9.1 in Chapter 9 (McGrew, this volume).

Similar schematic figures could be drawn to represent the relations between all the broad Gf-Gc abilities included in the comprehensive Gf-Gc theoretical model and the classification of all the individual subtests in each intelligence battery (see McGrew & Flanagan, 1996). The bridge between the Gf-Gc theory and assessment practice is the classification of the strong indicators (i.e., subtests) of the respective narrow abilities under the broad Gf ability in Figure 17.1. The six tests listed are taken from Tables 9.2 through 9.8 in Chapter 9 (McGrew, this volume). For readability purposes, only the strong indicators of Gf abilities are included in Figure 17.1 (the moderate and mixed test indicators are excluded).

Inspection of Figure 17.1 reveals a number of implications for practice. For example, when clinicians are attempting to measure the broad ability of Gf, they only have tests of the narrow abilities of General Sequential Reasoning (RG) (i.e., deductive reasoning) and Induction (I) from which to choose. Second, clinicians only have strong Gf indicators available in the WJ-R, KAIT, SB-IV, and Differential Ability Scales (DAS; Elliott, 1990) test batteries, with fewer options for measuring General Sequential Reasoning (i.e., only two tests). What does this mean for assessment?

If a clinician's instrument of choice is one of the Wechsler batteries, it is clear from a review of Figure 17.1 as well as Table 17.1 that the Wechsler scales do not include strong indicators of Gf

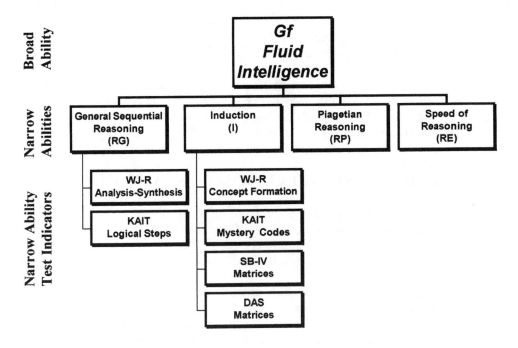

FIGURE 17.1. Strong test indicators of Gf.

abilities. Thus, clinicians would need to supplement their Wechsler battery by "crossing batteries"; that is, selecting tests from either the WJ-R, KAIT, SB-IV, or DAS. Summary figures similar to the one presented in Figure 17.1, as well as the information presented in Table 17.1 in this chapter and Tables 9.2 through 9.8 in Chapter 9 (McGrew, this volume), can be used by clinicians to identify the "holes" in their selected batteries that need to be "filled" through cross-battery assessment procedures.

To ensure that Gf construct underrepresentation is minimized when using the Wechsler batteries, a clinician would need to select at least one test of General Sequential Reasoning and one test of Induction from those listed in Figure 17.1. Of course, there are obvious measurement reasons (e.g., a common norm sample) for selecting the supplemental Gf tests from within the same battery (e.g., WJ-R Analysis–Synthesis and Concept Formation; KAIT Logical Steps and Mystery Codes).

Related to the need to fill the Gf hole in the Wechsler batteries, McGrew and Flanagan (1996) report a case study of an individual with WISC-III Verbal, Performance, and Full Scale scores of 79, 62, and 68, respectively. The individual had subtest scaled scores that ranged from 1 (Block Design and Object Assembly) to 9 (Digit Span and Coding). If the traditional interpretation of the Wechsler Block Design and Object Assembly tests as measures of both visual processing (Gv) and fluid intelligence (Gf) (Kaufman, 1994) had been followed, this individual would have been considered limited in Gv and Gf abilities. However, when the cross-battery approach was employed, the Block Design and Object Assembly tests were more appropriately interpreted as strong measures of Gv (McGrew & Flanagan, 1996), and the WISC-III was supplemented with two strong tests of Gf abilities (i.e., WJ-R Analysis–Synthesis and Concept Formation). As a result, this individual obtained an average standard score of 81 on the two Gf tests in comparison to standard scores (when converted to the same scale with a mean of 100 and standard deviation of 15) of 55 on the two Gv tests. In this case a difference between the individual's Gv (55) and Gf (81) abilities was detected, one that would have gone undetected through sole reliance on the tests within the WISC-III battery. This finding is particularly noteworthy given that Gf abilities are more strongly associated with academic achievement than are Gv abilities (see McGrew & Flanagan, 1996, for a summary). Thus, crossing the WISC-III and WJ-R batteries resulted in a more valid and comprehensive assessment of cognitive abilities.

The operationalization of the cross-battery approach is more involved than can be conveyed by this brief description. McGrew and Flanagan (1996) present information on how the various logical, technical, measurement, and procedural issues can be addressed in the form of a practical and valid approach to cross-battery assessment and interpretation.

IMPLICATIONS OF THE CROSS-BATTERY APPROACH

The "costs" of conducting cross-battery assessments are slightly increased testing time (i.e., 15–30 minutes depending on the test batteries used) and the need to have access to more than one intelligence battery. However, these practical and economic constraints are outweighed by the benefits of this approach, particularly with regard to its implications for practice, research, and test development.

First, the primary benefit of the cross-battery approach is the grounding of intellectual assessment and interpretation in contemporary and empirically supported theories of intelligence. The cross-battery approach provides a much needed and updated bridge between current intellectual theory and research and practice. Appropriately designed and conducted cross-battery assessments will result in more thorough assessments of an individual's broad Gf-Gc abilities.

Second, the cross-battery approach enhances the validity of the interpretations that can be drawn from assessments. By reducing the effects of construct irrelevant variance and construct underrepresentation in the measurement of the broad Gf-Gc abilities, the cross-battery approach increases the validity of the inferences that can be drawn regarding a person's functioning in the various Gf-Gc domains.

Third, regardless of a researcher's or clinician's preferred intelligence test battery, the conceptualization and implementation of cross-battery assessments within a common Gf-Gc theoretical framework will enhance communication between and among professionals and scholars. The field of intelligence testing abounds in the use of many different interpretive terms for cognitive abilities, some with little empirical support. Cross-battery assessments will help to shape researchers and clinicians toward the use of standard terms to interpret intelligence tests. In a sense, Carroll (1993a) has provided a cognitive "table of periodic elements" by which to identify and label the major broad and narrow human cognitive abilities. The cross-battery approach operationalizes the "table of human cognitive elements" into a standard nomenclature for use by researchers and practitioners in the field of intelligence testing.

Fourth, cross-battery assessments can facilitate a greater understanding of the relation between cognitive abilities and a variety of achievement criteria. Because cross-battery assessments are based on the most comprehensive and empirically supported model for the structure of human cognitive abilities, their use will likely result in a more valid means of assessing and interpreting intellectual functioning. Criterion-related inferences (i.e., predictive statements about different achievements) that are made from cross-battery assessments will be based on a more solid foundation. That is, excess "noise" in the predictor–criterion relation will be minimized through the reduction of construct irrelevant variance in the predictor (i.e., cognitive) constructs. Interpretive statements based on valid measures of Gf-Gc abilities can draw on the empirically established relations between specific Gf-Gc abilities and different achievement and vocational–occupational outcomes (see McGrew & Flanagan, 1996, for a summary). For example, there is a large body of literature that documents the importance of phonological awareness (a narrow indicator of Ga) in the early stages of reading (Felton & Pepper, 1995; McBride-Chang, 1995; Wagner & Torgesen, 1987). Likewise, there is an empirically established relationship between Gv and performance in mathematics (e.g., Ben-Chaim, Lappan, & Houang, 1989; Bishop, 1989; Friedman, 1995; Geary, 1993; Rasanen & Ahonen, 1995) as well as various occupations (e.g., Ghiselli, 1966; Humphreys, Lubinski, & Yao, 1993; Pearlman, Schmidt, & Hunter, 1980).

Properly conducted cross-battery assessments would include indicators of these important Gf-Gc abilities. Currently, only the WJ-R assesses Ga abilities; therefore, all other batteries should be augmented to include measurement of Ga, especially when referral concerns are related to difficulties in reading. Similarly, when referral concerns are related to difficulties in math, properly conducted cross-battery assessments would ensure that Gv indicators are included. Measures of Gv are well represented in tests such as the Wechslers and SB-IV but less represented on the WJ-R. An understanding of the strong Gf-Gc indicators that are included on all major intelligence test batteries (see Table 17.1) will assist practitioners in conducting cross-battery assessments.

Finally, cross-battery assessments may increase the chances of isolating important aptitude–treatment–interactions (ATIs). The cross-battery approach we have outlined has as one of its major pillars the use of the Gf-Gc model of intelligence, one of the most promising models currently available and therefore the one around which intelligence tests should be organized (Ysseldyke, 1990). The use of strong or pure indicators of the Gf-Gc constructs in this model may provide the opportunity to conduct more methodologically sound ATI research. "That is, we may now begin to address treatment relevance" (Ysseldyke, 1990, p. 273). The cross-battery assessment approach may facilitate better ATI research through the selection of better measures of the Gf-Gc constructs used in such research (see Flanagan, Andrews, & Genshaft, Chapter 23, this volume).

CONCLUSION

Until new intelligence test batteries are developed, or existing batteries are revised substantially, an empirically supported and theory-driven cross-battery assessment approach is needed to improve the practice of intelligence testing. It is clear from a review of the works of Carroll and Horn (presented in this volume) that we have learned much about the structure of human cognitive abilities. We now know that intelligence is a "many splendored thing" (McGrew, 1995). Unfortunately, most of our current intelligence batteries fall considerably short in their measurement of this complete array of cognitive abilities. Until intelligence batteries "catch up" with what is known about the structure of cognitive abilities and become more comprehensive, Gf-Gc conceptualized cross-battery assessments are necessary to provide a bridge between the extant theoretical knowledge and the practice of applied intellectual assessment and interpretation.

REFERENCES

Ben-Chaim, D., Lappan, B., & Houang, R. T. (1989). The role of visualization in middle school mathematics curriculum. *Focus on Learning Problems in Mathematics, 11*(1), 49–60.

Bishop, A. J. (1989). Review of research on visualization in mathematics education. *Focus on Learning Problems in Mathematics, 11*(1), 7–16.

Carroll, J. B. (1993a). *Human cognitive abilities: A survey of factor-analytic studies.* Cambridge, England: Cambridge University Press.

Carroll, J. B. (1993b). What abilities are measured by the WISC-III? [WISC-III Monograph]. *Journal of Psychoeducational Assessment,* 134–143.

Elliott, C. D. (1990). *The Differential Ability Scales: Introductory and technical handbook.* San Antonio, TX: Psychological Corporation.

Felton, R. H., & Pepper, P. P. (1995). Early identification and intervention of phonological deficits in kindergarten and early elementary children at risk for reading disability. *School Psychology Review, 24,* 405–414.

Flanagan, D. P., & McGrew, K. S. (1995a). The field of intellectual assessment: A current perspective. *The School Psychologist, 49,* 7, 14.

Flanagan, D. P., & McGrew, K. S. (1995b). *Will you evolve or become extinct? Interpreting intelligence tests from modern Gf-Gc theory.* Paper presented at the 27th annual convention of the National Association of School Psychologists, Chicago.

Flanagan, D. P., & McGrew, K. S. (1996). Interpreting intelligence tests from modern *Gf-Gc* theory: Joint confirmatory factor analyses of the WJ-R and the Kaufman Adolescent and Adult Intelligence Test (KAIT). Manuscript submitted for publication.

Friedman, L. (1995). The space factor in mathematics: Gender differences. *Review of Educational Research, 65*(1), 22–50.

Geary, D. C. (1993). Mathematical disabilities: Cognitive, neuropsychological, and genetic components. *Psychological Bulletin, 114*(2), 345–362.

Ghiselli, E. E. (1966). *The validity of occupational aptitude tests.* New York: Wiley.

Horn, J. L. (1991). Measurement of intellectual capabilities: A review of theory. In K. S. McGrew, J. K. Werder, & R. W. Woodcock, *Woodcock–Johnson Technical Manual* (pp. 197–232). Chicago: Riverside.

Horn, J. L. (1994). Theory of fluid and crystallized intelligence. In R. J. Sternberg (Ed.), *Encyclopedia of human intelligence* (pp. 443–451). New York: Macmillan.

Humphreys, L. G., Lubinski, D., & Yao, G. (1993). Utility of predicting group membership and the role of spatial visualization in becoming an engineer, physical scientist, or artist. *Journal of Applied Psychology, 78*(2), 250–261.

Kamphaus, R. W. (1993). *Clinical assessment of children's intelligence.* Boston: Allyn & Bacon.

Kaufman, A. S. (1979). *Intelligent testing with the WISC-R.* New York: Wiley.

Kaufman, A. S. (1990). *Assessing adolescent and adult intelligence.* Needham Heights, MA: Allyn & Bacon.

Kaufman, A. S. (1994). *Intelligent testing with the WISC-III.* New York: Wiley.

Kaufman, A. S., & Kaufman, N. L. (1993). *The Kaufman Adolescent and Adult Intelligence Test (KAIT) manual.* Circle Pines, MN: American Guidance Service.

Kavale, K. A., & Forness, S. R. (1984). A meta-analysis of the validity of Wechsler scale profiles and recategorizations: Patterns or parodies? *Learning Disability Quarterly, 7,* 136–152.

McBride-Chang, C. (1995). What is phonological awareness? *Journal of Educational Psychology, 87,* 179–192.

McDermott, P. A., Fantuzzo, J. W., Glutting, J. J., Watkins, M. W., & Baggaley, R. A. (1992). Illusions of meaning in the ipsative assessment of children's ability. *Journal of Special Education, 25,* 504–526.

McGhee, R. (1993). Fluid and Crystallized Intelligence: Confirmatory factor analysis of the Differential Abilities Scale, Detroit Tests of Learning Aptitude—3, and Woodcock–Johnson Psycho-Educational Battery—Revised. *Journal of Psychoeducational Assessment* [Monograph Series: WJ-R monograph], 20–38.

McGrew, K. S. (1995, March). Intelligence is a "many splendored" thing: Implications of theories of multiple intelligences. Presentation at the National Association of School Psychologists Convention, Chicago.

McGrew, K. S., & Flanagan, D. P. (1995). A "cross-battery" approach to intelligence test interpretation. *Communique, 24,* 28–29.

McGrew, K. S., & Flanagan, D. P. (1996). *An intelligence test desk reference (ITDR): A cross-battery approach to intelligence test interpretation.* Boston: Allyn & Bacon. Manuscript in preparation.

Messick, S. (1995). Validity of psychological assessment: Validation of inferences from persons' responses and performances as scientific inquiry into score meaning. *American Psychologist, 50,* 741–749.

Mueller, H. H., Dennis, S. S., & Short, R. H. (1986). A meta-exploration of WISC-R factor score profiles as a function of diagnosis and intellectual level. *Canadian Journal of School Psychology, 2,* 21–43.

Pearlman, K., Schmidt, F. L., & Hunter, J. E. (1980). Validity generalization results for tests used to predict job proficiency and training success in clerical occupations. *Journal of Applied Psychology, 65*(4), 373–406.

Rasanen, P., & Ahonen, T. (1995). Arithmetic disabilities with and without reading difficulties: A comparison of arithmetic errors. *Developmental Neuropsychology, 11*(3), 275–295.

Reynolds, C. R., & Kamphaus, R. W. (Eds.). (1990). *Handbook of psychological and educational assessment of children: Intelligence and achievement.* New York: Guilford Press.

Shaw, S. R., Swerdlik, M. E., & Laurent, J. (1993). Review of the WISC-III [WISC-III Monograph]. *Journal of Psychoeducational Assessment,* 151–160.

Sternberg, R. J. (1993). Rocky's back again: A review of the WISC-III [WISC-III Monograph]. *Journal of Psychoeducational Assessment,* 161–164.

Thorndike, R. L., Hagen, E. P., & Sattler, J. M. (1986). *Stanford–Binet Intelligence Scale, Fourth Edition.* Chicago: Riverside.

Wagner, R. K., & Torgesen, J. K. (1987). The nature of phonological processing and its causal role in the acquisition of reading skills. *Psychological Bulletin, 101,* 192–212.

Wechsler, D. (1974). *Wechsler Intelligence Scale for Children—Revised.* San Antonio, TX: Psychological Corporation.

Wechsler, D. (1991). *Wechsler Intelligence Scale for Children—Third edition.* San Antonio, TX: Psychological Corporation.

Woodcock, R. W. (1990). Theoretical foundations of the WJ-R measures of cognitive ability. *Journal of Psychoeducational Assessment, 8,* 231–258.

Woodcock, R. W. (in press). Extending *Gf-Gc* theory into practice. In J. J. McArdle & R. W. Woodcock (Eds.), *Human cognitive abilities in theory and practice.* Chicago: Riverside.

Woodcock, R. W., & Johnson, M. B. (1989). *Woodcock–Johnson Psycho-educational Battery—Revised.* Chicago: Riverside.

Ysseldyke, J. (1990). Goodness of fit of the Woodcock–Johnson Psycho-Educational Battery—Revised to the Horn–Cattell *Gf-Gc* theory. *Journal of Psychoeducational Assessment, 8,* 28–275.

Zachary, R. A. (1990). Wechsler's intelligence scales: Theoretical and practical considerations. *Journal of Psychoeducational Assessment, 8,* 276–289.

CHAPTER 18

Issues and Suggestions for Training Professionals in Assessing Intelligence

VINCENT C. ALFONSO

SARAH I. PRATT

$\mathbf{C}$OGNITIVE ASSESSMENT IS ONE of the primary activities of psychologists; therefore, competence in this area is essential. Competence in cognitive assessment requires quality training at the graduate level. The task of designing a graduate training program in cognitive assessment is increasingly difficult given two recent developments: (1) the proliferation of new and revised cognitive assessment instruments within the last decade, including the Wechsler Preschool and Primary Intelligence Scale—Revised (WPPSI-R; Wechsler 1989), Wechsler Intelligence Scale for Children—Third Edition (WISC-III; Wechsler, 1991), Stanford–Binet Intelligence Scale: Fourth Edition (SB-IV; Thorndike, Hagen, & Sattler, 1986), the Differential Ability Scales (DAS; Elliott, 1990), the Woodcock–Johnson Tests of Cognitive Ability—Revised (WJ-R COG; Woodcock & Johnson, 1989), and the Kaufman Adolescent and Adult Intelligence Test (KAIT; Kaufman & Kaufman, 1993), and (2) the advent of new and revised theories of intelligence, such as the modern Gf-Gc theory (Horn, 1991, 1994; Horn & Noll, Chapter 4, this volume), the three-stratum level theory of cognitive abilities (Carroll 1993, Chapter 7, this volume), and Gardner's multiple intelligences theory (Gardner, 1993; Chen & Gardner, Chapter 6, this volume), as well as models of personal competence (Greenspan, 1981; Greenspan & Driscoll, Chapter 8, this volume) and information processing (Das, Naglieri, & Kirby, 1994; Woodcock, 1993). As a result of these developments, psychologists are now faced with myriad options for test administration and interpretation. These developments as well as others make the practice of cognitive assessment, already a complex discipline, even more difficult to teach and to learn. Preparing graduate students to contend with this ever-expanding marketplace of assessment tools and interpretive strategies requires substantial commitments of time and resources on the part of cognitive assessment instructors, as well as much effort and dedication on the part of students in training.

This chapter addresses some of the major issues inherent in training graduate students to become competent users of cognitive assessment instruments. The first part of the chapter explains the importance of quality training in cognitive assessment through a review of past and recent surveys regarding the assessment activities of practitioners, researchers, and academicians, and a review of studies that have investigated examiner competency in the administration and scoring of cognitive assessment instruments. The second part of the chapter offers suggestions for designing a program of instruction in cognitive assessment. The recommendations proposed herein are based on current training practices in graduate school programs, the results of empirical studies that have evaluated these training practices, and suggestions of researchers and practitioners. Current ethical principles of psychologists and test user guidelines, which are discussed near the end of the chapter, served as an overarching framework in which the chapter was conceptualized.

THE IMPORTANCE OF QUALITY TRAINING IN COGNITIVE ASSESSMENT

Evidence from the Activities of Practitioners, Researchers, and Academicians

The importance of assessment has been demonstrated by surveys of the activities of practicing psychologists. One of the most traditional and enduring roles of the psychologist has been that of tester and assessment specialist (Hyman & Kaplinski, 1994; Matarazzo, 1990, 1992; Reynolds & Clark, 1984; Watkins, 1990). Psychological testing is conducted to assess human behavior in a variety of domains including cognitive, personality, and neuropsychological functioning (Brown & McGuire, 1976; Lubin, Larsen, & Matarazzo, 1984; Piotrowski & Keller, 1989). Testing and assessment are often used interchangeably; however, testing is only one of the many procedures that psychologists employ in conducting assessments that supplies information about an individual. Therefore, in the strictest sense, psychological testing is not synonymous with psychological assessment (Matarazzo, 1990, 1992). Nevertheless, there is no doubt that they are related and that "assessment activities remain the one common thread running throughout the discipline" (Reynolds & Clark, 1984, pp. 43–44).

The findings of many studies that have investigated assessment activities of psychologists demonstrate that cognitive assessment represents a major portion of assessment-related activity. Early surveys, such as those conducted by Sundberg (1961) and Lubin, Wallis, and Paine (1971), indicated that cognitive assessment instruments were ranked among the top 10 psychological instruments used by survey respondents. These surveys were conducted across assessment domains, including cognitive, personality, and achievement testing, across a variety of settings, and across psychological disciplines, including school and clinical psychology. Brown and McGuire (1976) found that in 1976, the Wechsler Adult Intelligence Scale (WAIS; Wechsler, 1955), the Wechsler Intelligence Scale for Children (WISC; Wechsler, 1949), and the Stanford–Binet (SB; Terman & Merrill, 1960) were among the most frequently used assessment instruments, ranking in the top 10 among *all* psychological instruments mentioned in their survey.

More recent surveys by Lubin et al. (1984) and Lubin, Larsen, Matarazzo, and Seever (1985) revealed that since 1935, cognitive assessment instruments have been ranked in the top 20 of all psychological assessment instruments in terms of frequency of use. Instruments such as the WAIS, WISC, and SB were among these top 20, with the WAIS ranking sixth or higher since its publication. In their survey of outpatient mental health facilities, Piotrowski and Keller (1989) found that the Wechsler Intelligence Scale for Children—Revised (WISC-R; Wechsler, 1974), the Wechsler Adult Intelligence Scale—Revised (WAIS-R; Wechsler, 1981), and the SB were ranked in the top 16 of the most frequently used psychological instruments. Similar results were reported by Craig and Horowitz (1990) in their survey of diagnostic practicum sites.

Several studies have found that school psychologists spend the majority of their time, up to 56%, engaged in assessment-related activities (Goh, Teslow, & Fuller, 1981; Hutton, Dubes, & Muir, 1992; Smith, 1984; Stinnett, Havey, & Oehler-Stinnett, 1994). Stinnett et al. surveyed school psychologists regarding their use of cognitive assessment instruments and compared their results to those of previous studies by Goh et al. and Hutton et al. The data indicated that, taken together, at least 74% of the psychologists in the three studies reported using the WISC-R and at least 53% reported using the WAIS-R as part of their routine practice. Fifty-seven percent of the respondents in the Stinnett et al. survey also reported using the WISC-III (Wechsler, 1991). Regarding the future of psychological assessment, Matarazzo (1992) stated, "I predict that several decades from now tests like the Binet and Wechsler scales . . . will still be in relatively wide use" (p. 1009).

Cognitive assessment has been a major focus of study and attention in psychological publications. In a recent review of articles published in school psychology journals such as the *Journal of School Psychology, School Psychology Review,* and *School Psychology Quarterly,* Little and Mink (1994) found that of 1,136 articles published between 1987 and 1992, 300, or 32.1%, were assessment related, with 202 of the 300 concerned with cognitive assessment. The findings of the Little and Mink study are consistent with those of previous studies conducted by O'Callaghan (1974) and Reynolds and Clark (1984). Although one may argue that the percentages reported by Little and Mink (1994) could be attributable to the "file drawer phenomenon" (Rosenthal, 1979), which generally refers to the publication of studies that demonstrate statistically significant results, or a publishing bias in favor of assessment-related research and articles, the data provide further evidence of the significant role that has been and continues to be played by cognitive assessment in the activities of psychologists.

It seems safe to assume, then, that a significant proportion of current students in graduate psychology programs ultimately use cognitive assessment instruments in their careers as professional psychologists. Therefore, it is imperative that graduate students receive training that will enable them to administer, score, and interpret properly cognitive assessment tools. The results of several studies that have investigated examiner competency in administration and scoring of intelligence tests follow.

Evidence Regarding Competence in Using Cognitive Assessment Instruments

Several studies have been conducted to evaluate the competence of psychologists and graduate students in psychology in the administration and scoring of cognitive assessment instruments. The results of several studies of competency in administration led Slate and Chick (1989) to state that "Despite educational training, [and] working in pairs, . . . student examiners continue to make errors that may affect the reliability and validity of major assessment instruments (p. 83). Table 18.1 presents the major findings of some of the studies that have investigated the competence of graduate students, master's- and doctoral-level school psychologists, and other professional psychologists to administer and score a variety of cognitive assessment instruments.

It is clear from an inspection of Table 18.1 that regardless of level of experience, use of real versus fabricated protocols, or amount of practice and feedback, errors in administration and scoring occur at alarmingly high rates (Bradley, Hanna, & Lucas, 1980; Miller & Chansky, 1972; Miller, Chansky, & Gredler, 1970; Ryan, Prifitera, & Powers, 1983; Slate & Chick, 1989; Slate & Jones, 1990a, 1990b; Slate, Jones, Coulter, & Covert, 1992). For example, Bradley et al. (1980) sent two fabricated WISC-R protocols to 63 members of the National Association of School Psychologists (NASP), who were instructed to calculate Verbal, Performance, and Full Scale IQs (FSIQs) for each protocol. One of the protocols was designed to be easy to score, while the other was designed to be more difficult to score. The standard deviations of the three IQ scores on the easy protocol ranged from 2.3 to 3.3, while the standard deviations on the difficult protocol ranged from 3.3 to 5.5, indicating moderate variability (error) in the IQ scores that the NASP members calculated for each of the protocols.

Warren and Brown (1972) reported that, collectively, 40 graduate students made 1,939 scoring and administration errors on 240 WISC and SB tests that they administered. In a more recent study,

TABLE 18.1. Description of Studies that Have Investigated Examiner Errors on Intelligence Tests

Study	Sample	Protocol (real or fabricated)	Instrument investigated	Major findings
Miller, Chanksy, & Gredler (1970)	32 graduate students	Fabricated	WISC	Obtained VIQ range of 81–99, PIQ range of 75–96, and FSIQ range of 76–93; on subtests, the range of scaled scores exceeded the standard error of measurement
Miller & Chanksy (1972)	64 doctoral- and master's-level psychologists	Fabricated	WISC	Obtained VIQ range of 75–95, PIQ range of 74–97, and FSIQ range of 78–95; on subtests, the range of scaled scores exceeded the standard error of measurement
Warren & Brown (1972)	40 graduate students	Real	WISC & Stanford–Binet	240 protocols examined; 1,939 errors were found on the 1873 subtests; the most frequent errors were failure to record response, failure to follow procedures, and in scoring and tabulating
Sherrets, Gard, & Langner (1979)	39 psychologists, interns, practicum students, school psychologists, and psychometricians	Real	WISC	200 protocols reviewed; 89% of examiners made at least one error. 46.5% of the protocols had at least one error; no significant differences regarding level of training; the most frequent errors were in addition (raw score, scaled scores, etc.)
Bradley, Hanna, & Lucas (1980)	63 members of NASP	Fabricated	WISC-R	*SDs* on the "difficult" protocol ranged from 3.3 to 5.5 and on the "easy" protocol from 2.3 to 3.3
Franklin, Stillman, Burpeau, & Sabers (1982)	33 school psychologists and graduate students	Fabricated	WAIS	Examiner errors on Information, Comprehension and Vocabulary, resulted in a large range of obtained scaled scores and IQs; the most frequent errors found were inaccurate point assignments and improper discontinuation
Slate & Chick (1989)	14 graduate students	Real	WISC-R	112 protocols were examined; no subtest was free of examiner error; 15.2 total errors on each protocol; errors on 66% of the WISC-R protocols resulted in FSIQ changes
Conner & Woodall (1983)	10 graduate students	Real	WISC-R	Each student assessed 15 individuals and received verbal and written feedback after each; a significant decrease was found in the total number of errors and in administrative errors, but not in the number of IQ, mathematical, or response scoring errors

(cont.)

TABLE 18.1. (continued)

Study	Sample	Protocol (real or fabricated)	Instrument investigated	Major findings
Ryan, Prifitera, & Powers (1983)	39 psychologists and graduate students	Real	WAIS-R	A range of *SDs* from 1.9 to 3.5 across the IQs
Slate & Jones (1990a)	26 graduate students	Real	WAIS-R	180 protocols were analyzed; 8.8 mistakes were found per protocol and when corrected 81% of the FSIQs changed; no improvement found over five practice administrations; most frequent errors were in recording responses verbatim, incorrect point assignment, and inappropriate questioning
Slate & Jones (1990b)	22 graduate students	Real	WAIS-R	149 protocols were analyzed, with 7.9 errors per protocol; overestimated 83% of FSIQs and underestimated 24% of FSIQs; most errors occurred on Vocabulary, Comprehension, and Similarities
Moon, Blakey, Gorsuch, & Fantuzzo (1991)	33 graduate students	Real	WAIS-R	20 administration requirements referenced in the manual were failed by at least 50% of the test administrators; after additional training, 11 specific administration requirements were failed by at least 24% of the test administrators
Slate, Jones, Coulter, & Covert (1992)	9 certified psychological examiners	Real	WISC-R	56 protocols were examined; an average of 38.4 errors per protocol was calculated when failure to record responses was counted as an error; errors on 81% of the WISC-R protocols resulted in FSIQ changes
Alfonso, Johnson, Patinella, & Rader (1995)	15 graduate students	Real	WISC-III	60 protocols examined; 468 errors were calculated with approximately 7.8 errors per protocol; the 5 most frequent errors were failure to query, failure to record responses verbatim, reporting FSIQs incorrectly, reporting VIQ incorrectly, and incorrect addition; IQs changed 77 times after correction

Slate and Jones (1990a) analyzed 180 WAIS-R protocols administered by 26 graduate students and found an average of 8.8 mistakes per protocol. Moreover, 81% of the FSIQs were affected when the protocols were corrected. Finally, Alfonso, Johnson, Patinella, and Rader (1995) reviewed 60 WISC-III protocols administered by 15 school psychology graduate students. They found that the students made a total of 468 scoring and administration errors, and that 77 IQ scores had to be adjusted after the errors were corrected.

The following general conclusions may be drawn from these studies and those reported in Table 18.1. First, most studies have found that whether using real or fabricated protocols, psychologists, regardless of training experience, make a significant number of errors in cognitive assessments of children, adolescents, and adults. Second, almost all studies investigating errors in the administration and scoring of cognitive assessment instruments have used the Wechsler scales. Virtually no studies have investigated competence in the administration and scoring of instruments such as the SB-IV, DAS, WJ-R COG, and KAIT. It is likely that errors in administration and scoring of these instruments occur with the same or similar frequency as the Wechsler scales given the minimal instruction provided on these newer instruments in most graduate training programs.

Third, scoring and administration errors usually consist of incorrect addition, incorrect point assignment, and failure to record responses verbatim. Less frequent errors include incorrect calculation of chronological age, incorrect discontinuation, and inappropriate questioning. Researchers have also observed the tendency of graduate students and psychologists to award more points to certain examinees than are warranted by their responses. It is suspected that a "halo effect" or some other type of positive bias may be operating in these instances (Babad, Mann, & Mar-Hayim, 1975; Sattler, Hillix, & Neher, 1970). Some examiners also err in providing inappropriate feedback to the test taker or allowing referral information about the client to influence their assignment or calculation of test scores (Slate & Hunnicutt, 1988). Fourth, scoring and administration errors seem to occur most often on tests that involve verbal expression on the part of the examinee, such as the Information, Vocabulary, Similarities, and Comprehension subtests of the Wechsler scales. However, errors also occur on "nonverbal" tests such as the Coding subtest of the Wechsler scales, which is particularly disconcerting given the objective criteria used to score these subtests. Finally, several studies have found that large differences in IQ scores result when protocols with errors are corrected.

These findings deserve attention because they indicate that psychologists and graduate students perhaps have been making unacceptable mistakes in the administration and scoring of the most frequently used cognitive assessment instruments for more than 30 years (e.g., Bradley et al., 1980; Conner & Woodall, 1983; Franklin, Stillman, Burpeau, & Sabers, 1982; Ryan et al., 1983; Sherrets, Gard, & Langner, 1979; Slate & Jones, 1990a, 1990b; Warren & Brown, 1972). Kaufman (1994) stated that, "more often than not, even experienced examiners will make unabashed errors on the test protocols . . . causing substantial difference between the scores on the record form and the scores the child truly earned" (p. 127). Therefore, it is logical to suspect that inappropriate diagnostic, placement, and educational planning decisions may occur as a result of tests that have been incorrectly administered or scored.

In their review of examiner errors on various Wechsler scales, Slate and Hunnicutt (1988) stated, "The primary cause of examiner error may be inadequate training and poor instructional design procedures" (p. 281). Moreover, they warned trainers that students most likely will not gain greater proficiency after receiving their graduate degrees if they lack mastery before completing their training. The studies regarding errors in administration and scoring by psychologists and graduate students in psychology perhaps provide the most compelling evidence for the need to develop a comprehensive training program that will produce the highest level of competence in cognitive assessment.

SUGGESTIONS FOR TRAINING

Basic Format and Structure of a Course in Cognitive Assessment

Many authors have discussed the important role of training programs in the instruction of cognitive assessment (e.g., Craig & Horowitz, 1990; Oakland & Zimerman, 1986; Slate & Hunnicutt, 1988). One of the most frequently cited complaints from internship supervisors is the inadequate basic assessment skills of interns, which is due, in part, to poor instruction at the university level (Drabman, 1985; Garfield & Kurtz, 1973; Shemberg & Keeley, 1974; Slate & Hunnicutt, 1988; Tipton, Watkins, & Ritz, 1991). University training programs have the considerable responsibility for preparing their students to administer, score, and interpret competently cognitive assessment instruments. Following are several format and content suggestions that school and clinical psychology trainers may wish to consider in their preparation of cognitive assessment courses.

Length of the Course

Although many institutions provide only one semester or three credits in cognitive assessment, a minimum of 1 year of course work in cognitive assessment is recommended (Oakland & Zimerman, 1986; Piotrowski & Zalewski, 1993). As is evident from the research on competency, trainers have not been successful at instructing students in the most basic aspects of cognitive assessment: administration and scoring (Fantuzzo, Sisemore, & Spradlin, 1983; Slate & Hunnicutt, 1988). This may be due, in part, to a lack of time in which to address adequately complex administration and scoring issues.

In addition to instruction in administration and scoring, instruction in interpretation of test results, integration of assessment data, and report writing are necessary components of a cognitive assessment course. Moreover, topics such as the debate regarding subtest analysis, the use of intelligence tests with very young children, and both new and revised theoretical foundations of intelligence tests also warrant significant classroom time for discussion (e.g., Bagnato & Neisworth, 1994; Bracken, 1994; Carroll, 1993; Horn, 1994; Kaufman, 1990, 1994; McDermott, Fantuzzo, & Glutting, 1990; McDermott, Fantuzzo, Glutting, Watkins, & Baggaley, 1992; Neisworth & Bagnato, 1992; Watkins & Kush, 1994; Woodcock, 1990). A perusal of the other chapters in this book demonstrates the considerable and rapid advancements in instrumentation, theory, and methodology that have taken place in the field of intellectual assessment in recent years. Therefore, in order to provide adequate instruction in administration, scoring, and interpretation as well as current advances in the field, more than one semester of cognitive assessment seems warranted.

Recognizing the number of issues that need to be addressed and skills that need to be taught in a cognitive assessment course, Oakland and Zimerman (1986) suggest that psychology departments "consider increasing the number of graduate hours awarded for this course from 3 to 4 to reflect its higher than average utilization of time, money, and other resources" (p. 58). Although it is recommended that graduate programs require, or at least offer, six credits in cognitive assessment, the suggestions proposed herein may be applied to either a one- or two-semester course. Regardless of the number of semesters, the format for this course, including lectures, labs, and use of a teaching assistant (TA), would be the same. What would differ is the content of the courses. For example, an introductory course may provide instruction in the administration, scoring, and interpretation of the most commonly used assessment devices as well as theories of intelligence, current issues affecting the field of applied intelligence testing and report writing. Additional courses in cognitive assessment may include instruction in administration, scoring and interpretation of *contemporary* and *nontraditional* assessment procedures (WJ-R, DAS, KAIT, Curriculum-Based Assessment, Dynamic Assessment, etc.), new and revised theories of intelligence (e.g., Gf-Gc and three-stratum level theory), emerging theoretical perspectives (e.g., Luria–Das PASS model), important topics that are necessary to move the field of intellectual assessment forward (e.g., the "Cross-Battery" Approach; Flanagan & McGrew, Chapter 17, this volume; McGrew & Flanagan, 1996), working with culturally diverse populations, integration of assessment data, and report writing, to name a few.

Time Commitment of Instructors and Students

Studies have found that cognitive assessment is one of the most time-consuming courses to teach and to learn (e.g., Oakland & Zimerman, 1986). Given the breadth of topics that should be covered in a cognitive assessment course, instructors will need to commit at least 14 hours per week to duties associated with teaching the course and students will need to devote at least 11 hours per week to activities associated with learning the course material. This is consistent with previous research findings regarding the time that is necessary to attend to classes, practice skills, and engage in self-study (Oakland & Zimerman, 1986). Table 18.2 provides a breakdown of the major responsibilities and time commitments expected from instructors, TAs, and students.

Instruction of the Course

In light of the time commitment required, cognitive assessment should be taught by a full-time faculty member rather than an adjunct faculty member who may not always be available to students. Ideally, the faculty member should possess considerable expertise in the area of cognitive assessment. This expertise may be demonstrated through research, publications, supervision, and/or field experience. It is recommended that a TA be provided to aid in activities such as direct instruction in administration and scoring of cognitive batteries, answering student questions, and observing practice administrations. The TA may direct a laboratory component of the course in which these duties are performed. The laboratory serves the dual purpose of providing the TA with supervisory experience and the students with support from an upper-level graduate student. The use of TAs in cognitive assessment courses for approximately 10 to 12 hours per week is time-efficient and aids in providing effective instruction to students in training (Oakland & Zimerman, 1986).

Training on Administration and Scoring of Cognitive Assessment Instruments

One of the hypotheses put forth by Slate and Hunnicutt (1988) as an explanation for examiner errors was carelessness on the part of the examiner. Many of the errors that examiners make are inexcusable oversights that cannot be attributed to legitimate differences of opinion on the scoring of items that require subjective judgment on the part of the examiner. It is for this reason that proper training in administration and scoring is critical. A variety of methods have been used to train graduate students in the administration and scoring of cognitive assessment instruments, including verbal feedback, written feedback, large numbers of practice administrations, and competency-based training models (Blakey, Fantuzzo, Gorsuch, & Moon, 1987; Boehm, Duker, Haesloop, & White, 1974; Fantuzzo et al., 1983; McQueen, Meschino, Pike, & Poelstra, 1994; Moon, Blakey, Gorsuch, & Fantuzzo, 1991; Moon, Fantuzzo, & Gorsuch, 1986; Slate & Jones, 1989; Slate, Jones, & Murray, 1991). Several of these methods are discussed in the following sections.

Practice Administrations and Feedback

Inconsistent results have been reported in the literature regarding the necessary amount of feedback and practice administrations. In 1972, Warren and Brown stated that "class discussion and feedback during the semester appear to have made little improvement in scoring accuracy " (p. 121). They

TABLE 18.2. Responsibilities and Time Commitments in Hours per Week of Instructors, Teaching Assistants, and Students

| | | | | | Responsibilities | | | | |
Participants	Read/grade test protocols and reports	Prepare for lectures and labs	Class lectures and discussion	Meet with students	Observe/conduct administration and scoring	Prepare exams	Conduct/ attend labs	Write reports	Read assignments	Total
Instructors	3.75	3.25	2.5	2.00	1.25	.75	.5			14
TAs	5.00	1.00		2.00	1.50		1.0			10.5
Students			2.0	.25	1.75		1.0	3.0	3.0	11.0

based this statement on the fact that graduate students showed no significant improvement in scoring accuracy between their first three and last three administrations of the SB and the WISC. Conner and Woodall (1983) found that although student errors decreased significantly with practice administrations, verbal feedback, and written feedback, scoring and administrative errors still accounted for 75% of the total errors committed.

Slate and Jones (1990a) reported that students did not demonstrate any significant improvements after five practice administrations of the WAIS-R but did show marked improvement after eight administrations. Despite improvement, however, errors were still plentiful. Slate et al. (1991) analyzed 150 WAIS-R protocols to determine the effectiveness of practice administrations in teaching the WAIS-R. They found that although failure to record information decreased over 10 administrations, no other improvements in administration or scoring were observed after 5 or 10 administrations. Based on evidence from empirical studies as well as practical experience, it is recommended that students be required to complete five to six practice administrations for each major cognitive assessment instrument covered in the course. This recommendation should be considered cautiously because it is improbable that students could complete five to six practice administrations if three or more major cognitive assessment instruments are taught. Therefore, students should be required to complete the practice administrations for two to three instruments per semester.

Performance Objectives and Checklists

Studies that incorporated behavioral objectives, criterion levels of accurate scoring and administration, and detailed training models have produced positive and consistent results (e.g., Boehm et al., 1974; Fantuzzo & Moon, 1984; Fantuzzo et al., 1983; Moon et al., 1986). In 1974, Boehm et al. reported that those students who had received a training program that consisted of studying the test manual, viewing a videotape of a correct administration of the SB, and reviewing and completing a set of testing "Guidelines" designed by the investigators, met the criterion of two consecutive SB administrations without *major* errors sooner than those students who had not received the training program. The training program students required an average of 7.9 SB administrations to meet the criterion whereas nontraining program students required an average of 9.5 SB administrations.

Fantuzzo et al. (1983) utilized a competency-based model to train several graduate students in the administration of the WISC-R. The authors constructed an instrument called the Criteria for Competent WISC-R Administration (CCWA). According to the authors, this instrument "is a thorough and comprehensive performance checklist, which consists of 198 items distributed across 15 sections (i.e., one section for each of the 12 subtests plus an Introduction, a Conclusion, and a General Considerations section)" (p. 226). The training program designed by Fantuzzo et al. required 15 hours of instruction. The program included studying the WISC-R manual, conducting a pretraining administration with written feedback on the CCWA, rating a videotaped WISC-R administration by an advanced student (using the CCWA), listening to a lecture on major pitfalls, rating student administrations through a one-way mirror, performing a second WISC-R administration with CCWA feedback, and completing a final WISC-R administration.

Results indicated a significant increase in accuracy from pretraining to final administration of the WISC-R. Specifically, the mean accuracy percentages on the CCWA for the eight participants increased from 60% to 97%. Fantuzzo et al. (1983) noted that "this training package serves as a competency-based model that can be easily adapted to the assessment of administration skills for commonly used educational and psychological tests" (p. 230). This training program has been adopted by others with positive results, including Blakey et al. (1987), who used the Criteria for Competent WAIS-R Administration and the Criteria for Competent WAIS-R Scoring (CCWS), tools similar to the CCWA mentioned above, for WAIS-R administration and scoring. Based on the foregoing evidence regarding the value of performance checklists, it is suggested that they be used in cognitive assessment courses.

Peer Training

One of the major differences between the Blakey et al. (1987) study and the Fantuzzo et al. (1983) study was the use of peer training. In the Fantuzzo et al. study, experimental and control groups were formed from the 32 graduate students who served as the examiners. The control group received minimal instruction (i.e., studied the WAIS-R manual and test materials) and the experimental group received in-depth training, including instruction using the CCWA and CCWS. At posttest, the experimental group earned an average competency score of 92.9% on the CCWA compared to 63.6% for the control group. No significant differences were obtained between the scores of the experimental and control groups on the CCWS. The experimental group then provided peer training to the control group. After receiving the peer training, the average competency score of the control group increased significantly to 96.2%. Recognizing the value of peer training, it is suggested that instructors include practice of administration with peers during the laboratory component of the course.

Instruction on Administration and Scoring Errors

Slate and Jones (1989) used a quasi-experimental design to determine if WISC-R administration and scoring performance could be improved through instruction on common mistakes. Their experimental group received detailed information regarding frequently made errors and rules that could be used to avoid these errors. Twenty-three graduate students served as the participants. Results indicated that the experimental group made fewer administration and scoring errors on the WISC-R than did the control group, which had not received the information on common errors. Therefore, cognitive assessment courses should include a lecture by the instructor on common errors in administration and scoring. In addition, it is suggested that TAs correct errors in administration and scoring observed during laboratory sessions.

Use of Laboratory Sessions

McQueen et al. (1994) investigated the effect of laboratory interventions designed to improve WISC-R administration and scoring performance. A control group received a traditional laboratory component consisting of basic instruction in administration, scoring, and report writing. An experimental group received a laboratory component that included not only instruction on scoring, administration and report writing, but also information on common errors, practicing calculations of chronological age, using a ruler to read tables, reviewing derived scores, using scoring criteria checklists, and other methods (see McQueen et al., 1994, for further details). The experimental group performed significantly better than the control group on academic criteria. Therefore, it is recommended that a cognitive assessment course include a 1-hour-per-week laboratory component. This represents the minimum amount of time required to allow students an adequate opportunity to practice skills and resolve administration and scoring issues.

Use of Audiovisual Aids

Another technique that seems to be helpful to students in training is the use of video equipment. Videotaping has been used as a means of training students in psychotherapy, as a tool in recording children's behavior, as an aid in conducting research, and as a means of teaching assessment skills

(Boehm et al., 1974; Fantuzzo et al., 1983; Harris, 1977; Primavera, Allison, & Alfonso, in press; Sigal et al., 1980). Training institutions should maintain a video library containing tapes of appropriate and inappropriate test administrations. Students could be required to videotape several test administrations in order to receive visual feedback. This suggestion would likely be easy for most programs to adopt as Oakland and Zimerman (1986) reported that 81% of the training institutions they surveyed indicated that "demonstration and observation . . . facilities are available in their building" (p. 56).

Competency Exam

Students should be given a competency exam some time during their course work. They could demonstrate their assessment skills on video or in person by administering partial or complete cognitive batteries. This competency exam could be administered and graded by the instructor or the TA. A criterion level of perfect scoring and administration would be most beneficial. Students should demonstrate competency in at least two to three cognitive assessment instruments that are introduced during their training.

A step-by-step flow chart regarding training in administration and scoring is provided in Figure 18.1 and represents an example of the sequence of steps that may be followed by graduate students in their preparation for competency exams in cognitive assessment. Although students are limited, to some extent, by the instruction and resources provided by their training institutions, they can do much to ensure that they are competent test users if they complete this course of study each time they set out to learn a new cognitive instrument.

In sum, the following conclusions may be drawn from the results of the studies that have investigated training methods in cognitive assessment. First, several practice administrations alone (with or without feedback) are not sufficient training, as this leads to the practice of making errors rather than developing competency in test administration. Second, training programs that incorporate behavioral objectives, administration and scoring checklists, peer trainers, training manuals, and videotaped testing sessions result in fewer errors and thus greater reliability of test scores. Third, although it is difficult to tease out the exact components of training programs that are most effective, it appears that a combination of methods represents the optimal means of training students.

ACCOUNTABILITY

Psychologists are guided by several documents that provide standards for the provision of reliable and valid assessment services to examinees. These documents include, but are not limited to, the American Psychological Association's (APA) *Ethical Principles of Psychologists and Code of Conduct* (1992), *Specialty Guidelines for the Delivery of Services by Clinical Psychologists, Counseling Psychologists, Industrial/Organizational Psychologists, and School Psychologists* (1981), *Guidelines for Computer Based Tests and Interpretations* (1987), and *Standards for Educational and Psychological Testing* (American Education Research Association, APA, & National Council on Measurement in Education, 1985).

In the domain of cognitive assessment, two particularly relevant sets of guidelines are the *Ethical Principles of Psychologists and Code of Conduct* (APA, 1992) and the *Standards for Educational and Psychological Testing* (APA, 1985). Although it is clear that "it is the individual responsibility of each psychologist to aspire to the highest possible standards of conduct" (APA, 1992, p. 1599), there are three groups, namely, university trainers, students in training, and test developers and publishers, who are each accountable, in their own way, for ensuring that psychologists are competent users of cognitive assessment instruments.

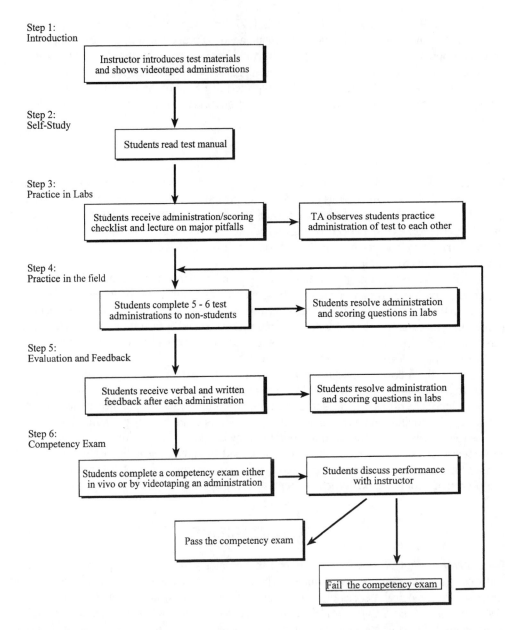

FIGURE 18.1. Preparing for competency exams in cognitive assessment. Adapted from Woodcock & Mather, 1989. Adapted by permission.

Responsibilities of University Trainers

Ethical Standard 6.01 (APA, 1992) states the following:

> Psychologists who are responsible for education and training programs seek to ensure that the programs are competently designed, provide the proper experiences, and meet the requirements for licensure, certification, or other goals for which claims are made by the program. (p. 1607)

University trainers are responsible for providing the instruction and resources necessary to produce students who demonstrate the highest level of competence in cognitive assessment. By selecting the components and designing the structure of cognitive assessment courses, they determine the extent of the training and knowledge that graduate students will obtain as part of their training. Ultimately, students rely on the expertise of university trainers in the development of their assessment skills.

Responsibilities of Students in Training

Ethical Standard 2.04a (APA, 1992) states the following:

> Psychologists who perform interventions or administer, score, interpret, or use assessment techniques are familiar with the reliability, validation, and related standardization or outcome studies of and proper applications and uses of, the techniques they use. (p. 1607)

The *Standards for Educational and Psychological Testing* (APA, 1985) add that "although the test developer should provide information on the strengths and weaknesses of the test, the ultimate responsibility for test use lies with the test user" (p. 41). Based on these standards, it is ultimately incumbent upon psychologists (or psychologists in training) to learn how to administer, score, and interpret properly the assessment instruments they will use in practice. Therefore, students are responsible for committing the time and effort that are required to gain proficiency in the use of cognitive assessment instruments.

Responsibilities of Test Developers and Publishers

Standard 5.4 (APA, 1985) states the following:

> Test manuals should identify any special qualifications that are required to administer a test and to interpret it properly. Statements of user qualifications should identify the specific training, certification, or experience needed. (p. 36)

Although test developers and publishers may not be directly involved in the training of students, they provide the necessary test materials and manuals, conduct workshops on the use of assessment instruments, and are responsible for attempting to safeguard their instruments against misuse. One of the themes that has been emphasized throughout this chapter is that many of the criticisms about psychological tests may be attributable to misuse of tests by the examiner rather than to some aspect of the tests themselves. Part of the responsibility of appropriate and accurate test use rests with test developers/publishers when they release their instruments for use with the public. The standard quoted above speaks to this responsibility.

The Test User Qualifications Working Group (TUQWoG; Eyde, Moreland, Robertson, Primoff, & Most, 1988) of the Joint Committee on Testing Practices (JCTP; Fremer, Diamond, & Camara, 1989), which includes many test publishers, was formed in response to the high level of test misuse. The JCTP was charged with establishing test user competencies, and has produced a list of 12 minimum competencies for proper use of tests, a sample crediting plan for individual intelligence tests, and a qualification form for test purchasers (Moreland, Eyde, Robertson, Primoff, & Most, 1995). Given that graduate students in training and psychologists in practice often make errors in basic assessments, which are then used in the more complex process of interpretation, integration, and reporting of data, it is important for test developers and publishers to continue working to ensure that tests are not misused or used by unqualified persons.

Test developers and publishers can also promote accurate administration and scoring of cognitive assessment instruments by constructing manuals that will help to minimize scoring errors. "Currently, the test manuals permit too much examiner judgment, and thus, subjectivity results in the scoring of individual responses," which may reduce the reliability of test scores (Slate & Hunnicutt, 1988, p. 284). A few test developers have attempted to address this issue in test manuals. For example, the WISC-III manual includes sample responses to verbal subtests in the same location as the actual items, which may lead to fewer errors (Alfonso et al., 1995). The SB-IV and KAIT use 0- or 1-point responses as opposed to 0, 1, and 2, which should lessen variability in scoring by reducing the number of scores that may be assigned to any given response. Also, some attempt at calculating the standard error of measurement for examiner errors would be helpful because it would provide information about the degree of variability in test scores attributable to examiner errors (Hanna, Bradley, & Holen, 1981). Finally, a monograph or note regarding the various types of commonly made errors would alert new examiners to possible pitfalls.

CONCLUSION

Based on surveys of the activities of psychologists and the volume of publications devoted to the subject of testing, it is clear that cognitive assessment is alive and well and worthy of continued study. Furthermore, the empirical studies reviewed in this chapter demonstrate clearly that there is a need to improve the training of professionals in the administration, scoring, and interpretation of cognitive assessment instruments. University trainers, students in training, and test developers and publishers are accountable particularly for ensuring competent and responsible test use. Suggestions that integrate science and practice and that are based on findings from relevant research, standards, and guidelines for professional practice and the experience of the authors were presented. In addition to recommending that contemporary tests, theories, and issues be incorporated into cognitive assessment courses, inclusion of the following course components was suggested: laboratory component, teaching assistant, video equipment, extensive instruction on administration and scoring of assessment instruments, instruction on common errors made by practitioners, administration and scoring checklists, and competency exams. The suggestions outlined in this chapter may be adopted and expanded to meet the particular requirements of cognitive assessment courses across a wide variety of training programs.

REFERENCES

Alfonso, V. C., Johnson, A., Patinella, L., & Rader, D. E. (1995, October). *Common WISC-III administration and scoring errors: Evidence from graduate students in training.* Paper presented at the annual convention of the New York Association of School Psychologists, Saratoga, NY.

American Psychological Association. (1981). *Specialty guidelines for the delivery of services by clinical psychologists, counseling psychologists, industrial/organizational psychologists, and school psychologists.* Washington, DC: Author.

American Psychological Association. (1987). *Guidelines for computer-based tests and interpretations.* Washington, DC: Author.

American Psychological Association. (1992). Ethical principles of psychologists and code of conduct. *American Psychologist, 47,* 1597–1611.

American Psychological Association, American Educational Research Association, & National Council on Measurement in Education. (1985). *Standards for educational and psychological testing.* Washington, DC: Author.

Babad, E. Y., Mann, M., & Mar-Hayim, M. (1975). Bias in scoring the WISC subtests. *Journal of Consulting and Clinical Psychology, 43,* 268.

Bagnato, S. J., & Neisworth, J. T. (1994). A national study of the social and treatment "invalidity" of intelligence testing in early intervention. *School Psychology Quarterly, 9,* 81–102.

Blakey, W. A., Fantuzzo, J. W., Gorsuch, R. L., & Moon, G. W. (1987). A peer-mediated, competency-based training package for administering and scoring the WAIS-R. *Professional Psychology: Research and Practice, 18,* 17–20.

Boehm, A. E., Duker, J., Haesloop, M. D., & White, M. A. (1974). Behavioral objectives in training for competence in the administration of individual intelligence tests. *Journal of School Psychology, 12,* 150–157.

Bracken, B. A. (1994). Advocating for effective preschool assessment practices: A comment on Bagnato and Neisworth. *School Psychology Quarterly, 9,* 103–108.

Bradley, F. O., Hanna, G. S., & Lucas B. A. (1980). The reliability of scoring the WISC-R. *Journal of Consulting and Clinical Psychology, 48,* 530–531.

Brown W. R., & McGuire, J. M. (1976). Current psychological assessment practices. *Professional Psychology, 7,* 475–484.

Carroll, J. B. (1993). *Human cognitive abilities: A survey of factor-analytic studies.* Cambridge, England: Cambridge University Press.

Conner, R., & Woodall, F. E. (1983). The effects of experience and structured feedback on WISC-R error rates made by student-examiners. *Psychology in the Schools, 20,* 376–379.

Craig, R. J., & Horowitz, M. (1990). Current utilization of psychological tests at diagnostic practicum sites. *The Clinical Psychologist, 43,* 29–36.

Das, J. P., Naglieri, J. A., & Kirby, J. R. (1994). *Assessment of cognitive processes: The PASS theory of intelligence.* Boston: Allyn & Bacon.

Drabman, R. (1985). Graduate training of scientist-practitioner-oriented clinical psychologists: Where we can improve. *Professional Psychology: Research and Practice, 16,* 623–633.

Elliott, C. D. (1990). *Differential Ability Scales: Administration and scoring manual.* San Antonio, TX: Psychological Corporation.

Eyde, L. D., Moreland, K. L., Robertson, G. J., Primoff, E. S., & Most, R. B. (1988). *Test user qualifications: A data-based approach to promoting good test use. Issues in Scientific Psychology.* Washington, DC: American Psychological Association, Science Directorate.

Fantuzzo, J. W., & Moon, G. W. (1984). Competency mandate: A model for teaching skills in the administration of the WAIS-R. *Journal of Clinical Psychology, 40,* 1053–1059.

Fantuzzo, J. W., Sisemore, T. A., & Spradlin, W. H. (1983). A competency-based model for teaching skills in the administration of intelligence tests. *Professional Psychology: Research and Practice, 14,* 224–231.

Franklin, M. R., Jr., Stillman, P. L., Burpeau, M. Y., & Sabers, D. L. (1982). Examiner error in intelligence testing: Are you a source? *Psychology in the Schools, 19,* 563–569.

Fremer, J., Diamond, E. E., & Camara, W. J. (1989). Developing a code of fair testing practices in education. *American Psychologist, 44,* 1062–1067.

Gardner, H. (1993). *Multiple intelligences: The theory in practice.* New York: Basic Books.

Garfield, S. L., & Kurtz, R. M. (1973). Attitudes toward training in diagnostic testing: A survey of directors of internship training. *Journal of Consulting and Clinical Psychology, 40,* 350–355.

Greenspan, S. (1981). Defining childhood social competence: A proposed working model. In B. K. Keough (Ed.), *Advances in special education* (Vol. 13, pp. 1–39). Greenwich, CT: JAI Press.

Goh, D. S., Teslow, C. J., & Fuller, G. B. (1981). The practice of psychological assessment among school psychologists. *Professional Psychology, 12,* 696–706.

Hanna, G. S., Bradley, F. O., & Holen, M. C. (1981). Estimating major sources of measurement error in individual intelligences scales: Taking our heads out of the sand. *Journal of School Psychology, 19,* 370–376.

Harris, J. (1977). Training in psychological assessment: A multidepartment enterprise. *Teaching of Psychology, 4,* 147–148.

Horn, J. L. (1991). Measurement of intellectual capabilities: A review of theory. In K. S. McGrew, J. K. Werder, & R. W. Woodcock, *WJ-R technical manual* (pp. 197–232). Chicago: Riverside.

Horn, J. L. (1994). Theory of fluid and crystallized intelligence. In R. J. Sternberg (Ed.), *Encyclopedia of human intelligence* (pp. 443–451). New York: Macmillan

Hutton, J. B., Dubes, R., & Muir, S. (1992). Assessment practices of school psychologists: Ten years later. *School Psychology Review, 21,* 271–284.

Hyman, I. A., & Kaplinski, K. (1994). Will the real school psychologist please stand up: Is the past a prologue for the future of school psychology?-Role and function. *School Psychology Review, 23,* 564–583.

Kaufman, A. S. (1990). *Assessment of adolescent and adult intelligence.* New York: Allyn & Bacon.

Kaufman, A. S. (1994). *Intelligent testing with the WISC-III.* New York: Wiley.

Kaufman, A. S., & Kaufman, N. L. (1993). *Kaufman Adolescent and Adult Intelligence Test: Manual.* Circle Pines, MN: American Guidance Service.

Little, S. G., & Mink, J. (1994). *Publication patterns in school psychology journals: 1987–1992.* Paper presented at the 102nd Annual Convention of the American Psychological Association, Los Angeles.

Lubin, B., Larsen, R. M., & Matarazzo, J. D. (1984). Patterns of psychological test usage in the United States: 1935–1982. *American Psychologist, 39,* 451–453.

Lubin, B., Larsen, R. M., Matarazzo, J. D., & Seever, M. (1985). Psychological test usage patterns in five professional settings. *American Psychologist, 40,* 857–861.

Lubin, B., Wallis, R. R., & Paine, C. (1971). Patterns of psychological test usage in the United States: 1935–1969. *Professional Psychology, 2,* 70–74.

Matarazzo, J. D. (1990). Psychological assessment versus psychological testing: Validation from Binet to school, clinic, and courtroom. *American Psychologist, 45,* 999–1017.

Matarazzo, J. D. (1992). Psychological testing and assessment in the 21st century. *American Psychologist, 47,* 1007–1018.

McDermott, P. A., Fantuzzo, J. W., & Glutting, J. J. (1990). Just say no to subtest analysis: A critique on Wechsler theory and practice. *Journal of Psychoeducational Assessment, 8,* 290–302.

McDermott, P. A., Fantuzzo, J. W., Glutting, J. J., Watkins, M. W., & Baggaley, A. R. (1992). Illusions of meaning in the ipsative assessment of children's ability. *Journal of Special Education, 25,* 504–526.

McGrew, K. S., & Flanagan, D. P. (1996). *An intelligence test desk reference (ITDR): The cross-battery approach to intelligence test interpretation.* Boston: Allyn & Bacon. Manuscript in preparation.

McQueen, W., Meschino, R., Pike, P., & Poelstra, P. (1994). Improving graduate student performance in cognitive assessment: The saga continues. *Professional Psychology: Research and Practice, 25,* 283–287.

Miller, C. K., & Chansky, N. M. (1972). Psychologists scoring of WISC protocols. *Psychology in the Schools, 9,* 144–152.

Miller, C. K., Chansky, N. M., & Gredler, G. G. (1970). Rater agreement on WISC protocols. *Psychology in the Schools, 7,* 190–193.

Moon, G. W., Blakey, W. A., Gorsuch, R. L., & Fantuzzo, J. W. (1991). Frequent WAIS-R administration errors: An ignored source of inaccurate measurement. *Professional Psychology: Research and Practice, 22,* 256–258.

Moon, G. W., Fantuzzo, J. W., & Gorsuch, R. L. (1986). Teaching WAIS-R administration skills: Comparison of the MASTERY model to other existing clinical modalities. *Professional Psychology: Research and Practice, 17,* 31–35.

Moreland, K. L., Eyde, L. D., Robertson, G. J., Primoff, E. S., & Most, R. B. (1995). Assessment of test user qualifications: A research-based measurement procedure. *American Psychologist, 50,* 14–23.

Neisworth, J. T., & Bagnato, S. J. (1992). The case against intelligence testing in early intervention. *Topics in Early Childhood Special Education, 12,* 1–20.

Oakland, T. D., & Zimerman, S. A. (1986). The course on individual mental assessment: A national survey of course instructors. *Professional School Psychology, 1,* 51–59.

O'Callaghan, S. (1974). Publication trends in school psychology: 1963–1973. *Journal of School Psychology, 12,* 269–275.

Piotrowski, C., & Keller, J. W. (1989). Psychological testing in outpatient mental health facilities: A national study. *Professional Psychology: Research and Practice, 20,* 423–425.

Piotrowski, C., & Zalewski, C. (1993). Training in psychodiagnostic testing in APA-approved Psy.D. and Ph.D. clinical psychology programs. *Journal of Personality Assessment, 61,* 394–405

Primavera, L. H., Allison, D. B., & Alfonso, V. C. (in press). Measurement of dependent variables. In R. Franklin, B. S. Gorman, & D. B. Allison (Eds.), *Single case designs.* Hillsdale, NJ: Erlbaum.

Reynolds, C. R., & Clark, J. H. (1984). Trends in school psychology research: 1974–1980. *Journal of School Psychology, 22,* 43–52.

Rosenthal, R. (1979). The "file drawer" problem and tolerance for null results. *Psychological Bulletin, 86,* 638–641.

Ryan, J. J., Prifitera, A., & Powers, L. (1983). Scoring reliability on the WAIS-R. *Journal of Consulting and Clinical Psychology, 51,* 149–150.

Sattler, J. M., Hillix, W. A., & Neher, L. A. (1970). Halo effect in examiner scoring of intelligence test responses. *Journal of Consulting and Clinical Psychology, 34,* 172–176.

Shemberg, K. M., & Keeley, S. M. (1974). Training practices and satisfaction with pre-internship preparation. *Professional Psychology, 5,* 98–105.

Sherrets, S., Gard, G., & Langner, H. (1979). Frequency of clerical errors on WISC protocols. *Psychology in the Schools, 16,* 495–496.

Sigal, J. J., Presser, B. G., Woodward, C. A., Santa-Barbara, J., Epstein, N. B., & Levin, S. (1980). Videotaped simulated families as a tool in family therapy outcome research. *International Journal of Family Therapy, 2,* 236–242.

Slate, J. R., & Chick, D. (1989). WISC-R examiner errors: Cause for concern. *Psychology in the Schools, 26,* 78–83.

Slate, J. R., & Hunnicutt, L. C. (1988). Examiner errors on the Wechsler Scales. *Journal of Psychoeducational Assessment, 6,* 280–288.

Slate, J. R., & Jones, C. (1989). Can teaching of the WISC-R be improved? Quasi-experimental exploration. *Professional Psychology: Research and Practice, 20,* 408–410.

Slate, J. R., & Jones, C. H. (1990a). Identifying students' errors in administering the WAIS-R. *Psychology in the Schools, 27,* 83–87.

Slate, J. R., & Jones, C. H. (1990b). Examiner errors on the WAIS-R: A source of concern. *The Journal of Psychology, 124,* 343–345.

Slate, J. R., Jones, C. H., Coulter, C., & Covert, T. L. (1992). Practitioners' administration and scoring of the WISC-R: Evidence that we do err. *Journal of School Psychology, 30,* 77–82.

Slate, J. R., Jones, C. H., & Murray, R. A. (1991). Teaching administration and scoring of the Wechsler Adult Intelligence Scale-Revised: An empirical evaluation of practice administrations. *Professional Psychology: Research and Practice, 22,* 375–379.

Smith, D. K. (1984). Practicing school psychologists: Their characteristics, activities, and populations served. *Professional Psychology: Research and Practice, 15,* 798–810.

Stinnett, T. A., Havey, J. M., & Oehler-Stinnett, J. (1994). Current test usage by practicing school psychologists: A national survey. *Journal of Psychoeducational Assessment, 12,* 331–350.

Sundberg, N. D. (1961). The practice of psychological testing in clinical services in the United States. *American Psychologist, 16,* 79–83.

Terman, L. M., & Merrill, M. A. (1960). *Stanford–Binet Intelligence Scale; Form L-M.* Chicago: Riverside.

Thorndike, R. L., Hagen, E. P., & Sattler, J. M. (1986). *Stanford–Binet Intelligence Scale: Fourth Edition.* Chicago: Riverside.

Tipton, R. M., Watkins, C. E., Jr., Ritz, S. (1991). Selection, training, and career preparation of pre-doctoral interns in psychology. *Professional Psychology: Research and Practice, 22,* 60–67.

Warren, S. A., & Brown, W. G., Jr. (1972). Examiner scoring errors on individual intelligence tests. *Psychology in the Schools, 9,* 118–122.

Watkins, C. E. (1990). What have surveys taught us about the teaching and practice of psychological assessment? *Journal of Personality Assessment, 56,* 426–437.

Watkins, M. W., & Kush, J. C. (1994). Wechsler subtest analysis: The right way, the wrong way, or no way? *School Psychology Review, 23,* 640–651.

Wechsler, D. (1949). *Wechsler Intelligence Scale for Children.* San Antonio, TX: The Psychological Corporation.

Wechsler, D. (1955). *Wechsler Adult Intelligence Scale: Manual.* San Antonio, TX: The Psychological Corporation.

Wechsler, D. (1974). *Wechsler Intelligence Scale for Children—Revised.* San Antonio, TX: The Psychological Corporation.

Wechsler, D. (1981). *Wechsler Adult Intelligence Scale—Revised.* San Antonio, TX: The Psychological Corporation.

Wechsler, D. (1989). *Wechsler Preschool and Primary Scale of Intelligence—Revised.* San Antonio, TX: Psychological Corporation.

Wechsler, D. (1991). *Wechsler Intelligence Scale for Children—Third Edition.* San Antonio, TX: The Psychological Corporation.

Woodcock, R. W. (1990). Theoretical foundations of the WJ-R measures of cognitive ability. *Journal of Psychoeducational Assessment, 8,* 231–258.

Woodcock, R. W. (1993). An information processing view of Gf-Gc theory. *Journal of Psychoeducational Assessment, Monograph Series: WJ-R Monograph,* 80–102.

Woodcock, R. W., & Johnson, M. B. (1989). *Woodcock–Johnson Tests of Cognitive Ability—Revised.* Chicago: Riverside.

Woodcock, R. W., & Mather, N. (1989). WJ-R tests of cognitive ability—standard and supplemental batteries: Examiner's manual. In R. W. Woodcock & M. B. Johnson, *Woodcock Johnson Psycho-Educational Battery—Revised.* Chicago: Riverside.

PART IV

EMERGING ISSUES
AND NEW DIRECTIONS
IN INTELLECTUAL ASSESSMENT

P ART IV OF THIS TEXTBOOK contains nine chapters that focus mainly on issues related to construct, predictive, and diagnostic validity of current intelligence test batteries. Each validity issue is discussed in terms of its implications for the general use and interpretation of cognitive ability tests, particularly with regard to special populations. Suggestions and recommendations regarding the appropriate use of intelligence tests with diverse groups as well as future research directions are provided by the authors of each chapter in this section. In Chapter 19, "Ontology, Structure, and Diagnostic Benefits of a Normative Subtest Taxonomy from the WISC-III Standardization Sample," Joseph J. Glutting, Paul A. McDermott, and Timothy R. Konold examine the drawbacks and methodological weaknesses of traditional approaches to determining whether a profile of scores on a given intelligence test battery is unique and, therefore, indicative of some type of psychopathology. In place of traditional methods of subtest/profile analysis that rely on univariate or linear multivariate analyses, the authors offer a nonlinear multivariate methodology that provides a core profile taxonomy that will allow researchers and practitioners to differentiate more accurately children with common subtest patterns from those with unusual patterns. Specifically, Glutting et al. provide a simple-to-use methodology for determining whether an individual's WISC-III profile is unique or commonplace in the population.

Two chapters in Part IV describe how confirmatory factor analysis (CFA) and structural equation modeling (SEM), a more general approach that subsumes CFA, can be used to understand the constructs that underlie intelligence tests as well as the genetic influences that might account for variations in intellectual abilities in the normal population, respectively. In Chapter 20, "Using Confirmatory Factor Analysis to Aid in Understanding the Constructs Measured by Intelligence Tests," Timothy Z. Keith provides an overview and introduction to CFA and demonstrates how this methodology can be used to (1) test the fit of formal theories of intelligence, (2) compare cognitive constructs across intelligence test batteries, and (3) compare the invariance of constructs measured by a single battery across different groups. In Chapter 21, "Contemporary Models for the Biometric Genetic Analysis of Intellectual Abilities," John J. McArdle and Carol A. Prescott discuss the emergence of the field of behavioral genetics (BG) and present research on genetic influences on cognitive abilities. In their presentation of structural models in behavioral genetics, they discuss the mathematical and statistical techniques through which these models have been formulated. In addition, they highlight fundamental issues regarding contemporary SEMs used in *biometric genetic analysis of intellectual abilities* (BGIA) research and attempt to bring further clarity to the methods, models, and results of BGIA by considering interpretations within the context of biometric theory. McArdle and Prescott present models using data from several studies of biological and adoptive families and twins to illuminate current trends in BG research. They conclude with a discussion of the implications for future research in BGIA.

Three chapters in Part IV focus on the psychometric quality of intelligence tests for use with special populations including individuals with specific learning disabilities (SLD), attention-deficit hyperactivity disorder (ADHD), and mental retardation as well as preschool-age children. In Chapter 22, "Diagnostic and Treatment Utility of Intelligence Tests," Daniel J. Reschly discusses the utility of intelligence tests for making educational placement decisions. In particular, he addresses the reliability and validity of diagnostic constructs (e.g., SLD) and the most popular assessment tools used to measure these constructs, as well as the diagnostic and treatment utility of traditional and nontraditional approaches to assessing intelligence. In Chapter 23, "The Functional Utility of Intelligence Tests with Special Education Populations," Dawn P. Flanagan, Ted J. Andrews, and Judy L. Genshaft review the extant literature on the predictive, discriminative, and treatment validity of intelligence tests for use with special education populations. In particular, they explore the utility of ability–achievement discrepancy procedures and subtest and profile analyses as an aid in making differential diagnoses. They conclude with a summary of the unique attributes of contemporary cognitive ability tests that may yield information that has greater treatment relevance than that provided by traditional methods. In Chapter 24, "The Utility of Intelligence Tests for Preschool Children," Bruce A. Bracken and Kathryn C. Walker begin with an historical account of the field of preschool assessment and discuss how past events have influenced current instrumentation and practice in this field. Next, they review all major intelligence tests that are used currently with preschool children according to specific criteria within the broad psychometric categories of reliability, validity, test floors and ceilings, and item gradients. Bracken and Walker provide the reader with suggestions and recommendations regarding the most appropriate uses of these instruments in light of their stated limitations. The information presented in Chapters 22–24 demonstrates a pressing need for test developers, publishers, researchers, and practitioners to consider more stringent guidelines and criteria for evaluating the technical quality of intelligence tests as well as alternative methods and approaches to establishing the functional utility of cognitive assessment instrumentation.

Two chapters in Part IV examine critically the validity of cognitive ability tests with diverse populations. In Chapter 25, "The Cognitive Assessment of Limited English Proficient and Bilingual Children," Emilia C. Lopez reviews several research, theory and practice issues related to the cognitive assessment of individuals from limited English proficient (LEP) and bilingual backgrounds. She highlights the importance of measuring language proficiency in these populations prior to determining the language(s) in which the cognitive assessment ought to be administered and discusses current and future trends in the assessment of cognitive abilities in LEP and bilingual children. Throughout this chapter, Lopez identifies inherent weaknesses in current intelligence tests for use with these populations and offers suggestions for circumventing such limitations. In Chapter 26, "The Triple Quandary of Race, Culture, and Social Class in Standardized Cognitive Ability Testing," Janet E. Helms provides an in-depth discussion of issues related to the cultural equivalence of cognitive ability tests across racial/cultural and social class groups, focusing particularly on African American test-takers. In addition, Helms reviews current efforts to develop and/or adapt existing measures of intelligence in an effort to eliminate the influences of race, culture, and socioeconomic status on cognitive test performance. Overall, Chapters 25 and 26 address a plethora of critical issues in the cognitive assessment of (multiply) disadvantaged groups and offer recommendations for reducing the extent to which the limitations of cognitive ability tests penalize members of such groups.

In the final chapter of this textbook (Chapter 27), Patti L. Harrison, Dawn P. Flanagan, and Judy L. Genshaft provide "An Integration and Synthesis of Contemporary Theories, Tests and Issues in the Field of Intellectual Assessment." They summarize the major contributions of this textbook, including modern theories of intelligence (Part II) and their applications (Part III) as well as information regarding the two validity questions that were raised most often in this textbook (Part IV)—Are intelligence tests valid for general test use and interpretation? and Are intelligence tests valid for use with special populations? In addition, they provide a comparative analysis of several important features (content, administration, interpretation, technical) of the major intelligence test batteries that were published at the time this textbook was being prepared. Overall, this chapter demonstrates the most salient ways in which the field of intellectual assessment has moved beyond traditional theories and instruments by providing and integration and synthesis of the information that was presented in Parts I through IV of this textbook.

JLG

CHAPTER 19

Ontology, Structure, and Diagnostic Benefits of a Normative Subtest Taxonomy from the WISC-III Standardization Sample

━━◦◦◦◦◦━━

JOSEPH J. GLUTTING

PAUL A. MCDERMOTT

TIMOTHY R. KONOLD

T HE INTERPRETATION OF SUBTEST SCORES on the *Wechsler Intelligence Scale for Children—Third Edition* (WISC-III; Wechsler, 1991) is among the most popular diagnostic activities in school and clinical child psychology. The enterprise seeks to determine whether the pattern of score elevations and depressions across component subtests from the WISC-III is indicative of unique cognitive abilities or suggestive of some form of psychopathology. Clinical tradition maintains that subtest patterns with peaks and valleys reflect unusual cognitive processes important to differential diagnosis and remediation. This legacy of interpretive relevance continues to be reflected in textbooks on intelligence testing, wherein despite the recent presentation of some notable limitations and caveats, page after page remains devoted to the identification of unusual subtest scores and the promotion of inferential hypotheses about them (cf. Kamphaus, 1993; Kaufman, 1994; Sattler, 1992) Given this intellectual climate, it seems reasonable to surmise that the vast majority of practitioners remain committed to the interpretation of subtest scores.

MOVING BEYOND TRADITIONAL SCHEMES OF ANALYSIS

The purpose of this chapter is to present a simple-to-use, yet *multivariate*, methodology for determining whether a child's WISC-III subtest profile is unusual or whether it actually is commonplace in the population. Specifically, the chapter introduces findings from an investigation that sought to identify the most representative subtest patterns from the standardization sample of the WISC-III ($N = 2,200$). The primary benefit of such a normative profile taxonomy is that it provides the best contrasts to date for testing hypotheses about subtest configurations believed to be unusual or clinically relevant. In other words, the taxonomy itself serves as a multivariate null hypothesis to which children's subtest scores can be compared to determine when their profiles are nomothetically exceptional.

Results are discussed in the context of leading research on the underlying arrangement of abilities measured by the WISC-III. Thereafter, two methods are presented for determining the relative rarity or uniqueness of WISC-III subtest patterns. Both methods compare children's subtest scores to the core profile taxonomy. The first method is more precise, but it is also mathematically complex. The second method is nearly as accurate and has the added advantage of being convenient to "everyday" clinical practice. A step-by-step worksheet is provided for the everyday method and a case study is presented using this procedure.

The mathematical and measurement advantages of the normative profile taxonomy make its methods suitable for replacing procedures currently used in practice. Accordingly, the methods presented here will help clinicians move beyond traditional systems of subtest analysis to techniques that better account for the multivariate nature of subtest profiles. However, clarification is necessary. Some individuals are confused about our methods of subtest analysis and their importance. Therefore, at several points, we swerve from the central theme of this chapter to clarify issues that have been presented to us. We begin by pointing out that our methods simply represent a better "mouse-trap" for comparing and contrasting subtest scores. By themselves, the methods do not directly resolve fundamental issues of whether subtest analysis is valid.

On the other hand, because our methods are both multivariate and *nonlinear,* they are more useful for conducting subtest comparisons than interpretive strategies that rely on univariate analysis or linear multivariate analysis. (Shortly, we discuss differences between univariate, linear multivariate, and nonlinear multivariate procedures.) The benefit to practitioners is that comparisons to our multivariate taxonomy have certain, clear-cut advantages over the most popular methods used to analyze subtest scores. The benefit to researchers is that they will be able to apply nonlinear multivariate methodology, rather than either univariate or linear multivariate methodologies, to theoretically and clinically interesting data sets.

Previously we identified several methodological problems that operate to essentially negate or equivocate much of the research on the profile analysis of children's ability scores (Glutting, McGrath, Kamphaus, & McDermott, 1992; McDermott, Fantuzzo, & Glutting, 1990). Among the factors are a concentration on exceptional samples and the circular use of subtest profiles for *both* the initial formation of diagnostic groups and the subsequent search for profiles that might inherently define these groups. The best alternative is to test heterogenous samples, *wait,* and later identify children having difficulty. Thereafter, a search would begin to uncover score patterns, background factors, and other signs that truly differentiate (i.e., accurately predict) those children who later experience academic, emotional, or behavioral difficulties from those who do not. The nonlinear multivariate methodology provided by the core profile taxonomy will help researchers in this effort by allowing them to more accurately differentiate children with common and ordinary subtest patterns from those who show unusual patterns. Thus, our methods can be used to advance scientific understanding because comparisons to the multivariate core profile types are clearly a superior methodology for identifying children who show unusual profiles. Once identified, children with unusual profiles can be compared and contrasted to those who do not have unusual profiles in order to investigate the diagnostic and treatment utility of subtest scores.

RATIONALE UNDERLYING SUBTEST ANALYSIS

Several lines of reasoning have been evoked to support the analysis of ability profiles. Prominent among the justifications is a belief that multidifferentiated constructions of intelligence provide greater insight into the nature and complexity of human ability, and that by evaluating multiple abilities, clinicians gain greater diagnostic precision. This position stands in direct opposition to the law of parsimony, that states fewer variables are to be preferred whenever their explanatory power equals that of a more complex model. Consequently, it is imperative for clinicians adopting the multidifferentiated perspective that their assessed variables possess either greater predictive validity or greater treatment validity than that obtainable from a more simplistic, or even a unitary, view of intelligence (Brody, 1985; Glutting, McDermott, Prifitera, & McGrath, 1994; Glutting et al., 1992; McDermott et al., 1990).

Theory is capable of decomposing intelligence into an infinite number of gradations (cf. Horn, 1988). Psychometrics, on the other hand, cease to differentiate ability beyond the level of subtest scores. A constellation of such terms as "subtest," "pattern," "profile," and "scatter"analysis are used to describe mechanisms for the systematic exploration and integration of results across the most finite scores available to clinicians. Wechsler (1958) can be credited with launching the analysis of children's subtest scores. His original hypothesis was that "a potential combination now being explored in a study of the WISC on childhood schizophrenics is the pattern, high Picture Completion, low Picture Arrangement, high Object Assembly, low Digit Symbol" (Wechsler, 1958, pp. 166–167). Since Wechsler's original pronouncement, and based primarily on inductive reasoning and logic, more than 75 patterns of subtest variation have been identified for the *Wechsler Intelligence Scale for Children* (WISC) (Wechsler, 1949) through to its most recent successor, the WISC-III (Bannatyne, 1974; Glasser & Zimmerman, 1967; Guilford, 1967; Kamphaus, 1993; Kaufman, 1994; Sattler, 1988; Selz & Reitan, 1979; Wechsler & Jaros, 1965).

The 75 patterns just mentioned have served as the foundation for popular methods of profile analysis and "hypothesis" generation. For example, on finding a putatively unusual subtest profile dominated by scores from the Arithmetic (AR), Information (IN), and Vocabulary (VO) subtests, clinicians compare obtained deviations to the recognized patterns. A hypothesis is generated when a match takes place between a child's profile and one or more patterns. Thus, unusual scores on AR, IN, and VO have been inductively associated with strengths or weaknesses in acquired knowledge (AR, IN, VO), long-term memory (AR, IN, VO), school learning (AR, IN, VO), fund of information (IN, VO), richness of early environment (IN, VO), and so forth (cf. Kaufman, 1979).

DECISION RULES

Today, clinical (vs. research) strategies for analyzing subtest scores can be divided conveniently into two major categories, although the two are not always distinct in their application. The first consists of examining statistical significance levels between one or more sets of subtest scores. The second documents variations in score base rates.

Psychologists are well versed in evaluating the *statistical significance* of WISC-III score differences (i.e., using such p values as $< .05, < .01$, etc.). Characteristically, a child's performance on one or more subtests is compared to either the group average (i.e., a normative approach) or the child's personal mean (an ipsative approach). Less well understood is that three factors influence whether *any* type of score comparison is likely to reach statistical significance, irrespective of whether the comparison takes place during clinical appraisals or research studies. Sample size is the first factor, uncontrolled sources of variance is the second, and the spacing of treatment conditions is the third (Keppel, 1973).

The most salient influence for WISC-III comparisons is sample size. In all, 2,200 children participated in the WISC-III standardization effort. This sample is substantial for the purpose of conducting statistical contrasts and the likelihood is quite high that children will show a "significant" score discrepancy.

Psychologists sometimes find it worthwhile to examine individual subtest scores. This practice has been facilitated in textbooks on intelligence testing as well as in many test manuals through the convenient tabling of critical values. As a preliminary matter to the main study in this chapter, we examined the number of children from the WISC-III standardization sample ($N = 2,200$) who showed at least one statistically significant subtest deviation. Scores from all 13 WISC-III subtests were compared one at a time to children's personal means. Statistically significant deviations were determined by tabled $p < .05$ critical values presented in the WISC-III manual (Table B.3, p. 264). We restricted our analysis to the identification of subtest weaknesses (i.e., children showing subtest scores significantly below their own mean). We did not investigate the number of strengths. Our analysis showed that 55.6% of the children had at least one statistically significant weakness. Thus, when statistical significance is employed as a guideline, clinicians are willing to identify some form of learning problem on the WISC-III, or to generate an interpretive hypothesis, for well over half the children in the United States.

The preceeding example may appear to be misleading. We directed the analysis to identify only subtest weaknesses and we were willing to identify a weakness when as few as one subtest score deviated from children's personal means. Psychologists typically are encouraged to develop hypotheses based on several subtests, not just one significant difference, and they are told to explore both strengths and weaknesses (Kaufman, 1994). Consequently, we repeated the analysis and directed it to the identification of children showing two or more subtest strengths or weaknesses. Results showed that 46.7% of the children in the WISC-III standardization sample had at least two statistically significant subtest differences from their personal means. Thus, results from the second analysis align with those from the first and demonstrate that clinicians are likely to identify an interpretive strength or weakness for nearly half of the children in the United States—and they will do so even when they avoid examining subtest scores in isolation.

A number of publications have addressed pitfalls associated with examining statistical significance levels (Cahan, 1986; Carver, 1978; McDermott & Watkins, 1985). Establishing the statistical significance of a score difference, whether it occurs between two IQs on an intelligence test, an IQ–achievement discrepancy, or across an entire profile of subtest scores, is important because it greatly enhances the probability that the difference is not merely a chance occurrence. However, as evident from analyses just presented for the WISC-III standardization sample, statistically significant differences can be quite common and ordinary. They simply reflect the distinct but natural variation of test scores and are not necessarily a reason for concern.

Recognizing the limitations of statistically significant score differences, textbooks on intelligence testing have recently begun to encourage an examination of *base rates* (Kamphaus, 1993; Kaufman, 1994; Sattler, 1988). The comparisons customarily start by subtracting a child's lowest WISC-III subtest score from their highest. The difference is then compared to cumulative percentages reported for the test's standardization sample (e.g., see WISC-III manual, Table B.5, p. 266). Thereafter, a decision is made regarding whether the child's obtained discrepancy is unusual. The advantage of base rates over statistical significance testing is that they provide the actual frequency of occurrence by which scores differ in the population (e.g., 10%, 5%, or 1% prevalence).

LIMITATIONS OF CURRENT METHODS

Statistical significance testing and the base rate approach suffer from three drawbacks. First, the methods rarely account for interdependencies among subtest scores.[1] As a result, some sets of subtests are prone to showing larger (or smaller) differences as a consequence of the magnitude of their correlations. Second, the methods are univariate. Only one subtest score at a time, one composite formed from several sets of subtests, or one difference score is compared to the appropriate mean. The comparisons must then be repeated as necessary. Third, *profiles* are quite unlike individual subtest scores or linear composites formed from groups of subtest scores.

APPROPRIATE STRATEGY

In actuality, univariate methodology cannot be used to analyze groups of subtest scores because profile analysis requires looking at more than one comparison at a time. Profiles are *integrated* sets of test scores and so require appropriate hypotheses and statistical treatments. Two classes of multivariate methods can be used to examine profiles. Cattell (1949) referred to the procedures as an *R* analysis or a *Q* analysis. Both account for intercorrelations among subtest scores. Moreover, the procedures are capable of completing multiple comparisons *simultaneously*—the typical situation during psychodiagnostic appraisals. Thus, multivariate methods better honor multidifferentiated views of intelligence, as well as, the full network of interrelationships that exist among such abilities (Tatsuoka & Lohnes, 1988; Thompson, 1991).

R analysis is based on the linear variation of test scores. Examples include factor, multiple regression, discriminant, and canonical analysis. *R* analysis is well understood because its methods are routinely taught in graduate programs. Furthermore, most of what we know about test scores comes from knowledge of their linear variation; it should come as no surprise that the majority of research conducted with Wechsler's tests has relied on *R* analysis.

By their nature, subtest profiles are doubly defined according to level (position toward the upper, central, or lower region of the ability continuum) and shape (the pattern of peaks and valleys across subtest scores). *R* analysis is based on linear modeling and is insensitive to differences in *both* profile level and shape. *Q* analysis respects each type of variation and is better able to address nonlinear, configural hypotheses (Cattell, 1949; Horst, 1941; Mosel & Roberts, 1954).

Given the above, a more appropriate approach to profile analysis would begin by applying *Q* methodology to group children simultaneously according to the level and shape of their subtest scores. A *normative* taxonomy of the most common subtest profiles/patterns would result when *Q* analysis is conducted with a test's standardization sample. The normative taxonomy would offer important diagnostic benefits because, as mentioned earlier, it could be used as a viable contrast, or *multivariate* "null hypothesis," for testing the validity of profiles believed to be unusual or clinically important. In such instances, the determination of an unusual profile would become plausible only when it could be demonstrated that a child's pattern of subtest scores is atypical of the most common patterns found in the population.

Normative taxonomies of the most common multivariate, or "core," subtest patterns have already been established and validated for standardization samples from the WISC-R (McDermott, Glutting, Jones, Watkins, & Kush, 1989), *Wechsler Adult Intelligence Scale—Revised* (WAIS-R; Wechsler, 1981) (McDermott, Glutting, Jones, & Noonan, 1989), *Wechsler Preschool and Primary Scale of Intelligence* (WPPSI; Wechsler, 1967) (Glutting & McDermott, 1990a), *Kaufman Assessment Battery for Children* (K-ABC; Kaufman & Kaufman, 1983) (Glutting et al., 1992), and *McCarthy Scales of Children's Abilities* (MSCA; McCarthy, 1972) (Glutting & McDermott, 1990b).

The normative taxonomy we previously developed for the WISC-R has become obsolete as a result of the WISC-III's publication. Therefore, we undertook a series of empirical studies to establish a new taxonomy of core subtest patterns within the WISC-III's national sample. We now summarize the culminating steps in that effort and relate the final taxonomy to known population prevalence for children's demographic and personal characteristics.

METHOD

Sample

The overall taxonomy was based on the entire sample of 2,200 children and adolescents used in the WISC-III's standardization study (Wechsler, 1991).[2] Subjects were selected according to a stratified quota system including 200 children at each of 11 age levels from 6 (6 years, 0 months) through 16 (16 years, 11 months), with equal numbers of males and females at each level. Quotas for distributions of children's race, education level of parents, geographic region, and educational placement (regular education vs. special education) were arranged to approximate distributions identified in the 1988 U.S. Census.

Profile Components

The WISC-III comprises 13 subtests. Ten are mandatory and contribute to two scale IQs: the Verbal Scale IQ (VIQ) which is composed of 5 subtests and the Performance Scale IQ (PIQ) which encompasses another 5 subtests. The VIQ and PIQ are combined to form the Full Scale IQ (FSIQ).

Factor analyses of the WISC-III's standardization sample (Wechsler, 1991) yielded four dimensions which form the basis for Index scores: (1) Verbal Comprehension Index (VCI), which includes scores from the Information, Similarities, Vocabulary, and Comprehension subtests; (2) Perceptual Organization Index (POI), which includes scores from the Picture Completion, Picture Arrangement, Block Design, and Object Assembly subtests; (3) Freedom from Distractibility Index (FDI), which includes scores from the Arithmetic and Digit Span subtests; and (4) Processing Speed Index (PSI), which includes scores from the Coding and Symbol Search subtests. All WISC-III scale IQs and the four factor Indexes have Ms of 100 and SDs of 15.

Each child's profile was based on standard scores (Ms = 10, SDs = 3) for 12 WISC-III subtests, including the mandatory five Verbal and five Performance subtests (Wechsler, 1991, p. 5). The supplementary subtests of Digit Span and Symbol Search were also included because they undergird the WISC-III's factor Indexes. The alternate Mazes subtest was not used. Both Digit Span and Symbol Search are regarded as primary components in most interpretation schemes, whereas Mazes traditionally has been excluded (e.g., see Bannatyne, 1974; Guilford, 1967; Witkin, Dyk, Faterson, Goodenough, & Karp, 1962).

Another deviation is needed from the primary presentation. Ipsatized scores are frequently recommended for WISC-III profile analysis (e.g., Kamphaus, 1993, p. 163; Kaufman, 1994, pp. 128–130; Sattler, 1988, pp. 167–169). They convey a certain intuitive appeal because, by removing every child's average performance from the profile, they appear to isolate and amplify individual differences. However, ipsative scores retain certain well-known mathematical properties that recommend against their use (see McDermott, Fantuzzo, Glutting, Watkins, & Baggaley, 1992, for a review and analysis.) Essentially, ipsatization substantially alters the original construct nature and interrelationships of the subtests, thereby reducing their attendant validity and reliability. Ipsatization automatically removes most of the common variance from subtests such that their mean intercorrelation tends to be negative and their mean correlation with an external variable approaches zero (Anastasi, 1988; Clemans, 1965; Hicks, 1970; McDermott et al., 1992). Moreover, as Clemans (1965) has emphasized, ipsative values contain no information not already reflected in standard scores and, in fact, contain less information because they do not reflect *level* differences among children. For example, given two children one with a high and the other a low ipsative score on the same subtests, there is no way of telling which child has more ability. Considering the intended purposes of the subtest taxonomy, ipsative scores would preclude future testing of levels hypotheses and, because of their algebraic properties (i.e., because each child's scores are altered by a different value and polytonic, no common metric exists across children), would preclude future application of profile classification procedures requiring nonipsatized values. Thus, ipsative scores were not used in our development of a subtest taxonomy.

Procedure

Cluster analysis (Q methodology) was used to sort the 2,200 profiles according to shape and level. Multiple methodologies exist for the identification of clusters. Hierarchical agglomerative clustering algorithms are the most popular in the social sciences (Blashfield & Aldenderfer, 1988; Milligan & Cooper, 1987). However, agglomerative analyses are prone to producing nested clusters that are ranked within hierarchies (Everitt, 1979). This situation exists because agglomerative algorithms make only one sweep through the data and are unable to compensate for a poor initial partition. By contrast, iterative-partitioning techniques correct improper assignments by making more than one sweep. Iterative algorithms also produce single-ranked clusters that are not nested; therefore, they are more likely to recover true structure (Bayne, Beauchamp, Begovich, & Kane, 1980; Milligan, 1980; Milligan & Sokal, 1980). The drawback to iterative methods is that users must specify the number of final clusters in advance of the actual analysis; otherwise, results are likely to be inferior to those from agglomerative algorithms (Milligan, 1980; Milligan & Cooper, 1987).

To overcome the problems just cited, our clustering strategy was a variation on the model suggested by Scheibler and Schneider (1985) for determining the most representative profile patterns in a population. The model was three staged and began with an agglomerative algorithm. Specifically, the aggregate sample of 2,200 children was partitioned by age levels to form 11 blocks of 200 children, and profiles for children comprising each block were clustered independently through Ward's (1963) agglomerative procedure. Clusters derived from the 11 independent analyses were pooled to form a proximity matrix of first-stage clusters that were themselves subject to second-stage clustering by Ward's method.

Second-stage clustering began with a similarity matrix whose diagonal elements held error sums of squares (*Ess*) statistic values for respective first-stage clusters, with off-diagonal elements corresponding to potential *Ess* statistics for merging each pair of first-stage clusters. Group centroids from the second-stage solution served as starting partitions ("seed points"; Anderberg, 1973) for the third-stage, iterative-partitioning analysis conducted using K-means passes.

The choice of similarity measure was the *Ess* statistic for the first- and second-stage agglomerative analyses and Euclidean distance for the third-stage, iterative-partitioning analysis. Correlation coefficients were rejected as similarity measures inasmuch as their sensitivity is constrained to differences in profile shape (Cattell, Coulter, & Tsujioka, 1966; Cronbach & Gleser, 1953; Sneath & Sokal, 1973). Alternatively, the *Ess* statistic and Euclidean distance simultaneously account for differences in profile shape and elevation (Aldenderfer & Blashfield, 1984).

Several stopping rules were employed during the first- and second-stage analyses. Appropriate agglomerative solutions were required to (1) correspond to a hierarchical step preceding an atypical inflection in the similarity measure, (2) have a ratio of within-profile-type (cluster) variances to variance for the full standardization sample < 1.0., (3) fulfill Mojena's (1977) first stopping rule, and (4) satisfy Wishart's (1982) *t*-test. Stopping during the third-stage, iterative-partitioning analysis occurred after 100 iterations.

Internal Criteria

Better practice in cluster analysis suggests results should be compared along criteria both internal and external to a derived solution (Aldenderfer & Blashfield, 1984). Results from the final solution were compared along four internal criteria.[3]

The first criterion addressed *replication rates*. It specified groups of similar profiles ("profile types") reasonably replicable from the first- to third-stage solutions. Replication is fundamental to developing cluster taxonomies with broad significance (Breckenridge, 1989; Overall & Klett, 1972). The most common method is to randomly halve samples, the first used to form clusters and the second to replicate solutions.

We employed an age-level replication criterion of 80%. Norms for IQ tests are age based. This means child performance is determined by comparison to norms for similarly aged children and not to the standardization sample as a whole. Consequently, rather than halving the sample and comparing solutions, the final (third-stage) taxonomy was deemed to have at least some applicability if it independently replicated across each of the 11 age-level analyses used to form first-stage solutions. Thus, replication for the final solution was determined by the number of first-stage solutions (independent experiments) in which it also emerged.

Successful replication does not necessarily mean a solution is valid, but failure to replicate is reason for rejecting it (Blashfield & Aldenderfer, 1988). The practical effect of nonreplication is that year-to-year fluctuations in profile types could be attributable to simple age changes rather than to substantial shifts in children's abilities. Consequently, replicability across age levels is essential for a normative taxonomy of ability scores.

The second criterion of *within-cluster cohesion* (Cormack, 1971) requires small score dispersions within clusters and, therefore, for individuals within a cluster to be maximally similar. Tryon and Bailey's (1970) homogeneity (H) coefficient was employed as our estimate of within-type cohesion.

The third criterion, *external isolation* (Cormack, 1971), requires large score differences between clusters (i.e., different clusters should be maximally dissimilar from one another). Cattell's (1949) r_p coefficient was calculated between profile types as our measure of external isolation. Both H and r_p are sensitive to profile shape and level and are interpreted similarly to correlation coefficients, where 0.0 indicates chance similarity and negative values indicate gross dissimilarity. Minimal criterion values have been established for H and r_p ($\leq .60$ and $\geq .40$, respectively) based on clustering and classification studies conducted with standardization samples from the WAIS-R, WISC-R, WPPSI, MSCA, and K-ABC (respectively, McDermott, Glutting, Jones, & Noonan, et al., 1989; McDermott, Glutting, Jones, Watkins, & Kush, 1989b; Glutting & McDermott, 1990a, 1990b; Glutting et al., 1992).

The fourth internal criterion specified that the overall taxonomy be representative of the national population of 6- to 16-year-olds. This requirement is known as full coverage and it means that the taxonomy must account for all profile variations and not discount outliers that happen to diverge from the norm. Outliers cause problems for clustering algorithms (Milligan, 1980). Reduced coverage, through deletion of outliers, has been proposed as a method for recovering true cluster structure (Edelbrock, 1979). Nevertheless, reduced coverage is methodologically improper for a *normative* taxonomy because deleted subjects will alter population *M*s and *SD*s for the variables being analyzed and affect the integrity of validity estimates based on the entire standardization sample.

Children's obtained deviation IQs for the FSIQ, VIQ, PIQ, and factor index scores (VCI, POI, FDI, PSI) were also used to describe and interpret the final taxonomy. In addition, we used prevalence of clinically abnormal VIQ/PIQ and FSIQ/PSI discrepancies within profile types to support interpretations regarding unusual profile configurations.

External Criteria

Upon obtaining a final taxonomy, the next step was to evaluate its external validity. Aldenderfer and Blashfield (1984) recommend that cluster solutions be compared and validated across demographic variables not used in the derivation of clusters. Thus, taking into consideration the prevalence distribution of each pertinent demographic variable (children's age, gender, ethnicity, region of the country, educational placements, and parent education levels), we conducted two-tailed tests of the standard error of proportional differences for all possible pairwise comparisons across levels of the criterion variables (Ferguson, 1981). The Type I error rate was apportioned by the Bonferroni correction (Stevens, 1986). By this approach, the expected prevalence for a given characteristic within a profile type (e.g., whites vs. African Americans) was based on its prevalence in the U.S. population, and unusual prevalence for a particular profile type was determined by statistically significant deviations from the general expectancy.

To achieve better balance in distributions of age intervals and in power for subsequent statistical tests, the original 11 age groups were reduced to 4 groups (i.e., 6–8, 9–11, 12–14, and 15–16 years). (Note that this arrangement pertained only to post hoc testing of age as an external criterion variable: As described earlier, development and replication of the typology itself considered variation separately within each of the 11 original age intervals.)

Consistent with the racial stratification used during the WISC-III's norming (Wechsler, 1991), children's ethnicity was coded as whites, blacks, Hispanics, and other race/ethnic groups. Parent education levels were stratified according to five levels: (1) eighth grade or less, (2) ninth through eleventh grade, (3) high school graduate or equivalent, (4) 1 through 3 years of college or technical training, and (5) 4 or more years of college. The average of two education levels was used when both parents lived with the child, and the education level of the parent living with the child was used when only one parent was in the home.

Approximately 7% of the WISC-III standardization sample was classified as learning disabled, speech/language impaired, emotionally disturbed, or physically impaired (Wechsler, 1991). Another 5% comprised children identified as gifted and talented. All special education groups, with the exception of gifted and talented children, were collapsed into one category so sufficient numbers would be available for statistical comparisons. To avoid confounds with general ability level, gifted and talented children were lumped with those from regular education. Giftedness was defined by overall ability above that of children in regular education. By contrast, all other special education groups tend to perform below children in regular education.

RESULTS

Typal Structure

First-stage clustering produced 110 profile groups (an average of 10.0 per analysis). These were submitted to second-stage agglomerative clustering based on an 110×110 similarity matrix and the solution at all hierarchical steps was evaluated against the stated internal criteria. The nine-cluster solution was the only one to satisfy all criteria, and therefore, it was submitted to a third-stage, iterative-partitioning analysis. Subject relocations ceased after 100 iterations during the third-stage analysis.

Table 19.1 displays, for each of the final nine core profile types, its average coefficient for within-type homogeneity, between-types similarity, and replication rate. The average H value (.66) satisfies the a priori criterion of $\geq .60$ and the average r_p (.26) satisfies the $< .40$ criterion. Moreover, the average H is nearly identical to that found for the previous WISC-R taxonomy (i.e., .66 for WISC-III vs. .63 for WISC-R) and the average r_p is somewhat superior (.26 for WISC-III vs. .33 for WISC-R). The types replicated 100% of the time across the 11 independent experiments and satisfied its a priori criterion of $\geq 80\%$. This rate is extremely high and noticeably superior to that for the WISC-R (84.4%).

Corresponding mean subtest scores, deviation IQs, and factor Indexes are presented in Table

TABLE 19.1. Prevalence and Psychometric Properties of WISC-III Core Profile Types

Cluster number	% population prevalence	Internal profile cohesion[a] (H)	External isolation[b] (r_p)	% Independent replications across 11 age blocks[c]
1	9.4	.55	.00	100%
2	13.3	.65	.27	100%
3	14.1	.64	.32	100%
4	13.2	.72	.43	100%
5	9.5	.70	.40	100%
6	9.9	.69	.34	100%
7	12.1	.68	.36	100%
8	9.7	.68	.27	100%
9	8.8	.62	−.08	100%
Averages	100.0	$H = .66$	$r_p = .26$	100%

Note. $N = 2,200$. From The Psychological Corporation, 1995. Reproduced by permission. All rights reserved.

[a]Internal cohesion values indicate the "tightness of fit" of profiles of standard scores within each profile type. If the patterns of children's profiles within each profile type were identical, the homogeneity value would be 1.0. Conversely, as the variability of profile patterns within a type approaches that for the entire WISC-III standardization sample, homogeneity drops toward 0.0. A negative value would indicate variability greater than that for the standardization sample.

[b]External isolation values are averages of the similarity coefficients between the mean standard score pattern for a given profile type and the mean pattern for every other profile type, where the similarity coefficient is calculated by Cattell's (1949) r_p formula. If the mean score pattern for a given type was identical to that of another type, r_p would equal 1.0. As the mean score patterns become more dissimilar and approach a degree of similarity that would approximate chance, r_p drops toward 0.0. A negative r_p results when mean score patterns between types are grossly dissimilar.

[c]A replication for a given profile type is defined as confirmation of the existence of that type within a first-stage clustering solution (i.e., within a solution for an age-level block of 200 children) using the same profile type confirmation criteria applied to the final solution involving all 2,200 children in the WISC-III standardization sample. Thus, a profile type confirmed in 6 out of 11 first-stage solutions has a 54.5% replication rate.

19.2, along with a descriptive name for each type. The types are arranged in order of descending FSIQs and names are assigned on the basis of this variation plus outstanding VIQ/PIQ, FSIQ/FDI, and FSIQ/PSI contrasts. Terminology such as "high" and "below average" are chosen to avoid confusion with standard WISC-III intelligence classifications such as "very superior," "low average," and "borderline" (Wechsler, 1991, p. 32), the latter referring to normal curve IQ distributions only and not to discrete subtest profile types.

Figure 19.1 illustrates the relative level and shape of each profile type. The primary distinction among types is general ability level (i.e., *g*). Also apparent, however, is that the profiles are *not* flat and nearly all tend to display secondary score differences within *g* levels. For instance, four profile types show subordinate VIQ/PIQ discrepancies, two types show secondary variation according to FSIQ/FDI discrepancies, and five types show FSIQ/PSI discrepancies.

It would be worthwhile to swerve again from our central premise. We just indicated that the WISC-III's *structure* is dominated by variation from a general factor (*g*), as well as, by secondary variation from the VIQ/PIQ dyad, the FDI, and the PSI. We are often asked whether our cluster analyses actually investigate a test's structure. The answer is yes, but the analyses do so indirectly. Cluster analysis and factor analysis (the most common method for identifying a test's structure) share certain similarities. Both operate to reduce a large set of variables into a smaller, more manageable number.

When factor analyses are directed to the WISC-III's subtests, the analyses compare how *subtest scores vary across children* and, thereby, directly answer questions about the test's structure. Cluster analysis, at least how we are engaging in the process, examines *how children vary across subtest scores;* it too can help to provide some evidence about the WISC-III's structure.

TABLE 19.2. Mean Subtest Score Patterns, Associated Deviation IQs, and Factor Indexes for WISC-III Core Profile Types

Profile type number	Mean subtest score[a]												Mean deviation quotient[b]			Mean factor Index[c]				Name and description
	PC	IN	CD	SM	PA	AR	BD	VO	OA	CM	SS	DS	FSIQ	VIQ	PIQ	VCI	POI	FDI	PSI	
1	13	14	13	14	13	14	15	14	14	13	13	13	126	123	124	122	123	121	116	High ability and depressed processing speed
2	13	13	10	13	11	12	12	12	13	12	13	10	114	116	110	116	112	109	101	Above-average ability; VIQ > PIQ and depressed processing speed
3	11	11	14	11	12	11	11	11	11	11	13	11	109	105	112	108	104	111	118	Slightly above average ability; PIQ > VIQ and elevated processing speed
4	10	11	9	11	11	10	10	10	11	9	11	10	102	104	99	105	100	95	98	Average ability
5	10	10	9	11	10	11	10	10	10	9	10	13	99	103	96	101	97	113	96	Average ability and elevated freedom from distractibility
6	11	9	7	8	8	9	8	10	8	11	8	8	92	90	97	90	101	91	87	Slightly below average ability
7	9	8	12	8	8	9	8	9	8	9	11	8	91	97	88	88	94	95	108	Slightly below average ability; PIQ > VIQ and elevated processing speed
8	7	9	8	8	8	8	6	6	9	6	9	7	86	92	82	93	82	92	89	Below-average ability and VIQ > PIQ
9	6	5	7	5	5	6	6	5	5	6	5	6	74	75	77	75	77	84	85	Low ability; elevated freedom from distractibility and elevated processing speed

Note. N = 2,200. Tabled values are rounded to nearest whole number for convenient presentation. WISC-III = Wechsler Intelligence Scale for Children—Third Edition; PC = Picture Completion; IN = Information; CD = Coding; SM = Similarities; PA = Picture Arrangement; AR = Arithmetic; BD = Block Design; VO = Vocabulary; OA = Object Assembly; CM = Comprehension; SS = Symbol Search; DS = Digit Span; FSIQ = Full Scale IQ; VIQ = Verbal Scale IQ; PIQ = Performance Scale IQ; PSI = Processing Speed Index; VCI = Verbal Comprehension Index; POI = Perceptual Organization Index; FDI = Freedom-from-Distractibility Index. Copyright 1995 by The Psychological Corporation. Reproduced by permission.

[a] The population standard score M = 10 and SD = 3 for each age group.

[b] Deviation quotients are conventional IQ equivalents specific to each age group, where the population M = 100 and SD = 15.

[c] Factor indexes are specific to each age group, where the population M = 100 and SD = 15.

Our cluster analysis reduced the original 2,200 profiles in the WISC-III standardization sample (one profile for each child) into a smaller number of groups. At the end of the analysis, children within a group (referred to as a "profile type") were optimally similar to one another with respect to the elevation and shape of their WISC-III subtest scores. Likewise, the distance between groups was also optimal such that each profile type was maximally different from one another as possible.

Once the constituent profile types had been identified (nine in the current case), it was possible to compare each and identify variables and constructs that made the greatest contribution to their variances. It would have been possible to compare types according to heuristically derived subtest groupings such as Bannatyne's (1974) ACID (Arithmetic, Coding, Information, and Digit Span) categorization. Instead, we concentrated on variables identified during factor analyses of the WISC-R and WISC-III (Kaufman, 1975; Macmann & Barnett, 1994; Roid, Prifitera, & Weiss, 1993; Wechsler, 1991). The reason for our concentration is threefold. First, constructs identified during factor analyses have the greatest theoretical importance because they directly address issues related to the WISC-III's structure. Second, the variables are derived empirically rather than speculatively. Third, practitioners are more likely to interpret factor-related scores than inductive scores because the former are readily available in the form of VIQs, PIQs, FDIs, and PSIs.

Our comparisons showed that the profile groups differed most on g (a variable repeatedly identified during factor analyses). This finding supports the FSIQ (i.e., the WISC-III's g-based estimate) as being important to the test's structure because not only does it emerge during factor

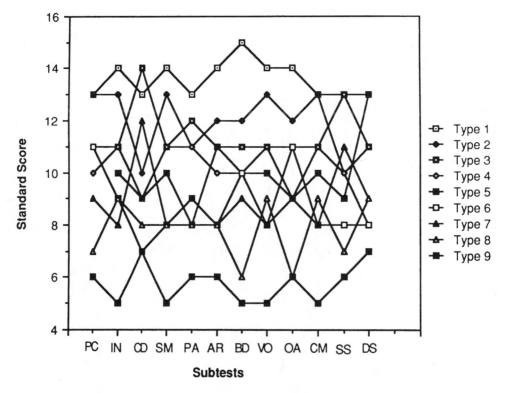

FIGURE 19.1. Core profile types in the WISC-III standardization sample. PC = Picture Completion; IN = information; CD = Coding; SM = Similarities; PA = Picture Arrangement; AR = Arithmetic; BD = Block Design; VO = Vocabulary; OA = Object Assembly; CM = Comprehension; SS = Symbol Search; DS = Digit Span.

analyses of how subtest scores vary across children, it is also reflected in how children themselves vary across subtest scores. By contrast, if the profile types did not vary on g, it would raise questions about the WISC-III's arrangement of scores in a hierarchical structure with g at its apex. Similarly, comparisons between types on VIQ/PIQ, FSIQ/FDI, and FSIQ/PSI were used to provide information about other sources of empirically derived score variation on the WISC-III.

Returning to the primary thesis, we see that inferences of secondary variation corresponding to the VIQ/PIQ dyad are supported by an examination of unusual prevalence distinctions (Table 19.3). Unusual VIQ/PIQ discrepancies are defined in the clinical sense as those that occur in no more than 3% of the child population. The comparisons make apparent that profile types 2, 3, 7, and 8 are defined not only by g variation but also by ancillary differences between the VIQ and PIQ. Similarly, the prevalence of severe FSIQ/FDI discrepancies (Table 19.4) shows types 5 and 9 contain FDI anomalies and the prevalence of severe FSIQ/PSI discrepancies (Table 19.5) shows types 1, 2, 3, 7, and 9 have PSI anomalies. Thus, secondary variation from the VIQ/PIQ dyad, the FDI factor, and the PSI factor represent other important features of the core profile types as well as the structure of abilities measured by the WISC-III.

Typal Membership

In addition to comparisons between the VIQ/PIQ, FSIQ/FDI, and FSIQ/PSI, the prevailing composition of each type was explained and validated in terms of demography and environment (children's age, sex, race, education placements, region of the country, and parent education levels). These latter contrasts help to validate the taxonomy because, unlike VIQ/PIQ, FSIQ/FDI, and FSIQ/PSI contrasts, the subtest scores comprising these variables were not used in the derivation of clusters. (See Aldenderfer & Blashfield, 1984, on the importance of validating taxonomies on the basis of variables

TABLE 19.3. Distribution and Prevalence of Verbal–Performance IQ Differences in WISC-III Core Profile Types

Profile type number	Percentage[a]			Prevalence[b]
	Severe VIQ > PIQ discrepancy	No severe difference	Severe PIQ > VIQ discrepancy	
1	3.6	92.8	3.6	n.s.
2	8.2	91.8	0.0	more VIQ > PIQ*
3	0.0	93.9	6.1	more PIQ > VIQ*
4	2.7	96.9	0.4	n.s.
5	3.3	96.7	0.0	n.s.
6	0.0	96.9	3.1	n.s.
7	0.0	90.6	9.4	more PIQ > VIQ**
8	7.5	92.5	0.0	more VIQ > PIQ*
9	4.7	95.3	0.0	n.s.

Note. $N = 2,200$. VIQ = Verbal Scale IQ; PIQ = Performance Scale IQ. The sum of percentages across each row is 100%. Copyright 1995 by The Psychological Corporation. Reproduced by permission. All rights reserved.
[a]Determinations of "severe" IQ differences in profile types is based on cut scores derived across the WISC-III normative sample, where VIQ–PIQ differences > 22 points comprise 3% of VIQ > PIQ differences and PIQ–VIQ differences > 24 points comprise 3% of PIQ > VIQ differences. The 3% criterion approximates differences nearly two standard deviations above and below the population mean respectively and is consistent with the standard established by McDermott, Glutting, Jones, & Noonan (1989).
[b]Identification of significant prevalence trends is based on tests of the standard error of proportional differences corrected for the number of simultaneous statistical contrasts by the Bonferroni method.
* $p < .01$, ** $p < .001$.

TABLE 19.4. Distribution and Prevalence of Full Scale IQ and FDI Differences in WISC-III Core Profile Types

Profile type number	Percentage[a]			Prevalence[b]
	Severe FSIQ > FDI discrepancy	No severe difference	Severe FDI > FSIQ discrepancy	
1	5.1	94.9	0.0	n.s.
2	5.2	94.9	0.0	n.s.
3	2.2	97.2	0.6	n.s.
4	4.5	95.5	0.0	n.s.
5	0.0	86.5	13.5	more FDI > FSIQ**
6	2.8	97.1	0.1	n.s.
7	0.1	97.2	2.7	n.s.
8	0.0	97.6	4.9	n.s.
9	0.5	91.2	8.3	more FDI > FSIQ*

Note. $N = 2,200$. FSIQ = Full Scale IQ; FDI = Freedom-from-Distractibility Index. The sum of percentages across each row is 100%. Copyright © 1995 by The Psychological Corporation. Reproduced by permission. All rights reserved.
[a]Determinations of "severe" IQ differences in profile types is based on cut scores derived across the WISC-III normative sample, where FSIQ–FDI differences > 21 points comprise 3% of FSIQ > FDI differences and FDI–FSIQ differences > 24 points comprise 3% of FDI > FSIQ differences. The 3% criterion approximates differences nearly two standard deviations above and below the population mean respectively, and is consistent with the standard established by McDermott, Glutting, Jones, Watkins, & Noonan (1989).
[b]Identification of significant prevalence trends is based on tests of the standard error of proportional differences corrected for the number of simultaneous statistical contrasts by the Bonferroni method.
* $p < .01$. ** $p < .0001$.

not used in the derivation of clusters.) For reader convenience, we summarize the distinguishing trends for each type. Unless indicated otherwise, only trends found to be statistically significant (i.e., $p < .05$, or less) are reported.

1. High ability and depressed processing speed (prevalence = 9.4%; FSIQ $M = 125.6$, $SD = 6.0$). The occurrence of unusual FSIQ > PSI discrepancies is nearly four times greater than that found in the general population (M difference = 9.2 points in favor of the FSIQ). More than 60% of the children are females and comparatively more whites are present (88.1% vs. 70.1% in the child population based on 1988 U.S. census data). The proportion of blacks is extremely small and less than 1/100th of the level anticipated from race/ethnicity distributions for the United States (0.1% vs. 15.3% for the child population). More than twice the expected number of children have parents who graduated college (44.7% vs. 18.7% for the population) and fewer parents than average failed to complete high school (1.4% vs. 18.1% for the population). More children come from the Northeast region, the percentage being slightly greater than 1.5 times the expected occurrence (27.2% vs. 17.9% for the population). In contrast to these findings, proportions for children's ages and educational placements (i.e., regular education vs. special education) conform to expected distributions. None of the nine core types show unusual variation in children's age levels or their educational placements.

2. Above-average ability; VIQ > PIQ and depressed processing speed (prevalence = 13.3%; FSIQ $M = 114.1$, $SD = 4.8$). Three profile types display atypical score variation from *both* the VIQ/PIQ dyad and the PSI (type numbers 2, 3, and 7). The frequency of unusual VIQ > PIQ discrepancies in profile type 2 is double the national propensity (M difference = 6.2 points in favor of the VIQ). This profile type has the second greatest disproportion of children evidencing atypical FSIQ/PSI anomalies. (Profile type 7 has the greatest disproportion.) The rate of FSIQ > PSI discrepancies in

TABLE 19.5. Distribution and Prevalence of Full Scale IQ and Processing Speed Index Differences in WISC-III Core Profile Types

Profile type number	Percentage[a]			Prevalence[b]
	Severe FSIQ > PSI discrepancy	No severe difference	Severe PSI > FSIQ discrepancy	
1	11.7	88.3	0.0	more FSIQ > PSI***
2	12.3	87.7	0.0	more FSIQ > PSI***
3	0.0	94.4	5.6	more PSI > FSIQ*
4	0.0	98.3	1.7	n.s.
5	2.4	97.6	0.0	n.s.
6	3.2	96.8	0.0	n.s.
7	0.0	88.8	11.2	more PSI > FSIQ***
8	0.0	99.9	0.1	n.s.
9	0.0	90.2	9.8	more PSI > FSIQ**

Note. $N = 2,200$. FSIQ = Full Scale IQ; PSI = Processing Speed Index. The sum of percentages across each row is 100%. Copyright © 1995 by The Psychological Corporation. Reproduced by permission. All rights reserved.

[a]Determinations of "severe" IQ differences in profile types is based on cut scores derived across the WISC-III normative sample, where FSIQ–PSI differences > 23 points comprise 3% of FSIQ > PSI differences and PSI–FSIQ differences > 26 points comprise 3% of PSI > FSIQ differences. The 3% criterion approximates differences nearly two standard deviations above and below the population mean respectively, and is consistent with the standard established by McDermott, Glutting, Jones, Watkins, & Noonan (1989).

[b]Identification of significant prevalence trends is based on tests of the standard error of proportional differences corrected for the number of simultaneous statistical contrasts by the Bonferroni method.

*$p < .05$. *** $p < .001$. *** $p < .0001$.

type 2 is more than four times larger than the population trend (*M* difference = 13.1 points in favor of the FSIQ). There are slightly more females and more whites than anticipated. The number of blacks and Hispanics is less than anticipated. More parents finished college and fewer parents failed to obtain high school diplomas than the general public. No unusual differences are present for educational placements or region of the country.

3. Above-average ability; PIQ > VIQ and elevated processing speed (prevalence = 14.1%; FSIQ *M* = 108.6, *SD* = 5.3). The incidence of unusual PIQ > VIQ discrepancies exceed the national trend by more than two and one-half times (*M* difference = 7.0 points in favor of the PIQ). Slightly more PSI > FSIQ differences are apparent than expected (*M* difference = 9.2 points in favor of the PSI). Males are predominant (65.5%). Slightly more whites are present than anticipated. The proportion of blacks and Hispanics is at their expectancy levels. The number of parents with college educations aligns with expectations and slightly more parents than normally predicted have some formal training beyond high school. No proportional differences are present for educational placements or region of the country.

4. Average ability (prevalence = 13.2%; FSIQ *M* = 101.6, *SD* = 4.4). Profile type 4 and profile type 6 are the only clusters defined solely by *g* level. Neither type shows unusual variation in the rate of children's VIQ/PIQ, FSIQ/FDI, or FSIQ/PSI discrepancies. Slightly more whites are present in profile type 4 than expected. Approximately half the anticipated number of blacks are present, but the proportion for Hispanics aligns with population trends. Parent educational levels conform to expectations and no unusual differences exist for children's educational placements or the region where they live.

5. Average ability and elevated freedom from distractibility (prevalence = 9.5%; FSIQ *M* = 99.2, *SD* = 5.1). Two profile types display atypical score FSIQ/FDI variation (type numbers 5 and 9). Interestingly, both types show a strength in the FDI. The frequencies of unusual VIQ/PIQ discrepancies in profile type 5 and the frequency of unusual FSIQ/PSI discrepancies align with their the national propensities. However, this type shows the greatest number of unusual FDI > FSIQ discrepancies; the rate is more than four times above that normally encountered for children in the United States (M difference = 14.2 points in favor of the FDI). No unusual differences are apparent for children's gender, age, race, parent educational levels, or children's educational placements. However, slightly more children than expected come from the Northeast region of the country.

6. *Slightly below average ability* (prevalence = 9.9%; FSIQ M = 92.4, SD = 5.5). Like profile type 4, profile type 6 is defined solely in terms of g level. No unusual variation is evident in the rate of children's VIQ/PIQ, FSIQ/FDI, or FSIQ/PSI discrepancies. This type shows a higher prevalence of females (70.6%). Whites and blacks are represented proportionately. However, the number of Hispanics is greater than the national average. Less than one-third the expected number of parents completed college, but the number graduating from high school equals the U.S. ratio. No unusual prevalence is indicated for educational placements or region of the country.

7. *Slightly below average ability; PIQ > VIQ and elevated processing speed* (prevalence = 12.1%; FSIQ M = 91.3, SD = 5.0). The occurrence of PIQ > VIQ discrepancies is more than three (3.1) times that for the aggregate population (M difference = 9.6 points in favor of the VIQ). This profile type also has the greatest disproportion of children evidencing atypical FSIQ/PSI anomalies. The rate of PSI > FSIQ discrepancies is more than four times larger than that found for the general public (M difference = 16.6 points in favor of the PSI). Differential expectations are present for gender, with females (67.0%) more prominent than males. Whites are slightly underrepresented. Blacks are represented proportionately, but more Hispanics are present than expected. Less than one-third of the anticipated number of parents completed college, but the number graduating from high school exceeds the national ratio. No unusual differences are evident for educational placements or region of the country.

8. *Below-average ability and VIQ > PIQ* (prevalence = 9.7%; FSIQ M = 86.0, SD = 4.7). More than two and one-half times the predicted number of children show VIQ > PIQ discrepancies (M difference = 10.2 points in favor of the VIQ). Distributions for gender are equitable. There are more blacks; the frequency is more than two times higher than the U.S. average. No difference in proportions is present for Hispanics. Lower parent educational levels are apparent. Proportionately fewer parents graduated from college and less than half the anticipated number of parents completed high school. No unusual differences exist for children's educational placements or the region where they live.

9. *Low ability; elevated freedom from distractibility and elevated processing speed* (prevalence = 8.%; FSIQ M = 73.6, SD = 6.4). Profile type 9 is the only one to display atypical score variation from *both* the PSI and FDI. The frequency of unusual FSIQ > FDI discrepancies is two and one-half times higher than expected (M difference = 10.0 points in favor of the FDI) and the frequency of unusual FSIQ > PSI discrepancies is three times higher (M difference = 11.0 points in favor of the FDI). These findings are intriguing. They suggest that children with low general ability are likely to show strengths in their FDIs and PSIs. Developmental improvement in both verbal and performance tasks has been tied to increases in processing speed (Kail, 1991). Consequently, psychologists may be inclined to interpret the results of children showing low general ability and concomitant elevations in their PSIs as indicting a potential for increasing general ability level. But, as found here, elevated PSIs (along with elevated FDI) are actually commonplace for children who obtain low general ability levels on the WISC-III. Psychologists need to be aware of this phenomenon and act accordingly. No irregularities are apparent for this type on gender. There are more blacks and Hispanics and fewer whites; the frequency of blacks is more than two and one-half times higher than the national average. Approximately one-tenth the anticipated number of parents graduated college and more than two and one-half times as many parents as expected failed to complete high school. There are slightly more children from the South than normally projected. Furthermore, a leaning is present for an overrepresentation in special education programs. However, the trend is significant at only $p < .10$.

DISCUSSION

The most commanding aspect of the core profile types is their distinctions by general ability level. This finding coincides with Macmann and Barnett's (1994) factor analyses for latent dimensions among WISC-III subtests. Their work suggests that a single ability dimension, as represented by the FSIQ, dominates all subtest variation. However, the core types cannot be explained by g variation alone. Four of the nine types (numbers 1, 2, 6, and 7) compel us to recognize individual subtest variation as ultimately reflected in VIQ/PIQ discrepancies. Two types (numbers 5 and 9) necessitate acknowledgment of the FDI and five types (numbers 1, 2, 3, 7, and 9) show variation according to the PSI. These latter findings align with research identifying between three and four secondary dimensions underlying the WISC-III (Wechsler, 1991; Roid et al., 1993; Sattler, 1992).

The current subtest taxonomy is remarkably similar to the one developed for the WISC-R. Both contain core profiles whose variance is dominated by g. Moreover, each analysis found second-stratum configurations conforming to the respective Verbal and Performance subtests. Thus, it is rather likely that the obtained parallels for Verbal subtests across certain profile types and for Performance subtests across other types stems from bifurcation of the Verbal Comprehension and Perceptual Organization dimensions which were discovered during factor analyses of the WISC-R and WISC-III (Kaufman, 1975; Kroonenberg & ten Berge, 1987; Roid et al., 1993; Wechsler, 1991).

Some factor-analytic solutions for the WISC-III proposed a third dimension (the Freedom-from-Distractibility factor) composed mainly of variance from the Digit Span and Arithmetic subtests (Wechsler, 1991; Roid et al., 1993). Other solutions failed to discover this factor (Sattler, 1992). We found conjoint subtest variation corresponding to the Freedom-from-Distractibility factor during our cluster analysis of the WISC-R standardization sample. Here too, we found similar variation during current development of the WISC-III taxonomy. Consequently, we infer that the FDI may have a role in assessing individuals because its component subtests are likely to deviate together in a given child's subtest profile.

Similarly, a number of WISC-III factor analyses demonstrated directional covariation of the Symbol Search and Coding subtests (Wechsler, 1991; Roid et al., 1993; Sattler, 1992). The current taxonomy comports rather convincingly with these findings and suggests reciprocal variation among subtests comprising the PSI.

Scientific Benefits

We have argued that our understanding of children's ability patterns has been hampered by an overreliance on R methodology. This chapter addressed the problem by applying Q methodology to isolate the nine *most common* (or core) subtest profiles for the WISC-III standardization sample. The normative taxonomy makes possible at least two kinds of scientific inquiry. First, given the set of most representative subtest profiles in the child population, we can reassess and extend our knowledge of how natural variation in child ability relates to such external phenomena as demography and environment. We have attempted to accomplish this with theoretically interesting characteristics of children comprising the WISC-III standardization sample.

Second, the normative taxonomy allows us to test the validity of WISC-III subtests believed to be atypical or clinically relevant. These methods, which we refer to as typological testing, are superior to conventional methods for analyzing subtest scores and they lay the groundwork for overcoming much of the surmise surrounding complex interrelationships among subtest scores. Moreover, for the first time, the taxonomy allows claims for the discovery of unusual subtest profiles to be evaluated against a viable, *multivariate* null hypothesis that the pattern is actually commonplace in the child population.

Methods of Subtest Comparison

Several strategies can be used to assess claims for whether a given profile is uncommon. However, we recommend two methods that have been useful in our own work. A profile is deemed uncommon in both methods when it is shown that a child's score pattern probably is *not* a member of a core type.

The first method is mathematically more accurate, but it also is more complex to calculate. Therefore, the first method may be more applicable to research than clinical practice. Each of the 9 core types is represented by its average (prototypical) score profile within the WISC-III standardization sample. Likelihood of core typal membership is determined by the $r_p(k)$ statistic (Tatsuoka & Lohnes, 1988, pp. 377), where a separate $r_p(k)$ value reflects both level and shape similar to each core type.[4] A value $> .16$ suggests reasonable similarity to a core type. If *all* nine $r_p(k)$ values for a profile are $< .16$, the null hypothesis may be rejected and the profile regarded as being appreciably distinct. Alternatively, the null hypothesis cannot be rejected and it must be concluded that the profile thought to be unusual actually represents a common or natural variation of normal intellectual abilities.

Case Example Using the Second Method

A somewhat less precise but more practical method is based on generalized distance theory (D^2) (Osgood & Suci, 1952). This second method is the one recommended for "everyday" decision making. It begins by comparing a child's profile to the *three* core types closest to his or her general ability level.[5] If the sum of the squared differences for a child's profile is > 120 for *each comparison*, the profile may be interpreted as being uncommon. By contrast, if any of the sums is < 120, the profile cannot be considered uncommon.

Directions for the practical everyday profiling procedure have been incorporated onto a convenient worksheet (see Appendix A). The following case example demonstrates the everyday method. A child, "Katie," obtained a WISC-III FSIQ of 100. The typological worksheet was used to compare her WISC-III scores to the core types (Table 19.6). Scanning down the far right-hand column, the examiner located the FSIQ closest to the one obtained by Katie. The best match occurred with profile type 5 (FSIQ = 99). Scores for the 12 corresponding WISC-III subtests were entered onto the worksheet at step 1. Next, Katie's WISC-III subtest standard scores were entered at step 2. The examiner then subtracted 12 times, once for each subtest comparison (step 3). The difference scores were squared (step 4) and added (step 5) to yield a total difference score of 104. The psychologist observed that the comparison fit a core type (i.e., a total difference < 120) and concluded that the profile was common. (If the first comparison had been found to be a poor match [i.e., show a total difference > 120], a second comparison [step 6], and maybe even a third comparison [step 7], would have occurred. A profile is deemed unusual only when *all three* comparisons show a total difference > 120 [step 8].)

The typological comparisons indicate that Katie's subtest pattern actually represents a normal variation of intellectual abilities. Interestingly, her profile shows several univariate subtest differences that are statistically significant and an infrequent univariate base rate (i.e., highest subtest score of 17, lowest subtest of 4 = 11, which then converts to a 3% base rate according to WISC-III manual, Table B.6, p. 266). Thus, the case example is informative because it demonstrates how common and ordinary variation can be misinterpreted as being diagnostically relevant when clinicians fail to account for nonlinear, *multivariate* aspects of a subtest profile.

Criteria for Unusual Profiles

Readers of our previous taxonomic studies have sometimes come to believe that we discovered a set of absolute criteria for identifying unusual subtest patterns. Actually, the WISC-III criteria are

TABLE 19.6. Case Study Number Two for Everyday Method to WISC-III Profile Analysis

Profile type number	Mean subtest score												
	PC	IN	CD	SM	PA	AR	BD	VO	OA	CM	SS	DS	FSIQ
1	13	14	13	14	13	14	15	14	14	13	13	13	126
2	13	13	10	13	11	12	12	13	12	13	10	11	114
3	11	11	14	11	12	11	11	11	11	11	13	11	109
4	10	11	9	11	11	10	10	11	9	11	10	8	102
5	10	10	9	10	8	11	10	10	9	10	9	13	99
6	11	9	7	8	9	8	10	8	11	8	8	8	92
7	9	8	12	8	9	8	9	8	9	8	11	9	91
8	7	9	8	8	8	8	6	9	6	9	7	9	86
9	6	5	7	5	6	6	5	5	6	5	6	7	74

Step 1. Enter standard scores for profile type whose FSIQ is nearest to child's FSIQ.

  10 10 9 10 8 11 10 10 9 10 9 13

Step 2. Enter child's standard scores.

  17 10 4 11 12 8 9 10 10 9 9 12

Step 3. Subtract to get 12 difference scores.

  −7 0 5 −1 −4 3 1 0 −1 1 0 1

Step 4. Square each of the 12 difference scores.

  49 0 25 1 16 9 1 0 1 1 0 1

Step 5. Sum the squared difference scores to get total = __104__.

Step 6. Repeat Steps 1 through 5 for the profile type whose FSIQ is *second nearest* to the child's FSIQ.

  Enter standard scores for profile type whose FSIQ is second nearest to child's FSIQ.

  — — — — — — — — — — — —

  Enter child's standard scores.

  — — — — — — — — — — — —

  Subtract to get 12 difference scores.

  — — — — — — — — — — — —

  Square each of the 12 difference scores.

  — — — — — — — — — — — —

  Sum the squared difference scores to get total = _____.

Step 7. Repeat Steps 1 through 5 for the profile type whose FSIQ is *third nearest* to the child's FSIQ.

  Enter standard scores for profile type whose FSIQ is third nearest to child's FSIQ.

  — — — — — — — — — — — —

  Enter child's standard scores.

  — — — — — — — — — — — —

  Subtract to get 12 difference scores.

  — — — — — — — — — — — —

  Square each of the 12 difference scores.

  — — — — — — — — — — — —

  Sum the squared difference scores to get total = _____.

Step 8. Determine whether profile is unusual.

Note. Copyright © 1995 by The Psychological Corporation. Reproduced by permission.

relative. They were obtained by first calculating dispersions for the $r_p(k)$ and D^2 statistics in the WISC-III standardization sample. The recommended critical values were then established according to properties associated with the dispersions. Table 19.7 presents a select accounting of critical values by method ($r_p(k)$ and D^2). The column labeled "Population percentage" makes clear that it is possible to adjust critical values so that a greater, or lesser, number of children possess unusual subtest profiles. However, it would be a mistake to conclude that the values are all equally viable.

The most appropriate critical values for the WISC-III are those associated with a prevalence of 5.0%. We enumerate two sources of support for this criterion. First, most assessment specialists would agree that a prevalence of 5.0% is sufficiently rare to be considered uncommon. Second, and perhaps more important, we developed computer programs to calculate $r_p(k)$ and D^2. The programs were used to return children from the WISC-III standardization sample to the core types. The new placements then were compared to children's original placements within the nine core types. Matches were nearly 100% when the lowest of each child's nine $r_p(k)$ values was $> .16$, but decreased when $r_p(k)$ was $< .16$. This second line of support is data analytic. It reveals children whose $r_p(k)$ values are $< .16$ bear little resemblance to the nine core types. Thus, empirical as well as heuristic considerations point to applying critical values associated with a prevalence of 5.0%.

CONCLUSION

Psychologists might naturally assume that we favor subtest analysis, given all the information we have presented here on the practical and scientific benefits of comparing WISC-III subtest scores to the core profile taxonomy. We are *not* currently in favor of subtest analysis and have said so elsewhere (cf. McDermott et al., 1990). Relatedly, we have often been asked what clinicians should do when presented with an unusual subtest profile identified by comparisons to the core profile taxonomy. Our recommendation is that the profile's consequential validity should be evaluated by examining relevant research studies to find evidentiary support for the profile's diagnostic and/or remedial utility. Perusal of the literature shows many testimonials and heuristic justifications; however, there is little to no empirical basis for interpreting hypotheses generated from subtest scores.

We and others have used empirical methodologies, including comparisons of theoretically and clinically interesting sets of subtest scores to core profiles for the WISC-R and K-ABC. So far, the evidence strongly recommends against the use of subtest analysis (Glutting et al., 1992; McDermott et al., 1992; Watkins & Kush, 1994). However, the utility of subtest scores is an empirical matter open

TABLE 19.7. Critical Values by Method for Identifying Percentages Who Fail to Fit a Core Profile Type

	Critical values	
Population percentage	$r_p(k)$	Generalized distance
1.0	$\leq .03$	> 157
2.0	$\leq .07$	> 141
3.0	$\leq .11$	> 132
5.0	$\leq .16$	> 120
7.0	$\leq .19$	≥ 112
10.0	$\leq .23$	≥ 103

Note. $r_p(k)$ values are rounded to the second decimal place for convenient presentation.
Copyright © 1995 by The Psychological Corporation. Reproduced by permission.

to further investigation, and, as shown here, it is one that the core subtest taxonomy will help to answer by providing a multivariate nonlinear methodology that is superior to univarite and multivariate linear methodologies for identifying unusual subtest profiles.

In light of the above, psychologists may question why they should compare subtest scores to the WISC-III taxonomy. We believe psychologists should refrain from interpreting subtest scores until substantial data-analytic evidence is offered on their behalf. On the other hand, we are compelled to reiterate an important point made during one of our previous studies (Glutting et al., 1992); namely, that psychologists who elect to differentially interpret subtest scores, and who do so without comparing them to the core subtest taxonomy, run a serious risk of mistaking common and ordinary phenomena as being rare, noteworthy, and possibly diagnostic. Such practice can only convolute decision making with the WISC-III and it is unlikely to help children.

NOTES

1. Salvia and Good (1982) present a univariate method of comparison that controls for intercorrelations among subtest scores. Nonetheless, the more popular procedure is to use Davis's (1959) formula for examining statistical significance levels. The formula does not control for intercorrelations and Davis's method is incorporated in such widely used comparison tables as found in the WISC-III manual (1991, p. 264), Sattler's (1988, p. 815) textbook on intelligence testing, as well as, other sources.

2. We gratefully acknowledge The Psychological Corporation, and in particular Aurellio Prifitera, for allowing us access to the WISC-III standardization data.

3. In our previous clustering of the WISC-R, K-ABC, and MSCA, we specified a fifth criterion dictated that the resultant taxonomy show reasonable *stability* across short time intervals. Unfortunately, it was not possible to assess profile stability for the WISC-III taxonomy. The Psychological Corporation was unable to locate archival data for the WISC-III test–retest sample at the time of our study. Therefore, we will publish stability analyses when the data is retrieved and made available to us.

4. Copies of computer programs used to calculate $r_p(k)$ and D^2 may be obtained from the Psychological Corporation. Both operate within the Statistical Package for the Social Sciences and can be applied to any sample. The programs read subtest standard scores from a data file, match children to the core types, and print either $r_p(k)$ (or generalized distance D^2) values for each child (one for each of the nine core types). The programs also identify the core type to which each child shows the best match. They then print the sample mean and standard deviation for $r_p(k)$ (or D^2) values corresponding to the best match. Furthermore, straightforward "select if(s)" can be incorporated into the program to identify subjects who fail to fit the core types.

5. Occasionally, it is necessary to make four, or even five, comparisons to the core profile taxonomy. Such a situation is likely to occur when (1) a child's subtest pattern is near types 4 and 5 or 6 and 7, and (2) when one of these types is the last of the three contrasts.

REFERENCES

Aldenderfer, M. S., & Blashfield, R. K. (1984). *Cluster analysis*. Beverly Hills, CA: Sage.

Anastasi, A. (1988). *Psychological testing* (6th ed.). New York: Macmillan.

Anderberg, M. (1973). *Cluster analysis for applications*. New York: Academic Press.

Bannatyne, A. (1974). Diagnosis: A note on recategorization of WISC scaled scores. *Journal of Learning Disabilities, 7,* 272–274.

Bayne, R., Beauchamp, J., Begovich, C., & Kane, V. E. (1980). Monte Carlo comparisons of selected clustering procedures. *Pattern Recognition, 12,* 51–62.

Blashfield, R. K., & Aldenderfer, M. S. (1988). The methods and problems of cluster analysis. In J. R. Nesselroade & R. B. Cattell (Eds.), *Handbook of multivariate experimental psychology* (2nd ed., pp. 447–473). New York: Plenum Press.

Breckenridge, J. N. (1989). Replicating cluster analysis: Method, consistency, and validity. *Multivariate Behavioral Research, 24,* 147–161.

Brody, N. (1985). The validity of tests of intelligence. In B. Wolman (Ed.), *Handbook of intelligence* (pp. 353–389). New York: Wiley.

Cahan, S. (1986). Significance testing of subtest score differences: The rules of the game. *Journal of Psychoeducational Assessment, 4,* 273–280.

Carver, R. P. (1978). The case against statistical significance testing. *Harvard Educational Review, 48,* 378–399.

Cattell, R. B. (1949). r_p and other coefficients of pattern similarity. *Psychometrika, 14,* 279–298.

Cattell, R. B., Coulter, M. A., & Tsujioka, B. (1966). The taxonomic recognition of types and functional emergents. In R. B. Cattell (Ed.), *Handbook of multivariate experimental psychology* (pp. 288–329). Chicago: Rand McNally.

Clemans, W. V. (1965). An analytical and empirical examination of some properties of ipsative measures. *Psychometric Monographs* (No. 14).

Cormack, R. M. (1971). A review of classification. *Journal of the Royal Statistical Society* (Series A), *134,* 321–367.

Cronbach, L. J., & Gleser, G. C. (1953). Assessing profile similarity. *Psychological Bulletin, 50,* 456–473.

Davis, F. B. (1959). Interpretation of differences among averages and individual test scores. *Journal of International Psychology, 50,* 162–170.

Edelbrock, C. (1979). Comparing the accuracy of hierarchical clustering algorithms: The problem of classifying everybody. *Multivariate Behavioral Research, 14,* 367–384.

Everitt, B. S. (1979). Unresolved problems in cluster analysis. *Biometrics, 35,* 169–181.

Ferguson, G. A. (1981). *Statistical analysis in psychology and education* (5th ed.). New York: McGraw-Hill.

Glasser, A. J., & Zimmerman, I. L. (1967). *Clinical interpretation of the Wechsler Intelligence Scale for Children (WISC).* New York: Grune & Stratton.

Glutting, J. J., & McDermott, P. A. (1990a). Patterns and prevalence of core profile types in the WPPSI standardization sample. *School Psychology Review, 19,* 471–491.

Glutting, J. J., & McDermott, P. A. (1990b). Score structures and applications of core profile types in the McCarthy Scales Standardization Sample. *Journal of Special Education, 24,* 212–233.

Glutting, J. J., McDermott, P. A., Prifitera, A., & McGrath, E. A. (1994). Core profile types for the WISC-III and WIAT: Development and their application in identifying multivariate IQ-achievement discrepancies. *School Psychology Review, 23,* 619–639.

Glutting, J. J., McGrath, E. A., Kamphaus, R. W., & McDermott, P. A. (1992). Taxonomy and validity of subtest profiles on the Kaufman Assessment Battery for Children. *Journal of Special Education, 26,* 85–115.

Guilford, J. P. (1967). *The nature of human intelligence.* New York: McGraw-Hill.

Hicks, L. E. (1970). Some properties of ipsative, normative, and forced normative measures. *Psychological Bulletin, 74,* 167–184.

Horn, J. (1988). Thinking about human abilities. In J. R. Nesselroade & R. B. Cattell (Eds.), *Handbook of multivariate experimental psychology* (2nd ed., pp. 645–685). New York: Plenum Press.

Horst, P. (1941). The prediction of personal adjustment. *Social Science Research Council Bulletin* (No. 48).

Kail, R. (1991). Developmental changes in speed of processing during childhood and adolescence. *Psychological Bulletin, 109,* 490–501.

Kamphaus, R. W. (1993). *Clinical assessment of children's intelligence.* Boston: Allyn and Bacon.

Kaufman, A. S. (1975). Factor analysis of the WISC-R at 11 age levels between 6½ and 16½ years. *Journal of Consulting and Clinical Psychology, 43,* 135–147.

Kaufman, A. S. (1979). *Intelligent testing with the WISC-R.* New York: Wiley.

Kaufman, A. S. (1994). *Intelligent testing with the WISC-III.* New York: Wiley.

Kaufman, A. S., & Kaufman, N. L. (1983). *Kaufman Assessment Battery for Children.* Circle Pines, MN: American Guidance Service.

Keppel, G. (1973). *Design and analysis: A researcher's handbook.* Englewood Cliffs, NJ: Prentice-Hall.

Kroonenberg, P. M., & ten Berge, J. M. F. (1987). Cross-validation of the WISC-R factorial structure using three-mode principal components analysis and perfect congruence analysis. *Applied Psychological Measurement, 11,* 195–210.

Macmann, G. M., & Barnett, D. W. (1994). Structural analysis of correlated factors: Lessons from the verbal-performance dichotomy of the Wechsler scales. *School Psychology Quarterly, 9,* 161–197.

McCarthy, D. (1972). *McCarthy Scales of Children's Abilities.* New York: Psychological Corporation.

McDermott, P. A., Fantuzzo, J. W., & Glutting, J. J. (1990). Just say no to subtest analysis: A critique on Wechsler theory and practice. *Journal of Psychoeducational Assessment, 8,* 290–302.

McDermott, P. A., Fantuzzo, J. W., Glutting, J. J., Watkins, M. W., & Baggaley, A. R. (1992). Illusions of meaning in the ipsative assessment of children's abilities. *Journal of Special Education, 25,* 504–526.

McDermott, P. A., Glutting, J. J., Jones, J. N., & Noonan, J. V. (1989). Typology and prevailing composition of core profiles in the WAIS-R standardization sample. *Psychological Assessment: A Journal of Consulting and Clinical Psychology, 1,* 118–125.

McDermott, P. A., Glutting, J. J., Jones, J. N., Watkins, M. W., & Kush, J. (1989). Identification and membership of core profile types in the WISC-R national standardization sample. *Psychological Assessment: A Journal of Consulting and Clinical Psychology, 1,* 292–299.

McDermott, P. A., & Watkins, M. W. (1985). *McDermott Multidimensional Assessment of Children.* New York: Psychological Corporation.

Milligan, G. W. (1980). An examination of the effect of six types of error perturbation on fifteen clustering algorithms. *Psychometrika, 45,* 325–342.

Milligan, G. W., & Cooper, M. C. (1987). Methodology review: Clustering methods. *Applied Psychological Measurement, 11,* 329–354.

Milligan, G. W., & Sokal, L. M. (1980). A two-stage clustering algorithm with robust recovery characteristics. *Educational and Psychological Measurement, 40,* 755–759.

Mojena, R. (1977). Hierarchical grouping methods and stopping rules: An evaluation. *Computer Journal, 20,* 359–363.

Mosel, J. N., & Roberts, J. B. (1954). The comparability of measures of profile similarity: An empirical study. *Journal of Consulting Psychology, 18,* 61–66.

Osgood, C. E., & Suci, G. J. (1952). A measure of relation determined by both mean differences and profile information. *Psychological Bulletin, 49,* 251–262.

Overall, J. E., & Klett, C. J. (1972). *Applied multivariate analysis.* New York: McGraw-Hill.

Roid, G. H., Prifitera, A., & Weiss, L. G. (1993). Replication of the WISC-III factor structure in an independent sample. In B. A. Bracken & R. S. McCallum (Eds.), *Journal of Psychoeducational Assessment* [Monograph Series, Advances in Psychoeducational Assessment: Wechsler Intelligence Scale for Children–Third Edition], 6–210. Germantown, TN: Psychoeducational Corporation.

Salvia, J., & Good, R. (1982). Significant discrepancies in the classification of pupils: Differentiating the concept. In J. T. Neisworth (Ed.), *Assessment in special edcuation* (pp. 77–82). Rockville, MD: Aspen.

Sattler, J. M. (1988). *Assessment of children* (3rd ed.). San Diego, CA: Author.

Sattler, J. M. (1992). *Assessment of children: WISC-III and WPPSI-R supplement.* San Diego, CA: Author.

Scheibler, D., & Schneider, W. (1985). Monte Carlo tests of the accuracy of cluster analysis algorithms—A comparison of hierarchical and nonhierarchical methods. *Multivariate Behavioral Research, 20,* 283–304.

Selz, M., & Reitan, R. M. (1979). Rules for neuropsychological diagnosis: Classification of brain function in older children. *Journal of Consulting and Clinical Psychology, 47,* 258–264.

Sneath, P., & Sokal, R. (1973). *Numerical taxonomy.* San Francisco: Freeman.

Stevens, J. (1986). *Applied multivariate statistics for the social sciences.* Hillsdale, NJ: Erlbaum.

Tatsuoka, M. M., & Lohnes, P. R. (1988). *Multivariate analysis* (2nd ed.). New York: Macmillan.

Thompson, B. (1991). Methods, plainly speaking: A primer on the logic and use of canonical correlation analysis. *Measurement and Evaluation in Counseling and Development, 24,* 80–95.

Tryon, R. C., & Bailey, D. E. (1970). *Cluster analysis.* New York: McGraw-Hill.

Ward, J. H., Jr. (1963). Hierarchical grouping to optimize an objective function. *American Statistical Association Journal, 58,* 236–244.

Watkins, M. W., & Kush, J. (1994). WISC-R subtest analysis: The right way, the wrong way, or no way? *School Psychology Review, 23,* 640–651.

Wechsler, D. (1949). *Wechsler Intelligence Scale for Children.* San Antonio, TX: Psychological Corporation.

Wechsler, D. (1958). *The measurement and appraisal of adult intelligence* (4th ed.). Baltimore: Williams & Wilkins.

Wechsler, D. (1967). *Wechsler Preschool and Primary Scale of Intelligence.* San Antonio, TX: Psychological Corporation.

Wechsler, D. (1981). *Wechsler Adult Intelligence Scale—Revised.* San Antonio, TX: Psychological Corporation.

Wechsler, D. (1991). *Wechsler Intelligence Scale for Children—Third edition: Manual.* San Antonio, TX: Psychological Corporation.

Wechsler, D., & Jaros, B. (1965). Schizophrenic patterns on the WISC. *Journal of Clincal Psychology, 21,* 288–291.

Wishart, D. (1982). *CLUSTAN users manual: Supplement* (3rd ed). Edinburgh, Scotland: Program Library Unit, Edinburgh University.

Witkin, H. A., Dyk, R. B., Faterson, H. G., Goodenough, D. R., & Karp, S. A. (1962). *Psychological differentiation.* New York: Wiley.

CHAPTER 20

Using Confirmatory Factor Analysis to Aid in Understanding the Constructs Measured by Intelligence Tests

TIMOTHY Z. KEITH

FACTOR ANALYSIS IS INEXORABLY LINKED with the development of intelligence theory and intelligence tests. Early intelligence theories and factor-analytic methods were developed in tandem, and the connection continues to this day. Carroll's (1993; Chapter 7, this volume) recent three-stratum theory of intelligence was developed, in part, through the use of exploratory factor analysis.

Until recently, the term "factor analysis" meant what we now call exploratory factor analysis (EFA). In its simplest form, EFA involves making a series of decisions about the method of factor extraction to use, the number of factors to retain, and the method of rotation to use. For researchers who do not wish to make these decisions, most computer programs will default to a common method if none is specified. The output from the analysis consists of factor loadings of each variable on each factor and, if an oblique rotation was used, correlations among the factors. The researcher then assigns names to the factors based on the loadings of the variables on the factors, along with relevant theory and previous research.

Of course, in the hands of an expert, EFA can be much more complex and elegant than the simple approach just described. A variety of extraction methods can be used, depending on the questions of interest; complex decision rules and expert judgment can be used to determine how many factors should be extracted; a variety of graphical and mathematical methods can be used to rotate the extracted factors to simple structure. For example, Carroll (1993; Chapter 3, this volume) outlines an approach to exploratory analysis that provides an elegant combination of consistency and judgment. Whether simple or complex, EFA involves judgment on the part of the researcher: judgment concerning the decisions required and judgment concerning the meaning of the extracted factors. It is this aspect of EFA that can be disconcerting to those wanting yes/no answers to questions, but it is also this requirement for thought that makes the approach so alluring and so powerful.

In its simplest form, confirmatory factor analysis (CFA) requires the researcher to decide, in advance, the nature of the factor structure underlying the data. He or she must specify the number of factors and the variables that load on each factor. So, for example, the researcher may specify that variable 1 loads on factor 1 but not on factor 2. The researcher may specify that factors are correlated or uncorrelated. The results of the analysis provide "fit statistics," which provide feedback as to the adequacy of the specified factor structure, or the degree to which the "model" (factor structure) "fits" (reproduces the covariances among) the data. In CFA, in other words, the researcher tests the adequacy of a particular factor structure by restricting the factor solution (thus the method is sometimes called restricted factor analysis; Allen & Thorndike, 1995) and seeing whether that restricted solution is consistent with the data. In contrast, in EFA, the researcher examines and imparts meaning to the best factor structure (given the decision rules used).

CFA is often described as a more theory-driven approach than EFA. This statement probably involves some overstatement. It is possible, for example, to use EFA in a theory-driven, hypothesis-testing manner (cf. Thorndike, 1990), just as it is possible to use CFA in a very exploratory, theory-absent manner. Nevertheless, the simple fact that CFA requires the specification of a model—and thus knowledge about the probable structure of the characteristic being measured—means that some sort of theory, formal or informal, strong or weak, is required. EFA can easily be conducted in the absence of theory, although theoretically driven analyses are almost invariably more complete and informative than atheoretical ones. EFA can be a valuable tool for *developing* theory, whereas CFA may be better suited for *testing* existing theory.

This chapter demonstrates the use of CFA, with particular attention to using CFA to understand the constructs measured by modern intelligence tests. It begins with a "simple" CFA model, and gradually moves to CFA methods that provide a more complete evaluation of the theories underlying tests (e.g., hierarchical analysis, the comparison of alternative models and multisample analyses). It demonstrates how the method can be used to test formal theories as well. The emphasis is on the use of CFA to *test hypotheses* about *theories*.

There are a number of computer programs available that conduct CFA. These programs generally are designed to conduct latent variable structural equation modeling (SEM); SEM includes and subsumes CFA (the "measurement model" in the jargon of SEM), and thus SEM programs also conduct CFA. The oldest and most widely know program is LISREL (LInear Structural RELations; Jöreskog & Sörbom, 1989), available on both mainframes and personal computers. Other common programs include EQS (Bentler & Wu, 1993) and CALIS (Covariance Analysis and LInear Structural equations; Hartmann, 1995). Most of the analyses presented in this chapter were conducted using Amos (Analysis of MOment Structures; Arbuckle, 1992, 1995), although a few were conducted using LISREL.

A SAMPLE CONFIRMATORY ANALYSIS

The Kaufman Adult and Adolescent Intelligence Test (KAIT) is a new measure of cognitive abilities for adolescents and adults ages 11 through adulthood (Kaufman & Kaufman, 1993). According to the manual, the KAIT is designed to measure intelligence according to the Horn–Cattell theory of intelligence, although only two of the Horn–Cattell factors (fluid and crystallized intelligence) are included in the KAIT model. In addition, the KAIT is designed to measure delayed recall, or a subject's memory for material learned earlier in the test. Thus, the KAIT includes 10 subtests designed to measure three abilities: Fluid Intelligence (Gf), Crystallized Intelligence (Gc), and Delayed Recall.

Figure 20.1 shows this "theory" of the KAIT in figural form. The 10 subtests are shown in rectangles, and the abilities that are designed to measure are enclosed in ellipses. Arrows or paths point from the abilities to the subtests in recognition of the implicit assumption that it is the abilities residing within the person that cause him or her to score a certain way on subtest. So, for example,

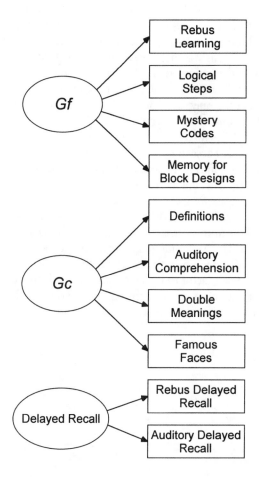

FIGURE 20.1. Theoretical structure of the KAIT.

subjects' levels of fluid intelligence are the primary determinant of their scores on the Mystery Codes subtest.

Figure 20.1 is the beginning of a confirmatory factor model as well; a more complete CFA model is shown in Figure 20.2.[1] In the jargon of CFA, the variables enclosed in rectangles (the subtests) are the *measured* variables, whereas the variables enclosed in ellipses (e.g., the KAIT abilities) are *unmeasured* variables, or *latent* variables, or *factors*. The paths from latent to measured variables represent the factor loadings. Notice that not all possible paths are drawn. Theoretically, the lack of a path from, say, Gf to Double Meanings means that the test authors believe Double Meanings does not measure Fluid Intelligence, or that a person's level of Fluid Intelligence does not affect his or her scores on the Double Meanings subtest. Rather, scores on Double Meanings are a reflection of Crystallized Intelligence, as indicated by the path drawn from Gc to Double Meanings. At a practical level, the path from Gc to Double Meanings means that the factor loading will be estimated in the analysis, and the lack of the path from Gf to Double Meanings means that the factor loading of Double Meanings on Gf will be constrained to zero.

Figure 20.2 includes information beyond that included in Figure 20.1. The curved, two-headed arrows between factors represent correlations. Although the KAIT manual does not say so explicitly, it is reasonable to expect that the abilities measured by the KAIT are not independent of (uncorrelated with) one another. Modern intelligence theories recognize this relation among factors (e.g., Carroll, 1993; Chapters 2 & 3, this volume), and CFAs of intelligence tests should generally specify correlated factors (unless the theory underlying the tests maintains that the factors are independent). The figure also includes small ellipses, labeled u1 through u10, with paths drawn to each of the subtests. The factors are not the only cause of a person's scores on the subtest; each subtest is also partially the result of other influences that are unique to each subtest, generally called unique or specific variances (cf. Keith & Reynolds, 1990). In addition, each subtest is also affected by errors of measurement (error variance). These unique and error variances, combined, are represented by u1 through u10; they are enclosed in ellipses because they are unmeasured. (These unique and error variances will hereafter be termed "unique variances.")

Several of the paths in Figure 20.2 have the value 1 beside them. The measured variables in the model have a defined scale, and that scale is whatever scale was used for each subtest (e.g., a raw score from 0 to 23). But none of the unmeasured variables (neither the factors nor the unique variances) has a predetermined scale. The 1's beside paths serve the purpose of setting the scales of the unmeasured variables by setting the path to 1.0. The path of 1.0 from Gf to Rebus Learning, for example, sets the scale of the Gf factor to be the same as the scale for Rebus Learning. Thus each factor includes one factor loading of 1.0, and the paths from each of the unique variances to the measured variables are set to 1.0 (to set the scale to be the same as the corresponding measured

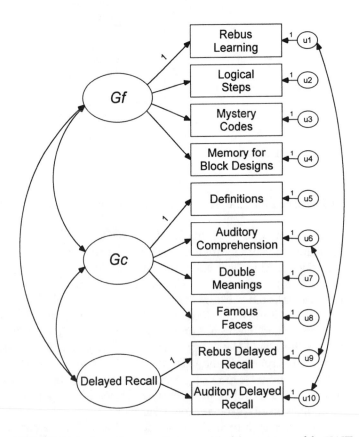

FIGURE 20.2. A confirmatory factor model of the structure of the KAIT.

variable). The use of 1.0 is arbitrary—any value could be used—and once all the parameters of the model are estimated using these constraints (called the unstandardized or metric solution), all values are restandardized (the standardized solution).

Finally, the model in Figure 20.2 includes a less common characteristic: correlations among the unique variances, as represented by the curved lines connecting several of the unique variances (e.g., u1 and u9). The Rebus Delayed Recall (RDR) test on the KAIT requires subjects to remember rebuses learned earlier in the test for the Rebus Learning (RL) subtest. Because RDR builds on RL, it seems likely that the unique variances affecting RDR will be related to those affecting RL. Similarly, the *error* variances affecting RDR may well be related to those affecting RL. These possibilities are built into the CFA model by specifying that the unique variances of the RDR and RL subtests are allowed to correlate.

The KAIT standardization data were used to estimate the model. The KAIT manual includes correlation matrices of subtests for the KAIT at each age level, along with an average correlation matrix for the entire sample (Kaufman & Kaufman, 1993, p. 136). The matrix for the entire standardization sample was used as input for the Amos computer program (Arbuckle, 1995). The average sample size ($N = 143$) for the different age groups was used as the sample size.

The results of the analysis are shown in Figure 20.3. First, notice the fit statistics for the model to the left of the figure. Because not all possible parameters are estimated, a CFA generally estimates an "overidentified" model (e.g., the path from Gf to Definitions was set to zero, as were many other paths). In an overidentified model, the number of parameters estimated is less than the number of

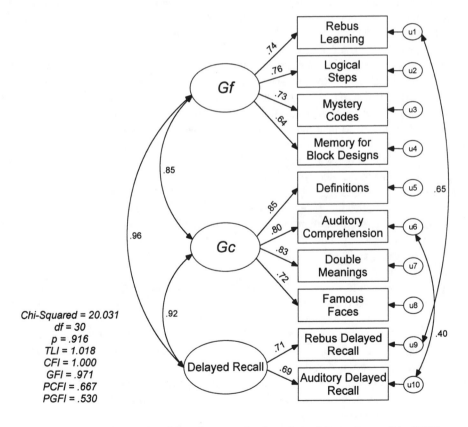

FIGURE 20.3. Results of a confirmatory factor analysis of the structure of the KAIT.

covariances used in estimation. As a result, the model has degrees of freedom. It is also possible to conduct the analysis in reverse: to estimate the correlation or covariance matrix from the numbers shown in the model. But because the model is overidentified, there may be several ways to estimate each covariance and the estimates of the covariances will not be identical to the covariance matrix used to estimate the model in the first place (see Kenny, 1979, for a discussion of overidentification; Chapters 3 & 9, this volume). The fit statistics shown in the figure are all measures of the degree to which the matrix *implied* by the model differs from the *actual* matrix.

Six fit statistics are shown in the figure, although there are dozens to choose from. Chi-squared (χ^2) is the most commonly reported fit statistic. It has the advantage of allowing a statistical test of the fit of the model; it can be used with the degrees of freedom to determine the probability that the model is correct. Thus a large χ^2 in comparison to the df (and a small probability, e.g., $< .05$) suggests that the actual and implied covariance matrices are significantly different, that the model provides a poor fit to the data, or that the model could not have produced the data. The model, therefore, is not a good representation of the "true" factor structure. In contrast, a small χ^2 in comparison to the df is insignificant ($p > .05$) and suggests that the model does provide a reasonable explanation of the data.

Although χ^2 fits well within the tradition of significance testing in psychology, it also has well-known problems as does the tradition of either/or significance testing itself (cf. Cohen, 1994). In particular, it is directly related to sample size, so that with large samples, virtually all χ^2s will be significant, even when the model is only trivially incorrect (see Bentler & Bonett, 1980; Tanaka, 1993, among others, for further discussion). With small samples, even inadequate models may have a good fit, as judged by χ^2. For this and other reasons, other fit statistics have been developed; the ones listed for this analysis were chosen because they highlight different dimensions of fit (Tanaka, 1993). The Tucker–Lewis Index (TLI) and the comparative fit index (CFI) both compare the fit of the model with that of a "null" model, one in which the measured variables are assumed to be unrelated; for both, values approaching 1.0 suggest a good fit. The TLI appears to be relatively unrelated to sample size, whereas the CFI is designed to estimate the fit in the population. The goodness of fit index (GFI) compares the model with a perfectly fitting (just-identified) model, which would have a value of 1.0. Thus, a GFI close to 1.0 also suggests a good fit. Also shown are the parsimony CFI (PCFI) and the parsimony GFI (PGFI), both of which adjust the values from which they were derived (CFI or GFI) by the degrees of freedom to take into account the complexity of the model and reward more parsimonious models. Like the indexes from which they are derived, larger values (closer to 1.0) are better, but the parsimony indexes are most useful for comparing several competing models. Other fit statistics will be introduced later in the chapter.

Briefly, all the fit statistics suggest that the KAIT model provides an excellent fit to the standardization data. χ^2 was small and insignificant, and the TLI, CFI, and GFI were all large (the PCFI and PGFI, again, are better for comparing competing models). Thus, the "theory" underlying the KAIT appears to fit the KAIT standardization data; the test appears to measure what the authors designed it to measure; and the structure of the KAIT appears valid. The next step, then, is to interpret the substantive results.

The paths from latent to measured variables show the factor loadings. They are all large, and examination of their standard errors and *t* values (shown in the detailed printout, but not included in the figure) shows they are all significant. Likewise, the factor correlations are large and significant, ranging from .96 for the correlation between the latent Delayed Recall and Gf factors to .85 between Gf and Gc. Finally, the correlations among unique variances suggests that there is a substantial correlation between the variance of the RL test that is not accounted for by the Gf factor and the variance of the RDR subtest that is not accounted for by the Delayed Recall factor ($r = .65$). Similarly, the unique and error variances of Auditory Comprehension and Auditory Delayed Recall (ADR) are substantially correlated, as well.

These substantive results are also generally supportive of the validity of the KAIT. One curious finding, however, is the magnitude of the correlation between the Delayed Recall and the Gf and Gc factors (.96 and .92, respectively), which are higher than the correlation between the two more intellectual factors, Gf and Gc (.85). Such a finding could be investigated by comparing this model with alternative models.

HIERARCHICAL CONFIRMATORY FACTOR ANALYSIS

Many modern theories of intelligence recognize an ability that is more general and broader than the specific abilities tested in first-order CFA. This *general* ability is often considered to subsume, affect, or partially cause the more narrow abilities, and is often symbolized as *g*, for general ability or intelligence. For example, Carroll's three-stratum theory of intelligence includes *g* as the most general, highest-order factor (Carroll, 1993). Although conceptually similar to Spearman's *g*, most modern theories assume that *g* is a *hierarchical* ability (cf. Burt, 1949, Vernon 1950). Most modern intelligence *tests* also tacitly recognize such a general, overall ability by summing subtests or subscales into an overall score. Although this general score may go by a variety of names—Full Scale IQ, General Cognitive Ability, or Broad Cognitive Ability—it generally represents an overall, general, summative ability.

If a general ability is recognized in formal theory and through the informal theory of the scoring of intelligence tests, it would also be valuable to test such a construct through CFA. One common approach has been to specify a single-factor model, such as the one shown in Figure 20.4. Such a model suggests that scores on the individual subtests are a product of a general factor and of unique and error variances. Although such an approach is fairly common (cf. Naglieri, Braden, & Gottling, 1993) and mirrors, to some degree, the common practice of isolating a *g* factor in EFA by examining the unrotated first factor in principal components or principal factors analysis, it is also an unsatisfying solution for several reasons. First, *g* is generally recognized as a *hierarchical* factor; a more realistic structure for the tests from Figure 20.4 is shown in Figure 20.5, in which the subtests are explained (in part) by first-order factors, and the first-order factors are, in turn, partially explained by a second-order *g* factor. Although it would be possible to conduct two analyses—one of the first-order factors (such as the previous analysis of the KAIT) and one of the second-order factor (e.g., Figure 20.4), it would be more satisfying to conduct the analysis is one step rather than two.

Second, if Figure 20.5 represents the *true* structure of the abilities measured by the six hypothetical tests, then Figure 20.4 represents an inadequate test of the second-order *g* factor. The presence of first-order factors means that the two verbal tests measure something in common other than general intelligence, the two spatial tests measure something in common other than *g*, and so on. To mirror adequately this structure, it is necessary to add correlated unique variances to Figure 20.4. That is, the second-order factor could be tested by specifying a correlation between u1 and u2, u3 and u4, and u5 and u6, in addition to the paths from *g* to each subtest. To reiterate, Figure 20.4 represents an inadequate, indirect test of a higher-order *g* factor.

There are several ways to test the model shown in Figure 20.5 and the presence of a *g* factor. Gustafsson and Balke (1993) and Carroll (e.g., 1995) load all subtests on both a *g* and more specific factors, with the factors orthogonal or uncorrelated. Such a method—a "nested factors" model (Mulaik & Quartetti, 1994)—is displayed graphically in Figure 20.6. But all CFA programs *can* analyze a hierarchical model such as the one shown in Figure 20.4; I prefer the more direct estimation of a hierarchical model, as shown in Figure 20.4 (see Jensen & Weng, 1993, for a more complete discussion of methods of estimating *g*; Mulaik & Quartetti, 1994, for a comparison of hierarchical and nested models).

Figure 20.7 shows a hierarchical model of the structure of the Differential Ability Scales (DAS;

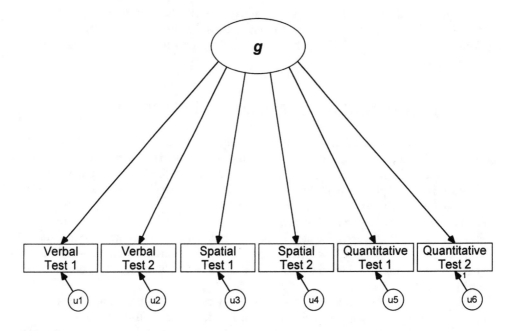

FIGURE 20.4. A general intelligence, or *g*, model of the structure of cognitive abilities. The model assumes that the six tests are reflections of general intelligence only, rather than more specific, shared abilities, such as verbal or spatial ability.

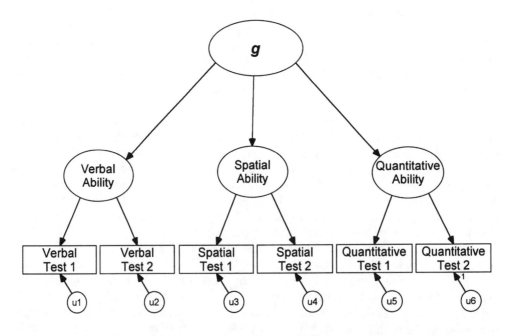

FIGURE 20.5. A hierarchical model of the structure of cognitive abilities. The model assumes that each test is a reflection of narrow, shared abilities (e.g., verbal ability), and that these narrow abilities are, in turn, partially a product of *g*.

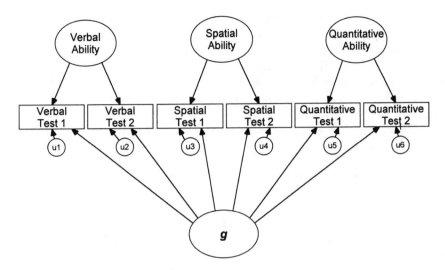

FIGURE 20.6. A nested-factors model. Although such a model may be considered an alternative to the hierarchical model, in that each test is assumed to be a product of both narrow, shared abilities and *g*, the model makes no assumptions about the relation of the narrow abilities to *g*.

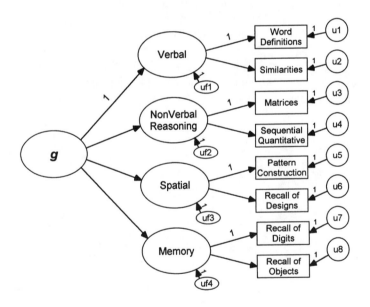

FIGURE 20.7. A hierarchical model of the structure of the DAS.

Elliott, 1990a).[2] In scoring the DAS, the "core" subtests (Word Definitions through Recall of Designs in the Figure) are added together to form Verbal, Nonverbal Reasoning and Spatial scores, and the Verbal, Nonverbal, and Spatial scores added together to form a General Cognitive Ability score. Thus, the core subtests are designed to measure both a *general* ability and more specific abilities. The informal theory underlying the test is clearly hierarchical in nature. Although Recall of Digits and Recall of Objects are not treated in the same manner, they presumably measure Memory skills, which also is affected by general intelligence. Thus, a fourth first-order factor (Memory) is included in the figure. The Speed of Information Processing subtest is not included in the analyses.

The figure is quite similar to the general hierarchical model from Figure 20.5 except for the presence of small ellipses (uf1 through uf4) pointing to the first-order factors. These represent the *unique* variances of each of the first-order factors. Just as the first-order factors are not the only causes of the scores on the subtests, *g* is not the only cause of a person's Verbal or Spatial ability; there is also something unique about Verbal ability as opposed to Spatial ability. This *unique factor* variance is recognized in the model through the presence of the latent variables uf1 through uf4.[3]

The model was estimated using the *averaged* covariance matrix from ages 6–17 from the DAS standardization data (from Keith, 1990). The sample size was set to 200 for the analysis (the average sample size for each age level). The results of the hierarchical CFA of the DAS are shown in Figure 20.8. The fit statistics suggest that the model provides an excellent fit to the data and thus support the structure of the DAS. The first-order factor loadings suggest that the core subtests are all good measures of their corresponding factors, although Recall of Designs may not be as good a measure of Spatial Abilities as is Pattern Construction. Although the loadings of Recall of Digits and Recall of Objects were significant, they were not large and thus do not form a strong Memory factor. This finding thus lends support to the author's decision not to add these two subtests together to create a Memory ability score.

The second-order factor loadings are perhaps even more interesting. In scoring the DAS, the Verbal, Nonverbal Reasoning, and Spatial ability scores are combined to create an overall score. The figure shows that the three corresponding latent factors are indeed strongly affected by *g*, thus supporting the hierarchical structure of the scale. Also of interest, the Nonverbal Reasoning factor had a very high loading, .98, on the second-order *g* factor. In fact, the 95% confidence interval of the standardized factor loading (.72–1.24) includes 1.0, suggesting that the Nonverbal Reasoning factor is indistinguishable from the second-order *g* factor. This finding, in turn, lends support to the claim that the nonverbal scale of the DAS should be considered a measure of Gf (Keith, 1990; McGrew, Chapter 9, this volume), given the evidence that Gf is often quite similar to *g* (e.g., Carroll, 1993; Gustafsson, 1984).

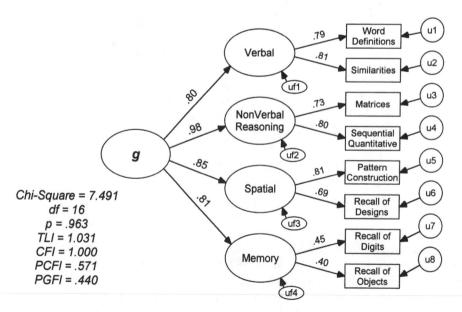

FIGURE 20.8. CFA solution for a hierarchical model of the structure of the DAS.

COMPARING ALTERNATIVE MODELS

The previous two sections have presented the basics of CFA, albeit a fairly sterile approach: the simple rejection of or support for a single model. Such an approach is problematic. The simple fact that a model does or does not fit the data provides only partial support for the validity of a test or theory. A model may fit the data well, but there may be other, competing models that fit the data as well or better. Or, a given model may provide an inadequate fit to the data but be the best model among the alternatives. Formal or informal theory may suggest several possible models to explain the test scores we observe; if all fit the data well, how is one to decide which is the *best* model? What is needed is the ability to compare competing models, or to compare a target model with one or several alternative models. "At best, a given model represents a tentative explanation of the data. The confidence with which one accepts such an explanation depends, in part, on whether other, rival explanations have been tested and found wanting" (Loehlin, 1992, p. 65).

Fortunately, the fit statistics used to evaluate a single model can be used to compare competing models, as well. If two models are nested—if one model can be derived from another by placing additional constraints on the model—the χ^2 for the two models can be compared. The χ^2 for the less constrained model (the model with smaller *df* and smaller χ^2) can be subtracted from the χ^2 for the more constrained model. The χ^2 difference ($\Delta\chi^2$) can then be compared to the change in degrees of freedom (Δdf) to determine whether the relaxation in the model results in a significant decrease in χ^2. If the $\Delta\chi^2$ is not significant, if one model is not significantly better than another, then scientists generally prefer the more parsimonious (more constrained) model. Likewise, some of the other fit statistics may be compared across models, although such comparison is generally a subjective one rather than a test of significance (see Hoyle & Panter, 1995). The parsimony fit indexes (e.g., PGFI and PCFI) may be especially useful for these purposes; they adjust the fit index by the complexity/parsimony of the model, with the higher number suggesting a better fitting, more parsimonious model. Comparisons of the parsimony fit indexes are also useful in that they do not require nested models. Finally, a highly constrained "baseline" model may be used instead of a null model in the calculation of fit indexes such as TLI and CFI. For example, a one-factor *g* model may provide a useful baseline model in CFAs of intelligence tests (Humphreys, 1990). Of course, with these alternative baseline models the resulting values will generally not approach the .90 cutoff often recommended for these fit statistics when null models are used.

Comparing Alternative Models for the KAIT

Figure 20.3 displayed the results of an initial CFA of the KAIT. The model fit the data well, and thus the model seems a good explanation of the KAIT standardization data. Nevertheless, questions concerning the structure, as displayed, are also reasonable. Because, for example, Rebus Delayed Recall asks examinees to recall material first learned in the Rebus Learning test, isn't RDR also a measure of Gf? Similarly, is Auditory Delayed Recall also a measure of Gc in addition to Delayed Recall? And why does the Delayed Recall factor correlate so highly with Gf and Gc? If it is indeed a measure of Delayed Recall, shouldn't it correlate at a lower level with these highly intellectual factors than they do with each other?

Figure 20.9 shows a model that tests the first two of these questions: whether the Delayed Recall subtests also measure Gf and Gc abilities. In addition to allowing RDR to load on the Delayed Recall factor, it was also allowed to load on the Gf factor; ADR loaded on both the Delayed Recall and the Gc factors. Otherwise, the model shown in Figure 20.9 is the same as that shown in Figure 20.3, with one exception: For the model to be properly identified, some sort of additional constraint was required for the Delayed Recall subtests. To allow estimation, the factor loadings for RDR and ADR on Delayed Recall were constrained to be equal.[4]

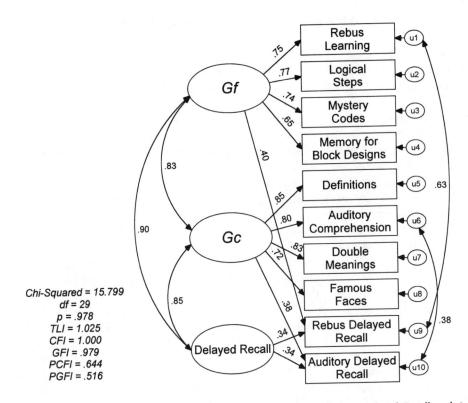

FIGURE 20.9. An alternative model of the structure of the KAIT. Rebus Delayed Recall and Auditory Delayed Recall are assumed to measure Gf and Gc, respectively, in addition to Delayed Recall ability.

TABLE 20.1. Comparison of Various CFA Models of the KAIT

Model (Figure)	$\chi^2(df)$	p	TLI	CFI	GFI	PCFI	PGFI	$\Delta\chi^2(\Delta df)^a$	p
Actual Structure (Fig. 20.3)	20.031(30)	.916	1.018	1.000	.971	.667	.530		
Delayed Recall and Gf-Gc (Fig. 20.9)	15.799(29)	.957	1.025	1.000	.979	.644	.516	4.232(1)	.0397
Gf-Gc (Fig. 20.10)	19.158(32)	.964	1.022	1.000	.975	.711	.567	3.359(3)	.3395
Gf-Gc and Shared Unique (No figure)	18.854(31)	.957	1.021	1.000	.975	.689	.549	.304(1)	.5814

^{a}All comparisons are with the preceding model.

   The results of this analysis are also shown in the figure. Like the earlier model, this variation provides an excellent fit to the averaged standardization data. But does the model provide any better fit than the structure as intended by the authors? The χ^2 for the model was 15.779 for Figure 20.9 versus 20.031 for Figure 20.3. As shown in Table 1, the change in χ^2 was 4.232, which given the change in df ($\Delta df = 1$), is significant ($p < .05$). Thus, specifying that RDR and ADR measure Gf and Gc in addition to Delayed Recall leads to a significant improvement in fit; Figure 20.9 may be a better explanation of the structure of the KAIT than Figure 20.3. The TLI and GFI also improved very slightly, but the model in Figure 20.9 is a less parsimonious explanation of the KAIT structure than is the model in Figure 20.3, and thus the PCFI and PGFI are slightly smaller for Figure 20.9 than for Figure 20.3.

But what about substantive interpretation? With the changes in the model, it appears that RDR is a slightly better measure of Gf than it is of Delayed Recall, although it provides a strong measure of neither ability. Likewise, ADR appears as good, or slightly better, a measure of Gc as it does of Delayed Recall, but appears a strong measure of neither ability. As in Figure 20.3, the Delayed Recall factor correlates with the Gf and Gc factors as highly or more highly than they correlate with each other, suggesting that a more intellectually laden name might be more appropriate (e.g., Glr, or general memory and learning).

Given the small paths from Delayed Recall to the two delayed recall subtests in Figure 20.9, it is reasonable to ask whether the two delayed recall subtests should be considered measures of fluid and crystallized ability only, and not measures of Delayed Recall. The results of the test of such a model are shown in Figure 20.10. This model is more constrained than the model shown in Figure 20.9, so the question of interest now becomes whether these constraints on the model result in a significantly *worse* fit to the data over the model in Figure 20.9.[5]

The fit statistics suggest that the model in Figure 20.10 provides as good a fit to the data as does that in Figure 20.9: The change in chi-squared was insignificant (see Table 20.1); the TLI and GFI decreased slightly, but because Figure 20.10 shows a more parsimonious model, PCFI and PGFI were larger. The substantive interpretation of the model in Figure 20.10 is straightforward. RDR and ADR provide measures of Gf and Gc abilities, respectively, that are almost as strong as the tests intended to measure those abilities.

One final model will be discussed before moving to another topic. The model in Figure 20.10 specifies that the primary reason for any correlation between RDR and ADR is because they assess Gf and Gc abilities, respectively, and Gf and Gc are, in turn, highly correlated ($r = .84$). If the two delayed recall subtests indeed measure anything in common (e.g., delayed recall ability) other than the highly correlated Gf and Gc abilities, the fit of the model should improve if the unique variances of the two tests are allowed to correlate. This change (relaxation) in the model, however, resulted in an insignificant decrease in χ^2 and little change in the other fit statistics (Table 20.1), thus suggesting that the correlation between Gf and Gc (and the correlated unique variance with Rebus Learning and Auditory Comprehension) adequately accounts for the correlation between RDR and ADR.

The model shown in Figure 20.10 can also be compared directly to the one in Figure 20.3. Although the two models appear to fit the data equally well, the model in Figure 20.10 is a more parsimonious explanation of the data. Taken together, these comparisons of models are not definitive, but do suggest that the RDR and ADR subtests of the KAIT should be considered additional measures of the abilities measured by the two primary KAIT scales (Fluid and Crystallized) rather than measures of Memory or Delayed Recall.

TESTING THE SIMILARITY OF FACTORS

CFA is also a useful method for testing the similarity of factors within a test or between two tests. Thus, CFA can be used to test whether two tests designed to measure the same factors (e.g., the Gf factors from the WJ-R and the KAIT) do, in fact, measure statistically indistinguishable factors. By the same token, the method can be used to test whether two tests designed to measure *different* abilities do, in fact, measure distinguishable factors.

What Does the K-ABC Measure?

The Kaufman Assessment Battery for Children (K-ABC; Kaufman & Kaufman, 1983) was designed to provide a more theoretically grounded measure of intelligence than did other tests commonly in use at the time, especially the Wechsler Intelligence Scale for Children—Revised (WISC-R; Wechsler, 1974). Based on the Luria–Das theory of brain functioning, the K-ABC was designed to assess novel problem-solving abilities through its Mental Processing subtests. Those subtests were also designed to assess two different aspects of mental processing: Simultaneous and Successive mental processing. In addition, the K-ABC was designed to assess skills and knowledge gained through schooling and experience through its Achievement subtests.

Although the K-ABC was designed to assess skills and abilities of a substantially different nature than tests such as the WISC-R, many researchers questioned whether the new test measured anything new (e.g., Anastasi, 1985; Page, 1985). In particular, Keith suggested that the Simultaneous Mental Processing Scale measured the same sorts of abilities as the Performance Scale of the WISC-R (Keith, 1985; Keith & Dunbar, 1984; Keith & Novak, 1987). He called those skills Nonverbal Reasoning, although the common name for the WISC-R factor is Perceptual Organization, and a more exact name might be Broad Visual Perception (or Gv) (cf. Carroll, 1993; McGrew, Chapter 9, this volume). In addition, Keith and others argued that the Achievement Scale was more likely a measure of Verbal Reasoning (or Verbal Comprehension) than academic achievement. Thus the question of interest was whether the K-ABC measured skills and abilities that were different from those measured by existing tests.

The data used to test the model were scores of 544 children (367 with complete information on all subtests used in this analysis) ages 6 to 12½ years who were referred for psychoeducational

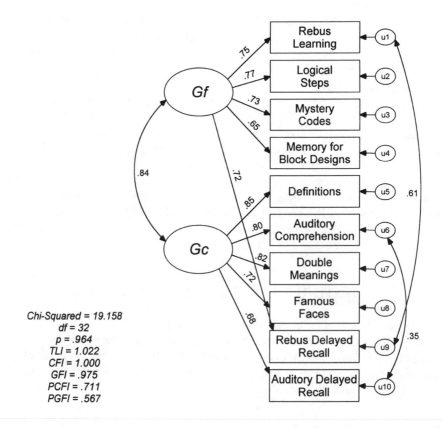

FIGURE 20.10. Another alternative model of the structure of the KAIT. The two Delayed Recall subtests (RDR and ADR) are assumed to measure Gf and Gc, not a separate Delayed Recall ability.

evaluation. The subjects were given both the K-ABC and the WISC-R as a part of a project designed to assess the validity of the K-ABC (for more information about the sample, see Keith & Novak, 1987).

Figure 20.11 shows a confirmatory factor model designed to test the question whether the abilities measured by the Simultaneous and Achievement Scales of the K-ABC are significantly different from those measured by the Performance and Verbal Scales of the WISC-R. The model shows the 11 WISC-R subtests (including Digit Span) loading only on Verbal Comprehension and Perceptual Organization factors, and the 13 K-ABC subtests loading only on Sequential, Simultaneous, and Achievement factors. Unlike most of the other models tested in this chapter, this model was *not* expected to provide a good fit to the data. Obviously, some of the K-ABC tests and the WISC-R tests measure similar abilities (e.g., the Arithmetic subtests from the two different scales), and forcing those subtests on separate factors will of course lead to a poor fit. Instead, the test of the similarity of the constructs will turn on a *comparison* of models.[6]

Figure 20.12 shows the results of the initial analysis of the K-ABC/WISC-R model. As expected,

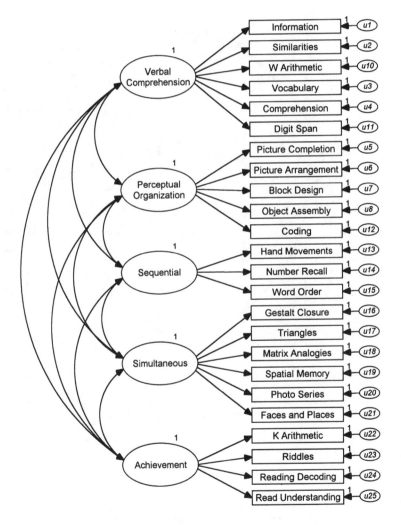

FIGURE 20.11. A confirmatory model to test the similarity in abilities measured by the K-ABC and the WISC-R.

the χ^2 was huge and significant but also unimportant. Of greatest interest are the correlations among first-order factors in general and the correlations between questioned factors in particular. If the Simultaneous scale of the K-ABC in fact measures something different from the Performance scale of the WISC-R, factors that mirror these scales should correlate no more highly than do other dissimilar scales. Instead, the two factors correlate 1.00, suggesting that the two factors are really measuring identical abilities. (The correlation is actually 1.009, an impossible value.) The correlation between the WISC-R verbal factor and the K-ABC Achievement factor was similarly high, .975. Indeed, given the standard error (.014), the 95% confidence interval for the correlation between Verbal and Achievement overlaps with 1.0 (.947–1.00), again suggesting that the two factors, rather than measuring different constructs, are measuring the same construct, verbal comprehension or reasoning.

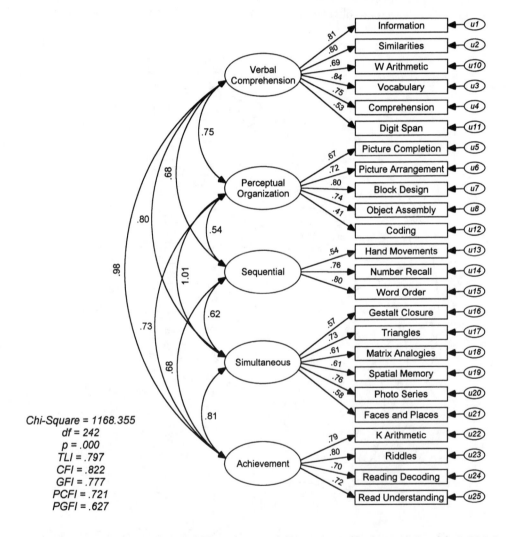

FIGURE 20.12. CFA solution to a test of the similarity in abilities measured by the K-ABC and the WISC-R. Of primary interest are the factor correlations, which suggest that the Verbal tests of the WISC-R and the Achievement tests of the K-ABC are measuring the same abilities, as are the WISC-R Performance tests and the K-ABC Simultaneous tests.

Thus, the initial analysis suggests that Simultaneous and Achievement Scales from the K-ABC are really measuring the same abilities as the Performance and Verbal Scales of the WISC-R, respectively. But this conclusion can be tested more directly by actually *setting* the correlations to 1.0 and seeing whether such constraints result in a significantly worse-fitting model. Figure 20.13 shows the results on this second step in the analysis: Both the correlations (Achievement/Verbal and Simultaneous/Performance) were set to 1.0. For this analysis, the names of the K-ABC factors were also changed to Verbal Reasoning and Nonverbal Reasoning to reflect the hypothesis, embodied by the model, that these scales measure the same abilities as the similarly named WISC-R scales. The χ^2 was again large, but the *change* in χ^2 was very slight, and was, in fact, insignificant ($\Delta\chi^2 = 3.467$ (2), $p = .18$). All other fit statistics were either unchanged or improved with the additional constraints shown in Figure 20.13. In other words, there is no significant *loss of fit* of the model when it is

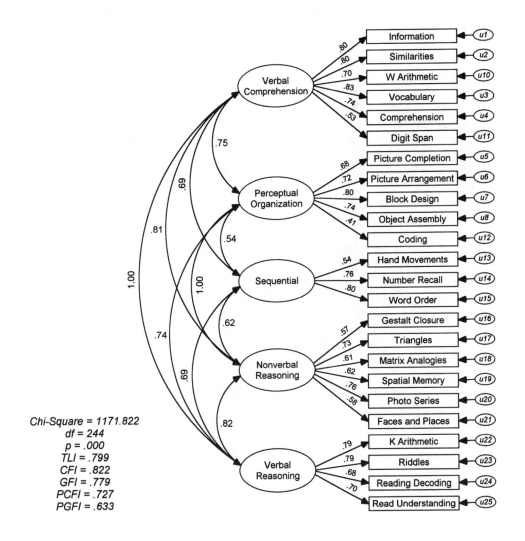

FIGURE 20.13. Further refinement of the WISC-R/K-ABC model. The WISC-R Perceptual/K-ABC Simultaneous (now called Nonverbal Reasoning) and WISC-R Verbal/K-ABC Achievement (relabeled Verbal Reasoning) correlations were constrained to 1.0, specifying that they measure the same underlying abilities. There was no loss of fit for this model over that shown in Figure 20.12.

assumed that (1) the underlying abilities measured by the K-ABC Simultaneous subtests are the same abilities as those measured by the WISC-R Performance subtests and (2) the underlying abilities measured by the K-ABC Achievement subtests are the same abilities as those measured by the WISC-R Verbal subtests. The alternative hypothesis, that the K-ABC measured something not measured by traditional intelligence tests, is not supported.

Do the Wechsler Performance Scales Measure Gf or Gv?

One current debate concerning the nature of constructs measured by modern tests concerns the nature of the construct measured by the Performance scales of the Wechsler tests. Briefly, clinical lore and research suggest that these tests, and especially Block Design, measure fluid intelligence (cf. Kaufman, 1994). Others contend—also with research backing—that the Performance scales are better considered measures of Broad Visualization (Carroll, 1993) or Visual Intelligence (McGrew, Chapter 9, this volume; see Kaufman, 1996; McGrew & Flanagan, 1996; Willis, 1996, for a summary of this debate).

CFA across tests can provide evidence to inform this debate, as well. Stone (1992) conducted a joint confirmatory factor analysis of the DAS and the WISC-R. His primary purpose was to compare models similar in structure to that guiding the WISC to those guiding the DAS (the DAS-type structure was more strongly supported). The data presented in Stone, however, can also be used to compare factors measured by the two tests and help answer questions about what is measured by the WISC-R Performance tests.

There is considerable evidence that the Nonverbal Reasoning scale of the DAS provides a strong and useful measure of Fluid Intelligence (e.g., Elliott, 1990b; Keith, 1990; McGrew, Chapter 9, this volume; Stone, 1992). The DAS Spatial Scale, in turn, may measure a mixture of Broad Visualization (Gv) and Short-Term Memory (Gsm). Thus, if the Wechsler Performance tests measure Gf, the corresponding factor should correlate more highly with the Nonverbal (Gf) factor of the DAS; if the tests measure Gv, the Performance factor should correlate more highly with the DAS Spatial factor.

Figure 20.14 presents a test of these competing hypotheses. The WISC-R factors, including a Performance factor labeled "Gf or Gv," are extracted separately from the DAS factors, including the Nonverbal Reasoning factor, here labeled Gf. The resulting correlations among factors are quite clear-cut: The WISC-R Performance factor correlates only .66 with the Gf (Nonverbal) DAS factor but has a perfect correlation (actually 1.02) with the DAS Spatial factor (Gv and Gsm). Comparisons of alternative models provides unsurprising (given these correlations) but decisive evidence. A model specifying the equivalence of the DAS Nonverbal and WISC-R Performance factor provided a significantly worse fit to the data (e.g., $\Delta\chi^2 = 30.190$ (1), $p < .01$, GFI = .887, PGFI = .575) than did the model shown, whereas a model specifying the equivalence of the WISC-R Performance and DAS Spatial factor provided no worse fit and a more parsimonious model ($\Delta\chi^2 = .124$ (1), $p > .05$). Thus, Stone's (1992) data, at least, strongly support the contention that the WISC-R Performance Scale measures the same abilities as the DAS Spatial Scale, and something quite different from the DAS Nonverbal Reasoning Scale. If the DAS Nonverbal Reasoning Scale is, in fact, a measure of Gf, the WISC-R Performance Scale seems to measure something other than Gf.

TESTING THE SIMILARITY OF FACTOR
STRUCTURE ACROSS GROUPS

An important subset of questions about the constructs measured by intelligence tests involve questions about whether the test measures the same constructs across groups. Does a multiage battery,

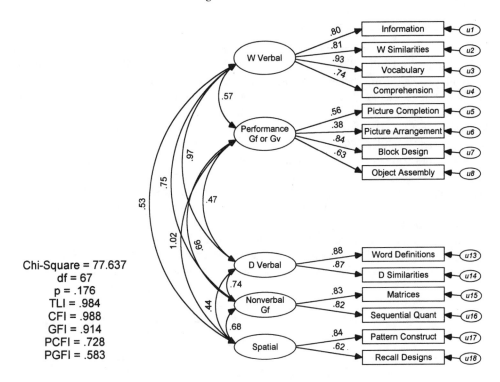

FIGURE 20.14. Similarities in the abilities measured by the DAS and the WISC-R. The factor correlations suggest that the WISC-R Performance tests should be considered as measures of Broad Visualization (Gv) rather than Fluid Intelligence (Gf).

for example, measure the same set of constructs for 8-year-olds as it does for 18-year-olds? Does a new intelligence test measure Gf and Gc abilities for white students but merely test-taking skills for minority students? These questions ask, in essence, whether the factor structure of the tests varies across groups. The method of *multisample* CFA (MCFA) provides an excellent method for answering such questions.

In MCFA, any of the parameters that are estimated or fixed in a model can be specified as being invariant across two or more groups. For example, suppose I wish to determine whether a set of tests measures the same constructs for boys and girls. I could specify that the factor loadings of that series of tests are the same for boys and girls, but I could also specify that the factor intercorrelations, the factor variances, and the unique and error variances are identical across groups. The resulting χ^2 and other fit statistics provide "a measure of the fit of all . . . models in all groups, including all constraints, to the data from all groups" (Jöreskog & Sörbom, 1989, p. 228). That is, the fit statistics test the adequacy of both the imposed factor structure and the equivalence of the factor structures across groups. Various degrees of equivalence can also be compared. I could begin by specifying that all possible parameters—factor loadings, factor correlations, factor variances, and subtest unique and error variances—were identical across groups, and could then gradually free those restrictions and see whether the fit improves. It is even possible to compare the equivalence of measurement across groups independent of a factor structure by comparing the equivalence of the covariance matrices for the two groups.[7] Because the factor structure is contained within and solved from the covariances, this comparison of matrices evaluates whether the test measures the same construct across groups without testing a particular factor structure.

Does the WISC-III Measure the Same Construct across Ages?

Keith and Witta (in press) used hierarchical MCFA to determine whether the Wechsler Intelligence Scale for Children—Third Edition (WISC-III; Wechsler, 1991) measured the same constructs across its 11-year age span. Their research asked whether the WISC-III measures the same constructs for 6-year-olds as for 8-year-olds, 10-year-olds, and so on. Their basic model is shown in Figure 20.15. According to the WISC-III manual, the WISC-III measures four components of intelligence: Verbal Comprehension, Perceptual Organization, Freedom from Distractibility, and Processing Speed (Wechsler, 1991); these components are built into the model as first-order latent factors. These four components are also reflections of overall, or Full Scale, intelligence; this aspect of the WISC-III "theory" is signified by the paths drawn from a second-order *g* to each of the first-order factors. What is different about the model shown is that a separate model was specified for each of 11 age levels in the standardization sample (ages 6 through 16 years), and various degrees of invariance specified across the age groups.

For the first analysis, all aspects of the factor structure (first- and second-order factor loadings, factor unique variances, and subtest unique and error variances) were specified as being invariant, or identical, across the 11 age groups. The results are also shown in the figure. The fit

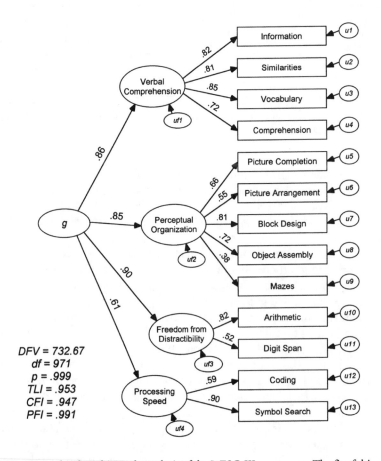

FIGURE 20.15. Hierarchical, multisample analysis of the WISC-III across ages. The fit of this model versus those allowing differences across ages suggests that the WISC-III measures the same abilities across its age span. Adapted from Keith & Witta. Adapted with permission.

statistics all suggest a good fit to the data (the DFV, or Differential Fit Value, is χ^2 with a sample size of 1,000 [see Muthn, 1989] the PFI is a transformation of the Bentler-Bonett Index [see Loehlin, 1992, p. 73]). More important, there were only small and insignificant improvements in fit when the specifications of invariance were relaxed. In the second set of analyses, the less important aspects of factorial invariance—factor unique variances and subtest unique and error variances (Marsh, 1993)—were allowed to vary across groups. That is, all ages were specified to have identical first- and second-order factor loadings, but the unique variances of the factors (uf1 through uf4) and the unique and error variances of the subtests (u1 through u13) were allowed to have different values for each age group. The fit statistics for this relaxed model and the initial model are shown in Table 20.2. As shown in the table, allowing the unique and error variances to differ across groups resulted in an decrease in the DFV, but this change was insignificant (ΔDFV = 130.70 [170], p > .05). The TLI and CFI increased slightly with the relaxation, but the PFI decreased substantially for this less parsimonious model. The third set of analyses specified that the WISC-III structure had the same *form* (i.e., same number of factors, same variables on each factor, etc.), but that the magnitude of *all* aspects of the factor structure were allowed to vary across the 11 age levels. Again, this further relaxation in the model did not result in a significant improvement of the fit. Cumulatively, the findings suggest that the WISC-III does indeed measure the same constructs across its entire age range.[8]

Is There Construct Bias in the K-ABC?

MCFA is also an excellent method for evaluating the presence and extent of construct bias in tests of intelligence. Keith et al. (1995) used MCFA to determine whether the K-ABC measures the same constructs for African-American and White students. A finding of differences across groups would suggest that different constructs are being measured, and thus that the K-ABC is biased against one group.

Keith et al. (1995) outlined a six-step process for testing increasingly lenient models as a method of determining both the extent of the bias in the test and the "location" of that bias. In the first step, the covariance matrices are compared for the two groups (in this case, Black and White children). Because any factor structure is contained within and solved from the original covariance matrix, a test of the equality of the covariance matrices tests whether the instrument (the K-ABC)

TABLE 20.2. Status of Different Hypotheses about the Structure of the WISC-III across 11 Age Levels

Hypothesis tested	DFV(*df*)	*p*	TLI	CFI	PFI	DFV change (*df*)	*p*
Factor structure identical across ages	732.67 (971)	.999	.953	.947	.991		
Factor loadings identical errors & unique variances vary	601.97 (801)	1.00	.954	.957	.838	130.70 (170)	.989
Factor structure similar (factor loadings, error, unique variances all vary)	510.66 (671)	1.00	.952	.962	.714	222.01 (300)	.999

Note. The changes in DFV (χ^2 with a sample size of 1,000) were calculated by comparing the DFV for each model with that from the model specifying identical factor structure across ages. Adapted from Keith & Witta, in press. Adapted with permission.

measures the same constructs across groups, without specifying the nature of those constructs. If the fit statistics lead to the rejection of this initial model, a confirmatory factor model is developed and used in all subsequent steps. Second, a CFA is conducted across the groups with *all* aspects of the model—factor loadings, factor correlations, factor variances, and unique and error variances—specified as invariant across the groups. This highly constrained CFA is no less constrained than the comparison of matrixes (everything is invariant) but in addition to testing for equality across groups also tests a specific factor model. Thus, the fit statistics from this second analysis provide a baseline for further comparisons in which the model is relaxed. In the third through sixth steps, these constrained parameters are gradually relaxed (e.g., the unique and error variances are allowed to be different for the two groups, then the factor variances, etc.).

Table 20.3 shows the results of these comparisons for Black and White 11–12-year-olds from the K-ABC standardization and sociocultural samples. The comparison of the matrix for Black with that of White children is shown in the first row of the table. Although several of the fit statistics suggested an adequate fit of the model to the data, the χ^2 was significant $(130.63[91], p = .004)$, suggesting the rejection of the hypothesis that the K-ABC measures identical constructs for Black and White children. It seemed prudent to conduct further tests, despite the mixed nature of the fit statistics.

Keith et al. (1995) next tested the theoretical structure of the K-ABC—as described in the K-ABC manual (Kaufman & Kaufman, 1983)—across ethnic groups. Table 20.3 also shows the results of the gradual relaxation of the models from all parameters invariant across groups (step 2) to all parameters free to vary in magnitude across ethnic groups (step 6). The last column shows the decrease in χ^2 with each relaxation. Allowing both the unique and error variances of the subtests (step 3) and allowing the factor variance to differ across groups (step 4) resulted in a significant decrease in χ^2, whereas allowing additional parameters to vary resulted in only insignificant decreases. The other fit statistics also suggest that step 4 provides a good mix of fit and parsimony. Thus, it appears that the differences in the matrices for Black and White students seen in the first step of

TABLE 20.3. Comparison of the Fit of Models Specifying Various Degrees of Equivalence of the K-ABC across Ethnic Groups for 11–12-Year-Olds

Model description	χ^2 (*df*)	*p*	TLI	CFI	PFI	χ^2 change (*df*)	*p*
Step 1. Covariance matrices invariant	130.63(91)	.004	.971	.983	.553		
Step 2. All parameters invariant	385.94(153)	<.001	.898	.900	.828		
Step 3. Unique/error variances vary	350.94(140)	<.001	.899	.909	.770	35.01(13)	<.001
Step 4. Unique/error variances and factor variances vary	340.21(137)	<.001	.900	.912	.758	10.73(3)	.013
Step 5. Unique/error variances, factor variances, and factor correlations vary (factor loadings invariant)	336.69(134)	<.001	.898	.913	.742	3.54(3)	.316
Step 6. All parameters vary between groups	329.33(124)	<.001	.889	.912	.689	7.34(10)	.693

Note. Adapted from Keith, DeGraff, Diamond, Fugate, Shadrach, & Stevens, 1995. The first model compares the equivalence of covariance matrices for Black and White children; all subsequent models compare factor structures.

the analysis are due to differences in the unique variances of the subtests and the unique variances of the factors, which are, in turn, relatively unimportant differences (Marsh, 1993, p. 851). Keith et al. (1995) also compared ages 7–8 and 9–10; even fewer differences were found across groups.

Keith et al. (1995) argued that the MCFA approach has several advantages over more traditional methods for assessing construct bias (e.g., comparison of factor loadings). Specifically, MCFA provides a more organized, more direct, more objective, and more complete analysis of bias over more traditional methods.

TESTING THEORIES OF INTELLIGENCE

Most of the examples used in this chapter are examples of CFA used to understand the constructs measured by specific tests. The method is equally applicable, however, for asking and answering questions about *theories* of intelligence.

Carroll's Three-Stratum Theory

Carroll's three-stratum theory of cognitive abilities presents a hierarchical model of intelligence with narrow-order abilities at the bottom, and the most general ability, *g*, at the apex. The theory is described in detail in Carroll (1993; Chapter 7, this volume) and in McGrew (Chapter 9, this volume). Bickley, Keith, and Wolfle (1995) tested Carroll's three-stratum theory across the 6–80 age range using data from the Woodcock–Johnson Psycho-Educational Battery—Revised (WJ-R; Woodcock & Johnson, 1989). Briefly, the authors found no significant difference in the *structure* of intelligence across the very wide age range and found that the three-stratum theory provided an excellent fit to the data. The research thus provided strong support for the three-stratum theory across the life-span.

Carroll speculated that there might well be *intermediate* factors between his second-stratum (e.g., Gf, Gc, and Gv) and third-stratum abilities but left the task of describing this intermediate structure up to other researchers. Bickley et al. (1995) addressed the possibility of intermediate factors, and tested one such model, but did not pursue the matter further. Several plausible models are pursued here as a method of demonstrating CFA's applicability to testing theory.

The basic three-stratum model, as tested by Bickley et al. (1995) with the WJ-R data, is shown in Figure 20.16. The data used were the average matrix for the 6–80 ages, as calculated via LISREL and reported in Bickley et al. (1995). The model represents what Carroll calls a "higher-stratum design" (p. 692), in which the subtests are designed to assess first-stratum abilities so that the first-order factors will reflect second-stratum abilities.[9] The only substantive difference between the model shown and Carroll's three-stratum model is that the Figure 20.16 has separate Gf and Gq factors, whereas Carroll specified quantitative abilities (Gq) as a part of fluid intelligence (Gf). The model also uses the same names for factors as McGrew (Chapter 9, this volume), which sometimes differ from those suggested by Carroll. The fit statistics shown along with the model suggest that Carroll's basic model indeed provides an excellent fit to the data.

Figure 20.17 tests Carroll's contention that Gq is a part of Gf rather than a separate second-stratum factor. Although such a specification results in a model that provides a slightly better fit to the data, the difference in fit is insignificant (see Table 20.4), and the model less parsimonious. Thus, the specification of Gq as a part of Gf does not find strong support in this analysis. Interestingly, however, this specification of an intermediate Gf factor *does* result in a near-unity loading of Gf on *g*, a not-uncommon finding in other research (e.g., Gustafsson, 1984).

The model shown in Figure 20.18 presents one possible set of intermediate factors between Carroll's second and third stratum (in the model, these are second-order factors and *g* is a third-or-

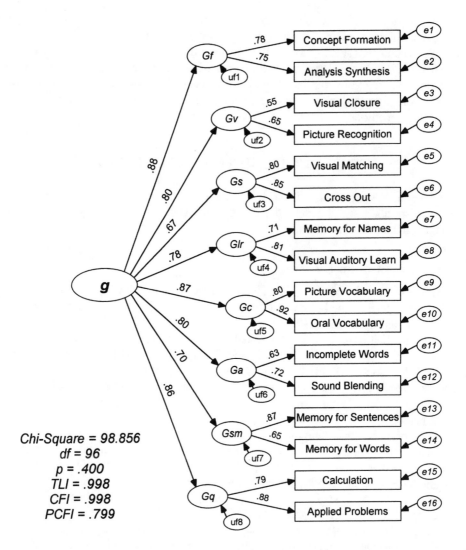

FIGURE 20.16. A test of Carroll's (1993) three-stratum theory across the life-span. The tests are from the WJ-R. Adapted from Bickley, Keith, & Wolfle, 1995. Adapted with permission.

TABLE 20.4. Comparison of the Fit of Models Testing Different Intermediate Level Factors in the Three-Stratum Theory

Model description	χ^2 (df)	p	TLI	CFI	PCFI	χ^2 change[a]	p
1. No intermediate factors	98.86(96)	.400	.998	.998	.799		
2. Gf subsumes Gq (strict Carroll)	97.01(95)	.424	.999	.999	.791	1.85(1)	> .05
3. Traditional intermediate factors	94.16(93)	.447	.999	.999	.775	4.70(3)	> .05
4. Cognitive performance model (Woodcock)	92.02(94)	.539	1.00	1.00	.783	6.84(2)	< .05

[a]Compared to the first model.

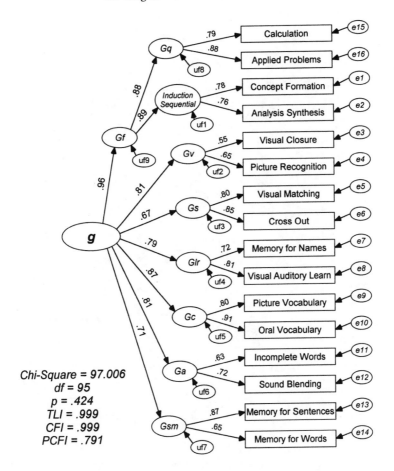

FIGURE 20.17. CFA used to test whether Quantitative Abilities are subsumed under Fluid Intelligence.

der factor). The model categorizes the second-stratum into intellectual, perceptual, and memory factors, what might be labeled "traditional intermediate factors." Although this categorization improves the fit of the model, the improvement is insignificant, suggesting that the more parsimonious model (Carroll's model, Figure 20.16) provides a better representation of the structure of cognitive abilities. The very high (1.0) factor loading of Memory on the hierarchical *g* factor also suggests the unsuitability of this model.

Figure 20.19 shows the results of a test of another possible set of intermediate factors. Woodcock (1993) proposed a "cognitive performance model" of abilities as a method of explaining how abilities work in concert to affect a person's overall functioning. Although Woodcock seemed to view the intermediate abilities and *g* (or cognitive performance) as *composites* rather than factors (and thus drew the paths *to* cognitive performance rather than from it), the model shown is consistent with Woodcock's categorization. Although not shown in the model, Woodcock also classified Gs as an internal facilitator–inhibitor.

As shown in the Figure 20.19 and Table 20.4, this categorization of second-stratum abilities into thinking abilities and acquired knowledge leads to an improvement in most of the fit statistics associated with the model (with the exception of the parsimony index). In particular, Woodcock's intermediate factors produced a significant decrease in χ^2, thus suggesting the division of some of

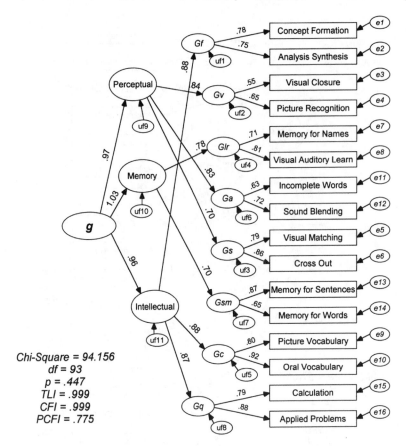

FIGURE 20.18. A test of possible intermediate factors between Carroll's stratum II and stratum III abilities. These "traditional" intermediate factors provide no improvement of fit over the model in Figure 20.16.

the second-stratum abilities into thinking and acquired knowledge as a worthwhile addition to the three-stratum theory.

SUMMARY

This chapter has provided an overview and introduction to the method of confirmatory factor analysis, with particular attention to the use of the method as an aid in understanding the constructs measured by modern tests of intelligence. The chapter has covered "simple" CFA: first-order confirmatory factor analysis, a method that is becoming fairly common in the factor-analytic/intelligence literature.

I believe, however, that additional uses of CFA are needed if we are really interested in understanding the constructs we are measuring. Thus, I encourage the comparison of *meaningful* alternative explanations to a researcher's pet theory through the testing and comparison of alternative factor models. This practice, too, is becoming more common, although alternative models are not always meaningful. For example, I argue that a single-factor model is generally not a meaningful alternative and does not represent modern thinking about the nature of *g* as a construct.

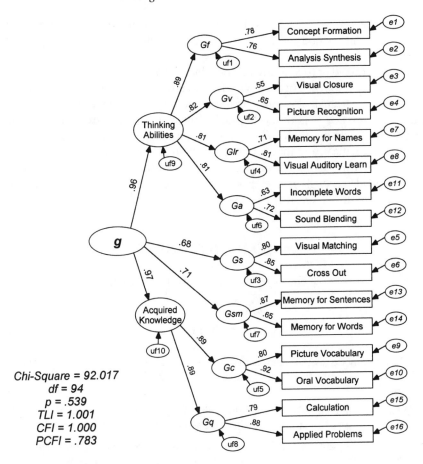

FIGURE 20.19. A test of Woodcock's Cognitive Performance Model as intermediate factors between Carroll's stratum II and stratum III abilities. The improvement of fit (over Figure 20.16) suggests that this model may provide viable intermediate factors.

Many modern theories of intelligence are hierarchical in nature, with the most prominent example being the three-stratum theory, a "meta-theory" developed and tested by John Carroll. Most tests of intelligence tacitly recognize this hierarchical nature of intelligence as well. I strongly believe that our research should therefore test these hierarchical notions of intelligence if we are to fully understand the constructs we are measuring. Put another way, a test of a first-order version of a hierarchical theory/test is an incomplete test of that theory. Furthermore, hierarchical analysis provides a more thorough understanding of the first-order abilities (Carroll, 1993). So, for example, with hierarchical analysis it becomes obvious that the supposed Freedom-from-Distractibility factor on the WISC-III is much too laden with g to measure the simple ability to tune out distractions (Keith & Witta, in press). This chapter has demonstrated several variations of hierarchical CFA, using second- and even third-order factors.

This chapter has demonstrated several other important uses of CFA: comparing the constructs measured across different tests and comparing the constructs measured by one test across different groups. Many of the most vexing problems in the intelligence field revolve around these issues, and CFA is an excellent method for answering these important questions. For example, multisample CFA provides an organized, effective method for testing for construct bias across groups. Finally, CFA provides a powerful method for testing theory, and especially for testing competing theories of intelligence.

I have not covered or tried to cover all possible uses of CFA; those uses are limited only by the imagination of the researcher. In addition, CFA is a subset of a more general approach—structural equation modeling—and that broader approach is also useful for understanding the nature of the constructs measured by tests of intelligence. To mention only two examples, SEM provides an excellent method for testing the stability over time of the *constructs* we measure, independent of the method of measurement, and multisample SEM provides an excellent method for evaluating the presence of *predictive* bias in our measurements (cf. McArdle, 1994). Nevertheless, I hope this chapter has provided enough of an overview to stimulate thought and further study, and to fire the imaginations of future CFA readers and researchers.

ACKNOWLEDGMENTS

I am grateful to Christine Diamond for her data and manuscript preparation assistance.

NOTES

1. The factor model tested is one that matches the intended structure of the KAIT. Other models (e.g., McGrew, Chapter 9, this volume; Flanagan & McGrew, 1995) are certainly plausible, but are not evaluated here.

2. Again, I here test one possible structure that fits fairly closely with the test author's intended structure. For other possible structures, see Keith, 1990; McGrew, Chapter 9, this volume; Stone, 1992.

3. In structural equation modeling, these are known as disturbances and represent all other causes not included in the model. Thus for the DAS example, uf1 represents all causes of Verbal ability other than *g*.

4. Without this constraint, this portion of the model would have been underidentified.

5. It may not be immediately obvious why the model in Figure 20.10 is a constrained version of that in Figure 20.9. Figure 20.10 is statistically identical to Figure 20.9 with the paths from Delayed Recall to the two delayed recall subtests set to zero, and the correlations between Delayed Recall and the other two factors set to zero.

6. There are several other aspects of the analysis that are different from previous examples. Instead of setting one factor loading per factor to 1.0 to set the metric of the factors, the factor variances were set to 1.0. This change has the effect of setting the metric by standardizing the factors. This approach was used to force the covariances among factors to be *correlations,* so that in the second step in the analysis certain factor correlations (rather than covariances) could be set to 1.0.

7. For many of the analyses discussed previously, the analysis of correlation and covariance matrices will generally produce the same results (fit statistics and standardized solution), despite the preference of most computer programs and statisticians to use covariance matrices. When comparing results across samples, as in multisample CFA, covariance matrices should be used, however. It is generally recognized that unstandardized coefficients are more appropriate for comparisons across groups in regression, and the same holds true for CFA and SEM. Because a correlation is a standardized covariance, its magnitude depending on both the covariance and the variances of the two variables involved, a difference in the same correlation across two groups could be a result of a difference in the original covariance, a difference in the variance in the variables correlated, or a difference in both. Most books and program manuals contain a discussion of these issues. Jöreskog and Sörbom (1989, pp. 47–49), Loehlin (1992, pp. 75–77), and Marsh (1993) are particularly useful.

8. Keith and Witta (in press) made a number of other comparisons across ages (e.g., the covariance matrices were compared, as were alternative factor structures), and alternative names were suggested for several factors. See the original article for details.

9. The distinction between *order* and *stratum* may not be apparent. According to Carroll (1993), "The *order* of a factor refers to the purely operational level of analysis at which it is found. The *stratum* of a factor would refer to an absolute measure of its degree of generality over the domain of cognitive abilities" (p. 577). According to Flanagan and McGrew (1995), the WJ-R does not provide a pure higher-stratum design, but rather confounds stratum I and II abilities. That is, some of the first-order factors (Figure 20.16) may indeed represent stratum II abilities, whereas others may better be considered stratum I abilities.

REFERENCES

Allen, S. R., & Thorndike, R. M. (1995). Stability of the WPPSI-R and WISC-III factor structure using cross-validation of covariance structure models. *Journal of Psychoeducational Assessment, 13,* 3–20.

Anastasi, A. (1985). Review of the test [*Kaufman Assessment Battery for Children*]. In J. V. Mitchell, Jr. (Ed.), *The ninth mental measurements yearbook* (pp. 769–771). Lincoln, NE: Buros Institute.

Arbuckle, J. (1992). *AMOS 3.1 documentation package.* Philadelphia: Temple University.

Arbuckle, J. (1995). *AMOS 3.5 user's guide.* Chicago: SmallWaters.

Bentler, P. M., & Bonett, D. G. (1980). Significance tests and goodness of fit in the analysis of covariance structures. *Psychological Bulletin, 88,* 588–606.

Bentler, P. M., & Wu, E. J. C. (1993). *EQS Windows user's guide.* Los Angeles: BMDP Statistical Software.

Bickley, P. G., Keith, T. Z., & Wolfle, L. M. (1995). The three-stratum theory of cognitive abilities: Test of the structure of intelligence across the life span. *Intelligence, 20,* 309–328.

Burt, C. L. (1949). The structure of the mind: A review of the results of factor analysis. *British Journal of Educational Psychology, 19,* 100–111, 176–199.

Carroll, J. B. (1993). *Human cognitive abilities: A survey of factor-analytic studies.* New York: Cambridge University Press.

Carroll, J. B. (1995). Review of the book [*Assessment of cognitive processes: The PASS theory of intelligence*]. *Journal of Psychoeducational Assessment, 13,* 397–409.

Cohen, J. (1994). The earth is round ($p < .05$). *American Psychologist, 49,* 997–1003.

Elliott, C. D. (1990a). *Differential Ability Scales..* San Antonio, TX: Psychological Corporation.

Elliott, C. D. (1990b). The nature and structure of children's abilities: Evidence from The Differential Ability Scales. *Journal of Psychoeducational Assessment, 8,* 376–390.

Gustafsson, J.-E. (1984). A unifying model for the structure of intellectual abilities. *Intelligence, 8,* 179–203.

Gustafsson, J.-E., & Balke, G. (1993). General and specific abilities as predictors of school achievement. *Multivariate Behavioral Research, 28,* 407–434.

Flanagan, D. P., & McGrew, K. S. (1995). *Interpreting intelligence tests from modern Gf-Gc theory: Joint confirmatory factor analysis of the WJ-R and Kaufman Adolescent and Adult Intelligence Test (KAIT).* Manuscript submitted for publication.

Hartmann, W. M. (1995). *The CALIS procedure release 6.11 extended user's guide.* Cary, NC: SAS Institute.

Hox, J. J. (1995). Amos, EQS, and LISREL for Windows: A comparative review. *Structural Equation Modeling, 2,* 79–91.

Hoyle, R. H., & Panter, A. T. (1995). Writing about structural equation models. In R. H. Hoyle (Ed.), *Structural equation modeling: Concepts, issues, and applications* (pp. 158–176). Thousand Oaks, CA: Sage

Humphreys, L. G. (1990). View of a supportive empiricist. *Psychological Inquiry, 1,* 153–155.

Jensen, A. R., & Weng, L. (1993). What is a good *g*? *Intelligence, 18,* 231–258.

Jöreskog, K. G., & Sörbom, D. (1989). *LISREL 7: A guide to the program and applications* (2nd ed.). Chicago: SPSS.

Kaufman, A. S. (1994). *Intelligent testing with the WISC-III.* New York: Wiley.

Kaufman, A. S. (1996, March). Wechsler and Horn: A reply to McGrew & Flanagan. *Communiqué, 24*(6), 15–17.

Kaufman, A. S., & Kaufman, N. L. (1983). *Kaufman Assessment Battery for Children.* Circle Pines, MN: American Guidance Service.

Kaufman, A. S., & Kaufman, N. L. (1993). *Kaufman Adolescent and Adult Intelligence Test.* Circle Pines, MN: American Guidance Service.

Keith, T. Z. (1985). Questioning the K-ABC: What *does* it measure? *School Psychology Review, 14,* 9–20.

Keith, T. Z. (1990). Confirmatory and hierarchical confirmatory analysis of the Differential Ability Scales. *Journal of Psychoeducational Assessment, 8,* 391–405.

Keith, T. Z., DeGraff, M., Diamond, C. M., Fugate, M. H., Shadrach, E. A., & Stevens, M. L. (1995). Using multi-sample confirmatory factor analysis to test for construct bias: An example using the K-ABC. *Journal of Psychoeducational Assessment, 13,* 347–364.

Keith, T. Z., & Dunbar, S. B. (1984). Hierarchical factor analysis of the K-ABC: Testing alternate models. *Journal of Special Education, 18,* 367–375.

Keith, T. Z., & Novak, C. G. (1987). Joint factor structure of the WISC-R and K-ABC for referred school children. *Journal of Psychoeducational Assessment, 4,* 370–386.

Keith, T. Z., & Reynolds, C. R. (1990). Measurement and design issues in child assessment research. In C. R. Reynolds & R. W. Kamphaus (Eds.), *Handbook of psychological and educational assessment of children: Vol. 1, Intelligence and achievement* (pp. 29–61). New York: Guilford Press.

Keith, T. Z., & Witta, E. L. (in press). Hierarchical and cross-age confirmatory factor analysis of the WISC-III: What does it measure? *School Psychology Quarterly.*

Kenny, D. A. (1979). *Correlation and causality.* New York: Wiley.

Loehlin, J. C. (1992). *Latent variable models: An introduction to factor, path, and structural analysis* (2nd ed.). Hillsdale, NJ: Erlbaum.

Marsh, H. W. (1993). The multidimensional structure of academic self-concept: Invariance over gender and age. *American Educational Research Journal, 30,* 841–860.

McArdle, J. J. (1994, September). *Contemporary statistical models for examining test bias.* Paper presented at the Human Cognitive Abilities in Theory and Practice conference, Charlottesville, VA.

McGrew, K. S., & Flanagan, D. P. (1995). The Wechsler Performance Scale debate: Fluid intelligence (Gf) or visual processing (Gv). *Communiqué, 24*(6), 14, 16.

Mulaik, S. A., & Quartetti, D. A. (1994, October). *First-order or higher-order g?* Paper presented at the annual meeting of the Society of Multivariate Experimental Psychology, Princeton, NJ

Muthén, B. O. (1989). Dichotomous factor analysis of symptom data. *Sociological Methods & Research, 18,* 19–65.

Naglieri, J. A., Braden, J. P., & Gottling, S. H. (1993). Confirmatory factor analysis of the planning, attention, simultaneous, successive (PASS) cognitive processing model for a Kindergarten sample. *Journal of Psychoeducational Assessment, 11,* 259–269.

Page, E. B. (1985). Review of the test [*Kaufman Assessment Battery for Children*]. In J. V. Mitchell, Jr. (Ed.), *The ninth mental measurements yearbook* (pp. 773–777). Lincoln, NE: Buros Institute.

Stone, B. J. (1992). Joint confirmatory factor analyses of the DAS and WISC-R. *Journal of School Psychology, 30,* 185–195.

Tanaka, J. S. (1993). Multifaceted conceptions of fit in structural equation models. In K. S. Bollen & J. S. Long (Eds.), *Testing structural equation models* (pp. 10–39). Newbury Park, CA: Sage.

Thorndike, R. M. (1990). Would the real factors of the Stanford–Binet Fourth Edition please come forward? *Journal of Psychoeducational Assessment, 8,* 412–435.

Vernon, P. E. (1950). *The structure of human abilities.* New York: Wiley.

Wechsler, D. (1974). *Wechsler Intelligence Scale for Children—Revised.* San Antonio, TX: Psychological Corporation.

Wechsler, D. (1991). *Wechsler Intelligence Scale for Children—Third edition.* San Antonio, TX: Psychological Corporation.

Willis, J. O. (1996, March). A practitioner's reaction to McGrew, Flanagan, & Kaufman. *Communiqué, 24*(6), 15, 17.

Woodcock, R. W. (1993). An information processing view of Gf-Gc theory. *Journal of Psychoeducational Assessment* [Monograph Series: *Woodcock–Johnson Psycho-Educational Battery—Revised*], 1, 80–102.

Woodcock, R. W., & Johnson, M. B. (1989). *Woodcock–Johnson Psycho-Educational Battery—Revised.* Chicago: Riverside.

CHAPTER 21

Contemporary Models for the Biometric Genetic Analysis of Intellectual Abilities

JOHN J. MCARDLE

CAROL A. PRESCOTT

RESEARCH ON THE GENETIC ASPECTS of intellectual behavior has taken many different forms. Scientific work in the late 19th and early 20th centuries established that key aspects of human intellectual functioning are influenced by genetic variation. Clinical research on cognitive deficits, especially research showing the effects of inbreeding and the genetic cause of Down's syndrome, has established the role for genetic regulation of impaired intellectual functioning (e.g., Lejeune & Turpin, 1957, cited in Medawar, 1959). Even minor genetic defects can produce dramatic physical and mental impairment. The search for specific genetic abnormalities linked to such disorders continues at a rapid pace (McKusick, 1994).

Researchers in many areas have questioned whether genetic factors might regulate aspects of behavior within the normal range of variation. This is a substantially different question from that of abnormalities arising from genetic factors. It requires its own methodology, and has led to the emergence of the field of behavioral genetics (BG). One of the most popular topics in the history of BG is the biometric genetic analysis of intellectual abilities (BGIA). This research was initiated by Galton's (1865) early work on the measurement of individual differences in physical and mental characteristics (Forrest, 1974; Johnson et al., 1985). Galton studied familial resemblance for intellectual achievement and reported that individuals born into higher social classes attained higher educational and social standing than individuals born into lower classes. Later, after Fisher's (1918, 1930) statistical exposition of quantitative rules of Mendellian inheritance, many researchers focused on a broader understanding of the familiality of various aspects of human intelligence (Burks, 1928; Cattell, 1937; DeFries et al., 1979; Loehlin, Horn, & Willerman, 1989; Munsinger, 1975; Scarr & Weinberg, 1978; Thorndike, 1905).

SELECTED BGIA STUDIES

There have been more than 100 studies reporting on genetic influences on intellectual abilities. In traditional BG analyses, pairs of relatives with known genetic relationships are studied and the correlations of their scores calculated. These correlations are then compared with expectations based on formal models of genetic and environmental influence. A variety of different statistical calculations are used in different studies to examine alternative biometric hypotheses (described in the next section).

The first comprehensive review of the BGIA literature was presented by Erlenmeyer-Kimling and Jarvik (1963). These researchers cited 52 studies of more than 30,000 pairings of relatives and summarized these results using the correlations reported in each study. The pattern of resemblance of various familial relationships led these researchers to suggest the existence of a strong genetic contribution to intelligence. The median correlation for identical twins (i.e., relatives with identical genetic makeup) was .87 compared with about .60 for fraternal twins and .50 for biological siblings and parent–offspring pairs (i.e., relatives with approximately half their genetic makeup in common). The observed resemblance among relatives also gave some evidence for the presence of a shared familial environment. For siblings reared apart, the correlations were somewhat lower (.75 for identical twins, .39 for siblings) than those for siblings reared together. Adopted individuals had low but still positive correlations of about .2 with their adoptive relatives.

A subsequent review by Bouchard and McGue (1981) included 111 studies selected from the published literature on the genetics of intelligence. Several studies included by Erlenmeyer-Kimling and Jarvik (1963) were excluded from this review on methodological grounds. Aside from the twin resemblance correlations, the more recent data summarized in this review suggested a smaller impact of genetic influence than reported previously. For example, the median correlation was .45 for siblings reared together and .24 for biological siblings reared apart compared to .30 for unrelated children reared together. These data suggest a greater role for family environment than evidenced previously.

Spousal resemblance for cognitive abilities, termed "assortative mating" in this literature, has also been studied in a variety of different ways (Cloninger, Rice, & Reich, 1979; Johnson, Ahern & Cole, 1980; Mascie-Taylor, 1989; Neale & McArdle, 1990; Phillips, Fulker, Carey, & Nagoshi, 1988; Zonderman, Vandenberg, Spuhler, & Fain, 1977). The results from most studies indicate a small but positive correlation between husbands and wives. This correlation has usually been interpreted as a tendency for individuals to choose spouses of somewhat similar intellectual abilities.

A variety of explanations have been advanced to address why more recent research has produced lower estimates of genetic influence on intelligence compared to previous research (e.g., Loehlin et al., 1989; Plomin & DeFries, 1980). These include more representative sampling and standardized assessment in modern studies, more stringent criteria for study inclusion in more recent reviews, and actual cohort changes in genetic variance. Earlier studies typically sampled individuals from a limited range of socioeconomic backgrounds, probably resulting in limited environmental variance, and this sampling may have resulted in a greater proportion of the observed variance being attributed to genetic sources.

In two recent examples of more advanced models applied to BGIA data, Loehlin (1989) and Chipeur, Rovine, and Plomin (1990) reanalyzed the summary data compiled by Bouchard and McGue (1981) using linear structural relations procedures (e.g., LISREL, discussed later). These analyses provided an overall model for all the data, an assessment of the goodness of fit of the data to this model, and an evaluation of the consistency of parameters estimated by different types of study designs. These researchers concluded that genetic sources accounted for about half the variance, environmental effects shared by siblings accounted for another quarter, and the remaining variance was due to a combination of experiences unique to individuals and measurement error. As before, these analyses also indicated that fraternal twins were more similar than siblings of different ages and that there was a moderate positive correlation between spouses for intellectual performance.

Given these methodological differences, and the discrediting of particular studies and methods, heritability ratios for intelligence of 70% to 80% reported in the past (e.g., Burt, 1966, 1969,

1972; Jensen, 1969) no longer appear tenable (but see Pedersen, Plomin, Nesselroade, & McClearn, 1992). Based on the current reviews, a heritability for intelligence of about 50% is now frequently cited (e.g., Plomin & Rende, 1990). The remaining literature has been widely accepted as demonstrating that familial resemblance for intelligence is largely genetic in origin. This consistency across studies has recently led some researchers to say, "Although much remains to be understood about the genetics of *g* (Plomin & Neiderhiser, 1991), additional quantitative genetic studies are no longer needed to document the importance of genetic influence" (Plomin et al., 1994, p. 107). These issues are re-examined in this report.

CONTROVERSY IN BGIA STUDIES

Studies of the genetic basis of intelligence have engendered a great deal of scientific and social debate. Galton's (1865) initial report, for example, was interpreted by some as evidence for genetic control over economic and social achievement, with little attention given to the striking group differences in educational opportunity. Soon afterwards, Cattell (1937) studied the intellectual attainment of a large number of families of 10-year-old children. He found that families with more children had lower intellectual attainment than families of smaller size, producing an overall negative correlation between family size and intellectual attainment. Cattell (1937, 1982) suggested that this was cause for "national concern." Critics (and Cattell himself) pointed out how these initial studies did not include unmarried persons or families with zero children. Furthermore, the longitudinal follow-ups did not appear to yield a "dysgenic trend" (e.g., Higgins, Reed, & Reed, 1962; Loehlin, 1984).

Results from animal research also suggested that variation in cognitive performance was associated with genetic variation. A variety of experimental studies demonstrated that *selective breeding* could lead to improved or diminished performance on learning tasks (e.g., "maze-bright" and "maze-dull" rats of Tryon, 1940; Cooper & Zubek, 1958; cf. Fulker, Whitlock, & Broadhurst, 1972; Henderson, 1982, 1986; Meredith, 1968). The clear results from animal studies may have influenced interpretations of the available human data (Dobzhansky, 1956, 1973; Medawar, 1959).

The misinterpretations of results from genetic studies of intellectual abilities have engendered social cost. In the early part of the 20th century, "eugenics" movements in England and the United States advocated applying the ideas of selective breeding to "improve" human populations. Scientific statements were used to defend public policies of restrictive immigration and sterilization that adversely affected minority groups (see Kelves, 1984, 1985). Around the time of World War II, this advocacy took another frightening turn: Eugenic concepts were used to justify the repressive activities of the German National Socialist Party (Kelves, 1985). Later, starting in the 1960s, controversy developed around charges of fraud in Cyril Burt's studies of identical twins reared apart (Burt, 1966; Jones, 1991). Controversy also arose and continues over ideas about racial differences on measures of intelligence (e.g., Chase, 1980; Fancher, 1985; Jencks et al., 1972; Jensen, 1969; Kamin, 1974; Mackenzie, 1980, 1984; Scarr, 1971, 1980; Taylor, 1980). Of central concern are the potential relationships among "race effects," "social class effects," and "genetic effects." These issues are often politicized in public policy debates (e.g., Ehrman, Omenn & Caspari, 1972; Jencks, 1980; Jensen, 1973; Kelves, 1985; Scarr, 1988; Scarr & Yee, 1980).

These BGIA controversies have been revived by the best-selling book, *The Bell Curve* (Herrnstein & Murray, 1994) and the widespread reactions it has provoked (Fraser, 1995; Jacoby & Glauberman, 1995). Advances in technology for gene location and gene cloning (Lander & Botstein, 1989; McKusick, 1994) may have added to the current controversies (Lee, 1993). It seems as if almost any discussion of this topic evokes a strong response from a large number of persons. In a fundamental way, a priori beliefs about the genetic basis of intellectual abilities differ widely among different people (Snyderman & Rothman, 1990). It follows that much of this debate is not scientific but represents a position of advocacy on one side of the issue or the other. We mention these concerns at the outset to underscore the distinction between scientific research, or *the gathering of facts,* and advocacy, or *the way these facts are used.* In this presentation, we focus mainly on the former, but we do not ignore the latter. The BGIA studies we discuss are not studies about eugenics, but we recognize that some aspects of these studies are important in the public debate.

STRUCTURAL MODELS IN BEHAVIOR GENETICS

Given the importance of the previous issues, a discussion of the current scientific models underlying BGIA results may be useful. During the last few decades substantial progress has been made in formulating such models using advanced mathematical and statistical techniques adapted from other areas of scientific research. A wide variety of BG analyses are now based on the simultaneous estimation of biometric parameters from multiple groups. The current methods grew out of "path analysis" models developed by the geneticist S. Wright (1921, 1934, 1982), the "factors of the correlation" decomposition of the statistician R.A. Fisher (1918, 1930), and the "multiple abstract variance analysis" of the psychologist R. B. Cattell (1953, 1960, 1982; also see Loehlin, 1965, 1978, 1984). In contemporary BG research, structural equation models (SEM) have been used to deal with some scientific aspects of these issues (Martin & Eaves, 1977; McArdle & Goldsmith, 1990; Loehlin, 1992; Neale & Cardon, 1992).

A few key features of these new techniques are highlighted here. We present a few basic BG models and then show the results when these models are fitted to real data. We emphasize interpretations relevant to intellectual abilities research, and we include other technical information only as references and footnotes. As a start, we introduce some key concepts about these models using the path diagrams of Figure 21.1: Figure 21.1a shows a traditional factor-analytic measurement model and Figure 21.1b shows a behavioral genetic model.[1] These models are related in a variety of ways that are discussed further here.

The factor-analytic model Figure 21.1a includes multiple observed performance variables (P), one unobserved or true score (T), and three unique variances (indicated by variable U and parameter u). Most critically, the single latent variable or true score (T drawn in an oval) is drawn as a common influence (by one headed arrows representing factor loadings l_j) on all the observed variables (P_j). Notice that each unique factor (U_j) is related to only one observed variable but not related to one another or to the common factor. From a SEM perspective, this structural model represents an explict mathematical hypothesis about the expected values of the correlations among the multiple measures (e.g., $R_{1,2} = L_1 \times L_2$). The adequacy of this structural model as a representation of the correlations among the observed variables can be evaluated using contemporary statistical techniques commonly known as confirmatory factor analysis (see Keith, Chapter 20, this volume; McArdle, 1996a).

One unusual feature of Figure 21.1a is the inclusion of an unobserved variable labeled $A + C + E$. This variable is included here to represent the theoretical biometric sources of the variance of the true score T. This modeling concept is expanded on (for one observed measure) in Figure 21.1b. In this second model the observed score P, now termed a "phenotype," is specified as a sum of the true score T plus error of measurement score U just as in Figure 21.1a. However, the $A+C+E$ that were not separated in Figure 21.1a are distinguished in model [1b]. For reasons detailed later, these three unobserved variables represent *additive genetic sources* (A), *common family environmental sources* (C), and *unique environmental sources* (E). The influences of these unobserved variables on the observed variables is indicated by the size of the factor loadings termed *a, c,* and *e* in Figure 21.1b. Other phenotypes could be included in a variety of ways (see McArdle & Goldsmith, 1990).

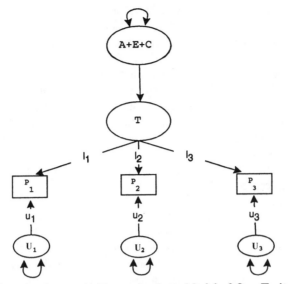

(a) A Psychometric–Factor Analytic Model of One Trait T

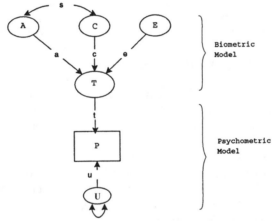

(b) A Biometric–Behavioral Genetic Model of One Performance P

FIGURE 21.1. Basic psychometric–biometric latent path models (see McArdle & Goldsmith, 1990).
Notes. P_m = observed performance on test m, T = unobserved trait or common factor score, U_m = unique factor score for test m, A = additive genetic component, C = shared family component, and E = nonshared-environmental component.

This separation of unobserved variables and their influences is the fundamental goal of BG analyses. The separation of these unobserved variables can be obtained from theoretical differences among relatives in different kinds of families, and the numerical values of these influences can be calculated from the associations observed in measurements of these relatives. Some of these technical issues are discussed in later sections. In this general SEM perspective, the goal of the BG analyses of Figure 21.1b is the same as the factor-analytic model of Figure 21.1a—BG analyses are designed to evaluate the adequacy of theories expressed as latent variable path models for multiple phenotypes.

The possibility of a correlation between the *A* and *C* variables is an important feature of contemporary BG models (this two-headed arrow is labeled *s* in Figure 21.1b). These correlations can be meaningful but they cannot be estimated without more extensive data collections and more complex models (Meredith, 1973; Neale & Cardon, 1992). Contemporary BG methods are important partly because they do include the possibility of evaluating these more complex models. Some of the models discussed in later sections of this chapter also include parent-to-child transmission of shared effects (termed *z*), the correlations between spouses (termed *m*), nonadditive genetic effects such as dominance (nonadditive effects of alleles at the same locus), and nonadditive effects of genes at different loci (Carey, 1986; Cloninger et al., 1979; Eaves, Fulker, & Heath, 1989; Heath, Kendler, Eaves, & Markell, 1990; Neale & Cardon, 1992).

In the next few sections we highlight basic issues about contemporary SEMs used in BGIA research. BGIA models can be estimated, evaluated, and presented in the same way as any other latent variable SEM (McArdle, 1986; McArdle & Goldsmith, 1990; McArdle & Prescott, 1992), but the interpretations must be considered in the context of biometric theory. We demonstrate how questions about the biometric bases of complex human characteristics are not simple questions that can be answered in terms of common statements such as "twin research shows it is largely genetic." A clearer understanding of the methods, models, and results from BGIA analysis may illuminate the complexity of genetic theory and the appropriateness of scientific inferences that can be made from such studies.

BASIC ISSUES IN BGIA MODELING STUDIES

Traditional Biometric Model Assumptions

Biometric genetic theory is used to define and specify the mathematical relations among the underlying components of measurements thought to represent a continuously distributed trait (e.g., Fisher, 1930; Falconer, 1990). By definition, the effects of individual *genes* (the DNA sequences on specific areas of the chromosome) combine to produce the underlying *genotype.* These genes are assumed to be (1) numerous, (2) additive in effect, (3) segregating independently (i.e., the probability of receiving one gene is independent of the probability of receiving others), (4) not sex-linked (transmitted via the X or Y chromosomes), and (5) not influencing characteristics used for spousal selection. With these asssumptions the underlying genotypic correlation between pairs of relatives is specified. This can also be cast as a structural model that posits that an observed score is a simple combination of unobserved genetic and nongenetic sources.[2] The model is identical to any regression or factor-analytic model in which the scores *A* and *E* may be correlated and the unknown coefficients are weights to be estimated (these are now labeled D_a and D_e to indicate deviations from the mean). In this basic model, *no interaction* of the two unobserved scores is considered.

These model assumptions lead to mathematical expectations about the correlations among pairs of relatives. If all resemblance between relatives in a family is due to genetic sources, the correlations between their scores are expected to be proportional to the correlations between their genetic backgrounds, and unrelated individuals would be uncorrelated. Assuming parents' genotypes are uncorrelated, the genotypes of first-degree relatives correlate (on average) at .50. First-degree relatives include fraternal (dizygotic or DZ) twins, ordinary siblings, and parent–child relationships. The genotypes of second-degree relatives (grandparents–grandchildren, aunt–niece, half siblings) are expected to correlate .25; third-degree relatives (cousins) .125, etc. Unrelated individuals living together, such as stepsiblings or parents and their adopted children would be expected to have zero genetic correlation. In the special case of identical (monozygotic or MZ) twins, the genotypes correlate 1.00. Of course, the sampling of subjects that are related or unrelated is a major concern of researchers in this area, and we return to these sampling issues later.

Nongenetic influences are considered as well. Most often, similarity in intellectual performance is expected to be correlated with similarity in relevant environments (e.g., home of rearing or social background). If true, the highest correlations would be found in scores from twins and similar-age siblings, lower correlations from parents and children, and still lower correlations from related individuals who have not lived together. Thus, under a purely environmental hypothesis, adoptees should be as similar to their adopting parents and siblings as any other children, and related individuals living in different environments would have scores with no correlation. A model that included both genetic and environmental sources of familial resemblance would produce estimates intermediate between these other two. All such models can include measurement error and the influence of experiences unique to particular individuals, so even MZ twins living together are not expected to have scores which correlate perfectly.

After the previous model coefficients are estimated at a specific value, it is possible to standardize the two unobserved variables, assume these two scores (A and E) are uncorrelated (orthogonal), and calculate the unobserved genetic variance (often calculated simply as D_a^2). To deal with variables of different scalings, it has become traditional to calculate the heritability ratio $h^2 = V_a / V_p$, so the heritability equals the unobserved additive genetic variance divided by the observed phenotypical variance. In some contexts this ratio is termed the "narrow" heritability because it includes only additive genetic variance. This kind of calculation may or may not take into account the common family environment (C) or the other factors described in Figure 21.1b. However, in most published BGIA studies this h^2 statistic is reported instead of the more fundamental coefficients (D_a and D_e). This simple reporting of heritability is a questionable practice.[3]

Models for Different Relative Groupings

Extensions of the genetic theory stated previously permit the estimation of BG structural coefficients from data from pairs of relatives. Figure 21.2a illustrates a latent path model for the most common design—the family design. In this model, additive genetic and shared environmental sources of resemblance are confounded. That is, any interpretation of family resemblance cannot be partitioned into separate genetic (A) and common family environment (C) components. In the adoption design of Figure 21.2b, these A and C components are (theoretically) separable, and the only source of parent-child resemblance is through cultural transmission, resulting in an estimate of common family effects (D_c). By comparing differences in resemblance among family members in the adoptive versus biological family designs, an estimate of the additive genetic parameter (D_a) is obtained. More complex models may be needed when considering the differences between adoptive versus biological families (see Munsinger, 1975; Turkheimer, 1991).

Figures 21.2c and 21.2d show models for resemblance between siblings or fraternal (DZ) twins and identical (MZ) twins. In this kind of model, pairs of DZ twins and pairs of full siblings are assumed to have the same genotypic correlation, even though the siblings can differ widely in chronological age. Unlike the family and adoption models, here we cannot estimate the effects of assortative mating or of the correlation between A and C. In most twin models these correlations are assumed to be zero although fixed estimates from other sources can be inserted. Using these assumptions, the twin design can provide estimates (of D_a and D_c) based on the difference between the resemblance between MZ and DZ pairs. The special case of MZ twins raised apart (MZA) allows a complete separation of these components.[4]

It is important to recognize that the previous models may not be reasonable representations of the underlying mechanisms. In the adoption data, for example, there may be a variety of effects of *selective placement*. If, for example, adoptive families were matched to biological families for educa-

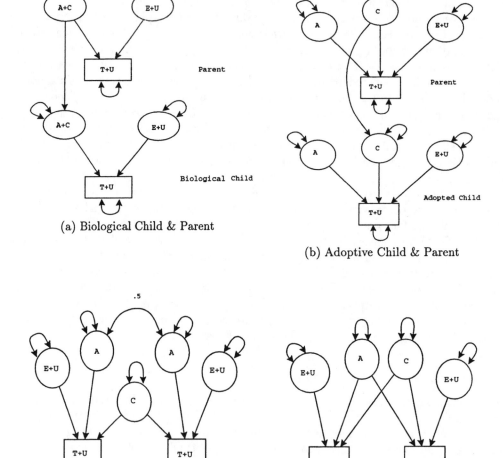

FIGURE 21.2. Biometric path models for separate family groups.

tional level, and if educational attainment is genetically influenced, there may be a correlation between the A's of the biological and adoptive parents. In this case it would be erroneous to conclude that all resemblance was due to cultural transmission alone. Similarly, in the twin data, if positive correlations between parents (assortative mating) is present but estimated as zero, the resulting estimate of additive genetic effects (D_a) will be biased downward and the common family effects (D_c) will be inflated. These and other interpretive issues require more advanced methodological treatments.

TABLE 21.1. Available Data from Seven Family Studies Using the WAIS

a. WAIS Data Sources and Sample Sizes

Study	Family studies		Adoption studies		Twin studies			Total
	HFS	IHD	MAS	TAP	LTS	NOR	NYT	
Individuals	415	526	854	759	150	160	152	3,016
Families	117	169	225	283	75	80	76	1,025
Fathers	117	169	225	283	0	0	0	794
Mothers	117	169	225	283	0	0	0	794
Biological child 1	117	119	119	116	0	0	0	471
Biological child 2	64	69	119	23	0	0	0	275
Adopted child 1	0	0	106	54	0	0	0	160
Adopted child 2	0	0	60	0	0	0	0	60
DZ twins	0	0	0	0	46	40	27	226
MZ twins	0	0	0	0	29	40	49	236

Note. HFS = Hawaii Family Study (Defries et al., 1979; Nagoshi & Johnson, 1985); IHD = Institute of Human Development (Berkeley) Study (Eichorn et al., 1981); MAS = Minnesota Adoption Study (Scarr & Weinberg, 1978); TAP = Texas Adoption Project (Horn et al., 1979; Loehlin et al., 1989); LTS = Louisville Twin Study (Vandenberg & Falkner, 1965; Block, 1968; Wilson, 1986); NOR = Norwegian Twin Study (Tambs et al., 1984); NYT = New York Twin Study (Jarvik et al., 1972).

b. Distribution of Age in Years in Combined Sample

Relative	Age–Score			Median	Minimum	Maximum
	Size N	Mean	(SD)			
Fathers	794	45.2	(6.5)	45	30	62
Mothers	794	42.6	(6.4)	42	28	60
Bio. child 1	471	18.6	(2.9)	18	13	31
Bio. child 2	275	18.2	(2.5)	18	13	26
Adop. child 1	160	19.5	(3.1)	19	15	32
Adop. child 2	60	17.8	(1.8)	17	15	22
DZ twins	226	36.5	(21.0)	32	12	82
MZ twins	236	44.5	(21.1)	45	12	81
Total	3,016	35.3	(15.1)	38	12	82

Notes. (1) Fathers and Mothers groups include spouse pairs whose children were too young to take the WAIS. (2) Child 1 is either the only child studied or the older of two biological or adopted children included. (3) Child 2 is the younger of two biological or adopted offspring.

BGIA Data on the WAIS Block Design

To illustrate some of these techniques we use some data we have collected from other researchers on the *Wechsler Adult Intelligence Scale* (WAIS; Wechsler, 1955; see McArdle & Horn, 1996). Table 21.1a presents the numbers of individuals and families from each of seven separate studies of relatives measured on the WAIS. These studies include two family studies, the Hawaii Family Study (DeFries et al., 1979) and the Berkeley Growth Study (Eichorn, Clausen, Haan, Honzik, & Mussen, 1981); two adoption studies, the Minnesota Adoption Study (Scarr & Weinberg, 1978) and the Texas

Adoption Project (Horn, Loehlin, & Willerman, 1979); and three twin studies, The Louisville Twin Study (Block, 1968; Vandenberg & Falkner, 1965), the New York Study of Aging (Jarvik, Kallmann, & Falek, 1962), and the Norwegian Twin Study (Tambs, Sundet, & Magnus, 1986).

These data are arranged by familial membership. There are 8 possible categories organized by relationship to a target individual: fathers (4 studies), mothers (4), older biological offspring (4), younger biological offspring (3), older adopted offspring (2), adopted offspring with older adopted siblings (1), adoptees with a sibling who was a biological offspring of the adopting parents (1), MZ twins (3), and DZ twins (3). For the purposes of the analyses in this chapter, individuals were selected from each family based on the availability of cognitive data. We combined the raw scores from these seven independent studies to form a total of $N = 3,016$ subjects from $N_f = 1,025$ families.

Table 21.1b presents summary characteristics for all subjects in each of the eight relative groups. Chronological age was obtained from self-reports at the time of testing; the mean age for the entire sample is 35.3 years ($SD = 15.1$) with a range of 12 to 82 years. Age variation is quite wide across the three twin samples but somewhat restricted among the parent and offspring groups.

Each of these seven studies used the full or partial WAIS. In this chapter we present analyses from scores on the Block Design (BD) measure. The BD subscale was originally developed by Kohs (1923), adapted by Wechsler (1955) for the WAIS, and has been widely used with only minor revisions since the 1930s. Low scores on the BD scale are widely used as indicators of neurological impairment (e.g., Lezak, 1976), BD scores show a rather dramatic decline over age (Botwinick, 1978), and BD is a relatively culture-free measure (Cattell, 1982; Matarazzo, 1980). It has been considered an indicator of Fluid Intelligence (Horn & McArdle, 1980), but more recent factor-analytic work suggests that BD is a better measure of General Visualization (g_v, McArdle & Horn, 1996; Woodcock, 1990).

The left-hand part of Table 21.2a displays score means, standard deviations, skewness, and kurtosis for raw BD scores. Compared to large normative samples, the high means for the parent and offspring groups may reflect a selection bias of volunteers for participation in studies of intellectual ability. In contrast to the data from parent–offspring groups, the twin data have greater score heterogeneity. This in part represents the greater age variation in these groups, as well as a greater range of ability. To examine non–age-related variation, we also calculated an Age-Adjusted Block Design (AABD) score created as a residual from an age-based polynomial equation.[5]

Table 21.2b presents sample sizes and correlations between pairs of relatives for raw and age-adjusted BD scores. For example, the correlation between spouses is based on 794 pairs of spouses from four different studies. The same individual may contribute to several pairings; for example, families with two offspring have four different parent–offspring pairings (mother–child 1, mother–child 2, etc.). Members of twin pairs show remarkably similar BD performance, whereas the correlations among other relative pairs are small. In general, the spouse and parent–offspring correlations increase after removing the age variation. Little change occurs for the sibling pairings due to the limited age variation within these groups, but the twin correlations decrease substantially.

Although rarely presented in BGIA studies, it is important to examine the raw scores in some detail. Figures 21.3a through 21.3d summarize some of the relations observed in these data. Figure 21.3a shows the correspondence between the age-partialed standardized BD scores of fathers and their biological children from 471 families. Figure 21.3b shows the scores for 275 pairs of biological siblings raised together, Figure 21.3c displays the data for the 92 unrelated sibling pairs, and Figure 21.3d shows the 118 MZ twin pairs. These figures illustrate the distribution characteristics of the current BD scale and the complexity of the data structure. One of the most obvious features of these plots is the ceiling of scores at the top end of the BD scale. This ceiling effect may be a feature of the WAIS–BD scaling, or it may reflect the generally high scores of the volunteer samples.

Illustrative Results from Twin Data

To illustrate contemporary approaches to BGIA, we first analyze WAIS–BD data from twin studies alone. The models presented in Figure 21.2 were traditionally estimated using simple algebraic expressions (see Goldsmith, 1983; Falconer, 1990). For example, an appropriate estimate of the additive genetic coefficient D_a could be estimated by a direct comparison of the MZ and DZ correlations (i.e., $D_a^2 = 2(r_{MZ} - r_{DZ})$). This popular calculation is based on a simple orthogonal A and E model (i.e., no r_{AE}), does not deal with differences in variance terms, and usually ignores statistical tests and confidence boundaries. To deal with these issues the model results reported in this chapter were obtained using computer programs designed for including multiple groups (e.g.,

TABLE 21.2. Basic Summary Statistics for WAIS Block Design Scores

a. Distributions of BD and AABD Scores in Total Sample

Relative	BD				AABD			
	Mean	(*SD*)	Skew.	Kurt.	Mean	(*SD*)	Skew.	Kurt.
Fathers	80.1	(15.2)	−.63	−.37	.35	(.66)	−.62	−.18
Mothers	74.5	(15.3)	−.19	−.72	.03	(.67)	−.18	−.69
Biological child 1	81.7	(15.1)	−.85	.28	.21	(.66)	−.84	.26
Biological child 2	81.3	(15.2)	−.80	−.07	.19	(.65)	−.81	−.05
Adopted child 1	77.0	(15.0)	−.49	−.42	−.00	(.65)	−.49	−.42
Adopted child 2	73.7	(13.8)	−.09	−.54	−.13	(.60)	−.09	−.51
DZ twins	63.2	(22.9)	−.39	−.63	−.32	(.77)	−.01	−.66
MZ twins	55.8	(25.1)	.04	−1.13	−.45	(.75)	.19	−.56
Total	75.5	(18.4)	−.82	.42	.05	(.71)	−.42	−.47

Notes. (1) Fathers and Mothers include spouse pairs whose children did not take the WAIS. (2) Child 1 is either only child studied or older of two children. (3) Child 2 is younger of two offspring. (4) Age-adjusted (AABD) scores calculated as residuals from polynomial (see note 5, p. 429).

b. Correlations of BD and AABD Scores for Different Relatives

Relative pair	Sample size of pairs	Raw score BD	AABD
1. Father and Mother	794	.156*	.186*
2. Father and biological child 1	471	.239*	.284*
3. Mother and biological child 1	471	.257*	.297*
4. Father and biological child 2	275	.254*	.299*
5. Mother and biological child 2	275	.218*	.238*
6. Father and adopted child 1	160	.040	.125
7. Mother and adopted child 1	160	.072	.147
8. Father and adopted child 2	60	−.119	−.086
9. Mother and adopted child 2	60	.111	.133
10. Biological children 1 and 2	275	.288*	.292*
11. Adopted children 1 and 2	60	.207	.200
12. Biological child 1 and adopted child 1	32	.256	.244
13. Fraternal DZ twins	113	.690*	.493*
14. Identical MZ twins	118	.888*	.767*

Note. Asterisk indicates a correlation which is significantly different from zero at $p > .05$.

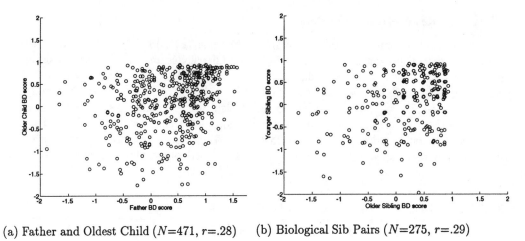

(a) Father and Oldest Child (N=471, r=.28)   (b) Biological Sib Pairs (N=275, r=.29)

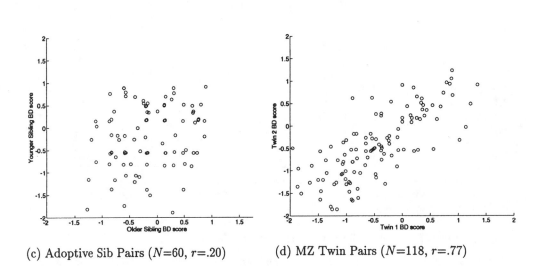

(c) Adoptive Sib Pairs (N=60, r=.20)   (d) MZ Twin Pairs (N=118, r=.77)

FIGURE 21.3. Paired similarity for age-adjusted block design (AABD) scores for separate family groups.

Mx by Neale, 1993; LISREL by Jöreskog & Sörbom, 1988).[6] We use this multiple group model-fitting approach because it (1) allows for a wide variety of mathematical models (e.g., the inclusion of r_{AE} components), and (2) provides an adequate statistical basis for calculation of parameters, standard errors, and fit indices. These computer calculations are somewhat complex and not described further here (but see McArdle & Goldsmith, 1990; Neale & Cardon, 1992).

Table 21.3 displays parameter estimates and goodness-of-fit indices for a series of models fit to the variance–covariance matrices of the age-adjusted block design scores from the three twin studies. The top section of the table (21.3a) displays estimates required to be equivalent across all studies. Results for models that allow some parameters to vary are shown separately for each study (in 21.3b–21.3d).

The first column of Table 21.3 shows results from an initial model requiring invariance of the

TABLE 21.3. Alternative Model Results for WAIS Block Design Scores from Twin Data

Parameters	Initial model estimates			Alternative models					
				No *A*		Equal *A*		All free	
	est	(se)	[var]	est	[var]	est	[var]	est	[var]
a. Invariant Group Parameters									
A Additive Genetic	15.7	(1.7)	[70%]	0	[00%]	12.2	[—]	—	[—]
C Common Environment	3.0	(8.1)	[2%]	13.7	[54%]	—	[—]	—	[—]
E Unique Environment	9.9	(0.6)	[28%]	12.7	[46%]	—	[—]	—	[—]
b. Adolescent Twins									
A Additive Genetic	—	(—)	[—]	—	[—]	==	[61%]	12.5	[62%]
C Common Environment	—	(—)	[—]	—	[—]	0	[0%]	0	[0%]
E Unique Environment	—	(—)	[—]	—	[—]	9.8	[39%]	9.8	[38%]
c. Adult Twins									
A Additive Genetic	—	(—)	[—]	—	[—]	==	[44%]	12.7	[48%]
C Common Environment	—	(—)	[—]	—	[—]	10.6	[34%]	10.2	[30%]
E Unique Environment	—	(—)	[—]	—	[—]	8.6	[22%]	8.5	[22%]
d. Older Adult Twins									
A Additive Genetic	—	(—)	[—]	—	[—]	==	[87%]	11.0	[68%]
C Common Environment	—	(—)	[—]	—	[—]	0	[0%]	0	[0%]
E Unique Environment	—	(—)	[—]	—	[—]	4.7	[13%]	7.6	[32%]
e. Goodness-of-Fit Indices									
NP Number of Parameters	3			2		.7		9	
DF Degrees of Freedom	15			16		11		9	
LR Likelihood Ratio	25.			.45		20.		11.	
RMS[*EA*] Root Mean Square	.054			.088		.059		.034	
Prob[*H₀*] Prob. Perfect Fit	.049			.00		.047		.25	
Prob[*H₁*] Prob. Close Fit	.39			.02		.32		.63	

Notes. (1) Number of twin pairs N_f = 231. (2) Scores are WAIS Age-Adjusted Block Design measurements. (3) Parameters are maximum-likelihood estimates from a six-group script fitted with the LISREL-7 modeling program (Jöreskog & Sörbom, 1988). (4) RMS[*EA*] and Prob values calculated by FITMOD program (Browne & Cudeck, 1993). (5) The 95% confidence boundaries for the initial estimates are: Additive Genetic *A* = 43% to 100%, Common Environment *C* = 0% to 100%, and Unique Environment *E* = 22% to 34%. (6) == indicates parameter is invariant over groups.

parameters across all three groups. The parameter estimates are the loadings for each variance component; the sum of the squares of these equals the total variance of the age-adjusted WAIS–AABD scores for the combined samples. Based on this invariance model, the additive genetic component is estimated at 15.7 with a standard error of 1.7, indicating, without statistical formality, that this D_a parameter is far different from zero. In contrast, the estimate for the common environmental parameter (D_c) is 3.0 with a standard error of 8.1, so this component is probably not different from zero. Finally the unique environmental parameter is estimated at 9.9 with a standard error of 0.6. The standardized proportions of variance are also estimated: additive genetic variance at 70%, common environmental variance at 2%, and unique environmental variance (plus measurement error) at 28%. Because *all* parameters are invariant over groups, these standardized estimates are invariant over groups also (but see later).

Section *e* of Table 21.3 shows the goodness-of-fit information for this model.[7] These are statistical indices which are used to test the empirical adequacy of specific aspects of the biometric theory. Without getting too bogged down in details, we can simply say these data include a total of 18 statistics: There are 2 variances and 1 covariance for each of the 6 groups of MZ and DZ twins. The model fitted here included 3 free parameters (D_a, D_c, and D_e), and this leaves 15 degrees of freedom (DF) to test the fit of the model to the data. The likelihood ratio test (LRT) obtained for these data is $LRT = 25$, and this can be compared to a chi-square distribution for variances and covariances. The probability of perfect fit ($p_{perfect} = .049$) is significant at the conventional $\alpha = .05$ level. However, the probability of close fit ($p_{close} = .39$, as indicated by the RMSEA[7]) is in an acceptable range. These results suggest that there is some minor differences (heterogeneity) between the effects in the different twin studies, but these differences are not large considering the small sample sizes.

In contemporary SEM, a series of nested models is used to provide a more formal statistical test of various hypotheses about the structure of similarity among family members (e.g., Heath, Neale, Hewitt, Eaves, & Fulker, 1989; McArdle & Goldsmith, 1990; Neale, Heath, Hewitt, Eaves, & Fulker, 1989). These comparisons are especially important in any evaluation of pattern hypotheses because the parameters of BGIA models are often (1) not in a comparable metric, (2) have different confidence boundaries, and (3) are highly correlated. We illustrate this kind of structural modeling approach using three alternatives.

The first alternative model is listed in the column labeled "No A." This model forces the coefficient associated with the additive genetic variable (A) to be equal to zero while the other two nonzero parameters are required to be invariant for all three groups. This model tests the hypothesis that all resemblance between twins is due to the environmental influences they share—that is, whether the additive genetic parameter can be parsimoniously set to zero. This model obtains a poor overall fit ($LRT = 45$ for $DF = 16$) as indicated by the probabilities associated with the test for perfect fit ($p = .00$) and close fit ($p = .02$). More important, relative to the initial model, this represents a substantial loss of fit relative to the initial model (difference $dLRT = 20$ on $dDF = 1$). From this result we conclude that the additive genetic effects are *not zero* for WAIS–BD.

The second alternative model differs from those used in traditional BGIA studies. It posits that the differences in variances and covariances across groups are due to fluctuation in the latent environmental variances; whereas, the contribution of the additive genetic component is equal over groups. This is likely when human migration or social change has occurred much more rapidly than any genetic selection for intellectual abilities. The additive genetic effect is estimated at 12.2 across all three groups. However, the groups differ in the estimates for the environmental components; the adolescent and older adult twin studies showing no evidence for common environmental effects, whereas the adult twin study attributes nearly one-third of the standardized variance to environments and experiences shared by twins. However, relative to the invariant model, this difference in fit is small and nonsignificant ($dLRT = 5$, $dDF = 4$, $p = .30$) so we conclude that genetic variance is equal across all groups.

The final model of Table 21.3 displays the results of a model that permits the parameters to vary across the three samples. This model suggests a small but significant heterogeneity among the twin groups ($dLRT = 14$, $dDF = 6$, $p = .03$). We could pursue these group differences in parameters, especially in the common family environment, but our small samples permit only limited precision.

One interesting piece of information from this analysis comes from a simple comparison of the standardized estimates (listed as percentages) across studies. For example, in the "Equal A" model, the estimates for the "heritability" differ substantially across groups—ranging from 44% to 87%— even though the absolute estimate of the genetic deviation ($D_a = 12.2$) is held constant over groups. This is just a small illustration of the problems of interpreting heritability coefficients.

ADVANCED ISSUES IN BGIA MODELING

The previous BGIA analyses can be expanded to include all the family and adoptee data described in Tables 21.1 and 21.2. Such analyses are important because they allow different kinds of model assumptions to be estimated and evaluated. The inclusion of these data allows us to expand the analyses to estimate parameters not available from the twin data alone, including assortative mating, parental transmission, covariance between components, and a second independent estimate of genetic contribution. We also examine the use of different statistical indicators, including models that use both covariances and means to account for unwanted sampling biases. These more advanced models require additional technical complexity, so some readers may wish to skip to the next section (p. 420).

BGIA Models Combining All Family Data

Figure 21.4 combines several aspects of the previously separate models for data with up to two parents and their biological offspring. The *circle-within-square* symbol designates a variable which may or may not be observed depending on the family configuration. Due to assortative mating in prior generations, the sources of variation for T may become correlated. We estimate R_s as the correlation between additive genetic and common environmental sources. We assume that within a person, A and C are uncorrelated with E. We assume that the U's are uncorrelated across persons within a family. The spousal resemblance for the phenotype is modeled through the correlations between the sources of their scores and this is separated into several different mathematically dependent components (i.e., R_γ is the correlation between spouse A's, R_ε is the correlation between spouse C's, etc.).

Score resemblance between parents and offspring comes from two sources. Each parent provides half of a child's genetic material, so the regression weights from the A's of parents to the A's of children are assigned a value of .5. We assume that the relevant genes segregate independently and there are negligible nonadditive effects. The residual genetic variation is due to genetic segregation and is here labeled *Seg* with a special variance [set at $.5 \times (1-R_\gamma)$]. This variable is correlated 1.0 between MZ twins and 0 for all other siblings. If parental genotypes are uncorrelated (i.e., $R_\gamma = 0$), the residual genetic variation is .5 and the correlation of the additive genetic variance of DZ twins and siblings is expected to be .5. However, to the extent that parental geneotypes are correlated, the residual variation is less than .5 and genetic correlation between siblings is increased.

A second source of parent–offspring resemblance in this model comes from what is termed "vertical" transmission—that is, the phenotype of the parent is correlated with that of the child through nongenetic sources. This can be modelled in several ways (Heath et al., 1990). Here we allow the true score of the parent (T) to contribute to the sibling common environment (C_p). This might occur if parents with more developed intellectual abilities provide environments for their children which promote intellectual development. The regression weights from the parental T's are labeled z_f and z_m and are separately estimable for fathers and mothers. These combine to produce the portion of the common environment that comes from the parents, C_p. The common environment for siblings also arises from nonparental sources and these are represented in the diagram as C_{sib}. Resemblance due to common environment may differ with type of relationship. For example, we test whether twins have more similar common environments than ordinary siblings by allowing an additional correlation between their environmental components which is not present for biological and adoptive siblings. For convenience, we model this as R_t, a correlation between the E scores of twins.

Three other aspects of this modeling approach are unusual:

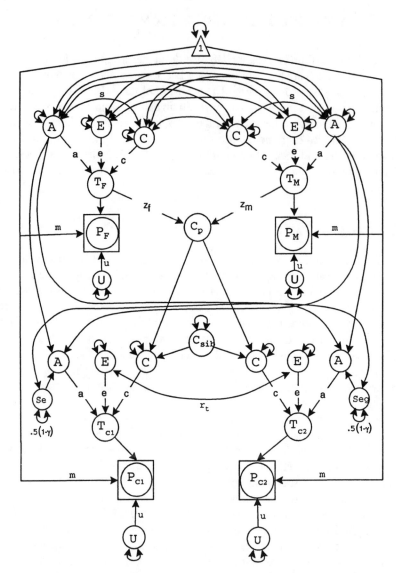

FIGURE 21.4. An overall structural model for multiple family groups. Circle designates an unobserved variable; circle within square designates a variable which is observed in some groups but not in others; triangle designates a unit constant.

1. We have included an estimate of the *uniqueness* of measurement within the model; here we fix the parameter at $R_u = .28$ based on other research.[8] Unique variance can inflate estimates of independent or nonshared environmental effects (D_e) and result in a loss of precision in statistical tests (e.g., McArdle & Goldsmith, 1990; compare Rowe & Plomin, 1981).

2. The means are included in these BG models by adding a constant (shown as a triangle in Figure 21.4) to the data set and analyzing cross-products matrices (see McArdle, 1986, for details). Previous research has shown how the inclusion of means is critical for models attempting to deal with nonrandom subject selection effects, and this may alter estimates of biometric parameters (see McArdle, 1986, 1994b).

3. The latent variable path model of Figure 21.4 is estimated using maximum-likelihood principles in the same way as a multiple group confirmatory factor analysis.[9] This general statistical approach is useful because it allows us to include results from other areas of statistical research within this BG context.

Illustrative Results Using All Family Data

Table 21.4 gives the overall results for the fully saturated mean and covariance models of WAIS–BD from 3,016 individuals. Section 21.4a presents the parameter estimates in score metric, 21.4b shows standardized parameter estimates, 21.4c shows estimates of correlations between various latent variables, and 21.4d presents goodness-of-fit information.

Model results for raw score covariances are displayed in the first column of Table 21.4. The mean is not included in this model and so is fixed at zero (row 1). The second row shows the estimated phenotypic score deviation ($D_p = 16.6$), and the measurement error is fixed at a value based on the previous estimate of unreliability. The estimates for the biometric parameters are listed next: additive genetic $D_a = 10.3$, common family environment $D_c = 5.8$, and unique environment $D_e = 10.9$. The parental transmission parameter is estimated at $B_z = 0.01$, and the assortative mating correlation is estimated at $R_\mu = .19$. Other correlations can be calculated, including the correlation between A and C ($R_s = .13$), and the specific twin environment correlation ($R_t = .32$). The variance components of this model are listed, but these calculations are a bit more complex and are discussed later. This model contains 6 parameters, yielding 45 degrees of freedom, and the goodness of fit is indexed by $LRT = 178$ with $RMSEA = .031$.

The second column of Table 21.4 shows similar results for AABD residual scores. The initial impact on the deviation is clear (now a .45 SD overall), and the corresponding parameter estimates are smaller. The resulting proportions of variance have changed slightly. The shared sibling environment has been reduced by 5% due to age effects, and this leads to a proportional increase in the unique environment. The fit of the model to the data is now excellent ($LRT = 50.5$ on $DF = 45$), indicating that the age differences in the data accounted for a large part of the misfit of the previous model.

The third column of Table 21.4 shows results for BD scores fitted using both means and covariances. In contrast to deviations around the mean *within a group*, all deviations around the *grand mean* of all groups are considered important here. This structural model fits very poorly ($LRT = 484$ on $df = 68$), and this indicates that the means in the separate groups are not equal. To counteract the obvious age differences (e.g., between parents and children), the mean and covariance model is refitted to the AABD residual scores and the fit is improved ($LRT = 340$ on $df = 68$). The fit of this last model indicates that the means in supposedly comparable samples are not equal ($dLRT = 290$ on $dDF = 13$, compared to the AABD covariance model). Nevertheless, the parameter estimates obtained from this model give us the best unbiased estimates of the effects under the requirement that the means are equal.[10] Overall, the biometric model of Figure 21.4 did not yield a perfect fit to the means and covariances ($LRT = 340$ on $DF = 68$), but we accept this misfit as part of the sampling bias inherent in using these data.

Assuming all scores are standardized, the estimated proportions of phenotypic variance for the age-adjusted mean and covariance models (column 4, Table 21.4) can be decomposed in the following way: (1) unique variance $P_w = 28\%$, (2) additive genetic $P_a = 46\%$, (3) shared sibling environment $P_c = 10\%$, (4) unique environment $P_e = 13\%$, (5) covariation between the additive genetic and shared environment latent variables $P_s = 3\%$, and (6) parental transmission $P_z = 0\%$. Although the heritability of 46% is largest, this entire pattern of results is needed to describe the result.

Confidence boundaries can (and should) be created for each parameter above from the point

TABLE 21.4. Alternative Model Fitting Results for WAIS Block Design Scores

Parameters		Covariances only		Means and covariances	
Symbol	Label	Raw score	Age adjusted	Raw score	Age adjusted
a. Biometric parameter estimates					
1. M_p	Phenotypic Mean	=0	=0	76.49	.17
2. D_p	Phenotypic Deviation	16.58	.45	17.40	.70
3. D_w	Unique Error	8.84	=.24	=9.27	=.37
4. D_a	Additive Genetic	10.33	.42	10.68	.48
5. D_c	Shared Environment	5.82	.19	7.40	.22
6. D_e	Unique Environment	10.89	.46	10.62	.45
7. B_z	Parental Transmission	.010	.29	.01	.14
8. R_μ	Assortative Mating	.19	.18	.18	.16
9. P_t	Shared Twin Environment	.46	.32	.45	.35
b. Variance components as percentages					
10. P_w	Unique Error	=28%	=28%	=28%	=28%
11. P_a	Additive Genetic	39%	39%	38%	46%
12. P_c	Shared Sib Environment	12%	7%	17%	10%
13. P_e	Unique Environment	15%	20%	9%	13%
14. P_s	Due to Corr a $\leftrightarrow$ c	6%	5%	7%	3%
15. P_z	Due to Parental Transmission	0%	1%	1%	0%
c. Calculated correlation estimates					
16. R_s	gene–environment	.13	.15	.13	.08
17. R_t	shared twin	.32	.23	.35	.24
18. R_γ	spouse a $\leftrightarrow$ a	.09	.08	.08	.08
19. R_ε	spouse c $\leftrightarrow$ c	.04	.03	.05	.02
20. R_α	spouse e $\leftrightarrow$ e	.08	.08	.07	.07
21. R_ω	spouse a $\leftrightarrow$ e	.09	.08	.07	.07
22. R_δ	spouse a $\leftrightarrow$ c	.06	.05	.06	.04
23. R_τ	spouse c $\leftrightarrow$ e	.06	.05	.05	.04
d. Goodness-of-fit indices					
24. NS	Number of Statistics	51	51	75	75
25. NP	Number of Parameters	6	6	7	7
26. DF	Degrees of Freedom	45	45	68	68
27. LR	Likelihood Ratio	178.	50.5	484.	340.
28. RMS[*EA*]	Root Mean Square	.031	.006	.045	.036
29. Prob[H_0]	Prob. Perfect Fit	.00	.27	.00	.00
30. Prob[H_1]	Prob. Close Fit	1.00	1.00	.98	1.00

Notes. (1) Number of Individuals N = 3,106, Number of families N_f = 1,025. (2) Parameters are maximum-likelihood estimates from the Mx modeling program (Neale, 1993). (3) Assortative mating is based on phenotypical assortment. (4) Parental transmission is from parental phenotypes to sibling shared environment parameter. (5) Shared twin standardized estimate is proportion of unique sib estimate that is shared within twin pairs (i.e., unique twin environment = unique sib × [1 – shared twin]). (6) RMS[*EA*] and Prob values calculated by FITMOD program (Browne & Cudeck, 1993).

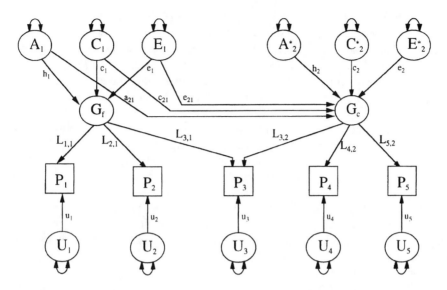

FIGURE 21.5. A psychometric genetic common factors model (adapted from McArdle & Goldsmith, 1980).

estimate and the estimated standard errors, or from the change in the fit.[11] In this example, the point estimate of the additive genetic variance is 46% but, due to sampling fluctuation, the 95% confidence interval for this proportion is 21% to 81%. This confidence range does not include zero, but it is surprisingly wide for a study that includes more than 3,000 observations. All other parameters should be evaluated in the same way.

The stability of critical parameters can be studied by refitting the model without the parameter. Four alternative models involving a single parameter were fitted to these AABD mean and covariance statistics: (1) removing the twin environment parameter (i.e., $P_t = 0$) produced a small but significant change in fit (overall $LRT = 345$ on $DF = 69$, so $dLRT = 5$ on $dDF = 1$); (2) removing parental transmission ($P \rightarrow C = 0$) yielded a nonsignificant change in fit ($dLRT = 1$ on $dDF = 1$); (3) no parental assortment ($R_\mu = 0$) yielded a larger and significant change in fit ($dLRT = 19$ on $dDF = 1$); (4) no additive genetic effect ($D_a = 0$) yielded the largest and significant change in fit ($dLRT = 36$ on $dDF = 1$). Two models requiring multiple constraints were also tested: (5) no shared environmental effects ($D_c = 0$, $P_s = 0$, and $P_z = 0$) yielded a small but significant change in fit ($dLRT = 25$ on $dDF = 3$); (6) no resemblance between family members (all six parameters zero) yielded a large and significant change in fit ($dLRT = 320$ on $dDF = 6$).

The main substantive results for the WAIS Block Design subscale are not startling—based on these models and assumptions, the additive genetic variance is sizable. Most important overall is the result that there is virtually no evidence for nongenetic transmission between parents and offspring for performance on the WAIS–BD task. That is, it seems that all parent–offspring resemblance can be parsimoniously modeled through genetic sources. There is limited evidence for the existence of gene–environment covariance, covariance among the latent variables of spouse pairs, and shared sibling environment (other than between twins).

Including a Psychometric Model

As mentioned earlier, it is possible to integrate a psychometric measurement model (Figure 21.1a) together with a biometric model (Figure 21.1b), and this is worth pursuing for a number of reasons.

In one approach, previously used by Loehlin and Vandenberg (1968) and Martin and Eaves (1977), the biometric components of each measure (e.g., A_m) could be formed into a higher-order common factor (e.g., A^*). McArdle and Goldsmith (1990) showed how a more restrictive model could be tested where the variables formed a single common factor of measurement (T), and this common factor itself had biometric components. Both of these common factor models allows the separation of measurement error or uniqueness (U_m) from the variance attributed to nonshared environmental effects (E).

Figure 21.5 illustrates a BGIA model from a twin analysis based on five scales from the Primary Mental Abilities (PMA) battery (from Loehlin & Vandenberg, 1968; McArdle & Goldsmith, 1990). This model is based on Cattell's original version of the Theory of Fluid and Crystallized Intelligence, or gf/gc theory (Cattell, 1987). In this theory, a general fluid intelligence factor (gf) supposedly reflected thinking, reasoning, and neurological efficiency and was assumed to have a strong biological and genetic basis. In contrast, a broad crystallized intelligence factor (gc) supposedly reflected knowledge, learning, and acculuration and was considered less heritable. In developmental progression, the gf factor was thought to be a precursor of the gc factor. To test some of these developmental concepts, the multivariate model included two common factors (labeled Gf and Gc here) and biometric components of these factor scores.

Using the same kind of SEM approach presented earlier, McArdle and Goldsmith (1990) concluded that there was a strong genetic component for each factor, there was no evidence that the gf was more highly heritable than the gc factor, and the overlap among these factors was due to both additive genetic (A) and common family environments (C). Perhaps more important, these multivariate data also allowed a test of the hypothesis that a single latent factor (F) could account for all the biometric and psychometric information in these data. Even with this relatively small sample of twins, this single-factor biometric model failed to produce a reasonable fit. The conclusion of this work was that although one common factor might seem to fit the internal correlations among the PMA scales, the external requirement of "proportional biometric relations" indicated that a one-factor model of intellectual ability is not acceptable. A similar result was presented dealing with aspects of the WAIS (McArdle & Goldsmith, 1984; McArdle & Horn, 1996). These illustrations shows how SEM–BG modeling research can help inform research about the construct validity of cognitive abilities (Goldsmith & Gottesman, 1977; McArdle & Prescott, 1992).

FUTURE QUESTIONS FOR BGIA STUDIES

The models used here illustrate some current trends in BG research. The measurement of different kinds of relative groups allows BG studies to make estimates of otherwise unidentifiable parameters. The family and twin studies have been cleverly designed to maximize genetic information and yet retain the power to reject alternative hypotheses about genetic and nongenetic transmission among relatives. These family and twin samples are not easy to obtain, and BG researchers continue to work hard to understand the sources of resemblance among different kinds of relatives. The integrative combination of multiple studies, as we have demonstrated here, allows additional parameters to be estimated and permits a more realistic appraisal of the confidence boundaries around these estimates.

In this specific application, we accumulated data from several studies of twins and biological and adoptive families, and we examined these data in a cumulative fashion. We formed a comprehensive SEM with explicit constraints to test various aspects of the relationships between parents and children. We added specific parameters from biometric theory, psychometric theory, and statistical theory. New SEM programs were used to calculate estimates, and traditional statistical theory was used to evaluate the goodness-of-fit between models and data.

Biometric analysis using a SEM approach has not escaped serious criticism, even from those doing the modeling (Goldsmith & McArdle, 1995b; Gottleib, 1991; Loehlin, 1992; Nesselroade & McArdle, in press; McArdle, 1987, 1994a, 1996a; McArdle & Gottesman, 1987; Prescott, Johnson, & McArdle, 1991; Thelen & Adolf, 1992). Persistent problems in BGIA research include the need to eliminate the historical dichotomy of "nature versus nurture" and clarify the appropriate scientific interpretations of BGIA results. Some problematic issues in BGIA research can be organized in terms of four key questions that follow.

Whom Should We Measure in BGIA Studies?

Most BGIA studies have not been carried out in the way presented here. Studies are frequently based on selected samples, using only one type of subject group. Twins or adoptees are commonly studied but may not be representative of the ability distribution of the general population. As shown here, different designs allow estimation of different sets of model parameters. Thus, reliance on only one study design may produce incomplete results. In fact, studies that include only twins have yielded different estimates of genetic and familial transmission effects on intelligence than studies based on adoptees and their families (e.g., Loehlin, 1989; Plomin & Loehlin, 1989). Other research using the simultaneous modeling of several types of relative groups has typically been limited by small, unrepresentative samples (e.g., Rodgers & Rowe, 1987; Rose et al., 1980; Rose, Harris, Christian, & Nance, 1979).

Volunteer bias and special twin effects have been a concern of several studies (e.g., Carey, Goldsmith, Tellegen, & Gottesman, 1978), but little has been done to overcome these problems. In some studies twins have been found to score significantly lower on measures of verbal ability than singletons from the same population (Record, McKeown, & Edwards, 1970). Subjects volunteering for research on cognitive abilities are frequently of above-average ability levels (Botwinick, 1978). Other possible selection effects include the selective placement of adoptees and the unintended narrowing of environmental variation within volunteer samples.

Another frequent problem with sample selection is the use of data obtained from subjects with decidedly different variation on such other variables as age. As observed in the current analyses, if twins and siblings show resemblance on a measure in part because of similarity in age, this will spuriously raise the similarity attributed to common environmental influences (i.e., studies with wide age spread will lead to larger estimates of D_c.) This may also reduce the apparent resemblance between parents and offspring, decreasing the ability to detect significant effects of parent to child transmission.

The distinction made between heritability estimates obtained through so-called direct (adoption study) and indirect (comparing resemblances of other relative pairs) methods (e.g., Plomin & Loehlin, 1989) also raises issues of subject sampling. For example, Loehlin (1989) included different genetic parameters for adoption and nonadoption family groups to improve the model fit to the Bouchard and McGue (1981) data. Although fitting such parameters is important for testing equivalence of data obtained under different designs, it must be remembered that this is a statistical adjustment rather than an explanation of the sources of the differences in the data. There is no current theory that says that genes work differently in different individuals based on their adoption (or twin) status. We should instead view such results as a clue to sampling biases or other confounds in the data such as selective placement or gene–environment correlation and include these as parameters in the SEM.

Continuing studies of cognitive change at different points in the lifespan (Schaie, Anderson, McClearn, & Money, 1975; Pedersen et al., 1992; Wilson, 1986) will need to recognize typical problems of longitudinal research. If, for example, variance is restricted in samples in which both twins are alive and continue to volunteer for testing, this may produce biased estimates of resemblance between individuals. Secular changes in environmental variance can produce changes in heritability estimates based on correlations, even in the absence of any changes of genetic variance. These and other sampling issues can have considerable impact on biometric interpretations of developmental processes.

What Should We Measure in BGIA Studies?

The use of a single IQ score is a continuing problem in BG research. Most BGIA researchers have treated intellectual abilities as if a single construct is sufficient to subsume the complex group of abilities required for intellectual functioning (e.g., g, IQ, or even a "first unrotated principal component"). However, when the same standards of goodness of fit used in the biometric components are applied to the measurement components of these models, multiple abilities are indicated (e.g., DeFries & Fulker, 1986; McArdle & Goldsmith, 1990; Pedersen, Plomin, & McClearn, 1994), although some notable research projects are exceptions to this rule (e.g., Jarvik et al., 1962; Jarvik, Blum, & Varma, 1972; DeFries et al., 1979). Bouchard and McGue (1981) recognized this problem, but the data on IQ presented in the literature were not reported in enough detail for these investigators to separate measures into even broad categories (e.g., verbal vs. spatial tests).

This leads us to ask, "What kinds of measurement variables are most appropriate for BGIA?" It sometimes seems that BG analyses are conducted on almost any available variable, followed by a highlighting of those variables with highest heritability. This is done, presumably, because variables with the highest heritability are believed to reflect phenomena with selective advantages and are therefore of potential biological importance. This argument seems at odds with evolutionary explanations—characteristics with the greatest importance have already undergone many generations of evolutionary selection (see Fisher, 1930; Wright, 1942; Medawar, 1959; Carey, 1991). In fact, the great majority of human genes are identical in all persons and therefore contribute no genetic variance (and thus zero heritability). Thus, despite the current search for behavioral traits with high heritability (i.e., intellectual abilities), the value of this goal is debatable on evolutionary grounds. In any case, it seems reasonable to suggest that a well-developed measurement model be presented for any construct (as in Figure 21.1a) before we should seriously investigate its biometric structure (as in Figure 21.1b; Prescott et al., 1992).

Often we are reminded about important genetic principles such as "[w]hat heredity determines are not fixed characters but developmental programs" (Dobzhansky, 1956, p. 344). Unfortunately, BGIA models have not yet reached this level of development. That is, most BGIA analyses do not often provide information about the developmental mechanisms by which individual differences in genotypes are related to individual differences in intellectual abilities (Ceci & Bruck, 1994). Timing of measurement is important because genetic and environmental variance may change over the course of development. Such developmental themes encourage the use of longitudinal measurement in biometric designs (Jarvik et al., 1962, 1972; Goldsmith, 1984; Goldsmith & McArdle, 1996; McArdle, Connell, & Goldsmith, 1980; McArdle, 1986, 1994a; Phillips & Fulker, 1989; Wilson, 1986; Vandenberg & Falkner, 1965). Although the temporal context does not by itself tell us about the causal directionality, longitudinal data collection may be a step in the right direction.

Scientific attempts to understand human behavioral development might be best started at the measurement of changes in the central nervous system (cited in Dalton & Bergenn, 1995). If so, there are probably many direct indicators of biological origin that would be more meaningful in a biometric analysis than higher-order intellectual abilities. Among many intellectual abilities, speed of processing has been considered to be related directly to neuronal characteristics of the central nervous system (Eysenck, 1986), and this would have some features related to a selective advantage. In the example used here, perhaps the speediness requirement of high BD scores is responsible for a large proportion of genetic variance; perhaps these results are related to the generally good health of attentive subjects (Elias, Schultz, Robbins, & Elias, 1989). These ideas lead to reasonable biological hypotheses for further multivariate biometric investigations.

Our own use of the WAIS–BD scale illustrates some serious limitations of measurement in BGIA research. In terms of factorial measurement, Block Design may reflect a General Visualization (g_v) component, but this is not yet well understood. Against this factorially complex background, our univariate results for the WAIS–BD scale can be seen as a stepping-stone toward understanding the biological features that lead to and support the expression and form of intellectual outcomes. In future BGIA studies, the most useful inferences about genetic effects will likely come in the context of well-developed biological and psychometric theory.

How Should We Interpret Heritability in BGIA Studies?

In practice, many BG researchers cite heritability coefficients and omit discussion of more fundamental structural results. Even when the genetic parameter is the largest, this does not imply that other sources of variation are unimportant. The calculation of heritability as a proportion suffers from oversimplification much like other common percentages. Explained variance (R^2) ratios and standardized regression weights (β) are often used in regression analysis to allow statistical comparisons among variables of different metrics. This is also true of the communalities of factor analysis models (also termed h^2). However, from a SEM perspective, the direct comparison of β and the size of the R^2 are *not* the central features of a regression analysis, nor is the communality h^2 the key feature of factor analysis. The key statistics in any structural model are the unstandardized parameters B, which describe the estimate of the effect of one variable upon another *as if the other variable were held constant.* This logic is most important in experimental designs with no possibility of a randomized control group—a key feature of all human BGIA studies.

In the SEM approach, we seek parameters that retain the same value under different conditions of sampling and measurement. The probable range of the associated parameter values, not the variance proportions, are the central results of structural regression or factor analyses (see Goldberger, 1972). Current BG models can provide information about how the additive genetic factors operate when considered separately from nongenetic factors, and vice versa. These BG parameters can help answer two questions: (1) For a specific genotype (A_1), what are the differences in outcome for different environments (E_1 vs. E_2 vs. E_x)? (2) For a specific environment (E_1), what are the differences in outcome for different genotypes (A_1 vs. A_2 vs. A_y)? As in any linear regression, resulting parameters (e.g., D_a and D_e) are obtained by averaging over all subgroups *as if these subgroups were homogeneous;* there is no specification in the typical path model for a *genotype × environment* interaction. In this context, the standard path-analytic models may not be complex enough to deal with the underlying complexity.

The importance of the genotype by environment interaction has a long history in BG research (Cattell, 1963; Eaves, 1984; Fulker et al., 1972; Jinks & Fulker, 1970; Rao & Morton, 1974). These ideas could improve our own models for the WAIS data, e.g., the BGIA models we fitted (Figure 21.4) could be compared for invariance under different and measurable environmental conditions (educational, social) to show how genotypes are affected by environments and vice versa. Various kinds of developmental models have been frequently discussed in the BGIA literature (Gottlieb, 1991; Scarr & McCartney, 1983; Thelen & Adolf, 1992; Waddington, 1953, 1962), so a dynamical systems view may be needed as well. In multivariate studies (e.g., the PMA models of Figure 21.5) BGIA analyses can also be redirected at, and can be most useful in providing, the search for *external validity* evidence for the existence of distinct intellectual ability factors (McArdle & Goldsmith, 1990; McArdle & Prescott, 1992). In any case, the popular reporting of heritability coefficients needs to be replaced by more complex modeling of *structural invariants.*

Will There Be Continuing Controversies in BGIA Studies?

A brief look at historical trends tells us the answer to this last question is yes. In response, some researchers will become more aware of the limitations and benefits of BG techniques and try to understand when BGIA studies are being used in a misguided fashion. Other researchers studying intellectual abilities will respond by avoiding BGIA studies altogether.

One heated debate that is likely to continue revolves around the issues of race differences in intellectual abilities (Jensen, 1969, 1973; Loehlin, Lindzey, & Spuhler, 1975; Scarr, 1971, 1980). Many BGIA researchers have instantly been labeled "fascist," presumably because some lay readers assume a direct linkage between genes and race, or fear that BGIA results provide a basis for considering racial differences as immutable or not deserving of social intervention (as discussed by Medawar, 1959; Scarr, 1971, 1980). The recent history includes Jensen's (1969, 1973) controversial reinterpretation of BGIA studies in terms of race differences and his creation of a "Spearman hypothesis" relating means and factor loadings between black and white groups (Jensen, 1985; see Cattell, 1985; Humphreys, 1985; Johnson & Nagoshi, 1985; Jones, 1985).

The most recent controversy was created, in part, by publication of *The Bell Curve* (Herrnstein & Murray, 1994). In discussing the large IQ score differences between racial groups, the authors suggest, "It seems highly likely to us that both genes and the environment have something to do with racial differences. What might the mix be? We are resolutely agnostic on this issue; as far as we can determine, the evidence does not yet justify an estimate" (p. 311). While there is seemingly little to argue about with this carefully worded statement, it unfortunately appears to place racial issues and genetic issues on unknown footing.

In contrast to Herrnstein and Murray (1994), there have been some compelling methodological studies that clearly show evidence against a genetic basis for these differences. For example, the analysis presented by Scarr, Pakstis, Katz, and Barker (1977) showed, "The test of a relationship between degree of African ancestry, estimated with the odds coefficients [of blood markers], and intellectual skills failed to provide evidence for genetic racial differences in intelligence. . . ." (pp. 84–85). Another key presumption in these kinds of arguments is that the physical differences between the races is directly related to genes. This is contraindicated by the extensive study of Cavalli-Sforza, Menozzi, and Piazza (1994):

> From a scientific point of view, the concept of race has failed to obtain any consensus; none is likely, given the gradual variation in existence. It may be objected that the racial stereotypes have a consistency that allows even the layman to classify individuals. However, the major stereotypes, all based on skin color, hair color and form, and facial traits, reflect differences that are not confirmed by deeper analysis with more reliable genetic traits and whose origin dates from recent evolution mostly under the effect of climate and perhaps sexual selection. (p. 19)

(See also Polednak, 1989; Storfer, 1990.)

Claims of the immutable nature of genetics and of IQ are often stated despite evidence to the contrary. For example, some scientific arguments about race and genes fail to consider the obvious covariates of nutritional and educational differences (Nichols & Anderson, 1973; Starfield et al., 1991) and basic concepts of cultural ethnicity (Jones, 1991). The complexity of generational changes in infant mortality, birth weight, health care, and family nurturing practices has been used to argue that ethnic and group disparities are neither endemic nor immutable (e.g., Starfield, 1991; Storfer, 1990). We can only hope that scientific information concerning genetics and group differences in intellectual abilities will be used more accurately in the future.

One of the newest and most controversial areas of research on genes and intellectual abilities comes directly from advances in technology for gene mapping. Rather than inferring genetic influence by studying resemblance among relatives, these methods attempt to locate the specific locations in the genome that code for specific functions. Some researchers have begun to apply this approach to intelligence by initiating a molecular genetic search for a small number of single genes of relatively large effect using a methodology termed "quantitative trait loci" (QTL).

> The most exciting direction for genetic research on cognitive ability is the possibility of harnessing the power of new molecular genetic techniques to identify some of the genes responsible for high heritability. The high heritability of *g*, its high reliability and stability, its key role in cognitive neuroscience, and its social importance as the best predictor of educational and occupational attainment (Jensen, 1980), make *g* a reasonable target for such a program of research. (Plomin et al., 1994, pp. 107–108)

The search for QTLs needs to be further understood in the BGIA context. Abnormalities in any of a large number of single genes may produce profound effects on central nervous system development (McKusick, 1994). But these genes are rare, often lethal, and unlikely to account for much of the variation in the normal population. Thus, studies of the extremes in behavior, most grossly in terms of high and low extreme groups, have provided a useful methodology to search for small correlations of gene locations and behavioral disorders. On the other hand, genetic theories about intellectual ability assume that a very large number of genes interacting in a complex way are involved in any of the phenotypes studied in BGIA. If we split up persons into extreme groups based on an IQ score, this newly constructed variable will not necessarily retain the internal or external validity of the original measure, so it may not be associated with the genetic sources of interest (see Nesselroade & Thompson, 1995; compare Thompson, Detterman, & Plomin, 1991). The current methodology of QTL analysis may require further refinements to be useful with the more complex variables of BGIA.

Assuming the search for the so-called "IQ genes" is a reasonable research goal, we can develop some predictions from prior research. For example, the cognitive models of hierarchical processing (Cattell, 1987; Horn, 1988; Sternberg, 1985; Carroll, 1993) may be re-expressed in these terms. Let us say these models postulate a *chain of events* in the relation between the expression of any single gene and the outcomes of individual differences in general intellectual functioning. In standard path-analytic terms, this model predicts that the impact of any gene (or any small area of the chromosome) on any global cognitive behavior is indirectly mediated through many circuitous paths. This means that the net effect of any single gene on any aggregate behavior is expected to be minuscule. To be sure, it is not that single genes have no important role in the behavioral outcomes of mental abilities but simply that from this kind of hierarchical processing perspective, the research on "IQ genes" appears to be a level of reductionism that is not now expected to produce large or important results for broad cognitive abilities (see Nesselroade & McArdle, in press). On the other hand, if QTL analyses do exhibit substantial effects, the classical hierarchical theory described earlier will require serious reconsideration.

If QTLs related to broad cognitive functioning are identified and considered important, the implications would be widespread. Thus far, psychologists, geneticists, and the general public have not dealt with the ramifications of the identification and cloning of a gene with a major contribution to any intellectual ability. In our view, the controversies over gene testing and gene therapy that would arise from such a discovery are likely to overshadow all previous debate concerning genetic contributions to intelligence. As stated elsewhere (e.g., Loehlin et al., 1975), we hope that the scientist and layman alike will remember that genetic differences are no excuse for racial, sexual, or any other form of discrimination.

The lack of scientific discussion surrounding these controversies suggests that scientists studying intellectual abilities should become more aware of behavioral genetic models and results. Despite the limitations outlined, the new BGIA models can provide information not available from any other study design and can illuminate questions beyond those concerned with genetic causality. We hope that the scientific modeling issues raised here offer a clearer way to deal with controversial issues in future scientific and social debates.

ACKNOWLEDGMENTS

The research was supported by grants from the National Institute on Aging (AG02695, AG04704, and AG07137). We thank all the researchers who provided these WAIS data for our NIA databank. These researchers include Dororthy Eichorn and Bill Meredith; Ron Johnson and Frank Ahern; Sandra Scarr and Richard Weinberg; Lissy Jarvick and Asenath LaRue; Steve Vandenberg, John Loehlin, Lindon Eaves, and Linda Corey; and Kristian Tambs. We also thank John L. Horn, Ronald C. Johnson, and John R. Nesselroade for their comments on various aspects of this report. The BG–WAIS analyses were initially presented at the Annual Meeting of the Behavior Genetic Association, Aussois, France, June 1990.

NOTES

1. In these path diagrams: (1) squares ($\square$) are used to represent observed or measured variables (e.g., P_1 and P_2); (2) circles ($\bigcirc$) are used to represent unobserved or theoretical variables (e.g., $E_{[t]}$ and F_t); (3) one-headed arrows ($\rightarrow$) are used to represent fixed regression coefficients (e.g., $F_1 \rightarrow P_1$), unlabeled one-headed arrows are assumed to have a numerical value of 1; (4) two-headed arrows ($\leftrightarrow$) are used to represent estimated variance or correlation coefficients (e.g., $F_t \leftrightarrow F_t = V_f$), unlabeled two-headed arrows are assumed to have a numerical value of 1, and (5) circles within squares are used in path diagrams to designate variables present for some groupings of persons but missing for others.

2. The standard BG model is expressed in the simple linear and additive form of a model written as

    $P_n = [D_a \times A_n] + [D_e \times E_n],$

    where for any individual n, the phenotype (P_n) is an observed (or manifest) score, and the additive genetic (A_n) and nongenetic or environmental (E_n) scores are unobserved (or latent) scores. The unknown coefficients D_a and D_e are weights to be estimated, and subsequently used to form variance components.

3. Heritability ratios (h^2) are formed to reflect the *explained variance due to genetic sources* relative to the total variance. The problems associated with the uses of such coefficients are similar to those encountered with R^2 indices in the analysis of variance. First, the variance attributed to the genetic sources (the numerator) may be affected by many other effects, including model misspecification and sampling biases. This variance will differ depending on whether only additive variance is used, if the correlations among spouses are not used, if the correlations among the genetic and nongenetic variables are not included, and if the range of genotypes are indirectly limited by sample selection. Second, the variance attributed to the phenotypes (the denominator) can be affected by subject sampling and bias. Some of these effects can be measured, but others are unavoidable and intrinsically confounded with genetic variability. The nongenetic or environmental variance is limited by the sample selection and model misspecification. Third, the likely confidence boundary around such indices is (1) typically nonsymmetric, (2) large, even in relatively large samples, and (3) not usually presented in research reports. These problems have been discussed in further detail by several other researchers (Chase, 1980; Feldman & Lewontin, 1975; Goldberger, 1977; Kempthorne, 1978; Scarr, 1971; Schonemann, 1995).

4. Other forms of possible "parameter bias" are specifically related to the assumptions about MZ twins. The standard twin model assumes that both kinds of twins have equal environments. But if the similarity of MZ pairs is in part due to sharing a more similar common environment, the additive

genetic effects will be raised spuriously (see Goldberger, 1977; cf. Carey et al., 1978; Scarr, Scarf, & Weinberg, 1980). Another special model is based on MZ twins who are "raised apart" (MZA). These MZA data have been given special status in the BG literature for a clear reason—true MZ twins are genetic replicates so, if raised in completely different environments, any observed correlation between the MZA pairs is a direct estimate of the unobserved genetic variance (see Burt, 1966; Bouchard, 1981). It follows that the BG model for MZA resemblance includes only the additive genetic (A) connection (i.e., no C). As in the adoption design (Munsinger, 1975; Turkheimer, 1991), the validity of this design requires assessing the degree to which MZAs were separated early and their environments were uncorrelated. It has now been thought that many "reared apart" pairs actually lived together for several years and then were raised by relatives, and this is thought to spuriously increase the genetic estimates. True MZA are very rare and only small samples have been found and measured.

5. The AABD score is the residual from an age polynomial model extracted from our study of 13,000 healthy adults ranging in age from 15–85 (McArdle & Horn, 1996). Z-scores were first formed using the mean = 67.54 and SD = 23.22, and then the polynomial used was based on A_n = Age$_n$ − 50.0, B_0 = −.052, B_1 = −.039, B_2 = −.00066, B_3 = 8.8 × 10^{-6}, and B_4 = 1.6 × 10^{-7}. The greatest reduction in variance due to age occurs in the twin groups, whereas the variances of the parent and offspring groups show little effect of age adjustment. The twin groups still retain the highest AABD variance. This is possibly due to other study differences.

6. McArdle, Connell, and Goldsmith (1980) originally showed how these twin models could be considered as special cases of the more general SEM with multiple groups, and how these could be fitted using the available LISREL program (Jöreskog & Sörbom, 1988). McArdle, Goldsmith, and Horn (1981) and McArdle and Goldsmith (1984) described how multivariate BG structural equation models could be fitted using the widely available LISREL programs, and how this approach allowed common factors to be included in a number of ways. This made special-purpose computer code (e.g., Martin & Eaves, 1977) unnecessary for these analyses, and LISREL input scripts are now available in many research articles (e.g., McArdle & Goldsmith, 1990; Neale & Cardon, 1992). The Mx computer program manual (Neale, 1993) also includes a wide variety of BG examples (also see Neale, Walters, Eaves, Maes, & Kendler, 1994).

7. An approximate likelihood ratio test (LRT) statistic is usually used for the evaluation of goodness of fit of the overall model to the data. These LRT indices and their differences ($dLRT$) are usually compared to a chi-square distribution for a probability interpretation of the adequacy of specific models. The LRT obtained is an index of the distance between the model and the data. All models here are fitted to the independent test statistics listed in Table 21.2. The associated chi-square test of fit examines a very rigid hypothesis of "perfect fit." As our sample sizes are relatively large (> 3,000), we add the RMSEA index of "close fit" proposed by Browne and Cudeck (1993).

8. The communality of BD with other WAIS scales is R_f = .72 (McArdle and Horn, 1996) so the standardized estimate R_u = (1 − R_f = .28 is used here. In terms of the raw score deviations, the D_p = 16.6, so the D_u = [$\sqrt{R_u}$ × D_p] = 8.84. In the univariate model these parameters for D_e and D_w are not unique, so the D_w is fixed. However, in the multivariate model the D_e for the common factor T may be simultaneously estimated along with the uniqueness for each variable (as in McArdle & Goldsmith, 1990).

9. The multiple group path diagram of Figure 21.4 can also be seen as one way we can accumulate the model parameters over many data groups. As presented here, each relative grouping provides a pattern of two, three, or four observations in a model. Although we cannot estimate all the parameters from a single group, we assume the model parameters are *invariant over groups,* and this provides a unique estimate for each of the model parameters. These planned missing-data structural analyses are virtually identical to previous cohort-sequential models of aging (see Horn & McArdle, 1980; McArdle & Hamagami, 1992; McArdle, 1994b). The model presented in Figure 21.4 also has several complex nonlinear constraints on the parameters. Although, in theory, these parameters can be built up using a series of linear constraints, this approach is tedious to program and slow to converge (due to matrix size). Cardon, Fulker, and Jöreskog (1991) show how the LISREL-8 program includes

capabilities for modeling such constraints. We used the Mx program (Neale, 1993) to estimate all models presented here.

10. This interpretation follows from standard statistical theory about selection effects (Little & Rubin, 1987; McArdle, 1994b). For example, in the covariance only AABD model, the estimate of additive genetic deviation $D_a = .42$, but in the mean and covariance AABD model the estimate of $D_a = .48$ is considered more appropriate because it accounts for the results on the observed (but not expected) mean differences. The standardized estimate of genetic influences also increases, from 38% to 46%. Although this increase is a function of the patterning of means in these data, increasing genetic similarity is not a necessary outcome of including the means. Because the largest part of this misfit was due to the need to account for equal AABD means across all groups ($dLRT = 289$ on $dDF = 23$), we accept this misfit as an indicator of nonrandom sample differences.

11. A confidence boundary (cb_p) for any structural parameter estimate (pe_p) can be formed in several different ways. One simple way is based on the 95% confidence boundary estimated from the standard error (se_p) of each parameter in the usual way: $cb_p = pe_p \pm 1.96 \times se_p$. If no standard errors are estimated, approximate standard errors can be formed from the parameter estimate and the loss in fit when the parameter is forced to equal zero: $se_p = pe_p / \sqrt{x^2}$. Bootstrap techniques can also be used to form empirical estimates of the likely range of parameter values.

REFERENCES

Block, J. B. (1968). Hereditary components in the performance of twins on the WAIS. In S. G. Vandenberg (Ed.), *Progress in human behavior genetics* (pp. 221–228). Baltimore: Johns Hopkins University Press.

Botwinick, J. (1978). *Aging and behavior: A comprehensive integration of research findings.* New York: Springer.

Bouchard, T. J. (1981). The study of mental ability using twin and adoption designs. *Twin Research 3: Intelligence, personality, and development* (21–23). New York: Liss.

Bouchard, T. J., & McGue, M. (1981). Familial studies of intelligence: A review. *Science, 212,* 1055–1059.

Browne, M., & Cudeck, R. (1993). Alternative ways of assessing model fit. In K. Bollen & S. Long (Eds.), *Testing Structural Equation Models* (pp. 136–162). Beverly Hills, CA: Sage.

Burks, B. S. (1928). The relative influence of nature and nurture on mental development: A comparative study of foster parent-foster child resemblance and true parent-true child resemblance. *Nature and nurture: Their influence upon intelligence. Twenty-Seventh Yearbook of the National Society for the Study of Education. Part I,* 216–316.

Burt, C. (1966). The genetic determination of differences in intelligence. *British Journal of Psychology, 57,* 137–153.

Burt, C. (1969). Intelligence and heredity: Some common misconceptions. *Irish Journal of Education, 3,* 75–94.

Burt, C. (1972). Inheritance of general intelligence. *American Psychologist, 1,* 175–190.

Cardon, L. R., Fulker, D. W. & Jöreskog, K. G. (1991). A LISREL model with constrained parameters for twin and adoptive families. *Behavior Genetics, 21,* 327–350.

Carey, G. (1986). A general multivariate approach to linear modeling in human genetics. *Annals of Human Genetics, 39,* 775–786.

Carey, G. (1991). Evolution and path models in human behavioral genetics. *Behavior Genetics, 21,* 433–444.

Carey, G., Goldsmith, H. H., Tellegen, A., & Gottesman, I. I. (1978). The limits of replication with twin data. *Behavioral Genetics, 8,* 299–313.

Carroll, J. B. (1993). *Human cognitive abilities: A survey of factor-analytic studies.* New York: Cambridge University Press.

Cattell, J. B. (1937). *The fight for our national intelligence.* London: King.

Cattell, R. B. (1953). Research design in psychological genetics, with special reference to the multiple variance method. *American Journal of Human Genetics, 5,* 76–93.

Cattell, R. B. (1960). The multiple abstract variance analysis equations and solutions for nature:nurture research on continuous variables. *Psychological Review, 67,* 353–372.

Cattell, R. B. (1963). The interaction of heredity and environmental influences. *British Journal of Statistical Psychology, 16,* 191–210.

Cattell, R. B. (1982). *The inheritance of personality and ability: Research methods and findings.* New York: Academic Press.

Cattell, R. B. (1985). Intelligence and *g*: An imaginative treatment of unimaginative data. *Behavioral and Brain Sciences, 8,* 227–228.

Cattell, R. B. (1987). *Intelligence: Their structure, growth, and action.* Boston: Houghton Mifflin (rev. by North Holland Press).

Cavalli-Sforza, L., Menozzi, P., & Piazza, A. (1994). *The history and geography of human genes.* Princeton, NJ: Princeton University Press.

Ceci, S. J., & Bruck, M. (1994). the bio-ecological theory of intelligence: A developmental-contextual perspective. In D. K. Detterman (Ed.), *Current topics in human intelligence, Volume 4: Theories of intelligence* (pp. 65–84). Norwood, NJ: Ablex.

Chase, A. (1980). *The legacy of Malthus: The social costs of the new scientific racism.* Chicago: University of Chicago Press.

Chipeur, H. M., Rovine, M., & Plomin, R. (1990). LISREL modelling: genetic and environmental influences on IQ revisted. *Intelligence, 14,* 11–29.

Cloninger, C. R., Rice, J., & Reich, T. (1979). Multifactorial inheritance with cultural transmission and assortative mating III. Family structure and the analysis of separation experiments. *American Journal of Human Genetics, 31,* 366–388.

Cooper, R. M., & Zubeck, J. P. (1958). Effects of enriched and restricted early environments on the learning ability of bright and dull rats. *Canadian Journal of Psychology, 12,* 159–164.

Dalton, T. C., & Bergenn, V. W. (1995). *Beyond heredity and environment: Myrtle McGraw and the maturation controversy.* Boulder, CO: Westview Press.

DeFries, J. C., & Fulker, D. W. (1986). Multivariate behavioral genetics and development: An overview. *Behavior Genetics, 16*(1), 1–10.

DeFries, J. C., Johnson, R. C., Kuse, A. R., McClearn, G. E., Plovina, J., Vandenberg, S. G., & Wilson, J. R. (1979). Familial resemblance for specific cognitive abilities. *Behavior Genetics, 9*(1), 23–43.

Dobzhansky, T. (1956). What is an adaptive trait? *American Naturalist, 90,* 337–347.

Dobzhansky, T. (1973). *Genetic diversity and human equality.* New York: Basic Books.

Eaves, L. J. (1984). The resolution of Genotype × Environment interaction in segregation analysis of nuclear families. *Genetic Epidemiology, 1,* 215–228.

Eaves, L. J., Fulker, D. W., & Heath, A. C. (1989). The effects of social homogamy and cultural inheritance on the covariances of twins and their parents: A LISREL model. *Behavior Genetics, 19,* 113–122.

Ehrman, L., Omenn, G., & Caspari, E. (1972). *Genetics, environment, and behavior: Implications for educational policy.* New York: Academic Press.

Eichorn, D. E., Clausen, J. A., Haan, N., Honzik, M. A., & Mussen, P. H. (Eds.). (1981). *Past and present in middle life.* New York: Academic Press.

Elias, M. F., Schultz, N. R., Robbins, M. A., & Elias, P. K. (1989). A longitudinal study of neuropsychological performance by hypertensives and normotensives: A third measurement time point. *Journal of Gerontology: Psychological Sciences, 44,* 25–28.

Erlenmeyer-Kimling, L., & Jarvik, L. F. (1963). Genetics and intelligence: A review. *Science, 142,* 1477–1479.

Eysenck, H. J. (1986). The theory of intelligence and the psychophysiology of cognition. In R. J. Sternberg (Ed.), *Advances in the psychology of human intelligence* (Vol. 3, pp. 1–34). Hillsdale, NJ: Erlbaum.

Falconer, D. S. (1990). *Introduction to quantitative genetics* (3rd ed.). Edinburg: Oliver & Boyd.

Fancher, R. E. (1985). *The intelligence men: Makers of the IQ controversy.* New York: Norton.

Feldman, M. W., & Lewontin, R. C. (1975). The heritability hangup. *Science, 190,* 1163–1168.

Fisher, R. A. (1918). The correlation between relatives on the supposition of Medellian inheritance. *Transaction of the Royal Society (Edinburgh), 52,* 399–433.

Fisher, R. A. (1930). *The genetical theory of natural selection.* Oxford, England: Clarendon.

Forrest, D. W. (1974). *Francis Galton: The life and work of a Victorian genius.* New York: Taplinger.

Fraser, S. (Ed.). (1995). *The bell curve wars: Race, intelligence, and the future of America.* New York: Basic Books.

Fulker, D. W., Whitlock, J., & Broadhurst, P. L. (1972). Studies in geneotype-environment interaction, I:

Methodology and preliminary multivariate analysis of a diallel cross of eight strains of rat. *Behavior Genetics, 2,* 261–287.

Galton, F. (1865). Heredity talent and character. *Macmillian's Magazine, 12,* 157–166, 318–327.

Goldberger, A. S. (1972). Introduction to structural equation modeling In A. S. Goldberger & O. D. Duncan (Eds.), *Structural equation modeling in the social sciences.* New York: Seminar Press.

Goldberger, A. S. (1977). Twin methods: A skeptical view. In P. Taubman (Ed.), *Kinometrics: Determinants of socioeconomic success within and between families* (pp. 299–329). Amsterdam: North-Holland.

Goldsmith, H. H. (1983). Genetic influences on personality from infancy to adulthood. *Child Development, 54,* 331–355.

Goldsmith, H. H. (1984). Continuity of personality: A genetic perspective. In R. N. Emde & R. J. Harmon (Eds.), *Continuities and discontinuities in development* (pp. 403–413). New York: Plenum Press.

Goldsmith, H. H., & Gottesman, I. I. (1977). An extension of construct validity for personality scales using twin-based criteria. *Journal of Research in Personality, 11,* 381–397.

Goldsmith, H. H., & McArdle, J. J. (1996). *Longitudinal biometric models for twin analyses: The case of childhood temperament.* Manuscript submitted for publication.

Gottlieb, G. (1991). Experiential canalization of behavioral development: Theory. *Developmental Psychology, 27,* 4–13.

Heath, A. C., Kendler, K. S., Eaves, L. J., & Markell, D. (1990). The resolution of cultural and biological inheritance: Informativeness of different relationships. *Behavior Genetics, 20,* 439–466.

Heath, A. C., Neale, M. C., Hewitt, J. K., Eaves, L. J., & Fulker, D. W. (1989). Testing structural equation models for twin data using LISREL. *Behavior Genetics, 19,* 9–35.

Henderson, N. D. (1982). Human behavior genetics. *Annual Review of Psychology, 33,* 403–440.

Henderson, N. D. (1986). Predicting relationships between psychological constructs and genetic character: An analysis of genetic influence on activity in mice. *Behavior Genetics, 16,* 201–220.

Herrnstein, R. J., & Murray, C. (1994). *The bell curve: Intelligence and class structure in American life.* New York: Free Press.

Higgins, J. V., Reed, E. W., & Reed, S. C. (1962). Intelligence and family size: A paradox resolved. *Eugenics Quarterly, 9,* 84–90.

Horn, J. L. (1988). Thinking about human abilities. In J. R. Nesselroade & R. B. Cattell (Eds.), *Handbook of multivariate experimental psychology* (2nd ed., pp. 645–685). New York: Plenum Press.

Horn, J. L., & McArdle, J. J. (1980). Perspectives on Mathematical and Statistical Model Building (MASMOB) in Research on Aging. In L. Poon (Ed.), *Aging in the 1980's: Psychological issues* (pp. 503–541). Washington, DC: American Psychological Association.

Horn, J. M., Loehlin, J. C., & Willerman, L. (1979). Intellectual resemblance among adoptive and biological relatives: The Texas Adoption Project. *Behavior Genetics, 9,* 177–207.

Humphreys, L. G. (1985). Race differences and the Spearman hypothesis. *Intelligence, 9,* 275–283.

Jacoby, R., & Glauberman, N. (Eds.). (1995). The Bell Curve debate: History, documents, opinions. New York: Times Books.

Jarvik L. F., Blum, J. E., & Varma, A. O. (1972). Genetic components and intellectual functioning during senescence: A 20-year study of aging twins. *Behavior Genetics, 2,* 159–171.

Jarvik, L. F., Kallman, F. J., & Falek, A. (1962). Intellectual changes in aged twins. *Journal of Gerontology, 17,* 289–294.

Jencks, C. (1980). Heredity, environment, and public policy reconsidered. *American Sociological Review, 45,* 723–736.

Jencks, C., Smith, M., Aclaud, A., Bane, M. J., Cohen, G., Gintes, H., Heyns, B., & Michelson, M. (1972). *Inequality: A reassessment of the effect of family and schooling in America.* New York: Basic Books.

Jensen, A. R. (1969). How much can we boost IQ and scholastic achievement? *Harvard Educational Review, 39,* 1–123.

Jensen, A. R. (1973). *Educability and group differences.* New York: Harper & Row.

Jensen, A. R. (1985). The nature of the black–white difference on various psychometric tests: Spearman's hypothesis. *Behavioral and Brain Sciences, 8,* 192–263 (with open peer commentary).

Jinks, J. L., & Fulker, D. W. (1970). Comparison of the biometrical, genetical, MAVA and classical approaches to the analysis of human behavior. *Psychological Bulletin, 73,* 311–349.

Johnson, R. C., Ahern, F. M., & Cole, R. E. (1980). Secular change in degree of assortative mating for ability? *Behavioral Genetics, 10,* 1–8.

Johnson, R. C., McClearn, G. E., Yuen, S., Nagoshi, C., Ahern, F. M., & Cole, R. E. (1985). Galton's data a century later. *American Psychologist, 40* (8), 875–892.

Johnson, R. C. & Nagoshi, C. T. (1985). Do we know enough about *g* to be able to speak of black–white differences. *Behavioral and Brain Sciences, 8,* 232–234.

Jones, J. M. (1991). Psychological models of race: What have they been and what should they be? In L. Garnets, J. Jones, D. Kimmel, S. Sue, & C. Tavris (Eds.), *Psychological Perspectives on Human Diversity in America* (pp. 7–46). Washington, DC: American Psychological Association.

Jones, L. V. (1985). Golly *g*: Interpreting Spearman's general factor. *Behavioral and Brain Sciences, 8,* 228.

Jöreskog, K. G., & Sörbom, D. (1988). *LISREL VII: A guide to the program and applications.* Chicago: SPSS.

Kamin, L. J. (1974). *The science and politics of I.Q.* Potomac, MD: Erlbaum.

Kelves, D. (1984, October 15). Annals of eugenics: A secular faith—II. *The New Yorker,* 52–125.

Kelves, D. (1985). *In the name of eugenics.* New York: Knopf.

Kempthorne, O. (1978). Logical, epistemological and statistical aspects of nature–nurture data interpretation. *Biometrics, 34,* 1–23.

Kohs, S. C. (1923). *Intelligence measurement: A psychological and statistical study based upon the blocks-design tests.* New York: Macmillan.

Lander, E. S., & Botstein, D. (1989). Mapping Medellian factor underlying quantitative traits using RFLP linkage maps. *Genetics, 121,* 185–199.

Lee, T.F. (1993). *Gene future: The promise and perils of the new biology.* New York: Plenum Press.

Lejeune, J., & Turpin, R. (1957). *C. R. Acad. Sci. Paris, 244,* 1833.

Lezak, M. D. (1976). *Neuropsychological assessment.* New York: Oxford University Press.

Little, R. T. A., & Rubin, D. B. (1987). *Statistical analysis with missing data.* New York: Wiley.

Loehlin, J. C. (1965). Some methodological problems in Cattell's multiple abstract variance analysis. *Psychological Review, 72,* 156–161.

Loehlin, J. C. (1978). Heredity–environment analyses of Jenk's I.Q. correlations. *Behavioral Genetics, 8,* 415–436.

Loehlin, J. C. (1984). R. B. Cattell and behavior genetics. *Multivariate Behavioral Research, 19,* 337–343.

Loehlin, J. C. (1989). Partitioning environmental and genetic contributions to behavioral development. *American Psychologist, 44,* 1285–1292.

Loehlin, J. C. (1992). *Genes and environment in personality development.* Newbury Park, CA: Sage.

Loehlin, J. C., Horn, J. M., & Willerman, L. (1989). Modeling IQ change: Evidence from the Texas Adoption Project. *Child Development, 60,* 993–1004.

Loehlin, J., Lindzey, G., & Spuhler, J. (1975). *Race differences in intelligence.* San Francisco: Freeman.

Loehlin, J. C., & Vandenberg, S. G. (1968). Genetic and environmental components in the covariation of cognitive abilities: An additive model. In S. G. Vandenberg (Ed.), *Progress in human behavior genetics* (pp. 261–286). Baltimore: Johns Hopkins University Press.

Mackenzie, B. (1980). Hypothesized genetic racial differences in IQ: A criticism of three proposed lines of evidence. *Behavior Genetics, 10*(2), 227–236.

Mackenzie, B. (1984). Explaining race differences in IQ: The logic, the methodology, and the evidence. *American Psychologist, 39,* 1214–1233.

Martin, N. G., & Eaves, L. J. (1977). The genetical analysis of covariance structure. *Heredity, 138,* 79–95.

Mascie-Taylor, C. G. N. (1989). Spouse similarity for IQ and personality and convergence. *Behavior Genetics, 19,* 223–228.

Matarazzo, J. D. (1980). *Wechsler's measurement and appraisal of adult intelligence.* New York: Oxford University Press.

McArdle, J. J. (1986). Latent variable growth within behavior genetic models. *Behavior Genetics, 16*(1), 163–200.

McArdle, J. J. (1987). Mixtures of behavioral genetics and developmental psychology. A review of Plomins' "Development, genetics, and psychology." *Contemporary Psychology, 32*(5), 433–435.

McArdle, J. J. (1994a). Appropriate questions about causal inference from "Direction of Causation" analyses. *Genetic Epidemiology, 11,* 477–482.

McArdle, J. J. (1994b). Structural factor analysis experiments with incomplete data. *Multivariate Behavioral Research, 29*(4), 409–454.

McArdle, J. J. (1995). Contemporary statistical models of test bias. In J. J. McArdle & R. W. Woodcock (Eds.), *Human abilities in theory and practice.* Mahwah, NJ: Erlbaum.

McArdle, J. J. (1996a). A workshop on contemporary behavioral genetics models and methods. *Contemporary Psychology, 41*(9), 886–887.

McArdle, J. J. (1996b). Current directions in structural factor analysis. *Current Directions in Psychological Science, 5,* 11–18.

McArdle, J. J., Connell, J., & Goldsmith, H. H. (1980). Latent variable approaches to measurement, structure, longitudinal stability, and genetic influences: Preliminary results from the study of behavioral style. *Behavior Genetics, 10,* 487.

McArdle, J. J., & Goldsmith, H. H. (1984). Multivariate biometric models of the WAIS. *Behavior Genetics, 14,* 609 [Abstract].

McArdle, J. J., & Goldsmith, H. H. (1990). Some alternative structural equation models for multivariate biometric analyses. *Behavior Genetics, 20*(5), 569–608.

McArdle, J. J., Goldsmith, H. H., & Horn, J. L. (1981) Genetic structural equation models of Fluid and Crystallized intelligence. *Behavior Genetics, 11*(6), 607 [Abstract].

McArdle, J. J., & Gottesman, I. I. (1987). Some models where independent / different: A response to Plomin and Daniels. *Behavioral and Brain Sciences, 10*(1), 31–32.

McArdle, J. J., & Hamagami, F. (1992). Modeling incomplete longitudinal and cross-sectional data using latent growth structural models. *Experimental Aging Research, 18*(3), 145–167.

McArdle, J. J., & Horn J. L. (1996). *A mega analysis of the WAIS: Adult intelligence across the life-span.* Mahwah, NJ: Erlbaum. Manuscript in preparation.

McArdle, J. J., & Prescott, C. A. (1992). Age-based construct validation using structural equation modeling. *Experimental Aging Research, 18*(3), 87–115.

McKusick, V. (1994). *Mendelian inheritance in man* (10th ed.). Baltimore: Johns Hopkins University Press.

Medawar, P. B. (1959). The future of man. *BBC Reith lectures.* Reprinted in *The threat and the glory: Reflections on science and scientists,* 1990. New York: HarperCollins.

Meredith, W. (1968). Factor analysis and the use of inbred strains. In S. G. Vandeenberg (Ed.), *Progress in human behavior genetics* (pp. 335–348). Baltimore: Johns Hopkins University Press.

Meredith, W. (1973). A model for analyzing heritability in the presence of correlated genetic and environmental effects. *Behavior Genetics, 3,* 271–277.

Munsinger, H. (1975). The adopted child's IQ: A critical review. *Psychological Bulletin, 82,* 623–659.

Nagoshi, C. T., & Johnson, R. C. (1985). Ethnic group-by-generation interactions in WAIS scores in the Hawaii Family Study of Cognition. *Intelligence, 9,* 259–264.

Neale, M. C. (1993). *Mx statistical modeling.* Unpublished program manual, Department of Human Genetics, Medical College of Virginia, Virginia Commonwealth University, Richmond.

Neale, M. C., & Cardon, L. R. (1992). *Methodology for genetic studies of twins and families.* London: Kluewer.

Neale, M. C., Heath, A. C., Hewitt, J. K., Eaves, L. J., & Fulker, D. W. (1989). Fitting genetic models with LISREL: Hypothesis testing. *Behavior Genetics, 19,* 37–49.

Neale, M. C., & McArdle, J. J. (1990). The analysis of assortative mating: A LISREL model. *Behavior Genetics, 20*(2), 287–296.

Neale, M. C., Walters, E. E., Eaves, L. J., Maes, H. H., & Kendler, K. S. (1994). Multivariate genetic analysis of twin–family data on fears: Mx Models. *Behavior Genetics, 24*(2), 119–139

Nesselroade, J. J., & McArdle, J. J. (in press). On the mismatching of levels of abstraction in mathematical–statistical model fitting. In M. D. Franzen & H. W. Reese (Eds.), *Life-span developmental psychology: Biological and neuropsychological mechanisms.* Hillsdale, NJ: Erlbaum.

Nesselroade, J. J., & Thompson, W. W. (1995). Selection and related threats to group comparison: An example comparing factorial structures of higher and lower ability groups of adult twins. *Psychological Bulletin, 117,* 271–284.

Nichols, P., & Anderson, V. E. (1973). Intellectual performance, race, and socioeconomic status. *Social Biology, 20,* 367–374.

Pedersen, N. L., Plomin, R., & McClearn, G. E. (1994). Is there G beyond g? *Intelligence, 18,* 133–143.

Pedersen, N. L., Plomin, R., Nesselroade, J. R., & McClearn, G. E. (1992). A quantitative genetic analysis of cognitive abilities during the second half of the life-span. *Psychological Science, 3,* 346–353.

Phillips, K., & Fulker, D. W. (1989). Quantitative genetic analysis of longitudinal trends in adoption designs with application to IQ in the Colorado Adoption Project. *Behavior Genetics, 19*, 621–658.

Phillips, K., Fulker, D. W., Carey, G., & Nagoshi, C. T. (1988). Direct marital assortment for cognitive and personality variables. *Behavior Genetics, 18*, 347–356.

Plomin, R., & DeFries, J. C. (1980). Genetics and intelligence: A review. *Intelligence, 4*, 15–24.

Plomin, R., & Loehlin, J. C. (1989). Direct and indirect heritability estimates: A puzzle. *Behavior Genetics, 19*, 331–342.

Plomin, R., McClearn, G. E., Smith, D. L., Vignetti, S., Chorney, M. J., Venditti, K., Kasarda, S., Thompson, L. A., Detterman, D. K., Daniels, J., Owen, M., & McGuffin, P. (1994). DNA markers associated with high versus low IQ: The IQ quantitative trait loci (QTL) project. *Behavior Genetics, 24*(2), 107–117.

Plomin, R., & Neiderhiser, J. M. (1991). Quantitative genetics, molecular genetics, and intelligence. *Intelligence, 15*, 369–387.

Plomin, R., & Rende, R. (1990). Human behavioral genetics. *Annual Review of Psychology, 42*, 161–190

Polednak, A. P. (1989). *Racial and ethnic differences in disease.* New York: Oxford University Press.

Prescott, C. A., Johnson, R. C., & McArdle, J. J. (1991). The genetics of television viewing [Letter]. *Psychological Science, 2*, 430–431.

Rao, D., & Morton, N. E. (1974). Path analysis of family resemblance in the presence of gene–environment interaction. *American Journal of Human Genetics, 26*, 767–772.

Record, R. G., McKeown, T., & Edwards, J. H. (1970). An investigation of the difference in measured intelligence between twins and single births. *Annals of Human Genetics, 34*, 11–20.

Rodgers, J. L., & Rowe, D. C. (1987). IQ similarity in twins, siblings, half-siblings, cousins, and random pairs. *Intelligence, 11*, 199–206.

Rose, R. J., Boughman, J. A., Corey, L. A., Nance, W. E., Christian, J. C., & Kang, K. W. (1980). Data from kinships of monozygotic twins indicate maternal effects on verbal intelligence. *Nature, 283*, 309–311.

Rose, R. J., Harris, E. L., Christian, J. C., & Nance, W. E. (1979). Genetic variance in nonverbal intelligence. *Science, 205*, 1153–1155.

Rowe, D. C., & Plomin, R. (1981). The importance of nonshared E_1 environmental influences in behavioral development. *Developmental Psychology, 17*, 517–531.

Scarr, S. (1971, December 17). Unknowns in the IQ equation: A review of three monographs. *Science, 174*, 1223–1228.

Scarr, S. (1980). {I.Q., race, social class and individual differences: New studies of old problems. Hillsdale, NJ: Erlbaum.

Scarr, S. (1988). Race and gender as psychological variables: Social and ethical issues. *American Psychologist, 43*(1), 56–59.

Scarr, S., & McCartney, K. (1983). How people make their own environments: A theory of geneotype environ-ment effects. *Child Development, 54*, 424–435.

Scarr, S., Pakstis, A. J., Katz, S. H., & Barker, W. B. (1977). Absence of a relationship between degree of white ancestry and intellectual skills within a black population. *Human Genetics, 39*, 69–86.

Scarr, S., Scarf, E., & Weinberg, R. A. (1980). Perceived and actual similarities in biological and adoptive families: Does perceived similarity bias genetic inferences? *Behavior Genetics, 10*, 445–458.

Scarr, S., & Weinberg, R. (1978). The influence of "family background" on intellectual attainment. *American Sociological Review, 43*, 674–692.

Scarr, S., & Yee, D. (1980). Heredity and educational policy: Genetic and environmental effects on IQ, aptitude, and achievements. *Educational Psychologist, 15*, 1–22.

Schaie, K. W., Anderson, V. E., McClearn, G. E., & Money, J. (Eds.). (1975). *Developmental human behavior genetics.* Lexington, MA: Lexington Books.

Schonemann, P. H. (1995). Heritability. In R. J. Sternberg (Ed.), *Encyclopedia of human intelligence* (pp. 528–536). New York: Macmillan.

Snyderman, M., & Rothman, S. (1990). *The IQ controversy, the media and public policy.* New Brunswick, NJ: Transaction.

Starfield, B., Shaspiro, S., Weiss, J., Liang, K-Y., Ra, K., Paige, D., & Wang, X. (1991). Race, family income and low birth weight. *American Journal of Epidemiology, 134*, 1167–1174.

Sternberg, R. J. (1985). Human intelligence: The model is the message. *Science, 230*, 1111–1118.

Storfer, M. D. (1990). *Intelligence and giftedness: The contribution of heredity and early environment*. San Francisco: Jossey-Bass.

Tambs, K., Sundet, J. M., & Magnus, P. (1986). Genetic and environmental contributions to the covariation between the Wechsler Adult Intelligence Scale (WAIS) subtests. *Behavior Genetics, 16*, 475–491.

Taylor, H. F. (1980). *The IQ game: A methodological inquiry into the heredity–environment controversy*. New Brunswick, NJ: Rutgers University Press.

Thelen, E., & Adolf, K. E. (1992). Arnold L. Gesell: The paradox of nature and nurture. *Developmental Psychology, 28*, 368–380.

Thompson, L. A., Detterman, D. K., & Plomin, R. (1991). Associations between cognitive abilities and scholastic achievement: Genetic overlap but environmental differences. *Psychological Science, 2*(3), 158–165.

Thorndike, E. L. (1905). The measurement of twins. *Journal of Philosophy, Psychology, and Scientific Method, 2*, 547–553.

Tryon, R. C. (1940). Genetic differences in the maze learning ability in rats. *Yearbook of the National Society for the Study of Education, 39*, 111–119.

Turkheimer, E. (1991). Individual and group differences in adoption studies of IQ. *Psychological Bulletin, 110*, 392–405.

Vandenberg, S. G. (Ed.). (1968). *Progress in human behavior genetics*. Baltimore: Johns Hopkins Press.

Vandenberg, S. G., & Falkner, F. (1965) Heredity factors in human growth. *Human Biology, 37*, 357–365.

Waddington, C. H. (1953). Genetic assimilation of an acquired character. *Evolution, 7*, 118–126.

Waddington, C. H. (1962). *New patterns in genetics and development*. New York: Columbia University Press.

Wechsler D. (1955). *Wechsler Adult Intelligence Scale*. San Antonio, TX: Psychological Corporation.

Wilson, R. (1986). Continuity and change in cognitive ability prfile. *Behavior Genetics, 16*, 45–60.

Woodcock, R. W. (1990). Theoretical foundations of the WJ-R measures of cognitive ability. *Journal of Psycho-Educational Assessment, 8*, 231–258.

Wright, S. (1921). Correlation and causality. *Journal of Agricultural Research, 20*, 557–585.

Wright, S. (1934). The method of path coefficients. *Annals of Mathematical Statistics, 5*, 161–215.

Wright, S. (1942). Statistical genetics and evolution. *Bulletin of the American Mathematical Society, 48*, 223–246.

Wright, S. (1982). On "Path analysis in genetic epidemiology: A critique." *American Journal of Human Genetics, 35*, 757–762.

Zonderman, A. B., Vandenberg, S. G., Spuhler, K. P., & Fain, P. R. (1977). Assortative mating for cognitive abilities. *Behavior Genetics, 7*, 261–271.

CHAPTER 22

Diagnostic and Treatment Utility of Intelligence Tests

—➤◦◦◦◦◄—

DANIEL J. RESCHLY

T HE UTILITY OF INTELLIGENCE TESTS can be approached from a number of different perspectives, including: (1) psychologists and other professionals who use the tests, (2) children and youth to whom the tests are administered, (3) corporations that publish the tests, (4) individuals and institutions that use the tests as part of decision making, and (5) the broader society that establishes policies involving intelligence as part of the basis for allocation of resources. Each of these perspectives is important in that significant interests are represented. In this chapter, the principal focus is on the utility of intelligence tests to children and youth, with secondary attention devoted to the institutions that use tests as part of decision making. This discussion begins with consideration of the reliability and validity of diagnostic constructs and the assessment procedures related to those constructs; proceeds to a brief treatment of current tests, their diagnostic uses, and treatment validity; and follows with a review of the diagnostic and treatment utility of alternative approaches to intellectual assessment.

OVERVIEW

Recognition of the importance of positive outcomes for human services' clients is pervasive in the literature of psychology and education (Cromwell, Blashfield, & Strauss, 1975; Heller, Holtzman, & Messick, 1982; Messick, 1989; Reschly & Tilly, 1993; Reschly & Ysseldyke, 1995). The pursuit of positive outcomes and the promotion of the welfare of clients is crucial to the ethical principles of psychologists (American Psychological Association [APA], 1992). The first line of the preamble announces, "Psychologists work to develop a valid and reliable body of scientific knowledge" (APA, 1992, p. 1599). It is clear that the purpose of this knowledge is to "contribute to the welfare of those with whom they interact professionally" (p. 1600). It is inconceivable that this principle would not apply to psychological assessment and the use of intelligence tests.

Outcomes Criteria

Reschly (1978, 1980, 1988a, 1988b) stressed the application of an outcomes criterion to problems related to alleged bias in assessment, overrepresentation of minority students in special education programs, and the value of assessment instruments and procedures for individuals. The outcomes criterion requires focusing on what does or does not happen after assessment activities are completed. Assessment that does not result in effective interventions is useless for the individual. Such assessment practices also may be biased or unfair as well if children and youth with minority characteristics are differentially exposed to ineffective programs as a result of assessment activities. The implications of an outcomes criterion are that judgments are made about assessment instruments and processes on the basis of what occurs with the client. The satisfaction of professionals with the completeness or richness of the descriptions of intellectual abilities, or greater understanding of the dynamics that presumably cause a learning or behavior problem, is regarded as useless if they do not translate into effective interventions for the client.

Context of Assessment and Consequential Validity

Heller et al. (1982) addressed the outcomes problem in several places in the National Academy of Sciences report on equity in classification of children and youth for special education programs. Specifically, they argued that intelligence and other kinds of tests cannot be evaluated apart from the context in which they are used. That context, in order to be in the best interests of children and youth, must emphasize prevention and early intervention, multiple attempts to resolve problems in natural contexts prior to a referral that may lead to the use of intelligence tests, and documented benefits of special programs that may be used after intelligence tests are used.

Messick (1989) emphasized consequential validity to refer to similar ideas; specifically, the consequences of test use must be examined as well as the nature of the tests. Moreover, test validity can never be considered apart from the consequences of test use. Tests that do not produce positive consequences must be regarded as highly questionable for the individual as well as for institutions such as schools.

Validity of Diagnostic Constructs

According to Cromwell et al. (1975), a diagnostic construct can be formed by two types of information, either alone or in combination: (1) historical or etiological information, and (2) currently assessable characteristics. The *reliability* of a diagnostic construct is determined by the consistency with which diagnoses are made by different professionals who have the same information which, in turn, is influenced by the objectivity and accuracy of the data collection procedures applied to historical–etiological information and currently assessable characteristics.

Reliable diagnostic constructs may have little or no utility. The utility or validity of a diagnostic construct for an individual is determined by its relationship to interventions or treatments and the known outcomes of applying or withholding those treatments or interventions. Consequences or outcomes for clients are stressed again by Cromwell et al. (1975). Validity of diagnostic constructs also can be determined by the degree to which there are relationships to broader prevention efforts and the results of those efforts. For the purposes of this chapter, however, the principal validity criterion for intelligence tests is the relationship to treatments for individuals and the outcomes of those treatments.

Summary

Context is crucial to the evaluation of measures of general intelligence. A context in which intellectual assessment is not related to interventions rarely is in the best interests of clients. Consideration of context compels examination of the decisions that are made with measures of intelligence and the outcomes of those decisions for individuals and institutions.

STANDARDIZED TESTING IN CURRENT PRACTICE

Aptitudes, intelligence, and achievement as kinds of tests are not easily distinguished. Distinctions among them, however, are essential to analyzing current test use because the most frequent current use involves a comparison of intelligence and achievement test performance. The traditional distinction was that achievement tests reflected the effects of past learning whereas aptitude and intelligence reflected the individual's potential for success. In this traditional view, both aptitude and intelligence were seen as relatively enduring traits of the individual, not easily modified by experience or special training. In some instances both aptitude and intelligence tests results were regarded as indications of innate capacity.

These traditional meanings of aptitude, intelligence, and achievement tests were rejected in all the leading measurement texts published in the last 15 years (Anastasi, 1988; Brown, 1983; Cronbach, 1990). All now are viewed as (1) tests of developed abilities, that is, they reflect the effects of experience; and (2) maximum performance measures, meaning that it is assumed that the individual is encouraged to try as hard as possible to do well.

The most important differences among aptitude, intelligence, and achievement have to do with *how* they are used and with assumptions about *antecedent experiences* (Anastasi, 1988; Brown, 1983). Achievement tests are assumed to measure past learning that occurred in a specific teaching or instructional situation. In contrast, aptitude has a future reference. The aptitude concept involves inferences about performance in future learning or training situations. Intelligence is usually seen as between achievement and aptitude on the continuum of test use and antecedent experiences. Intelligence has a present reference as a reflection of the effects of general, broad learning experiences. When intelligence tests are used in diagnoses, a future reference is assumed because predictions typically are made about the continuing status of the individual.

As a construct, aptitude often is used quite broadly, especially in theory and research on aptitude by treatment interactions (Cronbach & Snow, 1977; Snow, 1980, 1992). Here, aptitude is virtually any psychological characteristic of the person that predicts differences among people in later learning or training situations. Included in this very broad conception of aptitude are cognitive abilities and processes *and* personality and emotional characteristics (Snow, 1992).

Although standardized tests of intelligence, aptitude, and achievement have many common features, they vary significantly in frequency of use and purpose. Nearly all children and youth typically complete standardized achievement tests several times during their public school careers. Aptitude tests are used less frequently, most often in connection with college applications where most prospective college students take the Scholastic Aptitude Test or the American College Test (Anastasi, 1988, pp. 326–331; Cronbach, 1990, 264–269). Aptitude tests also are used in graduate and professional school applications, and as part of orientation and placement in the military. Achievement and aptitude testing is part of the experiences of most persons in technologically oriented societies around the world.

CURRENT USES OF INTELLIGENCE TESTS

Experience with devices characterized as intelligence tests is far from universal. Although group-administered intelligence tests exist, sometimes called tests of scholastic aptitude, most children and youth do not take such tests. Intelligence tests typically are administered only to those students who are referred by their teachers for consideration of (1) eligibility for an educationally related disability and (2) need for special education and related services.

In the United States, about 4.4 million children and youth between the ages of 6 and 17 are diagnosed as educationally disabled and in need of special education. This constitutes approximately 10.25% of the school age population in the United States (U.S. Department of Education, 1994; see Table 22.1). The vast majority of these students have disabilities that are mild in degree, which are understood best from a social system model of deviance (i.e., they do not have identifiable biological defects that cause the disability, their disability status typically is recognized first in a school setting, most are not regarded as disabled during the adult years, and they appear normal in most social roles and settings). It is this population with whom current intelligence tests are used most often, and against which the usefulness of alternatives is examined.

Preplacement Evaluation and Triennial Reevaluation

Federal regulations first implemented in August 1977 provide numerous protections to students and their parents in the referral, evaluation, and placement process. The protections associated with the preplacement evaluation and the reevaluation appear in Protection in Evaluation Procedures (34 C.F.R. § 300.530) section (Individuals with Disabilities Education Act [IDEA], 1990, 1991). Each child is entitled to a full and individual evaluation. Testing and evaluation materials and procedures must not be racially or culturally discriminatory, are provided and administered in the child's native language, have been validated for the specific purpose for which they are used, are administered by trained personnel, and assess specific areas of educational need and not just a single general intelligence quotient.

In addition, no single procedure can be used as the sole criterion for determining an educational program and the evaluation must be conducted by a multidisciplinary team. The child must be assessed in all areas related to the suspected disability, "including, if appropriate, health, vision, hearing, social and emotional status, general intelligence, academic performance, communicative status, and motor abilities" (34 C.F.R. § 300.532(f)) (IDEA, 1990, 1991). This clause in federal regulations is interpreted by some as requiring assessment of general intelligence with all referred students while others stress the limitation of "if appropriate" and suggest that general intelligence

TABLE 22.1. School Age Population (6–17) Diagnosed as Disabled

Category	6–11	12–17	Total	Percent of overall population
SLD	997,247 (41.55%)	1,249,940 (62.90%)	2,247,187 (51.22%)	5.25%
SP/L	889,257 (37.05%)	104,556 (5.26%)	993,813 (22.65%)	2.32%
MR	209,475 (8.73%)	258,406 (13.00%)	467,881 (10.66%)	1.09%
SED	137,423 (5.73%)	242,387 (12.20%)	379,810 (8.66%)	0.89%
Other[a]	166,724 (6.95%)	131,952 (6.64%)	298,676 (6.81%)	0.70%
Total	2,400,126	1,987,241 (100%)	4,387,367 (100%)	10.25%

Note. Data from U.S. Department of Education, 1994, Tables AA6, AA7, AA13, AA14 and AA27. Total estimated enrollment of children ages 6–17 = 42,845,380. SLD = specific learning disability; SP/L = speech and language; MR = mental retardation; and SED = seriously emotionally disturbed.

[a]"Other" is the prevalence of autism, deaf–blindness, deafness, hearing impairment, multiple disabilities, orthopedic impairment, other health impairment, traumatic brain injury, and visual impairment.

should be assessed only if it is clearly related to precisely defined referral questions (Reschly & Grimes, 1995).

Disability Diagnosis Criteria

Disability eligibility criteria have a profound influence on the use of intelligence tests. A conceptual definition of specific learning disabilities (SLD) appears in the IDEA (1991) regulations at Section 300.7 of the Code of Federal Regulations. Additional IDEA regulations regarding SLD were established, apparently reflecting congressional concern about possible excessive identification of students as SLD due to the absence of clarity in this diagnostic construct. The additional regulations (34 C.F.R. § 399.540), now in IDEA (1991), included several requirements, the most important of which to this discussion is the provision that a severe discrepancy must exist between achievement and intellectual ability that is not attributable to visual, hearing, or motor impairment, mental retardation, emotional disturbance, or environmental, cultural, or economic disadvantage.

SLD conceptual definitions and eligibility criteria also exist at the state level. The state conceptual definitions and eligibility criteria generally follow the federal regulations (Mercer, King-Sears, & Mercer, 1990). A critical issue on which states vary is the method to determine an intelligence–achievement discrepancy and the magnitude required for that discrepancy to be regarded as severe. Eligibility determination for SLD nearly always involves assessment of intellectual functioning. Given the numbers and proportions of students classified as SLD (see Table 22.1), it is highly likely that intelligence tests are given more for this purpose than any other.

Diagnosis of mental retardation (MR) among school-age children and youth probably constitutes the second most frequent purpose for which individually administered intelligence tests are used. The role of intelligence as one of the dimensions on which the MR diagnosis is based has been prominent for at least a century and predates the actual development of intelligence tests.

MR eligibility criteria, which vary significantly among the states (Patrick & Reschly, 1982), have changed since 1976 in the direction of more stringent IQ cutoff scores, greater emphasis on adaptive behavior, and explicit criteria to determine deficits in adaptive behavior. Controversial aspects of the MR eligibility criteria include the level of the IQ cutoff, the cutoff for adaptive behavior, the setting(s) in which adaptive behavior is examined, and the adjustments, if any, in the interpretation of IQ scores for children from non–middle-class environments.

The conventional MR conceptual definitions and eligibility criteria, like SLD, nearly always accord a prominent role to general intellectual functioning. Administration of an IQ test is regarded by nearly all professionals as essential to applying the MR eligibility criteria for persons at the mild level of MR. Use of IQ tests is far less important to the determination of eligibility with the moderate, severe, and profound levels of MR; indeed, the measurement scales for most current tests do not have sufficient range to assess functioning below a score of about 55 on IQ scales (assuming a mean = 100 and $SD = 15$; Reschly, 1992).

Although it is possible to develop diagnostic constructs of MR and SLD without using intellectual ability (Reschly, 1988c; Siegel, 1989), the conceptions that result typically are less complete representations of these diagnostic constructs. IQ testing is deeply embedded in the current classification system. As long as the diagnostic constructs of MR and SLD are used, it is highly likely that some form of intellectual assessment will be prominent in eligibility determination for special education.

Dominance of the Wechsler Scales

The profession of school psychology is responsible for IQ testing in most states when assessment of intellectual functioning is essential to determining disability eligibility and need for special education. It is quite likely that nearly all referred students suspected as meeting the criteria for mild MR or SLD, and many of the referrals for other kinds of problems as well, are administered one or more IQ tests. Although there are a number of technically adequate, individually administered IQ tests, most of which are taught in graduate school psychology programs, three instruments developed originally by Wechsler dominate the market: Wechsler Preschool and Primary Scale of Intelligence—Revised (WPPSI-R; Wechsler, 1989), Wechsler Intelligence Scale for Children—Third Edition (WISC-III; Wechsler, 1991), or Wechsler Adult Intelligence Scale—Revised (WAIS-R; Wechsler, 1981).

The average school psychologist administers a Wechsler scale, most often the WISC-III, about 10 times per month according to a survey of practicing school psychologists (Wilson & Reschly, 1996). There were 11 individually administered intelligence tests listed on this survey. Average test use per month approached two for only one other measure: the Stanford–Binet Intelligence Scale: Form L-M (Terman & Merrill, 1960) and Stanford–Binet Intelligence Scale—Fourth Edition (Thorndike, Hagen, & Sattler, 1986) combined. All other individually administered intelligence tests were used less than 1.5 times per month. Wechsler scales dominance is not a new phenomenon or restricted to school psychologists or to psychologists in the United States (Goh, Telzrow, & Fuller, 1981; Hutton, Dubes, & Muir, 1992; Lubin, Larsen, & Matarazzo, 1984; Oakland & Hu, 1992; Wade & Baker, 1977). An author of a rival individually administered test of intellectual ability titled his recent glowing review of the most commonly used of the Wechsler scales, "King WISC the Third Assumes the Throne," a grudging admission of the Wechsler scales' domination of the market (Kaufman, 1993).

An examination of current intelligence test use can focus almost exclusively on the Wechsler scales because other tests are used rarely or not at all by the typical practitioner. A major question facing publishers of rival individually administered intelligence tests is whether the Wechsler market domination can be changed. Clearly, that is a difficult enterprise.

Wechsler Scales as a Measure of g

The Wechsler scales, as well as a number of other comprehensive measures of general intellectual functioning, provide an excellent measure of the general factor of intelligence (g) (Spearman, 1927). A vast array of evidence supports the Wechsler scales as a measure of g (e.g., Kaufman, 1994a, 1994b; Sattler, 1988/1992; Witt & Gresham, 1985). Moreover, the diagnostic constructs of SLD and mild MR appear to reflect a conception of intelligence that is broad and comprehensive (Luckasson et al., 1992). The Wechsler Full Scale IQ score is an excellent measure of that hypothetical construct.

Factor Score, Scale, and Subtest Profile Interpretations

Applied psychology has an unfortunate tradition of highly speculative interpretation of scatter (i.e., differences within the individual's performance over different tests or subtests within the same test). This tradition can be traced to the psychoanalytic assumptions that all behaviors are related to multiple causes, the causes lie in the mostly unconscious dynamics of the personality, and useful insights into the emotional and intellectual makeup of the individual are revealed in the pattern of Wechsler subtest strengths and weaknesses (Holt, 1968; Rapaport, Gill, & Schafer, 1945/1946; Wechsler, 1955). For example, Wechsler (1955, pp. 172–173) described subtest patterns supposedly typical of persons with schizophrenia and adolescent sociopathy. This deeply dynamic (also highly speculative) methodology is less apparent now due to the overall decline in the popularity of psychoanalytic and other dynamic conceptions of personality. Moreover, it now is recognized that scatter (i.e., variations in verbal and performance IQs and over subtests) occurs with very high frequency

(Kaufman, 1976a, 1976b). Today, it is much less likely that intraindividual differences across the Wechsler IQ scales or subtests will be interpreted in terms of personality or emotional constructs.

Current practice often involves interpretation of the Wechsler factor scores, scale IQs, and subtest profiles as indications of cognitive strengths–weaknesses and as indications of neuropsychological status. For example, Kaufman (1994b) argued that Verbal–Performance scale variations were related to significant differences among persons in ethnic status (e.g., Hispanic origin and Native American Indian children obtain *on average* higher Performance than Verbal scores), brain injury, cognitive processing style, and gender. For example, patients with right hemisphere brain damage typically obtain Verbal scores 8 to 10 points higher than their Performance scores, which Kaufman (1994b) suggests as evidence for the "neuropsychological validity of the V–P dichotomy" (p. 201).

One does not have to look far in the current literature to find sharp criticism of this approach to Wechsler scale interpretation. Critics cite three lines of evidence in their vehement rejections of clinical interpretation of Wechsler factor scores, scale variations, and profile differences. The first line of evidence involves examination of the reliability of differences. Difference scores are inherently less reliable than the individual scores from which they are derived. An intuitive grasp of this concept might be facilitated by considering one's confidence in estimating the time interval for the December–January academic holiday. Assume that the start of the vacation period is somewhere between December 17 and December 20. The end of this holiday is somewhere between January 3 and January 6. Now how confident are you in estimating the beginning, the end, and the length of the holiday? In fact you are certain of being correct within 3 days of the beginning and 3 days of the end, but the length could vary by 6 days. In an analogous manner, if there is uncertainty or less than perfect reliability with each of the scores on which the difference is based, the reliability of the score difference has to be lower than the reliability of either of the scores.

Macmann and Barnett (Barnett & Macmann, 1992a, 1992b; Macmann & Barnett, 1985, 1992, 1994a, 1994b; Macmann, Barnett, Lombard, Belton-Kocher, & Sharpe, 1989) have done sophisticated analyses of the kinds of score differences that are frequently used in interpreting Wechsler factor score or Verbal–Performance scale differences. In several studies they have generated distributions of such scores based on the known reliability of the scales and the frequency of the differences in the factor or scale scores. The principal results are that (1) the WISC-III results are better interpreted as a single general factor rather than as two, three, or four factors; and (2) classifications based largely on discrepancy scores (e.g., SLD) are unstable, meaning that an individual's status is likely to change if the assessment procedures are repeated.

A second line of attack on traditional interpretations of the Wechsler scales focuses on the base rates of differences in the factor, Verbal–Performance scale, and subtest scores (Glutting, McGrath, Kamphaus, & McDermott, 1992; Glutting, McDermott, & Konold, Chapter 19, this volume; McDermott, Fantuzzo, & Glutting, 1990; McDermott, Fantuzzo, Glutting, Watkins, & Baggaley, 1992). Base rates refer to how frequently some characteristic or phenomenon occurs in the general population. These authors have established unequivocally that scatter (i.e., differences among the Wechsler factor, scale, or subtest scores) is more common than flat profiles or very small scale differences. Statistically, scatter is normal, just the opposite of the assumptions in the clinical tradition (Rapaport et al., 1945/1946; Wechsler, 1955). What is abnormal in terms of occurring infrequently is a flat profile of subtest scores or virtually equal verbal and performance scale IQs.

Norms for subtest and scale differences are available for the most widely used tests (Kaufman, 1976a, 1976b; Sattler, 1988/1992). The norms often are organized around the size of the difference between two scores that is statistically significant at the .05 or .01 levels. These results are widely misunderstood. For example, on a Wechsler scale the Verbal–Performance scale difference of about 15 points is statistically significant at the .01 level. Does this mean that only 1% of the standardization sample obtained Verbal and Performance scores at that magnitude of difference? No! In fact, nearly

25% of persons in the standardization sample obtained Verbal and Performance scores that were different by 15 points or more. The statistical significance indicates the likelihood that a difference of that magnitude would occur by chance. The .01 or .05 levels indicate that the difference is likely to be real, not whether the difference is unusual or unique. It is essential to keep in mind that real differences in profiles of scores do occur frequently, and that the stability of such differences is questionable. These points are addressed further in the later discussion of using presumed cognitive or neurological strengths to specify treatment methodology.

The third problem with the interpretation of the Wechsler factor scores, Verbal–Performance scale differences, and subtest profiles is their utility in decision making. There is little evidence to suggest that any of the factor, scale, or subtest profile differences can be used to improve decisions about individuals. It is widely assumed that these score differences have important implications for understanding the client and for differential educational programming (e.g., Kaufman, 1994a, 1994b). These implications are rarely specified precisely. Empirical tests of these interpretations are virtually nonexistent. The profile, scale, and factor score differences do provide opportunities for extensive interpretation of test results; however, despite the long tradition of this practice, empirical support does not exist for the accuracy or utility of these interpretations.

Diagnostic Validity of the Wechsler Scales

The least disputed use of current tests of intelligence including the Wechsler scales is in relation to measurement of general intellectual functioning, or as a measure of the general factor of intelligence. It is this general factor that appears to be essential to current conceptions of MR and SLD. The validity of the general factor is reasonably well established in terms of relationships to certain important criteria such as academic success and occupational attainment; however, the typical correlations of about .4 to about .7 are far from perfect. The general factor also has lower but statistically significant relationships to success within occupations and to a variety of other human conditions or performances varying from likelihood of law breaking to marital stability.

General factor measures also are related to a variety of indices of cognitive processing. Campione, Brown, and Ferrara (1982) provided an excellent discussion of these relationships. Although their review focused primarily on studies of persons with mild MR, the relationships they reported in the literature reviewed were interpreted as, for the most part, applying to all ranges of ability. According to Campione et al., performance on intellectual measures is positively related to the speed and efficiency of information processing, to the individual's knowledge base, to the spontaneous use of appropriate strategies in problem-solving tasks, to metacognitive operations whereby the individual exerts control over approaches to problem solving, and to the transfer of problem-solving skills to novel situations.

Perhaps the most salient result in the Campione et al. (1982) review was the interpretation of intellectual differences in terms of the capability of profiting from incomplete instruction. In general, the higher the level of intellectual ability, the greater the individual's capability of learning through indirect or incomplete instruction. Conversely, the lower the level of general intelligence, the greater the need for systematic, carefully sequenced, direct instruction.

It should be noted that the most widely used measures of intellectual functioning do not provide direct assessment of any of the cognitive processes. Rather, the complex types of items included on current measures require different cognitive processes to varying degrees. Furthermore, the scores on current measures, whether from subtests or from composite scales, cannot be interpreted directly, with few exceptions, as pure measures of any of the cognitive processes. Rather, these scores represent the products rather than the processes whereby individuals recall information, explain concepts, or solve problems.

Based on the evidence summarized in the preceding paragraphs, the Wechsler scales are valid as measures of diagnostic constructs involving learning ability and likely performance in an academic setting. Such performances, although narrow as such, have vast implications for coping capacity in a variety of other situations and contexts. Virtually all these relationships are correlational, however, and there typically is a large range of performance in academic settings or jobs for each IQ level.

Treatment Validity of the Wechsler Scales

Witt and Gresham's (1985) evaluation of the treatment validity of the WISC-R is equally pertinent to the WISC-III, "In short, the WISC-R lacks treatment validity in that its use does not enhance remedial interventions for children who show specific academic skill deficiencies. . . . For a test to have treatment validity, it must lead to better treatments (i.e., better educational programs, teaching strategies, etc.)" (p. 1717). Recently, similar concerns were expressed by Reschly and Ysseldyke (1995) and Macmann and Barnett (1994a, 1994b) who framed the relevant issues about Wechsler interpretation as follows: "What can be said with confidence?" "What can be said that might be helpful?" In fact, the results of the Wechsler scales and most traditional measures of intelligence have relatively little to say about specific interventions (see Flanagan, Andrews, & Genshaft, Chapter 23, this volume). The authors of the alternative measures focus to a greater extent on intervention issues of what to teach and/or how to teach it (see, e.g., Lidz, Chapter 15, this volume).

Treatment Validity of SLD and Mild MR Diagnostic Constructs

The validity of traditional measures including the Wechsler scales is dependent to an enormous degree on the validity of the diagnostic constructs with which they are so closely associated. Here the issues are (1) the validity of the diagnostic constructs of MR and SLD (recall the Cromwell et al., 1975, criteria) and (2) the availability of alternative methods of identifying children for special education services.

The SLD and MR diagnostic constructs have poor treatment validity according to Kavale's meta analyses and review of special education effects. The average benefits associated with diagnosis as SLD or MR are small (Kavale, 1990). Substantial evidence indicates that the same treatment goals and teaching strategies are adopted regardless of the category of mild disability (Reynolds & Lakin, 1987). For example, the top individual education plan goals typically are reading, then math, then written expression regardless of whether the disability is mild MR, SLD, or emotional–behavioral disorder (EBD), and the same teaching strategies are used regardless of disability category. Furthermore, programs for low-achieving students (e. g., Chapter I) and special education for students with mild disabilities are highly similar in terms of the needs of the students and the intervention methodology. Despite these similarities, markedly different levels of financial support are provided in special education and Chapter I, often on the basis of a few points on an intelligence test or the difference between intelligence and achievement tests that barely meets criteria for a discrepancy. Some students are called disabled (and lots more money spent on their education) while others remain in regular education with little assistance. Do these distinctions make sense?

It is difficult to justify the labeling process if program benefits are not clearly documented (Gallagher, 1972) and if differential treatment is not related to the category assigned (Cromwell et al., 1975; Heller et al., 1982). System reform efforts often involve noncategorical special education, with less emphasis on finding the right category or differential diagnosis among disabilities and more emphasis on determination of programming needs and design of interventions (Reschly 1988a, 1988b; Reschly & Ysseldyke, 1995; Reynolds & Lakin, 1987; Ysseldyke, 1987).

Although there are many tantalizing findings in the SLD research, few generalizations can be made beyond the observation that students with SLD have low achievement, most often in reading.

The same conclusion applies to students in Chapter I programs. Notably absent in the SLD research and practice is evidence for validated differential treatment based on the SLD diagnosis or the identification of reliable subtypes of SLD for whom matching treatment to subtype produces better outcomes (Epps, Ysseldyke, & McGue, 1984; Shinn, Tindal, Spira, & Marston, 1987; Shinn, Ysseldyke, Deno, & Tindal, 1986; Sleeter, 1986; Ysseldyke & Algozzine, 1983; Ysseldyke, Algozzine, & Epps, 1983; Ysseldyke, Algozzine, Shinn, & McGue, 1982; Ysseldyke, Thurlow, et al., 1983).

Recent literature suggests further that intelligence–achievement methods of identifying children as SLD have poor stability, uncertain validity, and overall negative effects on interventions for children with reading problems (Fletcher et al., 1994; Fletcher & Foorman, 1994; Shaywitz, Escobar, Shaywitz, Fletcher, & Makush, 1992; Shaywitz, Fletcher, Holahan, & Shaywitz, 1992). Lyon (1995) summarized these findings as follows: (1) exclusionary SLD definitions using intelligence–achievement discrepancies are invalid, (2) distinguishing between poor readers with and without intelligence–achievement discrepancies appears invalid because both groups show similar information processing and achievement profiles, (3) reading disabilities represent a persistent deficit rather than a developmental lag, and (4) children with poor reading differ from one another and from normal readers along a broad continuum that does not have a distinct "hump" that separates a group of poor readers from other poor readers or normal readers.

These authors (Fletcher et al., 1994; Shaywitz, Fletcher et al., 1992; Lyon, 1996) have suggested further that eligibility based on the intelligence–achievement discrepancy model hampers efforts at early intervention because kindergarten, first-, and many second-grade children with poor skills in phonological processing, letter naming, sound–symbol correspondence, and decoding often do not have sufficiently large intelligence–reading achievement discrepancies to meet SLD eligibility requirements. Assistance often is delayed until the discrepancy is sufficiently large to meet eligibility requirements, with valuable time lost and unnecessary failure experienced by children. These authors suggest changing eligibility requirements so that poor phonological processing skills per se would be sufficient to trigger most if not all of the additional resources now associated with SLD. A change of this nature likely would have an enormous impact on the use of traditional intelligence tests.

Alternative Delivery System Themes

Before leaving the discussion of current uses of intelligence tests, particularly the Wechsler scales, the trend in some states toward alternative delivery systems bears brief mention. These schemes have many common themes, including (1) the adoption of an outcomes criterion to determine the effectiveness of services, (2) use of functional assessment procedures that are directly related to defining problems in natural settings, monitoring progress, and evaluating outcomes, (3) systematic problem solving, (4) direct measures of academic and social–behavioral performance in natural settings, (5) frequent progress monitoring with changes in interventions when progress toward goals fails to meet expectations; and (6) systematic implementation of principles of instructional design and behavioral change (Reschly, 1988a, 1988b; Reschly & Tilly, 1993). System reforms may also involve (1) noncategorical classification schemes for students now classified in mild disability categories such as SLD, (2) combining remedial and special education programs such as Chapter I and resource pull-out programs, and (3) attempts to prevent disability classification through provision of services in general education, and delivery of special education in general education classrooms (Advocacy for Appropriate Educational Services, 1985; Cobb & Dawson, 1989; Heller et al., 1982; Knoff & Batsche, 1991; Kovaleski, 1988; Reschly, 1980, 1988a, 1988b; Reschly & Tilly, 1993; Reschly & Wilson, 1990, 1995; Reynolds & Lakin, 1987; Reynolds, Wang, & Walberg, 1987; Shapiro, 1989; Shinn, Tindal, & Stein, 1988: Will, 1988; Wilson, 1991; Ysseldyke, Reynolds, & Weinberg, 1984).

Noncategorical classification schemes have the greatest potential for changing the use of intelligence tests. When special education eligibility is determined by a combination of (1) large differences from typical levels of performance in relevant skills such as reading and (2) documented insufficiency of regular education interventions, there is no reason to use intelligence tests and, in fact, the school psychologists in this system do not use the Wechsler scales or any of its (mostly) ignored competitors (Tilly, Grimes, & Reschly, 1993).

Summary

Although intelligence test use, with a few exceptions, appears to be as prominent as ever, there are potentially huge changes that could change markedly and rapidly this long-standing approach to assessment. As noted, a noncategorical approach to special education eligibility can produce a system in which *no* intelligence tests are given by the vast majority of school psychologists (Tilly et al., 1993). Furthermore, if recent recommendations are adopted regarding the classification criteria for SLD (Lyon, 1996), use of intelligence tests may no longer be necessary for the SLD diagnosis. That, too, could markedly change the use of traditional individually administered intelligence tests. For now, it is clear that the validity of such tests is closely associated with the diagnostic constructs of SLD and MR.

ALTERNATIVE INSTRUMENTS AND USES

Instruments that might become alternatives to the Wechsler scales have a difficult marketing challenge in view of current assessment practices. The development and use of these intellectual assessment alternatives typically rests on one or some combination of the following rationales: (1) identification of weak cognitive processes with the purpose of overcoming these weaknesses through training procedures, (2) identification of cognitive strengths and weaknesses for the purpose of prescribing instructional procedures that capitalize on strengths and avoid weaknesses, and (3) better representation of the complex cognitive processes involved with human intellectual abilities or more complete coverage of the structure of intellectual abilities. Each of these purposes is represented in the alternative approaches described in other chapters in this volume.

Ability Training Approaches

There are two types of ability training approaches represented in this volume that also are prominent in the current literature. These approaches differ in terms of their degree of standardization and use of carefully constructed norms. Both types share the effort to improve cognitive skills or abilities as well as the assumption that these improvements will also translate to improved academic performance.

Cognitive Assessment System

The Cognitive Assessment System (CAS; Das & Naglieri, in press; Naglieri, Chapter 13, this volume) is closely related to Luria's theory regarding neurological organization, the different coding processes (simultaneous and successive), and the metacognitive operation of planning (Das, 1984; Das, Kirby, & Jarman, 1979; Naglieri & Das, 1988). The CAS is intended to provide a more complete description of intellectual abilities, improve diagnoses of learning problems, and identify weak cognitive abilities that can then be improved through educational procedures. The improvements in cognitive skills are believed to be important in and of themselves; that is, better planning skills are valuable as such, as well as translating into better academic performance.

The aims established by the CAS authors are similar to the claims made about three decades ago by several scholars involved with the early development of the field of SLD (Kirk, McCarthy, & Kirk, 1968). Psycholinguistic (PL) and perceptual–motor (PM) assessment and intervention are the oldest, best researched, and most controversial of the ability training models used currently with children and youth. These models made similar assumptions about cognitive processes, interventions, and anticipated effects on academic achievement.

The PL and PM models assumed that basic cognitive processes could be identified accurately and improved through systematic instruction. Transfer to improved school achievement was assumed in a chain of logic that proceeded through the following assumptions: (1) PL or PM processes were a prerequisite to successful school learning, and (2) untreated PL or PM process deficits would remain as barriers to, and improved PL or PM processes would lead to, more successful achievement.

The PL and PM models dominated thought and practice in SLD until about 1980. Reviews of research on the assessment of PL processes and the outcomes of PL interventions began to appear in the mid-1970s leading to diminished use. Hammill and Larsen (1974, 1978) and Newcomer, Larsen, and Hammill (1975) concluded that PL interventions had little positive effects on improving PL processes and no documented positive effects on school achievement. The conclusions about the effects of PL interventions were disputed by Minskoff (1975), and later by Lund, Foster, and McCall-Perez (1978) in a series of increasingly heated debates with Hammill and his associates. Later examination of the same body of literature using the technique of meta-analysis (Glass, 1983) led to slightly more positive conclusions about interventions with some PL processes (verbal expression, manual expression, visual closure, and auditory association) (Kavale, 1981, 1990), but no solid evidence has been provided confirming that improved PL processes lead to improved academic achievement.

The treatment validity evidence regarding the PM model is even more negative. Kavale and Mattson's (1983) meta-analysis of some 180 studies led to the disappointing conclusion that PM interventions had no effect on PM processes and no identifiable beneficial effects on school achievement. PM assessment and training appears to be a waste of teachers' and students' valuable time (Kavale, 1990).

We can anticipate similar questions about the CAS and other ability training procedures. Hard questions will be asked and empirically examined regarding improvements in the abilities and transfer of these improvements to academic performance. Transfer is the critical issue. Transfer to a narrow range of skills like those assessed initially by the test and then taught in the training procedures is likely to be seen as insufficient to justify changing now well-established assessment practices. Better or more complete representation of cognitive processes also is unlikely to be sufficient for the CAS to be used widely. Strong evidence of positive transfer will be required (e.g., showing that improved cognitive skills produce more efficient academic performance), and that is a very high standard that will be difficult to meet.

Dynamic Assessment

The ability training approach represented by dynamic assessment and its various forms (Feuerstein, Feuerstein, & Gross, Chapter 16, this volume; Feuerstein, Rand, & Hoffman, 1979; Haywood, Brown, & Wingenfeld, 1990; Jensen, Rand, Kaniel, & Tzuriel, 1988) is designed to identify the cognitive processes used by the child in a loosely structured situation that involves a testing–teaching–learning–testing procedure (Lidz, Chapter 15, this volume). The dynamic assessment approaches are, at best, loosely structured. None could be called standardized in the sense of uniformity of administration, scoring, and interpretation (Anastasi, 1988). The critical dynamic assessment assumptions are as follows (1) cognitive processes can be inferred from responses to test items, (2) weaknesses can be identified, (3) instruction can be designed to overcome the weaknesses and produce more sophisticated cognitive functioning, and (4) the improved cognitive functioning will transfer to other, nontesting and nontraining tasks such as academic skills.

Most dynamic assessment advocates recognize the necessity of going beyond the mere demonstration that test performance improves with coaching, or that all learners appear to have more potential than is demonstrated in actual performance. The real issues in the diagnostic utility of dynamic assessment are correctly regarded by them as the accurate classification of cognitive structures, the estimation of the modifiability of these structures, and the time/effort required to produce the modifications. These are, indeed, important diagnostic questions that, if answered accurately and followed with effective interventions, would certainly justify the substantially greater costs associated with dynamic assessment.

The evidence to date on these issues is not convincing. Accurate classification of cognitive structures appears to be problematic. The interjudge agreement regarding identification of categories of cognitive deficits by "world-class" dynamic assessment experts indicates low to moderate agreement for about half of the categories (Haywood et al., 1990). Agreement regarding kinds of deficits in cognitive structures is critical to the other diagnostic questions of modifiability and time/resources required. Reliability is a prerequisite to diagnostic utility for dynamic and traditional measures. Much work is still needed regarding the technical adequacy of dynamic assessment.

Before leaving this area, it is important to recognize the heroic efforts made by some of the leading scholars in this area to find ways to improve the cognitive functioning of children and youth. This enormous challenge is eclipsed only by the potential benefits of an intellectual assessment system that was useful for developing significantly better cognitive functioning and improved academic performance for children with learning problems.

Aptitude by Treatment Approaches

Three prominent treatment by aptitude interaction (ATI) models are used by many clinicians and educators today. All specify relationships between cognitive processes and the methodology used to teach cognitive and academic skills. The *modality* matching model generally focuses on three kinds of information processing strengths and weaknesses: (1) auditory, (2) visual, or (3) kinesthetic. Children experiencing difficulty in acquiring academic skills are assessed to determine strengths and weaknesses over these processes, and then an instructional method that utilizes the child's strengths is prescribed. The same procedures are used in the second and third models, cognitive style and neuropsychological. In the latter model, additional inference(s) are made about underlying brain functioning. The actual prescriptions for instructional methodology are highly similar across the three ATI models (Reschly & Gresham, 1989).

The ATI models see aptitudes as relatively unchanging, even to the point in the neuropsychological variation of cautioning against "teaching dead tissue" (Hartlage & Reynolds, 1981). Focusing interventions on deficit areas as is the case in the PL and PM models is seen as inefficient and perhaps futile. Aptitudes typically are assessed with conventional standardized measures of cognitive functions including individually administered measures of general intellectual functioning. Two well-standardized general intelligence measures have been developed with primary attention to diagnosing elements of cognitive style (Das & Naglieri, in press; Kaufman & Kaufman, 1983). The ATI models are used primarily to design instruction with an underlying assumption that process strengths will generalize to learner performance in instructional settings.

Modality matching, cognitive style determination, and neuropsychological assessment and intervention depend heavily on the existence of aptitude by treatment interactions (ATI). The ATI notion has enormous intuitive appeal. Reynolds (1992) described this process as follows: "Instruction is formatted around the child's best developed processes, avoiding those that are poorly developed or inept" (p. 10). According to a survey by Arter and Jenkins (1977), 99% of teachers believe that there are differences in how children process information, and that instruction will be more effective if instructional materials and methods are matched to modality or neuropsychological strengths.

The case for ATI was stated by Cronbach (1957) in a highly influential and widely cited article that appeared in the *American Psychologist,* the largest-circulation psychology journal in the world. Cronbach asserted that aptitudes could be measured accurately and that "for any potential problem, there is some best group of treatments to use and best allocation of persons to treatments" (p. 680). The allocation process meant matching individuals' aptitude strengths to treatments that utilize those strengths through differential stimulus properties or instructional methods.

Although the potential list of aptitudes that might be used in matching is nearly unlimited, the different instructional methodologies are much more limited. The typical matching procedure involves aptitudes such as auditory, visual, and kinesthetic processes; cognitive styles such as simultaneous and successive (Das et al., 1979) or sequential and simultaneous (Kaufman, Goldsmith, & Kaufman, 1984); or neuropsychological constructs such as right hemisphere and left hemisphere functioning. The different instructional methodologies prescribed for children with these aptitude strengths are highly similar (Reschly & Gresham, 1989). Phonic methods of teaching reading and overall emphasis on auditory cues are typically prescribed for children believed to have strengths in auditory processing, sequential or successive cognitive styles, or left hemisphere functions. Similarly, whole-word methods of teaching reading and visual cues are stressed for children with strengths in visual processing, simultaneous cognitive styles, or right hemisphere functioning.

For these models to have treatment validity, there must be an interaction between the presumed aptitude strength and instructional methodology. For example, children with right hemisphere strengths must learn more efficiently when instructional materials and methods are selected and presented in ways to utilize that strength and, conversely, such students must do less well if instructional methodology is not matched to strengths.

Unfortunately, the research to date does not support the existence of significant treatment by aptitude interactions. Some of the difficulties with ATI research were summarized by Cronbach (1975) in another *American Psychologist* article in which he expressed doubt about ever being able to use matching in clinical or educational settings. Based on 18 years of largely unsuccessful ATI research, Cronbach concluded that "once we attend to interactions, we enter a hall of mirrors that extends to infinity" (p. 119). The major problems in the ATI research were (1) nonexistent or very weak interactions, that is, matching strengths had, at best, small and inconsequential effects, (2) results over studies were enormously inconsistent, and (3) there were higher-order interactions, that is, complex three- and four-way interactions, that would be impossible to apply to practical clinical and educational problems.

The current research on modality matching and neuropsychological assessment and prescriptions fit the pattern described by Cronbach (1975). Matching presumed strengths with instructional methodologies does not lead to demonstrable differential gains in academic achievement, regardless of whether the aptitude strengths are conceptualized as modality preferences (Kavale & Forness, 1987, 1990; Kavale, 1990), cognitive styles (Ayres & Cooley, 1986; Ayres, Cooley, & Severson, 1988; Good, Vollmer, Creek, Katz, & Chowdhri, 1993), or neuropsychological functions (Reschly & Gresham, 1989; Teeter, 1987, 1989). Despite the negative evidence, the modality matching, cognitive style, and neuropsychological functioning approaches to assessment and intervention continue to be used widely in a variety of settings by psychologists and educators.

Improved Description and Interpretation of Intelligence

The final goal of the alternative methods is to provide a more complete representation and richer description of intellectual abilities. All the alternative assessment procedures share this goal to varying degrees. This goal is especially prominent in the Woodcock–Johnson Tests of Cognitive Ability (WJ-COG) (Woodcock, Chapter 12, this volume). The WJ-COG and the CAS are closely tied to the Horn–Cattell and Luria theoretical formulations of intelligence, respectively. These tests clearly are improvements over traditional tests such as the Wechsler scales in terms of providing opportunities to observe specific cognitive processes and to interpret performance using theoretical constructs such.

Richer description and more sophisticated interpretation may or may not be of any value to children and youth or to such institutions as schools where important resource allocation decisions must be made. Richer descriptions and more sophisticated interpretation may be more pleasing to the professionals who use the tests, but that is not a sufficient reason to adopt these measures. The challenge of demonstrating greater diagnostic and treatment validity remains for all of these approaches.

SUMMARY

The issue of diagnostic or treatment validity remains for all the alternative instruments and approaches. None of the new instruments are clearly superior to the Wechsler scales in terms of diagnostic utility and treatment validity. Several measures have promise. However, the requirements for new tests to obtain a share of the individual assessment market may be imposing and unfair for, indeed, being just as good as the Wechsler scales is unlikely to produce much change in current assessment practices. As a professional in a field that still is dominated to a large degree by intellectual assessment (Sarason, 1975; Wilson & Reschly, 1996), which, in turn, is dominated by one set of highly similar instruments, one can hope for a significant breakthrough that will substantially improve interventions for children and youth. Absent that kind of breakthrough, it is difficult not to question the continuation of traditional assessment practices that have, as their principal outcomes, the application of diagnostic constructs with questionable reliability and validity to children experiencing learning and behavior problems in educational settings.

REFERENCES

Advocacy for appropriate educational services for all children. (1985). Washington, DC: National Association of School Psychologists. (Reprinted in *School Psychology Review, 19*(4))

American Psychological Association. (1992). *Ethical principles of psychologists* (amended June 2, 1989). *American Psychologist, 47,* 1597–1611.

Anastasi, A. (1988). *Psychological testing* (6th ed.). New York: MacMillan.

Arter, J. A., & Jenkins, J. R. (1977). Examining the benefits and prevalence of modality considerations in special education. *Journal of Special Education, 11,* 281–298.

Ayres, R. R., & Cooley, E. J. (1986). Sequential versus simultaneous processing on the K-ABC: Validity in predicting learning success. *Journal of Psychoeducational Assessment, 4,* 211–220.

Ayres, R. R., Cooley, E. J., & Severson, H. H. (1988). Educational translation of the Kaufman Assessment Battery for Children: A construct validity study. *School Psychology Review, 17,* 113–124.

Barnett, D. W., & Macmann, G. M. (1992a). Aptitude–achievement discrepancy scores: Accuracy in analysis misdirected. *School Psychology Review, 21,* 494–508.

Barnett, D. W., & Macmann, G. M. (1992b). Decision reliability and validity: Contributions and limitations of alternative assessment strategies. *Journal of Special Education, 25,* 431–452.

Brown, F. G. (1983). *Principles of educational and psychological testing* (3rd ed.). New York: Holt, Rinehart, & Winston.

Campione, J. C., Brown, A. L., & Ferrara, R. A. (1982). Mental retardation and intelligence. In R. J. Sternberg (Ed.), *Handbook of human intelligence* (pp. 392–490). Cambridge, England: Cambridge University Press.

Cobb, C. T., & Dawson, M. M. (1989). The evolution of children's services: Approaching maturity. *School Psychology Review, 18,* 203–208.

Cromwell, R., Blashfield, R., & Strauss, J. (1975). Criteria for classification systems. In N. Hobbs (Ed.), *Issues in the classification of children* (pp. 4–25). San Francisco: Jossey-Bass.

Cronbach, L. J. (1957). The two disciplines of scientific psychology. *American Psychologist, 12,* 671–684.

Cronbach, L. J. (1975). Beyond the two disciplines of scientific psychology. *American Psychologist, 30,* 116–127.

Cronbach, L. J. (1990). *Essentials of psychological testing* (5th Ed.). New York: Harper & Row.

Cronbach, L. J., & Snow, R. E. (1977). *Aptitudes and instructional methods.* New York: Wiley (Halstead Press).

Das, J. P. (1984). Aspects of planning. In J. R. Kirby (Ed.), *Cognitive strategies and educational performance* (pp. 13–31). New York: Academic Press.

Das, J. P., Kirby, J. R., & Jarman, R. F. (1979). *Simultaneous and successive cognitive processes.* New York: Academic Press.

Das, J. P., & Naglieri, J. A. (in press). *Das–Naglieri: Cognitive Assessment System.* Chicago: Riverside.

Epps, S., Ysseldyke, J., & McGue, M. (1984). Differentiating SLD and non-SLD students: "I know one when I see one." *Learning Disability Quarterly, 7,* 89–101.

Feuerstein, R., Rand, Y., & Hoffman, M. (1979). *The dynamic assessment of retarded performers: The Learning Potential Assessment Device, theory, instruments, and techniques.* Baltimore: University Park Press.

Fletcher, J. M., & Foorman, B. R. (1994). Issues in the definition and measurement of learning disabilities: The need for early intervention. In G. R. Lyon (Ed.), *Frames of reference for assessment of learning disabilities: New views on measurement issues* (pp. 185–200). Baltimore: Paul H. Brooks.

Fletcher, J. M., Shaywitz, S. E., Shankweiler, D. P., Katz, L., Liberman, I. Y., Fowler, A., Francis, D. J., Stuebing, K. K., & Shaywitz, B. A. (1994). Cognitive profiles of reading disability: Comparisons of discrepancy and low achievement definitions. *Journal of Educational Psychology, 85,* 1–18.

Gallagher, J. (1972). The special education contract for mildly handicapped children. *Exceptional Children, 38,* 527–535.

Glass, G. V. (1983). Effectiveness of special education. *Policy Studies Review, 2,* 65–78.

Glutting, J. J., McGrath, E. A., Kamphaus, R. W., & McDermott, P. A. (1992). Taxonomy and validity of subtest profiles in the Kaufman Assessment Battery for Children. *Journal of Special Education, 26,* 85–115.

Goh, D. S., Telzrow, C. J., & Fuller, G. B. (1981). The practice of psychological assessment among school psychologists. *Professional Psychology, 12,* 696–706.

Good, R. H., Vollmer, M., Creek, R. J., Katz, L., & Chowdhri, S. (1993). Treatment utility of the Kaufman Assessment Battery for Children: Effects of matching instruction and student processing strength. *School Psychology Review, 22,* 8–26.

Hammill, D., & Larsen, S. (1974). The effectiveness of psycholinguistic training. *Exceptional Children, 41,* 5–14.

Hammill, D., & Larsen, S. (1978). The effectiveness of psycholinguistic training: A reaffirmation of position. *Exceptional Children, 44,* 402–414.

Hartlage, L. C., & Reynolds, C. R. (1981). Neuropsychological assessment and the individualization of instruction. In G. W. Hynd & J. E. Obrzut (Eds.), *Neuropsychological assessment and the school age child: Issues and procedures* (pp. 355–378). New York: Grune & Stratton.

Haywood, H. C., Brown, T., & Wingenfeld, S. (1990). Dynamic approaches to psychoeducational assessment. *School Psychology Review, 19,* 411–422.

Heller, K., Holtzman, W., & Messick, S. (Eds.). (1982). *Placing children in special education: A strategy for equity.* Washington, DC: National Academy Press.

Holt, R. R. (Ed.). (1968). *Diagnostic psychological testing.* New York: International Universities Press.

Hutton, J. B., Dubes, R., & Muir, S. (1992). Assessment practices of school psychologists: Ten years later. *School Psychology Review, 21,* 271–284.

Individuals with Disabilities Education Act, 20 U.S.C. ch. 33, §§ 1400–1485 (1990).

Individuals with Disabilities Education Act, 34 C.F.R. pt. 300 (1991).

Jensen, M. R., Rand, Y., Kaniel, S., & Tzuriel, D. (1988). Cultural difference and cultural deprivation: A theoretical framework for differential intervention. In R. M. Gupta & P. Coxhead (Eds.), *Cultural diversity and learning efficiency* (pp. 66–88). London: Macmillan.

Kaufman, A. (1976a). A new approach to interpretation of test scatter on the WISC-R. *Journal of Learning Disabilities, 9,* 160–168.

Kaufman, A. (1976b). Verbal performance IQ discrepancies on the WISC-R. *Journal of Consulting and Clinical Psychology, 44,* 739–744.

Kaufman, A. S. (1993). King WISC the third assumes the throne. *Journal of School Psychology, 31,* 345–354.

Kaufman, A. S. (1994a). *Intelligent testing with the WISC-III.* New York: Wiley.

Kaufman, A. S. (1994b). A reply to Macmann and Barnett: Lessons from the blind man and the elephant. *School Psychology Quarterly, 9,* 199–207.

Kaufman, A. S., Goldsmith, B. Z., & Kaufman, N. L. (1984). *K-SOS: Kaufman sequential or simultaneous.* Circle Pines, MN: American Guidance Service.

Kaufman, A., & Kaufman, N. (1983). *Kaufman Assessment Battery for Children* (K-ABC). Circle Pines, MN: American Guidance Service.

Kavale, K. A. (1981). Functions of the Illinois Test of Psycholinguistic Abilities (ITPA): Are they trainable? *Exceptional Children, 47,* 496–510.

Kavale, K. A. (1990). The effectiveness of special education. In T. B. Gutkin & C. R. Reynolds (Eds.). *The handbook of school psychology* (2nd ed., pp. 868–898). New York: Wiley.

Kavale, K. A., & Forness, S. R. (1987). Substance over style: Assessing the efficacy of modality testing and teaching. *Exceptional Children, 54,* 228–239.

Kavale, K. A., & Forness, S. R. (1990). Substance over style: A rejoinder to Dunn's animadversions. *Exceptional Children, 56,* 357–361.

Kavale, K. A., & Mattson, P. D. (1983). "One jumped off the balance beam": Meta-analysis of perceptual–motor training. *Journal of Learning Disabilities, 16,* 165–173.

Kirk, S. A., McCarthy, J., & Kirk, W. (1968). *Illinois Test of Psycholinguistic Abilities.* Champaign: University of Illinois Press.

Knoff, H. M., & Batsche, G. M. (1991). Integrating school and educational psychology to meet the educational and mental health needs of all children. *Educational Psychologist, 26,* 167–183.

Kovaleski, J. F. (1988). Paradigmatic obstacles to reform in school psychology. *School Psychology Review, 17,* 479–484.

Lubin, B., Larsen, R. M., & Matarazzo, J. D. (1984). Patterns of psychological test usage in the United States. *American Psychologist, 39,* 451–454.

Luckasson, R., Coulter, D. L., Polloway, E. A., Reiss, S., Schalock, R. L., Snell, M. E., Spitalnik, D. M., & Stark, J. A. (1992). *Mental retardation: Definition, classification, and systems of support* (9th ed.). Washington DC: American Association on Mental Retardation.

Lund, K., Foster, G., & McCall-Perez, F. (1978). The effectiveness of psycholinguistic training: A reevaluation. *Exceptional Children, 44,* 310–321.

Lyon, G. R. (1996). Learning disabilities. *The Future of Children: Special Education for Students with Disabilities, 6(1),* 54–76.

Macmann, G. M., & Barnett, D. W. (1985). Discrepancy score analysis: A computer simulation of classification stability. *Journal of Psychoeducational Assessment, 4,* 363–375.

Macmann, G. M., & Barnett, D. W. (1992). Redefining the WISC-R: Implications for professional practice and public policy. *Journal of Special Education, 26,* 139–161.

Macmann, G. M., & Barnett, D. W. (1994a). Structural analysis of correlated factors: Lessons from the verbal-performance dichotomy of the Wechsler scales. *School Psychology Quarterly, 9,* 161–167.

Macmann, G. M., & Barnett, D. W. (1994b). Some additional lessons from the Wechsler scales: A rejoinder to Kaufman and Keith. *School Psychology Quarterly, 9,* 223–236.

Macmann, G. M., Barnett, D. W., Lombard, T. J., Belton-Kocher, E., & Sharpe, M. N. (1989). On the actuarial classification of children: Fundamental studies of classification agreement. *Journal of Special Education, 23,* 127–149.

McDermott, P. A., Fantuzzo, J. W., & Glutting, J. J. (1990). Just say no to subtest analysis: A critique on Wechsler theory and practice. *Journal of Psychoeducational Assessment, 8,* 289–302.

McDermott, P. A., Fantuzzo, J. W., Glutting, J. J., Watkins, M. W., Baggaley, A. R. (1992). Illusions of meaning in the ipsative assessment of children's ability. *Journal of Special Education, 25,* 504–526.

Mercer, C. D., King-Sears, P., & Mercer, A. R. (1990). Learning disabilities definitions and criteria used by state education departments. *Learning Disability Quarterly, 13,* 141–152.

Messick, S. (1989). Validity. In R. Linn (Ed.), *Educational measurement* (3rd ed., pp. 13–103). New York: Macmillan.

Minskoff, E. (1975). Research on psycholinguistic training: Critique and guidelines. *Exceptional Children, 42,* 136–144.

Naglieri, J. A., & Das, J. A. (1988). Planning–arousal–simultaneous–successive (PASS): A model for assessment. *Journal of School Psychology, 26,* 35–48.

Newcomer, R., Larsen, S., & Hammill, D. (1975). A response to Minskoff. *Exceptional Children, 42,* 144–148.

Oakland, T., & Hu, S. (1992). The top 10 tests used with children and youth worldwide. *Bulletin of the International Test Commission, 19*(1), 99–120.

Patrick, J., & Reschly, D. (1982). Relationship of state educational criteria and demographic variables to school-system prevalence of mental retardation. *American Journal of Mental Deficiency, 86,* 351–360.

Rapaport, D., Gill, M. & Schafer, R. (1945/1946). *Diagnostic psychological testing* (Vol. I & II). Chicago: Yearbook.

Reschly, D. J. (1978). *Nonbiased assessment and school psychology.* Des Moines: Iowa Department of Public Instruction, Special Education Section. (ERIC Document Reproduction Service No. ED 157 240)

Reschly, D. J. (1980). School psychologists and assessment in the future. *Professional Psychology, 11,* 841–848.

Reschly, D. J. (1988a). Special education reform: School psychology revolution. *School Psychology Review, 17,* 459–475.

Reschly, D. J. (1988b). Obstacles, starting points, and doldrums notwithstanding: Reform/revolution from outcomes criteria. *School Psychology Review, 17,* 495–501.

Reschly, D. J. (1988c). Assessment issues, placement litigation, and the future of mild mental retardation classification and programming. *Education and Training of the Mentally Retarded, 23,* 285–301.

Reschly, D. J. (1992). Mental retardation: Conceptual foundations, definitional criteria, and diagnostic operations. In S. R. Hooper, G. W. Hynd, & R. E. Mattison (Eds.), *Developmental disorders: Diagnostic criteria and clinical assessment* (pp. 23–67). Hillsdale, NJ: Erlbaum.

Reschly, D. J., & Gresham, F. M. (1989). Current neuropsychological diagnosis of learning problems: A leap of faith. In C. R. Reynolds & E. Fletcher-Janzen (Eds.), *Handbook of clinical neuropsychology* (pp. 503–519). New York: Plenum Press.

Reschly, D. J., & Grimes, J. P. (1995). Intellectual assessment. In A. Thomas & J. Grimes (Eds.), *Best practices in school psychology III* (3rd ed., pp. 763–773). Washington, DC: National Association of School Psychologists.

Reschly, D. J., & Tilly, W. D. (1993). The WHY of system reform. *Communique, 22*(1), 1, 4–6.

Reschly, D. J., & Wilson, M. S. (1990). Cognitive processing versus traditional intelligence: Diagnostic utility, intervention implications, and treatment validity. *School Psychology Review, 19,* 443–458.

Reschly, D. J., & Wilson, M. S. (1995). School psychology faculty and practitioners: 1986 to 1991 trends in demographic characteristics, roles, satisfaction, and system reform. *School Psychology Review, 24,* 62–80.

Reschly, D. J., & Ysseldyke, J. E. (1995). School psychology paradigm shift. In A. Thomas & J. Grimes (Eds.), *Best practices in school psychology III* (3rd ed., 17–31). Washington, DC: National Association of School Psychologists.

Reynolds, C. R. (1992). Two key concepts in the diagnosis of learning disabilities and the habilitation of learning. *Learning Disability Quarterly, 15,* 2–12.

Reynolds, M. C., & Lakin, K. C. (1987). Noncategorical special education for mildly handicapped students. A system for the future. In M. C. Wang, M. C. Reynolds, & H. J. Walberg (Eds.), *The handbook of special education: Research and practice* (Vol. I, pp. 331–356). Oxford, England: Pergamon Press.

Reynolds, M. C., Wang, M. C., & Walberg, H. J. (1987). The necessary restructuring of special and regular education. *Exceptional Children, 53,* 391–398.

Sarason, S. (1975). The unfortunate fate of Alfred Binet and school psychology. *Teachers College Record, 77,* 579–592.

Sattler, J. M. (1992). *Assessment of children,* (3rd ed.). San Diego, CA: Author. (Original work published 1988)

Shapiro, E. S. (Ed.). (1989). *Academic skills problems: Direct assessment and intervention.* New York: Guilford Press.

Shaywitz, S. E., Escobar, M. D., Shaywitz, B. A., Fletcher, J. M., & Makush, R. (1992). Distribution and temporal stability of dyslexia in an epidemiological sample of 414 children followed longitudinally. *New England Journal of Medicine, 326,* 145–150.

Shaywitz, S. E., Fletcher, J. M., Holahan, J., & Shaywitz, B. A. (1992). Discrepancy compared to low achievement definitions of reading disability: Results from the Connecticut Longitudinal Study. *Journal of Learning Disabilities, 25,* 639–648.

Shinn, M. R., Tindal, G. A., Spira, D., & Marston, D. (1987). Practice of learning disabilities as social policy. *Learning Disabilities Quarterly, 10,* 17–28.

Shinn, M. R., Tindal, G. A., & Stein, S. (1988). Curriculum-based measurement and the identification of mildly handicapped students. *Professional School Psychology, 3,* 69–85.

Shinn, M. R., Ysseldyke, J. E., Deno, S. L., & Tindal, G. A. (1986). A comparison of differences between students labeled learning disabled and low achieving on measures of classroom performance. *Journal of Learning Disabilities, 19,* 545–552.

Siegel, L. S. (1989). IQ is irrelevant to the definition of learning disabilities. *Journal of Learning Disabilities, 22,* 469–479.

Sleeter, C. (1986). Learning disabilities: The social construction of a special education category. *Exceptional Children, 53,* 46–54.

Snow, R. E. (1980). Aptitude and achievement. In W. B. Schrader (Ed.), *Measuring achievement: Progress over a decade. New directions for testing and measurement* (pp. 39–60). San Francisco: Jossey-Bass.

Snow, R. E. (1992). Aptitude theory: Yesterday, today, and tomorrow. *Educational Psychologist, 27,* 5–32.

Spearman, C. (1927). *The abilities of man.* New York: Macmillan.

Teeter, P. A. (1987). Review of neuropsychological assessment and intervention with children and adolescents. *School Psychology Review, 16,* 582–583.

Teeter, P. A. (1989). Neuropsychological approaches to the remediation of educational deficits. In C. R. Reynolds & E. Fletcher-Janzen (Eds.), *Handbook of clinical child neuropsychology* (pp. 357–376). New York: Plenum Press.

Terman, L. M., & Merrill, M. A. (1960). *Stanford–Binet Intelligence Scale: Form L-M.* Boston: Houghton Mifflin.

Thorndike, R. L., Hagen, E. P., & Sattler, J. M. (1986). *Stanford–Binet Intelligence Scale: Fourth edition.* Chicago: Riverside.

Tilly, W. D., Grimes, J. P., & Reschly, D. J., (1993). Special education system reform: The Iowa story. *Communique, 22,* 1–4.

U.S. Department of Education. (1994). *Sixteenth annual report to Congress on the implementation of the Education of the Individuals with Disabilities Education Act.* Washington, DC: Author.

Wade, T. C., & Baker, T. B. (1977). Opinions and use of psychological tests: A survey of clinical psychologists. *American Psychologist, 32,* 874–882.

Wechsler, D. (1955). *The measurement and appraisal of adult intelligence* (4th ed.). Baltimore: Williams & Wilkins

Wechsler, D. (1981·). *Wechsler Adult Intelligence Scale—Revised.* San Antonio, TX: Psychological Corporation.

Wechsler, D. (1989). *Wechsler Preschool and Primary Scale of Intelligence—Revised.* San Antonio, TX: Psychological Corporation.

Wechsler, D. (1991). *Wechsler Intelligence Scale for Children—Third Edition.* San Antonio, TX: Psychological Corporation.

Will, M. (1988). Educating students with learning problems and the changing role of school psychologists. *School Psychology Review, 17,* 476–478.

Wilson, M. S. (1991). Support services professionals' evaluations of current services for students with learning disabilities and low achieving students without learning disabilities: More grist for the reform mill. *School Psychology Review, 17,* 67–80.

Wilson, M. S., & Reschly, D. J. (1996). Assessment in school psychology training and practice. *School Psychology Review, 25,* 9–23.

Witt, J. C., & Gresham, F. M. (1985). Review of the Wechsler Intelligence Scale for Children—Revised. In J. Mitchell (Ed.), *Ninth mental measurements yearbook* (pp. 1716–1719). Lincoln, NE: Buros Institute.

Ysseldyke, J. E. (1987). Classification of handicapped students. In M. C. Wang, M. C. Reynolds, & H. J. Walberg (Eds.), *The handbook of special education: Research and practice* (Vol. I, pp. 253–271). Oxford, England: Pergamon Press.

Ysseldyke, J. E., & Algozzine, B. (1983). SLD or not SLD: That's not the question! *Journal of Learning Disabilities, 16,* 29–31.

Ysseldyke, J. E., Algozzine, B., & Epps, S. (1983). A logical and empirical analysis of current practice in classifying students as handicapped. *Exceptional Children, 50,* 160–166.

Ysseldyke, J. E., Algozzine, B., Shinn, M., & McGue, M. (1982). Similarities and differences between low achievers and students classified learning disabled. *Journal of Special Education, 16,* 73–85.

Ysseldyke, J. E., Reynolds, M. C., & Weinberg, R. A. (1984). *School psychology: A blueprint for training and practice.* Minneapolis: National School Psychology Inservice Training Network, University of Minnesota.

Ysseldyke, J. E., Thurlow, M., Graden, J., Wesson, C., Algozzine, B., & Deno, S. (1983). Generalizations from five years of research on assessment and decision making: The University of Minnesota Institute. *Exceptional Education Quarterly, 4,* 75–93.

CHAPTER 23

The Functional Utility of Intelligence Tests with Special Education Populations

DAWN P. FLANAGAN

TED J. ANDREWS

JUDY L. GENSHAFT

T HIS CHAPTER EXAMINES THE FUNCTIONAL UTILITY of intelligence tests in special education service delivery, particularly with respect to eligibility determination. Functional utility as defined in this chapter refers to (1) the ability of intelligence tests to estimate current and future academic performance (i.e., predictive validity), (2) the ability of intelligence tests to distinguish between children with various psychoeducational diagnoses from children with no diagnoses as well as to make differential diagnoses (i.e., discriminative validity), and (3) the ability of intelligence tests to yield data that can be used to guide meaningful instructional programming for children with learning problems (i.e., treatment validity). This chapter differs from Reschly's (Chapter 22, this volume) in two ways. First, Reschly focuses on important issues related to the reliability and validity of *diagnostic constructs* (e.g., learning disabilities) whereas we review the extant literature regarding the functional utility of intelligence tests, particularly with respect to their ability to aid in making *differential diagnoses.* Second, while Reschly reviews mainly the *most popular* intellectual assessment tools that are used to aid in making educational placement decisions, this chapter highlights the unique characteristics of several major contemporary cognitive ability tests that may yield information that has greater treatment relevance than the most widely used (traditional and nontraditional) methods. This chapter, therefore, complements Reschly's chapter. Together, the information presented in both chapters demonstrates the need for continued efforts toward and alternative methods for establishing the functional utility of intelligence tests.

THE LINK BETWEEN PSYCHOLOGY
AND SPECIAL EDUCATION IN HISTORICAL PERSPECTIVE

Intellectual assessment, more than any other available scientific method, served as the foundation on which psychology emerged as an independent field of inquiry apart from physiology and philosophy in the latter part of the 19th century (see Thorndike, Chapter 1, this volume). Psychology in the schools, and by association intellectual assessment, can be traced to the work of Arnold Gessell (1880–1961). In 1915, Gesell was the first school psychologist appointed by the Connecticut State Board of Education (cf. Fagan, 1987). His appointment served as the catalyst for the creation of a special education program in Connecticut (Phillips, 1990). As a result of Gesell's work, the title "school psychologist" became associated with special education services, especially diagnostic and placement services. In November 1975, school psychology's association with special education was formally operationalized with the passage of Public Law (PL) 94-142, the Education for All Handicapped Children Act (reauthorized by Congress as the Individuals with Disabilities Education Act [IDEA] in 1990).

IDEA states that every child has a right to a comprehensive assessment of the nature and degree of his or her specific disability. Standardized, norm-referenced tests (e.g., intelligence tests) are often the primary tools utilized by psychologists who conduct psychoeducational assessments (Mercer, 1987; Reschly, Genshaft, & Binder, 1987; Stinnett, Havey, & Oehler-Stinnett, 1994; Wilson & Reschly, 1996). Of all the services that psychologists provide (e.g., assessment, intervention, and consultation), the practice of applied intelligence testing has generated the most discussion over the past several years, particularly in regard to the functional utility of commonly used cognitive assessment instruments (Batsche, 1992; Neisworth & Bagnato, 1992; Robinson-Zanartu, Sattler, Reschly, & Sandoval, 1994).

CRITICISMS OF TRADITIONAL INTELLIGENCE TESTS

In general, standardized, norm-referenced intelligence tests have been shown to be reliable, to have adequate criterion and concurrent validity (Anastasi, 1988; Jensen, 1980; Sattler, 1992), and to do an adequate job of surveying large groups of children and adolescents for educational planning, budgeting and screening for educational tracking purposes (e.g., special class placement) (Haywood, Brown, & Wingenfeld 1990). However, intelligence tests also have been criticized strongly for the following reasons. First, special education placement decisions that are based *solely* on intelligence test scores are not valid (e.g., Bracken, 1987; Flanagan & Alfonso, 1995; Ysseldyke, Reynolds, & Weinberg, 1984). Second, intelligence test scores do not appear to be related to instructional practices (Jenkins & Pany, 1978; Reschly, 1990, Chapter 22, this volume; Ysseldyke & Mirkin, 1982). Third, there is an overemphasis on product rather than process in traditional intelligence tests (i.e., the Wechsler and Binet scales) (Naglieri, Chapter 13, this volume; Wagner & Sternberg, 1984). Fourth, many intelligence tests were not developed from well-researched and empirically supported theoretical frameworks (Flanagan & McGrew, 1995a, 1995b, Chapter 17, this volume; Mackintosh, 1986; Naglieri, Chapter 13, this volume; Sternberg, 1986). Fifth, most intelligence tests do not assess the cognitive processes and abilities that are most closely associated with academic achievement and, therefore, do not yield much information that can be used to aid in diagnosing and treating learning disabilities (McGrew, 1993, 1994; Mather, 1993; Morris, 1993; Siegel, 1989). Sixth, some have claimed that intelligence tests may be biased against culturally and linguistically diverse populations (Cunningham, 1986; Elliott; 1988; Gould, 1981; Gregory & Lee; 1986; Helms, Chapter 26, this volume; Lopez, Chapter 25, this volume). Finally, the process of evaluating an individual's performance on traditional intelligence tests to understand better how he or she learns or fails to learn is considered an exercise in futility given the lack of empirical data supporting aptitude by treatment interactions (Good, Vollmer, Creek, Katz, & Chowdhri, 1993; Fuchs, Fuchs, Benowitz, & Barringer, 1987). The impact of such criticisms of intelligence tests was summarized aptly by Lezak (1988) when, after reviewing the utility of the traditional IQ score, she concluded that "the IQ—as concept and as score—has long ceased to be a useful scientific construct for organizing and describing our increasingly complex and sensitive behavioral observations" (p. 351).

Often these criticisms of intelligence tests are used to place blame on "traditional" assessment techniques for the limited success of special education. Given the fact that much ambiguity exists regarding the definition of such educational classifications as learning disabilities, it should come as no surprise that the research to date has shown that current psychological measures do not identify reliably these classification categories (see Reschly, Chapter 22, this volume). Because labeling continues to be a requirement for special education eligibility under IDEA, it continues to be difficult to make decisions when it is clear that a student has an instructional need but does not fit into a category that would allow special educational treatment. This dilemma has forced school psychologists and other members of multidisciplinary teams to create "override" rules to allow a child who is close to a state-established cutoff score to receive services. In extreme cases, for example, overinterpretation of subtest, factor, or VIQ–PIQ discrepancies has been promoted so that a child with learning difficulties can receive special services (see McDermott, Fantuzzo, & Glutting, 1990; Naglieri & Das, 1990, for a discussion).

The criticisms of traditional intelligence tests, especially for use with special education populations, are harsh indeed and convey a dismal outlook for the future practice of applied intelligence testing. However, the fact that *traditional* intelligence tests have certain inadequacies does not obviate the need to scrutinize closely the functional utility of new and revised instruments, especially as some newer intelligence batteries reflect recent advances in cognitive science and, therefore, should provide a better assessment of how children learn (see Harrison, Flanagan, & Genshaft, Chapter 27, this volume, McGrew, Chapter 9, this volume, for a summary). According to Heller, Holtzman, and Messick (1982), "The main purpose of assessment in education is to improve instruction and learning . . . a significant portion of children who experience difficulties in the classroom can be treated effectively through improved instruction" (p. 72). It is our contention that only through broader conceptualizations of human cognitive abilities that extend beyond those that are measured by traditional tests can a more valid understanding of the nature of children's cognitive characteristics be determined and more appropriate treatments identified.

THE FUNCTIONAL UTILITY OF INTELLIGENCE TESTS

Predictive Validity

Based on a review of the intellectual assessment literature, Sattler (1992) concluded that "standardized intelligence tests provide good indices of future levels of academic success and performance as defined by the majority culture" (p. 573). Similarly, Reschly and Grimes (1995) indicated that it is appropriate to use measures of current intellectual functioning to estimate current and likely future academic performance in light of the well-known substantial correlation between them (i.e., about .4 to .7 depending on the achievement criterion measure) . Many studies have shown that intelligence tests predict academic performance successfully and that their predictive utility is consistent across ethnic, gender, and special education groups (e.g., Roid, Prifitera, & Weiss, 1993; Sattler, 1992). The following section discusses the relationship between intelligence and achievement. Although general intelligence has been found to predict other criteria significantly (e.g., job performance) (Schmidt & Hunter, 1981), only academic achievement is discussed here given the emphasis in this chapter on special education eligibility. This section also discusses issues related to predicting achievement criteria from broad-based general ability scores and differential scholastic aptitude scores. In addition, given the prominence of ability–achievement discrepancy formulas (e.g., the predicted achievement method) in determining eligibility for specific learning disability (SLD) programming, issues related to the technical validity and clinical utility of various discrepancy procedures are presented.

This discussion on the predictive validity of intelligence tests is presented with one caveat. That is, intelligence tests are almost never given to a child prior to his or her exposure to a regular education curriculum with the intent being to predict that child's future academic performance within that curriculum. Therefore, "We will never have genuine predictive validity evidence matching our use of IQ tests because they are administered to students referred due to chronic and severe difficulties after, and only after, the student has been exposed for several years in the regular education curriculum" (Reschly, Kicklighter, & McKee, 1988, p. 43). Thus, the appropriate interpretation of a child's intelligence test score with respect to his or her current and future academic performance needs to take into account current developmental trends and the presence or absence of effective academic interventions (Reschly et al., 1988).

Intelligence and Academic Achievement

Demonstrating that intelligence is significantly related to important external criteria (e.g., academic achievement) is a central issue in intellectual assessment (Kamphaus, 1993). Typically, correlations between the broad-based scores of intelligence tests and measures of academic achievement are reported in test manuals as well as the extant assessment literature as evidence for an instrument's predictive validity. A sampling of this evidence is reported here.

The Wechsler Intelligence Scale for Children—Third Edition (WISC-III; Wechsler, 1991) Full Scale IQ correlated .74 with a group administered achievement test for 358 children (median age = 11 years). Similarly, the Kaufman Assessment Battery for Children (K-ABC; Kaufman & Kaufman, 1983) Mental Processing Composite correlated .65 with the California Achievement Test for a group of 45 school-age students (Childers, Durham, & Bolen; cited in Kaufman & Kaufman, 1983). A higher correlation of .82 was found between the Kaufman Adolescent Adult Intelligence Test (KAIT; Kaufman & Kaufman, 1993) Composite Intelligence Scale and the K-ABC Achievement Scale for 122 children ages 11 to 12. Correlations between the Stanford–Binet Intelligence Scale: Fourth Edition (SB-IV; Thorndike, Hagen, & Sattler, 1986) Test Composite and the Woodcock–Johnson Psycho-Educational Battery Tests of Achievement (WJ-ACH; Woodcock & Johnson, 1977) ranged from .57 to .81 for 40 students (mean age = 12 years, 10 months) (Delaney & Hopkins, 1987). Similar correlations ranging from .53 to .72 were found between the WJ-R Broad Cognitive Ability score (standard battery) and the Kaufman Test of Educational Achievement (K-TEA; Kaufman & Kaufman, 1985; cf. McGrew, Werder, & Woodcock, 1991). These studies show that intelligence accounts for approximately 25% to 65% of the variance in academic achievement. The findings reported above are consistent with the findings of a multitude of predictive validity investigations that have been reported in the literature. Few, if any, researchers in the field of intellectual assessment would dispute the fact that a full scale score from an intelligence test predicts academic achievement moderately to well.

Although it is clear that intelligence and achievement are related substantially, the interpretation of predictive validity coefficients is difficult for several reasons. First, it is often assumed erroneously that the following characteristics are inherent in the criterion measure: relevance, availability, reliability, and freedom from bias (Thorndike & Hagen, 1969). However, while the achievement measures used in the extant predictive validity literature are generally available and relevant, the degree to which they are reliable and free from bias varies. In general, the quality of criterion tests are likely to change across age and ability levels as a function of (1) the test's reliability, (2) the degree to which item bias was controlled, and (3) the consistency of the test construct (see Flanagan & Alfonso, 1995, for a discussion). Variations in theses characteristics of the criterion measure will have an impact on the interpretability of the validity coefficient.

Second, predictive validity coefficients are difficult to interpret in light of an assumption that the predictor (i.e., intelligence) is stable and, therefore, that an individual's relative standing in a group is static (cf. Flanagan & Alfonso, 1995; Neisworth & Bagnato, 1992). However, as limited information exists regarding the trait stability of the cognitive constructs that underlie intelligence tests, it should not be assumed that what is being measured will remain unchanged over time (see McGrew et al., 1991).

Third, the utility of predictive validity information is related to the worth of the behavior that is being predicted. If practitioners, for example, are interested in functional skills and planning instructional programs and interventions, knowledge of a moderate relationship between intelligence and later performance on an academic achievement test may not be very useful.

Fourth, predictive validity correlations may be inflated due to common content in the predictor (i.e., the predictor, an intelligence test, may contain *achievement-like* content). Knowledge of the composition of broad-based intelligence test scores, in particular, may have important implications for understanding the predictive validity literature more fully and for making appropriate interpretations regarding overall cognitive ability, especially in special education populations (this issue is discussed next). Overall, an understanding of the characteristics of the criterion and predictor measures described here enhance the usefulness of predictive validity information.

Broad-Based and Scholastic Aptitude Scores as Predictors of Achievement

Many measures of intelligence consist of several items and scales that measure academic achievement directly and/or require learned knowledge for successful completion (see Anastasi, 1988; Cunningham, 1986). For example, the Information, Arithmetic, and Vocabulary subtests on the Verbal Scale of the WISC-III directly assess information that is taught in schools. The Similarities and Comprehension subtests require children to draw on information they have been taught either formally in school or informally in other social settings (e.g., home) to formulate a response. An examination of the intercorrelations of the WISC-III Verbal subtests shows a relatively high degree of shared variance. For example, the correlation between the Information and Vocabulary subtests is .73 and the correlation between the Vocabulary and Similarities subtests is .70 (Wechsler, 1991). Based on these and similar findings, several authors have concluded that the Wechsler scales are, in large part, measures of academic achievement (see Anastasi, 1988; Cunningham, 1986; Sattler, 1992, for a review). However, because the knowledge that is necessary to respond correctly to verbal items on intelligence tests is dependent on accumulated knowledge and experience, that derives from living in mainstream American culture (or other highly industrialized societies), in addition to formal education, the Verbal scales of intelligence tests may be interpreted more appropriately as measures of crystallized intelligence, or Gc (see Carroll, Chapter 7, this volume; Horn & Noll, Chapter 4, this volume; and McGrew, Chapter 9, this volume, for a discussion).

Although most intelligence tests include a verbal scale or items and subtests that are similar to those on the Wechsler Verbal Scale, it appears that the extent to which academic achievement-like items contribute to a broad-based intelligence test score varies across instruments. Based on a series of joint factor analyses, Woodcock (1990) reported the factorial composition of the broad-based measures of intelligence provided by several major intelligence test batteries according to the approximate percentage that subtests measuring a particular cognitive factor contribute to the total broad score. He concluded that approximately 14% of the Broad Cognitive Ability (BCA) cluster of the Woodcock–Johnson—Revised Tests of Cognitive Ability (WJ-R COG; Woodcock & Johnson, 1989) is composed of achievement-like items, whereas about 50% of the Test Composite of the SB-IV and the Full Scale IQ of the Wechsler tests (i.e., Wechsler Intelligence Scale for Children—Revised [WISC-R; Wechsler, 1974] and Wechsler Adult Intelligence Scale [WAIS-R; Wechsler, 1981]) is composed of achievement-like items. (Given the similarities in content between the WISC-R and WISC-III, it can be assumed that approximately 50% of the WISC-III contains achievement-like content as well, although no empirical data are available to support this interpretation at this time.) This information appears to have relevance for interpreting predictive validity correlations and may aid in planning more appropriate instructional programs. For example, some broad-based scores from intelligence tests predict certain criteria (e.g., reading achievement) approximately equally, but, based on Woodcock's (1990) analyses, appear to contain a different weighted mix of cognitive abilities. Thus, although two scores may predict equally, the information gleaned from a broad-based score comprised of tasks of information processing may have greater relevance to intervention planning than the information obtained from a broad-based score consisting of only achievement-like tasks.

It cannot be assumed that all broad-based intelligence test scores are measures of " 'general intelligence,'—they are simply an average of whatever has been chosen by the test author to be included in that battery" (Woodcock, 1990, p. 250). Therefore, in order to understand which specific aspects of cognitive functioning account for the variance in the criterion measure, one must examine the composition of the broad-based score. The predictive utility of intelligence tests with regard to certain special education populations (e.g., learning disabled) depends, in part, on an under-standing of the component parts of broad-based scores, because inappropriate diagnostic conclu-sions and interventions may result when a broad-based ability measure includes subtests that have little or no relationship to the area of concern (McGrew, 1994).

To demonstrate the inherent differences among broad-based scores that contain varying mixes of cognitive abilities, a set of analyses using the cognitive clusters of the WJ-R COG are summarized. In a series of multiple regression studies (McGrew, 1993; McGrew & Hessler, 1995; McGrew & Knopik, 1993), using the WJ-R norm data (from age 5 through adulthood), the relationship between seven cognitive clusters and academic criteria (i.e., reading, mathematics, writing) was examined. The cognitive clusters of the WJ-R include Comprehension-Knowledge (Gc), Fluid Reasoning (Gf), Visual Processing (Gv), Auditory Processing (Ga), Processing Speed (Gs), Short-Term Memory (Gsm), and Long-Term Retrieval (Glr). (See Woodcock, Chapter 12, this volume, for a complete description of the WJ-R.) Results showed that the combined WJ-R cognitive clusters accounted for 50% to 70% of the variance in reading, mathematics and writing achievement.

In each of these studies, McGrew and his colleagues found that certain cognitive clusters had differential relationships with reading, mathematics, and written language achievement and that these relationships varied as a function of age. For example, the Gs and Ga cognitive clusters were highly associated with basic reading skills during the school-age years but showed a decreasing trend during the years following school (McGrew, 1993). These results were consistent with previous findings that demonstrated that the WJ-R Scholastic Aptitude clusters (which are composed of different combinations of the tests that constitute the seven Gf-Gc clusters) predicted achievement better than the WJ-R (Standard and Extended) BCA Clusters (i.e., better than global intelligence) (McGrew et al., 1991; see also McGrew, 1994, for a discussion of this research).

A review of the data reported in the *WJ-R Technical Manual* (McGrew et al., 1991) showed that the WJ-R scholastic aptitude clusters also predict achievement criteria better than the broad-based or general intelligence scores of existing cognitive batteries (e.g., K-ABC MPC, Wechsler Full Scale IQ, SB-IV Test Composite). According to McGrew et al., the tests that comprise the scholastic aptitude clusters are not *contaminated* with achievement-like content—a common misconception. These clusters predict achievement better than traditional broad-based general ability scores be-cause they include only those tests that are strongly related to the achievement criterion (as deter-mined through regression analyses). The higher predictive validity of scholastic aptitude clusters may suggest that cognitive instruments that are multidifferentiated may provide more insight (than less differentiated intelligence tests) into the broad and narrow cognitive abilities that are associated closely with academic achievement. This knowledge may, in turn, provide a necessary foundation from which to begin to investigate treatment relevance.

Overall, the available research provides preliminary support for the differential predictive validity of scholastic aptitude clusters when they are constructed from a pool of tests that measure a broad array of cognitive abilities. This research also shows the generally higher predictive power of scholastic aptitude clusters when compared to broad-based ability scores in the prediction of academic achievement. In light of this research, some have argued that appropriately designed scholastic aptitude clusters may be the best available measures to use when calculating ability–achievement discrepancies—the most commonly used quantitative method for determining eligibility for SLD programs (e.g., Mather, 1993). However, there are significant practical limitations to using scholastic aptitude scores in discrepancy formulas. First, an individual's disability in a specific area (e.g., auditory processing) may lower the (reading) aptitude cluster score to a level commensurate with (reading) achievement, rendering him or her ineligible for services in a system that only uses an ability–achievement model for identifying individuals with learning disabilities. In this type of identification system, use of scholastic aptitude clusters would serve to "penalize" an individual with a cognitive deficit. Second, most state criteria identification systems require the use of only one ability score (i.e., a broad-based or total test score from an individually administered intelligence test). The use of four scholastic aptitude cluster scores, such as those offered on the WJ-R, would be problematic in such systems. Unfortunately, practitioners are often constrained by state criteria and regulations and, as a result, unable to use or even "experiment" with alternatives to understanding an individual's cognitive and achievement strengths and weaknesses.

Ability–Achievement Discrepancy Procedures

The following discussion highlights important issues of technical validity that are necessary to consider when state regulations require that practitioners use ability–achievement discrepancy formulas when determining student eligibility for SLD programs. The limitations of the ability–achievement discrepancy procedure (i.e., a univariate regression method) are discussed and an alternative multivariate method is described that takes into account the multidifferentiated views of intelligence and the interrelationships that exist among cognitive and achievement abilities.

Issues of Technical Validity. Notwithstanding considerable variability and debate regarding the definition of SLD, the enactment of PL 94-142 led many states to adopt a discrepancy formula to satisfy a quantitative component of the *federal* definition of SLD (i.e., a severe discrepancy between ability and achievement). Because PL 94-142 did not provide procedural guidelines regarding what constitutes a significant discrepancy, numerous methods exist both within and across states creating inconsistency in the determination of a learning disability (Reynolds, 1984). Five methods for calculating ability–achievement discrepancies are used commonly (Evans, 1990; cf. Flanagan & Alfonso, 1993a, 1993b; Heath & Kush, 1991; Reynolds, 1981, 1984). Three of these methods, deviation from grade level, expectancy formulas, and scatter analysis are not recommended due to a multitude of limitations that are likely to result in inaccurate interpretations (see Berk, 1984; Heath & Kush, 1991; Reynolds, 1990). The remaining two methods, standard score differences (simple-difference method) and predicted-achievement methods (that account for regression effects) are more psychometrically sound, although the standard score approach does not take measurement error or the correlation between ability and achievement into account. Space limitations do not permit a comprehensive discussion of the uses, advantages, and limitations of these discrepancy methods (see McGrew, 1994; Reynolds, 1990; Ross, 1992a, 1992b for a review). However, practitioners who use discrepancy formulas routinely should ensure that the following three conditions are met before making interpretations and recommendations regarding special education placement.

First, if a discrepancy formula will be used to determine whether a significant difference exists between ability and achievement, *co-normed* ability and achievement tests should be administered.

The use of co-normed tests ensures that ability and achievement discrepancy scores do not contain error due to differences in norming samples (McGrew, 1994). Second, practitioners should ensure that the discrepancy formula they select takes into account the influence of *regression toward the mean*. Regression toward the mean is a phenomenon that occurs when comparing two test scores of instruments that are not correlated perfectly (Kamphaus, 1993; cf. McGrew, 1994; Reynolds, 1990). Essentially, regression toward the mean is defined as the tendency for extreme scores on Test A (e.g., intelligence) to be less extreme on Test B (e.g., achievement) when Tests A and B are related but not correlated perfectly. Because the relationship between intelligence and achievement is not perfect, practitioners cannot assume a one-to-one relationship between an individual's perform-ance on these tests, especially in situations in which the individual's performance on one test departs considerably from the mean (McGrew, 1994). Thus, when determining ability–achieve-ment discrepancies, procedures must be used that correct for regression effects. Predicted-achieve-ment methods that take into account regression to the mean and measurement error are considered the most psychometrically defensible approaches for quantifying ability–achievement discrepan-cies (Cone & Wilson, 1981; Evans, 1990; Heath & Kush, 1991; Reynolds, 1984). If practitioners determine ability–achievement discrepancies following the procedures outlined by the authors of the Wechsler tests/Wechsler Individual Achievement Test (WIAT; Psychological Corporation, 1992), WJ-R, and Differential Ability Scales (DAS; Elliott, 1990a), then they will meet this condi-tion.[1]

Third, practitioners should compare the size or magnitude of ability–achievement discrepan-cies to *discrepancy norms* to determine the *meaningfulness* of the discrepancy. This is important because the magnitude of an ability–achievement discrepancy can be *statistically* significant but not clinically meaningful. Discrepancy norms provide either actual or estimated percentages of indi-viduals (by age or grade) in the standardization sample who obtained ability–achievement discrep-ancies of various magnitudes. In general, if it is found that a discrepancy of a certain magnitude occurred in less than 5% of the standardization sample, it is considered unusual and may have clinical relevance with regard to the identification and treatment of learning problems. Conversely, if it is found that an ability–achievement discrepancy occurred in greater than 25% of the stand-ardization sample, it may not be meaningful, especially in the absence of additional sources of data, to corroborate the existence of a learning problem.

When determining the meaningfulness of an ability–achievement discrepancy, practitioners should compare discrepancy scores against *actual* distributions of discrepancy scores obtained from a nationally representative sample or *estimated* discrepancy norms, generated through the estimation of an individual's predicted or expected achievement score based on an estimate of the correlation between ability and achievement (McGrew, 1994, p. 215; see also McGrew et al., 1991). When actual aptitude–achievement discrepancy scores are available for persons in the norm sample, norms can be generated that allow a person's discrepancy score to be described in terms of percentile ranks and standard error of estimate units, based on real data, thereby allowing practitioners to determine the meaningfulness of the discrepancy (e.g., WJ-R). Estimated discrepancy norms are generated when tests are not co-normed (e.g., the WISC-III and WIAT are equated, see Psychological Corporation, 1992) or when the authors of co-normed tests do not provide actual discrepancy norms. The discrepancy norms that exist for the WJ-R tests of cognitive ability and tests of achievement, the DAS ability and achievement measures, and the WISC-III and WIAT are among the best available in the field of intellectual assessment and, therefore, the ones that should be used by practitioners. It is important to note that the WJ-R and WIAT measure a more comprehensive range of academic skills than the DAS and, therefore, may be more appropriate to use when assessing individuals with suspected learning disabilities.

Taken together, the most technically valid means of determining ability–achievement discrep-ancies is through procedures that employ co-normed (or equated) ability (or differentiated scholastic aptitude) and achievement measures using actual or estimated discrepancy norms. Practitioners are encouraged to review McGrew's (1994) hierarchy of discrepancy procedures to determine whether their approach to calculating ability–achievement discrepancies is technically valid. If necessary, practitioners should take appropriate steps toward improving the technical validity of the discrepancy procedures to which they adhere. Use of technically valid discrepancy procedures aids practitioners in making decisions regarding special education eligibility that are psychometrically defensible.

Beyond Univariate Regression. Although the technically valid discrepancy procedures described above have positive implications for practice, they are based on univariate regression and, as a result, have some notable limitations. For example, despite much discriminative validity research, it is still largely unknown whether children with significant ability–achievement discrepancies are substantively different from children who are low achievers (e.g., Algozzine, 1985; Fletcher, Francis, Rourke, Shaywitz, & Shaywitz, 1992; cf. Glutting McDermott, Prifitera, & McGrath, 1994; Siegel, 1992; Stanovich, 1991; Ysseldyke, Algozzine, Shinn, & McGue, 1982). In addition, univariate regression does not consider various areas of cognitive ability (e.g., verbal comprehension, perceptual organization, and processing speed) and academic achievement (e.g., reading, mathematics, and written language) *simultaneously,* which is most characteristic of psychoeducational evaluations (Glutting et al., 1994). Thus, according to Glutting et al., "We are compelled by this deficiency to seek analytic methods that better honor multidifferentiated views of intelligence as well as the full network of interrelationships that exist among such abilities. Otherwise, we will arrive at interpretations that may actually distort reality and serve to overlook relevant phenomena (Tatsuoka & Lohnes, 1988; Thompson, 1991)" (pp. 620–621).

To illustrate, we will use Swanson's (1991) definition of learning disabilities. According to Swanson, learning disabilities are based on the following premises: (1) disorders in information processing cause learning disabilities; (2) deficits in information processing reflect neurological, constitutional, and biological factors; and (3) the deficit manifests in specific cognitive ability, cognitive processing, and academic achievement areas (cf. Mather, 1993). Given this definition, any means of diagnosing a learning disability that is limited to univariate regression (e.g., ability–achievement discrepancy procedures) may limit the probability of finding an individual with a learning disability because "the very processing problems that act to suppress the reading [or other achievement] scores of these children also are likely to attenuate their FSIQs [Full Scale IQs]" (or any other broad-based ability score) (Glutting et al., 1994, p. 621; Mather, 1993).

There appear to be two ways to circumvent this problem. First, one could compare each broad cognitive ability or process score to each area of achievement, one at a time. However, this procedure leads to *increased error rates* which is a theoretical weakness of univariate regression (Glutting et al., 1994). Second, one could conduct *intra*cognitive analyses with an intelligence battery that assesses a broad range of cognitive abilities and processes to determine whether deficits exist in one or more cognitive processes (Mather, 1993). Following an intracognitive analysis, aptitude- or ability–achievement discrepancies could be conducted. Because it is assumed that learning disabilities arise from cognitive processing deficits, which, in turn, lead to difficulties in academic achievement (cf. Mather, 1993; Senf, 1978), the latter approach is logical and more technically valid and informative than the former. However, it is still limited by the negative features of univariate regression.

In an effort to move beyond univariate regression, Glutting et al. (1994) employed a multivariate method (*Q* analysis) for identifying WISC-III/WIAT ability–achievement discrepancies. Essentially, this approach treats ability and achievement test scores as an integrated profile that is represented by both linear and nonlinear components. This condition results, in part, because profiles are defined according to their *level* (high, average, and low performance on the score continuum), *shape* (pattern of high and low test scores), and *dispersion* (scatter of scores around their mean) (see

Glutting et al., 1994, for a detailed discussion). Using Q analysis with the WISC-III/WIAT linking sample/standardization data, Glutting et al. defined an empirical typology of the six most common WISC-III/WIAT profiles in the normal population. Consequently, questions about multivariate ability–achievement discrepancies can be made with respect to their uniqueness vis-à-vis *configural* (i.e., level and shape) rather than linear variation. Their typology provides an empirical basis (i.e., base rate data) for determining whether a profile of *multiple* abilities and achievements is unique or commonplace in the population.

Glutting et al.'s (1994) research demonstrated that almost 50% of children with univariate FSIQ-achievement discrepancies had multivariate IQ-achievement profiles that represented *normal* covariability in the population. This implies that practitioners may misdiagnosis children when they rely solely on univariate regression procedures. The normative typology developed by Glutting et al. (1994) allow "claims for the discovery of unusual ability and achievement profiles to be evaluated against a viable multivariate null hypothesis that the pattern actually is commonplace in the child population" (p. 630). Although this procedure is more psychometrically advanced than others and can aid in understanding complex ability and achievement interrelationships, it is not without limitations. Specifically, the WISC-III/WIAT typology has *not* been shown to have clinical utility (e.g., multivariate IQ-achievement profiles have not been shown to prescribe useful interventions) or predictive utility (e.g., multivariate IQ-achievement profiles have not been shown to predict the likelihood of developing a particular disorder) (see also Barnett & Macmann, 1992). Thus, much research is needed to determine the practical benefits of this multivariate methodology.

Discriminative Validity Research with Current Intelligence Test Batteries

Discriminative validity is defined as the ability of intelligence tests to make differential diagnoses and to discriminate between diagnostic (e.g., learning disabled, mentally retarded, and attention-deficit/hyperactivity disorder) and nondiagnostic (i.e., normal) groups. There appear to be two main approaches that researchers employ in an attempt to establish the discriminative validity of intelligence tests. The first approach is referred to as profile analysis and involves examining patterns of subtest score variation to determine whether a particular pattern (or profile) is indicative of some type of psychopathology or whether certain profiles have interpretive relevance for making differential diagnoses. Determining intraindividual variation (i.e., cognitive strengths and weaknesses) across intellectual tasks, a procedure referred to as subtest or ipsative analysis, provides the basis for identifying profiles that are believed to be unique in the population. Subtest analysis is conducted routinely by psychologists in an attempt to generate information that may aid in developing educational treatments and programs (e.g., Kaufman, 1976, 1979, 1994; Kaufman, Harrison, & Ittenbach, 1990; Sattler, 1992). In general, profile and subtest analyses are conducted conjointly in the test interpretation process. The second approach is referred to as discriminative validation and typically involves conducting discriminant function analyses or examining mean score differences to determine whether intelligence tests can be used to classify individuals according to distinct diagnostic categories or groups. These two approaches to establishing the discriminative validity of intelligence tests are discussed below.

Profile and Subtest Analysis

Several profiles, such as the ACID (Arithmetic, Coding, Information, and Digit Span subtests of the Wechsler Scales) profile, have been suggested in the literature as viable indicators of clinical diagnoses (e.g., learning disabilities) (e.g., Kaufman, 1994; Prifitera & Dersh, 1993; Sattler, 1988, 1992). As a result, practitioners conduct ipsative analyses routinely and look for these patterns (or profiles) of subtest scores in an attempt to aid them in making appropriate diagnostic decisions.

Although there is little scientific data to support the clinical practice of profile and subtest analysis (see Glutting, McDermott, & Konold, Chapter 19, this volume; Kamphaus, 1993; Kamphaus, Petoskey, & Morgan, Chapter 3, this volume; McDermott, Fantuzzo, Glutting, Watkins, & Baggaley, 1992; McGrew & Knopik, in press; Watkins & Kush, 1994), these diagnostic activities remain in widespread use because of their intuitive appeal and the ease with which they can be carried out using virtually any intelligence test battery (Mueller, Dennis, & Short, 1986). Therefore, the relevant literature on profile and subtest analysis is summarized in this section, focusing on the recent research that has been conducted using contemporary intelligence tests. In addition, the following discussion highlights an alternative method of examining profile variability (i.e., a non-linear multivariate methodology) and its implications for practice.

The Wechsler Scales. The Wechsler scales are the most frequently used assessment measures by psychologists (Reschly et al., 1987; Stinnett et al., 1994; Wilson & Reschly, 1996) and, as such, have been studied most often with respect to their ability to discriminate between diagnostic groups on the basis of intertest variability. Despite the frequency with which the Wechsler scales are used for conducting profile analyses, it is important to note that these scales were designed a priori as a measure of overall ability or "global intelligence" (Wechsler, 1991); they were not designed a priori to discriminate between groups based on subtest variability and they were not predicated on a theory of cognitive processing or neuropsychological functioning (McDermott et al., 1990). Nevertheless, as indicated by the following meta-analyses, numerous investigations focused on the utility of Wechsler scales in making differential diagnoses.

Kavale and Forness (1984) used meta-analytic procedures to summarize 94 research studies that examined the utility of the Wechsler scales in the differential diagnosis of learning disabilities. These authors found that there was no evidence for a recategorization, profile, factor cluster, or pattern which discriminates between children with learning disabilities and children without learning disabilities. Interestingly, Kavale and Forness (1984) also found that children in the learning disabled group showed average performance and less variability across subtests than children in the comparison group. As Reschly (1990) noted, "Profile analyses can produce differences that are reliable (i.e., not due to chance), but the differences may occur frequently in a normal population and therefore cannot be a unique or discriminating feature of any diagnosis" (p. 450). Based on their findings, Kavale and Forness (1984) concluded that "profile and scatter analysis is not defensible and that use of the Wechsler Scales should focus only on global intelligence assessment" (p. 136).

In an extension of the Kavale and Forness (1984) study, Mueller et al. (1986) conducted a meta-analysis of 66 studies reporting data from the WISC-R (Wechsler, 1974) for 119 different samples totaling over 13,740 children with a variety of psychoeducational diagnoses. Unlike the Kavale and Forness (1984) study, Mueller et al. included children with mental retardation and behavior/emotional disorders, in addition to children with learning disabilities, in their overall diagnostic group sample. Mueller et al. reported that "profile similarity appeared to be related most strongly to the mean Full Scale IQ of the samples" (p. 21). That is, different diagnostic groups could only be distinguished on the basis of an FSIQ (see also Glutting et al., Chapter 19, this volume). Like Kavale and Forness (1984), Mueller et al. concluded that there is no support for WISC-R profile analysis in differential psychoeducational diagnosis.

A few years later, McDermott et al. (1990), reviewed more than 70 profile analysis studies using the WISC-R and WAIS-R. They identified several methodological problems with these studies that rendered their findings of limited interpretive value. Following are examples of the methodological weaknesses inherent in the Wechsler profile analysis studies they reviewed: (1) an incorrect assumption exists that children in like diagnostic groups represent homogeneous categories, (2) there is circularity in using the Wechsler subtests to define diagnostic groups and to generate subsequent profiles (although common in the existing literature), (3) an incorrect assumption exists that pooling samples of different ages yields reasonable equitable measurement error for subtests across those age levels, (4) there is a statistical inadequacy associated with testing profiles through linear modeling (see also Sternberg, 1984), and (5) there is a failure to test hypotheses against a viable null hypothesis (i.e., against profiles that are commonplace in the normal population) (see also Glutting et al., Chapter 19, this volume; Watkins & Kush, 1994).

In addition to the methodological limitations of the studies they reviewed, McDermott et al. (1990) presented a multitude of weaknesses associated with conducting an *ipsative analysis*—the most popular method of profile and subtest analysis. This procedure involves uncovering significant *intra*cognitive strengths and weaknesses by removing the average ability element from each subtest score with the intent of isolating and exaggerating unique differential abilities (McDermott et al., 1990). That is, an ipsative analysis "produces a profile of positive and negative deviations from the average performance commonly interpreted as a pattern of cognitive strengths and weaknesses singularly characteristic of the child being examined" (Watkins & Kush, 1994, p. 640). The major weaknesses associated with ipsative analysis, as reported by McDermott et al., include the following: (1) ipsative scores have no construct validity, (2) ipsative scores have near zero (and typically negative) intercorrelations, (3) ipsative scores are not stable over time, (4) the properties of ipsative scores (e.g., their sum equals zero) make any attempt at remediation a "no win" situation, (5) ipsative scores have poor predictive validity, and (6) ipsative scores do not carry any additional information that is not already provided by normative scores. Based on the methodological weaknesses in the profile analysis studies they reviewed, coupled with a lack of support for the utility of the procedure (i.e., ipsative analysis), McDermott et al. (1990) concluded that psychologists should "just say 'no' to subtest analysis" (p. 299).

Despite such cautionary statements, Prifitera and Dersh (1993) conducted a base rate study of the WISC-III in which they examined subtest patterns among normal, learning disabled, and attention-deficit/hyperactivity disorder (ADHD) samples. Specifically, these authors examined the utility of the ACID, ACIDS, (ACID + Similarities), and Bannatyne profiles in differential diagnosis. The Bannatyne profiles are derived by regrouping the WISC-III subtests into three different groups: Group 1, spatial reasoning (Block Design, Object Assembly, and Picture Completion); Group 2, verbal conceptualization (Similarities, Vocabulary, and Comprehension); and Group 3, sequential processing (Arithmetic, Digit Span, and Coding). According to Bannatyne (1974), children with reading disabilities that are believed to be genetic in nature demonstrate a relative strength on the spatial reasoning subtests, moderate ability on the verbal conceptualization subtests, and a relative weakness on the sequential processing subtests.

Prifitera and Dersh's (1993) study included children with learning disabilities (LD) and ADHD. The LD sample was comprised of 99 children who were tested as part of the WISC-III's development and validation. The ADHD sample consisted of 65 children from two different mental health clinics. The performance of the LD and ADHD groups were compared against a portion of the WISC-III standardization sample ($N = 2,158$). An examination of the cumulative percentages of the normal (standardization), LD, and ADHD samples revealed that the prevalence of the ACID profile was rare in the general population (1.1% of the WISC-III standardization sample) as compared to the LD (5.1%) and ADHD (12.3%) clinical groups, χ^2 (2, $N = 2,322$). Prifitera and Dersh (1993) concluded that the results of their study "provide evidence for specific patterns of cognitive deficits in LD and ADHD children" and that these clinical groups showed "relatively poor performance on subtests that comprise the ACID profile and the third and fourth factors on the WISC-III" (p. 51).

Notwithstanding statistically significant findings, Prifitera and Dersh (1993) did not address adequately the *practical* (or *clinical*) significance of their results. For example, their findings demonstrate that in only 5 instances out of 100 children with a learning disability will exhibit the ACID profile and in only 12 instances out of 100 children with an attention-deficit disorder will exhibit the ACID profile. These results are less than favorable in regard to the clinical utility of the ACID profile for differentially diagnosing children with LD and ADHD (see also Kaufman, 1994). In addition, the cumulative percentages of the ACIDS and Bannatyne profiles were similar to those of the ACID profile in this investigation. Thus, contrary to the conclusion reached by Prifitera and Dersh, the results of their study do not support the use of the ACID, ACIDS, and Bannatyne profiles as an aid in making differential diagnoses.

Recently, Kaufman (1994) suggested replacing the ACID profile with the SCAD profile (Symbol Search, Coding, Arithmetic, and Digit Span), a merger of the four subtests that comprise the Processing Speed and Freedom-from-Distractibility factors of the WISC-III. Using the data provided by Prifitera and Dersh (1993), Kaufman found that approximately 85% of the combined LD and ADHD samples had higher Perceptual Organization (PO) than SCAD subtest sums as compared to 47% of the standardization sample. Kaufman concluded that "these differences won't diagnose the presence or absence of an exceptionality, and they certainly won't differentially diagnose learning-disabled children from other exceptional children. But groups of LD and ADHD children differ significantly from normal children in the magnitude of the discrepancy between PO and SCAD subtests (Prifitera & Dersh, 1993), and research findings indicate that large PO/SCAD differences are more likely to occur for abnormal than normal samples" (p. 220). However, Kaufman presented several lines of reasoning to substantiate the use of the SCAD profile to aid in identifying children with neurological impairment or with exceptionalities believed to be related to minimal brain dysfunction.

With the exception of Prifitera and Dersh's (1993) study and Kaufman's (1994) extended interpretation of their findings, the substantial empirical evidence that has been mounting for over a decade against the use of Wechsler profiles in differential diagnosis appears to have negated recent attempts to revitalize this practice. However, the practice of subtest analysis for the purpose of identifying cognitive strengths and weaknesses remains in widespread use despite its significant limitations from both a statistical and theoretical standpoint (see Glutting et al., Chapter 19, this volume). Regardless of its dominance in the realm of intelligence test interpretive procedures, the "fatal flaws" inherent in subtest (ipsative) analysis discussed above have led many to advocate replacing univariate and linear-multivariate procedure with an alternative; that is, *nonlinear-multivariate normative methods* (e.g., Glutting et al., Chapter 19, this volume; Watkins & Kush, 1994, p. 642).

Using multivariate methodology, McDermott, Glutting, Jones, Watkins, and Kush (1989) identified seven core profile types in the WISC-R standardization sample. These profiles were advanced as the normative standard (i.e., base rate) against which clinical WISC-R subtest profiles should be compared. This procedure allowed practitioners to make contrasts to determine whether a particular pattern of subtest scores is unique (i.e., rare) and therefore, potentially meaningful, or commonplace in the population. The normative profile taxonomy recommended by McDermott et al. was the best method available for making such comparisons using the WISC-R.

Following the development of the WISC-R normative profile taxonomy, Watkins and Kush (1994) were interested in knowing the relationship between these core profiles and the profiles of children commonly seen by psychologists. They applied the McDermott et al. (1989) WISC-R normative typology to WISC-R profiles exhibited by a large sample of children in special education programs ($N = 1,222$). Their findings showed that only 3.6% of the special education sample exhibited profiles that were unusual when compared to the normative core profile types. To determine whether the unique profiles represented in this portion of the special education sample ($n = 44$) were meaningful, a hierarchical clustering analysis was conducted. Results showed that no homogeneous clusters existed in this group. Because greater than 96% of the special education sample exhibited subtest profiles that were probabilistically similar to the WISC-R normative profiles and because the remaining portion of the sample had profiles that, although unique, represented random (rather than clinically relevant) subtest variation, this research does not support WISC-R subtest profile analysis. Watkins and Kush (1994) conclude that "discussions of the 'right' and 'wrong' ways to conduct subtest analysis be abandoned in favor of the conclusion that 'no way' exists to reliably identify unique Wechsler subtest profiles which reflect anything other than essentially random, meaningless, and uninterpretable subtest variation" (p. 648).

Despite the conclusions of Watkins and Kush (1994), Glutting et al. (Chapter 19, this volume) applied nonlinear multivariate methodology to create a normative profile taxonomy for the WISC-III. Although Glutting et al. are not in favor of Wechsler profile analysis, and indeed contributed significantly to the literature that argues against its use, their provision of a WISC-III normative profile taxonomy was warranted for the following reasons: (1) subtest analysis continues to be the most popular diagnostic activity; therefore, the best methods for testing hypotheses regarding subtest patterns that are believed to be unusual must be made available; (2) given its mathematical and measurement advantages over other methods, use of the WISC-III normative taxonomy provides a safeguard against overinterpretation (i.e., mistaking a common profile as one that is rare and possibly clinically relevant); and (3) because the utility of subtest scores is "an empirical matter open to further investigation," the superior methodology offered by the WISC-III taxonomy may advance scientific understanding (Glutting et al., Chapter 19, this volume). Thus, Glutting et al. provide the best method available to account for the multivariate nature of WISC-III subtest profiles, but they do not attempt to resolve basic issues regarding the appropriateness of conducting subtest analysis.

In sum, one unequivocal conclusion may be drawn from the aforementioned studies—the Wechsler scales were not designed with profile analysis in mind and, therefore, it is not surprising that empirical evidence does not support their use for this purpose. According to Kavale and Forness (1984), the Wechsler scales are conceived best as measures of general ability and, therefore, should be restricted to that purpose. Yet many psychologists are convinced that "the most valuable information about a child's mental abilities lies somewhere in between the global Full Scale IQ and the highly specific subtest scores" (Kaufman, 1994, p. 271). Until empirical evidence is available to support the diagnostic utility of the Wechsler scales, it appears that some combination of ingenuity, clinical experience and current theoretical and empirical research must guide the psychologist through the interpretation of an individual's performance on these intelligence tests. Kaufman's (1994) discussion of the use of the Wechsler SCAD profile (pp. 219–224) provides a good example of this delicate interpretive balance. We will now turn our discussion to contemporary and nontraditional measures of intelligence and their utility to aid in making differential diagnoses through profile and subtest analysis.

Differential Ability Scales. Elliott (1990a, 1990b) presents evidence that the diagnostic subtests of the DAS (Elliott, 1990b, Chapter 10, this volume) exhibit relatively high levels of reliable specific variance, a precursor for accurately identifying differences between subtests in profile analysis (McDermott et al., 1992). According to Elliott (1990b), "The DAS was designed primarily as a profile test. That is, it should yield reliable, focused, and interpretable scores at the cluster or subtest level" (p. 385) (see also Elliott, Chapter 10, this volume). In support of his assertion, Elliott (1990b) compared the mean specificities of the DAS Cluster scores, Core subtests, and Diagnostic subtests with the WISC-R subtests for a sample of school-age children. The mean specificity for the DAS Diagnostic subtests was .73, while the mean specificity for the WISC-R subtests was .30. The mean error variance was shown to be .13 for the DAS Diagnostic subtests and .22 for the WISC-R subtests. Based on these data, Elliott (1990b) concluded that the results "support the use of the DAS for analysis of cognitive strengths and weaknesses. To a greater extent than the subtests of other batteries, the subtests of the DAS have sufficient specific variance to make them individually interpretable and to make differences between them meaningful" (p. 385). This conclusion was substantiated recently following a comparison of the specificities of the DAS subtests with those of the subtests of all other major intelligence test batteries (Elliott, Chapter10, this volume). That is, intelligence tests such as the SB-IV (Thorndike et al., 1986), K-ABC (Kaufman & Kaufman, 1983), KAIT (Kaufman & Kaufman, 1993), and WJ-R generally have mean specificities that account for approximately 30–37% of the total variance. By contrast, the DAS has mean subtest specificities of .47 and .50 (range = .30–.82) for the Preschool and School-Age batteries, respectively, indicating that approximately 50% of the variance in the DAS subtests may be interpreted reliably as representing a unique cognitive function.

Given that interpretations regarding the unique ability that is assessed by a cognitive subtest can be made most confidently when it is based on the largest portion of that subtest's reliable variance, the subtests of the DAS appear to represent a great improvement over the subtests of other batteries with respect to subtest specificity. As such, it would appear that the practice of subtest and profile analysis could be carried out in a more psychometrically defensible manner with the DAS than with all other intelligence batteries. However, an examination of subtest specificity must be considered within the context of a "cognitive-subtest-mix" phenomenon. That is, specificities change as a function of the type and variety of cognitive tasks that are included in the test battery. Stated another way, as the total "mix" of subtests changes, the subtest uniqueness estimates change (McGrew, Untiedt, & Flanagan, in press).

For example, consider two intelligence test batteries that are similar in composition. Battery A includes two measures of fluid reasoning (e.g., an inductive and a deductive reasoning task) and two measures of crystallized intelligence (e.g., a measure of vocabulary and a measure of general information) whereas battery B contains the identical set of tests as battery A minus the deductive reasoning task. The specificity estimate for the inductive reasoning task in battery A would be smaller than the specificity estimate of this same task when it is included on battery B because it shares something in common with the deductive reasoning task (i.e., both tasks are strong indicators of the broad construct of fluid intelligence). Thus, the largest portion of the reliable variance in the inductive reasoning task on battery A is its *common* variance whereas the largest portion of the reliable variance on this same task when it is included on battery B is its *unique* variance. Despite the differences in specificity estimates that result as a function of the mix of subtests included in these batteries, the inductive reasoning task ought to be interpreted in the same manner *across* batteries (i.e., irrespective of the battery in which it is included).

More important, if the largest portion of a subtest's variance is its unique variance, it is likely that that subtest is underrepresented in the cognitive battery. Insufficient representation of a particular cognitive construct (referred to as *construct underrepresentation*) poses a threat to the construct validity of the instrument (Messick, 1995). This threat raises two important and interdependent questions: (1) Should subtest uniqueness estimates be derived from a broader theoretical framework in which estimates are calculated from joint intelligence battery designed research (McGrew et al., in press)? (2) When constructs are underrepresented, should assessments and interpretations follow from a broader theoretical and empirical foundation of the structure of intelligence (see McGrew & Flanagan, 1996)? Notwithstanding these inquiries, suffice it to say that *within-battery* specificity estimates are of limited utility in the interpretation of individual subtests because they are a function of the mix of tests that are included therein. Moreover, distinct variation alone is not enough evidence to support the interpretation of subtests as measures of unique constructs (McDermott & Watkins, 1985).

The renewed hope in profile analysis that the DAS seemed to offer because of its high subtest specificities is lost due to the arbitrariness of these estimates and the likelihood that the constructs that underlie subtests characterized by high specificities are underrepresented (see McGrew, Chapter 9, this volume). Thus, subtest analysis with the DAS (or any other intelligence test battery) is likely to fall prey to the same fallibilities as those previously discussed in regard to the Wechsler scales. Future research on subtest/profile analysis should be directed toward investigating the diagnostic utility of profiles at the *cluster/factor (common variance) level* within the context of current theory and research rather than at the *subtest (unique variance) level.*

Cross-Battery Assessment and Interpretation. The cross-battery approach to cognitive ability assessment and interpretation (Flanagan & McGrew, Chapter 17, this volume; McGrew & Flanagan, 1996) bypasses interpretation of individual subtests (and by association, subtest uniqueness). Rather, the cross-battery approach focuses on the broad and narrow cognitive ability strata to which subtests belong following from an integrated Horn–Carroll Gf-Gc theoretical model of the structure of intelligence (see McGrew, Chapter 9, this volume). In the cross-battery approach, the subtests of all major intelligence tests have been classified according to the broad and narrow stratum level abilities they measure via empirical analysis and expert consensus, respectively (McGrew, Chapter 9, this volume). Through this classification scheme and a set of psychometrically sound guiding principles, McGrew and Flanagan (1996) offer a means of augmenting intelligence test batteries that will result in empirically and theoretically directed interpretations of a broader range of cognitive abilities than that represented on any single intelligence battery. Moreover, construct underrepresentation is avoided in this approach since assessment is not restricted to one battery (e.g., Flanagan & McGrew, Chapter 17, this volume).

The cross-battery approach ensures that at least two strong (and qualitatively different) indicators of a particular broad cognitive domain (e.g., fluid intelligence) are administered before inferences are made about an individual's functioning in that area. If significant variations occur within a broad area, other similar narrow ability tests are administered to substantiate high–low score fluctuations. This approach effectively vitiates the need to rely on subtest uniqueness in the test interpretation process. Theoretically, in an appropriately designed test battery (i.e., one that operationalizes all known and empirically validated broad cognitive abilities through the provision of two or more strong, qualitatively different indicators of each ability) subtest uniqueness would always constitutes the *smallest* portion of a test's reliable variance. Therefore, in empirically and theoretically driven cross-battery assessments and interpretations, a consideration of unique variance plays a small part in the interpretive process.

Within the context of cross-battery interpretation, profile analysis would require testing hypotheses regarding Gf-Gc configurations that are believed to be unusual in the population. Future research that is predicated on the structural, developmental, neurocognitive, achievement (i.e., predictions of school performance) and heritability evidence that exists for approximately eight distinct Gf-Gc constructs (see Horn, 1994; Horn & Noll, Chapter 4, this volume) as well as a more appropriate (nonlinear multivariate) methodology for testing profile uniqueness (Glutting et al., Chapter 19, this volume) may reveal whether Gf-Gc cross-battery profiles have diagnostic utility.

Discriminative Validation Research

Woodcock–Johnson Psycho-Educational Battery—Revised. The WJ-R tests of cognitive ability measure seven broad abilities following from a modern version of the Horn–Cattell *Gf-Gc* theory of intelligence (Horn, 1991). This instrument appears to measure a broader range of cognitive abilities than any major intelligence test that was published at the time this chapter was being prepared (see McGrew, Chapter 9, this volume; Woodcock, 1990, Chapter 12, this volume). Although the previously mentioned cross-battery approach is more comprehensive in its operationalization of modern Gf-Gc theories of intelligence, the WJ-R also seems to offer promise with respect to profile analysis.

Initial discriminant function analysis research with the WJ-R, reported in its *Technical Manual* (McGrew et al., 1991), indicated that the combination of seven WJ-R broad cognitive clusters and four broad achievement clusters discriminated accurately between school-identified samples of students with no academic or developmental disability and students identified as either learning disabled, mentally retarded, or gifted. Although the results of this investigation were positive, they must be viewed cautiously because this study contained methodological weaknesses. For example, this study included unequal sample sizes, which can result in misleading significance tests under certain circumstances (e.g., when the homogeneity of variance–covariance matrices assumption is violated) in discriminant function analyses (cf. Tabachnick & Fidell, 1989).

In an attempt to circumvent the limitations of the aforementioned study, Evans, Carlsen, and McGrew (1993) examined the discriminative validity and classification accuracy of the WJ-R tests of cognitive ability and academic achievement. Specifically, this study investigated the ability of the WJ-R to discriminate between children who were nondisabled (i.e., normal), gifted, LD, or mentally retarded (MR). The study consisted of two groups (8- to 10-year-olds and 16- to 18-year-olds) with equal sample sizes within groups. Of the four categorical groups (i.e., normal, MR, LD, gifted), the group with the lowest number of subjects represented the sample size of the remaining groups. Thus, 23 participants were selected randomly for the gifted, LD, and norming samples for the 8- to 10-year-olds and 33 participants were selected randomly from the gifted, MR, and norming samples for the 16- to 18-year-olds. Analyses of variance with post hoc Tukey tests indicated significant differences within and between all four of the groups for 92 subjects ages 8 to 10 years and 132 subjects ages 16 to 18 years.

Results of discriminant function analyses showed that the WJ-R standard cognitive and achievement batteries effectively differentiated among and predicted (with high accuracy) membership of participants in both age groups into the four categorical groups. Overall classification accuracy for all subjects was 93.5% for the 8–10-year-old group and 89.1% for the 16–18-year-old group. Individual group accuracy ranged from 69.7% for the norming group (ages 16–18 years) to 100% for the MR and LD groups (ages 8–10 years). Classification accuracy in a subsequent cross-validation analysis was also high (i.e., 80.5% for the 8- to 10-year-olds and 72.0% for the 16- to 18-year-olds).

The major variables that were found to discriminate normal and exceptional students were acquired knowledge and achievement. In addition, significant cognitive factors on the discriminant functions included measures of processing speed (Gs), and auditory processing (Ga) for the 8- to 10-year-old group and long-term retrieval (Glr), short-term memory (Gsm), Gs, and Ga for the 16- to 18-year-old group. The classification functions presented by Evans et al. (1993) suggest that the WJ-R cognitive tests measure abilities that are important in the identification and classification of exceptional children—abilities that are not measured by other intelligence batteries (see Mather & Healey, 1990; McGhee, 1993; McGrew, Chapter 9, this volume; Woodcock, 1990). These findings must be replicated and cross validation of the "averaged" classification functions is needed in other groups of the same and different ages (Evans et al., 1993, p. 14) before the WJ-R may be used to aid in making differential diagnoses.

Kaufman Adolescent and Adult Intelligence Test. The KAIT is a new intelligence test battery that was developed from Horn and Cattell's (1966, 1967) original Gf-Gc conception of cognitive functioning (i.e., a two-factor, fluid-crystallized model; Kaufman & Kaufman, 1993) (see Flanagan, 1995; Kaufman & Kaufman, Chapter 11, this volume, for a critical review and complete description of the KAIT, respectively). In the KAIT manual, Kaufman and Kaufman (1993) present data regarding the diagnostic validity of their instrument. These authors compared mean IQs and subtest profiles of four clinical samples to matched controls derived from the standardization sample. The clinical groups were composed of individuals with neurological impairment (left and right hemisphere damage), clinical depression, Alzheimer's-type dementia, and reading disabilities.

Kaufman and Kaufman's (1993) research showed that the combined clinical samples ($N = 100$) obtained lower scores (approximately one-half a standard deviation) on 8 of the 10 KAIT subtests as compared to a matched control group. A comparison of the separate clinical samples to matched control groups yielded the following findings: (1) individuals with neurological impairment (left hemisphere damage) scored significantly lower than the control group on 6 of the 10 KAIT subtests, (2) individuals with neurological impairment (right hemisphere damage) scored significantly lower than the control group on 1 of the 10 KAIT subtests, (3) individuals with Alzheimer's-type dementia scored significantly lower than the control group on subtests that required a memory component, and (4) the scores of individuals with clinical depression and reading disabilities were not significantly different from those of the respective matched control groups.

Based on this investigation of the KAIT's diagnostic utility, Kaufman and Kaufman (1993) concluded that the Expanded Battery of the KAIT may be used to assist in clinical, neuropsychological, and psychoeducational assessment and diagnosis. In addition, they emphasized the utility of the Famous Faces subtest in this regard because it demonstrated the most consistent statistically significant mean score difference between the clinical and control groups. However, according to Flanagan, Alfonso, and Flanagan (1994), these recommendations are considered premature for the following reasons: (1) some of the clinical groups had small sample sizes (e.g., Alzheimer's-type dementia, $N = 8$), rendering the results highly speculative and of limited generalizability, (2) results of the combined clinical sample are misleading; that is, the differences between the combined clinical group and the matched control group were due to the samples of individuals with neurological damage (left hemisphere) and Alzheimer's-type dementia only; and (3) generating diagnostic and intervention decisions on the basis of one subtest (i.e., Famous Faces) is not a psychometrically sound practice.

Although the present data are encouraging, they do not substantiate the use of the KAIT for making differential diagnoses. At this time, the KAIT appears to be most useful as a measure of general and dichotomous (fluid and crystallized) abilities. However, the KAIT is a relatively new instrument and much research is needed before determining its utility as a diagnostic instrument (see Kaufman & Kaufman, Chapter 11, this volume for a summary of research that has been conducted subsequent to the publication of the KAIT). Like all previously mentioned tests, studies comparing KAIT profiles of large clinical samples against a viable null hypothesis are needed to determine whether this instrument is a useful diagnostic–prescriptive tool (see also Cicchetti, 1994).

Das–Naglieri Cognitive Assessment System. The Das–Naglieri: Cognitive Assessment System (DNCAS) has been in development since 1987 and is nearing completion (see Naglieri, Chapter 13, this volume). The DNCAS represents a cognitive functioning theory of intelligence (*PASS*—an acronym for *p*lanning, *a*ttention, *s*imultaneous, and *s*uccessive processes) that is based on the work of Luria (1966, 1970, 1973, 1976, 1980). Several discriminative validity studies were carried out with the experimental version of the DNCAS (Das & Naglieri, 1993) by Naglieri and his students (e.g., Bardos, 1987; Hurt & Naglieri, 1992; Reardon & Naglieri, 1992).

Specifically, Naglieri and his students examined the diagnostic utility of the DNCAS (experimental version) by contrasting the PASS profiles of individuals diagnosed as delinquent ($N = 30$; Hurt & Naglieri, 1992), MR ($N = 48$; Bardos, 1987), reading disabled (RD) ($N = 58$; Bardos, 1987), and ADHD ($N = 28$; Reardon & Naglieri, 1992). Each experimental group was matched to a normal control group on age, sex, race, socioeconomic status and area of residence. According to Naglieri, Das, and Jarman (1990), the results of these investigations demonstrated that groups of exceptional children differ from one another and from their matched controls in meaningful ways that are consistent with previous research findings. That is, the delinquent group demonstrated average performance in all areas with a deficiency in attention; the MR group performed significantly below average in all areas, with planning being the lowest score; the RD group had average scores on measures of simultaneous and successive processing, a depressed attention score, and a deficit in planning; and the ADHD group had an average score in simultaneous processing, low scores in successive processing and planning, and a deficit in attention (see Naglieri et al., 1990, for more details).

Although Naglieri's studies of contrasted groups offer some initial support for the discriminative validity of the DNCAS, the results of the aforementioned studies have been questioned on practical and methodological grounds. For example, it appears that the individuals in the RD group performed similarly on all four PASS processes (i.e., standard scores ranged from 83 to 89) and that their scores were farther below the population mean than they were different from each other (Reschly & Wilson, 1990). Use of this profile for diagnosing reading problems (see also Das, Mishra, & Kirby, 1994) may result in a high proportion of false positives and false negatives because, at this time, there is no way of knowing the likelihood that such a pattern is commonplace in the normal population. Moreover, recent independent factor-analytic research that has questioned the validity of the PASS model (e.g., Carroll, 1995; Kranzler & Weng, 1995a, 1995b) may negate further examination of how the PASS tasks relate to the many problems of school learning (Carroll, 1995). Because the forthcoming DNCAS may differ substantially from the experimental version that has been discussed in the literature for nearly a decade, future research with the published DNCAS will reveal its utility as a diagnostic tool.

In sum, few profile analysis and discriminative validity studies have provided convincing empirical evidence for the diagnostic utility of existing intelligence tests. Mather (1993), Mather and Healey (1990), and Ysseldyke (1990) offered a possible explanation to account for the lack of discriminative validity data supporting the utilization of intertest variability profiles. That is, research to date has not employed measures of intelligence based on the important cognitive processes that are related to learning. These authors suggest that the modern version of the Horn–Cattell Gf-Gc theory (e.g., Carroll, 1993; Horn, 1991) appears to offer the most viable framework from which to conduct this type of research. Based on their comments as well as the previous review of recent discriminative validity research, it appears that future research efforts should (1) incorporate tests that are based on cognitive processing theories of intelligence (e.g., Gf-Gc and PASS), (2) incorporate tests that measure a broad range of empirically validated cognitive processes, (3) examine profiles at the cluster/factor (common variance) level instead of at the subtest (unique variance) level, and (4) compare profiles to a viable null hypothesis using nonlinear multivariate methodology.

Treatment Validity

The belief that certain children, by virtue of their developmental characteristics, need specialized and individualized instruction in order to succeed academically is the foundation on which special education is based (Cole, Dale, Mills, & Jenkins, 1993). Individualized instruction entails asking a series of questions about a child's unique strengths and weaknesses, what educational goals should be established for the child, what specific learning principles appear to be relevant for the child, and what instructional approaches may be beneficial to the child (Knoblock, 1987). In effect, individualized instruction is based on the belief that aptitude by treatment interactions (ATIs) exist (Whitener, 1989).

The concept of ATI was introduced by Cronbach in his classic 1957 paper. In this paper, Cronbach argued that the reluctance of experimental psychology to consider individual differences has impeded the progress of psychological research. "The scientific problem is to locate interactions of individual differences among learners with instructional treatments, that is Aptitude × Treatment interactions" (Cronbach & Snow, 1977, p. 2).

Although many special educators have utilized the concept of ATI in an effort to enhance the quality of instruction received by children experiencing academic difficulties in the classroom, this research has not been positive. Although ATIs are valid (i.e., real as phenomena) and of theoretical and evaluative use, they are not understood well enough to be of practical utility at this time (Good et al., 1993; Reschly, 1990; Snow & Yalow, 1982; Ysseldyke & Mirkin, 1982). Some authors have argued that the ATI research literature is confounded by poor measures of aptitude and/or achievement (Andrews & Naglieri, 1994; Fuchs & Fuchs, 1986; Ysseldyke, 1990). According to Andrews and Naglieri (1994), "The lack of positive findings does not mean that the ATI concept is invalid, but that attempts to operationalize the concept have not been based on adequate theories of assessment for instructional planning" (p. 8).

With respect to attempts to operationalize the concept of ATI, Andrews and Naglieri (1994) suggested that traditional intelligence tests that are based on a verbal–nonverbal framework do not incorporate research findings from educational and cognitive psychology that indicate that a learner's cognitive strategies and prior knowledge are vital components of the instructional process. Recently, however, several authors (e.g., Das & Naglieri, 1993; Woodcock, 1993, Chapter 12, this volume) have operationalized theories of cognitive processing that may be helpful in providing empirical support for the ATI concept. For example, in a review of the WJ-R, Ysseldyke (1990) stated that because this instrument contains eight "relatively clean measures of specific factors, there is now an opportunity to use [it] in ATI investigations" (p. 273). That is, it is possible to examine the treatment relevance of the WJ-R by investigating "the extent to which knowledge of pupil performance on the various factors is prescriptively predictive of relative success in school" (Ysseldyke, 1990, p. 273). Given that there exists a substantial amount of construct and predictive validity evidence for the Gf-Gc factors underlying the WJ-R, it is unfortunate that studies of the effects of treatments based on the information yielded by this test have not been carried out to date.

In the field of intellectual assessment, some of the few ATI investigations currently under way are being conducted by Naglieri and his colleagues. Recently, Das, Naglieri, and Kirby (1994) and Naglieri (Chapter 13, this volume) described a theoretically based model of assessment that can be used to facilitate the teaching–learning process outlined by Meyers and Lytle (1986) and Lidz (1991, Chapter 15, this volume). These researchers joined others who have studied training of cognitive strategies and found beneficial effects of training in planning and goal setting, problem solving, and hypothesis generation (see Peterson, 1988).

For example, Cormier, Carlson, and Das (1990) used mediated learning to encourage planful solutions of problems in two groups of children, those who were already low in planning skills and those who were high in planning skills. These groups were defined on the basis of an experimental measure of planning. Cormier et al. found that subjects who were low in planning showed significantly more improvement than those who were already considered, on the basis on their performance on the experimental measure of planning, to be high in planning skills. Similarly, Naglieri and Gottling (1993; cf. Naglieri & Andrews, 1994) showed that students who performed poorly on the planning tasks comprising the DNCAS (Das & Naglieri, 1993) showed significantly greater improvement on a mathematics task than their counterparts with average planning ability when instruction was based on their cognitive processing status. The results of these studies are also consistent with those reported by Kar, Dash, Das, and Carlson (1993).

Despite the encouraging work in ATI research described previously, we are a long way from understanding whether the link between cognitive processing assessment and training is viable. For example, researchers have questioned the construct validity of the planning scale of the DNCAS recently, suggesting that it may measure *perceptual speed* rather than planning per se (e.g., Carroll, 1995). If this is the case, it would seem that instruction in how to be more planful may be an effective treatment in and of itself and perhaps irrelevant to an individual's profile of PASS strengths and weaknesses (see also Reschly & Wilson, 1990). Nevertheless, the studies presented here are important and need to be replicated. In addition, the positive effects that strategy training and mediating learning have on general cognitive ability need to be investigated and evidence regarding whether improvements in cognitive functioning transfer to academic skill acquisition needs to be documented. In this regard, dynamic assessment approaches appear to demonstrate promise (see Feuerstein, Feuerstein, & Gross, Chapter 16, this volume; Lidz, Chapter 15, this volume). However, empirical evidence for their claims is limited at this time. In sum, it is still the case that "the underlying concept [ATI] has not received an adequate test. Real life ATIs are transactional, multivariate, and developmental. This complexity needs to be reflected in our research before we can begin to understand school failure" (Speece, 1990, p. 146).

CONCLUSION

The purpose of this chapter was to examine the functional utility of intelligence tests in special education service delivery. In particular, the predictive, discriminative, and treatment utility of many traditional and contemporary intelligence tests was reviewed. It appears that newer tests and approaches to measuring cognitive processes and abilities that are grounded in theoretical and empirical research have the potential to aid practitioners in making diagnostic and instructional decisions. However, although preliminary studies with some newer tests are promising, a considerable amount of additional research is needed to demonstrate the diagnostic–prescriptive utility of these assessment methods.

The outcome of future diagnostic and treatment validity research will determine whether the utility of contemporary assessment methods can negate the negative impact that criticisms of *traditional* intelligence tests appear to have had on the use of *all* cognitive ability measures. Because traditional intelligence tests were not designed to evaluate instructional strategies for the purpose of remediating learning deficits, future research should focus on investigating the validity of nontraditional and/or contemporary cognitive assessment methods for this purpose. If there is greater recognition among researchers and practitioners of the *qualitative* ways in which traditional and contemporary cognitive tests differ, future research will likely investigate the utility of a broader range of new and alternative methods of cognitive assessment and perhaps demonstrate that cognitive ability tests are useful *for different purposes* (e.g., a measure of general ability, a prescriptive tool, and a diagnostic instrument).

NOTE

1. The correlation between the ability and achievement measures at separate age or grade levels is needed to account for the regression effect in ability–achievement comparisons. However, these correlations vary as a function of sample selection, age, and achievement criterion, introducing problems when practitioners wish to make comparisons between ability and achievement tests for which limited correlational information exists. Because approaches for estimating the effects of regression fall short of the accuracy desired (Reynolds, 1990), only co-normed (and equated) tests are recommended here as they offer the most optimal solution (see McGrew, 1994, for further discussion).

REFERENCES

Algozzine, B. (1985). Low achiever differentiation: Where's the beef? *Exceptional Children, 52*, 72–75.

Anastasi, A. (1988). *Psychological testing.* New York: Macmillan.

Andrews, T. J., & Naglieri, J. A. (1994). Aptitude–treatment interactions reconsidered. *Communique, 22*(6), 8–9.

Bannatyne, A. (1974). Diagnosis: A note on recategorization of the WISC scaled scores. *Journal of Learning Disabilities, 7*, 272–274.

Bardos, A. N. (1987). *Differentiation of normal, reading disabled, and developmentally handicapped students using the Das–Naglieri cognitive processing tasks.* Unpublished doctoral dissertation, Ohio State University, Columbus.

Barnett, D. W., & Macmann, G. M. (1992). Aptitude-achievement discrepancy scores: Accuracy in analysis misdirected. *School Psychology Review, 21,* 494–508.

Batsche, G. W. (1992). School psychology and America 2000: Where do we stand? *Communique, 20*(5), 2 & 27.

Berk, R. A. (1984). *Screening and diagnosis of children with learning disabilities.* Springfield, IL: Charles C. Thomas.

Bracken, B. A. (1987). Limitations of preschool instruments and standards for minimal levels of technical adequacy. *Journal of Psychoeducational Assessment, 4,* 313–326.

Carroll, J. B. (1993). *Human cognitive abilities: A survey of factor-analytic studies.* Cambridge, England: Cambridge University Press.

Carroll, J. B. (1995). Review of *Assessment of cognitive processes: The PASS theory of intelligence. Journal of Psychoeducational Assessment, 13,* 397–409.

Cicchetti, D. V. (1994). Guidelines, criteria, and rules of thumb for evaluating normed and standardized assessment instruments in psychology. *Psychological Assessment, 6*(4), 284–290.

Cole, K. N., Dale, P. S., Mills, P. E., & Jenkins, J. R. (1993). Interaction between early intervention curricula and student characteristics. *Exceptional Children, 60,* 17–28.

Cone, T. E., & Wilson, L. R. (1981). Quantifying a severe discrepancy: A critical analysis. *Learning Disability Quarterly, 4,* 359–371.

Cormier, P., Carlson, J. S., & Das, J. P. (1990). Planning ability and cognitive performance: The compensatory effects of a dynamic assessment approach. *Learning and Individual Differences, 2,* 437–449.

Cronbach, L. J. (1957). The two disciplines of scientific psychology. *American Psychologist, 12,* 671–684.

Cronbach, L. J., & Snow, R. E. (1977). *Aptitudes and instructional methods.* New York: Irvington.

Cunningham, G. K. (1986). *Educational and psychological measurement.* New York: Macmillan.

Das, J. P., Mishra, R. K., & Kirby, J. R. (1994). Cognitive patterns of children with dyslexia: A comparison between groups with high average and nonverbal intelligence. *Journal of Learning Disabilities, 27,* 235–242.

Das, J. P., & Naglieri, J. A. (1993). *Das–Naglieri: Cognitive assessment system: Experimental test battery.* Chicago: Riverside.

Das, J. P., Naglieri, J. A., & Kirby, J. (1994). *Assessment of cognitive processes: The PASS theory of intelligence.* Boston: Allyn & Bacon.

Delaney, E., & Hopkins, T. (1987). *Examiner's handbook: An expanded guide for Fourth Edition users.* Chicago: Riverside.

Elliott, C. D. (1990a). *The Differential Ability Scales: Introductory and technical handbook.* San Antonio, TX: Psychological Corporation.

Elliott, C. D. (1990b). The nature and structure of children's abilities: Evidence from the Differential Ability Scales. *Journal of Psychoeducational Assessment, 8,* 376–390.

Elliott, R. (1988). Tests, abilities, race, and conflict. *Intelligence, 12,* 333–350.

Evans, J. H., Carlsen, R. N., & McGrew, K. S. (1993). Classification of exceptional students with the Woodcock–Johnson Psycho-Educational Battery—Revised. *Journal of Psychoeducational Assessment* [Monograph Series: WJ-R Monograph], 6–19.

Evans, L. D. (1990). A conceptual overview of the regression discrepancy model for evaluating severe discrepancy between IQ and achievement scores. *Journal of Learning Disabilities, 23,* 406–411.

Fagan, T. K. (1987) Gesell: The first school psychologist. Part 1: The road to Connecticut. *School Psychology Review, 16,* 103–107.

Flanagan, D. P. (1995). A review of the Kaufman Adolescent and Adult Intelligence Test. In J. C. Conoley & J. C. Impara (Eds.), *The twelfth mental measurements yearbook* (pp. 527–530). Lincoln, NE: Buros Institute.

Flanagan, D. P., & Alfonso, V. C. (1993a). Differences required for significance between Wechsler Verbal and Performance IQs and WIAT subtests and composites: The predicted-achievement method. *Psychology in the Schools, 30,* 180–187.

Flanagan, D. P., & Alfonso, V. C. (1993b). WIAT subtest and composite predicted achievement values based on WISC-III Verbal and Performance IQs. *Psychology in the Schools, 30,* 310–320.

Flanagan, D. P., & Alfonso, V. C. (1995). A critical review of the technical characteristics of new and recently revised intelligence tests for preschool children. *Journal of Psychoeducational Assessment, 13,* 66–90.

Flanagan, D. P., Alfonso, V. C., & Flanagan, R. (1994). A review of the Kaufman Adolescent and Adult Intelligence Test: An advancement in cognitive assessment? *School Psychology Review, 23,* 512–525.

Flanagan, D. P., & McGrew, K. S. (1995a). The field of intellectual assessment: A current perspective. *The School Psychologist, 49,* 7, 14.

Flanagan, D. P., & McGrew, K. S. (1995b). *Will you evolve or become extinct? Interpreting intelligence tests from modern Gf-Gc theory.* Paper presented at the 27th annual convention of the National Association of School Psychologists, Chicago.

Fletcher, J. M., Francis, D. J., Rourke, B. P., Shaywitz, S. E., & Shaywitz, B. A. (1992). The validity of discrepancy-based definitions of reading disabilities. *Journal of Learning Disabilities, 25,* 555–561.

Fuchs, L. S., & Fuchs, D. (1986). Effects of systematic formative evaluation: A meta-analysis. *Exceptional Children, 53,* 199–208.

Fuchs, D., Fuchs, L. S., Benowitz, S., & Barringer, K. (1987). Norm-referenced tests: Are they valid for use with handicapped students? *Exceptional Children, 54,* 263–271.

Glutting, J. J., McDermott, P. A., Prifitera, A., & McGrath, E. A. (1994). Core profile types for the WISC-III and WIAT: Their development and application in identifying multivariate IQ-achievement discrepancies. *School Psychology Review, 23,* 619–639.

Good, R. H., Vollmer, M., Creek, R. J., Katz, L., & Chowdhri, S. (1993). Treatment utility of the Kaufman Assessment Battery for Children: Effects of matching instruction and student processing strength. *School Psychology Review, 22,* 8–26.

Gould, S. J. (1981). *The mismeasure of man.* New York: Norton.

Gregory, S., & Lee, S. (1986). Psychoeducational assessment of racial and ethnic minority groups: Professional implications. *Journal of Counseling and Development, 64,* 635–637.

Haywood, H. C., Brown, A. L., & Wingenfeld, S. (1990). Dynamic approaches to psychoeducational assessment. *School Psychology Review, 19,* 411–422.

Heath, C. P., & Kush, J. C. (1991). Use of discrepancy formulas in the assessment of learning disabilities. In J. E. Obrzut & G. W. Hynd (Eds.), *Neuropsychological foundations of learning disabilities: A handbook of issues, methods, and practice.* New York: Academic Press.

Heller, K. A., Holtzman, W. H., & Messick, S. (Eds.). (1982). *Placing children in special education: A strategy for equity.* Washington, DC: National Academy Press.

Horn, J. L. (1991). Measurement of intellectual capabilities: A review of theory. In K. S. McGrew, J. K. Werder, & R. W. Woodcock, *Woodcock–Johnson technical manual* (pp. 197–232). Allen, TX: DLM.

Horn, J. L. (1994). Theory of fluid and crystallized intelligence. In R. J. Sternberg (Ed.), *Encyclopedia of human intelligence* (pp. 443–451). New York: Macmillan.

Horn, J. L., & Cattell, R. B. (1966). Refinement and test of the theory of fluid and crystallized general intelligences. *Journal of Educational Psychology, 57,* 253–270.

Horn, J. L., & Cattell, R. B. (1967). Age differences in fluid and crystallized intelligence. *Acta Psychologica, 2,* 107–129.

Hurt, J., & Naglieri, J. A. (1992). Performance of delinquent and nondelinquent males on planning, attention, simultaneous, and successive cognitive processing tasks. *Journal of Clinical Psychology, 48,* 120–128.

Individuals with Disabilities Education Act. 20 U.S.C. ch. 33, § 602(a)(19).

Jenkins, J. R., & Pany, D. (1978). Standardized achievement tests: How useful for special education? *Exceptional Children, 44,* 448–453.

Jensen, A. R. (1980). *Bias in mental testing.* New York: Free Press.

Kamphaus, R. W. (1993). *Clinical assessment of children's intelligence.* Boston: Allyn & Bacon.

Kar, B. C., Dash, U. N., Das, J. P., & Carlson, J. (1993). Two experiments on the dynamic assessment of planning. *Learning and Individual Differences, 5,* 13–29.

Kaufman, A. S. (1976). A new approach to interpretation of test scatter on the WISC-R. *Journal of Learning Disabilities, 9,* 160–168.

Kaufman, A. S. (1979). Cerebral specialization and intelligence testing. *Journal of Research and Development in Education, 12,* 96–107.

Kaufman, A. S. (1994). *Intelligent testing with the WISC-III.* New York: Wiley.

Kaufman, A. S., Harrison, P. L., & Ittenbach, R. F. (1990). Intelligence testing in the schools. In T. B. Gutkin & C. R. Reynolds (Eds.), *The handbook of school psychology* (2nd ed., pp. 289–327). New York: Wiley.

Kaufman, A. S., & Kaufman, N. L. (1983). *Kaufman Assessment Battery for Children.* Circle Pines, MN: American Guidance Service.

Kaufman, A. S., & Kaufman, N. L. (1985). *Kaufman Test of Educational Achievement.* Circle Pines, MN: American Guidance Service.

Kaufman, A. S., & Kaufman, N. L. (1993). *Kaufman Adolescent and Adult Intelligence Test.* Circle Pines, MN: American Guidance Service.

Kavale, K. A., & Forness, S. R. (1984). A meta-analysis of the validity of Wechsler scale profiles and recategorizations: Patterns or parodies? *Learning Disability Quarterly, 7,* 136–152.

Knoblock, P. (1987). *Understanding exceptional children and youth.* Boston: Little, Brown.

Kranzler, J. H., & Weng, L. (1995a). Factor structure of the PASS cognitive tasks: A reexamination of Naglieri et al. (1991). *Journal of School Psychology, 33,* 143–157.

Kranzler, J. H., & Weng, L. (1995b). Reply to the commentary by Naglieri and Das on the factor structure of a battery of PASS cognitive tasks. *Journal of School Psychology, 33,* 169–176.

Lezak, M. D. (1988). IQ:R.I.P. *Journal of Clinical and Experimental Neuropsychology, 10,* 351–361.

Lidz, C. S. (1991). *Practitioner's guide to dynamic assessment.* New York: Guilford Press.

Luria, A. R. (1966). *Human brain and psychological processes.* New York: Harper & Row.

Luria, A. R. (1970). The functional organization of the brain. *Scientific American, 222,* 66–78.

Luria, A. R. (1973). *The working brain: An introduction to neuropsychology.* New York: Basic Books.

Luria, A. R. (1976). *Cognitive development: Its cultural and social foundations.* Cambridge, MA: Harvard University Press.

Luria, A. R. (1980). *Higher cortical functions in man (2nd ed.).* New York: Basic Books.

Luria, A. R. (1982). *Language and cognition.* New York: Wiley.

Mackintosh, N. J. (1986). The biology of intelligence? *British Journal of Psychology, 77,* 1–18.

Mather, N. (1993). Critical issues in the diagnosis of learning disabilities addressed by the Woodcock–Johnson Psycho-Educational Battery—Revised. *Journal of Psychoeducational Assessment* [Monograph Series: WJ-R Monograph], 103–122.

Mather, N., & Healey, W. C. (1990). Deposing aptitude–achievement discrepancy as the imperial criterion for learning disabilities. *Learning Disabilities, 1,* 40–48.

McDermott, P. A., Fantuzzo, J. W., & Glutting, J. J. (1990). Just say no to subtest analysis: A critique on Wechsler theory and practice. *Journal of Psychoeducational Assessment, 8,* 290–302.

McDermott, P. A., Fantuzzo, J. W., Glutting, J. J., Watkins, M. W., & Baggaley, R. A. (1992). Illusions of meaning in the ipsative assessment of children's ability. *Journal of Special Education, 25,* 504–526.

McDermott, P. A., Glutting, J. J., Jones, J. N., Watkins, M. W., & Kush, J. (1989). Core profile types in the WISC-R national sample: Structure, membership, and applications. *Psychological Assessment: A Journal of Consulting and Clinical Psychology, 1,* 292–299.

McDermott, P. A., & Watkins, M. W. (1985). *McDermott multidimensional assessment of children.* San Antonio, TX: Psychological Corporation.

McGhee, R. (1993). Fluid and crystallized intelligence: Confirmatory factor analysis of the Differential Abilities Scale, Detroit Tests of Learning Aptitude—3, and Woodcock–Johnson Psycho-Educational Battery—Revised. *Journal of Psychoeducational Assessment* [Monograph Series: WJ-R Monograph], 20–38.

McGrew, K. S. (1993). The relationship between the Woodcock–Johnson Psycho-Educational Battery—Revised Gf-Gc cognitive clusters and reading achievement across the life-span. *Journal of Psychoeducational Assessment* [Monograph Series: WJ-R Monograph], 39–53.

McGrew, K. S. (1994). *Clinical Interpretation of the Woodcock–Johnson—Revised Tests of Cognitive Ability—Revised.* Boston: Allyn & Bacon.

McGrew, K. S., & Flanagan, D. P. (1996). *An intelligence test desk reference (ITDR): A cross-battery approach to intelligence test interpretation.* Boston: Allyn & Bacon. Manuscript in preparation.

McGrew, K. S., & Hessler, G. L. (1995). The relationship between the WJ-R Gf-Gc cognitive clusters and mathematics achievement across the life-span. *Journal of Psychoeducational Assessment, 13,* 21–38.

McGrew, K. S., & Knopik, S. N. (1993). The relationship between the WJ-R Gf-Gc cognitive clusters and writing achievement across the life-span. *School Psychology Review, 22,* 687–695.

McGrew, K. S., & Knopik, S. N. (in press). The relationship between intra-cognitive scatter on the Woodcock–Johnson Psycho-Educational Battery—Revised and school achievement. *Journal of School Psychology.*

McGrew, K. S., Untiedt, S. A., & Flanagan, D. P. (in press). Uniqueness and general factor characteristics of the Kaufman Adolescent and Adult Intelligence Test. *Journal of Psychoeducational Assessment.*

McGrew, K. S., & Werder, J., & Woodcock, R. (1991). *Woodock–Johnson technical manual.* Chicago: Riverside.

Mercer, C. D. (1987). *Students with learning disabilities.* Columbus, OH: Merrill.

Messick, S. (1995). Validity of psychological assessment: Validation of inferences from persons' responses and performances as scientific inquiry into score meaning. *American Psychologist, 50,* 741–749.

Meyers, J., & Lytle, S. (1986). Assessment of the learning process. *Exceptional Children, 53*(2), 138–144.

Morris, R. (1993). Issues in empirical versus clinical identification of learning disabilities. In G. R. Lyon, D. B. Gray, J. F. Kavanagh, & N. A. Krasnegor (Eds.), *Better understanding learning disabilities: New views from research and their implications for education and public policies* (pp. 73–93). Baltimore: Brookes.

Mueller, H. H., Dennis, S. S., & Short, R. H. (1986). A meta-exploration of WISC-R factor score profiles as a function of diagnosis and intellectual level. *Canadian Journal of School Psychology, 2,* 21–43.

Naglieri, J. A., & Andrews, T. J. (1994). A cognitive approach to intervention design. *Communique, 22*(7), 17–18.

Naglieri, J. A., & Das, J. P. (1990). Planning, attention, simultaneous, successive cognitive processes as a model for intelligence. *Journal of Psychoeducational Assessment, 8,* 303–337.

Naglieri, J. A., Das, J. P., & Jarman, R. F. (1990). Planning, attention, simultaneous, and successive processes as a model for assessment. *School Psychology Review, 19,* 423–442.

Neisworth, J. T., & Bagnato, S. J. (1992). The case against intelligence testing in early intervention. *Topics in Early Childhood Special Education, 12,* 1–20.

Peterson, P. (1988). Selecting students and services for compensatory education: Lessons from aptitude–treatment interaction research. *Educational Psychologist, 23,* 313–352.

Phillips, B. N. (1990). *School psychology at a turning point: Ensuring a bright future for the profession.* San Francisco: Jossey-Bass.

Prifitera, A., & Dersh, J. (1993). Base rates of WISC-III diagnostic subtest patterns among normal, learning-disabled, and ADHD samples. *Journal of Psychoeducational Assessment* [Monograph Series: WISC-III Monograph], 43–55.

Psychological Corporation. (1992). *Wechsler individual achievement test manual.* San Antonio, TX: Author.

Reardon, S. M., & Naglieri, J. A. (1992). PASS cognitive processing characteristics of normal and ADHD males. *Journal of School Psychology, 30,* 151–163.

Reschly, D. J. (1990). Found: Our intelligences: What do they mean? *Journal of Psychoeducational Assessment, 8,* 259–267.

Reschly, D. J., Genshaft, J., & Binder, M. S. (1987). *The 1987 NASP survey: Comparison of practitioners, NASP leadership, and university faculty on key issues.* Washington, DC: National Association of School Psychologists. (ERIC Document Reproduction Service No. ED. 300 733)

Reschly, D. J., & Grimes, J. P. (1995). Best practices in intellectual assessment. In A. Thomas & J. Grimes (Eds.), *Best practices in school psychology—III* (pp. 763–773). Washington, DC: National Association of School Psychologists.

Reschly, D. J., Kicklighter, R., & McKee, P. (1988). Recent placement litigation part III: Analysis of differences in Larry P. Marshall and S-1 and implications for future practices. *School Psychology Review, 17,* 39–50.

Reschly, D. J., & Wilson, M. S. (1990). Cognitive processing versus traditional intelligence: Diagnostic utility, intervention implications, and treatment validity. *School Psychology Review, 19,* 443–458.

Reynolds, C. R. (1981). The fallacy of "two years below grade level for age" as a diagnostic criterion for reading disorders. *Journal of School Psychology, 19,* 350–358.

Reynolds, C. R. (1984). Critical measurement issues in learning disabilities. *Journal of Special Education, 18,* 451–476.

Reynolds, C. R. (1990). Conceptual and technical problems in learning disability diagnosis. In C. R. Reynolds & R. W. Kamphaus (Eds.), *Handbook of psychological and educational assessment of children: Intelligence and achievement* (pp. 571–592). New York: Guilford Press.

Robinson-Zanartu, C., Sattler, J. M., Reschly, D. J., & Sandoval, J. (1994). *IQ testing: The past or the future? The Sattler–Reschly Debate.* California State University-Sacramento and California Department of Education, Resources in Special Education.

Roid, G., Prifitera, A., & Weiss, L. G. (1993). The WISC-III and the fairness of predicting achievement across ethnic and gender groups. *Journal of Psychoeducational Assessment* [Monograph Series: WISC-III Monograph], 6–21.

Ross, R. P. (1992a). Accuracy in analysis of discrepancy scores: A nationwide study of school psychologists. *School Psychology Review, 21,* 480–493.

Ross, R. P. (1992b). Aptitude–achievement discrepancy scores: Accuracy in analysis ignored. *School Psychology Review, 21,* 509–514.

Sattler, J. M. (1988). *Assessment of children (third edition).* San Diego, CA: Author.

Sattler, J. M. (1992). *Assessment of children* (revised and updated third edition). San Diego, CA: Author.

Schmidt, F. L., & Hunter, J. E. (1981). Employment testing: Old theories and new research findings. *American Psychologist, 36,* 1128–1137.

Senf, G. M. (1978). Implications of the final procedures for evaluating specific learning disabilities. *Journal of Learning Disabilities, 11,* 11–13.

Siegel, L. S. (1989). IQ is irrelevant to the definition of learning disabilities. *Journal of Learning Disabilities, 22,* 469–479.

Siegel, L. S. (1992). An evaluation of the discrepancy definition of dyslexia. *Journal of Learning Disabilities, 25,* 618–629.

Snow, R. E., & Yalow, E. (1982). Education and intelligence. In R. J. Sternberg (Ed.), *Handbook of human intelligence* (pp. 493–585). Cambridge, England: Cambridge University Press.

Speece, D. L. (1990). Aptitude–treatment interactions: Bad rap or bad idea? *Journal of Special Education, 24,* 139–149.

Stanovich, K. E., (1991). Discrepancy definitions of reading disability: Has intelligence lead us astray? *Reading Research Quarterly, 26,* 7–29.

Sternberg, R. J. (1984). The Kaufman Assessment Battery for Children: An information-processing analysis and critique. *Journal of Special Education, 18,* 269–278.

Sternberg, R. J. (1986). Intelligence, wisdom, and creativity: Three is better than one. *Educational Psychologist, 21,* 175–190.

Stinnett, T. A., Havey, J. M., & Oehler-Stinnett, J. (1994). Current test usage by practicing school psychologists: A national survey. *Journal of Psychoeducational Assessment, 12,* 331–350.

Swanson, H. L. (1991). Operational definitions and learning disabilities: An overview. *Learning Disability Quarterly, 14,* 242–254.

Tabachnick, B. G., & Fidell, L. S. (1989). *Using multivariate statistics* (2nd ed.). New York: HarperCollins.

Tatsuoka, M. M., & Lohnes, P. R. (1988). *Multivariate analysis* (2nd ed.). New York: Macmillan.

Thompson, B. (1991). Methods, plainly speaking: A primer on the logic and use of canonical correlation analysis. *Measurement and Evaluation in Counseling and Development, 24,* 80–95.

Thorndike, R. L., & Hagen, E. (1969). *Measurement and evaluation in psychology and education* (3rd ed.). New York: Wiley.

Thorndike, R. L., Hagen, E. P., & Sattler, J. M. (1986). *Stanford–Binet Intelligence Scale, Fourth edition.* Chicago: Riverside.

Wagner, R., & Sternberg, R. (1984). Alternative conceptions of intelligence and their implications for education. *Review of Educational Research, 54,* 179–223.

Watkins, M. W., & Kush, J. C. (1994). Wechsler subtest analysis: The right way, the wrong way, or no way? *School Psychology Review, 23,* 640–651.

Wechsler, D. (1974). *Wechsler Intelligence Scale for Children—Revised.* San Antonio, TX: Psychological Corporation.

Wechsler, D. (1991). *Manual for the Wechsler Intelligence Scale for Children—Third Edition.* San Antonio, TX: Psychological Corporation.

Whitener, E. M. (1989). A meta-analytic review of the effect on learning of the interaction between prior achievement and instructional support. *Review of Educational Research, 59,* 65–86.

Wilson, M. S., & Reschly, D. J. (1996). Assessment in school psychology training and practice. *School Psychology Review, 25,* 9–23.

Woodcock, R. W. (1990). Theoretical foundations in the WJ-R measures of cognitive ability. *Journal of Psychoeducational Assessment, 8,* 231–258.

Woodcock, R. W. (1993). An information processing view of Gf-Gc theory. *Journal of Psychoeducational Assessment* [Monograph Series: WJ-R Monograph], 80–102.

Woodcock, R. W., & Johnson, M. B. (1977). *Woodcock–Johnson Psycho-Educational Battery.* Allen, TX: DLM.

Woodcock, R. W., & Johnson, M. B. (1989). *Woodcock–Johnson Psycho-Educational Battery—Revised.* Chicago: Riverside.

Ysseldyke, J. (1990). Goodness of fit of the Woodcock–Johnson Psycho-Educational Battery—Revised to the Horn–Cattell Gf-Gc theory. *Journal of Psychoeducational Assessment, 8,* 268–275.

Ysseldyke, J. E., Algozzine, B., Shinn, M. R., & McGue, M. (1982). Similarities and differences between low achievers and students labeled learning disabled. *Journal of Special Education, 16,* 73–85.

Ysseldyke, J., & Mirkin, P. (1982). The use of assessment information to plan instructional interventions: A review of the research. In C. Reynolds & T. Gutkin (Eds.), *The handbook of school psychology* (pp. 395–409). New York: Wiley.

Ysseldyke, J. E., Reynolds, M. C., & Weinberg, R. A. (1984). *School psychology: A blueprint for training and practice.* Minneapolis: National School Psychology Inservice Training Network, University of Minnesota.

CHAPTER 24

The Utility of Intelligence Tests for Preschool Children

BRUCE A. BRACKEN

KATHRYN C. WALKER

P RESCHOOL PSYCHOEDUCATIONAL and behavioral assessment is a practice with a long and important, but little known history; a history that has become increasingly important with the passage of recent legislation and the emphasis on early education. Preschool assessment practices and research have laid the groundwork for many important areas of psychology from applied clinical practice to more basic areas of child development, including language, cognitive, motor, and social development. Refinements in theories of intelligence, instrumentation, and practice have all benefited as a result of psychology's ongoing interest in assessing the abilities and behaviors of preschool children. This chapter addresses the historical evolution of preschool assessment and the consequent changes in and foibles related to preschool instrumentation and practice. For the purposes of this chapter, preschool assessment includes the ages of 2 through 8. Though most children begin school at 5 or 6 years of age, delayed 7- and 8-year-olds perform and behave much like preschool children; thus the limitations in instrumentation for these early childhood years are as germane as for the child who is truly a preschooler.

HISTORY OF PRESCHOOL INTELLIGENCE TESTING

Historically, and relative to other age levels, studies of preschool children's intellectual functioning have been fairly limited. Research interest in preschool development was stimulated by Charles Darwin's baby biographies. Darwin's (1877) reports illustrated the linkages between children's early and later behaviors and prompted further research into preschool behavior and child development. In the first couple decades of the 1900s educators and psychologists were limited in their ability to assess preschool intelligence because of a dearth of available, let alone sufficiently valid or reliable, instruments. Nearly all the instruments constructed to measure intellectual functioning at that time were designed for school-age children and adult populations (Goodenough, 1949).

Until early in the 20th-century intelligence was thought to be a fixed trait that was manifested through sensory functions (Anastasi, 1988; Kelley & Surbeck, 1991). Consequently, measures of intelligence consisted largely of tests of sensory and perceptual abilities and sensitivities. Alfred Binet was among the first to propose an assessment paradigm that posited reasoning, comprehension, and judgment as essential components of intellectual functioning (see Thorndike, Chapter 1, this volume). Binet and Simon's 1905 scale not only emphasized these cognitive attributes but introduced several subtests appropriate for children younger than 3 years of age. However, the 1908 revision of the original scale removed all the subtests intended for children younger than age 3. Over the years Binet and many others continued to revise and improve the original Binet scale, with subsequent forms evolving and giving way to the early Stanford edition and ultimately the most recent edition, the Stanford–Binet Intelligence Scale: Fourth Edition (SB-IV; Thorndike, Hagen, & Sattler, 1986). True to Binet's pioneering efforts, the SB-IV extends well into the preschool years, down to age 2. It is important to note, however, that the Kuhlmann (1922) revision of the Binet scale was extended even farther, down to 3 months. It is unfortunate for the Kuhlmann version that it had many limitations and did not compete well with the early Stanford instrument.

In addition to a shift in assessment paradigm from a sensory focus to a cognitive orientation, the concept of fixed intellectual abilities began to erode. The notion of fixed intelligence was widely accepted until Wellman's (1932) studies sparked the famous Wellman–Goodenough controversy. Over a period of several years, Wellman observed preschool children enrolled in child development laboratories and noted an increase in their intelligence over time. She contributed the increases in the children's intelligence to the beneficial experiences of the child development program to which the children were exposed; that is, to environmental influences.

Goodenough (1949), on the other hand, concluded that the Kuhlmann–Binet (Kuhlmann, 1922) used by Wellman was responsible for the observed changes in intelligence. The Kuhlmann–Binet was poorly standardized and limited in other ways as well. Goodenough further attributed Wellman's findings to faulty research design and instrumentation, and continued to defend the view of fixed intelligence. Since the Wellman–Goodenough controversy the influence of environment on intelligence has become widely accepted. And, in Goodenough's defense, it has also become widely accepted that all measures of cognitive ability have sources of measurement error that limit their accuracy and utility.

During the 1930s, the Binet scales were criticized for their adherence to the assessment of general intelligence, which was represented as a single global score. Researchers were beginning to hypothesize that intelligence comprised multifactored elements; for example, Thurstone's (1938) primary mental abilities arose from the factor analysis of a variety of cognitive measures. The relative importance of general intelligence versus specific or primary abilities continues to date with no foreseeable resolution (Azar, 1995).

During the early 1900s, preschool tests of intelligence were emerging; however, many of the scales were translations or adaptations of the original Binet (e.g., the Goddard, Kuhlmann, Yorkers–Bridges–Hardback, Stanford, and Herring adaptations or translations) (Stutsman, 1931). Between the 1920s and 1950s, a considerable number of psychological tests constructed for school-age children included downward extensions for preschool children. Among these scales are such notable contributions as the Goodenough Draw a Man Test (Goodenough, 1926), Merrill–Palmer Scale of Mental Tests (Stutsman, 1931), Leiter International Performance Scale (Leiter, 1948), Full Range Picture Vocabulary Test (Ammons & Holmes, 1949), Brenner Gestalt Test (Brenner, 1959), and several variations of the Sequin Form Board. However, all these tests lacked the technical qualities to warrant their continued use with preschool children, and they have largely disappeared from the assessment scene.

The 1960s was a decade of increased attention on child development and education. New tests for infants and preschool children were introduced, including the Wechsler Preschool and Primary Scale of Intelligence (WPPSI; Wechsler, 1967), the Illinois Test of Psycholinguistic Abilities (Kirk, McCarthy, & Kirk, 1968), and the Bayley Scales of Infant Development (Bayley, 1969). Also during this time period, the federally funded, community-based "grassroots" educational intervention program Head Start was initiated. Researchers such as Reissman (1962) and Jensen (1966) noted that children raised in poverty often suffered disproportionately poor school achievement. Further, the farther children from poverty progressed in school, the lower they tended to perform as compared to their more affluent peers on the norms of standardized tests (Hodges & Cooper, 1981). Project Head Start was established with the assumption that environment and education were primary determinants of mental ability. Furthermore, Head Start proposed that enrichment experiences could compensate for a child's limited exposure to educational experiences due to the detrimental effects of poverty (Lichtenstein & Ireton, 1984).

With the development of Head Start, program evaluation became a central element in early childhood education. Therefore, an ever increasing number of preschool assessment instruments were being developed to determine the efficacy of early childhood intervention programs cropping up across the country. Numerous measures were developed during the 1970s and still more in the 1980s, and test authors, publishers, and examiners began to address in earnest the measurement problems that had long plagued preschool assessment.

It is likely that in recent years no other variable has had as great an effect on preschool assessment as federal legislation. In 1975, Public Law (PL) 94-142, the Education for All Handicapped Children Act, was passed which mandated that all school-age children with disabilities must receive a free and appropriate education within the least restrictive environment. Public schools were thereby required to provide children with needed special education services, including psychological assessments. Under this law, states were required to serve disabled children between the ages of 3 and 5 years only to the extent that they served nondisabled children of the same ages. For example, if kindergarten programs were offered for 5-year-old children without disabilities, the state would be required to provide appropriate kindergarten experiences for 5-year-old children with disabilities.

Perhaps most critical to the preschool population was the Education of the Handicapped Act Amendments of 1986 (Public Law 99-457). As a downward extension of PL 94-142 this law mandated educational services for children between the ages of 3 to 5 years of age. In addition, PL 99-457 included incentives for states to provide free and appropriate services for children from birth through two years. One of the stipulations of PL 99-457 was that psychoeducational assessments must include a multidisciplinary team evaluation of the child's developmental areas including cognitive functioning (Benner, 1992). In 1990, PL 99-457 was subsumed by the Individuals with Disabilities Education Act—Part H (IDEA—Part H) for infants and toddlers, which provided funds for states to offer funds for early intervention programs. IDEA—Part H requires a comprehensive multidisciplinary evaluation in the areas of cognitive development, physical development, communication development, social or emotional development, and adaptive development. The culmination of legislation that collectively addressed the assessment of preschool children has further highlighted the need for adequate preschool assessment measures.

Recently, Bagnato and Neisworth (1994) conducted a survey of 223 members of the 1990–1991 membership of the joint Preschool Interest Group of the American Psychological Association (APA) Division 16 and the National Association of School Psychologists (NASP) in an effort to glean psychologists' impressions of current preschool assessment practices. Based on data offered by the respondents, Bagnato and Neisworth reported that early intelligence test results were considered useless "at an unacceptably high rate (43%)" (p. 96). Furthermore, Bagnato and Neisworth reported that more than 90% of children who were deemed "untestable" by the surveyed psychologists were found to qualify for services using other methods of assessment. Based on their data, Bagnato and Neisworth called for a discontinuation of early intelligence testing and advocated alternative assessment procedures.

In response to Bagnato and Neisworth's position, Bracken (1994) argued that preschool intelligence testing and alternative methods are not mutually exclusive activities. Rather, Bracken advocated that responsible clinicians tailor psychoeducational assessments to meet each child's needs. Furthermore, Bracken argued that the alternative practices advocated by Bagnato and Neisworth as superior to intelligence testing have not been empirically validated and may be equally or more problematic than traditional assessment approaches. Unfortunately, Bagnato and Neisworth did not sample respondents' opinions of alternative assessment practices to determine perceived problems with the various nontraditional assessment practices.

THE UTILITY OF INTELLIGENCE TESTING WITH PRESCHOOL CHILDREN

With the advent of PL 99-457, the assessment of preschool children's cognitive functioning has become a professional necessity. Psychologists and educators have become increasingly concerned with the predictive nature of preschool children's intelligence as well as with the utility of prematurely classifying preschool children into disability categories.

The emphasis of early assessment should not be on disability classification but rather to identify true delays and provide appropriate interventions for psychoeducational disorders or problems as early into the child's life as possible. Most psychologists would likely agree that assigning diagnostic classifications to children would be meaningless and unjustified without the consequent application of appropriate remedial interventions. Furthermore, psychoeducational interventions based on current test results are not justified if the diagnostic tests employed do not have a record of predicting important areas of psychological, social, or educational functioning.

The ability of tests to predict later functioning is an issue that has been widely investigated in past research. There is overwhelming evidence that intelligence tests predict more important life variables than any other psychological construct. Among the variables predicted by intelligence tests are such notables as academic achievement (Cassidy & Lynn, 1991; Paal, Skinner, & Reddig, 1988; Poteat, Wuensch, & Gregg, 1988; Stanton, Feehan, McGee, & Silva, 1990), adaptive behavior (Huberty, 1986), language development (Bracken, Howell, & Crain, 1993; Bracken, Prasse, & McCallum, 1984; Lindsay, Shapiro, Musselman, & Wilson, 1988), coping skills (Poon, Messner, Martin, Noble, Clayton, & Johnson, 1992), repeated criminal offenses (Denno, 1986), short-term memory (Miller & Vernon, 1992), nonorganic failure to thrive (Drotar & Sturm, 1988), activity level in early childhood (Halverson & Waldrop, 1976), delinquency (Siebert, 1962), leadership (Stogdill, 1948), employment (Hunter & Hunter, 1984), and many more.

In terms of the predictability and stability of preschool tests, tests tend to be better predictors the older the child (Bornstein & Sigman, 1986; Rose & Wallace, 1985) and the more severe the child's developmental delay (DuBose, 1976; Honzik, Hutchings, & Burnip, 1965; Vanderveer & Scheweid, 1974). Whereas assessments during the first 2 years have been reported to have little predictive ability (Bayley, 1949; Rubin & Balow, 1979), beyond age 2 the predictive abilities of preschool tests improve dramatically (Bloom, 1964; Honzik, 1938). For example, Clarke (1982) reported that the intelligence of children as young as 3 and 5 years correlated at a level of .40 with their assessed adult intelligence. It should be considered that the accuracy, stability, and predictive ability of preschool intelligence is diminished somewhat by both unique intra- and extraindividual difficulties associated with the assessment of young children (e.g., erratic and impulsive behaviors of preschool children and technical limitations of preschool instrumentation).

CRITERIA FOR TECHNICAL ADEQUACY OF PRESCHOOL INTELLIGENCE MEASURES

It has been noted that PL 99-457 has created an increased need for preschool instrumentation, including measures of intelligence. Concomitant with the increased need for preschool instrumentation is an increased demand for improved technical quality of preschool tests. However, there has been a lack of standardized criteria to establish precisely what levels of technical adequacy should be considered "acceptable." The *Standards for Educational and Psychological Testing* (APA, 1985) established general guidelines which were not intended to set specific criteria but rather were intended to "provide a frame of reference to assure that relevant issues are addressed" (p. 2). For example, the *Standards* state that test authors should provide estimates of reliabilities and standard errors of measurement so that test users have the necessary information to determine whether an instrument is suitable for its intended use. Although this standard indicates that manuals should provide evidence of reliability, information related to a desired level of reliability remains lacking.

Reliability is one of the primary qualities examiners should consider when selecting a test. As the sine qua non of technical adequacy, reliability sets the limits for validity. Both total test reliability and subtest reliabilities should meet standard criteria because information obtained through both sources are often used for diagnostic and screening purposes, as well as for making placement decisions. Because of the interpretive uses of subtest scores, Bracken (1987) suggested a median subtest internal consistency criterion of .80, which is consistent with Salvia and Ysseldyke's (1988) recommended criterion for individually administered screening devices. Total test scores are more frequently used in making placement decisions; therefore, because such important decisions are presumed to rest on sufficient reliable variance, Bracken suggested a .90 level of total test internal consistency. This criterion is commensurate with Salvia and Ysseldyke's and Nunnally's (1978) recommendations for a .90 level of internal consistency for total test scores.

Stability is a complex component of technical adequacy to consider when evaluating preschool intelligence measures. The variables that influence stability must be taken into consideration when setting a suitable criterion. Questions of how long assessed levels of behavior should remain stable (i.e., state vs. trait attributes), whether all abilities should be expected to remain equally stable, the extent to which environmental conditions differentially affect the stability of different constructs, and the extent to which children's normal course of development affects stability must be considered. However, because most cognitive characteristics are known to be quite stable, especially over short periods of times, a child's performance on intelligence tests should not change appreciably over a brief time interval (e.g., 2 to 4 weeks). Therefore, Bracken (1987) suggested that tests should meet a short-term stability criterion of .90 for the test's most reliable score, the total test score. The extent to which an instrument's stability approximates the .90 criterion, the more confidence examiners can have that the child's results reflect a stable estimate of ability. Remediation efforts based on test results are made with the assumption that the test has provided a stable estimate of the child's assessed abilities, and that only intervention will change the course of the child's progress.

Preschool instruments are especially vulnerable to the limitations of subtest and total test floors. An instrument's floor reflects the extent to which there are a sufficient number of easy items to discriminate levels of functioning between retardation and low average or average cognitive functioning. The McCarthy Scales of Children's Abilities (McCarthy, 1972) is one example of an instrument with exceptionally poor subtest floors. On the McCarthy the *average* child of 2½ years earns a raw score of *less than 1.0* on 7 of 17 entire subtests appropriate for that age (Bracken, 1991a; McCarthy, 1972). In addition, Parts II of both Verbal Memory and Numerical Memory yield mean raw scores that are less than 1. When discrimination between average and profoundly retarded levels of functioning is based on a mere fraction of a single item there is in reality no discrimination. Scales with floor problems produce spuriously inflated scores, and when a scale produces artifactually high scores the examiner gains only misleading information. For this reason, it is recommended that the subtest and total test floor extend at least two standard deviations below the mean to allow for the discrimination of children with average intelligence from children with mild, moderate, and more serious developmental delays.

Another crucial component of technical adequacy in preschool instrumentation is the subtest and/or total test item gradient. Item gradient refers to the magnitude of change in a child's standard score resulting from small incremental changes in raw scores. The smaller the change in standard scores as a result of incremental changes in raw scores, the more refined the measurement, and the more sensitive the measure is to minor differences in the child's true ability. An instrument with a steep item gradient (i.e., small raw score changes result in large standard score differences) offers only crude estimates of a child's true ability. Given scale scores with a mean of 10 and standard deviations of 3, Bracken (1987) suggested that a minimum criterion for item gradients should be no more than three raw score items associated with one standard deviation. That is, single items should be worth no more than one-third standard score standard deviation. To achieve a suitable item gradient a reasonably large number of nonredundant items must be distributed throughout the test.

As with the factors affecting a test's stability, test validation efforts are hindered by confounding factors such as criterion contamination. When examining criterion-related validity, an instrument's assessed validity depends in part on the criterion measure to which the scale is being compared. When the criterion measure is less valid than the predictor measure, the predictor test appears less valid than it actually is. Regardless of the problems associated with test validation, it is the test author's responsibility to provide evidence of validity so examiners can evaluate and determine whether the instrument is suitable for its intended purpose. Preferably, the manual should address issues related to construct, content, and criterion-related validity, including predictive, concurrent, and contrasted-groups validation where appropriate.

SPECIAL ISSUES IN THE ASSESSMENT OF PRESCHOOL CHILDREN

In addition to the limitations of the technical quality of preschool instruments, certain inherent characteristics of preschool children contribute to making the task of assessing this population a difficult endeavor. Preschool children comprise a unique population presenting behaviors that differ considerably from older children, adolescents, and adults. To the inexperienced or uneducated observer, the very nature of typical preschool behavior might be considered maladaptive. Although the unique characteristics of preschool children often render psychoeducational assessments difficult, these same characteristics make working with young children a very interesting and rewarding experience.

Very young children and older children who are language delayed or exceptionally shy typically do not possess or display well-developed expressive language skills; therefore, their ability to respond to traditional verbally loaded assessment devices is often limited (McCallum & Bracken, Chapter 14, this volume; Short, Simeonsson, & Huntington, 1990). As a result, examiners are often required to use alternative assessment practices or measures (e.g., third-party reports) when assessing preschool children (Lidz, 1991; Martin, 1991). However, it should be noted that preschool third-party scales reflect many of the same limitations as traditional instruments administered directly to the child (Bracken, Keith, & Walker, 1994). Some instruments, such as the Boehm Test of Basic Concepts—Preschool Version (Boehm, 1986), the Bracken Basic Concept Scale (Bracken, 1984), and the Peabody Picture Vocabulary Test—Revised (Dunn & Dunn, 1981) address this language barrier by presenting stimuli pictorially and relying on a nonverbal response mode (i.e., pointing) from the examinee.

There are other challenges examiners may encounter when evaluating preschool children. Common concerns include the typical preschool child's limited attention span, high energy and activity levels, and low tolerance to frustration. These characteristics pose special problems when conducting a comprehensive assessment that may require the child to attend and remain seated for 2 or more hours, with or without breaks. Another difficulty is encountered when young children have little interest in doing their best or have no concern about the outcome of the assessment. Preschool children often do not understand or appreciate the importance of performing at their optimal level to such foreign activities. In addition, preschool children often do not feel the same desire as older children to please the examiner by cooperating, attending, or participating fully.

Although there are characteristics inherent to this population that frequently pose problems for examiners, there are also common characteristics of preschool children that facilitate establishing rapport and conducting a successful evaluation. Due to the egocentric nature of young children, they often delight in the individual attention received when interacting with examiners. Test equipment too tends to be more colorful, novel, and stimulating at the preschool level, though this has not always been the case. Examiners can enhance the child's enjoyment of the evaluation by frequently offering warm complimentary statements and sincere words of encouragement. Moreover, young children often enjoy slapstick humor and respond well to absurd statements or those that challenge their egocentric self-perceptions (e.g., calling the child by another name, contradicting his or her knowledge of basic facts such as colors or familial relationships). Not only do such attempts at humor create an enjoyable atmosphere for the child, they also serve to relax the child and create a sense of mutual comfort between the examiner and examinee. Psychologists who rely on standard assessment techniques used for older children may have difficulty establishing and maintaining rapport with young children and may experience an increase in behavioral problems and boredom from the examinee. However, examiners who are bold enough to behave spontaneously and alter their traditional assessment styles are likely to enjoy a positive relationship with the examinee and, in turn, to obtain more valid results from the evaluation. When evaluations are done skillfully, preschool children frequently react with disappointment to the termination of sessions and look forward to subsequent meetings with the examiner.

ISSUES CONCERNING TRADITIONAL
PRESCHOOL INTELLECTUAL ASSESSMENT

The NASP adopted the position that multidisciplinary team assessment must include multiple sources of information, multiple procedures, and multiple settings to yield a comprehensive understanding of student's abilities. Further, the NASP endorsed the position that assessment practices must not be limited to any single methodology or theoretical framework (Bracken, Bagnato, & Barnett, 1991). Traditional psychoeducational assessment has undergone close scrutiny in the recent past; the primary concern seems related to the overreliance on intelligence tests at the expense of clinical skill, professional judgment, and the use of alternative assessment techniques (Bagnato & Neisworth, 1994; Bracken, 1994). As endorsed in the NASP preschool assessment position paper, practitioners should rely on multiple sources of information and their full armament of psychological skill when making diagnoses and placement decisions.

Clinical observations are a crucial aspect of a comprehensive preschool assessment (Bracken, 1991b). Practitioners should observe the child's nontest behaviors in a variety of contexts and question how typical the child's assessment behaviors were. If the examiner believes the child exhibited behaviors during testing that were incongruent with the child's normal functioning (e.g., the child appeared unusually sleepy, fidgety, or overly anxious), the validity of the test results should be questioned. Instruments such as the Bayley Scales of Infant Development—Revised (Bayley, 1993) are sensitive to this issue and ask parents to judge whether the child's assessment behavior was typical and whether the child performed as well as he or she could. In addition, the practitioner should be cognizant of the child's overall physical condition, which might indicate sensory or health-related reasons for a less than optimal assessment. Such behaviors and conditions which reduce the validity of test results should be identified through clinical observations made during multisource, multi-instrument, multiepisodic assessments. Before making important decisions about preschool children's futures, the examiner is ethically bound to secure a valid estimate of the child's true abilities.

In addition to clinical observations, a comprehensive assessment should include information obtained about the child from third-party respondents, typically the child's mother, father, or possibly a teacher or child-care provider. PL 99-457 encourages the participation of parents in the assessment process, and parents can provide valuable information about a child's typical functioning outside the assessment setting. Not only is parent-provided information useful, but parent-completed behavior rating scales can also facilitate a collaborative partnership between the assessment personnel and parents as suggested in the NASP's position paper on early childhood assessment (Bracken et al. 1991).

Just as using test results in isolation can be problematic, overreliance on clinical observations or third-party ratings can pose problems when making diagnoses and placement decisions. Clinical observations are less objective than standardized tests and they allow for disagreement and bias on the part of the professional. In addition, clinical observations have no published norms, percentile ranks, or standard scores such as those included with standardized measures of ability. As a result, practitioners are better equipped to defend classifications and recommendations when based on psychological and educational test data as opposed to only observational findings. Moreover, low to moderate levels of interparent agreement on third-party rating scales are common (Christensen, Margolin, & Sullaway, 1992; Earls, 1980; Lindholm & Touliatos, 1982; Miller, 1964; Novick, Rosenfeld, Bloch, & Dawson, 1966; Walker & Bracken, 1994). The lack of consistent parental agreement calls into question the utility of third-party scales with young children, especially when interpreted without collaborating data or supporting information.

Traditional intelligence tests have been criticized for excluding or underrepresenting preschool children from normative samples and failing to adequately assess young children with language, sensorimotor, and/or behavioral impairments (Bagnato & Neisworth, 1991), and because of limited technical adequacy (Barnett, Macmann, & Carey, 1992; Bracken, 1987; Bracken & Barnett, 1987; Flanagan & Alfonso, 1995; Meisels, 1987). In addition, psychologists who assess preschool children have been criticized for unduly focusing attention on categorical labels and for rigidly adhering to practices appropriate for older children (Bagnato & Neisworth, 1994). Such criticisms are serious and warrant further attention; however, as preschool instrumentation improves and as an increasing number of psychologists are trained to work specifically with preschool children these concerns become less pressing.

TRADITIONAL AND NONTRADITIONAL APPROACHES TO THE ASSESSMENT OF PRESCHOOL INTELLIGENCE

In recent years, many intelligence scales have been developed or revised for use with young children. Many of these instruments were constructed to address the limitations of previous preschool intelligence tests. Following is a brief review of several current and popular instruments designed to measure preschool cognitive functioning. There are additional comprehensive tests of cognitive ability that could be included in this section, but only the more technically sound or current preschool instruments were selected for presentation. For example, the Kaufman Assessment Battery for Children (K-ABC; Kaufman & Kaufman, 1983) extends down to 2½ years, but it has severely limited floors and item gradients, and low reliabilities at the preschool level (Bracken, 1985; 1987). Similarly, the McCarthy Scales of Children's Abilities (McCarthy, 1972) is outdated and therefore of little current use, especially given the finding that intelligence test norms "soften" at a rate of about 3 points per decade (Flynn, 1984); because the worldwide population appears to gain in intelligence at a rate of approximately 3 points per decade, existing norms become inflated at the same rate.

Commonly used and not so commonly used instruments and procedures with generally adequate technical adequacy are presented below. Each instrument is described and its technical adequacy is evaluated according to commonly accepted criteria. Because validity is such a relativistic characteristic and because the upper bounds of a test's validity as a predictor measure is bound to the criterion to which it is being compared (i.e., criterion contamination), validity will not be evaluated. Suffice it to say that all of the instruments addressed in this chapter have considerable evidence of validity reported in their respective examiner's or technical manuals. It is the examiner's responsibility to determine whether any individual test has sufficient evidence of validity for the specific purposes for which the examiner intends to use the test.

Bayley Scales

The newly revised Bayley Scales of Infant Development—Second Edition (BSID-II; Bayley, 1993) was designed to assess the "current developmental functioning of infants and children" between the ages of 1 month and 42 months (p. 1). The instrument is divided into three scales: the Mental Scale, the Motor Scale, and the Behavior Rating Scale. For the purposes of this chapter, only the Mental Scale is discussed. The BSID-II incorporates a flexible administration format and stimulating materials that capture infants' and young children's attention. The Bayley Mental Scale contains no subtests but, rather, provides a single global Index Score ($M = 100$, $SD = 15$); the Mental Scale also provides age equivalents, percentile ranks, and classifications.

The BSID-II manual reports internal consistency coefficients of .89 and .90 for ages 36 and 42 months, respectively, and an average reliability of .88 across all age levels. Therefore, the BSID-II possesses adequate internal consistency for making diagnoses and developing placement and/or treatment plans for infants and preschool children. Bayley test–retest reliability is reported as .91 for ages 24 and 36 months (no stability coefficients were reported for the 42-month age level); a stability coefficient of .87 is listed for the Mental Scale across all age levels. The BSID-II provides Index Scores as low as $3\frac{1}{3}$ standard deviations below the mean (i.e., Index Score = 50), thereby demonstrating sufficiently strong floors for the Mental Scale across all age levels. Similarly, the Bayley has excellent item gradients at all age levels except the first month.

In summary, the BSID-II appears to possess good quality technical adequacy for all its respective age levels. In addition to its psychometric quality, the BSID-II incorporates a flexible administration format and is composed of bright, colorful, and stimulating materials and tasks that are inherently interesting to infants and young children (e.g., bells, colorful rings, dolls, and plastic toys).

Bracken Basic Concept Scale

Though the Bracken Basic Concept Scale (BBCS; Bracken, 1984) is not a traditional intelligence test, it assesses an important aspect of preschool children's (ages 2,6 to 8,0) cognitive functioning, foundational language concepts. Concepts according to Kagan (1966) are the fundamental agents of intelligence, and the multitude of basic concepts embedded in the directions and items of common preschool intelligence tests attest to their importance and ubiquitous nature of basic language concepts (Bracken, 1986a; Kaufman, 1978). Concept acquisition as measured by the BBCS correlates as high or higher with other comprehensive preschool intelligence tests as the various intelligence tests correlate among themselves. For example, in independent studies the BBCS correlated .65 with the Broad Cognitive Ability score of the Woodcock–Johnson Psycho-Educational Battery—Revised Tests of Cognitive Ability (WJ-R COG; McGrew, Werder, & Woodcock, 1991); .91 with the SB-IV test composite (Howell & Bracken, 1992); and, .80 with the Differential Ability Scale's General Cognitive Ability score (McIntosh, Wayland, Gridley, & Barnes, 1995).

The BBCS is an individually administered instrument that measures understanding of such foundational content areas as colors, comparatives, directions and positions, textures and materials, quantities, familial and gender relations, sequences, shapes, sizes, social or emotional states, and characteristics, and time. The BBCS provides a total test score with a mean of 100 and a standard deviation of 15 and subtest scores ($M = 10$, $SD = 3$) for each of seven subtests.

The BBCS examiner's manual reports median subtest reliabilities for the 3-, 4-, 5-, and 7-year age levels that range from .84 to .93. Reliabilities are not reported for the half-year 2,6 age level and the average subtest reliability for the 6-year age level is .73. Therefore, the BBCS demonstrates sufficient median subtest reliabilities for all ages except 2,6 and 6,0. The BBCS possesses excellent total test internal consistencies for all age levels with reliabilities ranging between .94 and .98, and an average reliability of .97 across all age levels.

Tables 5.2 and 5.4 of the BBCS examiner's manual outlines the adequacy of the instrument's subtest and total test ceilings and floors. Although the BBCS lacks sufficient subtest floors for ages 2,6 through 3,6, it has adequate floors for all other age levels. The BBCS total test ceiling and floor will assess all but the most extreme 1% of the children tested at all age levels. Also, the BBCS item gradients meet the stated criterion at all age levels. Finally, the BBCS manual presents several validity studies including studies of criterion-related and content validity.

The BBCS was developed to incorporate a nonverbal pointing response to items of verbal/conceptual content. Children are instructed to select the correct option on a stimulus plate that contains the keyed response and three distracters. With the employment of a nonverbal response mode, the verbal conceptual component of intelligence is assessed while avoiding the limitation of preschool children's less well developed expressive language skills. Additional benefits of the BBCS lie in its curriculum-based nature. Not only is the BBCS a norm-referenced instrument, but it has a companion curriculum, the *Bracken Concept Development Program* (Bracken, 1986b), which provides instruction for all of the concepts assessed by the scale. Together the curriculum and scale permit curriculum-based assessment of important foundational language skills.

Although intelligence, as assessed by traditional intelligence tests is not "teachable," basic concepts can be taught effectively (Blai, 1973; Central Arkansas Education Center, 1972; Moers & Harris, 1978). Given the instrument's overall technical quality, brief administration time, functional skill assessment, and strong relationship with preschool measures of intelligence, the scale appears to be a useful instrument for the assessment of preschool children's cognitive abilities (Bagnato, Neisworth, & Munson, 1989).

Differential Ability Scales

The Differential Ability Scales (DAS; Elliott, 1990a) comprise both a cognitive and achievement battery for the assessment of children between ages 2½ through 17 years. For the purposes of this chapter, only the cognitive battery for preschool children (ages 2,6 through 5,11) is discussed (see Elliott, Chapter 10, this volume, for a complete description of the DAS). The DAS manual describes the conceptualization of the preschool cognitive battery which is divided into two levels. The Lower Level is appropriate for children between ages 2,6 through 3,5 and includes Core subtests of Block Building, Verbal Comprehension, Picture Similarities, and Naming Vocabulary and the Diagnostic subtests Recall of Digits and Recognition of Pictures. Together the Core subtests yield a General Conceptual Ability (GCA) composite score. The DAS was designed to provide a strong measure of general intellectual abilities (g); to accomplish that goal the Diagnostic subtests were separated from the Core subtests, with the latter subtests contributing more to g than the former and constituting the GCA (Elliott, 1990b, 1990c).

The Upper Level (ages 3,6 through 5,11) is composed of the Core subtests Verbal Comprehension and Naming Vocabulary, which purport to assess Verbal Ability. Also, Picture Similarities, Pattern Construction, and Copying are core subtests which together assess Nonverbal Ability. The Verbal Ability and Nonverbal Ability scales, and a sixth subtest Early Number Concepts contribute to the GCA composite score. In addition to the Upper Level Core subtests, the DAS includes the following Diagnostic subtests: Block Building, Matching Letter-Like Forms, Recall of Digits, Recall of Objects, and Recognition of Pictures.

DAS subtest scores are reported as T scores ($M = 50, SD = 10$) and the GCA Scores and Cluster Scores are reported as normalized standard scores ($M = 100, SD = 15$). Percentiles and age equivalents are also presented in the manual. The technical manual reports internal consistency coefficients for the DAS subtests ranging from .66 to .90, indicating moderate to good subtest reliability. For the GCA, internal consistency coefficients are reported as .90 for lower-level preschool children (i.e., children ages 2,6 to 4,11) and .94 for upper-level preschool children (i.e., children ages 3,6 to 6,11). The DAS appears to have sufficient total test reliability for making important decisions about preschool children. The DAS manual reports subtest stability coefficients ranging from .38 to .97 for ages 3,6 to 6,11. Total test stability coefficients are reported to range from .89 to .94. Some DAS subtests evidence weak stability estimates (retest interval 2 to 6 weeks) but the GCA remains very stable over such a brief time period.

DAS subtest floors extend to −3 standard deviations with the exception of a few subtests at specific age levels (i.e., the Recognition of Pictures subtest has an insufficient floor at age 3,0 to 3,2, Recall of Objects is insufficient at ages 4,0 to 5,2, Matching Letter-Like Forms is inadequate at 4,6 to 4,8, and Speed of Processing is limited at ages 6,0 to 6,2). The DAS appears to have excellent total test floors at all age levels, indicating adequate ability to discriminate children of average intellectual functioning from children of below average intelligence. Similarly, the DAS demonstrates excellent item gradients for all preschool ages at the subtest and total test levels.

The DAS, in general, displays good technical characteristics for its respective preschool age levels. In addition, the DAS incorporates colorful materials and stimulating tasks which naturally maintain children's interest. The combination of psychometric quality, stimulating materials, and a sound theoretical orientation (i.e., a robust measure of g) make the DAS an appropriate tool for the assessment of preschool intelligence (Elliott, 1990b, 1990c; Keith, 1990).

Stanford–Binet Intelligence Scale:Fourth Edition

The SB-IV (Thorndike, Hagen, & Sattler, 1986) is the fourth edition of the Stanford–Binet Intelligence Scale. The SB-IV purports to measure intelligence among individuals 2 years through 24 years of age. The SB-IV theoretical model is a three-tier conceptualization. The first tier measures g or general intellectual ability; the second level assesses crystallized abilities, fluid-analytic abilities, and short-term memory; and the third level assesses three primary intellectual abilities: verbal reasoning, quantitative reasoning, and abstract/visual reasoning.

The SB-IV produces total test and area standard scores ($M = 100, SD = 16$) and subtest scores ($M = 50, SD = 8$). The examiner's manual reports excellent total test (Composite SAS) internal consistencies that range from .95 to .97 at all preschool age levels. The SB-IV also possesses excellent stability with reliabilities of .91 and .90 for 5-year-olds and 8-year-olds, respectively for the Composite SAS. The SB-IV subtest floors are sufficiently strong to discriminate retarded level functioning at ages 4,0 to 6,0. However, the SB-IV possesses many inadequate subtest floors at the 2,0- to 4,0-year age levels. Similarly, the SB-IV has insufficient total test floors for ages 2,0 to 3,4 but has adequate total test floors for all other age levels. The examiner's manual reports that it "does not discriminate adequately among the lowest 10 to 15 percent of the 2-year-old group" (pp. 7–8). The SB-IV fails to meet the desired item gradient criterion for ages 2,0 through 2,7 but meets the criterion at all other age levels. It appears that the SB-IV possesses sound technical qualities for all preschool age levels except at the very youngest ages of 2 to 3 years.

As one of its unique features, the SB-IV was designed to allow for adaptive test administration. That is, the examiner uses the child's performance on the Vocabulary subtest as a guide to determine the level at which the child will likely be appropriately challenged on each subsequent subtest. Adaptive test administration allows the examiner to adjust the difficulty level of the activities to the child's level of functioning. With adaptive test administration, examiners are less likely to frustrate low-functioning or very young examinees and are more likely to appropriately challenge children who are of higher intellectual functioning.

Wechsler Preschool and Primary Scale of Intelligence—Revised

The WPPSI-R (Wechsler, 1989) is an individually administered instrument for use with preschool children between the ages of 3 and 7 years. The scale was developed based on the theoretical orientation of global and multidimensional abilities rather than unique, single-faceted abilities. The WPPSI-R is comprised of 12 subtests: Object Assembly, Information, Geometric Design, Comprehension, Block Design, Arithmetic, Mazes, Vocabulary, Picture Completion, Similarities, Animal Pegs, and Sentences. Each subtest yields a scale score with a mean of 10 and a standard deviation of 3. The WPPSI-R also comprises Verbal and Performance Scale IQs and a Full Scale IQ; IQs are set with means of 100 and standard deviations of 15. The WPPSI-R also provides percentiles, age equivalents, classifications, and prorated IQs when an examiner is unable to administer all subtests or invalidates one or more subtests.

The WPPSI-R examiner's manual reports internal consistency coefficients of .90 to .97 for ages 3 to 7 years, providing evidence of excellent total test reliability. Following a criterion of .80 subtest internal consistency, the WPPSI-R appears to have sufficient reliability at ages 3 to 5 years for the Verbal subtests; however, some Verbal subtest reliabilities for ages 5½, 6, 6½, and 7 years fall below the .80 criterion with some coefficients in the .50's. For the Performance subtests, the WPPSI-R demonstrates good subtest internal consistency for all subtests except Object Assembly for ages 3, 3½, 4, and 4½. However, Performance subtest internal consistencies fall below the .80 criterion for ages 5 years and above, with the exception of Block Design and Picture Completion subtests. Also, Object Assembly demonstrates insufficient reliability at all age levels with an average internal consistency of .63. When applying a stability criterion of .80 for subtests and .90 for scale scores, the WPPSI-R meets the criteria only for Block Design (.80), Information (.81), Verbal IQ (.90) and Full Scale IQ (.91). All other subtests and the Performance IQ evidence lower estimates of stability than the desired criterion.

The WPPSI-R has sufficiently strong subtest floors to distinguish functioning at the retarded level at all age levels except 3 years. Similarly, at the total test level, the WPPSI-R floors extend to at least 2 standard deviations below the mean at all ages except 3 years. The WPPSI-R evidences appropriate subtest and total test item gradients at all age levels. Thus, the WPPSI-R is sensitive to small incremental differences in ability at all age levels assessed by the instrument.

The WPPSI-R has technical adequacy strengths and weaknesses across its full range of ages. The scale has excellent reliability for the middle-most ages of four and five years but has weaker reliabilities for older preschool children. Conversely, the WPPSI-R has acceptable subtest and total test floors for all but the youngest age level (i.e., 3 years). Also, WPPSI-R stability tends to fall fairly consistently short of desired levels. Clinicians should consider these limitations and the age of their client when considering the WPPSI-R.

The Woodcock–Johnson Psycho-Educational Battery—Revised Tests of Cognitive Ability

The WJ-R COG (Woodcock & Johnson, 1989) is the cognitive component of the Woodcock–Johnson Psycho-Educational Battery—Revised. The battery was designed to assess cognitive abilities, scholastic aptitudes, and achievement. The WJ-R COG scale is divided into two parts: the Standard Battery and the Supplemental Battery, which may be used alone or in combination. The WJ-R COG purports to measure the following abilities: Broad Cognitive Ability, Cognitive Factors including Long-Term Retrieval, Short-Term Memory, Processing Speed, Auditory Processing, Visual Processing, Comprehension-Knowledge, and Fluid Reasoning, Oral Language, Differential Aptitudes including Oral Language, Reading, Mathematics, Written Language, and Knowledge, and Intra-Cognitive Discrepancies. The scale is standardized for use with individuals between the ages of 2 years through adult. The WJ-R COG provides standard scores ($M = 100$; $SD = 15$), percentile ranks, and classifications.

A brief section in the WJ-R COG is provided which describes beneficial techniques for the administration of the scale to preschool children. For preschool examinees, the WJ-R COG standard battery includes five tests which comprise the Early Development Scale: Memory for Names, Memory for Sentences, Incomplete Words, Visual Closure, and Picture Vocabulary. For our purposes, only the subtests that make up the Early Development Scale are included in our review of the WJ-COG (see Woodcock, Chapter 12, this volume, for a complete description of the WJ-R).

The WJ-R COG manual reports subtest internal consistency coefficients that range from .624 to .941 for 2-, 4-, and 6-year-old children, with an average reliability of .848 for across these ages. Early Development Scale reliabilities of .912, .955, and .957 are reported for children of ages 2, 4, and 6 years, respectively. The WJ-R COG demonstrates acceptable internal consistency at the subtest level and excellent reliability at the total test level. Test–retest reliability is reported in the WJ-R COG manual for only the Visual Matching and Cross-Out subtests which are appropriate only for children of 6-years and older. The stability coefficients at the 6-year age level are reported as .734 and .640 for the Visual Matching and Cross-Out subtests, respectively. A separate study investigating the stability of the WJ-R COG is reported; however, coefficients are not provided for respective age levels (McGrew, Werder, & Woodcock, 1991). Furthermore, examiners cannot be certain whether preschool respondents were appropriately represented in the sample. Without test–retest reliability data, practitioners cannot be certain that the scores they obtain on the WJ-R COG or the abilities they assess will remain stable for any period of time.

The WJ-R COG appears to possess sufficiently strong floors for preschool children; the Broad Cognitive Ability standard score for a child earning a raw score of "1" on each subtest ranges from $2\frac{1}{3}$ standard deviations below the mean (for children of 2 years of age) to $6\frac{1}{2}$ standard deviations below the mean (for age level 6–11). In addition, the WJ-R COG manual provides considerable evidence of content, criterion-related, and construct validity.

The WJ-R COG demonstrates appropriate technical quality for all its standardized age levels, with the exception of its limited evidence of stability. In addition, the WJ-R COG offers colorful materials and tasks that are stimulating to young examinees. It should be noted that scoring the WJ-R COG is extremely cumbersome; however, computerized scoring is available and requires the examiner only to enter subtest raw scores in order to obtain a comprehensive printout of data.

System to Plan Early Childhood Services

The system to plan early childhood services (SPECS; Bagnato & Neisworth, 1990) is not an intelligence test but a system designed to plan service delivery based on data derived from intelligence tests and other measures of preschool children's functioning. The service delivery program is unique because the intent of its authors was to provide a systematic linkage between assessment results and follow-up interventions. SPECS is comprised of three rating forms, Developmental Specs, Team Specs, and Program Specs.

Developmental Specs is a rating device that is completed by each member of the multidisciplinary or transdisciplinary team, using whatever data (assessment or otherwise) they have available upon which to base their ratings. Twelve team members are listed on the record form, including parents as equal team members, and a thirteenth category, "Other," allows for other appropriate individuals to be included in the "team" when appropriate. Categories rated by team members include typical preschool intellectual factors (i.e., Communication, Sensorimotor, and Cognition), as well as Physical and adaptive/affective behaviors (i.e., Self-Regulation and Self/Social). Each category includes two to four broad items (e.g., Receptive Language and Expressive Language comprise the Communication Domain) that are rated on a descriptive 1- to 5-scale.

Team Specs is a compilation of all the ratings generated by the respective multidisciplinary or transdisciplinary team members. One unique aspect of the Team Specs is that it does not use a simple numerical averaging strategy to quantify or typify the child's behaviors, but rather it requires all team members to discuss the rationale for their ratings and for the group to conclude with a consensus rating after all team members have contributed their views, ratings, and compromises. The resulting consensus ratings of the child's abilities are the bases on which program planning is developed.

The third and final aspect of SPECS is Program Specs. Program Specs is a fairly comprehensive list of primary service delivery options, each with individual service characteristics most appropriate for each individual primary service nested below. For example, the primary service delivery area *Behavior Therapy* has five nested issues that must be addressed: (1) Is an individual behavior management plan needed? (2) Are special reinforcement strategies needed? (3) Are special disciplinary techniques needed? (4) What types of behavior management strategies are warranted? (5) What number of specialized therapy sessions (e.g., school psychologist, counselor, or social worker) would be appropriate per week? Program Specs allows for the systematic identification of the types of services most needed, as well as the amount of service warranted, and the personnel best suited to provide the services.

In combination, Developmental Specs allows all team members to gather information in their typical professional modes (e.g., psychoeducational evaluations, social/home interviews, and pediatric medical visits) and incorporate these data into summary ratings. The individual summaries are then compiled through consensus into the Team Specs summary to provide a unified picture of the team's impressions of the child's psychosocial–physical strengths, weaknesses, and needs. Program Specs then allows for the systematic identification of services available to remediate the child's identified weaknesses. In total, SPECS provides a useful problem identification and service delivery model for preschool assessment.

As indicated previously, many of the newly developed or recently revised preschool tests illustrate higher standards of technical quality, have addressed the limitations of previous instrumentation, and more fully consider the truly unique characteristics of preschool children. However, psychometric limitations still remain among many preschool instruments, especially those intended for children below the age of 4 (Bracken, 1987). One of the most pressing preschool assessment problems has not been adequately addressed, the young child's inability to remain seated for very long periods of time or attend to materials for extended periods. Test authors and publishers are hard pressed to address this latter issue, however, because reduction in test length and a briefer administration ultimately compromise content sampling and scale technical characteristics. As always, clinical skill is what is needed most to produce a valid assessment by bridging the gap between examinee and instrumentation foibles.

Intelligence tests should be considered as only one facet of a multisource, multimethod evaluation. Flanagan and Alfonso (1995) followed up on Bracken's (1987) review of preschool intelligence

TABLE 24.1. Desirable Psychometric Criteria for Preschool Instruments

Criterion	Description
Internal consistency	.90 total test reliabilities .80 median subtest reliabilities
Test–retest reliability	.90 total test reliabilities for a 2–6-week interval
Floor	−2 standard deviations for total test and subtests, with −3 to −4 *SD* preferred
Ceiling	+2 standard deviations for total test and subtests, with +3 to +4 *SD* preferred
Item gradient	Change in single raw score equal to or less than change of 1/3 standard score standard deviation (i.e., three raw score points =/< 1 *SD*)
Norm table age divisions	For greater sensitivity, 1- to 2-month norm table divisions preferred over existing 3- to 4-month divisions
Predictive validity	Preschool tests should assess those skills that best predict future intellectual and/or academic abilities (e.g., language more than motor; reasoning more than imitation)
Skills assessed	Preschool tests should assess functional or remedial skills (e.g., basic concepts, language skills, and premath skills); skills that allow for intervention planning
Easily understood test directions	Preschool test directions should be short, simple, and easily understood; test directions should be more easily understood than the skill assessed by the subtest items
Test materials	Materials should be colorful, stimulating, easily handled, and inherently interesting and should maximize examinee participation and expression
Sample/teaching items	Test should allow for sample or teaching items to teach the nature of the assessment task or allow for failure without penalty until the child's understanding of the task demands is certain
Multicultural representation	Standardization sample and all test stimulus materials (e.g., pictures) should contain a representative proportion and nonstereotypical representation of ethnic groups and genders
Administration time	Less than 1 hour, unless the test is designed to be administered in more than one session
Response guessing factor	Items with multiple response options should have a sufficient number of options to decrease chance performance associated with guessing; discontinue rules should take into consideration chance level performance associated with guessing
Theoretical orientation	Preschool tests should reflect and be supported by a sound theoretical orientation (e.g., Crystallized vs. fluid intelligence)
Descriptive results	Tests should provide a full range of descriptors of the child's performance including standard scores, percentile ranks, classifications, and age equivalents
Interpretation	Test manuals should include a description of the ways in which the test is to be interpreted and suggest how the results can lead to intervention
Remediation	Test manuals should suggest direct linkages between attained test results and intervention strategies to remediate identified weaknesses or delays

tests and suggested that intelligence test data be used only as an aid in making educational decisions. In addition, Flanagan and Alfonso stated that intelligence test scores should be used only to report a child's current intellectual functioning because of inherent inadequacies of stability and criterion-related validity. Therefore, practitioners are cautioned about making predictive statements based solely on intelligence test scores.

RECOMMENDATIONS FOR THE DEVELOPMENT OF PRESCHOOL INTELLIGENCE TESTS

With the increased need for appropriate preschool intelligence measures comes an increased need for standards to guide test developers, publishers, and clinicians. Following are characteristics that are suggested as guidelines for future development of preschool intelligence tests. Some of the characteristics have been discussed previously but are reported in Table 24.1 (see opposite) in a complete and succinct listing of desirable test criteria.

REFERENCES

American Psychological Association. (1985). *Standards for educational and psychological testing.* Washington: Author.

Ammons, R. B., & Holmes, J. C. (1949). The Full-Range Picture Vocabulary Tests: III, Results for a preschool age population. *Child Development, 20,* 5–14.

Anastasi, A. (1988). *Psychological testing* (6th ed.). New York: Macmillan.

Azar, B. (1995). Searching for intelligence beyond 'g'. *The APA Monitor, 26*(1), 25.

Bagnato, S. J., & Neisworth, J. T. (1990). *SPECS: System to plan early childhood services.* Circle Pines, MN: American Guidance Services.

Bagnato, S. J., & Neisworth, J. T. (1991). *Assessment for early intervention: Best practices for professionals.* New York: Guilford Press.

Bagnato, S. J., & Neisworth, J. T. (1994). A national study of the social and treatment "invalidity" of intelligence testing for early intervention. *School Psychology Quarterly, 9*(2), 81–102.

Bagnato, S. J., Neisworth, J. T., & Munson, S. M. (1989). *Linking developmental assessment and early intervention: Curriculum-based assessment.* Rockville, MD: Aspen.

Barnett, D., W., Macmann, G. M., & Carey, K. T. (1992). Early interventions and the assessment of developmental skills: Challenges and directions. *Topics in Early Childhood Special Education, 12,* 21–43.

Bayley, N. (1949). Consistency and variability in the growth of intelligence from birth to eighteen years. *Journal of Genetic Psychology, 75,* 156–168.

Bayley, N. (1969). *Bayley Scales of Infant Development.* San Antonio, TX: Psychological Corporation.

Bayley, N. (1993). *Bayley Scales of Infant Development—Second Edition.* San Antonio, TX: Psychological Corporation.

Benner, S. M. (1992). *Assessing young children with special needs.* New York: Longman.

Blai, B. (1973). Concept learning–mastery in Harcum Junior College Laboratory Nursery School/Kindergarten. *Psychology, 10,* 35–36.

Bloom, B. S. (1964). *Stability and change in human characteristics.* New York: Wiley.

Boehm, A. E. (1986). *Manual for the Boehm Test of Basic Concepts—Preschool.* San Antonio: Psychological Corporation.

Bornstein, M. H., & Sigman, M. D. (1986). Continuity in mental development from infancy. *Child Development, 57,* 251–274.

Bracken, B. A. (1984). *Bracken Basic Concept Scale.* San Antonio, TX: Psychological Corporation.

Bracken, B. A. (1985). Critical review of the Kaufman Assessment Battery for Children (K-ABC). *School Psychology Review, 14,* 21–36.

Bracken, B. A. (1986a). Incidence of basic concepts in the directions of five commonly used American tests of intelligence. *School Psychology International, 7,* 1–10.

Bracken, B. A. (1986b). *Bracken concept development program.* San Antonio, TX: Psychological Corporation.

Bracken, B. A. (1987). Limitations of preschool instruments and standards for minimal levels of technical adequacy. *Journal of Psychoeducational Assessment, 4,* 313–326.

Bracken, B. A. (1991a). The assessment of preschool children with the McCarthy Scales of Children's Abilities. In B. A. Bracken (Ed.), *The psychoeducational assessment of preschool children* (pp. 53–85). Needham Heights, MA: Allyn & Bacon.

Bracken, B. A. (1991b). The clinical observation of preschool assessment behavior. In B. A. Bracken (Ed.), *The psychoeducational assessment of preschool children* (pp. 40–52). Needham Heights, MA: Allyn & Bacon.

Bracken, B. A. (1994). Advocating for effective preschool assessment practices: A comment on Bagnato and Neisworth. *School Psychology Quarterly, 9*(2), 103–108.

Bracken, B. A., & Barnett, D. W. (1987). The technical side of preschool screening and assessment. *Preschool Interests, 2,* 6–10.

Bracken, B. A., Bagnato, S. J., & Barnett, D. W. (1991). *Early childhood assessment.* Position statement adopted by the National Association of School Psychologists Delegated Assembly, March 24, 1991.

Bracken, B. A., Howell, K. K., & Crain, M. R. (1993). Prediction of Caucasian and African-American preschool children's fluid and crystallized intelligence: Contributions of maternal characteristics and home environment. *Journal of Clinical Child Psychology, 22,* 455–464.

Bracken, B. A., Keith, L. K., & Walker, K. C. (1994). Assessment of preschool behavior and social-emotional functioning: A review of thirteen third-party instruments. *Assessment in Rehabilitation and Exceptionality, 1,* 331–346.

Bracken, B. A., Prasse, D. P., & McCallum, R. S. (1984). Peabody Picture Vocabulary Test—Revised: An appraisal and review. *School Psychology Review, 13,* 49–60.

Brenner, A. (1959). A new gestalt test for measuring readiness for school. *Merrill–Palmer Quarterly, 6,* 1–25.

Cassidy, T., & Lynn, R. (1991). Achievement motivation, educational attainment, cycles of disadvantage and social competence: Some longitudinal data. *British Journal of Educational Psychology, 61,* 1–12.

Central Arkansas Education Center. (1972). *The detection and remediation of deficiencies in verbal understanding of first grade students.* Little Rock, AK: Author.

Christensen, A., Margolin, G., & Sullaway, M. (1992). Inter-parental agreement on child behavior problems. *Journal of Genetic Psychology, 92,* 103–110.

Clarke, A. M. (1982). Developmental discontinuities: An approach to assessing their nature. In L. A. Bond & J. M. Joffe (Eds.), *Facilitating infant and early childhood development* (pp. 58–77). Hanover, NH: University Press of New England.

Darwin, C. (1877). A biographical sketch of an infant. *Mind, 2,* 285–294.

Denno, D. W. (1986). Victim, offender, and situational characteristics of violent crime. *Journal of Criminal Law and Criminology, 77,* 1142–1158.

Drotar, D., & Sturm, L. (1988). Prediction of intellectual development in young children with early histories of nonorganic failure-to-thrive. *Journal of Pediatric Psychology, 13,* 281–296.

DuBose, R. F. (1976). Predictive value of infant intelligence scales with multiply handicapped children. *American Journal of Mental Deficiency, 81,* 388–390.

Dunn, L. M., & Dunn, L. M. (1981). *Peabody Picture Vocabulary Test—Revised.* Circle Pines, MN: American Guidance Service.

Earls, F. (1980). The prevalence of behavior problems in 3-year-old children. *Journal of the American Academy of Child Psychiatry, 19,* 439–452.

Education for All Handicaped Children Act of 1975, Pub. No. 94-142.

Education of the Handicapped Act Amendments of 1986, Pub. No. 99-457.

Elliott, C. D. (1990a). *The Differential Ability Scales: Administration and scoring manual.* San Antonio, TX: Psychological Corporation.

Elliott, C. D. (1990b). *The Differential Ability Scales: Introductory and technical handbook.* San Antonio, TX: Psychological Corporation.

Elliott, C. D. (1990c). The nature and structure of children's abilities: Evidence from the Differential Ability Scales. *Journal of Psychoeducational Assessment, 8,* 376–390.

Flanagan, D. P., & Alfonso, V. C. (1995). A critical review of the technical characteristics of new and recently revised intelligence tests for preschool children. *Journal of Psychoeducational Assessment, 13,* 66–90.

Flynn, J. R. (1984). The mean IQ of Americans: Massive gains 1932 to 1978. *Psychological Bulletin, 95,* 29–51.

Goodenough, F. L. (1926). *Measurement of intelligence by drawings.* Chicago: World Book.

Goodenough, F. L. (1949). *Mental testing.* New York: Rinehart.

Halverson, C. F. Jr., & Waldrop, M. F. (1976). Relations between preschool activity and aspects of intellectual and social behavior at age 7 1/2. *Developmental Psychology, 12*(2), 107–112.

Hodges, W., & Cooper, M. (1981). Head Start and Follow Through: Influences on intellectual development. *Journal of Special Education, 15*(3), 221–237.

Honzik, M. P. (1938). The constancy of mental test performance during the preschool period. *Journal of Genetic Psychology, 42,* 285–302.

Honzik, M. P., Hutchings, J. J., & Burnip, S. R. (1965). Birth record assessments and test performance at eight months. *American Journal of Diseases of Childhood, 109,* 416–426.

Howell, K. K., & Bracken, B. A. (1992). Clinical utility of the Bracken Basic Concept Scale as a preschool intellectual screener: Comparison with the Stanford–Binet for African-American children. *Journal of Clinical Child Psychology, 21*(3), 255–261.

Huberty, T. J. (1986). Relationship of the WISC-R factors to the Adaptive Behavior Scale—School Edition in a referral sample. *Journal of School Psychology, 24,* 155–162.

Hunter, J. E., & Hunter, R. F. (1984). Validity and utility of alternative predictors of job performance. *Psychological Bulletin, 96,* 72–98.

Jensen, A. R. (1966). Cumulative deficit in compensatory education. *Journal of School Psychology, 4,* 37–48.

Kagan, J. (1966). A developmental approach to conceptual growth. In H. J. Klausmeir & C. W. Harris (Eds.), *Analysis of concept learning* (pp. 97–116). New York: Academic Press.

Kaufman, A. S. (1978). The importance of basic concepts in individual assessment of preschool children. *Journal of School Psychology, 16,* 207–211.

Kaufman, A. S., & Kaufman, N. L. (1983). *Kaufman Assessment Battery for Children.* Circle Pines, MN: American Guidance Service.

Keith, T. Z. (1990). Confirmatory and hierarchical confirmatory analysis of the Differential Ability Scales. *Journal of Psychoeducational Assessment, 8,* 391–405.

Kelley, M. F., & Surbeck, E. (1991). History of preschool assessment. In B. A. Bracken (Ed.), *The psychoeducational assessment of preschool children* (2nd ed., pp. 1–17). Needham Heights, MA: Allyn & Bacon.

Kirk, S. A., McCarthy, J. J., & Kirk, W. D. (1968). *Illinois Test of Psycholinguistic Abilities.* Urbana: University of Illinois Press.

Kuhlmann, F. (1922). *A handbook of mental tests.* Baltimore: Warwick & York.

Leiter, R. G. (1948). *International Performance Scale.* Chicago: Stoelting.

Lichtenstein, R., & Ireton, H. (1984). *Preschool screening: Identifying young children with developmental and educational problems.* Orlando: Grune & Stratton.

Lidz, C. S. (1991). Issues in the assessment of preschool children. In B. A. Bracken (Ed.), *The Psychoeducational assessment of preschool children* (pp. 18–31). Needham Heights, MA: Allyn & Bacon.

Lindholm, B., & Touliatos, J. (1982). Checklist agreement among observers of children. *Psychology in the Schools, 19,* 548–551.

Lindsay, P. H., Shapiro, A., Musselman, C., & Wilson, A. (1988). Predicting language development in deaf children using subscales of the Leiter International Performance Scale. *Canadian Journal of Psychology, 42,* 144–162.

Martin, R. P. (1991). Assessment of social and emotional behavior. In B. A. Bracken (Ed.), *The psychoeducational assessment of preschool children, second edition* (pp. 450–464). Needham Heights, MA: Allyn & Bacon.

McIntosh, D. E., Wayland, S. J., Gridley, B., & Barnes, L. L. B. (1995). Relationship between the Bracken Basic Concept Scale and the Differential Ability Scales with a preschool sample. *Journal of Psychoeducational Assessment, 13,* 39–48.

McCarthy, D. (1972). *McCarthy Scales of Children's Abilities.* San Antonio, TX: Psychological Corporation.

McGrew, K. S., Werder, J. K., & Woodcock, R. W. (1991). *Woodcock–Johnson technical manual.* Chicago: Riverside.

Meisels, S. J. (1987). Uses and abuses of developmental screening and school readiness testing. *Young Children, 42,* 68–73.

Miller, L. C. (1964). Q-Sort agreement among observers of children. *American Journal of Orthopsychiatry, 34,* 71–75.

Miller, L. T., & Vernon, P. A. (1992). The general factor in short-term memory, intelligence, and reaction time. *Intelligence, 16,* 5–29.

Moers, F., & Harris, J. (1978). Instruction in basic concepts and first-grade achievement. *Psychology in the Schools, 15,* 84–86.

Novick, J., Rosenfeld, E., Bloch, D., & Dawson, D. (1966). Ascertaining deviant behavior in children. *Journal of Consulting Psychology, 30*(3), 230–238.

Nunnally, J. C. (1978). *Psychometric theory.* New York: McGraw-Hill.

Paal, N., Skinner, S., & Reddig, C. (1988). The relationship of non-verbal intelligence measures to academic achievement among deaf adolescents. *Journal of Rehabilitation of the Deaf, 21,* 8–11.

Poon, L. W., Messner, S., Martin, P., Noble, C. A., Clayton, G. M., & Johnson, M. A. (1992). The influences of cognitive resources on adaptation and old age. *International Journal on Aging and Human Development, 34,* 31–46.

Poteat, G., Wuensch, K., & Gregg, N. (1988). An investigation of differential prediction with the WISC-R. *Journal of School Psychology, 26,* 59–68.

Reissman, F. (1962). *The culturally deprived child.* New York: Harper & Row.

Rose, S. A., & Wallace, I. F. (1985). Visual recognition memory: A predictor of later cognitive functioning patterns. *Child Development, 56,* 843–852.

Rubin, R. A., & Balow, B. (1979). Measures of infant development and socioeconomic status as predictors of later intelligence and school achievement. *Developmental Psychology, 15,* 225–227.

Salvia, J., & Ysseldyke, J. E. (1988). *Assessment in special remedial education.* Boston: Houghton Mifflin.

Short, R. J., Simeonsson, R. J., & Huntington, G. S. (1990). Early intervention: Implications of Public Law 99-457 for professional child psychology. *Professional Psychology: Research and Practice, 21,* 88–93.

Siebert, L. A. (1962). Otis IQ scores of delinquents, *Journal of Clinical Psychology, 18,* 517.

Stanton, W., Feehan, M., McGee, R., & Silva, P. (1990). The relative value of reading ability and IQ as predictors of teacher-reported behavior problems. *Journal of Learning Disabilities, 23,* 514–517.

Stogdill, R. M. (1948). Personal factors associated with leadership: A survey of the literature. *Journal of Psychology, 25,* 35–71.

Stutsman, R. (1931). *Mental measurement of preschool children.* New York: World Book.

Thorndike, R. L., Hagen, L. P., & Sattler, J. M. (1986). *Stanford–Binet Intelligence Scale: Fourth edition.* Chicago: Riverside.

Thurstone, L. L. (1938). *Primary mental abilities.* Chicago: University of Chicago Press.

Vanderveer, B., & Scheweid, E. (1974). Infant assessment: Stability of mental functioning in young retarded children. *American Journal of Mental Deficiency, 79,* 1–4.

Walker, K. C., & Bracken, B. A. (1994). *Preschool behavior rating scales: Do parents agree on their child's behaviors?* Paper presented at the Mid-South Regional Annual Conference for School Psychologists, Huntsville, AL.

Wechsler, D. (1967). *Wechsler Preschool and Primary Scale of Intelligence.* San Antonio, TX: Psychological Corporation.

Wechsler, D. (1989). *Wechsler Preschool and Primary Scale of Intelligence—Revised.* San Antonio, TX: Psychological Corporation.

Wellman, B. L. (1932). Some new bases for interpretation of the IQ. *Journal of Genetic Psychology, 41,* 116–126.

Woodcock, R. W., & Johnson, M. B. (1989). *Woodcock–Johnson Psycho-Educational Battery—Revised.* Chicago: Riverside.

CHAPTER 25

The Cognitive Assessment of Limited English Proficient and Bilingual Children

—=⊸∘⊹∘⊷=—

EMILIA C. LOPEZ

THIS CHAPTER PRESENTS research, theory, and practice issues concerning the cognitive assessment of children from limited English proficient (LEP) and bilingual backgrounds. Current and future assessment trends are discussed while examining the unique problems inherent in measuring the cognitive skills of this population.

BACKGROUND AND DEFINITIONS

According to the U.S. Bureau of the Census (1990), 31.8 million Americans speak a language other than English at home, an increase from 23.1 million a decade ago. Spanish, French, German, Italian, Chinese, Tagalog, Polish, Korean, Vietnamese, and Portuguese are the 10 most common languages spoken in the United States. The largest groups of immigrants who speak a language other than English are Hispanics and Asian/Pacific Islanders. Spanish-speaking immigrants include individuals from Caribbean countries (e.g., Cuba, Dominican Republic, and Puerto Rico), Central American countries (e.g., Mexico and Honduras), and South American countries (e.g., Ecuador and Peru). Asian and Pacific Islanders are the fastest growing population of immigrants and are expected to constitute 4% of the population by the year 2000. The languages spoken by Asian and Pacific Islanders are diverse and include Cantonese, Chamorro, Hmong, Illocano, Japanese, Khmer, Korean, New Guinean, Mandarin, Tagalog, Thai, Vietnamese, and Yao (Cheng, Ima, & Labovitz, 1994).

The nation's linguistic diversity is reflected in our school systems where educators often work with significant numbers of children from LEP and bilingual backgrounds. In New York City, for example, there are individual schools in which more than 50 languages and dialects are spoken by the student population (New York City Public Schools, 1993). Similar profiles can be found in large metropolitan areas within the states of California, Texas, and Florida (Center for Research on Elementary and Middle Schools, 1990).

The term "limited English proficient" refers to individuals who (1) were not born in the United States and whose native language is other than English, or (2) come from environments in which a language other than English is dominant (U.S. Department of Education, 1994, p. 21). LEP children are typically described as dominant in their native language because their English-language skills are significantly less well developed. For the period 1992 to 1993, the U.S. Department of Education (1994) estimated that a total of 2,735,962 LEP students were enrolled in public and nonpublic schools in the United States. However, these statistics may not be accurate due to inconsistencies in the implementation of definitions, methods, and criteria found throughout the country. Methods used by different states to identify LEP students include student records, teacher observations, teacher interviews, referrals, parent information, student grades, home language surveys, informal assessments, language proficiency tests, achievement tests, and criterion-referenced tests. In addition, each state may use a different criteria for any one method (e.g., states using language proficiency tests to determine LEP classification may use different tests and different cutoff scores to identify LEP students) (U.S. Department of Education, 1994).

As children acquire more advanced skills in English, they may be described as *bilingual.* The term "bilingual" refers to children who have developed skills in some areas (i.e., listening, speaking, reading, and writing) in two languages. Balanced bilinguals are individuals who attain an equal level of proficiency in more than one language and in all aspects of language use (Hamayan & Damico, 1991). True balanced bilinguals are rare because first- and second-language skills rarely develop equally well across all areas. Instead, most bilingual children demonstrate varying degrees of language proficiency within English and their native languages (Hakuta, 1987).

Language proficiency is defined as "the degree of control one has over the language in question" (Hamayan & Damico, 1991, p. 42). Children first acquire proficiency in a second language at the basic interpersonal communicative skills (BICS) level (Cummins, 1984). BICS entails acquiring language skills needed to communicate in socially related situations with family, peers, teachers, and other school personnel. As LEP and bilingual children are exposed to academic types of activities in English, they acquire cognitive academic language proficiency skills (CALPS), or language skills that are needed in cognitively demanding classroom situations. CALPS provides LEP and bilingual children with the English language skills needed to participate during academic types of discussions as well as during writing and reading activities. The research indicates that second language learners need 2 to 3 years to acquire BICS and a minimum of 5 to 7 years to acquire CALPS in the second language.

LEGISLATIVE GUIDELINES AND PROFESSIONAL STANDARDS RELEVANT TO LEP AND BILINGUAL CHILDREN

LEP and bilingual students are often referred for special education testing because of low achievement levels and language difficulties (Figueroa, 1989; Ortiz, 1988). Within the special education context, cognitive measures are administered for the purposes of predicting achievement levels, classifying, placing, and determining curriculum or language intervention needs. Children receiving mental health services within clinical settings are often evaluated to determine treatment needs and plans. A number of legislative regulations and professional standards provide guidelines for educators and psychologists involved in assessing the cognitive abilities of children from LEP and bilingual backgrounds.

Diana v. State Board of Education (1970) is perhaps the most influential court case concerning assessment practices for this population of children (Figueroa, 1990). The suit was brought to court on behalf of a small group of Mexican-American children who had been placed in programs for the mentally retarded in California. It was argued that the children had been misclassified on the basis of culturally biased IQ tests administered in English. The court established that children must be assessed in their native or primary language for special education placement.

The Education for All Handicapped Children Act of 1975, or Public Law 94-142, provided all children with disabilities, including LEP and bilingual children with disabilities, with the right to a free and appropriate education. It also stressed that testing should be conducted in the native language or primary mode of communication unless it is clearly not possible to do so. In 1986, these same rights were extended to all children with disabilities between the ages of 3 to 5 years through Public Law 99-457 (Education of the Handicapped Amendments). Recently, Congress amended the Education for all Handicapped Children Act, now referred to as the Individuals with Disabilities Education Act (IDEA; 1990). IDEA emphasizes the use of nondiscriminatory assessment methods. Evaluation procedures should be selected and administered to prevent cultural or racial discrimination, and assessment tools must be validated for the purposes for which they are used (Hardman, Drew, Egan, & Wolf, 1993).

Professional standards in the field of psychology also provide general guidelines for psychological assessment. Chapter 13 of the Standards for Educational and Psychological Testing (American Educational Research Association, American Psychological Association, National Council on Measurement in Education, 1985), "Testing linguistic minorities," includes two guidelines particularly relevant to the cognitive assessment of children with LEP and bilingual profiles. Standard 13.4 refers to the need to establish the reliability and validity of translated tests with the linguistic groups to be tested. Standard 13.7 states that "English language proficiency should not be determined solely with tests that demand only a single linguistic skill" (p. 75) and suggests that a wider range of skills should be assessed. This last standard is relevant to cognitive assessment because the establishment of language proficiency is the first step in determining the language(s) that should be used to administer cognitive measures.

The American Psychological Association's (1990) *Guidelines for Providers of Psychological Services to Ethnic, Linguistic, and Culturally Diverse Populations* summons psychologists to acknowledge the influence of ethnicity and culture on behavior and to take those factors into account when working with ethnic/racial groups. The guidelines also urge psychologists to consider the validity of instruments or procedures utilized with minority populations and to interpret data within the context of the cultural and linguistic characteristics of individuals assessed.

Finally, the National Association of School Psychologists' (NASP) *Standards for the Provision of School Psychological Services* (NASP, 1992) also address nonbiased assessment issues relevant to individuals with LEP and bilingual backgrounds. Standard 3.5.3 states the following:

1. Assessment procedures are chosen to maximize the student's opportunities to be successful in the general culture, while respecting the student's ethnic background.

2. Multifaceted assessment batteries are used which include a focus on the student's strengths.

3. Communications are held in the client's dominant spoken language or alternative communication system. All student information is interpreted in the context of the student's socio-cultural background and the setting in which she/he is functioning.

4. Assessment techniques are used only by personnel professionally trained in their use and in a manner consistent with these *Standards*.

5. School psychologists promote the development of objective, valid, and reliable assessment techniques.

6. Interpretation of assessment results is based upon empirically validated research. (Thomas & Grimes, 1995, p. 1166)

Overall, legislative mandates and professional standards relevant to psychological assessment provide some general guidelines for educators and psychologists as to the implementation of appropriate assessment practices. The bottom line is that practitioners are left to implement those guidelines and mandates at a time when the fields of education and psychology are confronted with many questions regarding testing bias, a lack of assessment resources (e.g., shortage of instruments validated with a variety of language groups), and a questionable knowledge base as to how to assess children from LEP and bilingual backgrounds.

ASSESSMENT ISSUES AND PROCEDURES

Test Bias and Cognitive Assessment of LEP and Bilingual Children

Cognitive ability measures are considered biased when they do not predict equally for different group's achievements (Scarr, 1994). Test bias is measured by examining the external or predictive validity and the internal or construct validity of cognitive measures (Jensen, 1976). According to Figueroa (1990), "With children who are clearly not proficient in English, there are no research data on bias in intelligence tests" (p. 685). Because LEP children are usually excluded from normative samples, it is not surprising that we know little about the validity of cognitive measures with this population.

Major reviews of the literature on testing bias indicate that currently available measures of cognitive functioning do not appear to be biased towards English-proficient children from bilingual backgrounds (e.g., Reynolds & Kaiser, 1990). However, these findings remain highly controversial and questionable (see Helms, Chapter 26, this volume) because of a number of flaws in the empirical literature.

One major problem is that investigations related to test bias continue to fail to measure bilingual children's levels of language proficiency (e., g., Argulewicz & Abel, 1984; Bracken & Fouad, 1987; Dean, 1980; Mishra, 1981; Valencia, 1985). This is despite the fact that many of the test bias studies were conducted with samples of children who lived in homes in which a language other than English was spoken (e.g., Mexican-American children whose home language is Spanish). Studies that attempted to take some language factors into consideration (e.g., Valencia, Henderson, & Rankin, 1981) often used informal measures of language proficiency (e.g., teachers' judgments and children's preferences) with questionable validity (Lemmon & Goggin, 1989). In addition, the investigators typically failed to describe the characteristics of the informal assessment instruments that were utilized.

According to Figueroa (1990), "The literature on bilingualism, second-language acquisition, bilingual education, and the measurement of language proficiency are generally overlooked or omitted from considerations of bias in intelligence tests" (p. 685). A typical example of this point is that examiners' judgments were used in some test bias studies to determine the children's level of language proficiency in English (e.g., Valencia, 1985). These judgments were mostly based on informal conversations in which examiners attempted to establish the children's levels of language proficiency through context-embedded, interpersonal discussions (e.g., discussion about what the children like to do during the weekend) which are not highly correlated with the types of cognitively demanding, context-reduced tasks that are found in cognitive assessment measures (Cummins, 1984).

Studies on test bias also failed to control for other variables that interact with language and may have a considerable impact on cognitive functioning. Those variables include levels of acculturation (Anastasi & Cordova, 1953; Olmedo, 1981), cultural background (Armour-Thomas, 1992), quality of instruction (Campbell, Gersten, & Kolar, 1993), and educational history (e.g., English as a Second Language (ESL) immersion vs. bilingual programs) (Cummins, 1984).

In conclusion, the available data on test bias are highly questionable. Future studies need to explore the issue of test bias with LEP children. Test bias research is also needed to explore a number of important variables (e.g., levels of language proficiency and cultural issues) that may influence bilingual children's performance in measures of cognitive abilities.

Measurement of Language Proficiency with LEP and Bilingual Children

The first step in the process of assessing LEP and bilingual children is to determine their levels of language proficiency. Language proficiency data are useful in helping examiners to determine what language(s) will be utilized in the assessment of cognitive skills.

Best practices call for the assessment of a wide range of language skills while utilizing informal as well as formal assessment tools (Lopez, 1995). The level of proficiency should be established in each of the two languages using measures that tap both expressive and receptive skills across context-embedded, interpersonal situations (i.e., BICS) as well as context-reduced, academic conditions (i.e., CALPS). Among the informal measures recommended for the purposes of measuring language proficiency are language background questionnaires, informal observations, and language samples (Ramirez, 1990). To illustrate, evaluators can assess BICS in both languages through the collection of language samples in social situations that may include children communicating with peers, family members, or school personnel. As the children interact with others around them, the language samples can provide valuable information as to the use and understanding of language in numerous contexts (e.g., communicating with peers vs. with adults and discussing a variety of topics). The assessment of CALPS may incorporate the use of observations during classroom situations in which children are involved in discussing instructional issues and producing writing samples in each of the two languages.

A number of formal language proficiency measures are available in Spanish and English (for an annotated bibliography of communicative ability tests for students from Spanish and English language backgrounds, see Hamayan & Damico, 1991). However, formal measures of language proficiency are generally not available in other languages. According to Olmedo (1981), the language assessment measures currently available tend to be problematic because of the overemphasis on discrete aspects of language, the lack of instruments that assess an array of language proficiency skills, outdated norms, and questionable validity and reliability. Although informal measures provide evaluators with valuable qualitative data, the lack of guidelines for interpretation purposes can lead to questionable conclusions.

Applying the Language Proficiency Data to the Assessment of Cognitive Abilities

Once the language proficiency data are gathered, evaluators are faced with the challenge of determining which language(s) to use during the cognitive assessment process. The determination of what language(s) to use in assessing the cognitive skills of children with minimal exposure to English is relatively simple. In such cases, the data are useful because they quickly point out that the native language is clearly the most appropriate language to use in the assessment of cognitive skills.

Examiners working with bilingual children who have had more exposure to English will find themselves with very vague guidelines as to how to use the language proficiency data. School districts typically deal with this issue by determining language proficiency cutoff scores based on normed measures. In New York City, for example, a score below the 40th percentile on the English Language Assessment Battery (LAB) entitles a student to a bilingual psychological evaluation (New York City Public Schools, 1993).

Currently, the issue of how to use language proficiency data to determine what language(s) to use during cognitive assessment sessions warrants further empirical study. Among the variables that need further investigation are the utility of formal and informal measures to determine language proficiency levels and the implications of using language proficiency cutoff scores during assessment and classroom placement procedures. As a general rule, bilingual children's psychological evaluations should be conducted in both languages. The use of both languages seems particularly relevant given the fact that bilinguals rely on both languages in a variety of ways depending on the linguistic and communicative demands encountered in different settings (e.g., home, school) and contexts (Ascher, 1990).

Administering Intellectual Assessment Measures to LEP and Bilingual Children

The cognitive abilities of LEP and bilingual children should be assessed by personnel (e.g., school psychologists and clinical psychologists) who demonstrate high levels of proficiency in the children's native language and in English. In addition, assessment personnel should demonstrate knowledge of the children's cultural backgrounds to ensure that all assessment data are interpreted within the appropriate linguistic and cultural contexts.

A shortage of bilingual assessment professionals (e.g., school psychologists and special education teachers) has led to the frequent use of interpreters during assessment sessions (Ochoa, Delgado-Rivera, & Ford, 1994). The usual procedure is for the examiners to ask the interpreters to translate the test items as the assessment is in progress (e.g., Lopez, 1992). The use of interpreters to translate IQ questions during assessment sessions can result in errors whereby interpreters may omit, add, or substitute terms that may significantly change the content of the questions (Lopez, 1994; Valencia & Rankin, 1985). Asking interpreters to translate test items prior to the assessment sessions is an alternative procedure (Langdon, 1985). However, it is not a problem-free approach because it may not prevent the interpreters from significantly altering the content of the test items, thereby changing the validity and reliability of the test. In general, the practice of using interpreters during assessment sessions should be avoided because of the potential for misinterpretations of test data.

A number of procedures are recommended in the literature as to how to administer cognitive measures to LEP and bilingual children (Holtzman & Wilkinson, 1991). The cognitive strengths and weaknesses of LEP children should be established through their native language. Among the instruments available to assess LEP children are tests formally translated into languages other than English and nonverbal cognitive measures (e.g., the Universal Nonverbal Intelligence Test; see McCallum & Bracken, Chapter 14, this volume).

Several administration procedures are recommended for the cognitive assessment of bilingual children (Holtzman & Wilkinson, 1991). One option is for the evaluators to present every test item in both languages. This procedure may be confusing for some children as they must attend to two sets of directions in two different languages. A second option is to present the items in the most proficient language first with items that are failed presented in both languages. Although this procedure has the advantage of allowing the testers to probe for responses in both languages, it may provide test takers with cues as to the items that are being failed. A third alternative is for the examiners to start with the most proficient language and to switch to the second language when items are failed. Again, the disadvantage is that test takers may be cued as to failed items. The last option is to assess in the most proficient language first and reassess in the second language. Although time-consuming, this procedure may be useful because it allows examiners to determine strengths and weaknesses in each of the two languages. However, practice effects may lead to spuriously high scores on the second administration. Overall, these approaches provide general guidelines but should be used with caution because they lack empirical validation.

The instruments available to assess the intellectual abilities of bilingual children include traditional tests of cognitive abilities in English, tests formally translated into languages other than English, and nonverbal cognitive measures. Testing of the limits is a procedure that is recommended in assessing the psychological skills of both LEP and bilingual children (Sattler, 1992). Limits can be tested in both verbal and nonverbal subtests through modifications that may include providing the instructions in simpler terms in either or both languages, providing a demonstration of the task, extending or removing time limits, changing the presentation and response modes, and providing the children with prompts and feedback that aid in problem solving (McLoughlin & Lewis, 1986).

UTILITY OF COGNITIVE MEASURES FOR LEP AND BILINGUAL CHILDREN

The utility of cognitive measures available to assess LEP and bilingual children's strengths and weaknesses is addressed in this section of the chapter. The measures discussed include tests translated into other languages, traditional tests in English, and nonverbal tests.

Tests Translated to Other Languages

A Spanish version of the Wechsler Intelligence Scale for Children—Revised (WISC-R; Wechsler, 1974), the Escala de Inteligencia Wechsler Para Niños—Revisada, is available (EIWN-R; Wechsler, 1982). However, the translation for that test is limited because it is most appropriate for children from Cuban-American backgrounds. The Kaufman Assessment Battery for Children (K-ABC; Kaufman & Kaufman, 1983) also includes a translated version of selected subtests. Neither the EIWN-R nor the translated K-ABC subtests were normed in Spanish and testers must use the original English norms. The use of the original norms with translated tests is problematic because of a number of issues outlined by Geisinger (1994):

1. The lack of validation in the second language may mean that the instrument may not measure the same characteristics or skills as the original instrument.
2. The questions may have changed enough in meaning through the process of translation to affect the pattern of responses.
3. The two cultural groups may differ systematically in the underlying construct measured.
4. The use of the original norms violates two of the Standards for Educational and Psychological Testing (American Educational Research Association et al., 1985) that call for the use of norms developed for clearly described populations and evidence of test comparability when tests are translated into a different language.

Other versions of translated tests such as the WISC-R and the K-ABC were normed outside the United States (e.g., Mexico) (see Figueroa, 1990; Harrison, Flanagan, & Genshaft, Chapter 27, this volume, for a list of tests normed and standardized outside of the United States with Spanish-speaking populations). Among the limitations of these measures are questionable content validity (Bracken et al., 1990; Bracken & Fouad; 1987) and norming samples that exclude children living in the United States (Figueroa, 1990).

Translating a test for a new target population is problematic when the new target population significantly differs from the original population with which the assessment device was normed (Geisinger, 1994). Guidelines for the adaptation of existing cognitive measures with new target populations suggest a multistep process that includes (1) translating the measure, (2) using a panel of experts to review the items, (3) adapting the items, (4) piloting and field testing the adapted measure, (5) standardizing the scores, (6) performing validation research, (7) developing a manual, (8) training users, and (9) collecting reactions from users (Bracken & Barona, 1991; Bracken et al., 1990; Geisinger, 1994). Currently, the translated versions of most cognitive measures are limited because they are not available in a variety of languages and they were not developed following the recommended guidelines outlined above.

A Spanish version of the WISC-R which was developed following the recommended guidelines for the adaptation of available cognitive measures with new target populations is the Escala de Inteligencia Wechsler para Ninos—Revisada de Puerto Rico (EIWN-R-PR; Wechsler, 1992). The EIWN-R-PR was normed with 2,200 Spanish-speaking children in Puerto Rico. The test developers made numerous changes to the original Spanish version of the WISC-R (i.e., the EIWN-R) including adding and adapting items that are appropriate for the Puerto Rican culture. Although the EIWN-R-PR appears to be well developed and standardized, its limitation lies in a norming sample, which only includes Spanish-speaking children from Puerto Rico.

Traditional Cognitive Measures in English

Examiners assessing school-age bilingual children with proficiency in English typically use traditional cognitive measures in English. Those measures include the Wechsler Intelligence Scale for Children—Third Edition (WISC-III; Wechsler, 1991), the Stanford–Binet Intelligence Scale: Fourth Edition (SB:IV; Thorndike, Hagen, & Sattler, 1986), the K-ABC (Kaufman & Kaufman, 1983), the Woodcock–Johnson Tests of Cognitive Ability—Revised (WJ-R COG; Woodcock & Johnson, 1989), and the Kaufman Adolescent and Adult Intelligence Test (KAIT; Kaufman & Kaufman, 1993).

Although the test bias literature indicates that such traditional measures appear to be appropriate for children from bilingual backgrounds who are English proficient (e.g., Reynolds & Kaiser, 1990), many criticisms remain as to their appropriateness (Armour-Thomas, 1992; Cummins, 1984; Figueroa, 1990; Helms, Chapter 26, this volume; Olmedo, 1981). Among the concerns cited are (1) inadequate norms for bilingual children, (2) testing formats that do not allow examiners the opportunity to provide feedback or to probe into the bilingual children's quality of responses, (3) a product-oriented emphasis on scoring responses with little opportunity for testers to examine the process by which children arrived at their responses, (4) test items that tap information that many bilingual children may not be familiar with, perhaps due to their linguistically and culturally different backgrounds or to a lack of exposure to certain concepts, (5) the lack of a direct relationship between measures of cognitive performance and classroom-related situations, rendering such measures questionable in terms of their relevance for classroom interventions (e.g., in bilingual classrooms and ESL programs), (6) the underlying assumption that the bilingual children taking those tests have appropriate test-taking skills, (7) the assumption that the tasks contained in cognitive assessment tools actually measure the cognitive processes underlying intellectual behavior and that those cognitive processes are similar for all individuals regardless of linguistic or cultural backgrounds; and (8) the assumption that the processes measured by those tools are stable across tasks for all subjects. These concerns imply that traditional cognitive tests are limited in measuring the intellectual strengths and weaknesses of bilingual children. This conclusion is supported, in part, by empirical data suggesting that the IQ scores of English-proficient children from bilingual backgrounds are influenced by language history and use (e.g., languages spoken at home) (Figueroa, 1987).

Nonverbal Tests of Intelligence

Nonverbal measures of intelligence are frequently recommended for the assessment of both LEP and bilingual children because they may provide a language-free measure of children's cognitive abilities. The nonverbal tests available to assess LEP and bilingual children include the Standard Progressive Matrices (Raven, 1958), the Columbia Mental Maturity Scale (Burgemeister, Blum, & Lorge, 1972), the Leiter International Performance Scale (Leiter, 1979), and the Test of Nonverbal Intelligence—2 (TONI-2) (Brown, Sherbenou, & Johnson, 1990).

Some of the limitations of nonverbal measures of intelligence include inadequate psychometric properties, outdated norms, narrow focus in terms of abilities measured, reliance on extensive verbal directions, a failure to develop model-based tools, and low correlations with achievement measures (McCallum & Bracken, 1993). Although children from LEP and bilingual backgrounds perform better on nonverbal measures of intelligence (e.g., Kaufman & Kaufman, 1983; Pearce, 1983) there are some questions as to whether they are suitable for all culturally and linguistically different individuals. Anastasi (1988) noted that studies using measures such as the Standard Progressive Matrices with non-European cultural groups found that nonverbal measures of intelligence may not be valid for some cultural and linguistic groups. According to Berry (1994), "The understanding of such materials requires a form of literacy and acceptance that real-life objects and forms can be represented by lines on a two-dimensional paper surface. Both literacy and pictorial representations are cultural products that are learned in some cultures but not in others; moreover, styles of pictorial representation are known to vary greatly across cultures" (p. 319).

Another concern related to current nonverbal measures of intelligence is that most were not normed with populations of LEP and bilingual children with diverse language profiles. The Universal Nonverbal Intelligence Test (UNIT), a nonverbal measure that will be published in the near future, may address some of the limitations of currently available measures because it was developed to assess multiple areas of intelligence, it utilizes nonverbal directions, and it will include LEP children in the norming sample (see McCallum & Bracken, Chapter 14, this volume). Future validation studies with LEP and bilingual children are needed to provide evidence as to its utility.

FUTURE TRENDS IN THE ASSESSMENT OF LEP AND BILINGUAL CHILDREN

Given the many limitations of existing tests of intelligence (e.g., rigid testing formats, product-oriented emphasis, and outdated theoretical models), there is a call for alternative models of assessment. Models emphasizing multiple components of cognitive ability (Horn, 1991; Horn & Noll, Chapter 4, this volume), process assessment (Meyers, Pfeffer, & Erlbaum, 1985), and multiple intelligences (Gardner, 1983; Chen & Gardner, Chapter 6, this volume) may have some useful applications in the future for the cognitive assessment of LEP and bilingual children.

Multiple Components of Cognitive Ability Models

Cognitive measures typically emphasize a single general intelligence factor or measure of *g* (Flanagan & McGrew, 1995). New assessment instruments are now available emphasizing the modern Gf-Gc theory of intelligence (Horn, 1991; Horn & Noll, Chapter 4, this volume). Modern Gf-Gc theory has identified nine broad abilities that include fluid intelligence (Gf), crystallized intelligence (Gc), short-term acquisition and retrieval (Gsm), visual intelligence (Gv), auditory intelligence (Ga), long-term storage and retrieval (Glr), cognitive processing speed (Gs), correct decision speed (CDS), and quantitative knowledge (Gq). These broad abilities are based in part on factor-analytic research showing that intelligence is not made up of a single general factor but of a multitude of factors (see Horn, 1994, for a summary of validity evidence for the Gf-Gc factors).

The Woodcock–Johnson Tests of Cognitive Ability—Revised (in English) (Woodcock & Johnson, 1989) and the Batería Woodcock–Muñoz Pruebas de Habilidad Cognoscitiva—Revisada (i.e., the Woodcock–Muñoz Tests of Cognitive Ability—Revised in Spanish) (Woodcock & Muñoz-

Sandoval, 1996) are based on modern Gf-Gc theory and are recognized as batteries that measure multiple components of cognitive ability. A notable feature is that comparable scores were developed across the two batteries (i.e., Spanish and English) using Rasch Modeling Procedures.

In the future, tests of cognitive abilities measuring separate components of cognitive functioning will provide opportunities to explore the relationship between isolated cognitive variables and levels of language proficiency. For example, the research indicates that the processing of verbal information is influenced by the subjects' level of proficiency in the language of testing (Dornic, 1979). The use of tools that examine separate cognitive abilities may shed light on how language and culture influence the performance of bilinguals on short-term memory acquisition and retrieval tasks. Of course, the utility of measures such as the Woodcock–Muñoz Tests of Cognitive Ability–Revised in Spanish may continue to be limited by the reliance on standardized measures of intelligence that emphasize traditional testing formats.

Process Assessment Models

One of the most important goals of process assessment is to determine the extent to which cognitive functioning can be modified (Meyers et al., 1985). Process assessment is different from typical assessment procedures because it (1) focuses more on the learning processes children use in solving problems, (2) often advocates the use of materials that the children are actually using in the classroom, and (3) involves multiple samplings of children's learning.

Dynamic assessment procedures are process oriented and designed to measure cognitive functioning through the use of a test–teach–test approach (Feuerstein, Rand, & Hoffman, 1979; Feuerstein, Feuerstein, & Gross, Chapter 16, this volume; Lidz, Chapter 15, this volume). Examiners provide children with mediated experiences that include feedback and guidance. During these mediated experiences, examiners note the amount and type of assistance required by the subjects to answer the test questions. Both Feuerstein (Feuerstein et al., 1979) and Budoff (1975) developed dynamic assessment procedures that can be used with LEP and bilingual children. Dynamic assessment tools may provide assessors with the means to probe into the children's responses while also tapping into their cognitive potential. However, future studies are needed to establish their validity and reliability with populations of LEP and bilingual children in the United States.

Multiple Intelligences Models

Gardner's (1983) model of multiple intelligences examines intellectual skills from an ecological perspective. Gardner suggests that individuals are capable of cognitive functioning in at least seven relatively distinct areas including linguistic, musical, logical–mathematical, spatial, bodily kinesthetic, interpersonal, and intrapersonal skills (see Chen & Gardner, Chapter 6, this volume). He proposes that intelligence tests must measure how people function when they are able to draw upon their experience, feedback, and knowledge. Within this model, assessment is placed in the context of authentic domains and social environments. According to Kornhaber, Krechevsky, and Gardner (1990):

> [Assessment environments] should integrate curriculum and assessment and invite individuals to deploy their various competencies in the context of carrying out meaningful projects or activities. Such assessment should also make available a range of intrinsically interesting and motivating materials which would be used over time and which would be sensitive to individual differences. They should also be "intelligence-fair," that is, capable of engaging specific competencies without the need to rely on linguistic or logical means or abilities as an intermediary. (pp. 191–192)

Project Spectrum is applying Gardner's theoretical model into a more practical framework (Chen & Gardner, Chapter 6, this volume; Kornhaber et al., 1990). This project designed innovative and ecologically valid assessment tools targeted for children in early childhood. Children are exposed to classrooms that are equipped with a variety of materials such as games, puzzles, and musical instruments. Trained assessors use informal tools to measure children's learning and working styles through the monitoring of classroom activities.

Although the validity of such procedures needs to be established with LEP and bilingual children, they remain promising because they may provide examiners with more flexible, ecologically oriented testing formats. In addition, these procedures may provide testers with the opportunity to examine the relationship between LEP and bilingual children's classroom performance and the quality of instructional programs. This is of particular concern given research suggesting that bilingual students are exposed to a number of instructional problems including (1) bilingual educators and regular classroom educators with little training in second-language instructional techniques (Yates & Ortiz, 1991), (2) special education classrooms in which bilingual students are making little academic progress and are demonstrating significant drops in test scores (Campbell et al., 1993), and (3) special education (Commins & Miramontes, 1989) and bilingual programs (Wong Fillmore & Valdez, 1986) that utilize inadequate instructional techniques.

CONCLUSION

Many questions remain unanswered regarding the intellectual assessment of LEP and bilingual children. Empirical investigations are needed to address the interactions of numerous and complex variables including test bias, language proficiency, bilingualism, cultural background, and the process of second-language acquisition. Little progress has been made in terms of developing valid and reliable assessment measures for the assessment of LEP and bilingual children. There is also a lack of adequately normed tests in diverse languages.

Although new models of intellectual assessment appear promising, practitioners involved in assessing the intellectual skills of this population of children are basically faced with an incomplete puzzle in which many of the pieces are missing. The task of assessing children from LEP and bilingual backgrounds is daunting as examiners must apply a wide-angle lens to explore the internal (e.g., intellectual abilities and potential and motivation levels) as well as the external variables (e.g., home environment, school milieu, and instructional quality) that influence their cognitive functioning.

REFERENCES

American Psychological Association. (1990). *Guidelines for providers of psychological services to ethnic, linguistic, and culturally diverse populations.* Washington, DC: Author.

American Educational Research Association, American Psychological Association, National Council on Measurement in Education. (1985). *Standards for Educational and Psychological Testing.* Washington, DC: Author.

Anastasi, A. (1988). *Psychological testing* (6th ed.). New York: Macmillan.

Anastasi, A., & Cordova, F. (1953). Some effects of bilingualism upon the intelligence test performance of Puerto Rican children in New York. *Journal of Educational Psychology, 44,* 1–19.

Argulewicz, E. N., & Abel. R. R. (1984). Internal evidence of bias in the PPVT-R for Anglo-American and Mexican-American children. *Journal of School Psychology, 22,* 299–303.

Armour-Thomas, E. (1992). Intellectual assessment of children from culturally diverse backgrounds. *School Psychology Review, 21,* 552–565.

Ascher, C. (1990). *Assessing bilingual students for placement and instruction.* Washington, DC.: Office of Educational Research and Improvement. (ERIC Document Reproduction Service No. ED 322 273)

Berry, J. W. (1994). Cross-cultural variations in intelligence. In R. J. Sternberg (Ed.), *Encyclopedia of human intelligence* (pp. 316–322). New York: Macmillan.

Bracken, B. A., & Barona, A. (1991). State of the art procedures for translating, validating and using psychoeducational tests in cross-cultural assessment. *School Psychology International, 12,* 119–132.

Bracken, B. A., Barona, A., Bauermeister, J. J., Howell, K. K., Poggioli, L., & Puente, A. (1990). Multinational validation of the Spanish Bracken Basic Concept Scale for cross-cultural assessments. *Journal of School Psychology, 28,* 325–341.

Bracken, B. A., & Fouad, N. (1987). Spanish translation and validation of the Bracken Basic Concept Scale. *School Psychology Review, 16,* 94–102.

Brown, L., Sherbenou, R. J., & Johnson, S. K. (1990). *Test of Nonverbal Intelligence—2.* Austin, TX: Pro-Ed.

Budoff, M. (1975). Measuring learning potential: An alternative to the traditional intelligence test. In G. Gredler (Ed.), *Ethical and legal factors in the practice of school psychology: Proceedings of the First Annual Conference in School Psychology* (pp. 75–89). Philadelphia: Temple University Press.

Burgemeister, B. B., Blum, L. A., & Lorge, I. (1972). *Columbia Mental Maturity Scale* (3rd ed.). New York: Harcourt Brace Jovanovich.

Campbell, J., Gersten, R., & Kolar, C. (1993). *Quality of instruction provided to language minority students with learning disabilities: Five findings from micro-ethnographies* (Report No. 93–5). Eugene, OR: Eugene Research Institute.

Center for Research on Elementary and Middle Schools (1990). *The changing nature of the disadvantaged population: Current dimensions and future trends.* Baltimore: Johns Hopkins University Press.

Cheng, L. L., Ima, K., & Labovitz, G. (1994). Assessment of Asian and Pacific Islander students for gifted programs. In S. B. Garcia (Ed.), *Addressing cultural and linguistic diversity in special education* (pp. 30–45). Reston, VI: Council for Exceptional Children.

Commins, N. L., & Miramontes, O. B. (1989). Perceived and actual linguistic competence: A descriptive study of four low-achieving Hispanic bilingual students. *American Educational Research Journal, 26,* 443–472.

Cummins, J. (1984). *Bilingualism and special education.* Clevedon, England: Multilingual Matters.

Dean, R. S. (1980). Factor structure of the WISC-R with Anglos and Mexican-Americans. *Journal of School Psychology, 18,* 234–239.

Diana v. State Board of Education, Civ. Act. No. C-70-37 (N.D. Cal. 1970).

Dornic, S. (1979). Information processing in bilinguals: Some selected issues. *Psychological Research, 40,* 329–348.

Education for All Handicapped Children Act of 1975, P. L. No. 94-142. 20 U.S.C. Sec. 401.

Education of the Handicapped Act Amendments of 1986. Pub. L. No. 99-457.

Feuerstein, R., Rand, Y., & Hoffman, M. B. (1979). *The dynamic assessment of retarded performers: The Learning Potential Assessment Device, theory, instruments, and techniques.* Baltimore: University Park Press.

Figueroa, R. A. (1987). *Special education assessment of Hispanic pupils in California: Looking ahead to the 1990's.* Sacramento: California State Department of Education, Office of Special Education.

Figueroa, R. A. (1989). Psychological testing of linguistic-minority students: Knowledge gaps and regulations. *Exceptional Children, 56,* 111–119.

Figueroa, R. A. (1990). Assessment of linguistic minority group children. In C. R. Reynolds & R. W. Kamphaus (Eds.), *Handbook of psychological and educational assessment of children: Intelligence and achievement* (pp. 671–696). New York: Guilford Press.

Flanagan, D. P., & McGrew, K. S. (1995, March). *Will you evolve or become extinct? Interpreting intelligence tests from modern Gf-Gc theory.* Paper presented at the meeting of the National Association of School Psychologists, Chicago.

Gardner, H. (1983). *Frames of mind: The theory of multiple intelligences.* New York: Basic Books.

Geisinger, K. F. (1994). Cross-cultural normative assessment: Translation and adaptation issues influencing the normative interpretation of assessment instruments. *Psychological Assessment, 6,* 304–312.

Hakuta, K. (1987). Degree of bilingualism and cognitive ability in mainland Puerto Rican children. *Child Development, 58,* 1372–1388.

Hamayan, E. V., & Damico, J. S. (1991). Developing and using a second language. In E. V. Hamayan & J. S. Damico (Eds.), *Limiting bias in the assessment of bilingual students* (pp. 39–75). Austin: Pro-Ed.

Hardman, M. L., Drew, C. J., Egan, M. W., & Wolf, B. (1993). *Human exceptionality: Society, school, and family* (4th ed.). Boston: Allyn & Bacon.

Holtzman, W. H., & Wilkinson, C. Y. (1991). Assessment of cognitive ability. In E. V. Hamayan & J. S. Damico (Eds.), *Limiting bias in the assessment of bilingual students* (pp. 247–280) Austin: Pro-Ed.

Horn, J. L. (1991). Measurement of intellectual capabilities: A review of theory. In K. S. McGrew, J. K. Werder, & R. W. Woodcock (Eds.), *Woodcock-Johnson technical manual* (pp. 197–232). Allen, TX: DLM.

Horn, J. L. (1994). Theory of fluid and crystallized intelligence. In R. J. Sternberg (editor in chief), *Encyclopedia of human intelligence* (pp. 443–451). New York: Macmillan.

Individuals with Disabilities Education Act of 1990, Pub. L. No. 101-476, 602(a)(19). 20 U.S.C. Sec. 1400.

Jensen, A. R. (1976). Test bias and construct validity. *Phi Delta Kappan, 58,* 340–346.

Kaufman, A. S., & Kaufman, N. L. (1983). *Kaufman Assessment Battery for Children.* Circle Pines, MN: American Guidance Service.

Kaufman, A. S., & Kaufman, N. L. (1993). *Kaufman Adolescent and Adult Intelligence Test.* Circle Pines, MN: American Guidance Service.

Kornhaber, M., Krechebsky, M., & Gardner, H. (1990). Engaging intelligence. *Educational Psychologist, 25,* 177–199.

Langdon, H. W. (1985, February). *Working with interpreters and translators in a school setting.* Paper presented at the meeting of the Fordham University Bilingual Conference, New York.

Leiter, R. G. (1979). *Leiter International Performance Scale.* Chicago: Stoelting.

Lemmon, C. R., & Goggin, J. P. (1989). The measurement of bilingualism and its relationship to cognitive ability. *Applied Psycholinguistics, 10,* 133–155.

Lopez, E. C. (1992, April). *A survey of school interpreters.* Paper presented at the meeting of the National Association of School Psychologists, Nashville, TN.

Lopez, E. C. (1994, March). *Errors made by interpreters during on the spot translations of WISC-R questions.* Paper presented at the meeting of the National Association of School Psychologists, Seattle, WA.

Lopez, E. C. (1995). Best practices in working with bilingual children. In A. Thomas & J. Grimes (Eds.), *Best practices in school psychology III* (pp. 1111–1121). Washington, DC: National Association of School Psychologists.

McCallum, R. S., & Bracken, B. A. (1993, June). *The Universal Test of Nonverbal Intelligence: A test for all people.* Paper presented at the meeting of the International Testing Conference, Oxford, England.

McLoughlin, J. A., & Lewis, R. B. (1986). *Assessing special students* (2nd ed.). Columbus, OH: Merrill.

Meyers, J., Pfeffer, J., & Erlbaum, V. (1985). Process assessment: A model for broadening assessment. *Journal of Special Education, 19,* 73–89.

Mishra, S. P. (1981) Factor analysis of the McCarthy Scales for groups of white and Mexican-American children. *Journal of School Psychology, 19,* 178–182.

National Association of School Psychologists. (1992). *Standards for the Provision of School Psychological Services.* Silver Spring, MD: Author.

New York City Public Schools. (1993). *Answers to frequently asked questions about limited English proficient (LEP) students and bilingual ESL programs: Facts and figures 1992–1993.* New York: Author.

Ochoa, S. H., Delgado-Rivera, B., & Ford, L. (1994, August). *School psychology training pertaining to bilingual psychoeducational assessment.* Paper presented at the meeting of the American Psychological Association, Los Angeles.

Olmedo, E. S. (1981). Testing linguistic minorities. *American Psychologist, 36,* 1078–1085.

Ortiz, A. (1988). *Effective practices in assessment and instruction for language minority students: An intervention model.* Arlington, VA: U.S. Department of Education.

Pearce, N. (1983). A comparison of the WISC-R, Raven's Standard Progressive Matrices, and Meeker's SOI-screening for gifted. *Gifted Child Quarterly, 27,* 13–19.

Ramirez, A. G. (1990). Perspectives on language proficiency assessment. In A. Barona & E. E. Garcia (Eds.), *Children at risk: Poverty, minority status, and other issues in educational equity* (pp. 305–323). Washington, DC: National Association of School Psychologists.

Raven, J. C. (1958). *Standard Progressive Matrices.* London: H. K. Lewis.

Reynolds, C. R., & Kaiser, S. M. (1990). Bias in assessment of aptitude. In C. R. Reynolds & R. W. Kamphaus (Eds.), *Handbook of psychological and educational assessment of children: Intelligence and achievement* (pp. 611–653). New York: Guilford Press.

Sattler, J. M. (1992). *Assessment of children's intelligence and special abilities* (3rd ed.). San Diego, CA: Author.

Scarr, S. (1994). Culture-fair and culture-free tests. In R. J. Sternberg (Ed.), *Encyclopedia of human intelligence* (pp. 322–328). New York: Macmillan.

Thomas, A., & Grimes, J. (Eds.). (1995). *Best practices in school psychology III*. Washington, DC: National Association of School Psychologists.

Thorndike, R. L., Hagen, E. P., & Sattler, J. M. (1986). *Stanford–Binet Intelligence Scale: Fourth edition*. Chicago: Riverside.

U.S. Bureau of the Census. (1990). *Language spoken at home and ability to speak English for United States, regions and states: 1990* (Report No. CPH-L-133). Washington, DC: Author.

U.S. Department of Education. (1994). *Summary of the bilingual education state educational agency program survey of states' limited English proficient persons and available educational services (1992–1993): Final report*. Arlington, VA: Development Associates.

Valencia, R. R. (1985). Stability of the Kaufman Assessment Battery for Children for a sample of Mexican-American children. *Journal of School Psychology, 23,* 189–193.

Valencia, R. R., Henderson, R. W., & Rankin, R. J. (1981). Relationship of family constellation and schooling to intellectual performance of Mexican American Children. *Journal of Educational Psychology, 73,* 524–532.

Valencia, R. R., & Rankin, R. J. (1985). Evidence of content bias on the McCarthy Scales with Mexican American Children: Implications for test translation and nonbiased assessment. *Journal of Educational Psychology, 77,* 197–207.

Wechsler, D. (1974). *Wechsler Intelligence Scale for Children—Revised*. San Antonio, TX: Psychological Corporation.

Wechsler, D. (1982). *Escala de Inteligencia Wechsler para Ninos—Revisada*. Cleveland, OH: Psychological Corporation.

Wechsler, D. (1991). *Wechsler Intelligence Scale for Children—III*. San Antonio, TX: Psychological Corporation.

Wechsler, D. (1992). *Escala de Inteligencia Wechsler para Ninos—Revisada de Puerto Rico*. San Antonio, TX: Psychological Corporation.

Wong Fillmore, L., & Valdez, C. (1986). Teaching bilingual learners. In M. C. Wittrock (Ed.), *Handbook of research on teaching* (pp. 648–685). New York: Macmillan.

Woodcock, R. W., & Johnson, M. B. (1989). *Woodcock–Johnson Tests of Cognitive Ability—Revised*. Chicago: Riverside.

Woodcock, R. W., & Muñoz-Sandoval, A. F. (1996). *Bateria Woodcock–Muñoz Pruebas de Habilidad Cognosci-tiva—Revisada*. Chicago: Riverside.

Yates, J. R., & Ortiz, A. A. (1991). Professional development needs of teachers who serve exceptional language minorities in today's schools. *Teacher Education and Special Education, 14*(1), 11–18.

CHAPTER 26

The Triple Quandary of Race, Culture, and Social Class in Standardized Cognitive Ability Testing

JANET E. HELMS

AS IS ALSO THE CASE for most other applied psychological and educational interventions, psychologists' and psychometricians' attempts to develop universally applicable standardized cognitive ability tests (CATs) have never included adequately distinctive conceptualizations of the constructs of race, culture, and social class (Helms, 1992, 1994). Instead, the concepts have been treated as though they are interchangeable. Nevertheless, in spite of the inadequate operational definitions of the three constructs in existing literature (Helms, 1992), some information suggests that each of these domains of socialization may uniquely contribute to CAT performance (e.g., Grubb & Dozier, 1989; Robinson, 1994/1995). Yet conceptual models for managing the effects of race, culture, and social class on CAT performance are rudimentary at best and nonexistent at worst. Consequently, when test developers consider that they have controlled, eliminated, or reduced the effects of one of the members of the problematic triad, one or more of the others generally has been left to wander, apparently unbeknownst to the developers of such measures.

In the United States (the country of focus of this discussion), every person has psychological attributes that may be classified as racial, cultural, or socioeconomical in origin. Attributes emanating from each of these socialization categories may serve as an advantage or a disadvantage to a person's performance on CATs because such devices are constructed within racial, cultural, and socioeconomic contexts. For example, within racial or cultural groups, the CAT performance of poor people generally occurs under conditions of greater economic disadvantage than does the CAT performance of people who are economically better off. Consequently, the average CAT performance of economically advantaged people of the same racial classification tends to exceed that of their less well off racial counterparts because they have had greater exposure to the types of life experiences inherent to CATs. For similar reasons, people socialized in White Western or Anglo-Saxon-dominant American culture potentially enjoy greater CAT-relevant advantage than people socialized in other cultures, and people socialized in subjugated racial groups presumably experience greater disadvantage than those socialized in the subjugating group(s).

Therefore, a person may be multiply advantaged or disadvantaged when performance on cognitive ability tests is concerned, particularly to the extent that the combination of influences is allowed to vary unmonitored. When CAT construction and performance are concerned, America's nonWhite racial and continuously subjugated ethnic minorities (henceforth, visible racial/ethnic groups; VREGs)—especially African, Asian, Latino/Latina, and Native Americans—are most likely to be multiply (although not necessarily equivalently) disadvantaged because developers of CATs generally do not have intimate knowledge of these groups. Consequently, test developers may not be familiar enough with the differential racial, cultural, and/or socioeconomic socialization experiences of these groups to integrate their unique experiences of race, culture, and class into CATS or to remove them from such measures. Thus, CATs may not be culturally equivalent for VREGs and/or people of disadvantaged economic status and/or cultural heterogeneity.

Helms (1992) contends that cultural equivalence refers to whether CATs measure the same constructs across cultural groups as they do for respective CAT normative groups. Here, "cultural" is used to mean racial, ethnic cultural, and socioeconomic conditions of socialization. Based on her analysis of the general cross-cultural assessment literature, she proposed that the following types of cultural equivalence should be considered when developing and using CATs:

> (a) functional equivalence, the extent to which test scores have the same meaning in different cultural [racial, and socioeconomic] groups and measure psychological characteristics that occur with equal frequency within these groups; (b) conceptual equivalence, whether groups are equally familiar or unfamiliar with the content of test items and consequently assign the same meaning to them; (c) linguistic equivalence, whether the language used in tests has been equalized so that it has the same meaning to different cultural groups; and (d) (psycho)metric equivalence, the extent to which tests measure the same things at the same levels across cultural groups. (p. 1092)

To these more familiar forms of equivalence, she also adapted the following less known forms of cultural equivalence from Butcher (1982):

> [e] testing condition equivalence, assurance that the idea of testing as a means of assessing ability and the testing procedures are equally familiar and acceptable to Blacks [and other VREGs] and Whites; [f] contextual equivalence, evidence that in the various environments in which the person functions, the to-be-assessed cognitive ability is evaluated similarly; and [g] sampling equivalence, determination that samples of subjects representing each racial or ethnic [or cultural or socioeconomic] group are comparable at the test development, validation, and interpretation stages. (Helms, 1992, p. 1092)

Most efforts to enhance the applicability of CATs across societally defined demographic groups have attended to perhaps one of the forms of cultural equivalence generally with respect to race, culture, or socioeconomic status, but rarely all three categories of socialization or seven types of equivalence. The purpose of this chapter is to discuss the differential influence of race, culture, and social class on the cultural equivalence of CATs. In doing so, the differential relevance of each of the three potential contaminators of equivalence in test construction and individual performance is discussed.

The cultural equivalence issues of African American test takers are the primary focus of this discussion because African Americans are the group that is most often used to "prove" the equivalence of cognitive ability tests across racial/cultural and social class groups. Nevertheless, many of the issues raised may be pertinent to other VREGs as well, although not necessarily for identical reasons. In addition, contemporary efforts to develop and/or adapt measures to eliminate influences of race, culture, and socioeconomic status will be evaluated with a particular emphasis on the approaches discussed in this book. Finally, recommendations will be made for investigating the influences of racial, cultural, and socioeconomical factors so that they do not continue to unduly penalize members of multiply disadvantaged groups.

DEFINITIONAL AND CULTURAL EQUIVALENCE CONSIDERATIONS

Adequate consideration of the differential influences of the troublesome person–environment triad requires different operational definitions of culture, social class, and race, and independent consideration of their potential differential effects on CAT performance. Helms (1994; Helms & Cook, in press) contends that the efficacious use of race, culture, and social class requires a distinction between each of the three variables on demographic as well as psychological conceptual and measurement levels.

At the demographic conceptual level, in all three cases, characteristics typically have been defined by means of external environmental criteria which often are assumed to have implications for a person's quality of intellective functioning. In test construction and interpretation of CAT performance, demographic or sociologic qualities are typically "measured" at a nominal or categorical level. However, assignment of people to groups or demographic categories does not result in any obvious implications for CAT performance because placement in more or less "objective" categories does not permit verifiable hypotheses about how individuals within those groups might be expected to function in testing situations or otherwise. At best, knowledge of a person's demographic categories might potentially focus inquiry about the relevance of environmental factors to the testing process. Yet especially relevant to the issues of appropriate construction and usage of CATs as they pertain to VREGs are the psychological consequences to individuals who are socialized in one or more of the disadvantageous categories.

Although race, (ethnic) culture, and social class rarely have been defined on a conceptual level in the traditional CAT psychometric literature, psychological reactions could be defined as the person's internalized qualities or attributes that develop in response to being socialized in one or more of the relevant demographic domains. Helms and Cook (in press) use the modifier "psycho" to mean internalized psychological characteristics hypothesized to occur in response to sociodemographic socialization (e.g., psychorace); they use "socio" (e.g., sociorace) to mean variables assessed at a sociological or distal level.

Therefore, in the area of cognitive ability testing, pertinent psychological attributes could be evidenced by learning styles, information-processing strategies, perceptual processes, relevant attitudes, and so forth. Thus, psychological processes potentially define a person's range and variety of possible responses to stimuli. However, measurement of (as opposed to speculation about) psychological processes proposedly accrued through sociogroup socialization appears to be virtually nonexistent in the psychometric literature. In fact, even modern-day psychometricians typically have not used psychological processes as the basis for forming normative and comparison groups when constructing and validating CATs. Instead they have relied exclusively on preexisting demographic (e.g., age, race, and gender) categories for such purposes. Consequently, the subsequent consideration of the differential influences of demographic and psychological culture, social class, and race must be largely speculative.

The Wechsler Adult Intelligence Scale—Revised (WAIS-R; Wechsler, 1981) is used to illustrate possible differential psychological (psychoracial, psychocultural, and psychosocioeconomic) influences of sociogroup and cultural socialization on CAT performance. The WAIS-R is being used for this purpose because (1) it is readily available to most users of cognitive ability tests for comparison purposes, (2) it contains a wide variety of types of questions and other components (e.g., instructions), and (3) as a version of the test that was not intended to minimize bias due to race, culture, and socioeconomic status (SES), it offers many opportunities to speculate about the differential influences of such factors on test items. Most CATs contain some, if not all, similar components and/or item formats. Therefore, it should be possible to compare analogous components of other tests to form hypotheses about whether they have attended to issues of cultural equivalence with respect to all three members of the culture–SES–race triad.

Table 26.1 attempts to delineate some of the ways that these three factors may differently influence various aspects of performance on the WAIS-R. The first column refers to ways in which the test performance of persons of low SES might be adversely affected, virtually regardless of race; the culture column is intended to highlight some of the factors specific to African American culture that might negatively influence a person's test performance; the race column proposes possible CAT-relevant reactions to racial discrimination. Nevertheless, these descriptions are merely speculative and cannot be considered probative until they have been subjected to empirical investigation.

Culture and Acculturation

Culture may be defined as the customs, values, traditions, and behavioral practices (including information-processing strategies) that define a group (Helms, 1994). Its psychological consequence is acculturation or the learning of the culture(s) in which the person is expected to demonstrate competence (Helms, 1992). Traditionally, most CATs have been developed to reflect the intellective culture of (White) Americans of middle to upper SES (Katz, 1985; Stewart, 1971). Although he did not explicitly address issues of CAT performance, Alba (1990) provides evidence to suggest that by their third generation in this country, most White ethnic groups conform to and are socialized in White American culture, the dimensions of which have been specified elsewhere (Helms, 1992; Katz, 1985).

Examination of the content of the WAIS-R subtests suggests five places in which a person might be taught CAT-relevant cultural content including families, schools, religious institutions, occupations, and recreational activities. However, VREG people are likely to have experienced "nontraditional" cultural socialization with regard to each of these socialization sources. For example, African Americans as a group are socialized to be collectivistic (group-oriented) rather than individualistic (self-oriented). Consequently, as proposed in Table 26.1, they might be more likely to provide people-oriented responses to test items and expect to be socially engaged during the testing process.

Other proposed cultural predispositions include tendencies to perceive information "holistically" rather than "atomistically" (Willis, 1989), language differences (Terrell, Terrell, & Taylor, 1981), and valuing of creativity. As suggested in Table 26.1, conformance to one's primary cultural socialization in any of these domains is likely to result in lower CAT scores because such attributes are not valued or recognized by nonmembers of the culture as evidence of intelligent functioning.

For example, extrapolating from Willis's (1989) analysis of Hilliard's (1976) work, a reasonable conclusion is that Black Americans would perform better or at least more equivalently on subtests that emphasize skills in contextual interpretation, improvisation and creativity, memory for essence rather than facts, and divergent thinking, particularly if these competencies are assessed via people-oriented modalities. Willis's observations are somewhat supported by the relatively consistent findings in the literature that the smallest Black–White differences in performance occur on the Picture Arrangement (PA), Digit Span (DS), and Digit Symbol (DSy) subtests of the WAIS (Kaufman, 1990).

In the PA subtest, various picture arrangement sequences receive full credit. Thus, the combination of people focus, contextual interpretation, and creativity skills have an opportunity to contribute to higher scores. Also, PA, DS, and DSy each may reward memory, creativity, and improvisation to some extent. It has been my experience that people who do well on these tasks seem to use

TABLE 26.1. Analysis of Possible Differential Impact of Socioeconomic Status, Culture, and Race on African Americans' WAIS-R Performance

Test component	Hypothesized content and procedural biases		
	Socioeconomic	Culture	Race
Instructions	Short attention span may make it difficult to do test in single setting	Businesslike presentation violates cultural norms of sociability	"Objectivity" may elicit mistrust of the testing process
	Cooperation may be difficult to obtain if negative race-related motives are suspected	Creativity is considered to be intelligent; giving obvious responses may not be	Cooperation will be difficult to obtain if benefit is not obvious
	Mistrust of system may hurt performance; evasive answers to examinees' direct questions increase anxiety	Collectivistic orientation may influence performance; evasive answers may elicit even more creative responses	Racial-group stereotypes/expectations may decrease performance
Examiner	Different life opportunities can affect responses	Language and stylistic differences may be misinterpreted	Examiners of a different race may be suspect
Vocabulary	Defining words may be an atypical task and certain words may be unfamiliar	Certain words may be used infrequently or have different meanings	
	Items 8, 9, 11, 23, have a middle-class bias; items 12, 15, 21, 24, 25, 26, 29, are biased toward higher levels of education	Acceptable responses for items 8, 17, 18, 28, 29, might not be prevalent responses among intelligent African American people	
Picture Completion	One is accustomed to making do with imperfect things and has little exposure to others. So a doorknob or buckle tongue may not be perceived as missing; tennis, riding equipment, boats, violins, etc. may be unfamiliar	People-oriented responses are common. Thus, the hand is missing from the pitcher, the person is missing from the canoe; the person who stacked the wood is missing. Some things are either common or infrequent and therefore are not missing. Religious (especially) women may not play with cards	Task may be perceived as irrelevant because no VREG people or circumstances are portrayed
Block Design	Rapid manipulation of small objects may be an awkward activity particularly for heavy laborers	Figure-ground may be perceived differently; rotations may reflect perceptual differences or creativity. Timing may be stressful	
	The absence of similar toys during childhood make task unfamiliar		

(cont.)

TABLE 26.1. *(continued)*

| Test component | Hypothesized content and procedural biases | | |
	Socioeconomic	Culture	Race
Arithmetic	Education bias, e.g., substandard schooling may hinder performance	Being timed might be an impediment	
Object Assembly	Puzzle manipulation may be an uncommon recreational activity	Tendency to perceive "holistically" rather than "atomistically" may be a disadvantage; also, timing and creativity may not be appropriately rewarded	
Comprehension	Items 2, 4, 6, 8, 13 have middle-class bias	Items 12, 15 might be difficult because key terms (e.g., iron, swallow) have different or more prevalent people-oriented meanings. Different social customs might be operative (e.g., it's better to borrow from friends and relatives than a bank)	Exposure to racism may mean that different social rules are operative (e.g., banks may not lend money to Blacks)
Digit Symbol	Heavy laborers, outdoors persons, and under-schooled may be uncomfortable with pencils as a tool	Timing and lack of reward for creativity	Racial-group related academic performance expectations may influence performance
Similarities	Many of the stimuli may be unfamiliar due to lack of exposure	Pragmatic responses should be more common, but receive fewer WAIS points	

unusually efficient strategies for encoding and decoding information. These observations suggest that racial differences might be minimized even further by increasing the variety of correct responses throughout the subtests, updating some of the items and/or pictures in the PA, and finding ways to reward efficient "chunking" and other forms of creativity for the other two subtests.

In addition to possible incompatibility between their own-group(s) culture and the culture of CATs, the CAT performance of African Americans (and other VREGs) may be deleteriously affected by limited exposure or assimilation into the White American culture. Assimilation refers to the extent to which a person is integrated into the culture in which he or she is expected to be proficient as well as the quality of that integration (Helms, 1992, 1994). Acculturation means the person's acquisition or learning of culture(s). Presumably, if one is well integrated into a cultural group, one acquires cultural content through osmosis of some kind even if it is not directly taught. Likewise, presumably the greater one's exposure to the culture of CATs, the better one's performance on them.

Where African Americans are concerned, a long history of racial segregation means that most of them have been prone to receive their cultural socialization from members of their own racial group almost exclusively. That is, they attend schools, worship, and recreate in environments predominated by own-group members. Whereas in-group socialization is not peculiar to African Americans and, in fact, is probably unavoidable to some extent, VREGs are more disadvantaged by in-group socialization because it limits their amount of exposure to White culture—the culture of CATs. Moreover, if one's own group and White American culture are dissimilar, lack of access to White culture is apt to influence CAT performance in presumably negative ways.

Thus, perhaps an initial step in reducing potential cultural disadvantage in CATs is to discover the extent to which individual test takers have acculturated and/or received similar types of cultural information in those environments that would be expected to function in the role of acculturating or teaching the individual the relevant cultural content of CATs. Failure to consider a variety of potential culture-related psychological processes may contribute to cultural equivalence dilemmas of all types.

Unfortunately, existing measures of acculturation for most ethnic cultural groups are less than adequate, primarily because the acculturation theories on which such measures have been based do not treat acculturation as a cognitive process (Helms, in press). Consequently, existing acculturation measures generally consist of a polyglot of sociodemographic and ethnic preference items such as generation in this country, preferred language, and so forth (e.g., Suinn, Rickard-Figueroa, Lew, & Vigil, 1987). Furthermore, such characteristics typically are used to classify respondents rather than to identify acculturative processes that they use. Thus, in the general acculturation literature, acculturation is only measured at a nominal level, but in the psychometric literature, it has not been measured at all. Knowing, for example, that a person is the third generation of his or her family in this country actually reveals very little about the degree to which the person has learned the dominant culture (that is, for example, the culture of the WAIS-R). However, even this modicum of information might be more psychologically meaningful than knowing just the person's ethnic classification.

Be that as it may, not even inadequate measures of acculturation (see also Szapocznik, Scopetta, Kurtines, & Aranalde, 1978) have been used to study the acculturation issues of African or African American populations as such. To my knowledge, only one study in psychology (Landrine & Klonoff, 1994) addresses the acculturation issues of Black Americans in any domain of psychology. Instead, acculturation is treated as an indelible aspect of Asian and Latino/Latina American populations (regardless of their generation in this country) in the United States, and to the extent that the influence of acculturation on IQ scores is studied at all, such research focuses on Asian or Latino/Latina (and occasionally indigenous) populations—at least minimally. Thus, whereas acculturation theorists have avoided the question of whether Whites or Blacks (of any ethnicity) in this country differentially learn White culture, CAT psychometricians have avoided the question of whether differential cultural socialization is revealed in VREG people's test performance.

Obviously, such acculturation assessments cannot be adequately accomplished merely by comparing so-called racial groups because it is possible that people within groups may not have received similar cultural socialization. Rather, groups should be defined according to cultural dimensions assumed to be critical to satisfactory CAT performance. For example, if collectivism–individualism is considered a critical aspect of performance, cultural comparison groups should be formed by measuring this aspect of people's functioning.

Race, Racism, and Assimilation

Race, or at least psychorace, refers to the extent to which a person reacts to stimuli according to internalized norms acquired as a result of being socialized in one of the dominative or subjugated racial-classification groups that exist in the United States (Helms, 1994; Helms & Cook, in press). For members of both types of racial-classification groups, internalized norms might promote suspicion, mistrust, and rejection of out-group members and those aspects of behavior that are assumed to typify them. However, such reactions to out-group members and their culture presents a greater disadvantage for VREGs than for Whites because VREGs are less likely to have determined the content of CATs or the consequences of inadequate performance on such devices.

Moreover, as suggested in Table 26.1, because of such reactivity to out-group-related stimuli, VREG test takers may perceive test stimuli differently than the test constructors intended. For example, McCallum and Bracken (Chapter 14, this volume) use black and green human figures in an effort to create universal (i.e., culturally equivalent) symbols. Yet it is conceivable that for African Americans, "black" and "green" people are not the "universal" stimuli that the authors intended because of African Americans' long history of skin color discrimination. One rarely has to consider one's own skin color as a source of negative evaluation if one is a member of the White group. In other words, such figures may have different connotations for African Americans than they do for White Americans because of the two groups' different histories of sociopolitical socialization regarding skin color. Consequently, emotional reactivity to such stimuli might (probably) inhibit or (possibly) facilitate African Americans' performance on such measures relative to their White American counterparts, or other members of visible racial/ethnic groups who have not experienced similar histories of generational skin color oppression in this country.

Furthermore, it is reasonable to assume that more contact with White people produces greater exposure to the target culture, an argument that is often used to explain the differential test performance of Black adoptees raised in White rather than Black families (e.g., Scarr & Weinberg, 1976). However, VREGs' exposure to institutional racism and other forms of socioracial segregation and the consequent influence of such exposure on relevant group members' CAT performance has been infrequently investigated (Terrell et al., 1981). Terrell et al. found that African American test takers' "cultural mistrust" (perhaps more accurately, reactions to racism) interacted with racial classification of the examiner to influence the test takers' scores on the WAIS-R.

Therefore, if investigators wanted to move measurement of racial influences on CATs beyond nominal classification, the limited available literature suggests several possible avenues for doing so. For example, it might be useful to assess levels of test takers' amount and quality of interracial-group contact, subjective experiences of racism, and reactivity to racial stimuli. Such factors could be used to screen examinees for test appropriateness (i.e., conceptual equivalence), match examiners and examinees to minimize effects due to racial differences (i.e., testing situation equivalence), or weight responses to adjust for differential assimilation (i.e., psychometric equivalence).

Socioeconomic Status and Environmental Deprivation

SES, culture, and race often are irretrievably confounded in examinations of the psychometric properties of CATs. In fact, on a demographic or group level, racial classification and SES are often intertwined because of the country's history of depriving many of its VREGs of adequate financial recompense and resources. Thus, African and Native Americans and Latino/Latina Americans of color are more likely to exist under conditions of severe economic deprivation than their White counterparts (Frisby, 1992). Nevertheless, it may be possible to move beyond nominal categorizations of socioeconomic status to its person-relevant psychological implications.

SES may be defined as the amount and quality of economic resources available to a person. Ordinarily, it is inferred from indicators external to the person such as level of education, annual income, area of residency, and so forth. However, a potentially measurable consequence of economic deprivation may be that a person who receives his or her formative socialization under environmental circumstances of economic deprivation may not be exposed to the materials, intellectual customs and practices, and occupational experiences that perhaps enhance CAT performance. For example, a child who does not have regular access to the types of toys (e.g., blocks, mazes, and puzzles) that are often contained in CATs might encounter them for the first time in the testing situation. If such is the case, one would expect this deprivation to be reflected in the psychological consequence of deflated test performance. However, performance deficits in such instances would not truly reflect a person's aptitudes or abilities, but would reflect lack of conceptual and functional equivalence of those types of items for the person being tested.

In the psychological literature, years of education is one of the most frequently used indicators of social class. Education is also one of the primary means by which culture is taught. Generally speaking, levels of personal and/or familial income and/or occupational status determine the quality of one's educational experiences. Yet the number of years of education is a poor proxy for quality of education. Much evidence indicates that African Americans are not only disproportionately poor and unemployed but also are more likely than Whites to receive inferior educations. Across subtests of the WAIS-R, it seems evident that educational quality influences respondents' quality of performance at every stage of the process. Thus, strategies to assess the quality (rather than just the amount) of test takers' prior education need to be developed and used in the test construction process.

In addition, methodologies for adjusting test scores to compensate for differences in socioeconomic socialization ought to be developed. For example, with respect to the WAIS-R, previous research (e.g., Reynolds, Chastain, Kaufman, & McLean, 1987) suggests that if the test taker is illiterate or has minimal education, then her or his IQ score is not likely to exceed a Full Scale score of approximately 82. Therefore, one might use an IQ of 82 as the baseline for the amount of information a person could acquire under conditions of limited educational exposure to the culture of the WAIS-R. Presumably, the more and the better (i.e., culturally relevant) the test taker's education, the better he or she should perform beyond this baseline level. Thus, it might be possible to adjust scoring procedures to take into account differences in educational experiences.

Perhaps it should also be noted that quality of education is probably correlated with the quality of one's religious, work, and recreational activities as well such that superior educational attainment should be associated with other CAT-relevant life experiences that also reflect the dominant culture. In turn, if these other socialized life experiences and those that are dominant in White culture are the same, they should reinforce the cultural information taught in White culturally oriented schools as well as fill in gaps (e.g., religious teachings) that such institutions may have overlooked.

Summary and Implications

An obvious implication of the observations concerning the different influences of the culture–race–socioeconomic triad is that the operation of each of these factors may be implicit in the content of CATs even when they are not readily apparent. For instance, perhaps one is more likely to know the capital of Italy if one's religion comes from Italy; or one is more likely to know the distance from Paris to New York if one has had the opportunity to travel between these two places, and these two places have cultural significance to the person being tested. Similarly, if one's religion uses the *Koran* as its holy book, one might consider it sacrilegious to use "Mohammed" as an adjective, although apparently White culture more generally would not. Religious practices and travel preferences are probably cultural aspects of socialization, whereas the means to travel is seemingly socioeconomically related. Neither of these factors is necessarily racial.

A broader implication of the observation that culture, race, and SES are not necessarily synonymous is that controlling for culture or racial-group influences in test items will not automatically reduce the effects of SES and, conversely, controlling for socioeconomic effects will not automatically eliminate the influence of culture or racial-group socialization.

Of course, the implicit triadic components could interact to multiply suppress the quality—or at least evaluations of the quality—of an examinee's performance. Thus, a person who is of White middle to upper social class and is assimilated into White cultural institutions is likely to perform well on such measures, whereas a White person of low SES who is not assimililated into such institutions will likely do less well. However, it should be noted that middle-to-upper-class respondents of any racial group should be expected to perform better than the lower class within the relevant racial group because the culture of the test more closely parallels middle-class culture; to become middle-class, one must have some characteristics in common with other middle-class people.

Nevertheless, those VREGs who are of low SES *and* receive the bulk of their cultural socialization in predominantly VREG cultural institutions probably enter the testing process with a double, and perhaps a triple, disadvantage. Relative to Whites and their same VREG middle-class counterparts, they perhaps enter the testing situation with the double disadvantages of racial discrimination and cultural deviation, deficits whose severity depends on the quality and quantity of their White cultural socialization.

EVALUATION OF CULTURAL
EQUIVALENCE ENHANCEMENT STRATEGIES

Most attempts to reduce the effects of race, culture, or SES on CAT performance at the test-construction phase have involved examination of either response patterns of various sociodemographic groups (e.g., socioracial classifications) or differential outcomes (e.g., selection and placement) resulting from use of the tests across demographic groups. By means of increasingly sophisticated psychometric analyses of tests or test items, "cultural fairness" of such measures is "demonstrated," and cultural equivalence is inferred from the same between-group statistical indicators (e.g., regression lines, intercepts, means, factor patterns, and logits) ensuing from such analyses. However, Helms (1992) contends that culture fairness (as it is typically operationalized) and cultural equivalence may not be synonymous.

For the most part, analyses of culture fairness equate culture with the structural properties of the tests. Thus, similar between-group structure is interpreted as indicating lack of cultural bias and, by implication, the presence of cultural equivalence. However, analyses of cultural equivalence should locate culture within the person and her or his environment. Therefore, to develop tests that are culturally equivalent, one needs a model or models of how culture functions as well as a model of how culture interacts with manifested cognitive abilities. In such models, cultural equivalence would mean the interface between culture and cognitive functioning, and culturally equivalent CATs would deliberately incorporate the properties intrinsic to the interactions between intended test takers' cultural socialization and the content of the tests by which they are assessed.

Armour-Thomas (1992), interpreting Vygotsky's (1978) cultural model of cognitive development, suggests that culture shapes cognitive development (and expression) by means of three processes: (1) communicating knowledge as the culture defines it, (2) transmitting adaptive cognitive skills, and (3) recognizing and fostering culturally relevant cognitive potentials. Armour-Thomas further contends that culture arranges the occurrence or nonoccurrence of specific problem-solving environments and defines the frequency and patterning of relevant events in these learning environments. Consequently, the pragmatic implications for test constructors of culture's functions are that task difficulty, familiarity, and significance are determined by the test taker's cultural socialization, which presumably is manifested in their test performance.

If one conceptualizes CAT performance as the interaction between two primary factors, culture and cognitive ability, it is clear that most recent efforts to develop culture fair CATs have been preoccupied with cognitive ability to the virtual exclusion of consideration of cultural contributions to such abilities. Nevertheless, one or more of the following strategies have been used to reduce cultural bias in tests: (1) content modification, (2) heterogeneous sampling, and (3) item response theory. It is not clear that any of these approaches has been based on explicit models of culture, race, or social class. Yet it might be useful to consider briefly the implications of each of these approaches for the issues of cultural equivalence of CATs.

Content Modification

Theorists (e.g., Walsh & Betz, 1985) generally consider that evidence of content bias is the most significant reason why a CAT should not be used to assess the cognitive abilities of VREG test takers. Extrapolating from Walsh and Betz's discussion of test bias, content bias can be considered to be the extent to which test content is less familiar to VREG, less-than-middle class, and culturally collectivistic test takers than it is to White, middle-class, culturally individualistic test takers, the predominant group on whom such measures are devised. However, attempts to reduce bias due to differential familiarity have focused on the surface properties of tests rather than their underlying cultural characteristics. Walsh and Betz's definition also suggests that content bias is present if the test uses pictorial or linguistic materials that favor one (socioracial, social class, or sociocultural) group over another. Considerably more attention has been focused on the pictorial and linguistic aspects of culture-fair tests.

Familiarity

Criteria for assessing differential familiarity of test content are never specified. The strategy used to reduce this type of bias is to ask "expert" panelists presumably of relevant but unspecified racial, socioeconomic, and cultural characteristics, to evaluate items for appropriateness. However, descriptions of item development rarely specify what criteria panelists used in making such evaluations. For test developers themselves, ostensible group membership of panelists seems to be a sufficient indicator of relevant expertise.

Appropriate examination of familiarity as it pertains to (especially) functional cultural equivalence would involve assessment of the level of occurrence of the test constructs and/or test content in the environments of the persons being tested. For example, one strategy for making CATs more responsive to VREG cultures is to analyze unique cultural products (e.g., newspapers, magazines) from the various cultures. In considering cultural products, it should not be too difficult to develop strategies to examine overlap and discrepancies in the content of existing cultural products. One could, for instance, count the frequency of usage of vocabulary words in Black and White American newspapers, magazines, and popular literature and determine whether they had common meanings in these two sources. As a result of such analyses, words not occurring with equivalent frequency or having the same connotations in both sources would not be used as standard test items.

Also, cultural products could be content analyzed for the purpose of identifying cultural themes that might be related to various subtest items. For instance, wilderness skills or perceptivity (e.g., using nature to find directions and knowledge of plant characteristics) might not occur equally often in different cultural groups. This analysis could be guided by one of the theoretical models of cultural dimensions (e.g., Boykin, 1983; Katz, 1985; Stewart, 1971) or it could grow out of qualitative analyses of existing materials. In both cases, the criteria for the cultural evaluations should be clearly specified so that they could be used in subsequent equivalence investigations.

Pictorial

Developers of assessment devices that incorporate pictorial stimulus materials have used two strategies, cosmetic enhancement and minimalization. The Wechsler Intelligence Scale for Children (WISC-III; Wechsler, 1991) is perhaps the best example of a cosmetic enhancement approach to bias reduction. The pictures are in color, items have been updated, and some pictures of VREG people are included in the testing materials. Certainly, the use of color and the updating of items makes the WISC-III a more attractive and interesting task as does the inclusion of some ethnic content. However, it is not clear that such modifications enhance the cultural equivalence or reduce the cultural bias of the test because no culture-based framework for implementing the changes was explicated. In other words, although the test may *look* better than earlier versions, there is no evidence that it does or does not take into account pertinent cultural factors better than previous editions.

Linguistic

Minimalization is often used to compensate for linguistic bias in tests. McCallum and Bracken's (Chapter 14, this volume) Universal Nonverbal Intelligence Test is an example of a minimalization approach in that defining characteristics of pictorial materials are reduced by using "universal" (e.g., black and green human figures) stimuli. Yet as previously mentioned, the concept of universality across socioracial, cultural, and social class groups is too dubious to accept without confirmatory empirical examinations. In this case, confirmatory analyses would not be demonstrations that groups perform similarly on tests and/or items but rather that items have the same meaning to respondents and/or involve the same psychological processes regardless of the sociodemographic characteristics of the groups with whom the test is to be used.

Be that as it may, the most common method for addressing issues of linguistic equivalence or bias in tests has been providing versions of tests in alternate languages, especially Spanish (Woodcock & Muñoz-Sandoval, 1993, 1996). Thus, one can generally find Spanish-language versions of most standardized English-language tests, and the methodologies for creating such tests are becoming increasingly more sophisticated (Bracken & Barona, 1991). However, as McCallum and Bracken (Chapter 14, this volume) note, the varieties of languages (and language structures) used in the United States are too numerous to provide a measure that is adequately responsive to linguistic diversity.

For example, where African Americans (i.e., the group of Americans descended from enslaved peoples in the primarily southern United States) are concerned, the Smithsonian now recognizes Gullah and (presumably) its derivative language structures as a unique American language. However, no Gullah versions of CATs exist. To the extent that a person's primary language structure is something other than standard (White) American English, one is culturally disadvantaged with respect to CAT performance. The more disparate one's primary language is from the language used in CATs, the more disadvantaged one is. Nevertheless, quality of English-language usage or proficiency does not necessarily reveal the core dimensions of cultural socialization. If culture does contribute to different learning styles or information processing skills and/or strategies, it is important to ascertain how these strategies appear in CAT performance. Moreover, if language does signify a person's inherent cognitive abilities or information-processing strategies, tests should be developed to access the underlying strategies.

Perhaps only a few common strategies or components of ability exist across cultures as is suggested in the *WJ-R Technical Manual* (McGrew, Werder, & Woodcock, 1991) and by Hessler (1993). However, such equivalence should be determined by observing and assessing manifestations of the proposed strategies within the environmental contexts in which they occur prior to developing and translating supposedly common items. Otherwise, one risks forcing members of a cultural group to conform to singular representations of culture, which may inadequately fit their own internalized cultures.

Heterogeneous Sampling

There is still too much of a tendency for test developers to locate "culture" outside the United States (Elliott, 1990) while disregarding or minimizing its many varieties in this country. Nevertheless, to reduce test bias, most revisions of commonly used CATs do incorporate oversampling rather than representative sampling of underrepresented populations (e.g., Blacks, Latinos/Latinas) within the test-construction and norming process. For African Americans and other socioracial and cultural groups to truly influence the content of tests in a direction consistent with intelligent behavior in their cultures, it is necessary to over sample these groups. Thus, these more inclusive sampling strategies are an improvement over earlier standardization procedures because they permit the possibility that unmeasured cultural characteristics associated with sociodemographic member- ships may fortuitously effect the content of the tests. However, selection according to group mem- bership must not be misconstrued as constituting measurement of cultural criteria because a per- son's group designations may not reveal the person's cultural, social class, or racial socialization.

Moreover, truly representative sampling of people should be varied with respect to SES, geo- graphic regions, urbanicity, and cultural parameters within the nation or country. Also, repre- sentative sampling or construction of CAT tasks should involve assessment of skills that are common to VREG and White samples, lower-class and middle-class samples, and collectivistic and individu- alistic samples, for example. Alternatively, multiple "intelligent" responses to items could be deter- mined by interpreting the correctness of responses according to their meaning within the various groups in which test takers are socialized. Otherwise, including VREGs in normative samples creates the illusion of having reduced the cultural bias within a measure but probably does not cause tests to be much more culturally representative than they would be if these groups were not included.

Item Response Theory

With perhaps one exception, item response theory (IRT), metric equivalence in CATs remains an unexplored area. Whereas some theorists (e.g., Jensen, 1980; Gottfredson, 1988; Sackett & Wilk, 1994) argue that similar regression statistics across sociodemographic groups provide evidence of the fairness of CATs, in fact, such evidence generally is accrued after the test is a fait accompli. That is, the predictive validity of CATs across sociodemographic groups typically is based on summative scale scores of some kind and is usually judged from common between-group regression statistics (e.g., regression lines, slopes, and intercepts). To the extent that such measures do not *underpredict* the performance of target groups, they are judged to be sufficient measures of the cognitive ability assumed to exist in both the test and the predicted criteria.

However, the measurement model underlying such validity studies is classical measurement theory. As Hambleton, Swaminathan, and Rogers (1991) note, classical measurement theory con- ceptually cannot separate the characteristics of the person (e.g., psychorace, psychoclass, and psy- choculture) from the characteristics of the test items. Yet these person-level characteristics might be expected to differentially shape responses to CAT items.

IRT is intended to provide procedures for assessing both person and item characteristics. The simplest and most frequently used version of IRT in cognitive ability test construction is Rasch modeling (e.g., Elliott, 1990; Woodcock & Muñoz-Sandoval, 1993). Essentially, IRT is based on the premise that both the examinee's latent traits or abilities and item characteristics can be described separately. The various types of IRT models differ in the numbers of parameters or person–item characteristics (e.g., item difficulty estimates, item discrimination indices, adjustments for fortui- tious responses) used to assess the person's level of test performance. Rasch modeling uses only one parameter, item difficulty. Thus, strictly speaking, the virtually interchangeable use of the terms IRT and Rasch modeling is incorrect (e.g., Elliott, 1990; Woodcock & Muñoz-Sandoval, 1993).

Be that as it may, in IRT models, both abilities and item characteristics are inferred from examinees' performance on a test's items. High scorers on the items that make up a test are assumed to have "high ability" and conversely, low scorers have "low ability." Items are more "difficult" if fewer people at every ability level have more trouble responding to them correctly and less difficult if more people in the relevant sample can answer them correctly. Thus, the measurement and/or operational definition of person-item characteristics is test dependent.

Moreover, according to Hambleton et al. (1991), a common assumption of IRTs (including Rasch modeling) is that a set of test items measures only one ability. However, they note that this assumption may not be precisely met because a variety of person-level factors (e.g., cognitive processes, personality characteristics) as well as environmental forces (e.g., assimilation, racism) may influence CAT performance. Thus, Hambleton et al. contend that even when IRT is the basis by which tests are constructed, test performance may be affected by "level of motivation, test anxiety, ability to work quickly, tendency to guess when in doubt about answers, and cognitive skills in addition to the dominant one measured by the set of test items" (p. 9). Presumably, any of these potential performance hindrances may be elicited by the internalized culture, race, and socioeconomic socialization under which the test taker performs.

Thus, item response models do not resolve the issue of the psychometric cultural equivalence of CATs. Rather they create the illusion that the problem has been solved when, in fact, it has not been truly addressed. As is the case for other forms of equivalence, models of culture external to the test are needed to establish person as distinguished from item characteristics. In the absence of such models, neither cultural equivalence nor fairness of CATs can be "proven."

FUTURE DIRECTIONS

If culture, race, and socioeconomic socialization do contribute to cognitive or intellectual dimensions that differ from White American middle-to-upper-class cultural dimensions as many theorists argue (e.g., Grubb & Dozier, 1989; Willis, 1989), it is important to begin to conceptualize and measure these factors in more complex manners than CAT psychometricians typically have heretofore. At the very least, it is time to move beyond categorical operational definitions of cultural (racial and socioeconomic) factors at the test development phase.

Throughout this discussion, I have attempted to suggest some measurement strategies by which such movement might be encouraged. Table 26.2 summarizes these strategies. However, the general

TABLE 26.2. Person and Environmental Levels of Measurement of Sociodemographic Characteristics of CAT Test Takers

Dimension	Types of measures	
	Environment	Person
Ethnic culture	Linguistic community Community's cultural products Cultural composition Familial socialization	Language proficiency Collectivism–individualism Cognitive styles Cultural competence Learning styles Information processing
Racial classification	Racial segregation-integration Racial climate Intergroup contact Racial stereotyping	Internalized racism Racial identity Racism coping strategies Racism reactions
Socioeconomic status	Quality of education Interclass assimilation Access to resources Employment history	Literacy Familiarity with CAT materials Achievement motivation

intent of the table is to buttress the notion that legitimate claims to the cultural equivalence (or culture fairness) of CATs requires that researchers specify (1) which aspects of racial, cultural, and/or socioeconomic socialization are controlled or reduced; (2) how these factors were measured at both the person and environmental levels; and (3) the hypothesized psychological implications of these characteristics for CAT performance. Such specification should move the field closer to developing measures of the culture by cognitive abilities interactions that do not unduly penalize (especially) VREG persons.

In the interim, it seems only fair to warn CAT test takers and users that psychometricians do not have informed models for investigating the possible racial, cultural, and/or socioeconomic limitations of CATs. Consequently, a person's performance on such devices may be influenced in unknown ways depending on her or his degree of deviance from the racial–cultural–class standards that may be implicit to CATs. Such advisories might be particularly useful to VREG test takers because they are often misled into believing that CATs necessarily assess the same intellective constructs for them as they do for their more advantaged counterparts.

REFERENCES

Alba, R. D. (1990). *Ethnic identity: The transformation of white America.* New Haven: Yale University Press.

Armour-Thomas, E. (1992). Intellectual assessment of children from culturally diverse backgrounds. *School Psychology Review, 21,* 552–565.

Boykin, A. W. (1983). On academic performance and Afro-American children. In J. R. Spencer (Ed.), *Achievement and achievement motives* (pp. 324–371), Boston: Freeman.

Bracken, B. A., & Barona, A. (1991). State of the art procedures for translating, validating and using psychological tests in cross-cultural assessment. *School Psychology International, 12,* 119–132.

Butcher, J. N. (1982). Cross-cultural research methods in clinical psychology. In P. C. Kendall & J. N. Butcher (Eds.), *Handbook of research methods in clinical psychology* (pp. 273–308). New York: Wiley.

Elliott, C. D. (1990). *Differential Ability Scales.* San Antonio, TX: Psychological Corporation.

Frisby, C. L. (1992). Issues and problems in the influence of culture on the psychoeducational needs of African-American children. *School Psychology Review, 21,* 532–551.

Gottfredson, L. S. (1988). Reconsidering fairness: A matter of social and ethical priorities. *Journal of Vocational Behavior, 33,* 293–319.

Grubb, H. J., & Dozier, A. (1989). Too busy to learn: A "competing behaviors" explanation of cross-cultural differences in academic ascendency. *Journal of Black Psychology, 16*(1), 23–45.

Hambleton, R. K., Swaminathan, H., & Rogers, H. J. (1991). *Fundamentals of item response theory.* Newbury Park, CA: Sage.

Helms, J. E. (in press). Toward a methodology for measuring and assessing "racial" as distinguished from "ethnic" identity. In G. R. Sodowsky & J. Impara (Eds.), *Multicultural assessment.* Lincoln, NE: Buros Institute.

Helms, J. E. (1992). Why is there no study of cultural equivalence in standardized cognitive ability testing? *American Psychologist, 47*(9), 1083–1101.

Helms, J. E. (1994). The conceptualization of racial identity and other "racial" constructs. In E. J. Trickett, R. J. Watts, & D. Birman (Eds.), *Human diversity: Perspectives on people in context* (pp. 285–311). San Francisco: Jossey-Bass.

Helms, J. E., & Cook, D. A. (in press). *Using race and culture in counseling and psychotherapy: Theory and process.* Fort Worth, TX: Harcourt, Brace.

Hessler, G. L. (1993). *Use and interpretation of the Woodcock–Johnson Psycho-Educational Battery—Revised.* Chicago: Riverside.

Hilliard, A. G. (1976). A review of Leon Kamin's "The science and politics of I.Q.". *Journal of Black Psychology, 2*(2), 64–74.

Jensen, A. R. (1980). *Bias in mental testing.* New York: Free Press.

Katz, J. H. (1985). The sociopolitical nature of counseling. *The Counseling Psychologist, 13*(4), 615–624.

Kaufman, A. S. (1990). *Assessing adolescent and adult intelligence.* Boston: Allyn & Bacon.

Landrine, H., & Klonoff, E. A. (1994). The African-American Acculturation Scale: Development, reliability, validity. *Journal of Black Psychology, 20*(2), 104–127. Thousand Oaks, CA: Sage.

McGrew, K. S., Werder, J. K., & Woodcock, R. W. (1991). *Woodcock–Johnson technical manual.* Allen, TX: DLM.

Reynolds, C. R., Chastain, R. L., Kaufman, A. S., & McLean, J. E. (1987). Demographic characteristics and IQ among adults: Analysis of the WAIS-R standardization sample as a function of the stratification variables. *Journal of School Psychology, 25*, 323–342.

Robinson, D. N. (1994/1995, Winter). Hereditary monarchy in the republic of virtue. *Journal of Blacks in Higher Education, 2*(6), 117–122.

Sackett, P. R., & Wilk, S. L. (1994). Within-group norming and other forms of score adjustment in preemployment testing. *American Psychologist, 49*, 929–954.

Scarr, S., & Weinberg, R. A. (1976). IQ test performance of Black children adopted by White families. *American Psychologist, 31*, 726–739.

Stewart, E. C. (1971). *American cultural patterns: A cross-cultural perspective.* Pittsburgh: Regional Council for International Understanding.

Suinn, R. M., Rickard-Figueroa, K., Lew, S., & Vigil, P. (1987). The Suinn–Lew Asian self-identity acculturation scale: An initial report. *Educational and Psychological Measurement, 47*, 401–407.

Szapocznik, J., Scopetta, M. A., Kurtines, W., & Aranalde, M. D. (1978). Theory and measurement of acculturation. *Inter-American Journal of Psychology, 12*, 113–130.

Terrell, F., Terrell, S. L., & Taylor, J. (1981). Effects of race of examiner and cultural mistrust on the WAIS performance of Black students. *Journal of Consulting and Clinical Psychology, 49*, 750–751.

Vygotsky, L. S. (1978). *Mind in society: The development of higher psychological processes.* Cambridge, MA: Harvard University Press.

Walsh, W. B., & Betz, N. E. (1985). *Tests and assessment.* Englewood Cliffs, NJ: Prentice-Hall.

Wechsler, D. (1981). *Wechsler Adult Intelligence Scale—Revised.* San Antonio, TX: Psychological Corporation.

Wechsler, D. (1991). *Wechsler Intelligence Scale for Children—Third edition.* San Antonio, TX: Psychological Corporation.

Willis, M. G. (1989). Learning styles of African American children: A review of the literature and interventions. *Journal of Black Psychology, 16*(1), 47–65.

Woodcock, R. W., & Munoz-Sandoval, A. F. (1993). An IRT approach to cross-language test equating and interpretation. *European Journal of Psychological Assessment, 9*, 233–241.

Woodcock, R. W., & Muñoz-Sandoval, A. F. (1996). *Batería Woodcock–Muñoz Pruebas de habilidad cognoscitiva—Revisada.* Chicago: Riverside.

CHAPTER 27

An Integration and Synthesis of Contemporary Theories, Tests, and Issues in the Field of Intellectual Assessment

PATTI L. HARRISON

DAWN P. FLANAGAN

JUDY L. GENSHAFT

T HE PURPOSE OF THIS CHAPTER is to integrate and synthesize the information presented in this volume with respect to empirically supported theories of the structure of intelligence and personal competencies, new assessment technology, and current scientific knowledge of the validity of cognitive constructs and measures of intelligence. This information may provide a basis from which professionals can understand and appreciate the significant scientific advances that have been made recently in the field of intellectual assessment. In light of this new knowledge, professionals may choose to move beyond traditional tests and theories of intelligence and adopt new and improved measures and methods of assessing cognitive abilities that will allow them to make better informed decisions in everyday practice.

CURRENT PRACTICE

The Wechsler and Binet scales have a long history with respect to their development, use and interpretation. Part I of this volume describes the historical and theoretical origins of these instruments and traces the development and reconceptualizations of the original Binet–Simon and Wechsler–Bellevue Scales to their present-day editions. Professionals in the field of intellectual assessment have relied on the use of these instruments since the mid-1900s. It was not until the late 1970s and early 1980s that tests such as the Woodcock–Johnson Tests of Cognitive Ability (WJ-COG; Woodcock & Johnson, 1977) and the Kaufman Adolescent Battery for Children (K-ABC; Kaufman & Kaufman, 1983), respectively, added to the psychologist's choice of assessment instruments. The introduction of these tests represented a positive shift in the field because they focused on measurement of underlying cognitive processes rather than abilities and, therefore, were expected to provide more relevant and useful information for planning instructional programs and interventions. However, given the limited clinical interpretive information that was available for these instruments at the time of their publication coupled with a pervasive resistance to change current assessment practices, these cognitive processing measures did not gain widespread use (Harrison, Kaufman, Hickman, & Kaufman, 1988; McGrew, 1986, 1994; Reschly & Wilson, 1990). Although the WJ-COG and K-ABC had many spokespersons, the Wechsler and Binet scales continued to be used most widely.

There is no question that the study of the Wechsler scales, in particular, over the past several decades has contributed significantly to research and practice in school and clinical psychology as well as special education. However, in light of current advances in cognitive psychology, it is apparent that the most dependable and recent evidence of science supports models of intelligence that are more differentiated and complex than those that underlie these instruments (see Horn, 1991). The Wechsler scales were not developed from well-researched theoretical models of intelligence based on current scientific understanding of the structure of human cognitive abilities (see Carroll, 1993; Das, Naglieri, & Kirby, 1994; Gardner, 1983; Horn, 1991; Mackintosh, 1986; McGrew, 1993, 1994; Sternberg, 1986b, 1992, 1993). Nearly two decades ago, Kaufman (1979) stated that "One major limitation of intelligence tests [i.e., Wechslers and Binet] is their failure to grow conceptually with the advent of important advances in psychology and neurology. . . . impressive findings in the areas of cognitive development, learning theory, and neuropsychology during the past 25–50 years have not invaded the domain of the individual intelligence test" (p. 4). Today, the fact remains, "Presently available knowledge . . . would permit the development of tests and scales that would be much more adequate for their purposes than the Wechsler Scales" (Carroll, 1993, p. 702).

Despite the recent advances in theories of intelligence and their operationalization, described in Parts II and III of this volume, respectively, the Wechsler instruments remain the most widely used of all intelligence tests among practitioners (Harrison et al., 1988; Wilson & Reschly, 1996). Thus, it is still the case that dominant testing practices lag considerably behind current cognitive theories and research. Reminiscent of the 1970s and 1980s, it is likely that the limited amount of scientific evidence that is available to support the clinical utility of new instruments at this time as well as a continued resistance to change current practices contributes to the lack of growth in the field of intellectual assessment. Although there is currently a dearth of empirical support for the diagnostic and treatment validity of *all* intelligence batteries, recent studies with some newer tests have yielded positive preliminary findings (e.g., Das et al., 1994; Evans, Carlsen, & McGrew, 1993; Hessler, 1993; Mather, 1993; Naglieri & Andrews, 1994; see also Flanagan, Andrews & Genshaft, Chapter 23, this volume and Reschly, Chapter 22, this volume, for a review). However, additional research is needed to determine whether new instruments, by virtue of their technological and theoretical strengths, can circumvent the most salient weaknesses of traditional measures.

Contemporary and Emerging Theories of Intelligence

Several prominent theories of intelligence that encompass multiple cognitive abilities and competencies are presented in Part II of this volume and are summarized in Table 27.1. As may be seen in Table 27.1 many of these theories and their underlying assumptions depart significantly from traditional views of intelligence. For example, the triarchic theory of intelligence (Sternberg, Chapter 5, this volume) and the theory of multiple intelligences (Chen & Gardner, Chapter 6, this volume) focus, in part, on the external worlds of the individual as well as the creation of products that are valued in a culture. Therefore, both theoretical models may have significance for the development of assessment methods and procedures that are more relevant to multicultural populations than traditional paradigms. Other models of intelligence and personal competence appear to demon-

TABLE 27.1. Contemporary and Emerging Theoretical Perspectives

Theory	Theorist(s)	Ch.	Components	Assumptions	Examples of application
Fluid–Crystallized theory	John L. Horn Raymond B. Cattell	4	Fluid reasoning (Gf) Acculturation knowledge or crystallized intelligence (Gc) Short-term apprehension–retention (SAR, Gsm) Fluency of retrieval from long-term storage (TSR, Glr) Visual processing (Gv) Auditory processing (Ga) Processing speed (Gs) Correct decision speed (CDS) Quantitative knowledge (Gq)	Theory describes thinking capabilities that distinguish humans from other creatures. Theory describes abilities for which there are individual differences. Theory describes several types of distinct intelligences or cognitive abilities. Each of the distinct types of cognitive ability are equally important in explaining intelligent behavior (Horn, 1994).	Intelligence tests: Kaufman Assessment Battery for Children (Kaufman & Kaufman, 1983) Stanford–Binet Intelligence Scale: Fourth edition (Thorndike, Hagen, & Sattler, 1986) Woodcock–Johnson Tests of Cognitive Ability—Revised (Woodcock & Johnson, 1989) Kaufman Adolescent and Adult Intelligence Test (Kaufman & Kaufman, 1993) Universal Nonverbal Intelligence Test (McCallum & Bracken, in press) Other: Cross-Battery Approach to Measuring Gf-Gc Abilities (McGrew & Flanagan, 1996) Interpreting Gf-Gc abilities from an information processing model (Woodcock, 1993)

Triarchic theory of intelligence	Robert J. Sternberg	5	Componential (internal)
			  Metacomponents
			  Performance components
			  Knowledge–acquisition components
			
			Experiential (experience)
			  Ability to cope with novelty
			  Ability to automatize information
			
			Contextual (external)
			  Adaptation
			  Shaping
			  Selection
				Intelligence is understood by its relationship to the internal worlds, experience, and external worlds of individuals.	Teaching of learning of vocabulary from context (Sternberg, 1987)
					
					Teaching of insight skills (Davidson & Sternberg, 1984)
					
					"Practical intelligence in schools" (Gardner, Krechevsky, Sternberg, & Okagaki, 1994)
					
					Intelligence Applied (Sternberg, 1986a)
					
					Teaching subject matter areas (Sternberg, 1994)
					
					Testing common sense (Sternberg, Wagner, Williams, & Horvath, 1995)

(cont.)

TABLE 27.1. *(Cont.)*

Theory	Theorist(s)	Ch.	Components	Assumptions	Examples of application
Theory of multiple intelligences	Howard Gardner	6	Linguistic Logical–mathematical Musical Spatial Bodily-kinesthetic Interprsonal Intrapersonal	Intelligence defined as problem solving or creation of products valued in a culture. The seven intelligences are relatively autonomous, but do not function in isolation. The seven intelligences are not abstract, but are expressed in symbol systems. General intelligence (g) exists, but its explanatory and utility power is questioned. Multiple intelligences are shaped by culture and refined by education.	Alternative approaches to assessment (Gardner, 1984, 1986, 1993b) *Spectrum Preschool Assessment Activities* and *Observational Guidelines* (Chen, Isberg, & Krechevsky, in press) Harvard Project Zero (Gardner, 1993a)

Three-stratum theory of cognitive abilities	John B. Carroll	7	Stratum 3:
			  General intelligence (g)
			Stratum 2:
			  Fluid intelligence (Gf)
			  Crystallized intelligence (Gc)
			  General memory and learning (Gy)
			  Broad visual perception (Gv)
			  Broad auditory perception (Gu)
			  Broad retrieval ability (Gr)
			  Broad cognitive speediness (Gs)
			  Processing speed (Gt)
			Stratum 1:
			  Numerous level and speed factors
				Cognitive processes are required for the understanding and performance of tasks using these abilities.
				
				Theory intended to provide enumeration, identification, and structure of known cognitive abilities on a provisional basis.
				
				Theory provides structure of second-order factors subsumed by third-order factors and first-order factors subsumed by second order factors.
					Intended to provide guidance for future research
					
					Jonassen and Grabowski (1993) and Fleishman and Reilly (1992) described tests that measure factors.
					
					Flanagan and McGrew (Chapter 17, this volume) describe a cross-battery approach to assessment that operationalizes Carroll's second stratum.

TABLE 27.1. *(Cont.)*

Theory	Theorist(s)	Ch.	Components	Assumptions	Examples of application

Model of personal competence	Stephen Greenspan	8	Personal competence
			  Physical competence
			    Organ competence
			    Motor competence
			  Affective competence
			    Temperament
			    Character
			  Everyday competence
			    Social intelligence
			    Practical intelligence
			  Academic competence
			    Conceptual intelligence
			    Language
			
			In addition, some of the above competences can be categorized as follows:
			
			  Social competence
			    Temperament
			    Character
			    Social intelligence
			  Intellectual competence
			    Social intelligence
			    Conceptual intelligence
			    Language
				Aspects of competence, in addition to intelligence, contribute to solving problems/attaining goals.
				
				Competence is defined in terms of qualities that individuals bring to goals and by degree of success that individuals have in meeting goals.
					Nontraditional forms of assessment (Simeonsson, 1986)
					
					Framework for evaluating content coverage of scales (McGrew, 1994; Reschly, 1990)
					
					Devising individual education plans (Javel & Greenspan, 1983; Greenspan, 1982)
					
					Residential programming (Dunaway, Granfield, Norton, & Greenspan, 1992)
					
					Definition and conceptualization of the diagnostic construct of mental retardation (Greenspan, 1991; Greenspan & Granfield, 1992)

Neuropsychological Model of Intelligence	A. R. Luria J. P. Das	13	Attention Successive processing Simultaneous processing Planning	The cognitive activity of the brain may be described in terms of three functional units. Each functional unit is associated with specific neurological locations. Cognitive processing requires that these three functional systems work together. The collective participation of the three units is necessary to produce mental activity (Luria, 1973).	PASS model (Naglieri, 1989; Naglieri & Das, 1990) Kaufman Assessment Battery for Children (Kaufman & Kaufman, 1983) Das–Naglieri Cognitive Assessment Systems (Naglieri & Das, in press) PASS Remedial Program: PREP (training in simultaneous and successive processes) (Das, Naglieri, & Kirby, 1994)

strate more promise with respect to treatment relevance than traditional frameworks. For example, assessment procedures that are based on Greenspan's model of personal competence (Greenspan & Driscoll, Chapter 8, this volume) are particularly useful for devising individual education plans. Likewise, experimental tasks that measure the cognitive processes represented in Das and Naglieri's PASS Model (Naglieri, Chapter 13, this volume) may be useful in identifying and instructing individuals with poor planning ability.

Many of the theories presented in Table 27.1 encompass more cognitive abilities than traditional theories and have a considerable amount of structural evidence to support their multidimensionality. Current factor-analytic research has provided a clearer understanding of the general, broad, and narrow cognitive abilities that underlie intelligence tests (see Carroll, Chapter 7, this volume; Horn & Noll, Chapter 4, this volume; Keith, Chapter 20, this volume; Keith & Witta, in press; McGhee, 1993; McGrew, Werder, & Woodcock, 1991; Woodcock, 1990). The seminal work of Carroll (1993), which includes an extensive review and (re)analysis of most of the theoretical and empirical research on human cognitive functions and their measurement since the early 1900s, resulted in a three-stratum theoretical model of the nature of cognitive abilities that, according to Snow, may "define the taxonomy of cognitive differential psychology for many years to come" (cf. Carroll, 1993, p. back cover). Carroll's work served to provide additional support for one of the most widely recognized and well-researched theories of intelligence, the Horn–Cattell Fluid-Crystallized (Gf-Gc) model.

Given the substantial amount of empirical support for the Gf-Gc structure of intelligence (see Horn & Noll, Chapter 4, this volume, for a summary), it is not surprising that this model (in various stages of development) provided the foundation from which several tests of intelligence were constructed and interpreted. Tests that were premised on the Horn–Cattell Gf-Gc theoretical framework include the following: Woodcock–Johnson Psycho-Educational Battery, Tests of Cognitive Ability WJ-COG (Woodcock & Johnson, 1977), Kaufman Assessment Battery for Children K-ABC (Kaufman & Kaufman, 1983), Stanford–Binet Intelligence Scale: Fourth Edition (SB-IV; Thorndike, Hagen, & Sattler, 1986), Woodcock–Johnson Psycho-Educational Battery—Revised, Tests of Cognitive Ability (WJ-R COG; Woodcock & Johnson, 1989), Kaufman Adolescent and Adult Intelligence Test (KAIT; Kaufman & Kaufman, 1993), and the forthcoming Universal Nonverbal Intelligence Test (McCallum & Bracken, in press). Also, in light of the structural similarities between the most recently refined Horn–Cattell Gc-Gc model (Horn, 1991, 1994; Horn & Noll, Chapter 4, this volume) and the second stratum of Carroll's three-stratum theory, McGrew and Flanagan (1996) proposed a cross-battery approach to assessing and interpreting cognitive abilities based on an integrated Horn–Carroll theoretical framework (see McGrew, Chapter 9, this volume; Flanagan & McGrew, Chapter 17, this volume). Their approach is intended to provide practitioners with a means of augmenting any given intelligence test battery with empirically validated measures of Gf-Gc abilities, allowing for a broad-based cognitive assessment that is consistent with contemporary theory and research. Although it is clear that a psychometric approach to understanding intelligence is the most well-established and widely used in practical settings, other theoretical models have much to offer—no one conceptualization has answered all important questions about the structure of intelligence and none commands universal acceptance (Neisser et al., 1996).

The work that is currently being done in the area of theory development and validation presented in Part II of this volume demonstrates the importance of forms of intelligence that differ from those measured by standardized instruments (e.g., creativity, practical intelligence, social competence, and intra- and interpersonal skills) as well as the utility of and the growing need for an empirical foundation to guide test development and practice. Continued research and mounting validity evidence for the prominent and multidifferentiated theories presented in Table 27.1 will likely lead to informative alternatives to understanding, measuring and interpreting cognitive abilities, processes and personal competencies.

Contemporary Intelligence Tests

Several new instruments and techniques for assessing intelligence that are based on multidifferenti-ated theories of the structure of cognitive abilities have infiltrated the field of intellectual assessment in recent years. Much of this new assessment technology is described in Part III of this volume and is summarized in Tables 27.2 through 27.5. Some of these new instruments assess a greater breadth of broad cognitive abilities than traditional tests, such as the WJ-R COG (Woodcock & Johnson, 1989; Woodcock, Chapter 12, this volume). Others incorporate tests of cognitive processing, includ-ing the Differential Ability Scales (DAS; Elliott, 1990a, Chapter 10, this volume) and WJ-R COG, or were developed based on a theoretical model of information processing (e.g., Das–Naglieri Cogni-tive Assessment System, DNCAS; Naglieri & Das, in press; Naglieri, Chapter 13, this volume). Many new intelligence batteries were built (or are interpreted) from well-researched theoretical frame-works (e.g., the KAIT; Kaufman & Kaufman, 1993, Chapter 11, this volume) that reflect recent advances in psychometrics, neuropsychology and/or cognitive psychology (e.g., DNCAS, WJ-R COG). In addition, Part III of this volume presents dynamic assessment methods (Lidz, Chapter 15, this volume; and Feuerstein, Feuerstein, & Gross, Chapter 16, this volume) as alternatives to currently available technology as well as a cross-battery approach to assessment (see Flanagan & McGrew, Chapter 17). Both methods are theory driven; the former utilizes a "pretest–intervene–posttest" approach to understanding cognitive performance while the latter offers empirically supported procedures for assessing and interpreting cognitive abilities that may lead to improvements in the validity of the practice of intelligence testing.

The information included in Tables 27.2, 27.3, 27.4, and 27.5 provides a comparison of the major intelligence test batteries that were published at the time this book was being prepared, including the K-ABC (Kaufman & Kaufman, 1983), SB-IV (Thorndike et al., 1986), WJ-R COG, Wechsler scales (1981, 1989, 1991), DAS, and KAIT. In particular, these batteries were compared according to several important content (Table 27.2), administration (Table 27.3), interpretation (Table 27.4) and technical (Table 27.5) characteristics. Table 27.2 provides basic information about the age range of the batteries as well as the breadth of the independent lower-order composite scores yielded by each instrument. As may be seen in Table 27.2, some content features are unique to certain batteries. For example, the DAS has separately designed subtests for preschool children with varied printed and manipulative materials whereas preschool scales on other instruments represent down-ward extensions of scales designed for older subjects or do not include manipulatives for young children. Batteries such as the KAIT and WJ-R COG include controlled learning tests; that is, they measure learning with corrective feedback provided throughout the administration of the task. This type of test format allows the practitioner to view learning strategies and determine whether the individual benefits from instructional feedback. Because there is a strong theoretical relationship between intelligence and learning ability and intelligence is used to predict ability to learn in school, the inclusion of tests on cognitive batteries that assess learning ability, especially through high-level mental processing, is considered a positive feature (see Kaufman, 1979).

Table 27.2 also shows that both the KAIT and WJ-R COG allow for longitudinal follow-up with the same measures across the age range of the test. This condition results in a greater probability that the test's underlying constructs are invariant across the lifespan. Therefore, this feature is important when tests are used to monitor change over time (e.g., psychological reevaluations, longitudinal research). Tests such as the K-ABC, SB-IV, Wechsler instruments, and DAS include a nonverbal scale (or a nonverbal adaptation) which is considered useful when assessing language delayed and cul-turally diverse individuals. However, it is important to note that, with the exception of the K-ABC, each of these nonverbal scales requires receptive language despite the fact that no verbal responses are required. Also, even though the K-ABC can be administered nonverbally (e.g., through panto-mime), obtained scores are based on norms in which the directions were administered verbally. The

TABLE 27.2. Content Features of Intelligence Batteries

				Intelligence battery		
Content features	K-ABC (1983)	SB:IV (1986)	WJ-R (1989)	Wechsler Instruments (1981–1991)	DAS (1990)	KAIT (1993)
Age range of battery	Age 2-6 to 12-6	Age 2-0 to 23	Age 2-0 to 90+	WPPSI-R: Age 2-11 to 7-3 WISC-III: Age 6-0 to 16-11 WAIS-R: Age 16 to 74	Age 2-6 to 17-11	Age 11-0 to 85+
Broad measure of general intelligence	Mental Processing Composite (MPC)	Test Composite	Broad Cognitive Ability (BCA)	Full Scale IQ (FSIQ)	General Conceptual Ability (GCA)	Composite IQ
Total test composite limited to subtests with high factor loadings on the first principle factor (omits subtests with low loadings on this factor)	No	No	No	No	Yes	No
Independent lower-order composite scores	1. Sequential Processing 2. Simultaneous Processing 3. Verbal Intelligence (Achievement battery)[a]	1. Verbal Reasoning 2. Abstract/Visual Reasoning 3. Quantitative Reasoning 4. Short-Term Memory	1. Long-Term Retrieval 2. Short-Term Memory 3. Processing Speed 4. Auditory Processing 5. Visual Processing 6. Comprehension-Knowledge 7. Fluid Reasoning 8. Quantitative Ability (in WJ-R ACH)	WPPSI-R and WAIS-R 1. Verbal Scale 2. Performance Scale WISC-III 1. Verbal Comprehension 2. Perceptual Organization 3. Freedom from Distractibility 4. Processing Speed	Upper Preschool (Age 3-6 to 6-11) 1. Verbal Ability 2. Nonverbal Ability School Age (5-0 to 17-11) 1. Verbal Ability 2. Nonverbal Reasoning Ability 3. Spatial Ability	1. Fluid Scale (Gf) 2. Crystallized Scale (Gc) 3. Long-Term Retrieval (TSR; Delayed Recall subtests)
Nonverbal composite (requires no oral response)[b]	Yes	Yes[c]	No	Yes	Yes	No
Number of cognitive subtests normed at each age	Total: 10 Age 2-6 to 3: 5 Age 4: 7 Age 5: 7 Age 6 to 12: 8	Total: 15 Age 2-0 to 6: 8 Age 7 to 11: 12 Age 12 to 13: 15 Age 14: 14 Age 15 to 23: 13	Total: 21 Age 2-0 to 90+: 5 Age 4 to 90+: 21	WPPSI-R: 12 across age range WISC-III: 13 across age range WAIS-R: 11 across age range	Total: 17 Age 2-6 to 2-11: 7 Age 3-0 to 3-5: 8 Age 3-6 to 3-11: 9 Age 4-0 to 4-11: 11 Age 5-0 to 6-11: 16 Age 7-0 to 7-11: 15 Age 8-0 to 8-11: 11 Age 9-0 to 17-11: 10	Total: 10 Age 11-0 to 85+: 10

Differential aptitude measures for predicting specific achievement criteria	No	Yes 1. Oral Language Aptitude 2. Reading Aptitude 3. Mathematics Aptitude 4. Written Language Aptitude 5. Knowledge Aptitude	No	No	No
Controlled-learning tests[d]	No	Yes 1. Memory for Names 2. Analysis-Synthesis 3. Visual-Auditory Learning 4. Concept Formation	No	No	Yes 1. Rebus Learning
Tasks are unspeeded (except those intended to measure speed)	Yes	Yes	Yes	Yes	Yes
Separately designed subtests for preschool children with varied printed and manipulative materials	Yes	No	WPPSI-R: Yes[f] WISC-III: N/A WAIS-R: N/A	Yes	N/A
Allows longitudinal follow-up with same measures across the age range of the test[e]	No	Yes	Yes (within battery only)	No	Yes

Note: N/A means not applicable.

[a] See Kamphaus, & Reynolds, 1987.

[b] It is important to note that although no verbal response is required from the child on the subtests that comprise the nonverbal scales of intelligence tests, receptive language is required. The K-ABC is an exception; however, when the K-ABC subtests are administered nonverbally (e.g., pantomime), scores are based on norms in which directions were administered verbally.

[c] A special nonverbal adaptation of the SB:IV has been provided by Glaub and Kamphaus (1991).

[d] Tests that measure learning with corrective feedback provided throughout the administration of the task.

[e] The same set of tests used for young subjects are also used for older subjects.

[f] It is important to note that although the WPPSI-R includes novel subtests specifically designed for preschoolers, many of its subtests are downward extensions of WISC-R subtests.

TABLE 27.3. Administration Features of Intelligence Batteries

Administration features				Intelligence battery		
	K-ABC (1983)	SB:IV (1986)	WJ-R (1989)	Wechsler instruments (1981–1991)	DAS (1990)	KAIT (1993)
Tests of auditory processing and/or memory taped for standardized administration	No	No	Yes 1. Memory for Sentences 2. Incomplete Words 3. Memory for Words 4. Sound Blending 5. Sound Patterns 6. Listening Comprehension	No	No	Yes 1. Auditory Comprehension
Principle of selective testing by assessment purpose emphasized[a]	Yes	Yes	Yes	No	Yes	Yes
Comprehensive manual includes examiner training activities[b]	No	No	Yes	No	No	No
Spanish-language version	No	No	Bateria—R (Woodcock & Munoz-Sandoval, 1996)[c]	WISC-RM (Wechsler, 1984) EIWN-R-PR (Wechsler, 1993)[c]	No	No
Administration time	60 min	60–90 min	BCA—Early Development: 30–40 min BCA—Standard Scale: 40–50 min BCA—Extended Scale: 90–100 min	WPPSI-R: 50–70 min Optional subtests: 10–15 min WISC-III: 50–70 min Supplementary subtests: 10–15 min WAIS-R: 50–60 min	Core subtests: Ages 2-6 to 3-5: 25 min Ages 3-6 to 5-11: 40 min Ages 6-0 to 17-11: 45 min Diagnostic subtests: Ages 2-6 to 3-5: 10 min Ages 3-6 to 5-11: 25 min Ages 6-0 to 17-11: 20 min	Core Battery: 65 min Extended Battery: 90 min

[a] The phrase "selective testing" means that the test author's intent was not necessarily to require examiners to administer the entire battery, but rather to have them tailor the battery to referral concerns.
[b] Examiner training activities include an examiner training checklist, an observation test checklist, and so forth.
[c] Spanish norms provided by publisher.

Universal Nonverbal Intelligence Test (UNIT; McCallum & Bracken, Chapter 14, this volume), currently in development, will be the first test in the field to have norms developed based on a true nonverbal administration.

Table 27.3 highlights important administration features of cognitive batteries. For example, some newer measures of intelligence, such as the WJ-R COG and KAIT, include tests of auditory processing and/or memory on audiocassette to allow for standardized administration. The WJ-R and Wechsler scales have Spanish-language versions available, which are particularly useful in light of the changing demographics of the United States. Most tests have comprehensive technical manuals and, with the exception of the Wechsler scales, are premised on the principle of selective testing. That is, the test authors intent was to allow professionals to tailor the battery to referral concerns rather than administer the entire battery to each individual referred for a psychological evaluation. The utility of selective testing procedures may become apparent with the influx of a new generation of cognitive ability tests. Because it is likely that future assessment batteries will be more complex, differentiated, and comprehensive than traditional ones, as test developers strive to keep up with the advances in cognitive science and theory, selective testing procedures may become commonplace in the field of intellectual assessment.

Table 27.4 provides several interpretation features of contemporary batteries, including the types of scores yielded by each test (e.g., developmental level scores, proficiency level scores, and peer comparison scores) and the range of standard scores for the total test composite of each instrument. In addition, it may be seen from the information provided in Table 27.4 that tests such as the WJ-R COG, DAS, and Wechsler instruments provide the most technically valid aptitude–achievement discrepancy norms, which were derived from co-normed or, in the case of the Wechsler scales, equated measures of cognitive ability and achievement. This interpretive feature is particularly relevant to professionals who use aptitude–achievement discrepancy formulas to aid in identifying individuals with learning disabilities (see Flanagan, Andrews, & Genshaft, Chapter 23, this volume, for a discussion). Other important interpretation features that may enhance the "user friendliness" of a test battery include the immediate identification of significantly high or low scores, compared to the examinee's other scores, on the record form (i.e., separate tables are not needed) as well as the allocation of space on the record form for plotting confidence bands on a profile.

Finally, Table 27.5 presents many technical characteristics of intelligence tests, including norming characteristics, mean subtest floors across batteries and Rasch modeling features of various measures. With the exception of the Wechsler Adult Intelligence Scale—Revised (WAIS-R; Wechsler, 1981), all contemporary intelligence batteries employed Rasch modeling procedures for item analysis and scaling (see Ittenbach, Esters, & Wainer, Chapter 2, this volume for a brief discussion). However, only the DAS and WJ-R use a Rasch-based scale for measuring growth (see Elliott, 1990a; McGrew et al., 1991). Information pertaining to person and community variables in the norming plan as well as the size of the normative sample and the average number of subjects per year (or age group) is provided, allowing for a qualitative comparison across instruments. With respect to subtest floors, the information presented in Table 27.5 shows that only the WJ-R and DAS yield a mean floor at age 3 years, 0 months that is greater than 2 standard deviations below the normative mean (for a raw score of 1). A comparison of intelligence tests according to subtest and total test floors is critical for practitioners who work with preschool-age children (see Bracken, 1987; Bracken & Walker, Chapter 24, this volume; Flanagan & Alfonso, 1995). Likewise, for practitioners who work with culturally diverse populations, it is important to note that the authors of the K-ABC, Wechsler tests (1989, 1991), and DAS conducted bias analyses with minority samples.

The comparative features of new and recently revised intelligence tests presented in Tables 27.2 through 27.5 may provide a useful guide to aid professionals in selecting those instruments that can best meet the needs of the individuals with whom they assess and provide services. In addition,

TABLE 27.4. Interpretation Features of Intelligence Batteries

Interpretation features	Intelligence battery					
	K-ABC (1983)	SB:IV (1986)	WJ-R (1989)	Wechsler instruments (1981–1991)	DAS (1990)	KAIT (1993)
Types of derived scores:						
Developmental level scores	1. Subtest Age Equivalents	1. Subtest Age Equivalents	1. Subtest and Composite Age Equivalents 2. Subtest and Composite Grade Equivalents	1. Composite Test Age	1. Subtest Age Equivalents	1. Composite Test Age
Proficiency level scores[a]	No	No	1. Relative Mastery Index (RMI) 2. Developmental Level Band	No	No	No
Peer comparison scores	1. Percentile Rank 2. Standard Score	1. Percentile Rank 2. Standard Age Score	1. Percentile Rank 2. Standard Score	1. Percentile Rank 2. IQ/Index	1. Percentile Rank 2. Standard Score	1. Percentile Rank 2. Standard Score
College/university norms[b]	No	No	Yes	No	No	No
Conormed with tests of achievement	Yes 1. Reading 2. Mathematics 3. Knowledge (Faces & Places)	No	Yes 1. Reading 2. Mathematics 3. Written Language 4. Knowledge	No (Equated scores for WIAT) 1. Reading 2. Mathematics 3. Language 4. Writing	Yes 1. Basic Number Skills 2. Spelling 3. Word Reading	No
Aptitude–Achievement analysis based on *actual* discrepancy norms[c]	No	No	Yes	WPPSI-R: No WISC-III: No WAIS-R: No	No	No

Feature						
Aptitude–Achievement analysis based on *estimated* discrepancy norms (e.g., correction for regression procedures)	No	Yes	WPPSI-R: Yes (with WIAT) WISC-III: Yes (with WIAT) WAIS-R: Yes (with WIAT)	No	No	No
Significance of high or low scores, compared to examinee's other scores, immediately identifiable on Record Form (i.e., separate tables are not needed)	Yes	Yes	No	Yes	No	No
Range of standard scores for total test composite	40 to 160	Lower Pre-school (Age 2-6 to 3-5): 31 to 169 Upper Preschool (Age 3-6 to 6-11): 25 to 175 School-Age (6-0 to 17-11): 25 to 164	WPPSI-R: 41 to 160 WISC-III: 40 to 160 WAIS-R: 45 to 160	0 to 200	36 to 164	40 to 160
Confidence bands for composites centered on estimated true scores	Yes	Yes	WPPSI-R: No WISC-III: Yes WAIS-R: No	No	No	No
Confidence bands are plotted on profile	Yes	Yes	WPPSI-R: No WISC-III: Yes WAIS-R: No	Yes	No	Yes

[a] Quality of performance on age- or grade-level tasks.

[b] Refers to individuals who are enrolled in post-secondary educational institutions (grades 13.0 to 16.9). That is, separate grade norms are used to compare the individual to other college/university students whereas age norms include college *and* non-college individuals.

[c] Allows for a comparison of an individual's aptitude-achievement discrepancy with actual distributions of discrepancy scores obtained from a nationally representative sample (McGrew, 1994, p. 215; see also McGrew, Werder, & Woodcock, 1991).

TABLE 27.5. Technical Features of Intelligence Batteries

Technical features	Intelligence battery					
	K-ABC (1983)	SB:IV (1986)	WJ-R (1989)	Wechsler instruments (1981–1991)	DAS (1990)	KAIT (1993)
Rasch model used for item analysis and scaling	Yes	Yes	Yes	WPPSI-R: Yes WISC-III: Yes WAIS-R: No	Yes	Yes
Uses Rasch-based scale for measuring growth	No	No	Yes	No	Yes	No
Person variables in norming plan	1. Gender 2. Race/Ethnicity (confounding race and Hispanic origin) 3. Family SES (parent education)	1. Gender 2. Race/Ethnicity (confounding race and Hispanic origin) 3. Family SES (parent occupation and education)	1. Gender 2. Race 3. Hispanic origin 4. SES (occupation and education) (for adult sample only)	1. Gender 2. Race/Ethnicity (confounding race and Hispanic origin) 3. Family SES (occupation and education)	1. Gender 2. Race/Ethnicity (confounding race and Hispanic origin) 3. SES (parent education) 4. Educational enrollment (ages 2-6 to 5-11)	1. Gender 2. Race/Ethnicity (confounding race and Hispanic origin) 3. SES (educational level)
Community variables in norming plan	1. Location 2. Size	1. Location 2. Size	1. Location 2. Size 3. 13 community socioeconomic categories[d]	1. Location 2. Size	1. Location 2. Size	1. Location 2. Size
Size of norming sample for the broad measure of general intelligence	Ages 2-6 to 12-5 N = 2000 Average number per year: 222	Preschool ages 2-0 to 4-11 (N = 901) Average number per year: 300 School ages 5-0 to 17-11 (N = 3918)	BCA—Early Development Scale: Preschool ages 2–5 years N = 806 Average number per year: 201 BCA—Standard Scale School ages 6–19 years N = 2701	WPPSI-R: N = 1700 Average number per year: 283 WISC-III: N = 2200 Average number per year: 200	Preschool ages 2-6 to 4-11 N = 875 Average number per year: 350 School ages 5-0 to 17-11	School ages 11–19 (5 age groups) N = 650 Average number per age group: 130 Adult ages 20–85+ (8 age groups)

		Average number per year: 490 Adult ages 18-0 to 23-11 (N = 194)	Average number per year: 193 Adult ages 20-80+ years N=918 Average number for 7 age groups: 131	WAIS-R: N = 1880 Average number per age group: 209	N = 2600 Average number per year: 200	N = 1350 Average number per age group: 169
Norms weighted to correct sample mismatch to population	No	Yes	Yes	No	No	No
Age blocks in norm tables[a]	2-month blocks (age 2-6 to 5-11) 3-month blocks (age 6-0 to 12-6)	4-month blocks (age 2-0 to 5-11) 6-month blocks (age 6-0 to 10-11) 1-year blocks (age 11 to 17) 6-year block (age 18 to 23)	1-month blocks (age 2-0 to 18-11) 1-year blocks (age 19 to 90+)	WPPSI-R— 3-month blocks WISC-III— 4-month blocks WAIS-R— 2-year blocks (age 16 to 19); 5-year blocks (age 20 to 24; 65 to 74); 10-year blocks (age 25 to 64)	3-month blocks (age 2-6 to 7-11) 6-month blocks (age 8-0 to 17-11)	4-month blocks (age 11-0 to 16-11) 6-month blocks (age 17-0 to 18-11) 1-year blocks (age 19-0 to 20-11) 2-year blocks (age 21 to 24) 5-year blocks (age 25 to 84)
Grade-based norm tables available	No	No	Yes, by .1-year blocks (grades K.0 to 16.9)	No	No	No
Bias analyses conducted with minority samples	Yes	No	No	WPPSI-R: Yes WISC-III: Yes WAIS-R: No	Yes	No
Mean floor of subtests at age 3-0[b]	-1.1	-1.4	-3.5	WPPSI-R: -1.6 WISC-III: N/A WAIS-R: N/A	-2.4	N/A
General composite standard score for a child at age 3-0 obtaining a raw score of 1 on all subtests	77	75	31	WPPSI-R: 68 WISC-III: N/A WAIS-R: N/A	55	N/A
SEM provided for each subtest score level[c]	No	No	Yes	No	Yes	No

Note: N/A means not applicable.

[a] In most cases age blocks represent linear interpolations.

[b] Standard deviations below the mean for a raw score of 1.

[c] This is an interpretive feature of Rasch, representing an advance from the classical approach of assigning a single *SEM* to all scores obtained on a subtest.

[d] Distribution of values controlled in the set of communities: three levels of adult education, three classes of occupational status, and three classes of occupation. For colleges and universities: two types of institution and two sources of funding.

because these tables highlight many important strengths and limitations of contemporary measures, they may prove to be useful to test developers as a foundation from which to construct new instruments and improve intelligence test technology. Although it was not possible to include in Tables 27.2 through 27.5 all characteristics of intelligence tests that are useful, informative, and innovative, it is clear from the information that was summarized therein that all intelligence tests have important content, administration, interpretation and technical features that can inform practice and test development.

Validity Issues in the Field of Intellectual Assessment

Part IV of this volume focuses on issues related to the construct, predictive, diagnostic, and treatment validity of current intelligence test batteries. Each validity issue is discussed in terms of its implications for the general use and interpretation of cognitive ability tests, particularly with regard to special populations, including preschoolers and individuals from culturally and linguistically diverse backgrounds. Table 27.6 summarizes the major validity issues discussed in Part IV of this volume and highlights the salient conclusions and implications that follow from validation research that has been conducted recently in the field of intellectual assessment. In addition, Table 27.6 provides a listing of the representative research associated with each validity issue and includes examples of future research endeavors that may aid in substantiating the use of intelligence tests for various purposes.

As may be seen in Table 27.6, several validity issues focused on the utility of intelligence tests in making diagnostic and treatment decisions as well as differential diagnoses. The most commonly used interpretive procedure for identifying patterns of cognitive strengths and weaknesses that are believed to be unique and therefore, indicative of some type of psychopathology (i.e., subtest and profile analysis) has limited empirical support (see Flanagan, Andrews, & Genshaft, Chapter 23, this volume and Reschly, Chapter 22, this volume for a discussion). McDermott, Glutting and their colleagues (e.g., Glutting, McDermott, & Konold, Chapter 19, this volume; Glutting, McGrath, Kamphaus, & McDermott, 1992) suggested replacing subtest and profile analysis procedures that are based on univariate and linear multivariate methods with nonlinear multivariate normative methods (see Glutting et al., Chapter 19, this volume). Through nonlinear multivariate methodology, core profile types that are commonplace in the standardization samples of intelligence tests could be used as the standard (i.e., base rate) against which clinical subtest profiles could be compared. Although the normative profile taxonomies recommended by McDermott, Glutting, and colleagues represent the best available methods for making such comparisons, investigations are needed to determine the diagnostic and remedial utility of these profiles. There is also a need to investigate the relationship between cognitive profiles and external phenomena using contemporary and multidifferentiated tests and methods that are based on current theory and research (cross-battery approaches, tasks based on PASS processes, the WJ-R battery, etc.).

Table 27.6 also summarizes some important questions that were raised by Keith (Chapter 20, this volume) with respect to the construct validity of intelligence tests. For example, do intelligence tests measure the model specified by the test developer? Through a series of confirmatory factor analyses, Keith found varying degrees of support for the theoretical models underlying contemporary intelligence tests. In addition, he found considerable similarity across the models that underlie cognitive batteries, despite the fact that these tests were premised on different theoretical frameworks. Many intellectual tasks form a hierarchy of general, broad, and more specific abilities—if the cognitive tasks represented in factor analytic investigations are sufficient in breadth, then they form a model that is similar to Carroll's three-stratum theory of cognitive abilities. Future research in this area should be directed toward (1) investigating new and alternative theoretical models that may be used to interpret current and future cognitive ability tests and (2) using confirmatory factor-analytic

TABLE 27.6. Validity of Intelligence Tests for General Use and Interpretation

Validity issue	Relevant questions	Conclusions and implications	Representative research and literature	Future research needs
Chapter 19: Subtest profile analysis (Glutting, McDermott, & Konold)	What is the importance of statistical significance and base rates?	Large numbers of individuals have one or more statistically significant subtest deviations. Statistical significance data provide no information about the rarity of the subtest deviation. Base rates indicate the actual frequency of subtest deviations and, thus, if the deviations are unusual or rare.	Cahan, 1986; Carver, 1978; McDermott & Watkins, 1985; Kamphaus, 1993; Kaufman, 1994; Sattler, 1988	
	Is univariate, linear profile analysis less valid than multivariate, nonlinear profile analysis?	Yes, univariate, linear methods do not account for interdependencies among subtest scores but rather, consider one score at a time. Multivariate, nonlinear methods treat profiles as integrated intercorrelated sets of test scores and allow for multiple, simultaneous comparison of subtests.	Tatsuoka & Lohnes, 1988; Thompson, 1991	
	What subtest configurations are unusual or clinically relevant?	Research has identified core multivariate subtest profiles for the Wechsler scales, K–ABC, and McCarthy, and these core profiles should be used in practice to determine if a client's profile is rare and clinically relevant.	Glutting & McDermott, 1990a, 1990b; Glutting, McDermott, & Konold, Chapter 19, this volume; Glutting, McGrath, Kamphaus, & McDermott, 1992; McDermott, Glutting, Jones, Watkins, & Kush, 1989b; McDermott, Glutting, Jones, & Noonan, 1989a	Investigations of relationships between profiles and external phenomena. Investigations of diagnostic and remedial utility of profiles.

TABLE 27.6. *(Cont.)*

Validity issue	Relevant questions	Conclusions and implications	Representative research and literature	Future research needs
Chapter 20: Confirmation of theoretical models measured by intelligence tests (Keith)	Do intelligence tests measure the model specified by the test developer(s)?	Research with different intelligence tests shows varying degrees of support for the extent to which each test measures its underlying model.	Carroll, 1993, 1995; Elliott, 1990b; Flanagan & McGrew, 1996; Kaufman & Kaufman, 1983; Keith, Chapter 20, this volume; Keith, 1990; Kranzler & Weng, 1995a, 1995b; Naglieri, Braden, & Gottling, 1993; Ysseldyke, 1990	Investigations of various models of intelligence to guide development of new intelligence tests.
	Do intelligence tests measure models other than the ones specified?	Some models provide a better "fit" than the model intended for the test.	Keith, Chapter 20, this volume; Keith, 1985; Keith & Dunbar, 1984; Keith & Novak, 1987; McGrew, Chapter 9, this volume	Investigations to determine alternative models for interpreting current and new intelligence tests.
	Do intellectual tasks measure a hierarchy of general ability (g), broad, and more specific abilities?	Many intellectual tasks form a hierarchy of general, broad and more specific abilities.	Carroll, 1993, Chapter 7, this volume; Gustafsson & Balke, 1993; Keith, Chapter 20, this volume	Investigations to determine the extent to which intelligence tests operationalize empirically supported hierarchical models of intelligence.
	Do two or more intelligence tests measure similar models of intelligence?	There is similarity across many intelligence tests in the model of intelligence they measure, even when a new test is designed to measure a different model than existing tests.	Carroll, 1993, Chapter 7, this volume; Keith & Dunbar, 1984; Keith & Novak, 1987; Stone, 1992; Woodcock, 1990	Investigations to support cross battery approaches to test interpretation.
	Do intelligence tests measure the same model across different groups of people?	There is varying degree of support for the extent to which intelligence tests measure the same model across age groups, race or cultural groups, etc.	Carroll, 1993; Keith et al., 1995; Keith & Witta, in press	Investigations to support the use of confirmatory factor analysis to examine construct bias, stability, etc.
	Is there evidence to support the theoretical assumptions about a model of intelligence?	There is a varying degree of support for different theoretical models of intelligence.	Bickley, Keith, & Wolfe, 1995; Carroll, 1993, Chapter 7, this volume	Investigations to support contemporary theories of intelligence.

Chapter	Question	Finding	References	Future research
Chapter 21: Genetic analysis of intellectual abilities (McArdle & Prescott)	What is the nature of genetic influences on intelligence?	Genetic sources appear to account for about half of the variance in intelligence.	Bouchard & McGue, 1981; Chipeur, Rovine, & Plomin, 1990; Loehlin, 1989a, 1989b	Continuing research to investigate the many other sources of valuation in intelligence.
	What techniques are most useful for studying biometric genetic analysis of intellectual abilities?	Structural equation models are currently used to study these issues, but these techniques continue to have problems.	Goldsmith & McArdle, 1996; Loehlin, 1992; McArdle, 1987, 1994, in press	Research to address problems, including to whom and what and what should be measured and how heritability should be interpreted in biometric research.
Chapter 22: Diagnostic and treatment utility of intelligence tests (Reschly)	Are factor, scale, and subtests profiles related to differences in ethnic status, brain injury, cognitive style, gender and other characteristics of examinees?	Many types of profiles occur with great frequency, and little evidence supports the reliability or validity of using profiles to distinguish between diagnostic categories or other characteristics of examinees.	Barnett & Macmann, 1992; Glutting, McDermott, & Konold, Chapter 19, this volume; Macmann & Barnett, 1985	Research to support the diagnostic utility of profiles using new and alternative measures.
	Do measures of intelligence demonstrate any type of diagnostic validity?	Generally, overall scores from intelligence tests predict criteria such as academic success, occupational attainment, cognitive processing, and capability of profiting from instruction, and thus, may show validity for measuring diagnostic constructs (MR, LD) involving learning ability and academic performance.	Campione, Brown, & Ferrara, 1982	Research to support the diagnostic utility of new and alternative measures.
	Do diagnostic constructs such as MR and LD—and the use of intelligence tests in determining these diagnostic constructs—have implications for treatment or intervention?	Little evidence supports the validity of diagnostic constructs—or the use of intelligence tests—to implement effective treatment or intervention.	Fletcher & Foorman, 1994; Fletcher, et al., 1994; Shinn, Tindal, Spira, & Marston, 1987; Shinn, Ysseldyke, Deno, & Tindal, 1986; Ysseldyke, Algozzine, & Epps, 1983	Investigations to support treatment utility of noncategorical systems or other alternatives to diagnostic constructs. Research to investigate new intelligence tests and alternatives in terms of treatment implications.

TABLE 27.6. *(Cont.)*

Validity issue	Relevant questions	Conclusions and implications	Representative research and literature	Future research needs
Chapter 23: Utility of intelligence tests for individuals in special education groups (Flanagan, Andrews, & Genshaft)	How well do intelligence tests estimate current and future school performance?	Many studies have found that intelligence tests predict academic achievement, with good prediction across ethnic, gender, and special education groups.	McGrew & Hessler, 1995; Roid, Prifitera, & Weiss, 1993; Sattler, 1992	Predictive validity studies of broad and specific cognitive abilities, and whether the broad and specific abilities provide a foundation for investigating treatment validity.
	How valid are different methods for determining aptitude–achievement discrepancies and do the discrepancies relate to children's educational needs?	Many methods currently used are statistically incorrect. Most valid methods use co-normed tests, take into account regression to the mean, and compare discrepancy scores with actual discrepancies obtained by a norm sample. No evidence to support that children with aptitude–achievement discrepancies have different educational needs than children with low achievement.	Cone & Wilson, 1981; McGrew, 1994; Reynolds, 1984; Ysseldyke, Algozinne, Shinn, & McGue, 1982	Studies investigating multivariate methods of comparing various areas of cognitive ability and achievement simultaneously (Glutting, McDermott, Prifitera, & McGrath, 1994). Studies investigating the treatment utility of aptitude–achievement discrepancies.
	Do subtest scores on intelligence tests discriminate between children in different special education groups?	Evidence supports that subtest patterns or profiles do not discriminate between special education groups or between these groups and children who are not in special education.	Kamphaus, 1993; Kavale & Forness, 1984; McDermott, Fantuzzo, & Glutting, 1990; Watkins & Kush, 1994	Additional investigations with newer intelligence tests (DAS, DNCAS, WJ-R) and investigations of cross-battery approaches.
	How well do intelligence tests provide implications for effective interventions for students in special education?	There has been little support for aptitude by treatment interactions.	Cronbach & Snow, 1977; Good, Vollmer, Creek, Katz, & Chowdri, 1993	Additional investigations with newer intelligence tests and with cross-battery approaches.

552

Chapter	Question	Findings	References	Future directions
Chapter 24: Utility of intelligence tests with preschool children (Bracken & Walker)	How well do intelligence tests predict later functioning for preschool children?	Predictions of later functioning, including later intellectual function, become better with children's increasing age and for children whose disabilities become more severe.	Bornstein & Sigman, 1986; Clarke, 1982; DuBose, 1976; Vanderveer & Scheweid, 1974	Additional investigations with newer intelligence tests.
	Do most intelligence tests have adequate subtests or total test floors to use with young children?	Many intelligence tests may not have sufficient items to discriminate lower from average functioning young children.	Bracken, 1987; Bracken & Walker, Chapter 24, this volume; Flanagan & Alfonso, 1995	Development of new technically adequate intelligence tests for preschool children.
	What are limitations of intelligence tests with very young children or children with language delays?	Traditional, verbally loaded intelligence tests may have limited utility with many young children, and alternative assessments or non-verbal tests may be more useful.	Flanagan, Alfonso, Kaminer, & Rader, 1995; McCallum & Bracken, Chapter 14, this volume; Short, Simeonsson, & Huntington, 1990	Additional investigations with alternative techniques.
Chapter 25: Utility of intelligence tests for children with bilingual or limited English skills (Lopez)	Do intelligence tests predict equally well for bilingual/limited English proficient groups compared to English-speaking groups?	Some evidence suggests that test bias may not be present for most tests, but there are concerns that studies do not adequately control for examinees' levels of language proficiency and factors that may interact with language.	Figueroa, 1990; Helms, Chapter 26, this volume; Reynolds & Kaiser, 1990	Additional, comprehensive research of test bias with adequate controls for language proficiency and factors related to language.
	How should language proficiency be assessed before administration of intelligence tests?	Formal expressive and receptive language measures, informal observations, and language samples should be used.	Lopez, 1995; Ramirez, 1990	Investigations of how to use data about language proficiency to determine which language to use during intellectual assessment.

TABLE 27.6. *(Cont.)*

Validity issue	Relevant questions	Conclusions and implications	Representative research and literature	Future research needs
Chapter 25 *(cont.)*	How valid are translated intelligence tests, English intelligence tests, and nonverbal intelligence tests when administered to children with bilingual or limited English skills?	Most translated tests use English norms or norms for countries outside the U.S., which have limited validity for children in the U.S. English intelligence tests have many limitations for children with bilingual or limited English skills. Few nonverbal tests are available; these tests may measure skills that have cultural foundations, and these are not normed with children with bilingual or limited English skills.	Armour-Thomas, 1992; Berry, 1994; Geisinger, 1994; Helms, Chapter 26, this volume; McCallum & Bracken, Chapter 14, this volume	Development of new translated or nonverbal tests with appropriate norms. Validation studies for these tests.
Chapter 26: Influence of race, culture, and social class on intellectual assessment (Helms)	How do race, ethnic culture, and socioeconomic condition influence the cultural equivalence of intelligence tests (i.e., functional, conceptual, linguistic, and psychometric equivalence)?	Cultural predispositions and other factors may impact test responses (e.g., factors such as holistic and atomistic perceptions, expectations of creativity, contextual valuing of creativity, contextual interpretations, assimilation into the white American culture, people and self orientation, differential perceptions of test stimuli, cultural mistrust, race of examiner, etc). Few tests address how these factors could impact performance.	Helms, 1992, 1994; Katz, 1985; Terrell, Terrell, & Taylor, 1981; Willis, 1989	Empirical investigations to examine the influence of these factors on test performance and how these factors can be addressed in test development.

procedures to examine construct bias and the invariance of the structure of intelligence across age, race and cultural groups.

McArdle and Prescott (Chapter 21, this volume) discussed the nature of genetic influences on intelligence. They indicated that structural equation modeling (SEM), a more general approach that subsumes confirmatory factor analysis, can be used to understand the genetic influences that might account for variations in intellectual abilities in the normal population. In their presentation of structural models in behavior genetics, they highlighted fundamental issues regarding contemporary SEMs used in biometric genetic analysis of intellectual abilities (BGIA) research and attempted to clarify further the methods, models and results of BGIA by considering interpretations within the context of biometric theory. McArdle and Prescott presented models using data from several studies of biological and adoptive families and twins to demonstrate current trends in BG research. These researchers indicated that genetic sources account for approximately half of the variance in intelligence. Future research is needed in this area to address some of the problems associated with SEM techniques, including who should be tested and what should be measured as well as how heritability should be interpreted within behavioral genetics research.

The remaining chapters of Part IV in this volume focused on the validity of intelligence tests for use and interpretation with special populations, including special education groups, preschool children, individuals with bilingual or limited English skills, and individuals from various racial, cultural and social class backgrounds. Table 27.6 indicates that there are limitations to the use of intelligence tests with preschoolers, including poor test floors and an over reliance on expressive and receptive language demands. The latter characteristic also represents a limitation to the use of intelligence tests with linguistically diverse populations. Conducting an assessment of basic concepts or language proficiency prior to the administration of an intelligence test represents good practice when assessing young children and individuals with bilingual or limited English skills, respectively. This type of assessment is important because an individual's understanding of test directions is integral to the validity of the construct(s) that is measured by a given test (see Flanagan, Alfonso, Kaminer, & Rader, 1995). In the area of preschool assessment, there is a need for the development of new intelligence tests that are psychometrically superior to existing instruments as well as a need for continued research that examines the utility of alternatives to traditional cognitive assessment approaches.

Regarding the use of intelligence tests with linguistically diverse populations, there is a need for additional research of test bias that controls for language proficiency as well as other language-related factors. In addition, the development of new, translated, or nonverbal tests with appropriate norms is needed to enhance the availability, quality and breadth of instruments that may be used to assess the cognitive abilities of linguistically diverse populations. Finally, Helms (Chapter 26, this volume) demonstrated, through a thoughtful discussion of the influences of race, culture, and social class on intellectual performance, that a considerable amount of research is needed to understand (and improve) the cultural equivalence of intelligence tests, including functional, conceptual, linguistic and psychometric equivalences.

CONCLUSION

Current information regarding new theories and tests of intelligence as well as the empirical evidence for their utility was presented in this volume and integrated and synthesized in this chapter. This information is intended to provide a basis from which professionals can understand and appreciate the significant scientific advances that have been made recently in the field of intellectual assessment. In light of this new knowledge, professionals may choose to move beyond traditional tests and theories of intelligence and adopt new and improved measures and methods of assessing cognitive abilities that will allow them to make better informed decisions. The utilization of new instruments that are grounded in contemporary theory and research and up-to-date, empirically supported interpretations of older tests may lead to improvements in practice and serve to narrow the gap between applied intelligence testing and cognitive psychology.

ACKNOWLEDGMENTS

The authors gratefully acknowledge Mark Daniel, Colin Elliott, Alan Kaufman, Nadeen Kaufman, Kevin McGrew, Aurelio Prifitera, Jerome Sattler, Robert Thorndike, and Richard Woodcock for their review of and important contributions to Tables 27.2 through 27.5.

REFERENCES

Armour-Thomas, E. (1992). Intellectual assessment of children from culturally diverse backgrounds. *School Psychology Review, 21,* 552–565.

Barnett, D. W., & Macmann, G. M. (1992). Decision reliability and validity: Contributions and limitations of alternative assessment strategies. *Journal of Special Education, 25,* 431–452.

Berry, J. W. (1994). Cross-cultural variations in intelligence. In R. J. Sternberg (Ed.), *Encyclopedia of human intelligence* (pp. 316–322). New York: Macmillan.

Bickley, P. G., Keith, T. Z., & Wolfle, L. M. (1995). The three-stratum theory of cognitive abilities: Test of the structure of intelligence across the life span. *Intelligence, 20,* 309–328.

Bornstein, M. H., & Sigman, M. D. (1986). Continuity in mental development from infancy. *Child Development, 57,* 251–274.

Bouchard, T. J., & McGue, M. (1981). Familial studies of intelligence: A review. *Science, 212,* 1055–1059.

Bracken, B. A. (1987). Limitations of preschool instruments and standards for minimal levels of technical adequacy. *Journal of Psychoeducational Assessment, 4,* 313–326.

Cahan, S. (1986). Significance testing of subtest score differences: The rules of the game. *Journal of Psychoeducational Assessment, 4,* 273–280.

Campione, J. C., Brown, A. L., & Ferrara, R. A. (1982). Mental retardation and intelligence. In R. J. Sternberg (Ed.), *Handbook of human intelligence* (pp. 392–490). Cambridge, England: Cambridge University Press.

Carroll, J. B. (1993). *Human cognitive abilities: A survey of factor-analytic studies.* New York: Cambridge University Press.

Carroll, J. B. (1995). Review of *Assessment of cognitive processes: The PASS theory of intelligence. Journal of Psychoeducational Assessment, 13,* 397–409.

Carver, R. P. (1978). The case against statistical significance testing. *Harvard Educational Review, 48,* 378–399.

Chen, J. Q., Isberg, E., & Krechevsky, M. (in press). *Project spectrum early learning activities.* Cambridge, MA: Harvard Project Zero.

Chipeur, H. M., Rovine, M., & Plomin, R. (1990). LISREL modelling: genetic and environmental influences and IQ revisted. *Intelligence, 14,* 11–29.

Clarke, A. M. (1982). Developmental discontinuities: An approach to assessing their nature. In L. A. Bond & J. M. Joffe (Eds.), *Facilitating infant and early childhood development* (pp. 58–77). Hanover, NH: University Press of New England.

Cone, T. E., & Wilson, L. R. (1981). Quantifying a severe discrepancy: A critical analysis. *Learning Disability Quarterly, 4,* 359–371.

Cronbach, L. J., & Snow, R. E. (1977). *Attitudes and instructional methods.* New York: Wiley.

Das, J. P., Naglieri, J. A., & Kirby, J. R. (1994). *Assessment of cognitive processes: The PASS theory of intelligence.* Needham Heights: MA: Allyn & Bacon.

Davidson, J. E., & Sternberg, R. J. (1984). The role of insight in intellectual giftedness. *Gifted Child Quarterly, 28,* 58–64.

DuBose, R. F. (1976). Predictive value of infant intelligence scales with multiply handicapped children. *American Journal of Mental Deficiency, 81,* 388–390.

Dunaway, J., Granfield, J., Norton, K., & Greenspan, S. (1992). *Costs and benefits of privately-operated residential services for persons with mental retardation in Connecticut.* Storrs: Pappanikou Center of University of Connecticut.

Elliott, C. D. (1990a). *Differential Ability Scales: Introductory and technical handbook.* San Antonio, TX: Psychological Corporation.

Elliott, C. D. (1990b). The nature and structure of children's abilities: Evidence from the Differential Ability Scales. *Journal of Psychoeducational Assessment, 8,* 376–390.

Evans, J. H., Carlsen, R. N., & McGrew, K. S. (1993). Classification of exceptional students with the Woodcock–Johnson Psycho-Educational Battery—Revised. *Journal of Psychoeducational Assessment* [Monograph Series: WJ-R Monograph], 6–19.

Figueroa, R. A. (1990). Assessment of linguistic minority group children. In C. R. Reynolds & R. W. Kamphaus (Eds.), *Handbook of psychological and educational assessment of children: Intelligence and achievement* (pp. 671–696). New York: Guilford Press.

Flanagan, D. P., & Alfonso, V. C. (1995). A critical review of the technical characteristics of new and recently revised intelligence tests for preschool children. *Journal of Psychoeducational Assessment, 13,* 66–90.

Flanagan, D. P., Alfonso, V. C., Kaminer, T., & Rader, D. E. (1995). Incidence of basic concepts in the directions of new and revised American intelligence tests for preschool children. *School Psychology International, 16,* 345–364.

Flanagan, D. P., & McGrew, K. S. (1996). *Interpreting intelligence tests from modern Gf-Gc theory: Joint confirmatory factor analyses of the WJ-R and the Kaufman Adolescent and Adult Intelligence Test (KAIT).* Manuscript submitted for publication.

Fleishman, E. A., & Reilly, M. E. (1992). *Handbook of human abilities: Definitions, measurements, and job task requirements.* Palo Alto, CA: Consulting Psychologists Press.

Fletcher, J. M., & Foorman, B. R. (1994). Issues in the definition and measurement of learning disabilities: The need for early intervention. In G. R. Lyon (Ed.), *Frames of reference for assessment of learning disabilities: New views on measurement issues* (pp. 185–200). Baltimore: Paul H. Brooks.

Fletcher, J. M., Shaywitz, S. E., Shankweiler, D. P., Katz, L., Liberman, I. Y., Fowler, A., Francis, D. J., Stuebing, K. K., & Shaywitz, B. A. (1994). Cognitive profiles of reading disability: Comparisons of discrepancy and low achievement definitions. *Journal of Educational Psychology, 85,* 1–18.

Gardner, H. (1983). *Frames of mind: The theory of multiple intelligences.* New York: Basic Books.

Gardner, H. (1984). Assessing intelligence: A comment on "Testing intelligence without IQ test" by R. J. Sternberg. *Phi Delta Kappa, 65(10),* 699–700.

Gardner, H. (1986). The waning of intelligence tests. In R. Sternberg & D. Detterman (Eds.), *The acquisition of symbolic skills* (pp. 19–42). London: Plenum Press.

Gardner, H. (1993a). Assessment in context: The alternative to standardized testing. In H. Gardner (Ed.), *Multiple intelligences: The theory in practice* (pp. 161–183). New York: Basic Books.

Gardner, H. (1993b). *Frames of mind: The theory of multiple intelligences* (10th anniversary ed.). New York: Basic Books.

Gardner, H., Krechevsky, M., Sternberg, R. J., & Okagaki, L. (1994). Intelligence in context: Enhancing students' practical intelligence for school. In K. McGilly (Ed.), *Classroom lessons: Integrating cognitive theory and classroom practice* (pp. 105–127). Cambridge, MA: Bradford Books.

Geisinger, K. F. (1994). Cross-cultural normative assessment: Translation and adaptation issues influencing the normative interpretation of assessment instruments. *Psychological Assessment, 6,* 304–312.

Glaub, V. E., & Kamphaus, R. W. (1991). construction of a nonverbal adaptation of the Standford–Binet: Fourth Edition. *Educational and Psychological Measurement, 51,* 231–241.

Glutting, J. J., & McDermott, P. A. (1990a). Patterns and prevalence of core profile types in the WPPSI standardization sample. *School Psychology Review, 19,* 471–491.

Glutting, J. J., & McDermott, P. A. (1990b). Score structures and applications of core profile types in the McCarthy Scales Standardization Sample. *Journal of Special Education, 24,* 212–233.

Glutting, J. J., McDermott, P. A., Prifitera, A., & McGrath, E. A. (1994). Core profile types for the WISC-III and

WIAT: Development and their application in identifying multivariate IQ-achievement discrepancies. *School Psychology Review, 23,* 619–639.

Glutting, J. J., McGrath, E. A., Kamphaus, R. W., & McDermott, P. A. (1992). Taxonomy and validity of subtest profiles on the Kaufman Assessment Battery for Children. *Journal of Special Education, 26,* 85–115.

Goldsmith, H. H., & McArdle, J. J. (1996). *Longitudinal biometric models for twin analyses: The case of childhoop temperment. Manuscript submitted for publication.*

Good, R. H., Vollmer, M., Creek, R. J., Katz, L., & Chowdhri, S. (1993). Treatment utility of the Kaufman Assessment Battery for Children: Effects of matching instruction and student processing strength. *School Psychology Review, 22,* 8–26.

Greenspan, S. (1982). Personal competence as a guide to educational placement. *New Perspectives in Special Education, 3*(3), 1–3.

Greenspan, S. (1991). A universal approach to measuring disability severity: Implications of a model of general competence. In F. Hafferty, S. C. Hey, G. Kiger, & D. Pfeiffer (Eds.), *Translating disability: At the individual, institutional and societal levels* (pp. 127–132). Portland, OR: Society for Disability Studies.

Greenspan, S., & Granfield, J. M. (1992). Reconsidering the construct of mental retardation: Implications of a model of social competence. *American Journal on Mental Retardation, 96,* 442–453.

Gustafsson, J.-E., & Balke, G. (1993). General and specific abilities as predictors of school achievement. *Multivariate Behavioral Research, 28,* 407–434.

Harrison, P. L., Kaufman, A. S., Hickman, J. A., & Kaufman, N. L. (1988). A survey of tests used for adult assessment. *Journal of Psychoeducaitonal Assessment, 6,* 188–198.

Helms, J. E. (1992). Why is there no study of cultural equivalence in standardized cognitive ability testing? *American Psychologist, 47*(9), 1083–1101.

Helms, J. E. (1994). The conceptualization of racial identity and other "racial" constructs. In E. J. Trickett, R. J. Watts, & D. Birman (Eds.), *Human diversity: Perspectives on people in context* (pp. 285–311). San Francisco: Jossey-Bass.

Hessler, G. L. (1993). Clinical use of the Woodcock–Johnson Psycho-Educational Battery—Revised for the identification and instructional programming of types of learning disorders. *Journal of Psychoeducational Assessment,* [WJ-R Monograph], 123–135.

Horn, J. L. (1991). Measurement of intellectual capabilities: A review of theory. In K. S. McGrew, J. K. Werder, & R. W. Woodcock, *Woodcock–Johnson technical manual* (pp. 197–232). Chicago: Riverside.

Horn, J. L. (1994). Theory of fluid and crystallized intelligence. In R. J. Sternberg (Ed.), *Encyclopedia of human intelligence* (pp. 443–451). New York: Macmillan.

Javel, M. E., & Greenspan, S. (1983). Influence of personal competence profiles on mainstreaming recommendations of school psychologists. *Psychology in the Schools, 20,* 459–465.

Jonassen, D. H., & Grabowski, B. L. (Eds.). (1993). *Handbook of individual differences, learning, and instruction.* Hillsdale, NJ: Erlbaum.

Kamphaus, R. W. (1993). *Clinical assessment of children's intelligence.* Boston: Allyn & Bacon.

Kamphaus, R. W., & Reynolds, C. R. (1987). *Clinical and research applications of the K-ABC.* Circle Pines, MN: AGS.

Katz, J. H. (1985). The sociopolitical nature of counseling. *The Counseling Psychologist, 13*(4), 615–624.

Kaufman, A. S. (1979). *Intelligent testing with the WISC-R.* New York: Wiley.

Kaufman, A. S. (1994). *Intelligent testing with the WISC-III.* New York: Wiley.

Kaufman, A. S., & Kaufman, N. L. (1983). *Kaufman Assessment Battery for Children.* Circle Pines, MN: American Guidance Service.

Kaufman, A. S., & Kaufman, N. L. (1993). *Kaufman Adolescent and Adult Intelligence Test.* Circle Pines, MN: American Guidance Service.

Kavale, K. A., & Forness, S. R. (1984). A meta-analysis of the validity of Wechsler scale profiles and recategorizations: Patterns or parodies? *Learning Disability Quarterly, 7,* 136–152.

Keith, T. Z. (1985). Questioning the K-ABC: What does it measure? *School Psychology Review, 14,* 9–20.

Keith, T. Z. (1990). Confirmatory and hierarchical confirmatory analysis of the Differential Ability Scales. *Journal of Psychoeducational Assessment, 8,* 391–405.

Keith, T. Z., DeGraff, M., Diamond, C. M., Fugate, M. H., Shadrach, E. A., & Stevens, M. L. (1995). Using multi-sample confirmatory factor analysis to test for construct bias: An example using the K-ABC. *Journal of Psychoeducational Assessment, 13,* 347–364.

Keith, T. Z., & Dunbar, S. B. (1984). Hierarchical factor analysis of the K-ABC: Testing alternate models. *Journal of Special Education, 18,* 367–375.

Keith, T. Z., & Novak, C. G. (1987). Joint factor structure of the WISC-R and K-ABC for referred school children. *Journal of Psychoeducational Assessment, 4,* 370–386.

Keith, T. Z., & Witta, E. L. (in press). Hierarchical and cross-age confirmatory factor analysis of the WISC-III: What does it measure? *School Psychology Quarterly.*

Kranzler, J. H., & Weng, L. (1995a). Factor structure of the PASS cognitive tasks: A reexamination of Naglieri et al. (1991). *Journal of School Psychology, 33,* 143–157.

Kranzler, J. H. & Weng, L. (1995b). Reply to the commentary by Naglieri and Das on the factor structure of a battery of PASS cognitive tasks. *Journal of School Psychology, 33,* 169–176.

Loehlin, J. C. (1989). Partitioning environmental and genetic contributions to behavioral development. *American Psychologist, 44,* 1285–1292.

Loehlin, J. C. (1992). *Genes and environment in personality development.* Newbury Park, CA: Sage.

Lopez, E. C. (1995). Best practices in working with bilingual children. In A. Thomas & J. Grimes (Eds.), *Best practices in school psychology III* (pp. 1111–1121). Washington, DC: National Association of School Psychologists.

Luria, A. R. (1973). *The working brain: An introduction to neuropsychology.* New York: Basic Books.

Mackintosh, N. J. (1986). The biology of intelligence? *British Journal of Psychology, 77,* 1–18.

Macmann, G. M., & Barnett, D. W. (1985). Discrepancy score analysis: A computer simulation of classification stability. *Journal of Psychoeducational Assessment, 4,* 363–375.

Mather, N. (1993). Critical issues in the diagnosis of learning disabilities addressed by the Woodcock–Johnson Psycho-Educational Battery—Revised. *Journal of Psychoeducational Assessment,* [WJ-R Monograph], 103–122.

McArdle, J. J. (1987). Mixtures of behavioral genetics and developmental psychology. A review of Plomins' "Development, Genetics, and Psychology." *Contemporary Psychology, 32*(5), 433–435.

McArdle, J. J. (1994). Appropriate questions about causal inference from "Direction of Causation" analyses. *Genetic Epidemiology, 11,* 477–482.

McArdle, J. J. (in press). A workshop on contemporary behavioral genetics models and methods. *Contemporary Psychology.*

McCallum, S. A., & Bracken, B. A. (in press). *Universal Nonverbal Intelligence Test.* Chicago: Riverside.

McDermott, P. A., Fantuzzo, J. W., & Glutting, J. J. (1990). Just say no to subtest analysis: A critique on Wechsler theory and practice. *Journal of Psychoeducational Assessment, 8,* 290–302.

McDermott, P. A., Glutting, J. J., Jones, J. N., & Noonan, J. V. (1989a). Typology and prevailing composition of core profiles in the WAIS-R standardization sample. Psychological Assessment: *A Journal of Consulting and Clinical Psychology, 1,* 118–125.

McDermott, P. A., Glutting, J. J., Jones, J. N., Watkins, M. W., & Kush, J. (1989b). Identification and membership of core profile types in the WISC-R national standardization sample. Psychological Assessment: *A Journal of Consulting and Clinical Psychology, 1,* 292–299.

McDermott, P. A., & Watkins, M. W. (1985). *McDermott Multidimensional Assessment of Children.* New York: Psychological Corporation.

McGhee, R. (1993). Fluid and Crystallized Intelligence: Confirmatory factor analysis of the Differential Abilities Scale, Detroit Tests of Learning Aptitude-3, and Woodcock–Johnson Psycho-Educational Battery—Revised. *Journal of Psychoeducational Assessment,* [WJ-R Monograph], 20–38.

McGrew, K. S. (1986). *Clinical interpretation of the Woodcock–Johnson Tests of Cognitive Ability.* Orlando: Grune & Stratton.

McGrew, K. S. (1993). Intelligence testing and Gf-Gc theory. *Communique, 21*(5), 10–11.

McGrew, K. S. (1994). *Clinical interpretation of the Woodcock–Johnson—Revised Tests of Cognitive Ability—Revised.* Boston: Allyn & Bacon.

McGrew, K. S., & Flanagan, D. P. (1996). *An intelligence test desk reference (ITDR): A cross-battery approach to intelligence test interpretation.* Boston: Allyn & Bacon. Manuscript in preparation.

McGrew, K. S., & Hessler, G. L. (1995). The relationship between the WJ-R Gf-Gc cognitive clusters and mathematics achievement across the life-span. *Journal of Psychoeducational Assessment, 13,* 21–38.

McGrew, K. S., Werder, J. K, & Woodcock, R. W. (1991). *WJ-R technical manual.* Chicago: Riverside.

Naglieri, J. A. (1989). A cognitive processing theory for the measurement of intelligence. *Educational Psychologist, 24,* 185–206.

Naglieri, J. A., & Andrews, T. J. (1994). A cognitive approach to intervention design. *Communique, 22*(6), 8–9.

Naglieri, J. A., Braden, J. P., & Gottling, S. H. (1993). Confirmatory factor analysis of the planning, attention, simultaneous, successive (PASS) cognitive processing model for a Kindergarten sample. *Journal of Psychoeducational Assessment, 11,* 259–269.

Naglieri, J. A., & Das, J. P. (1990). Planning, attention, simultaneous, and successive (PASS) cognitive processes as a model for intelligence. *Journal of Psychoeducational Assessment, 8,* 303–337.

Naglieri, J. A., & Das, J. P. (in press). *Das-Naglieri Cognitive Assessment System interpretive and administration manuals.* Chicago: Riverside.

Neisser, U., Boodoo, G., Bouchard, T. J., Boykin, A. W., Brody, N., Ceci, S. J., Halpern, D. F., Loehlin, J. C., Perloff, R., Sternberg, R. J., & Urbina, S. (1996). Intelligence: Knowns and unknowns. *American Psychologist, 51*(2), 77–101.

Ramirez, A. G. (1990). Perspectives on language proficiency assessment. In A. Barona & E. E. Garcia (Eds.), *Children at risk: Poverty, minority status, and other issues in educational equity* (pp. 305–323). Washington, DC: National Association of School Psychologists.

Reschly, D. J. (1990). Best practices in adaptive behavior. In A. Thomas & J. Grimes (Eds.), *Best practices in school psychology—II* (pp. 29–42). Washington, DC: National Association of School Psychologists.

Reschly, D. J., & Wilson, M. S. (1990). Cognitive processing versus traditional intelligence: Diagnostic utility, intervention implications, and treatment validity. *School Psychology Review, 19,* 443–458.

Reynolds, C. R. (1984). Critical measurement issues in learning disabilities. *Journal of Special Education, 18,* 451–476.

Reynolds, C. R., & Kaiser, S. M. (1990). Bias in assessment of aptitude. In C. R. Reynolds & R. W. Kamphaus (Eds.), *Handbook of psychological and educational assessment of children: Intelligence and achievement* (pp. 611–653). New York: Guilford Press.

Roid, G., Prifitera, A., & Weiss, L. G. (1993). The WISC-III and the fairness of predicting achievement across ethnic and gender groups. *Journal of Psychoeducational Assessment* [Monograph Series: WISC-III Monograph], 6–21.

Sattler, J. M. (1988). *Assessment of children* (3rd ed.). San Diego, CA: Author.

Sattler, J. M. (1992). *Assessment of children* (rev. and updated 3rd ed.). San Diego, CA: Author.

Shinn, M. R., Tindal, G. A., Spira, D., & Marston, D. (1987). Practice of learning disabilities as social policy. *Learning Disabilities Quarterly, 10,* 17–28.

Shinn, M. R., Ysseldyke, J. E., Deno, S. L., & Tindal, G. A. (1986). A comparison of differences between students labeled learning disabled and low achieving on measures of classroom performance. *Journal of Learning Disabilities, 19,* 545–552.

Short, R. J., Simeonsson, R. J., & Huntington, G. S. (1990). Early intervention: Implications of Public Law 99-457 for professional child psychology. *Professional Psychology: Research and Practice, 21,* 88–93.

Simeonsson, R. J. (1986). *Psychological and developmental assessment of special children.* Boston: Allyn & Bacon.

Sternberg, R. J. (1986a). *Intelligence applied: Understanding and increasing your intellectual skills.* San Diego, CA: Harcourt Brace Jovanovich.

Sternberg, R. J. (1986b). Intelligence, wisdom, and creativity: Three is better than one. *Educational Psychologist, 21*(3), 175–190.

Sternberg, R. J. (1987). Most vocabulary is learned from context. In M. G. McKeown & M. E. Curtis (Eds.), *The nature of vocabulary acquisition* (pp. 89–105). Hillsdale, NJ: Erlbaum.

Sternberg, R. J. (1992). Ability tests, measurements, and markets. *Journal of Educational Psychology, 84,* 134–140.

Sternberg, R. J. (1993). Rocky's back again: A review of the WISC-III. *Journal of Psychoeducational Assessment,* [WISC-III Monograph], 161–164.

Sternberg, R. J. (1994). A triarchic model for teaching and assessing students in general psychology. *General Psychologist, 30*(2), 42–48.

Sternberg, R. J., Wagner, R. K., Williams, W. M., & Horvath, J. A. (1995). Testing common sense. *American Psychologist, 50,* 912–926.

Stone, B. J. (1992). Joint confirmatory factor analyses of the DAS and WISC-R. *Journal of School Psychology, 30,* 185–195.

Tatsuoka, M. M., & Lohnes, P. R. (1988). *Multivariate analysis* (2nd ed.). New York: Macmillan.

Terrell, F., Terell, S. L., & Taylor, J. (1981). Effects of race of examiner and cultural mistrust on the WAIS performance of Black students. *Journal of Consulting and Clinical Psychology, 49,* 750–751.

Thompson, B. (1991). Methods, plainly speaking: A primer on the logic and use of canonical correlation analysis. *Measurement and Evaluation in Counseling and Development, 24,* 80–95.

Thorndike, R. L., Hagen, E. P., & Sattler, J. M. (1986). *Stanford–Binet Intelligence Scale: Fourth edition.* Chicago: Riverside.

Vanderveer, B., & Scheweid, E. (1974). Infant assessment: Stability of mental functioning in young retarded children. *American Journal of Mental Deficiency, 79,* 1–4.

Watkins, M. W., & Kush, J. C. (1994). Wechsler subtest analysis: The right way, the wrong way, or no way? *School Psychology Review, 23,* 640–651.

Wechsler, D. (1981). *Wechsler Adult Intelligence Scale—Revised.* San Antonio, TX: Psychological Corporation.

Wechsler, D. (1984). *WISC-RM escala de inteligencia para nivel escolar Wechsler.* Mexico, DF: El Manual Moderno.

Wechsler, D. (1989). *Wechsler Preschool and Primary Scale of Intelligence—Revised.* San Antonio, TX: Psychological Corporation.

Wechsler, D. (1991). *Wechsler Intelligence Scale for Children—Third Edition.* San Antonio, TX: Psychological Corporation.

Wechsler, D. (1993). *Escala de Inteligencia Wechsler para Ninos—Revisada de Puerto Rico.* San Antonio, TX: Psychological Corporation.

Willis, M. G. (1989). Learning styles of African American children: A review of the literature and interventions. *Journal of Black Psychology, 16*(1), 47–65.

Wilson, M. S., & Reschly, D. J. (1996). Assessment in school psychology training and practice. *School Psychology Review, 25,* 9–23.

Woodcock, R. W. (1990). Theoretical foundations of the WJ-R measures of cognitive ability. *Journal of Psychoeducational Assessment, 8,* 231–258.

Woodcock, R. W. (1993). An information processing view of Gf-Gc theory. *Journal of Psychoeducational Assessment,* [Monograph Series: WJ-R Monograph], 80–102.

Woodcock, R. W. (in press). Extending Gf-Gc theory into practice. In J. J. McArdle & R. W. Woodcock (Eds.), *Human cognitive abilities in theory and practice.* Chicago: Riverside.

Woodcock, R. W., & Johnson, M. B. (1977). *Woodcock–Johnson Tests of Cognitive Ability.* Chicago: Riverside.

Woodcock, R. W., & Johnson, M. B. (1989). *Woodcock–Johnson Psycho-Educational Battery—Revised.* Chicago: Riverside.

Woodcock, R. W., & Munoz-Sandoval, A. F. (1996). *Bateria Woodcock–Munoz Pruebas de habilidad cognoscitiva—Revisada.* Chicago: Riverside.

Ysseldyke, J. (1990). Goodness of fit of the Woodcock–Johnson Psycho-Educational Battery—Revised to the Horn–Cattell Gf-Gc theory. *Journal of Psychoeducational Assessment, 8,* 28–275.

Ysseldyke, J. E., Algozzine, B., & Epps, S. (1983). A logical and empirical analysis of current practice in classifying students as handicapped. *Exceptional Children, 50,* 160–166.

Ysseldyke, J. E., Algozzine, B., Shinn, M. R., & McGue, M. (1982). Similarities and differences between low achievers and students labeled learning disabled. *Journal of Special Education, 16,* 73–85.

APPENDIX A

Ethical Principles of Psychologists and Code of Conduct (Ethical Standard 2)

2. EVALUATION, ASSESSMENT, OR INTERVENTION

2.01 Evaluation, Diagnosis, and Interventions in Professional Context

(a) Psychologists perform evaluations, diagnostic services, or interventions only within the context of a defined professional relationship. (See also Standard 1.03, Professional and Scientific Relationship.)

(b) Psychologists' assessments, recommendations, reports, and psychological diagnostic or evaluative statements are based on information and techniques (including personal interviews of the individual when appropriate) sufficient to provide appropriate substantiation for their findings. (See also Standard 7.02, Forensic Assessments.)

2.02 Competence and Appropriate Use of Assessment and Interventions

(a) Psychologists who develop, administer, score, interpret, or use psychological assessment techniques, interviews, tests, or instruments do so in a manner and for purposes that are appropriate in light of the research on or evidence of the usefulness and proper application of the techniques.

(b) Psychologists refrain from misuse of assessment techniques, interventions, results, and interpretations and take reasonable steps to prevent others from misusing the information these techniques provide. This includes refraining from releasing raw test results or raw data to persons, other than to patients or clients as appropriate, who are not qualified to use such information. (See also Standards 1.02, Relationship of Ethics and Law, and 1.04, Boundaries of Competence.)

2.03 Test Construction

Psychologists who develop and conduct research with tests and other assessment techniques use scientific procedures and current professional knowledge for test design, standardization, validation, reduction or elimination of bias, and recommendations for use.

2.04 Use of Assessment in General and With Special Populations

(a) Psychologists who perform interventions or administer, score, interpret, or use assessment techniques are familiar with the reliability, validation, and related standardization or outcome studies of, and proper applications and uses of, the techniques they use.

(b) Psychologists recognize limits to the certainty with which diagnoses, judgments, or predictions can be made about individuals.

(c) Psychologists attempt to identify situations in which particular interventions or assessment techniques or norms may not be applicable or may require adjustment in administration or interpretation because of factors such as individuals' gender, age, race, ethnicity, national origin, religion, sexual orientation, disability, language, or socioeconomic status.

2.05 Interpreting Assessment Results

When interpreting assessment results, including automated interpretations, psychologists take into account the various test factors and characteristics of the person being assessed that might affect psychologists' judgments or reduce the accuracy of their interpretations. They indicate any significant reservations they have about the accuracy or limitations of their interpretations.

2.06 Unqualified Persons

Psychologists do not promote the use of psychological assessment techniques by unqualified persons. (See also Standard 1.22, Delegation to and Supervision of Subordinates.)

2.07 Obsolete Tests and Outdated Test Results

(a) Psychologists do not base their assessment or intervention decisions or recommendations on data or test results that are outdated for the current purpose.

(b) Similarly, psychologists do not base such decisions or recommendations on tests and measures that are obsolete and not useful for the current purpose.

2.08 Test Scoring and Interpretation Services

(a) Psychologists who offer assessment or scoring procedures to other professionals accurately describe the purpose, norms validity, reliability, and applications of the procedures and any special qualifications applicable to their use.

(b) Psychologists select scoring and interpretation services (including automated services) on the basis of evidence of the validity of the program and procedures as well as on other appropriate considerations.

(c) Psychologists retain appropriate responsibility for the appropriate application, interpretation, and use of assessment instruments, whether they score and interpret such tests themselves or use automated or other services.

2.09 Explaining Assessment Results

Unless the nature of the relationship is clearly explained to the person being assessed in advance and precludes provision of an explanation of results (such as in some organizational consulting, preemployment or security screenings, and forensic evaluations), psychologists ensure that an explanation of the results is provided using language that is reasonably understandable to the person assessed or to another legally authorized person on behalf of the client. Regardless of whether the scoring and interpretation are done by the psychologist, by assistants, or by automated or other outside services, psychologists take reasonable steps to ensure that appropriate explanations of results are given.

2.10 Maintaining Test Security

Psychologists make reasonable efforts to maintain the integrity and security of tests and other assessment techniques consistent with law, contractual obligations, and in a manner that permits compliance with the requirements of this Ethics Code. (See also Standard 1.02, Relationship of Ethics and Law.)

APPENDIX B

Code of Fair Testing Practices in Education

PREPARED BY THE JOINT COMMITTEE ON TESTING PRACTICES

The Code of Fair Testing Practices in Education[*] states the major obligations to test takers of professionals who develop or use educational tests. The Code is meant to apply broadly to the use of tests in education (admissions, educational assessment, educational diagnosis, and student placement). The Code is not designed to cover employment testing, licensure or certification testing, or other types of testing. Although the code has relevance to many types of educational tests, it is directed primarily at professionally developed tests such as those sold by commercial test publishers or used in formally administered testing programs. The Code is not intended to cover tests made by individual teachers for use in their own classrooms.

The Code addresses the roles of test developers and test users separately. Test users are people who select tests, commission test development services, or make decisions on the basis of test scores. Test developers are people who actually construct tests as well as those who set policies for particular testing programs. The roles may, of course, overlap as when a state education agency commissions test development services, sets policies that control the test development process, and makes decisions on the basis of the test scores.

The Code presents standards for educational test developers and users in four areas:

A. Developing/selecting tests
B. Interpreting scores
C. Striving for fairness
D. Informing test takers

Organizations, institutions, and individual professionals who endorse the Code commit themselves to safeguarding the rights of test takers by following the principles listed. The Code is intended to be consistent with the relevant parts of the *Standards for Educational and Psychological Testing* (American Educational Research Association, American Psychological Association, and National Council on Measurement in Education, 1985). However, the code differs from the Standards in both audience and purpose. The Code is meant to be understood by the general public; it is limited to educational tests; and the

---

[*] The Code has been developed by the Joint Committee on Testing Practices, a cooperative effort of several professional organizations, that has as its aim the advancement, in the public interest, of the quality of testing practices. The Joint Committee was initiated by the American Educational Research Association, the American Psychological Association and the National Council on Measurement in Education. In addition to these three groups, the American Association for Counseling and Development/Association for Measurement and Evaluation in Counseling and Development, and the American Speech–Language-Hearing Association are now also sponsors of the Joint Committee. This is not copyrighted material. Reproduction and dissemination are encouraged.

primary focus is on those issues that affect the proper use of tests. The Code is not meant to add new principles over and above those in the Standards or to change the meaning of the Standards. The goal is rather to represent the spirit of a selected portion of the Standards in a way that is meaningful to test takers and/or their parents or guardians. It is the hope of the Joint committee that the Code will also be judged to be consistent with existing codes of conduct and standards of other professional groups who use educational tests.

A. DEVELOPING/SELECTING APPROPRIATE TESTS[*]

Test developers should provide the information that test users need to select appropriate tests.

Test Developers Should:

1. Define what each test measures and what the test should be used for. Describe the population(s) for which the test is appropriate.
2. Accurately represent the characteristics, usefulness, and limitations of tests for their intended purposes.
3. Explain relevant measurement concepts as necessary for clarity at the level of detail that is appropriate for the intended audience(s).
4. Describe the process of test development. Explain how the content and skills to be tested were selected.
5. Provide evidence that the test meets its intended purpose(s).
6. Provide either representative samples or complete copies of test questions, directions, answer sheets, manuals, and score reports to qualified users.
7. Indicate the nature of the evidence obtained concerning the appropriateness of each test for groups of different racial, ethnic, or linguistic backgrounds who are likely to be tested.
8. Identify and publish any specialized skills needed to administer each test and to interpret scores correctly.

Test users should select tests that meet the purpose for which they are to be used and that are appropriate for the intended test-taking populations.

Test Users Should:

1. First define the purpose for testing and the population to be tested. Then, select a test for that purpose and that population based on a thorough review of the available information.
2. Investigate potentially useful sources of information, in addition to test scores, to corroborate the information provided by tests.
3. Read the materials provided by test developers and avoid using tests for which unclear or incomplete information is provided.
4. Become familiar with how and when the test was developed and tried out.
5. Read independent evaluations of a test and of possible alternative measures. Look for evidence required to support the claims of test developers.
6. Examine specimen sets, disclosed tests or samples of questions, directions, answer sheets, manuals, and score reports before selecting a test.
7. Ascertain whether the test content and norms group(s) or comparison group(s) are appropriate for the intended test takers.

---

[*]Many of the statements in the Code refer to the selection of existing tests. However, in customized test programs test developers are engaged to construct new tests. In those situations, the test development process should be designed to help ensure that the completed tests will be in compliance with the Code.

8. Select and use only those tests for which the skills needed to administer the test and interpret scores correctly are available.

B. INTERPRETING SCORES

Test developers should help users interpret scores correctly.

Test Developers Should:

9. Provide timely and easily understood score reports that describe test performance clearly and accurately. Also explain the meaning and limitations of reported scores.
10. Describe the population(s) represented by any norms or comparison group(s), the dates the data were gathered, and the process used to select the samples of test takers.
11. Warn users to avoid specific, reasonably anticipated misuses of test scores.
12. Provide information that will help users follow reasonable procedures for setting passing scores when it is appropriate to use such scores with the test.
13. Provide information that will help users gather evidence to show that the test is meeting its intended purpose(s).

Test users should interpret scores correctly.

Test Users Should:

9. Obtain information about the scale used for reporting scores, the characteristics of any norms or comparison group(s), and the limitations of the scores.
10. Interpret scores taking into account any major differences between the norms or comparison groups and the actual test takers. Also take into account any differences in test administration practices or familiarity with the specific questions in the test.
11. Avoid using tests for purposes not specifically recommended by the test developer unless evidence is obtained to support the intended use.
12. Explain how any passing scores were set and gather evidence to support the appropriateness of the scores.
13. Obtain evidence to help show that the test is meeting its intended purpose(s).

C. STRIVING FOR FAIRNESS

Test developers should strive to make tests that are as fair as possible for test takers of different races, gender, ethnic backgrounds, or handicapping conditions.

Test Developers Should:

14. Review and revise test questions and related materials to avoid potentially insensitive content or language.
15. Investigate the performance of test takers of different races, gender, and ethnic backgrounds when samples of sufficient size are available. Enact procedures that help to ensure that differences in performance are related primarily to the skills under assessment rather than to irrelevant factors.
16. When feasible, make appropriately modified forms of tests or administration procedures available for test takers with handicapping conditions. Warn test users of potential problems in using standard norms with modified tests or administration procedures that result in non-comparable scores.

Test users should select tests that have been developed in ways that attempt to make them as fair as possible for test takers of different races, gender, ethnic backgrounds, or handicapping conditions.

Test Users Should:

14. Evaluate the procedures used by test developers to avoid potentially insensitive content or language.
15. Review the performance of test takers of different races, gender, and ethnic backgrounds when samples of sufficient size are available. Evaluate the extent to which performance differences may have been caused by inappropriate characteristics of the test.
16. When necessary and feasible, use appropriately modified forms of tests or administration procedures for test takers with handicapping conditions. Interpret standard norms with care in the light of the modifications that were made.

D. INFORMING TEST TAKERS

Under some circumstances, test developers have direct communication with test takers. Under other circumstances, test users communicate directly with test takers. Whichever group communicates directly with test takers should provide the information described below.

Test Developers or Test Users Should:

17. When a test is optional, provide test takers or their parents/guardians with information to help them judge whether the test should be taken, or if an available alternative to the test should be used.
18. Provide test takers the information they need to be familiar with the coverage of the test, the types of question formats, the directions, and appropriate test-taking strategies. Strive to make such information equally available to all test takers.

Under some circumstances, test developers have direct control of tests and test scores. Under other circumstances, test users have such control. Whichever group has direct control of tests and test scores should take the steps described below.

Test Developers or Test Users Should:

19. Provide test takers or their parents/guardians with information about rights test takers may have to obtain copies of tests and completed answer sheets, retake tests, have tests rescored, or cancel scores.
20. Tell test takers or their parents/guardians how long scores will be kept on file and indicate to whom and under what circumstances test scores will or will not be released
21. Describe the procedures that test takers or their parents/guardians may use to register complaints and have problems resolved.

The membership of the Working Group that developed the Code of Fair Testing Practices in Education and of the Joint Committee on Testing Practices that guided the Working Group was as follows: Theodore P. Bartell, John R. Bergan, Esther E. Diamond, Richard P. Duran, Lorraine D. Eyde, Raymond D. Fowler, John J. Fremer (Co-chair, JCTP and Chair, Code Working Group), Edmund W. Gordon, Jo-Ida C. Hansen, James B. Lingwall, George F. Madaus (Co-chair, JCTP), Kevin L. Moreland, Jo-Ellen V. Perez, Robert J. Solomon, John T. Stewart, Carol Kehr Tittle (Co-chair, JCTP), Nicholas A. Vacc, and Michael J. Zieky. Debra Boltas and Wayne Camara of the American Psychological Association served as staff liaisons. Additional copies of the Code may be obtained from the National Council on Measurement in Education, 1230 Seventeenth Street, NW, Washington, D.C. 20036. Single copies are free.

APPENDIX C

Code of Professional Responsibilities in Educational Measurement

PREPARED BY THE NCME AD HOC COMMITTEE
ON THE DEVELOPMENT OF A CODE OF ETHICS[*]

As an organization dedicated to the improvement of measurement and evaluation practice in education, the National Council on Measurement in Education (NCME) has adopted this Code to promote professionally responsible practice in educational measurement. Professionally responsible practice is conduct that arises from either the professional standards of the field, general ethical principles, or both.

[*] Cynthia B. Schmeiser, ACT, Chair; Kurt F. Geisinger, State University of New York; Sharon Johnson-Lewis, Detroit Public Schools; Edward D. Roeber, Council of Chief State School Officers; and William D. Schafer, University of Maryland. ©1995 National Council on Measurement in Education. Any portion of this Code may be reproduced and disseminated for educational purposes.

The purpose of the Code of Professional Responsibilities in Educational Measurement, hereinafter referred to as the Code, is to guide the conduct of NCME members who are involved in any type of assessment activity in education. NCME is also providing this Code as a public service for all individuals who are engaged in educational assessment activities in the hope that these activities will be conducted in a professionally responsible manner. Persons who engage in these activities include local educators such as classroom teachers, principals, and superintendents; professionals such as school psychologists and counselors; state and national technical, legislative, and policy staff in education; staff of research, evaluation, and testing organizations; providers of test preparation services; college and university faculty and administrators; and professionals in business and industry who design and implement educational and training programs.

This Code applies to any type of assessment that occurs as part of the educational process, including formal and informal, traditional and alternative techniques for gathering information used in making educational decisions at all levels. These techniques include, but are not limited to, large-scale assessments at the school, district, state, national, and international levels; standardized tests; observational measures; teacher-conducted assessments; assessment support materials; and other achievement, aptitude, interest, and personality measures used in and for education.

Although NCME is promulgating this Code for its members, it strongly encourages other organizations and individuals who engage in educational assessment activities to endorse and abide by the responsibilities relevant to their professions. Because the Code pertains only to uses of assessment in education, it is recognized that uses of assessments outside of educational contexts, such as for employment, certification, or licensure, may involve additional professional responsibilities beyond those detailed in this Code.

The Code is intended to serve an educational function: to inform and remind those involved in educational assessment of their obligations to uphold the integrity of the manner in which assessments are developed, used, evaluated, and marketed. Moreover, it is expected that the Code will stimulate thoughtful discussion of what constitutes professionally responsible assessment practice at all levels in education.

The Code enumerates professional responsibilities in eight major areas of assessment activity. Specifically, the code presents the professional responsibilities of those who:

1. Develop assessments
2. Market and sell assessments
3. Select assessments
4. Administer assessments
5. Score assessments
6. Interpret, use, and communicate assessment results
7. Educate about assessment
8. Evaluate programs and conduct research on assessments

Although the organization of the Code is based on the differentiation of these activities, they are viewed as highly interrelated, and those who use this Code are urged to consider the Code in its entirety. The index following this Code provides a listing of some of the critical interest topics within educational measurement that focus on one or more of the assessment activities.

GENERAL RESPONSIBILITIES

The professional responsibilities promulgated in this Code in eight major areas of assessment activity are based on expectations that NCME members involved in educational assessment will:

1. Protect the health and safety of all examinees;
2. Be knowledgeable about, and behave in compliance with, state and federal laws relevant to the conduct of professional activities;
3. Maintain and improve their professional competence in educational assessment;
4. Provide assessment services only in areas of their competence and experience, affording full disclosure of their professional qualifications;
5. Promote the understanding of sound assessment practices in education;
6. Adhere to the highest standards of conduct and promote professionally responsible conduct within educational institutions and agencies that provide educational services; and
7. Perform all professional responsibilities with honesty, integrity, due care, and fairness.

Responsible professional practice includes being informed about and acting in accordance with the *Code of Fair Testing Practices in Education* (Joint Committee on Testing Practices, 1988), the *Standards for Educational and Psychological Testing* (American Educational Research Association, American Psychological Association, NCME, 1985), or subsequent revisions, as well as all applicable state and federal laws that may govern the development, administration, and use of assessments. Both the *Standards for Educational and Psychological Testing* and the *Code of Fair Testing Practices in Education* are intended to establish criteria for judging the technical adequacy of tests and the appropriate uses of tests and test results. The purpose of this Code is to describe the professional responsibilities of those individuals who are engaged in assessment activities. As would be expected, there is a strong relationship between professionally responsible practice and sound educational assessments, and this Code is intended to be consistent with the relevant parts of both of these documents.

It is not the intention of NCME to enforce the professional responsibilities stated in the Code or to investigate allegations of violations to the Code. Since the Code provides a frame of reference for the evaluation of the appropriateness of behavior, NCME recognizes that the Code may be used in legal or other similar proceedings.

Section 1: Responsibilities of Those Who Develop Assessment Products and Services

Those who develop assessment products and services, such as classroom teachers and other assessment specialists, have a professional responsibility to strive to produce assessments that are of the highest quality. Persons who develop assessments have a professional responsibility to:

1.1. Ensure that assessment products and services are developed to meet applicable professional, technical, and legal standards.
1.2. Develop assessment products and services that are as free as possible from bias due to characteristics irrelevant to the construct being measured, such as gender, ethnicity, race, socioeconomic status, disability, religion, age, or national origin.
1.3. Plan accommodations for groups of test takers with disabilities and other special needs when developing assessments.
1.4. Disclose to appropriate parties any actual or potential conflicts of interest that might influence the developers' judgment or performance.
1.5. Use copyrighted materials in assessment products and services in accordance with state and federal law.
1.6. Make information available to appropriate persons about the steps taken to develop and score the assessment, including up-to-date information used to support the reliability, validity, scoring and reporting processes, and other relevant characteristics of the assessment.
1.7. Protect the rights to privacy of those who are assessed as part of the assessment development process.

1.8. Caution users, in clear and prominent language, against the most likely misinterpretations and misuses of data that arise out of the assessment development process.

1.9. Avoid false or unsubstantiated claims in test preparation and program support materials and services about and assessment or its use and interpretation.

1.10. Correct any substantive inaccuracies in assessments or their support materials as soon as feasible.

1.11. Develop score reports and support materials that promote the understanding of assessment results.

Section 2: Responsibilities of Those Who Market and Sell Assessment Products and Services

The marketing of assessment products and services, such as tests and other instruments, scoring services, test preparation services, consulting, and test interpretive services, should be based on information that is accurate, complete, and relevant to those considering their use. Persons who market and sell assessment products and services have a professional responsibility to:

2.1. Provide accurate information to potential purchasers about assessment products and services and their recommended uses and limitations.

2.2. Not knowingly withhold relevant information about assessment products and services that might affect an appropriate selection decision.

2.3. Base all claims about assessment products and services on valid interpretations of publicly available information.

2.4. Allow qualified users equal opportunity to purchase assessment products and services.

2.5. Establish reasonable fees for assessment products and services.

2.6. Communicate to potential users, in advance of any purchase or use, all applicable fees associated with assessment products and services.

2.7. Strive to ensure that no individuals are denied access to opportunities because of their inability to pay the fees for assessment products and services.

2.8. Establish criteria for the sale of assessment products and services, such as limiting the sale of assessment products and services to those individuals who are qualified for recommended uses and from whom proper uses and interpretations are anticipated.

2.9. Inform potential users of known inappropriate uses of assessment products and services and provide recommendations about how to avoid such misuses.

2.10. Maintain a current understanding about assessment products and services and their appropriate uses in education.

2.11. Release information implying endorsement by users of assessment products and services only with the users' permission.

2.12. Avoid making claims that assessment products and services have been endorsed by another organization unless an official endorsement has been obtained.

2.13. Avoid marketing test preparation products and services that may cause individuals to receive scores that misrepresent their actual levels of attainment.

Section 3: Responsibilities of Those Who Select Assessment Products and Services

Those who select assessment products and services for use in educational settings, or help others do so, have important professional responsibilities to make sure that the assessments are appropriate for their intended use. Persons who select assessment products and services have a professional responsibility to:

3.1. Conduct a thorough review and evaluation of available assessment strategies and instruments that might be valid for the intended uses.

3.2. Recommend and/or select assessments based on publicly available documented evidence of their technical quality and utility rather than on unsubstantiated claims or statements.

3.3. Disclose any associations or affiliations that they have with the authors, test publishers, or others involved with the assessments under consideration for purchase and refrain from participation if such associations might affect the objectivity of the selection process.

3.4. Inform decision makers and prospective users of the appropriateness of the assessment for the intended uses, likely consequences of use, protection of examinee rights, relative costs, materials and services needed to conduct or use the assessment, and known limitations of the assessment, including potential misuses and misinterpretations of assessment information.

3.5. Recommend against the use of any prospective assessment that is likely to be administered, scored, and used in an invalid manner for members of various groups in our society for reasons of race, ethnicity, gender, age, disability, language background, socioeconomic status, religion, or national origin.

3.6. Comply with all security precautions that may accompany assessments being reviewed.

3.7. Immediately disclose any attempts by others to exert undue influence on the assessment selection process.

3.8. Avoid recommending, purchasing, or using test preparation products and services that may cause individuals to receive scores that misrepresent their actual levels of attainment.

Section 4: Responsibilities of Those Who Administer Assessments

Those who prepare individuals to take assessments and those who are directly or indirectly involved in the administration of assessments as part of the educational process, including teachers, administrators, and assessment personnel, have an important role in making sure that the assessments are administered in a fair and accurate manner. Persons who prepare others for, and those who administer, assessments have a professional responsibility to:

4.1. Inform the examinees about the assessment prior to its administration, including its purposes, uses, and consequences; how the assessment information will be judged or scored; how the results will be kept on file; who will have access to the results; how the results will be distributed; and examinees' rights before, during, and after the assessment.

4.2. Administer only those assessments for which they are qualified by education, training, licensure, or certification.

4.3. Take appropriate security precautions before, during, and after the administration of the assessment.

4.4. Understand the procedures needed to administer the assessment prior to administration.

4.5. Administer standardized assessments according to prescribed procedures and conditions and notify appropriate persons if any nonstandard or delimiting conditions occur.

4.6. Not exclude any eligible student from the assessment.

4.7. Avoid any conditions in the conduct of the assessment that might invalidate the results.

4.8. Provide for and document all reasonable and allowable accommodations for the administration of the assessment to persons with disabilities or special needs.

4.9. Provide reasonable opportunities for individuals to ask questions about the assessment procedures or directions prior to and at prescribed times during the administration of the assessment.

4.10. Protect the rights to privacy and due process of those who are assessed.

4.11. Avoid actions or conditions that would permit or encourage individuals or groups to receive scores that misrepresent their actual levels of attainment.

Section 5: Responsibilities of Those Who Score Assessments

The scoring of educational assessments should be conducted properly and efficiently so that the results are reported accurately and in a timely manner. Persons who score and prepare reports of assessments have a professional responsibility to:

5.1. Provide complete and accurate information to users about how the assessment is scored, such as the reporting schedule, scoring process to be used, rationale for the scoring approach, technical characteristics, quality control procedures, reporting formats, and the fees, if any, for these services.

5.2. Ensure the accuracy of the assessment results by conducting reasonable quality control procedures before, during, and after scoring.

5.3. Minimize the effect on scoring of factors irrelevant to the purposes of the assessment.

5.4. Inform users promptly of any deviation in the planned scoring and reporting service or schedule and negotiate a solution with users.

5.5. Provide corrected score results to the examinee or the client as quickly as practicable should errors be found that may affect the inferences made on the basis of the scores.

5.6. Protect the confidentiality of information that identifies individuals as prescribed by state and federal law.

5.7. Release summary results of the assessment only to those persons entitled to such information by state or federal law or those who are designated by the party contracting for the scoring services.

5.8. Establish, where feasible, a fair and reasonable process for appeal and rescoring the assessment.

Section 6: Responsibilities of Those Who Interpret, Use, and Communicate Assessment Results

The interpretation, use, and communication of assessment results should promote valid inferences and minimize invalid ones. Persons who interpret, use, and communicate assessment results have a professional responsibility to:

6.1. Conduct these activities in an informed, objective, and fair manner within the context of the assessment's limitations and with an understanding of the potential consequences of use.

6.2. Provide to those who receive assessment results information about the assessment, its purposes, its limitations, and its uses necessary for the proper interpretation of the results.

6.3. Provide to those who receive score reports an understandable written description of all reported scores, including proper interpretations and likely misinterpretations.

6.4. Communicate to appropriate audiences the results of the assessment in an understandable and timely manner, including proper interpretations and likely misinterpretations.

6.5. Evaluate and communicate the adequacy and appropriateness of any norms or standards used in the interpretation of assessment results.

6.6. Inform parties involved in the assessment process how assessment results may affect them.

6.7. Use multiple sources and types of relevant information about persons or programs whenever possible in making educational decisions.

6.8. Avoid making, and actively discourage others from making, inaccurate reports, unsubstantiated claims, inappropriate interpretations, or otherwise false and misleading statements about assessment results.

6.9. Disclose to examinees and others whether and how long the results of the assessment will be kept on file, procedures for appeal and rescoring, rights examinees and others have to the assessment information, and how those rights may be exercised.

6.10. Report any apparent misuses of assessment information to those responsible for the assessment process.

6.11. Protect the rights to privacy of individuals and institutions involved in the assessment process.

Section 7: Responsibilities of Those Who Educate Others About Assessment

The process of educating others about educational assessment, whether as part of higher education, professional development, public policy discussions, or job training, should prepare individuals to understand and engage in sound measurement practice and to become discerning users of tests and test results. Persons who educate or inform others about assessment have a professional responsibility to:

7.1. Remain competent and current in the areas in which they teach and reflect that in their instruction.

7.2. Provide fair and balanced perspectives when teaching about assessment.

7.3. Differentiate clearly between expressions of opinion and substantiated knowledge when educating others about any specific assessment method, product, or service.

7.4. Disclose any financial interests that might be perceived to influence the evaluation of a particular assessment product or service that is the subject of instruction.

7.5. Avoid administering any assessment that is not part of the evaluation of student performance in a course if the administration of that assessment is likely to harm any student.

7.6. Avoid using or reporting the results of any assessment that is not part of the evaluation of student performance in a course if the use or reporting of results is likely to harm any student.

7.7. Protect all secure assessments and materials used in the instructional process.

7.8. Model responsible assessment practice and help those receiving instruction to learn about their professional responsibilities in educational measurement.

7.9. Provide fair and balanced perspectives on assessment issues being discussed by policymakers, parents, and other citizens.

Section 8: Responsibilities of those Who Evaluate Educational Programs and Conduct Research on Assessments

Conducting research on or about assessments or educational programs is a key activity in helping to improve the understanding and use of assessments and educational programs. Persons who engage in the evaluation of educational programs or conduct research on assessments have a professional responsibility to:

8.1. Conduct evaluation and research activities in an informed, objective, and fair manner.

8.2. Disclose any associations that they have with authors, test publishers, or others involved with the assessment and refrain from participation if such associations might affect the objectivity of the research or evaluation.

8.3. Preserve the security of all assessments throughout the research process as appropriate.

8.4. Take appropriate steps to minimize potential sources of invalidity in the research and disclose known factors that may bias the results of the study.

8.5. Present the results of research, both intended and unintended, in a fair, complete, and objective manner.

8.6. Attribute completely and appropriately the work and ideas of others.

8.7. Qualify the conclusions of the research within the limitations of the study.

8.8. Use multiple sources of relevant information in conducting evaluation and research activities whenever possible.

8.9. Comply with applicable standards for protecting the rights of participants in an evaluation or research study, including the rights to privacy and informed consent.

AFTERWORD

As stated at the outset, the purpose of the *Code of Professional Responsibilities in Educational Measurement* is to serve as a guide to the conduct of NCME members who are engaged in any type of assessment activity in education. Given the broad scope of the field of educational assessment as well as the variety of activities in which professionals may engage, it is unlikely that any code will cover the professional responsibilities involved in every situation or activity in which assessment is used in education. Ultimately, it is hoped that this Code will serve as the basis for ongoing discussions about what constitutes professionally responsible practice. Moreover, these discussions will undoubtedly identify areas of practice that need further analysis and clarification in subsequent editions of the Code. To the extent that these discussions occur, the Code will have served its purpose.

To assist in the ongoing refinement of the Code, comments on this document are most welcome. Please send your comments and inquiries to:

Dr. William J. Russell
Executive Officer
National Council on
Measurement in Education
1230 Seventeenth Street, NW
Washington, DC 20036-3078

SUPPLEMENTARY RESOURCES

The following list of resources is provided for those who want to seek additional information about codes of professional responsibility that have been developed and adopted by organizations having an interest in various aspects of educational assessment.

American Association for Counseling and Development (now American Counseling Association). (1988). *Ethical standards of the American Counseling Association.* Alexandria, VA: Author.

American Association for Counseling and Development (now American Counseling Association) & Association for Measurement and Evaluation in Counseling and Development (now Association for Assessment in Counseling). (1989). *Responsibilities of users of standardized tests: RUST statement revised.* Alexandria, VA: Author.

American Educational Research Association, American Psychological Association, & National Council on Measurement in Education. (1985). *Standards for educational and psychological testing.* Washington, DC: Author.

American Educational Research Association. (1992). *Ethical standards of the American Educational Research Association. Educational Researcher, 21*(7), 23–26.

American Federation of Teachers, National Council on Measurement in Education, & National Education Association. (1990). *Standards for teacher competence in educational assessment of students.* Washington, DC: Author.

American Psychological Association. (1992). *Ethical principles of psychologists and code of conduct.* Washington, DC: Author.

American Psychological Association President's Task Force on Psychology in Education. (in press). *Learner-centered psychological principles: Guidelines for school redesign and reform.* Washington, DC: Author.

Joint Advisory Committee. (1993). *Principles for fair assessment practices for education in Canada.* Edmonton, Alberta: Author.

Joint Committee on Testing Practices. (1988). *Code of fair testing practices in education.* Washington, DC: Author.

Joint Committee on Standards for Educational Evaluation. (1988). *The personnel evaluation standards: How to assess systems for evaluating educators.* Newbury Park, CA: Sage.

Joint Committee on Standards for Educational Evaluation. (1994). *The program evaluation standards: How to assess evaluations of educational programs.* Thousand Oaks, CA: Sage.

National Association of College Admission Counselors. (1988). *Statement of principles of good practice.* Alexandria, VA: Author.

INDEX TO THE CODE OF PROFESSIONAL RESPONSIBILITIES IN EDUCATIONAL MEASUREMENT

This index provides a list of major topics and issues addressed by the responsibilities in each of the eight sections of the Code. Although this list is not intended to be exhaustive, it is intended to serve as a reference source for those who use this Code.

Topic	Responsibility
Advertising	1.9, 1.10, 2.3, 2.11, 2.12
Bias	1.2, 3.5, 4.5, 4.7, 5.3, 8.4
Cheating	4.5, 4.6, 4.11
Coaching and Test Preparation	2.13, 3.8, 4.11
Competence	2.10, 4.2, 4.4, 4.5, 5.2, 5.5, 7.1, 7.8, 7.9, 8.1, 8.7
Conflict of Interest	1.4, 3.3, 7.4, 8.2
Consequences of Test Use	3.4, 6.1, 6.6, 7.5, 7.6
Copyrighted Materials, Use of	1.5, 8.6
Disabled Examinees, Rights of	1.3, 4.8
Disclosure	1.6, 2.1, 2.2, 2.6, 3.3, 3.7 4.1, 5.1, 5.4, 6.2, 6.3, 6.4, 6.6, 6.9, 8.2, 8.4, 8.5
Due Process	4.10, 5.8, 6.9
Equity	1.2, 2.4, 2.7, 3.5, 4.6
Fees	2.5, 2.6, 2.7
Inappropriate Test Use	1.8, 2.8, 2.9, 3.4, 6.8, 6.10
Objectivity	3.1, 3.2, 3.3, 6.1, 6.5, 7.2, 7.3, 7.9, 8.1, 8.2, 8.5, 8.7
Rights to Privacy	1.7, 3.4, 4.10, 5.6, 5.7, 6.11, 8.9
Security	3.6, 4.3, 7.7, 8.3
Truthfulness	1.10, 2.1, 2.2, 2.3, 2.11, 2.12, 3.2, 4.6, 7.3
Undue Influence	3.7
Unsubstantiated Claims	1.9, 3.2, 6.8

Author Index

Subject Index